Baseball
Prospectus
1997 Edition

Gary Huckabay

Clay Davenport

Rany Jazayerli

Chris Kahrl

Joseph S. Sheehan

Joseph S. Sheehan, Managing Editor

Table of Contents

About the Authors v
Dedications vi
From the Editor vii
Acknowledgements ix

Introduction

Welcome *by Keith Law* 3
Davenport Translations 5
Vladimir Projections 10
How to Use this Book for Rotisserie *by Keith Law* 12
1996: The Year In Review *by Keith Law* 16
Stop the Presses! 19

Teams

Atlanta Braves 23
Florida Marlins 37
Montreal Expos 54
New York Mets 68
Philadelphia Phillies 82

Chicago Cubs 97
Cincinnati Reds 112
Houston Astros 126
Pittsburgh Pirates 140
St. Louis Cardinals 154

Colorado Rockies 169
Los Angeles Dodgers 183
San Diego Padres 198
San Francisco Giants 211

Baltimore Orioles 225
Boston Red Sox 239
    Prospect Profile: Carl Pavano *by Bob Gajarsky* 254
Detroit Tigers 256
New York Yankees 272
Toronto Blue Jays 288

Chicago White Sox   305
Cleveland Indians   324
Kansas City Royals   340
Milwaukee Brewers   360
Minnesota Twins   373

California Angels   389
Oakland A's   402
Seattle Mariners   420
Texas Rangers   436

Arizona Diamondbacks   449
Tampa Bay Devil Rays   450

Labor

A History of the Labor War *by David Grabiner*   453
115 Years of Chicken Little:
The Business of Baseball *by Ted Frank*   456

Extra Innings

Support-Neutral Win-Loss Records *by Michael Wolverton* 465
Run Support *by Greg Spira*   470
Clutch: Myth or Adjective? *by Bob Gajarsky*   474
Defensive Average *developed by Sherri Nichols*   476
Internet Baseball Awards *by Greg Spira*   496

Index

501

About the Authors

Gary Huckabay is a baseball analyst and returning MBA student in Davis, California. In addition to his work on the *Baseball Prospectus* series, Gary has done research in support of arbitration cases and produced some of the world's most derivative comedy. Gary lives in Davis with his wife, Kathy, and manages the Fully Functional Disembodied Head of Rod Serling baseball and softball teams. Gary and the rest of the authors can be reached at info@baseballprospectus.com.

Clay Davenport has spent most of the last 15 years in Charlottesville, Virginia, as an undergraduate, a grad student and an employee at the University of Virginia. In his day job, he works as a meteorologist, studying the large scale transport and distribution of ozone. He is the coach of the University's academic competition team (#2 in the nation in 1996), and was himself a national champion in the 1980s. He is also the manager/catcher/pitcher/utilityman for the departmental softball team, and would not be highly rated by Equivalent Average. But he does the little things well.

Rany Jazayerli, 21, is a medical student at the University of Michigan in his spare time. When he's not having his heart broken by his beloved Royals, he can be found on I-94 driving to Chicago to visit his fiancée, or explaining to people that Islam is not a synonym for misogyny and terrorism.

Chris Kahrl is that rarest of birds, a happily ex-Californian. He's been a state champion horseman, an honor scholar at the University of Chicago, a guy who shovels horsecrap for money and a Teamster. Until the collapse of Daiwa Bank, he was a gaijin in the Chicago Foreign Bank League (16" softball - the barehanded game). He's currently finishing up his M.A. in history at Loyola University, while working full-time in publishing at the Oriental Institute Press. As a passionate fan of the Oakland A's, Chris grimly remembers the false hope of Billyball, and will be forever grateful to Dave Kingman for rejuvenating his interest in baseball during that fine summer of '84.

Joseph S. Sheehan is a magazine, book and newsletter editor in Orange County, California, where he lives with his wife, Sophia. In his time between *Baseball Prospectus* deadlines, he serves as Managing Editor of LAW OFFICE COMPUTING magazine. He has a B.A. in journalism from the University of Southern California. Joe is an American history aficionado, lifelong Yankee fan and avid Strat-O-Matic baseball player.

Dedications

Clay Davenport:

Before *Baseball Prospectus*, the DTs were published on the Internet along with commentary from fans of each particular team. Quite a few of the people who wrote the DT articles then are in this book, and Clay would like to publicly thank each and every one of them once again:

Kurtis Araki, Dave Bonar, Chuck Briese, Harold Brooks, Darin and Jason Brown, Jim Cowles, Hank Davis, Dave DeMers, Ken Emery, Jim Ferguson, Edward (Valentine) Fischer, Scott Fischthal, Ted Frank, Dave Geiser, Steve Geswein, Dave Hogg, Joe Huber, Gary Huckabay, Scot Hughes, Mark Jareb, Rany Jazayerli, Chris Kahrl, John-Paul Kastner, Mike Jones, Dorian Kim, Jonathan King, Natraj Kini, Dave Kirsch, Henry Koretzky, Sue Leopold, Chris Long, Nelson Lu, Tim Mavor, Dave Naehring, Brad Nathan, Sherri Nichols, Dave Nieporent, Gordon Niguma, Rodger Payne, John Perkins, Phil Ponebshek, Doug Riblet, John Rickert, Jake Roberts, Eric Roush, John Sandoval, Yaska Sankar, Tom Scudder, Dale Stephenson, Sean Sweda, Neal Traven, Roy White, Dylan Wilbanks, Michael Wong and Michael Wynblatt.

Those articles are still out there on the web. The 1993 articles can be found at ftp://ftp.baseball. org/pub/baseball/stats/DT/1993; the 1994 articles are at http://www.baseball.org/baseball/DT.

Rany Jazayerli:

Rany would like to dedicate this book to his parents, who have never understood my obsession with baseball but love me anyway; my brother Roukan, who patiently withstood my incessant babblings about the game as we grew up; and my fiancée Belsam, whose love for me is the greatest blessing I could have ever hoped to receive.

Chris Kahrl:

Chris would like to thank his parents for creating him in the first place, his wife for her attempts to be patient with his love of baseball ("Great, now I know which one is Robin Ventura."), Gary for bringing me aboard this project for what has been a bundle of fun, Joel Zuhars for making this all possible, Sherri Nichols for graciously taking the time to contribute to this book during a very rough time, Dave Pease and his crew of merry henchmen for the long hours they put in on the Web site and the cover, and Joe Sheehan for his annual ritual of nailing himself to a cross to edit this beast. I would not like to thank any of the various agents and publishers who have yet to figure out that baseball fans buy books, or Susan Fornoff.

From The Editor

In editing *Baseball Prospectus 1997*, I had a few small goals. Foremost among them was to include the St. Louis Cardinals, and as you'll see on page 154, I was able to achieve this. My primary goal, however, was simple: to make this the best baseball annual on the market, filling a gap that has existed since the demise of Bill James' *Baseball Book*. I believe that goal has been met.

We've made some improvements this year. First, there are 1,643 players listed in the Teams section, each with a full four-year Daveport Translation and comment. These 1,643 players are all included in the Index beginning on page 501. This Index was one of the most requested additions to the book, and I hope that it makes it easier for rotisserie, fantasy and table-game players to find that key player for their drafts and auctions.

Players are listed with the team with which they finished 1996. Albert Belle is listed with Cleveland, Alex Fernandez with the White Sox and so on. However, for players who changed teams through the third week of December, we have updated their Vladimir projection and, in some cases, their player comment to reflect their move.

At the end of every team section there is a single page with 65-75 players. These are players we elected to not comment on, and the stat lines are their 1996 Davenport Translations. The number of players listed varies with each organization, but generally this page includes players who had at least 100 at bats or 30 innings pitched at some level in 1996 and/or have a chance of appearing in the major leagues in 1997.

Another big addition to the book is the inclusion of guest essays from a variety of writers. The bulk of these are included in the back in the Labor and Extra Innings sections, and represent some fantastic work by some talented people.

We're particularly pleased to present the work of Sherri Nichols, whose pioneering effort in developing Defensive Average has made better baseball fans out of all who have seen it. Thanks, Sherri, for your work and allowing us to publish it.

Finally, in an effort to keep baseball fans abreast of all the organizations in MLB, we include essays on the expansion Arizona Diamondbacks and Tampa Bay Devil Rays.

On page ix, Gary Huckabay does the honors of thanking the many people who have given their time, energy and talent to this project. I would like to take a few paragraphs here to thank those who have been integral to my participation:

First, I'd like to thank the authorship group. *Baseball Prospectus 1997* would not be possible without the effort and dedication of Gary Huckabay, Rany Jazayerli, Chris Kahrl and Clay Davenport. It is a privilege to work with these guys, not to mention a heck of a lot of fun. Thanks to all of you.

The aforementioned guest essays add a lot to this year's edition, and without them the book would not be nearly as good. Thanks to Keith Law, Bob Gajarsky, David Grabiner, Ted Frank, Michael Wolverton and Greg Spira. Thanks also to Davids Tate and Pease, whose essays were unfortunate victims of a need to make page count.

Many have worked behind the scenes on the book and the Web site, among them Jeff and David Pease, Joel Zuhars and the staff at Ravenlock Media. Thanks for the support, guys.

I would not have been able to participate this year if not for the consideration of my employers. Thanks to Daryl Teshima and Jim Pawell for letting me pursue this opportunity. Thanks to Daryl as well for his feedback and encouragement, even though we continue to rip Eric Karros.

Many people have had a hand in putting me in a position to do this book. I am grateful to each and every one for the impact they've had on me over the years:

Pat McPartland, Jim McPartland, Jim Stafford, the Gonzalez family—especially Henry and Angie, Mike Regan, Mike Ervin, Derek Jacques, Matt McDonald, Richie Gonzalez, the ITBL (Mike Regan, Alex Lopez, Derek Jacques, Mike Sanchez, David Toro, Jose Mena, Eddie Kneafsey, Pete McCaffrey, Miguel Jimenez and Wayne), the members of the NABL, NASA and the OSL, the journalism school at USC—especially Ed Guthman and Jon Kotler, the "O" office at USC (Peggy, Karen, Irene, Margie, Laurie, Vickie, Adrienne, Denise and Arjun), Harold Richman—for developing the game that taught me the game, John Kreuz, Bill James—for his work and his wit, and the Elias Sports Bureau—especially Seymour, Steve and the night crew.

Most of all, I want to thank my mother, Maureen, who put me in a position to do something with my life; and my wife, Sophia, who believes I can do anything with it. Their love, support, patience and understanding make everything possible for me. I love you both.

Finally, thanks to you, the reader. Whether you've been reading rec.sport.baseball for years or are completely new to the book and the writers, thanks for supporting our effort to produce the best baseball book on the market. Enjoy, and be sure to give us feedback at info@baseballprospectus.com.

Joseph S. Sheehan
Placentia, Calif.
December 23, 1996

Acknowledgements

Hi. Thanks for buying *Baseball Prospectus 1997*. We really do appreciate your patronage and trust. We know how hard you work for your money, and we've asked you to lay out a fair amount of it for this book. We've chosen to put this project together over the last couple of years for one simple reason: no member of the authorship group has been happy with any of the available baseball annuals. The ones that claim to be analytical have severely flawed premises, sometimes strange goals and usually read something like wet plywood. The few that really do have value, like Ron Shandler's works or the STATS Handbooks, are primarily numbers with very little commentary.

There just wasn't anything out there that had good, solid baseball analysis and commentary that was worth reading.

So we decided to do it ourselves. Four years ago, an acquisitions editor for a book publisher approached me about doing a baseball annual, based primarily on what he had read on the Internet. I told him I'd do it, but labor problems and a house fire ended that project before it began. So in late 1995, I decided to make phone calls to Clay Davenport, Rany Jazayerli and Chris Kahrl, based on the work they had posted on Usenet. Rany told me that Joe Sheehan would probably be interested in getting involved, so I gave him a quick buzz and we were off. No word yet on whether Joe has forgiven Rany. It's a safe bet that more than once since then, each of us has decided that this probably wasn't a good idea. We didn't make any money off the book last year, and this project chews up as much time as we care to give to it. Not to mention lots that we don't care to give to it. But thanks to some amazing support from a very loyal reader base, and the very hard work of a lot of talented and dedicated people, we've managed to put together what we firmly believe is the very best baseball book available.

These are the 1500 words in the book where I get to write what I want, so I want to thank the core of the team for their continued effort, patience and damn fine work. So Chris, Joe, Rany, Clay, Dave and Keith—thanks. Thanks for putting up with the worried phone calls, the incessant badgering, the panicked e-mails, my rationalizations and bad jokes. Thanks for putting up with lapses like forgetting time zone differences, phone tag, late manuscript and 6 a.m. phone calls. Part of what makes doing this book worthwhile is the fact that I get to work with the lot of you. Even Joe.

The seven of us could not have put out a product like this by ourselves. We've had a lot of help. My deepest thanks, admiration and envy go to Jeff Pease for his cover art and graphics skills. There's a reason why I work in words and numbers rather than anything having to do with art, and it's nice to have people with real talent helping us out so generously. Similarly, this book would not be in your hands without the enthusiastic and skillful Joel Zuhars, who worked his tail off to get this book out the door. Furthermore, the gang at Ravenlock Media (Erik Brent, Bryce Lynn and the whole staff) have been beyond supportive, providing us with support and freedom that we didn't think we could get. And a special thanks to all the guest authors, who have provided some really fantastic stuff that I think makes this book a heckuva lot better than last year's. They're all bylined, and they're far too talented for us to hang onto them for too long with this pay, so enjoy them while you can.

This is starting to sound like Emma Thompson's speech at the Oscars, but bear with me. I would also like to thank everyone who ordered the Prospectus last year—I'm sorry we had a limited supply. The incredibly detailed and helpful letters we got from last year's customers were essential in putting together this year's book, and without the enthusiasm and excitement about the project that we all received from last year's customers, I know I wouldn't have been on board for this year. Some of the e-mail from the redbird.com address was rather unfriendly, but even that was in good fun.

Each of the authors gets space to do this sort of thank-you fest, and I'm chewing up valuable book space, so I want to get right into a whole bunch of special thanks. All of these people make this book better, and I'm extremely grateful. When there's a list this long, and I'm in this much of a hurry, deserving people will get omitted. In no particular order, and my apologies if you get left off due to Joe Sheehan's not liking you, thanks to: Angela Miller, Linda Acredolo, Betsy Amster, David Ungerer, Dennis Cleary, George Schofield, Chris Schofield, Kevin Schofield, John Skilton, Ron Shandler—who does very good work himself; see it at http://www.baseballhq.com, Rob Neyer for his consistently admirable column and encouragement, Ken Emery, Dorian Kim, Jeff and David Barton, John Samples at GU Press, Scott Davis—who knows more about pricing than anyone really should, Eitan Gerstner, Marc Lawrence, Billy Beane, Sean Lahman, Paul Andresen, Joe Lundy, David "That's vascularity, not stretchmarks" Kirsch, Craig Wright, Eric Walker, Randy Siverson, Marina Estabrook, Frank Samaniego, Eric Gelatt, Chris Redder, John Morrissey and the rest of the vaunted FFDHRS defense, featuring The Weasel [tm], Chih-Ling Tsai, Stephen Wolstenholme for his neural net experience, Gordon Niguma for his thankless work on last year's book, Susan Redmond and Gary Huckabay, Sr., who have the dubious distinction of being my parents, Sue Montoya for bending her schedule to fit my whims, Lee Saucerman and Janet Chambers for their patience and support, Dennis Cleary again because he's the funniest man I know, Gisela Cleary for introducing me to a woman who wore a T-shirt that exclaimed "I survived a Brown Recluse bite" (and had pictures to prove it), Rod Loewen, Richard Jacobsen, Joseph Dien, David and Keith Perry, Robert Giedt and Kyle Brink of Spectrum Holobyte, David Rakonitz, Romeo for trying to save our belongings at great personal risk to himself, John Baylis, Jim Mulliner, Craig Spearman, Ngaio Bealum, whose talents are completely wasted on SportsChannel Pacific, Dena Bealum, whose talents are largely wasted at her company, Mark Wolfson, whose talents make the Oakland A's broadcasts the very best in baseball, Jerry Gaskill, Ty Tabor and Doug Pinnick for their generosity and unparalleled musical gifts, Sean Sweda for agreeing to help me appear smarter than I am, Amy Haas, Jennifer Schofield for reminding me that idealism and optimism aren't completely lost causes, Tom Tippett for designing the only PC game actually suitable for a face-to-face league, Jerry Lee, Bill Davenport and Jan Hushbeck for their assistance above, beyond, over and past the call of duty or friendship, The *Baseball Prospectus* Mailing List and Dave Revue, Lori Conrad and Mel Tennyson, Sherry Williams for cheering us on, Mr. And Mrs. Richard Morrissey, Bill Rosen at Simon & Schuster, Roger Maynard, Brigit Kubiak, Dwight Perkins, Kris Perkins, Tim Feeley, Mary Feeley, Peter Spomer—who I learned my sense of humor from, Joe Donaghue, Mark R. Bureau and Ray DiPerna—who remind me why I love this damn game so much and why I spend so much time on it, Mark Montague, Keith Ferrar, Mr. And Mrs. Don Loewen, Craig and Lynn Stogner, Margie, Tiffany and Samantha Kyle, Mike Knorre at NW Direct, The 30-year old Erik Gaumer, Roberta Redmond, Jeff Lloyd, John Chu, Rick Suzuki, Kim Yang, Anthony Travers, Steve Tegenfeldt, Stephanie Rice, Tim Underwood, Al Differ, Edwin Daly, John Perkins, Roger Lustig, Keith Woolner and Mitch Plitnick for cleaning up my mess, Greg Coleman for his irrepressible spark and wit, and all the people who have helped with the book whom I've omitted because I'm sleep-deprived.

But most importantly, I'd like to thank Peter Collins for napping and allowing my only stolen base of the last two years. You might eventually hear the end of it.

I know it's standard practice for people to be disingenuous when talking to the public; after 18 months of political spin doctors, it's fairly tough to believe almost anything you see or read. But there's no attempt at manipulation here. I am genuinely thankful for all of the help and support these people and others have provided. Without that help, you wouldn't be reading this book, and we wouldn't be so proud of it.

Part of the contract of buying this book is that you read it carefully, and TELL US WHAT YOU LIKE AND DON'T LIKE. We really do read your comments, listen to your phone calls and try to put together the best baseball annual in the world. Send us e-mail at info@baseballprospectus.com. If you don't have e-mail, send us a letter—Baseball Prospectus, 121 Guaymas Place, Davis CA, 95616.

Enjoy. Baseball is about renewal, excellence and just plain fun. We hope this book contributes to all three of those for you. We've also conveniently made the book extremely heavy, in the event you get a chance to smack Bud Selig in the chops with it.

Live, from the birthplace of baseball's Lazlo Letters,

Gary Huckabay
Davis, Calif.
November 21, 1996

Introduction

Welcome

Welcome to the only comprehensive baseball annual to rise above the fluff that clogs up bookshelves across the country each spring. This is…*Baseball Prospectus 1997*.

Where do we get off saying that everything else is just fluff? Well, it's quite simple:

- Stats that actually tell you whether or not a player is any good. The Davenport Translation method takes ordinary stats—like those you might find in your Sunday paper—and takes out all the exogenous effects that, for example, make Andres Galarraga look like a real hitter instead of a stiff. The DTs strip away park effects, league effects and even year-to-year effects, to boil a hitter's statistics down to their essence: how good a player is relative to everybody else.

- Hard-hitting, accurate commentary. We pull no punches. We'll tell you we think Lou Piniella is an idiot for the way he mishandles young players. We'll tell you we think Dan Duquette is a pretty smart guy, despite the frying he takes in the Beantown media. We'll tell you Andres Galarraga (and Dante Bichette and Vinny Castilla) are really lousy hitters, but that Andruw Jones is even better than the hype. And we can back it up.

- Team-by-team organizational essays, including looks at both the Diamondbacks and Devil Rays. Want to know how your favorite team stacks up, this year and in the future? We cover every organization top to bottom, including the front office.

- Forecasts for hundreds of hitters. Vlad has the answer you seek. Vlad is a proprietary projection tool that uses DTs and several other key variables (age, career trend, park) to forecast a hitter's stats for the upcoming season. So let Vlad tell you whether Lance Johnson will have another eye-catching season.

- Guest essays. Questions about the labor situation? About run support's impact on pitchers? How to use this book for your rotisserie team? It's all covered.

So come on in. We bet you won't put this book down until you've devoured it, and then you'll agree with our assessment: Everything else really is just fluff.

Looking Backward

It's time to come clean. We did pretty damn well last year. Since this is our second printed edition, we thought it appropriate that we look back on our first edition and see how well we did with our prognostications.

We'll start with the highlights, of which these are just a few:

Todd Hundley

	AB	H	DB	TP	HR	BB	SB	BA	OBA	SA
1996 Projection	481	138	13	2	29	63	0	.287	.369	.503
Actual stats	540	140	32	1	41	79	1	.259	.356	.550

We said: "He's in danger of ruining his defensive reputation by turning into a good hitter. Last year was an excellent, if injury-filled, season; if he really has improved that much as a hitter, he could be batting cleanup by midseason." Hundley went on to set the single-season record for home runs hit by a catcher (only when playing as a catcher; don't you love parenthetical records?) and establish himself as the second-best hitting catcher in the NL. By the way, he was 27 last year.

Mariano Rivera

We said: "Skinny swingman who has good control of the corners of the strike zone. His K rate seemed to jump up a little as of late, and if that's a development rather than a fluke, this kid could really be something special." Special? Certainly the MVP of the World Champions. He also brought glamour to the setup role, even though several others had come before with similar results. Most importantly, he saved the Yankee starters by working two to three innings, two to three times a week. Rivera was the best reliever in the American League last year, and if the Yanks choose not to meet Wetteland's asking price, they'll face a tough decision on whether or not to move Rivera to the closer spot.

Jeff Fassero

We said: "He's one of the most underappreciated pitchers in baseball, and coming off a poor season, but is one of the 10 best left-handed starters in the game today. He's an extreme groundball pitcher who racks up strikeouts, a rare—and desirable—commodity. If his control improves a little and the Expos provide him with good run support, he could surprise everybody by winning 20 games this year." Well, he didn't win 20; he just turned in one of the five best starting pitching seasons in the NL in 1996. And of course, it got him traded to Seattle.

Jason Isringhausen and Bill Pulsipher

We said: "[Isringhausen's] workload is cause for concern." "Pulsipher's arm has been abused more than any other pitching prospect in the '90s, with the possible exception of Salomon Torres… His season ended early with a 'sprained' elbow, whatever that is, and I'd be very leery of him unless and until his workload comes down." BAM! Pulsipher missed the season after reconstructive elbow surgery, and Izzy struggled through five months before shutting it down for his own surgery. The Mets are enhancing their reputation for demolishing quality arms, and one has to worry about Paul Wilson (who also had surgery in October) and Juan Acevedo, who seems to have fallen off a cliff.

The Angels

I won't quote the whole essay, but this snippet ought to give you the idea: "That the Angels contended last year is undoubtedly a bad thing for the franchise's future. Rather than make the hard choices and build from the ground up around Salmon, Troy Percival, Brian Anderson and super-prospects Darin Erstad and Todd Greene, the Angels are now convinced their present collection of players is a contender.... Individually, [the Angels' pre-1996 moves] might not be damning. Collectively, they're signs the team can't tell a baseball player from Pocahontas, and that the Angels will regress to a .420-.450 level this year." Split the difference between .420 and .450 and you get .435, the Halos' winning percentage this year (70-91). In a sure foreshadowing that Scrooge McDuck was taking over the GM's spot, the Angels let Brian Anderson go in the spring by trying to save themselves $2.84 by cutting his salary by more than the allowed 20%. They never moved the overrated Garrett Anderson for pitching. Jim Abbott, in year one of a puzzling three-year deal, exploded. I could go on, but I'll leave the gory details to the essayists.

Of course, we did get a few things wrong. But owners of *BP '96* will notice that we didn't miss much. Here's a few of the larger errors we made:

Mike Lansing

	AB	H	DB	TP	HR	BB	SB	BA	OBA	SA
1996 Projection	410	111	23	3	8	33	27	.271	.325	.400
Actual stats	641	183	40	2	11	44	23	.285	.341	.406

We said: "Lansing is a terrific base stealer and has more power than your typical second baseman; in fact, the only major difference between him and his predecessor, Delino DeShields, is that DeShields reaches base more often. A lot more often. His age 27 season has come and gone, so don't look for any sudden improvement from Lansing. He's a useful but not irreplaceable cog in the Expos' lineup." We didn't strike out entirely here, but Lansing certainly improved his game last year. He upped his walk rate by over 50%, and got on base roughly 18% more often than DeShields last year, although D-squared had an unexpectedly awful year. All this doesn't make Lansing an All-Star, as some mediots claimed he should be, but if the improvements are real Lansing added four years to his career.

Kevin Elster

Does it even matter what we said? "He still can't hit much … Elster will probably make the Texas team as the veteran caddy at short in case Gil doesn't snap out of his [1995] second-half slump." The Elsteroid had an ungodly first half for such a lousy hitter. He pretty much fell apart down the stretch, but he had already fouled up every sabermetric projection system out there. One of the highlights of the '96 season for me came at Comiskey Park, when Chris Kahrl and I watched Elster have two extremely similar at bats. In each at bat, he got ahead in the count, ran the count full, hit a long foul home run over our heads (we were in the left-field foul area), and struck out.

Mike Bielecki

We said: "Might show up on someone's staff this year, might open a deli in Wilkes-Barre, PA. Either way, he'll be dealing meat." In five starts and 35 relief appearances, Bielecki was the most effective Braves' pitcher outside of the Cy Young troika and Mark Wohlers. He also threw two perfect but wasted innings in Game 4 of the Series, shutting down the Yanks' first three-run rally, but leaving before Jim Leyritz hit his second annual Dramatic Playoff Homer.

The Cardinals

This one hurts, so they made me write it. What can I say? We said they looked bad. We said they were "liable to get clobbered by teams who do the boring things like taking a walk and then hitting a home run, teams who display less fight but more baseball ability." The Cardinals won the NL Central, clobbered the arguably superior team (the Padres) in three games, and damn near slipped by the Braves until the sleeping giant from Atlanta woke up. Oops.

Now that you've seen the scoreboard from *BP '96*, go ahead and jump into *BP '97*. Some of the new features in this year's book include:

- Sherri Nichols' Defensive Average statistics for over 400 players

- An alphabetical index of all players in the book with full DTs and comments

- Special sections on the labor dispute and sabermetric tools

- The St. Louis Cardinals

Thanks for buying *Baseball Prospectus 1997*. Enjoy the book, and be sure to tell us what you think by e-mailing info@baseballprospectus.com.

--Keith Law

The Davenport Translations

In the beginning, there was batting average.

It was simple, which was important when you didn't have calculators or computers to do the math for player statistics. It was powerful, too: in the dead ball era, there weren't huge differences between players in power or walks. Some players were able to add extra value by stealing bases, but that's a hard way to get ahead: the run value of a stolen base simply isn't as great as an extra-base hit, and getting caught tears you down roughly twice as fast as a success moves you ahead. You could say with a lot of confidence that the best hitter in the game was the guy with the best batting average.

Then some batters, notably John McGraw and Roy Thomas in the 1890s, learned how to work walks from pitchers. They changed the rules to inhibit them, making foul balls strikes and two-strike foul bunts strikeouts; but ever since, there have always been a few guys in the game whose walks made them far more valuable than their batting average indicated.

Then came the live ball and the Bambino. Hitting, in terms of scoring runs and team success, became more and more synonymous with power. Changes in the ball and in stadium construction made home runs easier to hit; changes in gloves made singles somewhat tougher. Fan adulation and big paychecks went to the sluggers; the batting average champion was less and less of an offensive force.

Eventually, people's heads caught up with a little fact that their hearts had understood before: batting average didn't mean what it used to. A few adventurers started looking for something that would mean what batting average once had. Slugging average has been around since the teens, and legendary baseball executive Branch Rickey was an early disciple of on-base percentage. Other combinations ranging from simple to bizarre appeared; one that has real merit is simply adding the slugging average and on-base percentages together ("OPS"). With computers, it became possible to develop new combinations of traditional statistics that tracked run scoring better than any of the old ways. There was Thomas Boswell's Total Average. Bill James developed Runs Created, and with his insightful, acerbic and funny Baseball Abstracts did more than anyone else to popularize the "new statistics." Pete Palmer offered up Linear Weights, and used that to produce the megalithic Total Baseball encyclopedias.

But none of these metrics mean anything to most baseball fans.

Equivalent Average (EQA), like the statistics above, is a way to evaluate the offensive contributions of a baseball player. Instead of burning the bridges to the Triple Crown stats, as some in the statistical community are wont to do, we embrace them. Even a casual fan knows whether those numbers are good or bad. A more advanced fan knows what the records for those stats are for a season or a career, what it usually takes to lead the league and what it takes to stay in the league. Because they have that scale recognition, we don't ignore them: we co-opt them. Equivalent Average is deliberately designed to mirror batting average; its counterpart, Equivalent Runs, mirrors RBI.

The first question is, does it really follow batting average closely? Yes, it does. The mean EQA is defined as .260; that is the nearest round figure for major league batting average in the 20th century. For any given numerical rank, the figures for EQA and BA are very close; once you get past the extreme edges, the difference is almost always less than five points. Compare the rankings for all players with 4000 plate appearances:

Rk	Batting Average		Equivalent Average		Difference
1	Ty Cobb	.366	Babe Ruth	.378	-12
2	Rogers Hornsby	.358	Ted Williams	.372	-14
3	Joe Jackson	.356	Lou Gehrig	.353	+3
4	Ed Delahanty	.346	Ty Cobb	.351	-5
5	Tris Speaker	.345	Mickey Mantle	.351	-6
6	Ted Williams	.344	Rogers Hornsby	.349	-5
7	Billy Hamilton	.344	Dan Brouthers	.345	-1
8	Babe Ruth	.342	Joe Jackson	.343	-1
9	Dan Brouthers	.342	Pete Browning	.338	+4
10	Harry Heilmann	.342	Stan Musial	.337	+5
50	Kirby Puckett	.318	Sam Crawford	.315	+3
100	Frank Baker	.307	Joe Medwick	.306	+1
200	George Davis	.295	Johnny Bates	.295	0
300	Lou Finney	.287	Del Ennis	.288	-1
400	R. Bresnahan	.279	Dwayne Murphy	.282	-3
500	R. Stennett	.274	Bing Miller	.276	-2
600	Dode Paskert	.268	Mookie Wilson	.269	-1
700	Ted Sizemore	.262	Dave Cash	.262	0
800	Andy Thornton	.254	Ray Schalk	.251	+3
900	Arthur Irwin	.241	T. Corcoran	.234	+7

In addition, consider the following:

153 players have had a .300 BA. There have been 150 with a .300 EQA.

The single season record for EQA is also held by Babe Ruth; his 1920 season earns a .424. Rogers Hornsby holds the single-season record for batting average with….424.

Over the last ten years, most of which was a time of relatively low offense, the average league-leading BA has been .350. In that time, the average league-leading EQA has been .360.

Next question: are they accurate? Yes. Equivalent Runs are better at measuring team run scoring than Runs Created or Linear Weights when both get to use the same information. In addition, it does not suffer from RC's bias towards individuals with both a high on-base percentage and a high slugging percentage. EQR measures the difference in run scoring between a league that has this individual in it, and one which does not.

Table 1. Root mean square errors for predicted runs from various statistics.

1901-1992	AL	NL	Majors
Equivalent Runs	23.99	23.00	23.51
Linear Weights	24.94	23.96	24.46
Runs Created	25.62	24.27	24.97
Onbase plus slugging	27.52	26.37	26.96
Batting Average	47.32	42.97	45.24

1960-1992	AL	NL	Majors
Equivalent Runs	21.41	22.08	21.73
Linear Weights	21.54	21.82	21.68
Runs Created	22.85	22.68	22.79
Onbase plus slugging	23.42	23.47	23.44
Batting Average	41.77	39.85	40.87

So, EQAs use a familiar scale and are accurate. How do you calculate them?

Not easily. EQAs are a multi-step procedure.

There are many ways to estimate how many runs a given set of offensive statistics will produce. At the very beginning, equivalent average was simply two-thirds batting average plus one-third secondary average, an idea which came straight out of Bill James' 1986 Baseball Abstract (at the top of page 121). That original outline is still visible in the first step of the system, the Raw EQA:

$$RawEqA = \frac{1}{3} \times \frac{H + TB + BB + SB}{AB + CS + \frac{1}{3}SB + \frac{2}{3}BB}$$

It is, admittedly, an ugly function. That is partly because it is empirical; it is based not so much on theory but on what actually works. Another reason is due to its evolution: I added more information to the denominator to improve the correlation with run scoring. Placing stolen bases in the denominator is exceptionally odd, but it works to keep the ratings of players from non-caught stealing years in check.

In any event, RawEQA is closely related to the player's rate of run production compared to his league. I call the resulting estimate of run production Equivalent Runs (EQR).

If we set the league EQA (LgEQA) equal to the league RawEQA, then EQR are defined as

$$EqR = \left(2 * \frac{RawEqA}{LgEqA} - 1\right) \times \left(\frac{R}{AB + BB}\right)_{Lg} \times (AB + BB)_{Ind}$$

Properly speaking, this is not the number of runs which would score given this rate of production, but the number of runs added to the league total as a result of this player being in it. The first part shows that if a player has a RawEQA twice as high as the league, he will produce runs at 2*2-1 = 3 times the league rate. It also means that a .300 Raw EQA is more valuable in a league with a .220 EQA than in a .260 EQA league. Furthermore, a player with a RawEQA less than half that of the league will actually cost them runs: the league would be better if this player, and his outs, never appeared at all, even if they didn't get any more plate appearances. Most pitchers today fall into this category.

In order to compare individuals between seasons, it is necessary to adjust for the offensive level of the player's home park and his league, respectively. For park effects, I use a park factor based on how many runs score per game in each park, and how often each team plays in each park.

Adjusting for league offense is trickier, because there are really two separate adjustments. The league EQA varies from one year to the next, from a high of .266 in the 1930 NL to a low of .204 in the 1908 AL. Also, the number of runs produced by a given EQA varies with time; because of errors, especially, more runs were produced by a .300 EQA in Cobb's day than in ours. The effective park-adjusted equivalent runs (EPER) accounts for all this: it is defined as

$$EPER = EqR \times \frac{(AB - H + CS)_{Lg} \times .1723 \times DH}{R_{Lg}} \times \frac{1}{PF}$$

The numerator of the central element is the number of runs that a more-or-less average league this century would have scored, under modern relationships of runs to EQA. Comparing that to actual runs scored gives an idea of how inflated the EQR figure is for league effects that season. It can be calculated once and retained. I treat EPER as an acronym, and pronounce it to rhyme with "pepper." (Which is why I dropped the letter Q; in the case of purely park-adjusted equivalent runs, I didn't want to have to refer to Babe Ruth's "PEQR.")

The EPER measures total production after adjusting for park and league effects. The final measure I will introduce measures productivity, or production per out: the effective park-adjusted equivalent average, EPEQA, pronounced like "epic-kuh." It is defined as

$$EPEQA = \left[\frac{EPER}{5 \times (AB - H + CS)} \right]^{2/5}$$

If you trace a perfectly average player through all of these permutations, you will come up with an EPEQA of .2593. Why were these numbers (particularly 5 and 2/5) chosen? Because they are the numbers needed to convert the scale of runs per out to the scale of hits per at bat.

One final note: For the sake of convenience, throughout this book, whenever we talk about the EQA or EQR of an individual, we are really talking about his park- and league-adjusted values of EPEQA and EPER.

Translations

By far the most interesting spin-off of the EQA system is its use in Translations, estimating what a given statistical line in one league would look like if the same values were carried into another league. I believe very strongly that a player's statistics are a reflection of his skill, but distorted by three things: who his opponents are, where he plays and luck. The first refers to the skill level of his opponents; it should be obvious that any player will perform better against lower-skilled (i.e., minor league) opponents than against higher-skilled ones. Where refers to one's home field, as well as the other fields in the league; their dimensions and elevations influence the play of the game, as well as the outcome of discrete game events. Luck is just that; the line drives that get caught and the weak popups that fall in tend to even out in the long term, but this can take several hundred plate appearances. The fewer the at bats, the more careful you have to be in your conclusions.

What the Translations are designed to do is to estimate how much the Who and the Where are distorting the underlying performance of the individual, and like corrective lenses for vision, remove the distortion.

This involves a lot more than just normalizing and unnormalizing statistics. Ruth's home run rate in 1920, for instance, was 13.38 times the league average; taken at face value, it would imply 212 HR in 458 AB in the AL of 1996. I get around this problem by treating total offense, as measured by EQA, as a conserved quantity during translation: if Ruth's actual performance scores a .424 EQA against the standards of 1920, then the resulting line for, say, 1996, must score a .424 when measured against the standards of 1996.

To build a statistical line that produces a .424 EQA, I look at a multitude of player and league statistics: not only hits, walks, doubles, triples and home runs per at bat, but also ratios of each type of hit to the other, like singles to doubles, and at how much of the total offensive value is attributable to each part. All of this information is compared for the player, his league and the new league to which I am translating to produce a preliminary line. The EQA for that line is calculated; I then go into an iterative routine that makes successive changes in the statistical line, looking for the optimal fit between preserving the desired ratios and getting the EQA as close to the desired mark as possible. The procedure is complicated; trust me, you would not want to do this by hand. And it's not perfectly reversible. If I translated Ruth's 1920 stats to 1996, and translated those numbers back to 1920, they probably wouldn't match Ruth's stats exactly. But the value would still be the same. This is especially true when a player is well outside normal ranges of performance (Ruth's home runs, Wagner's doubles, Harmon Killebrew's double-to-homer ratio), or has none of something (like Canseco's 1988 season, with 34 doubles, 42 homers and 0 triples).

A refinement to the Translations is to not treat EQA as perfectly conserved, but to adjust it up or down depending on whether the new league is easier or tougher than the original league. We have a pretty good idea about how much more difficult the majors are compared to, say, AAA ball; it's easy to look up a large number of players who performed at each level and measure how much, on average, their performance changed. Using them, it is possible to translate the statistics of every player in organized ball to one standard league; to show everybody's ability to hit for average, power and so forth with the distortions of park and league removed.

That reference league, we decided in some jest, would be the American League of 1996. Last year's AL had more offense than any baseball fan under 60 has seen in their lives, at least at the major league level. An unprecedented number of players set career highs for home runs, for average and so on. Translating to the AL of 1996 tries to make the point that for most, the results are not without precedent; to show that they could have done just as well in previous seasons if only the prevailing conditions had been more favorable.

Translations, alas, can rarely be perfect. For one thing, players are not average; they have unique strengths and weaknesses. A league that increases offense 10% has a reason for doing so, and some players will be better suited to take advantage of it than others. If this happens, the translations won't take that advantage away; a player who takes better than average advantage of his home park has real game-winning value to his team. It would be inappropriate to simply

ply use the Translation to judge how a player would perform if he was traded to another park; his own unique characteristics need to be considered as well.

A typical player Translation looks like this:

ALEX OCHOA		**RF**		**1972**	**Age 25**												
Year	Team	Lge	AB	H	DB	TP	HR	BB	SB	CS	OUT	BA	OBA	SA	EQA	EQR	Peak
1993	Frederick	Caro	549	138	18	2	11	42	19	7	418	.251	.305	.352	.224	50	.250
1994	Bowie	East	532	148	17	1	13	45	17	8	392	.278	.334	.387	.245	58	.271
1995	Norfolk	Inter	128	40	4	1	3	15	5	2	90	.312	.385	.430	.277	18	.302
1995	Rochester	Inter	339	87	14	1	8	28	12	4	256	.257	.313	.375	.234	34	.255
1996	Norfolk	Inter	240	78	9	3	8	33	4	7	169	.325	.407	.488	.291	39	.312
1996	NY Mets	NL	292	92	20	2	5	20	3	3	203	.315	.359	.449	.270	38	.289
1997	*NY Mets*	*NL*	*502*	*135*	*36*	*5*	*12*	*44*	*8*	*0*	*367*	*.269*	*.328*	*.432*	*.273*	*71*	

The top line shows the player's name, primary position, baseball birth year and baseball age. The baseball birth year is based on a year that runs from July 1 to June 30 instead of Jan. 1 to Dec. 31. For players born before June 30, their actual birth year and baseball birth year are the same. Players born after July 1 are "credited" with the following year. Why go through this? So I can look at 1994 and Ochoa's given birth year of 1972, and say that he was 22 that year. The age listed is the player's baseball age for 1997.

All of the statistics listed are translated statistics, not actual ones—the book is big enough already. They represent the value a player's performance would have had, had he played exactly as well in the 1996 AL as he did in his real league. When looking at them, it would be good to remember that an average AL performance last year was a .277 batting average, .348 OBA (using only AB, H and BB), and a .445 slugging average, marks which in most years would be well above average. And, of course, a .260 EQA.

The column headings should be self-evident; the only truly unfamiliar terms, EQA and EQR, are described in this essay. "Peak" refers to the best EQA that can be reasonably expected from this player, either at age 27, or in the next three years for players already past 27. It is intended as a rough guide only to normal rates of growth, so that you can tell whether a player is progressing unusually quickly or slowly.

Outs are provided to help calculate combined EQAs. To get Ochoa's total EQA in 1996, for instance, you would add the EQRs (39+38=77); divide by the total number of outs (169+203=372); divide that by 5; lastly, the step that requires the scientific calculator, raise that to the 0.4 power. Voila: .280.

The "1997" line is a prediction; actually, two predictions. Vladimir, Gary Huckabay's neural net, predicts how the play-

er will perform in terms of the 1996 AL. The line printed is derived by translating that from the 1996 AL to my prediction of the league and park characteristics for 1997.

Pitcher translations are performed the same way as hitters; a pitching line is relatively easy to convert to a hitting line, which can be translated much the same way. Not quite exactly the same; better major league fielders will work to a pitcher's advantage, while they work against a hitter, but the principle is unchanged. Since real runs allowed are known—and I use total runs, not just earned runs—I can tell how much above or below his predicted run total a pitcher was and adjust the final total accordingly.

With batters, I rate players by EQA, set up so that the league average is always .260. For pitchers, I will use something which basically looks like an ERA, set up so that the league average is always 4.00 and all pitchers have the same proportion of earned to unearned runs. With hitters, I felt a free hand to set the standard league to the AL of 1996; people are unfamiliar enough with EQA that they cannot easily estimate it by looking at other statistics. I don't think that's true of pitchers; a given ERA value brings to mind definite values of hits, walks and so on. Setting the primary measure to 4.00 almost requires that hits, for instance, be set to a value appropriate to that ERA. Pitchers, then, have not been translated to the AL of 1996; they have been translated to a hypothetical season, one whose difficulty level is the same as the '96 AL, but has the following characteristics.

ERA, exactly 4.00.
Hits per nine innings, 9.00.
Home runs per nine innings, 1.00.
Walks per nine innings, 4.00. (I know that is too high, but I wanted an even value.)
Strikeouts per nine innings, exactly 6.00.

A pitcher's translation looks like this:

CALVIN MADURO	RSP		1975		Age 22												
YR TEAM	Lge	IP	H	ER	HR	BB	K	ERA	W	L	H/9	HR/9	BB/9	K/9	KW
1994 Frederick	Caro	136.0	165	90	17	80	92	5.96	5	10	10.92	1.12	5.29	6.09	.71
1995 Frederick	Caro	111.0	134	47	18	48	88	3.81	6	6	10.86	1.46	3.89	7.14	1.41
1995 Bowie	East	32.7	43	27	4	32	20	7.44	1	3	11.85	1.10	8.82	5.51	-.37
1996 Bowie	East	113.7	137	51	8	46	65	4.04	6	7	10.85	.63	3.64	5.15	.80
1996 Rochester	Inter	42.0	50	21	7	23	33	4.50	2	3	10.71	1.50	4.93	7.07	1.12
1996 Philadelphia	NL	15.0	13	5	1	5	10	3.00	1	1	7.80	.60	3.00	6.00	1.25

Combined ERA can be obtained from the translated earned runs and innings pitched. The "Win" and "Loss" column are derived from how much the pitcher worked (for decisions) and assumes average offensive support.

"KW" is a scale combining the player's ability to get strikeouts and avoid giving up walks. It is two times the strikeout rate, divided by league average strikeouts (6.00), minus walks divided by average walks (4.00). A league average pitcher scores 1.00; generally speaking, the higher the better. Other researchers have noted a fair correlation between this measure and future success; i.e., a pitcher with a good KW score is more likely to improve than a pitcher with a bad score.

Vladimir Projections

The projections in this book are radically different from those you'll find in other sources. For the most part, the numbers may be fairly similar to other works in most cases, but the method behind the projections is very different. The projection system we use in *Baseball Prospectus* is called the Vladimir Performance Projection system. The system is only for hitters at this point in time, but we are working on a system for pitcher projections that's accurate enough to publish. We're not there yet. In terms of projecting performance for pitchers, you might as well throw a few puppy entrails around and have a toothless Jim Nabors interpret them beneath the light of a gibbous moon. (Actually, you're best off betting on pitchers with good K rates and K/BB ratios to have continued success, as a general rule.)

How are the Vladimir projections different? Well, the long answer to that is extremely boring, so I'll try to do it in a way that won't send you screaming for a Danielle Steele novel. Most projection systems are based on a relatively simple statistical progression called linear regression. A player's past performance provides a pretty good line on which to base the next year's projected performance; players are generally projected to have a year in line with their past performance, adjusted to a "normal" career path, which is roughly a bell curve with the peak around ages 25-28. The Vladimir system is radically different in structure and execution.

The Vladimir system uses two tools in tandem to project hitter performance: A logic tree and a series of 26 neural nets. A neural net, simply put, is a tool designed to emulate the workings of the human brain. Nets are trained using series of the appropriate data, and weights are assigned to different data inputs according to frequency of resulting outputs. That's not a perfect definition, and it's not perfectly accurate technically, but it does give you an idea of what's going on within the system. Basically, we train the nets using historical performances of ballplayers with certain characteristics in their performances. Then, using a logic tree, players' histories are routed to the appropriate net. The player's career data is run through the net, and the system kicks out a projection of their next season. That's pretty simplified, but this isn't a book about neural nets or modeling. If you really want to learn a lot about Neural Nets, get on the World Wide Web or go to your local library and check around. There are some very good resources available.

Why should you care? The Vladimir system has roughly the same mean squared error as most of the other systems out there, but has a greater variance in its projections than any other published system. What does that mean? It means Vladimir was designed to look for players who are good candidates to break out or to completely collapse. Vladimir has projected the breakout seasons of John Olerud, Jeff Bagwell, Craig Biggio, Todd Hundley and many others. It's also missed quite a few. But by and large, it takes more chances than any other system, and still comes out with about the same error rate as other systems that basically just project an average. And isn't that why you project performances? Hell, every GM and fantasy player has a pretty good idea what most players are going to do during the season. Vladimir will point you in the direction of those players that are good candidates to deviate significantly from a typical career path. And that's where you want to be—making good gambles and letting others overpay for consistency.

Why are Vladimir's projections so high? One reason: we've benchmarked Vladimir's projections to the 1996 American League. Each year, we have to determine what baseline we want to use for projections and performances, because without context, statistics mean nothing and analysis means less. In 1988, Jose Canseco was the runaway AL MVP with a .307/.391/.569 performance while playing half his games in a fantastic pitcher's park. In 1996, that performance wouldn't have raised an eyebrow. The overall level of offense has been bouncing around like Howie Mandel on crack for the past ten years, and we have to choose a context in which to present our work, or else its value to you is greatly reduced. We've decided on the 1996 AL for this year; in addition to being recent, it allows you to see exactly how large the increase has been. In 1996, the AL hit .277/.350/.445. To give you some idea of how high that is, Joe Carter has never approached that OBP in any year, and his combined career OBP and SLG are lower than the AL as a whole in 1996.

Does Vladimir really expect Adrian Beltre to get 600 PA? Not necessarily. Predicting playing time is definitely more art than science. It is projected based on the idea of merit, and as those of you who have seen Kim Batiste disgracing a major league field are well aware, MLB is not a strict meritocracy. The projections presented are for the major league level, and adjusted for the park of the major league affiliate. If Vladimir projects Ben Grieve to hit .280/.360/.430, he may have to hit .330/.410/.600 at Edmonton in order to actually match the projection. In 1995, Vladimir told Lou Piniella that running Felix Fermin and Luis Sojo out to shortstop every day would cost his team the pennant. But Vladimir can't force managers and GMs to award playing time.

Why doesn't Vladimir project RBI? Simple. RBI aren't an individual performance metric—at least not a good one. RBI correlate better with the OBP of the two hitters before a hitter in the lineup than with any statistic of that hitter. If you want to have a good idea of how many runs someone is going to drive in, do this simple exercise: project how many total bases a hitter will have, multiply that number by the average OBP of the two hitters likely to precede him in the lineup, and add half their projected home runs. If Edgar Martinez is projected to have 280 total bases with 25 HR, and Ken Griffey and Alex Rodriguez are projected to have an aggregate .420 OBP, that comes to about 130 RBI. This assumes a full season and it's pretty crude, but it's fairly accurate, and face it—it's just kind of fun to speculate like that.

And that's why this book, and the Vladimir performance projection system, exists. We take it very seriously and will constantly try to improve it, but the bottom line is that it's fun, and it's right more often than my unaided guesses. We try to be honest—even when we know a projection is way off the mark we run it, unlike others in the field. Take them with a grain of salt, and expect a few misses, but by and large, I honestly believe this is the best system for projecting player performance out there, despite its delusions over the value of Andy Van Slyke.

How to Use This Book for Rotisserie

If you're reading this book for rotisserie purposes, you're either familiar with our methods and tools, or you're new to the *BP* way and are hoping that a hard analytical look at baseball will help your rotisserie team indirectly. This section of the book is targeted primarily to members of the latter group.

For those who've never seen a DT or a Vlad before, you might want to read this section before diving in. Some of the numbers you'll see later on in the book will require that you look at them with different eyes before digesting them. Clay and Gary have included more detailed description of the DTs and the Vlads, which I strongly recommend you read, but here's the quick 'n' dirty description.

Each player has DTs, or Davenport Translations, for the past four seasons. DTs are not real stats. To get at the essence of the player's performance, Clay adjusts their actual stats to remove exogenous effects, including ballpark, league and year effects. For example, Dodger Stadium deflates offensive output by around 20% relative to the norm. Any Dodger pitchers' stats must be adjusted to reflect the fact that they pitch in a very favorable stadium. Similar effects include higher offense in the AL vs. the NL, and increased offense in both leagues over the past three seasons.

In addition to the DTs, hitter entries also include a 1997 line. This line projects the player's 1997 stat line, should he play in the majors. Vlad, a proprietary neural-net forecasting tool, takes the DTs, the player's age, trend and other variables to produce a statistical forecast that is then adjusted to reflect ballpark and league effects. The 1997 projections assume the inflated offensive levels of the past few years will continue.

Furthermore, the commentary herein is written from a "real," not rotisserie, baseball perspective. At this point, Brian L. Hunter is not a good baseball player. However, as long as he can hit .280-.300 and steal 30-40 bases, he's a valuable player in rotisserie/fantasy leagues that use batting average and stolen bases. (He's a lot less valuable in OBA leagues and net stolen base leagues, but that's another story.) Thus, you need to read player comments with different lenses. Player comments shouldn't be looked at in a vacuum; a lousy hitter who'll steal 20 bases has value, and the only way he won't achieve that value is if he's so bad that he loses his job (cf. Coleman, Vince).

Trendspotting

With apologies to Spud et al, trendspotting is the term I use to describe how to look at a player's adjusted stats over four years and quickly determine whether or not the boy is going anywhere. The central tenet of trendspotting is that a

player's adjusted stats should increase as he climbs the minor league ladder. That's not as obvious a point as it seems. If you look at unadjusted stats, it may look like a pitcher who was awesome in the Southern League suddenly lost it when he moved up to the Pacific Coast League. As you may already know, the PCL is a terrific hitter's league, and pitchers who post ERAs below 4.00 there are the equivalent of 1994-95 vintage Greg Maddux. Once Clay has had his way with the stats, any outside factors disappear, allowing us to compare performances in the PCL and the Texas League (huge hitter's leagues) with performances in the International and Midwest Leagues (strong pitcher's leagues).

When examining veteran major leaguers' stats, remember that hitters that have steadily improved their EqAs and pitchers that have steadily improved their adjusted ERAs are still developing and should see further improvement, particularly if they're still young. I use the word "steadily" because many sudden improvements in adjusted stats are simply fluke years, like Travis Fryman's 1993 EqA of .303, 39 points above his second-best showing.

You can evaluate minor league prospects similarly. Players who move up a level should at least be able to hold their EqA or ERA; if those stats fall as the parent club promotes the player, then he's probably overmatched at the higher level. Players who move up a level and increase their EqA/ERA are keepers. Players who repeat levels, which isn't always their fault (who did Dave Hajek have to pay to get moved up to Houston?), must see increases in their EqA or they'll be doomed to a lifetime in the Peorias and Paducahs of the world.

Exhibit A: Future Hall of Famer Andruw Jones.

Year	Team	Lge	AB	H	DB	TP	HR	BA	OBA	SA	EQA
1995	Macon	S Atl	566	151	20	2	22	.267	.334	.426	.258
1996	Durham	Caro	251	72	6	1	13	.287	.374	.474	.283
1996	Grnvl	South	160	56	7	1	10	.350	.402	.594	.324
1996	Atlanta	NL	107	24	6	1	5	.224	.278	.439	.240

The 19-year-old darling of World Series Game 1 had a pretty impressive run through A ball and AA. After a phenomenal season as an 18-year-old in the slowest A league, the South Atlantic, he battered pitchers in the fast-A Carolina League and demolished the AA Southern League. (For comparison's sake, Chipper Jones' EqA for 1996 was .315, and Marquis Grissom's was .313.) Those increasing EqAs are about as good a sign of future stardom as you'll ever find. However, the sudden drop in EqA during his short trial in Atlanta indicates that he needs to make some adjustments before he'll develop into the .330/40-45 HR hitter we all believe he'll become. If anyone can do it, Andruw can, but Vlad has him at a very respectable .288/34 HR for 1997.

You can make some back-of-the-envelope adjustments if you're looking at midseason stats. First of all, players who move up a level and produce the same unadjusted results are, in general, improving their overall game. This is subject to park and league adjustments, so awareness of the tendencies of the AA and AAA leagues is useful as well.

A Note on Park Effects

More than one rotisserie player has asked proponents of park adjustments why s/he should care about park effects. After all, Dante Bichette may really be a bad hitter, but as long as he's in Colorado who cares? However, roto players should always be aware of the difference between ability and ballpark effects because players change teams so frequently.

Albert Belle appears Florida-bound as I write this. He beat the tar out of the ball in Jacobs Field, but, if he goes to Florida, he's moving to a lower-offense league and a park that suppressed home run production by roughly 5% versus the Jake. That's about three fewer homers and probably 10-15 fewer RBI before you consider the likelihood of runners actually being on base in Miami.

Players of Belle's roto stature don't change teams all that often, but plenty of starting hitters and pitchers move around like mercenaries (David Cone and David Wells come to mind). If you want to know what Bichette might hit if the Rockies do indeed trade him to make room for the kids they've got bubbling up, you need to understand park effects.

Lies, Damn Lies and RBI/Wins/Saves

Nearly every forecaster out there will dutifully provide you with forecast lines for the three horribly misleading statistics that most rotisserie leagues use: runs batted in, pitchers' wins and saves. You'll notice that Vlad doesn't forecast RBI, Clay doesn't even bother adjusting saves and we've got some severely adjusted won-loss records in the SNWL section. We spend less time on these stats because forecasts and adjustments on them aren't worth a sack of olestra. In fact, those stats, which led the BBWAA voters to rob Alex Rodriguez and Kevin Brown of the awards they clearly deserved, are in many cases completely misleading.

Joe Carter has 1280 RBI, ranking him fifth among players active in 1996, behind three sure Hall of Famers (Murray, Ripken and Dawson) and Harold Baines. He's knocked in 100 or more runs in seven of the last eight seasons and nine of the twelve full seasons he's been in the majors. Many, if not most, casual observers will talk about Joe Carter as a likely Hall of Famer. Many people also thought Bob Dole was young enough to be our President. Joe Carter is .261/.308/.470 on his career and has hit above .271 exactly

once (.302 in 1986, when he peaked a year early at age 26). He walked fewer times in 486 games in 1989-1991 than Barry Bonds did in 158 games last year. If Dante Bichette is the poster boy for park effects, Joe Carter is the poster boy for RBI. Not only is he not a Hall of Famer, he's not even a good player, and hasn't been in about a decade. That he has two rings and Fred McGriff only one is just an unfortunate coincidence.

Of course, Carter did get those RBI, and whether he got them by hook or by crook they still matter to your roto team. So how can you plan ahead in the RBI categories? By examining two factors: the player's slugging average, and the on-base percentages of anyone likely to be hitting in the four spots ahead of him in the lineup. When Roberto Alomar posted OBPs of .406, .408 and .386 in 1992-1994, Carter knocked in 119, 121 and 103 runs. When Alomar sunk to .354 in 1995, meaning he reached base roughly 25 fewer times over the full season, Carter's RBI total slumped to 76. That's not a full explanation, but it's not a coincidence.

Wins and saves are similarly fickle categories, but are a bit tougher to predict. Pitchers who win consistently benefit from three factors: good run support, good bullpens and their own ability. Pitchers like Kevin Brown, who was the best starter in baseball last year but received no run support and had a shoddy relief corps (except Robb Nen) to back him up, will have a lower ceiling on how many games they can win than Andy Pettitte or John Smoltz. There's still a tremendous amount of volatility in won/lost records—some pitchers do seem, anecdotally, to "pitch well enough to lose" with alarming frequency—but this strategy is the most solid I've seen.

As for saves, if you ignore the conventional wisdom you're miles ahead of the game. People will argue 'til they're blue in the face that closers for bad teams will get fewer save opportunities and thus fewer saves. That is, of course, about as smart as claiming you can lower taxes and balance the budget without touching spending. In 1996, the r-squared for the bivariate regression of winning percentage against team saves was 14%, but neither the intercept nor the regression coefficient pass the 95% confidence test. So don't waste your time chasing closers on good teams; focus on good closers, guys who show good control and low H/IP ratios. Personally, I chase closers who strike out a high percentage of hitters; while I believe this an excellent indicator of the closer's ability, particularly when combined with a high K/BB ratio, there is some interference in any analysis of the data. Every major league manager has been brought up to believe that closers should be guys who throw hard and get lots of strikeouts, so we haven't really had a recent example of a Maddux/Brown-type closer who gets most of his outs on ground balls.

The Rotisserie Year in Review

Into Your Arms

As if rotisserie baseball wasn't hard enough, even ordinarily reliable pitchers have been blowing up recently. Jose Rijo's fantastic voyage ended last year, and we won't see him again until 1998, if at all. Doug Drabek went into the toilet, although he did have the courtesy to win for me on my wedding day in '95, two weeks before I cut his sorry ass and his 5-plus ERA. But the latest moan emanating from the ranks of rotisserie players is the dearth of pitching. As evidence, they point to the inflated offense of the last three years.

What this entire argument fails to capture is one simple fact. In rotisserie, you are not competing against some predetermined threshold of "good," such as the nearly-extinct sub-3.00 ERA. If everyone else's team ERA is above 4.00 and you finish at 3.99, you win the category. It's simple and obvious, but not everyone has caught on yet.

The inflated offense and consequent rise in starters' ERAs have had a major impact on roto strategies: all of a sudden, middle relievers are moving up the chart of pitchers' dollar values. The "all-reliever" strategy, raised to legendary status by Dan Okrent, who earned a 10 for concept but a 3 for execution, has now gained significant value in a hybrid form. Several pre-season publications advocated a 3-and-6 rule: buy three quality, reliable starters; two closers; and four cheap ($1-2) relievers. If you couldn't get two closers, then stock up on quality setup men like Dave Veres, Julian Tavarez and Todd Jones, who would all pick up a few saves while adding 80-110 low-damage innings. In leagues where most teams carry five starters, a 3-and-6 strategist will punt wins but finish in the top 2-3 in saves, ERA and Ratio.

What the pundits didn't warn you about was who to pick as your relievers. The three setup men I named above are all extreme examples of a dangerous trend: the overworked middle reliever. Veres and Jones had never worked 100 innings in a season before, even in the minors. The sudden increase in workload—in this case, at the hands of the now-deposed Terry Collins—probably damaged their arms, and both missed significant time in '96 with injuries. When they pitched they were lousy, although Jones at least picked up 17 saves for owners who stuck with him.

So who's safe these days? Try to fill out your staffs with 40-60 IP guys, such as lefties who only face a few batters at a time (Fossas '95, Guthrie '96), or go with converted starters. Guys who started successfully in the minors and then serve in middle relief when they come up often record strong seasons, such as Hampton '94, Tavarez '95 and Lieber '96, who made a somewhat successful move to the rotation. Ugueth Urbina's value may shoot up due to rumors he'll close now that Rojas has left, and he's probably best suited

for the rotation, but he'll be a solid roto contributor in middle relief this year: he throws hard, has good control and nasty breaking stuff.

As for the small class of truly reliable starters, read on. The pitchers we like in baseball terms will also be solid rotisserie players, especially in ERA and Ratio. (Check out the adjusted K/IP numbers if your league uses strikeouts.)

Down in Flames

The 1996 season had perhaps the lowest real-life closer turnover in rotisserie history. Not only did 17 teams effectively have one closer all season long, but the teams that did change closers wound up with fewer saves, although there's certainly a correlation between the two facts. Four of the bottom five NL teams in saves changed closers: Colorado, Houston, Pittsburgh and the Cubs; similarly, the five AL teams who had closer battles (excluding the Angels, whose transition was inevitable) finished at the bottom in saves: Detroit, Oakland, Minnesota, Seattle and Toronto, whose spring training battle resulted in the very fortunate selection of Mike Timlin.

Unfortunately, major league managers have been completely brainwashed by the save statistic, an accounting anomaly rivaled only by the RBI and the pitcher's win for duplicity. Pitchers who rack up saves in bunches like John Wetteland earn the raves and the dollars even when they're not pitching particularly well. (How many times did you see Wetteland come in with a two- or three-run lead, give up a run, and earn the save? As Chris would say, "Bah!") Thus, organizations are now starting to groom closers-of-the-future like Terry Adams and T.J. Mathews, who may soon be supplanted by Steve Rain and Eric Ludwick, respectively. These teams would be better off breeding quality starters, but that's another story.

A few years back, we saw significant flux in the 12-to-15 or so teams that lacked closers, but now we're only seeing closer battles on a handful of weak teams. The outlook is similarly bleak. Three teams that might have had new closers in '97—the Mets, Dodgers and Cardinals—all re-signed the aging pieces of olestra currently filling the role for at least one more year, with Franco getting two years above Bobby Valentine's objections. Only three NL teams have serious closer question marks heading into 1997: the Astros, who suffer from a surfeit of candidates; the Pirates, who are currently considering the Natural Law Party's candidates; and the Expos, who will be without Mel Rojas. The San Francisco job will open up if Rod Beck is dealt. In the AL, the A's and Rangers are wide open, particularly since the Rangers let Mike Henneman go. The Royals will probably go with Jamie Bluma and/or Rick Huisman if Jeff Montgomery can't come back. The Yankees technically have no closer because Wetteland chose free agency over his $4 million option, and

Trader Dan Duquette and the Red Sox would dearly love to replace the hair-greying Heathcliff Slocumb with any of the former Expos on the market. That's about it.

The rotisserie ramifications are fairly simple. First of all, established closers will continue to command premium prices in auctions and trades, and may even see their prices go up unless several owners decide to punt the category entirely as a fiscal strategy. Second, middle relievers who pick up 5-10 saves are suddenly a lot more valuable. Focus on possible three-inning guys like Shaw or Terry Mathews, 8th-inning men like Jay Powell (who often come into save situations in the 8th, then finish the game if their team expands their lead), or every decent reliever in unsettled pens. In fact, the idiotic strategy of switching guys from the rotation to the bullpen and back seems to be back in vogue, as Dan Miceli, Francisco Cordova and Jon Ericks were all shuffled around Three Rivers in a quest for a closer. Touted starters who stink in the rotation could always be tried out in someone's pen. For example, in the unlikely event that the Reds move Jeff Brantley for any reason, Dave Burba could easily fill the job. Thinking ahead could nab you a few extra saves along the way.

Anna is a Speed Freak

The preseason pundits all predicted one trend correctly: speed shifted to the National League this year, with NL base-stealers grabbing more than 20% more bases than their AL counterparts. If you play in an AL-only league, they said, bid it up for Lofton and Goodwin, or face the consequences with Robertobobby Kelly and Keith Lockhart. Conversely, why bid yourself into oblivion on Vince Coleman when Al Martin and James Mouton would hang around a while longer?

In fact, the American League's stolen base dearth was compounded by a tremendous concentration at the top of the stolen base list. One out of every ten AL thefts had either Lofton or Goodwin as the perpetrator, and one of every five came from Lofton, Goodwin, Nixon, Knoblauch or Vizquel. To reach comparable percentages in the NL, you'd have to run your lists to four and eight players, respectively.

So where was the smart money in the NL? Focusing on Bagwell instead of Coleman? Well, yes and no. Coleman turned out to be a dud when the Reds figured out what we figured out a long time ago: Coleman can't steal first base, and really hasn't figured out any other way to get there. But the smart money in the National League was actually on the 20-25 SB/year guys, allowing their owners to take advantage of the tightly packed NL stolen base leader board.

The flaw in most preseason predictions about the abundance of stolen bases in the National League relies on a quick 'n' dirty scan of the prior year's top five-to-ten basestealers, plus the influx from the AL and/or the minors. You'll hear the same observation in retrospectives. But in rotisserie leagues with parity, categories are usually won by the less glamorous players, and that held particularly true in rotisserie leagues that used the National League, where stolen bases were–get this–more scarce than they were in AL-based leagues.

Witness:

American League		National League	
% of players	% of SB	% of players	% of SB
5%	36%	5%	33%
10%	53%	10%	54%
15%	65%	15%	69%
20%	73%	20%	78%
25%	80%	25%	85%

In business, the old adage is that twenty percent of your customers will provide 80% of your revenue. When they provide less, you're not getting enough revenue from your top customers—not enough concentration. Here we see that the National League, not the American, is more concentrated at every level after the 10% (31 or so players) mark. So once the top 64 basestealers were gone in 12-team NL leagues—only five or six per team—the stolen base category was largely decided, particularly since those players are rarely perfectly distributed.

The successful strategy for capturing stolen bases in a concentrated environment focuses on the large group of second-tier players, which in the 1996 NL roughly comprises those who fell between 15 and 30 steals. Only fourteen players topped 30 steals, while 27 players grabbed less than 30 but more than 15. Some were shockers—I doubt anyone drafted Luis Castillo, and if you did, shame on you for ignoring his '95 slugging average—but most were predictable regulars, bit players or touts: Mouton, Cangelosi, Morandini, Benard, Lansing, Devon White, Hollandsworth, Garcia, Owens, Curtis Goodwin and McCracken filled in the cracks between Grissom, Sanders, Jordan, Sosa and Bagwell.

The beauty of John Cangelosi is that he walks. Throughout this book, you'll notice a general reverence for hitters who control the strike zone. This is largely because hitters with poor plate discipline in the minors or in the early parts of their major league careers tend not to enjoy great success in the majors. A secondary benefit is that speedy bit players who draw a lot of walks can reach double digits in steals because they're on base more, yet they don't make you suffer through 500 at bats of .230 average. When the draft/auction hits the $1-2 range, these are the guys to target.

--Keith Law

1996: The Year in Review

The first full 162-game season in three years certainly proved to be a memorable one. We had the stretch runs in both wild card races, two shortstops who became the two best players in baseball, some dominant individual pitching performances, a number of ugly incidents involving players and umpires and the incredible story of the World Champion New York Yankees. But any analysis of the 1996 baseball season has to start in one place: beyond the outfield wall.

Offense

Unless you lived under a rock for the past 10 months, you probably noticed a dramatic surge in power production from major league hitters, even when compared to the relatively high-offense 1995 season. Despite the inevitable decline of mediot favorites like Henry Rodriguez and Kevin Elster, the season did, on the whole, produce an astounding number of high home run totals and shattered ERAs.

On the offensive side, the most notable aspect might have been the number of players who passed certain thresholds. Two players (Mark McGwire and Brady Anderson) reached the 50-homer mark; for comparison's sake, only two players had done that in the prior 15 full seasons. Seventeen players (eight in each league plus Greg Vaughn) hit 40 or more homers, including ten first-timers: Greg and Mo Vaughn, Brady Anderson, Andres Galarraga, Todd Hundley, Ellis Burks, Ken Caminiti, Sammy Sosa, Gary Sheffield and Vinny Castilla. And forty-three players topped the thirty-homer mark, representing nearly 7% of all players who appeared in the majors this year.

In fact, despite missing the first 30 games of the season, McGwire led the majors with 52 homers while flirting with an astounding .500 OBA and .800 SLG well into August. (He finished at .312/.467/.730, leading the majors in the latter two categories.) He wound up with one home run every eight at bats, and one every 10.5 plate appearances.

Of course, when the hitters are shining, the pitchers are fading. Only six pitchers (of those with at least 162 IP) posted ERAs below 3.00, and only half of those came in below 2.90. Juan Guzman's AL-leading 2.93 ERA was the worst to lead either league in 14 years. The AL average team ERA was 4.99 and no AL team posted an ERA under 4.3.

Comebacks

While 1996 will probably be remembered for the offensive explosion that has caused GMs to suggest raising the pitcher's mound, we'd do well to remember some truly remarkable comebacks.

The comebacks that get the most attention were comebacks from medical traumas. Brett Butler, one of the classiest men in baseball (the Mike Busch incident notwithstanding) and perhaps the most underappreciated player of the late '80s and early '90s, struggled through the first six weeks of the season before discovering that his tonsillitis was actually throat cancer. He vowed he'd return, even though all of his doctors claimed it was extremely unlikely. In an ending that could only have come out of Hollywood, Brett returned to the Dodgers' lineup in September and two days later received a well-deserved standing ovation at the Emmy Awards. Butler's comeback ended shortly thereafter with a broken hand, and, at this writing, it is unknown whether or not he will return in 1997. Should he retire as a player, he should be regarded as a top managerial candidate, if only because of his familiarity with the strike zone.

David Cone's odyssey, while just as scary from a medical perspective, ending a bit more happily. Cone, felled by an aneurysm in early May that looked certain to keep him off the mound for the season if not forever, returned to the floundering Yankees in early September and promptly pitched seven no-hit innings in Oakland before a very wise Joe Torre removed him before he threw 80 pitches. Mariano Rivera surrendered the no-hitter in the ninth, but the Yankee victory appeared to give the team just enough life to cling to their division lead over Baltimore. Cone came through yet again in October, providing the first decent performance by a Yankee starter in the World Series and helping the team take Game 3.

However, a few other comebacks that weren't as media-worthy merit recognition. Eric Davis, the man many compared to Willie Mays in the mid-to-late '80s, was plagued by injuries that forced him out of baseball after four seasons (1991-1994) below .237/.319/.415. (Of course, I owned him in 1991-92 fantasy leagues. That might explain everything.) He appeared in only 37 games with Detroit in 1994, and decided to take his aching neck home and call it a career. However, the 18 months or so of rest let Davis show us one more tantalizing glimpse of what might have been. His unadjusted .287/.394/.523 was arguably the second-best season of his career, behind his 1987 rabbit-ball-induced .293/.399/.593 and slightly ahead of his age-27 1989 campaign of .281/.367/.541. He walked 70 times last year, the second-highest total of his career. In fact, the only thing he did wrong all year was play too well: the Reds are saying they can't afford to bring the free-agent outfielder back in 1997.

A pair of apparently washed-up pitchers came back to the National League and produced impressive runs. Danny Darwin posted unadjusted ERAs of 6.30 and 7.45 in 1994-1995, and a spring training invitation by the Pirates in 1996 appeared to be a sign of the Pirates' desperation. Darwin responded with his best pitching since he left Houston after 1990 by posting a 3.02 ERA in 122.1 innings with the Pirates, who promptly did the smart thing and traded him for a marginal prospect. With Houston, Darwin moved back to the bullpen and looked more like the pitcher we saw in the prior two years, surrendering seven homers in 42.1 innings (compared to nine in Pittsburgh) with a 5.95 ERA.

Andy Benes was washed up at 28. His ERA had climbed every year for four straight seasons, and his 7-2 record during Seattle's amazing stretch run in 1995 masked his putrid 5.86 ERA. His arm was still considered a plus, but he was clearly on his way to the junk pile of failed #1 picks, pitching in the Northern League with Tyler Houston behind the plate and Jeff Jackson on deck. Benes picked up where he left off to start 1996, falling to an ugly 1-7 mark before he started his run. Thanks to some generous run support but also to improved performance, Benes went 17-3 to finish the season, lowering his ERA over two runs to 3.83. That doesn't justify the Cy Young votes he got, but Benes pitched as well as he had since 1990, and finally broke the whammy of the 15-win ceiling that threatened to follow him and John Smoltz to their graves.

The final comebackers I'll mention are the subjects of a tell-all book which I won't deign to name, but I think Dwight Gooden and Darryl Strawberry have to feel pretty good about how far back they came from the gutter of alcohol and drug abuse. Gooden's no-hitter, while not really a well-pitched game (he walked six), was an emotional highlight for his legions of fans in the Big Apple, and Darryl's spurts of power, including a bottom-of-the-ninth game-winner off Jeff Montgomery to snatch a victory from Kevin Appier, provided highlight film fodder that his unimpressive numbers wouldn't indicate. I'm not sanguine about their prospects for the future, but as a Yankee fan, I'd just like tell Darryl and Dwight, "Welcome back."

Up the Middle

Last year, we told you Barry Larkin was the best player in baseball. He was so overjoyed that he promptly went out and scored the first 30 HR/30 SB season ever by a shortstop (and only the second by an infielder). But speaking strictly of the 1996 season, Larkin wasn't even the best shortstop in baseball; that title went to the 20-year-old wunderkind (and real MVP) of Seattle, Alex Rodriguez. Two other middle infielders, Roberto Alomar and Chuck Knoblauch, had outstanding seasons as well.

These four players ranked 8th, 15th, 17th and 20th overall in EqA among players with at least 300 at bats (adjusted). Why is that remarkable? Because they play in the middle infield, an area of the diamond traditionally lacking in offensive content.

While four out of the top 20 players may not seem like a lot, since on average 25% of hitters are shortstops or second basemen, it is quite remarkable given the old baseball adage that the four players up the middle—middle infield, catcher and centerfield—should be fielders first, hitters second. In fact, all indications are that this trend is going to continue. Although such overachievers as Edgar Renteria and Mark Grudzielanek may come back down to earth a bit, they'll be joined by Derek Jeter, Royce Clayton (who'll be 27 next year), and the resurgent John Valentin and Craig Biggio in a growing cadre of strong hitters up the middle. And waiting in the wings are the talented Alex Gonzalez, whose role is uncertain with the Blue Jays' wholesale acquisition of the Pittsburgh Pirates, and Quilvio Veras, who is terribly underappreciated by the ordinarily level-headed Dave Dombrowski.

October and Everything After

Maybe it's just divine retribution for the agony of 1994, when the Yankees carried the best record into the strike and saw it go for naught. The Yanks were not the best team in the majors this season by any metric; they didn't have the best record, their starters were slightly above-average, and their hitters got on base at a good rate but hit for little power. You could only praise the bullpen as top-notch, and even that is a stretch: John Wetteland posted his worst season since 1992, and nearly put Joe Torre below Frank on the heart-transplant list; Jeff Nelson couldn't repeat his stellar 1995 season; and the Yankees ran an assortment of bodies through the rest of the pen (they threatened to call up Dave Eiland) before acquiring Graeme Lloyd, who went from goat to star in about eight weeks, thanks primarily to his ability to douse Ryan Klesko.

While the Yankees rolled on to the championship, a trio of other playoff teams were left to ponder their fates. Twenty percent of the Dodgers' playoff roster owns Rookie of the Year trophies (including Hollandsworth), but they remain a mediocre team. Without Butler in the lineup, the Dodgers have nobody to get on base for Piazza to drive in. The best pitchers in the majors can't win if the hitters don't score, and the Dodgers were predictably punished by a Braves team that was still not running on all cylinders.

Those same Braves have a different situation ahead of them. The new guard of stars, with Javy Lopez (26 in 1997), Ryan Klesko (26), Chipper Jones (25) and Andruw Jones (20) forming a frighteningly potent core to carry the team through the turn of the millenium. However, millions have already been committed in four-year deals for Marquis Grissom and Fred McGriff, who are both on the wrong side of 27. McGriff, in particular, is showing some real signs of decline, and should probably be moved to the first gullible GM who wanders by the office. In addition, Tom Glavine and Greg

Maddux will hit free agency next winter, and the fact that Schuerholz has decided to start negotiating an extension with Glavine instead of Maddux is a frightening sign. And rumors that Klesko may be moved to make room for Jermaine Dye may mean that the Braves won't shake their unfortunate reputation as losers, despite the well-deserved 1995 title.

The greatest turmoil lies on the shores of Lake Erie. Cleveland GM John Hart took advantage of an obviously drunk Joe McIlvaine to dump off an overpriced, out-of-shape Carlos Baerga for the underappreciated Jeff Kent and Jose Vizcaino, whom he recently turned into Matt Williams. (Imagine that: McIlvaine could have traded Kent, Vizcaino and Isringhausen for Matt Williams! Couldn't the Mets really use another potent bat in their lineup?) However, the fans went ballistic, since Baerga was a local favorite and very involved in the community. When the Indians didn't get out of the wild card round, falling in four games to Baltimore, mediots immediately began blaming the Baerga deal. While that's not terribly accurate—the pitching staff was woeful in the playoffs, and the Tribe avoided a sweep because Armando Benitez made a very bad decision that Albert Belle deposited in left field—media pressure can often cause smart GMs to do dumb things. Cleveland has already been active this off-season, and the best team in the AL merits very close attention.

And the MVP goes to...

No baseball season would be complete without a set of nonsensical postseason award selections to provide plenty of fodder for arguments to last us until pitchers and catchers report to Florida. Just when it looked like the mediots were heading for a successful balloting season, they went and screwed up one of the easiest awards of all.

Let's start with the Rookies of the Year. In the American League, it would have been nearly impossible for the mediots to screw it up. Derek Jeter posted an unadjusted .314/.370/.430 as a 22-year-old, and probably won over the last few skeptics with a hitting streak in the pressure of a pennant race. Jeter's unanimous selection was well-deserved. Mediots 1-0.

Unfortunately, in the National League, the voters couldn't have missed the mark by much more. Edgar Renteria and Todd Hollandsworth had roughly equal seasons offensively (.274 and .281 EqAs, respectively), but Renteria stole 16 of 18, controlled the strike zone better and provided solid defense at shortstop, which was actually his calling card from the minors. Hollandsworth, on the other hand, looked lost at times in left field; he didn't get to too many balls, and wasn't all that hot when he did get there. Jason Kendall's hitting was quite good for a rookie catcher straight out of AA, but his defense was really lacking. Renteria should have won. Mediots, 1-1.

The Cy Young awards should have been pretty clear-cut. Andy Pettite was widely considered the favorite in the American League on the strength of the oft-cited (but utterly meaningless) statistic that he was 13-3 after Yankee losses. Of course, that meant he was only 8-5 after Yankee wins, but no one liked to talk about that. More importantly, Pettite finished eighth in the league in ERA and gave up more than a hit an inning. Juan Guzman and Pat Hentgen both had better years, but wins count for a lot in Cy Young voting, and Guzman's injury knocked him out of the running. Hentgen put fewer guys on base and let fewer runners score in more innings. He's the right choice. Mediots, 2-1.

The National League Cy was so clear-cut, it's appalling that anyone could have gotten it wrong. Kevin Brown turned in one of the best pitching performances of the 1990s, posting a 1.89 ERA in a year when the league average was 4.21 and when the second-best NL ERA was 2.78 (Maddux). Unfortunately, the Marlins couldn't score a damn run for Brown, and he finished with a still-respectable but deceptive 17-11 record. The voters took one look at John Smoltz's 24 wins and that was it. Brown may never pitch that well again, and it'd be a damn shame if he retired without any hardware to commemorate his remarkable achievement. Mediots, 2-2.

Most Valuable Player awards seem to cause the most controversy. Is it for the best player, or just hitter? Or is it literally for the most valuable player? The value issue probably damaged Mike Piazza's hopes of an MVP award because he finally wore down in September, and the Dodgers faltered with him. Doesn't that prove that he was incredibly valuable to his team? Those who touted Ellis Burks, who probably had the best raw stats of any player in the NL this year, need a lesson in park effects. Barry Bonds' stats were impressive as always, but the highly-publicized chase for 40/40 cast his achievement in a slightly artificial light. Ken Caminiti posted an excellent season, certainly in league with the other candidates, but his success despite injury troubles and the now-famous Snickers incident pushed him over the top. I can't really argue with that. Mediots, 3-2.

Then the fun began. Alex Rodriguez, the barely-21 shortstop for Seattle who had one of the most impressive offensive seasons I've ever seen, was a shoo-in for the award as early as the All-Star break. His OPS was 1.045. It was the best season ever by a shortstop, and it was one of the best ever by a 20-year-old. But one damn voter, John Hickey, who won't be in my version of Profiles in Courage but would lead any copy of Profiles in Stupidity, listed A-Rod seventh on his ballot. No other voter had A-Rod lower than fourth. Juan Gonzalez, the Texas slugger whose season was superb but flatly inferior to Rodriguez', walked away with the award. Mediots, 3-3.

--Keith Law

Stop the Presses!

The essays and player comments in this book were submitted in early November, before most of the player movement had taken place. We have updated them as frequently and as thoroughly as possible during the editing and production stages, however it's possible some comments will be outdated by the time you read this.

In this section, we summarize the player movement from November through mid-December and look at its affect on the teams and players involved:

NL East: The Marlins improved their rotation by signing Alex Fernandez, a relative bargain, and acquiring hard-throwing Dustin Hermanson. However, throwing $25 million over five years to Moises Alou, who at age 31 isn't much better than Billy McMillon and is only likely to decline, was foolhardy. The Marlins do have several extraneous prospects (McMillon, Ralph Milliard) to trade in the spring or in July to fill any holes... The Braves haven't added or changed many players, but they did re-sign John Smoltz and extend Denny Neagle, both through 2000. Their next mission should be to dump Fred McGriff for something young, allowing Klesko and Andruw Jones to play every day, but at this writing the Crime Dog remains an overpaid Brave... The Expos created a huge hole in their rotation by dumping Jeff Fassero, but they may be reluctant to move Urbina back into a starting role with Rojas gone ... The Phillies pointelssly signed AARP members Rex Hudler, Mark Leiter and Mark Portugal to two-year deals; Portugal and Leiter could be blocking some decent pitching prospects as soon as September... The Mets extended Lance Johnson's contract. I'm guessing their division foes are not concerned.

NL Central: The Pirates deserve front-row status for some reasonably smart dumping. They traded overrated and perennially-injured Carlos Garcia and Orlando Merced (plus Dan Plesac) to Toronto for the Jays' entire AA roster, and then grabbed a few decent pitching prospects from Kansas City for Jeff King and Jay Bell. They could have probably gotten more for King, but these deals (plus the Neagle, Darwin and Hayes deals) lay an excellent foundation for a future division-winner... The Reds acquired Ruben Sierra for two no-name minor leaguers and enough cash to cover 80% of Sierra's salary. That's not necessarily a bad gamble, but if they're expected another Ron Gant or Eric Davis, they'll be disappointed. On the plus side, signing Kent Mercker, David Nied and Ricky Bones cheap is a smart move, as the odds are that one will get healthy and pitch well... The Astros traded their two worst hitters (Brian L. Hunter and Orlando Miller) and an overworked reliever (Todd Jones) to Detroit for some young pitching prospects. While Jose Lima, C.J. Nitkowski, and

Trever Miller haven't posted beautiful numbers, their peripherals are promising, they're all 24 and one or two should be useful major league pitchers... The Cardinals picked up Dennis Eckersley's option, and his ultimate collapse could happen at any minute. They also picked up options on Gaetti, Fossas and Honeycutt, and signed Delino (.224/.288/.298) DeShields. I'm not betting on a repeat... The Cubs have been pretty active, signing Mel Rojas for three years, Terry Mulholland for a yea, and Kevin Tapani for three. However, they lost Jaime Navarro, dumped their only third baseman who could hit (Leo Gomez) and re-signed Sandberg, McRae and Grace. Perhaps they'll get smart and swap their numerous left field prospects for something better than Ezra, but they're still just treading water.

NL West: The Dodgers, who have tried to convert Paul Konerko to third in the AFL this year, signed Todd Zeile to a three-year deal. Everyone who thinks he'll be something more than Tim Wallach, please raise your hand... The Padres have made a number of minor moves, swapping relievers around as if their well of arms constantly replenishes itself. However, one of those moves landed Quilvio Veras; if fully healthy, he should be one of the two or three best leadoff hitters in the NL... The Rockies have done little this offseason, other than sign Kirt Manwaring for an ungodly amount of money. He'll beat the tar out of the ball, collect some MVP votes, and the Rockies will finish in third... Why third? Ah, because of the Giants. First they trade Matt Williams for an excellent relief pitcher and two mediocre infielders; next they trade a so-so prospect for Mark Lewis, another mediocre infielder; then they trade a serviceable starter for J.T. Snow. Everyone out there who would trade a sack of olestra for J.T. Snow, please raise your hand.

AL East: The big movers and shakers have been fighting to spend each other into oblivion. The Yankees re-upped Joe Girardi for no apparent reason, then dealt Jimmy Leyritz to California for some shiny rocks. They lost out on Roger Clemens and John Wetteland and let Jimmy Key escape, replacing the latter two with the underrated David Wells and the overrated Mike Stanton. I'm not so sure the club isn't better off without Wetteland, who probably caused Frank Torre's heart problem in the first place, but I am sure they'll be better off if they can ditch Fielder and Hayes... The Orioles, desperately competing to stay in the race for Stupidest Offseason Move, threw $9 million over three years at Mike Bordick, who isn't a better fielder than Ripken and couldn't hit a wiffle ball 30 feet. They probably overpaid for Key, and certainly overpaid for the putrid Shawn Boskie, who should be making $4.75 an hour. They haven't addressed the catching problem, are subpar offensively at third and Brady Anderson will come back to earth. Gillick isn't done fouling things up yet... The Blue Jays traded half their farm system to Pittsburgh for two lousy hitters and an old reliever, then threw more money at Roger Clemens than anyone had ever thrown at a pitcher. Clemens is still a front-line pitcher, but he threw a lot of pitches last year (he topped 160 twice) and he'll be 38 when that contract is up. Toronto has improved its rotation as long as Clemens is healthy, but otherwise I don't think they're any better than they were last year... The Red Sox quietly consummated the long-rumored deal for pitcher Robinson Checo, but that means nothing in Red Sox nation, where citizens are splitting their ire between Clemens and Duquette. John Valentin will eventually be traded for pitching—if any is available... The Tigers are trying to keep their club OBP below the Giants', acquiring Brian (.297) Hunter, Orlando (.291) Miller, Matt (.252) Walbeck and Brian (.290) Johnson, while losing Frank Catalanatto, who projected to a .350+ OBP in the majors, in the Rule V draft. Todd Jones is a great pitcher if his arm stays attached; Dan Miceli is a hard thrower who had a hard time keeping the ball in Three Rivers; Willie Blair is a nice cog for the bullpen. The problem is that these guys will be entering games where the Tigers are losing 11-4.

AL Central: The White Sox signed Albert Belle and lost Alex Fernandez. In the short term, I'd rather have Belle, but that pitching hole is not even half-filled by Jaime Navarro... The Indians should be commended for not panicking this offseason, having re-upped Eric Plunk and signed Kevin Mitchell and Mike Jackson. However, who the heck is on second for the Tribe this year???... The Royals traded some better-than-marginal pitching prospects for Jay Bell and Jeff King. I'm not sure who in Kansas City thinks that they're in any position to be trading prospects, but I'll bet dimes to donuts they've had a lobotomy... The Twins didn't overpay for Tewksbury, and they paid less than market value for Terry Steinbach, who was coming off a career year. Bonus points for ditching Walbeck. They don't really have any gigantic holes, and with a few breaks they should contend in the Central this year... The Brewers have pretty much sat out the offseason.

AL West: Three cheers to Oakland for not overpaying for Steinbach (OK, maybe they tried to overpay, but at least it didn't work) and for grabbing Catalanatto in the Rule V draft. He could certainly start at second for them, with Batista keeping shortstop warm for Tejada for the next year or so. They lose points for not trading Brosius. They might still reacquire Canseco, but pitching is the real problem... The Mariners did very well to acquire Jeff Fassero, who (unlike Manto, Moyer and Mulholland) should be worth the prospects he cost. The left field hole will be filled by class-A Uberprospect Jose Cruz, Jr., so they hopefully won't be overpaying Mark Whiten for an unlikely repeat performance. If the Big Unit is healthy, the M's have to be the favorites... The Angels ditched J.T. Snow, and for that, they win a round of applause and a gold star. They cleared out Chili Davis as well, so now Darin Erstad can play in the majors, and they signed Dave Hollins. Then they inexplicably signed Eddie Murray, raising again the question of whether Erstad and Arias will play. They're not contenders, but they're showing signs of life... The Rangers addressed the bullpen weakness by signing John Wetteland. They also re-signed Mark McLemore for a lot of cash, and are threatening to do the same with Darryl Hamilton. They're probably not much better, and if they trade Darren Oliver, they could be a little worse.

Expansion teams: Both expansion teams went shopping this fall, and they snapped up the four 1996 first-round draft picks that were declared free agents on a technicality in July. Arizona shelled out a fortune for Travis Lee, the Golden Spikes-winning first baseman, who could potentially be a franchise player. The Diamondbacks also ponied up for Bobby Seay, while the Devil Rays signed John Patterson and Matt White. In light of the enormous risk involved in drafting high school pitchers, I'd sooner put the money in penny stocks—or into signing undrafted free agents.

Teams

Atlanta Braves

It took about ten minutes after Charlie Hayes squeezed the final out of the Series for the first talk radio imbecile to use the word "choke." The Braves didn't win the World Series, but they were once again the model franchise in major league baseball. Behind the pitching of Smoltz, Maddux, Glavine, et al, they were able to crank out a ho-hum 96 wins during the regular season, and slog into the final seven games. At this point, it's time to look to 1997 and beyond. No point in crying over Jeffrey Maier's team of destiny.

Are the Braves better off than they were a year ago? Not really. Atlanta fans should be fairly worried about the future, not so much because of a couple of late-season trades, but because of the lack of planning and foresight these trades demonstrate. For some reason known only to John Schuerholz' talking dog, the Braves brought back Terry Pendleton for the stretch run. Pendleton's older than Bob Hope, not as good a hitter and the left side of the infield is already populated by Blauser and Jones, two decent ballplayers, both of whom can outhit and out-field Terry Pendleton at either position. Pendleton doesn't push your club towards the postseason, he pushes it towards the offseason. He has no practical value; in fact, the opportunity cost of playing him is high enough so that you shouldn't take him if you get him for free.

Of course, the Braves didn't get him for free. They gave up Roosevelt Brown, a 20-year-old first base prospect who was hitting for power in Macon. He's not a blue chip prospect, but he's certainly worth more than the dessicated remains of Terry Pendleton, and he has the potential to be a major league power hitter.

No diagnosis went on here. For some reason, the Braves felt they needed something because something was wrong. When you go to a mechanic or doctor, do they just start ripping out parts or do they observe and test first? (Those of you who are with me in the FlatLine HMO need not comment here.) The Pendleton acquisition was pretty shortsighted and horrid. It pales in comparison, however, to the completely boneheaded trade for Denny Neagle.

The Braves extended Neagle's contract this winter, but at the time of the trade there was no guarantee they would do that. So let's look at what they dealt for. Neagle started six times for Atlanta down the stretch. He was signed for one more year. It has been proposed that he was acquired specifically to shut down left-handed bats in the playoffs. OK, let's assume that he'll start four times in the postseason, and that he'll pitch as expected. That's 45 games of Neagle over the

life of his contract, possibly 50. The Braves had reasonable pitching depth in the minors, and weren't in need of any more help in the rotation, so Neagle is addressing a problem that's insignificant at best. And what do they give up to get him? Jason Schmidt, a right-handed starter who's fully capable of pitching 200 quality innings in the major leagues as early as this year. They let Pittsburgh finish the Smiley/Neagle cycle. But that's not all. They also gave up Ron Wright, who is—and stop me if you've heard this—a power-hitting first base prospect. Wright, who is listed in the Pittsburgh section, slugged .600 in high A ball at the age of 20 and drew a bunch of walks. He's a genuine grade A prospect at first base.

For 50 games, tops, of Denny Neagle, who has a history of getting tired late in the year.

Does Schuerholz think that Fred McGriff's going to be productive into his mid-40s? How many first basemen with power is he going to ship off before he's done? Some have speculated that Dave Justice will play first in a couple of years when McGriff's pretty much done. Of course, Justice is no spring chicken himself, and his injury history certainly doesn't suggest someone with more longevity than, say, Alvin Davis. But enough of this depressing long-term gloom. What about 1997? What about the immediate future?

The immediate future is very bright. If you bought this book, you already know why. The Braves have the best prospect in 30 years, a young outfielder by the name of Andruw Jones. Jones is a good defensive center fielder, and he's probably one of the top five outfielders in baseball right now. A good comparison is probably Ken Griffey, Jr., but with more speed, more power and more defense. And he knows how to draw a walk.

The Atlanta rotation is still decent, and they have a lot of talent in the minors that could well turn out to be fantastic. Add in the impressive coaching staff and the first-class organization, and you've got a talented bunch of players firmly placed in an environment where they are expected and able to win. This is an organization that doesn't bend and turn on the whims of a tyrant owner or impetuous GM. The structure and organization is in place to support excellence, and in the short term they will be a great team.

There are some holes. Jeff Blauser has surprised everyone by being ineffectual, and the Braves still don't have a second baseman worth his salt. These are difficult holes to fill, but there are rumors of the Braves actually making a couple of minor deals to address these needs. An exceptionally strong pitching staff has made this organization grow complacent in terms of the offense it needs to win. Andruw Jones will improve it a great deal, but running Raffy Belliard and Mark Lemke out there has hamstrung the offense in the past, and they should be careful to avoid that in the future.

They're not the world champions, but they are, once again, the favorite to win the World Series this year. It's hard to argue with that much pitching. As this team moves into the egregiously-named Turner Park, they're in a good position to dominate the league again.

The Schuerholz/Cox/Mazzone triumvirate has been nothing short of outstanding, but most of the credit has been misplaced. Mazzone is nothing short of brilliant, and may be the most valuable person in all of baseball. He's managed to keep his pitchers excellent and healthy, and there's no one else in his job that's been able to do that. The farm system has, of late, been used primarily to develop trade currency. There's nothing wrong with that per se, but at some point you have to start producing quality and quantity. Andruw and Chipper Jones are both fantastic players, but the Braves don't have the depth anymore to throw away the likes of Roosevelt Brown for Terry Pendleton.

The Braves organization is run well, and if Schuerholz continues to step out of line, I expect his freedom of movement will be pretty quickly restricted. Ted Turner knows how to handle a leash. You may thank us for that visual later. "Let's play Barbarella again!"

DANNY BAUTISTA   **OF**   **1972**   **Age 25**

Year	Team	Lge	AB	H	DB	TP	HR	BB	SB	CS	OUT	BA	OBA	SA	EQA	EQR	Peak
1993	London	East	431	115	12	1	7	30	15	7	322	.267	.315	.348	.227	39	.254
1993	Detroit	AL	62	21	3	0	1	1	3	1	42	.339	.349	.435	.269	8	.300
1994	Toledo	Inter	99	24	5	0	2	6	2	2	77	.242	.286	.354	.211	8	.231
1994	Detroit	AL	99	23	4	1	4	3	1	2	78	.232	.255	.414	.215	8	.239
1995	Toledo	Inter	59	14	3	0	0	1	1	1	46	.237	.250	.288	.172	3	.187
1995	Detroit	AL	272	56	7	0	8	12	4	1	217	.206	.239	.320	.182	15	.197
1996	Detroit	AL	64	16	2	0	2	9	1	2	50	.250	.342	.375	.235	7	.253
1997	*Atlanta*	*NL*	*202*	*53*	*7*	*1*	*6*	*8*	*4*	*1*	*150*	*.262*	*.290*	*.396*	*.239*	*21*	

Paroled from Detroit to Atlanta, which is a good thing and a bad thing. Bautista went to a team that's good enough to realize he's worthless. No future, never was a prospect, and will be lucky to see the majors after 1997.

RAFAEL BELLIARD   **SS**   **1962**   **Age 35**

Year	Team	Lge	AB	H	DB	TP	HR	BB	SB	CS	OUT	BA	OBA	SA	EQA	EQR	Peak
1993	Atlanta	NL	80	19	4	0	0	5	0	0	61	.237	.282	.287	.187	5	.179
1994	Atlanta	NL	121	30	7	1	0	3	0	2	93	.248	.266	.322	.188	7	.178
1995	Atlanta	NL	181	40	1	1	0	8	2	2	143	.221	.254	.238	.150	6	.143
1996	Atlanta	NL	142	24	6	0	0	4	3	1	119	.169	.192	.211	.092	2	.082
1997	*Atlanta*	*NL*	*146*	*29*	*5*	*0*	*0*	*5*	*2*	*0*	*117*	*.199*	*.225*	*.233*	*.142*	*4*	

Defensive replacement nearing the end of the string. He's probably been the luckiest man in baseball over the past five years or so. Guys like Belliard are a dime a dozen, and that's only if you buy retail. Sure-handed fielder, but that won't be enough to keep him around much longer.

ESTEBAN BELTRE   **2B**   **1968**   **Age 29**

Year	Team	Lge	AB	H	DB	TP	HR	BB	SB	CS	OUT	BA	OBA	SA	EQA	EQR	Peak
1993	Nashville	AmA	494	141	21	3	8	37	16	4	357	.285	.335	.389	.249	55	.262
1994	Texas	AL	133	39	5	0	0	16	2	4	98	.293	.369	.331	.236	13	.244
1995	Texas	AL	92	20	9	0	0	4	0	0	72	.217	.250	.315	.182	5	.184
1996	Boston	AL	62	16	1	0	0	4	1	0	46	.258	.303	.274	.197	4	.198
1997	*Atlanta*	*NL*	*95*	*24*	*8*	*0*	*0*	*6*	*5*	*1*	*72*	*.253*	*.297*	*.337*	*.229*	*9*	

Generic backup utility infielder with a little speed. He'll bounce around from organization to organization at this point, trying to find a team with exactly the needs he can fill: pinch runner, occasional starter in the field.

JEFF BLAUSER   SS   **1966**   **Age 31**

Year	Team	Lge	AB	H	DB	TP	HR	BB	SB	CS	OUT	BA	OBA	SA	EQA	EQR	Peak
1993	Atlanta	NL	618	194	26	2	17	94	13	5	429	.314	.404	.445	.288	96	.295
1994	Atlanta	NL	386	102	21	3	7	43	1	3	287	.264	.338	.389	.243	42	.245
1995	Atlanta	NL	436	93	15	2	12	62	6	4	347	.213	.311	.339	.217	38	.215
1996	Atlanta	NL	271	68	14	1	10	42	5	0	203	.251	.351	.421	.261	35	.255
1997	*Atlanta*	*NL*	*260*	*66*	*13*	*1*	*9*	*32*	*8*	*2*	*196*	*.254*	*.336*	*.415*	*.262*	*34*	

Beavis' alter ego rebounded after two years of precipitous decline. Defense isn't bad enough to warrant the indignity of being subbed for by Raffy Belliard daily. His bat vanished after the age of 27, which happens more often than you'd think. Probably considered part of the problem at this point; Braves might be better served by putting Chipper back at shortstop.

JERMAINE DYE   RF   **1974**   **Age 23**

Year	Team	Lge	AB	H	DB	TP	HR	BB	SB	CS	OUT	BA	OBA	SA	EQA	EQR	Peak
1994	Macon	S Atl	530	151	18	1	15	30	10	5	384	.285	.323	.408	.246	58	.280
1995	Greenville	South	410	112	17	2	15	27	3	4	302	.273	.318	.434	.248	46	.278
1996	Richmond	Inter	143	33	4	1	6	6	2	0	110	.231	.262	.399	.220	12	.244
1996	Atlanta	NL	295	83	12	0	13	12	1	4	216	.281	.309	.454	.249	33	.275
1997	*Atlanta*	*NL*	*442*	*122*	*25*	*2*	*17*	*11*	*3*	*4*	*324*	*.276*	*.294*	*.457*	*.254*	*53*	

Grade B prospect. Walks approximately never, so even if he fulfills his potential he's not going really help a team. The most important thing a hitter can do is get on base, and Dye doesn't do that. Probably no more than about the sixth-best outfielder in the organization, if that. He's nothing more than a speed bump on the way to Andruw Jones. Will probably have a solid career as a marginal third outfielder, eventually serving time on someone's bench as a fourth outfielder.

OMAR GARCIA   1B   **1972**   **Age 25**

Year	Team	Lge	AB	H	DB	TP	HR	BB	SB	CS	OUT	BA	OBA	SA	EQA	EQR	Peak
1993	St. Lucie	Flor	503	155	15	3	6	51	13	4	352	.308	.372	.386	.262	62	.293
1994	Binghamton	East	254	85	11	2	5	21	2	2	171	.335	.385	.453	.282	36	.311
1994	Norfolk	Inter	234	58	9	2	0	19	5	3	179	.248	.304	.303	.205	17	.226
1995	Norfolk	Inter	442	136	21	4	4	25	3	2	308	.308	.345	.400	.253	49	.275
1996	Richmond	Inter	314	80	12	1	4	12	3	2	236	.255	.282	.338	.207	23	.221
1997	*Atlanta*	*NL*	*270*	*81*	*17*	*2*	*6*	*20*	*8*	*5*	*194*	*.300*	*.348*	*.444*	*.272*	*38*	

You watch this guy hit and wonder why he's not better. He'll have to get lucky to have a career now. It must be tough to be marginally talented in a great organization. Detroit mistook Danny Bautista for a prospect. Garcia needs to be a Cub.

TONY GRAFFANINO   2B   **1972**   **Age 25**

Year	Team	Lge	AB	H	DB	TP	HR	BB	SB	CS	OUT	BA	OBA	SA	EQA	EQR	Peak
1993	Durham	Caro	472	116	18	2	12	40	14	6	362	.246	.305	.369	.227	45	.255
1994	Greenville	South	459	136	22	1	9	50	16	4	327	.296	.365	.407	.266	59	.293
1995	Richmond	Inter	184	36	3	0	5	16	2	1	149	.196	.260	.293	.178	10	.193
1996	Richmond	Inter	361	101	25	1	7	35	8	4	264	.280	.343	.413	.255	43	.273
1996	Atlanta	NL	46	8	0	1	0	5	0	0	38	.174	.255	.217	.136	1	.149
1997	*Atlanta*	*NL*	*381*	*102*	*27*	*0*	*13*	*39*	*13*	*1*	*280*	*.268*	*.336*	*.441*	*.271*	*54*	

This is a good prospect. He hits fairly well, has a decent defensive rep and has consistently made the adjustments to move up. Why Atlanta insists on giving playing time to people like Lemke when they can run Graffanino out there is beyond me. He'll flirt with .300 for a couple of years in the majors, with some moderate power and a fair number of walks.

KEVIN GRIJAK   1B   **1971**   **Age 26**

Year	Team	Lge	AB	H	DB	TP	HR	BB	SB	CS	OUT	BA	OBA	SA	EQA	EQR	Peak
1993	Macon	S Atl	405	107	15	2	7	27	4	2	300	.264	.310	.363	.227	37	.250
1994	Durham	Caro	71	26	3	0	7	10	1	1	46	.366	.444	.704	.355	17	.386
1994	Greenville	South	356	93	11	1	11	23	1	1	264	.261	.306	.390	.232	34	.253
1995	Greenville	South	77	32	1	0	3	7	0	1	46	.416	.464	.545	.335	15	.359
1995	Richmond	Inter	323	101	14	2	14	27	1	2	224	.313	.366	.498	.284	48	.304
1997	*Atlanta*	*NL*	*496*	*143*	*25*	*1*	*30*	*31*	*0*	*1*	*354*	*.288*	*.330*	*.524*	*.285*	*77*	

Was reportedly going to be the "star scab" of 1995, despite his statements to the contrary. Of course, that's something like being the "hippest shriner." Shaky around the bag, but his power's for real. His top end could be one of the good low aver-age sluggers, and his low end is probably Kevin Maas or so. Will need to move on to have a career.

MARQUIS GRISSOM   **CF**   **1967**   **Age 30**

Year	Team	Lge	AB	H	DB	TP	HR	BB	SB	CS	OUT	BA	OBA	SA	EQA	EQR	Peak
1993	Montreal	NL	647	201	25	2	21	62	45	9	455	.311	.371	.453	.283	97	.294
1994	Montreal	NL	481	141	23	3	12	47	32	5	345	.293	.356	.428	.272	67	.278
1995	Atlanta	NL	557	145	22	2	13	54	23	8	420	.260	.326	.377	.240	59	.242
1996	Atlanta	NL	683	214	30	8	24	49	23	10	479	.313	.359	.486	.281	100	.279
1997	*Atlanta*	*NL*	*678*	*200*	*34*	*8*	*18*	*47*	*33*	*10*	*488*	*.295*	*.341*	*.448*	*.275*	*97*	

Valuable when he hits .300, and he did. He's not a real leadoff hitter; probably best suited to hit sixth or something. Consistently a very good defender, but Atlanta doesn't really have a need for him. I wouldn't put him on the field next year at the expense of Andruw Jones or David Justice. If it doesn't come down to that, I'd go ahead and run him out there. Not as much raw speed as people think, but takes a very good angle to the ball and knows how to run the bases well.

WES HELMS   **3B**   **1976**   **Age 21**

Year	Team	Lge	AB	H	DB	TP	HR	BB	SB	CS	OUT	BA	OBA	SA	EQA	EQR	Peak
1995	Macon	S Atl	562	138	13	1	11	41	1	1	425	.246	.297	.331	.209	43	.242
1996	Durham	Caro	260	74	8	1	10	11	1	0	186	.285	.314	.438	.251	29	.285
1996	Greenville	South	234	56	10	1	4	10	1	1	179	.239	.270	.342	.202	16	.229
1997	*Atlanta*	*NL*	*610*	*168*	*30*	*2*	*19*	*22*	*3*	*2*	*444*	*.275*	*.301*	*.425*	*.249*	*69*	

Has a bad case of Prospect disease: Hits well for the position he currently plays, but can't play it well enough to do so in the majors. As a third baseman, he hits well and projects to be darn good. Unfortunately, he fields the position about as well as Gimpy, the Diabetic Dwarf. Assuming he moves to first base, the lack of ability to get on base is enough to keep him from being a star. Young enough that he could learn to field. Will likely end up as an left fielder or first baseman.

DAMON HOLLINS   **OF**   **1974**   **Age 23**

Year	Team	Lge	AB	H	DB	TP	HR	BB	SB	CS	OUT	BA	OBA	SA	EQA	EQR	Peak
1994	Durham	Caro	496	122	15	0	17	38	7	4	378	.246	.300	.379	.226	46	.257
1995	Greenville	South	475	112	18	0	18	43	4	3	366	.236	.299	.387	.227	45	.255
1996	Richmond	Inter	149	29	8	0	0	16	1	2	122	.195	.273	.248	.162	6	.178

Good defensive outfielder with some pop. If he can start laying off pitches out of the strike zone, he could be a millionaire. Probably not in this organization, though.

ANDRUW JONES   **OF**   **1977**   **Age 20**

Year	Team	Lge	AB	H	DB	TP	HR	BB	SB	CS	OUT	BA	OBA	SA	EQA	EQR	Peak
1995	Macon	S Atl	566	151	20	2	22	57	26	7	422	.267	.334	.426	.258	71	.302
1996	Durham	Caro	251	72	6	1	13	35	7	2	181	.287	.374	.474	.283	39	.326
1996	Greenville	South	160	56	7	1	10	14	8	2	106	.350	.402	.594	.324	32	.375
1996	Atlanta	NL	107	24	6	1	5	8	3	0	83	.224	.278	.439	.240	12	.275
1997	*Atlanta*	*NL*	*577*	*166*	*34*	*2*	*34*	*65*	*26*	*8*	*426*	*.288*	*.360*	*.530*	*.303*	*107*	

A comparable prospect to Alex Rodriguez. He's going to be a slightly better hitter than Rodriguez, and probably will develop more strongly. I wouldn't trade him for Rodriguez or vice versa. Probably one of the top ten outfielders in baseball right now, and will be the very best within four years. The Vladimir projections aren't meant to be more than a one-year tool, and we all know that iterative modeling is a dicey proposition at best, but let's throw caution to the wind and let Vladimir project his entire career. Just for fun.

AB	H	2B	3B	HR	BB	SB	CS	BA	OBP	SLG
12022	3879	692	58	667	1482	243	102	.323	.397	.556

Works for me. Alex vs. Andruw will be the next generation's DiMaggio vs. Williams, but the arguments will be more equal. Why hasn't Atlanta offered him a 10-year, $50 million deal? I don't know. The scary part is that Andruw could take it, and be 30 when it ended.

CHIPPER JONES   **3B/SS**   **1972**   **Age 25**

Year	Team	Lge	AB	H	DB	TP	HR	BB	SB	CS	OUT	BA	OBA	SA	EQA	EQR	Peak
1993	Richmond	Inter	554	178	28	7	15	59	17	5	381	.321	.387	.478	.291	87	.326
1995	Atlanta	NL	533	143	20	2	24	79	6	3	393	.268	.363	.448	.270	74	.293
1996	Atlanta	NL	615	194	30	4	31	93	11	1	422	.315	.405	.528	.309	112	.331
1997	*Atlanta*	*NL*	*570*	*190*	*48*	*5*	*36*	*87*	*20*	*6*	*386*	*.333*	*.422*	*.625*	*.343*	*133*	

A very good ballplayer. I think the projection here is a little high, particularly if the Braves move him to shortstop as is the rumor du jour. I'm also not convinced that you can't get him out more effectively than is currently the case. Can he hit a pitch above the mid-thigh? If Keith Olbermann honestly thinks Chipper was the most valuable player in the NL last year, he's in need of some dopamine. I may be a small minority, but I like his defense a lot better at short than third.

DAVE JUSTICE   **RF**   **1966**   **Age 31**

Year	Team	Lge	AB	H	DB	TP	HR	BB	SB	CS	OUT	BA	OBA	SA	EQA	EQR	Peak
1993	Atlanta	NL	601	168	14	2	42	87	3	4	437	.280	.371	.519	.288	97	.295
1994	Atlanta	NL	364	117	15	2	20	75	2	3	250	.321	.437	.538	.319	72	.322
1995	Atlanta	NL	419	108	16	2	24	78	3	2	313	.258	.374	.477	.280	65	.278
1996	Atlanta	NL	144	47	5	0	7	23	1	1	98	.326	.419	.507	.306	25	.301
1997	*Atlanta*	*NL*	*340*	*95*	*18*	*3*	*18*	*56*	*3*	*1*	*246*	*.279*	*.381*	*.509*	*.300*	*61*	

Hard to believe that he'll be playing next year at only 31 years of age. His body's older than that, and his long injury history would scare the hell out of me as a GM. I also wouldn't be thrilled about that 1995 performance. This is an expensive, risky ballplayer to have on your club at this point, and I expect the Braves will ship his butt out of town for the first reasonable offer they get. Then again, it's always a better bet that a good ballplayer will get healthy than a bad ballplayer will get good.

GUS KENNEDY   **OF/1B**   **1974**   **Age 23**

Year	Team	Lge	AB	H	DB	TP	HR	BB	SB	CS	OUT	BA	OBA	SA	EQA	EQR	Peak
1995	Macon	S Atl	472	116	13	1	21	78	9	3	359	.246	.353	.411	.257	60	.287
1996	Durham	Caro	358	66	5	1	13	49	3	3	295	.184	.283	.313	.194	24	.214
1997	*Atlanta*	*NL*	*463*	*108*	*19*	*1*	*27*	*80*	*14*	*8*	*363*	*.233*	*.346*	*.454*	*.270*	*69*	

Blocky outfielder with arms roughly the size of Mark McGwire's. Lots of power and good plate discipline, but his defense and batting average need work. If one of the two comes around, he could be a valuable major leaguer. I'm betting on the batting average. Gus has a good eye and a vicious hitting stroke.

RYAN KLESKO   **LF/1B**   **1971**   **Age 26**

Year	Team	Lge	AB	H	DB	TP	HR	BB	SB	CS	OUT	BA	OBA	SA	EQA	EQR	Peak
1993	Richmond	Inter	355	98	10	1	21	47	3	2	259	.276	.361	.487	.278	53	.307
1994	Atlanta	NL	250	72	13	2	18	29	1	0	178	.288	.362	.572	.299	44	.325
1995	Atlanta	NL	336	105	22	2	24	51	4	3	234	.312	.403	.604	.319	67	.343
1996	Atlanta	NL	540	155	19	3	35	74	5	3	388	.287	.373	.528	.292	90	.308
1997	*Atlanta*	*NL*	*570*	*175*	*23*	*2*	*44*	*53*	*6*	*2*	*397*	*.307*	*.366*	*.586*	*.313*	*109*	

Bobby Cox does not believe Klesko is ever going to be able to hit lefties. Pinch hitting Terry Pendleton for Klesko is prima facie evidence that Bobby Cox has an appointment he wants to get to. Klesko doesn't hit lefties like he does righties, but he hasn't really gotten much of a shot either. Not as bad in the outfield as the media would have you believe, at least to my eye. Gets a decent break on the ball, but doesn't have a lot of speed.

MARK LEMKE   **2B**   **1966**   **Age 31**

Year	Team	Lge	AB	H	DB	TP	HR	BB	SB	CS	OUT	BA	OBA	SA	EQA	EQR	Peak
1993	Atlanta	NL	505	130	17	2	8	72	1	2	377	.257	.350	.347	.236	51	.242
1994	Atlanta	NL	357	107	9	0	5	44	0	3	253	.300	.377	.367	.253	41	.256
1995	Atlanta	NL	404	102	15	4	6	49	2	2	304	.252	.333	.354	.232	39	.231
1996	Atlanta	NL	506	129	8	0	8	59	4	2	379	.255	.333	.318	.222	44	.217
1997	*Atlanta*	*NL*	*448*	*116*	*15*	*1*	*5*	*51*	*4*	*1*	*333*	*.259*	*.335*	*.330*	*.235*	*45*	

Mr. Clutch. The Braves' pitching talent has made them cocky. No team is good enough that they shouldn't try to improve upon a player like this in their lineup. Currently a free agent, and rumored to be headed out of town, possibly and inexplicably to Los Angeles.

MARC LEWIS   **1975**   **OF**   **Age 22**

Year	Team	Lge	AB	H	DB	TP	HR	BB	SB	CS	OUT	BA	OBA	SA	EQA	EQR	Peak
1995	Utica	NY-P	274	66	8	1	5	13	8	4	212	.241	.275	.332	.204	20	.232
1995	Michigan	Midw	94	13	1	1	1	7	4	1	82	.138	.198	.202	.101	1	.111
1996	Macon	S Atl	251	70	7	1	5	16	10	4	185	.279	.322	.375	.239	26	.267
1996	Durham	Caro	266	68	5	0	6	21	11	4	202	.256	.310	.342	.224	24	.251
1997	*Atlanta*	*NL*	*492*	*136*	*33*	*2*	*11*	*34*	*25*	*15*	*371*	*.276*	*.323*	*.419*	*.256*	*61*	

Skinny right-handed kid who hits line drives. Power well develop, but probably not for a couple of years. No star potential, enough skills to make a run at the majors and possibly stick there. Certainly more valuable to a club than most of the detritus brought in during the season. Terry Pendleton? What, the trained ocelots cost too much?

JAVY LOPEZ   **C**   **1971**   **Age 26**

Year	Team	Lge	AB	H	DB	TP	HR	BB	SB	CS	OUT	BA	OBA	SA	EQA	EQR	Peak
1993	Richmond	Inter	386	115	16	1	17	16	2	4	275	.298	.326	.477	.263	49	.290
1994	Atlanta	NL	280	70	7	0	14	21	0	2	212	.250	.302	.425	.238	29	.259
1995	Atlanta	NL	337	107	9	3	15	18	0	1	231	.318	.352	.496	.279	48	.299
1996	Atlanta	NL	496	141	16	1	23	34	1	5	360	.284	.330	.460	.259	61	.273
1997	*Atlanta*	*NL*	*502*	*149*	*19*	*2*	*39*	*27*	*3*	*8*	*361*	*.297*	*.333*	*.576*	*.294*	*85*	

Wow. That projection looks awfully big. A Terry Steinbach for the next generation. Not exactly Greg Maddux's personal caddy. I don't understand the well-publicized preference of Maddux for catchers who can't hit – considering the run support he got, you'd think he'd want to hand Ryan Klesko the mask. Lopez is a very good and valuable ballplayer, and will be for the next five years.

DANNY MAGEE   **IF**   **1975**   **Age 22**

Year	Team	Lge	AB	H	DB	TP	HR	BB	SB	CS	OUT	BA	OBA	SA	EQA	EQR	Peak
1994	Macon	S Atl	371	93	13	1	1	16	5	4	282	.251	.282	.299	.192	23	.222
1995	Durham	Caro	273	68	8	1	4	11	4	2	207	.249	.278	.330	.203	19	.230
1996	Durham	Caro	348	92	7	1	10	17	8	3	259	.264	.299	.376	.228	32	.256
1997	*Atlanta*	*NL*	*449*	*123*	*21*	*3*	*19*	*8*	*13*	*7*	*333*	*.274*	*.287*	*.461*	*.255*	*54*	

Another young Atlanta prospect who won't draw a walk. As a class, stay away from them. If you're a rotisserie player, stockpile them and when one of them gets hyped, trade him to someone else in your league. Hard to fully develop without better plate discipline than this.

FRED McGRIFF   **1B**   **1964**   **Age 33**

Year	Team	Lge	AB	H	DB	TP	HR	BB	SB	CS	OUT	BA	OBA	SA	EQA	EQR	Peak
1993	Atlanta	NL	264	85	15	0	21	38	1	0	179	.322	.407	.617	.327	55	.325
1993	San Diego	NL	311	88	10	1	19	46	3	2	225	.283	.375	.505	.288	50	.286
1994	Atlanta	NL	435	143	20	1	37	56	7	3	295	.329	.405	.634	.329	91	.322
1995	Atlanta	NL	537	152	20	1	29	71	2	5	390	.283	.367	.486	.278	80	.269
1996	Atlanta	NL	630	189	28	1	30	75	6	3	444	.300	.374	.490	.286	97	.272
1997	*Atlanta*	*NL*	*582*	*163*	*22*	*2*	*31*	*68*	*6*	*3*	*422*	*.280*	*.355*	*.485*	*.284*	*91*	

If you bought this book, you already know more about Fred McGriff than I could write in 80 words. Instead, think of McGriff as an example of how statistics can be misused. Using their career numbers, Mark McGwire and Fred McGriff are very similar. And yet, they're two entirely different players. McGriff is this generation's Eddie Murray, quieting putting up very good numbers each year, staying healthy and being consistent. Mark McGwire, uh, doesn't do those things, but instead hits like Babe Ruth on a hot streak for three or four months at a time.

WONDERFUL MONDS   **OF**   **1973**   **Age 24**

Year	Team	Lge	AB	H	DB	TP	HR	BB	SB	CS	OUT	BA	OBA	SA	EQA	EQR	Peak
1994	Macon	S Atl	381	110	14	5	11	20	22	6	277	.289	.324	.438	.260	48	.291
1994	Durham	Caro	54	11	2	0	1	1	3	0	43	.204	.218	.296	.178	3	.198
1995	Durham	Caro	306	85	9	1	7	18	17	4	225	.278	.318	.382	.243	33	.268
1996	Greenville	South	112	32	6	1	2	7	5	2	82	.286	.328	.411	.251	13	.270
1997	*Atlanta*	*NL*	*524*	*148*	*28*	*5*	*11*	*17*	*37*	*5*	*381*	*.282*	*.305*	*.418*	*.260*	*66*	

Another relatively young Atlanta farmhand who hits pretty well and doesn't walk. At some point, you have to start looking at the organization, despite the two or three superprospects.

MIKE MORDECAI   **UT**   **1968**   **Age 29**

Year	Team	Lge	AB	H	DB	TP	HR	BB	SB	CS	OUT	BA	OBA	SA	EQA	EQR	Peak
1993	Richmond	Inter	209	55	6	1	2	15	7	1	155	.263	.312	.330	.223	18	.236
1994	Richmond	Inter	391	108	18	1	14	35	10	5	288	.276	.336	.435	.257	48	.268
1995	Atlanta	NL	76	21	3	0	4	10	0	0	55	.276	.360	.474	.275	11	.285
1996	Atlanta	NL	109	26	2	0	3	11	1	0	83	.239	.308	.339	.219	9	.220
1997	*Atlanta*	*NL*	*115*	*31*	*2*	*0*	*4*	*9*	*1*	*1*	*85*	*.270*	*.323*	*.391*	*.246*	*13*	

There is no line that accurately distinguishes between major leaguers and minor leaguers. Luck matters a great deal. There is no rhyme or reason to why Turner Ward has a job and Patrick Lennon doesn't. Hopefully for the Mordecai family, Mike is now perceived as a competent major league backup rather than a minor league journeyman.

ALDO PECORILLI   **1B**   **1971**   **Age 26**

Year	Team	Lge	AB	H	DB	TP	HR	BB	SB	CS	OUT	BA	OBA	SA	EQA	EQR	Peak
1993	Savannah	S Atl	546	151	15	2	14	63	7	5	400	.277	.351	.388	.250	62	.276
1994	St. Petersburg	Flor	528	146	17	1	21	51	8	5	387	.277	.340	.432	.257	65	.280
1995	Greenville	South	273	99	14	1	7	22	2	4	178	.363	.410	.498	.301	44	.321
1995	Richmond	Inter	134	37	3	0	6	19	0	0	97	.276	.366	.433	.268	18	.287
1996	Richmond	Inter	411	118	16	0	16	33	4	4	297	.287	.340	.443	.260	51	.274
1997	*Atlanta*	*NL*	*412*	*126*	*18*	*0*	*20*	*38*	*10*	*7*	*293*	*.306*	*.364*	*.495*	*.290*	*66*	

This guy can help a ballclub, and would start on many MLB teams. Lots of power to straightaway center, and hits balls away from him particularly well. Should have a major league career once he gets out from behind McGriff. I'd certainly rather have Aldo than Eric Karros.

TERRY PENDLETON   **3B**   **1961**   **Age 36**

Year	Team	Lge	AB	H	DB	TP	HR	BB	SB	CS	OUT	BA	OBA	SA	EQA	EQR	Peak
1993	Atlanta	NL	643	178	25	1	20	46	4	1	466	.277	.325	.412	.248	71	.236
1994	Atlanta	NL	311	80	17	2	8	17	2	0	231	.257	.296	.402	.233	30	.222
1995	Florida	NL	524	157	27	1	16	44	1	2	369	.300	.354	.447	.267	68	.254
1996	Atlanta	NL	164	34	5	0	4	16	2	1	131	.207	.278	.311	.194	11	.184
1996	Florida	NL	415	109	18	1	8	31	0	2	308	.263	.314	.369	.228	38	.217
1997	*Atlanta*	*NL*	*179*	*44*	*5*	*0*	*6*	*7*	*3*	*5*	*140*	*.246*	*.274*	*.374*	*.217*	*15*	

Peaked higher and later than I thought he would, but a bane to any organization at this point. His glove has deteriorated, his bat has disintegrated and his salary will buy you a lot of actual talent. Terry Pendleton is more valuable to a team than just a bag of charcoal briquets, though. After all, Terry can drive to the store to buy some if you run out. Overrated for 90% of his career.

EDDIE PEREZ   **C**   **1968**   **Age 29**

Year	Team	Lge	AB	H	DB	TP	HR	BB	SB	CS	OUT	BA	OBA	SA	EQA	EQR	Peak
1993	Greenville	South	84	26	4	0	5	3	1	0	58	.310	.333	.536	.285	13	.302
1994	Richmond	Inter	394	100	13	1	9	19	1	1	295	.254	.288	.360	.216	32	.224
1995	Richmond	Inter	333	91	12	0	7	15	1	1	243	.273	.305	.372	.227	30	.232
1996	Atlanta	NL	158	41	8	1	4	9	0	0	117	.259	.299	.399	.232	15	.235
1997	*Atlanta*	*NL*	*187*	*49*	*7*	*0*	*6*	*8*	*0*	*0*	*138*	*.262*	*.292*	*.396*	*.237*	*19*	

One of the many playful inhabitants of "Rip Taylor's Backup Catcher Safari." You drive through in your Ford Taurus and see them in their natural habitat. If Greg Maddux decides that he wants you call his game, though, you're gonna be employed a long time, even if you hit like Marc Sullivan or something.

LUIS POLONIA   **LF**   **1965**   **Age 32**

Year	Team	Lge	AB	H	DB	TP	HR	BB	SB	CS	OUT	BA	OBA	SA	EQA	EQR	Peak
1993	California	AL	581	163	21	6	1	51	50	17	435	.281	.339	.343	.241	62	.243
1994	NY Yankees	AL	357	117	23	6	1	38	19	11	251	.328	.392	.434	.279	52	.277
1995	Atlanta	NL	53	14	7	0	0	4	2	0	39	.264	.316	.396	.246	6	.243
1995	NY Yankees	AL	240	65	10	3	2	25	10	4	179	.271	.340	.363	.242	26	.236
1996	Baltimore	AL	176	43	5	1	2	10	8	6	139	.244	.285	.318	.202	13	.195
1997	*Atlanta*	*NL*	*234*	*63*	*5*	*3*	*0*	*16*	*18*	*8*	*179*	*.269*	*.316*	*.316*	*.229*	*23*	

A left-handed fifth outfielder with two skills: hitting hard-throwing right-handers, and pinch-running after a leadoff double by someone who runs like Ron Hassey. Not likely to be in the majors much longer.

ROB SASSER OF   1975 **Age 22**

Year	Team	Lge	AB	H	DB	TP	HR	BB	SB	CS	OUT	BA	OBA	SA	EQA	EQR	Peak
1995	Eugene	Nwern	229	59	4	1	7	16	5	2	172	.258	.306	.376	.230	22	.260
1996	Macon	S Atl	489	115	20	2	7	51	14	4	378	.235	.307	.327	.217	41	.242
1997	*Atlanta*	*NL*	*399*	*103*	*27*	*2*	*11*	*30*	*17*	*6*	*302*	*.258*	*.310*	*.419*	*.253*	*49*	

Line drive-hitting prospect. Aspires to be Hal Morris and might get there, but in a slightly different form. He could start walking a bunch and be Dave Magadan with more power. 1997 will be critical for him; if he can consolidate the strike zone judgment with a little power, he's a good prospect. If not, he'll fall by the wayside four or five years down the road.

RANDALL SIMON 1B   1975 **Age 22**

Year	Team	Lge	AB	H	DB	TP	HR	BB	SB	CS	OUT	BA	OBA	SA	EQA	EQR	Peak
1994	Macon	S Atl	369	101	12	1	9	7	4	3	271	.274	.287	.385	.225	32	.259
1995	Durham	Caro	435	114	12	1	17	35	4	2	323	.262	.317	.411	.243	47	.276
1996	Greenville	South	505	131	17	0	17	29	3	4	378	.259	.300	.394	.230	48	.257
1997	*Atlanta*	*NL*	*542*	*144*	*35*	*2*	*15*	*26*	*6*	*6*	*404*	*.266*	*.299*	*.421*	*.245*	*60*	

If you're going to be a real prospect at first base, you need to get on base more than this. Otherwise, your future probably lies in doing "wet work" for Ted Turner at the Fox News Channel. Of course, that pays pretty well too, and the fashionable brown shirts you have to wear to get in the Fox building can be pretty sharp, if you're going for that retro-teutonic thing.

DWIGHT SMITH PH/OF 1964 **Age 33**

Year	Team	Lge	AB	H	DB	TP	HR	BB	SB	CS	OUT	BA	OBA	SA	EQA	EQR	Peak
1993	Chicago Cubs	NL	316	96	17	3	12	30	7	5	225	.304	.364	.491	.281	47	.278
1994	Baltimore	AL	74	23	1	1	3	5	0	1	52	.311	.354	.473	.271	10	.265
1994	California	AL	122	32	5	1	5	7	2	3	93	.262	.302	.443	.241	13	.237
1995	Atlanta	NL	133	33	8	2	3	14	0	2	102	.248	.320	.406	.237	14	.230
1996	Atlanta	NL	155	32	4	0	3	18	1	3	126	.206	.289	.290	.186	9	.176
1997	*Atlanta*	*NL*	*162*	*43*	*8*	*3*	*3*	*17*	*4*	*2*	*121*	*.265*	*.335*	*.407*	*.257*	*20*	

This man has a very hard job. "Enjoy watching the game, Dwight? Well, we need you to get a base hit now, son. This guy's their closer, and I understand he's revered as a god in his home country—his name translates as 'hurler of liquid fire and vengeance.' Warm up, and go try to save our bacon with a line drive hard enough to score McGriff and his piano from second." A good hitter, robbed of a career by Don Zimmer.

PEDRO SWANN OF   1971 **Age 26**

Year	Team	Lge	AB	H	DB	TP	HR	BB	SB	CS	OUT	BA	OBA	SA	EQA	EQR	Peak
1993	Durham	Caro	189	56	5	0	5	16	4	5	138	.296	.351	.402	.250	22	.276
1993	Greenville	South	158	44	7	1	3	9	1	1	115	.278	.317	.392	.238	16	.262
1994	Greenville	South	445	122	18	0	12	46	9	4	327	.274	.342	.396	.250	51	.271
1995	Greenville	South	350	109	18	1	11	43	10	6	247	.311	.387	.463	.283	53	.302
1996	Greenville	South	132	37	3	0	3	15	3	2	97	.280	.354	.371	.247	15	.262
1996	Richmond	Inter	301	73	9	2	5	23	5	4	232	.243	.296	.336	.211	24	.223
1997	*Atlanta*	*NL*	*316*	*88*	*24*	*2*	*7*	*26*	*8*	*6*	*234*	*.278*	*.333*	*.434*	*.262*	*41*	

Good fourth outfielder. Plays solid defense, hits the ball fairly well, draws a few walks. He'll have to catch a break to have a major league career at this point. The musical chairs game that determines backup outfielders in baseball has precious little to do with ability and a hell of a lot to do with luck and perception. Pedro needs a little luck.

JEROME WALTON OF   1966 **Age 31**

Year	Team	Lge	AB	H	DB	TP	HR	BB	SB	CS	OUT	BA	OBA	SA	EQA	EQR	Peak
1993	Vancouver	PCL	177	51	8	1	2	15	3	2	128	.288	.344	.379	.245	19	.252
1994	Cincinnati	NL	69	22	1	0	2	5	1	3	50	.319	.365	.420	.254	8	.253
1995	Cincinnati	NL	166	50	13	1	8	19	8	6	122	.301	.373	.536	.290	28	.289
1996	Atlanta	NL	48	16	2	0	2	6	0	0	32	.333	.407	.500	.303	8	.300
1997	*Baltimore*	*AL*	*126*	*38*	*7*	*1*	*2*	*13*	*5*	*3*	*91*	*.302*	*.367*	*.421*	*.266*	*17*	

After his RoY stint with the Cubs, he fell out of favor in several organizations after being asked to do jobs he wasn't suited for. He's stuck with it, and can still help a team, but he needs a break. For some of these guys, it might actually be a good idea to hire a publicist. Walton can still help a team. The difference between him and a Stan Javier is maybe 5-10 runs of defense per year.

JUAN WILLIAMS   OF   1973   Age 24

Year	Team	Lge	AB	H	DB	TP	HR	BB	SB	CS	OUT	BA	OBA	SA	EQA	EQR	Peak
1993	Durham	Caro	412	81	10	1	8	33	7	5	336	.197	.256	.284	.173	21	.196
1994	Durham	Caro	406	80	6	0	14	45	4	5	331	.197	.277	.315	.192	27	.214
1995	Greenville	South	197	61	9	1	14	17	3	2	138	.310	.364	.579	.301	34	.332
1995	Richmond	Inter	135	37	4	0	5	18	1	2	100	.274	.359	.415	.257	17	.284
1996	Richmond	Inter	367	100	16	1	15	52	4	3	270	.272	.363	.444	.268	50	.291
1997	*Atlanta*	*NL*	*521*	*152*	*25*	*2*	*27*	*65*	*5*	*2*	*371*	*.292*	*.370*	*.503*	*.295*	*88*	

What does this guy have to do to be noticed? Williams can hit, with power, to all fields; he plays good defense; and he gets on base. A smart organization could work a deal with Atlanta for a bunch of prospects that would help both teams and all players involved. An organization that has shorter-term goals could snatch a bunch of really good prospects for very little. This is called "The Bonifay Horizon." Actually, that may be a Robert Ludlum novel. I get confused after watching Bud Selig.

JAMIE ARNOLD   RSP   1974   Age 23

YR	TEAM	LGE	IP	H	ER	HR	BB	K	ERA	W	L	H/9	HR/9	BB/9	K/9	KW
1993	Macon	S Atl	141.7	187	76	8	78	73	4.83	7	9	11.88	.51	4.96	4.64	.31
1994	Durham	Caro	130.0	165	92	23	103	61	6.37	4	10	11.42	1.59	7.13	4.22	-.37
1995	Durham	Caro	72.3	103	47	6	31	32	5.85	3	5	12.82	.75	3.86	3.98	.36
1995	Greenville	South	52.7	81	40	8	34	15	6.84	2	4	13.84	1.37	5.81	2.56	-.60
1996	Greenville	South	118.3	161	71	17	51	46	5.40	5	8	12.25	1.29	3.88	3.50	.20

Probably still a year away from earning a spot in Richmond, and that's if he can take a step forward again. Those three years without much progress are usually indicative of someone who's probably not going to make the bigs.

STEVE AVERY   LSP   1970   Age 27

YR	TEAM	Lge	IP	H	ER	HR	BB	K	ERA	W	L	H/9	HR/9	BB/9	K/9	KW
1993	Atlanta	NL	215.7	225	73	15	67	120	3.05	15	9	9.39	.63	2.80	5.01	.97
1994	Atlanta	NL	148.0	131	61	15	67	113	3.71	9	7	7.97	.91	4.07	6.87	1.27
1995	Atlanta	NL	170.7	164	77	21	65	125	4.06	9	10	8.65	1.11	3.43	6.59	1.34
1996	Atlanta	NL	129.3	147	60	9	51	75	4.18	7	7	10.23	.63	3.55	5.22	.85

Lefty starter, assumed to be gone with the acquisition of Neagle. K rate hasn't been what one would have expected after his minor league career, but still one of the better bets to be effective for some time. No pitcher is really a good bet for the future, but Avery's better than most.

MIKE BIELECKI   RRP   1960   Age 37

YR	TEAM	Lge	IP	H	ER	HR	BB	K	ERA	W	L	H/9	HR/9	BB/9	K/9	KW
1993	Rochester	Inter	45.3	60	31	4	22	25	6.15	1	4	11.91	.79	4.37	4.96	.56
1993	Cleveland	AL	69.0	91	42	8	27	40	5.48	3	5	11.87	1.04	3.52	5.22	.86
1994	Atlanta	NL	26.3	29	10	2	14	17	3.42	2	1	9.91	.68	4.78	5.81	.74
1995	California	AL	76.0	76	44	14	33	45	5.21	3	5	9.00	1.66	3.91	5.33	.80
1996	Atlanta	NL	74.0	65	20	8	39	62	2.43	6	2	7.91	.97	4.74	7.54	1.33

What a fine year. Nice to have one year like that to go out on. Cox used him masterfully, and he's not likely to ever do that well again. The one hope that his 1996 might be indicative of a few more good years: that K rate. That's quite a jump, and way out of line with his history.

PEDRO BORBON   LRP   1968   Age 29

YR	TEAM	Lge	IP	H	ER	HR	BB	K	ERA	W	L	H/9	HR/9	BB/9	K/9	KW
1993	Richmond	Inter	72.3	79	39	7	54	78	4.85	3	5	9.83	.87	6.72	9.71	1.56
1994	Richmond	Inter	76.0	74	27	3	50	68	3.20	5	3	8.76	.36	5.92	8.05	1.20
1995	Atlanta	NL	31.3	30	10	2	20	29	2.87	2	1	8.62	.57	5.74	8.33	1.34
1996	Atlanta	NL	34.7	28	9	1	9	27	2.34	3	1	7.27	.26	2.34	7.01	1.75

Bursting with pride after his dad agreed to be a high-profile scab. Lefty spot reliever with a good K rate; he'll be in the majors longer than I was in college.

ADAM BUTLER　　　**LRP**　　1974　**Age 23**

YR	TEAM	Lge	IP	H	ER	HR	BB	K	ERA	W	L	H/9	HR/9	BB/9	K/9	KW
1995	Eugene	Nwern	22.0	22	11	0	17	28	4.50	1	1	9.00	.00	6.95	11.45	2.08
1996	Macon	S Atl	13.7	8	3	2	4	12	1.98	2	0	5.27	1.32	2.63	7.90	1.98
1996	Durham	Caro	10.0	3	0	0	9	10	.00	1	0	2.70	.00	8.10	9.00	.97
1996	Greenville	South	32.7	39	20	6	19	22	5.51	1	3	10.74	1.65	5.23	6.06	.71

Lefty reliever who's been effective and struck out a bunch of guys in the minors. He looks like a darn good prospect, considering some of the left-handed relievers bouncing around the majors. May arrive in Atlanta as early as this year as a September callup.

BRAD CLONTZ　　　**RRP**　　1971　**Age 26**

YR	TEAM	Lge	IP	H	ER	HR	BB	K	ERA	W	L	H/9	HR/9	BB/9	K/9	KW
1993	Durham	Caro	65.3	86	35	5	40	50	4.82	3	4	11.85	.69	5.51	6.89	.92
1994	Greenville	South	41.0	40	13	6	16	38	2.85	3	2	8.78	1.32	3.51	8.34	1.90
1994	Richmond	Inter	24.0	22	5	1	11	17	1.88	2	1	8.25	.38	4.12	6.38	1.09
1995	Atlanta	NL	68.3	70	24	5	28	49	3.16	5	3	9.22	.66	3.69	6.45	1.23
1996	Atlanta	NL	80.0	78	45	11	39	43	5.06	3	6	8.77	1.24	4.39	4.84	.52

I have a letter from a *BP '96* reader asking: "Dear Gary: how can you possibly write an entire baseball book and not mention Brad Clontz's resemblance to the evil guy on 'The A Team?'" Well, to put it bluntly, I didn't write the Braves section last year. Clontz has a very unorthodox delivery, but it seems to serve him well against right-handers. If you want to know what his career path is going to be like, think Mark Eichhorn.

JOHN DETTMER　　　**RBP**　　1970　**Age 27**

YR	TEAM	Lge	IP	H	ER	HR	BB	K	ERA	W	L	H/9	HR/9	BB/9	K/9	KW
1993	Charlotte, FL	Flor	145.0	164	49	11	50	100	3.04	10	6	10.18	.68	3.10	6.21	1.29
1994	Tulsa	Texas	68.3	67	22	4	19	47	2.90	5	3	8.82	.53	2.50	6.19	1.44
1994	Oklahoma	AmA	45.0	60	30	8	16	24	6.00	2	3	12.00	1.60	3.20	4.80	.80
1994	Texas	AL	54.0	61	34	9	22	27	5.67	2	4	10.17	1.50	3.67	4.50	.58
1995	Rochester	Inter	78.0	101	48	10	25	39	5.54	3	6	11.65	1.15	2.88	4.50	.78
1996	Greenville	South	37.7	48	17	3	7	20	4.06	2	2	11.47	.72	1.67	4.78	1.17
1996	Richmond	Inter	57.0	73	24	8	15	22	3.79	3	3	11.53	1.26	2.37	3.47	.57

Escaped the SinewShredder [tm] of the Texas organization, and seems to have learned to pitch without that big fastball he used to have. Not a great bet for long-term success, but I think he's earned another shot at the majors. Anybody who can keep improving always deserves a shot. Wears men's clothes.

TOM GLAVINE　　　**LSP**　　1966　**Age 31**

YR	TEAM	Lge	IP	H	ER	HR	BB	K	ERA	W	L	H/9	HR/9	BB/9	K/9	KW
1993	Atlanta	NL	232.3	247	83	17	116	116	3.22	16	10	9.57	.66	4.49	4.49	.37
1994	Atlanta	NL	163.7	174	66	10	86	131	3.63	10	8	9.57	.55	4.73	7.20	1.22
1995	Atlanta	NL	194.0	185	62	9	81	113	2.88	15	7	8.58	.42	3.76	5.24	.81
1996	Atlanta	NL	230.7	227	76	13	105	157	2.97	17	9	8.86	.51	4.10	6.13	1.02

The Mike Mussina of the National League. Consistently enjoys the largest strike zone I've ever seen, and more power to him. Works the outside 5" of the zone masterfully, and seldom, if ever, gives in. Usually has a reverse platoon split that's pretty noticeable, but I didn't see anyone stack their lineup with lefties against him this year. The most likely of the big three to implode.

KERRY LIGTENBERG　　　**RSP**　　1971　**Age 26**

YR	TEAM	Lge	IP	H	ER	HR	BB	K	ERA	W	L	H/9	HR/9	BB/9	K/9	KW
1996	Durham	Caro	54.3	67	20	3	23	52	3.31	4	2	11.10	.50	3.81	8.61	1.92

I realize he's old for his level, but I see no reason to think this guy won't be able to pitch effectively in the majors. If GMs can give jobs to sentient turnips like Brad Pennington, then a guy like this deserves a bunch of shots to succeed.

KEVIN LOMON   **RSP**   **1972**   **Age 25**

YR	TEAM	Lge	IP	H	ER	HR	BB	K	ERA	W	L	H/9	HR/9	BB/9	K/9	KW
1993	Durham	Caro	74.0	98	40	7	45	43	4.86	3	5	11.92	.85	5.47	5.23	.37
1993	Greenville	South	72.3	83	39	5	41	50	4.85	3	5	10.33	.62	5.10	6.22	.80
1994	Richmond	Inter	138.3	174	67	12	69	81	4.36	7	8	11.32	.78	4.49	5.27	.63
1995	Richmond	Inter	55.0	76	26	2	40	45	4.25	3	3	12.44	.33	6.55	7.36	.82
1996	Richmond	Inter	134.7	161	74	11	60	85	4.95	6	9	10.76	.74	4.01	5.68	.89

A consistently mediocre starter; he'd probably get a shot in another organization, but this is like being a shortstop in the Orioles' system in about 1989. He'll probably fall into a MLB rotation for a couple years in 1998 or so. I think he's got the stuff to be more successful than he's been. Most pitchers surprise me when they break out; Lomon I expect it from.

GREG MADDUX   **RSP**   **1966**   **Age 31**

YR	TEAM	Lge	IP	H	ER	HR	BB	K	ERA	W	L	H/9	HR/9	BB/9	K/9	KW
1993	Atlanta	NL	256.0	243	75	15	79	189	2.64	20	8	8.54	.53	2.78	6.64	1.52
1994	Atlanta	NL	193.3	160	34	4	47	144	1.58	18	3	7.45	.19	2.19	6.70	1.69
1995	Atlanta	NL	201.0	156	28	8	38	160	1.25	20	2	6.99	.36	1.70	7.16	1.96
1996	Atlanta	NL	237.0	234	70	11	48	149	2.66	18	8	8.89	.42	1.82	5.66	1.43

I realize it's common to acknowledge this guy as the best pitcher of our generation, but he's not. Roger Clemens has still been more impressive. That said, Maddux could surpass Clemens, and the run he's on now is unequalled in history. Even Koufax's best five years aren't particularly close. Remember: Koufax pitched in the '60s in Dodger Stadium. Maddux is pitching in the new live ball era in a hitter's park. I was in Las Vegas for a wedding last year, and four out of 10 Las Vegans claim to have taught Greg everything he knows. Already a lock for the Hall of Fame, and a sheer joy to watch.

GREG McMICHAEL   **RRP**   **1967**   **Age 30**

YR	TEAM	Lge	IP	H	ER	HR	BB	K	ERA	W	L	H/9	HR/9	BB/9	K/9	KW
1993	Atlanta	NL	87.3	76	19	3	38	85	1.96	8	2	7.83	.31	3.92	8.76	1.94
1994	Atlanta	NL	58.0	66	25	1	25	44	3.88	3	3	10.24	.16	3.88	6.83	1.31
1995	Atlanta	NL	79.0	65	22	8	38	66	2.51	6	3	7.41	.91	4.33	7.52	1.42
1996	Atlanta	NL	85.0	86	31	4	34	68	3.28	5	4	9.11	.42	3.60	7.20	1.50

So Atlanta has Andruw Jones, three of the 10 best starting pitchers in baseball, and bullpen depth. That hardly seems fair. Obviously, what this sport needs is revenue sharing. That'll fix it. It couldn't be that some organizations are just better at this game than others. No, give Sal Bando and the current versions of Jim Frey some more money, and they'll be competing any day now. McMichael's a good pitcher, and that's not likely to change. Given to the Mets in a salary dump.

KEVIN MILLWOOD   **RSP**   **1975**   **Age 22**

YR	TEAM	Lge	IP	H	ER	HR	BB	K	ERA	W	L	H/9	HR/9	BB/9	K/9	KW
1994	Macon	S Atl	27.3	42	37	5	43	15	12.18	0	3	13.83	1.65	14.16	4.94	-1.89
1995	Macon	S Atl	86.3	117	78	13	80	51	8.13	2	8	12.20	1.36	8.34	5.32	-.31
1996	Durham	Caro	133.3	162	79	18	79	95	5.33	5	10	10.94	1.22	5.33	6.41	.80

<Crash> "Was that a strike, coach?" "Uh, no, Kev, that was the backstop." Guys like this can find their control, but it's about as likely as Jim Bakker's first prison tryst being voluntary.

DAMIAN MOSS   **LBP**   **1977**   **Age 20**

YR	TEAM	Lge	IP	H	ER	HR	BB	K	ERA	W	L	H/9	HR/9	BB/9	K/9	KW
1995	Macon	S Atl	126.3	181	88	17	100	101	6.27	4	10	12.89	1.21	7.12	7.20	.62
1996	Durham	Caro	75.7	63	25	10	52	61	2.97	5	3	7.49	1.19	6.19	7.26	.87
1996	Greenville	South	53.3	62	37	5	40	35	6.24	2	4	10.46	.84	6.75	5.91	.28

Still young, and may not have figured out what the pointy white thing is for yet. And I don't mean Dick Stockton's head.

DENNY NEAGLE   **LSP**   **1969**   **Age 28**

YR	TEAM	Lge	IP	H	ER	HR	BB	K	ERA	W	L	H/9	HR/9	BB/9	K/9	KW
1993	Pittsburgh	NL	79.3	85	45	10	47	71	5.11	3	6	9.64	1.13	5.33	8.05	1.35
1994	Pittsburgh	NL	135.7	134	69	18	61	114	4.58	6	9	8.89	1.19	4.05	7.56	1.51
1995	Pittsburgh	NL	207.0	217	75	19	61	133	3.26	14	9	9.43	.83	2.65	5.78	1.26
1996	Atlanta	NL	38.0	40	22	5	18	16	5.21	1	3	9.47	1.18	4.26	3.79	.20
1996	Pittsburgh	NL	179.3	188	57	20	49	114	2.86	13	7	9.43	1.00	2.46	5.72	1.29

Good bet to be a success for several years. One real big worry: In 1995, he pitched great for about the first 75% of the season, and then started to pitch like Todd Van Poppel on acid. I think Neagle will continue to be effective within very stringent boundaries. I wouldn't pitch him more than 180 innings next.

ERIC OLSZEWSKI   **RRP**   **1975**   **Age 22**

YR	TEAM	Lge	IP	H	ER	HR	BB	K	ERA	W	L	H/9	HR/9	BB/9	K/9	KW
1995	Macon	S Atl	70.3	72	42	4	69	59	5.37	3	5	9.21	.51	8.83	7.55	.31
1996	Durham	Caro	47.7	41	12	4	28	47	2.27	4	1	7.74	.76	5.29	8.87	1.64

Great young pitcher with lower back problems. That can mean one of two things: He'll either get healthy and be great, or he won't and he won't. I know which one my money's on.

JOHN SMOLTZ   **RSP**   **1967**   **Age 30**

YR	TEAM	Lge	IP	H	ER	HR	BB	K	ERA	W	L	H/9	HR/9	BB/9	K/9	KW
1993	Atlanta	NL	236.7	219	94	25	126	201	3.57	14	12	8.33	.95	4.79	7.64	1.35
1994	Atlanta	NL	132.0	122	60	15	60	105	4.09	7	8	8.32	1.02	4.09	7.16	1.36
1995	Atlanta	NL	189.0	169	62	15	86	171	2.95	14	7	8.05	.71	4.10	8.14	1.69
1996	Atlanta	NL	246.3	208	74	19	75	239	2.70	19	8	7.60	.69	2.74	8.73	2.23

The undeserving winner of the 1996 NL Cy Young award. A fine pitcher who's demonstrated the ability to pitch a huge number of innings effectively, which is the most valuable commodity in baseball. Has something of a reputation as a head case from years past, but it was without merit. On balance, I'm pretty happy to see him get the Cy. Hopefully Kevin Brown will get another shot at it.

TERRELL WADE   **LBP**   **1973**   **Age 24**

YR	TEAM	Lge	IP	H	ER	HR	BB	K	ERA	W	L	H/9	HR/9	BB/9	K/9	KW
1993	Macon	S Atl	72.7	77	17	1	50	71	2.11	6	2	9.54	.12	6.19	8.79	1.38
1993	Durham	Caro	29.3	31	13	3	25	29	3.99	2	1	9.51	.92	7.67	8.90	1.05
1993	Greenville	South	38.0	36	15	6	36	30	3.55	2	2	8.53	1.42	8.53	7.11	.24
1994	Greenville	South	95.7	105	54	9	78	83	5.08	4	7	9.88	.85	7.34	7.81	.77
1994	Richmond	Inter	22.3	26	9	1	18	22	3.63	1	1	10.48	.40	7.25	8.87	1.14
1995	Richmond	Inter	131.3	165	84	13	85	107	5.76	5	10	11.31	.89	5.82	7.33	.99
1996	Atlanta	NL	69.3	58	24	9	53	69	3.12	5	3	7.53	1.17	6.88	8.96	1.27

This is what a #1 starter in Detroit or Oakland looks like in the Braves' system. He needs to get those walks under control to really be effective, and his motion looks dangerous to me. That hip comes open early, and that tends to lead to a lot of stress on the shoulder. It's probably in Atlanta's best interest to get him to the majors and under the tutelage of Mazzone as soon as possible.

MARK WOHLERS   **RRP**   **1970**   **Age 27**

YR	TEAM	Lge	IP	H	ER	HR	BB	K	ERA	W	L	H/9	HR/9	BB/9	K/9	KW
1993	Richmond	Inter	27.7	24	6	0	15	32	1.95	2	1	7.81	.00	4.88	10.41	2.25
1993	Atlanta	NL	46.0	41	22	2	27	43	4.30	2	3	8.02	.39	5.28	8.41	1.48
1994	Atlanta	NL	50.7	52	30	1	38	54	5.33	2	4	9.24	.18	6.75	9.59	1.51
1995	Atlanta	NL	63.3	53	12	2	28	80	1.71	6	1	7.53	.28	3.98	11.37	2.79
1996	Atlanta	NL	76.3	72	25	8	27	87	2.95	5	3	8.49	.94	3.18	10.26	2.62

Closest thing to Troy Percival the National League has. The Braves' professional staff has done a fantastic job with him, and he's worked hard and responded. A great pitcher, likely to remain as such, and finds time in the offseason to do 15 different voices on "The Simpsons," including Chief Clancy Wiggum.

BRAD WOODALL   RSP   1969   Age 28

YR	TEAM	Lge	IP	H	ER	HR	BB	K	ERA	W	L	H/9	HR/9	BB/9	K/9	KW
1993	Durham	Caro	26.7	26	10	3	10	17	3.38	2	1	8.78	1.01	3.38	5.74	1.07
1993	Greenville	South	48.3	48	22	1	31	28	4.10	2	3	8.94	.19	5.77	5.21	.29
1993	Richmond	Inter	54.3	65	31	6	23	37	5.13	2	4	10.77	.99	3.81	6.13	1.09
1994	Richmond	Inter	174.7	177	57	15	66	114	2.94	12	7	9.12	.77	3.40	5.87	1.11
1995	Richmond	Inter	60.3	83	43	6	26	38	6.41	2	5	12.38	.90	3.88	5.67	.92
1995	Atlanta	NL	10.7	12	8	1	9	4	6.75	0	1	10.12	.84	7.59	3.38	-.77
1996	Richmond	Inter	126.7	133	52	10	50	61	3.69	8	6	9.45	.71	3.55	4.33	.56
1996	Atlanta	NL	20.0	27	16	4	6	18	7.20	0	2	12.15	1.80	2.70	8.10	2.02

Hasn't impressed in short stints with the big club, that's for sure. Probably about to begin the dreaded "Sanderson Voyage." Next stop: someplace like San Francisco, before continuing to Seattle, Milwaukee and finally, like all marginal starters before him, Detroit, home of the Sacred Marginal Starter Burial Grounds, where his ivory will litter the shifting sands.

Player	Age	Team	Lge	AB	H	DB	TP	HR	BB	SB	CS	OUT	BA	OBA	SA	EQA	EQR	Peak
JOE AYRAULT	24	Richmond	Inter	319	72	8	0	6	27	1	1	248	.226	.286	.307	.195	21	.209
LOU BENBOW	25	Richmond	Inter	253	56	4	0	2	18	2	2	199	.221	.273	.261	.171	12	.180
LUIS BRITO	25	Durham	Caro	317	76	6	1	3	9	3	1	242	.240	.261	.293	.182	17	.192
ROOSEVELT BROWN	20	Macon	S Atl	428	106	10	0	15	25	9	5	327	.248	.289	.376	.222	38	.253
MIGUEL CORREA	24	Durham	Caro	250	56	7	1	6	13	7	3	197	.224	.262	.332	.198	17	.213
	24	Greenville	South	227	47	9	1	5	9	1	1	181	.207	.237	.322	.178	12	.190
DARRON COX	28	Richmond	Inter	169	39	4	0	4	7	1	0	130	.231	.261	.325	.193	11	.195
KEITH DAUGHERTY	22	Macon	S Atl	338	69	8	0	8	20	2	1	270	.204	.249	.299	.175	17	.192
JOSE DELGADO	21	Macon	S Atl	358	88	8	0	1	21	8	4	274	.246	.288	.277	.189	21	.212
MIKE EAGLIN	23	Durham	Caro	475	103	11	1	9	43	10	5	377	.217	.282	.301	.194	31	.210
DEREK FOOTE	21	Macon	S Atl	342	72	5	0	12	23	1	0	270	.211	.260	.330	.193	22	.215
ANTON FRENCH	20	Durham	Caro	212	47	4	0	5	12	10	2	167	.222	.263	.311	.197	14	.225
ED GIOVANOLA	27	Atlanta	NL	83	19	2	0	0	9	1	0	64	.229	.304	.253	.187	5	.192
	27	Richmond	Inter	218	63	12	1	3	37	2	4	159	.289	.392	.394	.265	29	.271
RANDY HODGES	23	Macon	S Atl	286	56	6	1	2	14	4	3	233	.196	.233	.245	.142	9	.154
MANNY JIMENEZ	24	Greenville	South	479	121	17	1	3	22	7	4	362	.253	.285	.311	.200	32	.214
GEORGE LOMBARD	20	Macon	S Atl	459	99	8	2	12	28	10	7	367	.216	.261	.320	.190	29	.216
FERNANDO LUNAR	19	Macon	S Atl	351	53	4	0	5	16	1	1	299	.151	.188	.205	.056	1	.065
MIKE MAHONEY	23	Durham	Caro	367	82	9	1	8	20	2	1	286	.223	.264	.319	.190	23	.206
MARTY MALLOY	23	Greenville	South	437	126	21	1	4	45	7	5	316	.288	.355	.368	.246	48	.268
PABLO MARTINEZ	27	Richmond	Inter	266	70	11	2	1	14	10	4	200	.263	.300	.331	.216	22	.222
PASCUAL MATOS	21	Durham	Caro	220	43	4	1	5	6	3	0	177	.195	.217	.291	.160	9	.179
GATOR MCBRIDE	22	Greenville	South	295	73	14	3	4	23	3	2	224	.247	.302	.356	.220	25	.243
JASON MCFARLIN	26	Greenville	South	248	53	6	0	5	25	4	1	196	.214	.286	.298	.195	16	.202
BOBBY MOORE	30	Richmond	Inter	204	54	6	0	4	16	6	1	151	.265	.318	.353	.232	19	.227
BRETT NEWELL	23	Greenville	South	301	58	1	0	2	15	1	3	246	.193	.231	.216	.117	6	.127
RAMON NUNEZ	23	Durham	Caro	245	66	7	1	8	11	1	1	180	.269	.301	.404	.235	24	.255
	23	Greenville	South	171	32	2	0	4	7	1	1	140	.187	.219	.269	.144	6	.155
STEVE PEGUES	28	Richmond	Inter	170	57	7	1	7	8	0	0	113	.335	.365	.512	.290	26	.294
RAUL RODARTE	26	Greenville	South	179	55	5	0	6	13	0	1	125	.307	.354	.436	.264	22	.274
	26	Richmond	Inter	225	75	10	1	9	20	3	1	151	.333	.388	.507	.297	36	.310
ROBERT SMITH	22	Richmond	Inter	452	113	16	0	10	35	11	6	345	.250	.304	.352	.221	40	.244
SEAN SMITH	22	Durham	Caro	284	55	4	0	6	27	1	0	229	.194	.264	.271	.170	14	.188
DAVID TOTH	26	Greenville	South	384	96	19	1	10	49	2	2	290	.250	.335	.383	.240	41	.250
JOE TRIPPY	22	Macon	S Atl	460	109	14	4	4	43	17	8	359	.237	.302	.311	.209	36	.230
BEN UTTING	20	Macon	S Atl	340	65	6	1	1	16	6	2	277	.191	.228	.224	.129	8	.146
MIKE WARNER	25	Greenville	South	211	51	14	1	6	41	7	4	164	.242	.365	.403	.258	28	.272
GABE WHATLEY	24	Durham	Caro	166	47	4	0	3	27	3	3	122	.283	.383	.361	.254	20	.271
GLENN WILLIAMS	18	Macon	S Atl	188	32	3	1	3	13	2	1	157	.170	.224	.245	.135	5	.154

Player	Age	Team	Lge	IP	H	ER	HR	BB	K	ERA	W	L	H/9	HR/9	BB/9	K/9	KW
WINSTON ABREU	19	Macon	S Atl	49.7	74	37	5	37	33	6.70	2	4	13.41	.91	6.70	5.98	.32
BILLY BLYTHE	20	Macon	S Atl	99.7	172	118	8	148	47	10.66	1	10	15.53	.72	13.36	4.24	-1.93
JOE BOROWSKI	25	Atlanta	NL	26.3	32	13	4	16	13	4.44	1	2	10.94	1.37	5.47	4.44	.11
	25	Richmond	Inter	51.0	45	22	4	37	33	3.88	3	3	7.94	.71	6.53	5.82	.31
MICAH BOWIE	21	Durham	Caro	59.7	63	29	5	43	44	4.37	3	4	9.50	.75	6.49	6.64	.59
ANTHONY BRIGGS	22	Durham	Caro	111.0	149	85	12	79	52	6.89	3	9	12.08	.97	6.41	4.22	-.20
CHRIS BROCK	26	Richmond	Inter	143.3	146	84	19	78	93	5.27	6	10	9.17	1.19	4.90	5.84	.72
ANTONE BROOKS	22	Macon	S Atl	67.7	85	31	7	51	55	4.12	4	4	11.31	.93	6.78	7.32	.74
MATT BYRD	25	Greenville	South	84.3	113	67	12	46	48	7.15	2	7	12.06	1.28	4.91	5.12	.48
MIKE CATHER	25	Greenville	South	81.7	96	37	3	34	44	4.08	4	5	10.58	.33	3.75	4.85	.68
MAURICE CHRISTMAS	22	Macon	S Atl	68.7	126	56	12	33	34	7.34	2	6	16.51	1.57	4.33	4.46	.40
CHARLIE CRUZ	22	Macon	S Atl	64.0	101	50	10	49	49	7.03	2	5	14.20	1.41	6.89	6.89	.57
DERRIN EBERT	19	Durham	Caro	148.3	220	106	15	55	68	6.43	4	12	13.35	.91	3.34	4.13	.54
ROGER ETHERIDGE	24	Greenville	South	61.0	75	48	7	63	31	7.08	2	5	11.07	1.03	9.30	4.57	-.80
CHAD FOX	25	Richmond	Inter	89.3	97	51	9	61	72	5.14	4	6	9.77	.91	6.15	7.25	.88
JOSE GARCIA	21	Macon	S Atl	101.3	154	81	13	83	60	7.19	3	8	13.68	1.15	7.37	5.33	-.07
KEN GIARD	23	Durham	Caro	61.7	76	42	9	56	64	6.13	2	5	11.09	1.31	8.17	9.34	1.07
TOM HARRISON	24	Greenville	South	92.3	97	48	11	40	59	4.68	4	6	9.45	1.07	3.90	5.75	.94
MIKE HOSTETLER	26	Richmond	Inter	140.7	180	73	8	57	67	4.67	7	9	11.52	.51	3.65	4.29	.52
DWAYNE JACOBS	19	Macon	S Atl	66.7	115	99	3	104	42	13.37	1	6	15.53	.41	14.04	5.67	-1.62
RYAN JACOBS	22	Greenville	South	93.0	131	72	18	66	46	6.97	2	8	12.68	1.74	6.39	4.45	-.11
RAYMOND KING	22	Durham	Caro	74.3	118	55	4	24	36	6.66	2	6	14.29	.48	2.91	4.36	.73
	22	Macon	S Atl	60.7	87	40	5	30	35	5.93	2	5	12.91	.74	4.45	5.19	.62
MARK LEE	31	Richmond	Inter	33.3	33	10	3	14	30	2.70	3	1	8.91	.81	3.78	8.10	1.75
JOHN LEROY	21	Durham	Caro	100.0	104	47	7	69	64	4.23	5	6	9.36	.63	6.21	5.76	.37
	21	Greenville	South	41.7	48	16	5	21	27	3.46	3	2	10.37	1.08	4.54	5.83	.81
DEL MATHEWS	21	Durham	Caro	58.7	82	39	10	36	32	5.98	2	5	12.58	1.53	5.52	4.91	.26
ROD NICHOLS	31	Richmond	Inter	68.0	61	18	5	27	53	2.38	6	2	8.07	.66	3.57	7.01	1.44
JOHN ROCKER	21	Durham	Caro	52.3	71	24	5	34	30	4.13	3	3	12.21	.86	5.85	5.16	.26
	21	Macon	S Atl	88.3	121	75	10	89	59	7.64	2	8	12.33	1.02	9.07	6.01	-.26
MARTIN SANCHEZ	19	Macon	S Atl	88.0	151	74	11	77	51	7.57	2	8	15.44	1.12	7.88	5.22	-.23
CARL SCHUTZ	24	Richmond	Inter	67.0	91	41	4	34	43	5.51	2	5	12.22	.54	4.57	5.78	.78
RICK STEED	25	Greenville	South	93.0	110	47	4	51	50	4.55	4	6	10.65	.39	4.94	4.84	.38
ROD STEPH	26	Richmond	Inter	75.7	81	30	6	25	34	3.57	4	4	9.63	.71	2.97	4.04	.60
RACHAAD STEWART	21	Greenville	South	66.3	93	48	4	55	53	6.51	2	5	12.62	.54	7.46	7.19	.53
TOM THOBE	26	Richmond	Inter	69.7	92	54	6	47	33	6.98	2	6	11.89	.78	6.07	4.26	-.10
ISMAEL VILLEGAS	19	Macon	S Atl	59.0	114	57	10	29	33	8.69	1	6	17.39	1.53	4.42	5.03	.57

Florida Marlins

The Florida Marlins were baseball's greatest enigma in 1996. Most teams that go 80-82 are mediocre, lifeless teams with a collection of slightly above-average players trying to compensate for a number of obvious holes (also see Cubs, Chicago). Not the Marlins. With the most incongruous lineup in the game and three great pitchers struggling to save an otherwise second-rate pitching staff, they represent baseball's version of the age-old question: is the glass half empty or half full?

A pessimist can point to all the things that went wrong with the Marlins' season—and there were many:

• Charles Johnson, who looked like the second-best catcher in the NL at the start of the season, had a horrendous sophomore season, hitting just .218 with a .650 OPS.

• Quilvio Veras, who like Johnson was one of the NL's five best rookies in 1995, fared even worse, as he was demoted to Charlotte in mid-season.

• The veterans in the Marlins' lineup were no better: Greg Colbrunn hit .286 with 16 homers and only 25 walks, inadequate numbers for a first baseman, while Kurt Abbott and Terry Pendleton were absolute disasters at shortstop and third base. The Marlins, who had the fifth-best offense in the NL in 1995, finished ahead of only the Phillies in runs scored in 1996.

• The back end of the Marlins' pitching staff was brutal. Pat Rapp, the #4 starter, went 8-16 with a 5.10 ERA, and the Marlins were unable to find a fifth starter consistent enough to make even 10 starts. In addition, some of the bullpen members were hideously bad. Chris Hammond was a thorn in the Marlins' side all season, while youngsters like Kurt Miller, Marc Valdes and Matt Mantei all posted stratospheric ERAs. And the trade of John Burkett in mid-season exacerbated the problem by depriving the Marlins of a very dependable #3 starter.

That the Marlins had huge problems last year is evident. What looked like a slow start in April snowballed into a team-wide malaise that ultimately cost Rene Lachemann his job, turned away fans in south Florida in droves and had owner Wayne Huizenga openly hinting at major changes, possibly including selling the franchise.

But the optimist can easily point to the exceptional talent that the Marlins have managed to accumulate in just their fourth year of existence, and without stretching the facts make the case that the Marlins are poised for greatness. Consider that:

• Gary Sheffield is the best right fielder in the game, and quite possibly its best hitter: his 1.089 OPS led the NL, and his .465 OBP is exceeded only by Rogers Hornsby among right-handed hitters in the NL this century.

• Jeff Conine had another fine season, his third straight with at least a .360 OBP and a .480 slugging average, while continuing to swing back and forth between left field and first base as needed.

• Edgar Renteria, who should have won the NL Rookie of the Year Award, is already the second-best shortstop in the league, behind only Barry Larkin.

• Kevin Brown absolutely should have won the NL Cy Young award. His 1.89 ERA was a Madduxian 83 points better than his nearest competitor in either league.

• Al Leiter was possibly the best left-handed starter in baseball; his 2.93 ERA led all southpaws, and batters hit a feeble .202 against him, the lowest mark in the game.

• Robb Nen is the greatest reliever that no one knows about. Among the game's closers, only John Franco and Roberto Hernandez had lower ERAs than Nen, and only Mark Wohlers is younger.

So which half is it? Are the Marlins an underachieving team like the Orioles, with great players overshadowing a complete lack of depth? Or are they a truly good team which can attribute the problems last year to inexperience, youth and bad luck?

Well, if there is one underlying theme to the growing pains the Marlins had last year, it would be the difficult transition of replacing veterans with the best young talent that the Marlins have developed over the last five years. For every 20-year-old Renteria forcing his way into the everyday lineup, there was a 42-year-old Andre Dawson on his ninth pair of knees. Their undoing came because most of the youngsters were not quite ready, and the veterans signed to bridge the gap, guys like Pendleton and Joe Orsulak, were inadequate.

While GM Dave Dombrowski has taken a lot of flak for the Marlins' woeful season, give him credit for sticking to the original plan of slowly developing players and trading veterans for more prospects. The trade of Burkett ripped a hole out of the Marlins' staff, but their annual trade for a Rangers pitching prospect netted them Rick Helling, who pitched wonderfully after he was rescued from the criminal abuse he took in Texas. Helling's torrid September helped the Marlins post a 2.86 ERA that month, the best in the majors. Dombrowski also made shrewd pickups of Mark Hutton and Greg Zaun, who gave the team a boost as the season wound down, and who loom as potential solutions to the nagging problem of team depth.

The Marlins went 31-24 from August 1st on, a heartening sign for a team so committed to youth. By season's end, the Marlins were winning with Renteria and Luis Castillo, the two youngest regulars in the major leagues, at shortstop and second base; they had Helling and Hutton in the rotation, and rookie fireballer Jay Powell and 21-year-old southpaw Felix Heredia were setting up for Nen.

But Leyland's signing was quickly dwarfed by the wildest free agent shopping spree in baseball history. After their aggressive pursuit of Albert Belle failed, the Marlins decided to spread the wealth, and reeled in six quality players. Bobby Bonilla, while not the hitter Belle is, may actually be more valuable to the Marlins, because 1) he's a switch-hitter, helping to balance a lineup that swings almost entirely from the right side, and 2) he can play third base, filling the Marlins' biggest lineup hole. The signings of John Cangelosi and Jim Eisenreich upgraded Florida's bench tremendously, and are a terrific insurance policy in the event Sheffield gets injured or White begins to show his age. Alex Fernandez is a prime starter who, at worst, will rank behind only Tom Glavine as the best #3 starter in baseball. And Dennis Cook is a quality left-handed reliever who, along with Dustin Hermanson from San Diego, adds depth to what had been a top-heavy bullpen. The only mistake the Marlins made on the open market was paying too much for Moises Alou, who as a hitter is hardly better than Greg Colbrunn, the man he replaces. But even Alou will upgrade the Marlins' defense significantly, and if he remains healthy for a full season could put up numbers resembling his 1994 campaign.

So what does all of this mean? The media has already begun decrying these moves, criticizing the Marlins for trying to buy a pennant and reminding us how big spending for free agents rarely translates into success on the field. But the reality, as usual, is not that simple. Baseball history has taught us that signing one or two key players is not the panacea for a team unless it already has the talent to contend in place at other positions. The Marlins already had two of the 10 best starters in baseball, a top-of-the-line closer, the NL's best hitter and the most promising up-the-middle combination in baseball. The free agent signings may have shook up the baseball world, but they would mean little to the Marlins' playoff hopes if they hadn't already possessed championship talent at key positions. Unfortunately, if the Marlins do contend this year, the credit will be given to the deep pockets of Huizenga and not to the terrific job of player development done by Dombrowski's crew, which would be a shame.

Are the Marlins ready to make the big leap forward, or are they an over-hyped, bloated franchise making lots of noise but little progress? Last year in these pages, I wrote the Marlins "have everything in place to battle the Braves for dominance of the NL East for the rest of the decade." I believe that even more strongly this year. The Marlins went through growing pains last year, but they have too much talent to lie dormant any longer. This is the year the Marlins should reap the benefits of their patience, and prove that they had the right blueprint for success from the beginning.

KURT ABBOTT		3B/SS		1969		Age 28											
Year	Team	Lge	AB	H	DB	TP	HR	BB	SB	CS	OUT	BA	OBA	SA	EQA	EQR	Peak
1993	Tacoma	PCL	475	138	26	4	13	31	12	5	342	.291	.334	.444	.261	59	.279
1993	Oakland	AL	62	17	2	0	3	3	2	0	45	.274	.308	.452	.257	8	.276
1994	Florida	NL	344	83	15	2	9	21	3	0	261	.241	.285	.375	.221	30	.233
1995	Florida	NL	427	113	18	6	18	41	3	3	317	.265	.329	.461	.259	54	.269
1996	Charlotte-NC	Inter	69	25	8	1	4	7	1	0	44	.362	.421	.681	.348	16	.356
1996	Florida	NL	327	87	19	6	9	26	2	3	243	.266	.320	.443	.251	38	.257
1997	*Florida*	*NL*	*310*	*79*	*25*	*2*	*12*	*21*	*6*	*4*	*235*	*.255*	*.302*	*.465*	*.264*	*42*	

Swings a potent bat for a middle infielder, but he's a hacker and his defense at shortstop just didn't cut it. Renteria makes that all irrelevant, but now that Abbott's at third, his offense comes into question more. The Marlins have too many hitters just like Abbott, guys like White and Colbrunn, whose statistics look good superficially but don't stand up when considered in the context of the offensive levels of 1995-96. Abbott's chances of a breakout season have dwindled to almost nothing, and the Marlins should really consider alternatives at third base, be it by trade or free agency. Bonilla's acquisition should leave Abbott jobless.

ALEX ARIAS — 3B/SS — 1968 — Age 29

Year	Team	Lge	AB	H	DB	TP	HR	BB	SB	CS	OUT	BA	OBA	SA	EQA	EQR	Peak
1993	Florida	NL	254	69	5	1	2	30	1	1	186	.272	.349	.323	.230	24	.242
1994	Florida	NL	113	26	4	0	0	10	0	1	88	.230	.293	.265	.180	6	.189
1995	Florida	NL	221	61	9	1	4	24	1	0	160	.276	.347	.380	.247	24	.254
1996	Florida	NL	230	67	11	2	3	20	2	0	163	.291	.348	.396	.254	26	.256
1997	*Florida*	*NL*	*238*	*64*	*9*	*3*	*0*	*21*	*1*	*0*	*174*	*.269*	*.328*	*.332*	*.239*	*24*	

A very bland backup infielder who exacerbates the problems with the Marlins' infield situation. As a bench player, Arias' versatility is a real asset, but when he keeps getting 200 at bats a year his utter lack of secondary skills is a drain on the Marlins' offense. A consistent player, for better or for worse, and likely to spend yet another year as a part-time player.

DAVID BERG — SS — 1971 — Age 26

Year	Team	Lge	AB	H	DB	TP	HR	BB	SB	CS	OUT	BA	OBA	SA	EQA	EQR	Peak
1993	Elmira	NY-P	296	63	6	1	3	26	2	2	235	.213	.276	.270	.176	15	.193
1994	Kane County	Midw	454	112	18	4	9	44	4	3	345	.247	.313	.363	.226	42	.246
1995	Brevard Cty	Flor	414	125	13	1	5	61	6	2	291	.302	.392	.374	.265	53	.285
1996	Portland-ME	East	420	117	21	3	8	37	12	4	307	.279	.337	.400	.251	48	.264
1997	*Florida*	*NL*	*514*	*145*	*29*	*6*	*14*	*65*	*22*	*8*	*377*	*.282*	*.363*	*.444*	*.286*	*82*	

A virtual unknown, Berg possesses a tantalizing combination of talents for a shortstop. Vlad predicts his power/speed combination to improve dramatically next year, and there are least half a dozen teams that would improve with him as their starter. But he's too old to be considered a top prospect in an organization full of them, and he'll probably never get the chance to show what he can do.

JOSH BOOTY — 3B — 1975 — Age 22

Year	Team	Lge	AB	H	DB	TP	HR	BB	SB	CS	OUT	BA	OBA	SA	EQA	EQR	Peak
1995	Elmira	NY-P	296	56	7	0	6	15	2	2	242	.189	.228	.274	.152	11	.173
1995	Kane County	Midw	112	10	0	0	1	9	0	0	102	.089	.157	.116	-.143	-4	-.144
1996	Kane County	Midw	489	94	9	1	17	34	1	1	397	.192	.245	.319	.179	27	.200
1997	*Florida*	*NL*	*505*	*109*	*22*	*2*	*20*	*30*	*1*	*2*	*398*	*.216*	*.260*	*.386*	*.224*	*47*	

I hate to say it, but the record $1.6 million bonus the Marlins gave Booty to abandon his commitment to play quarterback at LSU may have been a waste. Let's recount what Booty has been through since he was drafted: a bout with mononucleosis, a .101 average at Kane County in 1995, a suspension for a grooved bat and persistent rumors that he was giving back the money and going back to LSU. After all that, his 1996 season has to look like a success; he stayed healthy all season and showed promising power. But Booty struck out 195 times in 128 games last year, and he's still four levels away from the major leagues. He's probably never going to make contact consistently enough to succeed above AA ball.

JERRY BROOKS — OF/1B — 1967 — Age 30

Year	Team	Lge	AB	H	DB	TP	HR	BB	SB	CS	OUT	BA	OBA	SA	EQA	EQR	Peak
1993	Albuquerque	PCL	402	112	15	1	10	19	2	2	292	.279	.311	.396	.237	40	.246
1994	Albuquerque	PCL	379	106	13	1	13	30	3	1	274	.280	.333	.422	.253	44	.259
1995	Indianapolis	AmA	329	92	15	1	14	25	3	1	238	.280	.331	.459	.262	42	.264
1996	Charlotte-NC	Inter	465	125	19	1	29	34	4	3	343	.269	.319	.501	.266	63	.264

Add Brooks to the list of veteran AAA hitters who clearly have the bat to play in the major leagues in some role, but are victims of age bias and the inertial forces that run the game. It makes too much sense for most teams to pay the minimum salary for a pinch-hitter who can do the job as well as a $750,000 veteran.

LUIS CASTILLO — 2B — 1976 — Age 21

Year	Team	Lge	AB	H	DB	TP	HR	BB	SB	CS	OUT	BA	OBA	SA	EQA	EQR	Peak
1995	Kane County	Midw	358	105	5	2	0	45	15	8	261	.293	.372	.318	.242	38	.279
1996	Portland-ME	East	429	120	13	5	1	58	34	14	323	.280	.366	.340	.249	50	.283
1996	Florida	NL	168	47	3	1	1	16	14	4	125	.280	.342	.327	.240	18	.273
1997	*Florida*	*NL*	*575*	*164*	*23*	*6*	*2*	*84*	*36*	*22*	*433*	*.285*	*.376*	*.357*	*.266*	*79*	

An obscene groundball hitter- his 4.59 G/F ratio led the major leagues. He still has hit into just four double plays in his entire career. His lack of power may hinder his development, but Castillo possesses incredible skills—he is one of the five fastest players in the game and a superb second baseman—for a 21-year-old. He's really an identical player to Quilvio Veras, only five years younger. Will probably lead the league in OBP multiple times in his career.

CHRIS CLAPINSKI   **SS**   **1972**   **Age 25**

Year	Team	Lge	AB	H	DB	TP	HR	BB	SB	CS	OUT	BA	OBA	SA	EQA	EQR	Peak
1993	Kane County	Midw	223	40	7	1	0	25	2	3	186	.179	.262	.220	.142	7	.160
1994	Brevard Cty	Flor	167	49	12	2	2	21	2	1	119	.293	.372	.425	.269	22	.299
1995	Portland-ME	East	214	49	7	1	5	25	3	1	166	.229	.310	.341	.219	19	.238
1996	Portland-ME	East	75	19	3	0	3	11	2	1	57	.253	.349	.413	.255	9	.274
1996	Charlotte-NC	Inter	363	94	13	1	9	47	8	4	273	.259	.344	.375	.244	40	.262

The Marlins have more up-the-middle prospects than any team in recent memory. Clapinski needs a change of scenery; he has no shot at a job in Florida, but like Berg, several teams could use a switch-hitting shortstop with his skills.

GREG COLBRUNN   **1B**   **1970**   **Age 27**

Year	Team	Lge	AB	H	DB	TP	HR	BB	SB	CS	OUT	BA	OBA	SA	EQA	EQR	Peak
1993	Montreal	NL	155	40	7	0	5	9	4	2	117	.258	.299	.400	.234	15	.254
1994	Florida	NL	155	46	5	0	7	11	1	1	110	.297	.343	.465	.267	20	.286
1995	Florida	NL	536	153	18	1	25	28	9	3	386	.285	.321	.463	.260	67	.275
1996	Florida	NL	524	158	24	2	17	31	3	5	371	.302	.341	.452	.262	65	.273
1997	*Florida*	*NL*	*555*	*161*	*22*	*1*	*29*	*30*	*5*	*3*	*397*	*.290*	*.326*	*.490*	*.282*	*84*	

Not a very good player. Colbrunn looks good in all the glamour categories, but it's almost impossible for a first baseman to be valuable without walking at least 50 times. The Marlins seem to realize this, and in all likelihood Jeff Conine will have taken Colbrunn's job by the time the season begins. Good defense and entering his age 27 season, so if he's ever going to have value it'll be now. Platoon splits have been all over the place.

JEFF CONINE   **LF/1B**   **1966**   **Age 31**

Year	Team	Lge	AB	H	DB	TP	HR	BB	SB	CS	OUT	BA	OBA	SA	EQA	EQR	Peak
1993	Florida	NL	607	179	23	2	13	60	2	2	430	.295	.358	.404	.258	73	.264
1994	Florida	NL	453	141	24	4	19	45	1	2	314	.311	.373	.508	.289	71	.292
1995	Florida	NL	498	156	24	2	27	72	2	0	342	.313	.400	.532	.306	89	.304
1996	Florida	NL	618	191	31	2	28	70	1	4	431	.309	.379	.502	.289	97	.283
1997	*Florida*	*NL*	*527*	*146*	*29*	*5*	*22*	*94*	*1*	*2*	*383*	*.277*	*.386*	*.476*	*.299*	*94*	

About as good as a player can be without having one outstanding skill. Conine has never hit .320, or bopped 30 homers, or walked 80 times, which in today's game is almost a prerequisite for greatness. He's an incredibly durable player, and about as consistent as the sun rising or Newt Gingrich annoying people.

ANDRE DAWSON   **OF/PH**   **1955**   **Age 42**

Year	Team	Lge	AB	H	DB	TP	HR	BB	SB	CS	OUT	BA	OBA	SA	EQA	EQR	Peak
1993	Boston	AL	461	127	25	1	16	20	2	1	335	.275	.306	.438	.247	51	.235
1994	Boston	AL	292	70	14	0	17	10	2	2	224	.240	.265	.462	.236	30	.224
1995	Florida	NL	229	60	10	2	9	12	0	0	169	.262	.299	.441	.244	25	.232
1996	Florida	NL	59	17	2	0	2	3	0	0	42	.288	.323	.424	.250	7	.237

I don't want to be cruel, but Dawson is not a deserving Hall of Famer. His career OBP of .323 is 21 points lower than any other outfielder in the Hall, and Dawson's power and (for a time) defense don't make up the difference. His 1987 MVP award is one of the most undeserving selections in history. A very good player for many years, but the Hall asks for greatness, and Dawson didn't have it.

TODD DUNWOODY   **OF**   **1975**   **Age 22**

Year	Team	Lge	AB	H	DB	TP	HR	BB	SB	CS	OUT	BA	OBA	SA	EQA	EQR	Peak
1994	Kane County	Midw	46	5	0	0	1	4	0	0	41	.109	.180	.174	-.088	0	-.109
1995	Kane County	Midw	513	135	11	3	14	41	16	6	384	.263	.318	.378	.237	52	.269
1996	Portland-ME	East	558	141	22	3	20	40	19	10	427	.253	.303	.410	.238	59	.266
1997	*Florida*	*NL*	*556*	*145*	*35*	*2*	*15*	*29*	*26*	*11*	*422*	*.261*	*.297*	*.412*	*.253*	*68*	

An all-around player who's been compared to Brady Anderson by some scouts. He still has some holes in his game, and Vlad remains unconvinced. But he's at the age where sudden development could happen at any time. The Marlins seem determined to sign an impact left fielder, but Dunwoody, McMillon and Kotsay give them three promising options from their own system. The Alou signing buries them all.

CRAIG GREBECK   **INF**   **1965**   **Age 32**

Year	Team	Lge	AB	H	DB	TP	HR	BB	SB	CS	OUT	BA	OBA	SA	EQA	EQR	Peak
1993	Chi. White Sox	AL	193	47	3	0	2	27	1	2	148	.244	.336	.290	.211	15	.214
1994	Chi. White Sox	AL	98	31	5	0	0	13	0	0	67	.316	.396	.367	.265	12	.264
1995	Chi. White Sox	AL	156	43	7	0	3	22	0	0	113	.276	.365	.378	.253	18	.247
1996	Florida	NL	96	21	1	0	1	5	0	0	75	.219	.257	.260	.162	4	.156
1997	*California*	*AL*	*100*	*24*	*4*	*0*	*3*	*16*	*0*	*0*	*76*	*.240*	*.345*	*.370*	*.247*	*11*	

A good role player for many years, with his best days behind him. He's a better player than he showed last year, but at 32, it's strictly non-roster invitee days ahead for Grebeck. Signed with the Angels.

TOMMY GREGG   **1B/OF**   **1964**   **Age 33**

Year	Team	Lge	AB	H	DB	TP	HR	BB	SB	CS	OUT	BA	OBA	SA	EQA	EQR	Peak
1993	Indianapolis	AmA	201	62	9	4	7	26	3	4	142	.308	.388	.498	.289	32	.287
1995	Charlotte-NC	Inter	130	51	7	1	9	21	5	0	79	.392	.477	.669	.372	33	.357
1995	Florida	NL	159	39	3	0	7	18	2	1	121	.245	.322	.396	.240	17	.232
1996	Charlotte-NC	Inter	406	108	14	1	19	49	7	1	299	.266	.345	.446	.265	54	.252
1997	*Florida*	*NL*	*222*	*56*	*13*	*1*	*9*	*24*	*5*	*1*	*167*	*.252*	*.325*	*.441*	*.270*	*32*	

Good hitter, adequate glove, no shot in hell of a job. See also Brooks, Jerry.

CHARLES JOHNSON   **C**   **1972**   **Age 25**

Year	Team	Lge	AB	H	DB	TP	HR	BB	SB	CS	OUT	BA	OBA	SA	EQA	EQR	Peak
1993	Kane County	Midw	509	131	15	2	17	48	4	1	379	.257	.321	.395	.240	54	.270
1994	Portland-ME	East	459	117	14	1	25	65	3	3	345	.255	.347	.453	.263	61	.291
1995	Florida	NL	323	84	14	1	12	49	0	2	241	.260	.358	.421	.258	41	.281
1996	Florida	NL	395	91	12	1	14	44	1	0	304	.230	.308	.372	.226	37	.242
1997	*Florida*	*NL*	*285*	*69*	*14*	*0*	*16*	*25*	*1*	*0*	*216*	*.242*	*.303*	*.460*	*.264*	*39*	

Calling his season a disaster would be an understatement. The Marlins waited all season for him to swing the bat like he had in 1994-95, but he looked lost at the plate all year. Hit only .250 when ahead in the count, which is just dumbfounding. To his credit, his defense was even better than in his rookie season: he threw out 48% of baserunners, and the Marlins' ERA with him behind the plate was 3.56, compared to 4.83 with Natal, Siddall and Zaun. Johnson's return to form is one of the keys to the Marlins' playoff hopes.

MARK KOTSAY   **OF**   **1976**   **Age 21**

Year	Team	Lge	AB	H	DB	TP	HR	BB	SB	CS	OUT	BA	OBA	SA	EQA	EQR	Peak
1996	Kane County	Midw	64	17	3	0	2	13	1	0	47	.266	.390	.406	.273	9	.310

To all the scouts who say that Kotsay "doesn't have any outstanding skills:" excuse me for asking, but isn't hitting a skill? Frank Thomas is slow and can't play defense, but I don't see anyone complaining…. Like Thomas, Kotsay was clearly the best hitter around in college, but was passed on by several teams (Thomas went seventh, Kotsay ninth) because their scouts had their heads buried in the sand. Of the eight teams that passed on Kotsay, chances are at least five of them will be kicking themselves in a few years. He's got everything you look for at the plate, average, power and patience. And like the cover says, everything else is fluff.

LOU LUCCA   **3B**   **1971**   **Age 26**

Year	Team	Lge	AB	H	DB	TP	HR	BB	SB	CS	OUT	BA	OBA	SA	EQA	EQR	Peak
1993	Kane County	Midw	438	107	15	1	6	48	2	4	335	.244	.319	.324	.215	36	.237
1994	Brevard Cty	Flor	470	136	17	1	13	67	3	4	338	.289	.378	.413	.266	62	.290
1995	Portland-ME	East	401	107	19	1	10	53	3	2	296	.267	.352	.394	.252	47	.269
1996	Charlotte-NC	Inter	271	64	9	1	6	13	0	2	209	.236	.271	.343	.200	19	.210

Lucca looked like a poor man's Dave Magadan for a couple of years, but last year played like a poor man's Kurt Abbott, and the Marlins already have the wealthy one.

BILLY McMILLON — OF — 1972 — Age 25

Year	Team	Lge	AB	H	DB	TP	HR	BB	SB	CS	OUT	BA	OBA	SA	EQA	EQR	Peak
1993	Elmira	NY-P	241	61	5	1	5	22	2	2	182	.253	.316	.344	.221	21	.249
1994	Kane County	Midw	520	123	14	1	15	69	3	1	398	.237	.326	.354	.229	50	.253
1995	Portland-ME	East	539	163	21	1	16	86	10	5	381	.302	.398	.434	.282	80	.306
1996	Charlotte-NC	Inter	347	114	22	0	16	37	4	2	235	.329	.393	.530	.303	59	.324
1996	Florida	NL	52	12	0	0	0	6	0	0	40	.231	.310	.231	.178	3	.181
1997	*Florida*	*NL*	*537*	*161*	*29*	*2*	*22*	*80*	*10*	*5*	*381*	*.300*	*.391*	*.484*	*.305*	*98*	

Has more to lose than anyone else if the Marlins go out and get a left fielder. McMillon has improved as a hitter every season, and while his defense is spotty, he can absolutely play in the major leagues. Won the International League batting title, and his left-handed swing is perfectly suited for the Marlins' predominantly right-handed lineup. A likely All-Star within three years if he gets a starting assignment. Future uncertain with Alou signing.

KEVIN MILLAR — 1B/3B — 1972 — Age 25

Year	Team	Lge	AB	H	DB	TP	HR	BB	SB	CS	OUT	BA	OBA	SA	EQA	EQR	Peak
1994	Kane County	Midw	500	141	17	1	18	61	2	1	360	.282	.360	.428	.264	65	.292
1995	Brevard Cty	Flor	493	145	19	1	17	62	3	2	350	.294	.373	.440	.273	68	.297
1996	Portland-ME	East	477	140	17	0	17	33	5	3	340	.294	.339	.436	.259	58	.277
1997	*Florida*	*NL*	*519*	*141*	*22*	*2*	*23*	*43*	*10*	*6*	*384*	*.272*	*.327*	*.455*	*.272*	*74*	

Another pure hitter with no outstanding talents away from the plate. Unlike Kotsay he doesn't have the benefit of a high draft position; Millar spent a year in the Northern League before the Marlins signed him as a free agent. The Marlins like his offensive potential enough to try him out at third base, where his path to the majors is less crowded, but it's still an experiment in progress. Needs a breakout season, and the decline in his walk rate is not promising.

RALPH MILLIARD — 2B — 1974 — Age 23

Year	Team	Lge	AB	H	DB	TP	HR	BB	SB	CS	OUT	BA	OBA	SA	EQA	EQR	Peak
1994	Kane County	Midw	537	144	20	2	8	56	5	4	397	.268	.337	.358	.235	53	.268
1995	Portland-ME	East	482	125	16	2	12	76	14	6	363	.259	.360	.376	.251	57	.282
1996	Charlotte-NC	Inter	251	63	13	1	5	37	5	2	190	.251	.347	.371	.244	28	.269
1996	Florida	NL	64	11	2	0	0	15	2	0	53	.172	.329	.203	.186	4	.206
1997	*Florida*	*NL*	*533*	*128*	*32*	*3*	*9*	*86*	*9*	*5*	*410*	*.240*	*.346*	*.362*	*.254*	*67*	

Poor Ralph. Like a normal prospect, he has developed slowly, steadily working his way up the minor league ladder. But as if Quilvio Veras wasn't enough of a roadblock, Milliard now has an overturned semi in the way in the person of Luis Castillo. Reminds me of a young Willie Randolph, but he's going to have to fight for playing time everywhere he goes.

RUSS MORMAN — 1B/OF — 1962 — Age 35

Year	Team	Lge	AB	H	DB	TP	HR	BB	SB	CS	OUT	BA	OBA	SA	EQA	EQR	Peak
1993	Buffalo	AmA	423	139	27	2	23	51	1	2	286	.329	.401	.565	.312	78	.301
1994	Edmonton	PCL	394	122	18	1	16	34	6	0	272	.310	.364	.482	.284	58	.269
1995	Charlotte-NC	Inter	173	52	5	1	6	14	2	1	122	.301	.353	.445	.267	23	.255
1995	Florida	NL	73	21	2	1	3	4	0	0	52	.288	.325	.466	.262	9	.247
1996	Charlotte-NC	Inter	289	89	12	1	15	30	2	2	202	.308	.373	.512	.289	46	.274

Good hitter, adequate glove, no shot in hell of a job. See also Gregg, Tommy.

BOB NATAL — C — 1966 — Age 31

Year	Team	Lge	AB	H	DB	TP	HR	BB	SB	CS	OUT	BA	OBA	SA	EQA	EQR	Peak
1993	Edmonton	PCL	64	18	2	0	3	7	0	0	46	.281	.352	.453	.268	9	.274
1993	Florida	NL	118	25	4	1	1	7	1	0	93	.212	.256	.288	.176	6	.182
1994	Edmonton	PCL	112	27	2	1	3	9	1	1	86	.241	.298	.357	.217	9	.219
1995	Charlotte-NC	Inter	194	59	8	0	4	13	0	0	135	.304	.348	.407	.256	22	.254
1996	Florida	NL	92	13	1	1	0	16	0	1	80	.141	.269	.174	.112	2	.110

At least he helped Marlin fans appreciate Charles Johnson more. The Marlins were supposed to have a pretty good bench last year, but too many spots were wasted on players with very narrow skills. Natal isn't a bad backstop, but couldn't the Marlins find someone able to play the field and hit better than your average pitcher?

JOSE OLMEDA   **3B**   **1968**   **Age 29**

Year	Team	Lge	AB	H	DB	TP	HR	BB	SB	CS	OUT	BA	OBA	SA	EQA	EQR	Peak
1993	Greenville	South	455	116	21	2	9	28	9	4	343	.255	.298	.369	.225	41	.237
1994	Richmond	Inter	394	89	18	3	5	30	12	3	308	.226	.281	.325	.205	29	.214
1995	Greenville	South	110	26	3	1	4	7	1	0	84	.236	.282	.391	.224	10	.230
1995	Richmond	Inter	249	65	10	2	2	18	2	1	185	.261	.311	.341	.220	21	.225
1996	Charlotte-NC	Inter	374	109	16	1	9	23	5	4	269	.291	.332	.412	.249	42	.252

Pint-sized switch-hitter who hit .320 in AAA. Not a prospect, but he wouldn't embarrass himself if he got a two-week stint in the majors because of injuries.

JOE ORSULAK   **OF**   **1962**   **Age 35**

Year	Team	Lge	AB	H	DB	TP	HR	BB	SB	CS	OUT	BA	OBA	SA	EQA	EQR	Peak
1993	NY Mets	NL	418	122	14	3	9	34	4	3	299	.292	.345	.404	.253	48	.243
1994	NY Mets	NL	294	77	2	0	8	20	4	2	219	.262	.309	.350	.223	26	.211
1995	NY Mets	NL	297	88	20	2	1	23	1	3	212	.296	.347	.387	.247	32	.235
1996	Florida	NL	221	51	6	1	2	19	1	1	171	.231	.292	.294	.193	14	.184

Yet another example of why batting average is such an overrated stat. Is there anything he does well other than hit singles? The Marlins should eat the last year of his contract, because he's wasting a roster spot that could better be filled by one of their youngsters, or even one of the veteran Brooks/Gregg/Morman trio.

MIKE REDMOND   **C**   **1971**   **Age 26**

Year	Team	Lge	AB	H	DB	TP	HR	BB	SB	CS	OUT	BA	OBA	SA	EQA	EQR	Peak
1993	Kane County	Midw	102	17	2	0	0	5	1	0	85	.167	.206	.186	.068	1	.077
1994	Kane County	Midw	315	75	3	0	2	22	2	2	242	.238	.288	.267	.181	17	.197
1995	Portland-ME	East	340	82	9	1	3	19	1	1	259	.241	.281	.300	.191	21	.206
1996	Portland-ME	East	398	103	11	0	5	23	3	2	297	.259	.299	.324	.209	30	.220

The Marlins have almost no catching depth in the minor leagues, which is why the pickup of Zaun was so important. Redmond predictably hits better his second year in a league, but there's no reason to think he'll ever be even a third-stringer in the major leagues.

EDGAR RENTERIA   **SS**   **1976**   **Age 21**

Year	Team	Lge	AB	H	DB	TP	HR	BB	SB	CS	OUT	BA	OBA	SA	EQA	EQR	Peak
1993	Kane County	Midw	396	69	1	0	2	27	3	3	330	.174	.227	.192	.096	5	.114
1994	Brevard Cty	Flor	456	115	13	1	1	33	4	5	346	.252	.303	.292	.198	30	.231
1995	Portland-ME	East	519	144	14	4	8	28	19	7	382	.277	.314	.366	.233	50	.270
1996	Charlotte-NC	Inter	132	33	3	0	3	9	7	2	101	.250	.298	.341	.222	12	.253
1996	Florida	NL	446	145	19	3	5	38	13	2	303	.325	.378	.415	.274	60	.313
1997	*Florida*	*NL*	*645*	*187*	*26*	*5*	*4*	*26*	*29*	*9*	*467*	*.290*	*.317*	*.364*	*.250*	*73*	

Will probably never hit 40 home runs. That's about the only limitation I would put on him. His age listed above is his official one, but it's generally accepted now that the Marlins pulled a fast one and had him claim he was a year older than he was so they could legally sign him. A fabulous shortstop; he, not Ordonez, will probably follow Barry Larkin on the list of Gold Glove winners. Between Jeter, Rodriguez and Renteria, the 2000s could be for shortstops what the 1950s were for center fielders.

JASON ROBERTSON   **OF**   **1971**   **Age 26**

Year	Team	Lge	AB	H	DB	TP	HR	BB	SB	CS	OUT	BA	OBA	SA	EQA	EQR	Peak
1993	Albany-NY	East	494	110	24	1	8	39	19	7	391	.223	.280	.324	.204	37	.225
1994	Albany-NY	East	447	95	8	4	11	45	13	5	357	.213	.285	.322	.204	33	.222
1995	Norwich	East	481	141	27	7	9	37	14	8	348	.293	.344	.435	.260	60	.279
1996	Portland-ME	East	342	85	12	2	10	28	9	3	260	.249	.305	.383	.232	34	.246

Not even the Marlins have three legitimate outfield prospects at every level. Here's one of the…er…illegitimate ones.

VICTOR RODRIGUEZ   **SS**   **1977**   **Age 20**

Year	Team	Lge	AB	H	DB	TP	HR	BB	SB	CS	OUT	BA	OBA	SA	EQA	EQR	Peak
1995	Kane County	Midw	486	100	6	1	0	32	7	3	389	.206	.255	.222	.145	15	.169
1996	Brevard Cty	Flor	451	118	13	2	1	30	10	4	337	.262	.308	.306	.210	34	.241

Al Gore has more power than Rodriguez, but he's an immensely talented shortstop with Renteria-like defense, and he's been young for the levels he's played at. Has a terrific upside, but there's no way to know if he'll reach it. His trade value right now is high, but the Marlins are content to develop him and worry about a Renteria-Rodriguez situation later.

NATE ROLISON   **1B**   **1977**   **Age 20**

Year	Team	Lge	AB	H	DB	TP	HR	BB	SB	CS	OUT	BA	OBA	SA	EQA	EQR	Peak
1996	Kane County	Midw	492	108	10	1	13	51	2	1	385	.220	.293	.323	.204	36	.236

The Marlins, who are one of baseball's most aggressive teams in the draft, offered him the largest signing bonus ever for a second-round pick. He has a potent bat and projects to have 30-homer power, but he's still several years away. The Marlins hope he'll be ready about the same time that Conine starts to decline.

MARC RONAN   **C**   **1970**   **Age 27**

Year	Team	Lge	AB	H	DB	TP	HR	BB	SB	CS	OUT	BA	OBA	SA	EQA	EQR	Peak
1993	St. Petersburg	Flor	89	26	2	0	1	6	0	0	63	.292	.337	.348	.234	8	.254
1993	Arkansas	Texas	288	58	10	0	7	26	1	1	231	.201	.268	.309	.186	17	.203
1994	Louisville	AmA	269	61	8	1	3	13	2	1	209	.227	.262	.297	.182	15	.195
1995	Louisville	AmA	225	44	7	0	0	17	4	2	183	.196	.252	.227	.145	7	.152
1996	Charlotte-NC	Inter	220	60	6	0	4	16	2	2	162	.273	.322	.355	.228	20	.238

Hit .305 for Charlotte, which leads me to formulate the Jazayerli Rule of Backup Catchers: Give any catcher 200 at bats a year for long enough, and he'll eventually have a good season just by chance.

JOHN ROSKOS   **1B**   **1975**   **Age 22**

Year	Team	Lge	AB	H	DB	TP	HR	BB	SB	CS	OUT	BA	OBA	SA	EQA	EQR	Peak
1994	Elmira	NY-P	145	34	1	0	4	21	0	0	111	.234	.331	.324	.221	13	.257
1995	Kane County	Midw	434	119	19	1	12	33	1	0	315	.274	.325	.406	.245	47	.278
1996	Portland-ME	East	405	102	19	2	8	59	3	2	305	.252	.347	.368	.242	44	.270

The Marlins think highly of Roskos, and he made the big jump from the Midwest League to AA without a hitch. If he were left-handed, the Marlins would be giving him the red carpet treatment, but as a right-hander he doesn't have anything that Colbrunn and Conine lack. Still two or three years away from consideration.

CHRIS SHEFF   **OF**   **1971**   **Age 26**

Year	Team	Lge	AB	H	DB	TP	HR	BB	SB	CS	OUT	BA	OBA	SA	EQA	EQR	Peak
1993	Kane County	Midw	475	118	14	2	6	46	14	5	362	.248	.315	.324	.219	41	.242
1994	Brevard Cty	Flor	127	49	9	2	2	16	4	1	79	.386	.455	.535	.333	25	.359
1994	Portland-ME	East	402	95	12	1	5	29	11	2	309	.236	.288	.308	.203	29	.220
1995	Portland-ME	East	487	132	18	4	14	64	15	4	359	.271	.356	.411	.261	62	.279
1996	Portland-ME	East	107	29	10	1	2	11	2	1	79	.271	.339	.439	.259	13	.274
1996	Charlotte-NC	Inter	283	69	10	0	11	22	5	1	215	.244	.298	.396	.233	28	.245
1997	*Florida*	*NL*	*310*	*79*	*15*	*1*	*10*	*40*	*21*	*7*	*238*	*.255*	*.340*	*.406*	*.269*	*45*	

Accept no substitutes. He has half of Sheffield's name, and fittingly, about half his talent. Sadly for Sheff, this is not the organization to be a second-rate prospect in.

GARY SHEFFIELD   **RF**   **1969**   **Age 28**

Year	Team	Lge	AB	H	DB	TP	HR	BB	SB	CS	OUT	BA	OBA	SA	EQA	EQR	Peak
1993	Florida	NL	242	72	7	2	11	32	10	3	173	.298	.380	.479	.287	38	.308
1993	San Diego	NL	264	80	11	1	11	22	4	1	185	.303	.357	.477	.278	38	.298
1994	Florida	NL	324	87	14	1	26	55	10	5	242	.269	.375	.559	.298	59	.315
1995	Florida	NL	223	76	8	0	17	59	16	3	150	.341	.479	.605	.355	56	.368
1996	Florida	NL	554	186	29	1	48	152	13	8	376	.336	.479	.652	.357	143	.366
1997	*Florida*	*NL*	*532*	*159*	*26*	*3*	*54*	*176*	*17*	*8*	*381*	*.299*	*.473*	*.664*	*.371*	*160*	

Vlad predicts him to break the major league record for walks, which is always nice to see. They don't call it "artificial intelligence" for nothing…as always, Sheffield is an MVP candidate if healthy. The Marlins absolutely cannot afford to lose him for any length of time if they hope to contend. Replace Sheffield with, say, Derek Bell in the Marlins' lineup last year, and the Marlins don't score 600 runs.

JESUS TAVAREZ CF 1971 Age 26

Year	Team	Lge	AB	H	DB	TP	HR	BB	SB	CS	OUT	BA	OBA	SA	EQA	EQR	Peak
1993	High Desert	Calif	439	104	13	4	6	39	19	6	341	.237	.299	.326	.215	37	.237
1994	Portland-ME	East	362	96	8	5	3	31	12	4	270	.265	.323	.340	.229	34	.248
1995	Charlotte-NC	Inter	142	40	7	1	1	10	5	4	106	.282	.329	.366	.234	14	.250
1995	Florida	NL	194	58	6	2	2	19	6	4	140	.299	.362	.381	.253	23	.269
1996	Florida	NL	116	27	3	0	0	8	4	1	90	.233	.282	.259	.184	6	.194

This is what a "tools guy" can aspire to be. Tavarez really had no worth with the acquisition of Devon White; his value stems from his speed and defense in center field, two commodities that White possesses in abundance. The Marlins were basically using his roster spot as a defensive replacement for Conine and Sheffield, and you can't waste a bench player on such a limited role.

QUILVIO VERAS 2B 1971 Age 26

Year	Team	Lge	AB	H	DB	TP	HR	BB	SB	CS	OUT	BA	OBA	SA	EQA	EQR	Peak
1993	Binghamton	East	462	134	18	4	3	82	27	12	340	.290	.397	.366	.266	62	.294
1994	Norfolk	Inter	477	124	20	3	1	57	29	12	365	.260	.339	.321	.231	47	.251
1995	Florida	NL	453	125	21	6	6	86	45	18	346	.276	.391	.389	.271	66	.290
1996	Charlotte-NC	Inter	104	31	5	1	2	13	5	2	75	.298	.376	.423	.272	14	.287
1996	Florida	NL	264	71	7	1	5	54	6	7	200	.269	.393	.360	.255	33	.270
1997	*San Diego*	*NL*	*388*	*107*	*26*	*5*	*2*	*77*	*51*	*28*	*309*	*.276*	*.396*	*.384*	*.283*	*66*	

A bizarre fall from grace for Veras, who's still a very good player. He was hitting about as well as in his much-heralded rookie season, but his base stealing, which was never all that good, went to pot. The Marlins' offense was scuffling and they needed a scapegoat, and they inexplicably chose Veras. Then again, it's hard to criticize the Marlins for replacing Veras with Castillo, who projects to be a much better player. He'll make the All-Star team a couple of times before he's through. Traded to San Diego, where he should be the starting second baseman.

DEVON WHITE CF 1963 Age 34

Year	Team	Lge	AB	H	DB	TP	HR	BB	SB	CS	OUT	BA	OBA	SA	EQA	EQR	Peak
1993	Toronto	AL	604	171	43	6	19	61	30	3	436	.283	.349	.469	.277	88	.272
1994	Toronto	AL	406	113	23	6	14	21	10	3	296	.278	.314	.468	.260	51	.250
1995	Toronto	AL	431	126	25	5	11	29	11	2	307	.292	.337	.450	.265	56	.252
1996	Florida	NL	567	164	37	5	19	45	19	6	409	.289	.342	.473	.271	78	.258
1997	*Florida*	*NL*	*553*	*147*	*39*	*6*	*14*	*43*	*26*	*4*	*410*	*.266*	*.319*	*.434*	*.270*	*78*	

It's hard to believe White was totally blameless in the Marlins' offensive collapse. He's aged with surprising grace, and his strikeouts have come down over the last three years. The Marlins were very grateful for his switch-hitting bat, which helped balance a lineup that leaned more to the right than Rush Limbaugh, but he hit .357 against left-handers and just .254 against righties, which didn't help the problem. As a team the Marlins went 20-12 against portsiders, but only 60-70 when facing right-handers. White's defense has slipped a little, but he's still among the best in the league. A big drop-off could come at any time.

DARRELL WHITMORE OF 1969 Age 28

Year	Team	Lge	AB	H	DB	TP	HR	BB	SB	CS	OUT	BA	OBA	SA	EQA	EQR	Peak
1993	Edmonton	PCL	264	79	13	1	8	20	7	4	189	.299	.349	.447	.266	34	.285
1993	Florida	NL	251	51	7	2	4	14	3	2	202	.203	.245	.295	.172	12	.186
1994	Edmonton	PCL	411	102	15	3	16	39	10	2	311	.248	.313	.416	.245	46	.258
1995	Florida	NL	59	12	2	0	1	5	0	0	47	.203	.266	.288	.177	3	.180
1996	Charlotte-NC	Inter	203	57	6	0	10	8	2	3	149	.281	.308	.458	.250	23	.255

He and ex-Marlin Nigel Wilson had a dozen chances to make the team, and failed them all. Could still be an All-Star someday. And Michael Jordan could win an Oscar for his role in "Space Jam."

GREG ZAUN   **C**   **1971**   **Age 26**

Year	Team	Lge	AB	H	DB	TP	HR	BB	SB	CS	OUT	BA	OBA	SA	EQA	EQR	Peak
1993	Bowie	East	268	79	6	0	4	25	3	4	193	.295	.355	.362	.243	28	.268
1993	Rochester	Inter	79	19	5	1	1	6	0	0	60	.241	.294	.367	.220	7	.244
1994	Rochester	Inter	397	90	12	3	7	53	3	1	308	.227	.318	.325	.217	34	.235
1995	Rochester	Inter	142	40	8	1	6	14	0	2	104	.282	.346	.479	.267	19	.284
1995	Baltimore	AL	105	28	3	0	4	16	1	1	78	.267	.364	.410	.259	13	.278
1996	Rochester	Inter	49	15	1	0	0	10	0	1	35	.306	.424	.327	.259	6	.274
1996	Baltimore	AL	109	26	8	1	1	11	0	0	83	.239	.308	.358	.222	10	.235
1997	*Florida*	*NL*	*290*	*75*	*14*	*1*	*6*	*33*	*0*	*1*	*216*	*.259*	*.334*	*.376*	*.252*	*35*	

The Practically Perfect Backup Catcher. Hits well from both sides of the plate, controls the running game pretty well and in the tradition of his uncle, Rick Dempsey, he's a pretty funny guy. His talents are much more valuable to an NL team, where pinch-hitters are more important and a switch-hitter off the bench is gold. With Johnson and Zaun, the Marlins shouldn't even think of carrying three catchers this season. Probably talented enough to make the transition to starter someday, much like Mike Stanley did.

JOEL ADAMSON   **LBP**   **1972**   **Age 25**

YR	TEAM	Lge	IP	H	ER	HR	BB	K	ERA	W	L	H/9	HR/9	BB/9	K/9	KW
1993	High Desert	Calif	116.3	169	68	13	28	49	5.26	5	8	13.07	1.01	2.17	3.79	.72
1993	Edmonton	PCL	23.7	36	16	4	16	5	6.08	1	2	13.69	1.52	6.08	1.90	-.89
1994	Portland, ME	East	82.3	109	51	9	44	43	5.57	3	6	11.91	.98	4.81	4.70	.36
1995	Charlotte, NC	Inter	107.3	123	49	13	33	67	4.11	6	6	10.31	1.09	2.77	5.62	1.18
1996	Charlotte, NC	Inter	94.3	105	38	13	38	68	3.63	5	5	10.02	1.24	3.63	6.49	1.26
1996	Florida	NL	11.7	18	8	1	9	6	6.17	0	1	13.89	.77	6.94	4.63	-.19

A member of the Marlins' organization since their inception, Adamson is on his last legs as a prospect. Held lefties to a .223 average in AAA, and the Marlins could use a situational left-hander. If anyone can use this guy well, it's Leyland.

ANTONIO ALFONSECA   **RSP**   **1972**   **Age 25**

YR	TEAM	Lge	IP	H	ER	HR	BB	K	ERA	W	L	H/9	HR/9	BB/9	K/9	KW
1993	Jamestown	NY-P	26.7	43	32	4	34	15	10.80	0	3	14.51	1.35	11.48	5.06	-1.18
1994	Kane County	Midw	75.0	101	45	7	31	46	5.40	3	5	12.12	.84	3.72	5.52	.91
1995	Portland, ME	East	89.7	92	40	7	51	58	4.01	5	5	9.23	.70	5.12	5.82	.66
1996	Charlotte, NC	Inter	69.3	83	37	5	29	42	4.80	3	5	10.77	.65	3.76	5.45	.88

As most of the western world knows by now, Alfonseca has six fingers on each hand; it's more a curiosity than a boon at this point, though. He no longer figures into the Marlins' plans after an uninspiring 1996, but if he ever makes the major leagues, I'm sure we'll hear the comparisons between him and Three-Finger Brown.

KEVIN BROWN   **RSP**   **1965**   **Age 32**

YR	TEAM	Lge	IP	H	ER	HR	BB	K	ERA	W	L	H/9	HR/9	BB/9	K/9	KW
1993	Texas	AL	229.3	235	90	15	86	148	3.53	14	11	9.22	.59	3.38	5.81	1.09
1994	Texas	AL	170.7	212	87	16	57	122	4.59	8	11	11.18	.84	3.01	6.43	1.39
1995	Baltimore	AL	169.7	154	54	9	52	117	2.86	13	6	8.17	.48	2.76	6.21	1.38
1996	Florida	NL	224.0	205	51	8	51	138	2.05	20	5	8.24	.32	2.05	5.54	1.34

His success in 1996 should not be all that surprising. If there's one lesson to learn from Brown's season, it is this: right-handed groundball starting pitchers who also rack up strikeouts are the rarest breed of pitcher in baseball, and quite possibly the best. Only three pitchers in baseball fit that description adequately: Brown, Greg Maddux and Joey Hamilton. All three will probably win at least 180 games in their career. Andy Ashby and Charles Nagy are trying to join the club, and the Rockies' Jamey Wright may be there in a few years. As a rule, these pitchers keep their pitch counts down, have minimal injury histories and can pitch effectively into their late 30s. Brown was denied the Cy Young last year, but he should be in contention for several more while he's with the Marlins.

WILL CUNNANE   **RSP**   **1974**   **Age 23**

YR	TEAM	Lge	IP	H	ER	HR	BB	K	ERA	W	L	H/9	HR/9	BB/9	K/9	KW
1994	Kane County	Midw	123.7	140	27	3	36	66	1.96	11	3	10.19	.22	2.62	4.80	.95
1995	Portland, ME	East	108.3	139	47	12	43	64	3.90	6	6	11.55	1.00	3.57	5.32	.88
1996	Portland, ME	East	140.0	172	67	14	41	74	4.31	7	9	11.06	.90	2.64	4.76	.93

A 165-pound experiment that should tell us whether a pitcher can survive in the big leagues with not even a hint of a fastball. Cunnane is polished like an apple on a teacher's desk, but for all his control he can't throw his fastball past Rookie League hitters. We should all root for him, because there's a little bit of Cunnane in all of us. Picked in the Rule V draft by San Diego.

VIC DARENSBOURG   **LRP**   **1971**   **Age 26**

YR	TEAM	Lge	IP	H	ER	HR	BB	K	ERA	W	L	H/9	HR/9	BB/9	K/9	KW
1993	Kane County	Midw	62.7	74	18	4	38	52	2.59	5	2	10.63	.57	5.46	7.47	1.12
1994	Portland, ME	East	135.0	167	76	19	79	75	5.07	6	9	11.13	1.27	5.27	5.00	.35
1996	Charlotte, NC	Inter	60.7	60	23	6	39	54	3.41	4	3	8.90	.89	5.79	8.01	1.22

Very similar to Adamson—he's a left-handed reliever with a favorable platoon split—but the Marlins only need one of these guys. Should make for quite a dogfight in spring training, if the Marlins don't settle the matter by signing Graeme Lloyd or something.

CHRIS HAMMOND   **LBP**   **1966**   **Age 31**

YR	TEAM	Lge	IP	H	ER	HR	BB	K	ERA	W	L	H/9	HR/9	BB/9	K/9	KW
1993	Florida	NL	186.3	211	96	18	88	104	4.64	9	12	10.19	.87	4.25	5.02	.61
1994	Florida	NL	72.7	74	24	5	29	37	2.97	5	3	9.17	.62	3.59	4.58	.63
1995	Florida	NL	158.7	160	63	17	60	113	3.57	10	8	9.08	.96	3.40	6.41	1.29
1996	Florida	NL	81.0	108	60	13	35	44	6.67	2	7	12.00	1.44	3.89	4.89	.66

A disastrous season, but there were warning signs for this; Hammond posted a 6.19 ERA over the last two months of 1995. His career has always been a bit of a riddle, and he may continue to alternate between Steve Carlton and Steve Dalkowski. Better suited to relief, but the Marlins aren't sure if they want him back in that role.

RICK HELLING   **RSP**   **1971**   **Age 26**

YR	TEAM	Lge	IP	H	ER	HR	BB	K	ERA	W	L	H/9	HR/9	BB/9	K/9	KW
1993	Tulsa	Texas	161.0	171	76	16	73	134	4.25	8	10	9.56	.89	4.08	7.49	1.48
1993	Oklahoma	AmA	10.3	6	1	0	4	15	.87	1	0	5.23	.00	3.48	13.06	3.48
1994	Oklahoma	AmA	127.7	159	85	18	56	77	5.99	4	10	11.21	1.27	3.95	5.43	.82
1994	Texas	AL	52.3	59	27	13	20	25	4.64	3	3	10.15	2.24	3.44	4.30	.57
1995	Oklahoma	AmA	106.0	135	68	13	56	70	5.77	4	8	11.46	1.10	4.75	5.94	.79
1995	Texas	AL	12.7	15	8	2	9	5	5.68	0	1	10.66	1.42	6.39	3.55	-.41
1996	Oklahoma	AmA	133.7	135	49	9	56	130	3.30	9	6	9.09	.61	3.77	8.75	1.98
1996	Florida	NL	26.3	17	5	2	9	23	1.71	3	0	5.81	.68	3.08	7.86	1.85
1996	Texas	AL	20.7	20	12	6	10	15	5.23	1	1	8.71	2.61	4.35	6.53	1.09

Helling, in a nutshell, encapsulates all that is wrong with the Rangers' organization, and all that has been wrong for their 36-year existence. The concept of patience is completely lost on them. Helling had a very promising start to his career in 1994, then had two disappointing starts in a row. The Rangers suddenly decided that his development would be better served if they moved him to the bullpen, sent him down to the minors and told the media that he wasn't ready and that promoting him had been a mistake.

Pitching is heavily dependent on confidence, and when the Rangers took that away from Helling, his stuff—which is wicked—didn't matter anymore. The Marlins greeted him with open arms, showed conviction in his ability and told him he had the stuff to succeed in the major leagues. They proved it by sticking him in the rotation in September and leaving him there. He's been a prospect for so long that the media's forgotten about him, but he'll catch their attention again if he wins 15 games out of the #4 rotation spot.

FELIX HEREDIA   LRP   1976   Age 21

YR	TEAM	Lge	IP	H	ER	HR	BB	K	ERA	W	L	H/9	HR/9	BB/9	K/9	KW
1994	Kane County	Midw	58.7	107	58	9	21	41	8.90	1	6	16.41	1.38	3.22	6.29	1.29
1995	Brevard Cty	Flor	82.0	137	66	10	51	55	7.24	2	7	15.04	1.10	5.60	6.04	.61
1996	Portland, ME	East	55.3	54	10	3	19	31	1.63	5	1	8.78	.49	3.09	5.04	.91
1996	Florida	NL	16.3	23	8	1	12	9	4.41	1	1	12.67	.55	6.61	4.96	.00

The Marlins may have the best Latin American development crew in the game. Either that or they've managed to forge a lot of birth certificates to make their prospects look younger. Heredia was the youngest pitcher in the Eastern League, but breezed through hitters there like so much riffraff. Throws in the low 90s with deceptive motion; how many left-handers do you know who can do that? Will probably stumble a little this year, if only because it seems implausible to expect a 21-year-old to make such a smooth transition to the major leagues. Has a tremendous upside.

LIVAN HERNANDEZ   RSP   1975   Age 22

YR	TEAM	Lge	IP	H	ER	HR	BB	K	ERA	W	L	H/9	HR/9	BB/9	K/9	KW
1996	Charlotte, NC	Inter	47.7	57	25	3	41	37	4.72	2	3	10.76	.57	7.74	6.99	.39
1996	Portland, ME	East	86.3	89	43	13	43	70	4.48	4	6	9.28	1.36	4.48	7.30	1.31

Once people stopped expecting him to throw a shutout every time out, Hernandez showed he might be worth the $4.5 million the Marlins signed him for. He started the year in AAA and went through a dead-arm period, but a demotion to AA coincided with the return of his 95 mph fastball, and he was untouchable for much of the second half. Remember that this was his first professional season and all the while he was dealing with language and culture differences. Has a classic pitcher's build and by the turn of the century he should one of baseball's best right-handers. Think Alex Fernandez.

BILL HURST   RRP   1970   Age 27

YR	TEAM	Lge	IP	H	ER	HR	BB	K	ERA	W	L	H/9	HR/9	BB/9	K/9	KW
1995	Brevard Cty	Flor	45.0	44	23	2	53	25	4.60	2	3	8.80	.40	10.60	5.00	-.98
1996	Portland, ME	East	45.3	48	20	3	37	34	3.97	3	2	9.53	.60	7.35	6.75	.41

Just happy to be playing pro ball. Hurst was a late-round pick by the Cardinals in 1989, and arm torments dogged his progress for three years before he succumbed to Tommy John surgery. The Marlins signed him out of a tryout camp two years ago, and he's been healthy and effective since then. Throws a noxious sinker, and the Marlins liked him enough to take a look-see at year's end. He's 27 and the next elbow twitch could be his last.

MARK HUTTON   RBP   1970   Age 27

YR	TEAM	Lge	IP	H	ER	HR	BB	K	ERA	W	L	H/9	HR/9	BB/9	K/9	KW
1993	Columbus, OH	Inter	125.3	110	49	14	70	91	3.52	8	6	7.90	1.01	5.03	6.53	.92
1993	NY Yankees	AL	22.0	25	15	2	19	13	6.14	1	1	10.23	.82	7.77	5.32	-.17
1994	Columbus, OH	Inter	32.7	34	15	6	15	22	4.13	2	2	9.37	1.65	4.13	6.06	.99
1995	Columbus, OH	Inter	49.7	64	46	7	32	19	8.34	1	5	11.60	1.27	5.80	3.44	-.30
1996	Florida	NL	55.0	50	21	6	23	27	3.44	3	3	8.18	.98	3.76	4.42	.53
1996	NY Yankees	AL	30.3	30	14	2	19	24	4.15	1	2	8.90	.59	5.64	7.12	.96

It's amazing how the Marlins succeed in taking pitchers other organizations have given up on, giving them a fair opportunity to succeed, and watching them do so. Like Helling, Hutton was never given a fixed role with the Yankees, jumping from the rotation to the bullpen and from the majors to AAA. Unless the Marlins decide to sign two or three starting pitchers, Hutton should have a spot waiting for him spring training. Never bet against an Australian.

ANDY LARKIN   RSP   1974   Age 23

YR	TEAM	Lge	IP	H	ER	HR	BB	K	ERA	W	L	H/9	HR/9	BB/9	K/9	KW
1993	Elmira	NY-P	74.0	104	52	2	40	47	6.32	2	6	12.65	.24	4.86	5.72	.69
1994	Kane County	Midw	124.3	156	54	7	42	79	3.91	7	7	11.29	.51	3.04	5.72	1.15
1995	Portland, ME	East	37.0	34	15	6	14	18	3.65	2	2	8.27	1.46	3.41	4.38	.61
1996	Brevard Cty	Flor	24.0	43	24	1	11	13	9.00	0	3	16.12	.38	4.12	4.88	.59
1996	Portland, ME	East	46.0	49	16	6	14	29	3.13	3	2	9.59	1.17	2.74	5.67	1.21

Coveted arm, but he can't stay healthy for an entire season and that's really hindered his progress. Larkin may be one of these Steve Ontiveros-type pitchers, who have terrific control and an idea what they're doing on the mound, but can't take the mound more than 15 times a year. Still young enough that he might reap rewards if the Marlins are patient with him.

AL LEITER   **LSP**   **1966**   **Age 31**

YR	TEAM	Lge	IP	H	ER	HR	BB	K	ERA	W	L	H/9	HR/9	BB/9	K/9	KW
1993	Toronto	AL	103.3	93	42	8	60	68	3.66	6	5	8.10	.70	5.23	5.92	.67
1994	Toronto	AL	112.0	121	52	5	68	98	4.18	6	6	9.72	.40	5.46	7.88	1.26
1995	Toronto	AL	182.7	158	61	14	112	153	3.01	13	7	7.78	.69	5.52	7.54	1.13
1996	Florida	NL	210.3	169	65	15	138	176	2.78	16	7	7.23	.64	5.90	7.53	1.03

One of the most unique pitchers in the game. He's not a groundball pitcher, but when he's on his game batters hit nothing but squibbers and ducksnorts. About as wild as a man can be and still be among the best pitchers in the league. Like Randy Johnson, Leiter turned his game around at age 29, but unlike Johnson, his control hasn't improved at all. Leiter has succeeded by not giving in when he puts runners on base, knowing that at worst he'll give up a bloop single. With runners in scoring position the last two years, batters have hit just .208 with a .302 slugging average. Nagging injuries at the start of his career have kept his arm fresh, and he still hasn't hit his ceiling. This could be the year he brings his walks below five per nine innings, and stakes his claim as the best left-hander in the National League.

MATT MANTEI   **RRP**   **1974**   **Age 23**

YR	TEAM	Lge	IP	H	ER	HR	BB	K	ERA	W	L	H/9	HR/9	BB/9	K/9	KW
1993	Bellingham	Nwern	21.0	36	21	3	17	19	9.00	0	2	15.43	1.29	7.29	8.14	.89
1994	Appleton	Midw	42.3	51	14	2	29	44	2.98	3	2	10.84	.43	6.17	9.35	1.58
1995	Portland, ME	East	10.3	12	3	0	6	12	2.61	1	0	10.45	.00	5.23	10.45	2.18
1995	Florida	NL	13.0	13	7	1	14	14	4.85	0	1	9.00	.69	9.69	9.69	.81
1996	Florida	NL	18.3	15	12	2	23	22	5.89	1	1	7.36	.98	11.29	10.80	.78

An intriguing Rule V find in the 1995 draft, Mantei didn't flinch at a promotion from the Midwest League to the majors. Has a genuine power arm and the stuff to dominate, but he's still wilder than a rodeo steer and it may be a few years before his control is up to snuff. I suspect it will eventually; hanging around Robb Nen, who was once as untamed as Mantei is, should help.

BRIAN MEADOWS   **RSP**   **1976**   **Age 21**

YR	TEAM	Lge	IP	H	ER	HR	BB	K	ERA	W	L	H/9	HR/9	BB/9	K/9	KW
1995	Kane County	Midw	126.3	209	98	14	58	67	6.98	3	11	14.89	1.00	4.13	4.77	.56
1996	Brevard Cty	Flor	127.7	172	91	20	40	51	6.42	4	10	12.13	1.41	2.82	3.60	.49
1996	Portland, ME	East	25.0	29	14	1	6	10	5.04	1	2	10.44	.36	2.16	3.60	.66

Extreme control pitcher who saw his strikeout rate go from bad to worse last year. His pitching style is a lot like Cunnane's, but Meadows doesn't disappear when he turns sideways. Sturdily-built pitchers rarely survive in the big leagues if they can't bring the cheese, and I doubt Meadows will prove to be an exception.

KURT MILLER   **RBP**   **1973**   **Age 24**

YR	TEAM	Lge	IP	H	ER	HR	BB	K	ERA	W	L	H/9	HR/9	BB/9	K/9	KW
1993	Tulsa	Texas	86.0	114	70	9	63	49	7.33	2	8	11.93	.94	6.59	5.13	.06
1993	Edmonton	PCL	43.3	39	17	2	39	15	3.53	3	2	8.10	.42	8.10	3.12	-.99
1994	Edmonton	PCL	118.0	147	78	15	77	49	5.95	4	9	11.21	1.14	5.87	3.74	-.22
1994	Florida	NL	20.0	24	15	3	9	10	6.75	1	1	10.80	1.35	4.05	4.50	.49
1995	Charlotte, NC	Inter	119.0	153	73	14	73	70	5.52	4	9	11.57	1.06	5.52	5.29	.38
1996	Charlotte, NC	Inter	63.3	74	31	6	33	31	4.41	3	4	10.52	.85	4.69	4.41	.30
1996	Florida	NL	46.7	60	38	5	38	27	7.33	1	4	11.57	.96	7.33	5.21	-.10

He's only 24, but Miller has been a prospect since the Bush administration. He had limitless potential as a 20-year phenom in 1992, and his decline since then is stunning because injuries have not appeared to play a role. He still shows flashes of his old self every fifth start or so, but the rest of the time he's backing up third base after walking the leadoff hitter and grooving a 3-1 fastball to the next. The Marlins tried him in relief, but that didn't work, and he was a complete disaster towards the end of the year. Maybe a 30% chance of ever having a good season.

ROBB NEN   **RRP**   **1970**   **Age 27**

YR	TEAM	Lge	IP	H	ER	HR	BB	K	ERA	W	L	H/9	HR/9	BB/9	K/9	KW
1993	Oklahoma	AmA	28.0	42	18	3	21	11	5.79	1	2	13.50	.96	6.75	3.54	-.51
1993	Florida	NL	33.0	35	25	6	24	26	6.82	1	3	9.55	1.64	6.55	7.09	.73
1993	Texas	AL	23.3	28	15	1	28	13	5.79	1	2	10.80	.39	10.80	5.01	-1.03
1994	Florida	NL	56.7	44	15	6	22	55	2.38	4	2	6.99	.95	3.49	8.74	2.04
1995	Florida	NL	64.7	64	23	6	28	61	3.20	4	3	8.91	.84	3.90	8.49	1.86
1996	Florida	NL	80.3	74	18	2	28	80	2.02	7	2	8.29	.22	3.14	8.96	2.20

Spending a year chewing the fat with Bryan Harvey must have done something to Nen, because their career paths have been remarkably similar. Both were wild as the cast of "Animal House" before undergoing a stunning conversion into disciplined power pitchers at the major league level. Nen was 24 when he went through his metamorphosis, and his stuff is so good now he can throw his fastball with control inside the strike zone, not just around it. If he avoids Harvey's injury history he could save 300 games before he's through. If he synchronizes a great season with the Marlins' peak in a few years, he could break Bobby Thigpen's save record of 57.

CLEMENTE NUNEZ   **RBP**   **1975**   **Age 22**

YR	TEAM	Lge	IP	H	ER	HR	BB	K	ERA	W	L	H/9	HR/9	BB/9	K/9	KW
1993	Elmira	NY-P	50.0	95	40	6	30	18	7.20	1	5	17.10	1.08	5.40	3.24	-.27
1994	Brevard Cty	Flor	89.3	107	51	12	35	51	5.14	4	6	10.78	1.21	3.53	5.14	.83
1995	Brevard Cty	Flor	109.3	134	58	6	34	57	4.77	5	7	11.03	.49	2.80	4.69	.86
1996	Portland, ME	East	90.7	124	66	16	40	38	6.55	3	7	12.31	1.59	3.97	3.77	.26

With Nunez, Meadows and Cunnane, the Portland staff had three virtually identical soft-tossing right-handers. You have to wonder if the trio's performance was affected by showing opposing hitters similar pitching styles so often. Nunez is one of many borderline Marlin pitching prospects who all have one thing going for them: they're all very young for their leagues. Nunez could easily surface and be a very good hurler three or four years for now. I doubt it will happen; he's a small guy and short right-handers have to pitch twice as well to get half the opportunities.

DONN PALL   **RRP**   **1962**   **Age 35**

YR	TEAM	Lge	IP	H	ER	HR	BB	K	ERA	W	L	H/9	HR/9	BB/9	K/9	KW
1993	Chi. White Sox	AL	57.7	63	21	5	13	30	3.28	4	2	9.83	.78	2.03	4.68	1.05
1993	Philadelphia	NL	17.0	16	6	1	4	11	3.18	1	1	8.47	.53	2.12	5.82	1.41
1994	NY Yankees	AL	35.0	43	15	3	10	21	3.86	2	2	11.06	.77	2.57	5.40	1.16
1995	Nashville	AmA	81.7	99	39	10	30	70	4.30	4	5	10.91	1.10	3.31	7.71	1.74
1996	Charlotte, NC	Inter	49.3	43	16	3	17	43	2.92	3	2	7.84	.55	3.10	7.84	1.84
1996	Florida	NL	18.3	18	14	3	10	8	6.87	1	1	8.84	1.47	4.91	3.93	.08

The Marlins' farm system is not nearly as deep with pitching prospects as it is with hitters, so journeymen like Pall had to be signed to fill the void. The quintessential tenth man, but he really deserves a job in the major leagues. He may not have the flash of, say, a Brad Pennington, but he doesn't walk anyone and keeps the ball in the park. As long as he's keeping hitters away from the three-run homer, he'll be effective even if they're batting .300 against him. Death on right-handed batters. His career is probably over.

YORKIS PEREZ   **LRP**   **1968**   **Age 29**

YR	TEAM	Lge	IP	H	ER	HR	BB	K	ERA	W	L	H/9	HR/9	BB/9	K/9	KW
1993	Harrisburg	East	40.7	56	26	4	26	44	5.75	2	3	12.39	.89	5.75	9.74	1.81
1993	Ottawa	Inter	18.7	16	10	0	9	14	4.82	1	1	7.71	.00	4.34	6.75	1.17
1994	Florida	NL	39.3	33	14	4	17	38	3.20	2	2	7.55	.92	3.89	8.69	1.93
1995	Florida	NL	45.7	37	25	6	32	42	4.93	2	3	7.29	1.18	6.31	8.28	1.18
1996	Charlotte, NC	Inter	10.0	7	4	1	4	11	3.60	1	0	6.30	.90	3.60	9.90	2.40
1996	Florida	NL	47.3	55	26	2	36	42	4.94	2	3	10.46	.38	6.85	7.99	.95

Perez's troubles last year stemmed directly from his difficulties with left-handed batters. Against right-handers he was as effective as usual, but left-handers went from hitting .157 in 1995 to .295 last year. Perez is one of the new specialist relievers, brought in specifically to get one or two lefties out and averaging barely two-thirds of an inning per appearance. He saw a higher percentage of left-handed batters than even Rick Honeycutt last year, which made his failure that much more acute. He wasn't that bad a pitcher overall—he gave only 10 extra-base hits all season—and I would chalk last year's numbers up to small sample size. A good, cheap pickup for 1997.

JAY POWELL   **RRP**   **1972**   **Age 25**

YR	TEAM	Lge	IP	H	ER	HR	BB	K	ERA	W	L	H/9	HR/9	BB/9	K/9	KW
1993	Albany, GA	S Atl	23.0	39	23	0	18	17	9.00	0	3	15.26	.00	7.04	6.65	.46
1994	Frederick	Caro	110.0	159	82	12	73	59	6.71	3	9	13.01	.98	5.97	4.83	.12
1995	Portland, ME	East	49.0	50	11	2	19	41	2.02	4	1	9.18	.37	3.49	7.53	1.64
1996	Florida	NL	70.3	76	38	5	43	46	4.86	3	5	9.73	.64	5.50	5.89	.59

Generally inconsistent all season, but he's got an arm. Powell was an Orioles first-rounder who they prepared for a career in relief by placing in the rotation. Traded to a franchise with an abundance of functioning brain cells, Powell's future suddenly brightened. He gets a lot of groundballs, and the early state of flux surrounding the Marlins' infield probably hurt. Should be Nen's top set-up man this year, but he did post a 5.15 ERA in the second half, so be wary.

PAT RAPP   **RSP**   **1968**   **Age 29**

YR	TEAM	Lge	IP	H	ER	HR	BB	K	ERA	W	L	H/9	HR/9	BB/9	K/9	KW
1993	Edmonton	PCL	99.0	87	33	9	44	74	3.00	7	4	7.91	.82	4.00	6.73	1.24
1993	Florida	NL	91.7	104	45	7	49	55	4.42	5	5	10.21	.69	4.81	5.40	.60
1994	Florida	NL	132.3	123	53	12	80	69	3.60	8	7	8.37	.82	5.44	4.69	.20
1995	Florida	NL	164.3	163	63	10	90	91	3.45	10	8	8.93	.55	4.93	4.98	.43
1996	Charlotte, NC	Inter	10.7	17	9	3	5	7	7.59	0	1	14.34	2.53	4.22	5.91	.91
1996	Florida	NL	161.0	196	89	12	108	77	4.98	7	11	10.96	.67	6.04	4.30	-.07

His ridiculous strikeout-to-walk ratios finally did him in. Let's repeat it one more time, kiddies: a pitcher's strikeout-to-walk ratio is the single most important prognosticator (besides age) for future success. Occasionally a pitcher will buck the trend for a few years, like Rapp did, by throwing a great sinker, keeping extra-base hits to a minimum, getting lots of double play balls, holding runners well…pretty much everything short of bribing the umpires. But it never lasts for long. Rapp is talented enough to adjust his pitching style and resurface, but the transition may take a few years.

TONY SAUNDERS   **LSP**   **1974**   **Age 23**

YR	TEAM	Lge	IP	H	ER	HR	BB	K	ERA	W	L	H/9	HR/9	BB/9	K/9	KW
1993	Kane County	Midw	71.3	96	26	4	43	51	3.28	5	3	12.11	.50	5.43	6.43	.79
1994	Brevard Cty	Flor	54.3	67	27	6	15	35	4.47	3	3	11.10	.99	2.48	5.80	1.31
1995	Brevard Cty	Flor	63.0	80	35	9	23	39	5.00	3	4	11.43	1.29	3.29	5.57	1.04
1996	Portland, ME	East	155.3	135	44	10	77	114	2.55	12	5	7.82	.58	4.46	6.61	1.09

Remember, pitching is supposed to be the weak underbelly of the Marlins' farm system. Are those numbers for real? Saunders is a virtual unknown - he wasn't listed among the Eastern League's Top 10 Prospects by Baseball America - but pitching in one of the best hitter's parks in AA, Saunders posted a 2.63 ERA, the same as Red Sox wunderkind Carl Pavano. Hitters flailed away for a .203 average, lower than against any other starter in the high minors. The Marlins have no plans for him any time soon, but talent like that doesn't sit on the farm for long. The Cubs were saying the same thing about Amaury Telemaco last year. In five seasons of pro ball, there isn't one shred of evidence that says Saunders can't pitch, so don't let the lack of attention fool you. An early front-runner for the 1998 Rookie of the Year.

CHRIS SEELBACH   **RSP**   **1973**   **Age 24**

YR	TEAM	Lge	IP	H	ER	HR	BB	K	ERA	W	L	H/9	HR/9	BB/9	K/9	KW
1993	Durham	Caro	114.0	157	91	15	105	70	7.18	3	10	12.39	1.18	8.29	5.53	-.23
1994	Greenville	South	84.3	77	27	4	53	62	2.88	6	3	8.22	.43	5.66	6.62	.79
1994	Richmond	Inter	58.0	73	35	6	44	29	5.43	2	4	11.33	.93	6.83	4.50	-.21
1995	Greenville	South	55.7	44	13	3	38	49	2.10	5	1	7.11	.49	6.14	7.92	1.10
1995	Richmond	Inter	67.7	77	43	8	51	56	5.72	3	5	10.24	1.06	6.78	7.45	.79
1996	Charlotte, NC	Inter	134.3	158	97	22	92	80	6.50	4	11	10.59	1.47	6.16	5.36	.25

Seelbach looked like a great pitcher when the Marlins swapped Alejandro Pena for him a year ago, but the Braves evidently knew what they were doing when they gave him up. The decline in his strikeout rate is alarming. Perhaps spending a season on the same team with Kurt Miller rubbed off on him. Has to re-establish himself as a prospect soon, because the Marlins have better pitchers coming up through the system.

MARC VALDES   **RSP**   **1972**   **Age 25**

YR	TEAM	Lge	IP	H	ER	HR	BB	K	ERA	W	L	H/9	HR/9	BB/9	K/9	KW
1994	Kane County	Midw	67.7	78	31	4	30	43	4.12	4	4	10.37	.53	3.99	5.72	.91
1994	Portland, ME	East	90.7	88	30	6	51	51	2.98	6	4	8.74	.60	5.06	5.06	.42
1995	Charlotte, NC	Inter	159.7	202	94	21	82	88	5.30	7	11	11.39	1.18	4.62	4.96	.50
1996	Portland, ME	East	60.0	65	22	5	17	36	3.30	4	3	9.75	.75	2.55	5.40	1.16
1996	Charlotte, NC	Inter	49.7	62	25	9	21	20	4.53	3	3	11.23	1.63	3.81	3.62	.26
1996	Florida	NL	48.7	66	30	5	28	12	5.55	2	3	12.21	.92	5.18	2.22	-.55

The Marlins were hoping for better. Valdes was a first-round draft pick and a very polished college pitcher at Florida. His velocity was never that great and the Marlins think his performance the last two years is a result of losing the movement on his other pitches. They're at a loss to fix it, though. He got straightened out a bit after a demotion to AA, and he pitched fine at times when the Marlins took a look at him late in the year. Won't last another month walking twice as many hitters as he strikes out, though.

BRYAN WARD   **LSP**   **1972**   **Age 25**

YR	TEAM	Lge	IP	H	ER	HR	BB	K	ERA	W	L	H/9	HR/9	BB/9	K/9	KW
1993	Elmira	NY-P	47.3	112	49	8	43	33	9.32	1	4	21.30	1.52	8.18	6.27	.05
1994	Kane County	Midw	49.3	57	28	5	29	39	5.11	2	3	10.40	.91	5.29	7.11	1.05
1995	Brevard Cty	Flor	62.3	94	35	8	26	47	5.05	3	4	13.57	1.16	3.75	6.79	1.32
1995	Portland, ME	East	66.7	80	40	10	37	54	5.40	2	5	10.80	1.35	5.00	7.29	1.18
1996	Portland, ME	East	136.7	182	87	22	43	91	5.73	5	10	11.99	1.45	2.83	5.99	1.29

At 24, he was one of the veterans of the Portland staff. Ward pitches like Saunders' reputation, a canny left-hander without great stuff. Ward is just good enough to be a career AAA pitcher, and in all likelihood he'll pitch 10 more years in the minor leagues and get 17 innings in the major leagues.

MATT WHISENANT   **LSP**   **1971**   **Age 26**

YR	TEAM	Lge	IP	H	ER	HR	BB	K	ERA	W	L	H/9	HR/9	BB/9	K/9	KW
1993	Kane County	Midw	60.3	85	49	4	72	43	7.31	2	5	12.68	.60	10.74	6.41	-.55
1994	Brevard Cty	Flor	144.3	157	79	12	106	80	4.93	6	10	9.79	.75	6.61	4.99	.01
1995	Portland, ME	East	119.3	120	53	8	79	82	4.00	7	6	9.05	.60	5.96	6.18	.57
1996	Charlotte, NC	Inter	117.7	139	85	13	117	79	6.50	4	9	10.63	.99	8.95	6.04	-.22

Scouts like to describe pitchers like Whisenant as having a "raw arm," which is fine when they're 19 years old. At 26, Whisenant's arm is rapidly growing stale. Took a big step backwards last year, and I doubt he can retrace his steps.

Player	Age	Team	Lge	AB	H	DB	TP	HR	BB	SB	CS	OUT	BA	OBA	SA	EQA	EQR	Peak
EARL AGNOLY	20	Kane County	Midw	208	44	6	1	1	10	1	2	166	.212	.248	.264	.157	8	.180
JOE AVERSA	28	Portland-ME	East	138	30	6	0	0	20	2	1	109	.217	.316	.261	.194	9	.194
MATT BRUNSON	21	Brevard Cty	Flor	414	83	10	1	1	58	14	6	337	.200	.299	.237	.180	23	.201
TODD CADY	23	Brevard Cty	Flor	351	71	5	0	8	34	2	3	283	.202	.273	.285	.179	19	.194
JOSE CAMILO	19	Kane County	Midw	99	18	1	0	4	7	3	0	81	.182	.236	.313	.182	6	.209
DENNIS CASTRO	23	Brevard Cty	Flor	231	56	7	1	4	15	0	2	177	.242	.289	.333	.204	17	.220
HAYWARD COOK	24	Brevard Cty	Flor	295	84	8	4	9	26	8	4	215	.285	.343	.431	.259	37	.278
TONY DARDEN	22	Brevard Cty	Flor	400	89	18	2	2	26	4	5	316	.222	.270	.292	.182	22	.201
MAT ERWIN	23	Brevard Cty	Flor	220	58	10	0	2	20	0	1	163	.264	.325	.336	.222	19	.241
JOE FUNARO	23	Kane County	Midw	303	85	10	1	7	30	3	1	219	.281	.345	.389	.249	34	.271
AMAURY GARCIA	21	Kane County	Midw	412	97	12	3	7	48	18	9	324	.235	.315	.330	.220	37	.247
LARRY GLOZIER	22	Kane County	Midw	83	15	1	1	0	15	1	1	69	.181	.306	.217	.168	4	.186
STEVE GOODELL	21	Kane County	Midw	291	74	8	1	8	23	1	0	217	.254	.309	.371	.228	27	.255
AARON HARVEY	23	Brevard Cty	Flor	369	91	12	1	7	20	7	4	282	.247	.285	.341	.210	28	.228
LIONEL HASTINGS	23	Portland-ME	East	295	62	9	1	5	13	3	1	234	.210	.244	.298	.174	15	.189
ERIK JOHNSON	30	Charlotte-NC	Inter	184	28	5	0	0	9	0	1	157	.152	.192	.179	-.065	-1	-.064
JAIME JONES	19	Kane County	Midw	243	56	7	1	7	14	4	1	188	.230	.272	.354	.209	19	.240
HECTOR KUILAN	20	Kane County	Midw	315	55	6	1	5	16	1	1	261	.175	.215	.248	.128	8	.146
QUINN MACK	30	Portland-ME	East	112	22	1	0	3	6	3	2	92	.196	.237	.286	.166	5	.163
SOMMER MCCARTNEY	23	Kane County	Midw	165	45	5	0	5	10	1	1	120	.273	.314	.394	.238	17	.260
DOUG O'NEILL	26	Portland-ME	East	245	58	7	1	6	23	6	2	189	.237	.302	.347	.220	21	.228
TOM OWEN	23	Brevard Cty	Flor	131	26	2	1	1	24	1	1	106	.198	.323	.252	.191	9	.209
SCOTT PODSEDNIK	20	Brevard Cty	Flor	398	99	8	1	1	40	10	5	304	.249	.317	.281	.205	29	.232
RENE RASCON	22	Kane County	Midw	193	29	3	0	3	13	0	0	164	.150	.204	.212	.088	2	.095
GLENN REEVES	22	Brevard Cty	Flor	500	143	21	2	9	57	4	3	360	.286	.359	.390	.254	59	.280
MARQUIS RILEY	25	Charlotte-NC	Inter	300	61	5	0	1	26	10	3	242	.203	.267	.230	.162	13	.171
RYAN ROBERTSON	23	Kane County	Midw	169	35	4	0	3	29	0	0	134	.207	.323	.284	.204	13	.220
MAXIMO RODRIGUEZ	22	Brevard Cty	Flor	279	59	8	0	5	17	2	2	222	.211	.257	.294	.176	14	.194
JASON SHANAHAN	22	Brevard Cty	Flor	382	74	15	1	3	32	1	1	309	.194	.256	.262	.161	16	.177
JOE SIDDALL	28	Charlotte-NC	Inter	188	47	9	1	3	12	1	1	142	.250	.295	.356	.217	16	.219
TONY TORRES	26	Portland-ME	East	128	32	5	0	2	12	2	1	97	.250	.314	.336	.220	11	.228
WALTER WHITE	24	Kane County	Midw	318	48	10	2	1	26	1	2	272	.151	.215	.204	.091	3	.099
POOKIE WILSON	25	Portland-ME	East	380	87	12	2	6	29	6	5	298	.229	.284	.318	.199	26	.210
RANDY WINN	22	Kane County	Midw	529	124	10	2	1	35	14	8	413	.234	.282	.267	.182	29	.201

Player	Age	Team	Lge	IP	H	ER	HR	BB	K	ERA	W	L	H/9	HR/9	BB/9	K/9	KW
NIGEL ALEJO	21	Brevard Cty	Flor	33.7	62	28	1	19	26	7.49	1	3	16.57	.27	5.08	6.95	1.05
MIGUEL BATISTA	25	Charlotte, NC	Inter	74.3	89	45	4	48	46	5.45	3	5	10.78	.48	5.81	5.57	.40
MITCHEL BOWEN	23	Brevard Cty	Flor	46.3	85	40	5	22	21	7.77	1	4	16.51	.97	4.27	4.08	.29
TRAVIS BURGUS	23	Kane County	Midw	84.7	102	30	2	51	70	3.19	6	3	10.84	.21	5.42	7.44	1.12
MIKE CARAVELLI	23	Brevard Cty	Flor	62.0	91	25	4	25	34	3.63	4	3	13.21	.58	3.63	4.94	.74
ANTONIO CASTRO	24	Kane County	Midw	58.0	69	40	3	41	40	6.21	2	4	10.71	.47	6.36	6.21	.48
DAN CHERGEY	25	Charlotte, NC	Inter	72.7	82	43	14	36	35	5.33	3	5	10.16	1.73	4.46	4.33	.33
SCOTT DEWITT	21	Kane County	Midw	126.7	196	107	11	77	75	7.60	3	11	13.93	.78	5.47	5.33	.41
MICHAEL DUVALL	21	Kane County	Midw	42.0	54	21	1	27	29	4.50	2	3	11.57	.21	5.79	6.21	.62
DANIEL EHLER	21	Brevard Cty	Flor	131.3	223	106	17	62	65	7.26	3	12	15.28	1.16	4.25	4.45	.42
RICK GARCIA	22	Kane County	Midw	48.0	79	51	4	52	30	9.56	1	4	14.81	.75	9.75	5.62	-.56
ROD GETZ	20	Kane County	Midw	102.7	184	86	11	53	53	7.54	2	9	16.13	.96	4.65	4.65	.39
GABE GONZALEZ	24	Brevard Cty	Flor	68.3	73	22	4	33	45	2.90	5	3	9.61	.53	4.35	5.93	.89
JUAN GONZALEZ	21	Brevard Cty	Flor	75.3	129	68	10	40	36	8.12	2	6	15.41	1.19	4.78	4.30	.24
DOUG HARRIS	26	Portland, ME	East	32.7	35	13	4	18	19	3.58	2	2	9.64	1.10	4.96	5.23	.51
VICTOR HURTADO	19	Brevard Cty	Flor	151.0	219	89	14	74	79	5.30	6	11	13.05	.83	4.41	4.71	.47
JAROD JUELSGAARD	28	Charlotte, NC	Inter	42.0	43	18	1	25	24	3.86	3	2	9.21	.21	5.36	5.14	.37
REYNOL MENDOZA	25	Charlotte, NC	Inter	88.3	106	53	15	43	33	5.40	4	6	10.80	1.53	4.38	3.36	.03
	25	Portland, ME	East	58.0	67	25	6	19	30	3.88	3	3	10.40	.93	2.95	4.66	.81
CHAD MILES	23	Brevard Cty	Flor	61.7	113	67	12	44	28	9.78	1	6	16.49	1.75	6.42	4.09	-.24
DAVID MILLER	22	Brevard Cty	Flor	73.7	121	60	17	38	30	7.33	2	6	14.78	2.08	4.64	3.67	.06
GREG MIX	24	Portland, ME	East	61.3	85	36	7	24	42	5.28	3	4	12.47	1.03	3.52	6.16	1.17
BOB PAILTHORPE	23	Kane County	Midw	62.0	97	40	3	40	47	5.81	2	5	14.08	.44	5.81	6.82	.82
MICHAEL PARISI	23	Brevard Cty	Flor	104.0	152	72	15	56	48	6.23	4	8	13.15	1.30	4.85	4.15	.17
GREGG PRESS	24	Brevard Cty	Flor	131.3	178	77	15	56	66	5.28	5	10	12.20	1.03	3.84	4.52	.55
GARY SANTORO	23	Kane County	Midw	29.0	38	14	0	15	22	4.34	1	2	11.79	.00	4.66	6.83	1.11
ROBBY STANIFER	24	Brevard Cty	Flor	42.7	70	21	5	15	24	4.43	2	3	14.77	1.05	3.16	5.06	.90
	24	Portland, ME	East	32.0	30	14	4	12	24	3.94	2	2	8.44	1.12	3.38	6.75	1.41
SHANNON STEPHENS	22	Kane County	Midw	92.0	124	47	11	33	53	4.60	4	6	12.13	1.08	3.23	5.18	.92
PAUL THORNTON	26	Portland, ME	East	72.0	78	40	6	53	47	5.00	3	5	9.75	.75	6.62	5.88	.30
PATRICK TREEND	24	Kane County	Midw	41.7	59	36	3	30	25	7.78	1	4	12.74	.65	6.48	5.40	.18
DANIEL VARDIJAN	19	Kane County	Midw	127.0	161	75	7	72	58	5.31	5	9	11.41	.50	5.10	4.11	.09
MICKEY WESTON	35	Charlotte, NC	Inter	100.7	125	58	10	50	38	5.19	4	7	11.18	.89	4.47	3.40	.01

Montreal Expos

The Montreal Expos are baseball's truest underdogs. Not the kind of underdog that everyone roots for, like the Mariners in 1995, but the underdog that no one even recognizes. The '95 Mariners made celebrities out of Bob Wolcott, Luis Sojo and Dave Niehaus, but the Expos are so unfashionable that Pedro Martinez can throw a perfect game for nine innings without anyone batting an eyelid.

How else can you explain why no one south of the border took notice when the Expos, who most pundits pegged to finish in the second division, went 88-74 and remained in wild card contention until the season's final weekend? If the New York Mets had been as successful, they would have issued commemorative caps and had a book deal in the works.

These Expos are not destiny's darlings. Destiny has, in fact, taken potshots at the Expos over the years: the strike that wiped out their most successful season ever, Moises Alou's freak ankle injury, Cliff Floyd's freak wrist injury, Rondell White being KO'ed by an unfriendly wall this season. Expos fans are resigned to the financial realities which led to the departures of Larry Walker, Marquis Grissom and John Wetteland. But the added insult of watching some of the best talent developed by their farm system—their one undeniable strength—fall to injury has made the script in Montreal read more like a Greek tragedy than a soap opera.

The tragedy is that despite struggling to overcome poverty, fate, and the Atlanta Braves, the Expos manage to fall just short every year. Their relative success stems from excelling at just about everything over which they have control. Their farm system, even on a smaller budget than many teams, is the envy of baseball. Just look at who has come out of Montreal since 1990: Grissom, Walker, White, Floyd, Delino DeShields, Mark Grudzielanek, Mike Lansing, Mel Rojas, Jeff Fassero and Wil Cordero. Along with Alou, John Wetteland and Sean Berry, who were all pilfered from other organizations at bargain-basement prices, these 13 players represent more talent than any other team developed over the same period. And the Expos are at it again; after a dry spell in 1995, their farm system pumped out Vladimir Guerrero and Ugueth Urbina this year.

The Expos also have one of baseball's best, if most unconventional, managers in Felipe Alou. He isn't held in awe the way Jim Leyland is, but Alou is a very similar manager who has succeeded in similarly difficult circumstances. Like Leyland, Alou coddles his pitching staff, never working his starters too hard and showing faith in rookie pitchers while not giving them roles that exceed their abilities. It's no surprise that pitchers like Urbina and Jose Paniagua had smooth transitions to the major leagues, while more-heralded rookies like Paul Wilson and Jimmy Haynes were getting their clocks cleaned.

But even more impressive than Alou's handling of rookies is his uncanny knack for salvaging other teams' discarded pitchers and converting them into dependable middle men. Consider the combined totals of Barry Manuel and Omar Daal last season: 173 IP, 144 hits, 63 walks, 144 strikeouts and a 3.63 ERA. How many fans even knew that Manuel and Daal were in the majors last season? Over the years, Alou has also helped Jeff Juden fulfill some of his considerable promise and given significant bullpen roles to the previously unwanted Tim Scott and the discarded Jeff Shaw. Most impressive of all, he molded Jeff Fassero, who had bounced around four organizations in the minor leagues, into one of the best left-handers in baseball. Alou's astute handling of his pitching staff is a huge reason why the Expos gave up the third-fewest runs in all of baseball last year.

Indeed, an offense that finished eleventh in the NL in runs scored was all that kept the Expos from the playoffs. Unfortunately for the Expos, they can't point to one or two players or positions as the culprit for their anemic output. Oh, sure, Shane Andrews could have reached base more often, and the Expos sorely needed more production from their bench than what Lenny Webster and Dave Silvestri provided. But what hurt the Expos most was that the heart of their offense failed with the loss of Rondell White for half the season. White's injury had a ripple effect on the rest of the lineup, forcing hitters into lineup slots that taxed their skills. Henry Rodriguez, perfectly suited for the #5 spot, took his .325 OBP to cleanup. The vastly overrated Mark Grudzielanek, who should never have batted higher than sixth all season, was used exclusively at the top of the lineup.

The loss of White also exposed the Expos' lack of a true franchise hitter. There was no Ken Caminiti or Mike Piazza to be the fulcrum on which the team's lineup balanced. The Expos were fooled into thinking that Rodriguez was that man, but his lack of plate discipline killed rallies and the RBI opportunities of the hitters behind him, and he predictably went into a tailspin around the All-Star Break. With White injured and Floyd unable to have the breakout season they sorely needed, Rodriguez' collapse forced the Expos to get production from every position to compensate for their lack of a meaty core. White's injury also forced super-sub F.P. Santangelo into the everyday lineup, leaving the Expos' bench punchless.

It is testimony to how well the Expos franchise has been constructed that despite an endless litany of small-market mantras, free-agent requiems and laments over injured players, they have gamely managed to remain competitive throughout the '90s. Last season was a big step in reclaiming the brilliance that was stolen from them in 1994, but the trade of Fassero proves that it is business as usual in Montreal. At the very least, the Expos were able to avoid the desperation fire sales of Wetteland and Grissom, trades which brought little talent in return. Chris Widger is a coveted catching prospect, and Matt Wagner, now that he's away from Lou Piniella, could develop into a 15-game winner by 1999.

The Expos can expect far greater contributions from White and Floyd next year, and if Urbina continues to develop he could help the Expos forget about the loss of Fassero. If Carlos Perez comes back or one of the other young arms steps up, and the Expos can get career years from Segui and Lansing, they will have what they need to contend in a loaded NL East. Otherwise, it may be another year of falling just short in Montreal.

ISRAEL ALCANTARA 3B 1973 Age 24

Year	Team	Lge	AB	H	DB	TP	HR	BB	SB	CS	OUT	BA	OBA	SA	EQA	EQR	Peak
1993	Burlington	Midw	478	105	13	0	15	15	3	3	376	.220	.243	.341	.189	29	.215
1994	West Palm Bch	Flor	483	136	17	1	18	25	6	2	349	.282	.317	.433	.251	55	.281
1995	West Palm Bch	Flor	139	38	3	1	4	8	2	0	101	.273	.313	.396	.241	14	.264
1995	Harrisburg	East	243	53	9	1	10	19	1	1	191	.218	.275	.387	.217	21	.239
1996	West Palm Bch	Flor	63	19	0	0	4	3	0	0	44	.302	.333	.492	.272	8	.300
1996	Harrisburg	East	221	44	2	0	7	13	1	1	178	.199	.244	.303	.173	11	.188

The Expos love his power potential, but there are cockroaches out there with more selectivity than Alcantara. Injuries hurt his progress last year, and at 24 he's going to have to develop in a hurry if he hopes to win a job someday.

MOISES ALOU RF/LF 1967 Age 30

Year	Team	Lge	AB	H	DB	TP	HR	BB	SB	CS	OUT	BA	OBA	SA	EQA	EQR	Peak
1993	Montreal	NL	494	147	29	4	20	45	15	5	352	.298	.356	.494	.281	74	.292
1994	Montreal	NL	430	147	28	3	24	48	7	5	288	.342	.408	.588	.320	83	.328
1995	Montreal	NL	351	100	17	0	16	34	3	3	254	.285	.348	.470	.269	48	.271
1996	Montreal	NL	548	155	25	2	21	55	7	4	397	.283	.348	.451	.266	72	.264
1997	*Florida*	*NL*	*547*	*150*	*27*	*3*	*26*	*51*	*10*	*6*	*403*	*.274*	*.336*	*.477*	*.281*	*84*	

Likely to be elsewhere by the time you read this. He's a good hitter, but with White, Guerrero and Floyd the Expos have better—and cheaper—alternatives. A very good right fielder, and more than adequate in center. He'll probably have another season like 1994 again. There's not much to say about Alou; he's about as consistently good as a player can be without being great.

SHANE ANDREWS 3B 1972 Age 25

Year	Team	Lge	AB	H	DB	TP	HR	BB	SB	CS	OUT	BA	OBA	SA	EQA	EQR	Peak
1993	Harrisburg	East	458	118	15	1	19	58	6	3	343	.258	.341	.419	.254	56	.284
1994	Ottawa	Inter	482	126	19	2	17	77	5	3	359	.261	.363	.415	.261	62	.288
1995	Montreal	NL	223	50	10	1	8	19	1	1	174	.224	.285	.386	.221	20	.239
1996	Montreal	NL	379	86	13	2	19	39	2	1	294	.227	.299	.422	.237	40	.254
1997	*Montreal*	*NL*	*273*	*68*	*14*	*1*	*13*	*31*	*4*	*2*	*207*	*.249*	*.326*	*.451*	*.267*	*38*	

His tendency to strike out continues to hinder his progress. His career average when he puts the ball in play is .324, but he has 187 Ks in just 595 ABs. He plays good defense and the Expos have no one waiting in the wings to take his spot, so he has at least one more chance to put his power to good use. He'll probably never be a great player, but even with all the strikeouts he's good enough to start for a few more years.

TONY BARRON OF 1967 Age 30

Year	Team	Lge	AB	H	DB	TP	HR	BB	SB	CS	OUT	BA	OBA	SA	EQA	EQR	Peak
1993	Albuquerque	PCL	250	58	10	0	7	24	4	3	195	.232	.299	.356	.218	22	.226
1994	Jacksonville	South	411	118	12	2	17	28	10	3	296	.287	.333	.450	.262	52	.269
1995	Harrisburg	East	107	33	4	0	9	9	0	0	74	.308	.362	.598	.306	19	.307
1995	Ottawa	Inter	151	38	6	0	10	14	0	1	114	.252	.315	.490	.259	20	.262
1996	Harrisburg	East	68	19	1	1	4	6	1	0	49	.279	.338	.500	.276	10	.276
1996	Ottawa	Inter	401	127	22	1	14	23	7	3	277	.317	.354	.481	.278	56	.276

A good hitter, but he's 30 years old and has no other recognizable skills. There are worse bench players in the major leagues, but that's little consolation for Barron—he isn't one of them and probably never will be.

YAMIL BENITEZ   **OF**   **1972**   **Age 25**

Year	Team	Lge	AB	H	DB	TP	HR	BB	SB	CS	OUT	BA	OBA	SA	EQA	EQR	Peak
1993	Burlington	Midw	421	104	11	2	13	22	8	3	320	.247	.284	.375	.221	37	.251
1994	Harrisburg	East	484	116	12	2	15	33	12	8	376	.240	.288	.366	.218	42	.244
1995	Ottawa	Inter	487	128	20	3	19	46	11	4	363	.263	.326	.433	.254	59	.280
1996	Ottawa	Inter	446	124	16	1	21	30	8	3	325	.278	.324	.460	.260	56	.283
1997	*Montreal*	*NL*	*501*	*133*	*20*	*2*	*24*	*28*	*11*	*3*	*371*	*.265*	*.304*	*.457*	*.264*	*66*	

A low-OBP slugger who's shown steady improvement, but at his peak will probably be no better than a fourth or fifth outfielder in the major leagues. He can no long rely on his .385 average in his brief debut in 1995 to attract attention, but I suspect he'll get another cup of coffee this year.

STEVE BIESER   **OF**   **1968**   **Age 29**

Year	Team	Lge	AB	H	DB	TP	HR	BB	SB	CS	OUT	BA	OBA	SA	EQA	EQR	Peak
1993	Reading	East	173	50	5	2	1	14	5	3	126	.289	.342	.358	.240	18	.253
1993	Scranton-WB	Inter	84	21	3	0	0	3	2	0	63	.250	.276	.286	.191	5	.200
1994	Scranton-WB	Inter	232	59	11	1	0	16	8	5	178	.254	.302	.310	.208	17	.216
1995	Scranton-WB	Inter	250	65	14	4	1	22	10	3	188	.260	.320	.360	.234	25	.240
1996	Ottawa	Inter	391	124	23	3	1	37	18	5	272	.317	.376	.399	.269	51	.272

Another aging hitter in the Ottawa outfield. Probably no worse a hitter than Luis Polonia, and almost certainly a better fielder. Such ringing endorsements are probably not going to get him to the majors.

GEOFFREY BLUM   **2B**   **1973**   **Age 24**

Year	Team	Lge	AB	H	DB	TP	HR	BB	SB	CS	OUT	BA	OBA	SA	EQA	EQR	Peak
1994	Vermont	NY-P	254	73	7	0	4	25	2	2	183	.287	.351	.362	.243	27	.273
1995	West Palm Bch	Flor	473	117	17	1	2	30	4	2	358	.247	.292	.300	.198	31	.219
1996	Harrisburg	East	407	90	18	1	1	53	5	3	320	.221	.311	.278	.197	28	.214

A glove man who draws the occasional walk, but Mike Lansing's not going anywhere. No prospect, but likely to be drawing a minor league paycheck for another couple of years.

HIRAM BOCACHICA   **SS**   **1976**   **Age 21**

Year	Team	Lge	AB	H	DB	TP	HR	BB	SB	CS	OUT	BA	OBA	SA	EQA	EQR	Peak
1995	Albany-GA	S Atl	406	109	16	6	3	43	20	8	305	.268	.339	.360	.241	43	.278
1996	West Palm Bch	Flor	282	94	17	2	4	31	11	2	190	.333	.399	.450	.292	44	.332
1997	*Montreal*	*NL*	*449*	*128*	*31*	*6*	*3*	*50*	*32*	*6*	*327*	*.285*	*.357*	*.401*	*.276*	*66*	

The Expos' next potential phenom. Bocachica is a great young hitter but an erratic fielder, and an elbow injury left him unable to play the field much this season. Offensively, the only skill he lacks is power, and he'll probably pick that up as he ages. I doubt he'll make it to the major leagues as a shortstop, but he should make it at some position and challenge for a batting title someday.

JIM BUCCHERI   **OF**   **1969**   **Age 28**

Year	Team	Lge	AB	H	DB	TP	HR	BB	SB	CS	OUT	BA	OBA	SA	EQA	EQR	Peak
1993	Tacoma	PCL	293	72	6	1	3	35	7	5	226	.246	.326	.304	.214	24	.228
1994	Tacoma	PCL	443	120	5	2	3	41	23	9	332	.271	.333	.312	.226	40	.238
1995	Ottawa	Inter	485	131	15	3	1	50	30	7	361	.270	.338	.320	.234	48	.244
1996	Ottawa	Inter	212	55	4	3	1	33	22	4	161	.259	.359	.321	.249	25	.256

Voted the best baserunner and defensive outfielder in the International League, Buccheri is—stop me if you've heard this before—a veteran AAA outfielder and is unlikely to ever expand on that role.

KEVIN CASTLEBERRY   **2B**   **1968**   **Age 29**

Year	Team	Lge	AB	H	DB	TP	HR	BB	SB	CS	OUT	BA	OBA	SA	EQA	EQR	Peak
1993	El Paso	Texas	330	87	7	3	2	27	7	1	244	.264	.319	.321	.221	28	.233
1994	El Paso	Texas	255	64	5	5	2	24	7	3	194	.251	.315	.333	.221	22	.230
1995	Ottawa	Inter	444	130	17	2	8	53	7	4	318	.293	.368	.394	.259	55	.266
1996	Ottawa	Inter	197	54	7	2	3	22	6	3	146	.274	.347	.376	.246	22	.249
1997	*Montreal*	*NL*	*177*	*48*	*8*	*3*	*2*	*17*	*6*	*2*	*131*	*.271*	*.335*	*.384*	*.257*	*22*	

His best chance at a Mike Mordecai-like career came and went last year. The Expos could use a left-handed hitting middle infielder, but they never called on Castleberry, who would make a fine bench player. Still might get a chance if Grudzielanek or Lansing go down with an injury this year.

RAUL CHAVEZ   **C**   **1973**   **Age 24**

Year	Team	Lge	AB	H	DB	TP	HR	BB	SB	CS	OUT	BA	OBA	SA	EQA	EQR	Peak
1993	Osceola	Flor	199	41	3	0	1	8	1	0	158	.206	.237	.236	.139	6	.159
1994	Jackson	Texas	256	53	3	0	2	16	1	0	203	.207	.254	.242	.152	9	.170
1995	Jackson	Texas	189	50	5	0	4	8	1	2	141	.265	.294	.354	.215	15	.239
1995	Tucson	PCL	101	22	5	0	0	8	0	1	80	.218	.275	.267	.171	5	.190
1996	Ottawa	Inter	200	47	5	0	3	13	0	1	154	.235	.282	.305	.192	12	.210

Chavez was acquired along with Dave Veres in the Sean Berry deal. Pay close attention, folks: it's not every day that you see a team trade for a backup catcher. A defensive specialist, but you knew that, right? If he didn't have a good defensive reputation, he probably would never have been signed.

DARRIN FLETCHER   **C**   **1967**   **Age 30**

Year	Team	Lge	AB	H	DB	TP	HR	BB	SB	CS	OUT	BA	OBA	SA	EQA	EQR	Peak
1993	Montreal	NL	404	106	18	1	10	40	0	0	298	.262	.329	.386	.240	42	.250
1994	Montreal	NL	288	75	15	1	11	29	0	0	213	.260	.328	.434	.253	34	.259
1995	Montreal	NL	358	106	19	1	12	37	0	1	253	.296	.362	.455	.272	49	.274
1996	Montreal	NL	398	106	13	0	14	32	0	0	292	.266	.321	.405	.243	42	.241
1997	*Montreal*	*NL*	*470*	*121*	*16*	*1*	*16*	*44*	*0*	*0*	*349*	*.257*	*.321*	*.398*	*.251*	*55*	

After years of steady improvement, Fletcher began his decline phase last year. The Expos have him on the block, but more likely than not he'll platoon with Widger for a year or two. Eventually he'll pack his bags and take his have-glove, will-travel show from team to team as a Greg Myers-like semi-backup.

CLIFF FLOYD   **OF/Martyr**   **1973**   **Age 24**

Year	Team	Lge	AB	H	DB	TP	HR	BB	SB	CS	OUT	BA	OBA	SA	EQA	EQR	Peak
1993	Harrisburg	East	396	130	11	2	25	50	18	6	272	.328	.404	.556	.313	75	.356
1993	Ottawa	Inter	128	29	3	1	2	16	2	1	100	.227	.312	.312	.211	10	.239
1994	Montreal	NL	337	95	18	3	5	29	9	3	245	.282	.339	.398	.251	39	.281
1995	Montreal	NL	70	10	1	0	1	7	2	0	60	.143	.221	.200	.113	1	.128
1996	Ottawa	Inter	78	23	2	1	1	7	1	1	56	.295	.353	.385	.249	9	.272
1996	Montreal	NL	231	57	13	4	6	31	6	1	175	.247	.336	.416	.254	28	.275
1997	*Montreal*	*NL*	*360*	*101*	*22*	*3*	*8*	*32*	*10*	*3*	*262*	*.281*	*.339*	*.425*	*.269*	*49*	

Still not the hitter he was before the injury. The Expos worked him back slowly last year, but if Floyd still has the talent, he's going to need a full season to show it. Will almost certainly hit for more power, but unless the wrist is healed it's unlikely he'll ever hit for a great average again. Maybe a 70% chance of returning to form. If he does it this year, the Expos could win the wild card.

BRAD FULLMER   **OF**   **1975**   **Age 22**

Year	Team	Lge	AB	H	DB	TP	HR	BB	SB	CS	OUT	BA	OBA	SA	EQA	EQR	Peak
1995	Albany-GA	S Atl	494	147	24	1	9	30	5	4	351	.298	.338	.405	.250	55	.284
1996	West Palm Bch	Flor	395	114	17	1	8	30	2	3	284	.289	.339	.397	.247	43	.277
1996	Harrisburg	East	99	26	3	1	3	3	0	0	73	.263	.284	.404	.229	9	.257
1997	*Montreal*	*NL*	*386*	*102*	*26*	*1*	*9*	*29*	*4*	*2*	*286*	*.264*	*.316*	*.407*	*.252*	*46*	

Fullmer was drafted as a third baseman, and his stroke has had observers comparing him to George Brett for years. Of course, Brett was already in the major leagues when he was 21…. His defense at third was reminiscent of Kevin Mitchell's, so the Expos have been searching for a position he can play. He could be another Hal Morris at the plate, but if he isn't able to play the outfield, his defensive liabilities may hinder his progress with the bat.

MARK GRUDZIELANEK   SS   1970   Age 27

Year	Team	Lge	AB	H	DB	TP	HR	BB	SB	CS	OUT	BA	OBA	SA	EQA	EQR	Peak
1993	West Palm Bch	Flor	310	82	12	3	3	13	9	5	233	.265	.294	.352	.218	26	.238
1994	Harrisburg	East	501	152	25	2	11	39	20	6	355	.303	.354	.427	.266	65	.285
1995	Ottawa	Inter	185	56	8	1	1	12	8	1	130	.303	.345	.373	.252	21	.265
1995	Montreal	NL	273	70	12	2	1	17	7	3	206	.256	.300	.326	.213	22	.223
1996	Montreal	NL	665	204	31	4	6	34	27	6	467	.307	.340	.392	.254	76	.264
1997	*Montreal*	*NL*	*504*	*142*	*41*	*3*	*9*	*32*	*27*	*6*	*368*	*.282*	*.325*	*.429*	*.269*	*69*	

Rodriguez, Jeter, Renteria, Grudzielanek…huh? Would someone please explain why Grudz was constantly lumped in with three guys who have a chance at Cooperstown? Oh, I forgot, he hit .300. Thanks for clearing that up. Never mind that he was 26 years old and can't play defense. Or that he has no secondary skills to speak of—Wade Boggs was the only other regular in baseball to hit .300 without either a .400 on-base or slugging average.

Grudzielanek's 26 walks were fewer than any hitter in Expos history (min: 600 PA). Even Andre Dawson was more patient at the plate. He has to hit .300 to have any value at all, and his defense may have Expos fans clamoring for Wil Cordero before long.

VLADIMIR GUERRERO   RF/CF   1976   Age 21

Year	Team	Lge	AB	H	DB	TP	HR	BB	SB	CS	OUT	BA	OBA	SA	EQA	EQR	Peak
1995	Albany-GA	S Atl	444	140	11	3	16	25	6	3	307	.315	.352	.462	.272	59	.314
1996	West Palm Bch	Flor	83	30	4	0	5	3	1	1	54	.361	.384	.590	.313	15	.354
1996	Harrisburg	East	429	147	25	5	17	46	13	5	287	.343	.406	.543	.312	78	.355
1997	*Montreal*	*NL*	*603*	*179*	*40*	*10*	*14*	*62*	*21*	*9*	*433*	*.297*	*.362*	*.466*	*.288*	*96*	

The bomb. He may always be in Andruw Jones' shadow, much like Tim Raines was always eclipsed by Rickey Henderson, but he's a legitimate All-Star candidate at 21. His minor league numbers are even more impressive than those of Floyd or White, and his defense is stellar. The Expos might be tempted to give him some AAA seasoning, but he's got more than enough flavor already. Alou is a smart enough manager to give Guerrero a shot at the starting job in spring training.

BOB HENLEY   C   1973   Age 24

Year	Team	Lge	AB	H	DB	TP	HR	BB	SB	CS	OUT	BA	OBA	SA	EQA	EQR	Peak
1993	Jamestown	NY-P	215	47	5	1	5	15	0	0	168	.219	.270	.321	.193	14	.219
1994	Burlington	Midw	357	98	8	1	16	41	1	1	260	.275	.349	.437	.262	46	.293
1995	Albany-GA	S Atl	369	96	12	1	4	70	1	1	274	.260	.378	.331	.245	41	.270
1996	Harrisburg	East	301	65	8	1	3	62	1	1	237	.216	.350	.279	.215	25	.233

Looks like a generic catching suspect, but check out those walk rates. Even if he never makes it to the major leagues, I'd sure love to see him as a hitting coach some day.

MIKE LANSING   2B   1968   Age 29

Year	Team	Lge	AB	H	DB	TP	HR	BB	SB	CS	OUT	BA	OBA	SA	EQA	EQR	Peak
1993	Montreal	NL	504	149	25	1	5	54	20	4	359	.296	.364	.379	.259	61	.273
1994	Montreal	NL	397	106	20	2	5	36	11	7	298	.267	.328	.365	.234	40	.243
1995	Montreal	NL	474	126	29	2	11	34	23	4	352	.266	.315	.405	.248	54	.254
1996	Montreal	NL	649	185	34	2	12	52	19	7	471	.285	.338	.399	.251	74	.253
1997	*Montreal*	*NL*	*632*	*175*	*23*	*2*	*16*	*44*	*28*	*9*	*466*	*.277*	*.324*	*.396*	*.257*	*78*	

Lansing's hot start (he hit .383 in April) was a big reason for the Expos' early success, but for the season he was about as average a player as anyone in baseball. He hits equally well against lefties, righties, during the day, at night, with a full moon or during a solar eclipse. Had trouble turning the double play last year, probably Grudzielanek's fault. Should keep his starting job for several more years; what you see is what you get.

JALAL LEACH   OF   1969   Age 28

Year	Team	Lge	AB	H	DB	TP	HR	BB	SB	CS	OUT	BA	OBA	SA	EQA	EQR	Peak
1993	Albany-NY	East	470	128	15	4	15	43	9	6	348	.272	.333	.417	.250	55	.269
1994	Columbus-OH	Inter	453	113	17	5	7	38	10	7	347	.249	.308	.355	.222	40	.235
1995	Columbus-OH	Inter	274	62	8	3	7	23	8	2	214	.226	.286	.354	.216	23	.225
1996	Harrisburg	East	274	84	16	2	6	18	3	3	194	.307	.349	.445	.264	35	.270
1996	Ottawa	Inter	103	32	2	0	3	9	0	0	71	.311	.366	.417	.266	13	.273

Leach, Barron and Bieser really are three different people, but only their mothers can tell them apart.

ROB LUKACHYK   OF/1B   1969   Age 28

Year	Team	Lge	AB	H	DB	TP	HR	BB	SB	CS	OUT	BA	OBA	SA	EQA	EQR	Peak
1993	El Paso	Texas	370	87	15	4	8	48	6	4	287	.235	.323	.362	.230	36	.246
1994	Bowie	East	382	105	15	3	10	43	20	4	281	.275	.348	.408	.261	49	.275
1995	Toledo	Inter	357	93	21	4	9	35	7	3	267	.261	.327	.417	.249	41	.258
1996	Harrisburg	East	95	30	3	0	5	10	3	1	66	.316	.381	.505	.294	15	.302
1996	Ottawa	Inter	249	65	11	3	9	15	7	1	186	.261	.303	.438	.248	29	.256

Picked up from the Tigers before last season, presumably because the Expos were attempting to corner the market on veteran minor league outfielders.

CHRIS MARTIN   SS   1968   Age 29

Year	Team	Lge	AB	H	DB	TP	HR	BB	SB	CS	OUT	BA	OBA	SA	EQA	EQR	Peak
1993	Harrisburg	East	407	116	15	1	8	37	9	3	294	.285	.345	.386	.250	46	.263
1994	Ottawa	Inter	385	92	13	0	6	35	4	3	296	.239	.302	.319	.208	29	.217
1995	Ottawa	Inter	425	111	16	1	4	47	21	4	318	.261	.335	.332	.235	42	.240
1996	Ottawa	Inter	458	119	20	1	9	35	18	8	347	.260	.312	.367	.231	45	.233

Veteran minor league shortstops, too.

DAN MASTELLER   1B   1968   Age 29

Year	Team	Lge	AB	H	DB	TP	HR	BB	SB	CS	OUT	BA	OBA	SA	EQA	EQR	Peak
1993	Nashville	South	124	32	2	0	3	10	1	1	93	.258	.313	.347	.221	11	.235
1993	Portland-OR	PCL	210	62	8	2	7	22	2	2	150	.295	.362	.452	.270	29	.284
1994	Salt Lake City	PCL	329	86	16	2	7	21	3	1	244	.261	.306	.386	.232	32	.241
1995	Salt Lake City	PCL	151	43	8	4	5	14	3	1	109	.285	.345	.490	.276	22	.283
1995	Minnesota	AL	199	48	8	0	5	18	1	2	153	.241	.304	.357	.219	17	.224
1996	Harrisburg	East	132	41	6	0	3	16	0	0	91	.311	.385	.424	.275	18	.277

The ex-replacement player used the Expos as a springboard to his new career in the independent Northeast League.

RYAN McGUIRE   1B   1972   Age 25

Year	Team	Lge	AB	H	DB	TP	HR	BB	SB	CS	OUT	BA	OBA	SA	EQA	EQR	Peak
1993	Ft Lauderdale	Flor	220	66	9	1	5	24	1	2	156	.300	.369	.418	.264	28	.296
1994	Lynchburg	Caro	503	116	13	0	9	67	6	4	391	.231	.321	.310	.213	41	.235
1995	Trenton	East	441	151	22	0	10	53	8	5	295	.342	.413	.460	.295	70	.320
1996	Ottawa	Inter	462	118	16	1	12	59	8	3	347	.255	.340	.372	.242	50	.259
1997	*Montreal*	*NL*	*421*	*123*	*25*	*1*	*13*	*74*	*7*	*1*	*299*	*.292*	*.398*	*.449*	*.298*	*73*	

One of the keys to the Cordero trade, McGuire, who hit like Mark Grace in 1995, had a pretty uninspiring season last year. I suspect he'll bounce back; he's young, has a great swing and leaving the Red Sox organization was a difficult transition. How exciting can it be to play baseball in Ottawa, anyway? Will probably be in the major leagues before the September callups.

SHERMAN OBANDO   RF   1970   Age 27

Year	Team	Lge	AB	H	DB	TP	HR	BB	SB	CS	OUT	BA	OBA	SA	EQA	EQR	Peak
1993	Bowie	East	60	14	1	0	3	9	1	0	46	.233	.333	.400	.247	7	.272
1993	Baltimore	AL	93	26	1	0	4	4	0	0	67	.280	.309	.419	.243	10	.264
1994	Rochester	Inter	410	132	27	4	20	30	1	1	279	.322	.368	.554	.299	68	.320
1995	Rochester	Inter	328	93	20	3	10	30	1	1	236	.284	.344	.454	.265	42	.279
1996	Montreal	NL	181	45	8	0	8	24	2	0	136	.249	.337	.425	.255	22	.265
1997	*Montreal*	*NL*	*338*	*102*	*21*	*2*	*15*	*33*	*1*	*1*	*237*	*.302*	*.364*	*.509*	*.297*	*57*	

The Expos overpaid for his services in the spring, then inexplicably relegated him to a reserve role after six weeks. Obando is not, as they say, into leather, but if he ever gets 400 at bats in the major leagues to show what he can do it won't matter. They said Geronimo Berroa would never pan out either. With the Expos' glut of outfielders, chances are Obando won't get that opportunity in Montreal.

HENRY RODRIGUEZ   **LF/1B**   **1968**   **Age 29**

Year	Team	Lge	AB	H	DB	TP	HR	BB	SB	CS	OUT	BA	OBA	SA	EQA	EQR	Peak
1993	Albuquerque	PCL	172	41	7	2	4	13	1	1	132	.238	.292	.372	.220	15	.231
1993	Los Angeles	NL	178	41	7	0	9	14	1	0	137	.230	.286	.421	.233	18	.245
1994	Los Angeles	NL	312	88	13	2	9	22	0	1	225	.282	.329	.423	.251	35	.261
1995	Los Angeles	NL	82	23	4	1	1	6	0	1	60	.280	.330	.390	.239	8	.245
1995	Montreal	NL	59	12	0	0	2	7	0	0	47	.203	.288	.305	.194	4	.186
1996	Montreal	NL	539	150	31	1	38	43	2	0	389	.278	.332	.551	.284	84	.287
1997	*Montreal*	*NL*	*619*	*157*	*29*	*3*	*23*	*42*	*2*	*1*	*463*	*.254*	*.301*	*.422*	*.250*	*72*	

The Larry Sheets of 1996. He hit 20 homers by the end of May, and made fools of just about every baseball analyst all season. But he had a ridiculous strikeout-to-walk ratio (160-37) and there was absolutely nothing in his record before the season that suggested he was anything more than a borderline major leaguer. The Expos are actively shopping him, and for once it's not just a financial decision; they don't think he can do it again either. The Vlad looks dead on; unless you like the way Ruben Sierra's career has gone, stay clear.

JON SAFFER   **OF**   **1974**   **Age 23**

Year	Team	Lge	AB	H	DB	TP	HR	BB	SB	CS	OUT	BA	OBA	SA	EQA	EQR	Peak
1993	Jamestown	NY-P	238	51	9	2	1	23	4	2	189	.214	.284	.282	.187	14	.215
1994	Vermont	NY-P	276	76	11	1	4	25	6	2	202	.275	.336	.366	.240	29	.273
1995	West Palm Bch	Flor	345	106	9	3	6	47	11	5	244	.307	.390	.403	.272	47	.305
1995	Harrisburg	East	78	18	4	0	0	6	1	1	61	.231	.286	.282	.186	5	.212
1996	Harrisburg	East	503	140	21	2	9	69	8	8	371	.278	.365	.382	.252	59	.278
1997	*Montreal*	*NL*	*481*	*121*	*27*	*2*	*10*	*62*	*13*	*8*	*368*	*.252*	*.337*	*.378*	*.252*	*59*	

Great on-base skills, and his power is developing. I don't know how he'll ever get an opportunity to play ahead of all the young studs in Montreal. He needs another year or two to develop, and lucky for him that's about the time he'll qualify for minor league free agency.

F.P. SANTANGELO   **UT**   **1968**   **Age 29**

Year	Team	Lge	AB	H	DB	TP	HR	BB	SB	CS	OUT	BA	OBA	SA	EQA	EQR	Peak
1993	Ottawa	Inter	465	122	19	1	4	60	13	5	348	.262	.347	.333	.235	47	.248
1994	Ottawa	Inter	430	110	22	1	6	57	6	6	326	.256	.343	.353	.235	44	.244
1995	Ottawa	Inter	276	70	13	2	3	32	5	2	208	.254	.331	.348	.231	27	.237
1995	Montreal	NL	101	31	5	1	1	13	1	1	71	.307	.386	.406	.269	13	.277
1996	Montreal	NL	400	111	19	5	7	53	4	2	291	.278	.362	.403	.259	50	.261
1997	*Montreal*	*NL*	*413*	*110*	*29*	*7*	*4*	*51*	*4*	*1*	*304*	*.266*	*.347*	*.400*	*.263*	*54*	

The more you see of Santangelo, the more you like. He has never hit .300 or popped even 10 homers in a season, but he can play seven positions and dominates the lower-profile stats. He never grounds into a double play and was hit by a pitch 11 times last year, not glamour stuff but the kind of production that helps win ballgames. Alou loves him, and used him as a pinch-hitter and defensive replacement so much that Santangelo played in all but 10 games last year while having fewer than 400 ABs. Tony Phillips Lite, and could really bump up his walk rate this year. Will probably get most of his playing time at third base, but can move anywhere in a crisis. For that reason, lots of table-game and rotisserie value.

RICK SCHU   **3B**   **1962**   **Age 35**

Year	Team	Lge	AB	H	DB	TP	HR	BB	SB	CS	OUT	BA	OBA	SA	EQA	EQR	Peak
1995	Oklahoma	AmA	405	107	14	2	13	43	5	2	300	.264	.335	.405	.249	46	.237
1996	Ottawa	Inter	403	108	19	2	12	43	6	2	297	.268	.339	.414	.253	48	.240

Rumors are that he'll play third base in Pittsburgh next year if the Pirates move Jeff King. Presumably, Jim Presley wasn't available.

DAVID SEGUI   **1B**   **1967**   **Age 30**

Year	Team	Lge	AB	H	DB	TP	HR	BB	SB	CS	OUT	BA	OBA	SA	EQA	EQR	Peak
1993	Baltimore	AL	454	128	20	0	15	61	2	1	327	.282	.367	.425	.266	60	.277
1994	NY Mets	NL	339	82	13	1	11	37	0	0	257	.242	.316	.383	.233	34	.239
1995	Montreal	NL	392	123	21	3	11	33	1	3	272	.314	.367	.467	.276	55	.279
1995	NY Mets	NL	77	27	3	1	2	13	1	3	53	.351	.444	.494	.304	14	.308
1996	Montreal	NL	425	122	26	1	12	64	3	4	307	.287	.380	.438	.273	60	.271
1997	*Montreal*	*NL*	*446*	*123*	*20*	*1*	*18*	*57*	*3*	*2*	*325*	*.276*	*.358*	*.446*	*.279*	*67*	

It's time for the Analogies section of the SAT. (Don't worry, it's only a sample question.)

Second Base: Lansing = First Base: ???

If you answered Segui, you know more than you need to about the Expos' infield. Segui, Lansing, Grudzielanek and Andrews are the most faceless foursome in baseball.

DAVE SILVESTRI   **SS**   **1968**   **Age 29**

Year	Team	Lge	AB	H	DB	TP	HR	BB	SB	CS	OUT	BA	OBA	SA	EQA	EQR	Peak
1993	Columbus-OH	Inter	444	119	21	2	20	68	5	6	331	.268	.365	.459	.271	63	.285
1994	Columbus-OH	Inter	408	102	15	1	23	79	13	7	313	.250	.372	.461	.274	62	.285
1995	Montreal	NL	74	20	4	0	3	10	2	0	54	.270	.357	.446	.272	10	.279
1996	Montreal	NL	165	33	1	0	2	36	2	1	133	.200	.343	.242	.201	12	.202
1997	*Montreal*	*NL*	*184*	*42*	*7*	*2*	*8*	*29*	*3*	*2*	*144*	*.228*	*.333*	*.418*	*.259*	*25*	

He picked a hell of a time to go into a slump. After waiting for years to get his first extended trial in the major leagues, Silvestri posted an EQA about 70 points off his norm and had as many extra-base hits as Danny Darwin. He still has the ability to be a power-hitting middle infielder, reminiscent of Bobby Grich, but he'll probably never get the opportunity.

ANDY STANKIEWICZ   **2B/SS**   **1965**   **Age 32**

Year	Team	Lge	AB	H	DB	TP	HR	BB	SB	CS	OUT	BA	OBA	SA	EQA	EQR	Peak
1993	Columbus-OH	Inter	338	79	11	3	1	30	9	5	264	.234	.296	.293	.198	23	.200
1994	Houston	NL	56	15	1	0	2	13	1	1	42	.268	.406	.393	.271	8	.269
1995	Tucson	PCL	85	20	3	0	1	13	2	1	66	.235	.337	.306	.220	8	.217
1995	Houston	NL	54	8	1	0	0	12	3	2	48	.148	.303	.167	.152	2	.150
1996	Montreal	NL	78	22	5	1	0	7	1	0	56	.282	.341	.372	.245	8	.236

Stankiewicz is Polish for "25th man."

SCOTT TALANOA   **1B/Hacker**   **1970**   **Age 27**

Year	Team	Lge	AB	H	DB	TP	HR	BB	SB	CS	OUT	BA	OBA	SA	EQA	EQR	Peak
1993	Beloit	Midw	273	74	7	0	17	57	2	1	200	.271	.397	.484	.291	46	.316
1994	El Paso	Texas	441	110	9	1	25	69	1	1	332	.249	.351	.444	.263	59	.281
1995	New Orleans	AmA	98	13	1	0	2	7	0	0	85	.133	.190	.204	.052	0	.056
1996	Harrisburg	East	143	30	4	0	9	28	0	0	113	.210	.339	.427	.252	18	.262
1996	New Orleans	AmA	81	15	2	0	1	9	2	0	66	.185	.267	.247	.168	4	.172

He's back, swinging for the moon and occasionally hitting one that far. Are we really sure that Talanoa and Joey Meyer are not, indeed, the same person? Hey, Paul White: now that Hector Villanueva has finally disappeared, you might want to start following Talanoa from organization to organization.

JOSE VIDRO   **3B**   **1975**   **Age 22**

Year	Team	Lge	AB	H	DB	TP	HR	BB	SB	CS	OUT	BA	OBA	SA	EQA	EQR	Peak
1993	Burlington	Midw	296	62	9	0	3	21	1	1	235	.209	.262	.270	.168	14	.198
1994	West Palm Bch	Flor	482	126	21	2	7	47	5	1	357	.261	.327	.357	.233	47	.269
1995	West Palm Bch	Flor	169	53	11	1	4	7	0	0	116	.314	.341	.462	.268	22	.304
1995	Harrisburg	East	254	65	13	1	5	18	2	4	193	.256	.305	.374	.224	23	.255
1996	Harrisburg	East	459	114	17	2	16	26	2	1	346	.248	.289	.399	.228	43	.255
1997	*Montreal*	*NL*	*537*	*141*	*29*	*3*	*9*	*34*	*4*	*5*	*401*	*.263*	*.306*	*.378*	*.239*	*56*	

Normally, a 22-year-old switch-hitting third baseman would attract my attention, but Vidro's lack of plate discipline is a big turn-off. His defense is good enough to get him the occasional start at shortstop, and he was making a concerted effort to take more pitches as the season went on. The Expos can afford to wait a year and see if he develops.

LENNY WEBSTER   **C**   **1965**   **Age 32**

Year	Team	Lge	AB	H	DB	TP	HR	BB	SB	CS	OUT	BA	OBA	SA	EQA	EQR	Peak
1993	Minnesota	AL	107	22	0	0	2	11	1	0	85	.206	.280	.262	.177	6	.180
1994	Montreal	NL	145	40	7	0	6	18	0	0	105	.276	.356	.448	.267	19	.265
1995	Philadelphia	NL	151	39	6	0	5	18	0	0	112	.258	.337	.397	.246	17	.241
1996	Montreal	NL	177	41	6	0	3	26	0	0	136	.232	.330	.316	.218	15	.210
1997	*Baltimore*	*AL*	*213*	*53*	*6*	*0*	*5*	*23*	*1*	*0*	*160*	*.249*	*.322*	*.347*	*.227*	*20*	

Earned tenure as a backup catcher last season, so in all likelihood he'll be garnering 150 at bats a year into the next century. Jazayerli's Rule of Backup Catchers suggests that one of these years, he'll hit .320 just by accident.

RONDELL WHITE   **CF**   **1972**   **Age 25**

Year	Team	Lge	AB	H	DB	TP	HR	BB	SB	CS	OUT	BA	OBA	SA	EQA	EQR	Peak
1993	Harrisburg	East	382	123	12	5	14	21	12	4	263	.322	.357	.490	.283	56	.316
1993	Ottawa	Inter	154	58	7	1	7	13	7	1	97	.377	.425	.571	.331	31	.370
1993	Montreal	NL	75	20	3	0	3	8	1	2	57	.267	.337	.427	.248	9	.278
1994	Ottawa	Inter	175	49	3	0	8	15	7	2	128	.280	.337	.434	.261	22	.288
1994	Montreal	NL	98	28	9	1	2	10	1	1	71	.286	.352	.459	.268	13	.295
1995	Montreal	NL	486	150	32	4	14	47	21	4	340	.309	.370	.477	.286	74	.311
1996	Montreal	NL	339	100	17	4	6	25	11	5	244	.295	.343	.422	.259	41	.277
1997	*Montreal*	*NL*	*525*	*160*	*51*	*8*	*17*	*57*	*24*	*9*	*374*	*.305*	*.373*	*.530*	*.307*	*97*	

The Franchise. Last year I wrote the Expos "need to offer Rondell White a six-year, $18-million contract." They did just that, even shaving a few million dollars off his price tag, in probably the shrewdest financial decision the Expos have ever made. If he plays that ball off the fence, the Expos are in the postseason. Vlad loves him—51 doubles! If the Expos' injury jinx doesn't hold and Guerrero makes it through the year unscathed, Montreal could have one of the best outfields in the league.

TAVO ALVAREZ   **RSP**   **1972**   **Age 25**

YR	TEAM	Lge	IP	H	ER	HR	BB	K	ERA	W	L	H/9	HR/9	BB/9	K/9	KW
1993	Ottawa	Inter	133.3	172	76	11	75	63	5.13	6	9	11.61	.74	5.06	4.25	.15
1995	Harrisburg	East	14.7	21	9	0	6	11	5.52	1	1	12.89	.00	3.68	6.75	1.33
1995	Ottawa	Inter	20.3	19	6	1	8	9	2.66	1	1	8.41	.44	3.54	3.98	.44
1995	Montreal	NL	37.0	47	27	2	17	15	6.57	1	3	11.43	.49	4.14	3.65	.18
1996	Ottawa	Inter	108.0	136	59	12	36	71	4.92	5	7	11.33	1.00	3.00	5.92	1.22
1996	Montreal	NL	20.7	19	8	0	14	8	3.48	1	1	8.27	.00	6.10	3.48	-.36

If he ever learns to control his appetite as well as his fastball, he'll be quite a pitcher. Alvarez has put a lot of effort into losing weight, and he's gone a long way toward stabilizing it over the last two years. He's never going to look like Pedro Martinez, and he'll probably always have injury troubles, a la Sid Fernandez. But this could be the year he turns the corner and establishes himself, probably as the junior member of Alou's bullpen.

DEREK AUCOIN   **RRP**   **1970**   **Age 27**

YR	TEAM	Lge	IP	H	ER	HR	BB	K	ERA	W	L	H/9	HR/9	BB/9	K/9	KW
1993	West Palm Bch	Flor	74.3	117	61	9	60	50	7.39	2	6	14.17	1.09	7.26	6.05	.20
1994	Harrisburg	East	43.0	41	18	5	36	35	3.77	3	2	8.58	1.05	7.53	7.33	.56
1995	Harrisburg	East	48.0	63	35	4	34	37	6.56	1	4	11.81	.75	6.38	6.94	.72
1996	Ottawa	Inter	72.3	77	33	6	64	58	4.11	4	4	9.58	.75	7.96	7.22	.41

Aucoin is a big guy in his own right, and once wrote a newspaper column evaluating the various restaurants he passed through in the minor leagues. His arm will give him more chances than most guys in his position, but he needs to tame his control before it chews up his career.

SHAYNE BENNETT   **RRP**   **1972**   **Age 25**

YR	TEAM	LGE	IP	H	ER	HR	BB	K	ERA	W	L	H/9	HR/9	BB/9	K/9	KW
1993	Ft Lauderdale	Flor	28.0	31	9	2	15	18	2.89	2	1	9.96	.64	4.82	5.79	.72
1994	Sarasota	Flor	43.3	52	31	2	34	21	6.44	1	4	10.80	.42	7.06	4.36	-.31
1995	Sarasota	Flor	53.3	61	25	5	30	49	4.22	3	3	10.29	.84	5.06	8.27	1.49
1996	Harrisburg	East	86.3	92	29	6	44	66	3.02	6	4	9.59	.63	4.59	6.88	1.15

Tossed in by the Red Sox for Rheal Cormier. Bennett is an Australian native who took to baseball late, and has come on strong as a relief prospect. He's considered a hard-nosed pitcher with a closer's mentality, which is what you'd expect from a former Australian Rules Football star. He may need another year of refinement, but don't bet against him.

KIRK BULLINGER   **RRP**   **1970**   **Age 27**

YR	TEAM	Lge	IP	H	ER	HR	BB	K	ERA	W	L	H/9	HR/9	BB/9	K/9	KW
1993	Springfield	Midw	45.7	36	19	6	27	42	3.74	3	2	7.09	1.18	5.32	8.28	1.43
1994	St. Petersburg	Flor	48.7	46	16	1	27	38	2.96	3	2	8.51	.18	4.99	7.03	1.09
1995	Harrisburg	East	61.0	75	23	5	31	33	3.39	4	3	11.07	.74	4.57	4.87	.48
1996	Harrisburg	East	42.0	52	15	5	22	21	3.21	3	2	11.14	1.07	4.71	4.50	.32
1996	Ottawa	Inter	14.3	11	5	3	11	7	3.14	1	1	6.91	1.88	6.91	4.40	-.26

Jim's little brother, and the bulk of the talent the Expos acquired for Ken Hill two years ago. He's a sinkerball pitcher who has managed to put up ERAs pleasantly out of line with his other stats. He's also 27 and has seen his K rate drop precipitously since 1994. Still has a shot, but it's a long one.

RHEAL CORMIER   LBP   1967   Age 30

YR	TEAM	Lge	IP	H	ER	HR	BB	K	ERA	W	L	H/9	HR/9	BB/9	K/9	KW
1993	St. Louis	NL	141.7	171	78	20	43	73	4.96	6	10	10.86	1.27	2.73	4.64	.86
1994	Louisville	AmA	21.0	21	9	3	10	11	3.86	1	1	9.00	1.29	4.29	4.71	.50
1994	St. Louis	NL	39.0	39	21	6	11	24	4.85	2	2	9.00	1.38	2.54	5.54	1.21
1995	Boston	AL	115.3	125	46	11	34	69	3.59	7	6	9.75	.86	2.65	5.38	1.13
1996	Montreal	NL	157.0	165	67	15	54	87	3.84	9	8	9.46	.86	3.10	4.99	.89

Well they finally got their man. No star potential, but has been very effective for several years by letting his fielders work for him. The Expos have good team defense, and left-handed groundball pitchers don't hit their prime until their 30s. Should continue to be effective indefinitely.

OMAR DAAL   LRP   1972   Age 25

YR	TEAM	Lge	IP	H	ER	HR	BB	K	ERA	W	L	H/9	HR/9	BB/9	K/9	KW
1993	Los Angeles	NL	35.0	37	19	6	26	19	4.89	2	2	9.51	1.54	6.69	4.89	-.04
1994	Albuquerque	PCL	32.3	35	15	5	20	24	4.18	2	2	9.74	1.39	5.57	6.68	.84
1994	Los Angeles	NL	13.3	13	5	1	6	8	3.38	1	0	8.78	.68	4.05	5.40	.79
1995	Albuquerque	PCL	50.3	52	21	4	32	42	3.75	3	3	9.30	.72	5.72	7.51	1.07
1995	Los Angeles	NL	20.3	31	15	1	17	10	6.64	1	1	13.72	.44	7.52	4.43	-.41
1996	Montreal	NL	85.7	75	33	10	44	71	3.47	6	4	7.88	1.05	4.62	7.46	1.33

Alou has never been a big fan of carrying a left-handed reliever just for the sake of having one, so it was surprising to see Daal even make the team in April. His pitching exceeded expectations and his strikeout rate suggests it's not a fluke. If he really is 25, he could be some pitcher.

MIKE DYER   RRP   1967   Age 30

YR	TEAM	Lge	IP	H	ER	HR	BB	K	ERA	W	L	H/9	HR/9	BB/9	K/9	KW
1993	Canton	East	85.7	105	66	10	69	57	6.93	2	8	11.03	1.05	7.25	5.99	.18
1993	Iowa	AmA	23.3	18	12	4	23	17	4.63	1	2	6.94	1.54	8.87	6.56	-.03
1994	Buffalo	AmA	33.3	35	10	2	19	23	2.70	3	1	9.45	.54	5.13	6.21	.79
1994	Pittsburgh	NL	15.3	15	11	1	14	12	6.46	1	1	8.80	.59	8.22	7.04	.29
1995	Pittsburgh	NL	74.3	79	34	9	36	47	4.12	4	4	9.57	1.09	4.36	5.69	.81
1996	Montreal	NL	75.0	79	34	7	40	44	4.08	4	4	9.48	.84	4.80	5.28	.56

The proverbial tenth man. He didn't do anything last year to raise or lower his status on the organizational ladder.

JEFF FASSERO   LSP   1963   Age 34

YR	TEAM	Lge	IP	H	ER	HR	BB	K	ERA	W	L	H/9	HR/9	BB/9	K/9	KW
1993	Montreal	NL	144.0	129	45	8	70	135	2.81	11	5	8.06	.50	4.38	8.44	1.72
1994	Montreal	NL	135.3	119	45	13	52	110	2.99	10	5	7.91	.86	3.46	7.32	1.57
1995	Montreal	NL	187.3	213	91	15	90	148	4.37	10	11	10.23	.72	4.32	7.11	1.29
1996	Montreal	NL	227.0	220	78	19	74	192	3.09	16	9	8.72	.75	2.93	7.61	1.80

A fine pitcher who finally received some overdue attention last year. Fassero has been in the majors for only six years, but he's 34, and some decline should be expected. He's a groundball/strikeout pitcher, extremely unusual for a left-hander and something that should make the transition to the Kingdome easier. Figuring in the league transition and the decline in the defense behind him, his ERA could easily climb a run this year. With the Mariners offense, of course, that still means he's a potential 20-game winner.

BEN FLEETHAM   RRP   1973   Age 24

YR	TEAM	Lge	IP	H	ER	HR	BB	K	ERA	W	L	H/9	HR/9	BB/9	K/9	KW
1994	Vermont	NY-P	23.3	32	16	0	24	17	6.17	1	2	12.34	.00	9.26	6.56	-.13
1994	Burlington	Midw	12.0	7	3	1	6	17	2.25	1	0	5.25	.75	4.50	12.75	3.12
1996	Delmarva	S Atl	17.3	14	5	3	10	18	2.60	1	1	7.27	1.56	5.19	9.35	1.82
1996	West Palm Bch	Flor	27.7	21	8	0	19	35	2.60	2	1	6.83	.00	6.18	11.39	2.25

If numbers count for anything, this guy could be real, real good. Fleetham was out of organized baseball in 1995, but the Expos re-signed him before last season. He blew through the low minors and was unfazed by a late promotion to Harrisburg. Almost nothing is known about him—he arrived so suddenly that no scouting reports on him are available— but if he is given a legitimate opportunity, look out.

SCOTT GENTILE RRP   1971   Age 26

YR	TEAM	Lge	IP	H	ER	HR	BB	K	ERA	W	L	H/9	HR/9	BB/9	K/9	KW
1993	West Palm Bch	Flor	119.0	175	92	15	75	86	6.96	3	10	13.24	1.13	5.67	6.50	.75
1994	West Palm Bch	Flor	59.3	56	16	1	26	69	2.43	5	2	8.49	.15	3.94	10.47	2.50
1995	Harrisburg	East	45.7	45	18	4	19	37	3.55	3	2	8.87	.79	3.74	7.29	1.49
1996	Harrisburg	East	22.0	17	8	2	17	17	3.27	1	1	6.95	.82	6.95	6.95	.58

He's supposed to be the Expos' future closer, but injuries have set him back the last two years. The rust showed last season. Throws very hard, and if he's healthy this spring he could squeeze onto the roster. Probably not a candidate to pick up saves until 1998.

ROD HENDERSON RSP   1971   Age 26

YR	TEAM	Lge	IP	H	ER	HR	BB	K	ERA	W	L	H/9	HR/9	BB/9	K/9	KW
1993	West Palm Bch	Flor	126.7	143	58	6	62	101	4.12	7	7	10.16	.43	4.41	7.18	1.29
1993	Harrisburg	East	27.0	24	10	0	19	19	3.33	2	1	8.00	.00	6.33	6.33	.53
1994	Harrisburg	East	10.7	7	2	1	6	12	1.69	1	0	5.91	.84	5.06	10.12	2.11
1994	Ottawa	Inter	115.3	141	68	17	83	85	5.31	5	8	11.00	1.33	6.48	6.63	.59
1995	Harrisburg	East	52.3	60	28	5	23	41	4.82	2	4	10.32	.86	3.96	7.05	1.36
1996	Ottawa	Inter	115.3	125	67	12	66	69	5.23	5	8	9.75	.94	5.15	5.38	.51

The number of pitchers with the talent to pitch in the major leagues easily surpasses the number who actually make it. Henderson is an example of why: injuries, injuries, injuries. His stuff is still good enough that he might yet make it, but three years ago he looked untouchable. At least a year away from competing for a job, most likely as a reliever.

JEFF JUDEN RRP   1971   Age 26

YR	TEAM	Lge	IP	H	ER	HR	BB	K	ERA	W	L	H/9	HR/9	BB/9	K/9	KW
1993	Tucson	PCL	156.0	167	79	9	93	124	4.56	7	10	9.63	.52	5.37	7.15	1.04
1994	Scranton-WB	Inter	24.7	30	25	5	23	23	9.12	0	3	10.95	1.82	8.39	8.39	.70
1994	Philadelphia	NL	27.3	30	22	4	14	21	7.24	1	2	9.88	1.32	4.61	6.91	1.15
1995	Scranton-WB	Inter	78.0	80	40	4	44	55	4.62	4	5	9.23	.46	5.08	6.35	.85
1995	Philadelphia	NL	61.7	52	25	6	36	42	3.65	4	3	7.59	.88	5.25	6.13	.73
1996	San Francisco	NL	41.3	40	20	7	23	31	4.35	2	3	8.71	1.52	5.01	6.75	1.00
1996	Montreal	NL	31.3	24	9	1	17	23	2.59	2	1	6.89	.29	4.88	6.61	.98

I really like this guy. He's a hulking beast, 6' 8" and 265 pounds of menace. The Astros brought him up when he was just 20, then gave up on him when he struggled for a few years. He began to put it together with the Phillies in 1995, but Lee Thomas sent him to San Francisco for waiver-wire bait Mike Benjamin. The Giants lost faith in him, so Alou picked him up at the break and Juden posted a 2.20 ERA. Throws a deadly splitter, gets groundballs and murders left-handers (.198 average). He's still only 26, and has both his health and a live arm. He could have the closer's job all to himself by June.

MARK LEITER RSP   1963   Age 34

YR	TEAM	Lge	IP	H	ER	HR	BB	K	ERA	W	L	H/9	HR/9	BB/9	K/9	KW
1993	Detroit	AL	106.3	109	51	17	49	73	4.32	6	6	9.23	1.44	4.15	6.18	1.02
1994	California	AL	95.0	94	42	12	38	69	3.98	6	5	8.91	1.14	3.60	6.54	1.28
1995	San Francisco	NL	191.7	195	83	20	71	116	3.90	11	10	9.16	.94	3.33	5.45	.98
1996	San Francisco	NL	135.7	151	81	24	62	103	5.37	5	10	10.02	1.59	4.11	6.83	1.25
1996	Montreal	NL	68.3	68	29	11	25	40	3.82	4	4	8.96	1.45	3.29	5.27	.93

The Expos and pitching coach Joe Kerrigan were given a lot of credit for Leiter's improvement after he was traded to Montreal, but that was hot air blown by reporters looking for a story. Leiter has always been a pretty good pitcher who's been dogged by the home run; all Kerrigan did was what any good pitching coach should: he told Leiter to throw strikes and keep the ball down, and Leiter listened. His pitching down the stretch got him a two-year deal with Philadelphia, which is good because Leiter has been an under-appreciated pitcher for many years and still has some gas left in the tank. Pedro Martinez gets all the flak for being a headhunter, but Leiter has now led his league in hit batters three straight years.

BARRY MANUEL   **RRP**   **1966**   **Age 31**

YR	TEAM	Lge	IP	H	ER	HR	BB	K	ERA	W	L	H/9	HR/9	BB/9	K/9	KW
1993	Oklahoma	AmA	23.3	27	17	1	19	17	6.56	1	2	10.41	.39	7.33	6.56	.35
1993	Rochester	Inter	18.0	16	7	2	9	9	3.50	1	1	8.00	1.00	4.50	4.50	.37
1994	Rochester	Inter	133.0	168	79	20	73	89	5.35	5	10	11.37	1.35	4.94	6.02	.77
1995	Ottawa	Inter	119.0	140	70	5	68	72	5.29	5	8	10.59	.38	5.14	5.45	.53
1996	Montreal	NL	84.0	71	28	10	33	54	3.00	6	3	7.61	1.07	3.54	5.79	1.04

The Billy Taylor of 1996, but pitching in Montreal he went completely unnoticed. There's no reason to think he can do it again, but there was no reason to think he could do it the first time.

PEDRO MARTINEZ   **RSP**   **1972**   **Age 25**

YR	TEAM	Lge	IP	H	ER	HR	BB	K	ERA	W	L	H/9	HR/9	BB/9	K/9	KW
1993	Los Angeles	NL	103.0	85	31	6	69	115	2.71	8	3	7.43	.52	6.03	10.05	1.84
1994	Montreal	NL	140.7	117	47	11	57	131	3.01	10	6	7.49	.70	3.65	8.38	1.88
1995	Montreal	NL	190.3	165	68	22	81	155	3.22	13	8	7.80	1.04	3.83	7.33	1.49
1996	Montreal	NL	212.3	192	82	18	88	192	3.48	14	10	8.14	.76	3.73	8.14	1.78

The Expos are stubbornly refusing to buck team policy and give him the four-year deal he wants, but they have to take the risk if they want to sign him at a price they can afford. He and Ismael Valdes are the two best 25-and-under pitchers in the game. Likely to post a sub-3.00 ERA at least three times in the next five years, and if the Expos are careful with him and don't let him leave town, he will almost certainly go down as the best pitcher in the team's history.

JOSE PANIAGUA   **RSP**   **1974**   **Age 23**

YR	TEAM	Lge	IP	H	ER	HR	BB	K	ERA	W	L	H/9	HR/9	BB/9	K/9	KW
1994	West Palm Bch	Flor	126.0	160	91	10	73	85	6.50	4	10	11.43	.71	5.21	6.07	.72
1995	Harrisburg	East	115.3	166	87	11	76	69	6.79	3	10	12.95	.86	5.93	5.38	.31
1996	Harrisburg	East	16.3	15	1	0	3	12	.55	2	0	8.27	.00	1.65	6.61	1.79
1996	Ottawa	Inter	80.3	78	34	7	32	50	3.81	5	4	8.74	.78	3.59	5.60	.97
1996	Montreal	NL	50.7	54	20	7	28	24	3.55	3	3	9.59	1.24	4.97	4.26	.18

A surprise addition to the staff in April after Carlos Perez went out for the year, Paniagua pitched admirably as a starter despite no experience above AA. He's an extreme groundball pitcher, and survived his trial-by-fire without very good control. He started to dominate hitters about a month after he was sent down to AAA, and last year's experience should really give him an edge for the #5 starter job this year. I like his future more than his numbers say I should.

MEL ROJAS   **RRP**   **1967**   **Age 30**

YR	TEAM	Lge	IP	H	ER	HR	BB	K	ERA	W	L	H/9	HR/9	BB/9	K/9	KW
1993	Montreal	NL	86.0	83	36	7	40	46	3.77	5	5	8.69	.73	4.19	4.81	.56
1994	Montreal	NL	82.0	71	29	11	28	78	3.18	6	3	7.79	1.21	3.07	8.56	2.09
1995	Montreal	NL	66.7	72	28	2	35	55	3.78	4	3	9.72	.27	4.73	7.43	1.29
1996	Montreal	NL	78.7	59	23	5	34	79	2.63	6	3	6.75	.57	3.89	9.04	2.04

Not a top-of-the-line closer, but he's definitely a luxury model. If he stays in Montreal, the Expos should have one of the best—and certainly most underrated—bullpens in the game. Left-handers hit just .147 against him, and he posted a 0.96 ERA after the break. Rojas was the undisputed closer, but Alou doesn't compartmentalize his pitchers like some managers do, and Mel's 34 appearances in non-save situations led all NL closers. Signed with the Cubs, where he'll start the year as the closer.

CURT SCHMIDT   **RRP**   **1970**   **Age 27**

YR	TEAM	Lge	IP	H	ER	HR	BB	K	ERA	W	L	H/9	HR/9	BB/9	K/9	KW
1993	West Palm Bch	Flor	56.0	84	41	6	35	41	6.59	2	4	13.50	.96	5.62	6.59	.79
1994	Harrisburg	East	65.7	60	18	5	38	55	2.47	5	5	8.22	.69	5.21	7.54	1.21
1995	Ottawa	Inter	48.7	47	13	1	24	32	2.40	4	1	8.69	.18	4.44	5.92	.86
1995	Montreal	NL	10.7	15	7	1	10	6	5.91	0	1	12.66	.84	8.44	5.06	-.42
1996	Ottawa	Inter	66.7	65	23	2	29	37	3.11	4	3	8.78	.27	3.92	5.00	.69

A control specialist who has had three great minor league campaigns in a row but doesn't light up the radar gun enough to get promoted. Probably won't ever be effective at the major league level.

EVERETT STULL   **RSP**   **1972**   **Age 25**

YR	TEAM	Lge	IP	H	ER	HR	BB	K	ERA	W	L	H/9	HR/9	BB/9	K/9	KW
1993	Burlington	Midw	70.3	86	47	9	76	50	6.01	2	6	11.00	1.15	9.73	6.40	-.30
1994	West Palm Bch	Flor	134.0	138	61	6	100	127	4.10	7	8	9.27	.40	6.72	8.53	1.16
1995	Harrisburg	East	116.0	138	91	15	95	103	7.06	3	10	10.71	1.16	7.37	7.99	.82
1996	Harrisburg	East	74.0	71	29	7	63	60	3.53	5	3	8.64	.85	7.66	7.30	.52
1996	Ottawa	Inter	68.0	89	50	7	48	58	6.62	2	6	11.78	.93	6.35	7.68	.97

Stull has a genuine power arm, but is wilder than Ross Perot talking about NAFTA. He's doubtful to ever harness his stuff as a starter, but a career spitting sunflower seeds beyond the outfield fence is still open.

UGUETH URBINA   **RSP**   **1974**   **Age 23**

YR	TEAM	Lge	IP	H	ER	HR	BB	K	ERA	W	L	H/9	HR/9	BB/9	K/9	KW
1993	Burlington	Midw	95.7	100	31	9	49	62	2.92	7	4	9.41	.85	4.61	5.83	.79
1993	Harrisburg	East	63.7	77	33	6	41	34	4.66	3	4	10.88	.85	5.80	4.81	.15
1994	Harrisburg	East	110.7	110	47	12	58	63	3.82	6	6	8.95	.98	4.72	5.12	.53
1995	Ottawa	Inter	63.0	54	24	1	35	47	3.43	4	3	7.71	.14	5.00	6.71	.99
1995	Montreal	NL	23.3	26	15	6	17	14	5.79	1	2	10.03	2.31	6.56	5.40	.16
1996	West Palm Bch	Flor	12.7	16	3	0	4	15	2.13	1	0	11.37	.00	2.84	10.66	2.84
1996	Ottawa	Inter	22.0	20	8	2	8	23	3.27	1	1	8.18	.82	3.27	9.41	2.32
1996	Montreal	NL	112.3	102	45	17	53	94	3.61	7	5	8.17	1.36	4.25	7.53	1.45

Urbina has terrific talent and an idea of what to do with it, but had an atrocious platoon split last year. Right-handers were handcuffed to a .153 average, but lefties hit .315 and pounded Urbina for a .511 slugging average. The Expos have talked about him as a possible replacement for Rojas, and he did post a 1.99 ERA out of the bullpen, but he won't survive for long if lefties continue to get the better of him. It may be just a one-year fluke, since he didn't have anywhere near the same split in AAA in 1995. If the Expos keep him in the rotation he might win 200 games before he's through.

DAVE VERES   **RRP**   **1967**   **Age 30**

YR	TEAM	Lge	IP	H	ER	HR	BB	K	ERA	W	L	H/9	HR/9	BB/9	K/9	KW
1993	Tucson	PCL	121.7	149	68	8	44	97	5.03	5	9	11.02	.59	3.25	7.18	1.58
1994	Tucson	PCL	22.3	17	5	0	12	16	2.01	2	0	6.85	.00	4.84	6.45	.94
1994	Houston	NL	40.0	40	12	4	10	26	2.70	3	1	9.00	.90	2.25	5.85	1.39
1995	Houston	NL	100.7	98	27	6	39	85	2.41	8	3	8.76	.54	3.49	7.60	1.66
1996	Montreal	NL	77.3	85	33	9	38	70	3.84	5	4	9.89	1.05	4.42	8.15	1.61

Did a terrible job of justifying his price tag (Sean Berry), running up a 5.44 ERA through the break. He pitched much better after that, but it probably wasn't enough to save his job. At 30, he may be forced to go to spring training as a non-roster invitee and hope for the best.

NEIL WEBER   **LSP**   **1973**   **Age 24**

YR	TEAM	Lge	IP	H	ER	HR	BB	K	ERA	W	L	H/9	HR/9	BB/9	K/9	KW
1993	Jamestown	NY-P	74.7	124	60	4	60	42	7.23	2	6	14.95	.48	7.23	5.06	-.12
1994	West Palm Bch	Flor	123.3	133	60	12	81	103	4.38	6	8	9.71	.88	5.91	7.52	1.03
1995	Harrisburg	East	140.3	185	101	20	109	93	6.48	4	12	11.86	1.28	6.99	5.96	.24
1996	Harrisburg	East	99.0	100	34	8	55	55	3.09	7	4	9.09	.73	5.00	5.00	.42

He's highly coveted because he's left-handed and throws 90. After years of battling his control, he finally scored a decisive victory last year. The Expos need to go slowly with him, because he still needs a lot of refinement. It would be an upset if he surfaced in 1997, but a good long-term gamble.

Player	Age	Team	Lge	AB	H	DB	TP	HR	BB	SB	CS	OUT	BA	OBA	SA	EQA	EQR	Peak
CARLOS ADOLFO	20	Delmarva	S Atl	520	132	12	3	10	37	7	3	391	.254	.303	.346	.219	44	.249
EDWARD BADY	23	W. Palm Bch	Flor	502	137	9	1	2	39	22	9	374	.273	.325	.307	.220	43	.240
MICHAEL BARRETT	19	Delmarva	S Atl	490	103	18	2	4	14	2	4	391	.210	.232	.280	.157	19	.181
YAMIL BENITEZ	23	Ottawa	Inter	446	124	16	0	22	30	8	3	325	.278	.324	.462	.260	56	.283
MO BLAKENEY	23	Delmarva	S Atl	115	26	1	0	2	5	1	2	91	.226	.258	.287	.172	6	.186
DANNY BRAVO	19	W. Palm Bch	Flor	141	26	3	1	0	13	2	2	117	.184	.253	.220	.139	4	.161
JOSH BRINKLEY	22	W. Palm Bch	Flor	278	70	7	1	6	24	1	1	209	.252	.311	.349	.221	24	.244
NATE BROWN	25	W. Palm Bch	Flor	295	62	7	1	4	27	6	2	235	.210	.276	.281	.185	17	.195
JOLBERT CABRERA	23	Harrisburg	East	359	80	14	1	3	21	7	3	282	.223	.266	.292	.184	20	.201
ORLANDO CABRERA	22	Delmarva	S Atl	542	130	16	1	13	42	21	8	420	.240	.295	.345	.218	46	.240
JASON CAMILLI	20	Delmarva	S Atl	455	92	8	1	3	49	10	6	369	.202	.280	.244	.169	22	.193
JESUS CAMPOS	22	Harrisburg	East	211	49	3	0	0	8	4	4	166	.232	.260	.246	.159	8	.174
	22	W. Palm Bch	Flor	153	37	6	1	0	11	4	2	118	.242	.293	.294	.198	10	.219
JHONNY CARVAJAL	21	W. Palm Bch	Flor	442	99	7	0	5	40	8	8	351	.224	.288	.274	.184	25	.206
SCOTT COOLBAUGH	30	Ottawa	Inter	177	36	10	1	3	23	1	1	142	.203	.295	.322	.203	13	.199
TRACE COQUILLETTE	22	W. Palm Bch	Flor	276	67	15	2	2	25	5	4	213	.243	.306	.333	.214	23	.236
WES DENNING	23	Delmarva	S Atl	370	79	12	3	5	33	12	5	296	.214	.278	.303	.195	25	.211
JOSE FERNANDEZ	21	Delmarva	S Atl	448	115	13	2	11	40	10	6	339	.257	.318	.368	.231	43	.258
JAIME GARCIA	24	Delmarva	S Atl	193	42	7	0	5	17	1	2	153	.218	.281	.332	.200	14	.214
MIKE GIARDI	23	W. Palm Bch	Flor	159	40	2	1	6	24	1	1	120	.252	.350	.390	.248	18	.270
MATT HAAS	24	W. Palm Bch	Flor	216	56	6	1	1	19	2	1	161	.259	.319	.310	.214	17	.228
DEREK HACOPIAN	26	W. Palm Bch	Flor	163	42	7	0	3	12	0	2	123	.258	.309	.356	.219	14	.227
BERT HEFFERNAN	31	Ottawa	Inter	202	59	6	1	1	15	1	2	145	.292	.341	.347	.233	19	.224
RAMSEY KOEYERS	21	Harrisburg	East	78	15	2	0	1	1	0	0	63	.192	.203	.256	.126	2	.139
JOSE MACIAS	22	Delmarva	S Atl	396	91	10	3	1	44	14	6	311	.230	.307	.278	.200	28	.220
FRANCISCO MATOS	26	Ottawa	Inter	310	71	14	2	2	18	3	3	242	.229	.271	.306	.189	19	.196
CHARLIE MONTOYO	30	Harrisburg	East	189	39	2	1	0	28	1	0	150	.206	.309	.228	.176	10	.174
FRANCISCO MORALES	23	W. Palm Bch	Flor	268	71	14	1	5	17	2	1	198	.265	.309	.381	.231	26	.252
DONALD OLSEN	24	Delmarva	S Atl	304	58	7	0	5	19	1	1	247	.191	.238	.263	.152	11	.163
PAUL OTTAVINIA	23	W. Palm Bch	Flor	145	30	1	1	1	11	1	1	116	.207	.263	.248	.159	6	.171
JOHN PACHOT	21	W. Palm Bch	Flor	165	29	5	0	1	2	0	0	136	.176	.186	.224	.084	1	.094
DAVE POST	22	W. Palm Bch	Flor	271	75	11	3	7	34	5	2	198	.277	.357	.417	.261	35	.286
DAVE RENTERIA	23	W. Palm Bch	Flor	110	19	2	1	0	8	1	1	92	.173	.229	.209	.113	2	.124
CHRIS SCHWAB	21	Delmarva	S Atl	451	94	18	1	8	35	1	2	359	.208	.265	.306	.184	26	.206
FERNANDO SEGUIGNOL	21	Delmarva	S Atl	435	94	7	2	8	37	5	5	346	.216	.278	.297	.187	26	.210
DAROND STOVALL	23	Harrisburg	East	278	58	5	0	9	29	7	3	223	.209	.283	.324	.203	21	.220
JULIAN YAN	30	Ottawa	Inter	137	25	3	1	3	11	0	0	112	.182	.243	.285	.164	6	.159

Player	Age	Team	Lge	IP	H	ER	HR	BB	K	ERA	W	L	H/9	HR/9	BB/9	K/9	KW
JASON BAKER	21	Delmarva	S Atl	137.3	173	82	8	111	81	5.37	5	10	11.34	.52	7.27	5.31	-.05
BOB BAXTER	27	Ottawa	Inter	78.3	109	49	7	32	50	5.63	3	6	12.52	.80	3.68	5.74	1.00
MIKE BELL	23	Delmarva	S Atl	52.7	54	15	2	27	32	2.56	4	2	9.23	.34	4.61	5.47	.67
JAKE BENZ	24	Harrisburg	East	34.7	46	28	6	32	19	7.27	1	3	11.94	1.56	8.31	4.93	-.43
DENIS BOUCHER	28	Ottawa	Inter	60.3	89	53	15	50	20	7.91	1	6	13.28	2.24	7.46	2.98	-.87
JOSE CENTENO	23	W. Palm Bch	Flor	53.0	78	34	6	28	34	5.77	2	4	13.25	1.02	4.75	5.77	.74
XAVIER CIVIT	23	Delmarva	S Atl	42.7	62	40	5	29	31	8.44	1	4	13.08	1.05	6.12	6.54	.65
JASON COLE	23	W. Palm Bch	Flor	54.7	72	28	4	28	29	4.61	3	3	11.85	.66	4.61	4.77	.44
FERNANDO DASILVA	24	W. Palm Bch	Flor	60.0	70	25	6	29	33	3.75	4	3	10.50	.90	4.35	4.95	.56
RICK DEHART	26	Harrisburg	East	40.0	51	18	4	24	22	4.05	2	2	11.48	.90	5.40	4.95	.30
TIMOTHY DIXON	24	W. Palm Bch	Flor	109.7	155	62	15	51	63	5.09	5	7	12.72	1.23	4.19	5.17	.68
JAYSON DUROCHER	21	W. Palm Bch	Flor	114.0	148	74	8	62	73	5.84	4	9	11.68	.63	4.89	5.76	.70
STEVE FALTEISEK	24	Harrisburg	East	105.7	126	58	9	60	46	4.94	5	7	10.73	.77	5.11	3.92	.03
	24	Ottawa	Inter	56.0	77	40	9	33	22	6.43	2	4	12.38	1.45	5.30	3.54	-.15
SCOTT FORSTER	24	Harrisburg	East	163.0	182	86	15	84	72	4.75	7	11	10.05	.83	4.64	3.98	.17
RUSSELL HANDY	21	Delmarva	S Atl	30.7	54	45	3	49	16	13.21	0	3	15.85	.88	14.38	4.70	-2.03
	21	W. Palm Bch	Flor	28.0	49	42	4	36	9	13.50	0	3	15.75	1.29	11.57	2.89	-1.93
BLAISE ILSLEY	32	Ottawa	Inter	43.3	51	24	9	20	18	4.98	2	3	10.59	1.87	4.15	3.74	.21
DAVE LEIPER	34	Ottawa	Inter	31.0	32	6	3	9	22	1.74	3	0	9.29	.87	2.61	6.39	1.48
SEAN LESLIE	22	Delmarva	S Atl	32.7	36	16	4	14	13	4.41	2	2	9.92	1.10	3.86	3.58	.23
ROBERT MARQUEZ	23	Delmarva	S Atl	38.3	63	29	5	32	27	6.81	1	3	14.79	1.17	7.51	6.34	.23
RAMIRO MARTINEZ	24	W. Palm Bch	Flor	37.3	57	22	2	20	32	5.30	1	3	13.74	.48	4.82	7.71	1.37
TROY MATTES	20	Delmarva	S Atl	145.0	209	100	19	76	83	6.21	5	11	12.97	1.18	4.72	5.15	.54
JASON MCCOMMON	24	Harrisburg	East	140.7	188	84	13	58	68	5.37	6	10	12.03	.83	3.71	4.35	.52
SCOTT MITCHELL	23	Delmarva	S Atl	63.7	101	37	9	36	42	5.23	3	4	14.28	1.27	5.09	5.94	.71
DAVID MORAGA	20	W. Palm Bch	Flor	110.7	167	82	10	70	70	6.67	3	9	13.58	.81	5.69	5.69	.47
TOMMY PHELPS	22	Harrisburg	East	43.7	47	15	3	24	17	3.09	3	2	9.69	.62	4.95	3.50	-.07
	22	W. Palm Bch	Flor	98.3	131	48	8	51	52	4.39	5	6	11.99	.73	4.67	4.76	.42
LOU POTE	24	Harrisburg	East	96.7	124	62	14	60	45	5.77	4	7	11.54	1.30	5.59	4.19	.00
JEREMY POWELL	20	Delmarva	S Atl	131.7	183	88	13	96	60	6.02	5	10	12.51	.89	6.56	4.10	-.27
RORY RHODRIGUEZ	25	W. Palm Bch	Flor	60.7	69	35	3	49	35	5.19	3	4	10.24	.45	7.27	5.19	-.09
BEN RIVERA	27	Ottawa	Inter	96.3	118	66	7	59	72	6.17	3	8	11.02	.65	5.51	6.73	.86
J.D. SMART	22	Delmarva	S Atl	129.7	225	96	18	49	60	6.66	4	10	15.62	1.25	3.40	4.16	.54
ANTHONY TELFORD	30	Ottawa	Inter	112.7	136	56	12	46	57	4.47	6	7	10.86	.96	3.67	4.55	.60
MICHAEL THURMAN	22	W. Palm Bch	Flor	99.7	152	60	5	37	50	5.42	4	7	13.73	.45	3.34	4.52	.67
JAVIER VAZQUEZ	20	Delmarva	S Atl	137.0	202	82	16	85	95	5.39	5	10	13.27	1.05	5.58	6.24	.68
CHRIS WEIDERT	22	W. Palm Bch	Flor	93.3	131	61	7	52	47	5.88	3	7	12.63	.67	5.01	4.53	.26
WALLY WHITEHURST	32	Ottawa	Inter	33.7	43	15	2	17	29	4.01	2	2	11.50	.53	4.54	7.75	1.45
JASON WOODRING	22	Delmarva	S Atl	50.7	60	20	3	25	24	3.55	3	3	10.66	.53	4.44	4.26	.31

New York Mets

The human shoulder consists of three bones that more or less come together: the upper arm, collarbone and shoulder blade (humerus, clavicle and scapula for the pedants out there). The shoulder blade consists mostly of a flat plate in the upper part of the back, but has a flange called the acromion that curls over the top of the shoulder. Feel the bone on top of your shoulder, towards the outside and back of it? The shoulder blade has a shallow indentation in which the upper arm rests; around the edge of this indentation, rising up like a sleeve around the ball of the arm is some cartilage called the "labrum." The joint is actually held in place by muscle. Underneath the large, cosmetically valuable deltoid are four small muscles which form the "rotator cuff." Tendons running between these muscles pass over the arm bone and actually hold the arm against the shoulder blade.

There isn't much room in the shoulder between the top of the arm bone and the acromion, and when you move your arm over your head, like you do when swimming or pitching a baseball, the gap narrows further. Normally, this isn't a problem. But when one or all of the muscles that make up the rotator cuff become weak, due to lack of conditioning, fatigue, injury or age, they can fail to hold the arm tightly against the shoulder blade; it slips. And if you're pulling your arm over your head, that slippage is going to be upwards, into an already narrow gap. That gap is not empty; the shoulder bursa, which provides a sort of lubricating fluid for the joint, is there, and so are some of those all-important rotator cuff tendons. When the arm bone slips and pinches these structures ("impingement syndrome") they become inflamed, giving rise to bursitis or tendinitis. And they swell, confining the space even further.

Continuing to pull the arm over the head without waiting for the rotator cuff muscles to restrengthen causes damage to accumulate. The labrum gets torn up from having the arm bone slide over it. The tendons behave like a rope sliding over a rock, getting small tears, fraying and eventually getting in the way of shoulder motion. The acromion builds up a calcium deposit where it's getting repeatedly banged into; this is a bone spur, a sharp little piece that can start ripping into the muscles of the rotator cuff itself, weakening them further or tearing through them completely.

The human elbow is less complicated, but no less vulnerable. Throwing puts two principal strains on an elbow. The act of throwing causes the three bones to bang together, sometimes with enough force to take a divot out of each other. These are the well-known bone chips or "loose bodies." The other problem comes when you throw a curve ball. Snapping your wrist over and outward twists the elbow towards the body (the "medial" side of the elbow) and stretches the ligament holding the bones together along that side ("medial collateral ligament"). Stretching it too hard causes small tears; stretch it hard while it's partially torn, and it will tear through completely.

I go into this discourse on overuse injuries of the arm because the Mets' pitcher conditioning program has been about as successful as the LAPD Handbook on Evidence Collection Procedure or the Jack Kevorkian CPR Manual. A year ago the Mets' Young Guns, Pulsipher, Isringhausen and Wilson, were going to lead them to the playoffs; this year, all three have been recovering from surgery to their arms. This was not due in any way, shape, or form, to bad luck. It was due to working too hard.

Pitcher injuries accumulate in one of two ways, usually both. One, overuse on any given day causes the rotator cuff muscles to fatigue, allowing the slippage that starts tears in the tendons. It only takes one outing to start the damage. Two, coming back too soon, before the muscles have recovered from their fatigue or the tears have healed, increases the damage. There is a definite age-related pattern to such injuries; they seem to be more common in a still-growing person, or until the early to mid-20s, stabilize, and then start becoming more common again in the mid-30s and thereafter as aging takes its toll.

Met management in recent years has had a philosophy about young pitchers: They need lots of work to strengthen their arms. They need to be tough, play-through-pain kind of guys who get mad when the manager takes them out. No organization has worked their pitchers harder in the minors, allowing them to throw more innings and to more batters, than the Mets have. What the minors didn't destroy, Dallas Green finished.

BENNY AGBAYANI   **LF**   **1972**   **Age 25**

Year	Team	Lge	AB	H	DB	TP	HR	BB	SB	CS	OUT	BA	OBA	SA	EQA	EQR	Peak
1993	Pittsfield	NY-P	176	37	4	1	2	15	2	1	140	.210	.272	.278	.179	9	.199
1994	St. Lucie	Flor	427	115	10	2	8	54	5	3	315	.269	.351	.358	.242	45	.267
1995	St. Lucie	Flor	164	49	6	2	3	22	5	2	117	.299	.382	.415	.272	23	.296
1995	Binghamton	East	304	80	9	1	2	34	7	2	226	.263	.337	.319	.227	28	.247
1996	Binghamton	East	55	9	0	0	2	9	1	0	46	.164	.281	.273	.183	3	.194
1996	Norfolk	Inter	337	92	12	5	8	31	10	3	248	.273	.334	.409	.252	40	.270
1997	*NY Mets*	*NL*	*384*	*99*	*18*	*6*	*9*	*41*	*13*	*3*	*288*	*.258*	*.329*	*.406*	*.267*	*53*	

He's hit the same for three straight years, and it's not enough to be an outfielder in the majors.

EDGARDO ALFONZO   **IF**   **1974**   **Age 23**

Year	Team	Lge	AB	H	DB	TP	HR	BB	SB	CS	OUT	BA	OBA	SA	EQA	EQR	Peak
1993	St. Lucie	Flor	511	142	10	2	13	51	14	7	376	.278	.343	.382	.247	57	.284
1994	Binghamton	East	516	143	22	1	15	58	10	6	379	.277	.350	.411	.256	63	.291
1995	NY Mets	NL	342	100	14	5	4	16	1	1	243	.292	.324	.398	.243	35	.272
1996	NY Mets	NL	379	105	16	1	5	29	2	0	274	.277	.328	.364	.236	37	.260
1997	*NY Mets*	*NL*	*402*	*115*	*24*	*3*	*8*	*34*	*6*	*3*	*290*	*.286*	*.342*	*.420*	*.274*	*57*	

His hitting projections have steadily slipped since reaching the majors, which is usually a very bad sign for one's future. Several factors help offset this for Alfonzo. He's still very young. He plays all of the infield positions and plays them well. That versatility has resulted in irregular playing time at changing positions. Stability has its virtues.

CARLOS BAERGA   **2B/3B**   **1969**   **Age 28**

Year	Team	Lge	AB	H	DB	TP	HR	BB	SB	CS	OUT	BA	OBA	SA	EQA	EQR	Peak
1993	Cleveland	AL	641	222	29	6	27	38	14	3	422	.346	.383	.537	.304	108	.326
1994	Cleveland	AL	443	140	29	2	20	10	7	2	305	.316	.331	.526	.282	64	.297
1995	Cleveland	AL	567	188	31	2	17	36	11	2	381	.332	.371	.483	.287	84	.299
1996	Cleveland	AL	423	112	18	0	12	16	1	1	312	.265	.292	.392	.228	39	.233
1996	NY Mets	NL	84	17	1	0	3	6	0	0	67	.202	.256	.321	.186	5	.190
1997	*NY Mets*	*NL*	*490*	*140*	*27*	*1*	*17*	*12*	*4*	*2*	*352*	*.286*	*.303*	*.449*	*.267*	*65*	

An embarrassing year for Carlos, who showed up for camp overweight and never recovered. In fact as the season went on he got worse, until he was swinging at every pitch thrown to him, regardless of location. The Indians were upset that he wouldn't accept playing third base, but he's told the Mets it's no problem. We'll see.

FLETCHER BATES   **RF**   **1974**   **Age 23**

Year	Team	Lge	AB	H	DB	TP	HR	BB	SB	CS	OUT	BA	OBA	SA	EQA	EQR	Peak
1995	Pittsfield	NY-P	293	84	6	2	8	32	7	4	213	.287	.357	.403	.257	36	.289
1996	Columbia	S Atl	519	124	11	5	14	50	6	3	398	.239	.306	.360	.223	47	.247

He had a really promising year at Pittsfield in '95 but couldn't keep it up, even if it does look exciting to have double figure numbers in doubles, triples, and homers (21-13-15 in real play). He's not exactly young for low-A, either.

RICO BROGNA   **1B**   **1970**   **Age 27**

Year	Team	Lge	AB	H	DB	TP	HR	BB	SB	CS	OUT	BA	OBA	SA	EQA	EQR	Peak
1993	Toledo	Inter	493	132	23	2	12	34	6	3	364	.268	.315	.396	.238	51	.259
1994	Norfolk	Inter	265	68	12	3	12	16	1	2	199	.257	.299	.460	.247	30	.265
1994	NY Mets	NL	133	47	11	2	7	8	1	0	86	.353	.390	.624	.325	26	.348
1995	NY Mets	NL	509	155	26	2	24	46	0	0	354	.305	.362	.505	.285	77	.301
1996	NY Mets	NL	194	53	9	1	8	22	0	0	141	.273	.347	.454	.265	26	.276
1997	*Philadelphia*	*NL*	*448*	*123*	*24*	*3*	*24*	*38*	*1*	*0*	*325*	*.275*	*.331*	*.502*	*.284*	*70*	

He shocked everyone with his hitting when he came over, and attributed it to hitting with his natural style instead of the forced pulling the Tigers were inflicting on him. Outside of '94, and then only with the Mets, it still wasn't that valuable for a first baseman, although being an excellent glove man helps. He needs a platoon partner badly. He missed most of the season with a torn labrum; must have hung out with the pitchers too long. Dealt to Philadelphia, where he's expected to at least platoon at first base.

BERTO CASTILLO   **C**   **1970**   **Age 27**

Year	Team	Lge	AB	H	DB	TP	HR	BB	SB	CS	OUT	BA	OBA	SA	EQA	EQR	Peak
1993	St. Lucie	Flor	341	83	9	0	8	25	0	1	259	.243	.295	.340	.211	26	.229
1994	Binghamton	East	325	75	8	0	7	37	1	1	251	.231	.309	.320	.210	25	.225
1995	Norfolk	Inter	225	60	9	1	5	27	2	2	167	.267	.345	.382	.245	25	.259
1996	Norfolk	Inter	347	71	9	1	10	39	1	1	277	.205	.285	.323	.199	25	.208

He's a great glove man, and should try hitting with it. Seriously, he gets high praise for calling a game and assisting the Met pitchers, so much so that they talk about him like he's the pitching coach. Which he may well become.

BRIAN DAUBACH   **1B**   **1972**   **Age 25**

Year	Team	Lge	AB	H	DB	TP	HR	BB	SB	CS	OUT	BA	OBA	SA	EQA	EQR	Peak
1993	Columbia	S Atl	398	99	10	1	7	39	2	1	300	.249	.316	.332	.218	33	.245
1994	St. Lucie	Flor	467	124	21	1	9	53	9	5	348	.266	.340	.373	.242	50	.266
1995	Binghamton	East	480	113	17	1	11	45	4	1	368	.235	.301	.344	.216	40	.235
1996	Binghamton	East	448	125	14	1	19	66	6	5	328	.279	.372	.442	.271	62	.290
1996	Norfolk	Inter	55	11	1	0	0	6	1	1	45	.200	.279	.218	.154	2	.167
1997	*NY Mets*	*NL*	*515*	*119*	*24*	*1*	*14*	*60*	*10*	*7*	*403*	*.231*	*.311*	*.363*	*.242*	*58*	

He's made slow progress, generally wiping out in his first exposure to new leagues, catching up later. That habit doesn't usually lead to success in the majors.

ALVARO ESPINOZA   **UT**   **1962**   **Age 35**

Year	Team	Lge	AB	H	DB	TP	HR	BB	SB	CS	OUT	BA	OBA	SA	EQA	EQR	Peak
1993	Cleveland	AL	268	81	10	0	7	10	2	2	189	.302	.327	.418	.250	29	.241
1994	Cleveland	AL	231	55	6	0	3	7	1	3	179	.238	.261	.303	.180	12	.172
1995	Cleveland	AL	145	39	2	0	3	2	0	2	108	.269	.279	.345	.204	10	.192
1996	Cleveland	AL	112	25	3	2	4	6	1	1	88	.223	.263	.393	.214	9	.204
1996	NY Mets	NL	138	45	7	2	4	6	0	2	95	.326	.354	.493	.276	19	.263
1997	*NY Mets*	*NL*	*291*	*73*	*12*	*4*	*3*	*0*	*1*	*1*	*219*	*.251*	*.251*	*.351*	*.215*	*23*	

The veteran shortstop-turned-utility infielder got into 17 games at first base, and even hit a little like one. He slugged .400 for the first time and had career highs in triples and homers, with 4 and 8. Don't expect that to happen again, Met fans.

CARL EVERETT   **OF**   **1970**   **Age 27**

Year	Team	Lge	AB	H	DB	TP	HR	BB	SB	CS	OUT	BA	OBA	SA	EQA	EQR	Peak
1993	High Desert	Calif	250	59	7	2	8	14	10	4	195	.236	.277	.376	.220	22	.240
1993	Edmonton	PCL	133	36	7	2	6	16	7	1	98	.271	.349	.489	.280	20	.305
1994	Edmonton	PCL	311	89	11	1	9	19	12	8	230	.286	.327	.415	.248	35	.266
1994	Florida	NL	51	11	0	0	2	3	4	0	40	.216	.259	.333	.213	4	.229
1995	Norfolk	Inter	268	81	13	3	7	22	9	4	191	.302	.355	.451	.271	36	.285
1995	NY Mets	NL	298	82	12	1	13	43	2	4	220	.275	.367	.453	.269	41	.284
1996	NY Mets	NL	198	51	9	1	1	24	5	0	147	.258	.338	.328	.232	19	.241
1997	*NY Mets*	*NL*	*182*	*46*	*9*	*3*	*8*	*11*	*17*	*9*	*145*	*.253*	*.295*	*.467*	*.267*	*27*	

After a good half-year in Norfolk and a strong September, the Mets convinced themselves he'd broken through. Back on Earth, he played himself onto the bench within a month and spent the rest of the year as a pinch-hitter and defensive replacement. A scout's favorite since he was with the Yankees.

MATT FRANCO   **3B/1B**   **1970**   **Age 27**

Year	Team	Lge	AB	H	DB	TP	HR	BB	SB	CS	OUT	BA	OBA	SA	EQA	EQR	Peak
1993	Orlando	South	246	74	13	0	8	27	2	3	175	.301	.370	.451	.272	34	.298
1993	Iowa	AmA	201	58	15	3	5	17	4	1	144	.289	.344	.468	.271	27	.294
1994	Iowa	AmA	444	122	26	2	13	53	2	2	324	.275	.352	.430	.261	56	.280
1995	Iowa	AmA	466	132	25	4	7	41	1	1	335	.283	.341	.399	.249	52	.263
1996	Norfolk	Inter	518	163	30	2	8	39	3	1	356	.315	.363	.427	.267	66	.278
1997	*NY Mets*	*NL*	*543*	*154*	*28*	*2*	*12*	*39*	*5*	*1*	*390*	*.284*	*.332*	*.409*	*.267*	*72*	

He has been, and is, a good hitter, even if he hasn't become the power hitter he was drafted to be. With the Cubs he was stuck behind Mark Grace so they tried him at third base; the charitable thing to say is, he improved this year. Needs to be on an AL team. Released.

BRYON GAINEY   **1B**   **1976**   **Age 21**

Year	Team	Lge	AB	H	DB	TP	HR	BB	SB	CS	OUT	BA	OBA	SA	EQA	EQR	Peak
1995	Columbia	S Atl	469	109	10	2	13	25	1	1	361	.232	.271	.345	.203	33	.234
1996	Columbia	S Atl	465	91	8	0	12	31	2	1	375	.196	.246	.290	.169	22	.192

Had 169 strikeouts against just 41 walks, which was an improvement over the previous year's 157-30. He can hit it a mile if he connects; since he rarely does, and would do so even less against high-level pitching, that point is moot.

BERNARD GILKEY   **LF**   **1967**   **Age 30**

Year	Team	Lge	AB	H	DB	TP	HR	BB	SB	CS	OUT	BA	OBA	SA	EQA	EQR	Peak
1993	St. Louis	NL	578	185	39	4	19	65	13	8	401	.320	.389	.500	.293	93	.305
1994	St. Louis	NL	385	98	19	1	7	44	14	7	294	.255	.331	.364	.236	40	.242
1995	St. Louis	NL	490	150	33	3	18	47	10	5	345	.306	.367	.496	.285	75	.287
1996	NY Mets	NL	600	204	43	3	34	81	14	9	405	.340	.419	.592	.324	121	.323
1997	*NY Mets*	*NL*	*610*	*181*	*39*	*3*	*30*	*68*	*14*	*8*	*437*	*.297*	*.367*	*.518*	*.306*	*113*	

A fabulous season has earned him a four-year contract worth $20 million. I'd say there's at least a 1 in 4 chance that he never posts a .300 EQA over the life of the contract, and 3 in 4 he doesn't have a season this good ever again. However, the scale is such that $5 million a year for better than average isn't an outrage.

JASON HARDTKE   **2B**   **1972**   **Age 25**

Year	Team	Lge	AB	H	DB	TP	HR	BB	SB	CS	OUT	BA	OBA	SA	EQA	EQR	Peak
1993	R. Cucamonga	Calif	521	140	22	3	10	40	3	3	384	.269	.321	.380	.235	51	.263
1994	Wichita	Texas	260	58	8	1	6	20	1	1	203	.223	.279	.331	.200	18	.221
1995	Binghamton	East	469	128	34	3	5	59	4	5	346	.273	.354	.390	.250	54	.272
1996	Binghamton	East	140	34	7	0	3	14	0	0	106	.243	.312	.357	.224	13	.240
1996	Norfolk	Inter	263	77	13	1	9	30	3	4	190	.293	.365	.452	.270	36	.289
1996	NY Mets	NL	58	12	5	0	0	2	0	0	46	.207	.233	.293	.164	3	.179
1997	*NY Mets*	*NL*	*374*	*97*	*27*	*2*	*13*	*29*	*2*	*1*	*278*	*.259*	*.313*	*.447*	*.268*	*51*	

Knee injuries have cost him his stolen base ability and great fielding range. He's still a fair second baseman who's shown major league ability, hitting a lot of doubles and taking some walks.

TODD HUNDLEY   **C**   **1969**   **Age 28**

Year	Team	Lge	AB	H	DB	TP	HR	BB	SB	CS	OUT	BA	OBA	SA	EQA	EQR	Peak
1993	NY Mets	NL	422	98	15	2	12	29	1	1	325	.232	.282	.363	.213	34	.228
1994	NY Mets	NL	293	70	9	1	16	29	2	1	224	.239	.307	.440	.246	34	.259
1995	NY Mets	NL	285	85	8	0	17	46	1	0	200	.298	.396	.505	.297	48	.309
1996	NY Mets	NL	563	158	29	1	46	86	1	3	408	.281	.376	.581	.303	103	.310
1997	*NY Mets*	*NL*	*587*	*154*	*31*	*2*	*30*	*86*	*3*	*5*	*438*	*.262*	*.357*	*.475*	*.289*	*98*	

When people talk about 1996, The Year of Living Dangerously in Bleacher Seats, they'll talk about him. He's had two things that together help explain his rise. He had bone chips removed from his wrist prior to the 1995 season, and he has learned how to take pitches, improving his walk rate from a dreadful once per 24 at bats to once per seven.

BUTCH HUSKEY   **1B/RF**   **1972**   **Age 25**

Year	Team	Lge	AB	H	DB	TP	HR	BB	SB	CS	OUT	BA	OBA	SA	EQA	EQR	Peak
1993	Binghamton	East	536	130	12	1	23	44	6	1	407	.243	.300	.397	.233	53	.261
1994	Norfolk	Inter	488	115	20	2	11	37	12	5	378	.236	.290	.352	.216	41	.238
1995	Norfolk	Inter	408	120	12	0	28	40	7	4	292	.294	.357	.529	.287	65	.312
1995	NY Mets	NL	92	18	2	0	3	11	1	0	74	.196	.282	.315	.198	6	.217
1996	NY Mets	NL	427	127	16	2	16	32	1	2	302	.297	.346	.457	.266	55	.285
1997	*NY Mets*	*NL*	*430*	*115*	*15*	*1*	*22*	*31*	*2*	*1*	*316*	*.267*	*.317*	*.460*	*.273*	*62*	

A player who often tried his best to live up to his name, he's listed as 6'3", 245, but has been a lot bigger than that. He can play third in an emergency. His hitting, like his weight, has been up and down to an extraordinary degree. He's capable of playing at the high points, say a .280 EQA, but has a tendency to fall a long way if he falls at all, chasing ever more unhittable pitches in an effort to get back up.

LANCE JOHNSON   **CF**   **1964**   **Age 33**

Year	Team	Lge	AB	H	DB	TP	HR	BB	SB	CS	OUT	BA	OBA	SA	EQA	EQR	Peak
1993	Chi. White Sox	AL	549	181	21	13	2	40	32	5	373	.330	.375	.426	.280	77	.278
1994	Chi. White Sox	AL	416	119	12	14	3	27	24	5	302	.286	.330	.404	.254	49	.249
1995	Chi. White Sox	AL	616	199	19	12	12	32	40	6	423	.323	.356	.451	.279	87	.269
1996	NY Mets	NL	709	253	33	20	11	42	43	12	468	.357	.393	.506	.303	118	.288
1997	*NY Mets*	*NL*	*706*	*208*	*20*	*20*	*7*	*32*	*45*	*9*	*507*	*.295*	*.325*	*.409*	*.273*	*98*	

Another aging veteran who had a phenomenal season in New York and was also rewarded with a contract extension. He led his league in hits and at bats for the second year in a row, and took home his fifth triples title with the most triples in a season since 1949. With numbers as far out of line as they were with his prior career, it's frightening to consider how much better he was on the road than at Shea: 73 more points of average and 133 of slugging.

CHRIS JONES   **OF/PH**   **1966**   **Age 31**

Year	Team	Lge	AB	H	DB	TP	HR	BB	SB	CS	OUT	BA	OBA	SA	EQA	EQR	Peak
1993	Colo. Springs	PCL	164	39	2	2	10	17	5	1	126	.238	.309	.457	.254	21	.261
1993	Colorado	NL	207	52	8	3	6	13	7	3	158	.251	.295	.406	.235	21	.240
1994	Colo. Springs	PCL	371	100	12	2	16	33	8	1	272	.270	.329	.442	.259	46	.261
1995	Norfolk	Inter	119	40	11	0	4	11	4	1	80	.336	.392	.529	.306	21	.303
1995	NY Mets	NL	187	55	5	2	9	15	2	1	133	.294	.347	.487	.275	26	.274
1996	NY Mets	NL	153	40	4	0	5	14	1	0	113	.261	.323	.386	.239	16	.234
1997	*NY Mets*	*NL*	*224*	*58*	*10*	*1*	*9*	*21*	*4*	*1*	*167*	*.259*	*.322*	*.433*	*.269*	*31*	

A fairy tale 1995, but it's back to mice and pumpkins. He's good enough defensively that there's no need to use him only as a pinch-hitter.

TERRENCE LONG   **CF**   **1976**   **Age 21**

Year	Team	Lge	AB	H	DB	TP	HR	BB	SB	CS	OUT	BA	OBA	SA	EQA	EQR	Peak
1995	Pittsfield	NY-P	195	45	4	0	5	13	4	2	152	.231	.279	.328	.203	14	.234
1995	Columbia	S Atl	190	36	0	1	2	23	3	2	156	.189	.277	.232	.161	8	.185
1996	Columbia	S Atl	494	131	15	4	11	28	13	4	367	.265	.305	.379	.232	48	.264
1997	*NY Mets*	*NL*	*507*	*127*	*18*	*6*	*10*	*29*	*22*	*8*	*388*	*.250*	*.291*	*.369*	*.242*	*56*	

He made some progress in his second year as a pro, even though his strikeout/walk ratio took a substantial dip. A first baseman when he was taken in the first round as compensation for Sid Fernandez, he's trying to make the rare conversion to center field. His range is pretty good for a converted first baseman, but nothing real special.

JOSE LOPEZ   **3B**   **1976**   **Age 21**

Year	Team	Lge	AB	H	DB	TP	HR	BB	SB	CS	OUT	BA	OBA	SA	EQA	EQR	Peak
1995	Columbia	S Atl	298	68	11	2	5	29	3	1	231	.228	.297	.329	.209	23	.241
1996	St. Lucie	Flor	423	115	10	2	12	35	9	5	313	.272	.328	.390	.242	45	.275
1997	*NY Mets*	*NL*	*509*	*130*	*19*	*2*	*13*	*46*	*14*	*7*	*386*	*.255*	*.317*	*.377*	*.251*	*61*	

He was named the best defensive third baseman in the league despite 37 errors, mostly on throws, and the fielding numbers back it up. His biggest problem in the eyes of Met brass, may be attitudinal; his manager yanked him from one game this season for not running out a ground ball.

TERRELL LOWERY   **OF**   **1971**   **Age 26**

Year	Team	Lge	AB	H	DB	TP	HR	BB	SB	CS	OUT	BA	OBA	SA	EQA	EQR	Peak
1993	Charlotte-FL	Flor	271	77	5	4	6	40	8	6	200	.284	.376	.399	.261	35	.289
1993	Tulsa	Texas	264	55	2	1	3	26	6	5	214	.208	.279	.258	.174	13	.192
1994	Tulsa	Texas	510	140	26	3	11	55	20	8	378	.275	.345	.402	.254	61	.276
1996	Binghamton	East	218	56	10	3	6	39	4	3	165	.257	.370	.413	.262	29	.276
1996	Norfolk	Inter	197	45	4	1	5	22	4	2	154	.228	.306	.335	.216	17	.227

A former member of the Loyola-Marymount basketball team that led the nation in scoring, he came back from a torn Achilles tendon that wiped out '95 like he'd never been away. He's had problems when promoted, and there's no sense of improvement from him, but given the injury…I'd let him play at Norfolk a little longer before passing judgment.

BRENT MAYNE   **C**   **1968**   **Age 29**

Year	Team	Lge	AB	H	DB	TP	HR	BB	SB	CS	OUT	BA	OBA	SA	EQA	EQR	Peak
1993	Kansas City	AL	206	54	9	0	3	19	3	1	153	.262	.324	.350	.229	19	.242
1994	Kansas City	AL	143	36	4	1	2	14	1	0	107	.252	.318	.336	.222	12	.230
1995	Kansas City	AL	311	83	20	1	1	25	0	1	229	.267	.321	.347	.225	27	.230
1996	NY Mets	NL	103	29	4	0	2	13	0	1	75	.282	.362	.379	.249	12	.251
1997	*NY Mets*	*NL*	*103*	*27*	*4*	*0*	*2*	*11*	*0*	*0*	*76*	*.262*	*.333*	*.359*	*.252*	*12*	

A light-hitting backup catcher who never, ever plays against a left-hander. Hitting like that and throwing out 1 of 24 bases-stealers is definitely a bad career move.

CARLOS MENDOZA   **LF**   **1975**   **Age 22**

Year	Team	Lge	AB	H	DB	TP	HR	BB	SB	CS	OUT	BA	OBA	SA	EQA	EQR	Peak
1996	Columbia	S Atl	325	97	5	1	1	46	11	5	233	.298	.385	.329	.251	37	.281
1997	*NY Mets*	*NL*	*511*	*143*	*10*	*2*	*1*	*55*	*23*	*6*	*374*	*.280*	*.350*	*.313*	*.252*	*60*	

He's a small Venezuelan outfielder. After hitting .328 in the Appalachian League last year he hit .337 in the Sally. He's got no power at all—he's only 5'11", 160—but he walked a lot, didn't strike out much, stole 31 bases and scored 61 runs in just 85 games in a low-scoring league. He's a good leadoff prospect, but he's a long ways away, 1999 at the earliest.

ALEX OCHOA   **RF**   **1972**   **Age 25**

Year	Team	Lge	AB	H	DB	TP	HR	BB	SB	CS	OUT	BA	OBA	SA	EQA	EQR	Peak
1993	Frederick	Caro	549	138	18	2	11	42	19	7	418	.251	.305	.352	.224	50	.250
1994	Bowie	East	532	148	17	1	13	45	17	8	392	.278	.334	.387	.245	58	.271
1995	Norfolk	Inter	128	40	4	1	3	15	5	2	90	.312	.385	.430	.277	18	.302
1995	Rochester	Inter	339	87	14	1	8	28	12	4	256	.257	.313	.375	.234	34	.255
1996	Norfolk	Inter	240	78	9	3	8	33	4	7	169	.325	.407	.488	.291	39	.312
1996	NY Mets	NL	292	92	20	2	5	20	3	3	203	.315	.359	.449	.270	38	.289
1997	*NY Mets*	*NL*	*502*	*135*	*36*	*5*	*12*	*44*	*8*	*0*	*367*	*.269*	*.328*	*.432*	*.273*	*71*	

He was taken from the Orioles for a year and a half of Bobby Bonilla. He has one of the best arms in the game. On top of that, he has raised his offensive level every year he's played. What's not to like about him? I think Vlad's got the power and walks right, but expect his batting average to be closer to .300 than .275.

REY ORDONEZ   **SS**   **1972**   **Age 25**

Year	Team	Lge	AB	H	DB	TP	HR	BB	SB	CS	OUT	BA	OBA	SA	EQA	EQR	Peak
1994	St. Lucie	Flor	321	95	19	1	3	14	7	3	229	.296	.325	.389	.243	33	.268
1994	Binghamton	East	193	46	9	1	1	5	3	2	149	.238	.258	.311	.187	11	.207
1995	Norfolk	Inter	447	94	20	2	3	30	9	7	361	.210	.260	.284	.175	23	.190
1996	NY Mets	NL	514	139	13	4	1	29	1	3	378	.270	.309	.317	.210	38	.225
1997	*NY Mets*	*NL*	*381*	*88*	*12*	*3*	*1*	*15*	*6*	*6*	*299*	*.231*	*.260*	*.286*	*.194*	*25*	

There is no question that he is an outstanding defensive shortstop. Everyone wants to compare him to Ozzie Smith, and the numbers are pretty similar for their first year in the league; while Ozzie had a much higher range factor, even a cursory look at 1978 shows that there were considerably more ground balls hit than there were in homer-happy, loft-the-ball 1996. Their relative position to other fielders is comparable. Ozzie hit better than this in his first year in the majors, but worse than this in his second, so their batting is also comparable. One advantage for Ozzie was that he was never as allergic to the base on balls as Ordonez (10 non-intentional walks) and developed that into a highly valuable skill. Ordonez' batting average is totally empty, and that was only .238 after April; I'm not convinced his leather can support his wood.

JAY PAYTON   **DH**   **1973**   **Age 24**

Year	Team	Lge	AB	H	DB	TP	HR	BB	SB	CS	OUT	BA	OBA	SA	EQA	EQR	Peak
1994	Pittsfield	NY-P	229	72	8	1	4	17	4	1	158	.314	.362	.410	.264	28	.296
1995	Binghamton	East	366	121	14	2	14	26	11	4	249	.331	.375	.495	.290	56	.320
1995	Norfolk	Inter	200	49	10	2	5	12	8	2	153	.245	.288	.390	.230	19	.255
1996	Norfolk	Inter	156	48	5	2	6	12	7	1	109	.308	.357	.481	.283	23	.307
1997	*NY Mets*	*NL*	*443*	*130*	*20*	*3*	*12*	*30*	*12*	*2*	*315*	*.293*	*.338*	*.433*	*.279*	*65*	

He's really a center fielder, but after having the medial collateral ligament in his throwing elbow repaired following the '95 season, followed by bone chip removal in the spring, he was kept away from having to throw the ball. He could still hit it, and continued in his high-average, moderate power, steal some bases way. He's fully recovered from the injuries and will be back in the outfield in '97.

ROBERTO PETAGINE   **1B**   **1971**   **Age 26**

Year	Team	Lge	AB	H	DB	TP	HR	BB	SB	CS	OUT	BA	OBA	SA	EQA	EQR	Peak
1993	Jackson	Texas	463	149	22	2	15	79	4	2	316	.322	.421	.475	.301	79	.332
1994	Tucson	PCL	243	69	8	0	10	32	2	1	175	.284	.367	.440	.270	33	.294
1995	Las Vegas	PCL	55	10	2	0	1	13	1	0	45	.182	.338	.273	.211	5	.226
1995	San Diego	NL	129	33	6	0	4	28	0	0	96	.256	.389	.395	.266	18	.284
1996	Norfolk	Inter	325	103	20	2	12	51	3	1	223	.317	.410	.502	.303	56	.320
1996	NY Mets	NL	102	26	3	0	4	10	0	2	78	.255	.321	.402	.235	10	.247
1997	*NY Mets*	*NL*	*486*	*136*	*25*	*1*	*19*	*90*	*4*	*3*	*353*	*.280*	*.392*	*.453*	*.300*	*87*	

He's spent the last three years on a minor-to-major league yo-yo, filling in for injured first basemen but never getting a real chance to play for himself. He's a good fielder, so that's not his problem. His problem is the perception that a first baseman has to be a big, brawny slugger and he's a slender guy who hits for average and draws walks. It's a valuable combination, but he just doesn't look right out there.

CHRIS SAUNDERS   **3B**   **1971**   **Age 26**

Year	Team	Lge	AB	H	DB	TP	HR	BB	SB	CS	OUT	BA	OBA	SA	EQA	EQR	Peak
1993	St. Lucie	Flor	468	110	11	2	6	35	3	3	361	.235	.288	.306	.196	31	.216
1994	Binghamton	East	512	129	15	0	11	39	4	3	386	.252	.305	.346	.218	43	.237
1995	Binghamton	East	451	110	17	3	9	40	2	3	344	.244	.305	.355	.220	39	.235
1995	Norfolk	Inter	58	14	2	1	3	9	1	1	45	.241	.343	.466	.262	8	.283
1996	Binghamton	East	523	146	20	2	15	65	4	2	379	.279	.359	.411	.260	65	.274

After three years in AA he discovered a hitting stroke. If it was real progress, and not just an older, wiser veteran beating up kid pitchers, he'll be worth having. He's excellent defensively.

PRESTON WILSON   **RF**   **1975**   **Age 22**

Year	Team	Lge	AB	H	DB	TP	HR	BB	SB	CS	OUT	BA	OBA	SA	EQA	EQR	Peak
1994	Columbia	S Atl	483	98	10	1	11	18	6	4	390	.203	.232	.296	.166	22	.191
1995	Columbia	S Atl	461	123	13	2	18	16	10	4	342	.267	.291	.421	.238	47	.271
1996	St. Lucie	Flor	87	14	2	0	1	7	1	0	73	.161	.223	.218	.119	2	.127

Mookie's stepson, and the Mets' first pick in 1992, has been one of the biggest first-round disasters in recent memory. A tremendous athlete, he's struck out 270 times with just 47 walks in the last three years; really just a little over two years, since this year was washed out by wrist and shoulder injuries. It's no real loss to the Mets; this guy, rated a Top 10 Prospect by Baseball America for three years in a row, isn't enough of a hitter.

JUAN ACEVEDO   **RSP**   **1970**   **Age 27**

YR	TEAM	Lge	IP	H	ER	HR	BB	K	ERA	W	L	H/9	HR/9	BB/9	K/9	KW
1993	Cent. Valley	Calif	105.0	128	58	8	64	74	4.97	5	7	10.97	.69	5.49	6.34	.74
1994	New Haven	East	160.0	169	56	18	55	117	3.15	11	7	9.51	1.01	3.09	6.58	1.42
1995	Colo. Springs	PCL	14.0	16	8	0	8	6	5.14	1	1	10.29	.00	5.14	3.86	.00
1995	Colorado	NL	66.0	71	39	13	25	35	5.32	3	4	9.68	1.77	3.41	4.77	.74
1996	Norfolk	Inter	99.3	120	62	14	66	69	5.62	4	7	10.87	1.27	5.98	6.25	.59

The Mets insisted on him when they traded Saberhagen to the Rockies, believing 1994 was the real Acevedo. It's hard to tell; he's had one injury after another ever since. This year, it was a stress fracture in his shin. Tomorrow?

PAUL BYRD   **RRP**   **1971**   **Age 26**

YR	TEAM	Lge	IP	H	ER	HR	BB	K	ERA	W	L	H/9	HR/9	BB/9	K/9	KW
1993	Charlotte, NC	Inter	75.7	90	43	9	40	44	5.11	3	5	10.70	1.07	4.76	5.23	.56
1994	Canton	East	125.0	166	78	12	71	78	5.62	5	9	11.95	.86	5.11	5.62	.59
1994	Charlotte, NC	Inter	34.7	36	18	6	14	12	4.67	2	2	9.35	1.56	3.63	3.12	.13
1995	Norfolk	Inter	80.7	82	29	7	32	52	3.24	5	4	9.15	.78	3.57	5.80	1.04
1995	NY Mets	NL	21.3	20	5	1	8	23	2.11	2	0	8.44	.42	3.38	9.70	2.39
1996	NY Mets	NL	46.0	52	21	7	26	28	4.11	2	3	10.17	1.37	5.09	5.48	.55

His fastball is his only good pitch, so the Mets tried to convert him to relief in 1995 (he wasn't exactly tearing through the league as a starter, so why not?) It worked in 1995, but not quite so good this year. Traded to Atlanta.

MARK CLARK	**RSP**	**1968**	**Age 29**												
YR TEAM	Lge	IP	H	ER	HR	BB	K	ERA	W	L	H/9	HR/9	BB/9	K/9	KW
1993 Charlotte, NC	Inter	12.0	10	4	0	4	10	3.00	1	0	7.50	.00	3.00	7.50	1.75
1993 Cleveland	AL	109.0	120	49	19	30	59	4.05	6	6	9.91	1.57	2.48	4.87	1.00
1994 Cleveland	AL	126.7	126	46	13	44	59	3.27	8	6	8.95	.92	3.13	4.19	.62
1995 Buffalo	AmA	33.7	42	14	0	14	15	3.74	2	2	11.23	.00	3.74	4.01	.40
1995 Cleveland	AL	125.3	141	63	12	45	69	4.52	6	8	10.12	.86	3.23	4.95	.84
1996 NY Mets	NL	208.0	233	91	20	67	125	3.94	12	11	10.08	.87	2.90	5.41	1.08

Pitched about as close to his 1993-96 average (3.91 ERA, 9.84 H/9, 0.94 HR/9, 2.99 BB/9, 4.93 K/9) as one can. He had problems in 1995, possibly the result of a broken wrist early in the year, and found himself traded to New York the day before Opening Day as the Mets tried to deal with the injuries sweeping their staff.

JOE CRAWFORD	**LSP**	**1970**	**Age 27**												
YR TEAM	Lge	IP	H	ER	HR	BB	K	ERA	W	L	H/9	HR/9	BB/9	K/9	KW
1993 St. Lucie	Flor	32.0	46	17	1	20	19	4.78	2	2	12.94	.28	5.62	5.34	.37
1994 St. Lucie	Flor	38.7	29	7	2	13	24	1.63	3	1	6.75	.47	3.03	5.59	1.11
1994 Binghamton	East	13.0	23	10	2	11	7	6.92	0	1	15.92	1.38	7.62	4.85	-.29
1995 Binghamton	East	56.7	55	16	5	21	31	2.54	4	2	8.74	.79	3.34	4.92	.81
1995 Norfolk	Inter	17.0	12	4	0	6	11	2.12	2	0	6.35	.00	3.18	5.82	1.15
1996 Binghamton	East	46.0	39	9	5	13	25	1.76	4	1	7.63	.98	2.54	4.89	.99
1996 Norfolk	Inter	92.0	105	40	10	29	56	3.91	5	5	10.27	.98	2.84	5.48	1.12

It took him three tries to get past St. Lucie, and three more to get past Binghamton. Normally, that would be Very Bad; here, though, there is a role change to consider. In a reverse of the normal move, he was starting for the first time in his six-year pro career. I don't believe older pitchers can be dismissed as casually as older hitters, so I think Mr. Crawford bears watching; he could be a real sleeper.

JERRY DIPOTO	**RRP**	**1968**	**Age 29**												
YR TEAM	Lge	IP	H	ER	HR	BB	K	ERA	W	L	H/9	HR/9	BB/9	K/9	KW
1993 Charlotte, NC	Inter	43.3	40	9	2	18	36	1.87	4	1	8.31	.42	3.74	7.48	1.56
1993 Cleveland	AL	55.7	60	18	0	33	43	2.91	4	2	9.70	.00	5.34	6.95	.98
1994 Charlotte, NC	Inter	32.3	40	12	1	15	22	3.34	2	2	11.13	.28	4.18	6.12	1.00
1994 Cleveland	AL	16.0	24	11	1	11	9	6.19	1	1	13.50	.56	6.19	5.06	.14
1995 NY Mets	NL	77.0	82	37	2	36	44	4.32	4	5	9.58	.23	4.21	5.14	.66
1996 NY Mets	NL	76.7	100	43	5	53	47	5.05	3	6	11.74	.59	6.22	5.52	.28

He went 7-2, but don't be fooled; those wins were vultured by letting half of his inherited runners score. His comeback from thyroid cancer is inspiring, but he's clearly not the pitcher he was in '94.

OCTAVIO DOTEL	**RSP**	**1974**	**Age 23**												
YR TEAM	Lge	IP	H	ER	HR	BB	K	ERA	W	L	H/9	HR/9	BB/9	K/9	KW
1996 Columbia	S Atl	97.0	131	64	10	72	78	5.94	3	8	12.15	.93	6.68	7.24	.74

Howe Sportsdata says he was born in November 1973, while Baseball America says he was 20 last season. Since his biggest problem is control, which is probably the most acquired skill a pitcher can have, the age makes a bigger difference. Does he realistically have five years to figure out where it's going, or two? The age is further clouded by a strained shoulder suffered this year; if he's 23, he doesn't have time to recover and impress anyone at a higher level.

NELSON FIGUEROA	**RSP**	**1974**	**Age 23**												
YR TEAM	Lge	IP	H	ER	HR	BB	K	ERA	W	L	H/9	HR/9	BB/9	K/9	KW
1996 Columbia	S Atl	162.3	170	64	13	86	110	3.55	10	8	9.43	.72	4.77	6.10	.84

A 30th round pick in '95 by way of Brandeis College and Brooklyn, no relation to Ed. He's a skinny guy who, in proper Met fashion, led his league in innings and complete games. However, he was so overwhelming at times, giving up just 119 hits in 185 innings including three one-hitters, two in consecutive starts, that I'm not certain his total workload was unreasonable. He throws six different pitches and led the league in every important category. Take a good look, but don't put his name on the 2001 Cy Young Award just yet.

JOHN FRANCO   **LRP**   **1961**   **Age 36**

YR	TEAM	Lge	IP	H	ER	HR	BB	K	ERA	W	L	H/9	HR/9	BB/9	K/9	KW
1993	NY Mets	NL	36.3	46	22	6	24	28	5.45	1	3	11.39	1.49	5.94	6.94	.83
1994	NY Mets	NL	49.0	47	17	2	23	39	3.12	3	2	8.63	.37	4.22	7.16	1.33
1995	NY Mets	NL	50.7	51	15	4	21	37	2.66	4	2	9.06	.71	3.73	6.57	1.26
1996	NY Mets	NL	53.0	59	14	2	26	43	2.38	4	2	10.02	.34	4.42	7.30	1.33

He did almost everything you'd want a reliever to do except get the first guy out: a .304 average, contributing to a wretched performance with inherited runners and eight blown saves. But he did have 28 saves, which bought him another two years with the Mets.

MIKE FYHRIE   **RSP**   **1970**   **Age 27**

YR	TEAM	Lge	IP	H	ER	HR	BB	K	ERA	W	L	H/9	HR/9	BB/9	K/9	KW
1993	Wilmington	Caro	24.7	42	17	3	13	12	6.20	1	2	15.32	1.09	4.74	4.38	.27
1993	Memphis	South	118.3	162	60	12	78	44	4.56	6	7	12.32	.91	5.93	3.35	-.37
1994	Memphis	South	61.3	78	31	5	27	30	4.55	3	4	11.45	.73	3.96	4.40	.48
1994	Omaha	AmA	82.3	100	50	13	41	33	5.47	3	6	10.93	1.42	4.48	3.61	.08
1995	Wichita	Texas	67.3	79	28	5	30	35	3.74	4	3	10.56	.67	4.01	4.68	.56
1995	Omaha	AmA	58.7	69	30	7	22	34	4.60	3	4	10.59	1.07	3.38	5.22	.89
1996	Norfolk	Inter	161.0	160	53	16	49	85	2.96	12	6	8.94	.89	2.74	4.75	.90

Somebody in Norfolk knows how to handle pitchers. I don't know if it was manager Bobby Valentine, pitching coach Bob Apodaca or even catcher Alberto Castillo, but Norfolk was where mediocre pitchers recovered their careers in 1996. The park may help; Fyhrie's always been tough on right-handed hitters, and Harbor Park is notoriously tough on left-handed ones.

MIKE GARDINER   **RSP**   **1966**   **Age 31**

YR	TEAM	Lge	IP	H	ER	HR	BB	K	ERA	W	L	H/9	HR/9	BB/9	K/9	KW
1993	Ottawa	Inter	23.7	19	7	2	12	20	2.66	2	1	7.23	.76	4.56	7.61	1.39
1993	Detroit	AL	11.3	12	4	0	8	4	3.18	1	0	9.53	.00	6.35	3.18	-.53
1993	Montreal	NL	36.7	44	27	3	23	20	6.63	1	3	10.80	.74	5.65	4.91	.22
1994	Detroit	AL	58.3	50	26	9	25	30	4.01	3	3	7.71	1.39	3.86	4.63	.58
1995	Toledo	Inter	15.0	22	8	1	17	9	4.80	1	1	13.20	.60	10.20	5.40	-.75
1995	Detroit	AL	13.0	25	15	4	2	7	10.38	0	1	17.31	2.77	1.38	4.85	1.27
1996	Norfolk	Inter	139.3	133	50	18	52	103	3.23	9	6	8.59	1.16	3.36	6.65	1.38

Norfolk Rejuvenation, Exhibit B, your honor. He came back from a debilitating sinus infection - you don't see that on the injury list too often. Fyhrie and Gardiner, between them, went 28-9 for the Tides this year.

ARNOLD GOOCH   **RSP**   **1977**   **Age 20**

YR	TEAM	LGE	IP	H	ER	HR	BB	K	ERA	W	L	H/9	HR/9	BB/9	K/9	KW
1995	Asheville	S Atl	76.7	96	31	7	60	47	3.64	5	4	11.27	.82	7.04	5.52	.08
1995	Columbia	S Atl	31.7	56	33	5	22	20	9.38	1	3	15.92	1.42	6.25	5.68	.33
1996	St. Lucie	Flor	151.0	159	76	11	72	102	4.53	7	10	9.48	.66	4.29	6.08	.95

The other guy the Mets got for Saberhagen, he made serious strides forward at St. Lucie, particularly in control. The DT is a little harsh on him because he gave up 26 unearned runs; that's what happens when a sinkerballer pitches in front of A-ball fielders.

MARK GUERRA   **RBP**   **1972**   **Age 25**

YR	TEAM	LGE	IP	H	ER	HR	BB	K	ERA	W	L	H/9	HR/9	BB/9	K/9	KW
1994	Pittsfield	NY-P	75.3	146	58	7	36	37	6.93	2	6	17.44	.84	4.30	4.42	.40
1995	St. Lucie	Flor	88.3	99	35	10	31	51	3.57	6	4	10.09	1.02	3.16	5.20	.94
1995	Binghamton	East	30.0	40	23	6	12	18	6.90	1	2	12.00	1.80	3.60	5.40	.90
1996	Binghamton	East	129.7	158	56	22	45	62	3.89	7	7	10.97	1.53	3.12	4.30	.65

A soft-tossing righty; if he doesn't spot the ball around the plate, he'll spot it going over his head. Norfolk's ability to suppress home runs should help him a lot, raising some unreasonable hopes in New York. He's done well, but I'm not real excited.

LINDSAY GULIN   **LSP**   **1977**   **Age 20**

YR	TEAM	Lge	IP	H	ER	HR	BB	K	ERA	W	L	H/9	HR/9	BB/9	K/9	KW
1996	Columbia	S Atl	93.3	130	52	8	82	74	5.01	4	6	12.54	.77	7.91	7.14	.40

When Nelson Figueroa had to miss a start for a minor non-arm-related injury, they called this guy up from extended spring training. He struck out 14 in seven innings and didn't go back to Florida.

PETE HARNISCH   **RSP**   **1967**   **Age 30**

YR	TEAM	Lge	IP	H	ER	HR	BB	K	ERA	W	L	H/9	HR/9	BB/9	K/9	KW
1993	Houston	NL	210.3	184	77	22	102	179	3.29	14	9	7.87	.94	4.36	7.66	1.46
1994	Houston	NL	94.3	101	53	13	47	58	5.06	4	6	9.64	1.24	4.48	5.53	.72
1995	NY Mets	NL	108.3	115	50	13	33	74	4.15	6	6	9.55	1.08	2.74	6.15	1.36
1996	St. Lucie	Flor	11.7	13	4	2	1	9	3.09	1	0	10.03	1.54	.77	6.94	2.12
1996	NY Mets	NL	191.3	210	98	31	78	101	4.61	9	12	9.88	1.46	3.67	4.75	.67

He fought through constant shoulder tendinitis in 1994 and 1995 and finally had surgery prior to last year. It wasn't a good year for him, but he did make 31 starts, he didn't have pain and he improved as the year went on. I think he'll improve on last year. I'd be very surprised if he ever pitches like 1993 again.

DOUG HENRY   **RRP**   **1964**   **Age 33**

YR	TEAM	Lge	IP	H	ER	HR	BB	K	ERA	W	L	H/9	HR/9	BB/9	K/9	KW
1993	Milwaukee	AL	55.7	65	31	7	28	40	5.01	2	4	10.51	1.13	4.53	6.47	1.02
1994	New Orleans	AmA	13.7	7	2	1	11	9	1.32	2	0	4.61	.66	7.24	5.93	.16
1994	Milwaukee	AL	31.3	29	12	6	24	19	3.45	2	1	8.33	1.72	6.89	5.46	.10
1995	NY Mets	NL	65.3	52	20	8	30	56	2.76	5	2	7.16	1.10	4.13	7.71	1.54
1996	NY Mets	NL	73.7	90	46	7	44	52	5.62	3	5	11.00	.86	5.38	6.35	.77

He was a better pitcher than this for most of the year; five innings in September cost him 12 hits, five homers, and 10 runs. Control is more important for him than most pitchers, since he has an unusually large split between pitching ahead or behind in the count.

JASON ISRINGHAUSEN   **RSP**   **1973**   **Age 24**

YR	TEAM	Lge	IP	H	ER	HR	BB	K	ERA	W	L	H/9	HR/9	BB/9	K/9	KW
1993	Pittsfield	NY-P	73.0	106	61	10	47	54	7.52	2	6	13.07	1.23	5.79	6.66	.77
1994	St. Lucie	Flor	91.7	92	31	4	38	45	3.04	6	4	9.03	.39	3.73	4.42	.54
1994	Binghamton	East	84.3	92	35	7	32	50	3.74	5	4	9.82	.75	3.42	5.34	.92
1995	Binghamton	East	38.3	31	13	2	15	45	3.05	3	1	7.28	.47	3.52	10.57	2.64
1995	Norfolk	Inter	81.0	75	16	3	34	64	1.78	8	1	8.33	.33	3.78	7.11	1.43
1995	NY Mets	NL	91.3	92	26	7	39	50	2.56	7	3	9.07	.69	3.84	4.93	.68
1996	NY Mets	NL	169.3	206	99	13	91	102	5.26	7	12	10.95	.69	4.84	5.42	.60

In 1995, he made 38 starts, more than any other pitcher in the last 10 years. It looks like a lot of organizations sort of lose their awareness of how many innings a guy has pitched when he moves up through three levels like that. The idea that front office people are incapable of adding three numbers wouldn't be a total surprise. He had a lot more trouble than most pitchers while working from the stretch; his OPS jumped 33% with men on base, while 6% is about normal. His injury list started in August with a pulled rib cage muscle, which isn't serious; then bone spurs in the elbow, a pretty easy thing to fix; then a torn labrum, which is pretty serious.

BOBBY JONES   **RSP**   **1970**   **Age 27**

YR	TEAM	Lge	IP	H	ER	HR	BB	K	ERA	W	L	H/9	HR/9	BB/9	K/9	KW
1993	Norfolk	Inter	156.0	170	71	10	51	103	4.10	8	9	9.81	.58	2.94	5.94	1.25
1993	NY Mets	NL	60.0	64	33	6	29	34	4.95	3	4	9.60	.90	4.35	5.10	.61
1994	NY Mets	NL	157.3	154	63	10	70	74	3.60	9	8	8.81	.57	4.00	4.23	.41
1995	NY Mets	NL	192.7	218	99	21	70	115	4.62	9	12	10.18	.98	3.27	5.37	.97
1996	NY Mets	NL	192.3	235	97	26	64	103	4.54	9	12	11.00	1.22	2.99	4.82	.86

Reliable, if mediocre, pitcher, he can probably get a little more mileage from his fluke 1994 campaign.

CORY LIDLE   **RSP**   **1972**   **Age 25**

YR	TEAM	Lge	IP	H	ER	HR	BB	K	ERA	W	L	H/9	HR/9	BB/9	K/9	KW
1994	Beloit	Midw	61.3	78	23	4	17	38	3.38	4	3	11.45	.59	2.49	5.58	1.24
1994	Stockton	Calif	37.3	71	32	2	18	25	7.71	1	3	17.12	.48	4.34	6.03	.92
1995	El Paso	Texas	100.7	126	45	7	47	66	4.02	5	6	11.26	.63	4.20	5.90	.92
1996	Binghamton	East	176.3	205	71	12	65	104	3.62	11	9	10.46	.61	3.32	5.31	.94

He started in '96 for the first time since 1993, when he worked for Pocatello's co-op team in the Pioneer League.

BOB MacDONALD   **LRP**   **1965**   **Age 32**

YR	TEAM	Lge	IP	H	ER	HR	BB	K	ERA	W	L	H/9	HR/9	BB/9	K/9	KW
1993	Detroit	AL	65.7	66	35	8	37	41	4.80	3	4	9.05	1.10	5.07	5.62	.61
1994	Birmingham	South	51.0	48	16	5	13	30	2.82	4	2	8.47	.88	2.29	5.29	1.19
1994	Calgary	PCL	29.3	35	21	3	17	22	6.44	1	2	10.74	.92	5.22	6.75	.95
1995	Columbus, OH	Inter	18.0	23	6	1	7	11	3.00	1	1	11.50	.50	3.50	5.50	.96
1995	NY Yankees	AL	46.3	48	19	6	23	41	3.69	3	2	9.32	1.17	4.47	7.96	1.54
1996	Norfolk	Inter	30.0	29	12	3	16	30	3.60	2	1	8.70	.90	4.80	9.00	1.80
1996	NY Mets	NL	18.3	18	9	2	11	11	4.42	1	1	8.84	.98	5.40	5.40	.45

"I'm a travelin' man, made a lot of stops…"

ETHAN McENTIRE   **LSP**   **1976**   **Age 21**

YR	TEAM	Lge	IP	H	ER	HR	BB	K	ERA	W	L	H/9	HR/9	BB/9	K/9	KW
1995	Pittsfield	NY-P	54.3	107	52	4	68	25	8.61	1	5	17.72	.66	11.26	4.14	-1.44
1995	Columbia	S Atl	26.3	39	18	5	32	18	6.15	1	2	13.33	1.71	10.94	6.15	-.68
1996	Columbia	S Atl	150.7	175	61	13	90	104	3.64	9	8	10.45	.78	5.38	6.21	.73

Another Bomber; it's easy to see why they led the league in ERA. He developed a clue about where the ball was going this season, and his prospects improved greatly.

DAVE MLICKI   **RRP**   **1968**   **Age 29**

YR	TEAM	Lge	IP	H	ER	HR	BB	K	ERA	W	L	H/9	HR/9	BB/9	K/9	KW
1993	Canton	East	21.0	19	2	0	10	16	.86	2	0	8.14	.00	4.29	6.86	1.21
1993	Cleveland	AL	13.7	10	5	3	7	7	3.29	1	1	6.59	1.98	4.61	4.61	.38
1994	Charlotte, NC	Inter	157.3	190	79	26	82	127	4.52	7	10	10.87	1.49	4.69	7.26	1.25
1995	NY Mets	NL	158.7	167	76	24	67	111	4.31	8	10	9.47	1.36	3.80	6.30	1.15
1996	NY Mets	NL	88.0	105	44	9	41	74	4.50	4	6	10.74	.92	4.19	7.57	1.47

A starter throughout his career, he really didn't do any better as a reliever.

ROBERT PERSON   **RBP**   **1969**   **Age 28**

YR	TEAM	Lge	IP	H	ER	HR	BB	K	ERA	W	L	H/9	HR/9	BB/9	K/9	KW
1993	High Desert	Calif	152.0	195	96	14	49	74	5.68	6	11	11.55	.83	2.90	4.38	.74
1994	Binghamton	East	145.0	146	68	19	89	95	4.22	8	8	9.06	1.18	5.52	5.90	.58
1995	Binghamton	East	61.7	54	24	5	31	50	3.50	4	3	7.88	.73	4.52	7.30	1.30
1995	Norfolk	Inter	30.0	34	17	3	17	28	5.10	1	2	10.20	.90	5.10	8.40	1.52
1995	NY Mets	NL	11.3	6	1	1	3	9	.79	1	0	4.76	.79	2.38	7.15	1.79
1996	Norfolk	Inter	40.7	36	14	7	26	27	3.10	3	2	7.97	1.55	5.75	5.98	.55
1996	NY Mets	NL	88.7	92	47	17	44	67	4.77	4	6	9.34	1.73	4.47	6.80	1.15

He was a shortstop when he started pro ball in 1989, and he's made slow, steady progress while learning to pitch. He throws hard (they don't move guys to pitcher who don't) and the long ball is a problem. His peripheral numbers don't look that bad in the majors; I think he'll rebound nicely. Traded to Toronto for John Olerud.

BILL PULSIPHER   **LSP**   **1974**   **Age 23**

YR	TEAM	Lge	IP	H	ER	HR	BB	K	ERA	W	L	H/9	HR/9	BB/9	K/9	KW
1993	Columbia	S Atl	37.3	46	19	1	17	17	4.58	2	2	11.09	.24	4.10	4.10	.34
1993	St. Lucie	Flor	85.7	79	28	4	53	80	2.94	6	4	8.30	.42	5.57	8.40	1.41
1994	Binghamton	East	181.7	212	93	20	116	125	4.61	9	11	10.50	.99	5.75	6.19	.63
1995	Norfolk	Inter	85.0	97	36	3	45	54	3.81	5	4	10.27	.32	4.76	5.72	.71
1995	NY Mets	NL	124.0	129	53	11	56	73	3.85	7	7	9.36	.80	4.06	5.30	.75

The Wild One, a.k.a. the Hard Working One. We said in the 1995 version of this book that he was a strong candidate for major surgery after he threw 201 innings in 28 starts at age 20, especially since his hit rates and walk rates weren't especially good. We repeated it last year, after he threw even more, 218 innings. Young pitchers in particular will get hurt facing more than 30 batters per game; he faced 30.3 and 30.2. Even an ox like him can't take that, and he wound up with two MCL tears in his elbow.

RICK REED   RSP   1965   Age 32

YR	TEAM	Lge	IP	H	ER	HR	BB	K	ERA	W	L	H/9	HR/9	BB/9	K/9	KW
1993	Oklahoma	AmA	33.0	42	16	2	5	19	4.36	2	2	11.45	.55	1.36	5.18	1.39
1993	Omaha	AmA	122.0	117	40	18	26	53	2.95	9	5	8.63	1.33	1.92	3.91	.82
1994	Indianapolis	AmA	135.3	163	70	21	31	71	4.66	6	9	10.84	1.40	2.06	4.72	1.06
1994	Oklahoma	AmA	11.0	11	4	0	0	7	3.27	1	0	9.00	.00	.00	5.73	1.91
1994	Texas	AL	16.7	17	10	3	7	12	5.40	1	1	9.18	1.62	3.78	6.48	1.21
1995	Indianapolis	AmA	128.7	133	55	15	41	82	3.85	7	7	9.30	1.05	2.87	5.74	1.19
1995	Cincinnati	NL	16.7	18	11	5	5	9	5.94	1	1	9.72	2.70	2.70	4.86	.94
1996	Norfolk	Inter	172.7	177	62	13	50	106	3.23	11	8	9.23	.68	2.61	5.53	1.19

The defense would call him for Exhibit C for Norfolk's healing properties, but he has pitched at roughly this level before.

CHRIS ROBERTS   LSP   1971   Age 26

YR	TEAM	Lge	IP	H	ER	HR	BB	K	ERA	W	L	H/9	HR/9	BB/9	K/9	KW
1993	St. Lucie	Flor	153.0	197	71	6	55	87	4.18	8	9	11.59	.35	3.24	5.12	.90
1994	Binghamton	East	157.7	195	80	12	101	94	4.57	8	10	11.13	.68	5.77	5.37	.35
1995	Norfolk	Inter	141.0	218	100	26	81	76	6.38	5	11	13.91	1.66	5.17	4.85	.32
1996	St. Lucie	Flor	5.3	2	0	0	4	1	.00	1	0	3.38	.00	6.75	1.69	-1.12
1996	Binghamton	East	43.0	56	36	5	44	22	7.53	1	4	11.72	1.05	9.21	4.60	-.77

A member of Binghamton's sterling 1994 rotation, he developed his labrum problems in 1995. He had it shaved last spring, but didn't pitch well.

JESUS SANCHEZ   LSP   1975   Age 22

YR	TEAM	Lge	IP	H	ER	HR	BB	K	ERA	W	L	H/9	HR/9	BB/9	K/9	KW
1995	Columbia	S Atl	141.7	226	103	14	88	103	6.54	4	12	14.36	.89	5.59	6.54	.78
1996	St. Lucie	Flor	83.0	67	22	9	35	58	2.39	7	2	7.27	.98	3.80	6.29	1.15

If there is hope for Met fans, he's it. He had surgery very similar to Pulsipher's in September of 1995, about seven months ahead of Pulse. He was deemed sufficiently recovered to pitch at midseason, and was absolutely dynamite for St. Lucie, showing big improvements over his pre-surgery game. He's very small for a pitcher, just 5' 10", 155.

BARRY SHORT   RRP   1974   Age 23

YR	TEAM	Lge	IP	H	ER	HR	BB	K	ERA	W	L	H/9	HR/9	BB/9	K/9	KW
1995	Columbia	S Atl	67.3	88	28	2	34	32	3.74	4	3	11.76	.27	4.54	4.28	.29
1996	St. Lucie	Flor	79.7	85	29	7	28	51	3.28	5	4	9.60	.79	3.16	5.76	1.13

I don't know why teams bother making one guy into a closer at A ball, but that's pretty much what he was.

JEFF TAM   RRP   1971   Age 26

YR	TEAM	Lge	IP	H	ER	HR	BB	K	ERA	W	L	H/9	HR/9	BB/9	K/9	KW
1993	Pittsfield	NY-P	31.0	73	28	1	14	16	8.13	1	2	21.19	.29	4.06	4.65	.53
1994	Columbia	S Atl	24.7	30	15	0	9	13	5.47	1	2	10.95	.00	3.28	4.74	.76
1994	St. Lucie	Flor	24.0	17	0	0	9	11	.00	3	0	6.38	.00	3.38	4.12	.53
1995	Binghamton	East	19.3	25	12	1	7	8	5.59	1	1	11.64	.47	3.26	3.72	.43
1996	Binghamton	East	58.3	57	17	6	21	35	2.62	4	2	8.79	.93	3.24	5.40	.99

And that's what he is, too. He recorded the feat, impressive in any league, of pitching 27 innings without a run for St. Lucie, despite less than overwhelming power numbers. After 34 saves in 1994, he spent most of 1995 on the DL but came back strong last season.

RICKY TRLICEK   RRP   1969   Age 28

YR	TEAM	Lge	IP	H	ER	HR	BB	K	ERA	W	L	H/9	HR/9	BB/9	K/9	KW
1993	Los Angeles	NL	61.7	63	29	3	28	40	4.23	3	4	9.19	.44	4.09	5.84	.92
1994	New Britain	East	22.3	16	3	0	9	10	1.21	2	0	6.45	.00	3.63	4.03	.44
1994	Pawtucket	Inter	25.3	21	9	2	16	16	3.20	2	1	7.46	.71	5.68	5.68	.47
1994	Boston	AL	23.0	28	16	5	17	7	6.26	1	2	10.96	1.96	6.65	2.74	-.75
1995	Canton	East	35.3	38	16	5	20	21	4.08	2	2	9.68	1.27	5.09	5.35	.51
1995	Phoenix	PCL	59.7	69	35	7	27	39	5.28	3	4	10.41	1.06	4.07	5.88	.94
1996	Norfolk	Inter	72.0	59	14	1	23	44	1.75	7	1	7.38	.12	2.88	5.50	1.11

Norfolk, exhibit D. He had good control of the ball for the first time in his career; the Red Sox obviously think he can continue.

DEREK WALLACE   **RRP**   **1972**   **Age 25**

YR	TEAM	Lge	IP	H	ER	HR	BB	K	ERA	W	L	H/9	HR/9	BB/9	K/9	KW
1993	Daytona	Flor	69.3	97	52	9	33	26	6.75	2	6	12.59	1.17	4.28	3.37	.05
1993	Orlando	South	87.3	122	61	13	40	51	6.29	3	7	12.57	1.34	4.12	5.26	.72
1994	Orlando	South	81.3	107	64	13	46	38	7.08	2	7	11.84	1.44	5.09	4.20	.13
1996	Norfolk	Inter	54.3	42	16	4	23	43	2.65	4	2	6.96	.66	3.81	7.12	1.42
1996	NY Mets	NL	24.3	32	12	2	17	13	4.44	1	2	11.84	.74	6.29	4.81	.03

A first round pick by the Cubs in 1992, he was another coal lump-turned-diamond in Norfolk. He added a split-finger pitch to his mid-90s fastball, and his game improved all over: more strikeouts, fewer hits and 26 saves in 30 tries.

PAUL WILSON   **RSP**   **1973**   **Age 24**

YR	TEAM	Lge	IP	H	ER	HR	BB	K	ERA	W	L	H/9	HR/9	BB/9	K/9	KW
1994	St. Lucie	Flor	33.7	38	25	5	23	28	6.68	1	3	10.16	1.34	6.15	7.49	.96
1995	Binghamton	East	111.7	106	30	6	31	97	2.42	9	3	8.54	.48	2.50	7.82	1.98
1995	Norfolk	Inter	62.0	67	25	3	29	57	3.63	4	3	9.73	.44	4.21	8.27	1.71
1996	NY Mets	NL	147.0	172	98	15	86	97	6.00	5	11	10.53	.92	5.27	5.94	.66

The crown jewel of young Met pitchers, Wilson was the first player picked in the 1994 draft. He took some lumps in Florida that year, but was dominating the following year. Everything he did was so impressive there was no way he could miss, but he did. He had control problems early in the year, then started having some tendinitis in his shoulder. He came back after only two weeks on the DL to pitch the rest of the season, after which he was diagnosed with a torn labrum and needed surgery.

Player	Age	Team	Lge	AB	H	DB	TP	HR	BB	SB	CS	OUT	BA	OBA	SA	EQA	EQR	Peak
JESUS AZUAJE	23	Binghamton	East	256	55	9	0	3	40	4	3	204	.215	.321	.285	.204	19	.221
TIM BOGAR	29	NY Mets	NL	91	21	4	0	0	9	1	3	73	.231	.300	.275	.183	5	.181
JOEL CHIMELIS	28	Norfolk	Inter	78	29	6	0	0	5	1	0	49	.372	.410	.449	.296	12	.298
BOB DALY	23	Columbia	S Atl	149	39	3	1	2	14	0	1	111	.262	.325	.336	.221	13	.243
	23	St. Lucie	Flor	187	46	3	0	3	11	1	1	142	.246	.288	.310	.198	12	.215
CESAR DIAZ	21	St. Lucie	Flor	252	57	6	1	8	16	5	1	196	.226	.272	.353	.210	20	.234
TRACY EDMONDSON	21	Columbia	S Atl	292	48	3	0	3	44	2	2	246	.164	.274	.205	.142	9	.159
COREY ERICKSON	19	Columbia	S Atl	218	42	5	0	2	14	2	1	177	.193	.241	.243	.145	7	.168
KEVIN FLORA	27	Norfolk	Inter	137	30	6	1	3	11	6	1	108	.219	.277	.343	.213	11	.220
PHIL GEISLER	26	Binghamton	East	361	84	11	1	10	29	4	2	279	.233	.290	.352	.214	29	.223
SHAWN GILBERT	31	Norfolk	Inter	502	126	21	1	9	47	12	6	382	.251	.315	.351	.225	46	.217
CHARLIE GREENE	25	Binghamton	East	339	75	7	0	4	16	1	0	264	.221	.256	.277	.170	16	.180
PEDRO GRIFOL	26	Binghamton	East	204	45	1	0	6	12	0	0	159	.221	.264	.314	.188	12	.194
RAFAEL GUERRERO	22	St. Lucie	Flor	266	60	4	0	4	18	2	0	206	.226	.275	.286	.184	15	.204
TYRONE HORNE	25	Binghamton	East	128	33	4	0	4	13	2	0	95	.258	.326	.383	.241	14	.254
CHRIS HOWARD	30	Norfolk	Inter	119	18	2	0	3	6	0	0	101	.151	.192	.244	.106	2	.102
SCOTT HUNTER	20	St. Lucie	Flor	486	118	13	0	4	34	25	7	375	.243	.292	.294	.204	35	.233
ANGEL JAIME	23	St. Lucie	Flor	297	71	6	0	4	30	6	3	229	.239	.309	.300	.206	22	.224
JOHN MAHALIK	24	Binghamton	East	221	50	8	1	3	23	4	1	172	.226	.299	.312	.207	17	.221
DWIGHT MANESS	22	Binghamton	East	408	92	12	4	6	46	17	4	320	.225	.304	.319	.215	34	.237
RYAN MILLER	23	St. Lucie	Flor	316	73	5	2	3	21	4	3	246	.231	.279	.288	.186	18	.203
KEVIN MORGAN	26	Binghamton	East	418	97	7	1	6	47	9	2	323	.232	.310	.297	.207	31	.215
	26	Norfolk	Inter	83	11	2	0	0	9	2	1	73	.133	.217	.157	.043	0	.058
GUILLERMO MOTA	22	St. Lucie	Flor	313	67	8	1	2	30	4	4	250	.214	.283	.265	.177	17	.195
SCOTT PAGANO	25	Binghamton	East	472	110	13	2	1	38	18	8	370	.233	.290	.275	.192	30	.203
JARROD PATTERSON	22	Columbia	S Atl	226	45	4	1	3	26	0	0	181	.199	.282	.265	.176	12	.194
ENOHEL POLANCO	20	Columbia	S Atl	309	57	7	1	1	13	2	1	253	.184	.217	.223	.116	6	.133
DANIEL RAMIREZ	22	Columbia	S Atl	148	29	3	0	1	9	2	1	121	.196	.242	.236	.143	5	.156
LUIS RIVERA	32	Norfolk	Inter	361	79	19	2	6	32	1	2	284	.219	.282	.332	.201	26	.192
KEVIN ROBERSON	28	Norfolk	Inter	218	57	10	2	7	15	0	1	162	.261	.309	.422	.241	23	.244
DAVID SANDERSON	23	St. Lucie	Flor	168	37	2	1	2	20	4	2	133	.220	.303	.280	.196	11	.215
JERAMIE SIMPSON	21	Columbia	S Atl	214	48	1	3	1	16	4	3	169	.224	.278	.271	.179	12	.201
	21	St. Lucie	Flor	226	45	7	3	1	16	11	6	187	.199	.252	.270	.171	11	.191
CARLOS SORIANO	21	Columbia	S Atl	185	38	1	0	1	13	2	1	148	.205	.258	.227	.147	6	.165
GARY THURMAN	31	Norfolk	Inter	457	120	21	4	9	42	17	8	345	.263	.325	.385	.240	49	.232
ANDY TOMBERLIN	29	Norfolk	Inter	131	42	4	1	7	9	1	2	91	.321	.364	.527	.288	20	.286
BRIAN TURNER	25	Binghamton	East	85	16	4	1	2	8	1	1	70	.188	.258	.329	.189	5	.201
	25	St. Lucie	Flor	102	19	2	0	2	9	0	0	83	.186	.252	.265	.159	4	.172
YOHANNY VALERA	19	Columbia	S Atl	382	69	6	0	6	13	1	1	314	.181	.208	.243	.121	8	.140
RANDY WARNER	22	St. Lucie	Flor	393	101	12	2	9	22	3	1	293	.257	.296	.366	.222	34	.246
DON WHITE	24	Binghamton	East	223	39	4	1	5	23	4	2	186	.175	.252	.269	.165	10	.177
VANCE WILSON	23	St. Lucie	Flor	319	72	7	1	7	28	1	2	249	.226	.288	.320	.200	22	.217
JULIO ZORRILLA	21	St. Lucie	Flor	410	92	6	1	0	24	12	8	326	.224	.267	.244	.165	18	.184

Player	Age	Team	Lge	IP	H	ER	HR	BB	K	ERA	W	L	H/9	HR/9	BB/9	K/9	KW
STEVE ARFFA	23	St. Lucie	Flor	29.3	35	15	3	12	13	4.60	1	2	10.74	.92	3.68	3.99	.41
LUIS ARROYO	22	St. Lucie	Flor	37.7	43	18	2	21	20	4.30	2	2	10.27	.48	5.02	4.78	.34
JOE ATWATER	21	St. Lucie	Flor	76.7	95	49	4	53	48	5.75	3	6	11.15	.47	6.22	5.63	.32
JOE AUSANIO	30	Norfolk	Inter	41.3	40	27	8	34	33	5.88	2	3	8.71	1.74	7.40	7.19	.54
JASON BULLARD	27	Norfolk	Inter	37.0	47	20	2	21	20	4.86	2	2	11.43	.49	5.11	4.86	.34
JOHN CARTER	24	Binghamton	East	102.7	127	55	9	67	35	4.82	4	7	11.13	.79	5.87	3.07	-.45
OSVALDO CORONADO	22	Columbia	S Atl	92.0	171	87	16	43	53	8.51	2	8	16.73	1.57	4.21	5.18	.68
CHRIS DEWITT	22	Columbia	S Atl	26.3	31	11	0	17	17	3.76	2	1	10.59	.00	5.81	5.81	.48
BRIAN EDMONDSON	23	Binghamton	East	106.3	140	64	15	48	61	5.42	4	8	11.85	1.27	4.06	5.16	.71
MARK FULLER	25	Binghamton	East	70.0	93	38	7	28	32	4.89	3	5	11.96	.90	3.60	4.11	.47
JEFF HOWATT	22	Columbia	S Atl	59.7	71	28	6	28	33	4.22	3	4	10.71	.91	4.22	4.98	.60
TOBY LARSON	23	Binghamton	East	44.3	62	33	5	18	18	6.70	1	4	12.59	1.02	3.65	3.65	.30
TOBY LARSON	23	St. Lucie	Flor	42.7	71	30	6	16	26	6.33	1	4	14.98	1.27	3.38	5.48	.98
MARK LEE	31	Norfolk	Inter	30.7	41	10	3	9	29	2.93	2	1	12.03	.88	2.64	8.51	2.18
JOSEPH LISIO	22	Columbia	S Atl	36.7	59	21	1	22	23	5.15	2	2	14.48	.25	5.40	5.65	.53
BLAS MINOR	30	NY Mets	NL	25.0	25	10	4	8	18	3.60	2	1	9.00	1.44	2.88	6.48	1.44
DAN MURRAY	22	St. Lucie	Flor	88.7	136	65	3	72	41	6.60	3	7	13.80	.30	7.31	4.16	-.44
ERICK OJEDA	20	Columbia	S Atl	48.3	81	40	10	22	28	7.45	1	4	15.08	1.86	4.10	5.21	.71
PHIL OLSON	22	Columbia	S Atl	79.7	80	41	9	47	35	4.63	4	5	9.04	1.02	5.31	3.95	-.01
PHIL OLSON	22	St. Lucie	Flor	44.3	73	28	7	26	20	5.68	2	3	14.82	1.42	5.28	4.06	.03
JASON PIERSON	25	Binghamton	East	49.3	61	20	6	20	31	3.65	3	2	11.13	1.09	3.65	5.66	.97
HECTOR RAMIREZ	24	Binghamton	East	52.3	55	30	3	29	36	5.16	2	4	9.46	.52	4.99	6.19	.82
RAFAEL ROQUE	24	Binghamton	East	56.0	75	51	7	47	34	8.20	1	5	12.05	1.12	7.55	5.46	-.07
RAFAEL ROQUE	24	St. Lucie	Flor	68.3	69	23	3	51	43	3.03	5	3	9.09	.40	6.72	5.66	.21
BILL SANTAMARIA	20	Columbia	S Atl	41.0	63	28	7	38	16	6.15	1	4	13.83	1.54	8.34	3.51	-.91
SCOTT SAUERBECK	24	Binghamton	East	43.0	54	23	4	15	22	4.81	2	3	11.30	.84	3.14	4.60	.75
SCOTT SAUERBECK	24	St. Lucie	Flor	87.7	123	41	2	40	45	4.21	5	5	12.63	.21	4.11	4.62	.51
RAMON TATIS	23	St. Lucie	Flor	65.7	85	38	6	51	33	5.21	3	4	11.65	.82	6.99	4.52	-.24
ANDY TRUMPOUR	22	Columbia	S Atl	116.0	131	57	11	56	58	4.42	6	7	10.16	.85	4.34	4.50	.41
RICH TURRENTINE	25	St. Lucie	Flor	46.0	37	18	0	57	46	3.52	3	2	7.24	.00	11.15	9.00	.21
MIKE WELCH	23	Binghamton	East	47.3	61	27	4	14	39	5.13	2	3	11.60	.76	2.66	7.42	1.81
SHANNON WITHEM	23	Binghamton	East	80.3	94	29	8	23	43	3.25	5	4	10.53	.90	2.58	4.82	.96
	23	Norfolk	Inter	41.0	58	22	6	10	25	4.83	2	3	12.73	1.32	2.20	5.49	1.28

Philadelphia Phillies

Like their Pennsylvania rivals, the Phillies are in the process of a rebuilding movement. Unlike the Pirates, who are sending their veteran players away for prospects, the Phils are sending their veterans to the infirmary, never to return.

This is the downside of a strategy that Thomas utilized in the late '80s and early '90s. The Philadelphia farm system had dried up and the money for impact free agents wasn't forthcoming. He picked up players who, for one reason or another, were out of favor in their organization and available cheap. Often, it was because the player was frequently injured, or had too limited a role or was an attitude problem with their current management. The genius of 1993 was in keeping the team healthy, in their prescribed roles and happy. They had talent, and it carried them to a league title.

Since then it hasn't happened. Dealing with that many risks is like juggling dinner plates; a talented juggler may be able to keep them going for a short while, but the longer it goes on the farther some of them start drifting, the whole system getting more unstable until it all crashes down around him. 1996 was the total, final collapse of that system. It started early, when the offseason pickup of Benito Santiago hinted that Daulton's knee rehabilitation wasn't going well. It continued in the spring when the entire starting rotation (Schilling, Munoz, Green, Greene, West) went on the DL. Daulton's knees wouldn't even let him play the outfield, and he went on the DL April 7; he said he'd be back in June, playing first base, but he never returned. Gregg Jefferies tore ligaments in his thumb at the same time; out two months. In early May, Lee Tinsley, though he was back in two weeks. May 21, it was Lenny Dykstra: gone for the year. Sid Fernandez at the end of the month. In June, Mike Grace and Kevin Jordan went down for the season, Fernandez came off the DL to play and went back on, Morandini was temporarily down. In July it was Glenn Murray and Mike Benjamin (again), both for the duration. August saw Mikes Mimbs and Lieberthal, as well as Bobby Munoz, say goodbye for the rest of the year. David West went back on right before the DL ended with expanded rosters; Scott Rolen and Jim Eisenreich would have with broken bones early in September. It wasn't just the sheer number of injuries, but that so many were season-ending.

1997 will see a younger Philadelphia team, which should reduce the number of injuries, but they don't have a good outlook. Schilling is the only proven star on the team, although Bottalico is close and Rolen will be. It will be a long year down by the Schuykill.

The Phillies revamped a decade-long problem in their scouting department a few years ago, but the results haven't shown at the higher levels yet. The Scranton/Wilkes-Barre Red Barons went 70-72 in the International League. Thirty-one players spent time on both the Scranton and Philadelphia rosters last year, not including Tommy Greene; as a result, no one in Scranton had a chance to build eye-catching numbers. In Reading, Scott Rolen was the eye-catcher early on, but the team drifted to a 66-75 finish. Catcher Bobby Estalella and left-handed starter Matt Beech were clearly the stars of the team after Rolen's promotion. The Clearwater Phillies were the most successful team in the organization, at 75-62 third in the FSL and reaching the finals, but no one on the team stands out as a great prospect. Likewise with the Piedmont club in the Sally League; 72-66 with no one looking very impressive. Aside from Rolen, the only Philly farmhand named as a top 10 prospect by Baseball America was Dave Coggin, a 19-year-old pitcher for Piedmont who was chosen more on potential than performance.

MANUEL AMADOR   **3B/2B**   **1976**   **Age 21**

Year	Team	Lge	AB	H	DB	TP	HR	BB	SB	CS	OUT	BA	OBA	SA	EQA	EQR	Peak
1994	Spartanburg	S Atl	354	79	8	1	6	26	2	1	276	.223	.276	.302	.190	22	.222
1995	Clearwater	Flor	339	89	11	2	8	20	3	1	251	.263	.304	.378	.229	32	.264
1996	Clearwater	Flor	178	46	4	0	6	17	1	1	133	.258	.323	.382	.236	18	.268
1997	*Philadelphia*	*NL*	*330*	*89*	*16*	*2*	*8*	*42*	*3*	*2*	*243*	*.270*	*.352*	*.403*	*.266*	*44*	

He'd be a better prospect in the middle infield (he played mostly shortstop in '94, second in '95 and third last year) but his defense keeps moving him down the defensive spectrum.

RUBEN AMARO   **RF**   **1965**   **Age 32**

Year	Team	Lge	AB	H	DB	TP	HR	BB	SB	CS	OUT	BA	OBA	SA	EQA	EQR	Peak
1993	Scranton-WB	Inter	422	122	27	2	10	33	18	3	303	.289	.341	.434	.265	55	.268
1993	Philadelphia	NL	50	17	3	2	1	6	0	0	33	.340	.411	.540	.313	9	.316
1994	Charlotte-NC	Inter	185	58	10	3	3	15	6	1	128	.314	.365	.449	.277	26	.275
1995	Buffalo	AmA	220	69	14	2	7	20	6	1	152	.314	.371	.491	.288	34	.282
1995	Cleveland	AL	61	13	1	0	2	4	1	3	51	.213	.262	.328	.182	4	.177
1996	Syracuse	Inter	52	13	0	0	0	9	4	1	40	.250	.361	.250	.225	5	.216
1996	Scranton-WB	Inter	181	48	8	2	2	15	5	1	134	.265	.321	.365	.236	18	.227
1996	Philadelphia	NL	121	40	7	0	3	10	0	0	81	.331	.382	.463	.284	17	.275

Back in Philadelphia again, although not for any good reason. A team with as many young, mediocre outfielders as the Phillies doesn't need an old, mediocre one.

MARLON ANDERSON   **2B**   **1974**   **Age 23**

Year	Team	Lge	AB	H	DB	TP	HR	BB	SB	CS	OUT	BA	OBA	SA	EQA	EQR	Peak
1995	Batavia	NY-P	317	77	6	1	4	12	8	4	244	.243	.271	.306	.193	20	.216
1996	Clearwater	Flor	262	69	7	2	3	14	14	1	194	.263	.301	.340	.227	24	.250
1996	Reading	East	318	78	12	1	3	23	12	4	245	.245	.296	.318	.210	25	.232

He's a speedy second baseman who puts the ball in play: no strikeouts or walks for him. He's good in the field and at stealing a base, but his hitting is awfully light.

MIKE BENJAMIN   **SS**   **1966**   **Age 31**

Year	Team	Lge	AB	H	DB	TP	HR	BB	SB	CS	OUT	BA	OBA	SA	EQA	EQR	Peak
1993	San Francisco	NL	148	31	5	0	5	11	0	0	117	.209	.264	.345	.198	10	.203
1994	San Francisco	NL	63	17	5	1	1	6	5	0	46	.270	.333	.429	.268	9	.269
1995	San Francisco	NL	189	45	3	0	4	10	10	1	145	.238	.276	.317	.208	14	.206
1996	Philadelphia	NL	105	24	5	0	5	14	3	1	82	.229	.319	.419	.246	12	.242

Strictly a fill-in player while Kevin Stocker mended.

STEVE CARVER   **1B**   **1973**   **Age 24**

Year	Team	Lge	AB	H	DB	TP	HR	BB	SB	CS	OUT	BA	OBA	SA	EQA	EQR	Peak
1995	Batavia	NY-P	223	57	4	1	6	13	1	0	166	.256	.297	.363	.221	19	.245
1996	Clearwater	Flor	452	121	14	0	19	46	1	1	332	.268	.335	.425	.253	54	.275
1997	*Philadelphia*	*NL*	*436*	*114*	*18*	*0*	*18*	*33*	*3*	*1*	*323*	*.261*	*.313*	*.427*	*.258*	*55*	

A right-handed first baseman. He may have been a little old for the Florida State League, but he hit pretty well against it, missing the league's home run title by one. He also missed more than his share of balls in the field, with nine errors in only 67 games.

WALT DAWKINS   **CF**   **1973**   **Age 24**

Year	Team	Lge	AB	H	DB	TP	HR	BB	SB	CS	OUT	BA	OBA	SA	EQA	EQR	Peak
1995	Batavia	NY-P	212	56	8	2	1	20	5	3	159	.264	.328	.335	.226	19	.250
1996	Clearwater	Flor	180	49	9	1	3	18	2	2	133	.272	.338	.383	.242	19	.263
1996	Reading	East	259	63	13	2	3	33	3	2	198	.243	.329	.344	.227	24	.247
1997	*Philadelphia*	*NL*	*464*	*120*	*27*	*3*	*8*	*48*	*8*	*5*	*349*	*.259*	*.328*	*.381*	*.250*	*55*	

The 5' 10", 190-pound Panamanian has been pushed aggressively through the Phillies' farm system, as much to keep him from learning losing habits as for talent. Seriously, his best asset is his good batting eye. He has very little power, doesn't steal well and just isn't fast enough to play center field in the majors.

DAVID DOSTER   2B   1971   Age 26

Year	Team	Lge	AB	H	DB	TP	HR	BB	SB	CS	OUT	BA	OBA	SA	EQA	EQR	Peak
1993	Spartanburg	S Atl	232	55	5	0	4	19	0	0	177	.237	.295	.310	.201	16	.222
1994	Clearwater	Flor	498	140	27	2	17	50	8	4	362	.281	.347	.446	.264	65	.287
1995	Reading	East	560	140	24	2	21	45	8	4	424	.250	.306	.412	.239	59	.255
1996	Scranton-WB	Inter	324	79	10	0	8	27	5	2	247	.244	.302	.349	.219	28	.231
1996	Philadelphia	NL	107	29	6	0	2	9	0	0	78	.271	.328	.383	.239	11	.252
1997	*Philadelphia*	*NL*	*290*	*73*	*14*	*1*	*11*	*25*	*9*	*2*	*219*	*.252*	*.311*	*.421*	*.258*	*37*	

He caught some attention with a big year in Florida in 1994, but this is the usual result of star seasons by 23-year-old players in A ball. He's spent the last two years regressing with the bat and in the field. The power's wonderful for a middle infielder, but he needs more.

LEN DYKSTRA   CF   1963   Age 34

Year	Team	Lge	AB	H	DB	TP	HR	BB	SB	CS	OUT	BA	OBA	SA	EQA	EQR	Peak
1993	Philadelphia	NL	664	209	43	4	22	138	31	10	465	.315	.433	.491	.310	125	.304
1994	Philadelphia	NL	326	93	27	4	6	74	14	3	236	.285	.417	.448	.295	56	.286
1995	Philadelphia	NL	256	66	14	1	2	36	8	4	194	.258	.349	.344	.238	27	.226
1996	Philadelphia	NL	139	38	6	2	4	28	2	1	102	.273	.395	.432	.279	21	.266
1997	*Philadelphia*	*NL*	*274*	*71*	*10*	*4*	*7*	*45*	*11*	*6*	*209*	*.259*	*.364*	*.401*	*.270*	*40*	

Lenny, Daulton and Kruk were the heart and soul of the '93 league champions. It's only taken three years to do them in. He had serious back surgery in midseason last year for a condition which has plagued him for several years.

JIM EISENREICH   OF   1959   Age 38

Year	Team	Lge	AB	H	DB	TP	HR	BB	SB	CS	OUT	BA	OBA	SA	EQA	EQR	Peak
1993	Philadelphia	NL	371	120	17	3	8	31	4	0	251	.323	.376	.450	.280	52	.267
1994	Philadelphia	NL	298	93	16	3	5	37	5	2	207	.312	.388	.436	.280	43	.266
1995	Philadelphia	NL	381	119	20	2	10	42	8	0	262	.312	.381	.454	.284	56	.270
1996	Philadelphia	NL	352	132	25	2	4	36	9	1	221	.375	.433	.491	.316	62	.300
1997	*Florida*	*NL*	*433*	*125*	*20*	*4*	*8*	*34*	*7*	*0*	*308*	*.289*	*.340*	*.409*	*.270*	*58*	

Rumors abounded all season that he was about to be traded, but the right deal never came around. He continued his remarkable post-Tourette's career with a fantastic season by anyone's standards. He can't hit lefties any more? So what?

BOBBY ESTALELLA   C   1975   Age 22

Year	Team	Lge	AB	H	DB	TP	HR	BB	SB	CS	OUT	BA	OBA	SA	EQA	EQR	Peak
1994	Spartanburg	S Atl	311	62	8	1	8	26	0	0	249	.199	.261	.309	.183	18	.212
1994	Clearwater	Flor	47	12	1	0	2	3	0	0	35	.255	.300	.404	.234	5	.267
1995	Clearwater	Flor	422	106	11	0	16	48	0	1	317	.251	.328	.391	.240	45	.272
1996	Reading	East	374	86	8	1	19	59	2	2	290	.230	.335	.409	.246	44	.275
1997	*Philadelphia*	*NL*	*396*	*97*	*20*	*1*	*20*	*56*	*1*	*0*	*299*	*.245*	*.338*	*.452*	*.273*	*58*	

In 1994, the grandson of '40s outfielder Bobby Estalella was an overweight catcher going nowhere. He then embarked on a rigorous training and dietary regimen (stir frying vegetables in his hotel room on road trips) that gave him the lowest body fat percentage of anybody in the Philly organization, making him an exceptionally solid 200 pounds. He's come on as a power hitter, but his average is low and strikeouts are high. His defense needs a lot of work; he is probably at least a year away from the majors, more likely two.

GREGG JEFFERIES   1B/LF   1968   Age 29

Year	Team	Lge	AB	H	DB	TP	HR	BB	SB	CS	OUT	BA	OBA	SA	EQA	EQR	Peak
1993	St. Louis	NL	570	207	23	3	18	72	40	8	371	.363	.435	.509	.321	109	.338
1994	St. Louis	NL	405	133	22	1	14	51	11	4	276	.328	.404	.491	.299	68	.311
1995	Philadelphia	NL	484	146	27	1	12	40	7	4	342	.302	.355	.436	.266	62	.272
1996	Philadelphia	NL	416	128	15	3	8	41	17	6	294	.308	.370	.416	.269	55	.271
1997	*Philadelphia*	*NL*	*543*	*168*	*31*	*2*	*16*	*56*	*35*	*9*	*384*	*.309*	*.374*	*.462*	*.297*	*92*	

Before the Andruw Jones hype goes overboard recall this man, who was also a two-time Minor League Player of the Year and whose hitting, at 18 and 19, was very comparable to Jones. He never really developed, and as a result his composite minor league DTs, .321/.364/.469 with a .282 EQA, are a great match for his major league composite, .314/.375/.462 with a .282 EQA. He's had the defensive problems, the media pressure of New York, repeated trades and injuries. This year he tore ligaments in his thumb and missed almost all of the first two months, and he still doesn't have a set position.

KEVIN JORDAN 1B 1970 Age 27

Year	Team	Lge	AB	H	DB	TP	HR	BB	SB	CS	OUT	BA	OBA	SA	EQA	EQR	Peak
1993	Albany-NY	East	526	144	24	1	17	38	5	2	384	.274	.323	.420	.249	59	.271
1994	Scranton-WB	Inter	320	90	14	1	12	28	0	1	231	.281	.339	.444	.259	40	.278
1995	Scranton-WB	Inter	418	126	24	3	6	30	2	0	292	.301	.348	.416	.259	50	.273
1995	Philadelphia	NL	54	10	0	0	2	2	0	0	44	.185	.214	.296	.155	2	.167
1996	Philadelphia	NL	134	39	8	0	4	6	2	1	96	.291	.321	.440	.254	16	.266
1997	*Philadelphia*	*NL*	*380*	*106*	*20*	*4*	*9*	*23*	*4*	*2*	*276*	*.279*	*.320*	*.424*	*.261*	*48*	

He hit pretty much like I expected him to, but that's ridiculous for a first baseman. The scary thing is that he was their best option at the time, before he tore up his knee in June and missed the rest of the year.

MIKE LIEBERTHAL C 1972 Age 25

Year	Team	Lge	AB	H	DB	TP	HR	BB	SB	CS	OUT	BA	OBA	SA	EQA	EQR	Peak
1993	Scranton-WB	Inter	389	99	11	0	8	26	1	0	290	.254	.301	.344	.217	32	.243
1994	Scranton-WB	Inter	300	66	7	0	3	21	1	1	235	.220	.271	.273	.175	15	.193
1994	Philadelphia	NL	80	22	3	1	1	4	0	0	58	.275	.310	.375	.230	7	.254
1995	Scranton-WB	Inter	287	78	15	1	7	44	1	2	211	.272	.369	.404	.259	36	.282
1995	Philadelphia	NL	47	12	1	0	0	6	0	0	35	.255	.340	.277	.211	4	.226
1996	Philadelphia	NL	169	45	5	0	8	12	0	0	124	.266	.315	.438	.249	19	.266

A first round pick, he's the favored starter now that Santiago's been deemed too expensive. He's better suited to a backup role.

WENDELL MAGEE LF 1973 Age 24

Year	Team	Lge	AB	H	DB	TP	HR	BB	SB	CS	OUT	BA	OBA	SA	EQA	EQR	Peak
1994	Batavia	NY-P	236	56	7	1	3	12	4	1	181	.237	.274	.314	.197	16	.220
1995	Clearwater	Flor	404	133	16	2	9	29	5	5	276	.329	.374	.446	.275	55	.303
1995	Reading	East	139	38	6	1	3	19	2	2	103	.273	.361	.396	.254	17	.278
1996	Reading	East	273	73	11	2	6	22	7	3	203	.267	.322	.388	.240	29	.261
1996	Scranton-WB	Inter	157	43	8	1	9	21	2	1	115	.274	.360	.510	.283	24	.308
1996	Philadelphia	NL	144	30	5	0	3	11	0	0	114	.208	.265	.306	.184	8	.199
1997	*Philadelphia*	*NL*	*522*	*150*	*28*	*3*	*17*	*38*	*7*	*4*	*376*	*.287*	*.336*	*.450*	*.273*	*73*	

Before *Baseball Prospectus*, the DTs were "published" over the Internet, with commentary by fans of the various teams. The people who did the Phils repeatedly emphasized how much Thomas and Fregosi liked "hard-nosed," "dirty uniform" types of players. Magee is one of those guys. He was cut by his high school team all three times he tried out and became a star running back in college, playing amateur ball in the summers. Unlike most prospects described as great athletes, he appears to know the difference between a ball and a strike. Hits for a good average, although he was overmatched in the bigs. He could use a year at AAA, but there's no one better in Philly.

MICKEY MORANDINI 2B 1966 Age 31

Year	Team	Lge	AB	H	DB	TP	HR	BB	SB	CS	OUT	BA	OBA	SA	EQA	EQR	Peak
1993	Philadelphia	NL	431	108	21	7	4	41	11	2	325	.251	.316	.360	.231	42	.236
1994	Philadelphia	NL	281	85	16	4	3	39	9	4	200	.302	.387	.420	.275	40	.277
1995	Philadelphia	NL	498	139	33	6	6	47	7	5	364	.279	.341	.406	.251	57	.249
1996	Philadelphia	NL	552	145	25	5	4	55	21	5	412	.263	.329	.348	.235	55	.230
1997	*Philadelphia*	*NL*	*290*	*73*	*16*	*5*	*2*	*29*	*22*	*9*	*226*	*.252*	*.320*	*.362*	*.247*	*34*	

Right on cue, he's steadily working his offense down from his high-water mark at (What age, class?) 28. He's a good enough defensive player that he can stick around for several years as a utility guy when he can no longer hit. That time isn't far off, and I had to suppress a giggle every time I read that he was a "good core player" to "build a future contender around."

GLENN MURRAY   **RF**   **1971**   **Age 26**

Year	Team	Lge	AB	H	DB	TP	HR	BB	SB	CS	OUT	BA	OBA	SA	EQA	EQR	Peak
1993	Harrisburg	East	490	124	13	2	25	51	10	4	370	.253	.323	.441	.254	60	.279
1994	Pawtucket	Inter	471	101	10	1	22	52	6	2	372	.214	.293	.380	.223	44	.242
1995	Pawtucket	Inter	341	81	8	0	23	34	4	4	264	.238	.307	.463	.250	41	.267
1996	Scranton-WB	Inter	145	51	8	1	7	22	5	0	94	.352	.437	.566	.334	30	.353
1996	Philadelphia	NL	98	20	3	0	2	8	1	1	79	.204	.264	.296	.180	5	.189
1997	*Philadelphia*	*NL*	*230*	*55*	*13*	*1*	*13*	*24*	*8*	*4*	*179*	*.239*	*.311*	*.474*	*.268*	*33*	

"Boom-boom" bangs the ball, unless he's thoughtfully providing a breeze for the spectators on those hot summer nights. He struck out over 100 times every year from 1991-95, and had picked up 65 in 79 games before a torn ligament in his wrist sidelined him.

JAMIE NORTHEIMER   **C**   **1973**   **Age 24**

Year	Team	Lge	AB	H	DB	TP	HR	BB	SB	CS	OUT	BA	OBA	SA	EQA	EQR	Peak
1994	Batavia	NY-P	149	32	4	1	2	11	0	2	119	.215	.269	.295	.178	8	.200
1995	Piedmont	S Atl	413	106	18	1	2	43	4	2	309	.257	.327	.320	.220	35	.242
1996	Clearwater	Flor	343	83	9	0	12	53	0	1	261	.242	.343	.373	.240	37	.262

Despite a .254 batting average, he finished third in the league in OBA, thanks to 60 walks and 16 HBPs in about 400 plate appearances. He's raised his offensive value two years in a row, which is good, but he's still in A ball at 23, which isn't. He had 22 passed balls and was below average at stopping baserunners, and that's not good either.

RICKY OTERO   **CF**   **1972**   **Age 25**

Year	Team	Lge	AB	H	DB	TP	HR	BB	SB	CS	OUT	BA	OBA	SA	EQA	EQR	Peak
1993	Binghamton	East	512	127	20	6	3	35	15	8	393	.248	.296	.328	.211	40	.236
1994	Binghamton	East	547	151	25	5	8	45	21	9	405	.276	.331	.384	.244	59	.269
1995	Norfolk	Inter	304	80	8	4	2	29	12	8	232	.263	.327	.336	.225	28	.246
1995	NY Mets	NL	51	7	2	0	0	4	2	1	45	.137	.200	.176	.068	0	.083
1996	Scranton-WB	Inter	180	51	11	5	1	28	10	4	133	.283	.380	.417	.272	26	.291
1996	Philadelphia	NL	422	120	12	7	2	38	13	9	311	.284	.343	.360	.239	44	.257
1997	*Philadelphia*	*NL*	*366*	*97*	*11*	*10*	*2*	*50*	*30*	*8*	*277*	*.265*	*.353*	*.366*	*.266*	*50*	

Tiny (5' 5", 150) Otero relies on speed and defense for his job. He worked IL pitchers for a lot of walks last year, which would be a very good thing for him try all the time. I think the Vlad line is incredibly optimistic.

J.R. PHILLIPS   **1B/OF**   **1970**   **Age 27**

Year	Team	Lge	AB	H	DB	TP	HR	BB	SB	CS	OUT	BA	OBA	SA	EQA	EQR	Peak
1993	Phoenix	PCL	499	115	16	0	24	48	5	3	387	.230	.298	.407	.233	50	.253
1994	Phoenix	PCL	355	97	18	2	23	42	4	3	261	.273	.350	.530	.283	56	.303
1995	San Francisco	NL	235	49	7	0	10	21	1	1	187	.209	.273	.366	.209	19	.221
1996	Scranton-WB	Inter	202	55	10	1	12	19	2	1	148	.272	.335	.510	.275	29	.286
1996	Philadelphia	NL	80	13	5	0	5	11	0	0	67	.162	.264	.412	.217	7	.225

He seems to have learned something about hitting at AAA; prior to 1994, that was too much for him. He hasn't transferred that skill to the majors, and it has a lot to do with his non-existent plate discipline. You don't have to give him a hittable pitch; in fact, you'd better not, because when he hits it he hits it very well. He fanned an incredible 51 times in 104 at bats last year, which would be an unusually bad strikeout rate for a pitcher.

DESI RELAFORD   **SS**   **1974**   **Age 23**

Year	Team	Lge	AB	H	DB	TP	HR	BB	SB	CS	OUT	BA	OBA	SA	EQA	EQR	Peak
1993	Jacksonville	South	483	110	11	3	8	47	10	6	379	.228	.296	.313	.204	36	.235
1994	Riverside	Calif	392	115	22	2	6	66	14	4	281	.293	.395	.406	.276	56	.314
1994	Jacksonville	South	148	30	4	2	4	21	5	1	119	.203	.302	.338	.218	13	.247
1995	Port City	South	372	111	9	2	8	40	16	5	266	.298	.367	.398	.264	47	.295
1995	Tacoma	PCL	115	28	5	1	2	13	5	0	87	.243	.320	.357	.237	12	.264
1996	Tacoma	PCL	320	64	7	0	5	23	9	4	260	.200	.254	.269	.169	15	.186
1996	Scranton-WB	Inter	86	20	2	1	1	8	5	1	67	.233	.298	.314	.215	7	.235
1997	*Philadelphia*	*NL*	*340*	*76*	*22*	*2*	*2*	*33*	*21*	*9*	*273*	*.224*	*.292*	*.318*	*.221*	*31*	

What is a minor league shortstop to do when the parent club has a phenomenal hitter who's younger than you? You can try to play second base, but that wasn't going too well. Or you can get traded, which is what happened here. He's very quick in the field, but he's hardly bigger than Ricky Otero, at 5' 8", 155. He's shown some ability to hit for average and work a walk; he's had trouble adjusting to every change in leagues, and his walks are down and strikeouts up since reaching AAA. He may simply be overmatched.

SCOTT ROLEN   **3B**   **1975**   **Age 22**

Year	Team	Lge	AB	H	DB	TP	HR	BB	SB	CS	OUT	BA	OBA	SA	EQA	EQR	Peak
1994	Spartanburg	S Atl	538	145	19	2	13	47	3	3	396	.270	.328	.385	.239	55	.275
1995	Clearwater	Flor	250	71	6	1	11	32	2	0	179	.284	.365	.448	.273	35	.310
1995	Reading	East	77	21	1	0	3	6	1	0	56	.273	.325	.403	.247	8	.281
1996	Reading	East	235	79	17	1	8	30	6	2	158	.336	.411	.519	.309	42	.347
1996	Scranton-WB	Inter	171	44	10	0	3	27	3	3	130	.257	.359	.368	.245	19	.274
1996	Philadelphia	NL	133	35	4	0	5	15	0	2	100	.263	.338	.406	.244	15	.275
1997	*Philadelphia*	*NL*	*539*	*151*	*34*	*2*	*18*	*57*	*9*	*3*	*391*	*.280*	*.349*	*.451*	*.279*	*81*	

The star of this organization. The Phillies convinced the high school point guard (he's from Indiana, what sport did you think he'd play?) to turn down a basketball scholarship to Georgia. His defensive skills draw raves from everyone, and his range factors have been good, but there always seems to be a couple of guys ahead of him. He's hit the ball very well, despite arm injuries the last two seasons: a broken wrist in 1995 and a broken forearm last year. The latter came on a hit-by-pitch, in what would have been his 131st at bat of the season. By staying at 130 he's officially a rookie for 1997.

BENITO SANTIAGO   **C**   **1965**   **Age 32**

Year	Team	Lge	AB	H	DB	TP	HR	BB	SB	CS	OUT	BA	OBA	SA	EQA	EQR	Peak
1993	Florida	NL	474	110	19	4	14	44	8	6	370	.232	.297	.378	.224	44	.225
1994	Florida	NL	337	89	13	1	11	29	1	2	250	.264	.322	.407	.242	36	.241
1995	Cincinnati	NL	272	81	15	0	13	27	2	2	193	.298	.361	.496	.281	40	.275
1996	Philadelphia	NL	494	137	20	1	32	55	2	0	357	.277	.350	.516	.282	75	.272
1997	*Toronto*	*AL*	*523*	*139*	*25*	*1*	*24*	*54*	*3*	*1*	*385*	*.266*	*.334*	*.455*	*.265*	*69*	

For years, Santiago was held up as a catcher whose real offensive value was a lot less than people thought it was. That hasn't been true the last two seasons as he's displayed a new-found patience and considerably more power. Defensively, he's not the catcher he was—elbow injuries have taken their toll—but he's still at least average.

GENE SCHALL   **1B**   **1970**   **Age 27**

Year	Team	Lge	AB	H	DB	TP	HR	BB	SB	CS	OUT	BA	OBA	SA	EQA	EQR	Peak
1993	Reading	East	290	90	8	2	14	22	1	1	201	.310	.359	.497	.282	42	.306
1993	Scranton-WB	Inter	143	34	3	1	4	19	3	1	110	.238	.327	.357	.232	14	.252
1994	Scranton-WB	Inter	473	132	28	2	16	48	6	1	342	.279	.345	.448	.265	62	.284
1995	Scranton-WB	Inter	331	102	20	2	13	49	2	2	231	.308	.397	.498	.295	55	.312
1995	Philadelphia	NL	65	14	2	0	0	7	0	0	51	.215	.292	.246	.174	3	.188
1996	Scranton-WB	Inter	376	104	11	3	16	48	1	0	272	.277	.358	.449	.269	51	.280
1996	Philadelphia	NL	69	20	5	1	2	13	0	0	49	.290	.402	.478	.293	11	.305
1997	*Philadelphia*	*NL*	*510*	*151*	*26*	*1*	*29*	*66*	*4*	*1*	*360*	*.296*	*.377*	*.522*	*.307*	*94*	

The first time this Philadelphia native and Villanova grad was called up, he flopped. In April, he got a chance to play when Jefferies got hurt, and went 5-for-26 before getting sent down. In Scranton he hit reasonably well, and when The Call came for the third time, he was finally ready, hitting .325 and slugging .625 over the final month. Vladimir is certainly impressed by him.

KEVIN SEFCIK SS/3B 1971 Age 26

Year	Team	Lge	AB	H	DB	TP	HR	BB	SB	CS	OUT	BA	OBA	SA	EQA	EQR	Peak
1993	Batavia	NY-P	294	73	15	1	2	20	8	3	224	.248	.296	.327	.212	23	.234
1994	Clearwater	Flor	534	149	30	5	4	46	17	7	392	.279	.336	.376	.244	57	.265
1995	Reading	East	515	128	14	2	5	34	9	6	393	.249	.295	.313	.204	37	.218
1996	Scranton-WB	Inter	182	58	8	3	0	15	7	2	126	.319	.371	.396	.266	23	.280
1996	Philadelphia	NL	119	35	6	3	0	11	2	0	84	.294	.354	.395	.257	14	.271

A year ago, it looked like 1994 was the fluke season. This year, it looks like 1995 is the one out of line. Next year…

KEVIN STOCKER SS 1970 Age 27

Year	Team	Lge	AB	H	DB	TP	HR	BB	SB	CS	OUT	BA	OBA	SA	EQA	EQR	Peak
1993	Scranton-WB	Inter	319	72	12	1	3	31	12	4	251	.226	.294	.298	.202	23	.221
1993	Philadelphia	NL	267	88	12	2	3	34	4	0	179	.330	.405	.423	.286	39	.312
1994	Philadelphia	NL	279	79	11	1	3	48	2	2	202	.283	.388	.362	.258	34	.277
1995	Philadelphia	NL	414	88	13	3	1	47	5	1	327	.213	.293	.266	.185	24	.195
1996	Philadelphia	NL	404	107	22	5	6	48	5	4	301	.265	.343	.389	.246	45	.256
1997	*Philadelphia*	*NL*	*361*	*95*	*22*	*4*	*5*	*43*	*7*	*3*	*269*	*.263*	*.342*	*.388*	*.259*	*46*	

He started last season like it was still 1995, which for him was a terrible place to be. Management thought he was getting lazy in the field as well, so they sent him upstate for a spell, just to remind him what the minors were like and how close he was to an extended trip. It must have worked; he hit .293 with 20 doubles after the break, compared to .200 with two doubles before.

REGGIE TAYLOR CF 1977 Age 20

Year	Team	Lge	AB	H	DB	TP	HR	BB	SB	CS	OUT	BA	OBA	SA	EQA	EQR	Peak
1996	Piedmont	S Atl	523	127	15	3	1	23	14	7	403	.243	.275	.289	.188	31	.216

He's only here because he was the Phillies' #1 pick in 1995. He is—all together now—a great athlete. He showed himself to be a very good outfielder down in Piedmont. He is not much of a hitter. You know this refrain too—he strikes out way too much (136) and he doesn't walk (29). When he does hit the ball, there's no power.

JON ZUBER 1B 1970 Age 27

Year	Team	Lge	AB	H	DB	TP	HR	BB	SB	CS	OUT	BA	OBA	SA	EQA	EQR	Peak
1993	Clearwater	Flor	508	146	29	2	8	44	4	3	365	.287	.344	.400	.251	58	.273
1994	Reading	East	511	136	21	2	9	62	2	2	377	.266	.346	.368	.241	54	.258
1995	Scranton-WB	Inter	429	119	17	3	4	50	1	1	311	.277	.353	.359	.243	45	.255
1996	Scranton-WB	Inter	419	123	19	3	4	57	3	1	297	.294	.378	.382	.261	52	.271
1996	Philadelphia	NL	93	24	2	0	2	7	1	0	69	.258	.310	.344	.223	8	.231
1997	*Philadelphia*	*NL*	*352*	*101*	*30*	*4*	*6*	*38*	*2*	*0*	*251*	*.287*	*.356*	*.446*	*.281*	*53*	

He weighed just 135 pounds coming out of high school, and jokes about being on a weight watch with John Kruk—Kruk to lose it, him to gain it. It hasn't helped him any in the power department, but the other parts of his game: average, strike zone judgment and defense, are good.

MATT BEECH LSP 1972 Age 25

YR	TEAM	Lge	IP	H	ER	HR	BB	K	ERA	W	L	H/9	HR/9	BB/9	K/9	KW
1994	Batavia	NY-P	16.0	13	4	0	17	16	2.25	2	0	7.31	.00	9.56	9.00	.61
1994	Spartanburg	S Atl	61.3	68	25	8	34	49	3.67	4	3	9.98	1.17	4.99	7.19	1.15
1995	Clearwater	Flor	75.3	109	52	8	42	60	6.21	2	6	13.02	.96	5.02	7.17	1.13
1995	Reading	East	73.3	74	29	8	40	53	3.56	4	4	9.08	.98	4.91	6.50	.94
1996	Reading	East	124.3	119	50	15	42	97	3.62	8	6	8.61	1.09	3.04	7.02	1.58
1996	Scranton-WB	Inter	14.3	10	5	3	2	11	3.14	1	1	6.28	1.88	1.26	6.91	1.99
1996	Philadelphia	NL	41.0	50	29	8	15	29	6.37	1	4	10.98	1.76	3.29	6.37	1.30

The University of Houston product has made a rapid rise through the tattered Philly farm system, pitching well at almost every stop. He's not reported to be a hard thrower, and still has gotten more than his share of strikeouts. An extreme fly-ball pitcher, he should at least contend for a starting role in the Philly rotation.

RON BLAZIER   **RRP**   **1972**   **Age 25**

YR	TEAM	Lge	IP	H	ER	HR	BB	K	ERA	W	L	H/9	HR/9	BB/9	K/9	KW
1993	Clearwater	Flor	135.3	205	91	14	59	67	6.05	5	10	13.63	.93	3.92	4.46	.50
1994	Clearwater	Flor	155.3	214	81	22	54	92	4.69	7	10	12.40	1.27	3.13	5.33	.99
1995	Reading	East	99.7	103	39	12	39	78	3.52	6	5	9.30	1.08	3.52	7.04	1.47
1996	Scranton-WB	Inter	39.7	36	12	1	12	31	2.72	3	1	8.17	.23	2.72	7.03	1.66
1996	Philadelphia	NL	38.3	50	27	6	13	22	6.34	1	3	11.74	1.41	3.05	5.17	.96

Undrafted in 1990, he's worked his way up the entire length of the farm system, making steady improvement as he went. In '95 he started relieving and excelled as Scranton's closer this year before moving up to Philadelphia—the first time he's ever been promoted in midseason.

TOBY BORLAND   **RRP**   **1969**   **Age 28**

YR	TEAM	Lge	IP	H	ER	HR	BB	K	ERA	W	L	H/9	HR/9	BB/9	K/9	KW
1993	Reading	East	49.0	46	16	2	25	56	2.94	3	2	8.45	.37	4.59	10.29	2.28
1993	Scranton-WB	Inter	27.7	35	19	4	25	21	6.18	1	2	11.39	1.30	8.13	6.83	.24
1994	Scranton-WB	Inter	50.3	41	10	3	26	51	1.79	5	1	7.33	.54	4.65	9.12	1.88
1994	Philadelphia	NL	33.3	33	9	1	17	24	2.43	3	1	8.91	.27	4.59	6.48	1.01
1995	Philadelphia	NL	73.7	78	30	3	43	52	3.67	4	4	9.53	.37	5.25	6.35	.80
1996	Philadelphia	NL	89.7	87	45	9	51	67	4.52	4	6	8.73	.90	5.12	6.72	.96

A tall sidearmer who frightens right-handed hitters, he got off to a shaky start, yielding five home runs in his first ten games, but settled down thereafter. His peripheral numbers make it clear that he really hasn't lost his effectiveness, despite the jump in ERA. Traded to New York, where he'll have a similar role.

RICKY BOTTALICO   **RRP**   **1970**   **Age 27**

YR	TEAM	Lge	IP	H	ER	HR	BB	K	ERA	W	L	H/9	HR/9	BB/9	K/9	KW
1993	Clearwater	Flor	17.0	24	7	0	7	15	3.71	1	1	12.71	.00	3.71	7.94	1.72
1993	Reading	East	66.7	69	20	5	34	49	2.70	5	2	9.32	.68	4.59	6.62	1.06
1994	Reading	East	39.3	34	12	7	14	37	2.75	3	1	7.78	1.60	3.20	8.47	2.02
1994	Scranton-WB	Inter	21.7	32	24	4	26	18	9.97	0	2	13.29	1.66	10.80	7.48	-.21
1995	Philadelphia	NL	85.0	52	18	7	48	77	1.91	7	2	5.51	.74	5.08	8.15	1.45
1996	Philadelphia	NL	65.7	51	20	7	29	65	2.74	5	2	6.99	.96	3.97	8.91	1.98

One of the most dominating pitchers around, he took over the closer's role last year and converted 34 of 38 save opportunities. His hit ratios are astounding; opposing batters are hitting just .182 off him in two of the most offensive-minded seasons the league has known.

CARLOS CRAWFORD   **RSP**   **1972**   **Age 25**

YR	TEAM	Lge	IP	H	ER	HR	BB	K	ERA	W	L	H/9	HR/9	BB/9	K/9	KW
1993	Kinston	Caro	142.0	204	104	12	75	78	6.59	4	12	12.93	.76	4.75	4.94	.46
1994	Canton	East	157.0	203	93	18	81	73	5.33	6	11	11.64	1.03	4.64	4.18	.23
1995	Canton	East	48.0	52	18	2	19	28	3.38	3	2	9.75	.38	3.56	5.25	.86
1995	Buffalo	AmA	28.7	40	22	2	17	15	6.91	1	2	12.56	.63	5.34	4.71	.24
1996	Scranton-WB	Inter	152.3	169	72	14	81	73	4.25	8	9	9.98	.83	4.79	4.31	.24

He's never done the things you expect of a true prospect, but he's been a reliable minor league workhorse. This year's performance was good enough to earn a closer look.

GLENN DISHMAN   **LSP**   **1971**   **Age 26**

YR	TEAM	Lge	IP	H	ER	HR	BB	K	ERA	W	L	H/9	HR/9	BB/9	K/9	KW
1993	Spokane	Nwern	69.7	84	25	4	7	45	3.23	5	3	10.85	.52	.90	5.81	1.71
1994	Wichita	Texas	154.7	180	71	8	60	120	4.13	8	9	10.47	.47	3.49	6.98	1.45
1994	Las Vegas	PCL	12.0	14	5	1	2	10	3.75	1	0	10.50	.75	1.50	7.50	2.12
1995	Las Vegas	PCL	99.7	87	27	13	29	58	2.44	8	3	7.86	1.17	2.62	5.24	1.09
1995	San Diego	NL	95.7	110	57	11	43	39	5.36	4	7	10.35	1.03	4.05	3.67	.21
1996	Las Vegas	PCL	146.3	172	84	17	57	93	5.17	6	10	10.58	1.05	3.51	5.72	1.03

Undrafted out of college since he has a very poor fastball, he proceeded to rocket through the Padre system on the strength of a great changeup, reaching the majors in only three years. Shortly thereafter, it came undone. His ERA soared, walks rose and strikeouts crashed; after an ineffective year at Las Vegas he found himself waived twice in a month, first to the Phillies in September and then to the Tigers.

SID FERNANDEZ   **LSP**   **1963**   **Age 34**

YR	TEAM	Lge	IP	H	ER	HR	BB	K	ERA	W	L	H/9	HR/9	BB/9	K/9	KW
1993	NY Mets	NL	115.3	87	38	19	48	78	2.97	8	5	6.79	1.48	3.75	6.09	1.09
1994	Baltimore	AL	115.3	100	48	24	49	92	3.75	7	6	7.80	1.87	3.82	7.18	1.44
1995	Baltimore	AL	29.0	33	20	8	17	31	6.21	1	2	10.24	2.48	5.28	9.62	1.89
1995	Philadelphia	NL	63.7	47	20	11	26	70	2.83	5	2	6.64	1.55	3.68	9.90	2.38
1996	Philadelphia	NL	61.7	54	21	5	31	67	3.06	4	3	7.88	.73	4.52	9.78	2.13

It's been five years now since El Sid last pitched as many as 20 games in a season. One of the most extreme flyball pitchers in the game, he survived one year in Camden Yards, but not the second, as home runs ate him alive. Back in the NL with its reasonably-sized outfields, he immediately went back to his 7-hit, 3.00-ERA form. He's still one heck of a good pitcher with one of the most deceptive deliveries around…when he's not injured, which is all too common. In '95 it was his shoulder, last year it was elbow ligaments. Signed with the Astros; the Dome is a great park for him.

STEVE FREY   **LRP**   **1964**   **Age 33**

YR	TEAM	Lge	IP	H	ER	HR	BB	K	ERA	W	L	H/9	HR/9	BB/9	K/9	KW
1993	California	AL	47.0	42	16	1	28	23	3.06	3	2	8.04	.19	5.36	4.40	.13
1994	San Francisco	NL	31.3	36	15	6	18	19	4.31	1	2	10.34	1.72	5.17	5.46	.53
1995	Philadelphia	NL	10.0	4	0	1	3	2	.00	1	0	3.60	.90	2.70	1.80	-.07
1995	Seattle	AL	11.7	15	5	0	6	7	3.86	1	0	11.57	.00	4.63	5.40	.64
1996	Scranton-WB	Inter	12.7	12	7	1	9	7	4.97	0	1	8.53	.71	6.39	4.97	.06
1996	Philadelphia	NL	34.0	40	17	4	21	11	4.50	2	2	10.59	1.06	5.56	2.91	-.42

He never had much stuff, but in '96 what little he had was gone. Batters knew he couldn't strike them out—even when he was ahead in the count or had two strikes, they slugged .500 off him.

WAYNE GOMES   **RRP**   **1973**   **Age 24**

YR	TEAM	Lge	IP	H	ER	HR	BB	K	ERA	W	L	H/9	HR/9	BB/9	K/9	KW
1994	Clearwater	Flor	93.3	104	69	8	102	79	6.65	3	7	10.03	.77	9.84	7.62	.08
1995	Reading	East	97.0	98	49	9	82	78	4.55	5	6	9.09	.84	7.61	7.24	.51
1996	Reading	East	59.7	57	31	7	56	58	4.68	3	4	8.60	1.06	8.45	8.75	.80

He worked as a starter in '94-'95, but that was just a ploy to get him more work; he's been projected as a reliever all along, and averaged less than five innings a game. A first-round pick in 1993, he's got a great fastball and curveball, but the BB/9 column only tells part of his story—how about an average of 1.5 wild pitches per nine innings over the last three years? How about six balks in one game?

MIKE GRACE   **RSP**   **1970**   **Age 27**

YR	TEAM	Lge	IP	H	ER	HR	BB	K	ERA	W	L	H/9	HR/9	BB/9	K/9	KW
1994	Spartanburg	S Atl	68.7	111	59	7	32	27	7.73	2	6	14.55	.92	4.19	3.54	.13
1995	Reading	East	137.7	151	59	15	45	90	3.86	8	7	9.87	.98	2.94	5.88	1.23
1995	Scranton-WB	Inter	15.7	19	3	0	4	11	1.72	2	0	10.91	.00	2.30	6.32	1.53
1995	Philadelphia	NL	10.7	11	3	0	4	6	2.53	1	0	9.28	.00	3.38	5.06	.84
1996	Philadelphia	NL	78.0	75	29	9	23	43	3.35	5	4	8.65	1.04	2.65	4.96	.99

He's been plagued with elbow trouble throughout his career. 1995 was the only year in his six-year pro career when he was healthy enough to get more than 15 starts or 90 innings; he missed 1993 entirely. When he's healthy he's good, and he got off to a 5-0 start with the Phillies last year; then he went and hurt his elbow again, requiring more surgery.

TOMMY GREENE   **RSP**   **1967**   **Age 30**

YR	TEAM	Lge	IP	H	ER	HR	BB	K	ERA	W	L	H/9	HR/9	BB/9	K/9	KW
1993	Philadelphia	NL	193.0	185	75	13	83	161	3.50	12	9	8.63	.61	3.87	7.51	1.53
1994	Philadelphia	NL	35.3	38	18	5	26	26	4.58	2	2	9.68	1.27	6.62	6.62	.55
1995	Clearwater	Flor	18.0	15	7	3	10	14	3.50	1	1	7.50	1.50	5.00	7.00	1.08
1995	Scranton-WB	Inter	26.0	21	7	1	9	16	2.42	2	1	7.27	.35	3.12	5.54	1.07
1995	Philadelphia	NL	34.7	41	26	6	23	21	6.75	1	3	10.64	1.56	5.97	5.45	.32
1996	Clearwater	Flor	24.3	30	9	3	7	17	3.33	2	1	11.10	1.11	2.59	6.29	1.45
1996	Scranton-WB	Inter	29.7	32	11	3	10	21	3.34	2	1	9.71	.91	3.03	6.37	1.37

He was another big part of the 1993 league champions, but since then he's had more starts (23-13) and innings (126-69) in minor league rehab assignments than major league work. He's continually beaten up on the minor leaguers, but hasn't made a return to form in the majors.

BRONSON HEFLIN   **RRP**   **1972**   **Age 25**

YR	TEAM	Lge	IP	H	ER	HR	BB	K	ERA	W	L	H/9	HR/9	BB/9	K/9	KW
1994	Batavia	NY-P	67.3	120	47	8	33	42	6.28	2	5	16.04	1.07	4.41	5.61	.77
1996	Reading	East	27.3	38	18	3	18	20	5.93	1	2	12.51	.99	5.93	6.59	.71
1996	Scranton-WB	Inter	35.7	28	9	4	6	19	2.27	3	1	7.07	1.01	1.51	4.79	1.22

How does a guy with his record suddenly decide to go 38 innings with only three walks, like he did in Scranton? The real question is, how long can he keep that pace up? Considering that he gave up three walks in only six innings in Philadelphia in September, the answer would seem to be, "not very."

RICH HUNTER   **RSP**   **1975**   **Age 22**

YR	TEAM	Lge	IP	H	ER	HR	BB	K	ERA	W	L	H/9	HR/9	BB/9	K/9	KW
1995	Piedmont	S Atl	91.0	106	42	12	32	46	4.15	5	5	10.48	1.19	3.16	4.55	.73
1995	Clearwater	Flor	51.3	79	27	5	12	33	4.73	2	4	13.85	.88	2.10	5.79	1.40
1995	Reading	East	20.0	18	5	1	7	13	2.25	2	0	8.10	.45	3.15	5.85	1.16
1996	Reading	East	66.0	75	23	6	17	29	3.14	4	3	10.23	.82	2.32	3.95	.74
1996	Scranton-WB	Inter	38.7	39	25	5	26	18	5.82	1	3	9.08	1.16	6.05	4.19	-.12
1996	Philadelphia	NL	69.7	86	49	10	40	28	6.33	2	6	11.11	1.29	5.17	3.62	-.09

He's a 14th-round pick who spent two years as a lousy reliever in the Appalachian League before going 19-2 at three stops in 1995. Throwing a fastball that doesn't reach 85, he relies on control and a very good changeup. He made the Phillies rotation out of spring due to the rash of injuries, didn't have his control and got hammered. He was demoted first to Scanton and later Reading, where he finally regained command. His lack of heat makes him doubtful for the majors, but he's still young.

RICARDO JORDAN   **LRP**   **1970**   **Age 27**

YR	TEAM	Lge	IP	H	ER	HR	BB	K	ERA	W	L	H/9	HR/9	BB/9	K/9	KW
1993	Dunedin	Flor	22.0	21	12	0	19	18	4.91	1	1	8.59	.00	7.77	7.36	.51
1993	Knoxville	South	33.7	35	15	3	23	26	4.01	2	2	9.36	.80	6.15	6.95	.78
1994	Knoxville	South	59.0	64	26	2	33	55	3.97	4	3	9.76	.31	5.03	8.39	1.54
1995	Syracuse	Inter	11.7	16	9	1	9	14	6.94	0	1	12.34	.77	6.94	10.80	1.86
1995	Toronto	AL	15.3	17	9	3	13	10	5.28	1	1	9.98	1.76	7.63	5.87	.05
1996	Scranton-WB	Inter	37.7	40	25	5	27	33	5.97	1	3	9.56	1.19	6.45	7.88	1.02
1996	Philadelphia	NL	24.0	20	5	0	14	15	1.88	2	1	7.50	.00	5.25	5.62	.56

Jordan was a closer in the minors, picking up 15+ saves in 1992 and 1994. In 1995, arm trouble derailed him and in 1996 he had a double-digit ERA into May. Then he started pulling it together, working his ERA down to 5 and change by August, then really getting it going in Philadelphia.

RYAN KARP   **LSP**   **1970**   **Age 27**

YR	TEAM	Lge	IP	H	ER	HR	BB	K	ERA	W	L	H/9	HR/9	BB/9	K/9	KW
1993	Greensboro	S Atl	95.3	100	28	3	55	77	2.64	8	3	9.44	.28	5.19	7.27	1.12
1993	Pr. William	Caro	43.3	45	19	5	20	21	3.95	3	2	9.35	1.04	4.15	4.36	.42
1993	Albany, NY	East	12.0	15	7	1	11	8	5.25	0	1	11.25	.75	8.25	6.00	-.06
1994	Reading	East	110.0	137	64	12	70	70	5.24	4	8	11.21	.98	5.73	5.73	.48
1995	Reading	East	43.7	49	17	5	19	28	3.50	3	2	10.10	1.03	3.92	5.77	.94
1995	Scranton-WB	Inter	76.3	87	40	7	42	62	4.72	3	5	10.26	.83	4.95	7.31	1.20
1996	Scranton-WB	Inter	39.0	36	11	1	18	25	2.54	3	1	8.31	.23	4.15	5.77	.88

He's never been able to recapture the glory he had at Greensboro, but I think I've talked about 23-year-olds in A ball before. He throws a fastball and changeup, and his ERA has usually been pretty sensitive to his walk rate.

RANDY KNOLL   **RSP**   **1977**   **Age 20**

YR	TEAM	Lge	IP	H	ER	HR	BB	K	ERA	W	L	H/9	HR/9	BB/9	K/9	KW
1996	Piedmont	S Atl	132.0	154	55	9	48	78	3.75	8	7	10.50	.61	3.27	5.32	.95
1996	Clearwater	Flor	18.7	21	8	3	4	14	3.86	1	1	10.12	1.45	1.93	6.75	1.77

Knoll, a third-rounder in 1995, got hammered in his professional debut, going 0-3 with an ERA approaching 9 in the Appalachian League. This year, he couldn't have been better, cutting through the SAL and then continuing to excel in four starts for Clearwater.

CALVIN MADURO **RSP** **1975** **Age 22**

YR	TEAM	Lge	IP	H	ER	HR	BB	K	ERA	W	L	H/9	HR/9	BB/9	K/9	KW
1994	Frederick	Caro	136.0	165	90	17	80	92	5.96	5	10	10.92	1.12	5.29	6.09	.71
1995	Frederick	Caro	111.0	134	47	18	48	88	3.81	6	6	10.86	1.46	3.89	7.14	1.41
1995	Bowie	East	32.7	43	27	4	32	20	7.44	1	3	11.85	1.10	8.82	5.51	-.37
1996	Bowie	East	113.7	137	51	8	46	65	4.04	6	7	10.85	.63	3.64	5.15	.80
1996	Rochester	Inter	42.0	50	21	7	23	33	4.50	2	3	10.71	1.50	4.93	7.07	1.12
1996	Philadelphia	NL	15.0	13	5	1	5	10	3.00	1	1	7.80	.60	3.00	6.00	1.25

Acquired for Todd Zeile, he became the first Aruban player to make a major league roster, although the Orioles' Kingsale was the first Aruban to play in a game. He broke out in his second year at Frederick, then held on to that value at higher leagues in 1996. He's regarded as a very intelligent pitcher, utilizing a decent fastball and good curves and changeups. This has the potential to be one of those palpably uneven trades talked about for years on end.

NELSON METHENEY **RRP** **1971** **Age 26**

YR	TEAM	Lge	IP	H	ER	HR	BB	K	ERA	W	L	H/9	HR/9	BB/9	K/9	KW
1993	Batavia	NY-P	22.7	33	12	3	13	8	4.76	1	2	13.10	1.19	5.16	3.18	-.23
1994	Spartanburg	S Atl	44.0	56	19	2	19	18	3.89	3	2	11.45	.41	3.89	3.68	.26
1994	Clearwater	Flor	57.0	90	46	9	26	22	7.26	1	5	14.21	1.42	4.11	3.47	.13
1995	Clearwater	Flor	62.7	84	38	4	34	27	5.46	2	5	12.06	.57	4.88	3.88	.07
1996	Clearwater	Flor	30.3	36	4	0	9	14	1.19	3	0	10.68	.00	2.67	4.15	.72
1996	Reading	East	36.0	51	26	7	24	13	6.50	1	3	12.75	1.75	6.00	3.25	-.42

25 years old. A ball. Go to Reading and get real.

MICHAEL MIMBS **LBP** **1969** **Age 28**

YR	TEAM	Lge	IP	H	ER	HR	BB	K	ERA	W	L	H/9	HR/9	BB/9	K/9	KW
1994	Harrisburg	East	140.7	149	67	12	81	106	4.29	7	9	9.53	.77	5.18	6.78	.97
1995	Philadelphia	NL	134.7	125	56	9	85	82	3.74	8	7	8.35	.60	5.68	5.48	.41
1996	Scranton-WB	Inter	27.7	28	7	2	8	16	2.28	2	1	9.11	.65	2.60	5.20	1.08
1996	Philadelphia	NL	98.7	120	60	12	51	50	5.47	4	7	10.95	1.09	4.65	4.56	.36

He and his twin brother Mark entered the Dodger organization in 1990. Mark is still there. Mike washed out with the Dodgers and spent 1993 as a St. Paul Saint, then the Phillies decided to take a chance on him. A year later, he's in the starting rotation. He relies on a well-placed changeup for success; if he doesn't place it well and has to come in with his BP fastball, the result is, well, BP.

LARRY MITCHELL **RRP** **1972** **Age 25**

YR	TEAM	Lge	IP	H	ER	HR	BB	K	ERA	W	L	H/9	HR/9	BB/9	K/9	KW
1993	Spartanburg	S Atl	97.3	149	65	5	75	67	6.01	3	8	13.78	.46	6.93	6.20	.33
1993	Clearwater	Flor	50.0	61	25	1	28	35	4.50	3	3	10.98	.18	5.04	6.30	.84
1994	Reading	East	151.0	156	84	6	129	93	5.01	7	10	9.30	.36	7.69	5.54	-.07
1995	Reading	East	119.3	145	77	16	86	81	5.81	4	9	10.94	1.21	6.49	6.11	.41
1996	Reading	East	52.7	58	35	2	52	52	5.98	2	4	9.91	.34	8.89	8.89	.74
1996	Scranton-WB	Inter	23.3	21	6	2	12	20	2.31	2	1	8.10	.77	4.63	7.71	1.41
1996	Philadelphia	NL	12.0	15	6	1	6	6	4.50	0	1	11.25	.75	4.50	4.50	.37

He started relieving this year, and the early returns from Reading were mixed; when his control was more real than imaginary, so was his success. He managed to get called up, and after 11 good games for the Red Barons it was Showtime.

BOBBY MUNOZ **RSP** **1968** **Age 29**

YR	TEAM	Lge	IP	H	ER	HR	BB	K	ERA	W	L	H/9	HR/9	BB/9	K/9	KW
1993	Columbus, OH	Inter	29.0	28	5	0	11	13	1.55	3	0	8.69	.00	3.41	4.03	.49
1993	NY Yankees	AL	45.0	51	23	1	28	35	4.60	2	3	10.20	.20	5.60	7.00	.93
1994	Scranton-WB	Inter	31.7	30	8	2	18	20	2.27	3	1	8.53	.57	5.12	5.68	.62
1994	Philadelphia	NL	102.3	104	36	8	44	55	3.17	7	4	9.15	.70	3.87	4.84	.64
1995	Philadelphia	NL	15.3	15	11	2	10	5	6.46	1	1	8.80	1.17	5.87	2.93	-.49
1996	Reading	East	25.7	27	11	3	10	21	3.86	2	1	9.47	1.05	3.51	7.36	1.58
1996	Scranton-WB	Inter	48.0	52	19	5	12	28	3.56	3	2	9.75	.94	2.25	5.25	1.19
1996	Philadelphia	NL	26.0	42	25	5	10	7	8.65	1	2	14.54	1.73	3.46	2.42	-.06

Another patient in the Phillies' private ward, Munoz started last season recovering from reconstructive elbow surgery. He pitched pretty well in 14 minor league starts, but couldn't throw the ball past anyone in six batting practice sessions for Philadelphia opponents.

RYAN NYE   **RSP**   **1973**   **Age 24**

YR	TEAM	Lge	IP	H	ER	HR	BB	K	ERA	W	L	H/9	HR/9	BB/9	K/9	KW
1994	Batavia	NY-P	59.0	92	34	6	25	42	5.19	3	4	14.03	.92	3.81	6.41	1.18
1995	Clearwater	Flor	146.7	209	83	13	50	82	5.09	6	10	12.82	.80	3.07	5.03	.91
1996	Reading	East	81.0	82	36	8	38	66	4.00	5	4	9.11	.89	4.22	7.33	1.39
1996	Scranton-WB	Inter	77.7	96	43	9	39	42	4.98	4	5	11.12	1.04	4.52	4.87	.49

Reading looked like a big step forward, but Scranton was the same old, same old.

JEFF PARRETT   **RRP**   **1962**   **Age 35**

YR	TEAM	Lge	IP	H	ER	HR	BB	K	ERA	W	L	H/9	HR/9	BB/9	K/9	KW
1993	Colorado	NL	73.0	71	37	6	52	62	4.56	3	5	8.75	.74	6.41	7.64	.95
1994	Wilmington	Caro	12.7	15	5	0	8	12	3.55	1	0	10.66	.00	5.68	8.53	1.42
1994	Omaha	AmA	36.7	36	18	2	17	31	4.42	2	2	8.84	.49	4.17	7.61	1.49
1995	St. Louis	NL	75.7	72	28	8	34	63	3.33	5	3	8.56	.95	4.04	7.49	1.49
1996	St. Louis	NL	41.3	43	18	2	24	37	3.92	3	2	9.36	.44	5.23	8.06	1.38
1996	Philadelphia	NL	23.7	26	4	0	13	19	1.52	3	0	9.89	.00	4.94	7.23	1.17

He must like Philadelphia. When he was here in 1989 he went 12-6 with a 2.98 ERA, then finished strong last year after coming over from the Cardinals. He spent '94 in the minors due to elbow injuries, but his split-fingered fastball was working as good as ever last season.

KEN RYAN   **RRP**   **1969**   **Age 28**

YR	TEAM	Lge	IP	H	ER	HR	BB	K	ERA	W	L	H/9	HR/9	BB/9	K/9	KW
1993	Pawtucket	Inter	23.7	19	8	1	21	18	3.04	2	1	7.23	.38	7.99	6.85	.29
1993	Boston	AL	48.7	43	17	2	31	50	3.14	3	2	7.95	.37	5.73	9.25	1.65
1994	Boston	AL	47.3	44	10	1	19	31	1.90	4	1	8.37	.19	3.61	5.89	1.06
1995	Trenton	East	15.7	28	14	2	6	13	8.04	0	2	16.09	1.15	3.45	7.47	1.63
1995	Boston	AL	30.7	31	15	4	24	33	4.40	1	2	9.10	1.17	7.04	9.68	1.47
1996	Philadelphia	NL	87.0	77	28	4	53	62	2.90	7	3	7.97	.41	5.48	6.41	.77

Once upon a time he was the Red Sox closer of the future. This year, he recovered from a disastrous 1995 that was as much a conflict with Kevin Kennedy as anything else. He was murderous on first batters faced, leading to an outstanding 4 of 21 mark in inherited runners scored.

CURT SCHILLING   **RSP**   **1967**   **Age 30**

YR	TEAM	Lge	IP	H	ER	HR	BB	K	ERA	W	L	H/9	HR/9	BB/9	K/9	KW
1993	Philadelphia	NL	229.0	241	103	24	82	179	4.05	12	13	9.47	.94	3.22	7.03	1.54
1994	Philadelphia	NL	81.3	88	37	10	35	54	4.09	4	5	9.74	1.11	3.87	5.98	1.02
1995	Philadelphia	NL	113.3	95	41	12	34	100	3.26	8	5	7.54	.95	2.70	7.94	1.97
1996	Clearwater	Flor	12.7	11	2	0	3	12	1.42	1	0	7.82	.00	2.13	8.53	2.31
1996	Scranton-WB	Inter	12.3	10	2	0	6	8	1.46	1	0	7.30	.00	4.38	5.84	.85
1996	Philadelphia	NL	178.7	160	60	16	65	159	3.02	13	7	8.06	.81	3.27	8.01	1.85

In 1995 he underwent surgery for a torn labrum, similar to what Met pitchers Jason Isringhausen and Paul Wilson underwent last September. Philly fans can be delighted that the results have been so successful for Curt Schilling; I'm not sure they'd be as pleased if it works for the other guys.

RUSS SPRINGER   **RRP**   **1969**   **Age 28**

YR	TEAM	Lge	IP	H	ER	HR	BB	K	ERA	W	L	H/9	HR/9	BB/9	K/9	KW
1993	Vancouver	PCL	53.7	61	34	6	41	33	5.70	2	4	10.23	1.01	6.88	5.53	.13
1993	California	AL	61.3	67	38	11	35	32	5.58	2	5	9.83	1.61	5.14	4.70	.28
1994	Vancouver	PCL	77.3	78	28	7	26	50	3.26	5	4	9.08	.81	3.03	5.82	1.18
1994	California	AL	46.0	49	21	8	15	27	4.11	2	3	9.59	1.57	2.93	5.28	1.03
1995	Vancouver	PCL	31.7	28	16	4	27	22	4.55	2	2	7.96	1.14	7.67	6.25	.17
1995	California	AL	53.0	56	29	10	26	38	4.92	2	4	9.51	1.70	4.42	6.45	1.05
1995	Philadelphia	NL	26.7	21	9	5	12	28	3.04	2	1	7.09	1.69	4.05	9.45	2.14
1996	Philadelphia	NL	95.7	111	54	11	47	83	5.08	4	7	10.44	1.03	4.42	7.81	1.50

He was once a top prospect for the Yankees, one of the principals in the Jim Abbott trade with the Angels. Results since then have been extremely mixed; he bounces around from one season to the next, with the only reliable figure being lots of gopher balls.

GARRETT STEPHENSON   **RSP**   **1972**   **Age 25**

YR	TEAM	Lge	IP	H	ER	HR	BB	K	ERA	W	L	H/9	HR/9	BB/9	K/9	KW
1993	Albany, GA	S Atl	148.3	194	76	9	63	87	4.61	7	9	11.77	.55	3.82	5.28	.80
1994	Frederick	Caro	97.7	111	61	12	49	90	5.62	4	7	10.23	1.11	4.52	8.29	1.64
1994	Bowie	East	33.3	53	22	2	15	23	5.94	1	3	14.31	.54	4.05	6.21	1.06
1995	Bowie	East	161.3	182	86	26	60	107	4.80	7	11	10.15	1.45	3.35	5.97	1.15
1996	Rochester	Inter	116.3	127	57	13	58	71	4.41	6	7	9.83	1.01	4.49	5.49	.71

When the Phillies traded Zeile and Inky to the Orioles, they thought they had gotten Cal Maduro and Don Florence. Trouble was, the O's had released Florence the day before, and so they settled on Stephenson to finish the trade. He's relied on a mediocre fastball, slow curve and changeup: less power than the Uzbekistani navy. Somehow, he avoids getting torched. Fear may be part of it; he's hit 29 batters the last two seasons. Even a poor fastball stings a little.

DAVID WEST   **LSP**   **1965**   **Age 32**

YR	TEAM	Lge	IP	H	ER	HR	BB	K	ERA	W	L	H/9	HR/9	BB/9	K/9	KW
1993	Philadelphia	NL	83.3	65	32	6	60	84	3.46	5	4	7.02	.65	6.48	9.07	1.40
1994	Philadelphia	NL	97.3	78	38	8	69	78	3.51	6	5	7.21	.74	6.38	7.21	.81
1995	Philadelphia	NL	37.3	33	14	5	22	22	3.38	2	2	7.96	1.21	5.30	5.30	.44
1996	Clearwater	Flor	20.3	26	9	2	15	12	3.98	1	1	11.51	.89	6.64	5.31	.11
1996	Scranton-WB	Inter	11.3	14	7	3	4	10	5.56	0	1	11.12	2.38	3.18	7.94	1.85
1996	Philadelphia	NL	28.0	33	15	0	14	19	4.82	1	2	10.61	.00	4.50	6.11	.91

It seems pretty obvious that the arm troubles of 1995 were not behind him.

SCOTT WIEGANDT   **LRP**   **1968**   **Age 29**

YR	TEAM	Lge	IP	H	ER	HR	BB	K	ERA	W	L	H/9	HR/9	BB/9	K/9	KW
1993	Reading	East	67.3	82	39	3	54	45	5.21	3	4	10.96	.40	7.22	6.01	.20
1994	Reading	East	47.7	54	22	4	26	25	4.15	2	3	10.20	.76	4.91	4.72	.35
1995	Scranton-WB	Inter	50.7	60	18	0	35	35	3.20	4	2	10.66	.00	6.22	6.22	.52
1996	Scranton-WB	Inter	60.3	64	17	3	40	38	2.54	5	2	9.55	.45	5.97	5.67	.40

While his DT-ERAs have improved steadily, there really hasn't been any change in his other numbers. That makes me real reluctant to recommend him.

MIKE WILLIAMS   **RSP**   **1969**   **Age 28**

YR	TEAM	Lge	IP	H	ER	HR	BB	K	ERA	W	L	H/9	HR/9	BB/9	K/9	KW
1993	Scranton-WB	Inter	92.0	101	32	8	27	43	3.13	6	4	9.88	.78	2.64	4.21	.74
1993	Philadelphia	NL	49.7	52	30	6	27	32	5.44	2	4	9.42	1.09	4.89	5.80	.71
1994	Philadelphia	NL	50.3	61	28	7	25	27	5.01	2	4	10.91	1.25	4.47	4.83	.49
1995	Philadelphia	NL.	86.0	76	29	10	35	50	3.03	6	4	7.95	1.05	3.66	5.23	.83
1996	Philadelphia	NL	166.7	192	97	25	83	91	5.24	7	12	10.37	1.35	4.48	4.91	.52

He did a good job for the Phillies in 1995, mostly in relief. So when injuries wiped out the real starting rotation in 1996, he got his chance to take a regular turn. This turned out to not be a good idea.

Player	Age	Team	Lge	AB	H	DB	TP	HR	BB	SB	CS	OUT	BA	OBA	SA	EQA	EQR	Peak
DOUG ANGELI	25	Reading	East	190	42	4	0	7	17	2	1	149	.221	.285	.353	.211	15	.222
HOWARD BATTLE	24	Scranton-WB	Inter	392	83	15	1	8	23	3	5	314	.212	.255	.316	.183	22	.195
GARY BENNETT	24	Scranton-WB	Inter	288	67	9	1	8	25	1	0	221	.233	.294	.354	.216	24	.231
ESSEX BURTON	27	Reading	East	386	107	15	4	1	33	26	7	286	.277	.334	.345	.240	40	.246
ROB BUTLER	26	Scranton-WB	Inter	299	71	14	5	4	22	2	3	231	.237	.290	.358	.213	24	.222
TODD COBURN	24	Piedmont	S Atl	163	29	2	0	2	12	1	0	134	.178	.234	.227	.131	4	.140
JONATHON CORNELIUS	22	Piedmont	S Atl	476	103	9	1	10	26	3	2	375	.216	.257	.303	.181	26	.199
BRIAN COSTELLO	21	Clearwater	Flor	287	54	10	1	3	16	3	2	235	.188	.231	.261	.148	10	.166
MARIO DIAZ	34	Scranton-WB	Inter	181	47	3	0	3	12	0	0	134	.260	.306	.326	.212	14	.202
ZACH ELLIOTT	22	Piedmont	S Atl	504	107	9	0	6	53	8	5	402	.212	.287	.266	.182	28	.201
STAN EVANS	25	Clearwater	Flor	250	57	3	1	3	29	6	3	196	.228	.308	.284	.200	18	.211
DAVID FISHER	26	Reading	East	173	42	5	0	4	10	4	2	133	.243	.284	.341	.210	13	.219
JOSE FLORES	23	Clearwater	Flor	290	63	6	3	2	30	7	1	228	.217	.291	.279	.193	19	.210
MATT GUILIANO	24	Clearwater	Flor	168	35	6	1	2	6	1	1	134	.208	.236	.292	.165	7	.176
	24	Reading	East	223	40	7	2	0	22	0	0	183	.179	.253	.229	.141	7	.151
JEFF GYSELMAN	25	Reading	East	130	19	2	0	0	12	0	1	112	.146	.218	.162	-.049	0	-.052
DAN HELD	25	Reading	East	505	114	11	3	21	53	3	4	395	.226	.299	.384	.225	47	.237
LARRY HUFF	24	Clearwater	Flor	501	131	16	3	1	54	19	6	376	.261	.333	.311	.225	45	.241
JARED JANKE	22	Piedmont	S Atl	405	81	8	0	7	18	1	1	325	.200	.234	.272	.154	15	.170
JEREMEY KENDALL	24	Clearwater	Flor	301	71	9	0	6	30	11	3	233	.236	.305	.326	.217	25	.231
	24	Reading	East	133	20	2	1	1	10	4	2	115	.150	.210	.203	.102	2	.107
JEFF KEY	21	Clearwater	Flor	354	81	12	1	5	15	8	2	275	.229	.260	.311	.191	22	.214
CHAD MCCONNELL	25	Reading	East	390	88	11	1	10	36	5	3	305	.226	.291	.336	.209	30	.220
ADAN MILLAN	24	Clearwater	Flor	363	94	10	1	12	46	1	1	270	.259	.342	.391	.246	41	.263
JASON MOLER	26	Reading	East	381	87	12	1	15	48	4	3	297	.228	.315	.383	.232	38	.240
TORREY PETTIFORD	23	Piedmont	S Atl	271	52	3	1	1	14	5	1	220	.192	.232	.221	.132	7	.142
KIRK PIERCE	23	Piedmont	S Atl	211	49	5	0	3	17	0	0	162	.232	.289	.299	.194	13	.210
SHANE PULLEN	23	Piedmont	S Atl	182	45	5	1	2	12	0	1	138	.247	.294	.319	.202	13	.221
MARK RAYNOR	23	Piedmont	S Atl	461	130	14	1	4	40	6	4	335	.282	.339	.343	.233	44	.253
EDDIE RIVERO	22	Piedmont	S Atl	208	53	6	2	4	15	2	1	156	.255	.305	.361	.224	18	.248
DAVID ROBINSON	23	Piedmont	S Atl	157	37	4	1	3	9	2	1	121	.236	.277	.331	.202	11	.220
AARON ROYSTER	23	Clearwater	Flor	297	79	5	1	11	21	2	2	220	.266	.314	.401	.238	30	.259
	23	Reading	East	234	54	5	0	4	27	3	2	182	.231	.310	.303	.206	18	.223
ERIC SCHREIMANN	21	Piedmont	S Atl	316	74	7	1	6	23	1	0	242	.234	.286	.320	.201	22	.226
SCOTT SHORES	24	Reading	East	404	85	14	4	10	41	14	5	324	.210	.283	.339	.210	33	.224
DAVE TOKHEIM	27	Scranton-WB	Inter	255	50	10	2	1	13	3	3	208	.196	.235	.263	.151	9	.154
RICKY WILLIAMS	19	Piedmont	S Atl	277	49	3	1	3	14	7	3	231	.177	.216	.227	.126	6	.143
RICK WRONA	32	Scranton-WB	Inter	175	37	5	0	5	8	1	1	139	.211	.246	.326	.184	10	.175

Player	Age	Team	Lge	IP	H	ER	HR	BB	K	ERA	W	L	H/9	HR/9	BB/9	K/9	KW
SCOTT BAKKUM	26	Scranton-WB	Inter	48.0	66	36	7	26	21	6.75	1	4	12.38	1.31	4.88	3.94	.09
JOE BARBAO	24	Clearwater	Flor	35.7	59	22	1	9	10	5.55	1	3	14.89	.25	2.27	2.52	.27
	24	Piedmont	S Atl	28.7	43	9	2	12	17	2.83	2	1	13.50	.63	3.77	5.34	.84
JASON BOYD	23	Clearwater	Flor	143.0	197	85	18	71	87	5.35	6	10	12.40	1.13	4.47	5.48	.71
ROB BURGER	20	Piedmont	S Atl	138.3	174	84	11	89	94	5.47	5	10	11.32	.72	5.79	6.12	.59
SILVIO CENSALE	24	Clearwater	Flor	111.0	147	73	8	74	73	5.92	4	8	11.92	.65	6.00	5.92	.47
DAVID COGGIN	19	Piedmont	S Atl	141.7	219	108	16	70	71	6.86	4	12	13.91	1.02	4.45	4.51	.39
TONY COSTA	25	Reading	East	141.7	159	96	18	110	82	6.10	5	11	10.10	1.14	6.99	5.21	-.01
ROBERT DODD	23	Reading	East	39.7	44	19	4	29	26	4.31	2	2	9.98	.91	6.58	5.90	.32
DONNIE ELLIOTT	27	Scranton-WB	Inter	99.7	104	51	11	71	76	4.61	5	6	9.39	.99	6.41	6.86	.68
TONY FIORE	24	Clearwater	Flor	114.3	125	65	7	76	58	5.12	5	8	9.84	.55	5.98	4.57	.03
	24	Reading	East	28.7	34	19	2	21	14	5.97	1	2	10.67	.63	6.59	4.40	-.18
BRIAN FORD	23	Piedmont	S Atl	45.7	98	39	6	27	22	7.69	1	4	19.31	1.18	5.32	4.34	.11
MARK FOSTER	24	Reading	East	70.7	87	48	6	54	41	6.11	2	6	11.08	.76	6.88	5.22	.02
MATT GROTT	28	Scranton-WB	Inter	83.3	93	40	16	30	52	4.32	4	5	10.04	1.73	3.24	5.62	1.06
CRAIG HOLMAN	27	Reading	East	43.0	46	19	6	17	25	3.98	3	2	9.63	1.26	3.56	5.23	.85
	27	Scranton-WB	Inter	60.7	75	36	9	42	30	5.34	3	4	11.13	1.34	6.23	4.45	-.07
TREVOR HUMPHRY	24	Clearwater	Flor	29.7	27	8	0	22	9	2.43	2	1	8.19	.00	6.67	2.73	-.76
JASON KERSHNER	19	Piedmont	S Atl	140.7	214	99	16	88	86	6.33	5	11	13.69	1.02	5.63	5.50	.43
KORY KOSEK	23	Clearwater	Flor	65.0	102	48	8	44	37	6.65	2	5	14.12	1.11	6.09	5.12	.18
CARLTON LOEWER	22	Reading	East	158.7	203	103	22	73	87	5.84	6	12	11.51	1.25	4.14	4.93	.61
LEN MANNING	24	Clearwater	Flor	90.0	115	57	9	83	56	5.70	3	7	11.50	.90	8.30	5.60	-.21
JAIME MENDES	23	Piedmont	S Atl	58.0	109	34	5	21	35	5.28	2	4	16.91	.78	3.26	5.43	1.00
MATT MURRAY	25	Scranton-WB	Inter	54.3	61	42	11	57	28	6.96	1	5	10.10	1.82	9.44	4.64	-.81
PETE NYARI	24	Piedmont	S Atl	45.3	54	31	4	30	37	6.15	1	4	10.72	.79	5.96	7.35	.96
RAFAEL QUIRICO	26	Reading	East	27.7	25	5	2	14	17	1.63	3	0	8.13	.65	4.55	5.53	.70
	26	Scranton-WB	Inter	61.7	51	24	8	32	42	3.50	4	3	7.44	1.17	4.67	6.13	.88
SHELBY RAMA	24	Clearwater	Flor	72.7	109	46	6	36	28	5.70	3	5	13.50	.74	4.46	3.47	.04
ANTHONY SHUMAKER	23	Clearwater	Flor	26.3	46	18	2	17	18	6.15	1	2	15.72	.68	5.81	6.15	.60
	23	Piedmont	S Atl	29.0	23	8	3	15	28	2.48	2	1	7.14	.93	4.66	8.69	1.73
JASON SIKES	20	Piedmont	S Atl	63.7	116	71	5	59	26	10.04	1	6	16.40	.71	8.34	3.68	-.86
BRIAN STUMPF	24	Clearwater	Flor	51.7	68	28	4	42	35	4.88	2	4	11.85	.70	7.32	6.10	.20
KEITH TROUTMAN	23	Reading	East	68.0	66	31	6	49	54	4.10	4	4	8.74	.79	6.49	7.15	.76
B.J. WALLACE	25	Clearwater	Flor	55.3	86	52	4	54	27	8.46	1	5	13.99	.65	8.78	4.39	-.73
TIM WALTON	23	Piedmont	S Atl	32.7	38	8	0	20	10	2.20	3	1	10.47	.00	5.51	2.76	-.46
DESTRY WESTBROOK	25	Clearwater	Flor	39.0	43	13	4	16	25	3.00	3	1	9.92	.92	3.69	5.77	1.00
	25	Reading	East	31.3	43	17	3	17	11	4.88	1	2	12.35	.86	4.88	3.16	-.17
GARY YEAGER	22	Piedmont	S Atl	69.7	98	30	3	29	36	3.88	4	4	12.66	.39	3.75	4.65	.61

Chicago Cubs

The Chicago Cubs entered the '96 season with ambitious goals, fearlessly announced. With the return of Ryne Sandberg, the expectation that Sammy Sosa would continue to blossom and the hope that the surprisingly successful rotation of '95 would continue to thrive in '96. Much was made of the return of Sandberg as a case of emotional closure, as it was the removal of one of the major scars of the Himes regime in the front office. Greg Maddux in a Braves' uniform was the other major accomplishment of Larry Himes; undoing that would have done a lot more good than a 36-year-old second baseman, but then Cubs fans usually aren't too choosy about good news. From all of their public statements, both players and management made it clear that the Cubs honestly believed that they would be capable of pushing for the Central Division title, or at least the wild card.

Were the expectations of success realistic? Even with the clever acquisitions of Scott Servais and Luis Gonzalez from an amazingly inept Houston franchise during the '95 season, or the successful rehabilitation of Jamie Navarro, was the expectation of contention fair to assume from this group of talent? Hardly. Without a single great offensive player, the Cubs lately have been in the awkward position of relying on their pitching staff to propel their team into respectability. The Cubs also have a problem with low expectations: sure, Scott Servais can't be a disappointment compared to Rick Wilkins or Joe Girardi (or Luis Gonzalez compared to Derrick May), but does that necessarily mean that a Servais or a Gonzalez is really any good? By measuring improvement in their lineups and roster in comparison to previous inadequate or disappointing rosters, the Cubs haven't paid attention to the coming decline of their core players (Grace, Sosa and McRae), the level of offensive production in the league around them or the level of talent available to their divisional rivals.

For example by July, the front office was getting disappointed with how the team was doing, and "unnamed sources" and Ed Lynch started fulminating about how this team needed shaking up. When push came to shove, what was the "major" change? They demoted Brian Dorsett, Todd Haney and Ozzie Timmons, and called up Terry Shumpert, Doug Glanville and Mike Hubbard. Ambition is relative.

The way in which the Cubs have attempted to be competitive indicates how organizations can claim they're competitive in the wild card age while not doing much to build a real contender. This may be deadly for the MacPhail regime, one that was ushered in with excitement and a sense of promise before the '95 season, as it has placed the Cubs in a lose-lose situation. On the one hand, if the Cubs feel they have to continue to publicly reiterate how serious they are about contending, they'll be engaged in a public relations campaign. They cannot fail to re-sign the popular veterans that got them to mediocrity in the first place for fear of a public backlash. On the other hand, if they are actually serious about building a team that can win for years to come, that means having the courage to not offer huge contracts to a first baseman without power or a second baseman with middling power and little range. It means making the important decisions about their various outfield prospects, or taking a shot at trying to pick up a good shortstop prospect.

The resulting public outcry at not re-signing a Grace or a Sandberg, of course, would be unthinkable in an organization still scarred by the public relations disasters of the Himes regime. Since they obviously lack the courage to do much more than continue plugging along with many of the same cast members as previous seasons, they'll continue to engage in that line of wishful thinking that wonders what might happen if everyone's lucky enough to have a great year all at the same time. That's the stuff of typical Cubbie pipe dreams, dreams that have Andy MacPhail making public promises to be aggressive in this year's free agent market, probably to get that third baseman the Cubs always need.

The Cubs are trapped in a cycle of promises that echo throughout the team's parent media feeds, leaving them incapable of having the strength of purpose to mimic really successful organizations, like the Indians or Braves, as they chase the "easily" attainable mirage of the wild card. They're stuck with the need to buy a free agent here or there to make them seem serious, while their overhyped stars become entrenched foundations of an organization that needs players better than they are to actually contend. It may make for better ratings than the miseries of the recent past, but it's a recipe for failure just the same.

As September rolled around and the Cubs' shot at the wild card waned, the organization tried at first to put a happy light on the slumping team's fortunes. Ed Lynch talked about how the Cubs could put up consecutive winning seasons for the first time since the Nixon administration, and how this was a major accomplishment. With inspiration like this, the team promptly blew its chance to reach this mighty goal, losing 14 of its last 16 games to finish 76-86. Lynch and Riggleman both blithely tried to wave off the flop, saying that the club's summer was a better indicator of what it was capable of. Brian McRae spearheaded the criticism of this make-believe. "After 162 games, that's what we did. We're a losing team."

The front office sheepishly shut up about how neato the season had been and started talking about what it had to do to improve, and Andy MacPhail apologized for not putting a better team on the field. Rather than talking about what might have been, the Cubs are talking about the need to acquire a major power hitter or a shortstop (possibly John Valentin). Are they sincere, or have they merely been embarrassed?

The Cubs' farm system isn't particularly strong. They need middle infield help badly, little of which is available in the system. They're rich in outfield prospects but none are outstanding, and having signed Brian McRae, Sammy Sosa and Mark Grace to long-term contracts, the Cubs have only left field to offer to Robin Jennings, Brooks Kieschnick and Pedro Valdes. The organization has produced most of the pitching staff, and there's further help on the way, particularly reliever Steve Rain. The Cubs waste a lot of time on "tools" prospects, notably Doug Glanville and Brant Brown.

1996 was not a good season for the teams of the Cubs' farm system. Neither Iowa (AAA) and Orlando (AA) could reach 70 wins, winding up well below .500. Iowa had an awful lineup, finishing seventh in the league in runs scored. The pitching staff finished last in strikeouts and first in home runs allowed. Orlando was little better, finishing at or near the bottom in almost every category; perhaps even more disappointing was that the Orlando squad was made up of many of the players who had dominated the Florida State League at Daytona the year before. At A ball, the results were only slightly better, as both Daytona and Rockford finished just over .500; nevertheless, neither team was particularly successful or strong in any area. Overall, the organization has an extreme paucity of power prospects.

The team has a few prospects who are outstanding or will get their big chance: the upper level outfielders, third baseman Kevin Orie, catcher Pat Cline, and pitchers Rain and Kerry Wood; in the distance are infielder Elinton Jasco and outfielder Terry Joseph. All should be part of the Cubs future, although only Wood might be a franchise player. There's a lot of work to be done, and so far the Cubs' drafts haven't been nearly productive enough.

BRET BARBERIE   **2B**   **1968**   **Age 29**

Year	Team	Lge	AB	H	DB	TP	HR	BB	SB	CS	OUT	BA	OBA	SA	EQA	EQR	Peak
1993	Florida	NL	382	106	16	2	5	38	2	3	279	.277	.343	.369	.240	39	.254
1994	Florida	NL	372	108	17	1	6	28	2	0	264	.290	.340	.390	.248	41	.259
1995	Baltimore	AL	239	59	10	0	4	36	3	3	183	.247	.345	.339	.231	24	.238
1996	Iowa	AmA	218	51	6	0	5	32	3	2	169	.234	.332	.330	.224	20	.226
1997	*Chicago Cubs*	*NL*	*224*	*59*	*18*	*1*	*4*	*21*	*4*	*2*	*167*	*.263*	*.327*	*.406*	*.255*	*28*	

Second base is the easiest position in baseball to stock, and Bret Barberie's big chance in Baltimore has come and gone. He lacks the skill to become a utility infielder, so his career is entering Casey Candaele territory.

BRANT BROWN   **1B/LF**   **1971**   **Age 26**

Year	Team	Lge	AB	H	DB	TP	HR	BB	SB	CS	OUT	BA	OBA	SA	EQA	EQR	Peak
1993	Daytona	Flor	267	81	6	3	5	10	4	3	189	.303	.329	.404	.247	29	.272
1993	Orlando	South	112	35	9	2	4	6	1	1	78	.312	.347	.536	.286	17	.316
1994	Orlando	South	481	120	25	3	6	39	7	7	368	.249	.306	.351	.219	41	.238
1995	Orlando	South	459	121	23	2	7	38	5	3	341	.264	.320	.368	.232	44	.248
1996	Iowa	AmA	351	107	22	1	10	23	6	5	249	.305	.348	.459	.267	46	.282
1996	Chicago Cubs	NL	70	22	0	0	5	3	3	3	51	.314	.342	.529	.277	10	.291
1997	*Chicago Cubs*	*NL*	*425*	*120*	*26*	*3*	*13*	*26*	*10*	*6*	*311*	*.282*	*.324*	*.449*	*.266*	*57*	

Just about the worst possible decision the Cubs could make is the one to make Brant Brown a regular. Despite his exciting month with the Cubs, he doesn't hit well enough to be a regular first baseman or left fielder, he's old and his major skill is his glovework at first. On a team that already has Mark Grace, that's less important than stocking up beach hats for clubhouse attendant Yosh Kawano.

SCOTT BULLETT   **OF**   **1969**   **Age 28**

Year	Team	Lge	AB	H	DB	TP	HR	BB	SB	CS	OUT	BA	OBA	SA	EQA	EQR	Peak
1993	Buffalo	AmA	418	120	13	5	1	42	27	12	310	.287	.352	.349	.245	46	.261
1993	Pittsburgh	NL	55	11	0	0	2	4	3	2	46	.200	.254	.309	.186	3	.184
1994	Iowa	AmA	534	160	22	2	15	24	21	10	384	.300	.330	.433	.257	64	.271
1995	Chicago Cubs	NL	152	43	4	6	4	14	7	3	112	.283	.343	.467	.269	21	.279
1996	Chicago Cubs	NL	166	36	4	0	3	12	6	3	133	.217	.270	.295	.188	10	.193
1997	*Chicago Cubs*	*NL*	*179*	*51*	*9*	*3*	*4*	*14*	*17*	*6*	*134*	*.285*	*.337*	*.436*	*.274*	*26*	

Bullett's major problem is that he hasn't given up the idea that he can be a major league regular. Sure, finding a fifth out-fielder who thumps his chest and says, "Fifth outfielder, and proud of it!" is pretty unlikely, but you have wonder if Scott Bullett actually notices what happens when he plays.

MIKE CARTER   **OF**   **1969**   **Age 28**

Year	Team	Lge	AB	H	DB	TP	HR	BB	SB	CS	OUT	BA	OBA	SA	EQA	EQR	Peak
1993	El Paso	Texas	73	23	1	1	2	4	4	2	52	.315	.351	.438	.266	9	.288
1993	New Orleans	AmA	374	102	15	4	4	21	19	8	280	.273	.311	.366	.233	37	.250
1994	Iowa	AmA	424	119	20	2	7	17	13	9	314	.281	.308	.387	.233	41	.247
1995	Iowa	AmA	429	138	13	2	9	20	13	10	301	.322	.352	.424	.260	52	.271
1996	Iowa	AmA	390	100	11	1	2	15	4	4	294	.256	.284	.305	.195	25	.200

After winning the American Association batting title in '95, you would think he might have been able to turn that into a Milt Thompson-type job somewhere. His career in the Cubs organization is probably over, because the man he was traded for (Bob Scanlan) is a distant memory to most people already, and Carter won't ever win a regular job.

PAT CLINE   **C**   **1975**   **Age 22**

Year	Team	Lge	AB	H	DB	TP	HR	BB	SB	CS	OUT	BA	OBA	SA	EQA	EQR	Peak
1995	Rockford	Midw	411	105	12	0	13	47	3	1	307	.255	.332	.380	.240	43	.273
1996	Daytona	Flor	443	113	14	1	17	48	5	1	331	.255	.328	.406	.246	50	.277

The catching prospect, as in the only one the Cubs have. Power, patience, the trite observation that he's "fast for a catch-er," the only gap is some concern that he needs to work on his footwork and release behind the plate to control the running game better.

BRIAN DORSETT   **C**   **1961**   **Age 36**

Year	Team	Lge	AB	H	DB	TP	HR	BB	SB	CS	OUT	BA	OBA	SA	EQA	EQR	Peak
1993	Indianapolis	AmA	281	83	18	0	18	29	2	0	198	.295	.361	.552	.296	47	.281
1993	Cincinnati	NL	64	17	3	0	2	4	0	0	47	.266	.309	.406	.238	7	.227
1994	Cincinnati	NL	219	55	5	0	6	24	0	0	164	.251	.325	.356	.229	21	.217
1995	Indianapolis	AmA	317	83	17	1	16	28	1	1	235	.262	.322	.473	.260	41	.247

Dorsett has come a long way from his early days in the A's organization when he was supposed to be John Orton. Instead, he wound up being Crash Davis, traveling from organization to organization, poking taters and being that third or fourth catcher in an organization. He's basically done, but considering some people left him for dead ten years ago he's had a nice little career.

RICKY FREEMAN   **1B**   **1972**   **Age 25**

Year	Team	Lge	AB	H	DB	TP	HR	BB	SB	CS	OUT	BA	OBA	SA	EQA	EQR	Peak
1995	Rockford	Midw	489	125	21	2	11	49	3	2	366	.256	.323	.374	.234	49	.255
1996	Daytona	Flor	483	132	19	2	15	33	6	4	355	.273	.320	.414	.245	53	.263

Too old to really be a prospect, Freeman is right out of the same mold as Brant Brown: the tools-oriented first baseman who doesn't actually have the one you want at first base: power.

DOUG GLANVILLE   **CF**   **1971**   **Age 26**

Year	Team	Lge	AB	H	DB	TP	HR	BB	SB	CS	OUT	BA	OBA	SA	EQA	EQR	Peak
1993	Daytona	Flor	243	62	6	0	3	24	9	6	187	.255	.322	.317	.217	21	.240
1993	Orlando	South	300	77	10	2	9	12	10	4	227	.257	.285	.393	.229	28	.252
1994	Orlando	South	491	119	15	1	6	27	15	9	381	.242	.282	.314	.200	34	.217
1995	Iowa	AmA	425	113	14	2	4	21	13	7	319	.266	.300	.336	.216	35	.232
1996	Iowa	AmA	381	115	21	2	3	17	14	8	274	.302	.332	.391	.246	41	.260
1996	Chicago Cubs	NL	84	20	5	1	1	4	2	0	64	.238	.273	.357	.214	7	.229
1997	*Chicago Cubs*	*NL*	*177*	*47*	*6*	*3*	*2*	*6*	*23*	*9*	*139*	*.266*	*.290*	*.367*	*.241*	*20*	

Glanville is a former first-round pick with great wheels, a good arm, good build and who also has a degree in engineering. Listen up, ladies: a young, athletic engineer. He's also a crummy baseball player. Although he's a fine defensive player who can poke the occasional wicked single against lefties, the Cubs were comparing him before last season to Kenny Lofton. Whatever they were drinking when they thought that one up, I'll take two.

LEO GOMEZ   **3B**   **1967**   **Age 30**

Year	Team	Lge	AB	H	DB	TP	HR	BB	SB	CS	OUT	BA	OBA	SA	EQA	EQR	Peak
1993	Baltimore	AL	245	50	7	0	11	34	0	1	196	.204	.301	.367	.219	22	.227
1994	Baltimore	AL	285	77	16	0	16	41	0	0	208	.270	.362	.495	.280	43	.287
1995	Baltimore	AL	128	31	4	0	5	18	0	1	98	.242	.336	.391	.240	14	.242
1996	Chicago Cubs	NL	370	90	15	0	18	57	1	4	284	.243	.344	.430	.254	46	.252
1997	*Chicago Cubs*	*NL*	*365*	*89*	*15*	*1*	*19*	*51*	*3*	*6*	*282*	*.244*	*.337*	*.447*	*.264*	*51*	

Last season, Leo Gomez showed both why you want to have him around, and why he can irritate the bejeezuz out of you once you've got him. He's very streaky at the plate. He'll have extended periods of uselessness that a team like the Cubs, scrapping for every run they can get, gets frustrated with easily. On the other hand, he was basically as effective as Steve Buechele had been in years past, and was a lot more available. On an organizational level, he does a nice job keeping a spot warm for Kevin Orie, and on a personal level it was nice to see him get over the ridiculous way he was handled by Clueless Phil Regan in Baltimore. Expected to head to Japan.

LUIS GONZALEZ   **LF**   **1968**   **Age 29**

Year	Team	Lge	AB	H	DB	TP	HR	BB	SB	CS	OUT	BA	OBA	SA	EQA	EQR	Peak
1993	Houston	NL	556	173	33	1	18	55	17	8	391	.311	.373	.471	.282	82	.297
1994	Houston	NL	402	114	29	3	9	55	14	11	299	.284	.370	.438	.268	55	.278
1995	Chicago Cubs	NL	269	80	18	3	8	42	4	4	193	.297	.392	.476	.286	42	.293
1995	Houston	NL	216	61	9	4	7	21	1	3	158	.282	.346	.458	.263	28	.269
1996	Chicago Cubs	NL	494	137	29	4	15	66	7	5	362	.277	.363	.443	.268	67	.270
1997	*Chicago Cubs*	*NL*	*496*	*140*	*44*	*6*	*9*	*74*	*10*	*6*	*362*	*.282*	*.375*	*.450*	*.285*	*79*	

The problem, or more precisely, the replacement-level problem. Luis Gonzalez is a fine little player, and one who can help a major league team. That's assuming that team has some power hitters at first or third, isn't carrying an automatic out at shortstop and has some great offensive players. The Cubs aren't that team. Re-signing Gonzalez for '96 was a mistake, because the Cubs are stuck with so many average players already, that carrying another one only makes the offensive problems worse. Gonzo is an exceptional defensive left fielder, and probably better off platooning for the rest of his career; he could easily put in another decade filling in a role like Jim Eisenreich has for Philadelphia. It just shouldn't be with a team as desperately in need of offensive help as the Cubs. Returned to Houston; good chance at a starting spot.

MARK GRACE   **1B**   **1964**   **Age 33**

Year	Team	Lge	AB	H	DB	TP	HR	BB	SB	CS	OUT	BA	OBA	SA	EQA	EQR	Peak
1993	Chicago Cubs	NL	611	201	37	2	16	80	7	3	413	.329	.407	.475	.296	99	.294
1994	Chicago Cubs	NL	417	131	23	3	7	54	0	1	287	.314	.393	.434	.280	59	.274
1995	Chicago Cubs	NL	567	190	46	3	18	72	5	2	379	.335	.410	.522	.308	100	.297
1996	Chicago Cubs	NL	563	189	31	2	11	68	2	3	377	.336	.407	.456	.291	86	.277
1997	*Chicago Cubs*	*NL*	*553*	*168*	*39*	*2*	*9*	*77*	*4*	*2*	*387*	*.304*	*.389*	*.430*	*.288*	*86*	

So now the Cubs give Grace the multi-year contract he's been kvetching for all these years, now that it's a very bad move. As has been said before, Grace is probably as good as a first baseman can get without hitting for power, but like Gonzalez he's a luxury that only a team that has genuine power can afford. He's not your typical Cub in that he consistently hits for better power on the road. Grace seems to have gotten a lot less aggressive throwing to second or third ahead of baserunners.

TODD HANEY   **2B**   **1966**   **Age 31**

Year	Team	Lge	AB	H	DB	TP	HR	BB	SB	CS	OUT	BA	OBA	SA	EQA	EQR	Peak
1993	Ottawa	Inter	515	143	27	1	4	39	8	5	377	.278	.329	.357	.233	49	.238
1994	Iowa	AmA	309	88	18	1	4	30	7	4	225	.285	.348	.388	.250	35	.252
1995	Iowa	AmA	335	105	19	2	4	32	2	2	232	.313	.373	.418	.268	43	.266
1995	Chicago Cubs	NL	76	32	5	0	3	8	0	0	44	.421	.476	.605	.358	17	.356
1996	Iowa	AmA	246	60	8	0	3	21	3	1	187	.244	.303	.313	.208	18	.203
1996	Chicago Cubs	NL	82	11	0	0	0	8	1	0	71	.134	.211	.134	-.084	-1	-.081
1997	*Chicago Cubs*	*NL*	*152*	*40*	*7*	*0*	*3*	*10*	*5*	*1*	*113*	*.263*	*.309*	*.368*	*.242*	*16*	

Your basic replacement-level second baseman. When it's somebody like Jody Reed, he does everything just a wee bit better than a guy like Todd Haney. Haney isn't a good defensive player, the sort of handicap that keeps him in AAA for years on end.

JOSE HERNANDEZ   **IF**   **1970**   **Age 27**

Year	Team	Lge	AB	H	DB	TP	HR	BB	SB	CS	OUT	BA	OBA	SA	EQA	EQR	Peak
1993	Canton	East	153	30	2	0	3	9	5	1	124	.196	.241	.268	.166	7	.182
1993	Orlando	South	270	79	7	1	8	19	5	2	193	.293	.339	.415	.255	32	.277
1994	Chicago Cubs	NL	134	34	3	3	1	10	2	2	102	.254	.306	.343	.217	11	.231
1995	Chicago Cubs	NL	247	62	10	3	14	16	1	0	185	.251	.297	.486	.255	30	.268
1996	Chicago Cubs	NL	335	82	13	1	10	28	3	0	253	.245	.303	.379	.229	32	.239
1997	*Chicago Cubs*	*NL*	*276*	*75*	*14*	*1*	*11*	*14*	*5*	*1*	*202*	*.272*	*.307*	*.449*	*.262*	*36*	

The new Luis Aguayo, with a better glove. Last year was his big chance to show he was capable of taking the everyday job at short, and he didn't win the job. He had problems at short, playing on his heels. You might think his power is a Wrigley illusion, but on his career, he's poked 14 of his 24 homers on the road. Like Aguayo before him, Hernandez is a superb spare part, but not cut out for regular playing time.

VEE HIGHTOWER   **OF**   **1972**   **Age 25**

Year	Team	Lge	AB	H	DB	TP	HR	BB	SB	CS	OUT	BA	OBA	SA	EQA	EQR	Peak
1994	Peoria	Midw	153	32	5	2	1	23	3	1	122	.209	.312	.288	.203	11	.225
1995	Rockford	Midw	252	64	6	0	7	31	9	3	191	.254	.336	.361	.239	27	.260
1996	Daytona	Flor	302	89	8	2	8	46	12	4	217	.295	.388	.414	.275	43	.294
1996	Orlando	South	76	5	0	0	0	3	2	0	71	.066	.101	.066	-.174	-4	-.173
1997	*Chicago Cubs*	*NL*	*435*	*121*	*21*	*6*	*10*	*78*	*25*	*10*	*324*	*.278*	*.388*	*.423*	*.286*	*71*	

A tall switch-hitter, Hightower has been used as a leadoff hitter. He's old to be a great prospect, and behind the outfield prospects the Cubs are excited about at higher levels. But with McRae saying he'd prefer to not lead off and no good leadoff prospect in the organization ahead of him (although Jasco is behind him), we may be hearing more about him soon.

TYLER HOUSTON   **C/UT**   **1971**   **Age 26**

Year	Team	Lge	AB	H	DB	TP	HR	BB	SB	CS	OUT	BA	OBA	SA	EQA	EQR	Peak
1993	Greenville	South	264	67	8	1	5	12	3	2	198	.254	.286	.348	.212	21	.235
1994	Richmond	Inter	317	75	14	1	4	16	2	2	244	.237	.273	.325	.197	21	.213
1995	Richmond	Inter	359	94	8	2	13	21	3	3	268	.262	.303	.404	.234	36	.251
1996	Chicago Cubs	NL	118	41	4	0	3	9	2	2	79	.347	.394	.458	.285	17	.300
1997	*Chicago Cubs*	*NL*	*358*	*93*	*10*	*0*	*17*	*11*	*0*	*0*	*265*	*.260*	*.282*	*.430*	*.243*	*38*	

I have no idea what he's doing differently. The ex-first rounder has gone from a total zero as a hitter to somebody who was an exceptional spare part this year. There's no reason to expect it to continue. Behind the plate, he has a lot in common with Mark Salas.

MIKE HUBBARD   **C**   **1971**   **Age 26**

Year	Team	Lge	AB	H	DB	TP	HR	BB	SB	CS	OUT	BA	OBA	SA	EQA	EQR	Peak
1993	Daytona	Flor	247	64	9	1	2	16	5	2	185	.259	.304	.328	.215	20	.236
1994	Orlando	South	366	98	8	2	11	30	4	3	271	.268	.323	.391	.239	38	.261
1996	Iowa	AmA	237	69	6	0	8	13	2	0	168	.291	.328	.418	.252	27	.266
1997	*Chicago Cubs*	*NL*	*340*	*94*	*11*	*1*	*15*	*17*	*0*	*0*	*246*	*.276*	*.311*	*.447*	*.261*	*43*	

Hubbard isn't an outstanding prospect, but the Cubs could do a lot worse than just letting Servais go to play a Houston-Hubbard platoon until Pat Cline arrives. As a hitter, Hubbard is about as dangerous as ex-Cub suspect Matt Walbeck, but he's got a good throwing arm so he may be Houston's defensive replacement.

TROY HUGHES   **OF**   **1971**   **Age 26**

Year	Team	Lge	AB	H	DB	TP	HR	BB	SB	CS	OUT	BA	OBA	SA	EQA	EQR	Peak
1993	Greenville	South	389	96	14	2	13	41	4	2	295	.247	.319	.393	.238	41	.262
1994	Richmond	Inter	234	49	8	1	1	28	4	1	186	.209	.294	.265	.186	14	.202
1995	Greenville	South	204	49	3	1	6	16	2	3	158	.240	.295	.353	.214	17	.228
1996	Orlando	South	464	125	18	1	18	42	2	2	341	.269	.330	.429	.252	54	.266
1997	*Chicago Cubs*	*NL*	*357*	*94*	*22*	*2*	*16*	*34*	*4*	*5*	*268*	*.263*	*.327*	*.471*	*.269*	*50*	

Hughes is a refugee from an Atlanta organization that can afford to give up on mediocre outfielders. A minor league veteran who's aging very well, at best he can get called up as a pinch-hitter if injuries wipe out a few starting outfielders.

ELINTON JASCO   **2B**   **1975**   **Age 22**

Year	Team	Lge	AB	H	DB	TP	HR	BB	SB	CS	OUT	BA	OBA	SA	EQA	EQR	Peak
1996	Rockford	Midw	483	128	9	4	2	47	22	7	362	.265	.330	.313	.225	44	.252
1997	*Chicago Cubs*	*NL*	*523*	*145*	*22*	*11*	*2*	*37*	*49*	*13*	*391*	*.277*	*.325*	*.373*	*.257*	*65*	

A second baseman from San Pedro de Macoris? I suspect that all the kids wanted to play with him. Jasco has some patience, but he's basically a speed merchant with no power. He'll have to hit to progress quickly, and there's probably no rush as long as the Cubs keep the Cult of Sandberg alive and well.

ROBIN JENNINGS   **OF**   **1972**   **Age 25**

Year	Team	Lge	AB	H	DB	TP	HR	BB	SB	CS	OUT	BA	OBA	SA	EQA	EQR	Peak
1993	Peoria	Midw	491	133	20	2	4	36	5	4	362	.271	.321	.344	.225	43	.252
1994	Daytona	Flor	494	134	17	2	12	42	2	5	365	.271	.328	.387	.238	51	.263
1995	Orlando	South	505	145	21	4	17	43	6	7	367	.287	.343	.446	.260	63	.283
1996	Iowa	AmA	342	99	14	4	17	35	2	0	243	.289	.355	.503	.282	51	.303
1996	Chicago Cubs	NL	59	14	4	0	0	3	1	0	45	.237	.274	.305	.195	4	.208
1997	*Chicago Cubs*	*NL*	*586*	*165*	*29*	*2*	*30*	*49*	*6*	*2*	*423*	*.282*	*.337*	*.491*	*.282*	*90*	

After the gains Jennings made in '95, '96 was a disappointment of sorts. Jennings suffered several nagging injuries, and rather than play him when Timmons was sent down, or when Sosa was injured, the Cubs avoided making a choice between their various outfield prospects. At this point, Jennings is the one who can hit and play center, whereas the others all have their problems. What's the point of having these guys have minor league careers if you don't use them to decide which ones are good and which ones are Doug Glanville? Jennings has an excellent throwing arm, but like Luis Gonzalez before him he may not be enough of a hitter to give the offense the help it needs. If he comes anywhere close to this projection, he'll be a fixture.

TERRY JOSEPH   **OF**   **1974**   **Age 23**

Year	Team	Lge	AB	H	DB	TP	HR	BB	SB	CS	OUT	BA	OBA	SA	EQA	EQR	Peak
1995	Williamsport	NY-P	271	68	7	4	2	23	6	3	206	.251	.310	.328	.216	22	.242
1996	Rockford	Midw	469	129	13	2	10	53	14	7	347	.275	.349	.375	.247	53	.272
1997	*Chicago Cubs*	*NL*	*500*	*134*	*19*	*7*	*10*	*63*	*23*	*12*	*378*	*.268*	*.350*	*.394*	*.262*	*66*	

His raw stats: 98 runs, 94 RBI, 69 walks and 25 HBPs! That's an offensive player. He's a tiny (5' 9") right-handed hitter, and given his age he needs to pushed hard up the chain. But with that kind of control of the strike zone, Joseph can be an offensive catalyst.

BROOKS KIESCHNICK   **LF/1B**   **1972**   **Age 25**

Year	Team	Lge	AB	H	DB	TP	HR	BB	SB	CS	OUT	BA	OBA	SA	EQA	EQR	Peak
1993	Orlando	South	94	31	3	0	3	6	1	1	64	.330	.370	.457	.277	13	.307
1994	Orlando	South	479	128	16	2	14	35	2	2	353	.267	.317	.397	.238	49	.263
1995	Iowa	AmA	521	156	20	1	25	62	2	2	367	.299	.374	.486	.284	79	.309
1996	Iowa	AmA	453	118	15	1	17	41	0	1	336	.260	.322	.411	.243	49	.261
1997	*Chicago Cubs*	*NL*	*493*	*149*	*20*	*1*	*27*	*53*	*0*	*0*	*344*	*.302*	*.370*	*.511*	*.300*	*85*	

The major platoon splits he had in '95 didn't continue; rather than get much better against left-handers, he got worse against right-handers. There's been some speculation that he was disappointed not to get a better shot at a job in '96, and let that affect his play at Iowa. He's a Klesko clone with the glove, save for an extremely good throwing arm left over from the pitching career the Cubs had him give up. This is a make or break season for Kieschnick.

DAVE MAGADAN   **3B/1B**   **1963**   **Age 34**

Year	Team	Lge	AB	H	DB	TP	HR	BB	SB	CS	OUT	BA	OBA	SA	EQA	EQR	Peak
1993	Florida	NL	235	68	7	0	6	47	0	1	168	.289	.408	.396	.274	33	.269
1993	Seattle	AL	232	64	8	0	3	38	2	0	168	.276	.378	.349	.252	27	.247
1994	Florida	NL	213	57	3	0	2	41	0	0	156	.268	.386	.310	.243	23	.233
1995	Houston	NL	370	126	16	0	6	78	2	1	245	.341	.455	.432	.307	64	.292
1996	Chicago Cubs	NL	173	45	6	0	4	31	0	2	130	.260	.373	.364	.248	20	.236
1997	*Chicago Cubs*	*NL*	*115*	*27*	*4*	*0*	*1*	*22*	*0*	*0*	*88*	*.235*	*.358*	*.296*	*.235*	*12*	

He's crossed the line to near uselessness as anything other than a pinch-hitter. When he puts on a glove, hide the children. On offense because he has so little power and is slower than most catchers, you have to ask yourself if he's really able to help a team more than Scott Bullett.

JASON MAXWELL   **SS**   **1972**   **Age 25**

Year	Team	Lge	AB	H	DB	TP	HR	BB	SB	CS	OUT	BA	OBA	SA	EQA	EQR	Peak
1994	Daytona	Flor	384	89	11	0	13	50	5	4	299	.232	.320	.362	.228	37	.251
1995	Daytona	Flor	404	98	6	1	11	54	7	4	310	.243	.332	.344	.229	39	.249
1996	Orlando	South	447	117	14	1	9	48	12	2	332	.262	.333	.358	.238	46	.255
1997	*Chicago Cubs*	*NL*	*432*	*118*	*22*	*1*	*10*	*36*	*30*	*4*	*318*	*.273*	*.329*	*.398*	*.265*	*57*	

He's not the worst shortstop prospect in the world; he isn't the best either. He does something of everything, was an FSL All-Star in '95, can field short and was given an AFL slot last fall. With Sanchez in trouble and Hernandez not looking reliable, Maxwell could win the shortstop job with the big league club if the Cubs don't make a move over the winter.

BRIAN McRAE   **CF**   **1968**   **Age 29**

Year	Team	Lge	AB	H	DB	TP	HR	BB	SB	CS	OUT	BA	OBA	SA	EQA	EQR	Peak
1993	Kansas City	AL	631	181	28	9	15	41	22	10	460	.287	.330	.431	.256	76	.270
1994	Kansas City	AL	434	115	23	5	4	54	24	7	326	.265	.346	.369	.248	50	.259
1995	Chicago Cubs	NL	590	174	38	6	13	54	22	7	423	.295	.354	.446	.270	80	.277
1996	Chicago Cubs	NL	638	180	31	4	18	80	30	8	466	.282	.362	.428	.269	88	.272
1997	*Chicago Cubs*	*NL*	*593*	*161*	*38*	*10*	*13*	*68*	*40*	*13*	*445*	*.272*	*.346*	*.435*	*.275*	*88*	

McRae set a career high in walks in '96, and has turned out to be a much better addition to the Cubs than anyone might have expected. Unfortunately, like so many of the Cubs' players, he's good but not great at what he does. He's grown into a much better player than he was with the Royals, but is it enough to justify the multiyear contract?

BOBBY MORRIS   **2B/1B**   **1973**   **Age 24**

Year	Team	Lge	AB	H	DB	TP	HR	BB	SB	CS	OUT	BA	OBA	SA	EQA	EQR	Peak
1994	Peoria	Midw	375	117	19	1	7	44	4	3	261	.312	.384	.424	.274	51	.306
1995	Daytona	Flor	355	100	14	1	3	33	12	4	259	.282	.343	.352	.241	37	.265
1996	Orlando	South	481	122	23	2	8	55	9	7	366	.254	.330	.360	.232	48	.252
1997	*Chicago Cubs*	*NL*	*505*	*137*	*33*	*2*	*11*	*51*	*22*	*10*	*378*	*.271*	*.338*	*.410*	*.263*	*67*	

His awful glove at second has kept him from being a solid prospect. When he was shifted to first base during this past season, his chance of being a major league regular officially died.

KEVIN ORIE   **3B**   **1973**   **Age 24**

Year	Team	Lge	AB	H	DB	TP	HR	BB	SB	CS	OUT	BA	OBA	SA	EQA	EQR	Peak
1993	Peoria	Midw	246	60	8	1	6	16	2	2	188	.244	.290	.358	.215	20	.243
1995	Daytona	Flor	420	94	11	1	10	36	3	2	328	.224	.285	.326	.202	30	.222
1996	Orlando	South	308	96	13	0	10	41	1	0	212	.312	.393	.451	.285	46	.310
1996	Iowa	AmA	49	10	0	0	2	7	0	0	39	.204	.304	.327	.209	4	.229
1997	*Chicago Cubs*	*NL*	*566*	*156*	*27*	*1*	*16*	*54*	*0*	*1*	*411*	*.276*	*.339*	*.412*	*.261*	*72*	

Injuries to each wrist have hampered his progress so far, but his march to be "The Man Who Replaced Santo" is up and running. He was being talked about as a September callup this season when he separated his shoulder, shutting him down a month early. Orie was named the best hitting prospect in the Southern League this year. He had a big AFL campaign and will probably win the regular job for the Cubs this spring. Since he's an ex-shortstop with a great arm, the feeling is that he'll be a good defensive player.

CHRIS PETERSEN   **SS**   **1971**   **Age 26**

Year	Team	Lge	AB	H	DB	TP	HR	BB	SB	CS	OUT	BA	OBA	SA	EQA	EQR	Peak
1993	Daytona	Flor	481	90	6	0	1	50	9	4	395	.187	.264	.206	.142	15	.156
1994	Orlando	South	385	79	10	1	2	37	5	5	311	.205	.275	.252	.167	18	.183
1995	Orlando	South	393	81	7	2	5	43	4	2	314	.206	.284	.272	.182	22	.195
1996	Orlando	South	157	44	3	3	2	15	2	2	115	.280	.343	.376	.242	17	.257
1996	Iowa	AmA	198	48	6	2	2	14	1	1	151	.242	.292	.323	.205	14	.216

Was he snorting his Wheaties to get out of Orlando this year? Petersen's best weapon is the bunt, and he's lost what little speed he had with age. Non-prospect.

REY SANCHEZ   **SS**   **1968**   **Age 29**

Year	Team	Lge	AB	H	DB	TP	HR	BB	SB	CS	OUT	BA	OBA	SA	EQA	EQR	Peak
1993	Chicago Cubs	NL	348	98	8	2	1	20	1	1	251	.282	.321	.325	.219	28	.231
1994	Chicago Cubs	NL	298	89	10	1	1	24	2	4	213	.299	.351	.349	.237	29	.247
1995	Chicago Cubs	NL	433	122	21	2	3	19	5	3	314	.282	.312	.360	.228	39	.233
1996	Chicago Cubs	NL	292	62	6	0	2	25	6	1	231	.212	.274	.253	.174	15	.175
1997	*Chicago Cubs*	*NL*	*283*	*69*	*16*	*1*	*2*	*18*	*10*	*2*	*216*	*.244*	*.289*	*.329*	*.222*	*25*	

Perspective: Rey Sanchez puts up a .272 OBP last season, and people are calling for his head on a pointed stick. Over on the south side, Ozzie Guillen puts up a .273 OBP, and it's being called another sturdy campaign from a good player. Sanchez is an exceptional defensive player, but unless his manager really likes him he won't play. Rey Ordonez should be following Sanchez' career closely, since it's what awaits him even if he learns to hit.

RYNE SANDBERG   **2B**   **1960**   **Age 37**

Year	Team	Lge	AB	H	DB	TP	HR	BB	SB	CS	OUT	BA	OBA	SA	EQA	EQR	Peak
1993	Chicago Cubs	NL	465	145	14	0	11	44	8	2	322	.312	.371	.413	.268	60	.255
1994	Chicago Cubs	NL	228	58	9	4	6	26	2	3	173	.254	.331	.408	.244	25	.231
1996	Chicago Cubs	NL	563	140	26	4	25	60	10	7	430	.249	.321	.442	.251	68	.238
1997	*Chicago Cubs*	*NL*	*345*	*84*	*17*	*2*	*13*	*43*	*11*	*6*	*267*	*.243*	*.327*	*.417*	*.257*	*45*	

Sandberg was much better than anyone would have expected after a year and a half off. That said, I think he'll crash and burn next year. People see the 25 homers and figure he's back, but he put up a .444 slugging percentage in a league where, counting pitchers, the slugging percentage was .408. That isn't outstanding. The real problem was that he was extremely tentative at the plate all season. While it's hard to be sure with the year off, Sandberg seemed to be that veteran player whose reflexes are shot and who works walks to compensate for slow wrists and age. It's a hunch, but if I'm the Cubs, I don't give Sandberg the $7.5 million, two-year contract he's asking for. [Ed. Note: Ryno is signed for 1997 only.]

SCOTT SERVAIS   **C**   **1967**   **Age 30**

Year	Team	Lge	AB	H	DB	TP	HR	BB	SB	CS	OUT	BA	OBA	SA	EQA	EQR	Peak
1993	Houston	NL	263	67	8	0	12	26	0	0	196	.255	.322	.422	.247	30	.256
1994	Houston	NL	252	51	12	1	10	14	0	0	201	.202	.244	.377	.201	18	.206
1995	Houston	NL	92	23	8	0	2	10	0	1	70	.250	.324	.402	.238	10	.238
1995	Chicago Cubs	NL	179	53	9	0	13	25	2	1	127	.296	.382	.564	.304	32	.307
1996	Chicago Cubs	NL	452	121	13	0	13	35	0	2	333	.268	.320	.383	.235	44	.234
1997	*Chicago Cubs*	*NL*	*455*	*122*	*17*	*1*	*19*	*34*	*0*	*5*	*338*	*.268*	*.319*	*.435*	*.256*	*56*	

An example of the problem. Yes, getting Servais and Gonzalez for Wilkins was a steal. The problem is, where does it get you? Servais has problems containing the running game and people who slugged under .400 in the NL are pretty bad.

SAMMY SOSA   **RF**   **1969**   **Age 28**

Year	Team	Lge	AB	H	DB	TP	HR	BB	SB	CS	OUT	BA	OBA	SA	EQA	EQR	Peak
1993	Chicago Cubs	NL	605	160	22	4	34	47	31	9	454	.264	.317	.483	.266	83	.285
1994	Chicago Cubs	NL	437	139	17	4	28	31	21	12	310	.318	.363	.568	.298	75	.314
1995	Chicago Cubs	NL	574	159	15	3	37	65	28	6	421	.277	.351	.507	.284	90	.295
1996	Chicago Cubs	NL	506	142	19	2	40	40	15	5	369	.281	.333	.563	.288	82	.295
1997	*Chicago Cubs*	*NL*	*606*	*177*	*24*	*5*	*45*	*61*	*28*	*9*	*438*	*.292*	*.357*	*.571*	*.309*	*116*	

After drawing (as promised) a career-high number of walks in '95, Sosa seemed to get back to some of his old bad habits at the plate in '96. He's still a very good, if erratic, outfielder. Last season saw people start talking about him as a superstar, which is unfortunate, because that's the point at which he's going to start disappointing people with unreasonable expectations. Sosa is a great second banana on a team that should have a better hitter than him.

OZZIE TIMMONS OF 1971 Age 26

Year	Team	Lge	AB	H	DB	TP	HR	BB	SB	CS	OUT	BA	OBA	SA	EQA	EQR	Peak
1993	Orlando	South	375	104	15	1	17	56	4	6	277	.277	.371	.459	.272	54	.300
1994	Iowa	AmA	445	117	22	1	23	38	0	2	330	.263	.321	.472	.258	56	.281
1995	Chicago Cubs	NL	173	46	10	1	8	16	2	0	127	.266	.328	.474	.265	23	.286
1996	Iowa	AmA	220	56	5	0	16	30	1	1	165	.255	.344	.495	.272	32	.288
1996	Chicago Cubs	NL	142	29	4	0	7	16	1	0	113	.204	.285	.380	.220	13	.231
1997	*Chicago Cubs*	*NL*	*356*	*97*	*15*	*2*	*30*	*35*	*0*	*0*	*259*	*.272*	*.338*	*.579*	*.301*	*64*	

This projection is on drugs. It's there for you to see, but it's about as reliable as Ronald Reagan's assessment of the weather. Timmons is a bad defensive player, and may make an excellent platoon mate for Brooks Kieschnick, but the chances that he could explode for this kind of season are remote. It's hard not to like him, because he's a good guy who works as an inner-city substitute teacher out of a belief in the need to set an example. Timmons still has to adapt to the part-time role of platoon outfielder. How many right-handed halves of platoons are reliably excellent at their jobs? Earl Weaver was always able to get fine seasons from guys like Gary Roenicke, and yet most right-handed platoon mates seem to have career patterns like "ace" pinch-hitters, where they alternately feast or famine from year to year. Just another reason to think Earl knows something that most people don't.

PEDRO VALDES OF 1973 Age 24

Year	Team	Lge	AB	H	DB	TP	HR	BB	SB	CS	OUT	BA	OBA	SA	EQA	EQR	Peak
1993	Daytona	Flor	231	60	7	1	8	8	2	2	173	.260	.285	.403	.227	21	.259
1994	Orlando	South	372	97	11	2	2	22	2	3	278	.261	.302	.317	.207	27	.231
1995	Orlando	South	439	128	22	2	8	36	2	3	314	.292	.345	.405	.252	50	.278
1996	Iowa	AmA	409	121	14	0	16	35	2	0	288	.296	.351	.447	.268	53	.291
1997	*Chicago Cubs*	*NL*	*645*	*195*	*29*	*2*	*17*	*26*	*5*	*6*	*456*	*.302*	*.329*	*.433*	*.264*	*82*	

Corner outfielder without a lot of power who gets touted because his swing is pretty... hmm…have we forgotten Derrick May that quickly? Iowa is a good home run park, and he wasn't overwhelming. Your basic tool-drool recipient. He'll have to improve every aspect of his game to be able to cut it offensively in right or left.

SCOTT VIEIRA C/1B 1974 Age 23

Year	Team	Lge	AB	H	DB	TP	HR	BB	SB	CS	OUT	BA	OBA	SA	EQA	EQR	Peak
1995	Williamsport	NY-P	216	51	3	0	5	18	1	0	165	.236	.295	.319	.205	16	.231
1996	Rockford	Midw	465	135	19	1	9	66	5	4	334	.290	.379	.394	.262	59	.290
1997	*Chicago Cubs*	*NL*	*509*	*147*	*26*	*1*	*12*	*68*	*8*	*6*	*368*	*.289*	*.373*	*.415*	*.275*	*73*	

He's not somebody who gets touted much, but this catcher from the University of Tennessee has been an outstanding hitter early on. He may get to skip Daytona, although the Cubs are usually very slow in making their promotions and rarely have a player skip a level.

TERRY ADAMS RRP 1973 Age 24

YR	TEAM	Lge	IP	H	ER	HR	BB	K	ERA	W	L	H/9	HR/9	BB/9	K/9	KW
1993	Daytona	Flor	61.7	86	48	4	56	27	7.01	2	5	12.55	.58	8.17	3.94	-.73
1994	Daytona	Flor	75.7	104	52	8	60	50	6.19	2	6	12.37	.95	7.14	5.95	.20
1995	Orlando	South	35.0	27	8	3	21	20	2.06	3	1	6.94	.77	5.40	5.14	.36
1996	Chicago Cubs	NL	99.0	88	30	6	57	68	2.73	8	3	8.00	.55	5.18	6.18	.77

He's got the big, wild heater and unlike many modern relievers, Adams can go several innings when he's on. He's already clamoring publicly for the closer's role. An organization can either say this is a nice, aggressive attitude, or label him an attitude problem because he should just accept whatever role he's given. Since Riggleman's style is usually low-key, it shouldn't be a problem.

DENNIS BAIR RSP 1975 Age 22

YR	TEAM	Lge	IP	H	ER	HR	BB	K	ERA	W	L	H/9	HR/9	BB/9	K/9	KW
1995	Williamsport	NY-P	34.3	42	13	1	5	18	3.41	2	2	11.01	.26	1.31	4.72	1.25
1995	Rockford	Midw	48.0	54	10	3	10	26	1.88	4	1	10.12	.56	1.88	4.88	1.16
1996	Daytona	Flor	157.0	195	84	12	63	92	4.82	7	10	11.18	.69	3.61	5.27	.86

Although Bair wasn't outstanding at Daytona, he's a good control pitcher with a dose of aggression (he hit 13 batters). Like any pitcher, if he stays healthy and can make the jump to AA, he'll become somebody to think about.

KENT BOTTENFIELD   RRP   1969   Age 28

YR	TEAM	Lge	IP	H	ER	HR	BB	K	ERA	W	L	H/9	HR/9	BB/9	K/9	KW
1993	Montreal	NL	81.7	96	47	12	43	32	5.18	3	6	10.58	1.32	4.74	3.53	-.01
1993	Colorado	NL	75.7	78	42	12	45	28	5.00	3	5	9.28	1.43	5.35	3.33	-.23
1994	Colo. Springs	PCL	29.0	31	13	5	14	14	4.03	1	2	9.62	1.55	4.34	4.34	.36
1994	Colorado	NL	24.3	26	12	1	12	14	4.44	1	2	9.62	.37	4.44	5.18	.62
1994	Phoenix	PCL	32.3	30	10	3	14	9	2.78	3	1	8.35	.84	3.90	2.51	-.14
1995	Toledo	Inter	126.7	171	84	17	75	58	5.97	4	10	12.15	1.21	5.33	4.12	.04
1996	Iowa	AmA	23.0	22	8	0	11	12	3.13	2	1	8.61	.00	4.30	4.70	.49
1996	Chicago Cubs	NL	60.0	61	21	3	24	29	3.15	4	3	9.15	.45	3.60	4.35	.55

That intriguing rarity—the pitcher the Expos let go early. Bottenfield was left for dead years ago, but throws his sinker and can reliably keep the ball in the infield. Like Rod Myers, he was used mostly in the middle innings when the Cubs were trailing. His role shouldn't be expanded, but he's a good addition to the bottom of a staff.

JIM BULLINGER   RBP   1966   Age 31

YR	TEAM	Lge	IP	H	ER	HR	BB	K	ERA	W	L	H/9	HR/9	BB/9	K/9	KW
1993	Iowa	AmA	70.7	65	24	3	52	68	3.06	5	3	8.28	.38	6.62	8.66	1.23
1993	Chicago Cubs	NL	16.3	18	8	1	11	10	4.41	1	1	9.92	.55	6.06	5.51	.32
1994	Chicago Cubs	NL	97.0	93	39	7	43	67	3.62	6	5	8.63	.65	3.99	6.22	1.07
1995	Chicago Cubs	NL	148.3	153	69	14	78	83	4.19	8	8	9.28	.85	4.73	5.04	.50
1996	Chicago Cubs	NL	129.0	145	87	14	80	79	6.07	4	10	10.12	.98	5.58	5.51	.44

Bullinger is an example of a team forgetting what made a player successful in the first place. When Bully was going good in '95, he was pitching on long rest out of the fifth slot of the rotation, and being handled carefully out of concern for a tender arm. It worked because he can't get his dandy curve to snap if he doesn't carry a light workload. The curve is also a problem because it can be intoxicating, both to Bullinger, as he overuses it, and to opposing batters, who deliriously send it onto Waveland Avenue when he starts losing control of it. He's only really suited for a job as a long reliever and spot starter, but Bullinger is convinced he should be a rotation regular, and has complained frequently and bitterly about being in the pen. Someone should tell him that winning games is considered important, even on the Cubs.

LARRY CASIAN   LRP   1966   Age 31

YR	TEAM	Lge	IP	H	ER	HR	BB	K	ERA	W	L	H/9	HR/9	BB/9	K/9	KW
1993	Minnesota	AL	55.3	59	18	1	17	32	2.93	4	2	9.60	.16	2.77	5.20	1.04
1994	Minnesota	AL	41.7	52	26	10	14	18	5.62	2	3	11.23	2.16	3.02	3.89	.54
1995	Chicago Cubs	NL	22.7	24	5	1	17	10	1.99	2	1	9.53	.40	6.75	3.97	-.36
1996	Iowa	AmA	45.0	41	12	9	17	27	2.40	4	1	8.20	1.80	3.40	5.40	.95
1996	Chicago Cubs	NL	23.0	16	4	2	12	13	1.57	3	0	6.26	.78	4.70	5.09	.52

Lefty relievers are like cats, just with twice as many lives. Casian isn't an outstanding pitcher, and his only gimmick is the occasional attempt to throw sidearm to lefties, which he keeps trying because he isn't consistently good at getting lefties out. It's enough for a major league career.

FRANK CASTILLO   RSP   1969   Age 28

YR	TEAM	Lge	IP	H	ER	HR	BB	K	ERA	W	L	H/9	HR/9	BB/9	K/9	KW
1993	Chicago Cubs	NL	138.7	162	75	20	55	81	4.87	6	9	10.51	1.30	3.57	5.26	.86
1994	Iowa	AmA	63.0	59	25	10	15	57	3.57	4	3	8.43	1.43	2.14	8.14	2.18
1994	Chicago Cubs	NL	22.7	26	12	3	7	18	4.76	1	2	10.32	1.19	2.78	7.15	1.69
1995	Chicago Cubs	NL	185.0	180	64	22	67	120	3.11	13	8	8.76	1.07	3.26	5.84	1.13
1996	Chicago Cubs	NL	181.0	209	96	26	62	121	4.77	8	12	10.39	1.29	3.08	6.02	1.23

Castillo was the Cubs' biggest disappointment, and his failure was probably the major reason for the firing of pitching coach Fergie Jenkins. Whereas Foster suffered a loss of velocity and Bullinger was fragile, Castillo had been so good in '95 that his fall from grace hit the Cubs harder than the others. He's a fun pitcher to watch when he's going well: a fast worker firing strikes with four pitches and finishing batters off with a circle change. He has a regular habit of improving in the second half.

MATT CONNOLLY   1969   Age 28

YR	TEAM	LGE	IP	H	ER	HR	BB	K	ERA	W	L	H/9	HR/9	BB/9	K/9	KW
1993	West Palm Bch	Flor	12.7	18	11	0	12	6	7.82	0	1	12.79	.00	8.53	4.26	-.71
1995	Daytona	Flor	49.7	48	13	1	14	54	2.36	4	2	8.70	.18	2.54	9.79	2.63
1995	Orlando	South	36.3	40	18	6	16	33	4.46	2	2	9.91	1.49	3.96	8.17	1.73
1996	Orlando	South	80.0	93	44	9	41	58	4.95	4	5	10.46	1.01	4.61	6.53	1.02

The continuing saga of this longshot continues. Connolly is a 6' 8" find from the independent leagues. He should surface in Chicago at some point this season, since he's outpitched most of the draft picks and prospects in the organization.

KEVIN FOSTER   RSP   1969   Age 28

YR	TEAM	Lge	IP	H	ER	HR	BB	K	ERA	W	L	H/9	HR/9	BB/9	K/9	KW
1993	Jacksonville	South	59.3	63	33	2	38	53	5.01	3	4	9.56	.30	5.76	8.04	1.24
1993	Scranton-WB	Inter	67.0	69	30	7	38	48	4.03	3	4	9.27	.94	5.10	6.45	.87
1994	Iowa	AmA	32.0	30	15	6	17	31	4.22	2	2	8.44	1.69	4.78	8.72	1.71
1994	Chicago Cubs	NL	79.3	74	28	7	43	71	3.18	6	3	8.39	.79	4.88	8.05	1.47
1995	Chicago Cubs	NL	166.0	148	77	31	79	130	4.17	9	9	8.02	1.68	4.28	7.05	1.28
1996	Iowa	AmA	109.3	118	54	21	62	73	4.45	5	7	9.71	1.73	5.10	6.01	.73
1996	Chicago Cubs	NL	87.0	97	54	15	43	46	5.59	3	7	10.03	1.55	4.45	4.76	.47

Foster opened the season in the rotation, but he'd lost velocity for some reason and that high fastball he routinely offers hitters was becoming a souvenir more regularly than usual. So the Cubs sent him down, he healed and he was back for the stretch.

GEREMIS GONZALEZ   RSP   1975   Age 22

YR	TEAM	Lge	IP	H	ER	HR	BB	K	ERA	W	L	H/9	HR/9	BB/9	K/9	KW
1994	Peoria	Midw	62.0	99	53	5	44	24	7.69	1	6	14.37	.73	6.39	3.48	-.44
1995	Rockford	Midw	55.3	84	49	5	38	24	7.97	1	5	13.66	.81	6.18	3.90	-.24
1995	Daytona	Flor	39.3	42	15	0	18	21	3.43	2	2	9.61	.00	4.12	4.81	.57
1996	Orlando	South	90.3	108	36	7	33	62	3.59	6	4	10.76	.70	3.29	6.18	1.24

Someone who just started drawing attention to himself this year, Gonzalez could easily wind up being a major surprise.

JASON HART   1972   Age 25

YR	TEAM	LGE	IP	H	ER	HR	BB	K	ERA	W	L	H/9	HR/9	BB/9	K/9	KW
1994	Peoria	Midw	33.3	36	17	5	10	21	4.59	2	2	9.72	1.35	2.70	5.67	1.21
1994	Daytona	Flor	34.0	33	11	2	9	30	2.91	3	1	8.74	.53	2.38	7.94	2.05
1995	Daytona	Flor	18.0	20	10	2	21	22	5.00	1	1	10.00	1.00	10.50	11.00	1.04
1995	Orlando	South	16.0	16	5	0	6	15	2.81	1	1	9.00	.00	3.38	8.44	1.97
1996	Orlando	South	67.7	69	27	11	33	57	3.59	4	4	9.18	1.46	4.39	7.58	1.43

Although he's a relatively unknown reliever with some talent, Hart is an extreme flyball pitcher, so Wrigley probably isn't the place where he'll have a future.

ROD MYERS   RRP   1969   Age 28

YR	TEAM	Lge	IP	H	ER	HR	BB	K	ERA	W	L	H/9	HR/9	BB/9	K/9	KW
1993	Rockford	Midw	76.0	83	23	4	25	38	2.72	5	3	9.83	.47	2.96	4.50	.76
1993	Memphis	South	60.0	80	45	8	42	31	6.75	2	5	12.00	1.20	6.30	4.65	-.02
1994	Memphis	South	63.7	55	21	4	40	42	2.97	5	2	7.77	.57	5.65	5.94	.57
1995	Omaha	AmA	46.3	52	23	4	25	33	4.47	2	3	10.10	.78	4.86	6.41	.92
1996	Chicago Cubs	NL	66.7	62	33	6	44	44	4.46	3	4	8.37	.81	5.94	5.94	.49

Maybe the Cubs thought they couldn't live without a pitcher named Myers. Snagged out of the Royals' organization in the Rule V draft, Rod is a fastball-slider type who mixes in the circle change for laughs. Although he was mostly used as a garbageman, finishing up blowouts or filling in for a shelled starter, Myers was reasonably effective. His slider is particularly tough on left-handed batters.

JAIME NAVARRO   **RSP**   **1967**   **Age 30**

YR	TEAM	Lge	IP	H	ER	HR	BB	K	ERA	W	L	H/9	HR/9	BB/9	K/9	KW
1993	Milwaukee	AL	214.3	251	115	21	84	119	4.83	10	14	10.54	.88	3.53	5.00	.78
1994	Milwaukee	AL	90.3	105	52	8	38	63	5.18	4	6	10.46	.80	3.79	6.28	1.15
1995	Chicago Cubs	NL	196.7	196	67	19	72	114	3.07	14	8	8.97	.87	3.29	5.22	.92
1996	Chicago Cubs	NL	233.3	247	100	24	92	138	3.86	13	13	9.53	.93	3.55	5.32	.89

He will not be a Cub in '97. He would routinely flip his lid each time he was pulled before the seventh inning and he also complained about the offense. In the end, he's come across as ungrateful to an organization that saved his career. However, he's fully recovered from the abuses of Phil Garner and should be able to help whatever team he winds up with. Signed with the White Sox in a de facto trade for Kevin Tapani.

BOB PATTERSON   **LRP**   **1959**   **Age 38**

YR	TEAM	Lge	IP	H	ER	HR	BB	K	ERA	W	L	H/9	HR/9	BB/9	K/9	KW
1993	Texas	AL	52.3	60	24	8	13	48	4.13	3	3	10.32	1.38	2.24	8.25	2.19
1994	California	AL	41.3	34	15	6	16	29	3.27	3	2	7.40	1.31	3.48	6.31	1.23
1995	California	AL	52.7	48	14	6	14	41	2.39	4	2	8.20	1.03	2.39	7.01	1.74
1996	Chicago Cubs	NL	53.3	48	16	6	27	46	2.70	4	2	8.10	1.01	4.56	7.76	1.45

"Country" was a genuine pleasure to watch. He can frighten people because his curve usually gets hit high and long for flyouts, and in Wrigley that can be especially scary. He's the kind of rubber arm that can pitch five days a week, as long as it isn't for too long. It's the Cubs' standards, of course, but he was probably their best free agent pickup last year.

MIKE PEREZ   **RRP**   **1965**   **Age 32**

YR	TEAM	Lge	IP	H	ER	HR	BB	K	ERA	W	L	H/9	HR/9	BB/9	K/9	KW
1993	St. Louis	NL	69.7	71	22	4	28	56	2.84	5	3	9.17	.52	3.62	7.23	1.51
1994	St. Louis	NL	32.0	49	28	5	13	19	7.88	1	3	13.78	1.41	3.66	5.34	.87
1995	Chicago Cubs	NL	70.3	73	26	8	32	44	3.33	5	3	9.34	1.02	4.09	5.63	.85
1996	Chicago Cubs	NL	26.3	30	12	2	16	19	4.10	1	2	10.25	.68	5.47	6.49	.80
1996	Iowa	AmA	29.7	44	23	4	21	16	6.98	1	2	13.35	1.21	6.37	4.85	.03

The Cubs gave up on him quickly, even though he was not pitching too badly. He completely came apart at Iowa, and may have to change organizations to pitch effectively again. He needs innings so that his curve and splitter can be effective, and he isn't cut out for modern usage patterns.

STEVE RAIN   **RRP**   **1975**   **Age 22**

YR	TEAM	Lge	IP	H	ER	HR	BB	K	ERA	W	L	H/9	HR/9	BB/9	K/9	KW
1995	Rockford	Midw	52.3	52	12	0	31	43	2.06	5	1	8.94	.00	5.33	7.39	1.13
1996	Orlando	South	35.7	39	15	5	14	35	3.79	2	2	9.84	1.26	3.53	8.83	2.06
1996	Iowa	AmA	24.3	20	9	3	11	19	3.33	2	1	7.40	1.11	4.07	7.03	1.33

He's been everything Terry Adams has been touted as. Like Adams, Rain is a sinker-slider pitcher, but unlike Adams, his slider has more bite and is more consistent, while his fastball has much less velocity. Rain is enormous (6' 6"), and has only been in the pen the last two years.

JON RATLIFF   **RBP**   **1972**   **Age 25**

YR	TEAM	Lge	IP	H	ER	HR	BB	K	ERA	W	L	H/9	HR/9	BB/9	K/9	KW
1994	Daytona	Flor	48.7	76	26	8	9	13	4.81	2	3	14.05	1.48	1.66	2.40	.39
1994	Orlando	South	57.0	87	46	5	37	15	7.26	1	5	13.74	.79	5.84	2.37	-.67
1994	Iowa	AmA	27.7	38	16	7	10	9	5.20	1	2	12.36	2.28	3.25	2.93	.16
1995	Orlando	South	128.3	164	69	11	59	72	4.84	6	8	11.50	.77	4.14	5.05	.65
1996	Iowa	AmA	89.7	117	62	9	44	49	6.22	3	7	11.74	.90	4.42	4.92	.54

Should Ratliff feel badly that he was picked in the Rule V draft before last season by the Tigers and then didn't get kept? Ratliff will always be infamous as the player drafted with the compensation pick the Cubs got for Greg Maddux. By that yardstick, he'll never be a success. Ratliff is a four-pitch starter, but '96 was a season lost to interorganizational shuffling and injury. He isn't a great prospect, but the Cubs will stubbornly hope for something to go right.

ROBERTO RIVERA   **LRP**   **1969**   **Age 28**

YR	TEAM	Lge	IP	H	ER	HR	BB	K	ERA	W	L	H/9	HR/9	BB/9	K/9	KW
1993	Kinston	Caro	30.0	56	30	4	9	20	9.00	0	3	16.80	1.20	2.70	6.00	1.32
1994	Orlando	South	42.0	51	14	2	18	24	3.00	3	2	10.93	.43	3.86	5.14	.75
1995	Orlando	South	62.7	59	17	5	17	26	2.44	5	2	8.47	.72	2.44	3.73	.63
1996	Orlando	South	15.3	24	13	2	9	10	7.63	0	2	14.09	1.17	5.28	5.87	.64
1996	Iowa	AmA	31.3	29	9	3	12	15	2.59	2	1	8.33	.86	3.45	4.31	.57

After '95, Rivera looked like he would have a great chance to win the left-handed spot relief job. That was derailed when the Cubs brought in Bob Patterson. Rivera relies on a good changeup, which means he's a lot like a few hundred other left-handed relievers.

KENNIE STEENSTRA   **RSP**   **1971**   **Age 26**

YR	TEAM	Lge	IP	H	ER	HR	BB	K	ERA	W	L	H/9	HR/9	BB/9	K/9	KW
1993	Daytona	Flor	71.7	78	28	4	20	44	3.52	5	3	9.80	.50	2.51	5.53	1.21
1993	Orlando	South	90.0	121	50	5	36	45	5.00	4	6	12.10	.50	3.60	4.50	.60
1994	Orlando	South	143.0	171	59	15	62	65	3.71	9	7	10.76	.94	3.90	4.09	.39
1995	Iowa	AmA	162.0	190	84	16	69	85	4.67	8	10	10.56	.89	3.83	4.72	.62
1996	Iowa	AmA	151.3	185	93	23	68	84	5.53	6	11	11.00	1.37	4.04	5.00	.65

He's a right-handed junkballer and doesn't fool anyone, but he's been durable and could luck into a start or two if there are enough injuries on the big league club.

BRIAN STEPHENSON   **RSP**   **1974**   **Age 23**

YR	TEAM	Lge	IP	H	ER	HR	BB	K	ERA	W	L	H/9	HR/9	BB/9	K/9	KW
1994	Peoria	Midw	37.0	51	19	4	10	18	4.62	2	2	12.41	.97	2.43	4.38	.85
1995	Daytona	Flor	131.7	176	87	11	80	77	5.95	5	10	12.03	.75	5.47	5.26	.39
1996	Orlando	South	117.7	151	80	14	71	77	6.12	4	9	11.55	1.07	5.43	5.89	.61

After initially thinking of Stephenson as a starter, the Cubs dabbled last season in converting him to relief. He's a '94 second-round draft choice out of UCLA who has the best curveball in the Cubs' minors. His fastball doesn't have much movement, so he's starting to struggle.

TANYON STURTZE   **RBP**   **1971**   **Age 26**

YR	TEAM	Lge	IP	H	ER	HR	BB	K	ERA	W	L	H/9	HR/9	BB/9	K/9	KW
1993	Huntsville	South	148.7	204	113	19	112	85	6.84	4	13	12.35	1.15	6.78	5.15	.02
1994	Huntsville	South	92.3	122	45	6	56	50	4.39	5	5	11.89	.58	5.46	4.87	.26
1994	Tacoma	PCL	60.3	70	29	4	41	24	4.33	3	4	10.44	.60	6.12	3.58	-.34
1995	Iowa	AmA	83.3	112	63	18	53	43	6.80	2	7	12.10	1.94	5.72	4.64	.12
1996	Iowa	AmA	69.0	88	41	6	45	43	5.35	3	5	11.48	.78	5.87	5.61	.40
1996	Chicago Cubs	NL	11.3	16	9	3	6	6	7.15	0	1	12.71	2.38	4.76	4.76	.40

One of the strangest fascinations with a non-prospect you'll see. Sturtze not only isn't a prospect, he's a genuinely lousy pitcher. He's got a 90+ heater that has no movement and no breaking pitch, so he routinely gets lit up. But the radar gun keeps him around; he's a burden to any minor league roster.

DAVE SWARTZBAUGH   **RBP**   **1968**   **Age 29**

YR	TEAM	Lge	IP	H	ER	HR	BB	K	ERA	W	L	H/9	HR/9	BB/9	K/9	KW
1993	Orlando	South	60.7	61	33	6	25	44	4.90	3	4	9.05	.89	3.71	6.53	1.25
1993	Iowa	AmA	83.7	90	49	15	53	63	5.27	3	6	9.68	1.61	5.70	6.78	.83
1994	Orlando	South	72.7	80	36	8	30	55	4.46	4	4	9.91	.99	3.72	6.81	1.34
1995	Orlando	South	26.7	23	9	1	10	28	3.04	2	1	7.76	.34	3.38	9.45	2.31
1995	Iowa	AmA	44.0	38	9	1	23	33	1.84	4	1	7.77	.20	4.70	6.75	1.07
1996	Iowa	AmA	112.7	118	60	21	48	86	4.79	5	8	9.43	1.68	3.83	6.87	1.33
1996	Chicago Cubs	NL	24.0	26	15	3	16	11	5.62	1	2	9.75	1.12	6.00	4.12	-.12

Whereas Sturtze gets press and tool drool from scouts, Swartzbaugh gets nothing. He routinely fools opposing hitters by spotting his fastball instead of overpowering them. The Cubs don't know what to do with him: they use him in relief and he succeeds; they put him in the rotation and he succeeds. It's downright embarrassing.

AMAURY TELEMACO   **RSP**   **1974**   **Age 23**

YR	TEAM	Lge	IP	H	ER	HR	BB	K	ERA	W	L	H/9	HR/9	BB/9	K/9	KW
1993	Peoria	Midw	123.7	168	78	12	73	78	5.68	5	9	12.23	.87	5.31	5.68	.56
1994	Daytona	Flor	69.7	75	37	6	32	45	4.78	3	5	9.69	.78	4.13	5.81	.90
1994	Orlando	South	57.3	64	29	7	30	38	4.55	3	3	10.05	1.10	4.71	5.97	.81
1995	Orlando	South	137.0	130	58	14	59	115	3.81	8	7	8.54	.92	3.88	7.55	1.55
1996	Iowa	AmA	47.7	42	18	5	25	35	3.40	3	2	7.93	.94	4.72	6.61	1.02
1996	Chicago Cubs	NL	97.0	107	58	19	40	56	5.38	4	7	9.93	1.76	3.71	5.20	.80

I really like his future. When his slider is on, he can be one of the best pitchers in the league. There should be no question about his status as a rotation starter or his chances of being a great pitcher. The Cubs need to just leave him alone, put him on the mound every five days and never let him go beyond 120 pitches until his 25th birthday.

STEVE TRACHSEL   **RSP**   **1971**   **Age 26**

YR	TEAM	Lge	IP	H	ER	HR	BB	K	ERA	W	L	H/9	HR/9	BB/9	K/9	KW
1993	Iowa	AmA	163.3	173	67	19	62	123	3.69	10	8	9.53	1.05	3.42	6.78	1.41
1993	Chicago Cubs	NL	19.0	16	9	5	5	13	4.26	1	1	7.58	2.37	2.37	6.16	1.46
1994	Chicago Cubs	NL	143.7	138	52	20	67	101	3.26	10	6	8.65	1.25	4.20	6.33	1.06
1995	Chicago Cubs	NL	160.7	172	90	24	90	105	5.04	7	11	9.63	1.34	5.04	5.88	.70
1996	Chicago Cubs	NL	201.0	185	70	29	78	115	3.13	14	8	8.28	1.30	3.49	5.15	.84

He finally beat the home field whammy. Entering the '96 season, Trachsel was 3-16 in Wrigley. He beat that by posting a 9-5 mark at home. He learned how to work the splitter into his repertoire against right-handed batters, and that's the biggest reason for his success. He put up 23 quality starts in 31 outings, one of the best marks in the NL. If Trachsel can remain at this level and Castillo can come back to where he was in '95, the Cubs won't miss Navarro.

WADE WALKER   **RSP**   **1972**   **Age 25**

YR	TEAM	Lge	IP	H	ER	HR	BB	K	ERA	W	L	H/9	HR/9	BB/9	K/9	KW
1994	Peoria	Midw	154.7	228	110	13	99	73	6.40	5	12	13.27	.76	5.76	4.25	-.02
1995	Daytona	Flor	121.0	137	52	8	52	82	3.87	7	6	10.19	.60	3.87	6.10	1.07
1996	Orlando	South	172.7	233	110	22	90	86	5.73	6	13	12.14	1.15	4.69	4.48	.32

Walker has been worked hard so far, and last year started to approach that dangerous threshold of facing 30 batters per start. He's got a mediocre fastball, relying on a sinker-slider combo to succeed. He isn't an outstanding prospect, and is probably a better candidate for a career-threatening injury.

TURK WENDELL   **RBP**   **1967**   **Age 30**

YR	TEAM	Lge	IP	H	ER	HR	BB	K	ERA	W	L	H/9	HR/9	BB/9	K/9	KW
1993	Iowa	AmA	142.3	151	75	9	62	101	4.74	7	9	9.55	.57	3.92	6.39	1.15
1993	Chicago Cubs	NL	22.0	25	12	0	11	15	4.91	1	1	10.23	.00	4.50	6.14	.92
1994	Iowa	AmA	159.3	148	48	13	41	105	2.71	12	6	8.36	.73	2.32	5.93	1.40
1994	Chicago Cubs	NL	15.0	22	18	3	11	9	10.80	0	2	13.20	1.80	6.60	5.40	.15
1995	Chicago Cubs	NL	60.3	70	30	10	29	45	4.48	3	4	10.44	1.49	4.33	6.71	1.16
1996	Chicago Cubs	NL	77.7	61	22	8	50	65	2.55	6	3	7.07	.93	5.79	7.53	1.06

The weird and woolly world of the Turk took a turn for the happier. His slider is an outstanding pitch, and he could easily continue to enjoy this kind of success. The real challenge for the Cubs is what they want to do with him. There are early rumors that they're thinking of moving him into the rotation so that Adams can be duly anointed the closer. He's capable of handling a return to the rotation, which will obviously mean a jump in his ERA.

KERRY WOOD   **RSP**   **1977**   **Age 20**

YR	TEAM	Lge	IP	H	ER	HR	BB	K	ERA	W	L	H/9	HR/9	BB/9	K/9	KW
1996	Daytona	Flor	103.0	86	51	9	91	98	4.46	5	6	7.51	.79	7.95	8.56	.87

The Cubs' top pick in the '95 draft, he was named the best pitching prospect in the Florida State League with the best fastball. He's wild and living almost entirely off a fastball that approaches 100 mph. The Cubs are being extremely careful with his arm, because they're convinced he could be the next Nolan Ryan.

Player	Age	Team	Lge	AB	H	DB	TP	HR	BB	SB	CS	OUT	BA	OBA	SA	EQA	EQR	Peak
GILBERT AVALOS	23	Daytona	Flor	288	65	7	0	1	18	11	4	227	.226	.271	.260	.178	15	.194
KELVIN BARNES	21	Rockford	Midw	442	97	10	3	11	32	12	2	347	.219	.272	.330	.203	32	.227
KEVIN BENTLEY	23	Daytona	Flor	257	62	6	1	5	17	4	2	197	.241	.288	.331	.207	19	.228
SAUL BUSTOS	23	Daytona	Flor	301	49	3	1	5	20	3	2	254	.163	.215	.229	.118	6	.128
DAVID CATLETT	22	Rockford	Midw	231	48	12	1	1	14	3	1	184	.208	.262	.281	.176	12	.192
DAN CHOLOWSKY	25	Orlando	South	148	34	1	0	4	20	2	2	116	.230	.321	.318	.214	12	.226
DEE DOWLER	24	Orlando	South	364	101	13	3	7	40	16	3	266	.277	.349	.387	.255	44	.273
KEVIN ELLIS	24	Daytona	Flor	485	118	10	1	16	23	3	2	369	.243	.278	.367	.214	39	.229
BRAD ERDMAN	26	Iowa	AmA	174	30	4	0	2	17	1	0	144	.172	.246	.230	.140	5	.147
PAUL FARIES	31	Iowa	AmA	119	31	3	2	0	15	5	1	89	.261	.343	.319	.233	12	.226
FELIX FERMIN	32	Iowa	AmA	121	34	3	1	0	5	1	0	87	.281	.310	.322	.216	9	.204
TREY FORKERWAY	25	Daytona	Flor	146	36	4	1	0	15	4	3	113	.247	.317	.288	.204	11	.214
	25	Orlando	South	165	39	6	1	3	9	0	1	127	.236	.276	.339	.201	12	.211
TROY FRYMAN	24	Orlando	South	205	46	13	1	1	17	1	1	160	.224	.284	.312	.196	14	.210
MARTY GAZAREK	23	Daytona	Flor	476	118	18	1	12	26	8	7	365	.248	.287	.366	.216	40	.235
DAVID JEFFERSON	21	Rockford	Midw	312	64	6	0	2	28	7	3	251	.205	.271	.244	.166	14	.186
KEITH KESSINGER	29	Iowa	AmA	190	45	4	0	5	23	0	1	146	.237	.319	.337	.219	16	.218
MARK KINGSTON	26	Orlando	South	126	26	6	0	3	20	1	1	101	.206	.315	.325	.213	11	.220
BRYN KOSCO	29	Iowa	AmA	81	20	2	0	2	6	0	0	61	.247	.299	.346	.215	7	.213
EDDIE LANTIGUA	22	Daytona	Flor	143	25	0	0	4	3	2	1	119	.175	.192	.259	.125	3	.137
JEREMY LEWIS	23	Rockford	Midw	379	85	15	1	6	35	6	2	296	.224	.290	.317	.203	28	.221
SHAWN LIVSEY	22	Daytona	Flor	198	58	9	2	3	21	9	3	143	.293	.361	.404	.263	25	.290
	22	Orlando	South	264	65	11	1	3	23	9	4	203	.246	.307	.330	.217	22	.240
ASHANTI MCDONALD	23	Rockford	Midw	209	43	3	1	1	15	3	1	167	.206	.259	.244	.158	8	.171
MATT MERULLO	30	Iowa	AmA	91	21	4	0	2	9	1	0	70	.231	.300	.341	.216	8	.214
JOSE MOLINA	21	Rockford	Midw	316	62	6	1	3	27	1	2	256	.196	.259	.237	.150	11	.169
JOSE NIEVES	21	Rockford	Midw	407	88	12	1	6	24	8	4	323	.216	.260	.295	.181	23	.203
HECTOR ORTIZ	26	Iowa	AmA	80	19	1	0	0	4	0	0	61	.237	.274	.250	.167	3	.172
	26	Orlando	South	222	46	4	0	1	22	1	1	177	.207	.279	.239	.163	10	.170
RICHARD PEREZ	23	Daytona	Flor	186	36	6	1	0	11	2	1	151	.194	.239	.237	.141	6	.154
	23	Rockford	Midw	86	20	2	0	3	8	1	0	66	.233	.298	.360	.221	8	.241
BO PORTER	23	Rockford	Midw	397	87	13	2	7	56	15	7	317	.219	.316	.315	.215	34	.233
SCOTT SAMUELS	25	Orlando	South	356	91	16	3	3	53	13	5	270	.256	.352	.343	.240	38	.254
TERRY SHUMPERT	29	Iowa	AmA	254	71	12	3	5	26	12	3	186	.280	.346	.409	.259	32	.257
JERREY THURSTON	24	Orlando	South	181	37	3	1	3	12	0	0	144	.204	.254	.282	.169	8	.181
STEVE WALKER	24	Daytona	Flor	228	67	9	0	10	15	11	3	164	.294	.337	.465	.270	31	.290
	24	Orlando	South	230	56	6	2	4	14	5	4	178	.243	.287	.339	.208	18	.223
GABE WHATLEY	24	Daytona	Flor	190	39	8	1	3	23	4	1	152	.205	.291	.305	.200	14	.214
HAROLD WILLIAMS	25	Orlando	South	262	67	4	0	9	23	1	1	196	.256	.316	.374	.231	25	.244

Player	Age	Team	Lge	IP	H	ER	HR	BB	K	ERA	W	L	H/9	HR/9	BB/9	K/9	KW
SHAWN BOX	23	Daytona	Flor	47.0	59	30	6	18	23	5.74	2	3	11.30	1.15	3.45	4.40	.61
DAROLD BROWN	22	Daytona	Flor	47.3	50	20	4	27	31	3.80	3	2	9.51	.76	5.13	5.89	.68
CHRIS BRYANT	20	Rockford	Midw	60.7	108	58	8	48	32	8.60	1	6	16.02	1.19	7.12	4.75	-.20
BEN BURLINGAME	26	Iowa	AmA	93.3	115	48	12	32	55	4.63	4	6	11.09	1.16	3.09	5.30	1.00
EARL BYRNE	23	Daytona	Flor	40.7	51	23	7	28	34	5.09	2	3	11.29	1.55	6.20	7.52	.96
	23	Orlando	South	33.3	42	27	5	30	22	7.29	1	3	11.34	1.35	8.10	5.94	-.04
MIKE CAMPBELL	32	Chicago Cubs	NL	35.3	30	16	7	13	16	4.08	2	2	7.64	1.78	3.31	4.08	.53
	32	Iowa	AmA	91.0	84	29	8	34	72	2.87	7	3	8.31	.79	3.36	7.12	1.53
FRED DABNEY	28	Iowa	AmA	62.0	82	37	8	34	28	5.37	2	5	11.90	1.16	4.94	4.06	.12
CHRIS DEWITT	22	Rockford	Midw	68.7	116	55	4	28	28	7.21	2	6	15.20	.52	3.67	3.67	.31
JAIRO DIAZ	20	Rockford	Midw	76.3	107	38	9	34	53	4.48	4	4	12.62	1.06	4.01	6.25	1.08
KYLE FARNSWORTH	20	Rockford	Midw	95.7	158	70	10	46	52	6.59	3	8	14.86	.94	4.33	4.89	.55
AL GARCIA	22	Daytona	Flor	42.3	57	21	2	9	20	4.46	2	3	12.12	.43	1.91	4.25	.94
	22	Orlando	South	109.0	169	69	18	38	48	5.70	4	8	13.95	1.49	3.14	3.96	.54
BRIAN GREENE	22	Daytona	Flor	49.7	61	28	7	25	27	5.07	2	4	11.05	1.27	4.53	4.89	.50
JOSE GUZMAN	33	Iowa	AmA	37.3	54	37	8	26	20	8.92	1	3	13.02	1.93	6.27	4.82	.04
BRANDON HAMMACK	23	Daytona	Flor	28.3	31	10	2	15	26	3.18	2	1	9.85	.64	4.76	8.26	1.56
	23	Rockford	Midw	28.0	28	13	0	24	28	4.18	1	2	9.00	.00	7.71	9.00	1.07
DAVID HUTCHESON	24	Orlando	South	77.7	96	43	9	33	44	4.98	4	5	11.12	1.04	3.82	5.10	.74
BARRY MARKEY	19	Rockford	Midw	83.0	130	50	11	21	25	5.42	3	6	14.10	1.19	2.28	2.71	.33
GARY MARSHALL	22	Rockford	Midw	39.3	52	23	4	25	22	5.26	1	3	11.90	.92	5.72	5.03	.25
JAVIER MARTINEZ	19	Rockford	Midw	51.7	62	27	6	39	33	4.70	3	3	10.80	1.05	6.79	5.75	.22
BRIAN MCNICHOL	22	Daytona	Flor	30.7	45	25	5	20	16	7.34	1	2	13.21	1.47	5.87	4.70	.10
JOE MONTELONGO	22	Daytona	Flor	91.0	100	54	7	50	56	5.34	4	6	9.89	.69	4.95	5.54	.61
TIM MOSLEY	21	Rockford	Midw	48.7	90	51	2	42	23	9.43	1	4	16.64	.37	7.77	4.25	-.52
SCOTT MOTEN	24	Iowa	AmA	40.7	59	45	8	25	15	9.96	1	4	13.06	1.77	5.53	3.32	-.28
	24	Orlando	South	50.0	66	38	8	36	26	6.84	2	4	11.88	1.44	6.48	4.68	-.06
JAY PETERSON	20	Rockford	Midw	80.7	109	56	11	50	55	6.25	3	6	12.16	1.23	5.58	6.14	.65
CARLOS PULIDO	24	Iowa	AmA	99.0	141	62	16	51	40	5.64	4	7	12.82	1.45	4.64	3.64	.05
CHAD RICKETTS	21	Rockford	Midw	75.3	116	68	11	38	44	8.12	2	6	13.86	1.31	4.54	5.26	.62
JAY RYAN	20	Daytona	Flor	59.7	83	44	11	44	35	6.64	2	5	12.52	1.66	6.64	5.28	.10
	20	Orlando	South	32.0	43	28	6	28	18	7.88	1	3	12.09	1.69	7.88	5.06	-.28
JUSTIN SPEIER	22	Daytona	Flor	34.3	37	19	4	25	25	4.98	2	2	9.70	1.05	6.55	6.55	.55
JASON STEVENSON	22	Daytona	Flor	108.3	161	60	11	36	62	4.98	5	7	13.38	.91	2.99	5.15	.97
GREG TWIGGS	24	Orlando	South	50.3	60	27	3	39	29	4.83	2	4	10.73	.54	6.97	5.19	-.01
ISMAEL VILLEGAS	19	Rockford	Midw	39.7	77	42	6	33	19	9.53	1	3	17.47	1.36	7.49	4.31	-.43
JEFF YODER	20	Rockford	Midw	132.3	186	80	14	63	78	5.44	5	10	12.65	.95	4.28	5.30	.70

Cincinnati Reds

Cincinnati (AP) – Owner Marge Schott was reprimanded by the league office today for her alleged interference in the day-to-day operations of the Cincinnati Reds. Ms. Schott, who signed an agreement with the commissioner's office stipulating that she would stay out of ballclub activities, had few words for reporters, but did state "You're a smart one, aren't you?" Apparently, Ms. Schott was trying to trade Barry Larkin to Milwaukee for clean-cut outfielder Turner Ward, because "Only fruits wear earrings." Upon learning of Ms. Schott's intent, acting commissioner Selig rescinded the reprimand. "It's her club, after all," said Selig, "and I'm not sure it was really her. It could have been Jimmy the Greek in drag. I can't tell them apart."

Age is catching up to this team fast, and they're not doing much to avoid its icy grasp. The best players on the team are old and aging fast. Barry Larkin, Reggie Sanders and Eric Davis will never see their primes again. Willie Greene's youngish, and there are some grade B prospects on the farm, but by and large this organization is in for a long, slow slide. They might be able to make a couple of grabs at the ring during the next three years, but they should have started rebuilding some time ago.

One strategy they might be able to make use of is mass trading. They've got competent replacements for a few of their marquee players, some of whom may really break out. (My software projects former prospect Keith Mitchell to have an enormous year, and I can't explain it.) If they can turn Barry Larkin into something resembling a farm system, maybe trade Taubensee while he's hot and get something for Reggie Sanders, they should probably do it. They've got some hole fillers, and they need to take a look at two to three years down the road instead of just living for the moment. I've always felt that you need a three-year and seven-year time horizon to run a baseball team well. This club has a three-week time horizon, and it gets a bit fuzzy after week two.

There's likely to be some fan outrage over such moves, but I'd rather suffer one year of fan anger than five years of fan disinterest. Considering some of the antics of this team's ownership, I don't think trying to build for the future is going to draw the wrath of the Cincinnati fans. There are quite a few grade B prospects in the Reds system, and all of them are likely to be passable on the major league level. By the time the Reds are ready to make another run at the division title, Barry Larkin will be a mediocre third baseman. Ship him off

and shoot for the moon. Pokey Reese can fill in for a year or two acceptably and people like Paul Bako, Steve Gibralter, Aaron Boone and Willie Greene are in the "let's see what sticks to the wall" category. Two of them are likely to become good major leaguers, and you could get luckier than that.

Even though the Reds are poised to grab at the wild card (read: they're not particularly good, but anyone can get lucky), they're not likely to do so without a healthy Jose Rijo. Considering that Rijo is approximately as likely to pitch for the Reds in 1997 as Don Gullett, that doesn't bode well for their postseason hopes. The best hope they have for making the playoffs is if Houston continues to make abominably stupid moves. But how many times can they really sign Derek Bell to a long-term deal anyway?

This team's diseases start and end at the top. As long as Marge Schott is the chief figurehead for ownership, this franchise is going to be in disarray. I'm not saying she should be stripped of her ownership; everyone has a right to be as ignorant and pathetic as they want to be. Hey, Trekkies need dates too. But at some point, the other members of ownership should probably do whatever they have to in order to secure the long-term stability of the franchise. Teams without solid management simply don't do well in the long run, and it's hard to have a good organization if the very top is as truly ill as this one is. It's sad that one has to mention these things so prominently when talking about a team, but c'est la vie.

Organization: If you leave her own rehabilitation up to Marge Schott, she's likely to come up with "Jew Night" or something equally clueless. The rest of the investors need to step up, make the necessary changes and decide what they want to do for the future. The Reds' farm system is somewhat stagnant at this point, but it's not in any trouble. While it's not producing any excellence, it is pushing out some decent quantity, and that's a start.

Baseball fans of America owe a huge debt to Ms. Schott and her lapdogs; it is because of them that we no longer have to sit through Ray Knight's homespun mental drool on ESPN's Baseball Tonight. It's kind of like the debt to Jimmy the Greek we can never repay: the man slugged Brent Musberger. But seriously—this organization is in a constant state of flux due to horrific top management, and there's no point in even taking a good look at it until that changes. That could be a long time. It's going to be a long winter, metaphorically, for fans of the Big Red Machine.

PAUL BAKO   **C**   **1972**   **Age 25**

Year	Team	Lge	AB	H	DB	TP	HR	BB	SB	CS	OUT	BA	OBA	SA	EQA	EQR	Peak
1994	Winston-Salem	Caro	296	51	5	1	2	30	1	1	246	.172	.248	.216	.131	8	.146
1995	Winston-Salem	Caro	262	74	7	2	7	40	2	1	189	.282	.377	.405	.265	34	.288
1996	Chattanooga	South	372	107	14	0	10	41	1	0	265	.288	.358	.406	.259	45	.277
1997	*Cincinnati*	*NL*	*504*	*147*	*28*	*1*	*16*	*64*	*5*	*2*	*359*	*.292*	*.371*	*.446*	*.287*	*79*	

Naturally, the second Bako started hitting, his defensive reputation started to slip. A good hitter who will get better, and I think he's fine behind the plate. The Reds probably have more depth at catcher and shortstop than any other organization. They've also got the most Marge Schott. Bako will start the year in Indianapolis and likely will stay there until September.

TIM BELK   **1B**   **1970**   **Age 27**

Year	Team	Lge	AB	H	DB	TP	HR	BB	SB	CS	OUT	BA	OBA	SA	EQA	EQR	Peak
1993	Winston-Salem	Caro	520	136	13	2	10	42	5	3	387	.262	.317	.352	.226	47	.246
1994	Chattanooga	South	433	132	25	2	12	59	8	4	305	.305	.388	.455	.283	65	.303
1995	Indianapolis	AmA	196	57	6	0	5	18	3	4	143	.291	.350	.398	.250	22	.262
1996	Indianapolis	AmA	448	129	24	1	15	32	5	2	321	.288	.335	.446	.261	56	.272
1997	*Cincinnati*	*NL*	*442*	*125*	*35*	*2*	*14*	*42*	*4*	*1*	*318*	*.283*	*.345*	*.466*	*.281*	*67*	

Marginal major league hitter without a position. He plays first base about as well as noted character actor Brian Dennehy. Maybe worse.

AARON BOONE   **3B**   **1973**   **Age 24**

Year	Team	Lge	AB	H	DB	TP	HR	BB	SB	CS	OUT	BA	OBA	SA	EQA	EQR	Peak
1995	Winston-Salem	Caro	410	105	13	1	13	41	7	3	308	.256	.324	.388	.240	43	.264
1995	Chattanooga	South	67	15	3	0	0	5	1	0	52	.224	.278	.269	.181	4	.197
1996	Chattanooga	South	561	159	33	4	17	30	15	6	408	.283	.320	.447	.256	68	.278
1997	*Cincinnati*	*NL*	*548*	*149*	*38*	*2*	*19*	*22*	*10*	*4*	*403*	*.272*	*.300*	*.453*	*.261*	*70*	

A remarkable swing. This guy can just flat out hit. If he can learn to walk a little bit he could really be something special. He'll probably start the year in Indianapolis, but is good enough to help a major league team right now. Supposedly a pretty good third baseman, but some question his arm strength.

BRET BOONE   **2B**   **1969**   **Age 28**

Year	Team	Lge	AB	H	DB	TP	HR	BB	SB	CS	OUT	BA	OBA	SA	EQA	EQR	Peak
1993	Calgary	PCL	268	76	9	1	8	25	2	4	196	.284	.345	.414	.252	31	.269
1993	Seattle	AL	274	72	12	2	14	19	2	2	204	.263	.311	.474	.256	34	.274
1994	Cincinnati	NL	388	127	22	2	13	29	3	3	264	.327	.374	.495	.287	58	.302
1995	Cincinnati	NL	523	145	30	2	17	47	4	1	379	.277	.337	.440	.259	65	.269
1996	Cincinnati	NL	526	125	19	3	12	37	2	2	403	.238	.288	.354	.212	42	.217
1997	*Cincinnati*	*NL*	*264*	*70*	*16*	*1*	*8*	*24*	*5*	*4*	*198*	*.265*	*.326*	*.424*	*.260*	*34*	

Anchors the "All-Disappointing Age 27 Team" along with Tim Salmon. Completely fell apart in 1996, and I have no idea why. His defense still looked reasonable, but his bat was slow, he swung at an awful lot of bad pitches and just generally didn't do a good job. I'd say he's a good candidate to bounce back, but I've been saying that about Delino DeShields and Brent Gates for too long to have any confidence in that statement.

JEFF BRANSON   **IF**   **1967**   **Age 30**

Year	Team	Lge	AB	H	DB	TP	HR	BB	SB	CS	OUT	BA	OBA	SA	EQA	EQR	Peak
1993	Cincinnati	NL	385	95	14	1	3	25	3	1	291	.247	.293	.312	.202	27	.210
1994	Cincinnati	NL	110	32	4	1	6	7	0	0	78	.291	.333	.509	.275	16	.281
1995	Cincinnati	NL	339	92	16	2	13	48	2	1	248	.271	.362	.445	.269	46	.271
1996	Cincinnati	NL	317	79	16	4	9	34	2	0	238	.249	.322	.410	.245	35	.244
1997	*Cincinnati*	*NL*	*259*	*64*	*15*	*1*	*10*	*46*	*2*	*1*	*196*	*.247*	*.361*	*.429*	*.275*	*39*	

Good, solid utility infielder. Good teams always have at least one guy like this. Of course, bad teams do too, but they're usually sitting behind complete sinkholes like Ozzie Guillen.

RAY BROWN   **1B**   **1973**   **Age 24**

Year	Team	Lge	AB	H	DB	TP	HR	BB	SB	CS	OUT	BA	OBA	SA	EQA	EQR	Peak
1995	Winston-Salem	Caro	463	122	15	0	19	49	2	1	342	.263	.334	.419	.251	54	.277
1996	Chattanooga	South	377	122	19	2	14	44	1	1	256	.324	.394	.496	.296	61	.321
1997	*Cincinnati*	*NL*	*570*	*170*	*31*	*2*	*24*	*49*	*4*	*2*	*402*	*.298*	*.354*	*.486*	*.290*	*91*	

Reasonable first base prospect; I'm not certain he'll be worse than Hal Morris next year. He's a good defender, has some pop, has hit for high average and power. Brown should have a good major league career, and it could start as early as this year if Hal Morris falters or gets hurt. A good analog might be Will Clark, at least on average.

STEVE CLAYBROOK   **OF**   **1973**   **Age 24**

Year	Team	Lge	AB	H	DB	TP	HR	BB	SB	CS	OUT	BA	OBA	SA	EQA	EQR	Peak
1996	Charleston-WV	S Atl	472	116	11	2	4	55	14	5	361	.246	.324	.303	.216	39	.235

If you're going to be a one-skill player you need to use that skill a lot. Claybrook draws a bunch of walks, but if he wants to make the majors he'll have to draw a bunch more. Either that, or learn a different skill—like brown-nosing. Hey, it worked for Joe Orsulak.

DECOMBA CONNER   **OF**   **1974**   **Age 23**

Year	Team	Lge	AB	H	DB	TP	HR	BB	SB	CS	OUT	BA	OBA	SA	EQA	EQR	Peak
1995	Charleston-WV	S Atl	330	85	8	3	6	32	9	3	248	.258	.323	.355	.232	32	.261
1996	Winston-Salem	Caro	522	131	6	2	16	37	15	6	396	.251	.301	.362	.225	47	.248
1997	*Detroit*	*AL*	*513*	*137*	*16*	*5*	*17*	*43*	*18*	*4*	*380*	*.267*	*.324*	*.417*	*.254*	*62*	

Popped 20 homers in the Carolina League, and has the swing to do it in the majors. I don't know if he does anything else well enough to make it that high. He's basically got two years to find out. If that fails, he can always go back to his comedy act where he wears a beret and smashes a bunch of melons.

ERIC DAVIS   **CF/LF**   **1962**   **Age 35**

Year	Team	Lge	AB	H	DB	TP	HR	BB	SB	CS	OUT	BA	OBA	SA	EQA	EQR	Peak
1993	Detroit	AL	76	20	0	1	7	15	2	1	57	.263	.385	.566	.302	14	.292
1993	Los Angeles	NL	384	95	12	0	16	47	29	5	294	.247	.329	.404	.255	48	.246
1994	Detroit	AL	120	22	4	0	3	19	5	0	98	.183	.295	.292	.203	9	.192
1996	Cincinnati	NL	428	127	15	0	28	75	19	8	309	.297	.402	.528	.304	78	.288
1997	*Cincinnati*	*NL*	*407*	*101*	*13*	*1*	*21*	*68*	*33*	*6*	*312*	*.248*	*.356*	*.440*	*.285*	*68*	

It was a real pleasure for me to watch ED have a great year. I still remember that month he had in 1987 like it was yesterday. Injuries can be cruel things. Here's hoping he can pull off at least one more great year, even if Ray Knight and Marge Schott are the primary beneficiaries. Only basestealer I've ever seen that was any better was Rickey Henderson.

BROOK FORDYCE   **C**   **1970**   **Age 27**

Year	Team	Lge	AB	H	DB	TP	HR	BB	SB	CS	OUT	BA	OBA	SA	EQA	EQR	Peak
1993	Norfolk	Inter	420	108	18	1	3	29	2	1	313	.257	.305	.326	.212	33	.232
1994	Norfolk	Inter	237	64	13	1	4	19	1	0	173	.270	.324	.384	.239	24	.256
1995	Buffalo	AmA	180	46	9	0	1	16	1	0	134	.256	.316	.322	.217	15	.228
1996	Indianapolis	AmA	384	107	18	2	15	29	2	1	278	.279	.329	.453	.259	48	.270
1997	*Cincinnati*	*NL*	*387*	*99*	*20*	*1*	*15*	*34*	*3*	*2*	*290*	*.256*	*.316*	*.429*	*.258*	*49*	

Probably good enough to be a backup in the bigs, but not in this organization. Extremely preppie-sounding name; very likely related to someone who went to school with George Bush and F. Scott Fitzgerald.

STEVE GIBRALTER   **OF**   **1973**   **Age 24**

Year	Team	Lge	AB	H	DB	TP	HR	BB	SB	CS	OUT	BA	OBA	SA	EQA	EQR	Peak
1993	Chattanooga	South	480	103	17	2	10	20	5	6	383	.215	.246	.321	.182	27	.206
1994	Chattanooga	South	477	126	18	2	15	48	6	4	355	.264	.331	.405	.246	53	.276
1995	Indianapolis	AmA	268	84	14	2	18	28	0	2	186	.313	.378	.582	.306	48	.338
1996	Indianapolis	AmA	457	116	25	1	11	31	2	2	343	.254	.301	.385	.228	43	.248
1997	*Cincinnati*	*NL*	*348*	*97*	*22*	*3*	*13*	*31*	*2*	*2*	*253*	*.279*	*.338*	*.471*	*.278*	*52*	

Last year, I didn't understand all the hype about this guy as a prospect. Vladimir projected his 1996 to be .268/.308/.417, which is fairly close to the .254/.301/.385 he posted. Of course, last year we were projecting that performance in the context of the 1995 NL, and this year we've averaged the 1995 and 1996 AL, so in reality the projection wasn't super, and neither was Gibralter. I realize he's still young, but he's got no star potential. Could be a fourth outfielder if everything breaks his way.

CURTIS GOODWIN   **OF**   **1973**   **Age 24**

Year	Team	Lge	AB	H	DB	TP	HR	BB	SB	CS	OUT	BA	OBA	SA	EQA	EQR	Peak
1993	Frederick	Caro	574	146	12	6	2	47	31	8	436	.254	.311	.307	.217	48	.247
1994	Bowie	East	609	165	14	5	3	36	34	6	450	.271	.312	.325	.226	54	.252
1995	Rochester	Inter	141	35	5	2	0	13	11	2	108	.248	.312	.312	.224	13	.248
1995	Baltimore	AL	291	79	13	3	1	15	21	4	216	.271	.307	.347	.233	28	.257
1996	Indianapolis	AmA	352	93	19	3	2	56	35	10	269	.264	.365	.352	.256	45	.278
1996	Cincinnati	NL	139	33	3	0	0	20	12	5	111	.237	.333	.259	.212	12	.231
1997	*Cincinnati*	*NL*	*421*	*108*	*21*	*6*	*1*	*55*	*73*	*17*	*330*	*.257*	*.342*	*.342*	*.266*	*60*	

Ray Knight was stunned that Goodwin didn't hit better. One can only assume Mr. Knight is also stunned by things like long division. Goodwin surprised me quite a bit this year, and he could really have some value if he hangs on to the majority of that increase in walks. Hitters don't often learn to walk. If Goodwin has done so, it's a testament to his hard work. He's at least earned a couple more seasons of serious PT at AAA.

WILLIE GREENE   **3B**   **1972**   **Age 25**

Year	Team	Lge	AB	H	DB	TP	HR	BB	SB	CS	OUT	BA	OBA	SA	EQA	EQR	Peak
1993	Indianapolis	AmA	345	90	12	0	21	52	2	3	258	.261	.358	.478	.272	50	.305
1993	Cincinnati	NL	50	8	1	1	2	3	0	0	42	.160	.208	.340	.169	2	.189
1994	Indianapolis	AmA	444	128	15	0	25	57	6	3	319	.288	.369	.491	.283	68	.312
1995	Indianapolis	AmA	331	80	10	1	18	40	3	2	253	.242	.323	.441	.251	40	.273
1996	Cincinnati	NL	293	74	6	4	19	39	0	1	220	.253	.340	.495	.270	42	.290
1997	*Cincinnati*	*NL*	*573*	*160*	*30*	*2*	*30*	*78*	*0*	*1*	*414*	*.279*	*.366*	*.496*	*.294*	*97*	

The Reds have two of the analyst community's former favorite prospects in Greene and Keith Mitchell. Aaron Boone is nibbling at Greene's heels, but I think Willie will hold on to the job and prosper. He's got quite a bit of power and his defense at third base looks pretty darn good to me. Knight may keep him in a platoon role, as Ray Knight is something of a dunderhead. (If this gets too technical, send us some e-mail.)

LENNY HARRIS   **UT**   **1965**   **Age 32**

Year	Team	Lge	AB	H	DB	TP	HR	BB	SB	CS	OUT	BA	OBA	SA	EQA	EQR	Peak
1993	Los Angeles	NL	163	40	6	1	2	18	3	1	124	.245	.320	.331	.222	14	.223
1994	Cincinnati	NL	101	32	3	1	0	7	6	2	71	.317	.361	.366	.256	12	.254
1995	Cincinnati	NL	199	43	9	3	2	17	8	1	157	.216	.278	.322	.206	15	.201
1996	Cincinnati	NL	308	90	16	2	5	24	11	5	223	.292	.343	.406	.254	36	.246
1997	*Cincinnati*	*NL*	*225*	*55*	*14*	*1*	*3*	*17*	*10*	*3*	*173*	*.244*	*.298*	*.356*	*.236*	*23*	

Inextricably linked in my mind with the late Mike Sharperson. His strong 1996 bought him a two-year contract. Harris is a reasonable hole filler, but you shouldn't be giving him 300 plate appearances.

THOMAS HOWARD   **OF**   **1965**   **Age 32**

Year	Team	Lge	AB	H	DB	TP	HR	BB	SB	CS	OUT	BA	OBA	SA	EQA	EQR	Peak
1993	Cincinnati	NL	144	41	7	2	5	14	5	5	108	.285	.348	.465	.264	19	.264
1993	Cleveland	AL	181	47	4	0	5	13	5	1	135	.260	.309	.365	.231	17	.233
1994	Cincinnati	NL	180	49	7	0	6	12	4	2	133	.272	.318	.411	.244	20	.243
1995	Cincinnati	NL	287	90	14	1	4	24	14	7	204	.314	.367	.411	.265	37	.260
1996	Cincinnati	NL	365	101	18	9	7	22	5	5	269	.277	.318	.433	.248	41	.239
1997	*Houston*	*NL*	*387*	*99*	*14*	*3*	*8*	*19*	*7*	*4*	*292*	*.256*	*.291*	*.370*	*.239*	*41*	

A reasonable fourth outfielder, but if your club has him in the outfield for half the season, you're probably not going to be a contender.

MIKE KELLY   OF   1970   Age 27

Year	Team	Lge	AB	H	DB	TP	HR	BB	SB	CS	OUT	BA	OBA	SA	EQA	EQR	Peak
1993	Richmond	Inter	433	104	9	0	18	38	9	4	333	.240	.301	.386	.230	42	.249
1994	Richmond	Inter	321	84	10	2	15	31	7	4	241	.262	.327	.445	.255	40	.273
1994	Atlanta	NL	78	22	10	1	2	3	0	1	57	.282	.309	.513	.263	10	.281
1995	Richmond	Inter	47	14	2	0	2	5	0	1	34	.298	.365	.468	.270	6	.283
1995	Atlanta	NL	138	27	5	1	3	12	6	3	114	.196	.260	.312	.190	9	.200
1996	Indianapolis	AmA	299	63	7	1	8	32	11	2	238	.211	.287	.321	.208	23	.217
1996	Cincinnati	NL	50	9	5	0	1	10	3	0	41	.180	.317	.340	.231	5	.243
1997	*Cincinnati*	*NL*	*167*	*38*	*4*	*1*	*6*	*16*	*17*	*3*	*132*	*.228*	*.295*	*.371*	*.249*	*20*	

Former Brave draft pick. Can't play baseball well, and that's something of an obstacle in his line of work. Could possibly have a big overrated season at age 27 this year, and then become a serious albatross to an organization bereft of intelligent life, but last I checked, Jim Frey's not currently employed.

BARRY LARKIN   SS   1964   Age 33

Year	Team	Lge	AB	H	DB	TP	HR	BB	SB	CS	OUT	BA	OBA	SA	EQA	EQR	Peak
1993	Cincinnati	NL	398	130	20	1	10	56	12	1	269	.327	.410	.457	.297	65	.295
1994	Cincinnati	NL	437	126	23	4	10	70	23	2	313	.288	.387	.428	.282	66	.277
1995	Cincinnati	NL	512	171	29	5	17	68	42	4	345	.334	.412	.510	.315	96	.304
1996	Cincinnati	NL	535	165	29	4	35	103	30	9	379	.308	.420	.574	.322	112	.306
1997	*Cincinnati*	*NL*	*572*	*167*	*39*	*4*	*20*	*99*	*44*	*16*	*421*	*.292*	*.396*	*.479*	*.306*	*109*	

The best shortstop in baseball, but he's worn that title for the final year. Interesting Hall of Fame case; I think he needs two more good years to make it. Others have made the case that he's simply not good enough; his career's not been long and he's been brittle. They're wrong. He's Cooperstown-bound. Still a fair defensive shortstop to my eye, and with that bat I'd run out him out there until he fielded like Abba with gout. Deadly basestealer; Larkin is usually my starting point for the inevitable "smartest player in baseball" arguments that fill the winters.

KEITH MITCHELL   OF   1970   Age 27

Year	Team	Lge	AB	H	DB	TP	HR	BB	SB	CS	OUT	BA	OBA	SA	EQA	EQR	Peak
1993	Richmond	Inter	362	82	19	1	4	45	7	3	283	.227	.312	.318	.213	30	.232
1994	Seattle	AL	128	29	1	0	5	18	0	0	99	.227	.322	.352	.225	12	.242
1995	Indianapolis	AmA	219	53	9	1	11	40	4	3	169	.242	.359	.443	.264	30	.279
1996	Indianapolis	AmA	377	116	17	3	16	66	8	1	262	.308	.411	.496	.304	66	.315
1997	*Cincinnati*	*NL*	*387*	*102*	*23*	*1*	*17*	*111*	*5*	*2*	*287*	*.264*	*.428*	*.460*	*.311*	*77*	

Wow. That projection is no typo. I don't see him doubling his walk rate all of a sudden, but then again my software's right more often than I am. Mitchell rotted behind Lonnie Smith in Atlanta, and has fought the "bad attitude" tag throughout his career. I still believe that this guy should have been in the majors at age 22. He's not a bad defensive outfielder, and he can most definitely hit. If he ends up somewhere in a full-time role, I fully expect him to be a legitimate MVP candidate. That won't happen, but it wouldn't surprise me.

KEVIN MITCHELL   OF/1B   1962   Age 35

Year	Team	Lge	AB	H	DB	TP	HR	BB	SB	CS	OUT	BA	OBA	SA	EQA	EQR	Peak
1993	Cincinnati	NL	333	117	18	2	21	30	1	0	216	.351	.405	.607	.326	66	.315
1994	Cincinnati	NL	320	107	16	1	32	65	2	0	213	.334	.447	.691	.356	80	.338
1996	Boston	AL	91	27	3	0	2	11	0	0	64	.297	.373	.396	.262	11	.250
1996	Cincinnati	NL	119	40	8	0	7	28	0	0	79	.336	.463	.580	.341	27	.323
1997	*Cleveland*	*AL*	*252*	*75*	*9*	*0*	*14*	*46*	*0*	*0*	*177*	*.298*	*.406*	*.500*	*.303*	*45*	

Kevin Mitchell can hit. He can't do anything else, except answer all those nagging questions we had about what a cross between Mike Tyson and the Michelin Man would look like. Can't field at all, carries a lot of baggage, can't stay healthy, but man, can this guy hit. That projection is low.

HAL MORRIS   **1B**   **1965**   **Age 32**

Year	Team	Lge	AB	H	DB	TP	HR	BB	SB	CS	OUT	BA	OBA	SA	EQA	EQR	Peak
1993	Cincinnati	NL	390	126	11	1	9	40	2	2	266	.323	.386	.426	.275	53	.278
1994	Cincinnati	NL	445	152	30	3	11	41	5	2	295	.342	.397	.497	.299	72	.297
1995	Cincinnati	NL	367	106	24	2	12	33	1	1	262	.289	.347	.463	.269	49	.263
1996	Cincinnati	NL	542	173	29	4	17	56	6	5	374	.319	.383	.482	.287	82	.277
1997	*Cincinnati*	*NL*	*492*	*147*	*32*	*4*	*13*	*35*	*1*	*1*	*346*	*.299*	*.345*	*.459*	*.280*	*72*	

I don't care much for this type of player. First basemen who don't walk and don't hit for power had better play superlative defense and hit .350. Morris doesn't do any of those things anymore, and yet he appears to have some value because of that high batting average. One year away from being part of the problem, and not helping the team at this point.

JOE OLIVER   **C**   **1966**   **Age 31**

Year	Team	Lge	AB	H	DB	TP	HR	BB	SB	CS	OUT	BA	OBA	SA	EQA	EQR	Peak
1993	Cincinnati	NL	488	119	19	0	17	34	0	0	369	.244	.293	.387	.226	45	.231
1995	Milwaukee	AL	336	90	15	0	14	27	2	4	250	.268	.322	.438	.249	39	.249
1996	Cincinnati	NL	294	73	11	1	11	31	2	0	221	.248	.320	.405	.243	32	.238
1997	*Cincinnati*	*NL*	*403*	*99*	*16*	*1*	*13*	*30*	*1*	*1*	*305*	*.246*	*.298*	*.387*	*.239*	*43*	

Oliver's done a pretty fair job of rebounding from some tough breaks. A reliable catcher; before 1995, this was the NL's version of Terry Steinbach. In a good situation right now, and Taubensee and he make good platoon mates. Credit where credit is due to Knight on handling these two. Of course, Ray Knight once said, and I quote: "Frank Thomas walks too much." Uh-huh.

ERIC OWENS   **UT**   **1971**   **Age 26**

Year	Team	Lge	AB	H	DB	TP	HR	BB	SB	CS	OUT	BA	OBA	SA	EQA	EQR	Peak
1993	Winston-Salem	Caro	498	114	15	1	8	47	11	5	389	.229	.295	.311	.204	37	.225
1994	Chattanooga	South	541	134	14	2	4	55	21	7	414	.248	.317	.303	.215	44	.234
1995	Indianapolis	AmA	437	134	20	6	13	55	31	10	313	.307	.384	.469	.288	70	.309
1996	Indianapolis	AmA	127	41	7	1	4	12	5	2	88	.323	.381	.488	.290	20	.305
1996	Cincinnati	NL	203	42	6	0	0	25	13	2	163	.207	.294	.236	.188	13	.198
1997	*Cincinnati*	*NL*	*283*	*75*	*17*	*2*	*5*	*26*	*18*	*6*	*214*	*.265*	*.327*	*.392*	*.259*	*37*	

He's earned his shot, having hit well two years in a row. Going to have to tangle with several others for the playing time he needs to develop. 1997 will be a very critical year for him, and it could turn on 25 PAs during spring training. This can be a vicious and unfair game.

EDDIE PEREZ   **3B/1B**   **1970**   **Age 27**

Year	Team	Lge	AB	H	DB	TP	HR	BB	SB	CS	OUT	BA	OBA	SA	EQA	EQR	Peak
1993	Vancouver	PCL	364	106	15	2	13	27	14	5	263	.291	.340	.451	.266	48	.289
1993	California	AL	181	46	6	2	5	10	5	3	138	.254	.293	.392	.229	17	.249
1994	Vancouver	PCL	218	59	10	1	7	31	7	3	162	.271	.361	.422	.264	29	.284
1994	California	AL	129	27	4	0	6	12	3	0	102	.209	.277	.380	.220	12	.236
1995	Vancouver	PCL	255	87	10	4	9	26	5	2	170	.341	.402	.518	.305	44	.322
1995	California	AL	72	13	5	1	1	12	0	2	61	.181	.298	.319	.194	5	.203
1996	Indianapolis	AmA	469	141	26	4	20	54	10	0	328	.301	.373	.501	.291	75	.302

Brought in as a favor to Daddy. Despite that, he played real well at Indianapolis last year, and earned at least a peek at spring training. The last 1000 PAs or so indicate he may have learned to hit.

POKEY REESE   **SS**   **1973**   **Age 24**

Year	Team	Lge	AB	H	DB	TP	HR	BB	SB	CS	OUT	BA	OBA	SA	EQA	EQR	Peak
1993	Chattanooga	South	348	67	14	2	3	22	5	2	283	.193	.241	.270	.160	14	.181
1994	Chattanooga	South	500	133	17	2	13	44	12	2	369	.266	.325	.386	.243	54	.272
1995	Indianapolis	AmA	348	81	16	0	11	38	8	4	271	.233	.308	.374	.228	34	.252
1996	Indianapolis	AmA	286	65	9	0	3	24	5	2	223	.227	.287	.290	.193	18	.209
1997	*Cincinnati*	*NL*	*230*	*60*	*11*	*1*	*6*	*16*	*8*	*5*	*175*	*.261*	*.309*	*.396*	*.247*	*27*	

Needs a change of scenery. He isn't going to be able to help this team during his career, and he could catch on somewhere else. Supposedly a pretty slick glove, but he's not going to displace Barry Larkin. With his luck, he'll be traded to Baltimore. Must have been some sort of mass murderer or telemarketer in a past life.

CHRISTIAN ROJAS   **OF**   **1975**   **Age 22**

Year	Team	Lge	AB	H	DB	TP	HR	BB	SB	CS	OUT	BA	OBA	SA	EQA	EQR	Peak
1996	Charleston-WV	S Atl	492	99	15	1	10	36	3	4	397	.201	.256	.297	.176	26	.197

Showed some power in the South Atlantic League, but that's like showing some range on "Melrose Place." Needs to hit for at least a reasonable average next year, whatever level he ends up at.

TOBY RUMFIELD   **1B**   **1973**   **Age 24**

Year	Team	Lge	AB	H	DB	TP	HR	BB	SB	CS	OUT	BA	OBA	SA	EQA	EQR	Peak
1993	Charleston-WV	S Atl	346	70	10	1	5	19	3	2	278	.202	.244	.280	.165	15	.187
1994	Winston-Salem	Caro	473	108	8	2	20	40	1	2	367	.228	.288	.381	.220	42	.246
1995	Chattanooga	South	281	72	8	1	8	26	0	2	210	.256	.319	.377	.232	27	.256
1996	Chattanooga	South	374	102	15	1	10	31	1	1	273	.273	.328	.398	.244	40	.266
1997	*Cincinnati*	*NL*	*439*	*119*	*21*	*2*	*13*	*35*	*1*	*1*	*321*	*.271*	*.325*	*.417*	*.259*	*55*	

Bulky first base prospect. He's shown improvement each year, and as long as someone does that you give them more playing time. Could really break out with some big power numbers. I like him more than his numbers would indicate. 1997 will be a make or break year for him.

REGGIE SANDERS   **RF**   **1968**   **Age 29**

Year	Team	Lge	AB	H	DB	TP	HR	BB	SB	CS	OUT	BA	OBA	SA	EQA	EQR	Peak
1993	Cincinnati	NL	508	144	15	2	22	58	23	8	372	.283	.357	.451	.272	71	.286
1994	Cincinnati	NL	406	109	19	6	19	47	19	8	305	.268	.344	.485	.273	59	.284
1995	Cincinnati	NL	500	160	35	5	31	75	30	10	350	.320	.409	.596	.322	103	.330
1996	Cincinnati	NL	294	77	15	1	15	47	20	7	224	.262	.364	.473	.278	46	.280
1997	*Cincinnati*	*NL*	*508*	*133*	*32*	*4*	*24*	*72*	*44*	*7*	*382*	*.262*	*.353*	*.482*	*.295*	*91*	

A very fine outfielder. That projection looks a little optimistic to me, but it's certainly not out of the question. At least two women in my cohort consider him to be nothing short of gorgeous; I haven't polled the guys. Will still be able to push a team closer to a championship for five to six more years; players with this set of skills tend to age particularly well. Don't be surprised to see the average drop and the walks skyrocket.

RUBEN SANTANA   **OF**   **1970**   **Age 27**

Year	Team	Lge	AB	H	DB	TP	HR	BB	SB	CS	OUT	BA	OBA	SA	EQA	EQR	Peak
1993	Jacksonville	South	510	146	13	1	20	36	8	4	368	.286	.333	.433	.256	61	.279
1994	Jacksonville	South	511	141	19	2	8	32	6	3	373	.276	.319	.368	.232	49	.249
1995	Chattanooga	South	574	164	19	6	13	49	2	3	413	.286	.342	.408	.251	65	.266
1996	Chattanooga	South	352	106	16	1	8	21	3	2	248	.301	.340	.420	.256	41	.266
1997	*Cincinnati*	*NL*	*546*	*158*	*26*	*2*	*17*	*25*	*6*	*5*	*393*	*.289*	*.320*	*.438*	*.264*	*70*	

Could help out several clubs as a utility outfielder, but that's not particularly likely. Four years in AA usually means no prospect, or possibly a stalker.

EDDIE TAUBENSEE   **C**   **1969**   **Age 28**

Year	Team	Lge	AB	H	DB	TP	HR	BB	SB	CS	OUT	BA	OBA	SA	EQA	EQR	Peak
1993	Houston	NL	293	76	11	1	9	26	1	0	217	.259	.320	.396	.240	31	.256
1994	Cincinnati	NL	180	54	8	2	8	18	2	0	126	.300	.364	.500	.286	28	.302
1995	Cincinnati	NL	223	66	12	2	10	25	2	2	159	.296	.367	.502	.284	34	.295
1996	Cincinnati	NL	334	99	14	0	14	30	2	4	239	.296	.354	.464	.269	45	.276
1997	*Cincinnati*	*NL*	*404*	*112*	*11*	*1*	*28*	*72*	*1*	*1*	*293*	*.277*	*.387*	*.517*	*.307*	*76*	

Will best be remembered for being the "bum half" of the Kenny Lofton trade, but that's not entirely fair. He's a good ballplayer in his own right, and is probably tougher to replace than Lofton. That projection would make him the 1997 version of Todd Hundley. It's fairly rare for hitters to take quantum leaps forward in more than one area. Vladimir projects Eddie to take a big step forward in isolated power and walk rate. Something to consider, anyway.

JUSTIN TOWLE   **UT**   **1974**   **Age 23**

Year	Team	Lge	AB	H	DB	TP	HR	BB	SB	CS	OUT	BA	OBA	SA	EQA	EQR	Peak
1994	Charleston-SC	S Atl	230	43	4	0	2	21	1	2	189	.187	.255	.230	.143	7	.163
1995	Charleston-WV	S Atl	368	94	13	1	8	36	2	2	277	.255	.322	.361	.229	35	.256
1996	Winston-Salem	Caro	369	86	7	1	13	79	7	2	285	.233	.368	.363	.250	45	.277
1997	*Cincinnati*	*NL*	*416*	*99*	*25*	*2*	*20*	*82*	*14*	*3*	*320*	*.238*	*.363*	*.452*	*.285*	*69*	

Boy, do I like this kid. He drew 93 walks in the Carolina League to go along with 17 stolen bases. Young players with plate discipline and speed are rare commodities. Add in power, and you've got a legitimate prospect. He's probably two years out, but Towle could really be a surprising player.

PAT WATKINS   **OF**   **1973**   **Age 24**

Year	Team	Lge	AB	H	DB	TP	HR	BB	SB	CS	OUT	BA	OBA	SA	EQA	EQR	Peak
1994	Winston-Salem	Caro	538	142	17	2	19	53	17	7	403	.264	.330	.409	.249	62	.279
1995	Winston-Salem	Caro	110	22	1	1	4	10	1	0	88	.200	.267	.336	.198	8	.218
1995	Chattanooga	South	370	106	19	1	13	32	4	3	267	.286	.343	.449	.263	47	.290
1996	Chattanooga	South	503	134	23	2	8	23	10	6	375	.266	.298	.368	.224	45	.243
1997	*Cincinnati*	*NL*	*438*	*117*	*25*	*1*	*11*	*26*	*15*	*8*	*329*	*.267*	*.308*	*.404*	*.251*	*52*	

Marginal prospect with marginal power. Top end, he could be the tail end of Milt Thompson's career. More likely? The tail end of Henry Block's.

JIMMY WHITE   **OF**   **1973**   **Age 24**

Year	Team	Lge	AB	H	DB	TP	HR	BB	SB	CS	OUT	BA	OBA	SA	EQA	EQR	Peak
1993	Osceola	Flor	461	118	6	5	11	47	13	7	350	.256	.325	.362	.233	46	.265
1994	Osceola	Flor	185	62	10	3	8	20	6	2	125	.335	.400	.551	.312	34	.349
1994	Jackson	Texas	216	61	5	3	9	12	1	2	157	.282	.320	.458	.255	26	.287
1997	*Cincinnati*	*NL*	*196*	*50*	*11*	*2*	*7*	*17*	*3*	*3*	*149*	*.255*	*.315*	*.439*	*.259*	*25*	

One year away from being no prospect. Defense might be enough to get him some brownie points and pull him up a level if he's on the edge.

BEN BAILEY   **RSP**   **1975**   **Age 22**

YR	TEAM	Lge	IP	H	ER	HR	BB	K	ERA	W	L	H/9	HR/9	BB/9	K/9	KW
1996	Chston., WV	S Atl	51.7	86	44	3	36	37	7.66	1	5	14.98	.52	6.27	6.45	.58
1996	Winston-Salem	Caro	90.3	107	35	11	44	53	3.49	6	4	10.66	1.10	4.38	5.28	.66

A lot of kids his age boost their K rate about one per nine innings. If Bailey can do that and continue his progress with his control, he'll be a very good prospect. If he doesn't, it may take him three or four more years to develop, if at all.

JEFF BRANTLEY   **RRP**   **1964**   **Age 33**

YR	TEAM	Lge	IP	H	ER	HR	BB	K	ERA	W	L	H/9	HR/9	BB/9	K/9	KW
1993	San Francisco	NL	110.7	121	59	20	60	74	4.80	5	7	9.84	1.63	4.88	6.02	.79
1994	Cincinnati	NL	63.3	48	17	6	34	59	2.42	5	2	6.82	.85	4.83	8.38	1.59
1995	Cincinnati	NL	68.3	56	19	11	25	55	2.50	6	2	7.38	1.45	3.29	7.24	1.59
1996	Cincinnati	NL	69.3	57	17	7	34	66	2.21	6	2	7.40	.91	4.41	8.57	1.75

Giants fans used to cringe when Brantley came into the game. More accurately, they used to start packing their stuff and heading for the parking lot. Since getting paroled to Cincinnati, Brantley's shown some sort of improvement each year and has really become a fine reliever. Hats off to him.

ADAM BRYANT   **RRP**   **1972**   **Age 25**

YR	TEAM	Lge	IP	H	ER	HR	BB	K	ERA	W	L	H/9	HR/9	BB/9	K/9	KW
1996	Chston., WV	S Atl	26.3	32	9	3	4	14	3.08	2	1	10.94	1.03	1.37	4.78	1.25
1996	Winston-Salem	Caro	30.0	45	13	1	14	11	3.90	2	1	13.50	.30	4.20	3.30	.05

Reds should have bumped him up another notch last year. He'll spend this year in AA, trying to consolidate his gains. The interesting thing about Adam Bryant: richer than Warren Buffett. No kidding. Rolling in dough.

DAVE BURBA RSP 1967 Age 30

YR	TEAM	Lge	IP	H	ER	HR	BB	K	ERA	W	L	H/9	HR/9	BB/9	K/9	KW
1993	San Francisco	NL	92.3	104	48	15	48	86	4.68	4	6	10.14	1.46	4.68	8.38	1.62
1994	San Francisco	NL	73.0	61	34	5	52	79	4.19	4	4	7.52	.62	6.41	9.74	1.64
1995	Cincinnati	NL	61.7	55	20	4	31	45	2.92	5	2	8.03	.58	4.52	6.57	1.06
1995	San Francisco	NL	43.0	40	24	6	29	42	5.02	2	3	8.37	1.26	6.07	8.79	1.41
1996	Cincinnati	NL	192.7	184	83	18	114	129	3.88	11	10	8.60	.84	5.33	6.03	.68

Dusty Baker must be kicking himself. The Reds have turned two virtual Giant castoffs into really valuable pitchers. Burba is not a good bet to maintain his success beyond 1997; his K rate wasn't particularly great and 1996 was the heaviest load he'd ever carried. If you've got him in a fantasy league and he's lighting up the league in July, go ahead and listen to trade offers.

HECTOR CARRASCO RRP 1970 Age 27

YR	TEAM	Lge	IP	H	ER	HR	BB	K	ERA	W	L	H/9	HR/9	BB/9	K/9	KW
1993	Kane County	Midw	127.3	193	99	14	100	74	7.00	3	11	13.64	.99	7.07	5.23	-.02
1994	Cincinnati	NL	54.7	44	14	3	35	38	2.30	5	1	7.24	.49	5.76	6.26	.64
1995	Cincinnati	NL	86.0	90	39	1	53	58	4.08	5	5	9.42	.10	5.55	6.07	.64
1996	Indianapolis	AmA	20.3	20	7	1	16	14	3.10	1	1	8.85	.44	7.08	6.20	.30
1996	Cincinnati	NL	73.0	61	31	6	51	52	3.82	4	4	7.52	.74	6.29	6.41	.57

Vicious, nasty stuff. If he can ever learn to throw it in the strike zone he'll be devastating. That might happen, but it won't be in 1997. More likely events include the release of Jerry Reinsdorf's new photo book, *Sex*.

TIM FORTUGNO LRP 1962 Age 35

YR	TEAM	Lge	IP	H	ER	HR	BB	K	ERA	W	L	H/9	HR/9	BB/9	K/9	KW
1993	Ottawa	Inter	37.7	31	16	5	37	34	3.82	2	2	7.41	1.19	8.84	8.12	.50
1994	Chattanooga	South	24.3	23	15	0	21	28	5.55	1	2	8.51	.00	7.77	10.36	1.51
1994	Cincinnati	NL	29.3	33	12	2	17	27	3.68	2	1	10.12	.61	5.22	8.28	1.46
1995	Vancouver	PCL	11.0	8	2	2	6	7	1.64	1	0	6.55	1.64	4.91	5.73	.68
1995	Chi. White Sox	AL	38.3	30	19	7	20	24	4.46	2	2	7.04	1.64	4.70	5.63	.70
1996	Chattanooga	South	10.0	6	0	0	5	7	.00	1	0	5.40	.00	4.50	6.30	.97
1996	Indianapolis	AmA	55.3	61	27	6	34	39	4.39	3	3	9.92	.98	5.53	6.34	.73

I'm convinced this guy could be Sandy Koufax if only I watched him every time he pitched. Every time I see the guy, he's Madduxesque—throws about nine different fastballs and changeups wherever he wants, and batters look more confused than Bob Dole's campaign manager trying to decide on a cotton candy color. His career is probably close to over.

KEVIN JARVIS RSP 1970 Age 27

YR	TEAM	Lge	IP	H	ER	HR	BB	K	ERA	W	L	H/9	HR/9	BB/9	K/9	KW
1993	Winston-Salem	Caro	126.3	159	72	13	73	63	5.13	5	9	11.33	.93	5.20	4.49	.20
1993	Chattanooga	South	34.0	30	6	0	15	13	1.59	3	1	7.94	.00	3.97	3.44	.15
1994	Indianapolis	AmA	126.7	140	48	14	45	80	3.41	8	6	9.95	.99	3.20	5.68	1.10
1994	Cincinnati	NL	17.7	21	12	4	7	9	6.11	1	1	10.70	2.04	3.57	4.58	.64
1995	Indianapolis	AmA	58.0	65	30	2	25	32	4.66	3	3	10.09	.31	3.88	4.97	.69
1995	Cincinnati	NL	78.7	91	50	13	39	30	5.72	3	6	10.41	1.49	4.46	3.43	.03
1996	Indianapolis	AmA	40.7	50	27	3	17	27	5.98	2	3	11.07	.66	3.76	5.98	1.05
1996	Cincinnati	NL	120.7	151	81	16	54	55	6.04	4	9	11.26	1.19	4.03	4.10	.36

Very possibly the next Jeff Bittiger. Not likely to ever really be effective, and his mechanics scare the hell out of me.

DOMINGO JEAN RRP 1969 Age 28

YR	TEAM	Lge	IP	H	ER	HR	BB	K	ERA	W	L	H/9	HR/9	BB/9	K/9	KW
1993	Albany, NY	East	56.3	48	23	2	41	31	3.67	3	3	7.67	.32	6.55	4.95	.01
1993	Columbus, OH	Inter	42.0	44	14	2	19	32	3.00	3	2	9.43	.43	4.07	6.86	1.27
1993	NY Yankees	AL	40.0	37	18	8	22	21	4.05	2	2	8.32	1.80	4.95	4.72	.34
1994	Tucson	PCL	17.7	19	10	3	13	14	5.09	1	1	9.68	1.53	6.62	7.13	.72
1995	Oklahoma	AmA	85.7	103	64	12	75	64	6.72	3	7	10.82	1.26	7.88	6.72	.27
1995	Tucson	PCL	12.7	14	7	1	8	13	4.97	0	1	9.95	.71	5.68	9.24	1.66
1996	Chattanooga	South	36.7	39	17	1	20	24	4.17	2	2	9.57	.25	4.91	5.89	.74

Yet another guy who used to have a great arm and can't find the strike zone. More likely to make an impact in the NBA than MLB. Probably safe for Domingo to invest in some extra padding for those many bus rides in his future. Has been switched to relief, so he won't officially be washed up until he's failed at that for two years.

CLINT KOPPE   **RSP**   **1974**   **Age 23**

YR	TEAM	Lge	IP	H	ER	HR	BB	K	ERA	W	L	H/9	HR/9	BB/9	K/9	KW
1995	Chston., WV	S Atl	131.0	212	90	15	73	69	6.18	4	11	14.56	1.03	5.02	4.74	.33
1996	Winston-Salem	Caro	85.0	102	42	11	36	31	4.45	4	5	10.80	1.16	3.81	3.28	.14
1996	Chattanooga	South	51.7	63	26	3	22	22	4.53	3	3	10.97	.52	3.83	3.83	.32

Grade C prospect. One big plus: he has adjusted well at each level as he's moved up, despite not having fantastic stuff or a huge K rate. He's more likely to succeed for a short time in the majors than a thousand guys like Brad Pennington.

DEREK LILLIQUIST   **LRP**   **1966**   **Age 31**

YR	TEAM	Lge	IP	H	ER	HR	BB	K	ERA	W	L	H/9	HR/9	BB/9	K/9	KW
1993	Cleveland	AL	63.3	66	18	6	22	42	2.56	5	2	9.38	.85	3.13	5.97	1.21
1994	Cleveland	AL	29.7	31	13	6	9	15	3.94	2	1	9.40	1.82	2.73	4.55	.83
1995	Albuquerque	PCL	12.7	17	3	1	4	8	2.13	1	0	12.08	.71	2.84	5.68	1.18
1995	Boston	AL	23.0	26	13	6	9	9	5.09	1	2	10.17	2.35	3.52	3.52	.29
1996	Indianapolis	AmA	49.7	52	16	3	13	42	2.90	4	2	9.42	.54	2.36	7.61	1.95

Can still get left-handers out, so he'll have a job longer than, say, anyone currently working on UPN.

CURT LYONS   **RSP**   **1975**   **Age 22**

YR	TEAM	Lge	IP	H	ER	HR	BB	K	ERA	W	L	H/9	HR/9	BB/9	K/9	KW
1994	Chston., WV	S Atl	55.7	84	35	3	33	33	5.66	2	4	13.58	.49	5.34	5.34	.44
1995	Winston-Salem	Caro	146.7	164	68	11	89	89	4.17	8	8	10.06	.67	5.46	5.46	.46
1996	Chattanooga	South	131.7	133	45	9	61	128	3.08	9	6	9.09	.62	4.17	8.75	1.87
1996	Cincinnati	NL	15.7	18	7	1	8	12	4.02	1	1	10.34	.57	4.60	6.89	1.15

Starting pitcher, and a good one. Reasonable control, good K rate, good stuff. My only concern is that his workload has been just shy of Cher's during shore leave. I don't like having 21-year-olds throw this many innings in a compressed time. He could develop into an exceptional starting pitcher; main danger might be that he gets hot and wins a spot in the rotation. If that happens and the Reds contend, he could be forced to do something stupid like pitch 220 innings at age 22.

PEDRO MARTINEZ   **LRP**   **1969**   **Age 28**

YR	TEAM	Lge	IP	H	ER	HR	BB	K	ERA	W	L	H/9	HR/9	BB/9	K/9	KW
1993	Las Vegas	PCL	80.7	86	37	8	49	51	4.13	4	5	9.60	.89	5.47	5.69	.53
1993	San Diego	NL	35.3	25	10	5	17	31	2.55	3	1	6.37	1.27	4.33	7.90	1.55
1994	San Diego	NL	67.0	54	26	4	55	49	3.49	4	3	7.25	.54	7.39	6.58	.35
1995	Tucson	PCL	31.7	41	21	2	16	19	5.97	1	3	11.65	.57	4.55	5.40	.66
1995	Houston	NL	21.0	32	18	3	19	16	7.71	0	2	13.71	1.29	8.14	6.86	.25
1996	Norfolk	Inter	53.7	49	25	4	26	31	4.19	3	3	8.22	.67	4.36	5.20	.64

Innovator who developed the Global Positioning Satellite System to help him find the strike zone. Although he's made millions in licensing fees, it doesn't always work. At least he's escaped the Mets' system, where pitchers are men and frayed labra roam free.

MIKE MORGAN   **RSP**   **1960**   **Age 37**

YR	TEAM	Lge	IP	H	ER	HR	BB	K	ERA	W	L	H/9	HR/9	BB/9	K/9	KW
1993	Chicago Cubs	NL	202.0	210	90	16	97	107	4.01	11	11	9.36	.71	4.32	4.77	.51
1994	Chicago Cubs	NL	82.3	111	60	12	44	54	6.56	2	7	12.13	1.31	4.81	5.90	.77
1995	Orlando	South	10.0	14	9	1	9	4	8.10	0	1	12.60	.90	8.10	3.60	-.82
1995	Chicago Cubs	NL	23.7	21	7	2	10	13	2.66	2	1	7.99	.76	3.80	4.94	.70
1995	St. Louis	NL	105.3	113	41	10	34	41	3.50	7	5	9.66	.85	2.91	3.50	.44
1996	Louisville	AmA	22.0	32	18	2	14	8	7.36	0	2	13.09	.82	5.73	3.27	-.34
1996	Cincinnati	NL	26.7	29	8	2	9	17	2.70	2	1	9.79	.68	3.04	5.74	1.15
1996	St. Louis	NL	102.7	120	56	14	49	48	4.91	4	7	10.52	1.23	4.30	4.21	.33

Only 37? I thought Morgan was at least 80 or so. Helped fill some gaps for the Cards last season, but his future is darker than Gordon Liddy's heart. He knows how to pitch, but it's hard to get people out when you walk nearly as many as you strike out, and he's pricier than the youngsters at this point. Will undoubtedly be dredged up and poured onto the mound a few times for somebody this year.

KIRT OJALA   **LSP**   **1969**   **Age 28**

YR	TEAM	Lge	IP	H	ER	HR	BB	K	ERA	W	L	H/9	HR/9	BB/9	K/9	KW
1993	Columbus, OH	Inter	119.0	158	83	13	91	68	6.28	4	9	11.95	.98	6.88	5.14	-.01
1994	Columbus, OH	Inter	138.7	172	74	12	61	68	4.80	6	9	11.16	.78	3.96	4.41	.48
1995	Columbus, OH	Inter	136.3	145	68	16	73	90	4.49	7	8	9.57	1.06	4.82	5.94	.78
1996	Indianapolis	AmA	127.3	158	66	14	49	77	4.66	6	8	11.17	.99	3.46	5.44	.95

Axiom: If a player's name is "Kirt" with an I, they won't help your ballclub.

MARK PORTUGAL   **RSP**   **1963**   **Age 34**

YR	TEAM	Lge	IP	H	ER	HR	BB	K	ERA	W	L	H/9	HR/9	BB/9	K/9	KW
1993	Houston	NL	201.7	206	69	11	100	127	3.08	14	8	9.19	.49	4.46	5.67	.77
1994	San Francisco	NL	135.0	136	60	17	57	81	4.00	8	7	9.07	1.13	3.80	5.40	.85
1995	Cincinnati	NL	76.3	81	31	7	28	30	3.66	4	4	9.55	.83	3.30	3.54	.35
1995	San Francisco	NL	102.7	111	51	10	43	57	4.47	5	6	9.73	.88	3.77	5.00	.72
1996	Cincinnati	NL	153.0	149	66	19	55	81	3.88	9	8	8.76	1.12	3.24	4.76	.78

I love anyone that drives Marge Schott this nuts. This includes Portugal in particular, although I must admit; I also have a soft spot for Simon Wiesenthal. Good control; irritates a lot of hitters by refusing to throw a ball over the middle of the plate for five or six innings at a time. I believe he'll stay healthy and league average, and that's a pretty good set of attributes for a starting pitcher. Mechanics are tighter than they were four years ago; Portugal's release point is much more consistent from pitch to pitch. I don't know how he went about doing this, but other guys should be seeking him out.

JASON ROBBINS   **RBP**   **1973**   **Age 24**

YR	TEAM	Lge	IP	H	ER	HR	BB	K	ERA	W	L	H/9	HR/9	BB/9	K/9	KW
1995	Winston-Salem	Caro	129.7	133	63	17	59	77	4.37	6	8	9.23	1.18	4.10	5.34	.76
1996	Chattanooga	South	70.0	92	44	9	50	52	5.66	3	5	11.83	1.16	6.43	6.69	.62

I really like this kid. He throws a fastball that's very hard to hit, one that tails a bit right at the end. He also throws it effortlessly. The numbers indicate he's a Grade B prospect, but I like him more than that. He'll struggle a bit more in the minors at each step, but could be a very impressive major league closer. Mr. Robbins is going to make a lot of money in MLB. Not as much as Jerry Colangelo, but a lot.

JOHN ROPER   **RSP**   **1972**   **Age 25**

YR	TEAM	Lge	IP	H	ER	HR	BB	K	ERA	W	L	H/9	HR/9	BB/9	K/9	KW
1993	Indianapolis	AmA	53.0	55	28	11	36	38	4.75	2	4	9.34	1.87	6.11	6.45	.62
1993	Cincinnati	NL	78.7	95	47	10	46	53	5.38	3	6	10.87	1.14	5.26	6.06	.71
1994	Indianapolis	AmA	54.3	52	14	0	15	29	2.32	4	2	8.61	.00	2.48	4.80	.98
1994	Cincinnati	NL	90.7	89	43	16	38	47	4.27	5	5	8.83	1.59	3.77	4.67	.61
1995	Indianapolis	AmA	40.0	48	24	9	21	20	5.40	1	3	10.80	2.03	4.72	4.50	.32
1996	Chattanooga	South	11.0	21	17	2	8	4	13.91	0	1	17.18	1.64	6.55	3.27	-.55

If your league levels starts losing letters, you might as well get to work on the résumé. Borderline prospect early in his career, and south of the border now.

JOHNNY RUFFIN   **RRP**   **1972**   **Age 25**

YR	TEAM	Lge	IP	H	ER	HR	BB	K	ERA	W	L	H/9	HR/9	BB/9	K/9	KW
1993	Birmingham	South	20.3	20	10	3	11	17	4.43	1	1	8.85	1.33	4.87	7.52	1.29
1993	Nashville	AmA	57.0	51	20	5	22	63	3.16	4	2	8.05	.79	3.47	9.95	2.45
1993	Cincinnati	NL	36.7	37	14	5	15	29	3.44	2	2	9.08	1.23	3.68	7.12	1.45
1994	Cincinnati	NL	68.0	59	22	7	33	41	2.91	5	3	7.81	.93	4.37	5.43	.72
1995	Indianapolis	AmA	47.0	30	17	4	44	51	3.26	3	2	5.74	.77	8.43	9.77	1.15
1995	Cincinnati	NL	13.0	5	2	0	12	10	1.38	1	0	3.46	.00	8.31	6.92	.23
1996	Cincinnati	NL	62.7	72	36	9	43	61	5.17	3	4	10.34	1.29	6.18	8.76	1.38

I'm not a major league pitcher, and I've had a pretty easy life so I can't really empathize completely, but this has got to be one of the most frustrating things in the world. You work your butt off your whole life to become one of the very best in the world at something, and then all of the sudden you simply lose it. Still throws nasty stuff, but has just completely lost the strike zone. Might look for it for several years. Great to watch, and I hope he can put it all back together. Ruffin can be great. He has that kind of ability, and I really enjoy watching him play.

ROGER SALKELD   **RSP**   **1971**   **Age 26**

YR	TEAM	Lge	IP	H	ER	HR	BB	K	ERA	W	L	H/9	HR/9	BB/9	K/9	KW
1993	Jacksonville	South	70.0	81	40	9	39	42	5.14	3	5	10.41	1.16	5.01	5.40	.55
1993	Seattle	AL	14.0	14	3	0	4	13	1.93	2	0	9.00	.00	2.57	8.36	2.14
1994	Calgary	PCL	63.0	66	39	9	46	46	5.57	2	5	9.43	1.29	6.57	6.57	.55
1994	Seattle	AL	59.7	70	35	6	46	45	5.28	3	4	10.56	.91	6.94	6.79	.53
1995	Indianapolis	AmA	113.0	102	55	13	73	75	4.38	6	7	8.12	1.04	5.81	5.97	.54
1995	Tacoma	PCL	14.0	9	3	0	9	10	1.93	2	0	5.79	.00	5.79	6.43	.70
1996	Cincinnati	NL	115.0	116	60	17	64	72	4.70	5	8	9.08	1.33	5.01	5.63	.63

Had a chance to be Roger Clemens once. That chance is gone. Like most pitchers, has lost some vicious off his fastball due to injury. One more data point to support the "There is no such thing as a pitching prospect" hypothesis.

PETE SCHOUREK   **LSP**   **1969**   **Age 28**

YR	TEAM	Lge	IP	H	ER	HR	BB	K	ERA	W	L	H/9	HR/9	BB/9	K/9	KW
1993	NY Mets	NL	127.3	171	84	14	61	70	5.94	4	10	12.09	.99	4.31	4.95	.57
1994	Cincinnati	NL	81.0	89	34	11	36	64	3.78	5	4	9.89	1.22	4.00	7.11	1.37
1995	Cincinnati	NL	185.3	165	61	17	60	143	2.96	14	7	8.01	.83	2.91	6.94	1.59
1996	Cincinnati	NL	67.0	79	42	7	31	47	5.64	2	5	10.61	.94	4.16	6.31	1.06

Wasn't as good as he looked in 1995 or as bad as he looked in 1996. With a little luck, he could pull a Mark Portugal, put his mechanics together and become a consistent starter. He's got good enough stuff so that he can be more than that, but his mechanics don't instill huge glops of confidence in me.

SCOTT SERVICE   **RRP**   **1967**   **Age 30**

YR	TEAM	Lge	IP	H	ER	HR	BB	K	ERA	W	L	H/9	HR/9	BB/9	K/9	KW
1993	Indianapolis	AmA	29.0	25	13	5	20	26	4.03	1	2	7.76	1.55	6.21	8.07	1.14
1993	Cincinnati	NL	40.0	38	17	6	19	39	3.83	2	2	8.55	1.35	4.28	8.77	1.86
1994	Indianapolis	AmA	55.0	39	12	1	33	60	1.96	5	1	6.38	.16	5.40	9.82	1.92
1995	Indianapolis	AmA	39.3	35	11	5	20	42	2.52	3	1	8.01	1.14	4.58	9.61	2.06
1995	San Francisco	NL	30.0	20	10	5	23	27	3.00	2	1	6.00	1.50	6.90	8.10	.97
1996	Indianapolis	AmA	45.7	39	16	5	15	48	3.15	3	2	7.69	.99	2.96	9.46	2.41
1996	Cincinnati	NL	48.0	51	18	7	22	40	3.38	3	2	9.56	1.31	4.12	7.50	1.47

Throws real hard. He reminds me of Eric Plunk of the Indians, and that's not a bad guess for what his next few years will hold.

JEFF SHAW   **RRP**   **1967**   **Age 30**

YR	TEAM	Lge	IP	H	ER	HR	BB	K	ERA	W	L	H/9	HR/9	BB/9	K/9	KW
1993	Montreal	NL	93.0	96	45	13	42	48	4.35	5	5	9.29	1.26	4.06	4.65	.53
1994	Montreal	NL	66.3	66	27	8	20	43	3.66	4	3	8.95	1.09	2.71	5.83	1.27
1995	Montreal	NL	61.3	60	30	4	31	40	4.40	3	4	8.80	.59	4.55	5.87	.82
1996	Cincinnati	NL	102.7	102	29	8	38	60	2.54	8	3	8.94	.70	3.33	5.26	.92

You just saw his peak, and it wasn't bad. He led the league in holds with 22, and will likely be able to make a few bucks the next few years as a reliable bullpen guy. Can continue to be successful in his current role, but stretched to go much beyond that.

JOHN SMILEY   **LSP**   **1965**   **Age 32**

YR	TEAM	Lge	IP	H	ER	HR	BB	K	ERA	W	L	H/9	HR/9	BB/9	K/9	KW
1993	Cincinnati	NL	103.7	120	64	15	42	58	5.56	4	8	10.42	1.30	3.65	5.04	.77
1994	Cincinnati	NL	156.7	167	69	18	51	104	3.96	9	8	9.59	1.03	2.93	5.97	1.26
1995	Cincinnati	NL	172.7	179	62	11	53	111	3.23	11	8	9.33	.57	2.76	5.79	1.24
1996	Cincinnati	NL	212.7	214	86	20	72	149	3.64	13	11	9.06	.85	3.05	6.31	1.34

Ray Knight may be mononeural, but he did do a reasonable job of finding the very edge of his pitching staff's workload limits. Smiley was pretty much maxed out last year, and he might have arm trouble next year as a result of it. In all probability, he'll be healthy and effective. Healthy, effective left-handed starters are likely to be a valuable commodity. That Neagle trade seems further back in history than "What's Happening."

LEE SMITH   **RRP**   **1958**   **Age 39**

YR	TEAM	Lge	IP	H	ER	HR	BB	K	ERA	W	L	H/9	HR/9	BB/9	K/9	KW
1993	St. Louis	NL	49.0	50	24	12	15	48	4.41	2	3	9.18	2.20	2.76	8.82	2.25
1994	Baltimore	AL	38.0	32	11	6	12	41	2.61	3	1	7.58	1.42	2.84	9.71	2.53
1995	California	AL	48.7	43	14	3	26	43	2.59	4	1	7.95	.55	4.81	7.95	1.45
1996	California	AL	10.7	8	3	0	3	6	2.53	1	0	6.75	.00	2.53	5.06	1.05
1996	Cincinnati	NL	44.3	50	18	4	27	31	3.65	3	2	10.15	.81	5.48	6.29	.73

Not done, but not particularly valuable. Can't bounce back and pitch effectively, and anyone that won't change his role for the genuine good of the team has a problem. And I'm not a big believer in clubhouse chemistry. Had a big reverse platoon split in 1996. Lefties hit only .222 against him.

GABE WHITE   **LSP**   **1972**   **Age 25**

YR	TEAM	Lge	IP	H	ER	HR	BB	K	ERA	W	L	H/9	HR/9	BB/9	K/9	KW
1993	Harrisburg	East	92.0	94	29	5	38	61	2.84	7	3	9.20	.49	3.72	5.97	1.06
1993	Ottawa	Inter	38.0	41	14	3	11	23	3.32	2	2	9.71	.71	2.61	5.45	1.16
1994	Ottawa	Inter	69.0	87	50	12	36	53	6.52	2	6	11.35	1.57	4.70	6.91	1.13
1994	Montreal	NL	23.3	24	14	4	13	16	5.40	1	2	9.26	1.54	5.01	6.17	.80
1995	Ottawa	Inter	57.7	67	32	11	24	31	4.99	2	4	10.46	1.72	3.75	4.84	.68
1995	Montreal	NL	25.7	26	18	7	11	22	6.31	1	2	9.12	2.45	3.86	7.71	1.61
1996	Indianapolis	AmA	64.7	77	24	5	17	42	3.34	4	3	10.72	.70	2.37	5.85	1.36

A good enough starting pitcher to be in any rotation in baseball. He'd be #5 in Atlanta, but #1 in Oakland and Detroit. May have a couple of rough transition years, but this guy can pitch. The home run trend is a bit troubling, but his peripheral stats all look either good or excellent. A keeper.

Player	Age	Team	Lge	AB	H	DB	TP	HR	BB	SB	CS	OUT	BA	OBA	SA	EQA	EQR	Peak
MARLON ALLEN	23	Winston-Salem	Caro	433	91	6	1	13	27	4	1	343	.210	.257	.319	.188	26	.205
AMADOR ARIAS	24	Winston-Salem	Caro	387	98	7	0	9	34	13	5	294	.253	.314	.341	.224	35	.240
DONALD BROACH	24	Chattanooga	South	359	91	7	1	6	33	13	5	273	.253	.316	.329	.222	32	.237
DAVID CONCEPCION	21	Charleston-WV	S Atl	121	21	2	1	0	8	1	0	100	.174	.225	.207	.111	2	.121
JAMES DAVIS	23	Charleston-WV	S Atl	332	86	8	1	3	25	3	1	247	.259	.311	.316	.213	26	.232
STEVE EDDIE	25	Winston-Salem	Caro	507	118	10	1	8	39	6	4	393	.233	.288	.304	.196	33	.207
GUILLERMO GARCIA	24	Chattanooga	South	208	63	6	0	7	9	2	2	147	.303	.332	.433	.255	24	.274
STEVEN GOODHART	23	Charleston-WV	S Atl	417	82	10	2	1	76	6	4	340	.197	.320	.237	.186	25	.202
BILLY HALL	27	Chattanooga	South	475	136	19	2	3	49	21	6	345	.286	.353	.354	.247	52	.253
MIKE HAMPTON	24	Charleston-WV	S Atl	504	105	12	2	11	47	9	3	402	.208	.276	.306	.193	33	.206
DANN HOWITT	32	Indianapolis	AmA	161	45	4	1	4	15	0	1	117	.280	.341	.391	.245	17	.232
DEE JENKINS	23	Winston-Salem	Caro	391	92	8	1	8	46	6	3	302	.235	.316	.322	.216	33	.234
ANDRE KING	22	Winston-Salem	Caro	268	46	3	2	6	29	7	3	225	.172	.253	.265	.165	12	.182
JOE KMAK	33	Indianapolis	AmA	150	42	3	0	2	27	2	0	108	.280	.390	.340	.256	18	.244
CLEVELAND LADELL	25	Chattanooga	South	414	101	13	4	5	25	20	8	321	.244	.287	.331	.212	33	.223
STEPHEN LARKIN	22	Charleston-WV	S Atl	220	55	3	1	5	28	2	2	167	.250	.335	.341	.228	21	.251
	22	Winston-Salem	Caro	120	19	2	0	2	12	2	1	102	.158	.235	.225	.131	3	.143
JAMES LOFTON	22	Winston-Salem	Caro	282	53	2	0	3	24	6	3	232	.188	.252	.227	.146	9	.162
RICKY MAGDALENO	21	Chattanooga	South	437	95	12	1	16	55	2	4	346	.217	.305	.359	.219	39	.245
LAMONT MASON	23	Charleston-WV	S Atl	203	39	1	1	1	22	4	2	166	.192	.271	.222	.154	8	.168
MIKE MEGGERS	25	Chattanooga	South	114	22	3	0	5	14	1	1	93	.193	.281	.351	.206	9	.217
NICK MORROW	24	Winston-Salem	Caro	434	102	7	2	14	50	12	3	335	.235	.314	.357	.228	42	.244
CHAD MOTTOLA	24	Cincinnati	NL	80	18	2	0	3	7	2	2	64	.225	.287	.362	.213	7	.227
	24	Indianapolis	AmA	370	97	20	2	9	25	9	5	278	.262	.309	.400	.237	38	.254
JASON PARSONS	23	Charleston-WV	S Atl	171	44	6	0	3	12	1	0	127	.257	.306	.345	.220	14	.240
ANTHONY PATELLIS	22	Charleston-WV	S Atl	234	37	5	0	3	11	2	1	198	.158	.196	.218	.092	3	.100
CHRIS SABO	34	Cincinnati	NL	128	34	7	1	3	19	2	0	94	.266	.361	.406	.261	16	.247
YURI SANCHEZ	22	Winston-Salem	Caro	362	67	6	1	5	36	4	3	298	.185	.259	.249	.157	15	.173
THOMAS SCOTT	23	Charleston-WV	S Atl	459	98	15	3	10	52	8	3	364	.214	.294	.325	.207	35	.225
JAY SORG	23	Charleston-WV	S Atl	290	62	1	0	2	21	1	2	230	.214	.267	.238	.155	11	.169
ROD THOMAS	22	Charleston-WV	S Atl	275	51	4	1	4	32	2	2	226	.185	.270	.251	.163	12	.181
TROVIN VALDEZ	22	Winston-Salem	Caro	347	75	5	2	3	19	11	6	278	.216	.257	.268	.171	17	.189
BRANDON WILSON	27	Indianapolis	AmA	315	73	5	3	4	41	9	5	247	.232	.320	.305	.213	26	.218
BRIAN WILSON	23	Charleston-WV	S Atl	322	58	5	0	2	33	4	3	267	.180	.256	.214	.138	9	.150

Player	Age	Team	Lge	IP	H	ER	HR	BB	K	ERA	W	L	H/9	HR/9	BB/9	K/9	KW
CEDRIC ALLEN	24	Chattanooga	South	25.0	36	22	4	13	9	7.92	1	2	12.96	1.44	4.68	3.24	-.09
	24	Winston-Salem	Caro	61.3	82	37	10	38	27	5.43	2	5	12.03	1.47	5.58	3.96	-.07
JUSTIN ATCHLEY	22	Charleston, WV	S Atl	74.7	142	55	10	36	43	6.63	2	6	17.12	1.21	4.34	5.18	.64
	22	Winston-Salem	Caro	61.7	86	48	13	23	34	7.01	2	5	12.55	1.90	3.36	4.96	.81
ALONSO BELTRAN	24	Winston-Salem	Caro	34.7	31	9	3	14	18	2.34	3	1	8.05	.78	3.63	4.67	.65
TRAVIS BUCKLEY	26	Chattanooga	South	49.0	67	39	6	15	30	7.16	1	4	12.31	1.10	2.76	5.51	1.15
	26	Indianapolis	AmA	116.3	138	67	22	48	48	5.18	5	8	10.68	1.70	3.71	3.71	.31
DAMON CALLAHAN	20	Charleston, WV	S Atl	84.0	160	85	7	58	47	9.11	1	8	17.14	.75	6.21	5.04	.12
GIOVANNI CARRARA	28	Indianapolis	AmA	44.3	31	5	2	14	37	1.02	5	0	6.29	.41	2.84	7.51	1.79
CLAY CARUTHERS	23	Winston-Salem	Caro	150.7	205	93	21	82	72	5.56	6	11	12.25	1.25	4.90	4.30	.21
JOHN COURTRIGHT	26	Chattanooga	South	56.3	59	17	4	14	26	2.72	4	2	9.43	.64	2.24	4.15	.83
DWAYNE CUSHMAN	24	Charleston, WV	S Atl	60.3	104	39	3	21	31	5.82	2	5	15.51	.45	3.13	4.62	.76
TOM DOYLE	26	Chattanooga	South	49.7	61	33	1	45	23	5.98	2	4	11.05	.18	8.15	4.17	-.65
TODD ETLER	22	Winston-Salem	Caro	69.3	85	31	8	25	40	4.02	4	4	11.03	1.04	3.25	5.19	.92
EDDY GARCIA	20	Charleston, WV	S Atl	87.7	134	63	4	83	41	6.47	3	7	13.76	.41	8.52	4.21	-.73
EMILIANO GIRON	24	Charleston, WV	S Atl	39.7	46	20	3	33	35	4.54	2	2	10.44	.68	7.49	7.94	.78
RICK LAPKA	24	Charleston, WV	S Atl	79.3	144	86	8	79	35	9.76	1	8	16.34	.91	8.96	3.97	-.92
BRIAN LOTT	24	Winston-Salem	Caro	131.3	191	98	20	68	58	6.72	4	11	13.09	1.37	4.66	3.97	.16
LARRY LUEBBERS	26	Chattanooga	South	64.0	73	30	6	30	28	4.22	3	4	10.27	.84	4.22	3.94	.26
	26	Indianapolis	AmA	68.0	84	44	7	33	29	5.82	3	5	11.12	.93	4.37	3.84	.19
SCOTT MACRAE	21	Charleston, WV	S Atl	101.0	172	81	4	78	46	7.22	3	8	15.33	.36	6.95	4.10	-.37
PETE MAGRE	25	Winston-Salem	Caro	52.7	51	22	6	42	23	3.76	3	3	8.72	1.03	7.18	3.93	-.48
SCOTT MCKENZIE	25	Chattanooga	South	43.7	58	24	7	27	20	4.95	2	3	11.95	1.44	5.56	4.12	-.02
MARCUS MOORE	25	Cincinnati	NL	26.3	27	18	3	24	24	6.15	1	2	9.23	1.03	8.20	8.20	.68
	25	Indianapolis	AmA	84.7	80	39	8	51	58	4.15	4	5	8.50	.85	5.42	6.17	.70
CHRIS MURPHY	24	Winston-Salem	Caro	111.0	182	85	20	52	55	6.89	3	9	14.76	1.62	4.22	4.46	.43
TONY NIETO	23	Winston-Salem	Caro	50.0	74	37	4	30	21	6.66	2	4	13.32	.72	5.40	3.78	-.09
JIM NIX	25	Chattanooga	South	81.7	93	42	6	54	68	4.63	4	5	10.25	.66	5.95	7.49	1.01
ROSS POWELL	28	Indianapolis	AmA	57.7	80	40	8	36	43	6.24	2	4	12.49	1.25	5.62	6.71	.83
CHRIS REED	22	Chattanooga	South	161.0	182	87	17	106	98	4.86	7	11	10.17	.95	5.93	5.48	.34
MIKE REMLINGER	30	Cincinnati	NL	27.3	24	15	4	22	17	4.94	1	2	7.90	1.32	7.24	5.60	.05
	30	Indianapolis	AmA	84.7	73	27	3	57	81	2.87	6	3	7.76	.32	6.06	8.61	1.36
JOHN RIEDLING	20	Charleston, WV	S Atl	114.3	195	112	3	96	50	8.82	2	11	15.35	.24	7.56	3.94	-.58
PAUL RUNYAN	24	Charleston, WV	S Atl	65.0	120	63	4	30	23	8.72	1	6	16.62	.55	4.15	3.18	.02
	24	Winston-Salem	Caro	33.3	44	11	3	12	8	2.97	3	1	11.88	.81	3.24	2.16	-.09
DAVID SOLOMON	24	Winston-Salem	Caro	47.3	63	32	4	36	19	6.08	2	3	11.98	.76	6.85	3.61	-.51
JEFF SPARKS	24	Charleston, WV	S Atl	73.0	117	67	5	66	52	8.26	2	6	14.42	.62	8.14	6.41	.10
JERRY SPRADLIN	29	Indianapolis	AmA	95.3	104	48	14	35	66	4.53	5	6	9.82	1.32	3.30	6.23	1.25
SCOTT SULLIVAN	25	Indianapolis	AmA	103.3	106	36	9	51	64	3.14	7	4	9.23	.78	4.44	5.57	.75
BRETT TOMKO	23	Chattanooga	South	146.0	153	68	21	63	119	4.19	8	8	9.43	1.29	3.88	7.34	1.47
BRIAN WARREN	29	Indianapolis	AmA	61.3	76	30	6	34	33	4.40	3	4	11.15	.88	4.99	4.84	.37
SCOTT WRIGHT	23	Charleston, WV	S Atl	57.3	76	29	1	31	29	4.55	3	3	11.93	.16	4.87	4.55	.30

Houston Astros

Over the last two seasons, the Houston Astros are a combined 3-22 against the National League Central champion. After a horrific 1-11 last year against Cincinnati, the Astros went out and handed the Central to the St. Louis Cardinals this year, going 2-11 against the Redbirds, including three three-game sweeps.

When the difference between winning and losing is this cut-and-dried, it begs the question: Why? Why did the Houston Astros have so much trouble with the Cardinals this year, and what can they do to fix it? The best way to answer this is to examine the 13 games the teams played and look for clues. St. Louis swept the Astros in Houston in May, in St. Louis in June, split a four-game series in St. Louis in August and swept in Houston, essentially burying the team, in the first week of September.

The biggest difference between the St. Louis games and the rest of Houston's season was their lack of hitting. In the 149 games not involving the Cardinals, Houston averaged 4.8 runs a game. Against the Cardinals, they scored just 3.0 runs per game. Their pitching and defense was essentially the same, allowing 4.9 runs per game to the Cardinals and 4.6 per game the rest of the time. So it's fair to say the main problem was the offense.

And they couldn't score because...? Because the Cardinals' staff murders right-handed batters, and Houston has no good left-handed hitters. Of the six pitchers who threw the most innings against the Astros, accounting for over 85% of the innings pitched, five were right-handers who were considerably more effective against right-handed batters, and they killed Houston:

Pitcher	Performance	1996 OPS split (L/R)
Todd Stottlemyre:	3-1, 1.91 in 33 IP	.820/.595
Andy Benes:	2-0, 2.70 in 20 IP	.762/.660
Alan Benes:	2-1, 3.00 in 15 IP	.907/.684
T.J. Mathews:	0-0, 3 holds in 8 IP	.679/.573
Dennis Eckersley:	0-0, 3 saves in 4.1 IP	.781/.686

The other pitcher to see significant time against Houston was Donovan Osborne, who, while left-handed, only allowed a .712 OPS to right-handed batters. He pitched extremely well in three starts against Houston, but his overall numbers (4.44 ERA in 26 1/3 innings) were ruined by a bad start on Labor Day: 3 1/3 IP, 7 ER in a game St. Louis went on to win anyway.

What made Houston so susceptible to the Cardinals' right-handers? First of all, Houston was a disproportionately right-handed hitting team. Their typical starting lineup consisted of seven righties, and they often started eight after the inexplic-

able Rick Wilkins/Kirt Manwaring trade. Their top left-handed hitters were Derrick May, who had a bad year and batted just .130 against St. Louis in 23 at bats; John Cangelosi, a switch-hitter whose injuries kept him out of the lineup for some of the games; and Bill Spiers, who hit .385 in 13 at bats against St. Louis but primarily played third base, where Sean Berry was one of the few Astros hitting the Cardinals well. Rick Wilkins hit .267 with a homer and a couple of walks in the first half games, but wasn't with the team in the second.

The Astro lineup was simply in an awful matchup against the Cardinal right-handers. While Jeff Bagwell (.429 OBP without much power) and Sean Berry (a historically "backwards" right-handed hitter who hit .313 with seven extra-base hits) played well, the rest of the lineup was brutal. Brian Hunter posted a .304 OBP, mostly in the leadoff spot. Craig Biggio and Derek Bell killed the offense, with OPSs of .341 and .510 respectively. Orlando Miller, despite a ninth-inning home run to win one game, wasn't much better at .186/.205/.326.

The inability of the Astro offense to score, particularly against right-handers, was crucial. Of the 13 games, nine were decided by one or two runs. The Astros went 1-8 in these. The Cardinal bullpen, notably the aforementioned Mathews and Eckersley, was a big part of Houston's downfall. They were 2-0 with four holds, four saves and no blown saves in the 13 games, posting an ERA of 2.28 in 23 2/3 innings. The numbers are even better if you exclude the back end of the bullpen like Jeff Parrett and Cory Bailey. St. Louis did not surrender one lead from the 6th inning onward.

Want an indication of just how unbalanced Houston's offense was? Tony Fossas and Rick Honeycutt, Tony LaRussa's geriatric but effective lefty specialists, made a combined four appearances in the 13 games, totaling 2 1/3 shutout innings.

While the Cardinal relievers were keeping things in order, the Astro bullpen was pumping out runs like Ron Jeremy working on Jennifer Peace, posting a 7.62 ERA in 26 innings. Houston led in five of their losses, and were tied in the seventh or later in two other games. The absence of John Hudek, ineffectiveness of an overworked Todd Jones and inability of the front office to find adequate replacements all contributed to the bullpen's demise.

How can the Astros make sure this never happens again? Well, it's unlikely that they'll have quite the same imbalance in 1997. Bob Abreu, a left-handed hitting left fielder, will probably be in the lineup, and it's possible Derek Bell will be gone, freeing right field for a lefty bat. A left-handed hitting infielder or catcher would help, but while the Astros have such players (Mitch Meluskey, Tim Forkner) in their system, it's unlikely that they will get significant playing time in 1997. Acquiring an effective middle reliever or two would also help.

In retrospect, a number of the Astros' woes might have been avoided with a few moves, or moves not made. First, re-signing Dave Magadan to play third base would have provided them with a cheap source of lefty OBP. By doing this, they could have kept Dave Veres, dealt to Montreal for Sean Berry, who would have been a boon in the bullpen. Finally, the Wilkins/Manwaring trade was idiotic. Despite Wilkins' protracted slump and perceived defensive inadequacies, he was still an above-average offensive catcher, and his lefty bat provided some much-needed balance. Having these players would have hampered LaRussa's ability to run right-handed relievers out at will and helped the Astros stay in some of the close games, possibly leading to an extra win or two.

Would it have been enough? We'll never know if Houston's September collapse would have been different had the Cardinals not shot past them early in the month, but it certainly would have given them more breathing room when the walls started closing in.

Organization: Drayton McLane is 80% of George Steinbrenner, alternately spending money like a drunken

sailor and whining about his situation in Houston. He does provide for the system, though, continuing to support a Venezuelan baseball academy that has cranked out prospects for six years, some of whom (Roberto Petagine, Bob Abreu, Richard Hidalgo) are now beginning to reach The Show.

The Astros have done a good job generating pitchers over the years, and for much of 1996 had three home-grown pitchers in the rotation (Shane Reynolds, Donne Wall and Darryl Kile). They haven't done as good a job with hitters, having been too easily fooled by gaudy stats inflated by the Texas and Pacific Coast leagues, and stubbornly giving jobs to thoroughly mediocre players such as Brian Hunter and Orlando Miller. The big trade with Detroit amounts to addition by subtraction. It clears out some of the stiffs like Hunter and Miller; the arms they received may pan out, but they're already ahead of the game.

Manager Terry Collins, who along with GM Gerry Hunsicker has to be blamed for the roster composition that led to the Cardinal bloodbath, is out, Larry Dierker is in. Dierker is something of an unknown, having done nothing more strenuous than call Astro games for the last 17 years. There are vague murmurs about him being something of a stathead, but until we see him with a real baseball team it's all just talk.

BOB ABREU — LF — 1974 — Age 23

Year	Team	Lge	AB	H	DB	TP	HR	BB	SB	CS	OUT	BA	OBA	SA	EQA	EQR	Peak
1993	Osceola	Flor	488	129	18	8	9	45	6	6	365	.264	.326	.389	.239	51	.275
1994	Jackson	Texas	413	122	17	4	18	40	8	5	296	.295	.358	.487	.278	60	.316
1995	Tucson	PCL	406	107	16	8	12	62	13	9	308	.264	.361	.431	.263	55	.294
1996	Tucson	PCL	486	126	9	8	15	77	20	11	371	.259	.361	.403	.257	62	.284
1997	Houston	NL	506	135	24	6	16	65	28	16	387	.267	.350	.433	.279	79	

Abreu is exactly what the Astros need, a left-handed hitting corner outfielder. His real-life numbers, and his rep, have been inflated by his parks, but he's very patient, good defensively and has shown improvement—better walk rates, better stolen base rates—every year. He didn't hit as well in 1996, but I doubt it's anything but a blip. He'll play left if Bell is around, right if he isn't, but only until Hidalgo comes up.

JEFF BAGWELL — 1B — 1968 — Age 29

Year	Team	Lge	AB	H	DB	TP	HR	BB	SB	CS	OUT	BA	OBA	SA	EQA	EQR	Peak
1993	Houston	NL	555	185	36	2	23	71	11	3	373	.333	.409	.530	.310	100	.327
1994	Houston	NL	419	161	29	2	43	72	14	4	262	.384	.475	.771	.383	119	.399
1995	Houston	NL	472	150	25	0	26	87	10	5	327	.318	.424	.536	.314	91	.322
1996	Houston	NL	604	204	45	2	36	145	18	7	407	.338	.466	.598	.345	142	.348
1997	Houston	NL	550	169	40	3	33	158	19	4	385	.307	.462	.571	.359	148	

Statheads love this guy, and he did have another good year, but his disappearing act in mid-season hurt the Astros. He had just a .431 SLG with six homers in June and July, in a lineup with little power to spare. He's the best first baseman in the league, maybe the best in baseball.

JEFF BALL   1B   1969   Age 28

Year	Team	Lge	AB	H	DB	TP	HR	BB	SB	CS	OUT	BA	OBA	SA	EQA	EQR	Peak
1993	Quad Cities	Midw	407	109	15	0	13	46	18	9	307	.268	.342	.400	.251	48	.269
1994	Jackson	Texas	370	114	19	2	14	32	6	4	260	.308	.363	.484	.280	54	.295
1995	Tucson	PCL	353	89	17	1	5	25	8	3	267	.252	.302	.348	.220	30	.229
1996	Tucson	PCL	427	128	18	1	19	33	9	5	304	.300	.350	.480	.274	60	.281

Bagwell, Jr. Bell's a converted third baseman who has roughly Tammy Faye Bakker's shot of beating out the incumbent. As a third baseman he deserves a job, but probably wouldn't hit as well. Expansion player.

DEREK BELL   RF   1969   Age 28

Year	Team	Lge	AB	H	DB	TP	HR	BB	SB	CS	OUT	BA	OBA	SA	EQA	EQR	Peak
1993	San Diego	NL	549	148	16	1	22	31	22	4	405	.270	.309	.423	.249	63	.266
1994	San Diego	NL	442	141	15	0	16	35	22	7	308	.319	.369	.462	.281	65	.296
1995	Houston	NL	473	171	22	2	9	39	23	8	310	.362	.410	.474	.301	77	.313
1996	Houston	NL	643	180	41	3	18	47	25	3	466	.280	.329	.437	.261	81	.267
1997	*Houston*	*NL*	*586*	*157*	*32*	*3*	*18*	*36*	*26*	*5*	*434*	*.268*	*.310*	*.425*	*.268*	*81*	

He drove in 113 runs, and thinks he deserves a multi-year deal for $4M per. To quote my esteemed co-author, BWA-HA-HA-HA-HA! Bell is awful, one of the worst right fielders in the league, and needs to be replaced immediately. There is no question that someone is going to pay this guy a lot of money to make 450 outs in the middle of their lineup this year. Pray it's not your team. Re-signed with the Astros for three years, $13 million. Brutal signing.

SEAN BERRY   3B   1966   Age 31

Year	Team	Lge	AB	H	DB	TP	HR	BB	SB	CS	OUT	BA	OBA	SA	EQA	EQR	Peak
1993	Montreal	NL	308	84	14	1	16	45	10	2	226	.273	.365	.481	.282	48	.289
1994	Montreal	NL	324	92	17	1	12	36	12	0	232	.284	.356	.454	.276	46	.278
1995	Montreal	NL	322	106	20	1	15	30	2	7	223	.329	.386	.537	.296	53	.294
1996	Houston	NL	442	131	33	0	20	29	11	6	317	.296	.340	.507	.277	64	.272
1997	*Houston*	*NL*	*446*	*127*	*29*	*2*	*17*	*51*	*17*	*9*	*328*	*.285*	*.358*	*.473*	*.293*	*76*	

Berry is the rare reverse-platoon player. He hits for average and power much better against right-handed pitchers over 1500 career at bats. He's another hitter the Royals decided to play, and keep, David Howard over, and despite some plate discipline problems is an average, maybe slightly above average third baseman. Good bet for 1997.

CRAIG BIGGIO   2B   1966   Age 31

Year	Team	Lge	AB	H	DB	TP	HR	BB	SB	CS	OUT	BA	OBA	SA	EQA	EQR	Peak
1993	Houston	NL	631	188	40	3	24	86	13	14	457	.298	.382	.485	.283	97	.290
1994	Houston	NL	452	151	46	3	8	69	35	4	305	.334	.422	.502	.317	86	.320
1995	Houston	NL	581	192	28	2	26	89	29	7	396	.330	.419	.520	.314	109	.312
1996	Houston	NL	628	192	25	3	17	83	21	7	443	.306	.387	.436	.280	92	.274
1997	*Houston*	*NL*	*579*	*161*	*37*	*2*	*16*	*100*	*27*	*12*	*430*	*.278*	*.384*	*.432*	*.294*	*101*	

Lost in the bidding war for his services last winter, and the excitement over his big year, was this: he's pretty damn old. I don't think last year is just a blip. Since moving to second base in 1992, Biggio has missed just 11 games, just four since 1993. Second basemen who play this much burn out, and I think we're starting to see that. Let's not forget he had a lot of mileage on him as a catcher prior to 1992 as well. He'll still be above average for another two or three years, but no superstar.

KARY BRIDGES   2B   1972   Age 25

Year	Team	Lge	AB	H	DB	TP	HR	BB	SB	CS	OUT	BA	OBA	SA	EQA	EQR	Peak
1993	Quad Cities	Midw	273	67	2	0	4	24	6	4	210	.245	.306	.297	.203	20	.228
1994	Quad Cities	Midw	458	120	14	3	1	32	7	4	342	.262	.310	.312	.211	35	.233
1995	Jackson	Texas	426	120	18	2	4	44	9	6	312	.282	.349	.362	.242	45	.263
1996	Jackson	Texas	344	102	9	1	4	30	3	3	245	.297	.353	.363	.244	36	.261
1996	Tucson	PCL	139	40	6	1	1	9	1	2	101	.288	.331	.367	.234	13	.251

He's a left-handed hitting second baseman, played well enough to get the callup to Tucson, but he has no future in Houston. As a left-handed middle infielder, he may be able to parlay one more good year into Bill Spiers' job, one I think he'd be good at. Rarely strikes out.

JOHN CANGELOSI   **OF**   **1963**   **Age 34**

Year	Team	Lge	AB	H	DB	TP	HR	BB	SB	CS	OUT	BA	OBA	SA	EQA	EQR	Peak
1993	Toledo	Inter	454	130	19	2	7	57	29	11	335	.286	.366	.383	.260	57	.254
1994	NY Mets	NL	113	29	4	0	0	20	4	1	85	.257	.368	.292	.235	11	.226
1995	Tucson	PCL	103	33	3	1	0	17	8	2	72	.320	.417	.369	.281	15	.268
1995	Houston	NL	215	76	4	2	3	53	18	5	144	.353	.481	.433	.323	43	.307
1996	Houston	NL	273	77	13	4	1	47	14	8	204	.282	.387	.370	.261	35	.247
1997	*Florida*	*NL*	*329*	*84*	*14*	*2*	*2*	*62*	*15*	*7*	*252*	*.255*	*.373*	*.328*	*.259*	*43*	

Vastly underrated player. Along with Bagwell, his absence and ineffectiveness torpedoed Houston's offense in the second half. He's cheap, good and probably the best fourth outfielder in baseball. He signed a two-year deal with the Marlins to be their fifth outfielder. Deserves 300 AB, won't get them

RAMON CASTRO   **C**   **1976**   **Age 21**

Year	Team	Lge	AB	H	DB	TP	HR	BB	SB	CS	OUT	BA	OBA	SA	EQA	EQR	Peak
1995	Auburn	NY-P	235	63	4	0	8	18	0	0	172	.268	.320	.387	.237	24	.274
1996	Quad Cities	Midw	325	73	6	0	7	23	1	0	252	.225	.276	.308	.192	20	.219

Young catching prospect with a good mix of offensive skills. He's still young enough that lots of bad things can happen to him, but there's so much to like here it's easy to envision him in the Dome, or Northern Virginia, in 1999.

ANDUJAR CEDENO   **SS**   **1970**   **Age 27**

Year	Team	Lge	AB	H	DB	TP	HR	BB	SB	CS	OUT	BA	OBA	SA	EQA	EQR	Peak
1993	Houston	NL	519	152	22	3	13	56	8	6	373	.293	.362	.422	.263	66	.286
1994	Houston	NL	348	95	19	0	12	34	1	1	254	.273	.338	.431	.256	42	.274
1995	San Diego	NL	397	89	17	1	7	33	4	3	311	.224	.284	.325	.201	28	.212
1996	Detroit	AL	179	35	5	2	7	4	2	1	145	.196	.213	.363	.185	11	.192
1996	San Diego	NL	157	38	2	0	4	11	2	2	121	.242	.292	.331	.207	12	.215
1997	*Detroit*	*NL*	*169*	*43*	*4*	*1*	*6*	*10*	*3*	*2*	*128*	*.254*	*.296*	*.396*	*.233*	*17*	

Cedeno finished the season one shy of Dave Kingman's record for most divisions in one season. I hate to write the guy off, but it's been two years of awful baseball, and he hasn't really been useful since 1993. Defense mediocre, offense gone.

ERIC CHRISTOPHERSON **C**   **1969**   **Age 28**

Year	Team	Lge	AB	H	DB	TP	HR	BB	SB	CS	OUT	BA	OBA	SA	EQA	EQR	Peak
1993	Shreveport	Texas	48	7	2	0	0	8	1	0	41	.146	.268	.188	.136	1	.136
1994	Shreveport	Texas	278	70	12	0	8	39	3	1	209	.252	.344	.381	.245	31	.259
1995	Phoenix	PCL	280	55	7	1	1	34	1	1	226	.196	.283	.239	.166	13	.172
1996	Tucson	PCL	222	59	10	2	6	21	2	0	163	.266	.329	.410	.249	25	.255

Former Giants prospect now beginning his tour of AAA. The Astros don't need him, although there's not much difference between him and Manwaring, and he's cheaper. He needs to get lucky, have some team's desperation match his hot streak, a la John Flaherty, to have a career.

DENNIS COLON   **1B**   **1974**   **Age 23**

Year	Team	Lge	AB	H	DB	TP	HR	BB	SB	CS	OUT	BA	OBA	SA	EQA	EQR	Peak
1993	Osceola	Flor	476	140	17	3	4	17	5	2	338	.294	.318	.368	.234	45	.270
1994	Jackson	Texas	387	103	14	2	7	18	5	2	287	.266	.299	.367	.224	34	.254
1995	Jackson	Texas	382	80	3	0	6	22	3	3	305	.209	.252	.264	.161	16	.181
1996	Jackson	Texas	435	112	13	1	11	22	0	2	325	.257	.293	.368	.219	37	.242

He appears to have found his home as Jackson's first baseman. Left-handed line drive hitter in the Hal Morris mode, but walks even less, has less power and doesn't hit as many singles. Remember this when he hits .360 this year and is touted as a prospect.

TONY EUSEBIO   **C**   **1967**   **Age 30**

Year	Team	Lge	AB	H	DB	TP	HR	BB	SB	CS	OUT	BA	OBA	SA	EQA	EQR	Peak
1993	Tucson	PCL	275	76	12	1	2	20	1	1	200	.276	.325	.349	.228	25	.238
1994	Houston	NL	162	50	9	1	5	10	0	1	113	.309	.349	.469	.270	21	.277
1995	Houston	NL	383	123	21	0	8	36	0	2	262	.321	.379	.439	.275	52	.278
1996	Tucson	PCL	52	20	3	0	0	3	0	0	32	.385	.418	.442	.297	8	.294
1996	Houston	NL	157	45	7	2	1	20	0	1	113	.287	.367	.376	.252	18	.250
1997	*Houston*	*NL*	*224*	*62*	*7*	*0*	*6*	*14*	*0*	*2*	*164*	*.277*	*.319*	*.388*	*.253*	*26*	

Eusebio is an underrated hitter, a big guy with real doubles power and some knowledge of the strike zone. He's not great defensively, but not awful, and definitely not so bad you need to give up his bat. Injuries to his left wrist and hadn't hampered him, but I think he'll be fine in 1997.

TIM FORKNER   **3B**   **1973**   **Age 24**

Year	Team	Lge	AB	H	DB	TP	HR	BB	SB	CS	OUT	BA	OBA	SA	EQA	EQR	Peak
1993	Auburn	NY-P	278	60	8	3	1	28	1	1	219	.216	.288	.277	.184	16	.209
1994	Quad Cities	Midw	445	117	16	2	6	46	3	3	331	.263	.332	.348	.230	42	.257
1995	Kissimmee	Flor	318	89	20	3	2	53	2	1	230	.280	.383	.381	.261	40	.288
1995	Jackson	Texas	122	31	6	0	4	17	1	2	93	.254	.345	.402	.247	14	.273
1996	Jackson	Texas	388	104	13	2	7	51	1	2	286	.268	.353	.366	.243	42	.264
1997	*Houston*	*NL*	*370*	*102*	*21*	*3*	*10*	*62*	*2*	*1*	*269*	*.276*	*.380*	*.430*	*.291*	*61*	

Dave Magadan redux. Forkner is a left-handed gap hitter with no real power and a good eye. The Astros really need some left-handed bats, even with the addition of Abreu in 1997, and Forkner could be their third baseman in 1998, when Berry gets too expensive.

CARLOS GUILLEN   **SS**   **1976**   **Age 21**

Year	Team	Lge	AB	H	DB	TP	HR	BB	SB	CS	OUT	BA	OBA	SA	EQA	EQR	Peak
1996	Quad Cities	Midw	117	35	2	1	3	13	7	3	85	.299	.369	.410	.267	16	.304
1997	*Houston*	*NL*	*379*	*99*	*10*	*2*	*6*	*32*	*18*	*8*	*288*	*.261*	*.319*	*.346*	*.246*	*43*	

Guillen is an injury-prone shortstop prospect—1994, left shoulder; 1995, right elbow—but he's a good hitter and defensive shortstop. Another product of the Venezuelan factory. Health is the only question, but it's a massive one.

RICKY GUTIERREZ   **IF**   **1970**   **Age 27**

Year	Team	Lge	AB	H	DB	TP	HR	BB	SB	CS	OUT	BA	OBA	SA	EQA	EQR	Peak
1993	Las Vegas	PCL	23	8	4	0	0	0	2	0	15	.348	.348	.522	.301	4	.332
1993	San Diego	NL	448	115	9	4	6	56	3	2	335	.257	.339	.335	.229	42	.249
1994	San Diego	NL	279	68	11	2	1	36	2	5	216	.244	.330	.308	.213	22	.227
1995	Tucson	PCL	230	59	11	2	1	27	7	4	175	.257	.335	.335	.229	22	.241
1995	Houston	NL	161	48	7	0	0	12	4	0	113	.298	.347	.342	.242	16	.256
1996	Houston	NL	226	68	9	1	1	25	5	1	159	.301	.371	.363	.255	26	.266

One of the better utility infielders in baseball. Gutierrez can play second, short and in a pinch, third. He's a decent hitter with some discipline and runs well enough to pinch-run. His complete lack of power keeps him on the bench, but he's not that much worse than Miller overall. I expect him to start for someone again, maybe as soon as this year.

DAVE HAJEK   **2B**   **1968**   **Age 29**

Year	Team	Lge	AB	H	DB	TP	HR	BB	SB	CS	OUT	BA	OBA	SA	EQA	EQR	Peak
1993	Jackson	Texas	338	91	15	1	5	19	4	2	249	.269	.308	.364	.227	30	.240
1994	Tucson	PCL	473	135	19	3	7	29	9	5	342	.285	.327	.383	.241	49	.250
1995	Tucson	PCL	488	138	28	2	5	39	9	5	355	.283	.336	.379	.243	51	.249
1996	Tucson	PCL	504	146	26	2	5	26	7	4	362	.290	.325	.379	.238	50	.241

Scab. Hajek has found his level as the Toros second baseman. He's just a slap hitter, OK defensively, no speed or power. Tucson makes him look good, but really he's nothing, not even as good as Gutierrez.

CHRIS HATCHER   **OF**   **1969**   **Age 28**

Year	Team	Lge	AB	H	DB	TP	HR	BB	SB	CS	OUT	BA	OBA	SA	EQA	EQR	Peak
1993	Jackson	Texas	371	90	10	1	13	14	4	4	285	.243	.270	.380	.214	30	.229
1994	Tucson	PCL	342	91	19	2	11	19	4	1	252	.266	.305	.430	.245	37	.259
1995	Tucson	PCL	284	71	11	1	13	39	5	2	215	.250	.341	.433	.257	36	.268
1996	Jackson	Texas	157	47	5	1	10	10	2	1	111	.299	.341	.535	.284	24	.290
1996	Tucson	PCL	345	97	14	1	17	15	9	5	253	.281	.311	.475	.259	43	.265

Hatcher is an outfielder who swings at everything, and hits enough to keep himself in a job. After a few years as a C prospect, he's now being passed by Abreu, Hidalgo, etc., and it looks like he'll never make the major leagues.

RICHARD HIDALGO   **RF**   **1976**   **Age 21**

Year	Team	Lge	AB	H	DB	TP	HR	BB	SB	CS	OUT	BA	OBA	SA	EQA	EQR	Peak
1993	Asheville	S Atl	414	97	10	1	9	21	9	6	323	.234	.271	.329	.199	28	.236
1994	Quad Cities	Midw	484	128	27	3	11	19	7	6	362	.264	.292	.401	.230	46	.269
1995	Jackson	Texas	494	125	19	2	15	31	7	5	374	.253	.297	.391	.229	47	.264
1996	Jackson	Texas	518	141	21	1	13	29	9	4	381	.272	.311	.392	.237	52	.269

Another Venezuelan, Hidalgo gets raves for his tools, including a cannon for an arm, but he's not anything earth-shattering. His plate discipline has not developed as hoped and he remains very thin, keeping his power down. Kind of an undernourished Alex Ochoa. He's still young, and probably arrives in September. I think he'll improve and have a career.

BRIAN L. HUNTER   **CF**   **1971**   **Age 26**

Year	Team	Lge	AB	H	DB	TP	HR	BB	SB	CS	OUT	BA	OBA	SA	EQA	EQR	Peak
1993	Jackson	Texas	535	146	14	2	11	36	21	8	397	.273	.319	.368	.235	53	.260
1994	Tucson	PCL	501	166	21	4	10	49	34	10	344	.331	.391	.449	.289	77	.314
1995	Tucson	PCL	151	43	3	1	1	16	8	2	110	.285	.353	.338	.244	16	.263
1995	Houston	NL	333	109	16	4	3	25	20	6	230	.327	.374	.426	.276	46	.297
1996	Houston	NL	538	157	28	1	6	23	30	9	390	.292	.321	.381	.244	57	.257
1997	*Detroit*	*AL*	*586*	*187*	*37*	*7*	*10*	*34*	*35*	*14*	*413*	*.319*	*.356*	*.457*	*.277*	*84*	

Hunter is just another empty average, courtesy of the Texas League and the PCL. He's a serviceable extra outfielder, but a bad regular and a pretty bad defensive outfielder. He needs to hit .320 to help, and he won't do that. A serious problem for the Astros. Traded to Detroit, where he'll get 300-400 ABs in at least a part-time role.

RUSS JOHNSON   **SS**   **1973**   **Age 24**

Year	Team	Lge	AB	H	DB	TP	HR	BB	SB	CS	OUT	BA	OBA	SA	EQA	EQR	Peak
1995	Jackson	Texas	484	114	11	0	10	46	7	3	373	.236	.302	.320	.209	37	.231
1996	Jackson	Texas	506	146	18	2	14	52	6	2	362	.289	.355	.415	.260	63	.283

Houston left Johnson in Jackson this year, despite a decent 1995 and a complete lack of shortstop prospects ahead of him. He improved across the board, although he did make twice as many errors, leading to some concern over his defense. Out of LSU, he got a late pro start and will need a good year at Tucson to stay ahead of Guillen. Miller trade makes him a sleeper in 1997.

KIRT MANWARING   **C**   **1966**   **Age 31**

Year	Team	Lge	AB	H	DB	TP	HR	BB	SB	CS	OUT	BA	OBA	SA	EQA	EQR	Peak
1993	San Francisco	NL	447	130	13	1	6	47	1	2	319	.291	.358	.365	.246	48	.253
1994	San Francisco	NL	320	81	18	1	1	30	1	1	240	.253	.317	.325	.216	26	.218
1995	San Francisco	NL	387	102	16	1	5	32	1	0	285	.264	.320	.349	.226	35	.225
1996	Houston	NL	83	19	3	0	0	4	0	0	64	.229	.264	.265	.168	4	.164
1996	San Francisco	NL	148	36	2	0	2	17	0	1	113	.243	.321	.297	.206	11	.202
1997	*Colorado*	*NL*	*280*	*82*	*6*	*0*	*7*	*15*	*0*	*1*	*199*	*.293*	*.329*	*.389*	*.224*	*24*	

A defensive replacement who's been masquerading as a regular for most of the '90s. He could fill the defensive replacement role behind Eusebio, giving the Astros an OK catching situation, but if he costs too much should be cut loose. "Too much," by the way, is $6.50 an hour. Manwaring's projected line from the Vlad for Houston: .251/.288/.332. Now that he's with Colorado: .293/.329/.389. Say thank you, Kirt. It's still a .223 EQA, and you still hit like John Leguizamo on NyQuil.

DERRICK MAY — LF — 1969 — Age 28

Year	Team	Lge	AB	H	DB	TP	HR	BB	SB	CS	OUT	BA	OBA	SA	EQA	EQR	Peak
1993	Chicago Cubs	NL	473	140	22	2	11	38	8	2	335	.296	.348	.421	.261	58	.280
1994	Chicago Cubs	NL	354	106	18	2	9	36	3	2	250	.299	.364	.438	.269	47	.284
1995	Houston	NL	215	70	14	1	10	22	4	0	145	.326	.388	.540	.306	38	.318
1995	Milwaukee	AL	113	28	3	1	1	5	0	1	86	.248	.280	.319	.195	7	.201
1996	Houston	NL	267	71	12	2	6	33	2	2	198	.266	.347	.393	.248	30	.255
1997	Houston	NL	286	76	18	1	9	27	2	3	213	.266	.329	.430	.269	40	

May's inability to be a productive power bat in the middle of the lineup was a big problem for a team desperate for lefty hitting. He has no business as a regular or even a platoon regular, but could have a career as a pinch-hitter. The type of player hurt by the new economics: he makes too much to keep in his role.

MITCH MELUSKEY — C — 1974 — Age 23

Year	Team	Lge	AB	H	DB	TP	HR	BB	SB	CS	OUT	BA	OBA	SA	EQA	EQR	Peak
1993	Columbus-GA	S Atl	353	73	11	1	3	26	0	0	280	.207	.261	.269	.167	16	.193
1994	Kinston	Caro	333	72	12	1	2	42	2	2	263	.216	.304	.276	.192	21	.218
1995	Kissimmee	Flor	272	58	12	1	4	23	2	0	214	.213	.275	.309	.192	17	.215
1996	Kissimmee	Flor	244	79	10	0	4	27	1	1	166	.324	.391	.414	.275	33	.303
1996	Jackson	Texas	137	39	6	0	1	17	0	0	98	.285	.364	.350	.245	15	.273
1997	Houston	NL	444	128	22	1	6	45	4	2	318	.288	.354	.383	.269	60	

He's a switch-hitting catcher with no power to speak of, but he does hit for average and walk a little. His bat will not support a position change, so he'll have to keep pace with Ramon Castro to play. I expect him to arrive in 1998 and have a career similar to Mike LaValliere.

ORLANDO MILLER — SS — 1969 — Age 28

Year	Team	Lge	AB	H	DB	TP	HR	BB	SB	CS	OUT	BA	OBA	SA	EQA	EQR	Peak
1993	Tucson	PCL	460	122	20	6	16	20	2	2	340	.265	.296	.439	.242	49	.260
1994	Tucson	PCL	332	76	12	2	9	17	3	2	258	.229	.266	.358	.206	25	.217
1995	Houston	NL	334	95	20	1	6	26	3	4	243	.284	.336	.404	.247	37	.256
1996	Houston	NL	477	129	24	2	16	20	2	7	355	.270	.300	.430	.238	49	.244
1997	Detroit	AL	504	136	27	3	13	31	4	5	373	.270	.312	.413	.243	54	

Below-average shortstop, has the job because of a lack of any other candidates. Russ Johnson will chase him, possibly as soon as this year, and he's not the type of player with a lot of bench value, so he could disappear as soon as he earns arbitration rights. Sent to Detroit, where he'll most likely be the starting SS, and has some roto value in that role.

RAY MONTGOMERY — OF — 1970 — Age 27

Year	Team	Lge	AB	H	DB	TP	HR	BB	SB	CS	OUT	BA	OBA	SA	EQA	EQR	Peak
1993	Jackson	Texas	349	93	11	1	10	35	7	3	259	.266	.333	.390	.244	38	.265
1993	Tucson	PCL	49	14	3	0	2	4	1	1	36	.286	.340	.469	.264	6	.287
1994	Tucson	PCL	327	73	13	3	7	34	4	2	256	.223	.296	.346	.214	27	.230
1995	Jackson	Texas	129	38	6	0	9	12	5	2	93	.295	.355	.550	.292	21	.309
1995	Tucson	PCL	284	75	9	0	11	23	4	2	211	.264	.319	.412	.244	31	.258
1996	Tucson	PCL	360	104	10	0	21	55	5	1	257	.289	.383	.492	.290	58	.301
1997	Houston	NL	535	142	18	2	25	96	7	5	398	.265	.377	.447	.293	92	

He finally started hitting in his third season at Tucson, and got a cup of coffee in Houston as a reward. Montgomery is walking more with age, but it's probably just the amount of time he's spent at AAA. He can't be written off yet, especially since the current Astro outfield defines mediocrity and they like him. Vlad does too.

JAMES MOUTON — OF — 1969 — Age 28

Year	Team	Lge	AB	H	DB	TP	HR	BB	SB	CS	OUT	BA	OBA	SA	EQA	EQR	Peak
1993	Tucson	PCL	536	147	27	4	16	64	24	10	399	.274	.352	.429	.263	71	.282
1994	Houston	NL	315	80	6	0	4	32	22	4	239	.254	.323	.311	.227	29	.240
1995	Houston	NL	308	88	18	2	5	29	22	7	227	.286	.347	.406	.260	39	.271
1996	Houston	NL	310	87	14	1	4	42	17	8	231	.281	.366	.371	.254	38	.260
1997	Houston	NL	384	104	28	2	14	49	33	10	290	.271	.353	.464	.294	68	

Mouton has earned a job as a platoon outfielder. He's good with the glove, can run and hits lefties well. He also has a lot of value as a bench player. Cangelosi/Mouton would have been the second-best left fielder in the division.

BRY NELSON   3B   1974   Age 23

Year	Team	Lge	AB	H	DB	TP	HR	BB	SB	CS	OUT	BA	OBA	SA	EQA	EQR	Peak
1994	Auburn	NY-P	267	74	8	1	7	9	1	1	194	.277	.301	.393	.232	25	.265
1994	Quad Cities	Midw	159	33	3	0	1	9	2	2	128	.208	.250	.245	.151	6	.171
1995	Kissimmee	Flor	411	129	29	3	5	18	9	5	287	.314	.343	.436	.262	50	.293
1996	Kissimmee	Flor	355	88	17	3	5	18	4	1	268	.248	.284	.355	.214	28	.236

He's been all over the diamond, a great thing for his managers, lousy for his development. Nelson played the outfield and infield in 1995, mostly third in 1996 and shortstop in the AFL. Shortstop is about the only position his bat will carry, but an erratic arm moved him to the outfield. Trapped between Jhonny Perez and Russ Johnson.

JHONNY PEREZ   SS   1977   Age 20

Year	Team	Lge	AB	H	DB	TP	HR	BB	SB	CS	OUT	BA	OBA	SA	EQA	EQR	Peak
1995	Kissimmee	Flor	224	60	6	0	6	19	14	4	168	.268	.325	.375	.243	25	.285
1996	Kissimmee	Flor	334	88	11	1	13	24	10	9	255	.263	.313	.419	.241	36	.278

Perez is a very young shortstop prospect, at least three years away but worth keeping an eye on. He's adding bulk and power with age, and a good 1997 at Jackson might vault him over Johnson in the pipeline.

OSCAR ROBLES   SS   1976   Age 21

Year	Team	Lge	AB	H	DB	TP	HR	BB	SB	CS	OUT	BA	OBA	SA	EQA	EQR	Peak
1995	Auburn	NY-P	231	57	5	0	1	30	3	1	175	.247	.333	.281	.211	18	.244
1996	Kissimmee	Flor	453	119	12	1	1	66	5	4	338	.263	.356	.300	.226	41	.257

Shortstop prospect #4, and the one with the best plate discipline. When a team has a glut of players at a position, they tend to do dumb things like convert them (see Sadler, Donnie) rather than let them develop at the position where they have the most value. The Astros have some interesting decisions to make with these shortstops.

BILL SPIERS   3B   1966   Age 31

Year	Team	Lge	AB	H	DB	TP	HR	BB	SB	CS	OUT	BA	OBA	SA	EQA	EQR	Peak
1993	Milwaukee	AL	344	87	8	4	3	32	9	6	263	.253	.316	.326	.217	29	.222
1994	Milwaukee	AL	214	53	8	2	0	19	6	1	162	.248	.309	.304	.212	17	.214
1995	Norfolk	Inter	43	10	1	0	0	8	0	1	34	.233	.353	.256	.202	3	.200
1995	NY Mets	NL	74	16	3	1	0	13	0	1	59	.216	.333	.284	.205	6	.204
1996	Houston	NL	224	60	11	1	6	23	6	0	164	.268	.336	.406	.254	27	.249
1997	*Houston*	*NL*	*260*	*61*	*5*	*0*	*5*	*21*	*10*	*2*	*201*	*.235*	*.292*	*.312*	*.226*	*24*	

He's a fair utility infielder, 80% of the player Lenny Harris is, and when your backup middle infielder is also a left-handed pinch-hitter, it really helps a manager. Despite this, he'll battle for the 25th spot on rosters the rest of his career.

MANUEL BARRIOS   RRP   1975   Age 22

YR	TEAM	Lge	IP	H	ER	HR	BB	K	ERA	W	L	H/9	HR/9	BB/9	K/9	KW
1994	Quad Cities	Midw	56.3	89	46	5	32	39	7.35	1	5	14.22	.80	5.11	6.23	.80
1995	Quad Cities	Midw	46.7	56	17	2	23	36	3.28	3	2	10.80	.39	4.44	6.94	1.21
1996	Jackson	Texas	62.7	66	27	4	38	57	3.88	4	3	9.48	.57	5.46	8.19	1.36

Emaciated (6' 0", 145 pounds) closer prospect. Despite the small workloads and considerable improvement over the last few years, Barrios' frame makes him an unlikely candidate for extended success.

DOUG BROCAIL   RRP   1967   Age 30

YR	TEAM	Lge	IP	H	ER	HR	BB	K	ERA	W	L	H/9	HR/9	BB/9	K/9	KW
1993	Las Vegas	PCL	47.3	48	19	4	19	25	3.61	3	2	9.13	.76	3.61	4.75	.68
1993	San Diego	NL	125.7	147	70	16	56	68	5.01	5	9	10.53	1.15	4.01	4.87	.62
1994	Las Vegas	PCL	12.0	19	9	1	3	7	6.75	0	1	14.25	.75	2.25	5.25	1.19
1994	San Diego	NL	16.7	21	11	1	7	10	5.94	1	1	11.34	.54	3.78	5.40	.85
1995	Tucson	PCL	15.7	16	6	1	6	14	3.45	1	1	9.19	.57	3.45	8.04	1.82
1995	Houston	NL	75.7	94	39	10	29	36	4.64	3	5	11.18	1.19	3.45	4.28	.56
1996	Houston	NL	52.3	62	29	7	28	30	4.99	2	4	10.66	1.20	4.82	5.16	.52

He's a mediocre middle reliever with a shaky past and even more uncertain future. No big splits in his record that would help define a role for him, so he's basically staff filler. He'll bounce around for five more years, adding to his pension. Avoid.

DANNY DARWIN   RBP   1956   Age 41

YR	TEAM	Lge	IP	H	ER	HR	BB	K	ERA	W	L	H/9	HR/9	BB/9	K/9	KW
1993	Boston	AL	225.7	187	70	31	59	133	2.79	17	8	7.46	1.24	2.35	5.30	1.18
1994	Boston	AL	76.7	93	41	11	27	53	4.81	4	5	10.92	1.29	3.17	6.22	1.28
1995	Texas	AL	35.0	35	20	11	8	22	5.14	2	2	9.00	2.83	2.06	5.66	1.37
1995	Toronto	AL	67.0	84	47	12	25	36	6.31	2	5	11.28	1.61	3.36	4.84	.77
1996	Houston	NL	41.0	47	29	7	14	24	6.37	1	4	10.32	1.54	3.07	5.27	.99
1996	Pittsburgh	NL	119.0	120	41	9	26	60	3.10	8	5	9.08	.68	1.97	4.54	1.02

Once removed from the mystical waters of the Allegheny, he reverted to form with the Astros. It was a great story while it lasted, but there's no way he could be expected to go too far beyond 100 innings. Darwin still could be effective as 1) a long reliever/spot starter or 2) a get-the-righty specialist.

DOUG DRABEK   RSP   1963   Age 34

YR	TEAM	Lge	IP	H	ER	HR	BB	K	ERA	W	L	H/9	HR/9	BB/9	K/9	KW
1993	Houston	NL	231.0	254	101	19	86	152	3.94	13	13	9.90	.74	3.35	5.92	1.14
1994	Houston	NL	160.0	138	50	15	58	113	2.81	12	6	7.76	.84	3.26	6.36	1.30
1995	Houston	NL	182.3	221	101	19	71	130	4.99	8	12	10.91	.94	3.50	6.42	1.26
1996	Houston	NL	174.3	218	95	21	77	121	4.90	8	11	11.25	1.08	3.98	6.25	1.09

The Astros bought out his option, surprise, and now he begins the employment hunt. His strikeout and walk data are pretty much unchanged, but the league now hits .280 against him and not .240. He still could help a team needing a #3 starter they can count on, and he'll probably be a bargain for some team, a la Tim Belcher. Recommended.

SCOTT ELARTON   RSP   1976   Age 21

YR	TEAM	Lge	IP	H	ER	HR	BB	K	ERA	W	L	H/9	HR/9	BB/9	K/9	KW
1994	Quad Cities	Midw	47.7	54	25	5	25	26	4.72	2	3	10.20	.94	4.72	4.91	.46
1995	Quad Cities	Midw	128.0	196	98	16	96	74	6.89	4	10	13.78	1.12	6.75	5.20	.05
1996	Kissimmee	Flor	152.0	196	78	20	77	95	4.62	7	10	11.61	1.18	4.56	5.62	.74

The 1994 #1 is 6' 8", but throws like he's much smaller, with good command and pitching smarts but not an overpowering fastball. He'll move to Jackson next year, and I expect him to hit trouble either there or in Tucson, as he makes the necessary adjustments at higher levels. Short-term prognosis is poor, but I like him long-term, say, 1999.

MIKE GRZANICH   RRP   1973   Age 24

YR	TEAM	Lge	IP	H	ER	HR	BB	K	ERA	W	L	H/9	HR/9	BB/9	K/9	KW
1993	Auburn	NY-P	74.7	141	71	13	46	37	8.56	1	7	17.00	1.57	5.54	4.46	.10
1994	Quad Cities	Midw	123.7	180	59	7	61	63	4.29	7	7	13.10	.51	4.44	4.58	.42
1995	Jackson	Texas	60.7	65	22	1	48	34	3.26	4	3	9.64	.15	7.12	5.04	-.10
1996	Jackson	Texas	66.0	66	45	10	55	66	6.14	2	5	9.00	1.36	7.50	9.00	1.12

Houston liked him enough to spend an AFL spot on him, but it's an open question why. He regressed badly in 1996, and continued to be ineffective in Arizona. 10:1 against his ever making the majors.

JOHN HALAMA   LSP   1972   Age 25

YR	TEAM	Lge	IP	H	ER	HR	BB	K	ERA	W	L	H/9	HR/9	BB/9	K/9	KW
1994	Auburn	NY-P	24.3	25	6	2	9	16	2.22	2	1	9.25	.74	3.33	5.92	1.14
1994	Quad Cities	Midw	44.3	75	32	2	26	23	6.50	1	4	15.23	.41	5.28	4.67	.24
1995	Quad Cities	Midw	54.0	67	19	9	30	37	3.17	4	2	11.17	1.50	5.00	6.17	.81
1996	Jackson	Texas	147.7	169	75	11	80	91	4.57	7	9	10.30	.67	4.88	5.55	.63

Halama is a tall lefty bopping between the rotation and the bullpen. He absolutely skewers the running game, with 14 pickoffs in 1996. Since the Astros seem confused about what to do with him, it's hard to predict his future.

MIKE HAMPTON   LSP   1973   Age 24

YR	TEAM	Lge	IP	H	ER	HR	BB	K	ERA	W	L	H/9	HR/9	BB/9	K/9	KW
1993	Jacksonville	South	79.7	82	42	3	44	62	4.74	4	5	9.26	.34	4.97	7.00	1.09
1993	Seattle	AL	17.7	27	17	3	18	8	8.66	0	2	13.75	1.53	9.17	4.08	-.93
1994	Houston	NL	40.7	47	17	4	20	23	3.76	3	2	10.40	.89	4.43	5.09	.59
1995	Houston	NL	148.0	153	69	14	62	104	4.20	8	8	9.30	.85	3.77	6.32	1.17
1996	Houston	NL	157.3	187	74	12	64	89	4.23	8	9	10.70	.69	3.66	5.09	.78

The small, young left-hander slipped a bit in his second year, particularly in the second half, finally being sidelined with shoulder tendinitis in September. Because of his size (5' 10") and his injury in spite of a small workload, I'm not optimistic about his future. Avoid.

XAVIER HERNANDEZ **RRP** **1966** **Age 31**

YR	TEAM	Lge	IP	H	ER	HR	BB	K	ERA	W	L	H/9	HR/9	BB/9	K/9	KW
1993 Houston	NL	93.0	81	33	7	38	97	3.19	6	4	7.84	.68	3.68	9.39	2.21
1994 NY Yankees	AL	40.7	47	22	6	22	37	4.87	2	3	10.40	1.33	4.87	8.19	1.51
1995 Cincinnati	NL	89.3	97	41	8	39	75	4.13	5	5	9.77	.81	3.93	7.56	1.54
1996 Houston	NL	73.3	74	36	11	33	69	4.42	4	4	9.08	1.35	4.05	8.47	1.81

Baseball's X-man hasn't been the same since throwing 207 innings in 1992-93 for Houston. 1996 was his best year since, and he was fantastic after the All-Star Break, so he may have turned the corner. Pick him up, but if he's on a 100-inning pace in June, look for a taker.

CHRIS HOLT **RSP** **1972** **Age 25**

YR	TEAM	Lge	IP	H	ER	HR	BB	K	ERA	W	L	H/9	HR/9	BB/9	K/9	KW
1993 Quad Cities	Midw	164.0	205	73	13	74	103	4.01	9	9	11.25	.71	4.06	5.65	.87
1994 Jackson	Texas	150.7	199	82	15	37	81	4.90	7	10	11.89	.90	2.21	4.84	1.06
1995 Jackson	Texas	29.3	31	8	3	8	21	2.45	2	1	9.51	.92	2.45	6.44	1.53
1995 Tucson	PCL	112.0	142	49	6	43	62	3.94	6	6	11.41	.48	3.46	4.98	.80
1996 Tucson	PCL	175.7	210	73	12	53	112	3.74	11	9	10.76	.61	2.72	5.74	1.23

Holt deserves a spot in the Houston rotation after his second good year at Tucson. He improved across the board in 1996, impressing the organization. Note, however, that he averaged almost seven innings a start, and might be an injury risk.

JOHN HUDEK **RRP** **1967** **Age 30**

YR	TEAM	Lge	IP	H	ER	HR	BB	K	ERA	W	L	H/9	HR/9	BB/9	K/9	KW
1993 Toledo	Inter	37.0	47	26	2	29	26	6.32	1	3	11.43	.49	7.05	6.32	.34
1993 Tucson	PCL	17.3	17	9	1	13	14	4.67	1	1	8.83	.52	6.75	7.27	.74
1994 Houston	NL	38.0	26	12	6	21	36	2.84	3	1	6.16	1.42	4.97	8.53	1.60
1995 Houston	NL	19.7	21	11	3	7	26	5.03	1	1	9.61	1.37	3.20	11.90	3.17
1996 Tucson	PCL	19.3	17	6	2	10	21	2.79	1	1	7.91	.93	4.66	9.78	2.09
1996 Houston	NL	15.3	14	5	2	6	12	2.93	1	1	8.22	1.17	3.52	7.04	1.47

Has anyone who has accomplished so little been relied on for so much? Hudek has a total of 75 fairly effective major league innings, yet the way the Astros fawn over his absence you'd think he was Christy Mathewson. When he's healthy, he's effective, but would you want to bet on his health?

TODD JONES **RRP** **1968** **Age 29**

YR	TEAM	Lge	IP	H	ER	HR	BB	K	ERA	W	L	H/9	HR/9	BB/9	K/9	KW
1993 Tucson	PCL	44.7	46	20	5	37	36	4.03	2	3	9.27	1.01	7.46	7.25	.55
1993 Houston	NL	36.0	31	13	5	18	24	3.25	2	2	7.75	1.25	4.50	6.00	.87
1994 Houston	NL	70.0	56	19	3	32	59	2.44	6	2	7.20	.39	4.11	7.59	1.50
1995 Houston	NL	98.3	98	36	9	61	87	3.29	7	4	8.97	.82	5.58	7.96	1.26
1996 Houston	NL	57.0	65	28	5	38	39	4.42	3	3	10.26	.79	6.00	6.16	.55

Not content with messing up Xavier Hernandez, the Astros have driven Jones, a hard thrower with wicked movement, into ineffectiveness and injury. Jones was saved from 100-inning seasons in 1994 and 1995 by the strike, and hasn't been effective since mid-1995, after tossing 54 innings in just ten weeks before the All-Star Break. He's going to scuffle for a while. Traded to Detroit; he's their best closer candidate, but still has to recover from the 1995-96 damage.

TIM KESTER **RBP** **1972** **Age 25**

YR	TEAM	Lge	IP	H	ER	HR	BB	K	ERA	W	L	H/9	HR/9	BB/9	K/9	KW
1993 Auburn	NY-P	82.0	105	45	3	35	43	4.94	4	5	11.52	.33	3.84	4.72	.61
1994 Osceola	Flor	118.3	201	102	12	45	55	7.76	3	10	15.29	.91	3.42	4.18	.54
1995 Quad Cities	Midw	137.7	219	96	11	31	73	6.28	4	11	14.32	.72	2.03	4.77	1.08
1996 Jackson	Texas	94.0	119	51	8	27	46	4.88	4	6	11.39	.77	2.59	4.40	.82

Used primarily out of the bullpen at Jackson, Kester had an OK year. He's tall, thin and doesn't throw very hard, so barring a sea change in the minds of player development people, he's probably going to be handling his own luggage for a while.

DARRYL KILE	RSP		1969		Age 28										
YR	TEAM	Lge	IP	H	ER	HR	BB	K	ERA	W	L	H/9	HR/9	BB/9	K/9	KW
1993 Houston	NL	166.7	162	67	13	88	137	3.62	10	9	8.75	.70	4.75	7.40	1.28
1994 Houston	NL	146.7	157	76	13	96	99	4.66	7	9	9.63	.80	5.89	6.07	.55
1995 Tucson	PCL	23.0	26	16	0	14	13	6.26	1	2	10.17	.00	5.48	5.09	.33
1995 Houston	NL	125.7	125	76	6	85	103	5.44	5	9	8.95	.43	6.09	7.38	.94
1996 Houston	NL	216.3	251	106	16	118	194	4.41	11	13	10.44	.67	4.91	8.07	1.46

Kile is as good as any pitcher this wild can be. He also led the league in hit batters with 16, meaning he put 346 runners on. In light of this, his ERA doesn't seem all that bad. No pitcher can be successful walking this many hitters, and Kile seems unlikely to be the exception. The number of pitches he throws makes him a major injury risk. Avoid.

DOUG MLICKI	RSP		1971		Age 26										
YR	TEAM	Lge	IP	H	ER	HR	BB	K	ERA	W	L	H/9	HR/9	BB/9	K/9	KW
1993 Osceola	Flor	138.3	190	91	23	88	87	5.92	5	10	12.36	1.50	5.73	5.66	.46
1994 Jackson	Texas	127.0	125	61	23	71	94	4.32	6	8	8.86	1.63	5.03	6.66	.96
1995 Jackson	Texas	88.0	83	39	7	43	62	3.99	5	5	8.49	.72	4.40	6.34	1.01
1995 Tucson	PCL	32.3	40	20	3	9	20	5.57	1	3	11.13	.84	2.51	5.57	1.23
1996 Tucson	PCL	129.7	169	74	9	54	80	5.14	5	9	11.73	.62	3.75	5.55	.91

Listed as "Douga" in the STATS Minor League Handbook, his little-known superhero persona. He's similar to his brother Dave, a Mets reliever, but doesn't throw as hard. That difference makes him the "other" Mlicki, which is not quite like being Mike Maddux or Tito Jackson, but I digress…. He's no better or worse than a dozen guys getting $50/day per diem, and needs some luck to prove it. Unlikely to happen in Houston.

ALVIN MORMAN	LRP		1969		Age 28										
YR	TEAM	Lge	IP	H	ER	HR	BB	K	ERA	W	L	H/9	HR/9	BB/9	K/9	KW
1993 Jackson	Texas	88.3	91	36	8	43	72	3.67	5	5	9.27	.82	4.38	7.34	1.35
1994 Tucson	PCL	69.3	79	39	6	34	42	5.06	3	5	10.25	.78	4.41	5.45	.71
1995 Tucson	PCL	45.7	46	19	6	24	32	3.74	3	2	9.07	1.18	4.73	6.31	.92
1996 Houston	NL	41.7	46	22	8	28	28	4.75	2	3	9.94	1.73	6.05	6.05	.50

Morman pitched very well after July, when Billy Wagner became the #1 lefty in the Houston bullpen. He does what you want a spot lefty to do: get lefties out and hold baserunners (2 SB, 1 CS all year). He's not ready for a bigger role, and might never be.

TONY MOUNCE	LSP		1975		Age 22										
YR	TEAM	Lge	IP	H	ER	HR	BB	K	ERA	W	L	H/9	HR/9	BB/9	K/9	KW
1995 Quad Cities	Midw	140.3	158	60	8	78	94	3.85	8	8	10.13	.51	5.00	6.03	.76
1996 Kissimmee	Flor	136.3	177	76	12	93	75	5.02	6	9	11.68	.79	6.14	4.95	.12

They're really high on him, but he's not overpowering and his strikeout rate dove in the jump to high A ball. Gets high marks for his intangibles, but without a better fastball or improved control he'll be more likely to make the majors as a pitching coach than a pitcher.

TYRONE NARCISSE	RSP		1972		Age 25										
YR	TEAM	Lge	IP	H	ER	HR	BB	K	ERA	W	L	H/9	HR/9	BB/9	K/9	KW
1993 Asheville	S Atl	134.0	223	107	15	91	67	7.19	4	11	14.98	1.01	6.11	4.50	-.03
1994 Osceola	Flor	129.3	195	110	12	78	67	7.65	3	11	13.57	.84	5.43	4.66	.20
1995 Jackson	Texas	148.7	156	73	10	77	80	4.42	8	9	9.44	.61	4.66	4.84	.45
1996 Jackson	Texas	116.0	162	87	15	73	73	6.75	3	10	12.57	1.16	5.66	5.66	.47

Narcisse has been a prospect since 1953. Kiki Cuyler was his first minor league manager. He's had some fair years, advancing oh-so-slowly through the system, and should make the majors in 2031.

GREGG OLSON	RRP		1967		Age 30										
YR	TEAM	Lge	IP	H	ER	HR	BB	K	ERA	W	L	H/9	HR/9	BB/9	K/9	KW
1993 Baltimore	AL	44.0	38	7	1	20	45	1.43	4	1	7.77	.20	4.09	9.20	2.05
1994 Richmond	Inter	10.7	9	3	1	9	11	2.53	1	0	7.59	.84	7.59	9.28	1.20
1994 Atlanta	NL	15.0	19	13	1	15	10	7.80	0	2	11.40	.60	9.00	6.00	-.25
1995 Buffalo	AmA	20.3	19	6	0	11	22	2.66	1	1	8.41	.00	4.87	9.74	2.03
1995 Kansas City	AL	30.0	24	9	3	17	21	2.70	2	1	7.20	.90	5.10	6.30	.82
1996 Detroit	AL	42.7	41	19	5	29	28	4.01	2	3	8.65	1.05	6.12	5.91	.44

He used to have the best curveball I'd ever seen. Olson's fought back from elbow injuries to be mediocre, and if he throws just a few more strikes could have a hell of a year. I think either 1997 or 1998 will be that year.

Houston Astros

BRONSWELL PATRICK   **RBP**   **1971**   **Age 26**

YR	TEAM	Lge	IP	H	ER	HR	BB	K	ERA	W	L	H/9	HR/9	BB/9	K/9	KW
1993	Tacoma	PCL	97.0	150	72	13	54	45	6.68	3	8	13.92	1.21	5.01	4.18	.14
1994	Huntsville	South	25.0	36	12	3	15	13	4.32	1	2	12.96	1.08	5.40	4.68	.21
1994	Tacoma	PCL	44.3	48	24	5	25	33	4.87	2	3	9.74	1.02	5.08	6.70	.96
1995	Tucson	PCL	78.0	82	30	4	28	56	3.46	5	4	9.46	.46	3.23	6.46	1.35
1996	Tucson	PCL	111.3	136	50	8	44	67	4.04	6	6	10.99	.65	3.56	5.42	.92

Patrick is starting his tenth year as a pro and has pitched in every role known to man, so you know he's a serious prospect. He was moderately effective in Tucson for two years. With his flexibility and ability to throw a good number of innings, he could be a decent long reliever in the majors. Cheap help if someone gives him a shot.

EDGAR RAMOS   **RSP**   **1975**   **Age 22**

YR	TEAM	Lge	IP	H	ER	HR	BB	K	ERA	W	L	H/9	HR/9	BB/9	K/9	KW
1994	Quad Cities	Midw	85.7	135	62	4	43	58	6.51	3	7	14.18	.42	4.52	6.09	.90
1995	Kissimmee	Flor	20.0	16	4	2	2	11	1.80	2	0	7.20	.90	.90	4.95	1.42
1996	Kissimmee	Flor	70.0	66	18	6	23	59	2.31	6	2	8.49	.77	2.96	7.59	1.79
1996	Jackson	Texas	61.0	68	38	2	39	43	5.61	2	5	10.03	.30	5.75	6.34	.68

He's an injury-prone right-hander. Ramos has been effective when he's been healthy, but elbow problems cut his 1995 short and a back injury took a chunk out of '96. Closed strong at Tucson. Lost in the Rule V draft.

SHANE REYNOLDS   **RSP**   **1968**   **Age 29**

YR	TEAM	Lge	IP	H	ER	HR	BB	K	ERA	W	L	H/9	HR/9	BB/9	K/9	KW
1993	Tucson	PCL	128.3	147	58	5	32	85	4.07	7	7	10.31	.35	2.24	5.96	1.43
1993	Houston	NL	10.7	12	4	0	7	10	3.38	1	0	10.12	.00	5.91	8.44	1.34
1994	Houston	NL	122.0	129	40	11	32	103	2.95	9	5	9.52	.81	2.36	7.60	1.94
1995	Houston	NL	186.0	210	82	16	53	158	3.97	11	10	10.16	.77	2.56	7.65	1.91
1996	Houston	NL	233.7	242	92	20	64	179	3.54	15	11	9.32	.77	2.47	6.89	1.68

Reynolds is a wonderful pitcher. They need to lock him up for four years, $16 million now, before they're fighting him in arbitration every year. He has good mechanics, control and no health questions. The National League's Alex Fernandez.

MARK SMALL   **RRP**   **1968**   **Age 29**

YR	TEAM	Lge	IP	H	ER	HR	BB	K	ERA	W	L	H/9	HR/9	BB/9	K/9	KW
1993	Jackson	Texas	75.3	85	37	9	57	46	4.42	4	4	10.15	1.08	6.81	5.50	.13
1994	Jackson	Texas	19.0	26	17	2	13	10	8.05	0	2	12.32	.95	6.16	4.74	.04
1994	Tucson	PCL	65.7	81	37	8	41	26	5.07	3	4	11.10	1.10	5.62	3.56	-.22
1995	Tucson	PCL	62.7	67	23	5	25	46	3.30	4	3	9.62	.72	3.59	6.61	1.30
1996	Tucson	PCL	36.3	33	14	3	22	29	3.47	2	2	8.17	.74	5.45	7.18	1.03
1996	Houston	NL	24.3	35	21	1	16	14	7.77	1	2	12.95	.37	5.92	5.18	.25

After almost two years of part-time closing at Tucson, Small broke camp with Houston to start 1996, pitched quite poorly and was sent back to the PCL when the Astros signed Xavier Hernandez. He's staff filler, might be back, but impossible to predict when and with whom.

BILLY WAGNER   **LBP**   **1972**   **Age 25**

YR	TEAM	Lge	IP	H	ER	HR	BB	K	ERA	W	L	H/9	HR/9	BB/9	K/9	KW
1993	Auburn	NY-P	23.0	31	21	3	36	16	8.22	1	2	12.13	1.17	14.09	6.26	-1.43
1994	Quad Cities	Midw	136.0	121	69	11	120	128	4.57	7	8	8.01	.73	7.94	8.47	.84
1995	Jackson	Texas	63.7	56	24	8	45	67	3.39	4	3	7.92	1.13	6.36	9.47	1.57
1995	Tucson	PCL	72.0	64	20	3	39	72	2.50	6	2	8.00	.38	4.88	9.00	1.78
1996	Tucson	PCL	69.3	64	26	2	40	70	3.37	5	3	8.31	.26	5.19	9.09	1.73
1996	Houston	NL	50.3	32	14	7	35	59	2.50	4	2	5.72	1.25	6.26	10.55	1.95

Wagner is a small left-hander with an explosive fastball, good curve and improving changeup. Dierker's handling of him is probably the single most important task facing the new manager. Wagner has been a starter, and a good one, in the minors. When we was called up to the Astros last July, they put him in the bullpen and his effectiveness, coupled with the injury/ineffectiveness of Hudek and Jones, won him the closer job.

Because of his size, I firmly believe that if he is used a starter he will injure himself and have a disappointing career. For 1997, I believe he would be best served in the Rivera role, throwing 100 high-leverage innings without being overused, a role I think he can handle. Using him as a closer would be a waste because he can handle a 95-110 inning workload, beyond a typical closer's total. If he's managed well, he'll be fabulous.

JAMIE WALKER   **LRP**   **1972**   **Age 25**

YR	TEAM	Lge	IP	H	ER	HR	BB	K	ERA	W	L	H/9	HR/9	BB/9	K/9	KW
1993	Quad Cities	Midw	113.0	178	101	15	64	71	8.04	3	10	14.18	1.19	5.10	5.65	.61
1994	Quad Cities	Midw	108.7	162	83	12	59	65	6.87	3	9	13.42	.99	4.89	5.38	.57
1995	Jackson	South	53.0	70	31	7	32	29	5.26	2	4	11.89	1.19	5.43	4.92	.28
1996	Jackson	Texas	92.7	103	32	7	48	65	3.11	6	4	10.00	.68	4.66	6.31	.94

Walker is another Astro prospect whose role keeps changing, from starter in 1992 and 1993 to the bullpen in 1995 through this July, and then back into the rotation. He pitched very well as a reliever this year. Lost in the Rule V draft.

DONNE WALL   **RSP**   **1968**   **Age 29**

YR	TEAM	Lge	IP	H	ER	HR	BB	K	ERA	W	L	H/9	HR/9	BB/9	K/9	KW
1993	Tucson	PCL	121.3	143	58	12	47	71	4.30	6	7	10.61	.89	3.49	5.27	.88
1994	Tucson	PCL	139.0	163	67	9	49	72	4.34	7	8	10.55	.58	3.17	4.66	.76
1995	Tucson	PCL	167.7	177	51	6	47	107	2.74	13	6	9.50	.32	2.52	5.74	1.28
1995	Houston	NL	24.0	35	18	5	8	15	6.75	1	2	13.12	1.88	3.00	5.62	1.12
1996	Tucson	PCL	49.7	67	25	2	10	29	4.53	3	3	12.14	.36	1.81	5.26	1.30
1996	Houston	NL	148.0	179	78	17	48	87	4.74	7	9	10.89	1.03	2.92	5.29	1.03

Despite a strong two months, Wall doesn't project as a long-term contributor, except perhaps to the United Way. Soft-tosser who will probably bounce up and down between AAA and the majors for the rest of the millennium without ever being good.

ANTHONY YOUNG   **RRP**   **1966**   **Age 31**

YR	TEAM	Lge	IP	H	ER	HR	BB	K	ERA	W	L	H/9	HR/9	BB/9	K/9	KW
1993	Norfolk	Inter	15.0	16	2	1	7	7	1.20	2	0	9.60	.60	4.20	4.20	.35
1993	NY Mets	NL	97.7	109	59	8	53	60	5.44	4	7	10.04	.74	4.88	5.53	.62
1994	Chicago Cubs	NL	112.7	107	52	13	56	61	4.15	6	7	8.55	1.04	4.47	4.87	.51
1995	Chicago Cubs	NL	41.0	47	17	5	17	13	3.73	3	2	10.32	1.10	3.73	2.85	.02
1996	Houston	NL	32.7	39	17	4	26	17	4.68	2	2	10.74	1.10	7.16	4.68	-.23

Young is now starting to pitch like the 0-16 guy he never really was, after years of observers insisting he had the ability to be successful. He still has the stuff, but probably needs 180 innings at AAA to get it back together.

Player	Age	Team	Lge	AB	H	DB	TP	HR	BB	SB	CS	OUT	BA	OBA	SA	EQA	EQR	Peak
JASON ADAMS	23	Quad Cities	Midw	235	55	7	0	3	22	3	3	183	.234	.300	.302	.200	16	.218
CHAD ALEXANDER	22	Quad Cities	Midw	453	110	14	1	12	44	9	5	348	.243	.310	.358	.224	41	.247
ADAN AMEZCUA	22	Kissimmee	Flor	275	75	12	1	1	23	0	0	200	.273	.329	.335	.225	24	.249
ANDY BOVENDER	23	Quad Cities	Midw	279	66	10	1	7	24	2	3	216	.237	.297	.355	.215	23	.234
R.J. BOWERS	22	Kissimmee	Flor	128	32	0	1	5	14	3	1	97	.250	.324	.383	.239	14	.262
	22	Quad Cities	Midw	236	54	11	0	5	25	4	5	187	.229	.303	.339	.211	19	.234
MIKE BRUMLEY	33	Tucson	PCL	279	60	9	4	5	37	7	2	221	.215	.307	.330	.216	24	.205
ARNIE CHAVERA	22	Quad Cities	Midw	190	42	9	1	3	15	0	0	148	.221	.278	.326	.199	13	.218
RYAN COE	23	Quad Cities	Midw	253	69	3	0	12	13	0	0	184	.273	.308	.427	.244	27	.267
JAY DAVIS	25	Tucson	PCL	100	31	6	1	1	5	3	1	70	.310	.343	.420	.260	12	.274
ALEJANDRO FREIRE	21	Kissimmee	Flor	396	100	10	1	14	22	7	4	300	.253	.292	.389	.227	37	.254
JERRY GOFF	32	Tucson	PCL	277	61	9	1	9	51	1	0	216	.220	.341	.357	.236	29	.224
JIMMY GONZALEZ	23	Kissimmee	Flor	215	36	2	0	6	23	1	0	179	.167	.248	.260	.156	9	.170
MIKE GROPPUSO	26	Jackson	Texas	113	26	2	1	2	10	1	0	87	.230	.293	.319	.205	8	.213
	26	Tucson	PCL	144	34	2	0	5	8	1	0	110	.236	.276	.354	.210	11	.218
CARLOS HERNANDEZ	20	Quad Cities	Midw	468	115	9	3	6	19	20	7	360	.246	.275	.316	.202	33	.230
RAY HOLBERT	25	Tucson	PCL	97	22	4	1	0	7	3	1	76	.227	.279	.289	.191	6	.202
RIC JOHNSON	22	Quad Cities	Midw	325	68	5	1	4	11	5	2	259	.209	.235	.268	.157	13	.173
FRANK KELLNER	29	Tucson	PCL	253	62	11	3	1	22	3	3	194	.245	.305	.324	.210	20	.208
RANDY KNORR	27	Houston	NL	88	18	2	0	2	6	0	1	71	.205	.255	.295	.172	4	.177
ROGER LUCE	27	Jackson	Texas	244	58	8	2	7	11	0	0	186	.238	.271	.373	.212	19	.218
JULIO LUGO	20	Quad Cities	Midw	406	109	10	0	10	23	12	6	303	.268	.308	.367	.229	38	.260
MARK MANWARREN	23	Kissimmee	Flor	163	32	4	0	2	14	9	2	133	.196	.260	.258	.176	9	.192
BUCK MCNABB	23	Jackson	Texas	286	78	11	3	1	38	7	3	211	.273	.358	.343	.242	30	.264
DONOVAN MITCHELL	26	Jackson	Texas	413	95	16	1	3	31	7	2	320	.230	.284	.295	.194	26	.203
MELVIN MORA	24	Jackson	Texas	257	66	4	1	4	14	3	4	195	.257	.295	.327	.206	19	.221
	24	Tucson	PCL	227	57	9	0	4	17	3	3	173	.251	.303	.344	.216	19	.231
GARY MOTA	25	Kissimmee	Flor	157	50	6	2	3	5	0	0	107	.318	.340	.439	.262	19	.276
NATE PETERSON	24	Jackson	Texas	328	83	8	0	4	26	1	1	246	.253	.308	.314	.209	24	.223
WES PRATT	23	Kissimmee	Flor	145	25	1	0	3	9	1	1	121	.172	.221	.241	.128	4	.138
ALAN PROBST	25	Jackson	Texas	182	42	4	1	6	16	1	0	140	.231	.293	.363	.219	16	.230
EDDIE PYE	29	Tucson	PCL	275	65	13	3	3	28	4	2	212	.236	.307	.338	.217	23	.215
KEN RAMOS	29	Tucson	PCL	385	94	17	2	4	39	6	5	296	.244	.314	.330	.216	32	.215
HASSAN ROBINSON	23	Quad Cities	Midw	381	92	8	1	1	9	7	3	292	.241	.259	.276	.175	19	.190
MARLON ROCHE	21	Quad Cities	Midw	284	67	4	1	4	20	3	5	222	.236	.286	.299	.191	18	.214
NOEL RODRIGUEZ	22	Kissimmee	Flor	302	74	9	0	7	24	0	1	229	.245	.301	.344	.214	24	.236
	22	Quad Cities	Midw	149	37	5	0	4	10	0	0	112	.248	.296	.362	.219	13	.243
TONY ROSS	21	Jackson	Texas	81	13	0	0	1	6	1	1	69	.160	.218	.198	.094	1	.081
	21	Kissimmee	Flor	199	44	6	1	2	14	5	1	156	.221	.272	.291	.189	12	.211
NELSON SAMBOY	19	Kissimmee	Flor	382	93	16	2	1	20	9	4	293	.243	.281	.304	.196	25	.227
VICTOR SANCHEZ	24	Jackson	Texas	212	45	6	0	10	14	3	1	168	.212	.261	.382	.212	17	.227
JAMIE SAYLOR	21	Kissimmee	Flor	185	36	3	1	2	10	4	3	152	.195	.236	.254	.150	7	.169
GARY TRAMMELL	23	Kissimmee	Flor	415	116	15	5	2	19	6	2	301	.280	.311	.354	.227	37	.246
CHRIS TRUBY	22	Quad Cities	Midw	373	83	7	1	8	20	4	4	294	.223	.262	.311	.186	22	.205

Player	Age	Team	Lge	IP	H	ER	HR	BB	K	ERA	W	L	H/9	HR/9	BB/9	K/9	KW
ERIC BELL	32	Tucson	PCL	120.3	171	96	7	61	47	7.18	3	10	12.79	.52	4.56	3.52	.03
ALBERTO BLANCO	20	Quad Cities	Midw	41.3	53	26	4	20	36	5.66	2	3	11.54	.87	4.35	7.84	1.52
RYAN CREEK	23	Jackson	Texas	129.3	148	90	9	149	99	6.26	4	10	10.30	.63	10.37	6.89	-.30
DONNIE DAULT	24	Kissimmee	Flor	35.3	39	25	5	27	31	6.37	1	3	9.93	1.27	6.88	7.90	.91
JIM DOUGHERTY	28	Tucson	PCL	58.0	65	29	1	33	43	4.50	3	3	10.09	.16	5.12	6.67	.94
DAVE EVANS	28	Tucson	PCL	105.3	118	65	9	58	65	5.55	4	8	10.08	.77	4.96	5.55	.61
KEVIN GALLAHER	27	Tucson	PCL	82.0	87	41	5	54	66	4.50	4	5	9.55	.55	5.93	7.24	.93
FREDDY GARCIA	19	Quad Cities	Midw	51.7	75	30	4	35	31	5.23	2	4	13.06	.70	6.10	5.40	.28
MIKE GUNDERSON	23	Quad Cities	Midw	68.0	98	63	9	81	37	8.34	1	7	12.97	1.19	10.72	4.90	-1.05
CHRIS HILL	21	Quad Cities	Midw	42.7	61	43	9	20	24	9.07	1	4	12.87	1.90	4.22	5.06	.63
RICH HUMPHREY	25	Jackson	Texas	59.3	59	20	7	22	31	3.03	4	3	8.95	1.06	3.34	4.70	.73
JOHN JOHNSTONE	27	Tucson	PCL	52.0	59	22	2	28	57	3.81	3	3	10.21	.35	4.85	9.87	2.08
DAN LOCK	23	Kissimmee	Flor	128.3	207	125	6	86	53	8.77	2	12	14.52	.35	6.03	3.72	-.27
NIUMAN LOIZ	22	Quad Cities	Midw	98.7	151	82	11	69	47	7.48	2	9	13.77	1.00	6.29	4.29	-.14
JOHANN LOPEZ	21	Kissimmee	Flor	85.7	142	57	8	50	51	5.99	3	7	14.92	.84	5.25	5.36	.47
JIM LYNCH	20	Quad Cities	Midw	51.3	65	30	4	63	32	5.26	2	4	11.40	.70	11.05	5.61	-.89
TOM MARTIN	26	Jackson	Texas	68.3	78	34	8	54	48	4.48	4	4	10.27	1.05	7.11	6.32	.33
HECTOR MERCADO	22	Kissimmee	Flor	70.3	97	49	7	63	50	6.27	2	6	12.41	.90	8.06	6.40	.12
PAUL O'MALLEY	23	Quad Cities	Midw	152.7	226	90	14	67	70	5.31	6	11	13.32	.83	3.95	4.13	.39
DEREK ROOT	21	Quad Cities	Midw	55.3	68	26	2	34	30	4.23	3	3	11.06	.33	5.53	4.88	.24
SEAN RUNYAN	22	Quad Cities	Midw	114.3	168	69	14	40	65	5.43	5	8	13.22	1.10	3.15	5.12	.92
TONY SHAVER	24	Kissimmee	Flor	56.0	73	28	5	32	26	4.50	3	3	11.73	.80	5.14	4.18	.11
BRIAN SIKORSKI	21	Quad Cities	Midw	143.3	185	88	16	91	94	5.53	6	10	11.62	1.00	5.71	5.90	.54
DOUG SIMONS	29	Jackson	Texas	115.3	147	52	11	45	62	4.06	6	7	11.47	.86	3.51	4.84	.73
	29	Tucson	PCL	39.3	52	21	1	19	22	4.81	2	2	11.90	.23	4.35	5.03	.59
ERIC SMITH	22	Quad Cities	Midw	65.0	87	36	6	34	37	4.98	3	4	12.05	.83	4.71	5.12	.53
ERIC STACHLER	23	Kissimmee	Flor	49.3	62	40	5	51	30	7.30	1	4	11.31	.91	9.30	5.47	-.50
BROCK STEINKE	21	Kissimmee	Flor	40.7	74	44	3	41	16	9.74	1	4	16.38	.66	9.07	3.54	-1.09
	21	Quad Cities	Midw	45.0	65	40	4	46	35	8.71	1	4	14.15	.87	10.02	7.62	.04
JEFF TABAKA	32	Tucson	PCL	40.3	40	13	2	26	42	2.90	3	1	8.93	.45	5.80	9.37	1.67
JULIEN TUCKER	23	Kissimmee	Flor	102.3	160	91	13	58	40	8.00	2	9	14.07	1.14	5.10	3.52	-.10
MICHAEL WALTER	21	Quad Cities	Midw	54.7	48	20	4	44	53	3.29	4	2	7.90	.66	7.24	8.73	1.10

Pittsburgh Pirates

An era is over in Pittsburgh; the last ties to the division championship teams of the early '90s have been cut. Manager Jimmy Leyland has gone to the Marlins; their best pitcher, Denny Neagle, is a Brave. They didn't have a best hitter, really, but Orlando Merced and Carlos Garcia are among the hitters who are gone, and the connection is tenuous for Jay Bell and Jeff King.

The Pirates are clearly hoping to duplicate the success of the San Diego Padres, who rose from their fire sale to a division title in a span of three years. The Padres at least kept a few good players, like Gwynn, and had the good fortune to make a great swindle with Houston. The Pirates are certainly trying the mega-trade approach, getting six players for three from the Jays, but none of them are major leaguers or even ready to contribute right now. The lack of talent in the majors, due to a combination of poor farm support, players who looked good coming through the minors but failed in Pittsburgh and a reliance on "proven" major league mediocrities has left them with little to trade. Silly contracts, like Bell's, have restricted the team's ability to trade the talent it has.

Cam Bonifay, the GM, has retained his position under the new Pirate ownership. He has continued to give sizable contracts to non-star players, such as Bell, Mike Kingery and now Al Martin, in a short-sighted strategy to remain "competitive," while delaying the retooling of the Pirates to a time when the players to be traded are clearly on the down side of their careers. Still, with a little luck the Pirates can have a strong team by the turn of the millennium. Trey Beamon has been an excellent hitter throughout his career, Jermaine Allensworth an exceptional fielder; Jason Schmidt and Ron Wright, acquired for Neagle, have great potential, as do Jimmy Anderson and Chad Hermansen from their own system. They have the unusual advantage of being able to draw off some Mexican players, thanks to a working arrangement with the Mexico City Red Devils, one that has already yielded a few pitchers. The following years will be more than lean; the prospective 1997 lineup looks AAA in every sense.

Pirate farm clubs tended to stay close to .500. The Calgary Cannons went 74-68, led on offense by Dale Sveum and in pitching by Joe Boever, who went 12-1 as a reliever. The Carolina Mudcats went 70-69 and sneaked into the playoffs after finishing second to Jacksonville in both halves of the Southern League season. They could furnish a number of players to the Pirate roster in 1997: pitchers Jimmy Anderson and Blaine Beatty, shortstop Lou Collier and outfielder T.J. Staton are cheap, available and good enough not to be a total embarrassment.

The Lynchburg Hillcats of the Carolina League finished dead last in the first half at 26-43, but improved to 39-31 in the second half and narrowly missed the playoffs. The Hillcats featured four players with good potential: last year's Rule Ver, Freddy Garcia, who tied for the league HR title with teammate Jose Guillen, also among the leaders in average and RBI; the aforementioned Jimmy Anderson, who went up to Carolina at midseason, and 1995's #1 draft pick Chad Hermansen, who came up from Augusta at the midway point. The Augusta Greenjackets went 71-70; after Hermansen moved up, the only bright spot on the team was the pitching of Elvin Hernandez.

JERMAINE ALLENSWORTH   **CF**   **1972**   **Age 25**

Year	Team	Lge	AB	H	DB	TP	HR	BB	SB	CS	OUT	BA	OBA	SA	EQA	EQR	Peak
1993	Welland	NY-P	274	70	11	1	1	18	6	2	206	.255	.301	.314	.210	21	.235
1994	Carolina	South	465	107	24	5	2	40	10	6	364	.230	.291	.316	.203	34	.224
1995	Carolina	South	224	56	11	2	1	24	8	4	172	.250	.323	.330	.223	20	.243
1995	Calgary	PCL	186	53	9	2	4	14	10	3	136	.285	.335	.419	.258	23	.279
1996	Calgary	PCL	351	107	18	2	9	37	19	4	247	.305	.371	.444	.280	51	.300
1996	Pittsburgh	NL	233	62	8	3	4	26	9	5	176	.266	.340	.378	.243	26	.261
1997	*Pittsburgh*	*NL*	*602*	*164*	*37*	*7*	*12*	*55*	*40*	*16*	*454*	*.272*	*.333*	*.417*	*.265*	*82*	

He's an outstanding center fielder whose offense is a puzzle: is the improvement in '95-'96 real, or just a favorable reaction to Calgary? I always get a little queasy recommending players whose performance is only worthwhile when playing in one particular stadium. He's fast, so naturally he's seen as a leadoff candidate, regardless of whether he's ever hit for average or drawn walks. This year at Calgary was the only season with good leadoff numbers.

RICH AUDE   **1B**   **1972**   **Age 25**

Year	Team	Lge	AB	H	DB	TP	HR	BB	SB	CS	OUT	BA	OBA	SA	EQA	EQR	Peak
1993	Carolina	South	428	114	15	2	16	46	5	2	316	.266	.338	.423	.254	52	.284
1993	Buffalo	AmA	67	26	5	0	5	11	0	0	41	.388	.474	.687	.369	17	.414
1994	Buffalo	AmA	531	152	30	3	18	44	7	3	382	.286	.341	.456	.265	69	.292
1995	Calgary	PCL	191	58	7	1	9	12	3	1	134	.304	.345	.492	.277	27	.301
1995	Pittsburgh	NL	110	27	5	0	3	7	1	2	85	.245	.291	.373	.217	9	.236
1996	Calgary	PCL	391	105	15	0	17	26	4	3	289	.269	.314	.437	.249	45	.267
1997	*Pittsburgh*	*NL*	*403*	*113*	*34*	*2*	*21*	*22*	*2*	*2*	*292*	*.280*	*.318*	*.531*	*.284*	*63*	

It seems he's been around forever. He hit a lot of doubles way back in 1990 and again in '92, and usually you'd expect some home run pop to develop from that. Not this time. Even in the years when he hit well, it wasn't good for a first baseman. He flopped in his one extended chance in Pittsburgh.

TREY BEAMON   **LF**   **1974**   **Age 23**

Year	Team	Lge	AB	H	DB	TP	HR	BB	SB	CS	OUT	BA	OBA	SA	EQA	EQR	Peak
1993	Augusta	S Atl	390	93	12	3	1	36	8	3	300	.238	.303	.292	.202	27	.232
1994	Carolina	South	451	142	14	6	7	35	13	5	314	.315	.364	.419	.267	58	.304
1995	Calgary	PCL	443	132	22	3	6	39	14	5	316	.298	.355	.402	.259	54	.290
1996	Calgary	PCL	378	100	11	2	5	51	12	2	280	.265	.352	.344	.243	41	.268
1996	Pittsburgh	NL	52	12	1	0	0	4	1	1	41	.231	.286	.250	.173	3	.188
1997	*Kansas City*	*AL*	*538*	*134*	*29*	*2*	*14*	*56*	*6*	*4*	*408*	*.249*	*.320*	*.388*	*.243*	*60*	

How a franchise hurts itself: you have a guy who's a dynamite hitter. He hits for a terrific average but not much power. The Pirates decide he's worthless if he can't hit for power. Beamon decides to accommodate them, tries to hit for more power and instead messes up his swing. He's supposed to spend the winter with the Pirates strength coach, still seeking that power. Hopefully, he'll return to the swing he had in 1994. Dumped on Kansas City, doesn't change his status much.

JAY BELL   **SS**   **1966**   **Age 31**

Year	Team	Lge	AB	H	DB	TP	HR	BB	SB	CS	OUT	BA	OBA	SA	EQA	EQR	Peak
1993	Pittsburgh	NL	623	197	33	6	11	86	13	8	434	.316	.399	.441	.284	93	.291
1994	Pittsburgh	NL	432	122	35	3	10	55	2	0	310	.282	.363	.447	.271	59	.273
1995	Pittsburgh	NL	536	140	25	3	14	61	2	4	400	.261	.337	.397	.245	59	.243
1996	Pittsburgh	NL	536	136	27	2	14	60	5	4	404	.254	.329	.390	.240	57	.236
1997	*Pittsburgh*	*NL*	*534*	*135*	*33*	*3*	*14*	*51*	*8*	*5*	*404*	*.253*	*.318*	*.404*	*.250*	*63*	

He signed a long-term contract for superstar money when he was 27 and coming off a good year. If you're me, you think this is as good as he gets. If you're Cam Bonifay, you think he's still four years from his peak. Now I certainly would not have thought he'd fall so far and fast, but I wouldn't have had a shortstop of his caliber signed for four years at over $5 million. Blame it on the strike if you want—he was a prominent union voice and was the lightning rod for fan grief in western Pennsylvania. Traded to Kansas City, where he'll be the starting shortstop.

D.J. BOSTON   1B   1972   Age 25

Year	Team	Lge	AB	H	DB	TP	HR	BB	SB	CS	OUT	BA	OBA	SA	EQA	EQR	Peak
1993	Hagerstown	S Atl	482	134	19	1	12	40	13	6	354	.278	.333	.396	.247	54	.277
1994	Dunedin	Flor	445	121	11	1	9	50	11	5	329	.272	.345	.362	.242	47	.267
1995	Knoxville	South	484	106	16	1	11	45	8	4	382	.219	.285	.324	.203	35	.220
1996	Syracuse	Inter	87	22	4	0	4	14	0	1	66	.253	.356	.437	.260	11	.276
1996	Carolina	South	331	90	13	2	8	41	3	2	243	.272	.352	.396	.252	39	.270
1997	*Pittsburgh*	*NL*	*355*	*95*	*24*	*1*	*11*	*29*	*6*	*2*	*262*	*.268*	*.323*	*.434*	*.263*	*46*	

A total disaster in his first trip to AA, he was doing fine at Syracuse before being traded to the Pirates and getting sent back to AA, where he pretty much continued his Syracuse season. He's a dreadful fielder, with 20 errors last year, and would have been a lot better off staying in an AL organization. He's a marginal pinch-hitter right now and could be a decent one with another step up in offense.

ADRIAN BROWN   CF   1974   Age 23

Year	Team	Lge	AB	H	DB	TP	HR	BB	SB	CS	OUT	BA	OBA	SA	EQA	EQR	Peak
1994	Augusta	S Atl	318	75	11	1	1	12	9	5	248	.236	.264	.286	.182	17	.205
1995	Augusta	S Atl	306	85	10	1	5	27	11	6	227	.278	.336	.366	.240	32	.269
1995	Lynchburg	Caro	221	52	3	2	1	12	7	3	172	.235	.275	.281	.186	13	.208
1996	Lynchburg	Caro	220	63	4	1	4	12	8	4	161	.286	.323	.368	.236	22	.261
1996	Carolina	South	348	98	9	2	3	20	17	6	256	.282	.321	.345	.231	33	.255
1997	*Pittsburgh*	*NL*	*505*	*149*	*17*	*5*	*7*	*22*	*35*	*13*	*369*	*.295*	*.324*	*.390*	*.257*	*62*	

Even if he didn't have a problem with joining a higher league in midseason, he's be pretty poor hitter. He has no power at all, and while he's not a big guy, at 6' 0", 185 he's not Ricky Otero, either. He is fast, has a good arm and puts the ball in play, hitting for a high but empty batting average. That being a combination easily overrated, he'll probably crack the big time in '98 or so, and his stolen bases will make him a good rotisserie pick.

LOU COLLIER   SS   1974   Age 23

Year	Team	Lge	AB	H	DB	TP	HR	BB	SB	CS	OUT	BA	OBA	SA	EQA	EQR	Peak
1993	Welland	NY-P	207	49	2	1	1	9	3	3	161	.237	.269	.271	.174	10	.200
1994	Augusta	S Atl	332	88	12	1	7	22	15	5	249	.265	.311	.370	.234	33	.265
1994	Salem, VA	Caro	158	32	1	1	4	12	3	3	129	.203	.259	.297	.178	9	.202
1995	Lynchburg	Caro	418	115	15	2	5	48	18	6	309	.275	.350	.356	.245	46	.275
1996	Carolina	South	454	122	17	2	3	40	18	5	337	.269	.328	.335	.231	43	.254
1997	*Pittsburgh*	*NL*	*566*	*158*	*26*	*1*	*5*	*39*	*34*	*10*	*418*	*.279*	*.326*	*.355*	*.248*	*64*	

A small guy, he's done reasonably well in his extended stays the last three years. Reportedly a good fielder, it doesn't show in the stats. The $5.5 million difference between his salary and Bell's would go a long way towards helping Bonifay meet McClatchy's payroll, especially since there's virtually no difference in their expected performance.

MIDRE CUMMINGS   OF   1972   Age 25

Year	Team	Lge	AB	H	DB	TP	HR	BB	SB	CS	OUT	BA	OBA	SA	EQA	EQR	Peak
1993	Carolina	South	238	64	11	1	6	14	3	2	176	.269	.310	.399	.237	24	.264
1993	Buffalo	AmA	238	68	10	1	9	23	5	1	171	.286	.349	.450	.268	32	.300
1994	Buffalo	AmA	187	59	11	3	3	15	4	0	128	.316	.366	.455	.279	26	.309
1994	Pittsburgh	NL	87	22	3	0	1	5	0	0	65	.253	.293	.322	.205	6	.226
1995	Calgary	PCL	156	38	7	1	1	7	1	1	119	.244	.276	.321	.197	10	.215
1995	Pittsburgh	NL	153	37	6	1	2	15	1	0	116	.242	.310	.333	.217	13	.236
1996	Calgary	PCL	365	101	17	1	9	21	5	2	266	.277	.316	.403	.242	38	.259
1996	Pittsburgh	NL	85	19	3	1	3	1	0	0	66	.224	.233	.388	.202	6	.216
1997	*Pittsburgh*	*NL*	*461*	*132*	*31*	*2*	*10*	*29*	*7*	*3*	*332*	*.286*	*.329*	*.427*	*.264*	*59*	

He's the reason I get queasy with one-park kind of guys. Outside of Buffalo and the disaster of '95, he's consistently hit .235, plus or minus a few points, including a .236 in 1991 and a .234 the next year. Notable: his walk/strikeout rate has plunged far more than most players as he's moved up.

ANGELO ENCARNACION   C   1973   Age 24

Year	Team	Lge	AB	H	DB	TP	HR	BB	SB	CS	OUT	BA	OBA	SA	EQA	EQR	Peak
1993	Salem-VA	Caro	238	47	7	1	2	13	1	1	192	.197	.239	.261	.151	9	.171
1994	Carolina	South	233	65	9	0	5	13	1	1	169	.279	.317	.382	.235	23	.263
1995	Calgary	PCL	78	17	2	0	1	2	1	0	61	.218	.237	.282	.167	3	.185
1995	Pittsburgh	NL	160	36	6	2	2	15	1	1	125	.225	.291	.325	.204	12	.225
1996	Calgary	PCL	260	76	10	0	5	11	5	1	185	.292	.321	.388	.243	27	.263
1997	*Pittsburgh*	*NL*	*299*	*77*	*7*	*0*	*6*	*13*	*4*	*2*	*224*	*.258*	*.288*	*.341*	*.221*	*26*	

The best defensive catcher in the PCL, and he showed a little life with the stick in a year interrupted for a month with the chicken pox. He's stuck behind Kendall and Osik; he was reportedly so disappointed at being sent back to Calgary that his wife had to talk him out of retiring.

CARLOS GARCIA   2B   1968   Age 29

Year	Team	Lge	AB	H	DB	TP	HR	BB	SB	CS	OUT	BA	OBA	SA	EQA	EQR	Peak
1993	Pittsburgh	NL	554	151	24	4	13	39	15	9	412	.273	.320	.401	.242	59	.256
1994	Pittsburgh	NL	416	117	15	2	6	22	16	8	307	.281	.317	.370	.234	41	.243
1995	Pittsburgh	NL	371	109	23	2	6	29	6	3	265	.294	.345	.415	.257	44	.263
1996	Pittsburgh	NL	396	114	17	4	6	28	13	5	287	.288	.335	.396	.249	45	.252
1997	*Toronto*	*AL*	*528*	*154*	*28*	*4*	*9*	*32*	*2*	*1*	*375*	*.292*	*.332*	*.411*	*.254*	*61*	

He's about as average as a player can get. He played a fair amount of shortstop and third base last year, along with his more familiar second base. A classic salary dump; a mediocre player signed for several years at more money than he's worth. At least he was still on the right side of 28 when signed, although some people aren't so sure that's true.

FREDDY GARCIA   3B   1973   Age 24

Year	Team	Lge	AB	H	DB	TP	HR	BB	SB	CS	OUT	BA	OBA	SA	EQA	EQR	Peak
1994	St. Catherine's	NY-P	272	68	3	0	10	25	1	1	205	.250	.313	.371	.229	26	.255
1995	Pittsburgh	NL	57	8	0	1	0	9	0	1	50	.140	.258	.175	.100	1	.111
1996	Lynchburg	Caro	488	138	16	2	18	38	2	1	351	.283	.335	.434	.257	59	.279
1997	*Pittsburgh*	*NL*	*560*	*139*	*24*	*1*	*20*	*41*	*1*	*0*	*421*	*.248*	*.300*	*.402*	*.243*	*61*	

He was a Rule V pick in 1994, and wasted all of 1995 sitting on the Pirate bench next to Leyland. He showed why the Pirates wanted to hang onto him, leading the Carolina League in home runs and doubles. To make it better, he easily showed the best range in the league; and to show you why he was in A ball, he led the league (not just third basemen, but the whole Carolina League) with 35 errors.

JOSE GUILLEN   RF   1976   Age 21

Year	Team	Lge	AB	H	DB	TP	HR	BB	SB	CS	OUT	BA	OBA	SA	EQA	EQR	Peak
1995	Erie	NY-P	260	68	4	0	9	8	0	2	194	.262	.284	.381	.219	22	.252
1996	Lynchburg	Caro	537	156	8	0	18	19	12	7	388	.291	.315	.406	.243	56	.276
1997	*Pittsburgh*	*NL*	*604*	*167*	*21*	*1*	*27*	*14*	*18*	*9*	*446*	*.276*	*.293*	*.449*	*.256*	*74*	

Garcia's teammate at Lynchburg and co-leader in home runs. The first thing you notice about Guillen is his arm: it's an absolute cannon, one of the best in all of baseball, like his good friend Raul Mondesi. He's only 5' 11" and 165 pounds, but he crushes the ball. He chased a Triple Crown for much of the year, finishing second in BA and RBI, and was the league's MVP. He has a chance to realize a common Latin American dream: to play right field for the Pirates, just like Clemente. It would help if he would learn the strike zone (73 K, 20 BB).

CHAD HERMANSEN   SS   1978   Age 19

Year	Team	Lge	AB	H	DB	TP	HR	BB	SB	CS	OUT	BA	OBA	SA	EQA	EQR	Peak
1995	Erie	NY-P	170	39	3	1	5	13	1	1	132	.229	.284	.347	.208	13	.247
1996	Augusta	S Atl	245	63	5	1	12	30	5	2	184	.257	.338	.433	.257	31	.301
1996	Lynchburg	Caro	259	66	4	2	8	25	2	1	194	.255	.320	.378	.235	26	.274
1997	*Pittsburgh*	*NL*	*605*	*165*	*34*	*5*	*16*	*58*	*10*	*6*	*446*	*.273*	*.336*	*.425*	*.264*	*80*	

The Pirates #1 pick in 1995, he was named the #1 prospect in the New York-Penn and Gulf Coast leagues in '95, and the #2 prospect in the SAL this year. Frequently compared to Cal Ripken, he's big, still growing at 6' 2", 185, has good power and knows what a walk is. He may not stay at short; he played the outfield in high school, there's concern he'll outgrow the position and he led all of professional baseball with 53 errors.

MARK JOHNSON　　**1B**　　**1968**　　**Age 29**

Year	Team	Lge	AB	H	DB	TP	HR	BB	SB	CS	OUT	BA	OBA	SA	EQA	EQR	Peak
1993	Carolina	South	407	87	11	2	13	59	3	1	321	.214	.313	.346	.221	37	.233
1994	Carolina	South	410	114	11	1	23	64	4	3	299	.278	.376	.478	.281	63	.292
1995	Pittsburgh	NL	224	47	6	1	13	39	4	2	179	.210	.327	.420	.246	27	.252
1996	Pittsburgh	NL	351	98	18	0	15	48	5	4	257	.279	.366	.459	.273	50	.275

Late bloomer? It took him three tries, until he was 26, to figure out AA pitching, and you could charitably call 1995 a year that should have been spent in Calgary. It's hard to imagine he'll do any better than this, and it's barely adequate for a first baseman.

JASON KENDALL　　**C**　　**1974**　　**Age 23**

Year	Team	Lge	AB	H	DB	TP	HR	BB	SB	CS	OUT	BA	OBA	SA	EQA	EQR	Peak
1993	Augusta	S Atl	376	89	11	1	2	16	3	2	289	.237	.268	.287	.181	20	.208
1994	Salem-VA	Caro	371	95	12	0	5	39	7	2	278	.256	.327	.329	.225	33	.255
1994	Carolina	South	48	11	1	0	0	2	0	0	37	.229	.260	.250	.159	2	.182
1995	Carolina	South	441	135	18	1	9	53	6	4	310	.306	.381	.413	.269	58	.302
1996	Pittsburgh	NL	423	129	22	5	3	39	4	2	296	.305	.364	.402	.261	51	.287
1997	*Pittsburgh*	*NL*	*532*	*166*	*24*	*3*	*7*	*35*	*6*	*2*	*368*	*.312*	*.354*	*.408*	*.270*	*70*	

He managed a rare feat for the Pirates: retaining the offensive performance he showed in the minors. His 1996 was a carbon copy of 1995. He showed steady improvement through the minors, and I'd expect him to resume an upward climb towards .300. His defense was puzzling: he was among the best at stopping baserunners at Carolina in '95, but surrendered more stolen bases than any catcher but Piazza while committing 18 errors. He's tough to strike out and easy to hit, with a 76-to-44 strikeout to HBP ratio over the last three years.

JEFF KING　　**1B/2B**　　**1965**　　**Age 32**

Year	Team	Lge	AB	H	DB	TP	HR	BB	SB	CS	OUT	BA	OBA	SA	EQA	EQR	Peak
1993	Pittsburgh	NL	626	187	34	1	11	68	7	5	444	.299	.367	.409	.263	79	.265
1994	Pittsburgh	NL	344	92	14	0	8	34	3	2	254	.267	.333	.378	.240	36	.239
1995	Pittsburgh	NL	451	120	25	2	18	60	6	3	334	.266	.352	.450	.266	61	.260
1996	Pittsburgh	NL	604	168	32	4	31	76	13	1	437	.278	.359	.498	.284	94	.273
1997	*Kansas City*	*AL*	*549*	*145*	*27*	*1*	*19*	*66*	*9*	*2*	*406*	*.264*	*.343*	*.421*	*.264*	*72*	

He played wherever he was asked in '96, although he hit and fielded much better at first than second. By setting career highs in doubles, triples, homers, runs, runs batted in, walks, stolen bases and total bases, he'll convince Cam Bonifay that players really do peak in their early 30s. Dealt to Kansas City, where he may play first, second or third.

MIKE KINGERY　　**CF**　　**1961**　　**Age 36**

Year	Team	Lge	AB	H	DB	TP	HR	BB	SB	CS	OUT	BA	OBA	SA	EQA	EQR	Peak
1993	Omaha	AmA	401	101	14	4	10	39	8	2	302	.252	.318	.382	.237	41	.225
1994	Colorado	NL	301	101	26	5	5	34	4	6	206	.336	.403	.505	.297	49	.281
1995	Colorado	NL	345	83	16	3	7	48	9	4	266	.241	.333	.365	.237	36	.225
1996	Pittsburgh	NL	280	70	11	2	3	26	2	1	211	.250	.314	.336	.219	24	.207
1997	*Pittsburgh*	*NL*	*172*	*40*	*9*	*1*	*2*	*19*	*4*	*1*	*133*	*.233*	*.309*	*.331*	*.228*	*16*	

Signing Kingery was the biggest joke of the 1995 offseason. I mean, the guy's had one good year since Reagan was president, and that was in Colorado (to be fair, he hit everywhere that season). He was horrible as a leadoff man (did you really think he'd hit .349 again?) and in the outfield.

NELSON LIRIANO　　**2B**　　**1964**　　**Age 33**

Year	Team	Lge	AB	H	DB	TP	HR	BB	SB	CS	OUT	BA	OBA	SA	EQA	EQR	Peak
1993	Colo. Springs	PCL	282	82	16	2	6	28	6	6	206	.291	.355	.426	.259	35	.258
1993	Colorado	NL	150	41	6	2	2	20	4	3	112	.273	.359	.380	.250	17	.251
1994	Colorado	NL	255	62	16	4	3	45	0	2	195	.243	.357	.373	.244	29	.238
1995	Pittsburgh	NL	262	75	11	1	5	27	2	2	189	.286	.353	.393	.252	30	.242
1996	Pittsburgh	NL	220	59	14	2	3	17	2	0	161	.268	.321	.391	.241	23	.229
1997	*Los Angeles*	*NL*	*168*	*40*	*9*	*1*	*2*	*18*	*4*	*1*	*129*	*.238*	*.312*	*.339*	*.243*	*19*	

A consistent and useful backup infielder, although the parts are starting to rust out. Picked up on waivers by the Dodgers.

AL MARTIN   **LF**   **1968**   **Age 29**

Year	Team	Lge	AB	H	DB	TP	HR	BB	SB	CS	OUT	BA	OBA	SA	EQA	EQR	Peak
1993	Pittsburgh	NL	490	141	25	5	20	49	14	7	356	.288	.353	.482	.275	71	.290
1994	Pittsburgh	NL	282	83	12	3	10	38	13	5	204	.294	.378	.465	.282	43	.293
1995	Pittsburgh	NL	445	126	24	3	13	49	16	9	328	.283	.354	.438	.265	59	.271
1996	Pittsburgh	NL	643	197	30	2	20	62	32	11	457	.306	.367	.453	.277	93	.280
1997	*Pittsburgh*	*NL*	*518*	*145*	*28*	*1*	*25*	*54*	*31*	*9*	*382*	*.280*	*.348*	*.483*	*.287*	*85*	

Apparently not learning from the problems they've had unloading middling players with expensive contracts, he's been signed to a two-year extension at a hefty raise, keeping him in Pittsburgh through 1999. There's nothing about him that says "better than your average outfielder," especially since he has got to stop playing against left-handed pitching.

TIM MARX   **C**   **1969**   **Age 28**

Year	Team	Lge	AB	H	DB	TP	HR	BB	SB	CS	OUT	BA	OBA	SA	EQA	EQR	Peak
1993	Augusta	S Atl	173	42	3	0	3	26	1	2	133	.243	.342	.312	.220	15	.236
1993	Salem-VA	Caro	44	7	0	0	0	6	0	0	37	.159	.260	.159	.096	1	.129
1994	Carolina	South	248	71	7	1	8	20	1	1	178	.286	.340	.419	.254	29	.269
1995	Calgary	PCL	182	48	8	1	1	19	2	2	136	.264	.333	.335	.226	17	.234
1996	Calgary	PCL	295	88	16	1	1	27	4	1	208	.298	.357	.369	.250	33	.256

If he hits like this year he could be a decent backup catcher. But not for this team.

ORLANDO MERCED   **RF**   **1967**   **Age 30**

Year	Team	Lge	AB	H	DB	TP	HR	BB	SB	CS	OUT	BA	OBA	SA	EQA	EQR	Peak
1993	Pittsburgh	NL	464	148	26	2	10	84	3	2	318	.319	.423	.448	.296	76	.308
1994	Pittsburgh	NL	393	109	21	2	10	47	4	1	285	.277	.355	.417	.260	49	.267
1995	Pittsburgh	NL	494	149	28	2	16	58	6	2	347	.302	.375	.464	.281	72	.283
1996	Pittsburgh	NL	463	136	20	1	18	56	6	4	331	.294	.370	.458	.275	66	.273
1997	*Toronto*	*AL*	*478*	*142*	*24*	*1*	*16*	*59*	*5*	*3*	*339*	*.297*	*.374*	*.452*	*.280*	*70*	

He had some good years at the plate, largely on the strength of his batting eye. In recent years, he's tried for more power with very little success, and he hasn't taken as many walks.

KEITH OSIK   **C**   **1969**   **Age 28**

Year	Team	Lge	AB	H	DB	TP	HR	BB	SB	CS	OUT	BA	OBA	SA	EQA	EQR	Peak
1993	Carolina	South	374	96	14	1	9	28	0	1	279	.257	.308	.372	.227	34	.243
1994	Buffalo	AmA	265	57	10	0	7	29	0	1	209	.215	.293	.332	.205	20	.217
1995	Calgary	PCL	295	89	13	1	11	21	2	1	207	.302	.348	.464	.270	39	.282
1996	Pittsburgh	NL	143	42	14	1	1	16	1	0	101	.294	.365	.427	.268	19	.275

Without fanfare, he's outhit Kendall each of the last two years. Given their ages, I'd be surprised if that extends more than perhaps one more year. He didn't do any better than Kendall at stopping baserunners, which indicts the pitching staff's ability to hold them. He'll play anywhere in an emergency, and got into games at third and left.

CHARLES PETERSON   **RF**   **1974**   **Age 23**

Year	Team	Lge	AB	H	DB	TP	HR	BB	SB	CS	OUT	BA	OBA	SA	EQA	EQR	Peak
1994	Augusta	S Atl	433	101	10	3	4	30	12	8	340	.233	.283	.298	.193	28	.220
1995	Lynchburg	Caro	408	109	8	3	7	41	18	8	307	.267	.334	.353	.236	42	.265
1995	Carolina	South	72	22	3	1	0	9	1	1	51	.306	.383	.375	.259	9	.291
1996	Carolina	South	473	125	19	0	8	42	20	6	354	.264	.324	.355	.235	47	.259
1997	*Pittsburgh*	*NL*	*497*	*123*	*29*	*1*	*11*	*42*	*17*	*6*	*380*	*.247*	*.306*	*.376*	*.241*	*54*	

A high-school football star and #1 draft pick in 1993. He's a great athlete, but hasn't displayed signs of being a good ballplayer. He didn't make any progress at the plate this year and led the league in outfield errors.

REED SECRIST   **3B**   **1970**   **Age 27**

Year	Team	Lge	AB	H	DB	TP	HR	BB	SB	CS	OUT	BA	OBA	SA	EQA	EQR	Peak
1993	Augusta	S Atl	276	66	7	1	6	20	2	1	211	.239	.291	.337	.209	21	.227
1994	Salem-VA	Caro	221	44	6	0	6	19	1	1	178	.199	.262	.308	.184	13	.196
1995	Lynchburg	Caro	400	114	13	2	18	51	2	2	288	.285	.366	.463	.274	57	.289
1996	Calgary	PCL	419	118	17	0	17	49	2	2	303	.282	.357	.444	.266	55	.277
1997	*Pittsburgh*	*NL*	*533*	*144*	*23*	*1*	*27*	*73*	*2*	*1*	*390*	*.270*	*.358*	*.469*	*.283*	*83*	

An old player to be reaching AAA, he played three very undistinguished seasons before coming around at Lynchburg in '95, and kept it up at Calgary last year. His best position is probably DH.

T.J. STATON   LF   1975   Age 22

Year	Team	Lge	AB	H	DB	TP	HR	BB	SB	CS	OUT	BA	OBA	SA	EQA	EQR	Peak
1994	Augusta	S Atl	130	26	5	1	0	8	2	1	105	.200	.246	.254	.156	5	.180
1995	Augusta	S Atl	410	111	13	2	6	23	12	6	305	.271	.309	.356	.226	37	.257
1996	Carolina	South	398	119	17	1	15	49	11	4	283	.299	.376	.460	.280	59	.314
1997	*Pittsburgh*	*NL*	*541*	*150*	*31*	*4*	*23*	*54*	*22*	*9*	*400*	*.277*	*.343*	*.477*	*.281*	*84*	

A big left-handed slugger, Staton made himself a prospect with a dynamite year in AA, improving in every phase of the game. Especially noteworthy was doubling his walk rate while not striking out more.

DALE SVEUM   IF   1964   Age 33

Year	Team	Lge	AB	H	DB	TP	HR	BB	SB	CS	OUT	BA	OBA	SA	EQA	EQR	Peak
1993	Calgary	PCL	118	31	5	0	6	21	0	1	88	.263	.374	.458	.273	17	.272
1993	Oakland	AL	81	16	1	1	3	17	0	0	65	.198	.337	.346	.229	8	.228
1994	Calgary	PCL	383	94	13	0	18	45	1	0	289	.245	.325	.420	.247	44	.242
1995	Calgary	PCL	402	102	18	0	14	47	2	1	301	.254	.332	.403	.246	45	.238
1996	Calgary	PCL	341	97	16	1	21	32	2	1	245	.284	.346	.522	.282	52	.268

Thought about retiring in the last couple of years, but decided to stick around for another Big Offense year.

DEREK SWAFFORD   2B   1975   Age 22

Year	Team	Lge	AB	H	DB	TP	HR	BB	SB	CS	OUT	BA	OBA	SA	EQA	EQR	Peak
1994	Welland	NY-P	67	22	2	1	1	4	3	2	46	.328	.366	.433	.271	9	.312
1994	Augusta	S Atl	194	35	7	2	1	10	6	3	161	.180	.221	.253	.144	6	.164
1995	Augusta	S Atl	467	112	11	2	4	27	22	8	363	.240	.281	.298	.199	32	.226
1996	Lynchburg	Caro	446	102	9	3	2	41	15	8	352	.229	.294	.276	.192	28	.215

Exceptional speed and range, but makes errors and doesn't hit.

SHON WALKER   1B/DH   1974   Age 23

Year	Team	Lge	AB	H	DB	TP	HR	BB	SB	CS	OUT	BA	OBA	SA	EQA	EQR	Peak
1993	Welland	NY-P	123	19	1	0	2	11	1	0	104	.154	.224	.211	.112	2	.127
1993	Augusta	S Atl	233	41	4	0	3	14	1	2	194	.176	.223	.232	.122	5	.140
1994	Augusta	S Atl	263	59	4	0	4	53	12	3	207	.224	.354	.285	.227	25	.258
1995	Augusta	S Atl	386	82	9	0	7	56	5	4	308	.212	.312	.290	.201	28	.225
1996	Lynchburg	Caro	336	93	7	2	12	42	1	2	245	.277	.357	.417	.259	42	.285

He set a national high school record by hitting 29 homers, was drafted in the first round, and spent the next few years out on the town. Missed the first month of the season in a custody battle for his infant son, and attributes his new-found dedication to the game to parenthood. He doesn't really have a position, trying first base out this year after showing abysmal range in right field.

JOHN WEHNER   3B/PH   1967   Age 30

Year	Team	Lge	AB	H	DB	TP	HR	BB	SB	CS	OUT	BA	OBA	SA	EQA	EQR	Peak
1993	Buffalo	AmA	338	87	18	2	8	42	16	3	254	.257	.339	.393	.253	41	.263
1994	Buffalo	AmA	339	105	18	2	8	34	16	5	239	.310	.373	.445	.278	49	.285
1995	Calgary	PCL	155	46	10	1	4	12	6	3	112	.297	.347	.452	.267	21	.268
1995	Pittsburgh	NL	109	34	1	1	1	11	2	1	76	.312	.375	.367	.256	13	.258
1996	Pittsburgh	NL	141	37	8	1	2	9	1	4	108	.262	.307	.376	.221	12	.219

The ultimate utility player, he also got into games at all three outfield positions, second base and even caught a couple of innings. With the Dodgers, where he'll battle for a roster spot.

TONY WOMACK   SS   1970   Age 27

Year	Team	Lge	AB	H	DB	TP	HR	BB	SB	CS	OUT	BA	OBA	SA	EQA	EQR	Peak
1993	Salem-VA	Caro	304	73	7	2	1	13	14	6	237	.240	.271	.286	.190	19	.205
1993	Carolina	South	249	68	4	1	1	16	12	3	184	.273	.317	.309	.221	21	.240
1994	Buffalo	AmA	425	97	8	1	1	23	31	7	335	.228	.268	.259	.186	25	.199
1995	Carolina	South	336	80	9	3	1	19	16	5	261	.238	.279	.292	.196	22	.208
1995	Calgary	PCL	105	25	3	1	0	12	5	3	83	.238	.316	.286	.206	8	.218
1996	Calgary	PCL	502	137	17	7	2	31	27	8	372	.273	.315	.347	.231	48	.241

A speedy, light-hitting shortstop who has somehow picked up three cups of coffee.

RON WRIGHT   **1B**   **1976**   **Age 21**

Year	Team	Lge	AB	H	DB	TP	HR	BB	SB	CS	OUT	BA	OBA	SA	EQA	EQR	Peak
1995	Macon	S Atl	553	141	9	0	25	50	1	0	412	.255	.317	.407	.241	59	.278
1996	Durham	Caro	247	63	5	1	15	31	0	0	184	.255	.338	.466	.264	33	.300
1996	Greenville	South	237	58	8	1	13	33	1	0	179	.245	.337	.451	.260	31	.296
1997	*Pittsburgh*	*NL*	*369*	*97*	*12*	*0*	*22*	*42*	*0*	*0*	*272*	*.263*	*.338*	*.474*	*.277*	*55*	

The minor leagues' premier slugger, probably for another year. He creates either a big fly or a big breeze when he goes to the plate, striking out 151 times this year but hitting 36 homers along the way. He does know how to take a walk at least, but is sssllllooowwww once he gets on. He'll need a year in AAA, and could push 50 HR if given a full year in the PCL. Anybody playing first in Pittsburgh is strictly a caretaker.

JIMMY ANDERSON   **LSP**   **1976**   **Age 21**

YR	TEAM	Lge	IP	H	ER	HR	BB	K	ERA	W	L	H/9	HR/9	BB/9	K/9	KW
1995	Albany, GA	S Atl	67.3	70	18	2	45	43	2.41	5	2	9.36	.27	6.01	5.75	.41
1995	Lynchburg	Caro	47.0	67	32	1	29	24	6.13	1	4	12.83	.19	5.55	4.60	.14
1996	Lynchburg	Caro	59.3	59	24	3	29	38	3.64	4	3	8.95	.46	4.40	5.76	.82
1996	Carolina	South	90.0	102	36	3	52	57	3.60	6	4	10.20	.30	5.20	5.70	.60

He's cruised through the minors with a 2.51 ERA. His attitude has been questioned, but not his arm: a fastball/slider combo that's left minor leaguers pounding balls into the dirt.

BLAINE BEATTY   **LSP**   **1964**   **Age 33**

YR	TEAM	Lge	IP	H	ER	HR	BB	K	ERA	W	L	H/9	HR/9	BB/9	K/9	KW
1993	Carolina	South	85.3	76	39	9	46	49	4.11	4	5	8.02	.95	4.85	5.17	.51
1993	Buffalo	AmA	34.7	53	23	2	12	13	5.97	1	3	13.76	.52	3.12	3.37	.35
1994	Chattanooga	South	179.7	175	69	19	70	127	3.46	11	9	8.77	.95	3.51	6.36	1.24
1995	Chattanooga	South	47.3	70	23	2	23	26	4.37	2	3	13.31	.38	4.37	4.94	.55
1995	Indianapolis	AmA	64.7	82	31	7	25	33	4.31	3	4	11.41	.97	3.48	4.59	.66
1996	Carolina	South	134.7	153	54	16	41	85	3.61	8	7	10.23	1.07	2.74	5.68	1.21

Left-handers can stick around forever. In his case, it isn't really fair. Buffalo '93 was the only time his real ERA has been over 4.31, including a 2.30 ERA in brief stints with the Mets in '89 and '91. He's got a 122-64 lifetime record, but gets left in the minors while strong-armed punks get chance after chance.

JOE BOEVER   **RRP**   **1961**   **Age 36**

YR	TEAM	Lge	IP	H	ER	HR	BB	K	ERA	W	L	H/9	HR/9	BB/9	K/9	KW
1993	Detroit	AL	22.3	15	7	1	12	14	2.82	1	1	6.04	.40	4.84	5.64	.67
1993	Oakland	AL	79.0	89	36	9	37	51	4.10	4	5	10.14	1.03	4.22	5.81	.88
1994	Detroit	AL	81.0	76	31	11	40	48	3.44	5	4	8.44	1.22	4.44	5.33	.67
1995	Detroit	AL	100.7	117	56	15	47	71	5.01	4	7	10.46	1.34	4.20	6.35	1.07
1996	Calgary	PCL	78.3	80	19	1	26	54	2.18	7	2	9.19	.11	2.99	6.20	1.32
1996	Pittsburgh	NL	15.0	17	9	2	7	5	5.40	1	1	10.20	1.20	4.20	3.00	-.05

He racked up a gaudy 12-1 record while controlling the ball better, and keeping it inside the park better, than he ever has in his life. That palm ball must work well in thin air.

TOM BOLTON   **LBP**   **1962**   **Age 35**

YR	TEAM	Lge	IP	H	ER	HR	BB	K	ERA	W	L	H/9	HR/9	BB/9	K/9	KW
1993	Detroit	AL	102.0	113	48	5	50	68	4.24	5	6	9.97	.44	4.41	6.00	.90
1994	Rochester	Inter	18.3	15	4	1	10	13	1.96	2	0	7.36	.49	4.91	6.38	.90
1994	Baltimore	AL	23.3	27	11	3	13	12	4.24	1	2	10.41	1.16	5.01	4.63	.29
1995	Nashville	AmA	96.7	114	50	10	44	72	4.66	5	6	10.61	.93	4.10	6.70	1.21
1996	Calgary	PCL	109.0	121	53	7	58	75	4.38	5	7	9.99	.58	4.79	6.19	.87

After an eight-year major league career, he's spent the last two in the minors. No telling how long he can go on bouncing from one organization to the next, refusing to die. Left-handers, like that damn rabbit, can hang around forever.

JASON CHRISTIANSEN   **LRP**   **1970**   **Age 27**

YR	TEAM	Lge	IP	H	ER	HR	BB	K	ERA	W	L	H/9	HR/9	BB/9	K/9	KW
1993	Salem, VA	Caro	63.7	56	28	5	35	43	3.96	4	3	7.92	.71	4.95	6.08	.79
1994	Carolina	South	35.3	36	10	3	20	34	2.55	3	1	9.17	.76	5.09	8.66	1.61
1994	Buffalo	AmA	32.0	21	8	4	19	35	2.25	3	1	5.91	1.12	5.34	9.84	1.95
1995	Pittsburgh	NL	55.7	49	23	5	39	47	3.72	3	3	7.92	.81	6.31	7.60	.96
1996	Pittsburgh	NL	45.0	55	29	7	23	33	5.80	2	3	11.00	1.40	4.60	6.60	1.05

He never had an ERA above 3.30 in the minors, but has never had one below 4 in the majors. He actually started to lose it in July of 1995; he was shut down last June with a sore shoulder, and later required arthroscopic surgery.

STEVE COOKE   **LSP**   **1970**   **Age 27**

YR	TEAM	Lge	IP	H	ER	HR	BB	K	ERA	W	L	H/9	HR/9	BB/9	K/9	KW
1993	Pittsburgh	NL	205.0	213	92	23	82	127	4.04	11	12	9.35	1.01	3.60	5.58	.96
1994	Pittsburgh	NL	134.0	153	69	20	59	69	4.63	6	9	10.28	1.34	3.96	4.63	.55
1996	Carolina	South	49.3	63	32	3	30	33	5.84	2	3	11.49	.55	5.47	6.02	.64

Threw 211 innings at age 23, got lit up at age 24, didn't pitch at all at age 25, failed comeback attempt at 26.

FRANCISCO CORDOVA   **RRP**   **1972**   **Age 25**

YR	TEAM	Lge	IP	H	ER	HR	BB	K	ERA	W	L	H/9	HR/9	BB/9	K/9	KW
1993	Mex Cy RD	Mexi	91.3	105	43	8	58	63	4.24	5	5	10.35	.79	5.72	6.21	.64
1994	Mex Cy RD	Mexi	126.7	149	49	11	57	87	3.48	8	6	10.59	.78	4.05	6.18	1.05
1995	Mex Cy RD	Mexi	99.0	134	48	8	47	73	4.36	5	6	12.18	.73	4.27	6.64	1.14
1996	Pittsburgh	NL	97.3	104	42	11	29	83	3.88	6	5	9.62	1.02	2.68	7.67	1.89

He went 13-0 for Mexico City in 1995 and got himself a year in Pittsburgh. He's from a remote part of Mexico where native languages are spoken and speaks no English and little Spanish, but certainly communicated well with Kendall.

ELMER DESSENS   **RBP**   **1972**   **Age 25**

YR	TEAM	Lge	IP	H	ER	HR	BB	K	ERA	W	L	H/9	HR/9	BB/9	K/9	KW
1994	Mex Cy RD	Mexi	104.7	151	45	7	42	43	3.87	6	6	12.98	.60	3.61	3.70	.33
1995	Carolina	South	139.7	188	60	11	35	52	3.87	8	8	12.11	.71	2.26	3.35	.55
1996	Carolina	South	11.0	16	7	1	5	5	5.73	0	1	13.09	.82	4.09	4.09	.34
1996	Calgary	PCL	32.3	39	12	5	18	12	3.34	2	2	10.86	1.39	5.01	3.34	-.14
1996	Pittsburgh	NL	25.3	40	20	2	6	11	7.11	1	2	14.21	.71	2.13	3.91	.77

He certainly doesn't have what people think of as a Mexican name, but that's where he's from. And he certainly doesn't have a fastball, but he gets people out. He pitched seven games in Mexico City this year (the Pirates were afraid it was too cold for him in Calgary) and went 7-0 with a 1.26 ERA. He'll give up hits and he won't strike anyone out, but at least he won't walk anyone.

MARIANO DE LOS SANTOS   **RRP**   **1971**   **Age 26**

YR	TEAM	Lge	IP	H	ER	HR	BB	K	ERA	W	L	H/9	HR/9	BB/9	K/9	KW
1993	Salem, VA	Caro	86.7	103	46	7	60	49	4.78	4	6	10.70	.73	6.23	5.09	.14
1993	Carolina	South	36.7	52	22	1	20	25	5.40	1	3	12.76	.25	4.91	6.14	.82
1994	Carolina	South	69.3	91	38	9	36	45	4.93	3	5	11.81	1.17	4.67	5.84	.78
1994	Buffalo	AmA	46.3	49	25	6	21	23	4.86	2	3	9.52	1.17	4.08	4.47	.47
1995	Carolina	South	25.0	31	15	5	18	15	5.40	1	2	11.16	1.80	6.48	5.40	.18
1995	Calgary	PCL	68.0	78	43	4	29	33	5.69	3	5	10.32	.53	3.84	4.37	.50
1996	Carolina	South	61.7	75	25	1	27	57	3.65	4	3	10.95	.15	3.94	8.32	1.79

He's been a starter with the Pirates since 1989 with two exceptions. In 1992, he worked as a closer in the SAL, picking up 12 saves, a 2.25 ERA and had the best strikeout rate of his career, at least until…1996, when he again switched to relief and blows Southern League hitters away. He's got a big body (5' 10", 200) and has no chance as a starter, but I think he could contribute in relief.

JOHN ERICKS RRP 1968 Age 29

YR	TEAM	Lge	IP	H	ER	HR	BB	K	ERA	W	L	H/9	HR/9	BB/9	K/9	KW
1994	Salem, VA	Caro	47.7	46	18	3	26	47	3.40	3	2	8.69	.57	4.91	8.87	1.73
1994	Carolina	South	52.0	51	22	2	28	50	3.81	3	3	8.83	.35	4.85	8.65	1.67
1995	Calgary	PCL	27.0	20	6	3	15	23	2.00	2	1	6.67	1.00	5.00	7.67	1.31
1995	Pittsburgh	NL	104.3	108	49	6	59	71	4.23	6	6	9.32	.52	5.09	6.12	.77
1996	Calgary	PCL	28.7	30	12	4	18	33	3.77	2	1	9.42	1.26	5.65	10.36	2.04
1996	Pittsburgh	NL	46.7	56	30	10	23	40	5.79	2	3	10.80	1.93	4.44	7.71	1.46

Drafted in 1988 by the Cardinals, he put his shoulder under the knife in 1992 and missed all of '93. He came to the Pirates and has shot through their system, apparently better than ever. He's very big (6' 7", 225) and throws very hard. He doesn't have an off-speed pitch to complement the fastball, though, and pitched much better in a relief role this year than he did from the rotation.

ELVIN HERNANDEZ RSP 1978 Age 19

YR	TEAM	Lge	IP	H	ER	HR	BB	K	ERA	W	L	H/9	HR/9	BB/9	K/9	KW
1995	Erie	NY-P	74.0	112	47	12	36	32	5.72	3	5	13.62	1.46	4.38	3.89	.20
1996	Augusta	S Atl	132.3	213	82	18	29	94	5.58	5	10	14.49	1.22	1.97	6.39	1.64

He went 17-5 this year with 171 strikeouts and 16 walks; yes, he really had a 10-1 K/BB ratio. He doesn't throw that hard right now, but he's awfully young and thin yet. He and Elmer Dessens could give a clinic on control.

JOHN HOPE RSP 1971 Age 26

YR	TEAM	Lge	IP	H	ER	HR	BB	K	ERA	W	L	H/9	HR/9	BB/9	K/9	KW
1993	Carolina	South	101.3	133	65	8	41	48	5.77	4	7	11.81	.71	3.64	4.26	.51
1993	Buffalo	AmA	20.7	31	15	4	4	6	6.53	1	1	13.50	1.74	1.74	2.61	.44
1993	Pittsburgh	NL	37.3	48	18	2	12	8	4.34	2	2	11.57	.48	2.89	1.93	-.08
1994	Buffalo	AmA	95.0	105	52	9	32	49	4.93	4	7	9.95	.85	3.03	4.64	.79
1994	Pittsburgh	NL	14.0	18	11	1	5	6	7.07	0	2	11.57	.64	3.21	3.86	.48
1995	Calgary	PCL	75.7	74	22	4	18	37	2.62	6	2	8.80	.48	2.14	4.40	.93
1996	Calgary	PCL	117.7	143	62	11	62	58	4.74	5	8	10.94	.84	4.74	4.44	.29
1996	Pittsburgh	NL	19.3	17	16	5	13	11	7.45	0	2	7.91	2.33	6.05	5.12	.19

He's been living right on the major league/AAA edge, but with no production in four major league calls he's probably doomed to the PCL for eternity.

JON LIEBER RBP 1970 Age 27

YR	TEAM	Lge	IP	H	ER	HR	BB	K	ERA	W	L	H/9	HR/9	BB/9	K/9	KW
1993	Wilmington	Caro	98.3	163	57	4	23	56	5.22	4	7	14.92	.37	2.11	5.13	1.18
1993	Carolina	South	30.7	43	14	3	14	21	4.11	1	2	12.62	.88	4.11	6.16	1.03
1994	Carolina	South	19.0	17	4	0	4	16	1.89	2	0	8.05	.00	1.89	7.58	2.05
1994	Buffalo	AmA	20.0	18	3	1	2	19	1.35	2	0	8.10	.45	.90	8.55	2.62
1994	Pittsburgh	NL	107.3	114	53	12	35	66	4.44	5	7	9.56	1.01	2.93	5.53	1.11
1995	Calgary	PCL	73.3	112	54	7	27	31	6.63	2	6	13.75	.86	3.31	3.80	.44
1995	Pittsburgh	NL	73.0	99	47	7	21	40	5.79	3	5	12.21	.86	2.59	4.93	1.00
1996	Pittsburgh	NL	140.7	156	60	18	40	82	3.84	8	8	9.98	1.15	2.56	5.25	1.11

A maddeningly inconsistent pitcher. He got a chance at the rotation after the All-Star break, and did as well as he had while relieving, so he'll probably get another chance at it.

ESTEBAN LOAIZA RSP 1972 Age 25

YR	TEAM	Lge	IP	H	ER	HR	BB	K	ERA	W	L	H/9	HR/9	BB/9	K/9	KW
1993	Salem, VA	Caro	95.7	128	53	7	48	38	4.99	4	7	12.04	.66	4.52	3.57	.06
1993	Carolina	South	39.3	43	17	6	17	29	3.89	2	2	9.84	1.37	3.89	6.64	1.24
1994	Carolina	South	139.3	201	76	18	53	91	4.91	6	9	12.98	1.16	3.42	5.88	1.10
1995	Pittsburgh	NL	172.0	198	97	20	70	76	5.08	7	12	10.36	1.05	3.66	3.98	.41
1996	Calgary	PCL	64.7	62	28	5	31	31	3.90	4	3	8.63	.70	4.31	4.31	.36
1996	Pittsburgh	NL	53.0	64	27	10	23	28	4.58	3	3	10.87	1.70	3.91	4.75	.61

Another product of the Pirates' Mexican connection, Loaiza was rushed to the majors in '95 and did about as well as could have been expected. He seemed to draw a lot of criticism for his attitude from Pirate management, and found himself back in Mexico City.

RICH LOISELLE   **RSP**   **1972**   **Age 25**

YR	TEAM	Lge	IP	H	ER	HR	BB	K	ERA	W	L	H/9	HR/9	BB/9	K/9	KW
1993	Waterloo	Midw	50.7	71	32	4	39	28	5.68	2	4	12.61	.71	6.93	4.97	-.07
1993	R. Cucamonga	Calif	73.0	116	55	5	36	37	6.78	2	6	14.30	.62	4.44	4.56	.41
1994	R. Cucamonga	Calif	139.7	177	76	13	96	78	4.90	6	10	11.41	.84	6.19	5.03	.13
1995	Memphis	South	72.3	94	47	6	44	37	5.85	3	5	11.70	.75	5.47	4.60	.17
1995	Las Vegas	PCL	25.7	33	20	5	12	14	7.01	1	2	11.57	1.75	4.21	4.91	.58
1996	Jackson	Texas	90.0	118	45	7	39	54	4.50	4	6	11.80	.70	3.90	5.40	.82
1996	Tucson	PCL	31.3	29	16	1	14	25	4.60	1	2	8.33	.29	4.02	7.18	1.39
1996	Calgary	PCL	48.0	62	23	3	21	33	4.31	2	3	11.62	.56	3.94	6.19	1.08
1996	Pittsburgh	NL	20.7	22	7	3	9	8	3.05	1	1	9.58	1.31	3.92	3.48	.18

He joined his third organization in two years when the Pirates traded Danny Darwin for him. It was the best year of his career by far, a combined 4.31 DT-ERA over four teams; it's worth mentioning that he got his control down, consistently, all year. The improvement could well be real, but it still doesn't make him a good pitcher.

DANNY MICELI   **RRP**   **1971**   **Age 26**

YR	TEAM	Lge	IP	H	ER	HR	BB	K	ERA	W	L	H/9	HR/9	BB/9	K/9	KW
1993	Memphis	South	53.3	62	30	8	49	51	5.06	2	4	10.46	1.35	8.27	8.61	.80
1994	Buffalo	AmA	22.7	17	4	3	8	28	1.59	3	0	6.75	1.19	3.18	11.12	2.91
1994	Pittsburgh	NL	27.0	28	16	5	14	25	5.33	1	2	9.33	1.67	4.67	8.33	1.61
1995	Pittsburgh	NL	58.0	59	25	7	33	50	3.88	3	3	9.16	1.09	5.12	7.76	1.31
1996	Pittsburgh	NL	86.3	97	56	15	54	58	5.84	3	7	10.11	1.56	5.63	6.05	.61

A closer in the minors, he failed disastrously in nine starts in '96. His trends, falling strikeouts with rising walks, are worrisome. Traded to the Tigers for Clint Sodowsky, he's in the bullpen mix there along with greater metropolitan Detroit.

RAMON MOREL   **RBP**   **1975**   **Age 22**

YR	TEAM	Lge	IP	H	ER	HR	BB	K	ERA	W	L	H/9	HR/9	BB/9	K/9	KW
1993	Welland	NY-P	60.3	126	55	9	37	27	8.20	1	6	18.80	1.34	5.52	4.03	-.04
1994	Albany, GA	S Atl	149.3	205	78	10	43	91	4.70	7	10	12.35	.60	2.59	5.48	1.18
1995	Lynchburg	Caro	65.3	97	39	2	21	32	5.37	2	5	13.36	.28	2.89	4.41	.75
1995	Carolina	South	64.0	78	29	4	16	26	4.08	3	4	10.97	.56	2.25	3.66	.66
1996	Carolina	South	58.7	85	40	3	19	32	6.14	2	5	13.04	.46	2.91	4.91	.91
1996	Pittsburgh	NL	42.7	56	23	4	23	19	4.85	2	3	11.81	.84	4.85	4.01	.12

Another skinny, soft-throwing, precision control Latin hurler: a Pirate specialty! He's knocked out scouts far more than the results justify, throwing four pitches with excellent control. Problem: they move too slowly to avoid being whacked.

STEVE PARRIS   **RBP**   **1968**   **Age 29**

YR	TEAM	Lge	IP	H	ER	HR	BB	K	ERA	W	L	H/9	HR/9	BB/9	K/9	KW
1993	Jacksonville	South	12.0	18	9	3	8	4	6.75	0	1	13.50	2.25	6.00	3.00	-.50
1994	Salem, VA	Caro	52.3	60	20	6	28	31	3.44	3	3	10.32	1.03	4.82	5.33	.57
1995	Carolina	South	82.7	72	21	2	24	65	2.29	7	2	7.84	.22	2.61	7.08	1.71
1995	Pittsburgh	NL	81.3	87	41	11	40	54	4.54	4	5	9.63	1.22	4.43	5.98	.89
1996	Carolina	South	25.0	27	10	1	7	16	3.60	2	1	9.72	.36	2.52	5.76	1.29
1996	Pittsburgh	NL	26.7	34	19	4	14	24	6.41	1	2	11.48	1.35	4.72	8.10	1.52

He first reached AAA in 1992, but following shoulder surgery found himself back in the A leagues. He's worked himself back and into the majors, throwing a big curve ball that minor leaguers flail at but major leaguers take. A victim of the postage stamp strike zone.

CHRIS PETERS   **LSP**   **1972**   **Age 25**

YR	TEAM	Lge	IP	H	ER	HR	BB	K	ERA	W	L	H/9	HR/9	BB/9	K/9	KW
1993	Welland	NY-P	21.7	43	19	0	30	13	7.89	0	2	17.86	.00	12.46	5.40	-1.32
1994	Augusta	S Atl	53.3	66	37	1	47	50	6.24	2	4	11.14	.17	7.93	8.44	.83
1995	Lynchburg	Caro	133.3	150	59	6	51	96	3.98	8	7	10.13	.41	3.44	6.48	1.30
1995	Carolina	South	13.0	10	2	0	4	5	1.38	1	0	6.92	.00	2.77	3.46	.46
1996	Carolina	South	85.0	84	33	4	40	50	3.49	5	4	8.89	.42	4.24	5.29	.71
1996	Calgary	PCL	25.3	20	2	0	10	13	.71	3	0	7.11	.00	3.55	4.62	.65
1996	Pittsburgh	NL	63.3	73	37	8	30	24	5.26	3	4	10.37	1.14	4.26	3.41	.07

After a couple of lousy seasons relieving in the low minors, the Pittsburgh area native and former Pirate ballboy entered the rotation in Lynchburg and didn't look back until he came home. He throws a nasty sinker/slider combo and gets a lot of groundballs.

DAN PLESAC   **LRP**   **1962**   **Age 35**

YR	TEAM	Lge	IP	H	ER	HR	BB	K	ERA	W	L	H/9	HR/9	BB/9	K/9	KW
1993	Chicago Cubs	NL	62.0	74	33	10	28	45	4.79	3	4	10.74	1.45	4.06	6.53	1.16
1994	Chicago Cubs	NL	54.3	62	27	9	18	50	4.47	3	3	10.27	1.49	2.98	8.28	2.02
1995	Pittsburgh	NL	59.0	54	21	3	32	51	3.20	4	3	8.24	.46	4.88	7.78	1.37
1996	Pittsburgh	NL	69.3	69	29	4	29	66	3.76	4	4	8.96	.52	3.76	8.57	1.91

Struggled early and late, but excelled through the middle of the season. He still throws a mean fastball when his shoulder isn't acting up on him. Dealt to Toronto, doesn't change his outlook except making him a candidate for a few more saves.

MATT RUEBEL   **LBP**   **1970**   **Age 27**

YR	TEAM	Lge	IP	H	ER	HR	BB	K	ERA	W	L	H/9	HR/9	BB/9	K/9	KW
1993	Albany, GA	S Atl	54.0	68	32	3	46	30	5.33	2	4	11.33	.50	7.67	5.00	-.25
1993	Salem, VA	Caro	29.0	36	29	5	41	18	9.00	0	3	11.17	1.55	12.72	5.59	-1.32
1994	Salem, VA	Caro	79.0	92	41	7	36	47	4.67	4	5	10.48	.80	4.10	5.35	.76
1994	Carolina	South	15.0	32	16	4	6	11	9.60	0	2	19.20	2.40	3.60	6.60	1.30
1995	Carolina	South	156.7	166	62	8	63	103	3.56	9	8	9.54	.46	3.62	5.92	1.07
1996	Calgary	PCL	72.0	87	36	8	35	39	4.50	4	4	10.88	1.00	4.38	4.88	.53
1996	Pittsburgh	NL	57.7	65	33	6	30	19	5.15	2	4	10.14	.94	4.68	2.97	-.18

The translations look harsher than normal on him because he's given up so many unearned runs. Had a heck of a fluke year in '95.

MATT RYAN   **RRP**   **1972**   **Age 25**

YR	TEAM	Lge	IP	H	ER	HR	BB	K	ERA	W	L	H/9	HR/9	BB/9	K/9	KW
1993	Welland	NY-P	14.0	16	13	0	18	13	8.36	0	2	10.29	.00	11.57	8.36	-.11
1994	Albany, GA	S Atl	36.7	43	15	0	12	29	3.68	2	2	10.55	.00	2.95	7.12	1.64
1994	Salem, VA	Caro	26.0	29	10	0	11	9	3.46	2	1	10.04	.00	3.81	3.12	.09
1995	Carolina	South	42.3	37	9	0	25	17	1.91	4	1	7.87	.00	5.31	3.61	-.12
1996	Calgary	PCL	50.0	67	32	4	34	28	5.76	2	4	12.06	.72	6.12	5.04	.15

He'd never had a real ERA above 2.33 before he got to Calgary, but he's also had an unusually large number of unearned runs. You can blame that on his sinker.

JASON SCHMIDT   **RSP**   **1973**   **Age 24**

YR	TEAM	Lge	IP	H	ER	HR	BB	K	ERA	W	L	H/9	HR/9	BB/9	K/9	KW
1993	Durham	Caro	101.7	152	75	12	71	69	6.64	3	8	13.46	1.06	6.29	6.11	.46
1994	Greenville	South	127.3	161	70	12	78	103	4.95	6	8	11.38	.85	5.51	7.28	1.05
1995	Richmond	Inter	108.3	114	41	3	65	82	3.41	7	5	9.47	.25	5.40	6.81	.92
1995	Atlanta	NL	25.0	27	15	2	20	17	5.40	1	2	9.72	.72	7.20	6.12	.24
1996	Richmond	Inter	43.0	40	15	2	24	34	3.14	3	2	8.37	.42	5.02	7.12	1.12
1996	Atlanta	NL	58.7	69	41	7	37	42	6.29	2	5	10.59	1.07	5.68	6.44	.73
1996	Pittsburgh	NL	37.3	40	16	2	24	23	3.86	2	2	9.64	.48	5.79	5.54	.40

The key guy in the Neagle trade, he pitched very well after coming over from the Braves. He pitched especially poorly in Atlanta, possibly due to the irregular schedule he pitched on as the fifth man in the Braves rotation. He came down with a stress fracture in his ribs in midseason, which may also have been part of his problem.

ZANE SMITH   **LSP**   **1961**   **Age 36**

YR	TEAM	Lge	IP	H	ER	HR	BB	K	ERA	W	L	H/9	HR/9	BB/9	K/9	KW
1993	Carolina	South	19.0	22	9	1	7	10	4.26	1	1	10.42	.47	3.32	4.74	.75
1993	Pittsburgh	NL	81.3	99	40	6	31	31	4.43	4	5	10.95	.66	3.43	3.43	.29
1994	Pittsburgh	NL	154.0	160	58	18	48	53	3.39	10	7	9.35	1.05	2.81	3.10	.33
1995	Boston	AL	111.3	138	62	6	26	47	5.01	5	7	11.16	.49	2.10	3.80	.74
1996	Pittsburgh	NL	82.7	104	46	7	28	41	5.01	4	5	11.32	.76	3.05	4.46	.73

A duplicate of '95, even though that wasn't anything you'd want a copy of. Started messing around with a knuckler; didn't help.

PAUL WAGNER RSP 1968 Age 29

YR	TEAM	Lge	IP	H	ER	HR	BB	K	ERA	W	L	H/9	HR/9	BB/9	K/9	KW
1993	Pittsburgh	NL	138.0	147	65	15	57	110	4.24	7	8	9.59	.98	3.72	7.17	1.46
1994	Pittsburgh	NL	119.0	135	60	7	61	80	4.54	6	7	10.21	.53	4.61	6.05	.86
1995	Pittsburgh	NL	163.7	171	81	17	85	107	4.45	8	10	9.40	.93	4.67	5.88	.79
1996	Pittsburgh	NL	81.3	86	42	10	47	71	4.65	4	5	9.52	1.11	5.20	7.86	1.32

If they gave extra credit for consistency he'd take a giant step forward. Unfortunately, his steps right now are backwards following a torn ligament in his elbow. He's questionable to pitch at all in 1997.

DAVID WAINHOUSE RRP 1968 Age 29

YR	TEAM	Lge	IP	H	ER	HR	BB	K	ERA	W	L	H/9	HR/9	BB/9	K/9	KW
1993	Calgary	PCL	14.3	10	5	2	9	6	3.14	1	1	6.28	1.26	5.65	3.77	-.16
1995	Portland, ME	East	23.3	41	20	4	10	12	7.71	1	2	15.81	1.54	3.86	4.63	.58
1995	Syracuse	Inter	22.7	32	13	1	15	15	5.16	1	2	12.71	.40	5.96	5.96	.50
1996	Carolina	South	46.7	49	20	3	36	25	3.86	3	2	9.45	.58	6.94	4.82	-.13
1996	Pittsburgh	NL	23.3	22	13	3	12	14	5.01	1	2	8.49	1.16	4.63	5.40	.64

Right-handers hit him like an average pitcher, left-handers hit him like an average Hall of Famer.

MARC WILKINS RRP 1971 Age 26

YR	TEAM	Lge	IP	H	ER	HR	BB	K	ERA	W	L	H/9	HR/9	BB/9	K/9	KW
1993	Albany, GA	S Atl	63.7	113	63	6	43	43	8.91	1	6	15.97	.85	6.08	6.08	.51
1994	Salem, VA	Caro	137.7	164	71	12	62	59	4.64	6	9	10.72	.78	4.05	3.86	.27
1995	Carolina	South	91.7	102	45	9	57	61	4.42	5	5	10.01	.88	5.60	5.99	.60
1996	Carolina	South	22.7	22	11	1	13	14	4.37	1	2	8.74	.40	5.16	5.56	.56
1996	Pittsburgh	NL	74.3	76	31	6	42	54	3.75	4	4	9.20	.73	5.09	6.54	.91

A stocky 5' 11", 200 pounds, he's never been highly regarded as a prospect but has done all right for himself. He's got a serious reverse platoon split, holding lefties to 297 fewer points of OPS than right-handed hitters.

Player	Age	Team	Lge	AB	H	DB	TP	HR	BB	SB	CS	OUT	BA	OBA	SA	EQA	EQR	Peak
MIKE ASCHE	24	Lynchburg	Caro	510	136	13	3	7	33	11	3	377	.267	.311	.345	.224	45	.241
TONY BEASLEY	29	Carolina	South	276	81	15	2	5	25	7	5	200	.293	.352	.417	.258	34	.257
JEFF BIGLER	26	Augusta	S Atl	134	33	4	0	1	24	0	1	102	.246	.361	.299	.225	12	.234
KEN BONIFAY	25	Carolina	South	280	66	13	1	6	35	3	2	216	.236	.321	.354	.226	26	.238
EDDIE BROOKS	23	Lynchburg	Caro	275	66	10	1	4	13	2	1	210	.240	.274	.327	.199	19	.216
STONEY BURKE	25	Lynchburg	Caro	94	16	3	0	0	6	0	0	78	.170	.220	.202	.096	1	.105
JERALD CLARK	32	Calgary	PCL	246	61	11	1	8	12	0	1	186	.248	.283	.398	.224	22	.213
JEFF CONGER	24	Carolina	South	182	40	5	1	3	14	7	2	144	.220	.276	.308	.198	13	.214
JAY CRANFORD	25	Carolina	South	277	71	11	1	3	40	4	2	208	.256	.350	.336	.235	28	.247
TIM EDGE	27	Carolina	South	157	37	6	0	4	13	1	0	120	.236	.294	.350	.216	13	.221
AARON EDWARDS	22	Augusta	S Atl	133	29	3	0	2	8	3	2	106	.218	.262	.286	.179	7	.196
RAMON ESPINOSA	24	Calgary	PCL	242	61	9	4	1	8	2	2	183	.252	.276	.335	.202	17	.217
JON FARRELL	24	Lynchburg	Caro	83	27	1	0	1	16	0	0	56	.325	.434	.373	.284	12	.303
MARK FARRIS	21	Augusta	S Atl	316	62	3	0	3	24	2	2	256	.196	.253	.234	.146	10	.163
MIKE FELDER	33	Calgary	PCL	80	21	1	0	1	3	0	0	59	.262	.289	.312	.201	5	.192
JOHN FINN	28	Calgary	PCL	192	44	10	1	0	23	2	3	151	.229	.312	.292	.200	13	.201
STEVEN FLANIGAN	24	Augusta	S Atl	149	27	5	0	0	3	1	0	122	.181	.197	.215	.093	2	.101
OVIDIO FRIAS	19	Augusta	S Atl	191	45	3	0	1	20	3	3	149	.236	.308	.267	.191	12	.220
WIKLEMAN GONZALEZ	22	Augusta	S Atl	450	104	14	2	4	46	2	2	348	.231	.302	.298	.200	31	.224
MARCUS HANEL	24	Carolina	South	337	57	13	1	5	12	1	1	281	.169	.198	.258	.123	7	.133
ERSKINE KELLEY	25	Lynchburg	Caro	352	88	11	3	5	22	6	4	268	.250	.294	.341	.213	28	.225
ROB LEARY	24	Carolina	South	113	20	2	1	4	19	1	1	94	.177	.295	.319	.201	8	.215
FREDDY MAY	20	Augusta	S Atl	422	80	6	3	5	57	9	7	349	.190	.286	.254	.175	22	.198
SERGIO MENDEZ	22	Augusta	S Atl	179	40	5	0	5	7	1	1	140	.223	.253	.335	.191	11	.210
	22	Lynchburg	Caro	139	34	4	1	3	6	0	0	105	.245	.276	.353	.208	10	.231
JOE MILLETTE	29	Calgary	PCL	108	21	6	0	0	8	0	1	88	.194	.250	.250	.148	4	.147
CHRIS MIYAKE	22	Augusta	S Atl	383	81	5	0	3	18	4	4	306	.211	.247	.248	.151	13	.166
ALEX PENA	18	Augusta	S Atl	172	24	4	1	0	5	1	0	148	.140	.164	.174	-.095	-2	-.094
KEVIN POLCOVICH	26	Calgary	PCL	333	82	18	2	1	19	6	4	255	.246	.287	.321	.203	24	.211
ELTON POLLOCK	23	Augusta	S Atl	486	108	8	2	6	54	11	5	383	.222	.300	.284	.197	33	.213
CHARLES RICE	20	Augusta	S Atl	194	32	3	1	2	14	2	1	163	.165	.221	.222	.118	4	.135
TONY ROBINSON	20	Lynchburg	Caro	97	14	3	0	0	14	2	1	84	.144	.252	.175	.112	2	.128
CHANCE SANFORD	24	Carolina	South	484	112	13	9	5	61	8	5	377	.231	.317	.326	.217	41	.232
STAN SCHREIBER	20	Augusta	S Atl	393	83	9	3	1	41	7	4	314	.211	.286	.257	.178	21	.202
BO SPRINGFIELD	20	Augusta	S Atl	195	46	3	2	0	23	2	1	150	.236	.317	.272	.198	13	.226
JON SWEET	24	Lynchburg	Caro	217	50	4	0	1	15	1	2	169	.230	.280	.263	.174	11	.187
STEVE THOBE	24	Lynchburg	Caro	367	74	6	0	9	25	2	2	295	.202	.253	.292	.173	18	.185
MORGAN WALKER	21	Augusta	S Atl	268	77	7	1	7	14	2	1	192	.287	.323	.399	.243	28	.272
BOOMER WHIPPLE	23	Augusta	S Atl	479	104	10	0	4	57	3	3	378	.217	.300	.263	.185	28	.201

Player	Age	Team	Lge	IP	H	ER	HR	BB	K	ERA	W	L	H/9	HR/9	BB/9	K/9	KW
JUAN AGOSTO	38	Calgary	PCL	25.3	28	13	4	14	8	4.62	1	2	9.95	1.42	4.97	2.84	-.30
BRONSON ARROYO	19	Augusta	S Atl	112.3	183	85	15	55	59	6.81	3	9	14.66	1.20	4.41	4.73	.47
BRETT BACKLUND	26	Calgary	PCL	36.7	45	21	4	20	13	5.15	2	2	11.05	.98	4.91	3.19	-.16
	26	Carolina	South	74.3	89	44	14	33	61	5.33	3	5	10.78	1.70	4.00	7.39	1.46
TODD BLYLEVEN	23	Lynchburg	Caro	50.7	57	18	5	20	23	3.20	4	2	10.12	.89	3.55	4.09	.47
MICHAEL BROWN	24	Lynchburg	Caro	62.7	97	64	7	66	43	9.19	1	6	13.93	1.01	9.48	6.18	-.31
DEREK BULLOCK	23	Augusta	S Atl	52.0	77	22	1	25	29	3.81	3	3	13.33	.17	4.33	5.02	.59
RAFAEL CHAVES	27	Lynchburg	Caro	28.7	40	18	4	12	14	5.65	1	2	12.56	1.26	3.77	4.40	.52
TIM COLLIE	22	Augusta	S Atl	25.7	39	13	2	7	11	4.56	1	2	13.68	.70	2.45	3.86	.67
KANE DAVIS	21	Lynchburg	Caro	140.3	186	87	14	77	80	5.58	5	11	11.93	.90	4.94	5.13	.48
JOHN DILLINGER	22	Lynchburg	Caro	119.0	118	64	12	77	77	4.84	5	8	8.92	.91	5.82	5.82	.49
JASON FARROW	22	Augusta	S Atl	64.0	92	35	4	49	45	4.92	3	4	12.94	.56	6.89	6.33	.39
AARON FRANCE	22	Lynchburg	Caro	54.3	85	52	7	43	28	8.61	1	5	14.08	1.16	7.12	4.64	-.23
KENNY GREER	29	Calgary	PCL	64.0	73	28	9	23	29	3.94	4	3	10.27	1.27	3.23	4.08	.55
JEFF HAVENS	23	Augusta	S Atl	36.3	73	29	3	19	24	7.18	1	3	18.08	.74	4.71	5.94	.81
JASON JOHNSON	22	Augusta	S Atl	69.3	120	53	3	38	46	6.88	2	6	15.58	.39	4.93	5.97	.76
	22	Lynchburg	Caro	39.0	65	37	6	17	19	8.54	1	3	15.00	1.38	3.92	4.38	.48
JEFF KELLY	21	Augusta	S Atl	69.3	112	52	6	41	38	6.75	2	6	14.54	.78	5.32	4.93	.31
	21	Lynchburg	Caro	67.0	90	46	8	33	39	6.18	2	5	12.09	1.07	4.43	5.24	.64
DENNIS KONUSZEWSKI	25	Carolina	South	74.0	112	56	12	43	43	6.81	2	6	13.62	1.46	5.23	5.23	.44
SEAN LAWRENCE	25	Carolina	South	76.0	89	38	12	42	59	4.50	4	4	10.54	1.42	4.97	6.99	1.09
JOE MASKIVISH	24	Augusta	S Atl	43.0	64	22	1	21	32	4.60	2	3	13.40	.21	4.40	6.70	1.13
BRIAN O'CONNER	19	Augusta	S Atl	29.3	49	17	3	13	20	5.22	1	2	15.03	.92	3.99	6.14	1.05
RICK PAUGH	24	Lynchburg	Caro	47.0	54	32	1	28	28	6.13	1	4	10.34	.19	5.36	5.36	.45
JASON PHILLIPS	22	Augusta	S Atl	76.7	110	42	4	44	42	4.93	4	5	12.91	.47	5.17	4.93	.35
	22	Lynchburg	Caro	65.3	94	48	3	47	43	6.61	2	5	12.95	.41	6.47	5.92	.36
KEVIN PICKFORD	21	Lynchburg	Caro	154.3	227	103	18	41	69	6.01	5	12	13.24	1.05	2.39	4.02	.74
MARC PISCIOTTA	25	Calgary	PCL	61.3	69	32	3	54	37	4.70	3	4	10.12	.44	7.92	5.43	-.17
MATT PONTBRIANT	24	Carolina	South	52.0	79	37	5	29	26	6.40	2	4	13.67	.87	5.02	4.50	.25
JOSE REYES	23	Augusta	S Atl	54.3	111	64	11	44	32	10.60	1	5	18.39	1.82	7.29	5.30	-.06
KEVIN RYCHEL	24	Carolina	South	33.7	36	19	3	13	15	5.08	2	2	9.62	.80	3.48	4.01	.47
MATT SPADE	23	Lynchburg	Caro	71.7	102	39	8	37	49	4.90	3	5	12.81	1.00	4.65	6.15	.89
SCOTT TAYLOR	29	Carolina	South	145.3	190	89	17	73	73	5.51	6	10	11.77	1.05	4.52	4.52	.38
MATT WILLIAMS	25	Lynchburg	Caro	36.7	45	26	9	36	31	6.38	1	3	11.05	2.21	8.84	7.61	.33
GARY WILSON	26	Calgary	PCL	152.7	203	87	18	59	72	5.13	6	11	11.97	1.06	3.48	4.24	.55
DANNY YOUNG	24	Augusta	S Atl	27.0	50	41	1	41	20	13.67	0	3	16.67	.33	13.67	6.67	-1.19
RYAN YOUNG	23	Augusta	S Atl	77.7	165	84	11	49	27	9.73	1	8	19.12	1.27	5.68	3.13	-.38

St. Louis Cardinals

The Cardinals deserve a world of credit, because they did what few people thought they could and exactly as they expected to. That doesn't happen very often, so what happened, why and who should get credit for what should be looked at carefully. Overnight successes or "buying" pennants is something that we're told is going to happen all the time these days, so when something that looks like that actually happens it needs to be looked at pretty carefully.

Before the '95 season began, the Cardinals were active in picking up veteran players: Ken Hill, Danny Jackson, Tom Henke, and Scott Cooper. With the exception of Henke, who retired, every one of them was a disastrous flop. You might think that kind of success would frighten Walt Jocketty away from free agents. Not in the least; before the '96 season began they'd been even more ambitious in player acquisition. They added a number of famous or well-regarded veteran players: Ron Gant, Gary Gaetti, Andy Benes, Dennis Eckersley, Todd Stottlemyre, Royce Clayton, Rick Honeycutt, Luis Alicea, Willie McGee, Pat Borders, Gregg Olson and Mike Gallego. But what drew the most attention, and indeed inspired many of the transactions, was the man most frequently hyped for baseball geniusdom, Tony LaRussa.

Frequently, it's perceived that the team that did the most or added the most players had done the most to improve, and nobody had been more active than the Cardinals. Naturally, they were the media's team of choice to win the National League Central. However, there were reasons to be worried. LaRussa had become available for a reason: he had run an Oakland team into the ground because of his unwillingness to give up on veterans of the '88-'90 teams and had become increasingly prone to fricasseeing players in the press, usually ones who weren't part of those glory years. Several reporters did their best to gloss over that sort of thing, pointing out that the failures of the last three LaRussa squads could be blamed on somebody else; as the Toronto Globe explained, now that he was with the Cardinals, "LaRussa has the money he wants, and the people he wants." That sentiment was echoed in papers around the country. Unfortunately, it's dead wrong, because in Oakland LaRussa wanted and got Bob Welch until his dying day, along with Dave Stewart, Ron Darling, Mike Gallego and others, and with the players he wanted, he put a lousy team on the field and lost games by the truckload.

There were other worries. Several of the free agents, particularly Gaetti, were coming off of seasons out of character with the general declines that had typified the '90s for them as a group. Ron Gant was still potentially fragile. Eckersley had been a poor reliever for several years and Andy Benes had been awful with Seattle down the stretch. When the Cardinals started out slowly, everyone wondered if all the changes had done any good. LaRussa started engaging in more weird sniping in the press, attacking other teams' players (like Gary Sheffield), and getting caught up in a major imbroglio with Ozzie Smith on the issue of playing time and what he'd promised to Smith behind closed doors. The team didn't have a leadoff hitter, to the point that LaRussa had experimented with batting Brian Jordan at the top of the order. On the other hand, LaRussa was doing things he wouldn't have thought of doing in previous seasons, like pulling Dennis Eckersley in a save situation with someone like Barry Bonds at the plate.

As is turned out the slow start meant nothing, and the Cardinals won the NL Central, in large part on the strength of beating their toughest rival, the Astros, 11 out of 13 times. No other first place team had drubbed another winning club as badly as the Cardinals had the Astros. If you're from Houston, sorry about re-opening that wound and pouring those sixty pounds of salt in.

What was really interesting is that nothing, absolutely nothing, went wrong for the Cardinals this year. The Benes brothers both came through. Eckersley pitched better than he had in several years. Gary Gaetti overcame a slow start to show he still has a pulse. Ron Gant was effective enough. Nobody flopped and several players exceeded expectations. That doesn't happen very often, so you might say the Cardinals had more than their fair share of luck. Nevertheless, tip your hat to them. It all worked like they wanted it to, and that translated into a fortunate matchup with a confused Padres team, and a brush with near-immortality against the Braves. Of course, they were squashed flat by the Braves after the Eck got in trouble with an obscenity-laced tirade directed at the Braves after he closed out Game 4 and Brian Jordan told reporters how sweet it would be after they'd beaten them. Those LaRussians, always a good-natured bunch.

As a result of the team's success, the media's love affair with LaRussa reached even more ludicrous proportions. Conveniently forgetting their predictions of easy success from the previous spring, LaRussa was touted as a genius for having rallied the team from its early slow going. People like Keith Olbermann were patting themselves on the back for having had the "courage" to pick the Cardinals before the season. Some commentators started saying Tony LaRussa was smarter than 99% of the people in this country. If that's true, public education is even worse off than you hear or I remember. He is what he was, a fine manager who usually takes advantage of every possible tactical situation, but who makes a lot of mistakes when it comes to judging talent or putting together a roster.

What does it all mean? The Cardinals, for all the attention they got, aren't a great team. Their offense, with nobody having a bad season by their standards and several enjoying career years, finished seventh in the NL in runs scored. Can they count on Gant's continued health or Gaetti's continued renaissance? Can they survive with a player like Royce Clayton in the leadoff slot? What made this team win was good defense and reliable pitching, but how long does any non-Braves pitching stay reliable? Certainly, if the only team that challenges is the Astros, and they can keep sacrificing live virgins in the loge area to keep the whammy they have on them, they'll be in great shape. That isn't exactly a sure thing. There's also the concern that like many intense managers of the past, such as Billy Martin or Leo Durocher, that LaRussa will start having a bad effect on the team if everything doesn't go right.

For all of the hijinks going on at the major league level, the Cardinals' farm system is in fine shape and getting better. In particular, it has an excellent group of pitching talent. Almost every first-round pick the Cardinals have had in the '90s has been spent on pitching, and unlike the infamous "Four Aces," all are still considered prospects. The question is whether or not they'll choose to use them, or trade them away for veteran hitting talent in the next few years as the declines or collapses of players like Gaetti and Gant come while the Cardinals still have the "win now" focus that all LaRussa teams have. That was the pattern in Oakland, where LaRussa's team traded away young pitchers like Jose Rijo, Tim Belcher and Kevin Tapani, among others.

There's also the concern that although LaRussa's pitching coach, Dave Duncan, has a well-established record of success working with veteran pitchers and in running a role-oriented bullpen, together they've gone fifteen years between developing young pitchers: Alan Benes was the second starting pitcher under the age of 30 that the LaRussa-Duncan tandem have trusted or developed since Britt Burns and Rich Dotson back in 1980 (the other was Storm Davis, who was in his fifth major league season by the time they got hold of him). It won't be surprising if they and their old friend Walt Jocketty choose to turn the organization's wealth of pitching into fodder for pennant-minded acquisitions. On the other hand, it will be very interesting if they choose to ignore their past habits and try to develop many of these young pitchers themselves.

All of that pitching talent hasn't necessarily translated into good minor league teams. The organization no longer observes the old Whiteyball mentality in its minor league development: none of their minor league teams came close to leading their leagues in steals or attempts. Louisville put up the second-worst record in AAA, scoring the fewest runs of any team at that level while also having the worst pitching staff in the league. Arkansas was also last in its league in scoring, although the team almost finished .500. On the other hand the two full-season A-ball teams, the ones overwhelmingly made up of Jocketty administration draft picks and signees, both posted winning records and finished first in their leagues in ERA. The quality of the offensive talent is also higher at the lower levels than it is at Arkansas or Louisville, with potentially outstanding prospects like infielder Placido Polanco, outfielder Kerry Robinson, and third baseman Chris Haas on the way up. The best position player prospects above A ball are first baseman Dmitri Young and catcher Elieser Marrero, both of whom should probably be in the big league lineup as regulars during the '97 season if the Cards want to start putting a younger, better team on the field.

LUIS ALICEA		**2B**		**1966**	**Age 31**												
Year	Team	Lge	AB	H	DB	TP	HR	BB	SB	CS	OUT	BA	OBA	SA	EQA	EQR	Peak
1993	St. Louis	NL	376	111	21	2	4	52	9	1	266	.295	.381	.394	.268	50	.275
1994	St. Louis	NL	209	59	10	4	6	33	4	4	154	.282	.380	.455	.275	31	.278
1995	Boston	AL	423	118	21	3	7	64	13	10	315	.279	.374	.392	.259	54	.257
1996	St. Louis	NL	391	105	25	3	6	56	9	3	289	.269	.360	.394	.257	48	.252
1997	*St. Louis*	*NL*	*322*	*82*	*18*	*1*	*4*	*46*	*7*	*2*	*242*	*.255*	*.348*	*.354*	*.253*	*39*	

A good example of replacement level talent. Alicea has excellent range, but because he was credited with 24 errors, a lot of people decided he was awful afield. Spending most of the year in the eighth slot, Alicea was given ten free passes. Why?

DAVID BELL 2B/3B 1973 Age 24

Year	Team	Lge	AB	H	DB	TP	HR	BB	SB	CS	OUT	BA	OBA	SA	EQA	EQR	Peak
1993	Canton	East	498	140	14	1	10	40	2	2	360	.281	.335	.373	.239	50	.272
1994	Charlotte-NC	Inter	491	139	14	2	17	40	2	3	355	.283	.337	.424	.253	57	.284
1995	Buffalo	AmA	261	72	10	1	8	25	0	2	191	.276	.339	.414	.250	30	.276
1995	Louisville	AmA	76	20	3	1	1	3	3	0	56	.263	.291	.368	.230	7	.251
1995	St. Louis	NL	145	37	6	2	2	6	1	2	110	.255	.285	.366	.214	12	.236
1996	Louisville	AmA	137	23	4	1	0	9	1	1	116	.168	.219	.212	.106	2	.111
1996	St. Louis	NL	147	32	3	0	2	12	1	1	116	.218	.277	.279	.180	8	.196
1997	*St. Louis*	*NL*	*368*	*99*	*20*	*1*	*8*	*23*	*1*	*1*	*270*	*.269*	*.312*	*.394*	*.248*	*41*	

Hasn't mastered utility infielder braggadocio like the immortal Mike Gallego. Bell is better at Gallego at everything you see on the field, but you could argue Bell needed some regular at bats in Louisville. The problem is that when Gallego was getting regular playing time because Alicea was slumping, that's exactly the situation where David Bell should have been getting playing time. As a regular, he isn't going to hit for that much power, but he's adapted well to second.

JEFF BERBLINGER 2B 1971 Age 26

Year	Team	Lge	AB	H	DB	TP	HR	BB	SB	CS	OUT	BA	OBA	SA	EQA	EQR	Peak
1993	Glens Falls	NY-P	143	36	3	0	2	9	3	2	109	.252	.296	.315	.205	10	.226
1993	St. Petersburg	Flor	71	13	0	0	0	5	2	1	59	.183	.237	.183	.110	1	.118
1994	Savannah	SAtl	507	143	18	3	9	44	11	3	367	.282	.339	.383	.247	56	.268
1995	Arkansas	Texas	333	92	11	1	6	43	12	7	248	.276	.359	.369	.249	38	.267
1996	Arkansas	Texas	506	133	21	3	11	48	16	6	379	.263	.327	.381	.241	54	.254

Described as the classic "scrapper," he took 25 pitches for the team in Savannah in '94. His defense gets good marks. Berblinger's too old to be a good prospect, but with the second base situation as confused as it is for the Dodgers—who acquired him after Detroit selected him in the Rule V draft—Berblinger could easily ride into the middle of the mess and emerge as the winner, a la Mike Bordick as the A's shortstop in '91. He played well in the AFL.

TERRY BRADSHAW CF 1969 Age 28

Year	Team	Lge	AB	H	DB	TP	HR	BB	SB	CS	OUT	BA	OBA	SA	EQA	EQR	Peak
1993	St. Petersburg	Flor	485	137	19	3	9	72	22	8	356	.282	.375	.390	.264	63	.283
1994	Arkansas	Texas	438	118	20	3	12	46	9	5	325	.269	.339	.411	.251	52	.265
1994	Louisville	AmA	80	19	3	0	4	7	4	1	62	.237	.299	.425	.244	9	.258
1995	Louisville	AmA	396	108	21	5	9	54	18	6	294	.273	.360	.419	.265	53	.275
1996	Louisville	AmA	403	121	18	1	12	46	19	7	289	.300	.372	.439	.275	57	.282

He's in the same situation as ex-Cardinal Allan Battle: he does several things well, but not outstanding. He hits right-handers well and can handle center field. He'd easily fill the Milt Thompson role on a roster, but he's left rotting in the minors because the hope is that he'll somehow be more than that.

ROYCE CLAYTON SS 1970 Age 27

Year	Team	Lge	AB	H	DB	TP	HR	BB	SB	CS	OUT	BA	OBA	SA	EQA	EQR	Peak
1993	San Francisco	NL	565	167	23	4	7	47	10	8	406	.296	.350	.388	.249	63	.271
1994	San Francisco	NL	389	95	13	5	4	36	21	3	297	.244	.308	.334	.226	36	.241
1995	San Francisco	NL	520	135	29	3	6	44	20	8	393	.260	.317	.362	.232	51	.245
1996	St. Louis	NL	502	145	20	4	6	39	27	14	371	.289	.340	.380	.246	56	.256
1997	*St. Louis*	*NL*	*477*	*140*	*29*	*4*	*5*	*36*	*28*	*9*	*346*	*.294*	*.343*	*.403*	*.269*	*65*	

An absolute disaster as the leadoff man. He had a .321 OBP on the season, .314 when batting leadoff. He handled the LaRussa-Smith war as well as you could hope. Clayton is an excellent defensive player, but the Cardinals are touting him as an up and coming young player, when he's at the peak of his career right now; to hope for more offense is unrealistic.

TRIPP CROMER SS 1968 Age 29

Year	Team	Lge	AB	H	DB	TP	HR	BB	SB	CS	OUT	BA	OBA	SA	EQA	EQR	Peak
1993	Louisville	AmA	312	85	6	2	12	18	1	2	229	.272	.312	.420	.242	33	.256
1994	Louisville	AmA	420	110	18	5	11	35	4	4	314	.262	.319	.407	.241	45	.250
1995	St. Louis	NL	347	79	13	0	7	19	0	0	268	.228	.268	.326	.194	22	.198
1996	Louisville	AmA	249	55	4	3	4	24	3	1	195	.221	.289	.309	.200	17	.202

All through the spring, in the war of words over Clayton or Smith for the shortstop's job, nobody cared a whit about the incumbent, poor old Tripp Cromer. Bears an uncanny resemblance to E.T., but with an Adam's apple that sticks out as far as his chin. Lost on waivers to the Dodgers.

St. Louis Cardinals

DARREL DEAK   2B   1970   Age 27

Year	Team	Lge	AB	H	DB	TP	HR	BB	SB	CS	OUT	BA	OBA	SA	EQA	EQR	Peak
1993	Arkansas	Texas	431	101	12	1	17	55	4	4	334	.234	.321	.385	.234	44	.255
1994	Louisville	AmA	488	127	17	1	18	52	1	1	362	.260	.331	.410	.247	55	.264
1995	Louisville	AmA	342	79	19	1	7	54	2	2	265	.231	.336	.354	.232	34	.244
1996	Louisville	AmA	170	40	2	0	8	24	2	1	131	.235	.330	.388	.240	19	.249

Mixed in with the general replaceability of most second basemen is that their development can easily be stunted by injuries. That would describe what's happened to Deak. His prospect status is two years out of date.

MIKE DiFELICE   C   1969   Age 28

Year	Team	Lge	AB	H	DB	TP	HR	BB	SB	CS	OUT	BA	OBA	SA	EQA	EQR	Peak
1993	St. Petersburg	Flor	100	22	1	0	0	10	0	0	78	.220	.291	.230	.166	4	.179
1994	Arkansas	Texas	203	48	9	0	3	12	0	0	155	.236	.279	.325	.199	14	.210
1995	Arkansas	Texas	177	42	7	1	1	20	0	1	136	.237	.315	.305	.206	13	.215
1995	Louisville	AmA	63	16	3	0	0	6	1	0	47	.254	.319	.302	.214	5	.223
1996	Louisville	AmA	253	72	8	0	9	22	0	2	183	.285	.342	.423	.254	30	.260

Should the Cardinals lose Pagnozzi to free agency, the catcher of last resort would be DiFelice. With Marrero just a level behind him, he's probably praying for a shot at that Backup Catchers' Union card.

MICAH FRANKLIN   OF   1972   Age 25

Year	Team	Lge	AB	H	DB	TP	HR	BB	SB	CS	OUT	BA	OBA	SA	EQA	EQR	Peak
1993	Charleston-WV	SAtl	363	91	5	1	15	36	3	1	273	.251	.318	.394	.238	38	.267
1993	Winston-Salem	Caro	71	14	1	0	2	9	0	0	57	.197	.287	.296	.190	5	.215
1994	Winston-Salem	Caro	156	46	4	0	15	23	4	0	110	.295	.385	.609	.318	31	.351
1994	Chattanooga	South	291	79	9	0	11	33	1	1	213	.271	.346	.416	.255	35	.282
1995	Calgary	PCL	353	94	15	0	20	45	3	2	261	.266	.349	.479	.271	50	.295
1996	Toledo	Inter	182	43	8	1	6	27	2	1	140	.236	.335	.390	.243	20	.260
1996	Louisville	AmA	298	70	16	2	14	42	2	2	230	.235	.329	.443	.253	37	.271
1997	*St. Louis*	*NL*	*391*	*106*	*13*	*1*	*21*	*45*	*2*	*1*	*286*	*.271*	*.346*	*.471*	*.272*	*55*	

He's jumped from organization to organization after strangely being left off the Pirates' 40-man roster after '95. Although he's an indifferent defender in either outfield corner, switch-hitters with this kind of power aren't common. He may have to wait for expansion to get his shot, but he's a good prospect.

GARY GAETTI   3B   1959   Age 38

Year	Team	Lge	AB	H	DB	TP	HR	BB	SB	CS	OUT	BA	OBA	SA	EQA	EQR	Peak
1993	California	AL	50	9	2	0	0	6	1	0	41	.180	.268	.220	.154	2	.151
1993	Kansas City	AL	282	74	16	1	16	18	0	2	210	.262	.307	.496	.259	36	.246
1994	Kansas City	AL	325	91	13	3	12	20	0	2	236	.280	.322	.449	.254	38	.240
1995	Kansas City	AL	521	143	24	0	40	48	3	3	381	.274	.336	.551	.283	81	.269
1996	St. Louis	NL	533	151	25	4	24	41	2	2	384	.283	.334	.480	.268	71	.255
1997	*St. Louis*	*NL*	*530*	*135*	*14*	*0*	*22*	*30*	*2*	*1*	*396*	*.255*	*.295*	*.406*	*.244*	*58*	

Gaetti's hot second half (.296/.347/.554) was a major part of the Cardinals' hot second half. He's still a solid defensive player and still can't resist hacking at off-speed stuff, but when he loses his ability to hammer the fastball he'll finally be done. It hasn't happened yet, and the Cardinals have decided to risk another year of Gaetti: he's been re-signed for '97.

MIKE GALLEGO   2B   1961   Age 36

Year	Team	Lge	AB	H	DB	TP	HR	BB	SB	CS	OUT	BA	OBA	SA	EQA	EQR	Peak
1993	NY Yankees	AL	414	128	21	1	13	54	3	2	288	.309	.389	.459	.284	62	.270
1994	NY Yankees	AL	311	78	17	1	7	39	0	1	234	.251	.334	.379	.239	33	.227
1995	Oakland	AL	122	31	0	0	0	9	0	1	92	.254	.305	.254	.183	7	.174
1996	St. Louis	NL	145	31	2	0	0	14	0	0	114	.214	.283	.228	.160	6	.151
1997	*St. Louis*	*NL*	*128*	*25*	*3*	*0*	*3*	*21*	*1*	*0*	*103*	*.195*	*.309*	*.289*	*.212*	*11*	

It should say something about how far he's fallen that I'd call this projection outrageously optimistic. He's washed up. When even Cardinal commentators point out he's lost his range, using him as a defensive replacement shows how silly a reliance on errors as a barometer of defensive skill can be. He does nothing better than either Alicea or David Bell, except that neither of them have Gallego's earlier affiliation with LaRussa. If the Cardinals changed their colors to green and red you could count on Mike Gallego being Santa's extra-grumpy little elf.

RON GANT LF 1965 Age 32

Year	Team	Lge	AB	H	DB	TP	HR	BB	SB	CS	OUT	BA	OBA	SA	EQA	EQR	Peak
1993	Atlanta	NL	621	177	24	3	38	76	22	8	452	.285	.363	.517	.288	100	.290
1995	Cincinnati	NL	423	122	18	3	32	80	19	7	308	.288	.402	.572	.313	84	.306
1996	St. Louis	NL	432	112	14	2	31	78	11	4	324	.259	.373	.516	.289	73	.279
1997	*St. Louis*	*NL*	*510*	*138*	*24*	*3*	*28*	*67*	*18*	*7*	*379*	*.271*	*.355*	*.494*	*.291*	*87*	

The gamble didn't work: Gilkey wound up having a much, much better season, while Gant continued to be injury-prone. His five-year contract has a chance of being the same kind of dead weight on an organization as those of Cecil Fielder, Danny Tartabull or Ruben Sierra. As the NLCS highlighted, he's an abysmal defensive player. If there's a major drop in offensive levels, Gant could be a prime candidate to be a flop immediately.

MIKE GULAN 3B 1971 Age 26

Year	Team	Lge	AB	H	DB	TP	HR	BB	SB	CS	OUT	BA	OBA	SA	EQA	EQR	Peak
1993	Springfield	Midw	467	113	15	1	18	26	4	2	356	.242	.282	.394	.224	42	.247
1994	St. Petersburg	Flor	477	112	19	1	11	25	2	4	369	.235	.273	.348	.203	34	.221
1995	Arkansas	Texas	240	69	11	1	11	11	3	1	172	.287	.319	.479	.264	31	.282
1995	Louisville	AmA	195	44	8	3	5	12	2	2	153	.226	.271	.374	.211	16	.226
1996	Louisville	AmA	427	110	22	3	16	31	7	2	319	.258	.308	.436	.247	49	.261

Should not be mistaken for a good prospect. When he was drafted, there was speculation that he was going to be moved to catcher. He should have done it, because as a third base prospect he's an impatient hacker with a strong arm. Has no platoon differential so he lacks a doesn't even have as a platoon player.

CHRIS HAAS 3B 1977 Age 20

Year	Team	Lge	AB	H	DB	TP	HR	BB	SB	CS	OUT	BA	OBA	SA	EQA	EQR	Peak
1996	Peoria	Midw	439	95	9	1	10	49	2	1	345	.216	.295	.310	.200	31	.231
1997	*St. Louis*	*NL*	*460*	*101*	*21*	*1*	*18*	*44*	*4*	*2*	*361*	*.220*	*.288*	*.387*	*.234*	*48*	

A first-round draft choice in '95 as one of the best high school players in the country, Haas is the organization's third base-man of the future. He had not completely adjusted to wood when he started last season. Haas made definite strides in the second half, but he's a good two years away from entering the Cardinals' big league plans.

SCOTT HEMOND C 1966 Age 31

Year	Team	Lge	AB	H	DB	TP	HR	BB	SB	CS	OUT	BA	OBA	SA	EQA	EQR	Peak
1993	Oakland	AL	221	62	14	0	9	34	14	4	163	.281	.376	.466	.284	35	.290
1994	Oakland	AL	200	47	9	0	4	17	7	6	159	.235	.295	.340	.211	16	.211
1995	St. Louis	NL	119	17	1	0	3	13	0	0	102	.143	.227	.227	.120	3	.123
1996	Louisville	AmA	154	40	8	1	3	14	1	2	116	.260	.321	.383	.233	15	.228

Although the number of ex-A's on the major league level has been much commented on, the number of ex-A's scrubs in the farm system is also remarkable. Dann Howitt, Joe Wolfe, Scott Hemond...why? None of them are worth much, and the Cardinals' farm isn't that hurting for talent. Are cronies, lackeys or people who know how you like your coffee that important to have around?

AARON HOLBERT SS/2B 1973 Age 24

Year	Team	Lge	AB	H	DB	TP	HR	BB	SB	CS	OUT	BA	OBA	SA	EQA	EQR	Peak
1993	St. Petersburg	Flor	468	119	14	1	4	25	24	10	359	.254	.292	.314	.209	36	.237
1994	Arkansas	Texas	238	67	9	3	3	13	6	3	174	.282	.319	.382	.238	24	.266
1995	Louisville	AmA	402	98	12	3	9	25	13	5	309	.244	.288	.356	.218	34	.240
1996	Louisville	AmA	444	114	15	4	4	26	19	11	341	.257	.298	.336	.215	37	.234

A first-rounder, the acquisition of Clayton should tell you what you need to know about his future. The Cardinals have started trying him at second base, which probably means a future as a utility infielder. He did not field the position well. The front office talks about getting him to hit the ball on the ground more, as if that will somehow make him a hitter who can make pitchers break a sweat. It's code for "can't hit, won't hit and we won't tell him."

KEITH JOHNS **SS** **1972** **Age 25**

Year	Team	Lge	AB	H	DB	TP	HR	BB	SB	CS	OUT	BA	OBA	SA	EQA	EQR	Peak
1993	Springfield	Midw	487	111	17	1	2	55	16	8	384	.228	.306	.279	.199	34	.223
1994	St. Petersburg	Flor	476	106	11	0	6	35	11	5	375	.223	.276	.284	.186	28	.205
1995	Arkansas	Texas	398	99	11	1	2	49	9	3	302	.249	.331	.296	.216	33	.235
1996	Arkansas	Texas	452	97	11	1	1	44	6	5	360	.215	.284	.250	.172	22	.185

Unlike Aaron Holbert, Johns has some patience at the plate. The speed that helped him steal 40 bases in '93 appears to have disappeared almost completely. Non-prospect.

BRIAN JORDAN **RF/CF** **1967** **Age 30**

Year	Team	Lge	AB	H	DB	TP	HR	BB	SB	CS	OUT	BA	OBA	SA	EQA	EQR	Peak
1993	Louisville	AmA	148	55	12	2	5	17	8	3	96	.372	.436	.581	.332	31	.346
1993	St. Louis	NL	230	75	10	4	12	15	5	5	160	.326	.367	.561	.296	38	.307
1994	St. Louis	NL	180	47	8	2	5	18	4	2	136	.261	.328	.411	.247	21	.252
1995	St. Louis	NL	497	151	19	3	23	28	20	8	354	.304	.341	.493	.276	71	.278
1996	St. Louis	NL	526	169	31	0	20	35	19	5	362	.321	.364	.494	.287	80	.285
1997	*St. Louis*	*NL*	*588*	*177*	*27*	*7*	*36*	*33*	*35*	*12*	*423*	*.301*	*.338*	*.554*	*.302*	*106*	

While the "Jordan for MVP" campaign was one of those ludicrous exercises in trying to single out one player on a team to blame for its success, his complaints about not winning a Gold Glove weren't any better. In the middle of the playoffs, he was bellyaching about how he sees Gold Glover Barry Bonds drop balls on SportsCenter all the time. If that's how players come to their conclusions about other players they play against, it might tell us a lot about how silly some of these reputations and awards are. His aggressive football mentality wound up mixing well with the classic LaRussa humorlessness, and Jordan was seen as the clubhouse "bridge" between LaRussa's collection of ex-A's and cronies and the veteran Cardinals. For an impatient hitter he's very good at crushing breaking pitches (like the home run he slammed off of Trevor Hoffman in the playoffs), but has problems with real gas.

RAY LANKFORD **CF** **1967** **Age 30**

Year	Team	Lge	AB	H	DB	TP	HR	BB	SB	CS	OUT	BA	OBA	SA	EQA	EQR	Peak
1993	St. Louis	NL	424	107	17	3	8	87	12	11	328	.252	.380	.363	.251	52	.261
1994	St. Louis	NL	423	115	23	4	20	64	10	9	317	.272	.368	.487	.277	64	.284
1995	St. Louis	NL	494	141	32	2	27	69	20	7	360	.285	.373	.522	.293	83	.295
1996	St. Louis	NL	563	164	35	7	23	85	29	7	406	.291	.384	.501	.295	96	.293
1997	*St. Louis*	*NL*	*538*	*141*	*31*	*8*	*25*	*107*	*47*	*17*	*414*	*.262*	*.384*	*.489*	*.302*	*104*	

It's hard to take the Jordan campaign for MVP seriously when he was pretty clearly not even the most valuable player in his outfield; Lankford was. Lankford couldn't hit left-handed pitching when he came up, and that hasn't changed. As a result, the Cardinals were a much, much worse team against lefties, finishing last in the majors in home runs hit against them while going 16-19. That was the worst mark against left-handers of any playoff team, and a big part of the difference was Ray Lankford.

He's starting to lose his range in center, which may lead the Cardinals to flip-flop him and Jordan in '97. A short, aggressive power source, Lankford routinely gets banged up during the course of a season. One of the worst decisions LaRussa made all year was keeping his regulars in games down the stretch after the Cardinals had clinched: Lankford tore his rotator cuff making a diving play in a meaningless extra-inning game with a week left in the season. It was an injury that seriously affected the Cardinals' playoff hopes.

JOHN MABRY **1B/RF** **1971** **Age 26**

Year	Team	Lge	AB	H	DB	TP	HR	BB	SB	CS	OUT	BA	OBA	SA	EQA	EQR	Peak
1993	Arkansas	Texas	540	147	20	1	15	30	6	7	400	.272	.311	.396	.235	53	.259
1994	Louisville	AmA	478	119	20	1	16	34	2	4	363	.249	.299	.395	.229	45	.249
1995	St. Louis	NL	395	123	19	0	6	29	0	2	274	.311	.358	.405	.258	46	.276
1996	St. Louis	NL	556	170	28	2	14	44	2	2	388	.306	.357	.439	.267	71	.282
1997	*St. Louis*	*NL*	*570*	*173*	*32*	*2*	*15*	*34*	*0*	*0*	*397*	*.304*	*.343*	*.446*	*.276*	*79*	

Mabry's reliable mediocrity would give the Cardinals some options, if they wanted them. They could move him to the outfield, now that Dmitri Young is ready, but the oufield is full with Jordan, Gant and Lankford. He's a strong-armed outfielder with good range. Although he's shown fine range at first, he still lacks the instincts at the position that leave him occasionally flat-footed on bunts or when he has to choose to cover the bag or charge the ball. As an upside, I could see him being Bill Buckner with healthy knees and a good glove, hanging around for years to come.

ELIESER MARRERO   C   1974   Age 23

Year	Team	Lge	AB	H	DB	TP	HR	BB	SB	CS	OUT	BA	OBA	SA	EQA	EQR	Peak
1994	Savannah	SAtl	441	110	9	1	17	34	3	2	333	.249	.303	.390	.231	43	.263
1995	St. Petersburg	Flor	392	79	8	0	11	21	6	2	315	.202	.242	.306	.177	21	.198
1996	Arkansas	Texas	377	94	10	1	16	30	7	3	286	.249	.305	.408	.238	39	.262
1997	*St. Louis*	*NL*	*410*	*100*	*15*	*2*	*13*	*30*	*14*	*6*	*316*	*.244*	*.295*	*.385*	*.241*	*45*	

The organization's catcher prospect. He's been named the best defensive catcher in his league each of the last two years. As a hitter he tries to pull everything, which compared to the Dann Bilardellos of the world is at least a plan of action. He might wind up being very similar to the man he'll eventually replace, Tom Pagnozzi. Hit fairly well in the AFL.

WILLIE McGEE   OF   1959   Age 38

Year	Team	Lge	AB	H	DB	TP	HR	BB	SB	CS	OUT	BA	OBA	SA	EQA	EQR	Peak
1993	San Francisco	NL	492	156	27	1	5	46	9	8	344	.317	.375	.407	.265	62	.252
1994	San Francisco	NL	159	46	3	0	5	17	3	0	113	.289	.358	.403	.261	20	.249
1995	Boston	AL	202	59	13	3	2	9	5	2	145	.292	.322	.416	.249	23	.238
1996	St. Louis	NL	317	101	15	2	5	22	4	2	218	.319	.363	.426	.267	40	.253
1997	*St. Louis*	*NL*	*292*	*85*	*16*	*2*	*2*	*15*	*7*	*2*	*209*	*.291*	*.326*	*.380*	*.254*	*34*	

A popular comeback to the scene of his glory days, but also someone who'd played for LaRussa in Oakland. McGee was a useful spare part, pinch-hitter and backup. He'll always be able to get the ball in play, but his days as a regular are long gone. Back in St. Louis in 1997.

MIGUEL MEJIA   OF   1975   Age 22

Year	Team	Lge	AB	H	DB	TP	HR	BB	SB	CS	OUT	BA	OBA	SA	EQA	EQR	Peak
1993	Albany-GA	SAtl	81	12	0	0	2	3	3	1	70	.148	.179	.222	.098	1	.103
1994	Albany-GA	SAtl	60	9	1	1	0	4	2	2	53	.150	.203	.200	.088	1	.101
1995	High Desert	Calif	117	23	3	1	0	11	6	3	97	.197	.266	.239	.167	5	.189

It used to be that pinch-runners had at least a prayer of being baseball players. Rod McCray could play baseball, so could Miguel Dilone; Herb Washington doesn't really count. What the Cardinals see in Mejia is beyond me; I can't explain why they'd pick him in the Rule V draft, much less why they'd keep him on the roster for the entire season. It effectively stuck them with a 24-man roster for the season, and there's a good chance that Miguel Mejia won't turn out to be even as good as the famous William Canate.

JOSE OLIVA   3B/DH   1971   Age 26

Year	Team	Lge	AB	H	DB	TP	HR	BB	SB	CS	OUT	BA	OBA	SA	EQA	EQR	Peak
1993	Richmond	Inter	420	99	16	3	20	37	1	3	324	.236	.298	.431	.237	45	.262
1994	Richmond	Inter	378	96	11	0	22	25	2	1	283	.254	.300	.458	.249	44	.270
1994	Atlanta	NL	60	18	5	0	6	8	0	1	43	.300	.382	.683	.322	13	.350
1995	Atlanta	NL	109	17	4	0	5	8	0	0	92	.156	.214	.330	.168	5	.177
1995	St. Louis	NL	74	9	1	0	2	6	0	0	65	.122	.188	.216	.068	0	.062
1996	Louisville	AmA	422	104	10	0	28	38	3	2	320	.246	.309	.469	.254	52	.267
1997	*St. Louis*	*NL*	*437*	*103*	*22*	*2*	*28*	*38*	*0*	*0*	*334*	*.236*	*.297*	*.487*	*.265*	*61*	

On the same roster as Mike Gulan, Oliva wound up DHing a lot. He's a poor defensive player and he lacks plate discipline, but with this kind of power he could help a major league team. At the plate, he tries to put everything in the air, so he's sort of Glenn Murray, but a third baseman. Picked up by the Mets, he's a longshot candidate for their third base job.

TOM PAGNOZZI   C   1963   Age 34

Year	Team	Lge	AB	H	DB	TP	HR	BB	SB	CS	OUT	BA	OBA	SA	EQA	EQR	Peak
1993	St. Louis	NL	337	91	13	1	8	24	1	0	246	.270	.319	.386	.237	34	.232
1994	St. Louis	NL	246	68	11	1	7	24	0	0	178	.276	.341	.415	.253	29	.245
1995	St. Louis	NL	221	48	14	1	2	13	0	1	174	.217	.261	.317	.186	13	.177
1996	St. Louis	NL	415	116	15	0	16	29	3	1	300	.280	.327	.431	.253	48	.240
1997	*St. Louis*	*NL*	*421*	*106*	*12*	*2*	*12*	*35*	*0*	*0*	*315*	*.252*	*.309*	*.375*	*.241*	*45*	

Like a lot of people, Pagnozzi seemed like he had his best year at the plate, setting a career high in home runs. There have been some talks about signing him to a multiyear contract, but his market value is probably at its highest now. He invariably misses about month to injury each season. His defense isn't what it was: the numerous knee injuries have affected his mobility behind the plate and cut into his ability to stop the running game. He's still good behind the plate, but his Gold Glove days are behind him.

PLACIDO POLANCO   **SS/2B**   **1976**   **Age 21**

Year	Team	Lge	AB	H	DB	TP	HR	BB	SB	CS	OUT	BA	OBA	SA	EQA	EQR	Peak
1995	Peoria	Midw	368	84	5	2	2	14	3	3	287	.228	.257	.269	.166	16	.191
1996	St. Petersburg	Flor	562	162	24	4	2	24	2	2	402	.288	.317	.356	.228	50	.259
1997	*St. Louis*	*NL*	*394*	*105*	*27*	*2*	*7*	*15*	*2*	*2*	*291*	*.266*	*.293*	*.398*	*.242*	*42*	

With the highly touted defensive skills of Luis Ordaz available, Polanco has been shifted around the infield. Polanco is a contact hitter without power, but he's young enough that he may develop some pop with time. He's someone to watch.

CHRIS RICHARD   **1B**   **1974**   **Age 23**

Year	Team	Lge	AB	H	DB	TP	HR	BB	SB	CS	OUT	BA	OBA	SA	EQA	EQR	Peak
1995	New Jersey	NY-P	295	64	7	0	4	35	2	2	233	.217	.300	.281	.192	19	.215
1996	St. Petersburg	Flor	489	143	18	3	18	53	4	2	348	.292	.362	.452	.272	67	.300

A left-handed hitter from San Diego, Richard works very hard at making himself a good hitter, having studied Tony Gwynn religiously while growing up. He was named the best defensive first baseman in the FSL. Assuming Dmitri Young gets himself entrenched at first by the time Richard makes the upper levels of the organization, he's probably doomed to be trade bait.

KERRY ROBINSON   **OF**   **1974**   **Age 23**

Year	Team	Lge	AB	H	DB	TP	HR	BB	SB	CS	OUT	BA	OBA	SA	EQA	EQR	Peak
1996	Peoria	Midw	457	146	13	8	3	39	24	13	324	.319	.373	.403	.265	59	.292

Robinson is one of the last remnants of the organization's historic commitment to speed. To put up an EqA like that at this level is extremely impressive. If he can hit like this, with his speed he'll be on the fast track to the majors.

DANNY SHEAFFER   **C**   **1962**   **Age 35**

Year	Team	Lge	AB	H	DB	TP	HR	BB	SB	CS	OUT	BA	OBA	SA	EQA	EQR	Peak
1993	Colorado	NL	213	53	6	1	4	12	2	2	162	.249	.289	.343	.210	16	.202
1994	Colorado	NL	109	22	3	0	1	12	0	2	89	.202	.281	.257	.166	5	.159
1995	St. Louis	NL	211	50	10	1	5	25	0	0	161	.237	.318	.365	.228	20	.216
1996	St. Louis	NL	200	47	8	3	2	12	2	3	156	.235	.278	.335	.201	14	.191

Still hanging around after being the man who was handed Rich Gedman's job in '87 while the owners were colluding to lower free agents' salaries. He doesn't do anything well, but it's easier to keep him around than pay for a new nameplate on the locker.

OZZIE SMITH   **SS**   **1955**   **Age 42**

Year	Team	Lge	AB	H	DB	TP	HR	BB	SB	CS	OUT	BA	OBA	SA	EQA	EQR	Peak
1993	St. Louis	NL	561	169	25	4	2	52	18	7	399	.301	.361	.371	.253	64	.241
1994	St. Louis	NL	386	103	16	2	4	43	5	3	286	.267	.340	.350	.235	38	.223
1995	St. Louis	NL	158	32	5	1	0	19	3	2	129	.203	.288	.247	.174	8	.164
1996	St. Louis	NL	233	68	10	2	2	28	6	4	169	.292	.368	.378	.254	28	.241

The greatest shortstop of all time? Not with Honus Wagner being so dominant back at the dawn of time, and with Alex Rodriguez looking like the second coming of Wagner, but a first-ballot Hall of Famer nonetheless. The Smith-LaRussa spat was an interesting exercise in how both men have gotten used to being treated, both by the press and by baseball people. LaRussa had gotten used to treating players however he wished in Oakland, attacking them in the press without being criticized for it. When he treated a local icon like Ozzie Smith shabbily, it blew up in his face because Smith wasn't going to put up with it. It won't be an incident either man will want to remember.

MARK SWEENEY   1B/OF   1970   Age 27

Year	Team	Lge	AB	H	DB	TP	HR	BB	SB	CS	OUT	BA	OBA	SA	EQA	EQR	Peak
1993	Palm Springs	Calif	252	82	13	2	3	31	4	3	173	.325	.399	.429	.281	36	.305
1993	Midland	Texas	190	59	8	0	8	25	1	0	131	.311	.391	.479	.291	30	.317
1994	Vancouver	PCL	343	89	9	2	7	54	2	2	256	.259	.360	.359	.244	38	.261
1995	Louisville	AmA	78	28	3	0	3	15	2	0	50	.359	.462	.513	.332	16	.351
1995	Vancouver	PCL	239	87	10	1	10	43	3	1	153	.364	.461	.540	.334	49	.351
1995	St. Louis	NL	79	22	2	0	2	11	1	1	58	.278	.367	.380	.253	9	.267
1996	St. Louis	NL	176	48	7	0	4	36	3	0	128	.273	.396	.381	.270	24	.281
1997	*St. Louis*	*NL*	*510*	*157*	*29*	*2*	*16*	*89*	*4*	*2*	*355*	*.308*	*.411*	*.467*	*.307*	*93*	

Sweeney can outhit John Mabry every day of the week, but Mabry was resorted to first in '95, so it's his job. The amazing thing is that the Angels gave him up for John Habyan during their '95 stretch drive, when he'd probably have taken J.T. Snow's job by now. Because he lacks the outstanding power you look for at first, he has to either hope that he gets a huge streak of luck, like Wally Joyner's '86, or get a break with a team with lousy alternatives, like the Angels. Because of Mabry and Dmitri Young, Sweeney has to humiliate himself in the outfield and be a fine pinch-hitter. It'll be a shame if his career winds up like those of Greg Gross or Dane Iorg.

DMITRI YOUNG   1B   1974   Age 23

Year	Team	Lge	AB	H	DB	TP	HR	BB	SB	CS	OUT	BA	OBA	SA	EQA	EQR	Peak
1993	St. Petersburg	Flor	279	84	9	1	7	22	2	2	197	.301	.352	.416	.258	33	.297
1993	Arkansas	Texas	169	39	9	1	3	10	3	2	132	.231	.274	.349	.206	13	.237
1994	Arkansas	Texas	463	120	21	1	10	34	0	1	344	.259	.310	.374	.228	43	.260
1995	Arkansas	Texas	366	96	12	3	10	28	2	2	272	.262	.315	.393	.236	37	.264
1996	Louisville	AmA	475	159	26	6	15	39	15	4	320	.335	.385	.509	.298	78	.329
1997	*St. Louis*	*NL*	*561*	*168*	*43*	*3*	*14*	*44*	*16*	*6*	*399*	*.299*	*.350*	*.462*	*.284*	*86*	

He won the batting title in the American Association. Apparently, somebody explained to him that eating everything in sight, like Cecil Fielder, wasn't a good idea until after you made the big leagues. Assuming he keeps that under control he could be the new Pedro Guerrero, because he's a hitting machine. In the field, he's made huge strides in the past year.

MANUEL AYBAR   RSP   1975   Age 22

YR	TEAM	Lge	IP	H	ER	HR	BB	K	ERA	W	L	H/9	HR/9	BB/9	K/9	KW
1995	Savannah	S Atl	97.3	120	60	11	55	58	5.55	4	7	11.10	1.02	5.09	5.36	.52
1995	St Petersburg	Flor	42.3	54	32	6	23	31	6.80	1	4	11.48	1.28	4.89	6.59	.97
1996	Arkansas	Texas	110.0	132	50	10	48	68	4.09	6	6	10.80	.82	3.93	5.56	.87
1996	Louisville	AmA	29.3	29	11	1	10	21	3.38	2	1	8.90	.31	3.07	6.44	1.38

A converted shortstop, Aybar has been consistently successful so far. The highest ERA he's posted at any level is 3.35.

CORY BAILEY   RRP   1971   Age 26

YR	TEAM	Lge	IP	H	ER	HR	BB	K	ERA	W	L	H/9	HR/9	BB/9	K/9	KW
1993	Pawtucket	Inter	61.7	52	18	1	39	47	2.63	5	2	7.59	.15	5.69	6.86	.86
1993	Boston	AL	15.3	12	5	0	13	11	2.93	1	1	7.04	.00	7.63	6.46	.24
1994	Pawtucket	Inter	57.7	47	21	4	45	43	3.28	4	2	7.34	.62	7.02	6.71	.48
1995	Louisville	AmA	57.0	52	26	6	38	43	4.11	3	3	8.21	.95	6.00	6.79	.76
1996	Louisville	AmA	32.3	32	21	1	26	23	5.85	1	3	8.91	.28	7.24	6.40	.32
1996	St. Louis	NL	56.0	60	19	1	36	34	3.05	4	2	9.64	.16	5.79	5.46	.37

Once upon a time, Bailey was a closer prospect with Boston. He's wild with a middling fastball; don't expect greatness.

BRIAN BARBER   RSP   1973   Age 24

YR	TEAM	Lge	IP	H	ER	HR	BB	K	ERA	W	L	H/9	HR/9	BB/9	K/9	KW
1993	Arkansas	Texas	127.7	183	76	21	83	91	5.36	5	9	12.90	1.48	5.85	6.42	.68
1994	Arkansas	Texas	33.3	35	14	5	21	39	3.78	2	2	9.45	1.35	5.67	10.53	2.09
1994	Louisville	AmA	82.0	79	47	7	54	84	5.16	3	6	8.67	.77	5.93	9.22	1.59
1995	Louisville	AmA	103.0	106	59	14	53	83	5.16	4	7	9.26	1.22	4.63	7.25	1.26
1995	St. Louis	NL	29.0	31	15	4	19	24	4.66	1	2	9.62	1.24	5.90	7.45	1.01
1996	Louisville	AmA	47.7	53	35	11	34	28	6.61	1	4	10.01	2.08	6.42	5.29	.16

A former first-round pick, Barber has been injury-prone. At this point, the question is whether or not this year's injured ulnar nerve in his right elbow has finally ruined his fastball. It's been a couple of seasons since he's had it consistently, and it may not be back.

RICHARD BATCHELOR **RRP** **1967** **Age 30**

YR	TEAM	Lge	IP	H	ER	HR	BB	K	ERA	W	L	H/9	HR/9	BB/9	K/9	KW
1993	Albany, NY	East	37.0	32	8	2	16	30	1.95	3	1	7.78	.49	3.89	7.30	1.46
1993	Columbus, OH	Inter	15.3	16	5	0	10	14	2.93	1	1	9.39	.00	5.87	8.22	1.27
1994	Louisville	AmA	78.0	83	33	7	40	44	3.81	5	4	9.58	.81	4.62	5.08	.54
1995	Louisville	AmA	81.0	87	34	5	26	53	3.78	5	4	9.67	.56	2.89	5.89	1.24
1996	Louisville	AmA	52.3	65	28	4	27	48	4.82	2	4	11.18	.69	4.64	8.25	1.59
1996	St. Louis	NL	14.3	10	1	0	2	9	0.63	2	0	6.28	.00	1.26	5.65	1.57

He racked up 28 saves in Louisville despite posting a mediocre ERA (4.12). The ERA tells you more about Batchelor's ability than the saves do about his pitching in tight situations, or whether he has major league makeup or lip balm or whatever. He was the compensation for Lee Smith, throws a good forkball and his control is fairly solid.

RIGO BELTRAN **LBP** **1970** **Age 27**

YR	TEAM	Lge	IP	H	ER	HR	BB	K	ERA	W	L	H/9	HR/9	BB/9	K/9	KW
1993	Arkansas	Texas	79.0	90	43	9	55	59	4.90	4	5	10.25	1.03	6.27	6.72	.67
1994	Arkansas	Texas	25.3	16	3	3	5	15	1.07	3	0	5.68	1.07	1.78	5.33	1.33
1994	Louisville	AmA	133.7	142	67	15	81	77	4.51	7	8	9.56	1.01	5.45	5.18	.36
1995	Louisville	AmA	125.3	155	72	12	50	80	5.17	5	9	11.13	.86	3.59	5.74	1.02
1996	Louisville	AmA	124.0	145	65	16	41	110	4.72	6	8	10.52	1.16	2.98	7.98	1.92

Beltran makes nobody's prospect lists, but lefties who fool this many people this often have to be able to do something right.

ALAN BENES **RSP** **1972** **Age 25**

YR	TEAM	Lge	IP	H	ER	HR	BB	K	ERA	W	L	H/9	HR/9	BB/9	K/9	KW
1993	Glens Falls	NY-P	29.3	54	25	3	23	15	7.67	1	2	16.57	.92	7.06	4.60	-.23
1994	Savannah	SAtl	21.0	29	6	2	11	14	2.57	1	1	12.43	.86	4.71	6.00	.82
1994	St. Petersburg	Flor	70.7	70	18	1	23	53	2.29	6	2	8.92	.13	2.93	6.75	1.52
1994	Arkansas	Texas	80.3	68	36	10	35	54	4.03	4	5	7.62	1.12	3.92	6.05	1.04
1994	Louisville	AmA	14.3	11	4	1	6	14	2.51	1	1	6.91	.63	3.77	8.79	1.99
1995	Louisville	AmA	52.7	40	14	6	20	47	2.39	4	2	6.84	1.03	3.42	8.03	1.82
1995	St. Louis	NL	16.3	24	13	2	5	18	7.16	0	2	13.22	1.10	2.76	9.92	2.62
1996	St. Louis	NL	189.7	197	108	27	105	115	5.12	8	13	9.35	1.28	4.98	5.46	.57

Benes deserves a lot of congratulations for this season. He showed that he can beat people with his great sinking fastball and that he had recovered fully from the injured forearm he suffered in 1995. He is the first starting pitcher prospect that Tony LaRussa and Dave Duncan have developed since Britt Burns and Rich Dotson during the Carter administration. They deserve credit for breaking their old bad habits; now let's see if they can do it with the large number of other talented young pitchers on the Cardinals' farm.

ANDY BENES **RSP** **1968** **Age 29**

YR	TEAM	Lge	IP	H	ER	HR	BB	K	ERA	W	L	H/9	HR/9	BB/9	K/9	KW
1993	San Diego	NL	224.0	209	101	25	110	173	4.06	12	13	8.40	1.00	4.42	6.95	1.21
1994	San Diego	NL	169.0	157	71	20	66	176	3.78	10	9	8.36	1.07	3.51	9.37	2.25
1995	San Diego	NL	117.3	129	61	11	55	114	4.68	5	8	9.89	.84	4.22	8.74	1.86
1995	Seattle	AL	63.7	68	33	7	35	45	4.66	3	4	9.61	.99	4.95	6.36	.88
1996	St. Louis	NL	226.7	223	94	28	96	140	3.73	13	12	8.85	1.11	3.81	5.56	.90

Since his big first half in '91, people have wondered what Andy Benes would do if he put together that big season people think he's capable of. This year didn't do anything to stop that talk. He was 2-7 with an ERA over 5.00 going into June, at which point he became almost unbeatable for the rest of the year. He could continue to be that effective if he really has learned how to change speeds and mix a good changeup into his power assortment; it's more likely that he'll continue to be frustratingly inconsistent.

KRIS DETMERS **LSP** **1974** **Age 23**

YR	TEAM	Lge	IP	H	ER	HR	BB	K	ERA	W	L	H/9	HR/9	BB/9	K/9	KW
1994	Madison	Midw	77.0	117	52	5	44	47	6.08	3	6	13.68	.58	5.14	5.49	.55
1995	St. Petersburg	Flor	131.3	150	71	17	79	107	4.87	6	9	10.28	1.16	5.41	7.33	1.09
1996	Arkansas	Texas	149.0	166	67	15	93	80	4.05	8	9	10.03	.91	5.62	4.83	.21

A 22nd round draft pick, Detmers has yet to disappoint at any level. Right now, he survives on an outstanding curveball and changeups. It's hoped that as he gets older he might pick up velocity. If not, his strikeout rate may drop further in Louisville, at which point he might stop being successful.

DENNIS ECKERSLEY   **RRP**   **1955**   **Age 42**

YR	TEAM	Lge	IP	H	ER	HR	BB	K	ERA	W	L	H/9	HR/9	BB/9	K/9	KW
1993	Oakland	AL	66.0	69	28	7	17	83	3.82	4	3	9.41	.95	2.32	11.32	3.19
1994	Oakland	AL	44.3	49	21	5	14	46	4.26	2	3	9.95	1.02	2.84	9.34	2.40
1995	Oakland	AL	50.0	54	24	5	12	40	4.32	3	3	9.72	.90	2.16	7.20	1.86
1996	St. Louis	NL	58.7	67	23	8	11	43	3.53	4	3	10.28	1.23	1.69	6.60	1.78

The man with a "heart of a lion." Does that mean Lee Smith has the heart of a sleeping rhino, or that Ron Davis had the heart of a lemur, or that Jeff Reardon had the dynamic personality of a tree sloth? Eckersley was still a reliably mediocre closer instead of falling over a cliff as was expected. He also had help, as there seemed to be many times when great catches by Ray Lankford or somebody got him off the hook. But hey, it worked. Don't be surprised when it stops working.

TONY FOSSAS   **LRP**   **1958**   **Age 39**

YR	TEAM	Lge	IP	H	ER	HR	BB	K	ERA	W	L	H/9	HR/9	BB/9	K/9	KW
1993	Boston	AL	39.3	37	22	4	17	40	5.03	2	2	8.47	.92	3.89	9.15	2.08
1994	Boston	AL	34.3	32	13	6	16	30	3.41	2	2	8.39	1.57	4.19	7.86	1.57
1995	St. Louis	NL	35.3	30	5	1	13	35	1.27	4	0	7.64	.25	3.31	8.92	2.14
1996	St. Louis	NL	46.3	45	17	7	25	32	3.30	3	2	8.74	1.36	4.86	6.22	.86

In the never ending shuffle in the LaRussian pen, Fossas put up a fine season as the middle inning setup man for the left-handed spot reliever, except on alternate Thursdays when the tides were high and the planet's gravitational pull affected his velocity.

JOHN FRASCATORE   **RBP**   **1970**   **Age 27**

YR	TEAM	Lge	IP	H	ER	HR	BB	K	ERA	W	L	H/9	HR/9	BB/9	K/9	KW
1993	Springfield	Midw	135.3	204	94	8	47	74	6.25	4	11	13.57	.53	3.13	4.92	.86
1994	Arkansas	Texas	71.7	87	36	4	22	46	4.52	4	4	10.93	.50	2.76	5.78	1.23
1994	Louisville	AmA	81.3	82	28	4	40	51	3.10	6	3	9.07	.44	4.43	5.64	.77
1995	Louisville	AmA	78.7	90	48	5	44	48	5.49	3	6	10.30	.57	5.03	5.49	.57
1995	St. Louis	NL	32.7	39	16	3	19	19	4.41	2	2	10.74	.83	5.23	5.23	.44
1996	Louisville	AmA	150.3	193	102	21	63	79	6.11	5	12	11.55	1.26	3.77	4.73	.63

The Cardinals have had a hard time deciding whether to use him in the rotation or as a closer. His fastball is considered the best in the organization, and with people like Matt Morris, Alan Benes and T.J. Mathews around, that's sort of impressive. They decided to keep trying him as a starter this year, and he was a dramatic failure. His breaking pitches are all still works in progress, which may dictate a return to the bullpen, because Frascatore isn't young.

RICK HONEYCUTT   **LRP**   **1954**   **Age 43**

YR	TEAM	Lge	IP	H	ER	HR	BB	K	ERA	W	L	H/9	HR/9	BB/9	K/9	KW
1993	Oakland	AL	40.0	34	16	2	22	22	3.60	2	2	7.65	.45	4.95	4.95	.41
1994	Texas	AL	25.7	35	17	4	10	18	5.96	1	2	12.27	1.40	3.51	6.31	1.23
1995	Oakland	AL	44.0	38	10	6	10	21	2.05	4	1	7.77	1.23	2.05	4.30	.92
1996	St. Louis	NL	45.7	45	13	3	11	26	2.56	4	1	8.87	.59	2.17	5.12	1.17

That year in Texas is interesting. Eckersley is quoted time and again about how only Tony LaRussa could have saved his career, and how only LaRussa could have made him successful as he's been. The same seems to be true for Honeycutt. Rick's ability to frighten Tony Gwynn in the playoffs was just one more reason that the Padres should have carried Rob Deer on their playoff roster: everyone goes out of their way to stock up on lefties in the pen on the old postseason roster, but how many teams stock up on lefty-mashing pinch-hitters? Earl Weaver always would...

DANNY JACKSON   **LBP**   **1962**   **Age 35**

YR	TEAM	Lge	IP	H	ER	HR	BB	K	ERA	W	L	H/9	HR/9	BB/9	K/9	KW
1993	Philadelphia	NL	204.0	223	95	12	104	116	4.19	11	12	9.84	.53	4.59	5.12	.56
1994	Philadelphia	NL	176.0	187	63	13	62	121	3.22	12	8	9.56	.66	3.17	6.19	1.27
1995	St. Louis	NL	100.3	120	71	9	57	47	6.37	3	8	10.76	.81	5.11	4.22	.13
1996	St. Louis	NL	35.7	35	16	3	19	24	4.04	2	2	8.83	.76	4.79	6.06	.82

If there's a reminder that not everything the Cardinals do recently is inspired by god, its the contract they gave to Danny Jackson. The slider doesn't slide nearly as well as it used to, and he's probably never going to be healthy for any length of time again: he still throws cross-body and at this point, miracles of modern microsurgery or no, there comes a point when you think he might not be able to pitch 100 innings again. He could have a big year as a middle reliever, but with the money he's making, it remains to be seen if the Cardinals have the willpower to take what they can get, instead of putting him into the rotation for one last hurrah.

MARCUS LOGAN   RBP   1972   Age 25

YR	TEAM	Lge	IP	H	ER	HR	BB	K	ERA	W	L	H/9	HR/9	BB/9	K/9	KW
1995	Savannah	SAtl	71.7	112	60	5	56	49	7.53	2	6	14.07	.63	7.03	6.15	.29
1996	St. Petersburg	Flor	117.3	155	55	14	68	72	4.22	6	7	11.89	1.07	5.22	5.52	.54

With a name right out of daytime soap operas, I'm sure that we'll hear how he's sleeping with the bullpen coach's sister's daughter's brother's aunt, but has a mysterious relationship with the guy with the eye patch.

KEVIN LOVINGIER   LRP   1972   Age 25

YR	TEAM	Lge	IP	H	ER	HR	BB	K	ERA	W	L	H/9	HR/9	BB/9	K/9	KW
1994	New Jersey	NY-P	44.7	50	15	5	29	42	3.02	3	2	10.07	1.01	5.84	8.46	1.36
1995	St Petersburg	Flor	19.3	13	4	0	13	10	1.86	2	0	6.05	.00	6.05	4.66	.04
1995	Savannah	S Atl	39.0	55	20	2	31	32	4.62	2	2	12.69	.46	7.15	7.38	.67
1996	Arkansas	Texas	58.3	63	27	4	59	60	4.17	3	3	9.72	.62	9.10	9.26	.81

His real life walk rate isn't nearly this bad, "only" around six men per nine. At any rate, lefties who strike out over a man per inning get noticed.

SEAN LOWE   RBP   1971   Age 26

YR	TEAM	Lge	IP	H	ER	HR	BB	K	ERA	W	L	H/9	HR/9	BB/9	K/9	KW
1993	St. Petersburg	Flor	114.7	184	92	11	84	69	7.22	3	10	14.44	.86	6.59	5.42	.16
1994	St. Petersburg	Flor	102.0	145	57	10	51	71	5.03	4	7	12.79	.88	4.50	6.26	.96
1994	Arkansas	Texas	17.3	15	3	0	11	8	1.56	2	0	7.79	.00	5.71	4.15	-.04
1995	Arkansas	Texas	117.0	146	75	2	80	65	5.77	4	9	11.23	.15	6.15	5.00	.13
1996	Arkansas	Texas	30.3	34	22	2	20	21	6.53	1	2	10.09	.59	5.93	6.23	.59
1996	Louisville	AmA	110.0	139	70	6	69	64	5.73	4	8	11.37	.49	5.65	5.24	.33

Lowe was the '92 first round pick, and although he hasn't turned out as well as other first rounders Alan Benes or Donovan Osborne, he still has the good fastball that got him picked in the first place.

ERIC LUDWICK   RBP   1972   Age 25

YR	TEAM	Lge	IP	H	ER	HR	BB	K	ERA	W	L	H/9	HR/9	BB/9	K/9	KW
1994	St. Lucie	Flor	134.3	190	110	10	100	59	7.37	3	12	12.73	.67	6.70	3.95	-.36
1995	Binghamton	East	133.0	123	47	11	82	100	3.18	9	6	8.32	.74	5.55	6.77	.87
1995	Norfolk	Inter	18.3	26	16	3	10	8	7.85	0	2	12.76	1.47	4.91	3.93	.08
1996	Louisville	AmA	57.7	61	23	4	32	61	3.59	3	3	9.52	.62	4.99	9.52	1.92
1996	St. Louis	NL	10.0	11	9	4	4	11	8.10	0	1	9.90	3.60	3.60	9.90	2.40

A survivor from the pitcher's charnel house that is the Mets' farm system. Like his '95 rotation mates Paul Wilson and Jason Isringhausen, he came down with an injury this year (a strained elbow). Ludwick is basically a fastball-slider pitcher. He's working on a curve and a changeup, but may shelve both pitches if he's converted to closer, which is where he was used in the AFL last fall.

T.J. MATHEWS   RRP   1970   Age 27

YR	TEAM	Lge	IP	H	ER	HR	BB	K	ERA	W	L	H/9	HR/9	BB/9	K/9	KW
1993	Springfield	Midw	142.3	156	60	9	41	84	3.79	8	8	9.86	.57	2.59	5.31	1.12
1994	St. Petersburg	Flor	60.3	63	23	2	31	48	3.43	4	3	9.40	.30	4.62	7.16	1.23
1994	Arkansas	Texas	89.0	96	36	10	34	67	3.64	5	5	9.71	1.01	3.44	6.78	1.40
1995	Louisville	AmA	63.3	62	31	2	36	44	4.41	3	4	8.81	.28	5.12	6.25	.81
1995	St. Louis	NL	28.3	23	6	1	13	25	1.91	2	1	7.31	.32	4.13	7.94	1.61
1996	St. Louis	NL	81.7	67	27	8	38	70	2.98	6	3	7.38	.88	4.19	7.71	1.52

He's a sinker-slider pitcher with a funky delivery who could easily improve if he perfects a breaking pitch to use against left-handed batters: he's worked on both the split-fingered fastball and the knuckle-curve. At this point, he's clearly a better pitcher than Eckersley, but he lacks charisma or makeup or Jeff Reardon's patented waterproof eyeliner and blush.

JEFF MATRANGA   RRP   1971   Age 26

YR	TEAM	Lge	IP	H	ER	HR	BB	K	ERA	W	L	H/9	HR/9	BB/9	K/9	KW
1993	Savannah	S Atl	90.3	105	28	11	20	53	2.79	7	3	10.46	1.10	1.99	5.28	1.26
1993	St Petersburg	Flor	25.0	29	11	2	9	17	3.96	2	1	10.44	.72	3.24	6.12	1.23
1994	St Petersburg	Flor	79.7	90	31	6	41	58	3.50	5	4	10.17	.68	4.63	6.55	1.03
1995	St Petersburg	Flor	59.0	63	29	3	28	50	4.42	3	4	9.61	.46	4.27	7.63	1.47
1996	Arkansas	Texas	73.0	62	20	7	40	68	2.47	6	2	7.64	.86	4.93	8.38	1.56

"Matranga, warrior chieftain of the Jujubee tribe." He's thin as a rail, and must do something silly to not get higher regard because he's barely moved through the chain despite fine pitching performances.

MATT MORRIS　　　**RSP**　　**1975**　**Age 22**

YR	TEAM	Lge	IP	H	ER	HR	BB	K	ERA	W	L	H/9	HR/9	BB/9	K/9	KW
1995	St Petersburg	Flor	30.3	29	18	2	16	22	5.34	1	2	8.60	.59	4.75	6.53	.99
1996	Arkansas	Texas	153.0	191	74	14	69	99	4.35	8	9	11.24	.82	4.06	5.82	.93

The Cardinals' '95 first-round draft choice out of Seton Hall. He consistently tops 90 on slow radar guns and his curve-ball is also outstanding. He's progressing extremely well, as he was named the best pitching prospect with the best fast-ball in the Texas League.

DONOVAN OSBORNE　　**LSP**　　**1969**　**Age 28**

YR	TEAM	Lge	IP	H	ER	HR	BB	K	ERA	W	L	H/9	HR/9	BB/9	K/9	KW
1993	St. Louis	NL	151.0	163	71	20	64	81	4.23	8	9	9.72	1.19	3.81	4.83	.66
1995	St. Louis	NL	112.0	111	50	17	43	73	4.02	6	6	8.92	1.37	3.46	5.87	1.09
1996	St. Louis	NL	195.3	198	77	22	74	117	3.55	12	10	9.12	1.01	3.41	5.39	.94

Osborne was probably the Cardinals' best starter last season, but since he wasn't somebody who came in with LaRussa that tended to be ignored. He had 23 quality starts in 30 starts, the third-best rate in the league and better than anybody in a Braves' uniform. With a pretty curve and a fastball he isn't afraid to throw inside, he can be a lot of fun to watch.

MARK PETKOVSEK　　**RBP**　　**1966**　**Age 31**

YR	TEAM	Lge	IP	H	ER	HR	BB	K	ERA	W	L	H/9	HR/9	BB/9	K/9	KW
1993	Buffalo	AmA	67.3	79	36	8	23	25	4.81	3	4	10.56	1.07	3.07	3.34	.35
1993	Pittsburgh	NL	32.3	43	23	7	12	14	6.40	1	3	11.97	1.95	3.34	3.90	.46
1994	Tucson	PCL	129.3	167	68	10	53	59	4.73	6	8	11.62	.70	3.69	4.11	.45
1995	Louisville	AmA	50.7	42	13	3	14	26	2.31	5	1	7.46	.53	2.49	4.62	.92
1995	St. Louis	NL	134.7	138	61	11	45	63	4.08	7	8	9.22	.74	3.01	4.21	.65
1996	St. Louis	NL	87.0	87	33	9	42	39	3.41	6	4	9.00	.93	4.34	4.03	.26

Petkovsek is one of my favorite pitchers to watch. His assortment of stuff generates a huge number of groundballs, so when he has a good infield behind him, as the Cardinals gave him, he can be very effective. Although it would be nice to see him return to the rotation regularly, with the young pitching talent and the expensive free agents the team has on hand he may still be stuck in the long relief/spot starter role. Basically, he'll continue to get used in the Gene Nelson role that LaRussa and Dave Duncan are familiar with.

BRADY RAGGIO　　**RSP**　　**1973**　**Age 24**

YR	TEAM	Lge	IP	H	ER	HR	BB	K	ERA	W	L	H/9	HR/9	BB/9	K/9	KW
1994	New Jersey	NY-P	23.3	36	8	1	7	12	3.09	2	1	13.89	.39	2.70	4.63	.87
1994	Madison	Midw	58.3	84	36	10	21	42	5.55	2	4	12.96	1.54	3.24	6.48	1.35
1995	Peoria	Midw	44.0	53	13	2	4	22	2.66	3	2	10.84	.41	.82	4.50	1.30
1995	St Petersburg	Flor	42.7	53	26	3	18	25	5.48	2	3	11.18	.63	3.80	5.27	.81
1996	Arkansas	Texas	148.3	175	64	17	59	101	3.88	8	8	10.62	1.03	3.58	6.13	1.15

Raggio's a human interest story: after the '92 season, he broke his knee into 13 pieces falling from a cliff. He was told he'd never play again. He spent all of '93 working out to get back. Although his stuff isn't the greatest, he's impressed people with his success so far.

BRITT REAMES　　**RSP**　　**1974**　**Age 23**

YR	TEAM	Lge	IP	H	ER	HR	BB	K	ERA	W	L	H/9	HR/9	BB/9	K/9	KW
1995	New Jersey	NY-P	25.7	24	7	2	19	25	2.45	2	1	8.42	.70	6.66	8.77	1.26
1995	Savannah	SAtl	45.7	65	33	10	23	37	6.50	1	4	12.81	1.97	4.53	7.29	1.30
1996	Peoria	Midw	143.7	131	42	7	54	104	2.63	11	5	8.21	.44	3.38	6.52	1.33

Reames was not a highly-touted prospect coming out of The Citadel last year, and being under 6' was another strike against him in most scouts' eyes. But he throws a knee-bending curve and spots his fastball well, so he blew the Midwest League out of the water this year, being named the best pitcher in the circuit. He'll have to continue to succeed like that to beat the biases against his relative lack of velocity and height.

BLAKE STEIN　　**RSP**　　**1974**　**Age 23**

YR	TEAM	Lge	IP	H	ER	HR	BB	K	ERA	W	L	H/9	HR/9	BB/9	K/9	KW
1995	Peoria	Midw	121.0	157	74	15	81	87	5.50	4	9	11.68	1.12	6.02	6.47	.65
1996	St. Petersburg	Flor	155.0	152	50	7	76	115	2.90	11	6	8.83	.41	4.41	6.68	1.12

A relative unknown drafted out of Spring Hill College in '95, Stein is a huge (6' 7") fireballer who bears watching in the future.

TODD STOTTLEMYRE   **RSP**   **1965**   **Age 32**

YR	TEAM	Lge	IP	H	ER	HR	BB	K	ERA	W	L	H/9	HR/9	BB/9	K/9	KW
1993	Toronto	AL	176.0	198	88	11	78	101	4.50	9	11	10.12	.56	3.99	5.16	.72
1994	Toronto	AL	140.3	143	51	17	53	103	3.27	10	6	9.17	1.09	3.40	6.61	1.35
1995	Oakland	AL	211.3	227	96	25	86	207	4.09	11	12	9.67	1.06	3.66	8.82	2.02
1996	St. Louis	NL	220.0	199	87	30	112	170	3.56	13	11	8.14	1.23	4.58	6.95	1.17

Collapse has been predicted for several seasons, but what probably deserves notice is that something happened in '94, when his strikeouts went up and haven't come down. The other thing to consider is that he may be using the split-finger more. It could be that he's more stable and less excitable than he used to be, in which case the uptight LaRussian competitiveness deserves credit. Whatever it is, Stottlemyre has now been an effective major league pitcher for three years in a row, and that's more than anybody thought he'd be when he was with the Blue Jays. It didn't help in the playoffs, of course, where the Toad did a convincing impression of Kenny Rogers, but the man has been successful.

Player	Age	Team	Lge	AB	H	DB	TP	HR	BB	SB	CS	OUT	BA	OBA	SA	EQA	EQR	Peak
GREG ALMOND	25	Peoria	Midw	281	57	6	0	3	20	1	0	224	.203	.256	.256	.160	11	.168
EFRAIN CONTRERAS	23	St Petersburg	Flor	82	13	3	1	1	9	0	0	69	.159	.242	.256	.148	3	.163
ROD CORREIA	28	Louisville	AmA	113	17	2	0	2	5	1	2	98	.150	.186	.221	.078	1	.076
DEE DALTON	24	Arkansas	Texas	349	74	10	1	6	35	3	2	277	.212	.284	.298	.191	22	.205
MIKE DIFELICE	27	Louisville	AmA	253	72	8	0	9	22	0	2	183	.285	.342	.423	.254	30	.260
TONY DIGGS	29	Arkansas	Texas	139	38	4	2	3	12	5	2	103	.273	.331	.396	.247	16	.244
	29	Louisville	AmA	315	64	12	2	6	35	5	4	255	.203	.283	.311	.195	21	.194
NATE DISHINGTON	21	Peoria	Midw	216	44	7	2	3	18	1	0	172	.204	.265	.296	.182	12	.203
PAUL ELLIS	27	Arkansas	Texas	160	37	1	0	3	20	0	0	123	.231	.317	.294	.205	12	.209
CHRIS FICK	26	Arkansas	Texas	456	108	15	1	16	61	2	3	351	.237	.327	.379	.235	47	.244
OSSIE GARCIA	22	Peoria	Midw	373	77	8	1	1	35	10	6	302	.206	.275	.241	.167	17	.183
SCARBOROUGH GREEN	22	Arkansas	Texas	305	54	3	2	3	35	14	5	255	.177	.262	.230	.161	13	.178
	22	St Petersburg	Flor	150	45	4	1	1	19	7	5	110	.300	.379	.360	.253	18	.277
ANDY HALL	22	Peoria	Midw	467	127	21	2	5	59	10	4	344	.272	.354	.358	.244	51	.270
RYAN HALL	24	St Petersburg	Flor	182	39	7	0	1	18	0	0	143	.214	.285	.269	.180	10	.191
DANN HOWITT	32	Louisville	AmA	145	37	6	1	3	17	4	2	110	.255	.333	.372	.239	15	.227
JOE JUMONVILLE	25	St Petersburg	Flor	104	16	3	1	0	8	0	0	88	.154	.214	.202	.088	1	.093
JASON LARIVIERE	22	Peoria	Midw	233	51	8	1	1	19	3	2	184	.219	.278	.275	.180	13	.199
	22	St Petersburg	Flor	150	46	3	0	4	16	1	1	105	.307	.373	.407	.265	19	.292
MIKE MATVEY	24	St Petersburg	Flor	430	110	9	2	2	43	2	3	323	.256	.323	.300	.210	33	.225
TRAVIS MCCLENDON	23	Peoria	Midw	160	26	6	0	0	13	1	2	136	.162	.225	.200	.098	2	.107
KEITH MCDONALD	23	St Petersburg	Flor	430	116	13	0	6	32	1	2	316	.270	.320	.342	.223	37	.243
JOE MCEWING	23	Arkansas	Texas	217	39	5	2	2	13	2	2	180	.180	.226	.249	.137	6	.148
RYAN MCHUGH	22	Peoria	Midw	247	58	11	1	6	25	4	2	191	.235	.305	.360	.223	22	.245
SHAWN MCNALLY	23	Peoria	Midw	448	111	10	2	8	44	5	4	341	.248	.315	.333	.218	38	.236
JUAN MUNOZ	22	Peoria	Midw	112	36	5	0	1	10	2	1	77	.321	.377	.393	.265	14	.292
	22	St Petersburg	Flor	348	86	11	2	2	34	3	3	265	.247	.314	.307	.209	26	.230
ISAIAS NUNEZ	22	Peoria	Midw	279	53	8	1	1	20	1	1	227	.190	.244	.237	.141	8	.156
LUIS ORDAZ	20	St Petersburg	Flor	442	121	10	1	5	29	6	3	324	.274	.318	.335	.222	38	.252
YUDITH OZORIO	21	St Petersburg	Flor	532	133	12	7	3	52	16	5	404	.250	.317	.316	.218	45	.244
JAVIER PAGES	24	St Petersburg	Flor	114	28	3	1	4	20	1	1	87	.246	.358	.395	.252	14	.268
MIGUEL RIVERA	22	Peoria	Midw	215	42	5	1	1	10	1	1	174	.195	.231	.242	.136	6	.151
BRIAN RUPP	24	Arkansas	Texas	356	96	11	1	4	32	4	3	263	.270	.330	.340	.227	32	.243
STEVE SANTUCCI	24	St Petersburg	Flor	363	83	5	1	8	25	2	3	283	.229	.278	.314	.194	23	.208
MIKE STEFANSKI	26	Louisville	AmA	128	26	5	1	2	12	1	2	103	.203	.271	.305	.185	8	.193
PAUL TORRES	25	Arkansas	Texas	314	75	8	0	10	40	1	1	240	.239	.325	.360	.229	30	.243
JOSE VELEZ	23	Arkansas	Texas	265	64	9	1	2	14	5	2	203	.242	.280	.306	.196	17	.213
RON WARNER	27	Arkansas	Texas	238	67	15	2	6	34	3	1	172	.282	.371	.437	.272	33	.279
CHRIS WIMMER	25	Louisville	AmA	351	85	9	2	2	20	10	2	268	.242	.283	.296	.197	23	.208
JOEL WOLFE	26	Arkansas	Texas	203	39	6	1	4	26	8	4	168	.192	.284	.291	.192	14	.200
JASON WOOLF	19	Peoria	Midw	378	88	10	4	2	44	13	6	296	.233	.313	.296	.208	29	.239

Player	Age	Team	Lge	IP	H	ER	HR	BB	K	ERA	W	L	H/9	HR/9	BB/9	K/9	KW
ARMANDO ALMANZA	23	Peoria	Midw	55.0	61	27	3	41	42	4.42	3	3	9.98	.49	6.71	6.87	.61
MATT ARRANDALE	26	Louisville	AmA	76.0	89	48	5	45	32	5.68	3	5	10.54	.59	5.33	3.79	-.07
COREY AVRARD	19	Peoria	Midw	94.7	131	78	8	75	64	7.42	2	9	12.45	.76	7.13	6.08	.25
MIKE BADOREK	27	Louisville	AmA	47.0	57	33	3	25	18	6.32	1	4	10.91	.57	4.79	3.45	-.05
ADAM BENES	23	Peoria	Midw	56.3	74	34	6	36	40	5.43	2	4	11.82	.96	5.75	6.39	.69
MIKE BUSBY	23	Louisville	AmA	70.0	95	55	10	57	45	7.07	2	6	12.21	1.29	7.33	5.79	.10
BRIAN CARPENTER	25	Arkansas	Texas	68.0	68	24	6	35	44	3.18	5	3	9.00	.79	4.63	5.82	.78
KEITH CONWAY	23	St Petersburg	Flor	62.7	75	19	2	35	49	2.73	5	2	10.77	.29	5.03	7.04	1.09
RICK CROUSHORE	25	Arkansas	Texas	98.7	120	68	17	67	70	6.20	3	8	10.95	1.55	6.11	6.39	.60
ROBERT DONNELLY	22	Peoria	Midw	53.3	57	27	4	31	47	4.56	3	3	9.62	.68	5.23	7.93	1.34
KEVIN FODERARO	23	Peoria	Midw	49.7	65	25	4	34	26	4.53	3	3	11.78	.72	6.16	4.71	.03
FRANK GARCIA	22	St Petersburg	Flor	28.3	42	12	2	24	18	3.81	2	1	13.34	.64	7.62	5.72	.00
KEITH GLAUBER	24	Peoria	Midw	57.0	66	31	3	34	50	4.89	2	4	10.42	.47	5.37	7.89	1.29
MATT GOLDEN	24	Arkansas	Texas	57.7	78	37	1	35	35	5.77	2	4	12.17	.16	5.46	5.46	.46
YATES HALL	23	St Petersburg	Flor	79.0	111	68	9	76	43	7.75	2	7	12.65	1.03	8.66	4.90	-.53
RICK HEISERMAN	23	St Petersburg	Flor	136.7	206	77	13	61	76	5.07	6	9	13.57	.86	4.02	5.00	.66
ERIK HILJUS	23	Arkansas	Texas	42.3	62	33	6	38	17	7.02	1	4	13.18	1.28	8.08	3.61	-.81
JOSE JIMENEZ	22	Peoria	Midw	148.7	205	83	9	69	81	5.02	7	10	12.41	.54	4.18	4.90	.59
CURTIS KING	25	St Petersburg	Flor	49.7	51	21	1	32	20	3.81	3	3	9.24	.18	5.80	3.62	-.24
JOHN KOWN	23	Peoria	Midw	67.3	103	35	3	26	29	4.68	3	4	13.77	.40	3.48	3.88	.42
JEFF MATULEVICH	26	Arkansas	Texas	54.7	51	30	5	38	42	4.94	2	4	8.40	.82	6.26	6.91	.74
BRIAN MAXCY	25	Louisville	AmA	59.0	70	33	4	42	44	5.03	3	4	10.68	.61	6.41	6.71	.64
KEVIN MCNEILL	25	St Petersburg	Flor	54.7	67	30	2	27	32	4.94	2	4	11.03	.33	4.45	5.27	.64
MANUEL MENDEZ	22	St Petersburg	Flor	60.7	76	28	5	48	39	4.15	3	4	11.27	.74	7.12	5.79	.15
JEFF MUTIS	29	Louisville	AmA	37.0	47	25	4	25	18	6.08	1	3	11.43	.97	6.08	4.38	-.06
CLIFF POLITTE	22	Peoria	Midw	133.7	137	50	11	62	95	3.37	9	6	9.22	.74	4.17	6.40	1.09
DAN PONTES	25	St Petersburg	Flor	105.7	149	63	12	50	53	5.37	4	8	12.69	1.02	4.26	4.51	.44
BRIAN REED	24	St Petersburg	Flor	61.0	67	28	3	46	55	4.13	3	4	9.89	.44	6.79	8.11	1.01
SCOTT SIMMONS	26	Louisville	AmA	95.3	107	49	16	48	48	4.63	5	6	10.10	1.51	4.53	4.53	.38
TOM URBANI	28	Louisville	AmA	42.0	44	18	5	18	22	3.86	3	2	9.43	1.07	3.86	4.71	.61
BEN VANRYN	24	Louisville	AmA	63.7	75	42	8	37	35	5.94	2	5	10.60	1.13	5.23	4.95	.34
MATTHEW WAGNER	21	Peoria	Midw	55.0	97	50	5	34	24	8.18	1	5	15.87	.82	5.56	3.93	-.08
CLINT WEIBL	21	Peoria	Midw	26.3	34	17	3	9	13	5.81	1	2	11.62	1.03	3.08	4.44	.71
TRAVIS WELCH	22	Peoria	Midw	35.7	39	17	5	22	21	4.29	2	2	9.84	1.26	5.55	5.30	.38
MIKE WINDHAM	24	St Petersburg	Flor	126.0	187	67	7	79	63	4.79	6	8	13.36	.50	5.64	4.50	.09

St. Louis Cardinals

Colorado Rockies

Cognitive dissonance is a very strange thing. We humans are really horrible about looking at ourselves and the way we make decisions. We pretty much act arbitrarily, than rationalize our decisions after the fact in an attempt to maintain our illusions of rationality. You'll have a hard time finding clearer examples of this than any two random ESPN or Fox talking heads discussing the Colorado Rockies. They'll bitch and moan about how easy it is to hit in Coors Field, saying things like "That's a fly ball out in any other ballpark, Tim McCarver." An inning and half later, they'll go into their four-minute monologue on why Ellis Burks should win the MVP. Do they just think that we're not paying attention? Do they really believe it?

Let me make one thing clear: I like Coors Field. I don't think it's an affront to baseball in the slightest, I don't think it cheapens the game and I don't think they should use a different baseball at high altitudes. I haven't been there, but it looks gorgeous and the fans there really seem to have a good time. Everyone I know that's been there says it's a great place to watch a ballgame. But there's no way you can possibly examine the Colorado Rockies without taking into the account the massive way in which Coors Field and the altitude in Denver affects the context of player performance.

Put another way, these guys actually have pretty decent pitching and just yucky hitting.

The context in which the Rockies operate is a lot different than that which other clubs operate in, so it makes sense to at least consider whether or not other ways of designing and building a franchise might be better. The orthodoxy among GMs has been basically to avoid planning at all costs, and make a run at the pennant when your job's at stake. Stathead analysts, on the other hand, have generally espoused pushing for a quantity of young players to always be on hand so you can take advantage of their peak years. It's entirely possible that an organization in Colorado may have to be run completely differently. It may be years before we really have any idea.

McMorris and crew are in a very interesting situation. They're pretty much rolling in dough, and they've got nothing in the farm system to speak of outside of a couple of B level prospects like Todd Helton. Usually, buying into a free agent market is a losing strategy–free agents have already seen their prime performance but haven't seen their prime paychecks. It might make sense, in the short term, to pay the big money for a free agent or two and stock the farm system for the future. The Rockies don't have the kind of talent in the minors that a Florida has, but they've got dough to spend and in the NL West, 88 wins could be a runaway victor in 1997.

There's also the issue of adding value. Run a few players through the organization, inflate their offensive stats and see if you can get other GMs to bite. Jim Frey was employed for a lot of years, and most GMs do underestimate the effects of park effects in general, and Coors Field specifically.

One thing is certain: The fans in Colorado have been exceptionally enthusiastic and supportive of their team, to a level which embarrasses me as an A's fan. They deserve a champion, and I find myself rooting for the unlikely success of futureless waifs like Galarraga, Castilla and Bichette. They'll be in the NL West hunt in 1997, along with the other huggable elves in the division.

There is no hitter on this team that can reasonable be expected to be one of the top thirty hitters in baseball next year. Not one. There are several pitchers that can be expected to be among the best though, particularly in the bullpen. Steve Reed leaps to mind. Colorado inflates offense by roughly 68% over an average NL park, and more than that over a median park. It makes average hitters look not just good, but like superstars. The Rockies did demonstrate an ability to take advantage of their home park to a greater extent than their opponents, and that has real value. I would also expect that trend to continue; if you play half your games in a place where fastballs drop less and curveballs break less, you're going to have a hard time recalibrating for road trips.

What's on the farm? Not a lot. Todd Helton, a few Matt Stairs/Geronimo Berroa types, an overrated shortstop prospect and some bad coaches. Neifi Perez is likely to take the shortstop job if they can unload Walt Weiss, and Helton will likely be with the big club to stay by midseason or so. The bullpen is as strong as ever, despite the need to use it heavily because of all those extra batters. Bullpen depth means more here, and you can make a good argument that the Rockies will be at a permanent disadvantage because of the need to carry another two pitchers.

I think their primary disadvantage right now comes from weak management. Baylor bullied his way into the managerial job, and although he's done a hell of a job handling the pitching staff, the hitters just haven't developed particularly well once you get past the emperor's clothes.

There is still time for this organization to avoid becoming Cubs West. The Cubs haven't learned a thing about park effects in 80 years; the Rockies have to be a bit quicker.

ERIC ANTHONY **OF**   **1968** **Age 29**

Year	Team	Lge	AB	H	DB	TP	HR	BB	SB	CS	OUT	BA	OBA	SA	EQA	EQR	Peak
1993	Houston	NL	497	128	18	2	17	57	3	4	373	.258	.334	.404	.245	56	.259
1994	Seattle	AL	262	62	14	1	10	23	5	2	202	.237	.298	.412	.236	27	.244
1995	Cincinnati	NL	137	38	4	0	6	15	2	1	100	.277	.349	.438	.263	18	.268
1996	Cincinnati	NL	126	32	5	0	8	24	0	1	95	.254	.373	.484	.278	19	.281
1996	Colorado	NL	61	13	2	0	3	10	0	1	49	.213	.324	.393	.232	6	.237
1997	*Colorado*	*NL*	*172*	*51*	*8*	*0*	*9*	*20*	*0*	*0*	*129*	*.297*	*.370*	*.500*	*.262*	*23*	

Hit the lottery. A hitter traded to Colorado. It could make him a rich man if he gets any playing time. Anthony is a serviceable fourth outfielder with some pop, but he never took that step up to stardom. Could slug .500 in Coors Field, but that's true of almost every player in this book, a third of the Manhattan phone directory and roughly a fifth of Arlington National Cemetery.

JASON BATES **UT**   **1971** **Age 26**

Year	Team	Lge	AB	H	DB	TP	HR	BB	SB	CS	OUT	BA	OBA	SA	EQA	EQR	Peak
1993	Colo. Springs	PCL	438	95	11	1	11	41	5	4	347	.217	.284	.322	.200	31	.220
1994	Colo. Springs	PCL	443	102	12	1	9	55	3	3	344	.230	.315	.323	.213	36	.232
1995	Colorado	NL	318	75	15	3	7	44	2	4	247	.236	.329	.368	.231	32	.248
1996	Colorado	NL	158	28	5	1	1	24	1	1	131	.177	.286	.241	.167	7	.175
1997	*Colorado*	*NL*	*131*	*35*	*4*	*0*	*3*	*14*	*4*	*1*	*97*	*.267*	*.338*	*.366*	*.224*	*12*	

In the 1996 version of this tome, I wrote about Bates: "The trend is up, and as long as a guy keeps getting better, you gotta keep running him out there." He's stopped now, and getting under 200 PA at age 25 doesn't do a lot for one's development. No prospect; get used to it in this organization.

DANTE BICHETTE **LF/RF**   **1964** **Age 33**

Year	Team	Lge	AB	H	DB	TP	HR	BB	SB	CS	OUT	BA	OBA	SA	EQA	EQR	Peak
1993	Colorado	NL	533	153	35	3	20	35	11	6	386	.287	.331	.477	.266	71	.265
1994	Colorado	NL	481	140	25	2	27	26	19	7	348	.291	.327	.520	.277	70	.271
1995	Colorado	NL	569	177	27	2	37	29	10	7	399	.311	.344	.561	.291	91	.280
1996	Colorado	NL	622	174	31	2	27	50	22	10	458	.280	.333	.466	.265	83	.252
1997	*Colorado*	*NL*	*665*	*208*	*30*	*5*	*31*	*28*	*36*	*11*	*468*	*.313*	*.341*	*.513*	*.267*	*86*	

A league average hitter. That's better than I expected. You gotta be happy for this guy. The guy he was swapped for, Kevin Reimer, was probably the better hitter and probably still is. Bichette's put up one genuinely good year and he's rich. In addition, he makes all the right noises about wanting to improve, and he looked like he was trying to be more selective. Don't get me wrong—this is not someone I'd want to acquire if I were a GM, but Bichette is durable, a good baserunner and an average hitter. Basically, he's Joe Carter with cooler hair.

ELLIS BURKS **CF/LF**   **1965** **Age 32**

Year	Team	Lge	AB	H	DB	TP	HR	BB	SB	CS	OUT	BA	OBA	SA	EQA	EQR	Peak
1993	Chi. White Sox	AL	507	146	24	4	21	64	7	7	368	.288	.368	.475	.277	74	.279
1994	Colorado	NL	149	46	7	2	13	18	3	1	104	.309	.383	.644	.322	31	.321
1995	Colorado	NL	274	66	7	4	13	41	5	2	210	.241	.340	.438	.258	35	.252
1996	Colorado	NL	602	188	35	6	35	65	24	5	419	.312	.379	.565	.308	110	.297
1997	*Colorado*	*NL*	*625*	*198*	*35*	*7*	*30*	*83*	*25*	*10*	*437*	*.317*	*.397*	*.539*	*.289*	*98*	

MVP? Not in this reality. There's a weird phenomenon going on in the media when it comes to Rockies' hitters. The talking heads usually say something like "Well, you know, it's easy to hit in Coors, but wow! Here's another guy with 40 HR, and you don't do that without talent." Vinny Castilla is proof that yes, on occasion you do. The media doesn't understand just how vast the effects of Coors Field are. Burks is a good ballplayer. He's not clearly in the top half of NL outfielders.

PETE CASTELLANO   OF   1970   Age 27

Year	Team	Lge	AB	H	DB	TP	HR	BB	SB	CS	OUT	BA	OBA	SA	EQA	EQR	Peak
1993	Colo. Springs	PCL	295	77	11	1	10	32	2	3	221	.261	.333	.407	.246	33	.266
1993	Colorado	NL	70	11	1	0	3	9	1	1	60	.157	.253	.300	.174	4	.189
1994	Colo. Springs	PCL	115	34	8	1	3	12	1	1	82	.296	.362	.461	.273	16	.292
1995	Colo. Springs	PCL	326	75	13	1	9	24	1	0	251	.230	.283	.359	.213	26	.224
1996	Colo. Springs	PCL	357	108	20	1	13	38	0	1	250	.303	.370	.473	.279	52	.291
1997	Colorado	NL	470	150	36	3	22	47	0	0	320	.319	.381	.549	.286	70	

A comparable hitter to the other Colorado outfielders other than Walker; good enough to start in the majors. Defense is suspect, but I'd rather pay him than Dante Bichette. Even if Castellano doesn't hit quite as well, which isn't likely, he's a heck of a lot cheaper and that money can go towards a couple dozen prospects.

VINNY CASTILLA   3B   1968   Age 29

Year	Team	Lge	AB	H	DB	TP	HR	BB	SB	CS	OUT	BA	OBA	SA	EQA	EQR	Peak
1993	Colorado	NL	333	77	8	4	9	18	2	4	260	.231	.271	.360	.206	25	.217
1994	Colo. Springs	PCL	76	15	3	1	1	6	0	0	61	.197	.256	.303	.178	4	.188
1994	Colorado	NL	130	42	9	1	3	8	2	1	89	.323	.362	.477	.280	18	.289
1995	Colorado	NL	519	146	25	2	29	35	1	6	379	.281	.327	.505	.268	70	.274
1996	Colorado	NL	618	168	21	0	36	41	5	2	452	.272	.317	.481	.262	79	.265
1997	Colorado	NL	644	178	28	0	37	36	6	4	470	.276	.315	.492	.247	71	

Interesting ballplayer. Reminds me a physics class. Why? A stone at rest has very little energy, but put it at altitude and it's got lots of potential energy. That's what Coors Field buys the Rockies. Castilla's basically a league average hitter or worse, but he looks a lot better than he really is. If the Rockies' management team can start leveraging that perception into real value, the Rockies could really build a dynasty.

ALAN COCKRELL   OF   1963   Age 34

Year	Team	Lge	AB	H	DB	TP	HR	BB	SB	CS	OUT	BA	OBA	SA	EQA	EQR	Peak
1993	Charlotte-NC	Inter	282	77	10	1	8	24	0	0	205	.273	.330	.401	.245	31	.240
1994	Colo. Springs	PCL	261	67	8	1	10	27	1	1	195	.257	.326	.410	.245	29	.237
1995	Colo. Springs	PCL	344	92	10	1	12	30	0	2	254	.267	.326	.407	.243	37	.231
1996	Colo. Springs	PCL	354	96	15	2	13	48	1	1	259	.271	.358	.435	.264	47	.251
1997	Colorado	NL	372	109	14	1	18	42	0	1	264	.293	.365	.481	.262	46	

Included as an illustration. That projection for Cockrell, without park adjustment, is .264/.344/.425; that's just barely short of league average. That's a huge difference. There's nothing wrong, per se, with having an extreme park like this; it just demands a shift in the way teams think about their strategy and tactics. Considering that very few clubs have done that before, I'm wondering whether or not Coors will be enough to make management come around.

STEVE DECKER   C   1966   Age 31

Year	Team	Lge	AB	H	DB	TP	HR	BB	SB	CS	OUT	BA	OBA	SA	EQA	EQR	Peak
1994	Edmonton	PCL	250	86	10	0	11	25	0	1	165	.344	.404	.516	.304	42	.307
1995	Florida	NL	136	32	2	1	3	20	1	0	104	.235	.333	.331	.226	13	.225
1996	San Francisco	NL	124	29	0	0	1	17	0	0	95	.234	.326	.258	.197	8	.193

Jerry Willard: The Next Generation. Okay, maybe not quite that good. But comparable. Got caught in the semi-prospect trap, and rotted away instead of developed. It happens.

JUSTIN DRIZOS   UT   1974   Age 23

Year	Team	Lge	AB	H	DB	TP	HR	BB	SB	CS	OUT	BA	OBA	SA	EQA	EQR	Peak
1995	Portland-OR	Nwern	242	45	8	1	3	40	2	1	198	.186	.301	.264	.186	15	.210
1996	Asheville	S Atl	461	107	12	1	14	54	3	1	355	.232	.313	.354	.223	42	.247
1997	Colorado	NL	355	95	18	1	16	58	4	3	263	.268	.370	.459	.257	44	

Be warned: The Vladimir projection system has trouble with players who play in Asheville. Drizos won't hit that well, and beating up on that competition at that age isn't all that terribly impressive. He probably wouldn't have gotten any ink in this book if he were in any other organization. Most of the Rockie prospects are roughly as impressive as Dinner Theatre Othello [tm].

ANGEL ECHEVARRIA OF 1971 Age 26

Year	Team	Lge	AB	H	DB	TP	HR	BB	SB	CS	OUT	BA	OBA	SA	EQA	EQR	Peak
1993	Cent. Valley	Calif	357	78	8	1	5	30	3	2	281	.218	.279	.289	.186	21	.205
1994	Cent. Valley	Calif	193	52	5	0	5	7	1	1	142	.269	.295	.373	.223	17	.242
1994	New Haven	East	210	50	3	0	7	13	2	2	162	.238	.283	.352	.210	16	.228
1995	New Haven	East	473	144	18	1	23	50	6	2	331	.304	.371	.493	.286	72	.306
1996	Colo. Springs	PCL	409	124	11	1	15	36	3	2	287	.303	.360	.445	.269	54	.284
1997	*Colorado*	*NL*	*624*	*198*	*33*	*3*	*27*	*50*	*6*	*4*	*430*	*.317*	*.368*	*.510*	*.272*	*83*	

Middle of the road defensive outfielder who would look like a star in Coors. The Rox have about four of these guys at various levels. If they're smart, they'll start converting them into value. It's more likely that they'll start turning them into Turner Ward and Dann Howitt. In marketing, we might call this "adding value." Well, perhaps not.

JAY GAINER 1B 1967 Age 30

Year	Team	Lge	AB	H	DB	TP	HR	BB	SB	CS	OUT	BA	OBA	SA	EQA	EQR	Peak
1993	Colo. Springs	PCL	285	70	6	0	9	20	2	1	216	.246	.295	.361	.219	24	.228
1994	Colo. Springs	PCL	275	55	8	1	7	24	2	2	222	.200	.264	.313	.186	17	.191
1995	Colo. Springs	PCL	349	88	8	1	20	40	2	2	263	.252	.329	.453	.256	44	.259
1996	Colo. Springs	PCL	330	69	9	0	12	35	5	1	262	.209	.285	.345	.210	27	.208

Some random schmuck on Usenet was raving about this guy two years ago. One would assume that his medication's worn off by now. Very few organizations have a burning need for a first baseman who hits .234 in Colorado Springs. A comparable number: VFW members yearning for a Richard Simmons Menthol Rub.

ANDRES GALARRAGA 1B 1961 Age 36

Year	Team	Lge	AB	H	DB	TP	HR	BB	SB	CS	OUT	BA	OBA	SA	EQA	EQR	Peak
1993	Colorado	NL	466	161	28	3	21	30	2	3	308	.345	.385	.554	.305	79	.290
1994	Colorado	NL	415	128	15	0	30	25	7	3	290	.308	.348	.561	.293	68	.279
1995	Colorado	NL	546	139	23	2	28	37	9	2	409	.255	.302	.458	.251	65	.239
1996	Colorado	NL	615	168	29	2	41	46	13	7	454	.273	.324	.527	.274	90	.261
1997	*Colorado*	*NL*	*618*	*183*	*27*	*2*	*34*	*33*	*8*	*5*	*182*	*.296*	*.333*	*.526*	*.252*	*85*	

Has resurrected his career nicely, going from complete and total waste of a roster spot to just a partial waste of a roster spot. A first baseman who hits near the league average isn't a strength, Mr. Gebhard. One is truly terrified to think what someone like Sam Horn would have done with the same opportunity. Andres is a player who will fervently push a team towards mediocrity. That said, if I played standard rotisserie ball, I'd probably grab him if I had the chance. He stays healthy, and the OBPs in front of him are going to be 35 points higher than they would be elsewhere. Yet one more reason to play Scoresheet Baseball instead. (This gratuitous plug not paid for – I'm just a satisfied client.)

DERRICK GIBSON OF 1975 Age 22

Year	Team	Lge	AB	H	DB	TP	HR	BB	SB	CS	OUT	BA	OBA	SA	EQA	EQR	Peak
1995	Asheville	S Atl	520	140	9	3	24	24	14	7	387	.269	.301	.437	.245	58	.279
1996	New Haven	East	460	113	16	2	14	28	4	6	353	.246	.289	.380	.220	40	.246
1997	*Colorado*	*NL*	*500*	*142*	*28*	*4*	*26*	*31*	*13*	*6*	*358*	*.284*	*.326*	*.532*	*.251*	*82*	

One of the four best hitters in the organization, along with Walker, Helton and Burks. A year away. Will be a pretty good hitter before figuring in Coors. And Coors has never seen a really good hitter in the home purples. Has a chance to be a great hitter, but he's not a grade A prospect. When Colorado has a grade A prospect, "A great pall will hang o'er the skies, and the 61st shall smite and be smote." – John 3:36.

TODD HELTON 1974 1B Age 23

Year	Team	Lge	AB	H	DB	TP	HR	BB	SB	CS	OUT	BA	OBA	SA	EQA	EQR	Peak
1995	Asheville	S Atl	210	45	7	1	1	20	0	0	165	.214	.283	.271	.179	11	.200
1996	New Haven	East	334	108	18	2	7	46	2	3	229	.323	.405	.452	.288	51	.318
1996	Colo. Springs	PCL	70	22	2	1	2	10	0	0	48	.314	.400	.457	.289	11	.321
1997	*Colorado*	*NL*	*602*	*186*	*31*	*5*	*15*	*71*	*6*	*2*	*416*	*.309*	*.382*	*.452*	*.279*		

The next hitter to take a shot at .400. A large portion of the reason is his talent. Be careful; this is exactly the sort of player who is likely to be overrated. Mark Grace is a comparable ballplayer, and a good bet in terms of a career path, except Helton will hit for a higher average and is more likely to quit mid-career rather than appear in a film with Jim Belushi.

DAVID KENNEDY   **1B**   **1971**   **Age 26**

Year	Team	Lge	AB	H	DB	TP	HR	BB	SB	CS	OUT	BA	OBA	SA	EQA	EQR	Peak
1993	Boise	Nwern	261	54	7	1	7	45	1	0	207	.207	.324	.322	.217	23	.240
1995	New Haven	East	503	156	14	1	23	43	3	1	348	.310	.364	.479	.281	73	.300
1996	Colo. Springs	PCL	330	75	15	0	11	34	1	1	256	.227	.299	.373	.222	30	.234
1997	*Colorado*	*NL*	*386*	*116*	*25*	*1*	*21*	*43*	*3*	*1*	*271*	*.301*	*.371*	*.534*	*.278*	*55*	

A good enough hitter to have a major league career. This is, of course, contingent on Commissioner Selig's plan to move all the franchises to Denver.

QUINTON McCRACKEN   **OF**   **1970**   **Age 27**

Year	Team	Lge	AB	H	DB	TP	HR	BB	SB	CS	OUT	BA	OBA	SA	EQA	EQR	Peak
1993	Cent. Valley	Calif	481	115	12	4	2	55	24	8	374	.239	.317	.293	.213	39	.232
1994	New Haven	East	559	145	20	3	5	44	22	10	424	.259	.313	.333	.222	49	.237
1995	New Haven	East	231	82	10	3	2	19	17	5	154	.355	.404	.450	.295	36	.312
1995	Colo. Springs	PCL	235	73	10	3	4	23	12	4	166	.311	.372	.430	.274	33	.289
1996	Colorado	NL	278	71	11	4	3	34	12	5	212	.255	.337	.356	.238	29	.247
1997	*Colorado*	*NL*	*248*	*71*	*15*	*6*	*2*	*21*	*27*	*5*	*182*	*.286*	*.342*	*.419*	*.252*	*29*	

This should be McCracken's peak year. Don't blink.

JAYHAWK OWENS   **C**   **1969**   **Age 28**

Year	Team	Lge	AB	H	DB	TP	HR	BB	SB	CS	OUT	BA	OBA	SA	EQA	EQR	Peak
1993	Colo. Springs	PCL	169	44	5	1	6	18	3	2	127	.260	.332	.408	.247	19	.264
1993	Colorado	NL	85	16	3	0	3	7	1	0	69	.188	.250	.329	.189	5	.203
1994	Colo. Springs	PCL	249	55	8	3	5	30	2	2	196	.221	.305	.337	.213	21	.224
1995	Colo. Springs	PCL	215	56	8	2	11	19	2	1	160	.260	.321	.470	.259	27	.269
1996	Colorado	NL	178	37	8	1	3	27	3	1	142	.208	.312	.315	.211	15	.217

Owens is kind of the poor man's Scott Bradley. He could actually hit much better than that .239 average; it could surge up to .250 or so, with all the power and plate discipline you've come to expect. Accept no substitutes.

NEIFI PEREZ   **SS**   **1975**   **Age 22**

Year	Team	Lge	AB	H	DB	TP	HR	BB	SB	CS	OUT	BA	OBA	SA	EQA	EQR	Peak
1993	Bend	Nwern	302	64	6	1	3	7	6	5	243	.212	.230	.268	.154	11	.180
1994	Cent. Valley	Calif	511	105	13	4	1	26	4	3	409	.205	.244	.252	.151	18	.175
1995	New Haven	East	438	110	23	1	7	22	3	1	329	.251	.287	.356	.215	35	.244
1996	Colo. Springs	PCL	560	156	22	6	8	23	13	8	412	.279	.307	.382	.232	53	.260
1997	*Colorado*	*NL*	*560*	*151*	*38*	*7*	*11*	*30*	*14*	*8*	*417*	*.270*	*.307*	*.421*	*.225*	*50*	

Hit .316 at Colorado Springs, which doesn't really tell you much. Hasn't developed much in terms of average, power, plate discipline, baserunning or defense. Had better get his ass in gear if he wants to stick in the bigs. He's basically Ozzie Guillen right now, but there's not going to be two teams stupid enough to run someone like that out there every day. Oh yeah, the Mets.

BEN PETRICK   **OF**   **1977**   **Age 20**

Year	Team	Lge	AB	H	DB	TP	HR	BB	SB	CS	OUT	BA	OBA	SA	EQA	EQR	Peak
1996	Asheville	S Atl	469	95	11	1	11	59	7	4	378	.203	.292	.301	.196	32	.226

Showed good plate discipline at age 19 in Asheville and hit the ball hard. If he can bump the batting average up one notch this year while retaining the walks and power, he'll be a good prospect. If he can do it in three years, he'll be an OK prospect.

JEFF REED   **C**   **1963**   **Age 34**

Year	Team	Lge	AB	H	DB	TP	HR	BB	SB	CS	OUT	BA	OBA	SA	EQA	EQR	Peak
1993	San Francisco	NL	124	35	1	0	7	17	0	1	90	.282	.369	.460	.273	17	.267
1994	San Francisco	NL	104	19	2	0	1	12	0	0	85	.183	.267	.231	.151	4	.147
1995	San Francisco	NL	117	33	2	0	0	22	0	0	84	.282	.396	.299	.245	12	.232
1996	Colorado	NL	336	84	15	1	7	45	1	2	254	.250	.339	.363	.236	34	.224
1997	*Colorado*	*NL*	*226*	*61*	*7*	*1*	*6*	*25*	*0*	*3*	*168*	*.270*	*.343*	*.389*	*.224*	*20*	

Competent backup catcher with offense a little better than Matheny from the left side. Career lights getting dim; Reed's about where Mike LaValliere was three years ago—two years away from lots of golf.

JOHN VANDERWAL　　**PH**　　　**1966**　**Age 31**

Year	Team	Lge	AB	H	DB	TP	HR	BB	SB	CS	OUT	BA	OBA	SA	EQA	EQR	Peak
1993	Montreal	NL	220	53	7	3	6	30	5	2	169	.241	.332	.382	.241	24	.246
1994	Colorado	NL	110	26	3	0	5	17	2	1	85	.236	.339	.400	.247	13	.249
1995	Colorado	NL	100	32	5	1	5	16	1	1	69	.320	.414	.540	.310	19	.308
1996	Colorado	NL	149	33	4	2	4	20	1	2	118	.221	.314	.356	.220	13	.217
1997	*Colorado*	*NL*	*142*	*40*	*10*	*1*	*6*	*21*	*0*	*4*	*106*	*.282*	*.374*	*.493*	*.259*	*18*	

No worse a hitter than Dante Bichette, really. Slapped with the Dave Hansen/Dwight Smith label, which is more difficult to shake than that burning sensation one gets while urinating. Or is that just me?

EDGARD VELAZQUEZ　　**OF**　　**1976**　**Age 21**

Year	Team	Lge	AB	H	DB	TP	HR	BB	SB	CS	OUT	BA	OBA	SA	EQA	EQR	Peak
1994	Asheville	S Atl	456	95	11	1	9	20	4	4	365	.208	.242	.296	.170	22	.198
1995	Salem-VA	Caro	505	136	19	3	12	39	5	4	373	.269	.322	.390	.238	52	.275
1996	New Haven	East	502	144	22	2	18	48	4	1	359	.287	.349	.446	.266	65	.303
1997	*Colorado*	*NL*	*579*	*185*	*33*	*4*	*18*	*50*	*11*	*6*	*400*	*.320*	*.374*	*.484*	*.268*	*74*	

This is probably my favorite Rockies prospect, which is something like having a favorite episode of "Who's the Boss?" Edgard has moved up steadily, gotten slightly better at all facets of the game each year and hasn't made any bad trade-offs along the way. A lot of times, a guy's average might jump up at the expense of his power, or his selectivity might jump at the expense of batting average. Velazquez sure looks like a great hitter to me, both in person and on paper. Helton will hit for a higher average and get more press, but I think Velazquez will be the better offensive player.

LARRY WALKER　　**RF/CF**　　**1967**　**Age 30**

Year	Team	Lge	AB	H	DB	TP	HR	BB	SB	CS	OUT	BA	OBA	SA	EQA	EQR	Peak
1993	Montreal	NL	507	141	22	4	25	87	25	6	372	.278	.384	.485	.290	84	.302
1994	Montreal	NL	402	131	37	2	21	53	14	4	275	.326	.404	.585	.320	79	.327
1995	Colorado	NL	487	136	25	3	33	53	12	2	353	.279	.350	.546	.291	80	.293
1996	Colorado	NL	268	67	15	2	16	22	14	2	203	.250	.307	.500	.268	38	.265
1997	*Colorado*	*NL*	*603*	*196*	*36*	*4*	*36*	*48*	*43*	*6*	*413*	*.325*	*.375*	*.577*	*.297*	*99*	

Strained a hip flexor while opening a jar of Smucker's strawberry preserves during Halloween. He won't miss any time, but he'll be playing through an injury. Walker is still capable of having an MVP year, but it seems like he's always playing through something nagging, like a telemarketer or something. I think he'll be healthy this year and have a big season; look for him to dramatically outperform the projection above, or to match it if he ends up on a new team.

WALT WEISS　　**SS**　　　**1964**　**Age 33**

Year	Team	Lge	AB	H	DB	TP	HR	BB	SB	CS	OUT	BA	OBA	SA	EQA	EQR	Peak
1993	Florida	NL	513	137	14	2	1	86	6	2	378	.267	.372	.308	.237	52	.236
1994	Colorado	NL	422	99	11	3	1	61	10	5	328	.235	.331	.282	.210	33	.206
1995	Colorado	NL	422	96	15	2	1	100	11	2	328	.227	.375	.280	.232	43	.225
1996	Colorado	NL	509	125	14	2	7	83	7	2	386	.246	.351	.322	.232	50	.221
1997	*Colorado*	*NL*	*483*	*129*	*19*	*3*	*2*	*94*	*11*	*4*	*358*	*.267*	*.386*	*.331*	*.233*	*47*	

The best defensive shortstop I've ever seen, circa 1988. Injuries have robbed him of what was once absurd range. As his defensive skills have deteriorated, he's become a smarter ballplayer, and I wish him well. I don't think he'd help many teams right now as a starting shortstop, but he's learned to draw a bunch of walks, and right there he's better than guys like Bordick or DiSarcina.

ERIC YOUNG　　**2B**　　　**1967**　**Age 30**

Year	Team	Lge	AB	H	DB	TP	HR	BB	SB	CS	OUT	BA	OBA	SA	EQA	EQR	Peak
1993	Colorado	NL	487	118	14	5	4	68	31	14	383	.242	.335	.316	.227	47	.237
1994	Colorado	NL	228	59	10	1	7	41	15	6	175	.259	.372	.404	.265	32	.272
1995	Colorado	NL	361	104	17	7	6	51	25	9	266	.288	.376	.424	.274	52	.276
1996	Colorado	NL	558	160	19	3	7	52	37	15	413	.287	.348	.369	.249	64	.247
1997	*Colorado*	*NL*	*463*	*141*	*20*	*5*	*9*	*78*	*59*	*21*	*343*	*.305*	*.405*	*.428*	*.271*	*65*	

Colorado learned the wrong lesson here. They learned "Eric Young is valuable." The real lesson was "second basemen this good are pretty easy to find." A bad basestealer, but a step up from the Joey Cora detritus of the world at the plate. A potentially disastrous free agent signing soon. Much more valuable in rotisserie than in real life, not unlike gutted plucked chickens.

GARVIN ALSTON   **RRP**   **1972**   **Age 25**

YR	TEAM	Lge	IP	H	ER	HR	BB	K	ERA	W	L	H/9	HR/9	BB/9	K/9	KW
1993	Cent. Valley	Calif	103.7	127	67	11	78	62	5.82	4	8	11.03	.95	6.77	5.38	.10
1994	Cent. Valley	Calif	77.7	102	48	9	53	54	5.56	3	6	11.82	1.04	6.14	6.26	.55
1995	New Haven	East	62.0	57	23	2	32	56	3.34	4	3	8.27	.29	4.65	8.13	1.55
1996	Colo. Springs	PCL	32.7	43	18	3	31	29	4.96	2	2	11.85	.83	8.54	7.99	.53

K/W rate certainly didn't justify his callup. He does strike a lot of guys out, but if he becomes a successful pitcher in the bigs it'll be a surprise.

ROGER BAILEY   **RSP**   **1971**   **Age 26**

YR	TEAM	Lge	IP	H	ER	HR	BB	K	ERA	W	L	H/9	HR/9	BB/9	K/9	KW
1993	Cent. Valley	Calif	99.0	142	64	9	61	58	5.82	4	7	12.91	.82	5.55	5.27	.37
1994	New Haven	East	143.3	185	73	10	76	82	4.58	7	9	11.62	.63	4.77	5.15	.52
1995	Colo. Springs	PCL	15.7	13	6	0	10	6	3.45	1	1	7.47	.00	5.74	3.45	-.29
1995	Colorado	NL	80.7	77	36	8	45	29	4.02	4	5	8.59	.89	5.02	3.24	-.18
1996	Colo. Springs	PCL	46.0	56	27	5	25	22	5.28	2	3	10.96	.98	4.89	4.30	.21
1996	Colorado	NL	83.3	82	46	6	57	38	4.97	4	5	8.86	.65	6.16	4.10	-.17

Yes, if there's one thing that history has taught us, it's that long-term success in the big leagues is best accomplished by walking more guys than you strike out. Yessiree.

BOBBY BEVEL   **LRP**   **1974**   **Age 23**

YR	TEAM	Lge	IP	H	ER	HR	BB	K	ERA	W	L	H/9	HR/9	BB/9	K/9	KW
1995	Portland, OR	Nwern	23.3	32	15	0	24	14	5.79	1	2	12.34	.00	9.26	5.40	-.51
1996	Asheville	S Atl	56.3	85	30	5	43	33	4.79	2	4	13.58	.80	6.87	5.27	.04

Bevel posted a pretty decent season at Asheville against significantly younger competition. He'll need to advance quickly to have a career.

HEATH BOST   **RRP**   **1975**   **Age 22**

YR	TEAM	Lge	IP	H	ER	HR	BB	K	ERA	W	L	H/9	HR/9	BB/9	K/9	KW
1995	Asheville	S Atl	21.0	26	7	2	5	10	3.00	1	1	11.14	.86	2.14	4.29	.89
1995	Portland, OR	Nwern	14.3	21	7	2	0	14	4.40	1	1	13.19	1.26	.00	8.79	2.93
1996	Asheville	S Atl	67.3	64	14	4	28	55	1.87	6	1	8.55	.53	3.74	7.35	1.51

What we have here, folks, is a monster. Hard thrower who throws a very heavy ball. Walked 16 unintentionally in 82 innings last year, allowing only 50 hits and striking out 109. Hasn't been overworked, so his arm isn't likely to fall off in the very near future. Will probably hit the majors to stay later this year, and he's pitched roughly like Troy Percival for the past couple of years. Absolute Grade A Prospect.

MARK BROWNSON   **RBP**   **1975**   **Age 22**

YR	TEAM	Lge	IP	H	ER	HR	BB	K	ERA	W	L	H/9	HR/9	BB/9	K/9	KW
1995	Asheville	S Atl	84.0	137	60	15	45	54	6.43	3	6	14.68	1.61	4.82	5.79	.72
1995	Salem, VA	Caro	14.3	17	8	0	13	7	5.02	1	1	10.67	.00	8.16	4.40	-.58
1996	New Haven	East	132.0	166	74	11	56	115	5.05	6	9	11.32	.75	3.82	7.84	1.66

Another talented Rockie pitching prospect. Good K rates, K/W ratios. I've seen this guy pitch, and he reminds me a bit of Mark Gubicza. Slight of build, mechanics are apparently very solid. Grade B prospect.

ALBERT BUSTILLOS   **RSP**   **1968**   **Age 29**

YR	TEAM	Lge	IP	H	ER	HR	BB	K	ERA	W	L	H/9	HR/9	BB/9	K/9	KW
1993	Albuquerque	PCL	28.0	32	11	4	16	13	3.54	2	1	10.29	1.29	5.14	4.18	.11
1994	San Antonio	Texas	58.3	92	32	4	24	25	4.94	2	4	14.19	.62	3.70	3.86	.36
1994	Albuquerque	PCL	40.0	52	27	4	18	21	6.07	1	3	11.70	.90	4.05	4.72	.56
1995	Colo. Springs	PCL	125.3	137	60	16	43	69	4.31	6	8	9.84	1.15	3.09	4.95	.88
1996	Colo. Springs	PCL	136.3	160	72	24	57	77	4.75	6	9	10.56	1.58	3.76	5.08	.75

Journeyman minor leaguer out of the Dodger organization. Probably good enough to bounce around the vaunted Oakland/Detroit circuit as a fifth starter, but so is Senor Wences. 'Zalright.

MIKE DeJEAN　　　**RRP**　　　**1971**　　**Age 26**

YR	TEAM	Lge	IP	H	ER	HR	BB	K	ERA	W	L	H/9	HR/9	BB/9	K/9	KW
1993	Greensboro	S Atl	15.0	28	14	2	11	9	8.40	0	2	16.80	1.20	6.60	5.40	.15
1994	Tampa	Flor	30.3	47	17	2	17	17	5.04	1	2	13.95	.59	5.04	5.04	.42
1994	Albany, NY	East	22.3	26	14	1	19	10	5.64	1	1	10.48	.40	7.66	4.03	-.57
1995	Norwich	East	72.3	74	32	7	42	45	3.98	4	4	9.21	.87	5.23	5.60	.56
1996	New Haven	East	20.7	23	9	2	10	9	3.92	1	1	10.02	.87	4.35	3.92	.22
1996	Colo. Springs	PCL	38.0	49	19	3	25	25	4.50	2	2	11.61	.71	5.92	5.92	.49

Probably no worse than a lot of teams' #9 or #10 pitcher. On the cusp of the go/no go decision as far as baseball is concerned. Hard to develop a lot as a pitcher in the PCL, except in terms of personal psychoses.

MIKE FARMER　　　**LRP**　　　**1969**　　**Age 28**

YR	TEAM	Lge	IP	H	ER	HR	BB	K	ERA	W	L	H/9	HR/9	BB/9	K/9	KW
1993	Reading	East	94.3	134	58	19	45	48	5.53	3	7	12.78	1.81	4.29	4.58	.45
1994	Cent. Valley	Calif	25.3	33	16	4	14	18	5.68	1	2	11.72	1.42	4.97	6.39	.89
1994	New Haven	East	13.3	8	2	2	6	9	1.35	1	0	5.40	1.35	4.05	6.08	1.01
1995	New Haven	East	100.7	139	66	10	44	60	5.90	3	8	12.43	.89	3.93	5.36	.80
1996	Colo. Springs	PCL	53.7	50	21	4	30	23	3.52	3	3	8.39	.67	5.03	3.86	.03
1996	Colorado	NL	28.3	27	18	7	15	14	5.72	1	2	8.58	2.22	4.76	4.45	.29

Bullpen fodder. Probably more valuable in Colorado than elsewhere, because you need an extra pitcher per game. Farmer is pretty much the definition of an extra pitcher in the bigs. Has some value, and is likely to have a Buddy Groom-like career. If he were right-handed, he'd probably be thinking about exploring some Amway options.

SCOTT FREDRICKSON　　　**RRP**　　　**1968**　　**Age 29**

YR	TEAM	Lge	IP	H	ER	HR	BB	K	ERA	W	L	H/9	HR/9	BB/9	K/9	KW
1993	Colo. Springs	PCL	24.0	23	12	3	21	16	4.50	1	2	8.62	1.12	7.88	6.00	.03
1993	Colorado	NL	28.7	30	20	3	20	19	6.28	1	2	9.42	.94	6.28	5.97	.42
1995	Colo. Springs	PCL	71.0	63	27	2	54	63	3.42	5	3	7.99	.25	6.85	7.99	.95
1996	Colo. Springs	PCL	60.3	66	44	8	47	53	6.56	2	5	9.85	1.19	7.01	7.91	.88

Smooth. Consistent. Pretty bad. Somewhere, there's a GM thinking, "If I could only find someone who'd walk six guys a game." Get to the phone, Mr. Frey. We've found your man.

TODD GENKE　　　**RRP**　　　**1971**　　**Age 26**

YR	TEAM	Lge	IP	H	ER	HR	BB	K	ERA	W	L	H/9	HR/9	BB/9	K/9	KW
1993	Batavia	NY-P	28.3	73	32	4	14	12	10.16	0	3	23.19	1.27	4.45	3.81	.16
1994	Spartanburg	S Atl	56.7	69	25	5	24	29	3.97	3	3	10.96	.79	3.81	4.61	.58
1995	Piedmont	S Atl	44.3	68	36	4	27	21	7.31	1	4	13.80	.81	5.48	4.26	.05
1996	Salem, VA	Caro	78.0	95	38	7	38	37	4.38	4	5	10.96	.81	4.38	4.27	.33

25 in A ball. For the fourth time. *Billy Madison* wasn't any good as a movie; I can't imagine it's much better in real life.

JOHN HABYAN　　　**RRP**　　　**1964**　　**Age 33**

YR	TEAM	Lge	IP	H	ER	HR	BB	K	ERA	W	L	H/9	HR/9	BB/9	K/9	KW
1993	Kansas City	AL	14.0	13	6	1	5	10	3.86	1	1	8.36	.64	3.21	6.43	1.34
1993	NY Yankees	AL	41.7	47	18	5	18	30	3.89	3	2	10.15	1.08	3.89	6.48	1.19
1994	St. Louis	NL	46.7	50	14	2	24	43	2.70	3	2	9.64	.39	4.63	8.29	1.61
1995	California	AL	32.7	35	12	2	13	25	3.31	2	2	9.64	.55	3.58	6.89	1.40
1995	St Louis	NL	39.3	34	14	0	19	31	3.20	2	2	7.78	.00	4.35	7.09	1.28
1996	Colorado	NL	24.3	29	13	3	16	21	4.81	1	2	10.73	1.11	5.92	7.77	1.11

An effective reliever, and I expect him to remain as such. He's fighting some nagging injuries, but has a history of being able to overcome such things. Of course, being a good reliever in Colorado means a 4.50 ERA or so. Habyan will probably do better than that. Picked up by the Mets.

RYAN HAWBLITZEL   **RBP**   **1971**   **Age 26**

YR	TEAM	Lge	IP	H	ER	HR	BB	K	ERA	W	L	H/9	HR/9	BB/9	K/9	KW
1993	Colo. Springs	PCL	153.0	202	97	16	64	71	5.71	6	11	11.88	.94	3.76	4.18	.45
1994	Colo. Springs	PCL	153.3	176	84	18	67	86	4.93	7	10	10.33	1.06	3.93	5.05	.70
1995	Colo. Springs	PCL	78.7	80	34	8	24	36	3.89	5	4	9.15	.92	2.75	4.12	.69
1996	Colo. Springs	PCL	110.7	126	61	16	37	61	4.96	5	7	10.25	1.30	3.01	4.96	.90
1996	Colorado	NL	14.7	16	9	2	7	6	5.52	1	1	9.82	1.23	4.30	3.68	.15

Borderline fifth starter/bullpen guy. The longest of shots to have more than one good year, but it could happen. Pitched in Colorado for four straight years; probably feels like he's having some sort of horrible nightmare; in reality, he's building up quite a karma account.

DWAYNE HENRY   **RRP**   **1962**   **Age 35**

YR	TEAM	Lge	IP	H	ER	HR	BB	K	ERA	W	L	H/9	HR/9	BB/9	K/9	KW
1993	Seattle	AL	54.3	55	34	6	38	36	5.63	2	4	9.11	.99	6.29	5.96	.41
1995	Toledo	Inter	45.0	49	22	4	31	44	4.40	2	3	9.80	.80	6.20	8.80	1.38
1996	Colo. Springs	PCL	37.3	40	30	5	35	27	7.23	1	3	9.64	1.21	8.44	6.51	.06
1996	Toledo	Inter	18.0	21	16	3	15	19	8.00	0	2	10.50	1.50	7.50	9.50	1.29

You have to admire Henry's perseverance. Year after year, more guys reach first base off him than Divine Brown. And yet, year after year he's back, trying to get better. He doesn't of course, but he sure hasn't given up. Sisyphus.

DARREN HOLMES   **RRP**   **1966**   **Age 31**

YR	TEAM	Lge	IP	H	ER	HR	BB	K	ERA	W	L	H/9	HR/9	BB/9	K/9	KW
1993	Colorado	NL	64.7	53	23	6	27	56	3.20	4	3	7.38	.84	3.76	7.79	1.66
1994	Colorado	NL	28.7	32	20	5	26	30	6.28	1	2	10.05	1.57	8.16	9.42	1.10
1995	Colorado	NL	65.7	53	17	3	33	53	2.33	5	2	7.26	.41	4.52	7.26	1.29
1996	Colorado	NL	76.3	69	27	6	33	62	3.18	5	3	8.14	.71	3.89	7.31	1.46

An extremely good pitcher, value disguised but enhanced by pitching in Colorado. There are many good and promising pitchers in this organization. It'll be extremely interesting to see how things play out for them over time.

BOBBY JONES   **LRP**   **1972**   **Age 25**

YR	TEAM	Lge	IP	H	ER	HR	BB	K	ERA	W	L	H/9	HR/9	BB/9	K/9	KW
1993	Beloit	Midw	124.7	190	84	11	86	67	6.06	4	10	13.72	.79	6.21	4.84	.06
1994	Stockton	Calif	130.7	161	93	14	83	97	6.41	4	11	11.09	.96	5.72	6.68	.80
1995	New Haven	East	68.0	72	27	5	44	54	3.57	4	4	9.53	.66	5.82	7.15	.93
1995	Colo. Springs	PCL	38.7	43	28	5	37	43	6.52	1	3	10.01	1.16	8.61	10.01	1.18
1996	Colo. Springs	PCL	83.3	82	43	8	73	63	4.64	4	5	8.86	.86	7.88	6.80	.30

Seems driven by some sort of holy internal fire to sabotage himself. Good stuff, but simply can't throw it for strikes. Rarely, one of these guys will find the strike zone and become dominant, but Jones doesn't strike out enough guys for me to believe that he'll be able to do that. Even if he does improve his control, I don't think he's going to get over that hump and pitch more than a few innings in the majors.

JAMES KAMMERER   **LSP**   **1974**   **Age 23**

YR	TEAM	Lge	IP	H	ER	HR	BB	K	ERA	W	L	H/9	HR/9	BB/9	K/9	KW
1995	Portland, OR	Nwern	30.7	34	9	0	15	9	2.64	2	1	9.98	.00	4.40	2.64	-.22
1996	Asheville	S Atl	37.0	48	20	0	26	24	4.86	2	2	11.68	.00	6.32	5.84	.36

Starting pitcher starting his career a bit late. He's basically got two years to show significant improvement.

MIKE KUSIEWICZ   **LSP**   **1977**   **Age 20**

YR	TEAM	Lge	IP	H	ER	HR	BB	K	ERA	W	L	H/9	HR/9	BB/9	K/9	KW
1995	Asheville	S Atl	107.3	119	43	8	52	59	3.61	7	5	9.98	.67	4.36	4.95	.56
1996	Salem, VA	Caro	21.0	20	13	3	15	12	5.57	1	1	8.57	1.29	6.43	5.14	.11
1996	New Haven	East	70.0	96	39	4	35	48	5.01	3	5	12.34	.51	4.50	6.17	.93

Good looking left-handed starter with decent control and good stuff. Will probably start the year at Colorado Springs. Gets batters out with a plus, well-spotted fastball and a sharp breaking ball. Has plenty of time to get better; overwork is his main danger.

CURT LESKANIC   **RRP**   **1968**   **Age 29**

YR	TEAM	Lge	IP	H	ER	HR	BB	K	ERA	W	L	H/9	HR/9	BB/9	K/9	KW
1993	Wichita	Texas	40.0	44	21	3	25	30	4.72	2	2	9.90	.68	5.62	6.75	.84
1993	Colo. Springs	PCL	40.7	36	17	3	30	30	3.76	3	2	7.97	.66	6.64	6.64	.55
1993	Colorado	NL	56.0	54	32	7	33	28	5.14	2	4	8.68	1.12	5.30	4.50	.17
1994	Colo. Springs	PCL	123.0	112	39	6	66	82	2.85	9	5	8.20	.44	4.83	6.00	.79
1994	Colorado	NL	22.3	25	11	2	12	16	4.43	1	1	10.07	.81	4.84	6.45	.94
1995	Colorado	NL	96.3	76	25	6	39	93	2.34	8	3	7.10	.56	3.64	8.69	1.99
1996	Colorado	NL	74.0	71	37	10	43	64	4.50	4	4	8.64	1.22	5.23	7.78	1.29

Still throws well and had a better than average year. Will be an effective reliever for several more years, provided Don Baylor doesn't use his arm up. There was some speculation that Leskanic's arm was tired this year after the heavy load in 1995, so there is cause for concern. Barring injury, one of the better relievers in either league.

CHRIS MACCA   **RRP**   **1975**   **Age 22**

YR	TEAM	Lge	IP	H	ER	HR	BB	K	ERA	W	L	H/9	HR/9	BB/9	K/9	KW
1995	Portland, OR	Nwern	30.7	35	17	2	23	23	4.99	1	2	10.27	.59	6.75	6.75	.56
1996	Asheville	S Atl	30.0	26	5	3	16	25	1.50	3	0	7.80	.90	4.80	7.50	1.30
1996	New Haven	East	31.7	23	5	0	22	25	1.42	4	0	6.54	.00	6.25	7.11	.81

Cut through the South Atlantic and Eastern Leagues like Cecil Fielder through a smorgie line. Dynamite stuff. Will probably be in the majors to stay by the end of the year. The Rockies don't have much in the way of hitting prospects, but they've got a bunch of young pitchers who might really be something special. I wonder if they know that.

DOUG MILLION   **LSP**   **1976**   **Age 21**

YR	TEAM	Lge	IP	H	ER	HR	BB	K	ERA	W	L	H/9	HR/9	BB/9	K/9	KW
1994	Bend	Nwern	49.7	63	23	5	27	37	4.17	3	3	11.42	.91	4.89	6.70	1.01
1995	Salem, VA	Caro	101.3	120	67	6	98	61	5.95	3	8	10.66	.53	8.70	5.42	-.37
1996	Salem, VA	Caro	96.3	89	32	1	76	67	2.99	7	4	8.31	.09	7.10	6.26	.31
1996	New Haven	East	50.0	61	23	2	49	30	4.14	3	3	10.98	.36	8.82	5.40	-.40

The much vaunted prospect continues to have success in the minors, but there are some danger signs. K rate is showing signs of decay and his control isn't coming around just yet. Nonetheless, still a high grade B prospect and will start the year at Colorado Springs. If he gets hot for five or six consecutive starts, he'll be in the majors.

JOEL MOORE   **RRP**   **1973**   **Age 24**

YR	TEAM	Lge	IP	H	ER	HR	BB	K	ERA	W	L	H/9	HR/9	BB/9	K/9	KW
1993	Bend	Nwern	78.3	99	34	3	31	44	3.91	5	4	11.37	.34	3.56	5.06	.79
1994	Cent. Valley	Calif	117.7	167	73	8	81	58	5.58	4	9	12.77	.61	6.20	4.44	-.07
1995	New Haven	East	143.0	189	72	10	82	79	4.53	7	9	11.90	.63	5.16	4.97	.37
1996	New Haven	East	28.3	42	18	4	7	11	5.72	1	2	13.34	1.27	2.22	3.49	.61

Battling for a career at this point; Moore's indistinguishable from the 100 or so guys hoping to catch on and get a chance to make an MLB roster. A longshot at best to help a major league club.

MIKE MUNOZ   **LRP**   **1966**   **Age 31**

YR	TEAM	Lge	IP	H	ER	HR	BB	K	ERA	W	L	H/9	HR/9	BB/9	K/9	KW
1993	Colo. Springs	PCL	35.0	42	7	0	13	24	1.80	3	1	10.80	.00	3.34	6.17	1.22
1993	Colorado	NL	17.7	19	9	1	11	15	4.58	1	1	9.68	.51	5.60	7.64	1.15
1994	Colorado	NL	45.0	35	17	3	34	29	3.40	3	2	7.00	.60	6.80	5.80	.23
1995	Colorado	NL	44.0	46	28	8	30	32	5.73	2	3	9.41	1.64	6.14	6.55	.65
1996	Colo. Springs	PCL	12.3	8	2	0	7	11	1.46	1	0	5.84	.00	5.11	8.03	1.40
1996	Colorado	NL	44.7	48	23	4	19	38	4.63	2	3	9.67	.81	3.83	7.66	1.60

Reliable arm out of the pen; won't hurt you in that role, nor be able to expand on it. Could go to another club and take a big step forward. He's got an awfully big platoon split; right-handers hit .963 against him last year. OK, OK, it was only .352.

DAVID NIED   **RRP**   **1969**   **Age 28**

YR	TEAM	Lge	IP	H	ER	HR	BB	K	ERA	W	L	H/9	HR/9	BB/9	K/9	KW
1993	Colo. Springs	PCL	14.0	21	12	3	8	9	7.71	0	2	13.50	1.93	5.14	5.79	.64
1993	Colorado	NL	85.3	92	42	7	50	43	4.43	4	5	9.70	.74	5.27	4.54	.19
1994	Colorado	NL	121.0	127	56	14	57	68	4.17	6	7	9.45	1.04	4.24	5.06	.63
1995	Colo. Springs	PCL	29.0	27	12	0	28	19	3.72	2	1	8.38	.00	8.69	5.90	-.21
1996	Salem, VA	Caro	39.0	39	22	4	24	28	5.08	2	2	9.00	.92	5.54	6.46	.77
1996	Colo. Springs	PCL	60.3	104	71	15	39	42	10.59	1	6	15.51	2.24	5.82	6.27	.63

Destined to be a trivia answer at SABR's 50th anniversary convention, along with Nigel Wilson. Has fought some tenacious arm problems and has an uphill battle at this point. If healthy, he's serviceable Rotation Helper [tm].

LANCE PAINTER   **LRP**   **1968**   **Age 29**

YR	TEAM	Lge	IP	H	ER	HR	BB	K	ERA	W	L	H/9	HR/9	BB/9	K/9	KW
1993	Colo. Springs	PCL	127.7	152	68	11	57	72	4.79	6	8	10.72	.78	4.02	5.08	.69
1993	Colorado	NL	38.3	47	21	5	14	15	4.93	2	2	11.03	1.17	3.29	3.52	.35
1994	Colo. Springs	PCL	67.0	73	29	4	34	49	3.90	4	3	9.81	.54	4.57	6.58	1.05
1994	Colorado	NL	73.7	83	41	9	32	38	5.01	3	5	10.14	1.10	3.91	4.64	.57
1995	Colo. Springs	PCL	24.0	29	15	3	13	11	5.62	1	2	10.88	1.12	4.88	4.12	.16
1995	Colorado	NL	45.3	48	17	8	14	31	3.38	3	2	9.53	1.59	2.78	6.15	1.36
1996	Colorado	NL	50.7	48	26	10	29	40	4.62	3	3	8.53	1.78	5.15	7.11	1.08

Lefty reliever, about four years away from boarding the Tony Fossas Train. "Step up and step aboard, your seat is to the left…." Another Rockie with a pronounced platoon split. If he gets injured at this point, his career is likely over.

STEVE REED   **RRP**   **1966**   **Age 31**

YR	TEAM	Lge	IP	H	ER	HR	BB	K	ERA	W	L	H/9	HR/9	BB/9	K/9	KW
1993	Colo. Springs	PCL	11.3	8	1	0	4	8	.79	1	0	6.35	.00	3.18	6.35	1.32
1993	Colorado	NL	82.3	74	37	12	38	48	4.04	4	5	8.09	1.31	4.15	5.25	.71
1994	Colorado	NL	64.0	73	26	8	31	47	3.66	4	3	10.27	1.12	4.36	6.61	1.11
1995	Colorado	NL	82.0	56	15	8	27	69	1.65	8	1	6.15	.88	2.96	7.57	1.78
1996	Colorado	NL	74.0	58	25	10	25	43	3.04	5	3	7.05	1.22	3.04	5.23	.98

A monster fully capable of having a Troy Percival year at any moment. His stuff reminds me of the unfortunate former reliever for the Red Sox, Jeff Gray, who was actually a darn good pitcher. Reed is at the top of the second tier of closers right now, just behind Percival and ahead of Wetteland.

BRYAN REKAR   **RSP**   **1972**   **Age 25**

YR	TEAM	Lge	IP	H	ER	HR	BB	K	ERA	W	L	H/9	HR/9	BB/9	K/9	KW
1993	Bend	Nwern	65.0	110	38	10	13	33	5.26	3	4	15.23	1.38	1.80	4.57	1.07
1994	Cent. Valley	Calif	100.0	136	48	3	41	60	4.32	5	6	12.24	.27	3.69	5.40	.88
1995	New Haven	East	74.3	79	27	5	21	62	3.27	5	3	9.57	.61	2.54	7.51	1.87
1995	Colo. Springs	PCL	44.7	29	6	0	17	35	1.21	5	0	5.84	.00	3.43	7.05	1.49
1995	Colorado	NL	84.3	84	37	10	30	52	3.95	5	4	8.96	1.07	3.20	5.55	1.05
1996	Colo. Springs	PCL	116.3	132	54	13	47	61	4.18	6	7	10.21	1.01	3.64	4.72	.66
1996	Colorado	NL	59.3	74	44	9	30	21	6.67	2	5	11.22	1.37	4.55	3.19	-.08

Had a promising future at one point, but appears to have lost the strike zone in 1996. Probably just a one-year aberration, but you never know with that particular affliction.

ARMANDO REYNOSO   **RSP**   **1966**   **Age 31**

YR	TEAM	Lge	IP	H	ER	HR	BB	K	ERA	W	L	H/9	HR/9	BB/9	K/9	KW
1993	Colo. Springs	PCL	20.7	18	7	1	10	18	3.05	1	1	7.84	.44	4.35	7.84	1.52
1993	Colorado	NL	185.3	189	79	20	82	110	3.84	11	10	9.18	.97	3.98	5.34	.79
1994	Colorado	NL	52.0	49	23	5	26	23	3.98	3	3	8.48	.87	4.50	3.98	.20
1995	Colo. Springs	PCL	21.3	14	2	1	8	15	.84	2	0	5.91	.42	3.38	6.33	1.27
1995	Colorado	NL	93.0	101	45	11	42	35	4.35	5	5	9.77	1.06	4.06	3.39	.11
1996	Colorado	NL	167.7	170	69	22	62	74	3.70	10	9	9.13	1.18	3.33	3.97	.49

Best noted for his riotous Martin Lawrence impersonation and his four fully functional tendons. Knows how to pitch–better than league average last year, despite throwing about as hard as Vanna White at this point. I don't know how he gets people out but he does, a la Steve Ontiveros. Traded to the Mets, where his role will depend on the health of four other guys.

KEVIN RITZ   **RSP**   **1965**   **Age 32**

YR	TEAM	Lge	IP	H	ER	HR	BB	K	ERA	W	L	H/9	HR/9	BB/9	K/9	KW
1994	Colo. Springs	PCL	32.7	25	4	2	9	23	1.10	4	0	6.89	.55	2.48	6.34	1.49
1994	Colorado	NL	73.3	81	39	5	42	49	4.79	3	5	9.94	.61	5.15	6.01	.72
1995	Colorado	NL	172.0	150	62	14	77	104	3.24	11	8	7.85	.73	4.03	5.44	.81
1996	Colorado	NL	211.7	205	96	20	120	88	4.08	12	12	8.72	.85	5.10	3.74	-.03

His peripheral numbers last year stunk up the joint like George Wendt in the elevator at "Freddy Floret's World of Broccoli." He did manage to get people out, but he was living right on the edge. He could just as easily have had a nice puffy ERA. Could detonate big in 1997.

BRUCE RUFFIN   **LRP**   **1964**   **Age 33**

YR	TEAM	Lge	IP	H	ER	HR	BB	K	ERA	W	L	H/9	HR/9	BB/9	K/9	KW
1993	Colorado	NL	137.7	132	53	9	83	119	3.46	9	6	8.63	.59	5.43	7.78	1.24
1994	Colorado	NL	55.3	51	22	6	35	60	3.58	3	3	8.30	.98	5.69	9.76	1.83
1995	Colorado	NL	33.0	24	5	1	21	20	1.36	4	0	6.55	.27	5.73	5.45	.39
1996	Colorado	NL	68.3	50	23	5	34	63	3.03	5	3	6.59	.66	4.48	8.30	1.65

Has really put it all together. I think it's astounding that Ruffin has become as good as he has. He used to leave that breaking ball up at the belt occasionally and spoil a fantastic outing with a longball. Now he still has great stuff, but he uses it exceptionally well. Few guys can improve like that. It takes a lot of hard work, and my hat's off to him. Should retain lots of value for 1997 and 1998.

MIKE SAIPE   **RSP**   **1974**   **Age 23**

YR	TEAM	Lge	IP	H	ER	HR	BB	K	ERA	W	L	H/9	HR/9	BB/9	K/9	KW
1994	Bend	Nwern	70.7	95	56	9	44	36	7.13	2	6	12.10	1.15	5.60	4.58	.13
1995	Salem, VA	Caro	78.7	76	32	7	42	65	3.66	5	4	8.69	.80	4.81	7.44	1.28
1996	New Haven	East	127.7	134	51	12	54	94	3.60	8	6	9.45	.85	3.81	6.63	1.26

He's certainly earned a good long look in Colorado Springs this year, and will likely be fighting for a rotation spot at spring training 1998. Decent prospect all around. If his K rate jumps by one, he could be a monster.

BILL SWIFT   **RSP**   **1962**   **Age 35**

YR	TEAM	Lge	IP	H	ER	HR	BB	K	ERA	W	L	H/9	HR/9	BB/9	K/9	KW
1993	San Francisco	NL	223.3	214	77	20	79	152	3.10	16	9	8.62	.81	3.18	6.13	1.25
1994	San Francisco	NL	107.3	109	43	10	41	58	3.61	7	5	9.14	.84	3.44	4.86	.76
1995	Colorado	NL	105.3	107	45	10	50	59	3.84	6	6	9.14	.85	4.27	5.04	.61
1996	Colorado	NL	18.3	20	8	1	6	4	3.93	1	1	9.82	.49	2.95	1.96	-.08

When healthy he can pitch, even today. Of course, we're speaking strictly in hypotheticals at this point. Logged more surgery hours than frequent flier miles over the past few years. Probably got some sort of co-marketing thing going with VISA and Dr. Frank Jobe.

MARK THOMPSON   **RSP**   **1971**   **Age 26**

YR	TEAM	Lge	IP	H	ER	HR	BB	K	ERA	W	L	H/9	HR/9	BB/9	K/9	KW
1993	Cent. Valley	Calif	63.3	55	15	4	19	50	2.13	5	2	7.82	.57	2.70	7.11	1.69
1993	Colo. Springs	PCL	30.7	29	9	1	14	17	2.64	2	1	8.51	.29	4.11	4.99	.64
1994	Colo. Springs	PCL	132.0	147	57	9	70	69	3.89	8	7	10.02	.61	4.77	4.70	.37
1995	Colo. Springs	PCL	58.7	65	31	3	31	34	4.76	3	4	9.97	.46	4.76	5.22	.55
1995	Colorado	NL	51.7	63	31	6	25	26	5.40	2	4	10.97	1.05	4.35	4.53	.42
1996	Colorado	NL	169.0	164	77	21	86	83	4.10	9	10	8.73	1.12	4.58	4.42	.33

Not a bad year, and certainly better than one would have expected given his career history. Unlikely to maintain it, either in terms of success or number of innings.

JOHN THOMSON   **RSP**   **1974**   **Age 23**

YR	TEAM	Lge	IP	H	ER	HR	BB	K	ERA	W	L	H/9	HR/9	BB/9	K/9	KW
1994	Asheville	S Atl	78.3	87	35	4	48	47	4.02	4	5	10.00	.46	5.51	5.40	.42
1994	Cent. Valley	Calif	44.0	50	18	0	24	27	3.68	3	2	10.23	.00	4.91	5.52	.61
1995	New Haven	East	119.7	158	72	10	70	64	5.42	5	8	11.88	.75	5.26	4.81	.29
1996	New Haven	East	90.3	96	34	8	35	64	3.39	6	4	9.56	.80	3.49	6.38	1.25
1996	Colo. Springs	PCL	65.7	73	36	6	33	50	4.93	3	4	10.01	.82	4.52	6.85	1.15

Took a big step forward in 1996, and he'll fight to maintain it in 1997. Could be a darn good pitcher if he can just control his stuff a little bit more, and I think he'll do it. Look for him to be in a rotation somewhere in two-and-a-half years.

JAMEY WRIGHT   **RSP**   **1975**   **Age 22**

YR	TEAM	Lge	IP	H	ER	HR	BB	K	ERA	W	L	H/9	HR/9	BB/9	K/9	KW
1994	Asheville	S Atl	122.7	229	116	7	87	61	8.51	3	11	16.80	.51	6.38	4.48	-.10
1996	New Haven	East	41.3	34	6	0	16	40	1.31	5	0	7.40	.00	3.48	8.71	2.03
1996	Colo. Springs	PCL	55.3	53	15	3	28	32	2.44	4	2	8.62	.49	4.55	5.20	.60
1996	Colorado	NL	91.0	91	43	7	48	38	4.25	5	5	9.00	.69	4.75	3.76	.07

Long term, I'm concerned about the number of innings he threw in 1996. Short term, look for him to strike out a lot more guys next year and completely shut down right-handed hitters. A good bet to be an effective starter for the next three or four years. You'll particularly enjoy watching Raul Mondesi trying to hit against him; the visual is something akin to what Jim Carrey might look like trying to play racquetball with a wet baguette.

Player	Age	Team	Lge	AB	H	DB	TP	HR	BB	SB	CS	OUT	BA	OBA	SA	EQA	EQR	Peak
EFRAIN ALAMO	19	Asheville	S Atl	258	47	4	0	5	18	3	4	215	.182	.236	.256	.146	9	.167
BLAKE BARTHOL	23	Salem-VA	Caro	387	101	7	1	11	31	5	2	289	.261	.316	.370	.231	37	.252
STEVE BERNHARDT	25	New Haven	East	86	23	0	0	0	4	0	1	64	.267	.300	.291	.194	5	.205
	25	Salem-VA	Caro	208	55	8	1	1	11	2	2	155	.264	.301	.327	.210	16	.223
JORGE BRITO	30	Colo. Springs	PCL	157	49	9	0	7	22	0	1	109	.312	.397	.503	.295	26	.289
CLINT BRYANT	22	Asheville	S Atl	239	48	5	1	4	28	4	3	194	.201	.285	.280	.185	14	.203
JEFF CARTER	32	Colo. Springs	PCL	160	35	3	0	2	21	3	3	128	.219	.309	.275	.194	11	.183
JOHN CLIFFORD	22	Asheville	S Atl	326	58	7	1	1	19	7	3	271	.178	.223	.215	.120	7	.132
BRIAN CULP	25	Salem-VA	Caro	125	22	1	0	1	14	1	0	103	.176	.259	.208	.137	4	.146
EARL CUNNINGHAM	26	Asheville	S Atl	136	32	3	0	7	5	2	1	105	.235	.262	.412	.222	12	.232
	26	Salem-VA	Caro	89	14	0	0	1	8	1	0	75	.157	.227	.191	.100	1	.092
SALVADOR DUVERGE	20	Asheville	S Atl	360	56	6	0	3	24	3	4	308	.156	.208	.197	.078	3	.089
BRETT ELAM	23	Asheville	S Atl	429	85	6	1	4	37	2	2	346	.198	.262	.245	.156	17	.170
JOHN FANTAUZZI	24	Salem-VA	Caro	100	26	7	0	0	14	1	0	74	.260	.351	.330	.235	10	.253
DAVID FEUERSTEIN	22	Asheville	S Atl	531	127	20	3	1	32	7	4	408	.239	.282	.294	.191	33	.211
CHAD GAMBILL	21	Salem-VA	Caro	418	110	10	1	7	29	3	3	311	.263	.311	.342	.219	35	.246
VICENTE GARCIA	21	New Haven	East	303	62	7	1	3	25	1	1	242	.205	.265	.264	.167	14	.186
RAY GIANNELLI	30	Colo. Springs	PCL	117	22	3	0	3	21	1	1	96	.188	.312	.291	.199	9	.196
JOHN GIUDICE	25	New Haven	East	121	29	4	1	3	9	2	2	94	.240	.292	.364	.217	10	.231
	25	Salem-VA	Caro	387	105	11	1	14	39	5	4	286	.271	.338	.413	.251	45	.264
PETE GONZALEZ	26	Colo. Springs	PCL	86	13	4	0	2	16	1	1	74	.151	.284	.267	.176	5	.185
	26	New Haven	East	122	21	0	0	2	13	1	1	102	.172	.252	.221	.137	4	.143
DAVID GROSECLOSE	23	Asheville	S Atl	263	51	9	0	1	34	5	4	216	.194	.286	.217	.159	11	.171
KEITH GRUNEWALD	24	New Haven	East	360	79	9	2	3	22	1	1	282	.219	.264	.281	.175	18	.187
MIKE HIGGINS	25	Salem-VA	Caro	226	47	3	0	5	21	1	2	181	.208	.275	.288	.181	13	.192
NATE HOLDREN	24	Salem-VA	Caro	437	112	8	0	14	25	7	3	328	.256	.297	.371	.224	39	.240
KYLE HOUSER	21	Salem-VA	Caro	454	95	7	2	1	59	5	4	363	.209	.300	.240	.176	24	.197
TRENT HUBBARD	30	Colo. Springs	PCL	186	52	9	3	6	26	6	5	139	.280	.368	.457	.271	27	.264
LINK JARRETT	24	New Haven	East	168	31	2	0	2	12	1	1	138	.185	.239	.232	.135	5	.147
	24	Salem-VA	Caro	100	19	2	1	0	7	0	1	82	.190	.243	.230	.133	3	.143
POOKIE JONES	24	Salem-VA	Caro	345	88	8	0	6	25	7	3	260	.255	.305	.330	.216	28	.231
TERRY JONES	25	Colo. Springs	PCL	491	123	5	2	1	36	19	8	376	.251	.302	.275	.198	33	.208
TAL LIGHT	22	Asheville	S Atl	213	62	6	0	9	16	3	2	153	.291	.341	.446	.262	27	.289
	22	Salem-VA	Caro	240	53	4	0	10	16	1	1	188	.221	.270	.363	.207	18	.229
CHAN MAYBER	23	Salem-VA	Caro	271	50	0	0	2	24	9	4	225	.185	.251	.207	.138	8	.151
ROGER MILLER	29	New Haven	East	263	61	5	1	3	24	0	0	202	.232	.296	.293	.195	17	.193
JOHN MYROW	24	New Haven	East	416	101	9	2	4	27	8	2	317	.243	.289	.303	.200	28	.214
GARRETT NEUBART	22	Asheville	S Atl	293	72	7	1	1	24	12	3	224	.246	.303	.287	.205	21	.225
	22	Salem-VA	Caro	89	28	1	2	0	11	3	3	64	.315	.390	.371	.258	11	.286
ELVIS PENA	19	Salem-VA	Caro	356	71	5	2	1	53	13	7	292	.199	.303	.233	.180	20	.206
HARVEY PULLIAM	28	Colo. Springs	PCL	280	69	8	0	9	30	2	2	213	.246	.319	.371	.231	27	.233
WILL SCALZITTI	23	Salem-VA	Caro	275	48	4	0	6	14	0	1	228	.175	.215	.255	.130	7	.141
CHRIS SEXTON	24	New Haven	East	460	95	9	1	1	64	6	3	368	.207	.303	.237	.178	25	.191
MARK STRITTMATTER	27	Colo. Springs	PCL	158	32	5	1	2	16	2	1	127	.203	.276	.285	.183	9	.188
JAMIE TAYLOR	25	New Haven	East	374	89	13	1	8	40	1	1	286	.238	.312	.342	.219	32	.231
FORRY WELLS	25	New Haven	East	315	71	13	1	7	41	1	1	245	.225	.315	.340	.218	27	.231
BILLY WHITE	27	Colo. Springs	PCL	282	60	8	1	3	30	2	1	223	.213	.288	.280	.187	17	.191
MATT WHITLEY	24	Asheville	S Atl	383	77	6	0	1	34	4	4	310	.201	.266	.225	.149	13	.159

Player	Age	Team	Lge	IP	H	ER	HR	BB	K	ERA	W	L	H/9	HR/9	BB/9	K/9	KW
KEITH BARNES	21	Asheville	S Atl	83.7	111	49	5	46	42	5.27	3	6	11.94	.54	4.95	4.52	.27
ROBBIE BECKETT	23	New Haven	East	44.7	44	30	7	55	41	6.04	2	3	8.87	1.41	11.08	8.26	-.02
JOHN BURKE	26	Colo. Springs	PCL	60.3	71	36	3	34	43	5.37	2	5	10.59	.45	5.07	6.41	.87
LUIS COLMENARES	19	Asheville	S Atl	54.0	82	44	7	36	31	7.33	1	5	13.67	1.17	6.00	5.17	.22
	19	Salem, VA	Caro	29.3	30	19	4	27	30	5.83	1	2	9.20	1.23	8.28	9.20	1.00
BRENT CROWTHER	24	New Haven	East	79.0	123	64	10	39	40	7.29	2	7	14.01	1.14	4.44	4.56	.41
	24	Salem, VA	Caro	46.7	55	21	3	20	19	4.05	2	3	10.61	.58	3.86	3.66	.26
MARC D'ALESSANDRO	20	Asheville	S Atl	131.0	244	109	15	83	65	7.49	3	12	16.76	1.03	5.70	4.47	.06
BILL EDEN	23	New Haven	East	38.3	54	26	6	29	31	6.10	1	3	12.68	1.41	6.81	7.28	.72
NEIL GARRETT	21	Asheville	S Atl	113.3	182	74	16	56	66	5.88	4	9	14.45	1.27	4.45	5.24	.64
LUTHER HACKMAN	21	Salem, VA	Caro	99.3	96	53	3	87	56	4.80	5	6	8.70	.27	7.88	5.07	-.28
TOM KRAMER	28	Colo. Springs	PCL	106.0	122	59	15	58	64	5.01	5	7	10.36	1.27	4.92	5.43	.58
SCOTT LAROCK	23	Salem, VA	Caro	73.7	77	34	4	41	38	4.15	4	4	9.41	.49	5.01	4.64	.30
CHANDLER MARTIN	22	Asheville	S Atl	74.3	88	29	3	45	40	3.51	5	3	10.65	.36	5.45	4.84	.25
	22	Salem, VA	Caro	62.3	79	49	5	66	40	7.07	2	5	11.41	.72	9.53	5.78	-.46
PATRICK MCCLINTON	24	Salem, VA	Caro	58.3	64	26	2	28	32	4.01	3	3	9.87	.31	4.32	4.94	.57
SEAN MURPHY	23	Asheville	S Atl	71.3	78	40	4	61	44	5.05	3	5	9.84	.50	7.70	5.55	-.07
CHRIS NEIER	24	New Haven	East	74.7	111	62	9	55	40	7.47	2	6	13.38	1.08	6.63	4.82	-.05
ROD PEDRAZA	26	Colo. Springs	PCL	26.7	37	21	3	6	10	7.09	1	2	12.49	1.01	2.03	3.38	.62
	26	New Haven	East	112.3	134	48	10	30	55	3.85	6	6	10.74	.80	2.40	4.41	.87
MATT POOL	22	Salem, VA	Caro	123.3	165	72	9	57	63	5.25	5	9	12.04	.66	4.16	4.60	.49
SCOTT RANDALL	20	Asheville	S Atl	134.0	162	60	14	74	74	4.03	7	8	10.88	.94	4.97	4.97	.41
BRIAN ROSE	23	Asheville	S Atl	59.7	73	34	5	24	40	5.13	3	4	11.01	.75	3.62	6.03	1.11
STEPHEN SHOEMAKER	23	Salem, VA	Caro	78.0	66	43	6	78	71	4.96	4	5	7.62	.69	9.00	8.19	.48
JEFF SOBKOVIAK	24	Salem, VA	Caro	70.3	72	28	7	35	35	3.58	4	4	9.21	.90	4.48	4.48	.37
MIKE VAVREK	22	Salem, VA	Caro	135.0	175	82	15	79	69	5.47	5	10	11.67	1.00	5.27	4.60	.22
JAKE VIANO	22	New Haven	East	41.0	45	27	6	29	24	5.93	2	3	9.88	1.32	6.37	5.27	.16
MIKE ZOLECKI	24	New Haven	East	83.3	94	59	13	82	62	6.37	3	6	10.15	1.40	8.86	6.70	.02

Colorado Rockies

Los Angeles Dodgers

A myocardial infarction brought the Tommy Lasorda era to an end in 1996, and 1997 brings with it the boredom of Bill Russell for Dodger fans. The real concern for Dodger fans is simple: When is Fred Claire going to pull it together? The Dodgers, despite having a fantastic rotation and a bushel of Rookie of the Year awards, are just not a very strong team. Why not? Part of the reason is that baseball writers wouldn't know a good rookie if he bit them on the ass; if one did that, it would almost certainly cost him a bunch of votes. The other part is that the Dodgers have made a whole bunch of really bad personnel decisions in the last few years, and they have one big bias: they've been acquiring and playing players with low on-base percentages.

No one in the Dodger lineup for most of the year except Mike Piazza was particularly strong at getting on base. That's not enough. You can't realistically run Greg Gagne, Mike Blowers, Raul Mondesi, Delino DeShields, Eric Karros and the pitcher out there and expect to score an adequate number of runs. Sure, Gagne and Mondesi had surprisingly good years, and DeShields was at least a reasonable bet to bounce back somewhat. But they got breaks on Gagne and Mondesi and still scored only 703 runs. League average was 759. Part of that is park effects, and the average excluding Colorado is only 743. Accounting for all that, the Dodgers had a mediocre offense to go with slightly better than average pitching.

Now we get to another piece of the same problem: Mike Piazza was responsible for somewhere around 125 of those runs, using whatever flavor of RC or EqR you like. That leaves a whopping 578 runs or so for the rest of the offense. Let's call pitchers worth perhaps 18 runs per year, just to make the math easy. That leaves 560 runs produced by the non-battery parts of the offense. That's putrid. The heart of the problem is this: No one on this team except Piazza is a particularly good hitter. No pitching staff can make up for the relentless lack of oomph in the Dodger lineup. Do the Dodgers recognize the problem? Hard to say. They've got some decent prospects in their system, like Paul Konerko, Karim Garcia and Adrian Beltre. Will they get a chance to play as time goes on? Or will Fred Claire fall in love with another 30-year-old free agent with a middling to fair OBP? [Ed. Note: the Dodgers signed Todd Zeile, who defines this concept.] Who can tell at this point?

I think offensive help is on the way, but it won't arrive until 1998. Look for Mondesi to head somewhere else if Fred Claire grows a brain; Mondesi's perceived value is way higher than his actual value; sort of like Demi Moore, but with beefier legs. The Dodgers need help in the infield, and Wilton Guerrero just isn't going to cut it. They may be best off trading some of that pitching for a real middle infielder who can actually hit. Delino DeShields just isn't going to come around in a Dodger uniform and Greg Gagne, even at his peak, isn't a good hitter. Teams with great guys at the corners can get away with that. Todd Zeile, Raul Mondesi, Eric Karros and Todd Hollandsworth do not qualify as great guys at the corners. They're barely passable if you want to contend.

With Lasorda gone, one naturally wonders whether the days of pitcher abuse have also passed. I don't think so. The Dodgers' success at developing good young pitchers has made them a bit arrogant, and probably deservedly so. Ismael Valdes' career hangs in the balance here, but why should they worry about that if they think they can dig up two or three more just like him? The pitcher/team relationship in baseball is an unnatural one; often the conflict between the best interests of the two is extremely stark, and it's almost always the pitcher who pays the price. The outcry over Roger Clemens merely mentioning that he might sit out his last start provides a quick insight to which side public opinion would be on should that conflict become part of the public discourse.

What will 1997 bring? Probably more of the same weak offense and great pitching, although a major injury is almost certain to jump up and bite the Dodger rotation somewhere along the line. Valdes' heavy use has actually been more in terms of innings than batters faced per start; I think they're pushing the envelope with him. I'm betting that Astacio will get hurt this season and at least one of the bullpen flamethrowers will go down hard as well. The Dodgers are one of the few teams with enough pitching depth to overcome that kind of setback. Their offense is far more vulnerable. If Piazza gets hurt, their season is over on the spot.

This farm system is pretty well stocked. There's useful players falling out of trees around these parts, but only at particular positions. Of course, none of that matters if the new manager continues the playing time patterns of Tommy Lasorda, and Fred Claire doesn't apply any pressure to actually play the good players. Dodger fans who watched Mike Blowers jog out to third every day must have been seething, particularly with Dave Hansen on the bench. Of course with Adrian Beltre on the horizon, that hole may be filled as early as 1998.

Organization: The Dodger organization has the most stability of any franchise, both as a matter of practice and principle. Management is almost exclusively developed from within; carpetbagging is something for other teams to do. This isn't necessarily a positive or a negative, but it can be helpful in terms of retaining talented people, provided you can identify them. This club still finds and produces more good pitchers than any other, and that's extremely valuable, even if the big club wouldn't know the value of OBP if it came up and bit them on the ass.

Part of the developmental cycle in the Dodger chain is the extreme park effects. Albuquerque is an extreme hitters' paradise, almost the exact opposite of Chavez Ravine. This can lead to some unexpected flops, at least as far as the organization is concerned. Human brains aren't particularly good at dealing with a lot of contradicting context when evaluating situations; we need to use tools to really do a good job of that. I believe the Dodger organization is still relying a bit too much on intuition and not enough on solid analysis. This is true of most organizations, but I'm surprised that LA isn't ahead of the curve here.

One foible about the Dodger minor league system: it has two tracks. If you're promising, you'll shoot through the minor league system like a meteor. If they don't think you're going to be an impact player, you'll rot in San Antonio or something. This means that your real prospects often get to the majors faster, but it also means that some guys who might have developed better didn't get a shot. It also means that managers invest more heavily in rapid-rising prospects, even when they shouldn't. That leads to weird sunk cost situations, and you end up with people like Eric Karros signing long-term deals without being very talented because someone's mentally tied to him being good.

Loved to hate you, Tommy. Enjoy your retirement. You were a good foe.

BILLY ASHLEY   LF/PH   1971   Age 26

Year	Team	Lge	AB	H	DB	TP	HR	BB	SB	CS	OUT	BA	OBA	SA	EQA	EQR	Peak
1993	Albuquerque	PCL	464	112	16	1	20	32	4	2	354	.241	.290	.409	.231	46	.255
1994	Albuquerque	PCL	377	116	11	2	29	48	5	3	264	.308	.386	.578	.309	70	.335
1995	Los Angeles	NL	221	56	4	0	9	28	0	0	165	.253	.337	.394	.245	25	.262
1996	Los Angeles	NL	114	25	4	1	9	23	0	0	89	.219	.350	.509	.276	18	.291
1997	*Los Angeles*	*NL*	*208*	*48*	*14*	*1*	*10*	*23*	*0*	*0*	*160*	*.231*	*.307*	*.452*	*.269*	*30*	

Bad fielder with a slugger's rep. Wasn't really much of a prospect, but has, in my opinion, greatly improved and could outperform that projection given an opportunity. I think he's learned to walk and will be a valuable major leaguer. Not as valuable as Barry Bonds, but probably more than Werner Klemperer.

ADRIAN BELTRE   3B   1978   Age 19

Year	Team	Lge	AB	H	DB	TP	HR	BB	SB	CS	OUT	BA	OBA	SA	EQA	EQR	Peak
1996	Savannah	S Atl	264	79	7	1	13	28	2	1	186	.299	.366	.481	.281	39	.329
1996	San Bernardino	Calif	238	53	7	1	7	14	2	2	187	.223	.266	.349	.201	17	.235
1997	*Los Angeles*	*NL*	*520*	*134*	*20*	*6*	*24*	*53*	*6*	*2*	*388*	*.258*	*.326*	*.458*	*.280*	*81*	

The Dodgers have a number of very good prospects, and may actually start deserving their annual Rookie of the Year awards soon. Beltre is a leading candidate for one. He'll spend the year adjusting to AA and AAA, and probably be a September callup in 1998. The Dodgers tend to fast-track their real prospects, and let the others take the Brian Traxler career path. Beltre's the real deal.

MIKE BLOWERS   3B   1965   Age 32

Year	Team	Lge	AB	H	DB	TP	HR	BB	SB	CS	OUT	BA	OBA	SA	EQA	EQR	Peak
1993	Seattle	AL	385	113	24	3	18	47	2	4	276	.294	.370	.512	.286	60	.288
1994	Seattle	AL	270	77	10	0	10	25	2	2	195	.285	.346	.433	.259	33	.259
1995	Seattle	AL	442	117	21	1	26	54	2	1	326	.265	.345	.493	.274	64	.268
1996	Los Angeles	NL	329	94	20	1	7	41	0	0	235	.286	.365	.416	.264	42	.254
1997	*Los Angeles*	*NL*	*411*	*103*	*25*	*1*	*14*	*50*	*0*	*0*	*308*	*.251*	*.332*	*.418*	*.271*	*59*	

Not a smart acquisition. Dave Hansen's probably a better player, but he's dripping with imaginary Lasorda albumin that forces one to be a pinch hitter. Signing a 30-year-old coming off a career year that wasn't that great is smarter than sending your kid to Neverland for a weekend, but that's not setting the bar real high. Blowers isn't a real bad player, just not particularly worth the money as a starter. The unlikely Bermanism of Mike "I really" Blowers isn't really called for.

BRETT BUTLER **CF** **1957** **Age 40**

Year	Team	Lge	AB	H	DB	TP	HR	BB	SB	CS	OUT	BA	OBA	SA	EQA	EQR	Peak
1993	Los Angeles	NL	630	195	24	8	2	95	33	15	450	.310	.400	.383	.272	87	.258
1994	Los Angeles	NL	436	146	14	8	10	76	25	7	297	.335	.434	.472	.309	79	.294
1995	Los Angeles	NL	152	46	5	2	0	26	9	1	107	.303	.404	.362	.275	21	.261
1995	NY Mets	NL	381	126	15	7	1	48	17	6	261	.331	.406	.415	.284	56	.269
1996	Los Angeles	NL	135	39	1	1	0	11	7	3	99	.289	.342	.311	.230	13	.217
1997	*Los Angeles*	*NL*	*403*	*112*	*17*	*6*	*2*	*50*	*15*	*5*	*296*	*.278*	*.358*	*.365*	*.272*	*57*	

We all know the story. Most of his skills are still intact, and he hasn't had any significant orthopedic problems in his career. Can still help a team in some role for two more years. I enjoyed his interviews during recovery—they actually had some substance. I admire anyone who can really examine his own belief system like that. Still can't throw well. Re-signed with the Dodgers, but still might retire.

ROGER CEDENO **CF** **1975** **Age 22**

Year	Team	Lge	AB	H	DB	TP	HR	BB	SB	CS	OUT	BA	OBA	SA	EQA	EQR	Peak
1993	San Antonio	Texas	487	135	11	5	5	45	18	9	361	.277	.338	.351	.237	49	.277
1994	Albuquerque	PCL	373	101	14	2	4	47	20	8	280	.271	.352	.351	.244	41	.283
1995	Albuquerque	PCL	362	97	17	5	3	50	18	12	276	.268	.357	.367	.246	41	.280
1996	Albuquerque	PCL	123	22	1	2	1	14	5	3	104	.179	.263	.244	.163	6	.182
1996	Los Angeles	NL	218	58	11	0	3	27	4	1	161	.266	.347	.358	.242	23	.271
1997	*Los Angeles*	*NL*	*361*	*94*	*18*	*6*	*4*	*38*	*19*	*13*	*280*	*.260*	*.331*	*.377*	*.259*	*48*	

Future leadoff hitter, and likely to be a pretty fair one. Will have a peak not unlike Butler's. The Dodger brass apparently has some issues with him. If he can learn to steal bases properly, he can be a championship caliber leadoff hitter.

DAVE CLARK **PH/LF** **1963** **Age 34**

Year	Team	Lge	AB	H	DB	TP	HR	BB	SB	CS	OUT	BA	OBA	SA	EQA	EQR	Peak
1993	Pittsburgh	NL	284	79	10	1	12	42	1	0	205	.278	.371	.447	.274	40	.268
1994	Pittsburgh	NL	227	69	10	0	11	25	2	2	160	.304	.373	.493	.285	35	.274
1995	Pittsburgh	NL	199	56	5	0	4	26	2	2	145	.281	.364	.367	.249	22	.236
1996	Pittsburgh	NL	216	60	12	2	8	34	2	1	157	.278	.376	.463	.279	32	.265
1997	*Los Angeles*	*NL*	*172*	*43*	*7*	*1*	*8*	*20*	*2*	*2*	*131*	*.250*	*.328*	*.442*	*.274*	*26*	

One of my favorite players. Was good enough to be a minor star, but never really had the opportunity to show what he could do during his prime. Since then, he's been a useful ballplayer, providing steady defense, solid on-base percentages and some pop. A consummate professional, and his work ethic is evident in his performance. If there's a contending team with an obvious hole, they could certainly fill it adequately with Clark. Wouldn't surprise me to see him hit 20 homers and .285 in a platoon outfield role, even at his advanced age.

CHAD CURTIS **OF** **1969** **Age 28**

Year	Team	Lge	AB	H	DB	TP	HR	BB	SB	CS	OUT	BA	OBA	SA	EQA	EQR	Peak
1993	California	AL	589	172	25	3	8	74	45	17	434	.292	.371	.385	.263	77	.282
1994	California	AL	454	116	21	4	12	38	23	10	348	.256	.313	.399	.241	49	.254
1995	Detroit	AL	588	159	28	3	23	70	26	14	443	.270	.348	.446	.264	79	.274
1996	Detroit	AL	401	106	21	1	10	53	16	10	305	.264	.350	.397	.251	48	.257
1996	Los Angeles	NL	108	25	3	0	3	18	2	1	84	.231	.341	.343	.232	11	.237
1997	*Cleveland*	*AL*	*515*	*135*	*32*	*1*	*15*	*78*	*29*	*20*	*400*	*.262*	*.359*	*.416*	*.261*	*70*	

Never developed. If you're not a better player at 28 than at 24, you're atypical. I don't know what happened here; I'd be interested to hear why people think Curtis never developed. Drop me some e-mail at info@baseballprospectus.com. This much I can say: He's a reliable outfielder who's not going to really help you or hurt you offensively, and he does play some decent defense.

DELINO DESHIELDS **2B** **1969** **Age 28**

Year	Team	Lge	AB	H	DB	TP	HR	BB	SB	CS	OUT	BA	OBA	SA	EQA	EQR	Peak
1993	Montreal	NL	499	154	20	5	3	80	36	8	353	.309	.404	.387	.280	73	.300
1994	Los Angeles	NL	331	89	12	2	3	60	25	6	248	.269	.381	.344	.259	42	.274
1995	Los Angeles	NL	440	123	19	3	9	69	33	12	329	.280	.377	.398	.268	61	.278
1996	Los Angeles	NL	596	146	12	8	6	60	41	11	461	.245	.314	.322	.225	55	.230
1997	*St Louis*	*NL*	*540*	*140*	*23*	*12*	*6*	*92*	*69*	*22*	*422*	*.259*	*.367*	*.380*	*.276*	*84*	

Since we're on the topic of failed development…Delino's gone right into the tank. I think he needs a change of scenery. He's a better player than he showed last year, but he's shown the same lack of growth Curtis has, only worse. This is more common in middle infielders than outfielders, but still. I mean, a quick graph of those EqAs looks like a graph of Apple's stock price.

CHAD FONVILLE **SS/2B** **1971** **Age 26**

Year	Team	Lge	AB	H	DB	TP	HR	BB	SB	CS	OUT	BA	OBA	SA	EQA	EQR	Peak
1994	San Jose	Calif	293	84	8	3	1	29	11	4	213	.287	.351	.345	.242	31	.263
1995	Los Angeles	NL	317	94	5	0	1	27	17	4	227	.297	.352	.322	.240	32	.257
1996	Albuquerque	PCL	94	19	1	0	0	8	4	0	75	.202	.265	.213	.159	4	.164
1996	Los Angeles	NL	206	45	5	1	0	19	6	2	163	.218	.284	.252	.179	11	.190
1997	*Los Angeles*	*NL*	*263*	*67*	*6*	*2*	*0*	*17*	*17*	*2*	*198*	*.255*	*.300*	*.293*	*.235*	*26*	

Fleet and worthless. A tools player who lacks only four of them. Can't hit, no power, no plate discipline and as has been stated many times, you can't steal first. Dodger fans seem to love the guy, but hey, Jim Carrey has a job down there, so talent obviously isn't an issue in that part of the country.

GREG GAGNE **SS** **1962** **Age 35**

Year	Team	Lge	AB	H	DB	TP	HR	BB	SB	CS	OUT	BA	OBA	SA	EQA	EQR	Peak
1993	Kansas City	AL	543	154	33	3	12	37	10	9	398	.284	.329	.422	.250	62	.241
1994	Kansas City	AL	373	93	20	3	7	28	9	15	294	.249	.302	.375	.219	33	.208
1995	Kansas City	AL	436	118	27	4	7	38	3	5	323	.271	.329	.399	.242	47	.230
1996	Los Angeles	NL	443	121	13	2	11	56	3	2	324	.273	.355	.386	.251	51	.238
1997	*Los Angeles*	*NL*	*424*	*94*	*15*	*1*	*11*	*47*	*5*	*6*	*336*	*.222*	*.299*	*.340*	*.232*	*44*	

Had a great year, probably a career year, at age 34. Can still play defense pretty well. Would probably be better suited for another team though. It's hard to carry his typical low OBP when your entire team is pretty much an OBP sink, even after park effects. 18 months away from being a backup somewhere.

KARIM GARCIA **OF** **1976** **Age 21**

Year	Team	Lge	AB	H	DB	TP	HR	BB	SB	CS	OUT	BA	OBA	SA	EQA	EQR	Peak
1993	Bakersfield	Calif	468	105	13	3	16	23	3	1	364	.224	.261	.368	.207	35	.246
1994	Vero Beach	Flor	459	117	16	4	23	34	5	2	344	.255	.306	.458	.251	54	.294
1995	Albuquerque	PCL	466	135	17	4	21	38	10	4	335	.290	.343	.479	.272	65	.314
1996	San Antonio	Texas	131	32	4	1	4	9	1	1	100	.244	.293	.382	.223	12	.253
1996	Albuquerque	PCL	319	81	11	5	12	27	5	2	240	.254	.312	.433	.247	36	.281
1997	*Los Angeles*	*NL*	*358*	*89*	*13*	*3*	*14*	*25*	*8*	*4*	*273*	*.249*	*.298*	*.419*	*.259*	*47*	

The Dodger brass thinks he's got a weight problem, an attitude problem, blah blah blah…. What he's got is a bat. A pretty much indifferent outfielder in Albuquerque with the glove, but he's a reasonable major league hitter right now. I like him somewhat, but anybody that doesn't walk once per 10 at bats needs to work on it. Will be up for good at the first sign of an outfield injury.

WILTON GUERRERO **SS/2B** **1975** **Age 22**

Year	Team	Lge	AB	H	DB	TP	HR	BB	SB	CS	OUT	BA	OBA	SA	EQA	EQR	Peak
1994	Vero Beach	Flor	408	108	10	2	2	27	13	9	309	.265	.310	.314	.212	32	.244
1995	San Antonio	Texas	393	130	12	4	1	25	18	11	274	.331	.371	.389	.260	47	.295
1996	Albuquerque	PCL	412	119	15	7	2	25	19	8	301	.289	.330	.374	.242	43	.270
1997	*Los Angeles*	*NL*	*526*	*147*	*17*	*7*	*2*	*28*	*27*	*15*	*394*	*.279*	*.316*	*.350*	*.249*	*61*	

Wears the "prospect" label well. In my bloated opinion, he's absolutely no prospect. Doesn't play the middle infield particularly well, and with his bat he's got no value anywhere else. Could hit .320 in the majors and be worthless. The Dodger brass would be wise to advise him to get on base more if he wants to play in the bigs. No matter what, his defense looks pretty ugly in the middle of the diamond.

DAVE HANSEN **PH/3B** **1969** **Age 28**

Year	Team	Lge	AB	H	DB	TP	HR	BB	SB	CS	OUT	BA	OBA	SA	EQA	EQR	Peak
1993	Los Angeles	NL	111	42	1	0	5	23	0	1	70	.378	.485	.523	.338	23	.360
1994	Los Angeles	NL	46	16	4	0	0	6	0	0	30	.348	.423	.435	.295	7	.314
1995	Los Angeles	NL	189	58	5	0	3	31	0	0	131	.307	.405	.381	.272	25	.282
1996	Los Angeles	NL	107	25	2	0	0	12	0	0	82	.234	.311	.252	.187	6	.190
1997	*Los Angeles*	*NL*	*115*	*32*	*7*	*1*	*3*	*25*	*0*	*0*	*83*	*.278*	*.407*	*.435*	*.307*	*22*	

A very good hitter, and perfectly acceptable major league third baseman. Tarred with the "pinch hitter" brush, and that's a damn shame. Was a better player than Blowers the last three years and will continue to be so. I'd forgive him if he goes postal, power-shaves Bill Russell's scrotum and sits him in a tub of cheap aftershave. Ooohh…that tingles.

BRIAN HARMON **OF** **1976** **Age 21**

Year	Team	Lge	AB	H	DB	TP	HR	BB	SB	CS	OUT	BA	OBA	SA	EQA	EQR	Peak
1995	Yakima	Nwern	62	13	1	0	0	9	0	0	49	.210	.310	.226	.175	3	.201
1996	Savannah	S Atl	251	52	6	0	8	40	0	1	200	.207	.316	.327	.213	21	.243
1997	*Los Angeles*	*NL*	*404*	*89*	*16*	*1*	*11*	*62*	*1*	*1*	*316*	*.220*	*.324*	*.347*	*.246*	*47*	

Low-average, high-walk power hitter. One of the building blocks of a successful franchise. They don't typically command high salaries, but produce runs more effectively than the expensive mediocrities like Joe Carter. Still, these are old player's skills, and players with this skill set don't typically age well. Will probably arrive in Albuquerque in 1998. Harmon is definitely a prospect that bears watching.

TODD HOLLANDSWORTH **LF/CF** **1973** **Age 24**

Year	Team	Lge	AB	H	DB	TP	HR	BB	SB	CS	OUT	BA	OBA	SA	EQA	EQR	Peak
1993	San Antonio	Texas	488	123	17	4	17	31	16	6	371	.252	.297	.408	.237	51	.269
1994	Albuquerque	PCL	493	121	20	2	16	44	11	6	378	.245	.307	.391	.233	50	.261
1995	Los Angeles	NL	106	27	3	0	5	11	2	1	80	.255	.325	.425	.249	12	.273
1996	Los Angeles	NL	496	155	27	3	14	47	18	6	347	.312	.372	.464	.281	73	.306
1997	*Los Angeles*	*NL*	*534*	*146*	*36*	*2*	*17*	*49*	*22*	*9*	*397*	*.273*	*.334*	*.444*	*.282*	*84*	

I guess he'd get my Rookie of the Year vote…if I were a heroin addict trying to work him for dimebag money. Not a bad player, and probably will be fairly decent, but likely will spend his time in the majors being on the fringe of useful. I'd trade him and anyone who looks like him for Edgar Renteria. Not a bad defensive outfielder, but his offensive skills don't fill one with glee.

ERIC KARROS **1B** **1968** **Age 29**

Year	Team	Lge	AB	H	DB	TP	HR	BB	SB	CS	OUT	BA	OBA	SA	EQA	EQR	Peak
1993	Los Angeles	NL	628	160	22	2	25	44	0	1	469	.255	.304	.416	.238	65	.251
1994	Los Angeles	NL	415	117	18	1	16	36	2	0	298	.282	.339	.446	.262	52	.272
1995	Los Angeles	NL	572	182	27	3	36	69	3	4	394	.318	.392	.565	.308	103	.315
1996	Los Angeles	NL	628	176	25	1	38	60	7	0	452	.280	.343	.505	.279	93	.281
1997	*Los Angeles*	*NL*	*536*	*141*	*28*	*2*	*26*	*51*	*6*	*2*	*397*	*.263*	*.327*	*.468*	*.283*	*85*	

A right-handed Tino Martinez without the defense. Has already been the most overrated player in baseball for a couple of years, and I think he'll be able to regain that crown in a year or so. Any first baseman who gets on base at a clip less than league average is not someone you want to make long-term plans around.

WAYNE KIRBY **OF** **1964** **Age 33**

Year	Team	Lge	AB	H	DB	TP	HR	BB	SB	CS	OUT	BA	OBA	SA	EQA	EQR	Peak
1993	Charlotte-NC	Inter	77	22	5	1	3	4	3	1	56	.286	.321	.494	.269	11	.269
1993	Cleveland	AL	468	137	23	5	8	41	16	4	335	.293	.350	.415	.261	58	.260
1994	Cleveland	AL	192	56	4	0	6	13	10	3	140	.292	.337	.406	.255	23	.249
1995	Cleveland	AL	190	42	12	2	1	13	10	3	151	.221	.271	.321	.203	14	.197
1996	Los Angeles	NL	195	57	11	1	1	19	3	2	140	.292	.355	.374	.249	22	.236
1997	*Los Angeles*	*NL*	*193*	*49*	*8*	*2*	*1*	*13*	*6*	*3*	*147*	*.254*	*.301*	*.332*	*.236*	*20*	

Fifth outfielder/defensive replacement/left-handed pinch hitter/pinch runner. Worth a roster spot, and likely will bounce around filling one for a couple more years.

PAUL KONERKO   **1B**   **1976**   **Age 21**

Year	Team	Lge	AB	H	DB	TP	HR	BB	SB	CS	OUT	BA	OBA	SA	EQA	EQR	Peak
1994	Yakima	Nwern	268	66	7	1	5	25	0	0	202	.246	.311	.336	.217	22	.254
1995	San Bernardino	Calif	451	105	9	0	14	47	1	0	346	.233	.305	.346	.218	38	.251
1996	San Antonio	Texas	489	145	15	1	26	67	1	2	346	.297	.381	.491	.287	76	.327
1997	*Los Angeles*	*NL*	*530*	*142*	*21*	*1*	*28*	*88*	*1*	*0*	*388*	*.268*	*.372*	*.470*	*.301*	*96*	

One year away from being better than Karros. Two years away from being a lot better than Karros. Three years away from making people forget Karros. Converted catcher with power in the Klesko/Canseco/McGwire class. Going to be a star. If he were still a catcher, grade A prospect. At first base, a grade B prospect whom I like much more than the numbers.

RYAN LUZINSKI   **C**   **1974**   **Age 23**

Year	Team	Lge	AB	H	DB	TP	HR	BB	SB	CS	OUT	BA	OBA	SA	EQA	EQR	Peak
1993	Yakima	Nwern	251	59	7	1	4	26	2	1	193	.235	.307	.319	.210	19	.242
1993	Bakersfield	Calif	149	37	5	1	3	9	1	1	113	.248	.291	.356	.215	12	.247
1994	Vero Beach	Flor	385	94	11	1	12	31	1	1	292	.244	.300	.371	.224	34	.254
1995	Vero Beach	Flor	138	44	4	0	6	8	1	0	94	.319	.356	.478	.279	19	.313
1995	San Antonio	Texas	147	33	2	0	2	12	1	1	115	.224	.283	.279	.183	8	.204
1996	San Bernardino	Calif	117	36	5	0	4	8	3	1	82	.308	.352	.453	.271	16	.298
1996	San Antonio	Texas	106	29	6	0	0	11	1	0	77	.274	.342	.330	.232	10	.256
1997	*Los Angeles*	*NL*	*286*	*72*	*7*	*0*	*6*	*18*	*4*	*1*	*215*	*.252*	*.296*	*.339*	*.236*	*29*	

Took a big step forward, and if he can improve half that much in the next two years he may force the Dodgers to move Piazza to another position. Defensive reputation is great, but that'll fade if he continues to hit. That projection is low in terms of bases on balls; I expect Ryan will draw a fair number more than that. Note, however, that my software has a much better track record than my mouth. Given to Baltimore this winter.

RAUL MONDESI   **RF**   **1971**   **Age 26**

Year	Team	Lge	AB	H	DB	TP	HR	BB	SB	CS	OUT	BA	OBA	SA	EQA	EQR	Peak
1993	Albuquerque	PCL	410	91	11	2	11	17	8	5	324	.222	.253	.339	.194	27	.215
1993	Los Angeles	NL	88	27	3	1	4	5	3	1	62	.307	.344	.500	.280	13	.309
1994	Los Angeles	NL	445	144	27	7	18	23	11	7	308	.324	.357	.537	.290	70	.315
1995	Los Angeles	NL	551	169	23	5	29	40	23	4	386	.307	.354	.525	.291	88	.311
1996	Los Angeles	NL	655	208	40	7	26	40	12	7	454	.318	.357	.519	.287	100	.303
1997	*Los Angeles*	*NL*	*665*	*207*	*37*	*13*	*27*	*18*	*17*	*8*	*466*	*.311*	*.329*	*.528*	*.301*	*116*	

Lots of raw speed, a high batting average, good power, no walks. Playing in a big media market. This is the prototype for an overpriced and overrated player. Everyone raves about his arm, and they should, but watch him make a straight ahead throw. He can turn and throw exceptionally well, but if he has the play entirely in front of him, he adds this release hitch that gives the runner an extra 10 feet. A good ballplayer, but not a great one, and will not age gracefully.

MIKE PIAZZA   **C**   **1969**   **Age 28**

Year	Team	Lge	AB	H	DB	TP	HR	BB	SB	CS	OUT	BA	OBA	SA	EQA	EQR	Peak
1993	Los Angeles	NL	564	186	21	2	37	55	3	3	381	.330	.389	.571	.310	102	.331
1994	Los Angeles	NL	419	142	14	0	27	39	1	3	280	.339	.395	.566	.310	75	.327
1995	Los Angeles	NL	453	166	16	0	35	46	1	0	287	.366	.425	.634	.339	96	.353
1996	Los Angeles	NL	579	209	13	0	40	90	0	3	373	.361	.447	.591	.336	122	.344
1997	*Los Angeles*	*NL*	*609*	*205*	*15*	*0*	*36*	*67*	*0*	*2*	*406*	*.337*	*.402*	*.539*	*.331*	*128*	

One of the best three or four players in baseball, along with Alex Rodriguez and two of the other monsters in any given year. Bad defensive reputation, but who cares? He's not that bad back there and he hits like a beast. Every year. A truly magnificent ballplayer, and if he gets five more years at catcher he will be the very best ever. The most textbook right-handed swing in baseball. You know how hard it is to finish a swing the way he does without opening up your hip? It's damn hard—requires a lot of strength and discipline.

ADAM RIGGS **2B** **1973** **Age 24**

Year	Team	Lge	AB	H	DB	TP	HR	BB	SB	CS	OUT	BA	OBA	SA	EQA	EQR	Peak
1995	San Bernardino	Calif	541	168	22	2	18	46	13	5	378	.311	.365	.458	.276	76	.305
1996	San Antonio	Texas	518	142	22	3	14	36	12	4	380	.274	.321	.409	.247	57	.268
1997	*Los Angeles*	*NL*	*492*	*122*	*22*	*1*	*13*	*42*	*18*	*7*	*377*	*.248*	*.307*	*.376*	*.253*	*61*	

He gets very little attention, but is probably the Dodgers' best second base option for 1997. Plays fairly slick defense, won't hurt you with the bat right now and will get a heck of a lot better. This guy is a ballplayer. Has amazing range to his left for a second baseman. Grade B prospect, but you'll not find a better one.

J.P. ROBERGE **3B/OF** **1973** **Age 24**

Year	Team	Lge	AB	H	DB	TP	HR	BB	SB	CS	OUT	BA	OBA	SA	EQA	EQR	Peak
1995	San Bernardino	Calif	449	109	10	0	13	27	13	4	344	.243	.286	.352	.216	37	.239
1996	San Antonio	Texas	237	67	10	1	6	14	7	2	172	.283	.323	.409	.249	27	.270
1996	Albuquerque	PCL	152	42	4	1	3	13	2	0	110	.276	.333	.375	.242	16	.263
1997	*Los Angeles*	*NL*	*414*	*112*	*15*	*3*	*11*	*27*	*6*	*2*	*304*	*.271*	*.315*	*.401*	*.263*	*54*	

Another vaguely defined prospect; can hit well enough to help a team at third base, but just barely, and is unlikely to do it well enough to make the bigs. Probably will bounce up and down to the bigs a couple of time, but would have been better off staying in Duran Duran.

WILLIE ROMERO **OF** **1975** **Age 22**

Year	Team	Lge	AB	H	DB	TP	HR	BB	SB	CS	OUT	BA	OBA	SA	EQA	EQR	Peak
1993	Yakima	Nwern	52	12	0	0	0	0	1	0	40	.231	.231	.231	.141	1	.155
1993	Bakersfield	Calif	78	25	3	0	1	2	2	1	54	.321	.338	.397	.251	9	.291
1994	Bakersfield	Calif	263	65	11	1	6	15	8	3	201	.247	.288	.365	.221	23	.254
1994	Vero Beach	Flor	128	27	1	0	3	8	0	1	102	.211	.257	.289	.172	6	.198
1995	San Antonio	Texas	387	100	13	1	8	37	9	6	293	.258	.323	.359	.230	37	.262
1996	San Antonio	Texas	455	128	27	3	7	33	17	9	336	.281	.330	.400	.247	51	.276
1997	*Los Angeles*	*NL*	*488*	*127*	*25*	*3*	*9*	*30*	*17*	*11*	*372*	*.260*	*.303*	*.379*	*.250*	*58*	

Improved little by little, and he needs to keep it up for two more years to have a legitimate case for big league playing time. Defense is a big plus—the Dodgers are apparently very high on his glovework, so he might see the bigs more easily than some others.

ERIC STUCKENSCHNEIDER **1B/UT** **1972** **Age 25**

Year	Team	Lge	AB	H	DB	TP	HR	BB	SB	CS	OUT	BA	OBA	SA	EQA	EQR	Peak
1994	Yakima	Nwern	202	54	8	2	3	33	8	3	151	.267	.370	.371	.256	25	.283
1996	Savannah	S Atl	519	140	16	3	15	90	20	8	387	.270	.378	.399	.265	70	.284

A man among boys at A ball…. Maybe I shouldn't put it quite like that. Way too old for his level, but played fantastic and showed great plate discipline. He needs to get to AAA this year to have a good shot at a career, but unlike most old "prospects," I like his chances.

MILT THOMPSON **OF** **1959** **Age 38**

Year	Team	Lge	AB	H	DB	TP	HR	BB	SB	CS	OUT	BA	OBA	SA	EQA	EQR	Peak
1993	Philadelphia	NL	348	93	14	2	4	45	7	3	258	.267	.351	.353	.242	37	.229
1994	Philadelphia	NL	225	64	5	0	4	26	6	2	163	.284	.359	.360	.249	25	.236
1995	Houston	NL	136	33	8	0	3	16	4	2	105	.243	.322	.368	.233	14	.218
1996	Los Angeles	NL	52	7	1	0	0	6	1	1	46	.135	.224	.154	.033	0	-.042

Done. A professional ballplayer for a long time, and consistently performed up to expectations. He'll be missed.

PEDRO ASTACIO **RSP** **1970** **Age 27**

YR	TEAM	Lge	IP	H	ER	HR	BB	K	ERA	W	L	H/9	HR/9	BB/9	K/9	KW
1993	Los Angeles	NL	180.3	175	73	15	88	118	3.64	11	9	8.73	.75	4.39	5.89	.87
1994	Los Angeles	NL	146.0	149	72	19	61	102	4.44	7	9	9.18	1.17	3.76	6.29	1.16
1995	Los Angeles	NL	102.0	110	50	12	37	72	4.41	5	6	9.71	1.06	3.26	6.35	1.30
1996	Los Angeles	NL	208.0	223	80	18	86	115	3.46	13	10	9.65	.78	3.72	4.98	.73

Throws that patented, elbow-rending Dodger curveball along with a plus fastball. Has been worked hard at a young age, and his K rate plummeted in 1996. I realize Pedro's not a superstar, but he is not going to just ride the wave this year. Look for him to bring the K rate back up and be fantastic, or to go down with a horrible arm injury of some sort.

NATE BLAND   **LSP**   **1975**   **Age 22**

YR	TEAM	Lge	IP	H	ER	HR	BB	K	ERA	W	L	H/9	HR/9	BB/9	K/9	KW
1993	Yakima	Nwern	54.3	74	37	3	32	25	6.13	2	4	12.26	.50	5.30	4.14	.06
1994	Bakersfield	Calif	45.0	63	28	10	34	12	5.60	2	3	12.60	2.00	6.80	2.40	-.90
1995	Bakersfield	Calif	106.7	163	78	13	71	29	6.58	3	9	13.75	1.10	5.99	2.45	-.68
1996	Savannah	S Atl	23.7	34	10	0	15	13	3.80	2	1	12.93	.00	5.70	4.94	.22
1996	Vero Beach	Flor	84.7	117	44	5	49	50	4.68	4	5	12.44	.53	5.21	5.31	.47

Touring our nation's wonderful A ball leagues. Formerly the guitarist for Thin Lizzy, but lost his job to Gary Moore. You may remember his solo hit, "Precious and Few." Not within a light year of being a prospect.

BILLY BREWER   **LRP**   **1968**   **Age 29**

YR	TEAM	Lge	IP	H	ER	HR	BB	K	ERA	W	L	H/9	HR/9	BB/9	K/9	KW
1993	Kansas City	AL	38.3	31	13	6	22	29	3.05	3	1	7.28	1.41	5.17	6.81	.98
1994	Kansas City	AL	38.0	27	7	4	17	24	1.66	3	1	6.39	.95	4.03	5.68	.89
1995	Kansas City	AL	46.3	51	23	9	21	31	4.47	2	3	9.91	1.75	4.08	6.02	.99
1996	Albuquerque	PCL	29.3	26	9	4	25	26	2.76	2	1	7.98	1.23	7.67	7.98	.74
1996	Columbus, OH	Inter	24.3	26	17	4	22	22	6.29	1	2	9.62	1.48	8.14	8.14	.68

A serviceable reliever whose career hasn't really started yet; he'll be bouncing from organization to organization for some time to come. Can help a lot of major league clubs if he's healthy.

WILLIAM BRUNSON   **LBP**   **1970**   **Age 27**

YR	TEAM	Lge	IP	H	ER	HR	BB	K	ERA	W	L	H/9	HR/9	BB/9	K/9	KW
1993	Charleston, WV	S Atl	102.3	166	84	14	71	61	7.39	2	9	14.60	1.23	6.24	5.36	.23
1994	Winston-Salem	Caro	148.7	188	80	20	79	86	4.84	7	10	11.38	1.21	4.78	5.21	.54
1995	San Bernardino	Calif	74.0	79	21	4	28	45	2.55	6	2	9.61	.49	3.41	5.47	.97
1995	San Antonio	Texas	72.0	120	49	5	31	38	6.12	2	6	15.00	.62	3.88	4.75	.61
1996	San Antonio	Texas	38.3	38	13	2	21	32	3.05	3	1	8.92	.47	4.93	7.51	1.27
1996	Albuquerque	PCL	51.3	48	21	6	28	38	3.68	3	3	8.42	1.05	4.91	6.66	.99

Right on the cusp of being good enough to break into the majors. There's no difference between this guy and the Jim Corsis and Alan Millses of the world except a little luck. Brunson will likely be in the majors in 1998, and will likely be effective.

JIM BRUSKE   **RRP**   **1965**   **Age 32**

YR	TEAM	Lge	IP	H	ER	HR	BB	K	ERA	W	L	H/9	HR/9	BB/9	K/9	KW
1993	Jackson	Texas	87.7	101	35	7	37	59	3.59	6	4	10.37	.72	3.80	6.06	1.07
1993	Tucson	PCL	61.3	75	29	4	24	33	4.26	3	4	11.01	.59	3.52	4.84	.73
1994	Tucson	PCL	36.7	45	17	2	11	21	4.17	2	2	11.05	.49	2.70	5.15	1.04
1995	Albuquerque	PCL	107.7	121	42	7	52	90	3.51	7	5	10.11	.59	4.35	7.52	1.42
1996	Albuquerque	PCL	58.7	57	24	3	27	41	3.68	4	3	8.74	.46	4.14	6.29	1.06
1996	Los Angeles	NL	13.0	18	7	2	4	11	4.85	0	1	12.46	1.38	2.77	7.62	1.85

Journeyman who's been good enough to have a job, but just never really took advantage of his limited opportunities. Bud Selig and his ilk have their collective eyes on guys like this for the next scab folly.

DAN CAMACHO   **RSP**   **1974**   **Age 23**

YR	TEAM	Lge	IP	H	ER	HR	BB	K	ERA	W	L	H/9	HR/9	BB/9	K/9	KW
1994	Bakersfield	Calif	19.7	12	2	0	18	16	.92	2	0	5.49	.00	8.24	7.32	.38
1995	San Bernardino	Calif	59.7	74	29	7	39	50	4.37	3	4	11.16	1.06	5.88	7.54	1.04
1995	San Antonio	Texas	10.0	11	2	0	10	7	1.80	1	0	9.90	.00	9.00	6.30	-.15
1996	San Bernardino	Calif	66.3	80	43	10	60	45	5.83	2	5	10.85	1.36	8.14	6.11	.00
1996	Vero Beach	Flor	48.7	45	16	5	38	36	2.96	3	2	8.32	.92	7.03	6.66	.46
1996	San Antonio	Texas	15.0	13	5	0	21	9	3.00	1	1	7.80	.00	12.60	5.40	-1.35

To quote Sun Tzu, "Throw the %^$^%ing ball over the #$%@#$%ing plate, you #$%@$^!!!" (*The Art of War*, Billy Martin commemorative edition.)

TOM CANDIOTTI   **RSP**   **1958**   **Age 39**

YR	TEAM	Lge	IP	H	ER	HR	BB	K	ERA	W	L	H/9	HR/9	BB/9	K/9	KW
1993	Los Angeles	NL	207.0	204	79	13	94	150	3.43	13	10	8.87	.57	4.09	6.52	1.15
1994	Los Angeles	NL	149.7	158	71	9	68	96	4.27	8	9	9.50	.54	4.09	5.77	.90
1995	Los Angeles	NL	186.3	200	87	19	75	127	4.20	10	11	9.66	.92	3.62	6.13	1.14
1996	Los Angeles	NL	150.0	185	87	18	57	70	5.22	6	11	11.10	1.08	3.42	4.20	.54

If he's healthy, he can be in any rotation in baseball, post a league average ERA and soak up 175 innings. What don't we know about Tom Candiotti?

SCOTT CHAMBERS   **LRP**   **1976**   **Age 21**

YR	TEAM	Lge	IP	H	ER	HR	BB	K	ERA	W	L	H/9	HR/9	BB/9	K/9	KW
1995	Yakima	Nwern	24.0	40	22	5	18	20	8.25	1	2	15.00	1.88	6.75	7.50	.81
1996	Vero Beach	Flor	11.0	8	6	2	7	14	4.91	0	1	6.55	1.64	5.73	11.45	2.39

Hard thrower who'll spend most of 1997 in San Antonio looking for his control. If he finds it… he'll be a prospect. (Stop me if you've heard this before.) His motion looks as wild on Crispin Glover on ecstasy; I expect he'll improve under good tutelage.

DARREN DREIFORT   **RRP**   **1972**   **Age 25**

YR	TEAM	Lge	IP	H	ER	HR	BB	K	ERA	W	L	H/9	HR/9	BB/9	K/9	KW
1994	San Antonio	Texas	32.3	43	15	0	17	24	4.18	2	2	11.97	.00	4.73	6.68	1.04
1994	Los Angeles	NL	29.7	46	20	0	19	21	6.07	1	2	13.96	.00	5.76	6.37	.68
1996	Albuquerque	PCL	81.3	79	36	6	60	60	3.98	5	4	8.74	.66	6.64	6.64	.55
1996	Los Angeles	NL	23.3	26	13	2	14	21	5.01	1	2	10.03	.77	5.40	8.10	1.35

Seems to have come back from the injury fairly well; now he's got a much tougher battle ahead of him—learning to pitch and control his stuff. There's a good chance he won't be able to do it. Often compared to a young Todd Worrell, but Worrell had a bit more control than this at the same age. Did not attend Pepperdine University.

JOEY EISCHEN   **LRP**   **1970**   **Age 27**

YR	TEAM	Lge	IP	H	ER	HR	BB	K	ERA	W	L	H/9	HR/9	BB/9	K/9	KW
1993	Harrisburg	East	108.7	141	63	13	77	84	5.22	4	8	11.68	1.08	6.38	6.96	.72
1993	Ottawa	Inter	38.3	37	16	3	20	23	3.76	2	2	8.69	.70	4.70	5.40	.63
1994	Ottawa	Inter	58.3	62	39	8	49	48	6.02	2	4	9.57	1.23	7.56	7.41	.58
1995	Albuquerque	PCL	15.3	8	0	0	5	13	.00	2	0	4.70	.00	2.93	7.63	1.81
1995	Ottawa	Inter	14.7	11	3	0	10	11	1.84	2	0	6.75	.00	6.14	6.75	.72
1995	Los Angeles	NL	20.3	20	8	1	13	14	3.54	1	1	8.85	.44	5.75	6.20	.63
1996	Detroit	AL	24.7	26	8	2	15	15	2.92	2	1	9.49	.73	5.47	5.47	.46
1996	Los Angeles	NL	42.7	52	24	4	25	32	5.06	2	3	10.97	.84	5.27	6.75	.93

Eischen can pitch, but no one's ever sure of when. One day, you get an unhittable selection of pitches, the next day you get Bob Tewksbury without control. Every outing's like a blind date. But in Detroit, he's a staff ace.

KRIS FOSTER   **RBP**   **1975**   **Age 22**

YR	TEAM	Lge	IP	H	ER	HR	BB	K	ERA	W	L	H/9	HR/9	BB/9	K/9	KW
1995	Yakima	Nwern	46.7	52	31	3	50	30	5.98	2	3	10.03	.58	9.64	5.79	-.48
1996	San Bernardino	Calif	73.3	68	36	5	63	49	4.42	4	4	8.35	.61	7.73	6.01	.07

Critical year for Foster. Could take a big step forward or could flounder. I think he's a prospect, but to be quite honest, that's nothing more than a gut feeling. I have no evidence to support it, no logic behind it. Think of Kris Foster as Bob Dole's Tax Plan or Bill Clinton's Foreign Policy, but carbon-based.

MARK GUTHRIE   **LRP**   **1966**   **Age 31**

YR	TEAM	Lge	IP	H	ER	HR	BB	K	ERA	W	L	H/9	HR/9	BB/9	K/9	KW
1993	Minnesota	AL	21.0	20	9	2	17	16	3.86	1	1	8.57	.86	7.29	6.86	.46
1994	Minnesota	AL	51.3	62	33	7	20	37	5.79	2	4	10.87	1.23	3.51	6.49	1.29
1995	Los Angeles	NL	19.3	20	10	1	11	17	4.66	1	1	9.31	.47	5.12	7.91	1.36
1995	Minnesota	AL	42.7	44	16	5	17	48	3.38	3	2	9.28	1.05	3.59	10.12	2.48
1996	Los Angeles	NL	71.0	72	19	3	28	49	2.41	6	2	9.13	.38	3.55	6.21	1.18

Makes your bullpen full and light. Fills a need, and will likely do so for several years to come. He's finally found the role he can excel at, and his pitches are too good for him not to succeed.

MIKE HARKEY   RBP   1967   Age 30

YR	TEAM	Lge	IP	H	ER	HR	BB	K	ERA	W	L	H/9	HR/9	BB/9	K/9	KW
1993	Chicago Cubs	NL	154.7	187	91	17	61	65	5.30	6	11	10.88	.99	3.55	3.78	.37
1994	Colorado	NL	92.0	114	49	9	43	36	4.79	4	6	11.15	.88	4.21	3.52	.12
1995	California	AL	62.7	75	25	11	17	28	3.59	4	3	10.77	1.58	2.44	4.02	.73
1995	Oakland	AL	66.7	74	38	11	33	28	5.13	3	4	9.99	1.49	4.46	3.78	.15
1996	Albuquerque	PCL	113.0	132	58	10	49	72	4.62	6	7	10.51	.80	3.90	5.73	.94

"Albuquerque's on the line. They say you're a $%^head, brainless and should be ground up for food."
"Bastards. Grab Mike Harkey off waivers and send his ass down there. That'll put the fear of God in 'em."

MATT HERGES   RBP   1970   Age 27

YR	TEAM	Lge	IP	H	ER	HR	BB	K	ERA	W	L	H/9	HR/9	BB/9	K/9	KW
1993	Bakersfield	Calif	80.0	82	46	7	64	59	5.18	3	6	9.23	.79	7.20	6.64	.41
1994	Vero Beach	Flor	100.3	130	45	12	45	46	4.04	5	6	11.66	1.08	4.04	4.13	.37
1995	San Bernardino	Calif	45.3	64	26	3	20	22	5.16	2	3	12.71	.60	3.97	4.37	.46
1995	San Antonio	Texas	24.7	39	17	2	20	16	6.20	1	2	14.23	.73	7.30	5.84	.12
1996	San Antonio	Texas	75.7	94	37	3	39	38	4.40	4	4	11.18	.36	4.64	4.52	.35
1996	Albuquerque	PCL	32.7	30	8	2	17	12	2.20	3	1	8.27	.55	4.68	3.31	-.07

Got people out at two levels last year, but I'm not sure how. Doesn't throw real hard, doesn't have great control and his breaking pitches didn't impress me. Of course, I don't have to hit off the guy. He's a journeyman, and probably no prospect, but I think he's earned an invite to camp.

JOE LAGARDE   RRP   1975   Age 22

YR	TEAM	Lge	IP	H	ER	HR	BB	K	ERA	W	L	H/9	HR/9	BB/9	K/9	KW
1993	Yakima	Nwern	58.0	101	33	6	29	26	5.12	2	4	15.67	.93	4.50	4.03	.22
1994	Vero Beach	Flor	96.0	113	55	7	54	50	5.16	4	7	10.59	.66	5.06	4.69	.30
1995	Bakersfield	Calif	19.3	20	7	1	16	16	3.26	1	1	9.31	.47	7.45	7.45	.62
1995	San Bernardino	Calif	107.3	144	74	9	87	65	6.20	4	8	12.07	.75	7.30	5.45	-.01
1996	Vero Beach	Flor	40.0	47	17	1	29	33	3.83	2	2	10.57	.22	6.53	7.43	.84
1996	San Antonio	Texas	28.3	32	7	0	15	18	2.22	2	1	10.16	.00	4.76	5.72	.71
1996	Albuquerque	PCL	11.3	12	5	2	10	9	3.97	1	0	9.53	1.59	7.94	7.15	.40

Currently undergoing that starter to reliever transition. Contrary to what you've heard, you don't have to go to Sweden, but it is a long and painful process nonetheless. Good stuff; will have to find some control to go with it, but he's got a few years to do so.

RICH LINARES   RRP   1973   Age 24

YR	TEAM	Lge	IP	H	ER	HR	BB	K	ERA	W	L	H/9	HR/9	BB/9	K/9	KW
1993	Vero Beach	Flor	97.3	112	37	7	41	62	3.42	6	5	10.36	.65	3.79	5.73	.96
1995	Bakersfield	Calif	59.3	76	17	2	24	36	2.58	5	2	11.53	.30	3.64	5.46	.91
1996	San Bernardino	Calif	56.0	64	24	2	22	37	3.86	3	3	10.29	.32	3.54	5.95	1.10

Has pitched consistently and well. Will spend the season in San Antonio. I like him; throws well low in the strike zone and doesn't give up a lot of home runs. His stuff isn't the most overpowering in the world, but he's a quick learner, and I expect him to get to the majors and have success there. Perhaps not in this organization, but I expect it to happen.

JESUS MARTINEZ   LSP   1974   Age 23

YR	TEAM	Lge	IP	H	ER	HR	BB	K	ERA	W	L	H/9	HR/9	BB/9	K/9	KW
1993	Bakersfield	Calif	126.7	171	93	13	85	76	6.61	4	10	12.15	.92	6.04	5.40	.29
1994	Vero Beach	Flor	79.7	100	64	10	56	52	7.23	2	7	11.30	1.13	6.33	5.87	.38
1995	San Antonio	Texas	124.3	153	69	8	90	72	4.99	5	9	11.08	.58	6.51	5.21	.11
1996	San Antonio	Texas	145.7	183	93	8	119	104	5.75	5	11	11.31	.49	7.35	6.43	.30

"I hate playing in September, because everyone you face has brought up Chico Pascual Jesus Perez Martinez Sanchez, a skinny kid, from the minors and you don't know where they're going to throw the ball." – Don Baylor, 1984. Baylor's a yutz of a manager, but he nailed this one.

RAMON MARTINEZ   **RSP**   **1968**   **Age 29**

YR	TEAM	Lge	IP	H	ER	HR	BB	K	ERA	W	L	H/9	HR/9	BB/9	K/9	KW
1993	Los Angeles	NL	206.3	214	82	16	128	123	3.58	13	10	9.33	.70	5.58	5.37	.39
1994	Los Angeles	NL	167.0	167	76	19	71	112	4.10	9	10	9.00	1.02	3.83	6.04	1.06
1995	Los Angeles	NL	201.7	189	87	20	98	124	3.88	11	11	8.43	.89	4.37	5.53	.75
1996	Los Angeles	NL	166.3	167	70	12	102	118	3.79	9	9	9.04	.65	5.52	6.38	.75

29, my pink ass. Appears to have rebounded a little from his overwork, but I still think he's going to go down at any moment due to tendon strain. Lasorda worked him like a limber hooker for years, and eventually the piper is going to be paid. I expect he'll miss the better part of one of the next two years, then come back and pitch well out of the bullpen in about 2000.

ONAN MASAOKA   **LBP**   **1978**   **Age 19**

YR	TEAM	Lge	IP	H	ER	HR	BB	K	ERA	W	L	H/9	HR/9	BB/9	K/9	KW
1995	Yakima	Nwern	42.0	36	26	3	61	41	5.57	2	3	7.71	.64	13.07	8.79	-.34
1996	Savannah	S Atl	53.3	83	46	9	50	45	7.76	1	5	14.01	1.52	8.44	7.59	.42

Part of the Dodgers' international outreach program that they've used exceptionally well. Has nasty stuff and probably will get to the majors, but it's going to be a couple of years. Star of a little-known porn film last year, "Onan the Barbarian." Right now, approximately 5% of you are laughing hysterically, 85% are going on to Mitch McNeely, and 10% are checking out your video library. To the 5%: Fight the power.

MITCH McNEELY   **LRP**   **1974**   **Age 23**

YR	TEAM	Lge	IP	H	ER	HR	BB	K	ERA	W	L	H/9	HR/9	BB/9	K/9	KW
1995	Yakima	Nwern	43.7	73	35	1	20	17	7.21	1	4	15.05	.21	4.12	3.50	.14
1996	Vero Beach	Flor	43.0	39	13	0	18	24	2.72	3	2	8.16	.00	3.77	5.02	.73

Pitched well in his stint at Vero Beach; headed for California and then San Antonio. Good mechanics; he'll have success if he can keep the ball down.

MARK MIMBS   **LSP**   **1969**   **Age 28**

YR	TEAM	Lge	IP	H	ER	HR	BB	K	ERA	W	L	H/9	HR/9	BB/9	K/9	KW
1993	San Antonio	Texas	61.0	62	23	1	28	55	3.39	4	3	9.15	.15	4.13	8.11	1.67
1993	Albuquerque	PCL	17.0	17	15	0	18	9	7.94	0	2	9.00	.00	9.53	4.76	-.79
1995	Albuquerque	PCL	100.0	102	30	8	31	87	2.70	8	3	9.18	.72	2.79	7.83	1.91
1996	Albuquerque	PCL	143.3	152	69	14	56	109	4.33	7	9	9.54	.88	3.52	6.84	1.40

Good enough to be starting outside of Atlanta or Los Angeles. Of course there's no pitching in the majors; a lot of it's hiding in Richmond and Albuquerque. I really think Mimbs can be a very good major league starter, and he'll likely get a chance to prove it at some point.

TONY NAKASHIMA   **LBP**   **1978**   **Age 19**

YR	TEAM	Lge	IP	H	ER	HR	BB	K	ERA	W	L	H/9	HR/9	BB/9	K/9	KW
1996	Savannah	S Atl	31.7	30	14	3	27	22	3.98	2	2	8.53	.85	7.67	6.25	.17

Quick. Name the nine countries that have not produced a Dodger pitcher. If I were O'Malley, I'd fight the internationalization of the draft like it were life and death. Baseball's collective ownership is doing everything it can to eliminate the incentives to invest in your own business. If the Dodgers are smart enough to make this sort of investment, they should be able to do so.

HIDEO NOMO   **RSP**   **1969**   **Age 28**

YR	TEAM	Lge	IP	H	ER	HR	BB	K	ERA	W	L	H/9	HR/9	BB/9	K/9	KW
1995	Los Angeles	NL	185.0	142	56	16	92	211	2.72	14	7	6.91	.78	4.48	10.26	2.30
1996	Los Angeles	NL	223.3	198	85	24	104	206	3.43	14	11	7.98	.97	4.19	8.30	1.72

A very fine pitcher, and responsible for shutting me up about the caliber of play in Japan, for which many are eternally grateful. I'm beginning to wonder about the caliber of play in Detroit, though. You know about Nomo; takes forever to release the ball, and baserunners can actually trot to the next bag. I'd have loved to see Eric Davis in his prime against this guy. He'd go 1 for 9 with about five walks per series, and might not even stop at second base when he stole it. Just make the turn and go to third.

ANTONIO OSUNA   **RRP**   **1973**   **Age 24**

YR	TEAM	Lge	IP	H	ER	HR	BB	K	ERA	W	L	H/9	HR/9	BB/9	K/9	KW
1993	Bakersfield	Calif	16.0	24	10	2	5	14	5.62	1	1	13.50	1.12	2.81	7.88	1.92
1994	San Antonio	Texas	42.0	26	5	0	24	39	1.07	5	0	5.57	.00	5.14	8.36	1.50
1995	Albuquerque	PCL	17.7	13	7	3	11	17	3.57	1	1	6.62	1.53	5.60	8.66	1.49
1995	Los Angeles	NL	44.0	42	20	6	24	42	4.09	2	3	8.59	1.23	4.91	8.59	1.64
1996	Los Angeles	NL	81.7	73	30	6	39	75	3.31	5	4	8.04	.66	4.30	8.27	1.68

You can succeed without great control, but if Osuna could just get on top of that fastball a little bit more, he might be completely unhittable. Right-handers hit him as if they were Raffy Belliard's sick cousin Willy.

CHAN HO PARK   **RRP**   **1973**   **Age 24**

YR	TEAM	Lge	IP	H	ER	HR	BB	K	ERA	W	L	H/9	HR/9	BB/9	K/9	KW
1994	San Antonio	Texas	91.0	114	59	6	73	74	5.84	3	7	11.27	.59	7.22	7.32	.63
1995	Albuquerque	PCL	103.7	86	48	11	87	92	4.17	6	6	7.47	.95	7.55	7.99	.77
1996	Los Angeles	NL	107.3	91	44	8	82	105	3.69	6	6	7.63	.67	6.88	8.80	1.22

Still two years away from finding his control. A patient team will kill guys like this, while the Cubs will simply go down quietly, swinging at pitches near their Adam's apple.

JULIO PARRA   **RRP**   **1975**   **Age 22**

YR	TEAM	Lge	IP	H	ER	HR	BB	K	ERA	W	L	H/9	HR/9	BB/9	K/9	KW
1995	San Bernardino	Calif	60.7	83	40	7	38	41	5.93	2	5	12.31	1.04	5.64	6.08	.62
1995	Vero Beach	Flor	35.7	48	23	3	27	26	5.80	1	3	12.11	.76	6.81	6.56	.48
1996	Savannah	S Atl	13.7	13	5	3	9	11	3.29	1	1	8.56	1.98	5.93	7.24	.93
1996	Vero Beach	Flor	19.0	15	3	2	8	12	1.42	2	0	7.11	.95	3.79	5.68	.95

Pitched real well and actually started to show some control and finesse on a few pitches. Parra's a keeper, and he'll be in the majors for good by 1998. His stuff isn't in the same category as Osuna's, but he can make the hitters get a bit uncomfortable. Not likely to be a closer.

JOSE PRADO   **RRP**   **1972**   **Age 25**

YR	TEAM	Lge	IP	H	ER	HR	BB	K	ERA	W	L	H/9	HR/9	BB/9	K/9	KW
1993	Vero Beach	Flor	49.3	51	32	4	38	24	5.84	2	3	9.30	.73	6.93	4.38	-.27
1994	Bakersfield	Calif	145.3	185	72	9	73	94	4.46	7	9	11.46	.56	4.52	5.82	.81
1995	San Antonio	Texas	129.3	151	77	12	82	81	5.36	5	9	10.51	.84	5.71	5.64	.45
1996	San Antonio	Texas	29.3	36	22	3	30	17	6.75	1	2	11.05	.92	9.20	5.22	-.56

The reward for pitching tepidly in San Antonio is another glorious year there. He hasn't taken that step up, and will be hard pressed to get significant playing time at Albuquerque. Six-year free agent, will probably end up with the Angel organization.

SCOTT RADINSKY   **LRP**   **1968**   **Age 29**

YR	TEAM	Lge	IP	H	ER	HR	BB	K	ERA	W	L	H/9	HR/9	BB/9	K/9	KW
1993	Chi. White Sox	AL	54.3	61	28	3	21	46	4.64	3	3	10.10	.50	3.48	7.62	1.67
1995	Chi. White Sox	AL	38.7	44	19	7	18	14	4.42	2	2	10.24	1.63	4.19	3.26	.04
1996	Los Angeles	NL	51.0	57	18	2	22	42	3.18	4	2	10.06	.35	3.88	7.41	1.50

Back to where he was before his rather unfriendly illness. He'll get back another mph or two on his fastball this year, and I expect him to pick up right where he left off. One of the few guys I ever saw who made Harold Baines look completely lost at the plate.

GARY RATH   **LSP**   **1973**   **Age 24**

YR	TEAM	Lge	IP	H	ER	HR	BB	K	ERA	W	L	H/9	HR/9	BB/9	K/9	KW
1994	Vero Beach	Flor	56.7	63	26	5	31	38	4.13	3	3	10.01	.79	4.92	6.04	.78
1995	San Antonio	Texas	105.3	113	44	8	62	70	3.76	6	6	9.66	.68	5.30	5.98	.67
1995	Albuquerque	PCL	37.0	42	24	4	24	21	5.84	1	3	10.22	.97	5.84	5.11	.24
1996	Albuquerque	PCL	170.0	159	69	12	106	100	3.65	10	9	8.42	.64	5.61	5.29	.36

Pitched effectively all year at Albuquerque and will be battling for the fifth spot in the Dodger rotation. Control comes and goes. There's still something wrong with his release point. That's not necessarily a bad thing; better than just sucking. Release points can be found and mechanics can be fixed. Just sucking, a la Sean Bergman, is considerably harder to overcome.

DAN RICABAL RBP 1973 Age 24

YR	TEAM	Lge	IP	H	ER	HR	BB	K	ERA	W	L	H/9	HR/9	BB/9	K/9	KW
1994	Yakima	Nwern	25.0	25	4	0	13	16	1.44	3	0	9.00	.00	4.68	5.76	.75
1995	San Bernardino	Calif	63.3	69	31	7	43	39	4.41	3	4	9.81	.99	6.11	5.54	.32
1996	Savannah	S Atl	48.7	48	23	6	26	43	4.25	2	3	8.88	1.11	4.81	7.95	1.45
1996	Vero Beach	Flor	27.3	17	6	2	22	26	1.98	2	1	5.60	.66	7.24	8.56	1.04

Control issues, but definitely has the stuff to make the bigs. Had some soreness in 1995, seems to have recovered nicely and will probably spend the year in glorious San Antonio, Texas.

FELIX RODRIGUEZ RSP 1973 Age 24

YR	TEAM	Lge	IP	H	ER	HR	BB	K	ERA	W	L	H/9	HR/9	BB/9	K/9	KW
1993	Vero Beach	Flor	114.7	128	75	19	92	62	5.89	4	9	10.05	1.49	7.22	4.87	-.18
1994	San Antonio	Texas	123.7	130	75	11	111	93	5.46	5	9	9.46	.80	8.08	6.77	.24
1995	Albuquerque	PCL	48.0	49	22	5	32	42	4.12	2	3	9.19	.94	6.00	7.88	1.12
1995	Los Angeles	NL	10.0	13	3	2	6	5	2.70	1	0	11.70	1.80	5.40	4.50	.15
1996	Albuquerque	PCL	101.3	99	52	15	70	52	4.62	5	6	8.79	1.33	6.22	4.62	-.01

Seems to have blown his clutch and is kind of spinning in place. He's been effective during those games where he hasn't walked ten guys. But you kind of need to get rid of those games in order to be a good starter. Will fight for a rotation spot, but I think Rath's likely to beat him out for it, at least by June.

RUDY SEANEZ RRP 1969 Age 28

YR	TEAM	Lge	IP	H	ER	HR	BB	K	ERA	W	L	H/9	HR/9	BB/9	K/9	KW
1993	Las Vegas	PCL	18.0	22	11	2	13	11	5.50	1	1	11.00	1.00	6.50	5.50	.21
1994	Albuquerque	PCL	20.7	25	10	3	15	22	4.35	1	1	10.89	1.31	6.53	9.58	1.56
1994	Los Angeles	NL	23.3	25	6	2	12	17	2.31	2	1	9.64	.77	4.63	6.56	1.03
1995	Los Angeles	NL	34.3	42	25	5	21	26	6.55	1	3	11.01	1.31	5.50	6.82	.90
1996	Albuquerque	PCL	18.3	24	13	0	13	16	6.38	1	1	11.78	.00	6.38	7.85	1.02

Seanez doesn't throw 141 mph anymore and he still can't find the strike zone. At some point, you just have to give up. I mean, how long is "it feels so good when I stop" a good reason to do something? The Dodgers need to just say no.

JODY TREADWELL RSP 1969 Age 28

YR	TEAM	Lge	IP	H	ER	HR	BB	K	ERA	W	L	H/9	HR/9	BB/9	K/9	KW
1993	Albuquerque	PCL	97.7	104	40	7	62	79	3.69	6	5	9.58	.65	5.71	7.28	1.00
1994	Albuquerque	PCL	149.0	139	55	10	74	97	3.32	10	7	8.40	.60	4.47	5.86	.84
1995	Albuquerque	PCL	117.7	116	47	16	43	72	3.59	7	6	8.87	1.22	3.29	5.51	1.01
1996	Albuquerque	PCL	17.0	27	13	3	12	13	6.88	1	1	14.29	1.59	6.35	6.88	.71

Injured most of the year, but is still a good candidate to end up in a rotation somewhere. If he shows he's healthy he could be trade bait. Earned a rotation spot three years ago, but doesn't break 90, so the Dodgers just kind of ignored him. Can help most of the teams in the AL.

ISMAEL VALDES RSP 1974 Age 23

YR	TEAM	Lge	IP	H	ER	HR	BB	K	ERA	W	L	H/9	HR/9	BB/9	K/9	KW
1994	San Antonio	Texas	49.3	63	23	5	15	40	4.20	2	3	11.49	.91	2.74	7.30	1.75
1994	Albuquerque	PCL	42.0	42	15	1	17	33	3.21	3	2	9.00	.21	3.64	7.07	1.45
1994	Los Angeles	NL	27.3	23	9	2	13	26	2.96	2	1	7.57	.66	4.28	8.56	1.78
1995	Los Angeles	NL	192.7	180	68	18	66	135	3.18	13	8	8.41	.84	3.08	6.31	1.33
1996	Los Angeles	NL	220.3	236	87	20	74	153	3.55	13	11	9.64	.82	3.02	6.25	1.33

Looks something like Speed Racer. One of my favorite pitchers, and probably the most consistent starter I can think of off the top of my head. (See Michael Wolverton's excellent Support Neutral Won/Loss Reports on page 465.) He's been overworked, and I'm hopeful for Ismael's sake that Bill Russell will take it easy on his arm. He's only 23 this coming year, and those innings in 1995 were compressed into a short season.

TODD WORRELL   **RRP**   **1960**   **Age 37**

YR	TEAM	Lge	IP	H	ER	HR	BB	K	ERA	W	L	H/9	HR/9	BB/9	K/9	KW
1993	Los Angeles	NL	38.3	47	26	6	16	30	6.10	1	3	11.03	1.41	3.76	7.04	1.41
1994	Los Angeles	NL	40.7	40	19	4	16	41	4.20	2	3	8.85	.89	3.54	9.07	2.14
1995	Los Angeles	NL	60.3	55	14	5	24	55	2.09	6	1	8.20	.75	3.58	8.20	1.84
1996	Los Angeles	NL	64.3	75	27	5	21	58	3.78	4	3	10.49	.70	2.94	8.11	1.97

The Pride of Biola College, Worrell pitched great all year and there's little reason to believe things will be any different during 1997. 65 innings is about his limit, but he's very effective under that threshold. Good to see him come back from those injuries. Sometimes it takes a few years, and most pitchers don't ever really get that chance.

Player	Age	Team	Lge	AB	H	DB	TP	HR	BB	SB	CS	OUT	BA	OBA	SA	EQA	EQR	Peak
CLIFF ANDERSON	25	Albuquerque	PCL	182	41	5	1	4	20	2	2	143	.225	.302	.330	.210	14	.221
	25	S. Bernardino	Calif	229	59	9	1	8	11	4	3	173	.258	.292	.410	.232	23	.245
ALEX ASENCIO	22	Vero Beach	Flor	412	102	10	4	3	26	8	3	313	.248	.292	.313	.205	30	.226
TODD BARLOK	24	Vero Beach	Flor	399	96	15	1	6	49	4	3	306	.241	.324	.328	.220	35	.235
HENRY BLANCO	24	San Antonio	Texas	315	80	9	1	5	27	2	2	237	.254	.313	.337	.218	26	.234
MIKE BUSCH	27	Albuquerque	PCL	139	37	3	0	10	20	0	1	103	.266	.358	.504	.278	21	.285
	27	Los Angeles	NL	85	20	5	0	4	6	0	0	65	.235	.286	.435	.236	9	.239
MIKE CARPENTIER	21	Vero Beach	Flor	213	44	4	0	5	17	2	2	171	.207	.265	.296	.181	12	.202
JUAN CASTRO	24	Los Angeles	NL	135	29	5	3	0	11	1	0	106	.215	.274	.296	.188	8	.200
KYLE COONEY	23	S. Bernardino	Calif	406	95	9	0	11	19	4	4	315	.234	.268	.337	.199	28	.215
ALEX CORA	20	Vero Beach	Flor	218	51	4	2	1	12	3	2	169	.234	.274	.284	.183	12	.207
BRAD DANDRIDGE	24	Albuquerque	PCL	78	17	2	0	2	3	0	0	61	.218	.247	.321	.183	4	.198
	24	San Antonio	Texas	181	49	4	0	3	12	3	2	134	.271	.316	.343	.223	16	.237
EDDIE DAVIS	23	S. Bernardino	Calif	549	122	17	1	21	46	16	12	439	.222	.282	.372	.216	47	.235
CHRIS DEMETRAL	26	Albuquerque	PCL	205	44	4	0	4	37	3	2	163	.215	.335	.293	.213	17	.221
CHRIS DURKIN	25	Vero Beach	Flor	210	56	4	0	15	25	2	0	154	.267	.345	.500	.277	31	.292
KEVIN GIBBS	22	Vero Beach	Flor	441	115	11	6	2	58	30	11	336	.261	.347	.327	.237	46	.262
GERONIMO GIL	20	Savannah	S Atl	285	63	6	0	6	6	0	1	223	.221	.237	.305	.171	14	.195
MANUEL GONZALEZ	20	S. Bernardino	Calif	167	42	4	2	0	9	5	4	129	.251	.290	.299	.197	11	.224
	20	Savannah	S Atl	242	50	8	1	1	16	6	3	195	.207	.256	.260	.166	11	.189
RAFAEL GROSS	21	S. Bernardino	Calif	362	73	11	1	5	12	15	7	296	.202	.227	.279	.164	16	.181
JUAN HERNAIZ	21	Savannah	S Atl	512	134	12	3	12	17	18	7	385	.262	.285	.367	.222	45	.249
CARLOS HERNANDEZ	29	Albuquerque	PCL	228	45	5	0	5	11	4	2	185	.197	.234	.285	.164	10	.164
KEN HUCKABY	25	Albuquerque	PCL	279	65	11	1	3	17	0	0	214	.233	.277	.312	.194	18	.204
KEITH JOHNSON	25	San Antonio	Texas	528	139	21	3	10	19	12	5	394	.263	.289	.371	.223	46	.235
TITO LANDRUM	25	S. Bernardino	Calif	158	36	4	0	2	16	4	2	124	.228	.299	.291	.199	11	.209
	25	Vero Beach	Flor	125	28	3	0	2	9	1	0	97	.224	.276	.296	.189	8	.200
PAUL LODUCA	24	Vero Beach	Flor	460	133	10	0	6	62	4	1	328	.289	.374	.350	.251	52	.268
BILLY LOTT	25	Albuquerque	PCL	409	92	11	1	15	43	5	4	321	.225	.299	.367	.220	37	.233
BRIAN MAJESKI	24	Vero Beach	Flor	213	50	6	1	1	26	8	4	167	.235	.318	.286	.207	16	.221
ORESTE MARRERO	26	Albuquerque	PCL	431	103	15	1	12	34	2	3	331	.239	.295	.362	.217	36	.226
RAFAEL MARTINEZ	20	Vero Beach	Flor	364	65	6	1	6	36	1	2	301	.179	.252	.250	.151	13	.172
JOSE MATEO	19	Savannah	S Atl	323	48	2	0	2	26	5	2	277	.149	.212	.173	.059	1	.070
RON MAURER	28	Albuquerque	PCL	217	49	7	1	5	28	2	2	170	.226	.314	.336	.217	19	.219
DAN MELENDEZ	25	San Antonio	Texas	194	44	5	0	2	19	0	0	150	.227	.296	.284	.191	12	.201
TRAVIS MEYER	22	Savannah	S Atl	198	53	5	1	3	17	0	0	145	.268	.326	.348	.228	18	.252
MIKE MOORE	25	San Antonio	Texas	204	47	9	2	2	17	6	2	159	.230	.290	.324	.208	16	.219
GREGORY MORRISON	20	Savannah	S Atl	312	70	7	2	4	15	2	2	244	.224	.260	.298	.180	17	.204
ANDY OWEN	22	Vero Beach	Flor	352	88	16	0	5	31	3	2	266	.250	.311	.338	.218	30	.241
RICK PARKER	33	Albuquerque	PCL	171	43	5	2	0	21	5	3	131	.251	.333	.304	.218	15	.207
JOSE PIMENTEL	21	Savannah	S Atl	483	125	12	2	7	22	20	9	367	.259	.291	.335	.214	39	.239
TOM PRINCE	31	Albuquerque	PCL	91	33	2	0	6	14	0	1	59	.363	.448	.582	.333	19	.320
LUKE PROKOPEC	18	Savannah	S Atl	259	50	6	0	4	21	0	2	211	.193	.254	.263	.157	10	.185
BRIAN RICHARDSON	20	Albuquerque	PCL	348	72	10	1	8	31	3	1	277	.207	.272	.318	.191	22	.216
EDUARDO RIOS	23	San Antonio	Texas	248	66	8	1	5	19	2	1	183	.266	.318	.367	.231	24	.251
JUAN SOSA	20	Savannah	S Atl	389	90	12	0	7	23	6	5	304	.231	.274	.316	.194	25	.221
DANILO SOTELO	21	Vero Beach	Flor	247	56	11	1	5	25	2	1	192	.227	.298	.340	.213	20	.238
CHAD TOWNSEND	24	S. Bernardino	Calif	422	108	8	1	16	37	1	1	315	.256	.316	.393	.237	43	.254
REGGIE WILLIAMS	30	Albuquerque	PCL	344	83	15	1	6	35	13	4	265	.241	.311	.343	.224	32	.220
ERVAN WINGATE	22	S. Bernardino	Calif	381	104	8	0	9	23	3	4	281	.273	.314	.365	.227	35	.251
BRUCE YARD	24	San Antonio	Texas	156	47	12	1	1	7	0	0	109	.301	.331	.410	.250	17	.268
	24	Vero Beach	Flor	198	49	6	0	2	16	1	1	150	.247	.304	.308	.204	14	.219

Player	Age	Team	Lge	IP	H	ER	HR	BB	K	ERA	W	L	H/9	HR/9	BB/9	K/9	KW
ALVIN BROWN	25	S. Bernardino	Calif	61.0	45	31	2	71	52	4.57	3	4	6.64	.30	10.48	7.67	-.06
JULIO COLON	23	San Antonio	Texas	32.7	41	21	2	22	12	5.79	1	3	11.30	.55	6.06	3.31	-.41
	23	Vero Beach	Flor	36.7	51	22	3	26	35	5.40	1	3	12.52	.74	6.38	8.59	1.27
JOHN DAVIS	22	Savannah	S Atl	96.0	105	48	10	83	68	4.50	5	6	9.84	.94	7.78	6.38	.18
ERIC GAGNE	20	Savannah	S Atl	95.7	144	65	15	63	73	6.11	3	8	13.55	1.41	5.93	6.87	.81
JOSE GARCIA	24	Albuquerque	PCL	73.7	87	37	9	47	27	4.52	4	4	10.63	1.10	5.74	3.30	-.34
RYAN HENDERSON	26	San Antonio	Texas	57.3	69	30	2	39	39	4.71	3	3	10.83	.31	6.12	6.12	.51
DAN HUBBS	25	Albuquerque	PCL	71.7	79	38	4	54	65	4.77	3	5	9.92	.50	6.78	8.16	1.03
JOE JACOBSEN	24	San Antonio	Texas	52.3	72	34	4	32	33	5.85	2	4	12.38	.69	5.50	5.68	.52
MIKE JUDD	21	Savannah	S Atl	48.0	58	26	3	23	34	4.88	2	3	10.88	.56	4.31	6.38	1.05
BILLY NEAL	24	Vero Beach	Flor	97.7	109	37	6	54	54	3.34	6	5	9.84	.54	4.88	4.88	.41
EDDIE OROPESA	24	S. Bernardino	Calif	141.0	141	59	8	90	83	3.77	8	8	9.00	.51	5.74	5.30	.33
JEFF PALUK	23	S. Bernardino	Calif	62.7	81	37	9	36	43	5.31	3	4	11.63	1.29	5.17	6.18	.77
TOM PRICE	24	S. Bernardino	Calif	74.7	103	35	8	5	38	4.22	4	4	12.42	.96	.60	4.58	1.38
DAVE PYC	25	Albuquerque	PCL	33.7	46	29	4	22	21	7.75	1	3	12.30	1.07	5.88	5.61	.40
	25	San Antonio	Texas	87.7	123	47	6	36	52	4.83	4	6	12.63	.62	3.70	5.34	.86
DENNIS REYES	19	S. Bernardino	Calif	149.0	176	86	10	90	110	5.19	6	11	10.63	.60	5.44	6.64	.86
KEN SIKES	23	S. Bernardino	Calif	82.0	91	46	10	65	40	5.05	3	6	9.99	1.10	7.13	4.39	-.32
DAVE SPYKSTRA	22	Savannah	S Atl	83.0	126	63	11	64	58	6.83	2	7	13.66	1.19	6.94	6.29	.36
RICKY STONE	21	Savannah	S Atl	25.7	51	20	3	13	17	7.01	1	2	17.88	1.05	4.56	5.96	.85
	21	Vero Beach	Flor	100.3	134	61	13	63	53	5.47	4	7	12.02	1.17	5.65	4.75	.17
BRANDON WATTS	23	San Antonio	Texas	114.0	155	70	21	91	66	5.53	4	9	12.24	1.66	7.18	5.21	-.06
ERIC WEAVER	22	Albuquerque	PCL	44.0	57	29	4	27	30	5.93	2	3	11.66	.82	5.52	6.14	.66
	22	San Antonio	Texas	111.7	122	51	7	61	58	4.11	6	6	9.83	.56	4.92	4.67	.33

San Diego Padres

The San Diego Padres are on the brink of a major collapse, and unless they address their problems, they are going to find themselves back at the bottom of the National League West faster than you can say "Valenzuela." Despite the popular local notion that this is a team built around players that are at their peak, they actually field one of the oldest lineups in the game, and have no fewer than five starting players who are staring a collapse in the face, including the entire outfield.

The Padre offense in 1996 was built around the late-arriving career years of 31-year-old Steve Finley and 33-year-old Ken Caminiti. Both players posted career highs in almost every statistical category while playing above average defense. With them, the Padres fielded 36-year-old Tony Gwynn, 34-year-old Wally Joyner, 37-year-old Rickey Henderson and 33-year-old Jody Reed. While all four players showed some decline, only Reed drove off the cliff, posting a .622 OPS and showing greatly diminished range.

All six of these players are under contract for 1997, with only Reed not expected to be a starter. Four of them are under contract for 1998, meaning the Padres have a chance to be one of the oldest teams since the 1983 Phillies if they keep it up.

Actually, the Phillies give us an interesting comparison, but a more recent vintage. The 1993 National League champions were an old team, also built around a few unexpectedly great seasons: A comparison:

Pos.	Player	Age	OPS prior	1993 OPS
C	Darren Daulton	31	.736	.874
1B	John Kruk	32	.839	.905
2B	Mariano Duncan	30	.666	.721
SS	Kevin Stocker	23	rookie	.826
3B	Dave Hollins	27	.799	.814
LF	Pete Incaviglia	29	.753	.848
CF	Len Dykstra	30	.770	.902
RF	Jim Eisenreich	34	.714	.808

Pos.	Player	Age	OPS prior	1993 OPS
C	John Flaherty	28	.614	.778
1B	Wally Joyner	34	.806	.781
2B	Jody Reed	33	.716	.622
SS	Chris Gomez	25	.675	.694
3B	Ken Caminiti	33	.731	1.029
LF	Rickey Henderson	37	.847	.754
CF	Steve Finley	31	.723	.885
RF	Tony Gwynn	36	.837	.841

No one on the Phillies had a Caminiti year, although Daulton's, adjusted for offense level and park, is close. Both teams had career years from their center fielders, a young player at shortstop and a scar at second base. The 1994 Phillies went on to collapse, as Kruk, Hollins, Incaviglia and Dykstra all declined precipitously. The Padres might be able to avoid this fate, however, because their pitching staff is far more reliable than the collection of surgeries-in-waiting the Phillies used.

In addition to the offensive decline, the top two starters on that 1993 team, Tommy Greene and Curt Schilling, underwent surgery in 1994, and a third was traded (Terry Mulholland). The bullpen, effective in 1993 behind Mitch Williams and Larry Andersen, wasn't as good despite a big year from free agent Doug Jones, due to the losses of David West (injury), Roger Mason (trade) and Andersen (age).

The Padres are unlikely to suffer the same fate. Their rotation is deep in young arms, with Andy Ashby, Joey Hamilton—the best pitcher no one knows about—Scott Sanders and a number of candidates for the #4 and #5 spots, all under 28. They also have an incredibly deep bullpen, led by the best closer in the National League, Trevor Hoffman. More importantly, they seem to recognize the need to get younger, dealing relief prospect Dustin Hermanson to Florida for Quilvio Veras, a 26-year-old second baseman who can get on base and field. Kevin Towers, the Padre GM, has not been afraid to make deals to improve the team in his year of service, and what he does about making the Padre lineup younger will make or break this team in the next three years.

Organization: As mentioned, Towers is new to the job but has shown a willingness to make a move. The farm system is still chock full of arms stockpiled during the Randy Smith era, an excess that enabled them to make the Greg Vaughn and Veras trades. Like many teams with AAA franchises in the Pacific Coast League, they do a better job of producing major league pitchers than hitters: the last impact hitter the Padre system produced was Roberto Alomar, although Derrek Lee threatens that record.

In the new Padre era of good feeling, owner John Moores has been primarily hands-off, allowing his baseball staff to make decisions and not forcing them to operate under the salary constraints that hampered Smith. The next step is to put more money into scouting and development, to keep the system full and enable the Padres to replace their aging stars, because however much they spend on player development, it still costs less to develop a player to fill a hole than to sign one after he's just had his career year. Resources, combined with what appears to be a sane, if not brilliant, general manager, could make the Padres a perennial contender.

DUSTIN ALLEN   **1B**   **1973**   **Age 24**

Year	Team	Lge	AB	H	DB	TP	HR	BB	SB	CS	OUT	BA	OBA	SA	EQA	EQR	Peak
1995	Clinton	Midw	143	35	6	0	5	10	0	0	108	.245	.294	.392	.227	13	.250
1996	Clinton	Midw	260	64	6	1	9	54	2	3	199	.246	.376	.381	.255	33	.277
1996	R. Cucamonga	Calif	209	54	8	1	7	30	2	1	156	.258	.351	.407	.255	26	.277
1997	*San Diego*	*NL*	*458*	*112*	*20*	*3*	*16*	*87*	*5*	*5*	*351*	*.245*	*.365*	*.406*	*.274*	*69*	

Allen is a first baseman with wonderful walk rates and nothing else. He's been old for his leagues and is now trapped behind Derrek Lee, so even if he develops no one will know. Still, if I'm going to bet on a long shot, it's going to be one who knows the strike zone.

GABE ALVAREZ   **3B**   **1974**   **Age 23**

Year	Team	Lge	AB	H	DB	TP	HR	BB	SB	CS	OUT	BA	OBA	SA	EQA	EQR	Peak
1995	R. Cucamonga	Calif	215	65	10	1	5	23	0	0	150	.302	.370	.428	.269	28	.301
1996	Memphis	South	380	90	14	1	9	55	2	2	292	.237	.333	.350	.230	37	.253
1997	*San Diego*	*NL*	*403*	*95*	*23*	*3*	*14*	*60*	*4*	*5*	*313*	*.236*	*.335*	*.412*	*.262*	*55*	

He was a college shortstop, and ripped up the California League in 1995. Moved to a new position and a new level in 1996, he struggled. There's a lot here to like, and I expect Alvarez to have a big start at Memphis and quickly move to Las Vegas. At that point he'll be blocked by Caminiti, but at worst he should be starting for someone by mid-1998.

STONEY BRIGGS   **OF**   **1972**   **Age 25**

Year	Team	Lge	AB	H	DB	TP	HR	BB	SB	CS	OUT	BA	OBA	SA	EQA	EQR	Peak
1993	Waterloo	Midw	434	102	8	2	9	23	9	4	336	.235	.274	.325	.200	30	.224
1994	R. Cucamonga	Calif	424	100	13	1	13	44	7	6	330	.236	.308	.363	.223	39	.246
1995	Memphis	South	397	97	12	4	9	38	11	4	304	.244	.310	.363	.228	38	.248
1996	Memphis	South	465	124	19	3	12	52	18	6	347	.267	.340	.398	.252	55	.269

Tweener, improving each year but not enough to get noticed, and with the Padres that's hard. He should move up to AAA this year, since Vegas' 1996 outfield was loaded with veterans like Jim Tatum, Ira Smith, Doug Dascenzo and [insert reverential pause] Rob Deer. If he's really a player, there's some opportunity here.

JULIO BRUNO   **2B**   **1973**   **Age 24**

Year	Team	Lge	AB	H	DB	TP	HR	BB	SB	CS	OUT	BA	OBA	SA	EQA	EQR	Peak
1993	R. Cucamonga	Calif	200	52	6	1	3	12	6	3	151	.260	.302	.345	.220	17	.250
1993	Wichita	Texas	251	66	12	1	3	13	2	2	187	.263	.299	.355	.219	21	.249
1994	Las Vegas	PCL	438	95	18	2	5	24	3	3	346	.217	.258	.301	.180	24	.201
1995	Memphis	South	200	52	4	2	3	8	2	1	149	.260	.288	.345	.213	16	.235
1995	Las Vegas	PCL	136	28	5	1	0	9	1	2	110	.206	.255	.257	.157	5	.172
1996	Memphis	South	86	19	7	1	0	4	1	1	68	.221	.256	.326	.188	5	.207
1996	Las Vegas	PCL	294	71	11	0	3	17	5	3	226	.241	.283	.310	.197	20	.214

Again managed to move up a level despite displaying no talent whatsoever, this time when Homer Bush broke his leg. Bruno's maximum is defensive replacement, but he's now just an injury or two away from accumulating pension time. Do you think Tim Barker or Kevin Castleberry or Brad Tyler has an opinion on this?

HOMER BUSH   **2B**   **1973**   **Age 24**

Year	Team	Lge	AB	H	DB	TP	HR	BB	SB	CS	OUT	BA	OBA	SA	EQA	EQR	Peak
1993	Waterloo	Midw	485	142	12	2	5	14	16	7	350	.293	.313	.357	.230	44	.261
1994	R. Cucamonga	Calif	162	48	8	2	0	7	4	1	115	.296	.325	.370	.240	16	.268
1994	Wichita	Texas	249	71	9	2	4	10	12	4	182	.285	.313	.386	.240	26	.270
1995	Memphis	South	440	121	9	3	6	17	22	7	326	.275	.302	.350	.226	40	.249
1996	Las Vegas	PCL	114	36	8	1	2	4	3	3	81	.316	.339	.456	.262	14	.286

If he hadn't gotten hurt (broken leg), he might have been the Padre second baseman by July. This is an indictment of Jody Reed, not an endorsement of Bush. Like Bruno, he's moved up without being particularly impressive. He can hit for average but little else, and steal bases, but his ability to do so after the injury is a big question mark. The acquisition of Veras probably buries him.

KEN CAMINITI   3B   1963   Age 34

Year	Team	Lge	AB	H	DB	TP	HR	BB	SB	CS	OUT	BA	OBA	SA	EQA	EQR	Peak
1993	Houston	NL	556	151	20	0	17	57	7	4	409	.272	.339	.399	.249	63	.243
1994	Houston	NL	416	123	25	2	20	49	4	3	296	.296	.370	.510	.287	65	.277
1995	San Diego	NL	548	178	26	0	31	77	10	5	375	.325	.408	.542	.310	101	.295
1996	San Diego	NL	571	197	34	1	44	85	9	5	379	.345	.430	.639	.339	126	.322
1997	*San Diego*	*NL*	*570*	*172*	*25*	*1*	*33*	*98*	*10*	*6*	*404*	*.302*	*.404*	*.523*	*.320*	*117*	

Caminiti had one of the best stretch drives of my lifetime, hitting .359/.456/.797 after August 1, playing good defense and getting a big hit every 11 minutes. MVP cases can be made for a handful of players, and I didn't vote for Caminiti, but he's not a bad pick.

His future is uncertain. He's a better player now than we had any reason to expect, but he'll be coming off rotator cuff surgery and he's 34. Vlad's been too good to doubt, but I don't think we'll see those levels again.

ARCHI CIANFROCCO   UT   1967   Age 30

Year	Team	Lge	AB	H	DB	TP	HR	BB	SB	CS	OUT	BA	OBA	SA	EQA	EQR	Peak
1993	Ottawa	Inter	190	54	12	0	5	9	3	1	137	.284	.317	.426	.249	21	.260
1993	San Diego	NL	283	71	8	1	12	21	2	0	212	.251	.303	.413	.239	30	.248
1994	Las Vegas	PCL	109	28	7	1	1	11	0	1	82	.257	.325	.367	.230	10	.235
1994	San Diego	NL	146	32	5	0	5	6	2	0	114	.219	.250	.356	.201	10	.207
1995	Las Vegas	PCL	314	87	12	1	10	17	4	0	227	.277	.314	.417	.247	34	.249
1995	San Diego	NL	121	34	5	0	6	13	0	2	89	.281	.351	.471	.266	16	.268
1996	San Diego	NL	196	57	13	3	2	11	1	0	139	.291	.329	.418	.252	22	.251
1997	*San Diego*	*NL*	*189*	*48*	*8*	*1*	*5*	*8*	*1*	*1*	*142*	*.254*	*.284*	*.386*	*.238*	*20*	

He's exactly what he was a year ago: a good bench player. No reason to believe he can't be the same in 1997, or 2001.

BEN DAVIS   C   1977   Age 20

Year	Team	Lge	AB	H	DB	TP	HR	BB	SB	CS	OUT	BA	OBA	SA	EQA	EQR	Peak
1996	R. Cucamonga	Calif	355	59	6	1	4	23	0	0	296	.166	.217	.223	.111	6	.128

Calcium deposits in his elbow ripped apart his season, killing his numbers and forcing him to DH for two months. Long-term this might be a blessing, saving him 500 or so innings behind the plate, but right now he needs those for his development. His defense is reportedly good, and the Padres remain very high on him, but he's got a terribly long road ahead. High school catchers do not have good track records.

ROB DEER   OF   1961   Age 36

Year	Team	Lge	AB	H	DB	TP	HR	BB	SB	CS	OUT	BA	OBA	SA	EQA	EQR	Peak
1993	Boston	AL	143	28	5	1	8	21	2	0	115	.196	.299	.413	.235	15	.224
1993	Detroit	AL	327	75	9	0	17	40	3	1	253	.229	.313	.413	.241	36	.229
1995	Las Vegas	PCL	219	57	12	1	13	29	2	1	163	.260	.347	.502	.276	33	.263
1995	Vancouver	PCL	84	26	4	0	5	16	0	0	58	.310	.420	.536	.313	16	.297
1996	Las Vegas	PCL	260	55	9	1	17	51	4	1	206	.212	.341	.450	.260	35	.247
1996	San Diego	NL	52	10	4	0	4	15	0	0	42	.192	.373	.500	.281	9	.267
1997	*San Diego*	*NL*	*305*	*63*	*9*	*0*	*18*	*47*	*1*	*2*	*244*	*.207*	*.312*	*.413*	*.253*	*39*	

Deer wasn't originally in the book, but I was convinced to include him by some colleagues. [Note to RDFC: Can I have my wife back now?] He's still 80% of the player he was, but that's just a marginal bench player. He could help a lefty-heavy team needing power, perhaps Kansas City or Minnesota.

STEVE FINLEY   CF   1965   Age 32

Year	Team	Lge	AB	H	DB	TP	HR	BB	SB	CS	OUT	BA	OBA	SA	EQA	EQR	Peak
1993	Houston	NL	555	153	16	10	10	36	16	5	407	.276	.320	.395	.243	59	.245
1994	Houston	NL	380	109	16	4	12	34	12	6	277	.287	.345	.445	.264	50	.262
1995	San Diego	NL	583	186	25	7	12	67	30	11	408	.319	.389	.448	.285	88	.279
1996	San Diego	NL	675	212	44	9	32	65	19	8	471	.314	.374	.548	.300	116	.289
1997	*San Diego*	*NL*	*651*	*184*	*35*	*11*	*16*	*70*	*26*	*4*	*471*	*.283*	*.352*	*.444*	*.287*	*104*	

Another in the 30+ brigade that won the division. Finley's been a good player with doubles power, good defense and good stolen base rates, but 1996 was out of line. His defense is beginning to slip, so I think 1997 is the year Finley slides back from part of the solution to part of the problem.

JOHN FLAHERTY   **C**   **1968**   **Age 29**

Year	Team	Lge	AB	H	DB	TP	HR	BB	SB	CS	OUT	BA	OBA	SA	EQA	EQR	Peak
1993	Pawtucket	Inter	367	91	13	0	7	28	0	1	277	.248	.301	.341	.214	29	.226
1994	Toledo	Inter	152	38	7	1	7	7	2	1	115	.250	.283	.447	.240	16	.251
1995	Detroit	AL	355	87	22	1	12	18	0	0	268	.245	.282	.414	.229	34	.234
1996	Detroit	AL	152	38	10	0	5	8	1	0	114	.250	.287	.414	.233	15	.235
1996	San Diego	NL	270	85	9	0	10	13	2	3	188	.315	.346	.459	.267	35	.269
1997	*Detroit*	*NL*	*386*	*97*	*14*	*0*	*13*	*25*	*2*	*1*	*290*	*.251*	*.297*	*.389*	*.231*	*37*	

Flaherty has an eerie ability to get hot at exactly the right time to make himself seem useful. He won the catching job in Detroit in 1995 with a hot April and May, and was awful afterwards. He was traded to San Diego this past June, right when Brian Johnson had started killing the ball, and hit a couple of quick homers before embarking on a 29-game hitting streak that locked up the job. Stiff.

CHRIS GOMEZ   **SS**   **1971**   **Age 26**

Year	Team	Lge	AB	H	DB	TP	HR	BB	SB	CS	OUT	BA	OBA	SA	EQA	EQR	Peak
1993	Toledo	Inter	283	68	9	1	1	24	4	1	216	.240	.300	.290	.199	19	.219
1993	Detroit	AL	129	34	8	1	0	10	2	1	96	.264	.317	.341	.223	11	.245
1994	Detroit	AL	297	77	13	0	10	33	5	3	223	.259	.333	.404	.247	34	.268
1995	Detroit	AL	432	97	20	2	12	41	4	1	336	.225	.292	.363	.218	37	.234
1996	Detroit	AL	128	31	3	0	2	18	1	1	98	.242	.336	.312	.219	11	.231
1996	San Diego	NL	338	93	16	1	3	43	2	2	247	.275	.357	.355	.243	36	.256
1997	*San Diego*	*NL*	*310*	*76*	*18*	*2*	*7*	*39*	*4*	*2*	*236*	*.245*	*.330*	*.384*	*.256*	*39*	

He quietly improved last year, bumping up his walk rate and average, although his power slipped. He wore down as the season went on, a common affliction among middle infielders playing their first full season. He was signed to a two-year deal, so he'll be the shortstop in 1997. Recommended until Melo arrives.

TONY GWYNN   **RF**   **1960**   **Age 37**

Year	Team	Lge	AB	H	DB	TP	HR	BB	SB	CS	OUT	BA	OBA	SA	EQA	EQR	Peak
1993	San Diego	NL	505	185	40	3	8	44	12	1	321	.366	.417	.505	.312	88	.297
1994	San Diego	NL	434	175	28	1	15	55	5	0	259	.403	.470	.576	.350	94	.332
1995	San Diego	NL	559	218	27	2	12	43	15	5	346	.390	.434	.510	.319	99	.303
1996	San Diego	NL	470	173	27	1	4	45	9	4	301	.368	.423	.455	.301	75	.286
1997	*San Diego*	*NL*	*574*	*193*	*27*	*2*	*10*	*43*	*13*	*3*	*384*	*.336*	*.382*	*.443*	*.299*	*94*	

Age and injuries are beginning to take their toll on Gwynn, and he's falling back to "good" from the "fantastic" level of 1994-95. He'll slap singles to left through the end of the millennium, but it'll be his ability to hit doubles, walk a bit and not be awful in right field that will determine whether he's contributing. He has at least one more year as an asset, but if the Achilles tendon injury is as bad as it now appears, that's probably it.

RICKEY HENDERSON   **LF**   **1959**   **Age 38**

Year	Team	Lge	AB	H	DB	TP	HR	BB	SB	CS	OUT	BA	OBA	SA	EQA	EQR	Peak
1993	Oakland	AL	333	119	19	1	22	91	29	5	219	.357	.495	.619	.366	89	.349
1993	Toronto	AL	165	38	3	1	5	36	19	1	128	.230	.368	.352	.265	23	.251
1994	Oakland	AL	303	84	9	0	8	73	21	6	225	.277	.418	.386	.282	48	.268
1995	Oakland	AL	418	135	31	1	12	74	33	10	293	.323	.425	.488	.309	78	.294
1996	San Diego	NL	487	127	17	2	10	132	30	14	374	.261	.418	.366	.273	73	.260
1997	*San Diego*	*NL*	*468*	*119*	*21*	*2*	*10*	*129*	*27*	*1*	*350*	*.254*	*.415*	*.372*	*.298*	*85*	

The decision to acquire Vaughn and move Rickey out of left field and the leadoff spot showed complete and total ignorance of why the Padres were scoring any runs at all—guys at the top of the lineup on base, and why their offense wasn't very good—a pitiful 5 through 8 while Gwynn and/or Joyner was hurt, 6 through 8 afterward. Bochy deserves a lot of credit for having the guts to start Henderson regularly, rotating out Vaughn, Finley and Gwynn as necessary. Henderson played in his most games since 1989, and even if his power really is gone he's an asset to any team. I think the power will bounce back, and I expect him to be the second-best left fielder in the league in 1997.

BRIAN JOHNSON   **C**   **1968**   **Age 29**

Year	Team	Lge	AB	H	DB	TP	HR	BB	SB	CS	OUT	BA	OBA	SA	EQA	EQR	Peak
1993	Las Vegas	PCL	402	115	21	2	10	37	0	0	287	.286	.346	.423	.258	49	.273
1994	Las Vegas	PCL	50	9	2	0	1	7	0	1	42	.180	.281	.280	.174	3	.181
1994	San Diego	NL	94	24	4	1	3	6	0	0	70	.255	.300	.415	.237	10	.245
1995	San Diego	NL	211	56	7	0	4	14	0	0	155	.265	.311	.355	.224	18	.229
1996	San Diego	NL	247	70	13	1	8	7	0	0	177	.283	.303	.441	.247	27	.249
1997	*Detroit*	*AL*	*268*	*71*	*11*	*1*	*10*	*16*	*0*	*0*	*197*	*.265*	*.306*	*.425*	*.245*	*29*	

He's an above average backup catcher with a lousy defensive reputation, one not entirely supported by the available data. Johnson was hitting well through June, but his playing time and hitting fell off after the Flaherty trade. He's a better player than a bunch of guys (Matheny, Manwaring, Flaherty) with better paychecks. He's trade bait, since the Padres want to give Sean Mulligan his job.

WALLY JOYNER   **1B**   **1962**   **Age 35**

Year	Team	Lge	AB	H	DB	TP	HR	BB	SB	CS	OUT	BA	OBA	SA	EQA	EQR	Peak
1993	Kansas City	AL	502	149	36	3	18	69	5	6	359	.297	.382	.488	.285	78	.276
1994	Kansas City	AL	361	109	19	3	8	47	3	2	254	.302	.382	.438	.276	51	.263
1995	Kansas City	AL	474	155	20	0	17	70	3	2	321	.327	.414	.477	.299	78	.284
1996	San Diego	NL	450	132	27	0	10	74	4	3	321	.293	.393	.420	.275	64	.261
1997	*San Diego*	*NL*	*468*	*122*	*21*	*0*	*14*	*79*	*4*	*5*	*351*	*.261*	*.367*	*.395*	*.272*	*68*	

Joyner gets way too much playing time against left-handers, who he just can't hit anymore (.666 OPS since 1992). If used strictly in a platoon role, he's above average, and can really help a team like San Diego that needs the OBP. He died in August and September, a bad sign for a 34-year-old.

TIM KILLEEN   **C**   **1971**   **Age 26**

Year	Team	Lge	AB	H	DB	TP	HR	BB	SB	CS	OUT	BA	OBA	SA	EQA	EQR	Peak
1993	Madison	Midw	255	50	8	0	8	31	0	0	205	.196	.283	.322	.198	18	.218
1994	Modesto	Calif	373	81	11	1	13	41	3	1	293	.217	.295	.357	.216	32	.236
1995	Memphis	South	237	56	10	0	9	26	1	0	181	.236	.312	.392	.235	24	.251
1996	Memphis	South	230	59	7	4	10	23	0	1	172	.257	.324	.452	.254	28	.267

He's a left-handed hitting catcher with pop, but hasn't been able to get noticed yet, which speaks poorly for his defense. With Mulligan ahead of him and Davis behind him, Killeen might be unable to advance no matter how he plays.

GREG LAROCCA   **2B**   **1973**   **Age 24**

Year	Team	Lge	AB	H	DB	TP	HR	BB	SB	CS	OUT	BA	OBA	SA	EQA	EQR	Peak
1994	Spokane	Nwern	162	39	4	1	1	9	2	1	124	.241	.281	.296	.192	10	.213
1994	R. Cucamonga	Calif	86	12	2	1	1	6	2	1	75	.140	.196	.221	.101	1	.120
1995	R. Cucamonga	Calif	470	131	24	2	7	35	6	2	341	.279	.329	.383	.242	49	.266
1996	Memphis	South	456	118	17	2	7	43	4	4	342	.259	.323	.351	.226	42	.246

A converted shortstop who struggled to get over the AA wall but didn't fall back. The prospects ahead of him aren't exactly Knoblauch and Alomar, but the Veras trade hurts him. Very little chance of a career.

DEREK LEE   **1B**   **1976**   **Age 21**

Year	Team	Lge	AB	H	DB	TP	HR	BB	SB	CS	OUT	BA	OBA	SA	EQA	EQR	Peak
1993	R. Cucamonga	Calif	73	16	2	1	1	7	0	1	58	.219	.287	.315	.194	5	.234
1994	R. Cucamonga	Calif	447	102	12	1	7	34	9	7	352	.228	.283	.306	.195	29	.228
1995	R. Cucamonga	Calif	507	133	12	0	18	39	6	3	377	.262	.315	.393	.237	52	.274
1996	Memphis	South	514	143	23	1	32	55	9	4	375	.278	.348	.514	.280	78	.319
1997	*San Diego*	*NL*	*639*	*155*	*44*	*3*	*33*	*65*	*15*	*5*	*489*	*.243*	*.312*	*.476*	*.274*	*96*	

Lee has had a very odd development cycle. While improving almost every area of his game the past three years, including power, walks and hitting for average, his strikeout rate has gone haywire. From one K every 4.65 AB in 1994 to one every 3.87 in 1995 to a ridiculous 1 every 2.94 this year. Now strikeouts aren't any worse than other types of outs when it comes to producing runs, but developmentally they're a concern. Lee's a good prospect, but I'm not as high on him as most people.

SCOTT LIVINGSTONE   **1B/3B**   **1966**   **Age 31**

Year	Team	Lge	AB	H	DB	TP	HR	BB	SB	CS	OUT	BA	OBA	SA	EQA	EQR	Peak
1993	Detroit	AL	308	95	10	2	3	21	1	2	215	.308	.353	.383	.250	33	.256
1994	San Diego	NL	182	51	12	1	2	8	2	2	133	.280	.311	.390	.234	18	.235
1995	San Diego	NL	204	73	11	0	7	18	2	1	132	.358	.410	.515	.308	35	.306
1996	San Diego	NL	176	54	4	1	2	12	0	1	123	.307	.351	.375	.246	19	.241
1997	*San Diego*	*NL*	*239*	*69*	*9*	*1*	*4*	*7*	*0*	*0*	*170*	*.289*	*.309*	*.385*	*.250*	*27*	

As consistent as a player with 200 at bats a year can be. Livingstone might be the best pinch-hitter in the National League, and can play third or first once a week to give people a rest. He's not as valuable in San Diego as he might be in, say, Cleveland, with right-handed hitters on the corners, but that's quibbling.

LUIS LOPEZ   **SS/2B**   **1971**   **Age 26**

Year	Team	Lge	AB	H	DB	TP	HR	BB	SB	CS	OUT	BA	OBA	SA	EQA	EQR	Peak
1993	Las Vegas	PCL	476	121	24	2	7	26	4	0	355	.254	.293	.357	.219	40	.242
1994	San Diego	NL	238	67	16	1	2	19	3	2	173	.282	.335	.382	.242	25	.263
1996	Las Vegas	PCL	67	12	2	0	1	3	0	0	55	.179	.214	.254	.131	2	.135
1996	San Diego	NL	141	26	1	0	3	10	0	0	115	.184	.238	.255	.147	5	.155
1997	*San Diego*	*NL*	*77*	*15*	*3*	*0*	*0*	*3*	*1*	*0*	*62*	*.195*	*.225*	*.234*	*.153*	*3*	

Lopez was a promising shortstop two years ago, but a blown-out knee cost him a crucial year, and it's doubtful he'll ever be a starter in the majors. A shame, since he looked like he was going to be a player.

GARY MATTHEWS   **OF**   **1975**   **Age 22**

Year	Team	Lge	AB	H	DB	TP	HR	BB	SB	CS	OUT	BA	OBA	SA	EQA	EQR	Peak
1994	Spokane	Nwern	197	32	3	1	0	12	1	2	167	.162	.211	.188	.065	1	.077
1995	Clinton	Midw	440	94	14	2	2	55	10	4	350	.214	.301	.268	.191	28	.219
1996	R. Cucamonga	Calif	437	100	15	5	6	46	3	4	341	.229	.302	.327	.209	34	.233

He's a young outfielder who has displayed patience and doubles/triples power in A ball. He's not Vladimir Guerrero, but I like his chances to improve in AA. Watch him.

JUAN MELO   **SS**   **1977**   **Age 20**

Year	Team	Lge	AB	H	DB	TP	HR	BB	SB	CS	OUT	BA	OBA	SA	EQA	EQR	Peak
1995	Clinton	Midw	492	122	17	0	6	26	5	5	375	.248	.286	.319	.200	34	.235
1996	R. Cucamonga	Calif	500	128	18	2	7	13	3	4	376	.256	.275	.342	.204	35	.236

Melo's a Dominican shortstop who's adding strength as he gets older, and it shows. He has real power, and has shown he can hit for average. Plate discipline and defense are a question—he'll probably end up as a second baseman—but if he doesn't improve the patience, he'll be Roberto Mejia. I think he'll get better.

VINCE MOORE   **OF**   **1972**   **Age 25**

Year	Team	Lge	AB	H	DB	TP	HR	BB	SB	CS	OUT	BA	OBA	SA	EQA	EQR	Peak
1993	Durham	Caro	328	86	7	1	10	26	12	4	246	.262	.316	.381	.238	34	.266
1994	Wichita	Texas	135	19	1	0	3	15	3	1	117	.141	.227	.215	.122	3	.135
1995	R. Cucamonga	Calif	304	61	6	0	11	27	4	2	245	.201	.266	.329	.195	21	.211
1996	R. Cucamonga	Calif	221	56	8	1	6	32	6	1	166	.253	.348	.380	.250	26	.267
1996	Memphis	South	145	29	10	1	1	17	5	2	118	.200	.284	.303	.197	10	.210

The sole remaining part of the bounty for Fred McGriff. Moore, put simply, can't hit. He's had a couple of decent years in A-ball, but gets beaten like a Republican in Massachusetts whenever he steps up to AA. McGriff, you may have heard, is still fairly good.

SEAN MULLIGAN   **C**   **1970**   **Age 27**

Year	Team	Lge	AB	H	DB	TP	HR	BB	SB	CS	OUT	BA	OBA	SA	EQA	EQR	Peak
1993	R. Cucamonga	Calif	268	61	7	1	5	24	1	1	208	.228	.291	.317	.201	19	.219
1994	R. Cucamonga	Calif	246	67	9	1	8	19	0	0	179	.272	.325	.415	.247	27	.264
1994	Wichita	Texas	213	70	6	0	3	11	2	1	144	.329	.362	.399	.260	25	.280
1995	Las Vegas	PCL	332	80	12	1	7	27	0	0	252	.241	.298	.346	.215	27	.227
1996	Las Vegas	PCL	355	94	15	2	17	29	1	1	262	.265	.320	.462	.257	44	.267

Brian Johnson redux. He's a right-handed hitter with OK power, no plate discipline, average or below average defensive reputation. He'll be the backup in San Diego after Johnson is traded. Good cheap NL roto pick.

JODY REED **2B** **1963** **Age 34**

Year	Team	Lge	AB	H	DB	TP	HR	BB	SB	CS	OUT	BA	OBA	SA	EQA	EQR	Peak
1993	Los Angeles	NL	456	129	21	1	3	45	1	2	329	.283	.347	.353	.238	46	.233
1994	Milwaukee	AL	398	105	13	0	5	57	5	3	296	.264	.356	.334	.237	40	.228
1995	San Diego	NL	460	126	17	1	5	65	5	3	337	.274	.364	.348	.244	50	.232
1996	San Diego	NL	509	130	12	0	5	65	1	5	384	.255	.340	.308	.218	43	.207
1997	*San Diego*	*NL*	*181*	*45*	*5*	*0*	*3*	*27*	*3*	*4*	*140*	*.249*	*.346*	*.326*	*.242*	*20*	

When a player like this goes bad he kills you. Reed lost what little doubles power he had, walked less and lost more range. Of course, he was still the second-best second baseman in the division. Veras' arrival means that Reed won't be the starter in 1997, but since he's signed he might be on the roster. End of the line.

CRAIG SHIPLEY **UT** **1963** **Age 34**

Year	Team	Lge	AB	H	DB	TP	HR	BB	SB	CS	OUT	BA	OBA	SA	EQA	EQR	Peak
1993	San Diego	NL	232	56	5	0	5	14	11	3	179	.241	.285	.328	.211	18	.206
1994	San Diego	NL	244	83	14	2	5	13	6	5	166	.340	.374	.475	.282	35	.271
1995	Houston	NL	238	68	9	1	3	11	5	1	171	.286	.317	.370	.236	23	.223
1996	San Diego	NL	94	31	2	0	2	3	6	0	63	.330	.351	.415	.273	12	.260
1997	*San Diego*	*NL*	*213*	*61*	*8*	*2*	*5*	*8*	*5*	*0*	*152*	*.286*	*.312*	*.413*	*.264*	*27*	

Shipley is another part of a pretty good Padre bench. He can play five positions—none particularly well—pinch-hit against lefties and righties and pinch-run for catchers and Gwynns. Arbitration-eligible, which could price him out of his role.

TODD STEVERSON **OF** **1972** **Age 25**

Year	Team	Lge	AB	H	DB	TP	HR	BB	SB	CS	OUT	BA	OBA	SA	EQA	EQR	Peak
1993	Dunedin	Flor	414	96	16	1	12	38	8	5	323	.232	.296	.362	.219	36	.246
1994	Knoxville	South	436	112	16	3	11	68	12	5	329	.257	.357	.383	.252	52	.278
1996	Las Vegas	PCL	301	65	10	2	11	43	5	3	239	.216	.314	.372	.228	30	.245

He add an awful year, meaning we might get to add his name to the list of players ruined by Rule V. Steverson got 70 at bats total in 1995 while rotting on Detroit's bench. He hasn't yet recovered, although his walk rate is still good. Don't give up on him yet.

JIM TATUM **OF/3B** **1968** **Age 29**

Year	Team	Lge	AB	H	DB	TP	HR	BB	SB	CS	OUT	BA	OBA	SA	EQA	EQR	Peak
1993	Colorado	NL	97	18	3	0	1	6	0	0	79	.186	.233	.247	.140	3	.148
1994	Colo. Springs	PCL	420	124	20	1	18	41	2	1	297	.295	.358	.476	.276	60	.288
1995	Colo. Springs	PCL	90	26	4	0	5	6	0	1	65	.289	.333	.500	.269	12	.274
1996	Las Vegas	PCL	231	74	12	1	11	22	3	0	157	.320	.379	.524	.299	38	.300
1996	Pawtucket	Inter	66	17	2	0	4	8	1	0	49	.258	.338	.470	.268	9	.271

Oh, well. He's still the same major league hitter he's been for four years, but it now looks like his chance has passed. Guys like this are available all over AAA, and the sooner GMs realize it, the sooner they can spend money wisely and build better, cheaper teams. Tatum has been rumored to be headed to Japan.

JASON THOMPSON **1B** **1971** **Age 26**

Year	Team	Lge	AB	H	DB	TP	HR	BB	SB	CS	OUT	BA	OBA	SA	EQA	EQR	Peak
1993	Spokane	Nwern	248	64	11	1	6	23	1	1	185	.258	.321	.383	.236	25	.260
1994	R. Cucamonga	Calif	257	84	10	1	11	30	1	1	174	.327	.397	.502	.298	42	.324
1994	Wichita	Texas	222	57	11	0	9	26	0	0	165	.257	.335	.428	.253	27	.275
1995	Memphis	South	493	134	12	1	20	59	5	2	361	.272	.350	.422	.259	62	.277
1996	Las Vegas	PCL	385	106	15	0	19	48	6	3	282	.275	.356	.462	.271	54	.285
1996	San Diego	NL	50	12	1	0	3	1	0	0	38	.240	.255	.440	.227	5	.240
1997	*San Diego*	*NL*	*420*	*116*	*21*	*1*	*17*	*47*	*7*	*6*	*310*	*.276*	*.349*	*.452*	*.281*	*65*	

Thompson is an old first base prospect who got two weeks in San Diego when Joyner was hurt and didn't embarrass himself. He's not a long-term solution. For one year or so, he's as good as Joyner for about 1/25th the cost. Of course, you'd have to find someone to take Joyner, and Hawk Harrelson is broadcasting these days.

GREG VAUGHN | LF | 1966 | Age 31

Year	Team	Lge	AB	H	DB	TP	HR	BB	SB	CS	OUT	BA	OBA	SA	EQA	EQR	Peak
1993	Milwaukee	AL	580	164	28	2	36	94	10	5	421	.283	.383	.524	.295	99	.302
1994	Milwaukee	AL	369	92	19	1	20	51	8	4	281	.249	.340	.469	.265	51	.267
1995	Milwaukee	AL	391	86	17	1	18	55	9	4	309	.220	.316	.407	.240	44	.239
1996	Milwaukee	AL	374	104	15	0	31	58	5	2	272	.278	.375	.567	.301	68	.295
1996	San Diego	NL	145	32	4	1	10	26	3	1	114	.221	.339	.469	.264	20	.259
1997	*San Diego*	*NL*	*583*	*145*	*22*	*1*	*31*	*81*	*9*	*6*	*444*	*.249*	*.340*	*.449*	*.276*	*89*	

He had 12 good weeks at exactly the right time, and will make $15 million for his trouble. I'm all for players making whatever they can, but where is it written that one good year wipes out all the mediocre ones? Vaughn's Vlad looks dead on, although I don't think he'll play that much. With his defense, it's not enough. Avoid. Staying with the Padres.

SEAN WATKINS | 1B | 1975 | Age 22

Year	Team	Lge	AB	H	DB	TP	HR	BB	SB	CS	OUT	BA	OBA	SA	EQA	EQR	Peak
1996	Clinton	Midw	58	11	1	0	1	7	0	0	47	.190	.277	.259	.170	3	.186
1996	R. Cucamonga	Calif	365	84	13	2	5	43	0	1	282	.230	.311	.318	.210	28	.234

This is not the organization to be a mediocre first base prospect in. Watkins, like a number of the Padre minor leaguers, has a good walk rate but no power. This will short-circuit his career, oh, now.

ANDY ASHBY | RSP | 1968 | Age 29

YR	TEAM	Lge	IP	H	ER	HR	BB	K	ERA	W	L	H/9	HR/9	BB/9	K/9	KW
1993	Colo. Springs	PCL	38.7	42	18	2	16	28	4.19	2	2	9.78	.47	3.72	6.52	1.24
1993	Colorado	NL	55.0	78	43	5	38	31	7.04	1	5	12.76	.82	6.22	5.07	.14
1993	San Diego	NL	68.3	79	42	14	32	43	5.53	3	5	10.40	1.84	4.21	5.66	.83
1994	San Diego	NL	160.3	147	64	16	57	112	3.59	10	8	8.25	.90	3.20	6.29	1.30
1995	San Diego	NL	189.3	191	72	18	78	135	3.42	12	9	9.08	.86	3.71	6.42	1.21
1996	San Diego	NL	147.7	154	54	17	46	74	3.29	10	6	9.39	1.04	2.80	4.51	.80

He fought shoulder problems all season, but pitched as well as ever when he was healthy. The culprit may have been a heavy workload early in the season, an average of over 7 IP/start through May. The decline in his strikeout rate appears to be a vestige of the injury. Ashby's thin, and his motion isn't exactly smooth, so I would be wary of continued problems. Watch him carefully in spring training.

SEAN BERGMAN | RBP | 1970 | Age 27

YR	TEAM	Lge	IP	H	ER	HR	BB	K	ERA	W	L	H/9	HR/9	BB/9	K/9	KW
1993	Toledo	Inter	110.7	135	61	10	70	74	4.96	5	7	10.98	.81	5.69	6.02	.58
1993	Detroit	AL	39.7	46	25	6	26	20	5.67	1	3	10.44	1.36	5.90	4.54	.04
1994	Toledo	Inter	146.3	158	70	15	68	120	4.31	7	9	9.72	.92	4.18	7.38	1.41
1994	Detroit	AL	17.7	21	8	2	7	12	4.08	1	1	10.70	1.02	3.57	6.11	1.15
1995	Detroit	AL	137.7	155	72	17	70	86	4.71	6	9	10.13	1.11	4.58	5.62	.73
1996	San Diego	NL	111.3	125	57	14	43	75	4.61	5	7	10.10	1.13	3.48	6.06	1.15

He may have found the role he was born for after getting his clock cleaned in the rotation in the first half. Bergman pitched well out of the bullpen—admittedly, mostly in lost causes—for three months, and may have a similar role in 1997. Roto players: he's as good a candidate as any for ten vulture wins.

ANDRES BERUMEN | RRP | 1971 | Age 26

YR	TEAM	Lge	IP	H	ER	HR	BB	K	ERA	W	L	H/9	HR/9	BB/9	K/9	KW
1993	High Desert	Calif	82.3	92	38	8	38	51	4.15	4	5	10.06	.87	4.15	5.57	.82
1993	Wichita	Texas	23.7	41	18	2	16	12	6.85	1	2	15.59	.76	6.08	4.56	.00
1994	Las Vegas	PCL	70.3	81	51	4	65	41	6.53	2	6	10.36	.51	8.32	5.25	-.33
1995	San Diego	NL	43.7	41	26	3	41	38	5.36	2	3	8.45	.62	8.45	7.83	.50
1996	Las Vegas	PCL	66.3	69	43	4	66	48	5.83	2	5	9.36	.54	8.95	6.51	-.07

I still like him—good build, good fastball—but he better start finding home plate if he wants to eat more meals with utensils and fewer that come with plastic toys. He'll be back in the majors in 1997, but probably with another organization.

WILLIE BLAIR   **RRP**   **1966**   **Age 31**

YR	TEAM	Lge	IP	H	ER	HR	BB	K	ERA	W	L	H/9	HR/9	BB/9	K/9	KW
1993	Colorado	NL	143.7	169	72	18	57	79	4.51	7	9	10.59	1.13	3.57	4.95	.76
1994	Colorado	NL	77.7	91	46	8	45	62	5.33	3	6	10.55	.93	5.21	7.18	1.09
1995	San Diego	NL	112.3	119	55	11	55	75	4.41	5	7	9.53	.88	4.41	6.01	.90
1996	San Diego	NL	86.3	84	47	13	37	59	4.90	4	6	8.76	1.36	3.86	6.15	1.09

Blair survived Colorado and has gotten a hell of a lot better the last two years, doing a much better job of finding the strike zone. I wouldn't want to move him from his current role, since this is the first time he's had consistent, extended success. Let him take 80 low-leverage innings in 1997, then see if you can move him up.

DOUG BOCHTLER   **RRP**   **1971**   **Age 26**

YR	TEAM	Lge	IP	H	ER	HR	BB	K	ERA	W	L	H/9	HR/9	BB/9	K/9	KW
1993	Cent. Valley	Calif	42.0	43	19	2	32	30	4.07	2	3	9.21	.43	6.86	6.43	.43
1993	Colo. Springs	PCL	47.0	63	31	3	31	30	5.94	2	3	12.06	.57	5.94	5.74	.43
1993	Las Vegas	PCL	36.7	49	19	2	14	24	4.66	2	2	12.03	.49	3.44	5.89	1.10
1994	Las Vegas	PCL	94.3	103	48	9	58	72	4.58	4	6	9.83	.86	5.53	6.87	.91
1995	Las Vegas	PCL	34.0	28	13	5	29	29	3.44	2	2	7.41	1.32	7.68	7.68	.64
1995	San Diego	NL	44.3	41	17	6	23	41	3.45	3	2	8.32	1.22	4.67	8.32	1.61
1996	San Diego	NL	64.3	49	22	7	45	60	3.08	4	3	6.85	.98	6.30	8.39	1.22

Bochtler's a hard-throwing righty with a funky delivery. Had, literally, one bad inning all year, a horrific three-homer, one-out performance against Cincinnati in June, at the end of a one-month stretch where Bochy used him only on days ending in "Y." If used normally, he's wonderfully effective. His dominance of lefties—just a .597 OPS—was important, since Bochy essentially did without a left-handed reliever all season. He closed strong: just 12 hits allowed in 31 innings after the All-Star Break. Excellent setup material.

SHANE DENNIS   **LSP**   **1972**   **Age 25**

YR	TEAM	Lge	IP	H	ER	HR	BB	K	ERA	W	L	H/9	HR/9	BB/9	K/9	KW
1994	Spokane	Nwern	63.7	105	44	7	32	40	6.22	2	5	14.84	.99	4.52	5.65	.75
1994	Springfield	Midw	15.0	7	1	1	11	6	.60	2	0	4.20	.60	6.60	3.60	-.45
1995	Clinton	Midw	76.3	85	52	7	47	52	6.13	2	6	10.02	.83	5.54	6.13	.66
1995	R. Cucamonga	Calif	69.3	77	27	9	30	49	3.50	5	3	10.00	1.17	3.89	6.36	1.15
1996	R. Cucamonga	Calif	53.3	62	18	6	22	34	3.04	4	2	10.46	1.01	3.71	5.74	.98
1996	Memphis	South	107.0	96	31	12	53	95	2.61	8	4	8.07	1.01	4.46	7.99	1.55

Despite not having a great fastball, Dennis blew through the Southern League after a promotion from A ball. Left-hander, best control pitcher in the organization. Most guys like this do not rush to the majors, but get hung up somewhere where they get hit hard and have to scratch and claw their way back to prospect status. Dennis might be the exception, but I expect him to find reality in AAA.

BUBBA DIXON   **LRP**   **1972**   **Age 25**

YR	TEAM	Lge	IP	H	ER	HR	BB	K	ERA	W	L	H/9	HR/9	BB/9	K/9	KW
1994	Spokane	Nwern	39.0	41	8	0	32	40	1.85	3	1	9.46	.00	7.38	9.23	1.23
1995	R. Cucamonga	Calif	126.0	136	56	15	62	85	4.00	7	7	9.71	1.07	4.43	6.07	.92
1996	R. Cucamonga	Calif	15.0	21	13	3	5	13	7.80	0	2	12.60	1.80	3.00	7.80	1.85
1996	Memphis	South	58.7	61	30	7	33	56	4.60	3	4	9.36	1.07	5.06	8.59	1.60

Like Dennis, Dixon is a lefty without a good fastball. His best pitch is a changeup, not something I like to see in a relief prospect. He needs one more good year, preferably at AAA, to open eyes. I'm doubtful.

CADE GASPAR   **RSP**   **1974**   **Age 23**

YR	TEAM	Lge	IP	H	ER	HR	BB	K	ERA	W	L	H/9	HR/9	BB/9	K/9	KW
1995	Lakeland	Flor	26.7	37	30	8	12	18	10.12	0	3	12.49	2.70	4.05	6.08	1.01
1995	Lakeland	Flor	85.7	127	59	8	60	70	6.20	3	7	13.34	.84	6.30	7.35	.88
1996	R. Cucamonga	Calif	101.3	127	56	12	58	66	4.97	4	7	11.28	1.07	5.15	5.86	.67

Gaspar fought elbow and shoulder injuries in 1996, so he spent most of the year without his good fastball. He pitched well after a DL stint, and should be back on the prospect track at Memphis this year. He's still at least two years out, and has yet to pitch impressively at any level.

JOEY HAMILTON RSP 1971 Age 26

YR	TEAM	Lge	IP	H	ER	HR	BB	K	ERA	W	L	H/9	HR/9	BB/9	K/9	KW
1993	Wichita	Texas	80.0	120	61	4	54	36	6.86	2	7	13.50	.45	6.07	4.05	-.17
1993	Las Vegas	PCL	43.3	45	18	0	27	26	3.74	3	2	9.35	.00	5.61	5.40	.40
1994	Las Vegas	PCL	55.7	62	18	2	28	27	2.91	4	2	10.02	.32	4.53	4.37	.32
1994	San Diego	NL	105.7	100	34	8	38	57	2.90	8	4	8.52	.68	3.24	4.85	.81
1995	San Diego	NL	199.7	201	81	18	73	111	3.65	12	10	9.06	.81	3.29	5.00	.85
1996	San Diego	NL	208.7	217	90	19	102	162	3.88	12	11	9.36	.82	4.40	6.99	1.23

He had an OK year overall, but Hamilton showed development as his strikeout rate jumped, and he continued to eat up starts and innings. I'd look for him to explode on the league this year and be no worse than its third-best starter. Hamilton gets strikeouts and groundballs, a lethal combination.

DENNY HARRIGER RSP 1970 Age 27

YR	TEAM	Lge	IP	H	ER	HR	BB	K	ERA	W	L	H/9	HR/9	BB/9	K/9	KW
1993	Binghamton	East	155.3	200	69	10	56	67	4.00	9	8	11.59	.58	3.24	3.88	.48
1994	Las Vegas	PCL	148.3	193	89	14	58	73	5.40	6	10	11.71	.85	3.52	4.43	.60
1995	Las Vegas	PCL	166.7	174	71	14	76	88	3.83	10	9	9.40	.76	4.10	4.75	.56
1996	Las Vegas	PCL	154.7	178	74	12	66	83	4.31	8	9	10.36	.70	3.84	4.83	.65

He seems to have settled in as the #2 starter in Las Vegas. Harriger gets overlooked because he's small and doesn't throw hard, but could help most teams as a #4 starter. The Padres, who are fairly deep in starters, aren't his best opportunity, but any number of other teams should be jumping. Might get a shot if Sanders is traded.

KENNY HENDERSON RSP 1973 Age 24

YR	TEAM	Lge	IP	H	ER	HR	BB	K	ERA	W	L	H/9	HR/9	BB/9	K/9	KW
1996	Clinton	Midw	23.3	39	15	0	7	16	5.79	1	2	15.04	.00	2.70	6.17	1.38
1996	R. Cucamonga	Calif	15.7	19	11	1	12	9	6.32	1	1	10.91	.57	6.89	5.17	.00

Henderson hasn't impressed anyone yet, but is just 24 and has fought injury problems. He's got a long road ahead, but keep the name in mind.

DUSTIN HERMANSON RRP 1973 Age 24

YR	TEAM	Lge	IP	H	ER	HR	BB	K	ERA	W	L	H/9	HR/9	BB/9	K/9	KW
1994	Wichita	Texas	19.3	16	1	0	8	22	.47	2	0	7.45	.00	3.72	10.24	2.48
1995	Las Vegas	PCL	34.3	31	17	5	32	38	4.46	2	2	8.13	1.31	8.39	9.96	1.22
1995	San Diego	NL	32.0	36	24	8	26	17	6.75	1	3	10.12	2.25	7.31	4.78	-.23
1996	Las Vegas	PCL	43.3	40	16	3	32	44	3.32	3	2	8.31	.62	6.65	9.14	1.38
1996	San Diego	NL	14.0	18	13	3	5	10	8.36	0	2	11.57	1.93	3.21	6.43	1.34

He won't have to deal with the Vegas-San Diego shuttle anymore, having been dealt to Florida for Quilvio Veras. I have to figure Dave Dombrowski gets a nice Christmas present from him, since Hermanson was one of many good Padre relief prospects, but in Miami unquestionably deserves to be Robb Nen's setup man. Recommended.

FERNANDO HERNANDEZ RSP 1971 Age 26

YR	TEAM	Lge	IP	H	ER	HR	BB	K	ERA	W	L	H/9	HR/9	BB/9	K/9	KW
1993	Kinston	Caro	45.3	44	16	2	27	33	3.18	3	2	8.74	.40	5.36	6.55	.84
1993	R. Cucamonga	Calif	88.0	97	46	8	75	84	4.70	4	6	9.92	.82	7.67	8.59	.95
1993	Canton	East	70.7	23	0	2	9	6	.00	8	0	2.93	.25	1.15	.76	-.03
1994	Wichita	Texas	118.7	142	83	15	97	69	6.29	4	9	10.77	1.14	7.36	5.23	-.09
1995	Memphis	South	61.3	82	47	5	53	57	6.90	2	5	12.03	.73	7.78	8.36	.84
1995	Las Vegas	PCL	35.7	38	24	3	35	36	6.06	1	3	9.59	.76	8.83	9.08	.82
1996	Memphis	South	136.7	143	76	9	99	117	5.00	6	9	9.42	.59	6.52	7.70	.94

Hernandez isn't notable except for his home run rate, which is consistently low. He has some control issues to work out, but I think there's enough here to keep an eye on. Signed by Detroit, so he might end up in the majors this year.

TREVOR HOFFMAN   **RRP**   **1968**   **Age 29**

YR	TEAM	Lge	IP	H	ER	HR	BB	K	ERA	W	L	H/9	HR/9	BB/9	K/9	KW
1993	Florida	NL	34.7	25	11	6	22	25	2.86	3	1	6.49	1.56	5.71	6.49	.74
1993	San Diego	NL	53.0	58	28	6	27	51	4.75	2	4	9.85	1.02	4.58	8.66	1.74
1994	San Diego	NL	54.3	41	13	4	24	63	2.15	5	1	6.79	.66	3.98	10.44	2.48
1995	San Diego	NL	52.7	50	23	11	18	47	3.93	3	3	8.54	1.88	3.08	8.03	1.91
1996	San Diego	NL	85.0	57	18	7	38	97	1.91	7	2	6.04	.74	4.02	10.27	2.42

He's the best closer in the National League, second only to Troy Percival overall. Needs lots of work to stay effective, and Bochy gets it for him—Hoffman had the most innings of any 30-save pitcher in baseball. Excellent bet for three more years at this level.

BRAD KAUFMAN   **RSP**   **1972**   **Age 25**

YR	TEAM	Lge	IP	H	ER	HR	BB	K	ERA	W	L	H/9	HR/9	BB/9	K/9	KW
1993	Spokane	Nwern	44.7	68	55	9	48	27	11.08	1	4	13.70	1.81	9.67	5.44	-.60
1994	Springfield	Midw	126.7	152	64	11	85	76	4.55	6	8	10.80	.78	6.04	5.40	.29
1995	Memphis	South	136.3	163	114	19	114	92	7.53	3	12	10.76	1.25	7.53	6.07	.14
1996	Memphis	South	164.0	184	80	20	97	118	4.39	8	10	10.10	1.10	5.32	6.48	.83

The little light went on. Kaufman, a big, hard-throwing right-hander, hadn't had any success until this year, when he discovered the strike zone and all the joys within. B, B- prospect, but one that I'd bet on.

MARC KROON   **RRP**   **1973**   **Age 24**

YR	TEAM	Lge	IP	H	ER	HR	BB	K	ERA	W	L	H/9	HR/9	BB/9	K/9	KW
1993	Columbia	S Atl	103.3	162	76	9	95	72	6.62	3	8	14.11	.78	8.27	6.27	.02
1994	R. Cucamonga	Calif	128.3	157	78	14	101	100	5.47	5	9	11.01	.98	7.08	7.01	.57
1995	Memphis	South	106.7	105	48	12	77	94	4.05	6	6	8.86	1.01	6.50	7.93	1.02
1996	Memphis	South	43.3	38	17	5	32	41	3.53	3	2	7.89	1.04	6.65	8.52	1.18

Another Randy Smith holdover, finally converted to relief this year. Smith collected pitchers with good fastballs, both through the draft and trades, and had lots of success: Hoffman, Bochtler, Sanders, Hermanson. Kroon is a product of that mindset. A thumb injury to his left (non-throwing) hand is not serious. Recommended, especially with Hermanson out of the picture.

HEATH MURRAY   **LSP**   **1973**   **Age 24**

YR	TEAM	Lge	IP	H	ER	HR	BB	K	ERA	W	L	H/9	HR/9	BB/9	K/9	KW
1994	Spokane	Nwern	82.3	141	55	9	22	39	6.01	3	6	15.41	.98	2.40	4.26	.82
1995	R. Cucamonga	Calif	81.7	91	34	5	50	52	3.75	5	4	10.03	.55	5.51	5.73	.53
1995	Memphis	South	72.0	93	35	1	54	55	4.38	4	4	11.62	.12	6.75	6.88	.60
1996	Memphis	South	161.0	176	76	14	71	113	4.25	8	10	9.84	.78	3.97	6.32	1.11

The organization is very high on him, despite an average repertoire. He gets high marks for working fast, command and makeup, along with a plus fastball. He started strong, finished awful, not a good sign. He will probably start the year at Las Vegas, and a good three months will have him in San Diego.

MIKE OQUIST   **RBP**   **1968**   **Age 29**

YR	TEAM	Lge	IP	H	ER	HR	BB	K	ERA	W	L	H/9	HR/9	BB/9	K/9	KW
1993	Rochester	Inter	140.7	154	57	20	59	103	3.65	9	7	9.85	1.28	3.77	6.59	1.25
1993	Baltimore	AL	11.3	12	4	0	5	8	3.18	1	0	9.53	.00	3.97	6.35	1.12
1994	Rochester	Inter	47.7	58	21	5	20	30	3.97	3	2	10.95	.94	3.78	5.66	.94
1994	Baltimore	AL	59.0	68	31	6	32	38	4.73	3	4	10.37	.92	4.88	5.80	.71
1995	Rochester	Inter	11.3	17	7	0	8	9	5.56	0	1	13.50	.00	6.35	7.15	.79
1995	Baltimore	AL	54.0	49	21	6	42	27	3.50	3	3	8.17	1.00	7.00	4.50	-.25
1996	Las Vegas	PCL	132.0	134	44	12	57	89	3.00	10	5	9.14	.82	3.89	6.07	1.05

Tweener. Oquist isn't impressive to watch, but his major league ERA is 4.92 in 131 innings, including a decent year of mop-up for the Orioles in 1995. He pitched well for Las Vegas, and will get more chances elsewhere. No star potential, long-term outlook uncertain. He needs to get lucky. Famous worldwide as the "Macarena" choreographer.

SCOTT SANDERS **RBP** **1969** **Age 28**

YR	TEAM	Lge	IP	H	ER	HR	BB	K	ERA	W	L	H/9	HR/9	BB/9	K/9	KW
1993	Las Vegas	PCL	141.3	156	75	19	77	127	4.78	7	9	9.93	1.21	4.90	8.09	1.47
1993	San Diego	NL	50.7	57	29	4	29	36	5.15	2	4	10.12	.71	5.15	6.39	.84
1994	San Diego	NL	109.3	104	54	10	58	102	4.45	5	7	8.56	.82	4.77	8.40	1.61
1995	San Diego	NL	88.3	84	43	15	39	79	4.38	5	5	8.56	1.53	3.97	8.05	1.69
1996	San Diego	NL	141.0	125	50	11	60	137	3.19	10	6	7.98	.70	3.83	8.74	1.96

He could start the All-Star Game. He's that good. Sanders hasn't been able to stay healthy, but when he's pitched he's been effective. He bumped it up another notch last year, avoiding injury and figuring out left-handed hitters, who had killed him previously. Highly recommended. Get him. Traded to Seattle for Sterling Hitchcock. He'll be the #4 starter in Seattle; his prognosis is a little less bright in the better hitter's park, but I still expect him to be well above average.

BOB TEWKSBURY **RSP** **1961** **Age 36**

YR	TEAM	Lge	IP	H	ER	HR	BB	K	ERA	W	L	H/9	HR/9	BB/9	K/9	KW
1993	St. Louis	NL	206.7	275	97	16	43	94	4.22	11	12	11.98	.70	1.87	4.09	.90
1994	St. Louis	NL	154.3	184	84	18	37	74	4.90	7	10	10.73	1.05	2.16	4.32	.90
1995	Texas	AL	130.0	158	57	7	23	53	3.95	7	7	10.94	.48	1.59	3.67	.82
1996	San Diego	NL	203.3	233	104	17	61	111	4.60	10	13	10.31	.75	2.70	4.91	.96

Tewksbury is still an OK #4 starter, but the Padres bought out his option anyway. He'll sign late, as teams explore all their better options before seeking him out as an innings-muncher/pitching coach. His control is something I'd like to expose young pitchers to if I had a team with young starters going nowhere, like Detroit or Pittsburgh. Not at all recommended in Strat or roto leagues.

FERNANDO VALENZUELA **LSP** **1961** **Age 36**

YR	TEAM	Lge	IP	H	ER	HR	BB	K	ERA	W	L	H/9	HR/9	BB/9	K/9	KW
1993	Baltimore	AL	177.7	172	83	18	87	80	4.20	10	10	8.71	.91	4.41	4.05	.25
1994	Philadelphia	NL	44.0	42	14	8	11	18	2.86	3	2	8.59	1.64	2.25	3.68	.66
1995	San Diego	NL	90.0	105	50	16	42	52	5.00	4	6	10.50	1.60	4.20	5.20	.68
1996	San Diego	NL	168.7	187	72	17	83	84	3.84	10	9	9.98	.91	4.43	4.48	.39

A great story, but he's doing it with mirrors. His strikeout and walk rates deteriorated badly in the second half, despite which his ERA improved. Now, I'm not going to say he can't do it again, but it ain't bloody likely. Still a decent hitter for a 41…er…"36"-year-old.

DARIO VERAS **RRP** **1973** **Age 24**

YR	TEAM	Lge	IP	H	ER	HR	BB	K	ERA	W	L	H/9	HR/9	BB/9	K/9	KW
1993	Bakersfield	Calif	12.0	14	10	1	10	8	7.50	0	1	10.50	.75	7.50	6.00	.12
1993	Vero Beach	Flor	47.3	69	25	3	21	24	4.75	2	3	13.12	.57	3.99	4.56	.52
1994	R. Cucamonga	Calif	71.3	75	25	7	33	37	3.15	5	3	9.46	.88	4.16	4.67	.52
1995	Memphis	South	75.7	95	39	9	37	54	4.64	3	5	11.30	1.07	4.40	6.42	1.04
1996	Memphis	South	40.0	44	13	4	10	34	2.92	3	1	9.90	.90	2.25	7.65	1.99
1996	Las Vegas	PCL	38.0	41	14	1	9	24	3.32	2	2	9.71	.24	2.13	5.68	1.36
1996	San Diego	NL	28.3	26	9	3	12	20	2.86	2	1	8.26	.95	3.81	6.35	1.16

I'll always have a place in my heart for Veras, who was left out to dry by Bruce Bochy on the final day of the season when he didn't want to use any of his regular relievers. Veras threw three shutout innings to help clinch the division. He has good control, and while he doesn't throw as hard as Bochtler or Kroon, deserves a spot in the Padre bullpen.

TIM WORRELL **RRP** **1968** **Age 29**

YR	TEAM	Lge	IP	H	ER	HR	BB	K	ERA	W	L	H/9	HR/9	BB/9	K/9	KW
1993	Las Vegas	PCL	81.0	94	46	13	34	70	5.11	3	6	10.44	1.44	3.78	7.78	1.65
1993	San Diego	NL	98.0	108	58	11	55	50	5.33	4	7	9.92	1.01	5.05	4.59	.27
1994	San Diego	NL	14.3	10	5	0	6	13	3.14	1	1	6.28	.00	3.77	8.16	1.78
1995	R. Cucamonga	Calif	19.7	30	17	2	8	11	7.78	0	2	13.73	.92	3.66	5.03	.76
1995	Las Vegas	PCL	22.7	24	15	1	20	16	5.96	1	2	9.53	.40	7.94	6.35	.13
1995	San Diego	NL	13.3	17	7	2	8	12	4.72	0	1	11.48	1.35	5.40	8.10	1.35
1996	San Diego	NL	118.3	116	40	9	50	87	3.04	8	5	8.82	.68	3.80	6.62	1.25

He came back from a torn elbow ligament to pitch well for the Padres, particularly in the first half as part of the under-rated bullpen. Worrell has a rather dramatic drop in effectiveness after 45 pitches, so at this point he's best used as a reliever, at least until his stamina returns. He could have a monster year in the Rivera role.

Player	Age	Team	Lge	AB	H	DB	TP	HR	BB	SB	CS	OUT	BA	OBA	SA	EQA	EQR	Peak
GORDON AMERSON	19	Clinton	Midw	411	76	8	1	9	47	4	2	337	.185	.269	.275	.174	21	.201
JEFF BARRY	27	Memphis	South	232	52	2	0	4	24	3	3	183	.224	.297	.284	.192	15	.197
DARRYL BRINKLEY	27	Memphis	South	208	59	6	0	8	19	8	3	152	.284	.344	.428	.261	26	.269
	27	R. Cucamonga	Calif	257	81	16	1	7	16	9	5	181	.315	.355	.467	.274	35	.279
CESARIN CARMONA	19	Clinton	Midw	328	57	5	1	2	34	4	3	274	.174	.251	.213	.134	9	.154
CRAIG COLBERT	31	Las Vegas	PCL	198	45	4	0	5	8	2	1	154	.227	.257	.323	.190	12	.182
EDUARDO CUEVAS	22	Clinton	Midw	321	80	12	2	2	16	9	3	244	.249	.285	.318	.205	23	.227
RANDY CURTIS	25	R. Cucamonga	Calif	363	82	9	2	5	59	10	3	284	.226	.334	.303	.220	32	.232
DOUG DASCENZO	32	Las Vegas	PCL	318	79	12	2	1	30	12	7	246	.248	.313	.308	.212	25	.201
NATHAN DUNN	21	Clinton	Midw	174	41	7	1	1	23	5	1	134	.236	.325	.305	.218	15	.243
ANTONIO FERNANDEZ	23	R. Cucamonga	Calif	470	122	10	0	9	31	1	1	349	.260	.305	.338	.216	38	.235
RICARDO GAMA	23	R. Cucamonga	Calif	417	96	16	1	6	27	6	3	324	.230	.277	.317	.197	28	.214
CHRIS GWYNN	31	San Diego	NL	92	17	1	0	2	11	0	0	75	.185	.272	.261	.168	4	.164
RICH HILLS	22	Clinton	Midw	449	102	13	0	9	38	2	2	349	.227	.287	.316	.199	31	.219
RICCARDO INGRAM	29	Las Vegas	PCL	407	90	13	1	8	46	5	4	321	.221	.300	.317	.205	31	.204
EARL JOHNSON	24	Memphis	South	343	81	7	4	3	14	10	7	269	.236	.266	.306	.189	21	.202
JAMES JOHNSON	23	Clinton	Midw	445	102	8	2	1	40	21	8	351	.229	.293	.263	.191	28	.208
JAMIE KEEFE	22	Clinton	Midw	114	33	2	0	3	28	4	1	82	.289	.430	.386	.286	18	.314
MIKE MARTIN	23	Clinton	Midw	214	33	1	0	2	23	0	0	181	.154	.236	.187	.097	3	.105
JOHN MASSARELLI	30	Memphis	South	209	53	13	2	2	10	6	2	158	.254	.288	.364	.221	18	.217
	30	R. Cucamonga	Calif	108	27	7	2	0	12	3	1	82	.250	.325	.352	.231	11	.228
LEROY MCKINNIS	23	R. Cucamonga	Calif	329	73	14	1	3	29	1	1	257	.222	.285	.298	.191	21	.208
JOHN POWERS	22	Clinton	Midw	247	56	7	2	1	27	1	2	193	.227	.303	.283	.193	16	.213
CHRIS PRIETO	23	R. Cucamonga	Calif	218	44	7	1	2	31	10	4	178	.202	.301	.271	.196	15	.214
RANDY READY	36	Las Vegas	PCL	105	31	2	0	4	21	0	1	75	.295	.413	.429	.283	16	.268
DAN ROHRMEIER	30	Memphis	South	487	163	19	0	27	66	2	3	327	.335	.414	.540	.312	89	.306
MANDY ROMERO	28	Memphis	South	305	80	8	0	10	35	2	1	226	.262	.338	.387	.244	33	.246
RICO ROSSY	32	Las Vegas	PCL	413	92	17	1	4	64	5	3	324	.223	.327	.298	.212	33	.201
PAUL RUSSO	26	Las Vegas	PCL	225	51	11	1	4	22	2	1	175	.227	.296	.338	.211	18	.220
MARCOS SANCHEZ	21	Clinton	Midw	128	24	2	1	3	11	1	0	104	.188	.252	.289	.173	6	.194
GARY SCOTT	27	Las Vegas	PCL	216	52	11	1	3	29	0	1	165	.241	.331	.343	.226	20	.232
MIKE SHARPERSON	34	Las Vegas	PCL	112	31	3	0	2	18	1	0	81	.277	.377	.357	.254	13	.241
IRA SMITH	28	Las Vegas	PCL	250	54	9	1	5	20	3	2	198	.216	.274	.320	.195	17	.197
JASON TOTMAN	23	Clinton	Midw	127	25	6	1	0	17	1	0	102	.197	.292	.260	.181	7	.195
CHAD TREDAWAY	24	Las Vegas	PCL	195	40	6	1	5	16	3	1	156	.205	.265	.323	.194	13	.208
	24	R. Cucamonga	Calif	84	18	0	0	2	5	0	0	66	.214	.258	.286	.174	4	.185
JORGE VELANDIA	21	Memphis	South	400	91	9	1	9	25	3	4	313	.228	.273	.322	.194	26	.218
DICKIE WOODRIDGE	25	R. Cucamonga	Calif	142	36	3	1	2	18	0	0	106	.254	.338	.331	.227	13	.240
MARK WULFERT	23	Clinton	Midw	471	112	13	2	15	53	13	5	364	.238	.315	.369	.231	47	.251

Player	Age	Team	Lge	IP	H	ER	HR	BB	K	ERA	W	L	H/9	HR/9	BB/9	K/9	KW
PAUL ABBOTT	28	Las Vegas	PCL	26.7	26	11	4	15	30	3.71	2	1	8.78	1.35	5.06	10.12	2.11
JIM BARON	22	R. Cucamonga	Calif	78.7	93	36	9	41	53	4.12	4	5	10.64	1.03	4.69	6.06	.85
TODD BUSSA	23	Clinton	Midw	31.0	30	7	0	10	31	2.03	2	1	8.71	.00	2.90	9.00	2.27
TIM CAMPBELL	23	Clinton	Midw	56.7	57	28	6	24	42	4.45	3	3	9.05	.95	3.81	6.67	1.27
BRIAN CARMODY	20	Clinton	Midw	65.7	103	47	6	28	29	6.44	2	5	14.12	.82	3.84	3.97	.37
CHRIS CLARK	21	Clinton	Midw	69.3	119	62	6	66	47	8.05	2	6	15.45	.78	8.57	6.10	-.11
DERA CLARK	21	Memphis	South	42.0	55	23	6	15	30	4.93	2	3	11.79	1.29	3.21	6.43	1.34
CRAIG CLAYTON	25	Clinton	Midw	33.0	36	10	2	10	18	2.73	3	1	9.82	.55	2.73	4.91	.95
	25	R. Cucamonga	Calif	25.7	36	15	4	9	18	5.26	1	2	12.62	1.40	3.16	6.31	1.31
MATT CLEMENT	21	Clinton	Midw	84.7	85	32	4	67	69	3.40	5	4	9.04	.43	7.12	7.33	.66
	21	R. Cucamonga	Calif	51.0	64	32	7	31	47	5.65	2	4	11.29	1.24	5.47	8.29	1.40
KEITH DAVIS	23	R. Cucamonga	Calif	137.7	184	96	13	91	77	6.28	4	11	12.03	.85	5.95	5.03	.19
TODD ERDOS	22	R. Cucamonga	Calif	60.7	66	27	2	44	51	4.01	3	4	9.79	.30	6.53	7.57	.89
MIKE FREITAS	26	Memphis	South	63.0	87	39	8	31	26	5.57	2	5	12.43	1.14	4.43	3.71	.13
HAL GARRETT	21	Clinton	Midw	42.7	57	30	5	40	38	6.33	1	4	12.02	1.05	8.44	8.02	.56
	21	R. Cucamonga	Calif	46.3	45	10	3	24	35	1.94	4	1	8.74	.58	4.66	6.80	1.10
A. HAMMERSCHMIDT	24	R. Cucamonga	Calif	74.0	109	49	5	23	37	5.96	2	6	13.26	.61	2.80	4.50	.80
GREG HARRIS	32	R. Cucamonga	Calif	30.7	45	22	5	12	21	6.46	1	2	13.21	1.47	3.52	6.16	1.17
RUSTY KILGO	29	Memphis	South	68.3	91	34	7	21	42	4.48	4	4	11.99	.92	2.77	5.53	1.15
BRANDON KOLB	22	Clinton	Midw	155.0	222	95	10	99	87	5.52	6	11	12.89	.58	5.75	5.05	.25
SCOTT LEWIS	30	Las Vegas	PCL	141.7	169	78	21	49	88	4.96	6	10	10.74	1.33	3.11	5.59	1.09
CHRIS LOGAN	25	R. Cucamonga	Calif	64.7	82	35	4	42	35	4.87	3	4	11.41	.56	5.85	4.87	.16
JOEY LONG	25	Las Vegas	PCL	32.0	37	17	2	26	19	4.78	2	2	10.41	.56	7.31	5.34	-.05
ROB MATTSON	29	Memphis	South	150.7	195	83	20	64	64	4.96	7	10	11.65	1.19	3.82	3.82	.32
ERIC NEWMAN	23	Clinton	Midw	96.7	130	78	12	86	68	7.26	3	8	12.10	1.12	8.01	6.33	.11
JAKE REMINGTON	20	Clinton	Midw	72.0	127	67	4	33	37	8.38	1	7	15.88	.50	4.12	4.62	.51
JIM SAK	22	Clinton	Midw	57.3	58	32	3	58	45	5.02	2	4	9.10	.47	9.10	7.06	.08
TODD SCHMITT	26	Memphis	South	36.7	43	23	1	24	34	5.65	1	3	10.55	.25	5.89	8.35	1.31
PETE SMITH	30	Las Vegas	PCL	159.3	187	86	17	57	77	4.86	7	11	10.56	.96	3.22	4.35	.64
RUSSELL SPEAR	18	Clinton	Midw	43.7	73	45	4	53	28	9.27	1	4	15.05	.82	10.92	5.77	-.81
RUSS SWAN	32	Las Vegas	PCL	118.7	142	65	16	59	58	4.93	5	8	10.77	1.21	4.47	4.40	.35
LUIS TORRES	20	Clinton	Midw	57.3	97	50	11	34	41	7.85	1	5	15.23	1.73	5.34	6.44	.81
RYAN VANDEWEG	22	R. Cucamonga	Calif	131.7	175	64	14	60	81	4.37	7	8	11.96	.96	4.10	5.54	.82
KEVIN WALKER	19	Clinton	Midw	64.3	103	50	11	43	27	6.99	2	5	14.41	1.54	6.02	3.78	-.24
PETE WALKER	27	Las Vegas	PCL	26.3	34	17	6	17	19	5.81	1	2	11.62	2.05	5.81	6.49	.71
BRETT WALTERS	21	R. Cucamonga	Calif	122.0	161	61	15	45	56	4.50	6	8	11.88	1.11	3.32	4.13	.55
DARELL WHITE	24	R. Cucamonga	Calif	49.0	76	38	1	29	27	6.98	1	4	13.96	.18	5.33	4.96	.32

San Diego Padres

San Francisco Giants

Well, it could have been worse. I mean, Williams could have been traded for Joe Carter, Ed Sprague and a Blue Jay Outfield Prospect [tm]. In a trade that makes remarkably little sense for either team, the Giants sent third baseman Matt Williams to the Indians for Jeff Kent, Jose Vizcaino, Julian Tavarez and some cash. This is the first big move for Bob Quinn's hand-picked replacement, GM Brian Sabean. Sabean's defense of his actions tells you something about what he's going to be like as a top manager; at his press conference he stated, quite unambiguously, "I am not an idiot." This is roughly like saying "I'm not a racist": It doesn't really do anything to convince the people you're talking with.

Sabean's got a tough but doable task in front of him. The Giants are coming off an extremely unpleasant season during which virtually nothing went right. Of course, a lot of what went wrong was the result of bad management, but the Giants also didn't get many breaks. Glenallen Hill got to see what it's like to touch your forearm with the back of the same hand, Matt Williams broke his foot with a foul ball and Robby Thompson's decline reached heretofore unimaginable depths. The pitching staff was somewhat less than exceptional, despite the resurgence of closer Rod Beck, and the entire city seems to be focusing more on the Giants' move into Pacific Bell Park than on actually going to see them play in 3Com.

So what next? The Giants actually have a good amount of quality and quantity in their farm system; there are a bunch of players that can be acceptable major leaguers, and a few that have a chance to be very good. Furthermore, there are a lot of players in this system with good plate discipline and some power. There aren't many Royce Claytons running around to look good and play poorly. The Giants aren't in a particularly tough division, so it's possible they could be the best team in the division as early as September or so. The Dodgers have more star-quality talent in their minors, but the Giants are light years ahead of the Rockies in terms of talent, and pretty much even with the Padres, Derrek Lee notwithstanding.

They've also got a pretty decent guy to build upon. Barry Bonds is already past his prime, but he's going to be a better player at 35 than 99% of players ever were. They can plan to build a winning organization; building the infrastructure now and executing in 1998 and 1999. In last year's book, I wrote that I expected them to be a very surprising team in 1997. Well, the Williams trade sure surprised me, and the signings of stopgaps like Javier and Dunston pretty much threw me for a loop. The Giants have a bunch of youngsters who could develop into something; if the Giants devote some resources towards developing their youth, I think they've got the material here to build a darn good team.

Of course, to do that they need to put together a cogent plan and execute it well. There are a couple of obstacles in the way of that. Owner Peter Magowan seems to have his energies entirely focused on the new ballpark and the business end of things. That's probably not where his focus should be. The hiring of Sabean from within the organization leads one to believe that they're pretty happy with the way the organization runs. My question is simple: Why are they happy? This club hasn't been a serious contender or money machine for several years. There is a cycle of failure here that could keep dozens of sociologists on talk shows for a decade. Every year it's the same thing: No coherent plan, a couple of minor free agent signings that don't address the real needs of the team and a completely lack of understanding of how to translate minor league performances. This is not an organization that just needs to promote a company man.

The Giant organization's biggest threat is not on the field, it's in the front office. In Colorado, they're learning to how run the baseball side of things, but they're learning with a big ol' pile of cash. Eventually, Jerry McMorris and company will figure out how to deal with the baseball stuff – that'll only add to their ability to win. And in LA, the Dodgers are investing time, knowledge and money into developing young talent. Meanwhile, the Giants are twiddling their thumbs and concentrating on a new park.

A new park isn't enough. The Giants' management team needs to take a careful look at what they want to do and figure out how to do it. If they're not capable of that, then no new park is going to help this franchise in the long run. Baseball does not have to run in cycles of success and failure; it has done so because of mediocre-to-bad management. No current organization exemplifies the problems poor management causes more than the San Francisco Giants.

Organization: Dusty Baker runs the big club with a seat of the pants philosophy; he's run a couple of pitchers into the ground, played little ball when he shouldn't and hasn't really demonstrated anything that would lead one to believe that he's the right guy to bring this club out of the basement. Nonetheless, he's popular and respected. The Giants don't really seem to understand the drastic effects Phoenix and San Francisco have on performance, but this is a common failing in front offices across the country. The Giants do have a bunch of good to very good prospects in their system, including guys like Dante Powell and Don Denbow. One real nice bonus for Giants fans: almost all of their serious hitting prospects have a good batting eye. That's pretty uncommon, and it's a nice thing to have in a farm system.

RICH AURILIA   **SS**   **1972** **Age 25**

Year	Team	Lge	AB	H	DB	TP	HR	BB	SB	CS	OUT	BA	OBA	SA	EQA	EQR	Peak
1993	Charlotte-FL	Flor	463	135	13	2	8	67	9	7	336	.292	.381	.380	.259	58	.290
1994	Tulsa	Texas	469	104	12	2	13	49	7	6	371	.222	.295	.339	.210	38	.232
1995	Shreveport	Texas	234	76	12	1	5	25	7	2	160	.325	.390	.449	.286	35	.311
1995	Phoenix	PCL	256	64	6	0	6	34	2	1	193	.250	.338	.344	.231	25	.252
1996	San Francisco	NL	323	79	6	1	3	29	3	1	245	.245	.307	.297	.204	23	.218
1997	*San Francisco*	*NL*	*339*	*91*	*16*	*1*	*5*	*37*	*6*	*5*	*253*	*.268*	*.340*	*.366*	*.252*	*40*	

A make or break year for him, and he probably won't get a shot now that the Giants have acquired the estimable Jose Vizcaino. He's not a horrible shortstop prospect, and has a good defensive rep, but he didn't take that step forward with the bat last year that would have secured the job. Of course, he didn't get a good shot at it, given the way his playing time broke down, but he certainly didn't impress anyone enough to earn any breaks for this year. If he doesn't make a big advance this year, he probably won't have a significant career. I still think he can hit. He just didn't, and might not.

KIM BATISTE   **3B/Really, Genuinely Bad Baseball Player**   **1968**   **Age 29**

Year	Team	Lge	AB	H	DB	TP	HR	BB	SB	CS	OUT	BA	OBA	SA	EQA	EQR	Peak
1993	Philadelphia	NL	158	45	7	1	5	5	0	1	114	.285	.307	.437	.245	17	.260
1994	Philadelphia	NL	210	50	4	0	2	4	1	1	161	.238	.252	.286	.172	10	.178
1995	Bowie	East	98	34	4	0	4	5	1	0	64	.347	.379	.510	.297	15	.306
1995	Rochester	Inter	261	67	9	1	3	10	4	4	198	.257	.284	.333	.205	19	.209
1995	Scranton-WB	Inter	122	27	3	0	4	4	1	0	95	.221	.246	.344	.194	8	.199
1996	Phoenix	PCL	163	46	4	1	13	7	1	1	118	.282	.312	.558	.278	24	.280
1996	San Francisco	NL	131	28	5	0	3	7	3	3	106	.214	.254	.321	.185	8	.185

There are worse ideas for a ballclub than signing Kim Batiste. Perhaps a "Win your child a night at Neverland Ranch with Michael Jackson" promotion. That could be worse, I guess. Or perhaps "Painful Rectal Itch Night." Released.

MARVIN BENARD   **CF**   **1971** **Age 26**

Year	Team	Lge	AB	H	DB	TP	HR	BB	SB	CS	OUT	BA	OBA	SA	EQA	EQR	Peak
1993	Clinton	Midw	370	105	10	1	5	45	18	5	270	.284	.361	.357	.252	43	.278
1994	Shreveport	Texas	467	143	25	1	6	30	15	7	331	.306	.348	.403	.256	55	.278
1995	Phoenix	PCL	375	102	10	2	8	48	9	8	281	.272	.355	.373	.245	42	.263
1996	San Francisco	NL	499	128	17	4	5	64	20	10	381	.257	.341	.337	.233	50	.246
1997	*San Francisco*	*NL*	*436*	*122*	*19*	*4*	*7*	*48*	*4*	*0*	*314*	*.280*	*.351*	*.390*	*.267*	*58*	

He's learned from his prototype, Stan Javier. They're basically the same player, but Javier had a higher potential upside at the same age. Benard won't kill your lineup, but he won't help it any. Good fourth outfielder, and should help teams for a few years in that role. He has no place on this team, though.

BARRY BONDS   **LF**   **1965** **Age 32**

Year	Team	Lge	AB	H	DB	TP	HR	BB	SB	CS	OUT	BA	OBA	SA	EQA	EQR	Peak
1993	San Francisco	NL	579	209	36	3	53	138	26	10	380	.361	.484	.708	.372	160	.375
1994	San Francisco	NL	404	131	16	1	39	81	27	8	281	.324	.437	.658	.345	98	.343
1995	San Francisco	NL	533	169	31	6	38	130	26	9	373	.317	.451	.612	.340	126	.333
1996	San Francisco	NL	544	176	25	3	45	160	33	7	375	.324	.477	.629	.356	142	.344
1997	*San Francisco*	*NL*	*569*	*172*	*22*	*5*	*37*	*147*	*34*	*6*	*403*	*.302*	*.446*	*.554*	*.346*	*142*	

Insanely great. No longer the best player in baseball on a one-year basis, but only because he plays left field instead of shortstop. In career value, he has passed all left fielders except Williams, Musial and Henderson. He'll pass Henderson in about two years, Musial in three and Williams in seven. By the time his career ends, he will displace Ted Williams in those "best player ever" discussions between Ruth and Wagner. Believe it or not, Bonds is still underrated.

JAY CANIZARO 2B 1974 Age 23

Year	Team	Lge	AB	H	DB	TP	HR	BB	SB	CS	OUT	BA	OBA	SA	EQA	EQR	Peak
1994	San Jose	Calif	478	114	10	1	13	38	6	3	367	.238	.295	.345	.214	39	.243
1995	Shreveport	Texas	455	132	20	3	14	54	13	5	328	.290	.365	.440	.271	63	.304
1996	Phoenix	PCL	363	87	16	1	7	43	11	3	279	.240	.320	.347	.228	35	.252
1996	San Francisco	NL	121	24	4	1	2	11	0	2	99	.198	.265	.298	.176	6	.195
1997	*San Francisco*	*NL*	*336*	*81*	*22*	*3*	*6*	*39*	*17*	*9*	*264*	*.241*	*.320*	*.378*	*.249*	*41*	

A very disappointing 1996 campaign, but a large part of that is probably a problem with my perception. Shreveport was the home of a lot of big numbers in 1995, and so I probably got more excited about Jay than I should have. I really like his swing, but his results haven't been real impressive. Still young enough to develop. Nearly came to blows in the dugout with Kim Batiste during a televised game last year; is this indicative of some sort of problem? Defense hasn't improved from mediocre.

JACOB CRUZ OF 1973 Age 24

Year	Team	Lge	AB	H	DB	TP	HR	BB	SB	CS	OUT	BA	OBA	SA	EQA	EQR	Peak
1994	San Jose	Calif	121	27	5	0	0	7	0	1	95	.223	.266	.264	.166	5	.187
1995	Shreveport	Texas	473	138	18	1	16	53	8	4	339	.292	.363	.436	.268	63	.296
1996	Phoenix	PCL	435	112	18	2	8	58	5	5	328	.257	.345	.363	.239	46	.259
1996	San Francisco	NL	79	19	3	0	3	13	0	1	61	.241	.348	.392	.244	9	.265

Another big 1995 at Shreveport. Cruz is a very good defensive outfielder with some patience and some power. He'll be a good player. Probably not a superstar, but he'll be able to push a team towards a championship in his peak years. Those years probably start in 1998, provided he can get enough playing time to develop in 1997. I'd rather have him out there than Glenallen Hill.

DON DENBOW OF 1973 Age 24

Year	Team	Lge	AB	H	DB	TP	HR	BB	SB	CS	OUT	BA	OBA	SA	EQA	EQR	Peak
1994	Everett	Nwern	238	52	2	1	8	27	1	1	187	.218	.298	.336	.210	19	.234
1995	Burlington	Midw	336	54	3	0	9	33	5	1	283	.161	.236	.250	.147	12	.162
1996	Burlington	Midw	318	83	8	1	16	64	10	3	238	.261	.385	.443	.279	49	.303
1996	San Jose	Calif	100	36	6	1	5	13	1	1	65	.360	.434	.590	.331	20	.358
1997	*San Francisco*	*NL*	*499*	*136*	*28*	*1*	*23*	*70*	*18*	*6*	*369*	*.273*	*.362*	*.471*	*.291*	*85*	

Walks and bat speed are a winning combination. Denbow's beaten up on younger competition, and probably was moved up too slowly by the Giants organization. He can most definitely hit, and probably will rip through AA like a hot knife through butter. His hands stay back better than the vast majority of hitters; he strikes me as someone who's going to crush breaking balls low in the strike zone. Giants should have sent him to Shreveport early last year.

SHAWON DUNSTON SS 1963 Age 34

Year	Team	Lge	AB	H	DB	TP	HR	BB	SB	CS	OUT	BA	OBA	SA	EQA	EQR	Peak
1994	Chicago Cubs	NL	338	98	13	1	13	21	3	7	247	.290	.331	.450	.255	40	.246
1995	Chicago Cubs	NL	483	145	29	5	15	16	8	4	342	.300	.323	.474	.264	61	.251
1996	San Francisco	NL	292	89	12	2	5	17	7	0	203	.305	.343	.411	.260	35	.247
1997	*Chicago Cubs*	*NL*	*307*	*85*	*17*	*1*	*7*	*13*	*6*	*1*	*223*	*.277*	*.306*	*.407*	*.251*	*35*	

I didn't like this signing at the time, because I thought Dunston was rarely healthy and rarely good. That's not a lot of overlap to play with. He wasn't healthy, and he's never really been good, even in his prime. Part Of The Problem, despite his fantastic arm. Fittingly, he's back with the Cubs.

KURT EHMANN SS 1971 Age 26

Year	Team	Lge	AB	H	DB	TP	HR	BB	SB	CS	OUT	BA	OBA	SA	EQA	EQR	Peak
1993	San Jose	Calif	451	105	12	1	5	55	6	4	350	.233	.316	.297	.207	34	.228
1994	Shreveport	Texas	435	103	8	0	4	26	6	2	334	.237	.280	.283	.187	25	.202
1995	Shreveport	Texas	135	31	1	0	2	20	1	1	105	.230	.329	.281	.206	10	.219
1995	Phoenix	PCL	214	52	5	1	0	24	6	2	164	.243	.319	.276	.205	16	.220
1996	Phoenix	PCL	134	24	7	1	0	11	0	1	111	.179	.241	.246	.141	4	.147

Seems to have shed those unflattering home runs from his game, while also managing to hit for a poor average. That's impressive. One look at this guy, and you'll understand why they could afford to ship off Mike Benjamin.

GLENALLEN HILL   **RF**   **1965**   **Age 32**

Year	Team	Lge	AB	H	DB	TP	HR	BB	SB	CS	OUT	BA	OBA	SA	EQA	EQR	Peak
1993	Chicago Cubs	NL	89	32	6	0	10	7	1	0	57	.360	.406	.764	.358	22	.359
1993	Cleveland	AL	177	43	8	1	7	12	7	2	136	.243	.291	.418	.238	19	.240
1994	Chicago Cubs	NL	278	88	11	1	11	33	18	5	195	.317	.389	.482	.294	46	.292
1995	San Francisco	NL	510	144	29	3	27	45	21	5	371	.282	.341	.510	.281	77	.275
1996	San Francisco	NL	387	112	19	0	21	38	5	3	278	.289	.353	.501	.279	57	.269
1997	*San Francisco*	*NL*	*443*	*120*	*22*	*1*	*23*	*41*	*10*	*4*	*328*	*.271*	*.333*	*.481*	*.281*	*69*	

Spent this past season entertaining viewers with a sickening break of his wrist. Brrr, that was ugly. A moderate power hitter without much else going for him. Slightly above average with the bat, slightly below with the glove, and the best that most former Blue Jay prospects can hope to aspire to. A placeholder for a real outfielder, not someone you count on to build a team around.

JESUS IBARRA   **UT**   **1973**   **Age 24**

Year	Team	Lge	AB	H	DB	TP	HR	BB	SB	CS	OUT	BA	OBA	SA	EQA	EQR	Peak
1994	Everett	Nwern	262	52	5	1	7	23	0	0	210	.198	.263	.305	.183	15	.204
1995	Burlington	Midw	455	138	12	1	26	61	0	1	318	.303	.386	.505	.293	74	.323
1996	San Jose	Calif	510	135	18	0	16	49	3	1	376	.265	.329	.394	.243	55	.264

Is Ibarra still in the Giants organization? I have one report that says he's been shipped off, and another that claims he's still with the club. A decent young hitter with power and patience, both of which should increase with time. His ultimate defensive position is something of a mystery; I honestly believe that despite his appearance, he could probably play a middle infield spot. Whether the Giants are going to do that or put him in the outfield is unknown.

STAN JAVIER   **CF**   **1964**   **Age 33**

Year	Team	Lge	AB	H	DB	TP	HR	BB	SB	CS	OUT	BA	OBA	SA	EQA	EQR	Peak
1993	California	AL	240	73	11	4	4	28	11	1	168	.304	.377	.433	.280	35	.277
1994	Oakland	AL	426	122	18	0	13	50	23	7	311	.286	.361	.420	.267	58	.262
1995	Oakland	AL	452	136	21	2	10	50	37	5	321	.301	.371	.423	.279	66	.269
1996	San Francisco	NL	280	78	16	0	5	28	12	2	204	.279	.344	.389	.254	33	.242
1997	*San Francisco*	*NL*	*315*	*81*	*16*	*2*	*5*	*29*	*27*	*6*	*240*	*.257*	*.320*	*.368*	*.257*	*40*	

Career as a fine fourth outfielder is nearing its end. He's got three years of diminishing playing time left, unless he somehow develops some power or something. An excellent basestealer until 1996; I don't know whether or not to blame Dusty Baker for that, or whether or not Javier just doesn't have it anymore. A fine defensive outfielder who could have helped more than he did during his prime if he'd be given the shot.

MARCUS JENSEN   **C**   **1973**   **Age 24**

Year	Team	Lge	AB	H	DB	TP	HR	BB	SB	CS	OUT	BA	OBA	SA	EQA	EQR	Peak
1993	Clinton	Midw	345	86	14	1	10	54	1	1	260	.249	.351	.383	.247	39	.280
1994	San Jose	Calif	434	97	8	0	8	51	1	0	337	.224	.305	.297	.201	31	.225
1995	Shreveport	Texas	332	94	20	4	6	37	0	0	238	.283	.355	.422	.261	41	.288
1996	Phoenix	PCL	404	97	18	1	6	42	1	1	308	.240	.312	.334	.216	33	.235
1997	*San Francisco*	*NL*	*359*	*89*	*18*	*1*	*10*	*55*	*1*	*0*	*270*	*.248*	*.348*	*.387*	*.262*	*47*	

Nagging injuries have hindered his development, but he's still a damn sight better than Kirt Manwaring, who has mercifully been shipped off. Could develop into a catcher with Don Slaught's offensive value or so; when your defensive skills are as good as Jensen's, that's a valuable thing. Will hit 20 homers some season, probably in about five years.

DAX JONES   **OF**   **1971**   **Age 26**

Year	Team	Lge	AB	H	DB	TP	HR	BB	SB	CS	OUT	BA	OBA	SA	EQA	EQR	Peak
1993	Shreveport	Texas	449	122	15	2	5	28	8	4	331	.272	.314	.347	.225	40	.248
1994	Phoenix	PCL	392	96	18	3	4	22	12	5	301	.245	.285	.337	.210	31	.228
1995	Phoenix	PCL	399	95	16	2	3	32	9	7	311	.238	.295	.311	.202	28	.217
1996	Phoenix	PCL	296	83	15	3	7	19	11	5	218	.280	.324	.422	.251	34	.265
1996	San Francisco	NL	59	11	0	0	2	8	2	2	50	.186	.284	.288	.185	4	.197
1997	*San Francisco*	*NL*	*279*	*70*	*13*	*2*	*9*	*15*	*14*	*7*	*216*	*.251*	*.289*	*.409*	*.247*	*33*	

Not a prospect, and has been passed in the organization by basically everyone. Is now at the stage of his career where he'll be scrambling for minor league playing time, much less worrying about making the majors. Probably studying his Swedish/English dictionary so he can go to Europe and play there. "Horst Borgen, ma'am?"

DARRYL KENNEDY   **C**   **1969**   **Age 28**

Year	Team	Lge	AB	H	DB	TP	HR	BB	SB	CS	OUT	BA	OBA	SA	EQA	EQR	Peak
1993	Charlotte-FL	Flor	362	96	14	0	4	41	3	3	269	.265	.340	.337	.230	34	.246
1994	Charlotte-FL	Flor	187	51	4	1	2	23	1	1	137	.273	.352	.337	.236	18	.249
1994	Tulsa	Texas	72	15	0	0	2	7	1	0	57	.208	.278	.292	.189	4	.200
1995	Tulsa	Texas	198	47	7	1	3	16	0	0	151	.237	.294	.328	.207	15	.216
1996	Phoenix	PCL	191	53	9	1	3	12	2	1	139	.277	.320	.382	.237	19	.243

Stolen from the Texas system, but I have a feeling they left the window open and the keys in the ignition. Not likely to help a major league ballclub any millennium soon.

TOM LAMPKIN   **C**   **1964**   **Age 33**

Year	Team	Lge	AB	H	DB	TP	HR	BB	SB	CS	OUT	BA	OBA	SA	EQA	EQR	Peak
1993	New Orleans	AmA	84	27	2	0	3	18	5	3	60	.321	.441	.452	.301	15	.301
1993	Milwaukee	AL	164	35	7	0	5	21	7	2	131	.213	.303	.348	.222	15	.220
1994	Phoenix	PCL	445	118	24	4	8	41	6	4	332	.265	.327	.391	.241	47	.236
1995	San Francisco	NL	79	23	0	0	2	10	2	0	56	.291	.371	.367	.258	9	.249
1996	San Francisco	NL	180	43	7	0	6	22	1	5	142	.239	.322	.378	.226	17	.215
1997	*San Francisco*	*NL*	*160*	*37*	*6*	*0*	*6*	*22*	*0*	*0*	*123*	*.231*	*.324*	*.381*	*.249*	*19*	

Lefty backup catcher, draws a few walks, has fair defensive skills. As likely to be in the majors as not for each of the next four years.

DAVE McCARTY   **1B/OF**   **1970**   **Age 27**

Year	Team	Lge	AB	H	DB	TP	HR	BB	SB	CS	OUT	BA	OBA	SA	EQA	EQR	Peak
1993	Portland-OR	PCL	143	51	4	0	8	24	3	1	93	.357	.449	.552	.331	29	.360
1993	Minnesota	AL	351	77	14	2	3	22	3	4	278	.219	.265	.296	.181	19	.196
1994	Salt Lake City	PCL	183	39	6	1	3	31	1	2	146	.213	.327	.306	.211	15	.226
1994	Minnesota	AL	132	35	8	2	1	7	2	1	98	.265	.302	.379	.229	12	.245
1995	Indianapolis	AmA	143	47	8	1	8	17	0	0	96	.329	.400	.566	.314	26	.332
1995	Phoenix	PCL	149	49	12	1	5	17	1	1	101	.329	.398	.523	.302	25	.318
1995	Minnesota	AL	55	12	4	1	0	4	0	1	44	.218	.271	.327	.190	3	.200
1996	San Francisco	NL	178	40	2	0	6	20	2	1	139	.225	.303	.337	.214	15	.222
1997	*San Francisco*	*NL*	*136*	*37*	*6*	*1*	*5*	*11*	*2*	*2*	*101*	*.272*	*.327*	*.441*	*.267*	*19*	

Good thing he's got an education, 'cause he can't play this game. Long swing, slow bat, no future in baseball. Anyone who's watched him or seen his results knows that; the question is why they didn't tell Dusty.

DOUG MIRABELLI   **C**   **1971**   **Age 26**

Year	Team	Lge	AB	H	DB	TP	HR	BB	SB	CS	OUT	BA	OBA	SA	EQA	EQR	Peak
1993	San Jose	Calif	382	91	15	1	1	54	0	2	292	.238	.333	.291	.210	30	.232
1994	Shreveport	Texas	264	57	3	0	5	33	2	1	208	.216	.303	.284	.195	18	.212
1995	Shreveport	Texas	131	39	10	0	1	18	1	0	92	.298	.383	.397	.268	17	.287
1995	Phoenix	PCL	66	10	0	0	1	11	1	0	56	.152	.273	.197	.142	2	.136
1996	Shreveport	Texas	395	113	14	0	19	69	0	1	283	.286	.392	.466	.285	61	.301
1996	Phoenix	PCL	47	13	6	0	0	4	0	0	34	.277	.333	.404	.248	5	.258
1997	*San Francisco*	*NL*	*502*	*124*	*20*	*2*	*15*	*73*	*2*	*1*	*379*	*.247*	*.343*	*.384*	*.259*	*64*	

Posted a big year in Shreveport in 1996, and is considered by some in the organization to be a better receiver than Jensen. If true, he'll reach the bigs in late 1997. If not, he'll probably get converted to another position and fade out of baseball. Make or break year. If he can retain a little of that 1996 performance, he'll make the bigs and stay there. Might even make a few bucks.

ALEX MORALES   **UT**   **1974**   **Age 23**

Year	Team	Lge	AB	H	DB	TP	HR	BB	SB	CS	OUT	BA	OBA	SA	EQA	EQR	Peak
1995	Bellingham	Nwern	270	71	11	2	6	24	11	5	204	.263	.323	.385	.240	29	.268
1996	Burlington	Midw	144	30	4	0	5	21	7	1	115	.208	.309	.340	.225	14	.248
1996	San Jose	Calif	56	9	1	0	1	11	3	1	48	.161	.299	.232	.182	3	.191

Supposedly can play any defensive position well. If he can hit 15% better, that might be enough, but I wouldn't bet on it.

BILL MUELLER 3B/2B 1971 Age 26

Year	Team	Lge	AB	H	DB	TP	HR	BB	SB	CS	OUT	BA	OBA	SA	EQA	EQR	Peak
1993	Everett	Nwern	211	55	6	1	1	27	4	3	159	.261	.345	.313	.225	19	.249
1994	San Jose	Calif	456	129	17	4	6	88	2	4	331	.283	.399	.377	.265	60	.288
1995	Shreveport	Texas	343	104	14	1	2	49	5	3	242	.303	.390	.367	.262	42	.280
1995	Phoenix	PCL	170	46	12	3	3	19	0	0	124	.271	.344	.429	.258	21	.277
1996	Phoenix	PCL	438	120	12	4	4	42	2	3	321	.274	.338	.347	.232	41	.244
1996	San Francisco	NL	207	70	13	2	0	26	0	0	137	.338	.412	.420	.286	30	.302
1997	San Francisco	NL	410	119	24	4	5	55	4	3	294	.290	.374	.405	.278	60	

A very nice little ballplayer. Gets on base well, which is something the Giants sorely and desperately need, can fill in competently at second baseman, and is a dynamite third baseman. I don't think losing Matt Williams was the end of the world; not because of what they got back, but because I really like Bill Mueller. Could develop into Dave Magadan with a little power and good defense. Will draw 100 walks during the 1999 season. Main concern: throwing motion is awkward and looks to me like it could cause elbow problems.

DANTE POWELL OF 1974 Age 23

Year	Team	Lge	AB	H	DB	TP	HR	BB	SB	CS	OUT	BA	OBA	SA	EQA	EQR	Peak
1994	Everett	Nwern	171	49	6	0	5	12	11	2	124	.287	.333	.409	.258	21	.294
1995	San Jose	Calif	512	113	14	4	9	37	18	6	405	.221	.273	.316	.199	36	.223
1996	Shreveport	Texas	522	137	16	1	19	67	32	14	399	.262	.346	.406	.255	66	.282
1997	San Francisco	NL	493	112	19	1	23	91	38	11	392	.227	.348	.410	.273	76	

Hit well in Shreveport in 1996, and will get a chance to do so in the desert this year. Will arrive for good in September and be a very good outfielder for a long time. His numbers aren't insanely high, but there is no reason to think he won't develop pretty well. Probably not a superstar, but probably a good step up from Glenallen Hill. Could have a similar peak to Ray Lankford.

STEVE SCARSONE IF 1966 Age 31

Year	Team	Lge	AB	H	DB	TP	HR	BB	SB	CS	OUT	BA	OBA	SA	EQA	EQR	Peak
1993	Phoenix	PCL	69	16	1	0	3	7	1	0	53	.232	.303	.377	.229	7	.233
1993	San Francisco	NL	105	28	6	0	3	6	0	1	78	.267	.306	.410	.235	10	.241
1994	San Francisco	NL	105	29	6	0	3	11	0	2	78	.276	.345	.419	.250	12	.253
1995	San Francisco	NL	239	68	10	3	12	21	3	2	173	.285	.342	.502	.275	34	.272
1996	San Francisco	NL	287	64	12	1	5	28	1	3	226	.223	.292	.324	.202	21	.198
1997	San Francisco	NL	229	58	10	1	6	23	3	3	174	.253	.321	.384	.249	27	

Fifth infielder who can probably hang around for another four or five years somewhere. Not a bad player, but certainly not someone you're going to spend a lot on. Could probably handle an expanded role; if not on the ballclub, then probably on this fall's wonderful CBS Comedy Monday lineup.

BENJI SIMONTON 1B 1972 Age 25

Year	Team	Lge	AB	H	DB	TP	HR	BB	SB	CS	OUT	BA	OBA	SA	EQA	EQR	Peak
1993	Clinton	Midw	325	79	10	1	11	31	4	3	249	.243	.309	.382	.230	32	.256
1994	Clinton	Midw	251	67	10	1	12	43	5	2	186	.267	.374	.458	.277	38	.306
1994	San Jose	Calif	269	77	9	0	13	26	0	1	193	.286	.349	.465	.268	36	.297
1995	San Jose	Calif	231	60	7	2	7	33	3	0	171	.260	.352	.398	.255	28	.278
1995	Shreveport	Texas	111	35	7	2	4	10	2	1	77	.315	.372	.523	.293	18	.318
1996	Shreveport	Texas	487	117	13	1	21	92	5	2	372	.240	.361	.400	.256	62	.274
1997	San Francisco	NL	481	115	19	1	27	97	6	2	368	.239	.367	.451	.285	80	

J. R. Phillips with plate discipline. Defense is more suspect than David Keith in a Columbo episode, and since he's already playing first, he's not likely to find another place to hide that leather. Hits well enough so that there's no excuse for Desi Wilson and Dave McCarty to be on the big club, except for their unparalleled five-alarm chili.

ROBBY THOMPSON   **2B**   **1962**   **Age 35**

Year	Team	Lge	AB	H	DB	TP	HR	BB	SB	CS	OUT	BA	OBA	SA	EQA	EQR	Peak
1993	San Francisco	NL	514	170	28	1	22	53	9	3	347	.331	.393	.518	.302	87	.291
1994	San Francisco	NL	131	28	9	2	2	16	3	1	104	.214	.299	.359	.221	12	.211
1995	San Francisco	NL	345	82	11	0	10	46	1	2	265	.238	.327	.357	.229	33	.217
1996	San Francisco	NL	231	50	11	1	5	26	2	2	183	.216	.296	.338	.209	18	.199
1997	*San Francisco*	*NL*	*99*	*24*	*5*	*0*	*3*	*11*	*1*	*1*	*76*	*.242*	*.318*	*.384*	*.247*	*12*	

Stick a fork in him.

RICK WILKINS   **C**   **1967**   **Age 30**

Year	Team	Lge	AB	H	DB	TP	HR	BB	SB	CS	OUT	BA	OBA	SA	EQA	EQR	Peak
1993	Chicago Cubs	NL	457	141	17	1	32	56	2	1	317	.309	.384	.560	.305	81	.317
1994	Chicago Cubs	NL	320	77	25	2	8	45	4	3	246	.241	.334	.406	.246	37	.252
1995	Chicago Cubs	NL	166	33	2	0	6	37	0	0	133	.199	.345	.319	.224	16	.227
1995	Houston	NL	42	12	1	0	1	11	0	0	30	.286	.434	.381	.284	6	.282
1996	Houston	NL	263	60	9	2	6	49	0	1	204	.228	.349	.346	.234	27	.233
1996	San Francisco	NL	162	49	7	0	9	23	0	2	115	.302	.389	.512	.292	26	.290
1997	*Houston*	*NL*	*424*	*107*	*23*	*1*	*18*	*73*	*0*	*1*	*318*	*.252*	*.362*	*.439*	*.284*	*68*	

A fantastic acquisition for the Giants for two reasons. Wilkins has some offensive value, and has at least once demonstrated that he can be a very good hitter. The primary reason that getting Wilkins was a good idea is that they got a negative Kirt Manwaring in the deal, and negative Kirt Manwaring is usually one of the two or three best players in the league.

KEITH WILLIAMS   **OF**   **1972**   **Age 25**

Year	Team	Lge	AB	H	DB	TP	HR	BB	SB	CS	OUT	BA	OBA	SA	EQA	EQR	Peak
1993	Everett	Nwern	302	84	11	2	10	29	8	4	222	.278	.341	.427	.258	37	.288
1994	San Jose	Calif	522	151	19	4	19	50	2	2	373	.289	.351	.450	.267	68	.294
1995	Shreveport	Texas	282	85	13	1	10	22	4	2	199	.301	.352	.461	.271	38	.295
1995	Phoenix	PCL	82	23	2	1	2	5	0	0	59	.280	.322	.402	.243	9	.263
1996	Phoenix	PCL	398	100	16	2	13	49	2	1	299	.251	.333	.399	.245	44	.263
1997	*San Francisco*	*NL*	*464*	*135*	*27*	*3*	*16*	*40*	*6*	*3*	*332*	*.291*	*.347*	*.466*	*.284*	*71*	

Good hitter who still has a chance to develop into something more than that. The Giants have a few guys like this, but Williams is a better bet than most of them to take a big step up. His low performance points in the past have apparently been caused by nagging injuries. If he gets a chance to play, I think he'll perform about as well as projected, and that's pretty darn well. If he doesn't take that step forward, he could well fall into Dax Jones' career path. And that ain't no nature walk.

MATT WILLIAMS   **3B**   **1966**   **Age 31**

Year	Team	Lge	AB	H	DB	TP	HR	BB	SB	CS	OUT	BA	OBA	SA	EQA	EQR	Peak
1993	San Francisco	NL	595	185	31	2	42	37	1	3	413	.311	.351	.582	.297	100	.305
1994	San Francisco	NL	451	125	16	2	44	40	1	0	326	.277	.336	.614	.299	79	.301
1995	San Francisco	NL	295	105	16	0	26	34	2	0	190	.356	.422	.675	.346	67	.344
1996	San Francisco	NL	415	129	14	1	23	43	1	2	288	.311	.376	.516	.291	66	.285
1997	*Cleveland*	*AL*	*555*	*164*	*21*	*2*	*47*	*40*	*1*	*1*	*392*	*.295*	*.343*	*.595*	*.301*	*97*	

New GM Brian Sabean has shipped Williams and his baldness to Cleveland for Jose Vizcaino, Julian Tavarez and Jeff Kent. I don't mind the trading of Williams, but Sabean should have been able to do better than that. Tavarez looks like the real thing, and Jeff Kent's been underrated, but none of those three guys is going to make a significant different in the future of this franchise. Williams' injuries are similar to Mark McGwire's in terms of impact – they're not likely to impede him in the long term. I see no reason why Williams won't continue to be a great but slightly overrated power hitter. If he continues his trend of drawing walks, he'll be a legitimate MVP candidate. I also don't like the trade from Cleveland's perspective.

DESI WILSON   **1B**   **1968**   **Age 29**

Year	Team	Lge	AB	H	DB	TP	HR	BB	SB	CS	OUT	BA	OBA	SA	EQA	EQR	Peak
1993	Charlotte-FL	Flor	530	156	20	3	6	44	15	5	379	.294	.348	.377	.250	59	.264
1994	Tulsa	Texas	504	136	12	0	9	38	11	7	375	.270	.321	.347	.227	46	.235
1995	Shreveport	Texas	494	138	22	2	6	37	9	5	361	.279	.330	.368	.237	49	.243
1996	Phoenix	PCL	403	126	20	4	6	19	11	3	280	.313	.344	.427	.263	49	.265
1996	San Francisco	NL	121	34	1	0	2	13	0	2	89	.281	.351	.339	.231	11	.233
1997	*San Francisco*	*NL*	*284*	*78*	*11*	*1*	*4*	*19*	*19*	*4*	*210*	*.275*	*.320*	*.363*	*.255*	*34*	

Low power, middling average, no walks first baseman. No prospect with extreme prejudice, despite the penchant of Mike Krukow to remind us of how much he looks like Fred McGriff. Thank God 3Com doesn't have an organist. The theme from I Love Lucy could have driven the sanest of men to acts of unspeakable violence. Hopefully, he'll end up in Comiskey, so Nancy Faust can torture the denizens of Reinsdorf's 3rd ring.

PHILIP BAILEY   **LBP**   **1974**   **Age 23**

YR	TEAM	Lge	IP	H	ER	HR	BB	K	ERA	W	L	H/9	HR/9	BB/9	K/9	KW
1995	Bellingham	Nwern	48.0	86	23	5	20	22	4.31	2	3	16.12	.94	3.75	4.12	.44
1996	San Jose	Calif	65.7	88	28	4	26	34	3.84	4	3	12.06	.55	3.56	4.66	.66

Good-looking youngster who survives on guile and an average fastball. Unlikely to advance much past AA.

LORENZO BARCELO   **RSP**   **1978**   **Age 19**

YR	TEAM	Lge	IP	H	ER	HR	BB	K	ERA	W	L	H/9	HR/9	BB/9	K/9	KW
1995	Bellingham	Nwern	37.0	71	34	4	26	19	8.27	1	3	17.27	.97	6.32	4.62	-.04
1996	Burlington	Midw	132.7	177	75	23	60	87	5.09	6	9	12.01	1.56	4.07	5.90	.95

Flamethrowing "18"-year-old who could well turn into something special, provided his age isn't more fictional than Cecil Fielder's listed 240 pounds.

JOSE BAUTISTA   **RRP**   **1965**   **Age 32**

YR	TEAM	Lge	IP	H	ER	HR	BB	K	ERA	W	L	H/9	HR/9	BB/9	K/9	KW
1993	Chicago Cubs	NL	109.0	106	34	12	38	60	2.81	8	4	8.75	.99	3.14	4.95	.87
1994	Chicago Cubs	NL	68.3	77	28	10	24	42	3.69	4	4	10.14	1.32	3.16	5.53	1.05
1995	San Francisco	NL	100.7	121	70	24	35	41	6.26	3	8	10.82	2.15	3.13	3.67	.44
1996	Phoenix	PCL	36.7	42	16	1	8	15	3.93	2	2	10.31	.25	1.96	3.68	.74
1996	San Francisco	NL	68.3	67	28	10	21	24	3.69	4	4	8.82	1.32	2.77	3.16	.36

That's as good a year as you're going to get out of Bautista. If Dusty can keep doing it, he's probably deserving of some sort of medal. Bautista's got basically nothing left in his arm, but these things do eventually heal up. If he can hang on for two more years, I'll bet his arm will come all the way back and he'll have a late-career burst of effectiveness.

ROD BECK   **RRP**   **1969**   **Age 28**

YR	TEAM	Lge	IP	H	ER	HR	BB	K	ERA	W	L	H/9	HR/9	BB/9	K/9	KW
1993	San Francisco	NL	76.0	63	19	12	21	83	2.25	6	2	7.46	1.42	2.49	9.83	2.65
1994	San Francisco	NL	48.3	48	15	10	17	36	2.79	3	2	8.94	1.86	3.17	6.70	1.44
1995	San Francisco	NL	57.7	63	29	7	26	38	4.53	3	3	9.83	1.09	4.06	5.93	.96
1996	San Francisco	NL	60.7	58	20	9	15	42	2.97	5	2	8.60	1.34	2.23	6.23	1.52

Bounced back from an aberrant 1995. No reason to believe he won't continue to be excellent. Voted "The Major Leaguer who most resembles the authorship group." Looks like a cross between Al Hrabosky and a NASCAR driver. Throws some nasty stuff when he's on, and even pitched OK when bouncing back on short rest. I think Dusty's learned his lesson, and Beck should be a good closer for years to come. The long ball is really the only problem.

DARIN BLOOD   **RSP**   **1975**   **Age 22**

YR	TEAM	Lge	IP	H	ER	HR	BB	K	ERA	W	L	H/9	HR/9	BB/9	K/9	KW
1995	Bellingham	Nwern	59.0	105	39	3	44	44	5.95	2	5	16.02	.46	6.71	6.71	.56
1996	San Jose	Calif	153.7	161	50	4	84	122	2.93	11	6	9.43	.23	4.92	7.15	1.15

Grade A- Prospect, but was worked like a Henny Youngman punch line in 1996. If the organization can back off a bit, and Blood develops normally, he's a good rotation starter. K rate was spectacular, and K/W ratio pretty solid for a guy his age. Mechanics are average.

STEVE BOURGEOIS　　**RBP**　　**1973**　　**Age 24**

YR	TEAM	Lge	IP	H	ER	HR	BB	K	ERA	W	L	H/9	HR/9	BB/9	K/9	KW
1993	Everett	Nwern	63.7	89	49	8	51	44	6.93	2	5	12.58	1.13	7.21	6.22	.27
1994	Clinton	Midw	91.3	123	60	17	73	55	5.91	3	7	12.12	1.68	7.19	5.42	.01
1994	San Jose	Calif	32.7	46	21	4	28	18	5.79	1	3	12.67	1.10	7.71	4.96	-.28
1995	Shreveport	Texas	129.7	166	54	10	69	79	3.75	7	7	11.52	.69	4.79	5.48	.63
1995	Phoenix	PCL	32.3	37	14	2	17	21	3.90	2	2	10.30	.56	4.73	5.85	.77
1996	Phoenix	PCL	91.3	109	41	6	52	53	4.04	5	5	10.74	.59	5.12	5.22	.46
1996	San Francisco	NL	40.7	60	31	4	25	15	6.86	1	4	13.28	.89	5.53	3.32	-.28

Earned his shot in the bigs, and will be in the fight for a rotation spot out of spring training, provided he can lift his arm over his head. Less than sterling stuff, but he can work the hitters fairly well and he's done a creditable job through AA and AAA. Unlikely to be a star, but could be a decent #4 starter.

DAN CARLSON　　**RSP**　　**1970**　　**Age 27**

YR	TEAM	Lge	IP	H	ER	HR	BB	K	ERA	W	L	H/9	HR/9	BB/9	K/9	KW
1993	Shreveport	Texas	90.3	104	33	10	42	58	3.29	6	4	10.36	1.00	4.18	5.78	.88
1993	Phoenix	PCL	64.7	75	42	11	39	38	5.85	2	5	10.44	1.53	5.43	5.29	.41
1994	Phoenix	PCL	142.0	164	62	19	70	100	3.93	8	8	10.39	1.20	4.44	6.34	1.00
1995	Phoenix	PCL	124.7	132	53	11	80	85	3.83	7	7	9.53	.79	5.78	6.14	.60
1996	Phoenix	PCL	137.7	136	50	18	59	100	3.27	9	6	8.89	1.18	3.86	6.54	1.21

Has certainly pitched well enough to earn a spot in the Giants' rotation, but the organization has just never been very high on him. He's consistently been very effective, his peripheral numbers are solid and he's been healthy. If he's not dying of bursitis in March, he could help just about any team in baseball, at least as a #5 starter. In San Francisco, I see no reason why he couldn't anchor the rotation. Of course, the Giants management and I overlap roughly as often as Madeline Murray O'Hair and Bishop Pederast.

MARINO CASTILLO　　**RRP**　　**1971**　　**Age 26**

YR	TEAM	Lge	IP	H	ER	HR	BB	K	ERA	W	L	H/9	HR/9	BB/9	K/9	KW
1993	Clinton	Midw	60.7	82	34	4	26	35	5.04	3	4	12.16	.59	3.86	5.19	.77
1994	San Jose	Calif	93.7	133	52	11	36	54	5.00	4	6	12.78	1.06	3.46	5.19	.86
1995	San Jose	Calif	51.0	57	13	2	18	33	2.29	5	1	10.06	.35	3.18	5.82	1.15
1995	Shreveport	Texas	33.7	44	18	5	17	27	4.81	2	2	11.76	1.34	4.54	7.22	1.27
1996	San Jose	Calif	10.3	10	1	1	0	12	.87	1	0	8.71	.87	.00	10.45	3.48
1996	Shreveport	Texas	45.7	55	21	7	20	44	4.14	2	3	10.84	1.38	3.94	8.67	1.91

Ready for the bigs right now, and probably will be pushing Rod Beck for a job within 18 months. Relentlessly effective reliever who throws a very heavy ball, a la Bryan Harvey. I think about four guys hit the ball hard off him in San Jose. Could have been five.

DOUG CREEK　　**LBP**　　**1969**　　**Age 28**

YR	TEAM	Lge	IP	H	ER	HR	BB	K	ERA	W	L	H/9	HR/9	BB/9	K/9	KW
1993	Arkansas	Texas	131.0	172	83	17	73	92	5.70	5	10	11.82	1.17	5.02	6.32	.85
1993	Louisville	AmA	13.3	11	4	0	10	8	2.70	1	0	7.43	.00	6.75	5.40	.11
1994	Arkansas	Texas	83.0	110	55	10	48	47	5.96	3	6	11.93	1.08	5.20	5.10	.40
1994	Louisville	AmA	25.7	35	21	2	26	14	7.36	1	2	12.27	.70	9.12	4.91	-.64
1995	Arkansas	Texas	31.3	26	10	4	20	42	2.87	2	1	7.47	1.15	5.74	12.06	2.59
1995	Louisville	AmA	28.0	22	10	1	24	25	3.21	2	1	7.07	.32	7.71	8.04	.75
1996	San Francisco	NL	48.3	45	36	11	37	33	6.70	1	4	8.38	2.05	6.89	6.14	.33

All over the road, at least in terms of results. I've never thought much of him, but he has had some limited success in short stints at AAA. That's not really all that rare of a skill. The BP after his name is something of a double entendre as far as I'm concerned.

RICH DELUCIA   **RRP**   **1965**   **Age 32**

YR	TEAM	Lge	IP	H	ER	HR	BB	K	ERA	W	L	H/9	HR/9	BB/9	K/9	KW
1993	Calgary	PCL	40.7	43	23	6	24	30	5.09	2	3	9.52	1.33	5.31	6.64	.89
1993	Seattle	AL	42.7	46	20	5	25	50	4.22	2	3	9.70	1.05	5.27	10.55	2.20
1994	Indianapolis	AmA	40.7	25	9	3	28	46	1.99	4	1	5.53	.66	6.20	10.18	1.84
1994	Cincinnati	NL	10.7	9	5	4	6	14	4.22	0	1	7.59	3.38	5.06	11.81	2.67
1995	St. Louis	NL	80.3	65	32	9	43	68	3.59	5	4	7.28	1.01	4.82	7.62	1.34
1996	San Francisco	NL	61.3	63	39	8	37	48	5.72	2	5	9.24	1.17	5.43	7.04	.99

Winner of one of the first Binaca Blast Deep Drive Derbies, for allowing an astonishing number of home runs in an equally astonishing number of innings. Can be effective in a limited role; that role has now become so limited that he may not be worth the roster spot, much less the money. Does do a good job inducing groundballs a lot of the time.

MARK DEWEY   **RRP**   **1965**   **Age 32**

YR	TEAM	Lge	IP	H	ER	HR	BB	K	ERA	W	L	H/9	HR/9	BB/9	K/9	KW
1993	Buffalo	AmA	27.3	24	8	2	8	16	2.63	2	1	7.90	.66	2.63	5.27	1.10
1993	Pittsburgh	NL	25.0	16	6	0	13	13	2.16	2	1	5.76	.00	4.68	4.68	.39
1994	Pittsburgh	NL	51.0	61	19	4	23	28	3.35	4	2	10.76	.71	4.06	4.94	.63
1995	San Francisco	NL	31.3	33	11	2	19	29	3.16	2	1	9.48	.57	5.46	8.33	1.41
1996	San Francisco	NL	82.3	81	35	9	49	50	3.83	5	4	8.85	.98	5.36	5.47	.48

Nicknamed "Puffy" by his cruel Orphan Master, and has used that inner turmoil to drive himself to new heights of performance. Dewey's pitched fairly well now for four years, and despite less than glittering peripheral numbers, he'll probably continue to do so.

SHAWN ESTES   **LSP**   **1973**   **Age 24**

YR	TEAM	Lge	IP	H	ER	HR	BB	K	ERA	W	L	H/9	HR/9	BB/9	K/9	KW
1993	Appleton	Midw	71.3	124	85	4	68	38	10.72	1	7	15.64	.50	8.58	4.79	-.55
1994	Appleton	Midw	17.3	21	12	2	22	17	6.23	1	1	10.90	1.04	11.42	8.83	.09
1995	Burlington	Midw	13.0	16	8	2	15	14	5.54	0	1	11.08	1.38	10.38	9.69	.63
1995	San Jose	Calif	44.0	40	12	2	23	39	2.45	4	1	8.18	.41	4.70	7.98	1.48
1995	Shreveport	Texas	20.0	17	5	2	13	16	2.25	2	0	7.65	.90	5.85	7.20	.94
1995	San Francisco	NL	17.0	17	12	2	6	13	6.35	1	1	9.00	1.06	3.18	6.88	1.50
1996	Phoenix	PCL	103.3	94	35	8	48	77	3.05	7	4	8.19	.70	4.18	6.71	1.19
1996	San Francisco	NL	68.7	66	26	3	46	53	3.41	5	3	8.65	.39	6.03	6.95	.81

The one name that came up a lot when people shopped actual first base talent to the Giants, and Bob Quinn turned them away as fast as they came. Probably the staff ace at the start of the 1997 season, and barring idiocy by the Giants in handling him, he should have a long and productive career. Of course, with pitchers you never really know. Careers are fragile things. One minute you're watching Eric Davis wave ineffectually, the next minute you're on Frank Jobe's Christmas card list.

OSVALDO FERNANDEZ   **RSP**   **1970**   **Age 27**

YR	TEAM	Lge	IP	H	ER	HR	BB	K	ERA	W	L	H/9	HR/9	BB/9	K/9	KW
1994	Riverside	Calif	76.0	81	32	8	48	53	3.79	4	4	9.59	.95	5.68	6.28	.67
1995	Port City	South	144.0	171	83	7	81	124	5.19	6	10	10.69	.44	5.06	7.75	1.32
1996	San Francisco	NL	170.3	196	84	19	72	93	4.44	9	10	10.36	1.00	3.80	4.91	.69

The Painmaker. Responsible for the ingestion of more Maalox in the Bay Area than a mass Taxpayer Compliance Audit. Decent stuff, and wholly random. From pitch to pitch, you don't know what you're going to get, much less from hitter to hitter or game to game. Definitely has the stuff to succeed, but so does Reggie Harris.

KEITH FOULKE   **RSP**   **1973**   **Age 24**

YR	TEAM	Lge	IP	H	ER	HR	BB	K	ERA	W	L	H/9	HR/9	BB/9	K/9	KW
1994	Everett	Nwern	16.7	23	4	0	4	11	2.16	2	0	12.42	.00	2.16	5.94	1.44
1995	San Jose	Calif	155.3	204	87	18	46	108	5.04	7	10	11.82	1.04	2.67	6.26	1.42
1996	Shreveport	Texas	167.3	171	58	17	54	107	3.12	12	7	9.20	.91	2.90	5.75	1.19

Wow. Dominated AA like John Harrington's "Xena: Warrior Princess" leather fantasy. The Giants will be tempted to call him up to the bigs by June, and they'll give in to that by July if Foulke does anything like he did last year. He's still probably a year and a half away from being ready to consistently get people out in the big leagues.

AARON FULTZ	LSP		1974		Age 23										
YR	TEAM	Lge	IP	H	ER	HR	BB	K	ERA	W	L	H/9	HR/9	BB/9	K/9	KW
1993	Clinton	Midw	126.3	177	74	11	86	85	5.27	5	9	12.61	.78	6.13	6.06	.49
1994	Ft Myers	Flor	150.0	238	110	15	83	103	6.60	5	12	14.28	.90	4.98	6.18	.81
1996	San Jose	Calif	93.3	114	47	7	64	65	4.53	4	6	10.99	.67	6.17	6.27	.55

Strikes out enough guys to be successful, and walks enough not to be. Something has to give, but it probably won't happen for a couple of years. Will start and spend the season in AA.

MARK GARDNER	RSP		1962		Age 35										
YR	TEAM	Lge	IP	H	ER	HR	BB	K	ERA	W	L	H/9	HR/9	BB/9	K/9	KW
1993	Omaha	AmA	45.7	35	14	7	24	37	2.76	3	2	6.90	1.38	4.73	7.29	1.25
1993	Kansas City	AL	92.0	86	52	17	40	56	5.09	4	6	8.41	1.66	3.91	5.48	.85
1994	Florida	NL	91.3	91	43	13	38	52	4.24	5	5	8.97	1.28	3.74	5.12	.77
1995	Florida	NL	102.3	109	53	14	52	78	4.66	5	6	9.59	1.23	4.57	6.86	1.14
1996	San Francisco	NL	178.7	201	92	27	73	127	4.63	9	11	10.12	1.36	3.68	6.40	1.21

A very bright acquisition by Quinn. He has a history of moderate success, and his career peripheral numbers would certainly indicate that he's capable of having more for a few years. Nearing the end of his career and has been pretty darn valuable; at least more than his reputation.

CHAD HARTVIGSON	LSP		1971		Age 26										
YR	TEAM	Lge	IP	H	ER	HR	BB	K	ERA	W	L	H/9	HR/9	BB/9	K/9	KW
1994	Everett	Nwern	33.7	49	19	7	18	25	5.08	2	2	13.10	1.87	4.81	6.68	1.02
1995	San Jose	Calif	73.3	100	38	5	33	41	4.66	3	5	12.27	.61	4.05	5.03	.66
1996	San Jose	Calif	93.3	108	40	10	36	72	3.86	5	5	10.41	.96	3.47	6.94	1.45

Pitched well, but he was 25 in A ball. I'm extremely dubious. Let's see how Shreveport treats him.

JULIAN HEREDIA	RRP		1970		Age 27										
YR	TEAM	Lge	IP	H	ER	HR	BB	K	ERA	W	L	H/9	HR/9	BB/9	K/9	KW
1993	Midland	Texas	81.7	82	38	10	32	62	4.19	4	5	9.04	1.10	3.53	6.83	1.40
1994	Midland	Texas	90.3	94	42	11	48	78	4.18	5	5	9.37	1.10	4.78	7.77	1.39
1995	Vancouver	PCL	68.7	80	36	10	31	61	4.72	3	5	10.49	1.31	4.06	8.00	1.65
1996	Phoenix	PCL	65.7	70	33	11	30	48	4.52	3	4	9.59	1.51	4.11	6.58	1.16

Pulled from the Angels' system, Heredia could be a rubber armed bullpen filler for someone; he pitches well enough to help a major league club and he wouldn't be expensive. Has not yet been invited to camp, but might still be.

SANTOS HERNANDEZ	RBP		1973		Age 24										
YR	TEAM	Lge	IP	H	ER	HR	BB	K	ERA	W	L	H/9	HR/9	BB/9	K/9	KW
1994	Clinton	Midw	42.0	59	25	6	16	30	5.36	2	3	12.64	1.29	3.43	6.43	1.29
1995	Burlington	Midw	57.7	65	26	4	28	55	4.06	3	3	10.14	.62	4.37	8.58	1.77
1996	Burlington	Midw	60.0	53	15	6	17	49	2.25	5	2	7.95	.90	2.55	7.35	1.81

Did to the Midwest League what Wilt Chamberlain once did to singles bars. Grade B prospect who could reach the majors as early as late this year. The Giants made a big mistake in not promoting him; the winds shift with the sound of "attitude problems," which is usually so much rubbish.

CHRIS HOOK	RBP		1969		Age 28										
YR	TEAM	Lge	IP	H	ER	HR	BB	K	ERA	W	L	H/9	HR/9	BB/9	K/9	KW
1993	Chattanooga	South	152.0	179	81	8	87	90	4.80	7	10	10.60	.47	5.15	5.33	.49
1994	Phoenix	PCL	84.3	103	37	5	38	49	3.95	5	4	10.99	.53	4.06	5.23	.73
1995	San Francisco	NL	52.0	58	31	7	34	36	5.37	2	4	10.04	1.21	5.88	6.23	.61
1996	Phoenix	PCL	120.7	136	63	18	63	57	4.70	5	8	10.14	1.34	4.70	4.25	.24
1996	San Francisco	NL	13.7	16	11	3	15	4	7.24	0	2	10.54	1.98	9.88	2.63	-1.59

I didn't think he could pitch, and I still don't. He might be successful for short stretches, but by and large, he's not reliable and has never really flashed any brilliance. Then again, we just re-elected Bill Clinton. I wish I didn't look so much like him.

FAUSTO MACEY   **RSP**   **1976**   **Age 21**

YR	TEAM	Lge	IP	H	ER	HR	BB	K	ERA	W	L	H/9	HR/9	BB/9	K/9	KW
1994	Everett	Nwern	22.7	41	14	2	10	11	5.56	1	2	16.28	.79	3.97	4.37	.46
1995	San Jose	Calif	148.7	198	84	19	68	61	5.09	6	11	11.99	1.15	4.12	3.69	.20
1996	Shreveport	Texas	142.7	184	85	23	67	52	5.36	6	10	11.61	1.45	4.23	3.28	.04

No Prospect isn't a strong enough term. Can't dent wet bread.

RUSS ORTIZ   **RRP**   **1974**   **Age 23**

YR	TEAM	Lge	IP	H	ER	HR	BB	K	ERA	W	L	H/9	HR/9	BB/9	K/9	KW
1995	Bellingham	Nwern	29.7	31	5	2	18	31	1.52	3	0	9.40	.61	5.46	9.40	1.77
1996	San Jose	Calif	33.3	20	1	0	24	40	.27	4	0	5.40	.00	6.48	10.80	1.98
1996	Shreveport	Texas	24.7	24	13	0	26	24	4.74	1	2	8.76	.00	9.49	8.76	.55

Struck out 3.74 guys per inning at San Jose, so the Giants decided to move him to Shreveport. That number should come down under 3 there, and his walk numbers will likely step up a bit. Could be the next Rob Dibble, could be the next Brad Pennington. I can't call this one.

MARK PETERSON   **LRP**   **1971**   **Age 26**

YR	TEAM	Lge	IP	H	ER	HR	BB	K	ERA	W	L	H/9	HR/9	BB/9	K/9	KW
1993	San Jose	Calif	71.0	117	37	6	13	32	4.69	3	5	14.83	.76	1.65	4.06	.94
1994	San Jose	Calif	31.7	45	17	5	9	18	4.83	2	2	12.79	1.42	2.56	5.12	1.07
1994	Shreveport	Texas	51.0	64	24	2	11	23	4.24	3	3	11.29	.35	1.94	4.06	.87
1996	Shreveport	Texas	51.0	66	23	5	14	27	4.06	3	3	11.65	.88	2.47	4.76	.97

No relation to Adam Peterson, the famed minor league no-hit artist. A generic reliever trying to catch on somewhere with someone. Unlikely to ever make the bigs.

JIM POOLE   **LRP**   **1966**   **Age 31**

YR	TEAM	Lge	IP	H	ER	HR	BB	K	ERA	W	L	H/9	HR/9	BB/9	K/9	KW
1993	Baltimore	AL	48.0	33	13	2	23	30	2.44	4	1	6.19	.38	4.31	5.62	.80
1994	Baltimore	AL	20.7	29	11	4	11	17	4.79	1	1	12.63	1.74	4.79	7.40	1.27
1995	Cleveland	AL	49.7	41	17	7	18	41	3.08	4	2	7.43	1.27	3.26	7.43	1.66
1996	Cleveland	AL	26.7	26	10	2	15	18	3.38	2	1	8.78	.68	5.06	6.08	.76
1996	San Francisco	NL	23.0	17	6	2	14	16	2.35	2	1	6.65	.78	5.48	6.26	.72

Lefty control freak who's been pretty darn good at a limited job. Dave Leiper doesn't have a job, and Jim Poole does. Will be doing this for at least five more years, and probably will stay effective at it. Rick Honeycutt, Jr.

BOBBY RECTOR   **RSP**   **1975**   **Age 22**

YR	TEAM	Lge	IP	H	ER	HR	BB	K	ERA	W	L	H/9	HR/9	BB/9	K/9	KW
1995	Burlington	Midw	117.7	165	80	9	78	66	6.12	4	9	12.62	.69	5.97	5.05	.19
1996	San Jose	Calif	147.7	189	71	14	51	92	4.33	7	9	11.52	.85	3.11	5.61	1.09

Pitched fair in San Jose, and a grade B- prospect. Not likely to remain healthy unless his motion gets some work from a good pitching coach. His landing spot varies pretty significantly, and he makes the adjustment with his shoulder in mid-pitch. That's not a long term strategy. I think he knows how to pitch, though; appeared to have a brain out there.

KIRK RUETER   **LBP**   **1971**   **Age 26**

YR	TEAM	Lge	IP	H	ER	HR	BB	K	ERA	W	L	H/9	HR/9	BB/9	K/9	KW
1993	Harrisburg	East	55.0	56	10	5	11	27	1.64	5	1	9.16	.82	1.80	4.42	1.02
1993	Ottawa	Inter	40.7	50	19	7	7	22	4.20	2	3	11.07	1.55	1.55	4.87	1.24
1993	Montreal	NL	82.3	90	31	5	28	30	3.39	5	4	9.84	.55	3.06	3.28	.33
1994	Montreal	NL	92.0	102	51	11	31	46	4.99	4	6	9.98	1.08	3.03	4.50	.74
1995	Ottawa	Inter	111.3	138	52	8	37	55	4.20	6	6	11.16	.65	2.99	4.45	.73
1995	Montreal	NL	45.3	41	14	3	13	25	2.78	3	2	8.14	.60	2.58	4.96	1.01
1996	Ottawa	Inter	14.3	22	6	3	4	2	3.77	1	1	13.81	1.88	2.51	1.26	-.21
1996	Phoenix	PCL	23.7	26	10	2	14	12	3.80	2	1	9.89	.76	5.32	4.56	.19
1996	Montreal	NL	78.0	89	37	11	29	26	4.27	4	5	10.27	1.27	3.35	3.00	.16
1996	San Francisco	NL	22.3	20	5	0	7	14	2.01	2	0	8.06	.00	2.82	5.64	1.18

The Anti-Anthony Young. Younger than most people think, but pitches like an old man. Will probably be out of baseball before he's 30. Not a good bet to maintain long-term success, but a better bet than any show that currently contains Ted Danson.

TIM SCOTT RRP 1967 Age 30

YR	TEAM	Lge	IP	H	ER	HR	BB	K	ERA	W	L	H/9	HR/9	BB/9	K/9	KW
1993	Montreal	NL	33.3	33	14	4	23	34	3.78	2	2	8.91	1.08	6.21	9.18	1.51
1993	San Diego	NL	36.3	40	12	1	20	29	2.97	3	1	9.91	.25	4.95	7.18	1.16
1994	Montreal	NL	52.0	52	14	0	22	34	2.42	4	2	9.00	.00	3.81	5.88	1.01
1995	Montreal	NL	62.0	54	25	6	28	51	3.63	4	3	7.84	.87	4.06	7.40	1.45
1996	Montreal	NL	45.3	42	15	3	25	32	2.98	3	2	8.34	.60	4.96	6.35	.88
1996	San Francisco	NL	20.0	24	16	5	10	9	7.20	0	2	10.80	2.25	4.50	4.05	.22

Effective, underrated reliever, and a very valuable setup man. Giants should probably sign him to a relatively long-term deal and make good use of his talents. It's not easy to find players this good. Scott's never gotten the recognition he deserves, and there's no reason to suspect he will now. A very good pitcher. Released, picked up by the Reds.

STEVE SODERSTROM RSP 1972 Age 25

YR	TEAM	Lge	IP	H	ER	HR	BB	K	ERA	W	L	H/9	HR/9	BB/9	K/9	KW
1994	San Jose	Calif	35.3	43	21	2	33	27	5.35	1	3	10.95	.51	8.41	6.88	.19
1995	Shreveport	Texas	105.3	121	54	7	66	79	4.61	5	7	10.34	.60	5.64	6.75	.84
1996	Phoenix	PCL	160.7	177	78	14	73	65	4.37	8	10	9.91	.78	4.09	3.64	.19
1996	San Francisco	NL	13.7	16	10	1	8	8	6.59	1	1	10.54	.66	5.27	5.27	.44

Struggling starting pitcher who pitched fairly well in Phoenix, and he'll be given a decent look in Spring Training. Clubs usually have five or six guys like this vying for two rotation spots and two bullpen spots. That's gotta get old, but that's what's in Steve's future. He does strike out enough guys so that he could break out if he finds his control; there are worse pitchers to take a flyer on.

WILLIAM VANLANDINGHAM RSP 1971 Age 26

YR	TEAM	Lge	IP	H	ER	HR	BB	K	ERA	W	L	H/9	HR/9	BB/9	K/9	KW
1993	San Jose	Calif	142.3	199	102	8	98	121	6.45	4	12	12.58	.51	6.20	7.65	1.00
1994	Shreveport	Texas	46.7	49	21	5	16	33	4.05	2	3	9.45	.96	3.09	6.36	1.35
1994	Phoenix	PCL	27.0	21	11	0	17	25	3.67	2	1	7.00	.00	5.67	8.33	1.36
1994	San Francisco	NL	82.3	72	32	4	51	52	3.50	5	4	7.87	.44	5.57	5.68	.50
1995	San Francisco	NL	120.3	132	54	14	50	86	4.04	6	7	9.87	1.05	3.74	6.43	1.21
1996	San Francisco	NL	180.0	200	109	17	95	85	5.45	7	13	10.00	.85	4.75	4.25	.23

Everything pretty much went straight to hell. Not only did William stink up the place like rancid cheese, he had to live with that haircut. I normally would say he's likely to bounce back, but I think something's wrong with his arm. His K rate went down faster than Heidi Fleiss, and he just wasn't fooling anyone. I still think he has a future, but it might be two or three years down the road now.

ALLEN WATSON LSP 1971 Age 26

YR	TEAM	Lge	IP	H	ER	HR	BB	K	ERA	W	L	H/9	HR/9	BB/9	K/9	KW
1993	Louisville	AmA	114.3	107	41	13	43	79	3.23	8	5	8.42	1.02	3.38	6.22	1.23
1993	St. Louis	NL	83.7	96	52	12	38	48	5.59	3	6	10.33	1.29	4.09	5.16	.70
1994	St. Louis	NL	116.0	125	63	15	64	69	4.89	5	8	9.70	1.16	4.97	5.35	.54
1995	Louisville	AmA	22.7	21	8	1	9	17	3.18	2	1	8.34	.40	3.57	6.75	1.36
1995	St. Louis	NL	113.3	125	59	16	51	44	4.69	5	8	9.93	1.27	4.05	3.49	.15
1996	San Francisco	NL	184.0	192	92	27	85	112	4.50	9	11	9.39	1.32	4.16	5.48	.79

A generic bottom of the rotation starter. Fairly reliable, won't hurt you, but you don't build a team around him. As long as you understand his role, Watson can definitely help a team. He has fought an assortment of injuries, but what pitcher hasn't? If he were in the Mets chain, they'd probably have broken him by now. "Get out there, you weasely little #$%#$!! Did I tell you you could come out?" — D. Green. Traded to the Angels for J.T. Snow, probably #4 starter in Anaheim.

Player	Age	Team	Lge	AB	H	DB	TP	HR	BB	SB	CS	OUT	BA	OBA	SA	EQA	EQR	Peak
JOSE ALGUACIL	23	San Jose	Calif	277	67	8	2	1	18	9	4	214	.242	.288	.296	.198	19	.216
JOHNNY BESS	26	Shreveport	Texas	179	43	7	2	6	17	1	1	137	.240	.306	.402	.234	18	.243
BOBBY BONDS	26	San Jose	Calif	429	100	11	2	10	32	10	3	332	.233	.286	.338	.211	34	.218
MALCOLM CEPEDA	23	Burlington	Midw	218	28	6	1	0	32	1	1	191	.128	.240	.165	.078	2	.084
PABLO CORDERO	23	Burlington	Midw	81	6	2	0	0	4	1	0	75	.074	.118	.099	-.161	-4	-.160
REY CORUJO	24	San Jose	Calif	192	48	6	1	4	14	0	0	144	.250	.301	.354	.219	16	.235
DEIVI CRUZ	21	Burlington	Midw	526	133	13	1	9	25	6	2	395	.253	.287	.333	.208	39	.234
ROBERTO DELEON	25	Shreveport	Texas	267	58	9	2	4	22	0	1	210	.217	.277	.311	.191	17	.203
WILSON DELGADO	20	San Jose	Calif	472	115	15	4	2	36	4	1	358	.244	.297	.305	.202	33	.230
ANDRES DUNCAN	24	Phoenix	PCL	106	22	7	1	1	7	1	0	84	.208	.257	.321	.189	7	.205
	24	Shreveport	Texas	197	48	6	1	2	19	5	2	151	.244	.310	.315	.213	16	.229
PEDRO FELIX	19	Burlington	Midw	326	74	6	1	5	12	2	1	253	.227	.254	.298	.179	17	.206
TIM FLOREZ	26	Phoenix	PCL	364	96	24	2	4	33	1	3	271	.264	.325	.374	.233	36	.242
JOEL GALARZA	22	San Jose	Calif	297	80	7	0	8	18	5	2	219	.269	.311	.374	.232	28	.255
TIM GARLAND	27	San Jose	Calif	561	160	13	4	5	40	25	10	411	.285	.333	.349	.236	56	.243
MARK GULSETH	24	Burlington	Midw	441	101	22	1	6	70	2	1	341	.229	.335	.324	.223	40	.239
EDWARDS GUZMAN	19	San Jose	Calif	375	91	14	3	1	30	2	2	286	.243	.299	.304	.201	26	.232
BRETT KING	23	Shreveport	Texas	469	102	16	2	7	46	14	5	372	.217	.287	.305	.200	33	.217
BRIAN MANNING	21	Burlington	Midw	116	30	2	1	3	17	1	0	86	.259	.353	.371	.247	13	.277
RAUL MARVAL	20	Burlington	Midw	161	27	8	0	0	4	1	0	134	.168	.188	.217	.083	1	.091
	20	San Jose	Calif	139	29	4	0	0	7	0	0	110	.209	.247	.237	.144	4	.162
CRAIG MAYES	26	San Jose	Calif	479	142	19	2	3	20	3	4	341	.296	.325	.363	.232	44	.241
CALVIN MURRAY	24	Phoenix	PCL	311	69	13	3	4	41	9	4	246	.222	.312	.322	.215	26	.230
	24	Shreveport	Texas	174	43	4	0	6	23	5	3	134	.247	.335	.374	.239	19	.254
DAN PELTIER	28	Phoenix	PCL	266	68	5	2	1	27	0	1	199	.256	.324	.301	.210	20	.212
GARY PHILLIPS	24	Shreveport	Texas	341	76	13	2	3	22	2	3	268	.223	.270	.299	.184	19	.197
JEFF POOR	22	Burlington	Midw	370	76	5	0	3	37	4	0	294	.205	.278	.243	.164	16	.181
HIRAM RAMIREZ	23	Burlington	Midw	338	73	7	0	9	40	1	0	265	.216	.299	.317	.205	25	.223
DEREK REID	26	San Jose	Calif	357	116	9	2	12	26	12	2	243	.325	.371	.462	.283	52	.294
	26	Shreveport	Texas	120	27	1	0	4	11	2	1	94	.225	.290	.333	.208	9	.216
ARMANDO RIOS	24	Shreveport	Texas	338	90	13	1	11	41	8	5	253	.266	.346	.408	.253	41	.271
JON SBROCCO	25	San Jose	Calif	370	105	10	3	2	53	14	6	271	.284	.374	.343	.250	42	.264
	25	Shreveport	Texas	84	20	0	1	1	10	3	0	64	.238	.319	.298	.217	7	.229
CHRIS SINGLETON	23	Shreveport	Texas	506	140	27	5	5	25	19	7	373	.277	.311	.379	.236	50	.257
MICHAEL SORROW	22	Burlington	Midw	233	47	4	1	0	32	0	0	186	.202	.298	.227	.168	11	.187
BRUCE THOMPSON	23	Burlington	Midw	378	62	3	0	1	47	8	5	321	.164	.256	.180	.119	8	.130
DAN TOPPING	19	Burlington	Midw	135	26	3	0	3	15	0	0	109	.193	.273	.281	.178	7	.204
JOHN WATSON	22	Burlington	Midw	326	75	9	1	1	22	10	3	254	.230	.279	.273	.186	19	.204
KEVIN WATSON	23	Burlington	Midw	80	9	1	1	3	8	0	0	71	.112	.193	.262	.117	2	.123
TERRY WEAVER	23	Burlington	Midw	223	39	7	1	1	22	1	2	186	.175	.249	.248	.142	7	.156
TODD WILSON	26	San Jose	Calif	323	90	12	1	4	12	2	1	234	.279	.304	.359	.224	28	.232
KEN WOODS	25	Phoenix	PCL	207	52	8	1	2	18	3	2	157	.251	.311	.329	.216	17	.228
	25	Shreveport	Texas	293	75	12	1	1	27	10	5	223	.256	.319	.314	.217	24	.229

Player	Age	Team	Lge	IP	H	ER	HR	BB	K	ERA	W	L	H/9	HR/9	BB/9	K/9	KW
SHAWN BARTON	33	Phoenix	PCL	46.0	52	22	1	23	22	4.30	2	3	10.17	.20	4.50	4.30	.31
MANUEL BERMUDEZ	19	Burlington	Midw	116.3	148	77	16	94	59	5.96	4	9	11.45	1.24	7.27	4.56	-.30
JOSEPH BLASINGIM	23	Burlington	Midw	57.0	70	41	12	45	38	6.47	2	4	11.05	1.89	7.11	6.00	.22
JASON BRESTER	19	Burlington	Midw	135.7	177	83	18	82	89	5.51	5	10	11.74	1.19	5.44	5.90	.61
JAMIE BREWINGTON	24	Phoenix	PCL	104.3	124	77	14	84	61	6.64	3	9	10.70	1.21	7.25	5.26	-.06
TROY BROHAWN	23	Shreveport	Texas	142.7	182	97	30	69	68	6.12	5	11	11.48	1.89	4.35	4.29	.34
ANDY CARTER	27	Phoenix	PCL	75.0	95	51	5	45	41	6.12	2	6	11.40	.60	5.40	4.92	.29
EDWIN CORPS	23	Shreveport	Texas	64.3	81	44	6	36	32	6.16	2	5	11.33	.84	5.04	4.48	.23
JOE FONTENOT	19	San Jose	Calif	128.0	155	78	7	88	78	5.48	5	9	10.90	.49	6.19	5.48	.28
DENNYS GOMEZ	25	San Jose	Calif	25.0	33	25	0	19	17	9.00	0	3	11.88	.00	6.84	6.12	.33
JASON GROTE	21	Burlington	Midw	120.0	181	83	21	71	64	6.22	4	9	13.57	1.58	5.32	4.80	.27
LEE HANCOCK	29	Phoenix	PCL	33.3	41	16	0	16	15	4.32	2	2	11.07	.00	4.32	4.05	.27
BOBBY HOWRY	22	Shreveport	Texas	142.0	182	89	18	78	47	5.64	5	11	11.54	1.14	4.94	2.98	-.24
JEFF HUTZLER	23	Burlington	Midw	120.3	171	78	10	43	49	5.83	4	9	12.79	.75	3.22	3.66	.42
RICH HYDE	27	Shreveport	Texas	30.3	40	26	4	17	21	7.71	1	2	11.87	1.19	5.04	6.23	.82
JEFF KEITH	24	Burlington	Midw	44.7	55	33	6	50	26	6.65	1	4	11.08	1.21	10.07	5.24	-.77
BRIAN KNOLL	22	Burlington	Midw	67.3	96	46	6	44	35	6.15	2	5	12.83	.80	5.88	4.68	.09
KEVIN LAKE	23	Burlington	Midw	83.3	132	59	13	49	53	6.37	3	6	14.26	1.40	5.29	5.72	.58
JEFF MARTIN	23	San Jose	Calif	54.0	59	32	4	34	34	5.33	2	4	9.83	.67	5.67	5.67	.47
MIKE MCMULLEN	22	Burlington	Midw	49.0	57	22	4	36	22	4.01	2	3	10.40	.73	6.57	3.83	-.36
STEVE MINTZ	27	Phoenix	PCL	53.7	61	32	6	31	28	5.37	2	4	10.23	1.01	5.20	4.70	.27
JASON MYERS	22	San Jose	Calif	106.7	158	67	10	44	52	5.65	4	8	13.33	.84	3.71	4.39	.53
RANDY PHILLIPS	25	Shreveport	Texas	63.7	85	34	6	30	26	4.81	3	4	12.02	.85	4.24	3.68	.16
RICKY PICKETT	26	Shreveport	Texas	44.7	39	20	4	43	42	4.03	2	3	7.86	.81	8.66	8.46	.65
SHAWN PURDY	27	Shreveport	Texas	47.7	52	22	3	22	19	4.15	2	3	9.82	.57	4.15	3.59	.16
CARL SCHRAMM	26	San Jose	Calif	63.3	73	27	5	30	42	3.84	4	3	10.37	.71	4.26	5.97	.92
JIM STOOPS	24	Burlington	Midw	53.0	53	24	3	51	43	4.08	3	3	9.00	.51	8.66	7.30	.27
ANDY TAULBEE	23	Shreveport	Texas	126.3	185	86	11	66	46	6.13	4	10	13.18	.78	4.70	3.28	-.08
BENJAMIN TUCKER	22	San Jose	Calif	60.0	78	48	8	43	19	7.20	2	5	11.70	1.20	6.45	2.85	-.66
CARLOS VALDEZ	24	Phoenix	PCL	55.7	62	31	4	40	31	5.01	2	4	10.02	.65	6.47	5.01	.05
DOUG VANDERWEELE	26	Phoenix	PCL	84.0	98	46	13	44	34	4.93	4	5	10.50	1.39	4.71	3.64	.04
MIKE VILLANO	24	San Jose	Calif	79.3	62	10	2	40	85	1.13	8	1	7.03	.23	4.54	9.64	2.08

San Francisco Giants

Baltimore Orioles

With the New York Yankees becoming a team of nice guys, great comeback stories and "underappreciated team players" with all the heartwarming goodness of a Berenstein Bears special, the major leagues' hottest soap opera set moved south to Baltimore. Owner Peter Angelos has run through three managers in three years, convinced a noted former general manager to come out of retirement to run the team and got another well-thought-of former GM to take a job as assistant GM. And while they made the playoffs this year, after the owner overruled his hired hands and refused to allow some mid-season trades for sorely-needed prospects, they didn't win a title.

Perhaps no team has endured such a struggle to discover who is in charge. Peter Angelos is, ultimately, The Boss; as the man who signs the checks, he gets the last word. Pat Gillick, the former Blue Jay GM, inherited a team that was ninth in run scoring and second in runs allowed in 1995; after a whirlwind offseason (Baines, Goodwin, Brown, McDonald, Moyer, Manto, Gomez, Barberie, Obando out; Alomar, McDowell, Surhoff, Myers, Wells, Mercker in), he got the scoring up to fourth, but the pitching collapsed to twelfth. He wanted to trade Bobby Bonilla for mediocre prospects at mid-season, but Angelos wouldn't let him; he wanted to replace Hoiles at catcher, but was blocked there too. Davey Johnson got it from above and below; Angelos fired pitching coach Pat Dobson without consulting Johnson, and was reportedly trying to goad him into quitting (firing would still leave him liable for Johnson's contract). He had various disputes with players, especially with Bonilla over playing DH and even took on Cal Ripken.

Many players, it seems, were taking their cues not from manager Johnson but from Ripken. Cal was targeted throughout the year, by Angelos for not being a fiery enough leader and by the attempts to move him to third base, even though the always comical Manny Alexander was the only other option at shortstop; these attempts will resume in the spring. This four-way bid for control kept the Baltimore papers in business, but did little for the clubhouse atmosphere; departing players such as Greg Zaun and Luis Polonia ripped the team once they left. It appears that all will be back in 1997, ensuring more plot twists, character assassination and meddling on a team that is rapidly aging and has little farm system support.

On the field, the Orioles set a new major league record by hitting 257 home runs; several times in September they fielded a lineup in which all nine players had at least 20 homers. Often, this was attributed to Camden Yards being a bandbox,

yet...the O's scored more runs (511-438) and allowed more (462-441) in road games, even though they had one less game on the road. The O's hit more home runs (136-121) on the road than at home as well, although their pitchers surrendered more (108-101) at home. The most surprising of the Oriole home run hitters, Brady Anderson, had a colossal home/road split (19-31); Bobby Bonilla (9-19) and Cal Ripken (10-16) had substantial road-favoring splits. Only Alomar (14-6) gained more than three home runs from Camden Yards.

This is not to say that Camden Yards isn't a great hitting park; over the previous three years, it had been 9% better than an average AL park for scoring, and 18% better for homers, as Mike Mussina would quickly point out. The idea that they used the park to set the record is clearly erroneous. They were a terrific slugging team in a year that aided sluggers like never before.

The Orioles' farm system isn't going to produce much help except pitching, but two of their best prospects suffered injuries and two were traded to Philadelphia for a month of Todd Zeile and Pete Incaviglia. The Rochester Red Wings went 72-69, fourth best in the International League, and made it into the championship series. The offense was led by Joe Hall, Clay Bellinger and Scott McClain; only the latter is a prospect. The pitching staff only had two pitchers reach 100 innings, and their top winner had just 7. The best pitcher they had, Rocky Coppinger, was promoted before the All-Star break. The Bowie BaySox were an absolute disaster, staggering in at 54-88, with the worst defense and second-worst offense in the Eastern League. Several players had good power but couldn't get on base; the only good prospect, Calvin Maduro, went to the Phillies in the Zeile/Inky trade. The Carolina League's Frederick Keys were a little more successful, at 67-72. The prospects here are better: Johnny Isom led the league in RBI, Eugene Kingsale is a very fast center fielder, Dave Dellucci is a high-average hitter, and pitcher Chris Fussell was tearing up the league before shoulder injuries shut him down. The Orioles didn't have a low- or mid-A club last year, and so had a second high-A club, High Desert in the California League. The Mavericks did better than any other team in the system, going 76-64, but play in such an extreme hitter's park that all results have to be looked at with extreme skepticism. Normally noteworthy accomplishments, like Mike Berry's league-leading .361 BA and .477 OBA, and Chris Kirgan's league-leading 35 HR and 131 RBI, aren't so special here, especially from 25- and 23-year olds, respectively. Only one relief pitcher, Matt Snyder, showed any promise.

MANNY ALEXANDER   SS   1971   Age 26

Year	Team	Lge	AB	H	DB	TP	HR	BB	SB	CS	OUT	BA	OBA	SA	EQA	EQR	Peak
1993	Rochester	Inter	474	109	21	5	6	26	14	4	369	.230	.270	.333	.204	34	.224
1994	Rochester	Inter	429	102	21	4	6	17	20	5	332	.238	.267	.347	.211	34	.229
1995	Baltimore	AL	243	59	10	1	3	21	11	4	188	.243	.303	.329	.217	21	.233
1996	Baltimore	AL	68	7	0	0	0	3	3	3	64	.103	.141	.103	-.140	-2	-.136
1997	*Baltimore*	*AL*	*145*	*35*	*6*	*1*	*0*	*6*	*8*	*4*	*114*	*.241*	*.272*	*.297*	*.194*	*9*	

One of the most useless seasons in major league history. He has never performed at any level at any time in a way that would make you believe he was major league material. When he got a chance to pinch-run for Cal, early in the season, he got picked off. He got a chance to play shortstop for a week while Cal played third base and hit two balls out of the infield all week. The bloom may finally be off his rose, particularly after he accused the Oriole front office of not playing him because he was Dominican. No, Manny; you're not playing because you're not good.

ROBERTO ALOMAR   2B   1968   Age 29

Year	Team	Lge	AB	H	DB	TP	HR	BB	SB	CS	OUT	BA	OBA	SA	EQA	EQR	Peak
1993	Toronto	AL	598	202	35	6	21	84	50	11	407	.338	.419	.522	.317	115	.334
1994	Toronto	AL	396	124	23	4	9	52	18	7	279	.313	.393	.460	.288	62	.299
1995	Toronto	AL	522	162	23	7	15	48	30	3	363	.310	.368	.467	.287	80	.294
1996	Baltimore	AL	593	199	43	4	23	91	17	6	400	.336	.424	.538	.317	113	.320
1997	*Baltimore*	*AL*	*613*	*201*	*35*	*7*	*18*	*87*	*23*	*4*	*416*	*.328*	*.411*	*.496*	*.307*	*108*	

It appears that the reason Alomar was punished so lightly by the league office for spitting is that the umpire did so much to provoke it, which raises a question. There are certain words, names and phrases that a player can say to an umpire which will get him immediately ejected. What happens when the umpire uses such phrases to a player? It's a shame that this episode had to detract from an outstanding season.

BRADY ANDERSON   CF   1964   Age 33

Year	Team	Lge	AB	H	DB	TP	HR	BB	SB	CS	OUT	BA	OBA	SA	EQA	EQR	Peak
1993	Baltimore	AL	565	153	36	8	16	86	22	9	421	.271	.367	.448	.273	82	.271
1994	Baltimore	AL	453	118	23	4	13	57	27	1	336	.260	.343	.415	.264	60	.259
1995	Baltimore	AL	558	151	36	9	18	88	25	7	414	.271	.370	.464	.279	85	.269
1996	Baltimore	AL	583	177	39	5	51	77	21	8	414	.304	.385	.650	.323	122	.307
1997	*Baltimore*	*AL*	*624*	*173*	*49*	*8*	*28*	*79*	*20*	*1*	*452*	*.277*	*.358*	*.516*	*.289*	*102*	

There are those who will say that Brady Anderson took advantage of Camden Yards. Those people will have to explain how Anderson hit 31 home runs on the road, the second-best total ever behind Ruth's 32 in 1927, and equal to Maris' 31 in 1961. Anderson moved in on the plate (getting hit 22 times), tried to loft the ball and did. And he did it despite nagging leg injuries all season and a mysterious diagnosis of appendicitis in July that apparently went away on its own.

CLAY BELLINGER   SS/1B   1969   Age 28

Year	Team	Lge	AB	H	DB	TP	HR	BB	SB	CS	OUT	BA	OBA	SA	EQA	EQR	Peak
1993	Phoenix	PCL	401	87	13	1	6	35	4	4	318	.217	.280	.299	.189	25	.202
1994	Phoenix	PCL	331	78	10	1	6	19	4	1	254	.236	.277	.326	.201	23	.212
1995	Phoenix	PCL	274	68	10	1	3	27	2	1	207	.248	.316	.325	.216	22	.224
1996	Rochester	Inter	465	136	26	2	15	35	6	3	332	.292	.342	.454	.265	60	.271

The Orioles didn't have a high-level shortstop prospect in the organization, so Bellinger and Eddie Zosky were picked up to play for Rochester. Bellinger, who'd been slowly improving as a hitter, suddenly starting hitting for both average and power, and actually deserved some playing time at first for his hitting. If he can hold any of this extra value, he becomes a very useful utility man at the major league level.

MIKE BERRY   3B   1971   Age 26

Year	Team	Lge	AB	H	DB	TP	HR	BB	SB	CS	OUT	BA	OBA	SA	EQA	EQR	Peak
1993	Burlington	Midw	97	20	0	0	1	16	0	0	77	.206	.319	.237	.184	6	.203
1994	Burlington	Midw	346	97	8	1	9	44	3	1	250	.280	.362	.387	.255	41	.277
1995	Visalia	Calif	373	98	16	1	8	45	5	3	278	.263	.342	.375	.243	40	.260
1995	West Palm Bch	Flor	83	13	2	1	1	11	0	0	70	.157	.255	.241	.148	3	.162
1996	High Desert	Calif	453	134	24	2	10	75	3	2	321	.296	.396	.424	.278	65	.293

Yes, it was a great year. The three strikes are: 25-year-old in A ball, in his second year in league, in an extreme hitter's park. He's not as good as he looks.

BOBBY BONILLA **RF** **1963** **Age 34**

Year	Team	Lge	AB	H	DB	TP	HR	BB	SB	CS	OUT	BA	OBA	SA	EQA	EQR	Peak
1993	NY Mets	NL	517	142	20	2	36	80	3	2	377	.275	.372	.530	.292	87	.286
1994	NY Mets	NL	410	120	18	1	22	60	1	3	293	.293	.383	.502	.289	66	.279
1995	NY Mets	NL	329	113	24	4	20	35	0	3	219	.343	.407	.623	.325	66	.309
1995	Baltimore	AL	239	82	12	4	11	23	0	2	159	.343	.401	.565	.312	43	.296
1996	Baltimore	AL	599	176	27	5	29	76	1	3	426	.294	.373	.501	.286	93	.272
1997	Florida	NL	474	127	21	1	26	71	3	3	350	.268	.363	.481	.291	80	

It was no surprise that his EQA dropped to around .290; that's more his normal level. He started the season very slowly, becoming embroiled in a controversy over whether he would play DH or in the field. When he went to the outfield, he started to hit. Coincidence? Selfish player dogging it to get what he wanted? The media had a field day. He signed a four-year, $23 million deal with Florida, a risky proposition for a 34-year-old.

BRENT BOWERS **OF** **1971** **Age 26**

Year	Team	Lge	AB	H	DB	TP	HR	BB	SB	CS	OUT	BA	OBA	SA	EQA	EQR	Peak
1993	Knoxville	South	577	126	17	2	5	22	21	9	460	.218	.247	.281	.174	29	.192
1994	Knoxville	South	481	126	17	7	5	24	9	4	359	.262	.297	.358	.221	41	.240
1995	Syracuse	Inter	309	77	14	3	6	13	4	1	233	.249	.280	.372	.218	26	.234
1996	Bowie	East	234	71	8	1	8	16	7	2	165	.303	.348	.449	.269	31	.283
1996	Rochester	Inter	209	66	6	3	4	15	6	2	145	.316	.362	.431	.270	27	.284

Got to walk through the Orioles' revolving door in left field, hitting a very empty .308 while there. Seemingly rejuvenated by a trip back to AA, he continued to hit well in Rochester. He runs well enough to play center field; it's not clear where he fits into the Phillies' outfield.

DANNY CLYBURN **RF** **1974** **Age 23**

Year	Team	Lge	AB	H	DB	TP	HR	BB	SB	CS	OUT	BA	OBA	SA	EQA	EQR	Peak
1993	Augusta	S Atl	472	109	10	2	8	27	2	2	365	.231	.273	.311	.191	29	.220
1994	Salem-VA	Caro	458	102	8	0	14	17	2	2	358	.223	.251	.332	.189	28	.215
1995	High Desert	Calif	157	35	1	0	7	14	1	0	122	.223	.287	.363	.216	13	.241
1995	Winston-Salem	Caro	233	59	8	1	10	13	2	2	176	.253	.293	.425	.236	24	.264
1996	Bowie	East	372	93	10	3	16	15	3	2	281	.250	.279	.422	.231	36	.255
1997	Baltimore	AL	560	145	25	3	25	27	4	2	417	.259	.293	.448	.245	62	

It is indicative of the state of the Oriole farm system that he is one of the most highly touted position players they have. Pretty good power, but a low batting average, horrendous strike zone judgment (88 K, 17 BB), and terrible in the field (ever seen a sub-.900 fielding percentage in the outfield? Look no further). He's big and strong, but so are the guys delivering beer to the stadium.

BRENT COOKSON **OF** **1970** **Age 27**

Year	Team	Lge	AB	H	DB	TP	HR	BB	SB	CS	OUT	BA	OBA	SA	EQA	EQR	Peak
1993	San Jose	Calif	241	59	4	1	13	32	7	3	185	.245	.333	.432	.254	30	.277
1994	Shreveport	Texas	214	70	14	1	12	17	3	1	145	.327	.377	.570	.307	38	.329
1995	Phoenix	PCL	208	58	5	0	15	24	3	2	152	.279	.353	.519	.283	32	.298
1995	Omaha	AmA	139	52	8	0	5	18	0	0	87	.374	.446	.540	.329	27	.351
1996	Pawtucket	Inter	257	66	9	1	16	24	2	2	193	.257	.320	.486	.262	34	.272
1996	Rochester	Inter	114	30	3	0	6	10	2	1	85	.263	.323	.447	.255	14	.262
1997	Baltimore	AL	403	121	15	0	22	53	3	1	283	.300	.382	.501	.292	65	

He's under six feet tall, weighs around 200 pounds and doesn't look real firm. Nonetheless, he runs fairly well, plays the corner positions in the outfield well and has been pounding the ball everywhere he's played—everywhere except a brief stop in Kansas City in 1995. He's picked up the dreaded "career minor leaguer" label.

KEVIN CURTIS   **OF**   **1973**   **Age 24**

Year	Team	Lge	AB	H	DB	TP	HR	BB	SB	CS	OUT	BA	OBA	SA	EQA	EQR	Peak
1993	Albany-GA	S Atl	193	36	2	0	6	29	2	1	158	.187	.293	.290	.192	13	.219
1994	Albany-GA	S Atl	70	14	1	0	1	7	0	1	57	.200	.273	.257	.163	3	.181
1995	High Desert	Calif	393	90	9	0	14	42	3	3	306	.229	.303	.359	.220	35	.242
1996	Bowie	East	474	115	16	0	17	48	2	1	360	.243	.312	.384	.232	47	.252
1997	*Baltimore*	*AL*	*452*	*108*	*16*	*1*	*22*	*55*	*3*	*2*	*346*	*.239*	*.321*	*.425*	*.247*	*52*	

People get excited when a guy hits .293/.389/.521 in the minors. When you hit like that in High Desert, though, it's only worth about a hundred bucks…in Confederate money. He is not nearly enough of a hitter for an outfielder or first baseman, his position in 1995.

TOMMY DAVIS   **1B**   **1973**   **Age 24**

Year	Team	Lge	AB	H	DB	TP	HR	BB	SB	CS	OUT	BA	OBA	SA	EQA	EQR	Peak
1994	Albany-GA	S Atl	225	56	5	1	4	16	1	2	171	.249	.299	.333	.210	17	.234
1995	Frederick	Caro	514	137	20	2	15	40	4	1	378	.267	.319	.401	.242	54	.267
1996	Bowie	East	537	135	22	2	13	37	5	4	406	.251	.300	.372	.224	48	.244
1997	*Baltimore*	*AL*	*554*	*147*	*27*	*2*	*16*	*45*	*6*	*4*	*411*	*.265*	*.321*	*.408*	*.244*	*60*	

The Orioles' first pick in the 1994 draft, he has a lot in common with Danny Clyburn. Power. No walks. Lots of strikeouts. Dreadful fielder; attempting to play third base in '94, he had the lowest range factor at the position and led the league in errors.

DAVID DELLUCCI   **OF**   **1974**   **Age 23**

Year	Team	Lge	AB	H	DB	TP	HR	BB	SB	CS	OUT	BA	OBA	SA	EQA	EQR	Peak
1995	Frederick	Caro	101	27	0	0	2	11	1	1	75	.267	.339	.327	.226	9	.255
1996	Frederick	Caro	193	54	3	1	4	33	2	3	142	.280	.385	.368	.256	23	.282
1996	Bowie	East	259	71	11	1	2	25	3	3	191	.274	.338	.347	.232	25	.254
1997	*Baltimore*	*AL*	*466*	*135*	*18*	*1*	*5*	*76*	*3*	*3*	*334*	*.290*	*.389*	*.365*	*.260*	*57*	

He's only 5'10", which partly explains why he lasted until the 10th round of the 1995 draft after leading the SEC in hitting at .410. He's done pretty well for himself in two professional seasons, hitting for average and showing a willingness to take a walk. Power is lacking, although that wasn't a problem in college, and he plays all three outfield positions.

CESAR DEVAREZ   **C**   **1970**   **Age 27**

Year	Team	Lge	AB	H	DB	TP	HR	BB	SB	CS	OUT	BA	OBA	SA	EQA	EQR	Peak
1993	Frederick	Caro	128	32	4	0	2	11	1	2	98	.250	.309	.328	.211	10	.230
1993	Bowie	East	177	39	6	1	0	5	3	1	139	.220	.242	.266	.161	7	.174
1994	Bowie	East	252	74	9	2	6	8	4	1	179	.294	.315	.417	.248	27	.265
1995	Rochester	Inter	240	55	9	1	1	9	2	1	186	.229	.257	.287	.176	12	.186
1996	Rochester	Inter	225	62	7	1	4	10	3	1	164	.276	.306	.369	.229	21	.238

A good defensive catcher, but getting up in years without getting his hitting up. He did a credible job in 1994, but that was a season when his team played on small college fields since Bowie's stadium hadn't been finished. Results from that year have to be taken with a handful of salt.

MIKE DEVEREAUX   **OF**   **1963**   **Age 34**

Year	Team	Lge	AB	H	DB	TP	HR	BB	SB	CS	OUT	BA	OBA	SA	EQA	EQR	Peak
1993	Baltimore	AL	530	136	30	3	17	47	3	2	396	.257	.317	.421	.245	59	.240
1994	Baltimore	AL	301	60	7	2	9	22	1	2	243	.199	.254	.326	.185	18	.179
1995	Chi. White Sox	AL	338	109	20	1	12	25	6	6	235	.322	.369	.494	.283	50	.268
1995	Atlanta	NL	55	14	3	0	1	3	2	0	41	.255	.293	.364	.228	5	.214
1996	Baltimore	AL	325	76	13	2	8	34	8	2	251	.234	.306	.360	.226	30	.215
1997	*Baltimore*	*AL*	*122*	*30*	*4*	*0*	*3*	*10*	*5*	*3*	*95*	*.246*	*.303*	*.352*	*.221*	*11*	

He's loved in Baltimore; memories of 1992 die hard, and he's a genuine class act in the community. But a lot of people who should have known better convinced themselves that what he did for the White Sox and in the playoffs represented a return to an earlier level of performance. It was, but people betting on that to be more than a one-year event are working from their hearts, not heads.

Teams 229

JIM FOSTER   **C**   **1972**   **Age 25**

Year	Team	Lge	AB	H	DB	TP	HR	BB	SB	CS	OUT	BA	OBA	SA	EQA	EQR	Peak
1994	Albany-GA	S Atl	444	110	17	1	8	46	2	1	335	.248	.318	.345	.223	39	.246
1995	Frederick	Caro	448	115	22	3	6	48	1	1	334	.257	.329	.359	.232	43	.252
1996	Frederick	Caro	286	63	10	1	6	34	3	1	224	.220	.303	.325	.210	23	.226

He committed only one error this year, breaking Cal Ripken's league record for fielding percentage by a catcher. Cal, Senior's, that is, set way back in 1958.

JOE HALL   **OF**   **1966**   **Age 31**

Year	Team	Lge	AB	H	DB	TP	HR	BB	SB	CS	OUT	BA	OBA	SA	EQA	EQR	Peak
1993	Nashville	AmA	431	123	26	4	11	54	10	7	314	.285	.365	.441	.269	59	.274
1994	Birmingham	South	71	14	6	0	0	14	0	0	57	.197	.329	.282	.205	5	.211
1994	Nashville	AmA	73	21	5	0	4	16	0	0	52	.288	.416	.521	.307	14	.310
1995	Toledo	Inter	334	110	14	1	13	38	3	1	225	.329	.398	.494	.298	54	.295
1996	Rochester	Inter	489	137	23	5	19	67	10	6	358	.280	.367	.464	.275	71	.270

He had a perfectly normal Joe Hall season for Rochester. Despite being the best hitter at Rochester, when judged over the last three years and not just this season, he was about the only guy the Orioles didn't try for their essentially vacant left field and designated hitter jobs.

JEFFREY HAMMONDS   **OF**   **1971**   **Age 26**

Year	Team	Lge	AB	H	DB	TP	HR	BB	SB	CS	OUT	BA	OBA	SA	EQA	EQR	Peak
1993	Bowie	East	95	26	2	0	3	9	2	2	71	.274	.337	.389	.242	10	.269
1993	Rochester	Inter	152	45	5	1	5	7	5	2	109	.296	.327	.441	.258	18	.284
1993	Baltimore	AL	106	34	7	0	4	2	4	0	72	.321	.333	.500	.282	15	.307
1994	Baltimore	AL	250	73	18	2	8	17	4	0	177	.292	.337	.476	.272	34	.295
1995	Baltimore	AL	179	44	11	1	4	9	4	2	137	.246	.282	.385	.223	16	.240
1996	Rochester	Inter	128	34	4	1	3	19	2	1	95	.266	.361	.383	.253	15	.266
1996	Baltimore	AL	249	58	11	1	9	23	3	3	194	.233	.298	.394	.227	24	.239
1997	*Baltimore*	*AL*	*224*	*63*	*12*	*2*	*6*	*8*	*6*	*3*	*164*	*.281*	*.306*	*.433*	*.247*	*25*	

He was labeled the "next Rickey Henderson" by people who had no idea what they were talking about. He's never shown any indication that he can tell the difference between a strike and a ball, which was painfully obvious last summer in Baltimore. He was "being more patient" and taking walks, but he was taking pitches in the strike zone to do it, taking his strikeout rate to a new personal high. In addition, repeated injuries have robbed him of his speed.

CHRIS HOILES   **C**   **1965**   **Age 32**

Year	Team	Lge	AB	H	DB	TP	HR	BB	SB	CS	OUT	BA	OBA	SA	EQA	EQR	Peak
1993	Baltimore	AL	425	136	22	0	35	72	1	1	290	.320	.419	.619	.330	90	.333
1994	Baltimore	AL	332	81	8	0	19	63	2	0	251	.244	.365	.440	.268	47	.266
1995	Baltimore	AL	355	91	14	1	21	68	1	0	264	.256	.376	.479	.281	55	.276
1996	Baltimore	AL	410	108	13	0	26	57	0	1	303	.263	.353	.485	.274	59	.265
1997	*Baltimore*	*AL*	*386*	*100*	*13*	*0*	*24*	*62*	*0*	*0*	*286*	*.259*	*.362*	*.479*	*.276*	*57*	

An arthritic problem in his shoulder and an extremely slow start had the Oriole front office talking about acquiring a new catcher, but they never did. His recovery after the All-Star break played a large role in the Orioles' drive to the playoffs. He was criticized all year for throwing out only 23% of baserunners, but the remaining catchers on the team, supposedly defensive specialists, only had a 19% rate. He has an exceptionally large split between hitting ahead or behind in the count.

PETE INCAVIGLIA   **OF**   **1964**   **Age 33**

Year	Team	Lge	AB	H	DB	TP	HR	BB	SB	CS	OUT	BA	OBA	SA	EQA	EQR	Peak
1993	Philadelphia	NL	374	105	15	2	25	26	1	1	270	.281	.327	.532	.277	55	.276
1994	Philadelphia	NL	247	59	8	1	14	19	1	0	188	.239	.293	.449	.244	28	.239
1996	Philadelphia	NL	275	68	7	2	16	34	2	0	207	.247	.330	.462	.261	36	.248
1997	*Baltimore*	*AL*	*288*	*71*	*8*	*0*	*14*	*21*	*1*	*1*	*218*	*.247*	*.298*	*.420*	*.237*	*30*	

After spending a year in Japan, he was dismayed by the changes that have shaken the Phillies since 1993. He went over to Baltimore to help them against left-handed pitching down the stretch, homered in his first two games for the Birds, then spent the rest of the month playing behind a slumping Eddie Murray.

JOHNNY ISOM   **LF**   **1974**   **Age 23**

Year	Team	Lge	AB	H	DB	TP	HR	BB	SB	CS	OUT	BA	OBA	SA	EQA	EQR	Peak
1996	Frederick	Caro	496	128	10	1	15	34	4	3	371	.258	.306	.373	.227	46	.250
1997	*Baltimore*	*AL*	*540*	*147*	*20*	*2*	*16*	*42*	*6*	*4*	*397*	*.272*	*.325*	*.406*	*.245*	*59*	

He missed winning the 1995 Appalachian League batting title by one hit, then moved to Frederick this year to lead the Carolina League with 104 RBI. He's unimpressive in the outfield, and an early shoulder injury impaired his throwing all year. He's a decidedly sub-par outfielder at this stage.

EUGENE KINGSALE   **OF**   **1977**   **Age 20**

Year	Team	Lge	AB	H	DB	TP	HR	BB	SB	CS	OUT	BA	OBA	SA	EQA	EQR	Peak
1996	Frederick	Caro	170	41	4	3	0	17	9	2	131	.241	.310	.300	.215	14	.250
1997	*Baltimore*	*AL*	*434*	*113*	*16*	*11*	*2*	*43*	*39*	*5*	*326*	*.260*	*.327*	*.362*	*.248*	*50*	

He is extremely fast, running 60 yards in less than 6.3 seconds. He's used that speed to steal 58 bases in a pro career that's consisted of just 505 total at bats in three seasons; last year was shortened by a shoulder injury incurred on a head-first slide. He became the first player from Aruba to play in the major leagues when used as a defensive replacement in September, beating Calvin Maduro by a couple of days.

EDDY MARTINEZ   **SS**   **1978**   **Age 19**

Year	Team	Lge	AB	H	DB	TP	HR	BB	SB	CS	OUT	BA	OBA	SA	EQA	EQR	Peak
1996	Frederick	Caro	248	46	0	0	2	19	5	3	205	.185	.243	.210	.130	6	.152
1997	*Baltimore*	*AL*	*480*	*115*	*12*	*1*	*5*	*33*	*9*	*5*	*370*	*.240*	*.288*	*.300*	*.197*	*32*	

Eddy got a lot of attention in spring training 1995, when the then-17-year-old hit an inside-the-park grand slam. He went on to have a good year at Bluefield, but not this year. His batting average was just .221 in Frederick when he was sent down to Bluefield again, where he continued to hit .221. He's already got a great defensive reputation, but the 6' 2", 150-(!) pound kid needs to do some growing up and out.

SCOTT McCLAIN   **3B**   **1972**   **Age 25**

Year	Team	Lge	AB	H	DB	TP	HR	BB	SB	CS	OUT	BA	OBA	SA	EQA	EQR	Peak
1993	Frederick	Caro	449	105	13	1	8	60	6	3	347	.234	.324	.321	.218	39	.245
1994	Bowie	East	442	101	17	1	11	64	4	2	343	.229	.326	.346	.226	42	.249
1995	Bowie	East	266	73	9	0	13	22	1	1	194	.274	.330	.455	.259	33	.282
1995	Rochester	Inter	202	48	6	0	8	23	0	1	155	.238	.316	.386	.232	20	.253
1996	Rochester	Inter	472	129	19	2	16	61	6	4	347	.273	.356	.424	.261	60	.279
1997	*Baltimore*	*AL*	*556*	*153*	*23*	*4*	*14*	*72*	*5*	*2*	*405*	*.275*	*.358*	*.406*	*.259*	*69*	

He opened the 1995 season in Rochester, and hit just like he had in 1993 and 1994. Sent back down to Bowie, he raised his offense to a major league level, and continued to do so last year in Rochester. That's a good thing for him, because his glovework has always been excellent—best in his league twice in the last four years, according to Baseball America's tools survey. And just his luck: now that he appears on the verge of reaching the major leagues, the Orioles decide Cal Ripken is moving to third base.

EDDIE MURRAY   **DH**   **1956**   **Age 41**

Year	Team	Lge	AB	H	DB	TP	HR	BB	SB	CS	OUT	BA	OBA	SA	EQA	EQR	Peak
1993	NY Mets	NL	623	183	20	1	30	50	2	2	442	.294	.346	.474	.271	84	.257
1994	Cleveland	AL	434	110	19	1	18	31	7	3	327	.253	.303	.426	.242	47	.230
1995	Cleveland	AL	445	152	18	0	25	40	5	1	294	.342	.396	.551	.311	79	.295
1996	Cleveland	AL	335	87	8	1	12	34	3	0	248	.260	.328	.397	.245	37	.232
1996	Baltimore	AL	231	60	11	0	11	28	1	0	171	.260	.340	.450	.262	30	.249
1997	*California*	*AL*	*341*	*80*	*14*	*0*	*11*	*34*	*0*	*0*	*261*	*.235*	*.304*	*.372*	*.230*	*33*	

The first day Murray was with the Orioles last season, he brought his career EQR total up to 1990, tying him with Lou Gehrig among first basemen. A couple of weeks later, he became the 15th player in history to reach 2000; shortly thereafter was the 500th home run. The end is very, very close.

WILLIS OTANEZ   **3B**   **1973**   **Age 24**

Year	Team	Lge	AB	H	DB	TP	HR	BB	SB	CS	OUT	BA	OBA	SA	EQA	EQR	Peak
1993	Bakersfield	Calif	331	77	5	1	9	18	1	2	256	.233	.272	.335	.199	23	.227
1994	Vero Beach	Flor	486	127	13	1	20	48	2	1	360	.261	.328	.416	.248	55	.278
1995	Vero Beach	Flor	363	88	9	0	12	25	1	1	276	.242	.291	.366	.218	31	.240
1995	San Antonio	Texas	102	24	3	1	1	6	0	1	79	.235	.278	.314	.192	6	.212
1996	Bowie	East	520	135	18	1	22	40	3	4	389	.260	.312	.425	.243	57	.264

He's small (5' 10", 150) but hits with good power, especially when he's more patient. Reports say he's a very good defensive third baseman; his statistics don't match.

RAFAEL PALMEIRO   **1B**   **1965**   **Age 32**

Year	Team	Lge	AB	H	DB	TP	HR	BB	SB	CS	OUT	BA	OBA	SA	EQA	EQR	Peak
1993	Texas	AL	612	194	38	2	46	78	20	2	420	.317	.394	.611	.323	124	.326
1994	Baltimore	AL	435	137	24	0	25	54	6	3	301	.315	.391	.543	.304	77	.302
1995	Baltimore	AL	559	178	30	2	42	63	3	1	382	.318	.387	.605	.316	108	.310
1996	Baltimore	AL	631	187	38	2	41	96	8	0	444	.296	.389	.558	.307	116	.297
1997	*Baltimore*	*AL*	*622*	*189*	*32*	*2*	*40*	*86*	*9*	*1*	*434*	*.304*	*.388*	*.555*	*.307*	*114*	

He's been one of baseball's most consistent hitters these last four years, and at a high level. Marylanders complain when he's left off the All-Star team every year, but his performance just isn't quite up to that of a few others in the league. He's good, and with his defense may well rate ahead of Thomas and Vaughn, but you have to admit that the AL is loaded at first.

MARK PARENT   **C**   **1962**   **Age 35**

Year	Team	Lge	AB	H	DB	TP	HR	BB	SB	CS	OUT	BA	OBA	SA	EQA	EQR	Peak
1993	Rochester	Inter	338	80	10	0	13	40	0	1	259	.237	.317	.382	.232	34	.225
1993	Baltimore	AL	54	14	1	0	5	4	0	0	40	.259	.310	.556	.276	8	.264
1994	Chicago Cubs	NL	102	29	4	0	3	14	0	1	74	.284	.371	.412	.261	13	.247
1995	Pittsburgh	NL	235	55	7	0	15	26	0	0	180	.234	.310	.455	.250	28	.237
1996	Detroit	AL	104	25	4	0	8	3	0	0	79	.240	.262	.510	.248	12	.235
1997	*Philadelphia*	*NL*	*145*	*33*	*6*	*0*	*5*	*16*	*0*	*0*	*112*	*.228*	*.304*	*.372*	*.236*	*15*	

The August pickup became Scott Erickson's personal catcher over the final month and got good results from him. That's good. He hit just .188 for the Orioles in 33 plate appearances. That's bad.

BILLY RIPKEN   **2B**   **1965**   **Age 32**

Year	Team	Lge	AB	H	DB	TP	HR	BB	SB	CS	OUT	BA	OBA	SA	EQA	EQR	Peak
1993	Texas	AL	134	28	5	0	0	11	0	1	108	.209	.269	.246	.158	5	.157
1994	Texas	AL	82	26	6	0	0	3	2	0	56	.317	.341	.390	.254	9	.253
1995	Buffalo	AmA	460	136	28	1	6	33	5	3	327	.296	.343	.400	.251	52	.246
1996	Baltimore	AL	136	32	5	0	3	9	0	0	104	.235	.283	.338	.205	10	.199

He teamed up with Manny Alexander and Jeff Huson to give the Orioles three weak-hitting middle infielders on the bench, this on a team with big brother Cal and Alomar. He wouldn't have played, but for his name; maybe he could go into business with Chris Gwynn and Craig Griffey.

CAL RIPKEN   **SS**   **1961**   **Age 36**

Year	Team	Lge	AB	H	DB	TP	HR	BB	SB	CS	OUT	BA	OBA	SA	EQA	EQR	Peak
1993	Baltimore	AL	646	171	25	3	28	69	1	3	478	.265	.336	.443	.257	80	.244
1994	Baltimore	AL	443	138	17	3	13	33	1	0	305	.312	.359	.451	.272	59	.258
1995	Baltimore	AL	554	149	33	2	19	52	0	1	406	.269	.332	.439	.255	67	.242
1996	Baltimore	AL	644	183	36	2	28	59	1	2	463	.284	.344	.477	.270	88	.257
1997	*Baltimore*	*AL*	*637*	*162*	*28*	*1*	*16*	*64*	*0*	*0*	*475*	*.254*	*.322*	*.377*	*.235*	*64*	

The "move to third" faction succeeded for a week last year, and is as loud as ever in the offseason as the Orioles pursue free agent shortstops. He did have a sore shoulder late in the year that noticeably affected his throwing, but all statistics indicate that he was still average to above average as a shortstop. His continuing offensive slide was halted, at least for the moment, but Vladimir has little confidence in him for 1997.

MEL ROSARIO   **C**   **1973**   **Age 24**

Year	Team	Lge	AB	H	DB	TP	HR	BB	SB	CS	OUT	BA	OBA	SA	EQA	EQR	Peak
1993	Spokane	Nwern	144	28	1	0	3	2	1	0	116	.194	.205	.264	.137	4	.157
1993	Waterloo	Midw	108	22	3	1	4	5	3	1	87	.204	.239	.361	.198	8	.227
1995	South Bend	Midw	464	117	16	2	14	23	0	4	351	.252	.287	.386	.221	40	.243
1996	High Desert	Calif	160	43	4	0	7	16	2	0	117	.269	.335	.425	.256	19	.277
1996	Bowie	East	164	33	4	0	3	6	3	1	132	.201	.229	.280	.161	7	.172

The switch-hitting catcher who supposedly came of age at High Desert last year. 23-year-olds who start to hit in A ball are rarely worth a second look, even when they translate well. His poor strike zone command (K/W ratio over 3 at High Desert) killed him when he moved up; the pitchers in AA had him for lunch, striking him out 43 times against only six walks.

MARK SMITH   **LF**   **1970**   **Age 27**

Year	Team	Lge	AB	H	DB	TP	HR	BB	SB	CS	OUT	BA	OBA	SA	EQA	EQR	Peak
1993	Rochester	Inter	492	130	16	1	13	39	4	4	366	.264	.318	.380	.234	48	.254
1994	Rochester	Inter	443	106	17	1	18	34	3	2	339	.239	.294	.404	.230	43	.247
1995	Rochester	Inter	367	97	17	2	12	26	5	2	272	.264	.313	.420	.245	40	.258
1995	Baltimore	AL	105	25	3	0	4	12	3	0	80	.238	.316	.381	.239	11	.252
1996	Rochester	Inter	135	47	9	1	8	14	7	1	89	.348	.409	.607	.331	28	.344
1996	Baltimore	AL	78	19	3	0	4	3	0	2	61	.244	.272	.436	.224	7	.234

Aside from last year's performance in Rochester, which just demonstrates that anyone can have a good month, he's a .235 EQA hitter, plus or minus 10. That's incredibly consistent, which under other circumstances might be considered a good thing. But when it is that far below league average, and even more importantly, when it comes at ages 23-26, when most major leaguers improve substantially, it's a bad thing.

B.J. SURHOFF   **3B/OF**   **1965**   **Age 32**

Year	Team	Lge	AB	H	DB	TP	HR	BB	SB	CS	OUT	BA	OBA	SA	EQA	EQR	Peak
1993	Milwaukee	AL	560	162	41	3	9	40	12	7	405	.289	.337	.421	.254	66	.257
1994	Milwaukee	AL	134	34	11	2	5	16	0	1	101	.254	.333	.478	.263	18	.262
1995	Milwaukee	AL	413	131	24	3	14	37	7	3	285	.317	.373	.492	.287	63	.281
1996	Baltimore	AL	541	162	26	6	22	47	0	1	380	.299	.355	.492	.279	78	.269
1997	*Baltimore*	*AL*	*536*	*149*	*21*	*4*	*23*	*51*	*4*	*2*	*389*	*.278*	*.341*	*.461*	*.266*	*71*	

He had a career high in home runs last year, which makes him about as special as a Danielle Steele TV movie, but he also set a career high for strikeouts. He had 79 last year, 30 more than in any previous season. He struck out 32 times more than he walked, more than in his entire nine-year career prior to '96 (323 K, 294 BB, +29). He took more pitches than is his custom; his ground/fly ratio was down quite a bit. Can you say, "swinging for the fences?"

TONY TARASCO   **OF**   **1971**   **Age 26**

Year	Team	Lge	AB	H	DB	TP	HR	BB	SB	CS	OUT	BA	OBA	SA	EQA	EQR	Peak
1993	Richmond	Inter	382	124	12	3	16	38	15	7	265	.325	.386	.497	.293	61	.323
1994	Atlanta	NL	134	37	4	0	6	11	5	0	97	.276	.331	.440	.263	17	.287
1995	Montreal	NL	448	117	18	4	15	56	20	3	334	.261	.343	.420	.261	58	.280
1996	Rochester	Inter	105	26	4	0	2	17	3	2	81	.248	.352	.343	.237	11	.249
1996	Baltimore	AL	84	20	1	0	2	7	5	3	67	.238	.297	.321	.210	7	.223
1997	*Baltimore*	*AL*	*288*	*81*	*12*	*2*	*9*	*36*	*12*	*3*	*210*	*.281*	*.361*	*.431*	*.270*	*40*	

Tarasco was traded for Sherman Obando last spring, even though the Orioles' assistant GM and former Expo GM Kevin Malone knew that he had a bad shoulder. Surprise: it was worse than we thought. He spent most of the season on the DL, was limited to DH in Rochester when he did play and was ineffective even then.

BRAD TYLER   **2B**   **1969**   **Age 28**

Year	Team	Lge	AB	H	DB	TP	HR	BB	SB	CS	OUT	BA	OBA	SA	EQA	EQR	Peak
1993	Bowie	East	458	110	22	9	13	77	14	6	354	.240	.350	.413	.256	58	.274
1994	Rochester	Inter	320	80	14	5	7	37	5	2	242	.250	.328	.391	.242	35	.255
1995	Rochester	Inter	371	92	12	2	16	68	7	3	282	.248	.364	.420	.263	50	.274
1996	Rochester	Inter	392	104	16	6	13	66	13	5	293	.265	.371	.436	.271	56	.278

What he does: hit for decent power, draw walks, steal 10-15 bases, play all of the infield positions. What he doesn't do: hit for average, field those positions. It's an unfortunate fact of life for Brad that while a , good-field, no-hit infielder like Billy Ripken or Alvaro Espinoza can get a major league utility job, a good-hit poor-field infielder of equal value cannot.

B.J. WASZGIS   **C**   **1971**   **Age 26**

Year	Team	Lge	AB	H	DB	TP	HR	BB	SB	CS	OUT	BA	OBA	SA	EQA	EQR	Peak
1993	Albany-GA	S Atl	314	89	13	1	8	20	2	0	225	.283	.326	.408	.248	34	.274
1993	Frederick	Caro	112	24	1	0	3	8	1	0	88	.214	.267	.304	.187	7	.206
1994	Frederick	Caro	446	120	10	2	16	56	3	1	327	.269	.351	.408	.255	54	.278
1995	Bowie	East	453	110	12	0	12	63	2	2	345	.243	.335	.349	.231	44	.247
1996	Rochester	Inter	310	80	9	0	11	41	2	2	232	.258	.345	.394	.247	35	.261
1997	*Baltimore*	*AL*	*264*	*70*	*11*	*1*	*10*	*35*	*3*	*1*	*195*	*.265*	*.351*	*.428*	*.261*	*34*	

Converted to catcher in 1993, he's been advanced slowly by the Orioles as his defense develops. He doesn't stand out in any way: break down his game into its components, and they're all OK, nothing special. That might be enough to get a job with the Orioles next year.

TODD ZEILE   **3B**   **1966**   **Age 31**

Year	Team	Lge	AB	H	DB	TP	HR	BB	SB	CS	OUT	BA	OBA	SA	EQA	EQR	Peak
1993	St. Louis	NL	592	173	29	1	21	79	4	3	422	.292	.376	.451	.276	84	.282
1994	St. Louis	NL	422	115	19	1	21	57	1	3	310	.273	.359	.472	.272	60	.275
1995	St. Louis	NL	130	39	3	0	6	20	1	0	91	.300	.393	.462	.288	20	.285
1995	Chicago Cubs	NL	301	69	11	1	10	20	0	0	232	.229	.277	.372	.214	25	.213
1996	Philadelphia	NL	516	145	17	0	23	73	1	1	372	.281	.370	.448	.273	72	.267
1996	Baltimore	AL	118	29	6	0	6	15	0	0	89	.246	.331	.449	.257	15	.251
1997	*Los Angeles*	*NL*	*466*	*119*	*23*	*1*	*18*	*51*	*1*	*1*	*348*	*.255*	*.329*	*.425*	*.272*	*67*	

Major league organizations seem to have been victimized by a mimetic disease that causes them to believe that Todd Zeile is a valuable major league ballplayer, even though his hitting is essentially average and his fielding anywhere is dreadful. Signed by the Dodgers, he'll represent an improvement over what they've run out there the last two years. Health history makes him a safe roto pick.

ARMANDO BENITEZ   **RRP**   **1973**   **Age 24**

YR	Team	Lge	IP	H	ER	HR	BB	K	ERA	W	L	H/9	HR/9	BB/9	K/9	KW
1993	Albany, GA	S Atl	46.7	45	11	3	27	49	2.12	4	1	8.68	.58	5.21	9.45	1.85
1993	Frederick	Caro	12.3	10	1	0	6	18	.73	1	0	7.30	.00	4.38	13.14	3.28
1994	Bowie	East	66.0	49	27	7	49	77	3.68	4	3	6.68	.95	6.68	10.50	1.83
1995	Rochester	Inter	20.0	13	3	2	8	30	1.35	2	0	5.85	.90	3.60	13.50	3.60
1995	Baltimore	AL	48.0	35	25	8	38	56	4.69	2	3	6.56	1.50	7.12	10.50	1.72
1996	Baltimore	AL	13.7	8	4	2	6	19	2.63	1	1	5.27	1.32	3.95	12.51	3.18

A big, intimidating, hard-throwing Dominican, he's either not quite hard enough or too straight with it to avoid costly home runs. An elbow injury in April kept him out most of the year; when he returned in September, he wasn't allowed to face more than a couple of batters at a time.

CARLOS CHAVEZ   **RRP**   **1973**   **Age 24**

YR	TEAM	Lge	IP	H	ER	HR	BB	K	ERA	W	L	H/9	HR/9	BB/9	K/9	KW
1993	Albany, GA	S Atl	28.3	45	24	4	24	17	7.62	1	2	14.29	1.27	7.62	5.40	-.11
1995	Frederick	Caro	75.3	74	39	5	52	78	4.66	3	5	8.84	.60	6.21	9.32	1.55
1996	Bowie	East	76.0	80	44	8	64	60	5.21	3	5	9.47	.95	7.58	7.11	.47

The results aren't spectacular, yet he's shown that he's tough to hit in the minor leagues, with a good fastball and a slurve. Walks are a problem.

ROCKY COPPINGER   **RSP**   **1974**   **Age 23**

YR	Team	Lge	IP	H	ER	HR	BB	K	ERA	W	L	H/9	HR/9	BB/9	K/9	KW
1995	Frederick	Caro	62.7	59	17	4	33	66	2.44	5	2	8.47	.57	4.74	9.48	1.97
1995	Bowie	East	77.7	67	30	8	51	47	3.48	5	4	7.76	.93	5.91	5.45	.34
1995	Rochester	Inter	32.0	25	4	3	22	16	1.12	4	0	7.03	.84	6.19	4.50	-.05
1996	Rochester	Inter	69.7	69	30	5	47	67	3.88	4	4	8.91	.65	6.07	8.66	1.37
1996	Baltimore	AL	125.7	118	58	22	63	101	4.15	7	7	8.45	1.58	4.51	7.23	1.28

The Orioles' best prospect a year ago, he held his own when called up in June and pitched his best ball in the heat of the pennant race. He's shown himself to be an extreme flyball pitcher, with a ratio of groundballs to flyballs like Sid Fernandez. Like Sid Fernandez, he didn't find Baltimore to be a friendly environment, and gave up 20% more hits and home runs and 60% more runs at home. Again like Sid Fernandez, he's had weight problems.

ARCHIE CORBIN   **RRP**   **1968**   **Age 29**

YR	Team	Lge	IP	H	ER	HR	BB	K	ERA	W	L	H/9	HR/9	BB/9	K/9	KW
1993	Harrisburg	East	67.0	52	29	0	71	69	3.90	4	3	6.99	.00	9.54	9.27	.71
1994	Buffalo	AmA	21.3	16	11	0	21	21	4.64	1	1	6.75	.00	8.86	8.86	.74
1995	Calgary	PCL	57.7	69	48	6	60	48	7.49	1	5	10.77	.94	9.36	7.49	.16
1996	Rochester	Inter	42.3	45	21	5	30	39	4.46	2	3	9.57	1.06	6.38	8.29	1.17
1996	Baltimore	AL	27.0	21	5	2	23	19	1.67	3	0	7.00	.67	7.67	6.33	.19

Corbin was recommended to the Orioles by Bonilla and Alomar, who had trouble hitting off him in winter ball. So did everyone else—his fastball is terrific—but working him for a walk was relatively easy. Somehow, he managed to compile a great ERA while posting lousy peripheral numbers.

SCOTT ERICKSON   **RSP**   **1968**   **Age 29**

YR	Team	Lge	IP	H	ER	HR	BB	K	ERA	W	L	H/9	HR/9	BB/9	K/9	KW
1993	Minnesota	AL	218.3	257	114	17	82	120	4.70	10	14	10.59	.70	3.38	4.95	.80
1994	Minnesota	AL	144.3	165	74	13	64	102	4.61	7	9	10.29	.81	3.99	6.36	1.12
1995	Minnesota	AL	88.3	96	47	10	34	45	4.79	4	6	9.78	1.02	3.46	4.58	.66
1995	Baltimore	AL	108.0	108	35	6	37	61	2.92	8	4	9.00	.50	3.08	5.08	.92
1996	Baltimore	AL	222.3	249	106	18	72	97	4.29	12	13	10.08	.73	2.91	3.93	.58

He pitched well in September for the second straight year, which seems to impress them more than the other five months. He throws a hard sinker that generates a lot of groundballs, but has been criticized for being too concerned with his strikeouts and radar gun reading.

CHRIS FUSSELL   **RSP**   **1976**   **Age 21**

YR	Team	Lge	IP	H	ER	HR	BB	K	ERA	W	L	H/9	HR/9	BB/9	K/9	KW
1996	Frederick	Caro	76.7	86	38	9	58	65	4.46	4	5	10.10	1.06	6.81	7.63	.84

Fussell didn't start pitching until his junior year in high school, but has progressed quickly. The Orioles' ninth-round pick in 1994 dominated the Appalachian League in 1995, going 9-1 with a 2.19 ERA and 98 Ks in 66 innings, making him the league's top prospect. He started out very strong in Frederick last year, but started to fade as the All-Star break approached and missed the rest of the season with a shoulder injury.

JIMMY HAYNES   **RBP**   **1973**   **Age 24**

YR	Team	Lge	IP	H	ER	HR	BB	K	ERA	W	L	H/9	HR/9	BB/9	K/9	KW
1993	Frederick	Caro	152.3	172	79	14	92	109	4.67	7	10	10.16	.83	5.44	6.44	.79
1994	Bowie	East	159.7	177	64	17	64	129	3.61	10	8	9.98	.96	3.61	7.27	1.52
1994	Rochester	Inter	12.7	20	10	3	8	12	7.11	0	1	14.21	2.13	5.68	8.53	1.42
1995	Rochester	Inter	157.0	169	69	17	69	117	3.96	9	8	9.69	.97	3.96	6.71	1.25
1995	Baltimore	AL	23.3	12	4	2	13	22	1.54	3	0	4.63	.77	5.01	8.49	1.57
1996	Rochester	Inter	27.7	31	16	5	22	20	5.20	1	2	10.08	1.63	7.16	6.51	.38
1996	Baltimore	AL	91.3	113	65	12	60	63	6.41	3	7	11.14	1.18	5.91	6.21	.59

A starter during his ascent through the minors, Haynes started 1996 full of promise and finished it full of questions. He was hit hard in virtually every outing, he had no control and was throwing huge numbers of pitches; he averaged close to 20 pitches per inning during the season. He did a little better out of the bullpen, but not much.

RICK KRIVDA   **LSP**   **1970**   **Age 27**

YR	Team	Lge	IP	H	ER	HR	BB	K	ERA	W	L	H/9	HR/9	BB/9	K/9	KW
1993	Bowie	East	114.0	138	49	13	65	83	3.87	7	6	10.89	1.03	5.13	6.55	.90
1993	Rochester	Inter	31.0	23	6	3	20	19	1.74	3	0	6.68	.87	5.81	5.52	.39
1994	Rochester	Inter	154.0	159	67	12	91	101	3.92	9	8	9.29	.70	5.32	5.90	.64
1995	Rochester	Inter	95.3	101	40	12	45	62	3.78	6	5	9.53	1.13	4.25	5.85	.89
1995	Baltimore	AL	75.3	72	30	8	27	53	3.58	4	4	8.60	.96	3.23	6.33	1.30
1996	Rochester	Inter	42.3	52	20	6	20	28	4.25	2	3	11.06	1.28	4.25	5.95	.92
1996	Baltimore	AL	82.3	84	37	12	41	53	4.04	4	5	9.18	1.31	4.48	5.79	.81

Krivda is a standard soft-tossing lefty in the mold of Jamie Moyer (today's Moyer, not like he was in the '80s). He's performed well at every location, including his stints in the majors, but always looks like he's right on the edge of getting creamed.

TERRY MATHEWS	RRP	1965	Age 32											
YR Team	Lge	IP	H	ER	HR	BB	K	ERA	W	L	H/9	HR/9	BB/9	K/9	KW
1993 Jackson	Texas	92.0	134	59	13	47	53	5.77	3	7	13.11	1.27	4.60	5.18	.58
1993 Tucson	PCL	30.7	39	11	1	14	27	3.23	2	1	11.45	.29	4.11	7.92	1.61
1994 Edmonton	PCL	79.3	81	31	4	29	39	3.52	5	4	9.19	.45	3.29	4.42	.65
1994 Florida	NL	42.3	42	13	4	13	19	2.76	3	2	8.93	.85	2.76	4.04	.66
1995 Florida	NL	81.0	73	28	9	33	64	3.11	6	3	8.11	1.00	3.67	7.11	1.45
1996 Florida	NL	54.7	63	31	7	32	43	5.10	2	4	10.37	1.15	5.27	7.08	1.04
1996 Baltimore	AL	18.7	19	5	3	7	13	2.41	1	1	9.16	1.45	3.38	6.27	1.25

With a shortage of arms in the bullpen, the Orioles dealt Greg Zaun to Florida to get Mathews, who was having a bad year in Florida after a couple of good ones. He went back to being good once he came to Baltimore.

ROGER McDOWELL	RRP	1961	Age 36											
YR Team	Lge	IP	H	ER	HR	BB	K	ERA	W	L	H/9	HR/9	BB/9	K/9	KW
1993 Los Angeles	NL	66.0	81	31	2	38	26	4.23	3	4	11.05	.27	5.18	3.55	-.11
1994 Los Angeles	NL	41.3	52	24	3	26	28	5.23	2	3	11.32	.65	5.66	6.10	.62
1995 Texas	AL	84.7	81	28	4	36	49	2.98	6	3	8.61	.43	3.83	5.21	.78
1996 Baltimore	AL	59.7	65	25	6	24	19	3.77	4	3	9.80	.91	3.62	2.87	.05

Early season problems for the Orioles, such as Mills' continuing recuperation, Benitez' injury and Jimmy Myers' ineffectiveness left McDowell as the only reliable right-handed pitcher in the pen. Davey Johnson wound up using him every day it seemed, for two or even three innings at a time, a staggering pace that didn't seem possible to sustain. It wasn't. He started experiencing pain in his shoulder in June, and was eventually diagnosed with torn cartilage.

MIKE MILCHIN	LRP	1968	Age 29											
YR Team	Lge	IP	H	ER	HR	BB	K	ERA	W	L	H/9	HR/9	BB/9	K/9	KW
1993 Louisville	AmA	107.0	112	50	17	55	66	4.21	6	6	9.42	1.43	4.63	5.55	.69
1995 Albuquerque	PCL	78.3	89	33	3	38	45	3.79	5	4	10.23	.34	4.37	5.17	.63
1996 Salt Lake City	PCL	20.7	21	7	0	13	15	3.05	1	1	9.15	.00	5.66	6.53	.76
1996 Minnesota	AL	22.3	27	15	5	13	18	6.04	1	1	10.88	2.01	5.24	7.25	1.11
1996 Baltimore	AL	11.0	12	5	0	6	10	4.09	0	1	9.82	.00	4.91	8.18	1.50

Milchin has been plagued by injuries throughout his career and underwent Tommy John surgery in 1994. He recovered from that, then had to have bone chips removed from his elbow.

ALAN MILLS	RRP	1967	Age 30											
YR Team	Lge	IP	H	ER	HR	BB	K	ERA	W	L	H/9	HR/9	BB/9	K/9	KW
1993 Baltimore	AL	99.0	78	31	14	55	70	2.82	7	4	7.09	1.27	5.00	6.36	.87
1994 Baltimore	AL	45.0	40	19	6	26	43	3.80	3	2	8.00	1.20	5.20	8.60	1.57
1995 Baltimore	AL	23.7	28	16	4	18	16	6.08	1	2	10.65	1.52	6.85	6.08	.32
1996 Baltimore	AL	54.3	38	20	10	37	49	3.31	4	2	6.29	1.66	6.13	8.12	1.17

He suffered from shoulder problems in 1994 and '95 and finally had surgery to repair them, with his recovery extending well into 1996. When he did come back, his velocity was back and his slider looked sharper than ever. He still suffered from control problems, which cost him greatly. When he was ahead in the count and could throw the slider, hitters had only a .303 OPS off him. Behind in the count, it was four times that; a doubling is about normal.

MIKE MUSSINA	RSP	1969	Age 28											
YR Team	Lge	IP	H	ER	HR	BB	K	ERA	W	L	H/9	HR/9	BB/9	K/9	KW
1993 Baltimore	AL	166.3	157	67	20	52	120	3.63	10	8	8.49	1.08	2.81	6.49	1.46
1994 Baltimore	AL	174.0	154	44	17	47	96	2.28	14	5	7.97	.88	2.43	4.97	1.05
1995 Baltimore	AL	218.7	184	63	23	55	157	2.59	17	7	7.57	.95	2.26	6.46	1.59
1996 Baltimore	AL	243.3	252	104	27	75	198	3.85	14	13	9.32	1.00	2.77	7.32	1.75

Mussina had a tough year despite winning 19 games. His hits allowed were up considerably, and a lot of them—63, in fact—were doubles. There is a strong perception that the changes in the Orioles' outfield defense, such as Bonilla's play in right and Anderson's move from left field, contributed to his problems; the statistical evidence is mixed. He also encountered some tragedy close to home; he coaches basketball for his hometown high school in Montoursville, Pa., the same school whose French class was on TWA Flight 800.

JIMMY MYERS   **RRP**   **1969**   **Age 28**

YR	Team	Lge	IP	H	ER	HR	BB	K	ERA	W	L	H/9	HR/9	BB/9	K/9	KW
1993	Shreveport	Texas	43.0	62	16	1	28	17	3.35	3	2	12.98	.21	5.86	3.56	-.28
1993	Phoenix	PCL	53.3	67	28	2	28	16	4.72	3	3	11.31	.34	4.72	2.70	-.28
1994	Carolina	South	10.3	9	3	0	9	5	2.61	1	0	7.84	.00	7.84	4.35	-.51
1994	Memphis	South	58.0	81	43	4	45	28	6.67	2	4	12.57	.62	6.98	4.34	-.30
1995	Rochester	Inter	60.0	76	26	2	38	26	3.90	4	3	11.40	.30	5.70	3.90	-.12
1996	Rochester	Inter	50.0	56	16	1	17	17	2.88	4	2	10.08	.18	3.06	3.06	.25
1996	Baltimore	AL	14.0	17	10	3	4	6	6.43	1	1	10.93	1.93	2.57	3.86	.64

A minor league closer, boasting 99 career saves, he started the 1996 season in Baltimore. He had been a strong ground-ball pitcher who prevented the home run, but after giving up four in 14 innings and letting seven of nine inherited runners score, he found himself back in Rochester.

RANDY MYERS   **LRP**   **1963**   **Age 34**

YR	Team	Lge	IP	H	ER	HR	BB	K	ERA	W	L	H/9	HR/9	BB/9	K/9	KW
1993	Chicago Cubs	NL	72.7	68	23	7	34	83	2.85	5	3	8.42	.87	4.21	10.28	2.37
1994	Chicago Cubs	NL	39.7	42	17	3	20	30	3.86	2	2	9.53	.68	4.54	6.81	1.13
1995	Chicago Cubs	NL	55.0	50	21	7	32	53	3.44	3	3	8.18	1.15	5.24	8.67	1.58
1996	Baltimore	AL	59.0	57	18	6	31	72	2.75	5	2	8.69	.92	4.73	10.98	2.48

Much of what was said for Alan Mills applies to Myers as well: a fastball/slider pitcher whose OPS allowed is four times higher when behind in the count. He was very inconsistent, overpowering in one game, blowing a two-run lead in the next; he converted 31 of 38 saves, which was roughly average. He did have some sharp words for Davey Johnson down the stretch, upset on one occasion where he was pulled in favor of Mills, and a few days later when sent to replace a cruising Mills.

JESSE OROSCO   **LRP**   **1957**   **Age 40**

YR	Team	Lge	IP	H	ER	HR	BB	K	ERA	W	L	H/9	HR/9	BB/9	K/9	KW
1993	Milwaukee	AL	55.0	50	20	2	20	69	3.27	4	2	8.18	.33	3.27	11.29	2.95
1994	Milwaukee	AL	38.7	30	18	4	26	35	4.19	2	2	6.98	.93	6.05	8.15	1.20
1995	Baltimore	AL	48.3	30	13	4	28	58	2.42	4	1	5.59	.74	5.21	10.80	2.30
1996	Baltimore	AL	54.7	42	16	5	29	50	2.63	4	2	6.91	.82	4.77	8.23	1.55

Two games in April, on consecutive nights, resulted in 2.1 innings of work, 80 pitches, three home runs and 12 runs. Outside of those two games, he pitched like a half-time Mariano Rivera, limiting opponents to 1.69 runs and 5.40 hits per nine innings.

BILLY PERCIBAL   **RSP**   **1974**   **Age 23**

YR	Team	Lge	IP	H	ER	HR	BB	K	ERA	W	L	H/9	HR/9	BB/9	K/9	KW
1994	Albany, GA	SAL	143.7	213	95	11	128	79	5.95	5	11	13.34	.69	8.02	4.95	-.35
1995	High Desert	Calif	113.7	123	50	10	71	66	3.96	7	6	9.74	.79	5.62	5.23	.34
1995	Bowie	East	12.7	9	0	0	9	5	.00	1	0	6.39	.00	6.39	3.55	-.41

In 1994, in a not particularly good season at Albany, Billy Percibal made my Death List: the top 10 most overworked pitchers at a young age. Bill Pulsipher was #1 and Percibal was #5. Half the pitchers on the list have had surgery in the last two years, including Percibal, who missed all of 1996 following two operations on his elbow.

ARTHUR RHODES   **LRP**   **1970**   **Age 27**

YR	Team	Lge	IP	H	ER	HR	BB	K	ERA	W	L	H/9	HR/9	BB/9	K/9	KW
1993	Rochester	Inter	25.7	27	11	5	19	27	3.86	2	1	9.47	1.75	6.66	9.47	1.49
1993	Baltimore	AL	86.0	86	51	16	53	51	5.34	4	6	9.00	1.67	5.55	5.34	.39
1994	Rochester	Inter	85.0	77	36	7	43	71	3.81	5	4	8.15	.74	4.55	7.52	1.37
1994	Baltimore	AL	52.7	47	24	7	31	46	4.10	3	3	8.03	1.20	5.30	7.86	1.30
1995	Baltimore	AL	76.0	64	40	12	49	77	4.74	3	5	7.58	1.42	5.80	9.12	1.59
1996	Baltimore	AL	52.7	46	21	6	25	60	3.59	3	3	7.86	1.03	4.27	10.25	2.35

The starter who never quite worked out has done some impressive work out of the bullpen, jumping out to a 9-0 start in 1996 before being sidelined with shoulder inflammation. He was back at the end of the season, but limited to one-batter situations.

NERIO RODRIGUEZ   **RBP**   **1973**   **Age 24**

YR	Team	Lge	IP	H	ER	HR	BB	K	ERA	W	L	H/9	HR/9	BB/9	K/9	KW
1996	Frederick	Caro	100.3	100	43	11	55	78	3.86	6	5	8.97	.99	4.93	7.00	1.10
1996	Rochester	Inter	14.0	11	2	0	4	5	1.29	2	0	7.07	.00	2.57	3.21	.43
1996	Baltimore	AL	16.7	17	8	2	8	12	4.32	1	1	9.18	1.08	4.32	6.48	1.08

After three years as a struggling catcher, he decided to change to the other end of the battery. He showed a surprising array of pitches and control for someone in his first season as a pitcher, almost leading the Carolina League in ERA (he was 2/3 of an inning short of qualifying; he could have given up five runs in those 2/3 of an inning and still won the title) and pitching respectably in the majors.

ALVIE SHEPHERD   **RRP**   **1974**   **Age 23**

YR	Team	Lge	IP	H	ER	HR	BB	K	ERA	W	L	H/9	HR/9	BB/9	K/9	KW
1996	Frederick	Caro	86.0	130	69	14	63	72	7.22	2	8	13.60	1.47	6.59	7.53	.86

The O's first pick in 1995, he's a big (6' 7"), hard-throwing pitcher from Nebraska. Despite his high heat, he's never done very well. Even in college he gave up a lot of runs, although Oriole management tried to dismiss that as resulting from coming in to relieve without warming up, since he also played first base. The results so far aren't encouraging, but it was his first year of pro ball; I'll cut him some slack. For now.

MATT SNYDER   **RRP**   **1975**   **Age 22**

YR	Team	Lge	IP	H	ER	HR	BB	K	ERA	W	L	H/9	HR/9	BB/9	K/9	KW
1996	High Desert	Calif	65.7	60	25	6	44	57	3.43	4	3	8.22	.82	6.03	7.81	1.10

He's interesting for the contrasts presented with Alvie Shepherd. He wasn't a high draft choice; as far as I can determine, he wasn't drafted at all. He's under 6' tall. But he's been in thorough control of professional hitters, piling up 8 saves and a 1.04 ERA in Bluefield in '95, and coming back with 20 saves and a 3.75 ERA this year; that ERA may not look impressive, but in this park it is.

DAVID WELLS   **LSP**   **1963**   **Age 34**

YR	Team	Lge	IP	H	ER	HR	BB	K	ERA	W	L	H/9	HR/9	BB/9	K/9	KW
1993	Detroit	AL	185.3	181	78	27	51	144	3.79	11	10	8.79	1.31	2.48	6.99	1.71
1994	Detroit	AL	110.0	109	40	11	27	69	3.27	7	5	8.92	.90	2.21	5.65	1.33
1995	Detroit	AL	130.0	113	39	16	40	82	2.70	10	4	7.82	1.11	2.77	5.68	1.20
1995	Cincinnati	NL	71.3	76	30	6	21	45	3.79	4	4	9.59	.76	2.65	5.68	1.23
1996	Baltimore	AL	223.7	236	102	28	57	126	4.10	12	13	9.50	1.13	2.29	5.07	1.12

Wells proved to be a disappointment for the Orioles, struggling for most of the season trying to find a groove. It wasn't as bad as people think—the AL of 1996 makes pitching stats difficult to compare with prior seasons—but it does add to the Orioles' pitcher paranoia.

ESTEBAN YAN   **RBP**   **1974**   **Age 23**

YR	Team	Lge	IP	H	ER	HR	BB	K	ERA	W	L	H/9	HR/9	BB/9	K/9	KW
1994	Macon	S Atl	145.7	219	108	19	56	73	6.67	4	12	13.53	1.17	3.46	4.51	.64
1995	West Palm Bch	Flor	119.0	183	77	5	49	64	5.82	4	9	13.84	.38	3.71	4.84	.69
1996	Bowie	East	14.7	21	12	2	10	12	7.36	0	2	12.89	1.23	6.14	7.36	.92
1996	Rochester	Inter	69.0	77	32	6	26	50	4.17	4	4	10.04	.78	3.39	6.52	1.33

He's completed six seasons of pro ball in three different organizations at the young age of 22. He was exclusively a starter in previous years, but his performance was never impressive. Last year, he made great strides, especially at Rochester, cutting his hits and raising his strikeouts without sacrificing control.

Player	Age	Team	Lge	AB	H	DB	TP	HR	BB	SB	CS	OUT	BA	OBA	SA	EQA	EQR	Peak
CARLOS AKINS	21	Frederick	Caro	152	39	2	1	4	29	4	2	115	.257	.376	.362	.253	19	.283
WADY ALMONTE	21	Frederick	Caro	292	73	5	1	9	18	1	2	221	.250	.294	.366	.218	25	.245
ROLO AVILA	22	Bowie	East	239	61	10	0	2	17	6	3	181	.255	.305	.322	.213	19	.235
	22	High Desert	Calif	290	77	9	1	3	15	7	3	216	.266	.302	.334	.217	24	.239
JUAN BAUTISTA	21	Bowie	East	449	99	14	2	3	19	12	6	356	.220	.252	.281	.174	22	.194
HARRY BERRIOS	24	Bowie	East	127	24	1	0	6	14	5	1	104	.189	.270	.339	.205	10	.219
	24	Frederick	Caro	164	33	4	0	4	10	4	1	132	.201	.247	.299	.179	9	.191
GREG BLOSSER	25	Rochester	Inter	117	27	4	1	2	12	1	1	91	.231	.302	.333	.211	9	.222
BRYAN BOGLE	23	High Desert	Calif	485	126	17	2	16	24	7	4	363	.260	.295	.402	.232	47	.252
JARVIS BROWN	29	Rochester	Inter	206	43	5	4	4	20	6	1	164	.209	.279	.330	.206	16	.204
CHRIS BRYANT	23	High Desert	Calif	231	55	4	1	4	24	1	1	177	.238	.310	.316	.209	18	.228
BARTT CARNEY	22	High Desert	Calif	115	22	1	2	1	11	3	2	95	.191	.262	.261	.167	5	.186
ERIC CHAVEZ	25	Frederick	Caro	431	108	10	1	15	62	2	1	324	.251	.345	.383	.245	48	.258
HOWIE CLARK	22	Bowie	East	465	120	25	2	4	53	3	4	349	.258	.334	.346	.229	44	.253
TOM D'AQUILA	23	Frederick	Caro	135	17	1	0	1	21	4	2	120	.126	.244	.156	.091	2	.098
BIEN FIGUEROA	32	Rochester	Inter	157	47	3	0	2	14	2	1	111	.299	.357	.357	.246	17	.234
DENIO GABRIEL	20	Frederick	Caro	135	19	0	1	0	10	2	3	119	.141	.200	.156	-.078	-1	-.071
JESSE GARCIA	22	High Desert	Calif	455	98	13	2	7	42	11	4	361	.215	.282	.299	.194	30	.214
MIKE GARGIULO	21	Frederick	Caro	164	28	3	0	2	13	1	0	136	.171	.232	.226	.128	4	.142
KEITH GORDON	27	Bowie	East	313	78	9	1	5	20	10	6	241	.249	.294	.332	.211	25	.216
	27	Rochester	Inter	105	25	3	0	5	10	0	2	82	.238	.304	.410	.230	10	.235
KRIS GRESHAM	25	Bowie	East	132	25	6	0	0	9	1	1	108	.189	.241	.235	.139	4	.144
ROY HODGE	25	High Desert	Calif	389	86	11	1	6	34	4	3	306	.221	.284	.301	.192	25	.203
CHRIS KIRGAN	23	High Desert	Calif	521	128	9	1	23	39	1	1	394	.246	.298	.399	.231	51	.252
DAVID LAMB	20	High Desert	Calif	456	90	15	2	2	37	2	2	368	.197	.258	.252	.157	18	.179
CHIP LAWRENCE	21	Frederick	Caro	134	27	1	0	0	7	2	1	108	.201	.241	.209	.127	3	.141
JASON LECRONIER	23	Frederick	Caro	94	19	0	0	3	9	0	0	75	.202	.272	.298	.184	5	.202
	23	High Desert	Calif	134	26	0	1	3	3	0	0	108	.194	.212	.276	.144	4	.154
LINCOLN MARTIN	24	Frederick	Caro	432	100	8	5	2	43	9	3	335	.231	.301	.287	.199	30	.214
DOMINGO MARTINEZ	28	Rochester	Inter	118	42	3	0	7	11	0	1	77	.356	.411	.559	.315	21	.317
DOUG NEWSTROM	24	High Desert	Calif	397	99	16	2	8	56	7	4	302	.249	.342	.360	.238	42	.255
BILLY OWENS	25	Rochester	Inter	202	49	9	0	5	12	2	1	154	.243	.285	.361	.215	17	.227
MATT RALEIGH	25	High Desert	Calif	83	20	2	0	5	11	1	0	63	.241	.330	.446	.257	11	.271
RICK SHORT	23	Frederick	Caro	482	130	9	0	6	25	5	3	355	.270	.306	.326	.213	37	.232
RAY SUPLEE	25	High Desert	Calif	347	82	8	1	5	22	1	1	266	.236	.282	.308	.194	22	.205
JIM WAWRUCK	26	Rochester	Inter	206	56	11	4	1	15	3	1	151	.272	.321	.379	.237	21	.247
MIKE WOLFF	23	Frederick	Caro	356	78	6	0	7	14	3	1	279	.219	.249	.295	.175	18	.191
EDDIE ZOSKY	28	Rochester	Inter	343	84	19	3	3	23	3	1	260	.245	.292	.344	.213	27	.215

Player	Age	Team	Lge	IP	H	ER	HR	BB	K	ERA	W	L	H/9	HR/9	BB/9	K/9	KW
JOEL BENNETT	26	Bowie	East	50.7	43	20	6	21	36	3.55	3	3	7.64	1.07	3.73	6.39	1.20
BRIAN BREWER	24	Bowie	East	52.7	68	39	10	34	26	6.66	2	4	11.62	1.71	5.81	4.44	.03
	24	High Desert	Calif	67.0	75	40	7	55	35	5.37	2	5	10.07	.94	7.39	4.70	-.28
ROCCO CAFARO	23	Bowie	East	95.3	145	66	14	46	41	6.23	3	8	13.69	1.32	4.34	3.87	.20
SCOTT CONNER	24	Bowie	East	75.3	98	53	12	45	44	6.33	2	6	11.71	1.43	5.38	5.26	.41
	24	Frederick	Caro	54.7	63	31	8	36	32	5.10	2	4	10.37	1.32	5.93	5.27	.27
BRAD CRILLS	24	High Desert	Calif	70.0	79	34	9	30	28	4.37	4	4	10.16	1.16	3.86	3.60	.24
GREG DEAN	22	High Desert	Calif	94.3	105	51	5	81	47	4.87	4	6	10.02	.48	7.73	4.48	-.44
JIM DEDRICK	28	Rochester	Inter	65.0	86	49	13	50	31	6.78	2	5	11.91	1.80	6.92	4.29	-.30
STEVE DIXON	26	Rochester	Inter	32.7	29	13	1	27	26	3.58	2	2	7.99	.28	7.44	7.16	.53
TODD DYESS	23	Frederick	Caro	85.3	118	67	8	53	62	7.07	2	7	12.45	.84	5.59	6.54	.78
RADHAMES DYKHOFF	21	Frederick	Caro	55.7	89	46	8	30	52	7.44	1	5	14.39	1.29	4.85	8.41	1.59
TOM EDENS	35	Rochester	Inter	64.7	76	37	8	30	30	5.15	3	4	10.58	1.11	4.18	4.18	.35
DON FLORENCE	29	Rochester	Inter	82.7	111	53	10	40	44	5.77	3	6	12.08	1.09	4.35	4.79	.51
SHANE HALE	27	Bowie	East	124.3	166	81	18	65	64	5.86	4	10	12.02	1.30	4.71	4.63	.37
F'CISCO HERNANDEZ	19	Frederick	Caro	40.0	53	27	6	28	27	6.07	1	3	11.93	1.35	6.30	6.07	.45
MARCUS HOSTETLER	26	Bowie	East	52.7	59	28	4	27	33	4.78	2	4	10.08	.68	4.61	5.64	.73
AARON LANE	25	Bowie	East	46.3	52	37	7	30	26	7.19	1	4	10.10	1.36	5.83	5.05	.23
CHRIS LEMP	25	Bowie	East	44.0	60	27	4	30	26	5.52	2	3	12.27	.82	6.14	5.32	.24
MATT MARENGHI	23	High Desert	Calif	155.7	203	89	23	61	70	5.15	6	11	11.74	1.33	3.53	4.05	.47
STEVE MONTGOMERY	22	High Desert	Calif	65.3	82	40	7	39	48	5.51	2	5	11.30	.96	5.37	6.61	.86
JULIO MORENO	20	Frederick	Caro	144.3	201	86	16	56	101	5.36	6	10	12.53	1.00	3.49	6.30	1.23
ROBERT MORSEMAN	22	Frederick	Caro	43.3	64	37	5	40	35	7.68	1	4	13.29	1.04	8.31	7.27	.35
OSCAR MUNOZ	26	Rochester	Inter	107.7	104	51	16	49	70	4.26	6	6	8.69	1.34	4.10	5.85	.93
TIM OLSZEWSKI	22	High Desert	Calif	57.3	73	39	4	47	23	6.12	2	4	11.46	.63	7.38	3.61	-.64
SIDNEY PONSON	19	Frederick	Caro	97.0	116	57	7	40	76	5.29	4	7	10.76	.65	3.71	7.05	1.42
DAN REED	21	High Desert	Calif	46.0	53	21	6	26	27	4.11	2	3	10.37	1.17	5.09	5.28	.49
TODD REVENIG	27	Bowie	East	57.0	50	17	6	23	29	2.68	4	2	7.89	.95	3.63	4.58	.62
JOE RHODES	21	High Desert	Calif	110.7	130	63	11	75	50	5.12	5	7	10.57	.89	6.10	4.07	-.17
JASON ROGERS	23	Frederick	Caro	102.0	156	90	9	82	60	7.94	2	9	13.76	.79	7.24	5.29	-.04
BRIAN SACKINSKY	25	Rochester	Inter	65.0	77	24	11	22	31	3.32	4	3	10.66	1.52	3.05	4.29	.67
FRANCISCO SANEAUX	22	High Desert	Calif	90.3	92	52	10	103	62	5.18	4	6	9.17	1.00	10.26	6.18	-.51
CHRIS SAURITCH	24	High Desert	Calif	47.0	50	24	8	38	25	4.60	2	3	9.57	1.53	7.28	4.79	-.22
KEITH SHEPHERD	28	Rochester	Inter	90.0	95	46	11	48	81	4.60	4	6	9.50	1.10	4.80	8.10	1.50
BRIAN SHOUSE	27	Rochester	Inter	48.0	55	23	6	21	37	4.31	2	3	10.31	1.12	3.94	6.94	1.33
HUT SMITH	23	High Desert	Calif	45.7	59	25	6	18	21	4.93	2	3	11.63	1.18	3.55	4.14	.49
MARK TRANBARGER	26	Bowie	East	50.7	74	36	5	43	34	6.39	2	4	13.14	.89	7.64	6.04	.10
GARY WHITE	23	High Desert	Calif	46.0	59	26	8	30	21	5.09	2	3	11.54	1.57	5.87	4.11	-.10

Baltimore Orioles

Boston Red Sox

After a fantastic job of accumulating talent in the first sixteen months in his Boston Red Sox' general manager, Dan Duquette saw all of his work go down the tubes in a 6-19 start to the Sox' season. While the Red Sox recovered to be the second-best team in the division from May through the end of the year (just two games worse than the Yankees) the .240 opening had buried them.

A good team that loses 19 of 25 in June is said to be going through a slump. Moves may be made, controversies erupt, but management can console itself with the knowledge that they have a good team, and that the current stretch is just a down period, not the team's actual level. Key to this mindset is that when this team sees its overall record, it's not reflective of just the slump, but the entire season to date. A team like Boston that starts slow, never has that success to fall back on and is prone to making decisions based on insufficient evidence that reverberate throughout the season and beyond.

Boston simply had their slump at a bad time. In April, no one hit at all as the Sox posted the lowest OBP and second lowest SLG in the league. The pitching, except for Roger Clemens and Heathcliff Slocumb, was awful. They weren't getting lucky, with an 0-6 record in one-run games. But what got all the attention was the defense, as measured by errors. Wil Cordero and Dwayne Hosey, in particular, were the fall guys for a stretch of embarrassing Red Sox losses. Hosey looked awkward in center field, and a 2-for-19 slump got him sent to Pawtucket. Cordero made six errors in the first three weeks and was the topic of daily speculation about a move to left field.

Duquette, who only likes to make player moves on days that end in "y," continued his pattern of turning the bench over every few days in an effort to quell the slump and improve the defense. The Hosey fiasco had a serious secondary effect: panicked over their center field situation, the Red Sox moved Donnie Sadler, a top shortstop prospect, to center field at the end of April. While Sadler was a fair center fielder, his hitting suffered and he eventually moved back to short. Allowing a three-week bad spell by your major league center fielder to affect player development decisions like this is horrific management, and alone should call Duquette's status among the stathead community to be questioned.

By the second week of May, the Red Sox were playing the kind of baseball expected of them. Mo Vaughn, John Valentin and Wil Cordero started hitting. Tim Naehring was activated and hit well until the All-Star break. Tom Gordon and Tim Wakefield started pitching better and the bullpen improved.

The Sox played .500 ball for two months, but it wasn't enough to make them wild card contenders, so Duquette began getting what he could for his older players. He did a fantastic job, turning Jamie Moyer, Jeff Manto, Kevin Mitchell and Mike Stanton into Darren Bragg, Arquimedez Pozo, Roberto Mejia, Mark Brandenburg and Kerry Lacy. Bragg and Brandenburg made immediate contributions, while Pozo and Lacy could have an impact in 1997. Bragg alone is worth all four of the players Boston coughed up, giving the Red Sox a serviceable center fielder and above average leadoff hitter.

The additions of Bragg and Jeff Frye, who hit well and played a fair second base, a tremendous hot streak by Clemens and good stretches by Gordon and Wakefield helped the Red Sox storm back into wild card contention with a 22-7 August. But the loss of Jose Canseco (back) and John Valentin (shoulder) short-circuited the offense, and they couldn't make up the last few games they'd spotted the league in April, finishing four games behind Baltimore in the wild card chase.

So at the end of the year, do you remember the great five months of baseball? The best record in the league after the All-Star break? The adjustments Kevin Kennedy made to right the ship and yank the team into contention? Nope. All that was recalled was that the Red Sox started 6-19 and someone had to go down for it. Kennedy, predictably, was fired, amidst talk of his "not having the team prepared" and "being too soft." This just one year removed from a division title.

The Red Sox currently stand one player away from being the best team in the division. That player is future Hall of Famer and free agent Roger Clemens. Clemens is insisting on a four-year contract, terms Duquette is balking at, but that other teams will be all too eager to give Clemens. Although he is perceived as a disappointment over the last few years because of low win totals, much of that can be traced to awful run and bullpen support, circumstances he has no control over. There are very few pitchers you can reasonably give four-year contracts to, but Clemens is on the short list. He is in excellent physical condition, has a tremendous work ethic and is still one of the five best pitchers in the league.

Clemens, added to Gordon, Suppan, Wakefield and Sele would give the Red Sox the deepest rotation in the division, maybe the league, in front of an above-average bullpen and potentially excellent offense. What the Red Sox do at catcher (Stanley/Haselman/Hatteberg), second base (Frye/Cordero/Pozo), third base (Valentin/Naehring/Pozo) and the corner outfield spots will tell us a lot about new manager Jimy

Williams, and give us a clue as to whether we should keep expecting good things out of Dan Duquette.

Duquette has always been able to identify and collect talent. His 1996 performance was erratic, and while we know he has the ability to find baseball players, there comes a time when you have to convert the talent into a baseball team. This is that time for the Red Sox. They have a lot of cheap hitting help available in the minors in players like Bo Dodson, Rudy Pemberton and Adam Hyzdu. By spending wisely on one top-tier second baseman or third baseman (via trade, because there's nothing available on the free agent market), re-signing Clemens and adding a quality left-handed reliever, this team can win 95-100 games without an unreasonable payroll.

Organization: The turnover in the Sox organization is not limited to players. In a revolving door reminiscent of the mid-1980s Yankees, the Red Sox have gone through pitching coaches at the major league level like Bud Selig picking through lead negotiators, with five in two years. Of course, with this kind of commitment to the coaching staff, the Kennedy firing makes more sense. A lack of patience seems to define the organization.

Under Duquette, the Red Sox have populated their AAA and AA teams with minor league veterans who can hit, but are positionless. If they were a prospect in 1993, there's a good chance they're buried in Pawtucket or Trenton. Any of these guys, most notably Rudy Pemberton, could help a team looking for 200 at bats out of a fifth outfielder/DH type. The organization has been able to produce some grade A prospects, however, in shortstop Nomar Garciaparra and pitchers Jeff Suppan and Carl Pavano.

It is easier to beat Duquette to a waiver claim than to get respect as a hitting prospect in Trenton, a pitcher's park in a pitcher's league. Both Trenton and Pawtucket favor pitchers, making it difficult to project the Sox' arms until they get to Boston, and a good reason to watch Pavano carefully. All in all, the system has improved in the last few years, as Duquette's staff has pumped money into scouting and drafting. Young pitchers such as Paxton Crawford, Andy Yount and Bobby Rodgers will all be getting noticed in 1997 as they advance to high A ball and AA.

ANDY ABAD OF/1B 1973 Age 24

Year	Team	Lge	AB	H	DB	TP	HR	BB	SB	CS	OUT	BA	OBA	SA	EQA	EQR	Peak
1994	Sarasota	Flor	362	93	9	0	5	38	2	5	274	.257	.327	.323	.217	30	.244
1995	Sarasota	Calif	59	14	1	0	0	5	2	1	46	.237	.297	.254	.186	3	.204
1995	Trenton	East	301	74	13	2	5	32	4	4	231	.246	.318	.352	.224	27	.247
1996	Sarasota	Flor	211	57	11	1	3	33	5	2	156	.270	.369	.374	.255	26	.277
1996	Trenton	East	222	61	17	1	4	30	4	2	163	.275	.361	.414	.261	28	.284
1997	Boston	AL	439	119	44	2	6	52	5	2	322	.271	.348	.421	.257	54	

Abad is a left-handed hitter, developing power slowly while keeping the rest of his game together. A tweener, he can help if his defense in the outfield is really good, or he turns the doubles into homers or walks more. As is, he's going to be hard-pressed to make the majors, and he's in the wrong organization for a first baseman/outfielder.

RICHIE BORRERO C 1973 Age 24

Year	Team	Lge	AB	H	DB	TP	HR	BB	SB	CS	OUT	BA	OBA	SA	EQA	EQR	Peak
1993	Utica	NY-P	123	14	1	0	1	8	1	0	109	.114	.168	.146	-.115	-2	-.115
1994	Sarasota	Flor	146	25	3	0	4	9	0	0	121	.171	.219	.274	.145	5	.163
1995	Michigan	Midw	72	15	2	0	2	4	0	0	57	.208	.250	.319	.183	4	.198
1995	Sarasota	Flor	100	18	5	0	0	4	0	0	82	.180	.212	.230	.113	2	.128
1996	Sarasota	Flor	94	22	3	0	3	5	1	1	73	.234	.273	.362	.209	7	.226
1996	Trenton	East	74	23	3	2	3	7	2	1	52	.311	.370	.527	.293	12	.317

Borrero's been a pro for seven years without ever getting 300 AB in a year. Neat trick. He also never hit until this year, but when someone has the month of their life in a place like Trenton, it gets your attention. There was clearly some improvement in 1996, and until I know why, I'd want to hold onto him. Six-year free agent, unsigned at this writing.

DARREN BRAGG   **CF/RF**   **1970**   **Age 27**

Year	Team	Lge	AB	H	DB	TP	HR	BB	SB	CS	OUT	BA	OBA	SA	EQA	EQR	Peak
1993	Jacksonville	South	469	119	19	2	11	73	12	6	356	.254	.354	.373	.247	54	.269
1994	Calgary	PCL	483	145	21	2	15	62	20	8	346	.300	.380	.445	.279	71	.298
1995	Tacoma	PCL	216	66	11	2	5	23	8	2	152	.306	.372	.444	.278	31	.295
1995	Seattle	AL	146	36	6	1	3	18	9	0	110	.247	.329	.363	.246	16	.258
1996	Tacoma	PCL	73	21	6	0	3	14	1	0	52	.288	.402	.493	.298	13	.308
1996	Boston	AL	220	54	12	1	3	36	6	4	170	.245	.352	.350	.238	24	.248
1996	Seattle	AL	196	54	13	1	7	33	8	5	147	.276	.380	.459	.277	30	.288
1997	*Boston*	*AL*	*414*	*121*	*27*	*2*	*13*	*62*	*18*	*12*	*305*	*.292*	*.384*	*.461*	*.278*	*62*	

Bragg escaped from Seattle in the Jamie Moyer deal and established himself as Boston's leadoff hitter and center field-er. He's been a major league hitter for three years now, and should finally get a full season to prove it. Excellent corner outfielder, stretched in center. Should be platooned.

JOSE CANSECO   **DH/LF**   **1965**   **Age 32**

Year	Team	Lge	AB	H	DB	TP	HR	BB	SB	CS	OUT	BA	OBA	SA	EQA	EQR	Peak
1993	Texas	AL	235	64	14	1	12	17	6	4	175	.272	.321	.494	.265	32	.268
1994	Texas	AL	436	128	19	2	33	70	14	7	315	.294	.391	.573	.308	83	.306
1995	Boston	AL	400	126	22	1	27	43	4	0	274	.315	.381	.577	.310	73	.304
1996	Boston	AL	357	100	19	1	28	62	3	1	258	.280	.387	.574	.307	67	.296
1997	*Boston*	*AL*	*457*	*128*	*18*	*1*	*34*	*66*	*2*	*2*	*331*	*.280*	*.371*	*.547*	*.293*	*77*	

This just in: he's still a fantastic hitter. Final numbers, while good, were hurt by his decision to try and play after back surgery in August. Hit just .204/.143 during the comeback. The back is still a concern, but Canseco's one of the most con-sistent hitters in baseball, and a good bet to match his Vlad. Bad long-term bet.

TODD CAREY   **3B**   **1972**   **Age 25**

Year	Team	Lge	AB	H	DB	TP	HR	BB	SB	CS	OUT	BA	OBA	SA	EQA	EQR	Peak
1993	Ft Lauderdale	Flor	450	100	10	2	5	22	2	2	352	.222	.258	.287	.175	22	.195
1994	Lynchburg	Caro	372	75	9	1	9	41	1	2	299	.202	.281	.304	.190	23	.210
1995	Sarasota	Flor	89	27	3	0	4	7	1	1	63	.303	.354	.472	.273	12	.297
1995	Trenton	East	240	68	7	1	9	25	2	3	175	.283	.351	.433	.260	30	.282
1996	Trenton	East	454	114	25	2	18	43	4	2	342	.251	.316	.434	.248	52	.265
1997	*Boston*	*AL*	*374*	*100*	*23*	*1*	*14*	*28*	*3*	*4*	*278*	*.267*	*.318*	*.447*	*.249*	*43*	

Another tweener, and like Abad, behind some pretty good players. Boston has Valentin, Naehring, Pozo and possibly Cordero as third base candidates. Carey's got real power, and a left-handed hitting third baseman with power and a fair glove is going to get a shot somewhere; probably not Boston, probably in 1998.

WIL CORDERO   **2B**   **1972**   **Age 25**

Year	Team	Lge	AB	H	DB	TP	HR	BB	SB	CS	OUT	BA	OBA	SA	EQA	EQR	Peak
1993	Montreal	NL	483	124	30	2	11	42	10	3	362	.257	.316	.395	.240	51	.269
1994	Montreal	NL	421	126	28	2	16	46	14	3	298	.299	.368	.489	.286	65	.316
1995	Montreal	NL	525	156	33	2	11	42	7	4	373	.297	.349	.430	.262	65	.284
1996	Boston	AL	197	55	10	0	4	11	2	1	143	.279	.317	.391	.239	20	.257
1997	*Boston*	*AL*	*619*	*193*	*36*	*2*	*13*	*37*	*13*	*5*	*431*	*.312*	*.351*	*.439*	*.265*	*78*	

I know everyone's down on him, so keep this in mind: He's still just 25, and was developing fine until Felipe Alou moved him to left field in August of 1995. He was awful after that, got off to a horrendous start for Boston this year while doing OJT at second, then got hurt right when he was scorching the ball (4/1-4/21: .159/.183/.217; 4/22-5/20 (the injury): .387/.426/.534). He's a young right-handed hitter with power in Fenway. If they give him a position and leave him alone, he'll have a .300/.380/.470 year, and get better after that. Highly recommended.

TONY DeROSSO   **3B**   **1976**   **Age 21**

Year	Team	Lge	AB	H	DB	TP	HR	BB	SB	CS	OUT	BA	OBA	SA	EQA	EQR	Peak
1995	Michigan	Midw	393	83	7	1	11	30	4	1	311	.211	.267	.318	.192	25	.222
1996	Sarasota	Flor	425	105	11	1	15	28	8	1	321	.247	.294	.384	.228	40	.259
1997	*Boston*	*AL*	*493*	*120*	*16*	*2*	*18*	*40*	*9*	*4*	*377*	*.243*	*.300*	*.394*	*.230*	*48*	

Young, with developing power. DeRosso improved his game this year while being converted from first base to third. He hit much better in the second half, a good sign. If he can hold his gains in AA this year, he'll have a career.

BO DODSON   **1B**   **1971**   **Age 26**

Year	Team	Lge	AB	H	DB	TP	HR	BB	SB	CS	OUT	BA	OBA	SA	EQA	EQR	Peak
1993	El Paso	Texas	337	94	18	2	8	39	1	2	245	.279	.354	.415	.257	41	.283
1994	New Orleans	AmA	264	69	7	0	4	43	2	2	197	.261	.365	.333	.239	28	.260
1995	El Paso	Texas	222	72	13	2	7	33	1	0	150	.324	.412	.495	.303	38	.324
1995	New Orleans	AmA	210	59	4	1	9	37	0	0	151	.281	.389	.438	.278	31	.297
1996	Pawtucket	Inter	279	91	11	1	11	32	3	0	188	.326	.395	.491	.297	45	.313
1997	*Boston*	*AL*	*529*	*171*	*30*	*2*	*25*	*78*	*1*	*0*	*358*	*.323*	*.410*	*.529*	*.308*	*94*	

Hitter, trapped in AAA behind that Vaughn guy and about six Red Sox DHs. Brewers, who let him go last winter, could-n't use a left-handed hitter with power, could they? Dodson's not a real good risk at this point, because there's a serious lack of opportunity for him. Could help the Devil Rays in 1998.

JEFF FRYE   **2B**   **1967**   **Age 30**

Year	Team	Lge	AB	H	DB	TP	HR	BB	SB	CS	OUT	BA	OBA	SA	EQA	EQR	Peak
1994	Oklahoma	AmA	69	19	0	0	2	7	2	0	50	.275	.342	.362	.246	7	.255
1994	Texas	AL	209	71	19	3	1	29	6	1	139	.340	.420	.474	.305	36	.312
1995	Texas	AL	314	88	16	2	4	24	3	3	229	.280	.331	.382	.240	32	.242
1996	Oklahoma	AmA	186	43	6	0	2	25	9	1	144	.231	.322	.296	.219	16	.217
1996	Boston	AL	415	115	25	2	4	54	18	4	304	.277	.360	.376	.256	50	.255
1997	*Boston*	*AL*	*382*	*106*	*18*	*1*	*4*	*45*	*13*	*5*	*281*	*.277*	*.354*	*.361*	*.245*	*42*	

Picked up off the scrap heap right before the season started, he stepped in after Cordero's injury and had a good year, one not out of line with his career. Sox have been unable to fill second base since losing Jody Reed in the expansion draft, going through Scott Fletcher, Tim Naehring, Luis Alicea, Wil Cordero and now Frye. They could do worse than to run him out there again in 1997. Future depends on what they do with Cordero, and may be undecided well into spring train-ing.

AARON FULLER   **OF**   **1972**   **Age 25**

Year	Team	Lge	AB	H	DB	TP	HR	BB	SB	CS	OUT	BA	OBA	SA	EQA	EQR	Peak
1993	Utica	NY-P	182	36	0	0	1	15	8	2	148	.198	.259	.214	.154	7	.171
1994	Sarasota	Flor	428	106	14	1	3	74	25	7	329	.248	.359	.306	.237	45	.261
1995	Visalia	Calif	188	39	5	1	1	15	4	4	153	.207	.266	.261	.167	9	.181
1995	Trenton	East	210	43	7	3	1	14	10	3	170	.205	.254	.281	.180	12	.196
1996	Sarasota	Flor	451	127	14	2	8	56	17	7	331	.282	.361	.375	.253	53	.271

Small slap-hitting outfielder with good plate discipline. He had a good year, but was old for the FSL. Probably a non-prospect, but as a real center fielder is in the right organization, and a good start at Trenton could have him in Boston by June. He might be a valuable roto pickup for the steals.

NOMAR GARCIAPARRA   **SS**   **1974**   **Age 23**

Year	Team	Lge	AB	H	DB	TP	HR	BB	SB	CS	OUT	BA	OBA	SA	EQA	EQR	Peak
1994	Sarasota	Flor	107	29	6	0	2	9	3	1	79	.271	.328	.383	.242	11	.278
1995	Trenton	East	536	149	17	5	11	45	24	8	395	.278	.334	.390	.248	61	.278
1996	Pawtucket	Inter	173	58	11	1	14	15	2	1	116	.335	.388	.653	.327	35	.361
1996	Boston	AL	87	21	1	3	4	3	5	0	66	.241	.267	.460	.248	10	.273
1997	*Boston*	*AL*	*551*	*155*	*30*	*2*	*22*	*44*	*27*	*6*	*402*	*.281*	*.334*	*.463*	*.267*	*74*	

Garciaparra added muscle last winter and it showed. He also suffered some injuries (ankle, left knee) that cut into his playing time. Has already moved Valentin to third, or possibly out of Boston, and will join the AL's list of good young shortstops in 1997. Good defensive player.

MIKE GREENWELL LF   1964   Age 33

Year	Team	Lge	AB	H	DB	TP	HR	BB	SB	CS	OUT	BA	OBA	SA	EQA	EQR	Peak
1993	Boston	AL	542	172	37	6	16	57	5	3	373	.317	.382	.496	.291	85	.289
1994	Boston	AL	328	88	22	1	12	38	2	2	242	.268	.344	.451	.263	43	.257
1995	Boston	AL	485	149	24	4	17	39	9	5	341	.307	.359	.478	.277	69	.267
1996	Boston	AL	293	84	19	1	7	18	4	0	209	.287	.328	.430	.256	35	.243
1997	*Boston*	*AL*	*287*	*86*	*11*	*0*	*10*	*21*	*3*	*1*	*202*	*.300*	*.347*	*.443*	*.264*	*36*	

An era closes. Greenwell gets lumped in with the string of Red Sox left fielders (Williams to Yasztremski to Rice), but he doesn't deserve to be in that company. He was never as big a contributor as perceived due to bad defensive play, a lack of real power and the high standard of contemporary left fielders. There's a good chance he'll catch on with someone as a pinch-hitter/fifth outfielder, and he could contribute in that role for years. Off to Japan.

BILL HASELMAN C   1966   Age 31

Year	Team	Lge	AB	H	DB	TP	HR	BB	SB	CS	OUT	BA	OBA	SA	EQA	EQR	Peak
1993	Seattle	AL	139	38	5	0	7	13	2	1	102	.273	.336	.460	.263	18	.268
1994	Calgary	PCL	158	46	4	0	12	27	1	0	112	.291	.395	.544	.305	29	.308
1994	Seattle	AL	83	16	7	1	1	3	1	0	67	.193	.221	.337	.180	5	.180
1995	Boston	AL	153	39	6	0	6	17	0	2	116	.255	.329	.412	.243	17	.241
1996	Boston	AL	235	63	11	1	8	19	4	2	174	.268	.323	.426	.250	27	.244
1997	*Boston*	*AL*	*243*	*61*	*9*	*0*	*13*	*31*	*0*	*0*	*182*	*.251*	*.336*	*.449*	*.257*	*30*	

Nice to see him finally get some playing time. He backed up Stanley and became the regular when Stanley's neck problem ended his season. Not the best combination, since they're both slow right-handed hitters with power and just fair defensive skills, but it beats carrying a Manwaring. Stanley's expected to see more time at DH in 1997, so Haselman, Hatteberg or McKeel stands to benefit. I'll bet on a Haselman/Hatteberg platoon.

SCOTT HATTEBERG C   1970   Age 27

Year	Team	Lge	AB	H	DB	TP	HR	BB	SB	CS	OUT	BA	OBA	SA	EQA	EQR	Peak
1993	New Britain	East	239	66	8	0	8	39	1	2	175	.276	.378	.410	.264	31	.288
1993	Pawtucket	Inter	53	8	0	0	1	7	0	0	45	.151	.250	.208	.125	1	.144
1994	New Britain	East	71	18	3	1	1	6	0	1	54	.254	.312	.366	.223	6	.242
1994	Pawtucket	Inter	242	54	8	0	7	30	1	1	189	.223	.309	.343	.217	21	.232
1995	Pawtucket	Inter	257	67	11	1	7	39	1	0	190	.261	.358	.393	.254	31	.268
1996	Pawtucket	Inter	292	74	8	0	12	56	1	1	219	.253	.374	.404	.262	38	.272
1997	*Boston*	*AL*	*209*	*56*	*8*	*0*	*10*	*34*	*0*	*1*	*154*	*.268*	*.370*	*.450*	*.270*	*29*	

The Red Sox have some serious depth at catcher, with three guys no worse than a good #2, a decent #3 in Delgado and a B prospect on the way (McKeel). Hatteberg would make a good platoon partner for Haselman, and that's probably what the Sox will do in 1997.

ADAM HYZDU LF   1972   Age 25

Year	Team	Lge	AB	H	DB	TP	HR	BB	SB	CS	OUT	BA	OBA	SA	EQA	EQR	Peak
1993	San Jose	Calif	168	65	6	1	11	21	1	0	103	.387	.455	.631	.352	38	.394
1993	Shreveport	Texas	308	59	9	0	6	21	1	2	251	.192	.243	.279	.161	13	.180
1994	Winston-Salem	Caro	214	54	6	1	10	16	1	3	163	.252	.304	.430	.239	23	.264
1994	Chattanooga	South	136	34	5	0	4	9	0	1	103	.250	.297	.375	.221	12	.245
1995	Chattanooga	South	324	85	9	1	13	43	2	1	240	.262	.349	.417	.256	40	.278
1996	Trenton	East	391	130	18	1	23	51	2	4	265	.332	.410	.560	.313	73	.336
1997	*Boston*	*AL*	*558*	*164*	*28*	*2*	*29*	*76*	*3*	*3*	*397*	*.294*	*.379*	*.507*	*.288*	*88*	

Hyzdu has apparently mastered AA after over 1000 at bats. Another corner outfielder, but a pretty good defensive one. He's being converted to catcher this winter, a move that works only slightly more often than Bud Selig smiles. Vlad loves him, I'm more skeptical because of the position change.

REGGIE JEFFERSON **DH/LF** **1969** **Age 28**

Year	Team	Lge	AB	H	DB	TP	HR	BB	SB	CS	OUT	BA	OBA	SA	EQA	EQR	Peak
1993	Cleveland	AL	373	100	11	2	13	31	1	2	275	.268	.324	.413	.245	41	.263
1994	Seattle	AL	162	53	7	0	9	17	0	0	109	.327	.391	.537	.304	28	.321
1995	Boston	AL	122	36	7	0	6	9	0	0	86	.295	.344	.500	.277	17	.289
1996	Boston	AL	382	129	30	4	18	25	0	0	253	.338	.378	.579	.310	67	.318
1997	Boston	AL	434	138	32	2	19	44	0	0	296	.318	.381	.532	.297	71	

Quietly had his second great year in three. Another Boston left field/DH type, setting them up perfectly for two-platoon baseball that's not going to happen. He's probably the best of the bunch, but may price himself out of the job and be elsewhere in 1997. Recommended.

T.R. LEWIS **OF** **1971** **Age 26**

Year	Team	Lge	AB	H	DB	TP	HR	BB	SB	CS	OUT	BA	OBA	SA	EQA	EQR	Peak
1993	Bowie	East	496	149	21	1	6	34	12	5	352	.300	.345	.383	.249	55	.275
1994	Bowie	East	73	17	2	0	3	6	1	0	56	.233	.291	.384	.226	7	.247
1994	Rochester	Inter	177	52	7	0	6	16	4	1	126	.294	.352	.435	.266	23	.289
1995	Bowie	East	319	91	14	1	6	36	8	2	230	.285	.358	.392	.257	39	.275
1995	Rochester	Inter	79	22	5	0	4	7	1	1	58	.278	.337	.494	.270	11	.291
1996	Pawtucket	Inter	277	83	15	1	13	34	1	1	195	.300	.376	.502	.288	44	.304
1997	Boston	AL	408	132	20	2	8	26	2	1	277	.324	.364	.441	.270	53	

Another decent hitter Duquette picked up. Lewis has been a pro for eight years, putting up more or less the same numbers for the last four. He's not a bad player, but there's no compelling reason to add him to a roster and he's not going to beat someone out of a job. Great chance to be a Devil Ray.

JOSE MALAVE **LF** **1971** **Age 26**

Year	Team	Lge	AB	H	DB	TP	HR	BB	SB	CS	OUT	BA	OBA	SA	EQA	EQR	Peak
1993	Lynchburg	Caro	326	90	15	1	7	32	1	1	237	.276	.341	.393	.247	36	.272
1994	New Britain	East	488	148	26	3	24	48	4	4	344	.303	.366	.516	.287	76	.312
1995	Pawtucket	Inter	323	85	7	1	21	31	0	1	239	.263	.328	.486	.265	43	.284
1996	Pawtucket	Inter	156	40	5	0	7	12	1	1	117	.256	.310	.423	.242	17	.255
1996	Boston	AL	102	24	2	0	4	1	0	0	78	.235	.243	.373	.201	7	.212
1997	Boston	AL	494	130	24	2	37	56	1	0	364	.263	.338	.545	.282	77	

Malave has regressed since the big 1994 and 1995, and at 26 it's an open question whether he'll have a career. Has to hit to keep a job since he definitely doesn't get there on defense. Vlad likes his chances, but I wonder who he's going to take those 494 at bats from?

WALT McKEEL **C** **1972** **Age 25**

Year	Team	Lge	AB	H	DB	TP	HR	BB	SB	CS	OUT	BA	OBA	SA	EQA	EQR	Peak
1993	Lynchburg	Caro	256	55	12	1	4	23	0	0	201	.215	.280	.316	.195	17	.219
1994	Sarasota	Flor	140	36	4	1	3	13	1	0	104	.257	.320	.364	.232	13	.256
1994	New Britain	East	167	29	5	1	1	7	0	0	138	.174	.207	.234	.112	3	.123
1995	Sarasota	Flor	208	67	6	0	9	22	4	2	143	.322	.387	.481	.289	32	.315
1995	Trenton	East	87	22	2	1	2	8	1	1	66	.253	.316	.368	.228	8	.246
1996	Trenton	East	482	142	13	1	15	55	2	2	342	.295	.367	.419	.265	62	.283
1997	Boston	AL	494	135	18	1	16	64	3	2	361	.273	.357	.411	.256	60	

The organization raves about him, and now that he's started to hit a little he's in the mix. Has been quoted as saying a key to his improvement is a better grasp of the strike zone, a positive indicator. Seems ticketed for Pawtucket in 1997, but any problems in Boston could have him in the majors. Recommended, but be patient.

ROBERTO MEJIA   **2B**   **1972**   **Age 25**

Year	Team	Lge	AB	H	DB	TP	HR	BB	SB	CS	OUT	BA	OBA	SA	EQA	EQR	Peak
1993	Colo. Springs	PCL	282	71	8	1	11	17	7	3	214	.252	.294	.404	.234	28	.261
1993	Colorado	NL	227	48	12	2	6	16	3	1	180	.211	.263	.361	.206	17	.230
1994	Colo. Springs	PCL	273	63	15	1	5	21	5	3	212	.231	.286	.348	.211	22	.234
1994	Colorado	NL	116	27	6	1	4	16	3	1	90	.233	.326	.405	.245	13	.269
1995	Colo. Springs	PCL	139	35	7	0	3	7	0	1	105	.252	.288	.367	.216	11	.233
1995	Colorado	NL	51	7	0	0	1	1	0	1	45	.137	.154	.196	-.094	-1	-.101
1996	Indianapolis	AmA	386	114	21	7	13	33	12	4	276	.295	.351	.487	.278	56	.297
1996	Pawtucket	Inter	74	17	3	0	0	6	3	1	58	.230	.287	.270	.191	5	.210
1997	*Boston*	*AL*	*407*	*105*	*29*	*8*	*9*	*32*	*9*	*4*	*306*	*.258*	*.312*	*.435*	*.247*	*46*	

Plate discipline is still a problem for Mejia, acquired for Kevin Mitchell in July. The unsettled second base situation in Boston means he has to be considered an option. He's still young enough to have a career, but his next chance is probably his last.

TIM NAEHRING   **3B**   **1967**   **Age 30**

Year	Team	Lge	AB	H	DB	TP	HR	BB	SB	CS	OUT	BA	OBA	SA	EQA	EQR	Peak
1993	Pawtucket	Inter	207	59	7	0	7	34	0	1	149	.285	.386	.420	.271	29	.282
1993	Boston	AL	127	42	6	0	3	11	1	0	85	.331	.384	.449	.283	18	.295
1994	Boston	AL	298	82	18	1	7	30	1	3	219	.275	.341	.413	.250	34	.257
1995	Boston	AL	438	139	29	2	11	78	0	2	301	.317	.421	.468	.298	73	.301
1996	Boston	AL	426	119	11	0	18	49	2	1	308	.279	.354	.432	.263	55	.261
1997	*Boston*	*AL*	*413*	*119*	*15*	*1*	*15*	*77*	*2*	*2*	*296*	*.288*	*.400*	*.438*	*.280*	*62*	

Naehring started the year where he left off 1995, but back spasms and a bum knee ruined his second half. He gained free agency in the labor agreement and probably won't be back in Boston in 1997. He should be a starter somewhere, contributing a good OBP, doubles power and if his back lets him, good defense.

TROT NIXON   **OF**   **1974**   **Age 23**

Year	Team	Lge	AB	H	DB	TP	HR	BB	SB	CS	OUT	BA	OBA	SA	EQA	EQR	Peak
1994	Lynchburg	Caro	272	60	5	0	9	37	5	2	214	.221	.314	.338	.220	24	.250
1995	Sarasota	Flor	279	81	6	2	7	39	4	3	201	.290	.377	.401	.264	36	.295
1995	Trenton	East	97	17	2	1	2	6	1	1	81	.175	.223	.278	.151	4	.167
1996	Trenton	East	452	109	9	3	10	45	6	4	347	.241	.310	.341	.218	39	.241
1997	*Boston*	*AL*	*303*	*79*	*11*	*3*	*8*	*33*	*7*	*4*	*228*	*.261*	*.333*	*.396*	*.243*	*33*	

The back injury that ruined his 1994 season has apparently had a residual effect. Nixon still has good plate discipline, but no longer hits for power. This has killed his prospect status, and with the hitters ahead of him, he'll be hard-pressed to get it back.

TROY O'LEARY   **OF**   **1970**   **Age 27**

Year	Team	Lge	AB	H	DB	TP	HR	BB	SB	CS	OUT	BA	OBA	SA	EQA	EQR	Peak
1993	New Orleans	AmA	397	109	24	1	9	46	6	2	290	.275	.350	.408	.256	48	.279
1994	New Orleans	AmA	232	78	15	3	10	33	8	1	155	.336	.419	.556	.322	46	.344
1994	Milwaukee	AL	66	18	0	1	2	5	1	1	49	.273	.324	.394	.239	7	.257
1995	Boston	AL	403	128	34	6	11	29	5	3	278	.318	.363	.514	.288	62	.303
1996	Boston	AL	494	125	25	5	15	46	3	2	371	.253	.317	.415	.243	54	.252
1997	*Boston*	*AL*	*376*	*117*	*31*	*4*	*13*	*26*	*13*	*5*	*264*	*.311*	*.356*	*.519*	*.286*	*58*	

O'Leary is the poster boy for Duquette's waiver-wire fetish. He was claimed from Milwaukee in March of 1995 and had a fine season. He slipped in 1996, partially as a result of increased playing time against lefties, who he can't hit at all (.550 OPS in 1996, .541 career, vs. .819 and .839 against RHP). Can contribute as a platooner, but his role in Boston is tenuous.

RUDY PEMBERTON   OF   1970   Age 27

Year	Team	Lge	AB	H	DB	TP	HR	BB	SB	CS	OUT	BA	OBA	SA	EQA	EQR	Peak
1993	London	East	477	122	16	1	15	23	8	6	361	.256	.290	.388	.225	43	.245
1994	Toledo	Inter	365	107	10	1	12	18	21	6	264	.293	.326	.425	.257	44	.275
1995	Toledo	Inter	233	82	12	2	8	17	6	3	154	.352	.396	.524	.304	39	.320
1996	Oklahoma	AmA	71	17	1	0	2	3	2	3	57	.239	.270	.338	.195	5	.199
1996	Pawtucket	Inter	397	124	19	2	24	20	12	5	278	.312	.345	.552	.291	63	.302
1997	*Boston*	*AL*	*634*	*195*	*41*	*2*	*21*	*30*	*18*	*5*	*444*	*.308*	*.339*	*.478*	*.272*	*85*	

Hit .512/.556/.780 in a late season callup, giving him a heck of a Strat card. Pemberton has no plate discipline, although when you hit .300 with this much power we can overlook that. Rudy's just a one-trick pony, but he's figured out the International League and deserves some kind of job in the majors. Over the last two years, he has hit righties better than lefties, a good sign if you just want to hand him a DH job.

GREG PIRKL   1B/DH/RRP?   1971   Age 26

Year	Team	Lge	AB	H	DB	TP	HR	BB	SB	CS	OUT	BA	OBA	SA	EQA	EQR	Peak
1993	Calgary	PCL	434	116	10	1	18	14	2	2	320	.267	.290	.419	.235	43	.260
1994	Calgary	PCL	342	95	9	0	18	23	1	1	248	.278	.323	.462	.259	42	.281
1994	Seattle	AL	53	14	3	0	6	1	0	0	39	.264	.278	.660	.290	9	.313
1995	Tacoma	PCL	177	54	5	1	15	14	1	1	124	.305	.356	.599	.302	31	.323
1996	Tacoma	PCL	352	107	14	1	21	15	1	1	246	.304	.332	.528	.280	51	.295

After not being able to crack a lineup for four years, Pirkl was designated for assignment by Veterans 'R Us in the Pacific Northwest to make room for Jeff Manto. I'm not making this up. The Red Sox picked him up and are trying to make a pitcher out of him. They seem to like these little experiments, moving scab OF Ron Mahay to pitching and pitcher Roy Padilla now an outfielder. Check back in 1998.

ARQUIMEDEZ POZO   3B/2B   1974   Age 23

Year	Team	Lge	AB	H	DB	TP	HR	BB	SB	CS	OUT	BA	OBA	SA	EQA	EQR	Peak
1993	Riverside	Calif	519	157	26	3	12	37	5	4	366	.303	.349	.434	.262	64	.302
1994	Jacksonville	South	458	126	16	1	15	34	7	4	336	.275	.325	.413	.247	51	.281
1995	Tacoma	PCL	455	135	15	3	13	29	3	2	322	.297	.339	.429	.257	54	.288
1996	Tacoma	PCL	372	103	9	2	16	38	3	2	271	.277	.344	.441	.261	47	.288
1996	Boston	AL	58	10	2	1	1	2	1	0	48	.172	.200	.293	.152	2	.169
1997	*Boston*	*AL*	*489*	*143*	*20*	*3*	*22*	*30*	*4*	*2*	*348*	*.292*	*.333*	*.481*	*.267*	*64*	

Pozo stagnated after the strong season as a 19-year-old, but he's still a good prospect. Decent plate discipline and fair power, only in his first season as a third baseman. Future uncertain, but he's the best second baseman the Red Sox have and that's his best position. A Garciaparra/Pozo double play combination could be excellent. Recommended.

DONNIE SADLER   SS/2B   1975   Age 22

Year	Team	Lge	AB	H	DB	TP	HR	BB	SB	CS	OUT	BA	OBA	SA	EQA	EQR	Peak
1995	Michigan	Midw	459	118	16	4	9	63	16	7	348	.257	.347	.368	.244	51	.278
1996	Trenton	East	467	123	19	5	6	34	24	5	349	.263	.313	.364	.236	47	.263
1997	*Boston*	*AL*	*494*	*135*	*23*	*6*	*11*	*51*	*33*	*6*	*365*	*.273*	*.341*	*.411*	*.259*	*63*	

As mentioned, Sadler was jerked around by the Boston development people this year, moving to center field for a month in May, then back to shortstop after his replacement was injured. He was hitting .317 at the time of the move, slumped afterward, but there should be no long-term effects. Sadler's playing second base in the Arizona Fall League, and it looks like he'll be there in 1997. He's a fair prospect, and since the Red Sox are always desperate to add speed, could be in Boston this year.

DAMIAN SAPP   C   1976   Age 21

Year	Team	Lge	AB	H	DB	TP	HR	BB	SB	CS	OUT	BA	OBA	SA	EQA	EQR	Peak
1995	Utica	NY-P	114	17	2	0	1	10	0	1	98	.149	.218	.193	.077	1	.091
1996	Michigan	Midw	354	112	11	1	17	29	2	1	243	.316	.368	.497	.286	53	.326
1997	*Boston*	*AL*	*424*	*118*	*28*	*2*	*16*	*44*	*6*	*2*	*308*	*.278*	*.346*	*.467*	*.268*	*57*	

Because you can never have too many catchers.... Sapp is a 1995 draft pick. It's early, but he looks like a hitter. The jump to AA will tell us everything. Two years out, recommended anyway.

BILL SELBY **3B/2B** **1970** **Age 27**

Year	Team	Lge	AB	H	DB	TP	HR	BB	SB	CS	OUT	BA	OBA	SA	EQA	EQR	Peak
1993	Lynchburg	Caro	403	90	12	1	6	23	1	1	314	.223	.265	.303	.184	23	.200
1994	Lynchburg	Caro	357	99	13	0	14	24	2	1	259	.277	.323	.431	.251	41	.269
1994	New Britain	East	112	29	1	0	2	14	0	1	84	.259	.341	.321	.223	10	.238
1995	Trenton	East	473	139	21	2	15	42	3	4	338	.294	.351	.442	.264	60	.279
1996	Pawtucket	Inter	261	62	11	3	10	23	0	2	201	.238	.299	.418	.234	27	.244
1996	Boston	AL	94	25	3	0	3	9	1	1	70	.266	.330	.394	.242	10	.252

Selby's utility infield material and can help a team in that role. Good secondary skills; not enough to hold a regular job, but with three right-handed hitters at second, short and third, the Red Sox can use a guy like this.

MIKE STANLEY **C** **1963** **Age 34**

Year	Team	Lge	AB	H	DB	TP	HR	BB	SB	CS	OUT	BA	OBA	SA	EQA	EQR	Peak
1993	NY Yankees	AL	436	144	17	1	32	61	1	1	293	.330	.412	.594	.323	87	.317
1994	NY Yankees	AL	296	93	16	0	20	40	0	0	203	.314	.396	.571	.312	55	.301
1995	NY Yankees	AL	402	111	25	1	21	58	1	1	292	.276	.367	.500	.283	62	.269
1996	Boston	AL	393	103	19	1	23	69	2	0	290	.262	.372	.491	.284	62	.269
1997	*Boston*	*AL*	*369*	*102*	*10*	*0*	*19*	*67*	*0*	*0*	*267*	*.276*	*.388*	*.458*	*.280*	*56*	

Stanley picked up his end of a dual option after Boston declined theirs. He's still a pretty good player, but the neck problems make him a question mark. Boston's deep behind the plate and is talking about making Stanley the DH. Considering the many options they have for that spot, this seems wasteful. Stanley loses a lot of value if used as a DH.

LEE TINSLEY **CF** **1969** **Age 28**

Year	Team	Lge	AB	H	DB	TP	HR	BB	SB	CS	OUT	BA	OBA	SA	EQA	EQR	Peak
1993	Calgary	PCL	441	116	17	7	12	45	20	6	331	.263	.331	.415	.253	53	.271
1994	Boston	AL	144	32	1	0	3	19	12	0	112	.222	.313	.292	.223	13	.236
1995	Boston	AL	344	101	17	1	8	40	18	8	251	.294	.367	.419	.267	46	.278
1996	Boston	AL	191	45	6	1	3	13	6	8	154	.236	.284	.325	.197	13	.202
1996	Philadelphia	NL	52	7	0	0	0	5	1	4	49	.135	.211	.135	-.100	-1	-.089
1997	*Seattle*	*AL*	*178*	*45*	*8*	*0*	*8*	*29*	*8*	*7*	*140*	*.253*	*.357*	*.433*	*.262*	*25*	

Tinsley has found his niche as a pinch-runner/defensive replacement after a year as a mediocre starter. He's got plenty of use left as a bench player, with speed, some plate discipline and a lefty bat. Traded to Seattle, where he may be the regular left fielder. If so, he'll be replacement-level.

JOHN VALENTIN **SS** **1967** **Age 30**

Year	Team	Lge	AB	H	DB	TP	HR	BB	SB	CS	OUT	BA	OBA	SA	EQA	EQR	Peak
1993	Boston	AL	469	131	40	3	13	52	3	3	341	.279	.351	.461	.268	63	.279
1994	Boston	AL	302	95	24	2	10	42	3	1	208	.315	.398	.507	.300	51	.307
1995	Boston	AL	526	162	34	2	31	82	20	5	369	.308	.401	.557	.312	101	.315
1996	Boston	AL	522	150	29	3	12	63	9	10	382	.287	.364	.423	.262	67	.260
1997	*Boston*	*AL*	*552*	*168*	*43*	*2*	*20*	*82*	*3*	*2*	*386*	*.304*	*.394*	*.498*	*.293*	*90*	

A bum right shoulder dragged him down from "superstar" to "above average." His value drops if he's a third baseman, and if he's in Boston, that's where he'll play. Very likely to be traded. Still wildly underrated.

MO VAUGHN **1B** **1968** **Age 29**

Year	Team	Lge	AB	H	DB	TP	HR	BB	SB	CS	OUT	BA	OBA	SA	EQA	EQR	Peak
1993	Boston	AL	542	163	27	1	34	82	4	2	381	.301	.393	.542	.304	97	.320
1994	Boston	AL	395	122	22	1	27	57	4	3	277	.309	.396	.575	.311	74	.323
1995	Boston	AL	556	172	29	3	42	69	11	4	388	.309	.386	.599	.314	107	.322
1996	Boston	AL	628	199	23	1	44	95	2	0	429	.317	.407	.567	.316	120	.319
1997	*Boston*	*AL*	*620*	*196*	*24*	*0*	*45*	*87*	*4*	*1*	*425*	*.316*	*.400*	*.573*	*.313*	*116*	

Mo can hit a little, and is now almost as good against lefties as righties. His defense has improved as well. None of this makes him an MVP, or even a candidate, but he's a good first baseman and will be one for a while.

TYRONE WOODS   DH   1970   Age 27

Year	Team	Lge	AB	H	DB	TP	HR	BB	SB	CS	OUT	BA	OBA	SA	EQA	EQR	Peak
1993	Harrisburg	East	327	82	9	1	15	32	2	1	246	.251	.318	.422	.245	37	.267
1994	Harrisburg	East	137	42	11	1	5	11	1	1	96	.307	.358	.511	.284	21	.305
1994	Ottawa	Inter	302	69	7	0	7	26	1	1	234	.228	.290	.321	.202	21	.216
1995	Rochester	Inter	241	59	11	1	8	24	2	2	184	.245	.313	.398	.236	25	.250
1996	Trenton	East	372	116	11	1	23	51	4	2	258	.312	.395	.532	.303	65	.315

Woods is listed here just to make the point that he is not a prospect, so when you hear his name this spring, ignore it. Just a good AA hitter, and he's found his level.

ALAN ZINTER   1B   1968   Age 29

Year	Team	Lge	AB	H	DB	TP	HR	BB	SB	CS	OUT	BA	OBA	SA	EQA	EQR	Peak
1993	Binghamton	East	449	115	15	2	23	81	1	0	334	.256	.370	.452	.273	65	.288
1994	Toledo	Inter	482	113	21	3	20	66	9	3	372	.234	.327	.415	.247	57	.257
1995	Toledo	Inter	344	80	12	2	14	37	3	1	265	.233	.307	.401	.235	36	.241
1996	Pawtucket	Inter	362	94	14	2	24	57	3	1	269	.260	.360	.508	.283	57	.285
1997	*Boston*	*AL*	*466*	*119*	*20*	*2*	*27*	*105*	*5*	*4*	*351*	*.255*	*.392*	*.481*	*.285*	*76*	

If you play at a level long enough, you master it. Zinter's been in the International League for 1200 at bats and finally had a good year. Unless he moves back to catcher he has no shot a career.

STAN BELINDA   RRP   1967   Age 30

YR	TEAM	Lge	IP	H	ER	HR	BB	K	ERA	W	L	H/9	HR/9	BB/9	K/9	KW
1993	Kansas City	AL	27.0	29	10	2	8	26	3.33	2	1	9.67	.67	2.67	8.67	2.22
1993	Pittsburgh	NL	40.7	37	16	5	15	29	3.54	3	2	8.19	1.11	3.32	6.42	1.31
1994	Kansas City	AL	48.7	43	25	5	26	36	4.62	2	3	7.95	.92	4.81	6.66	1.02
1995	Boston	AL	68.3	52	18	5	29	57	2.37	6	2	6.85	.66	3.82	7.51	1.55
1996	Boston	AL	28.7	28	16	2	21	17	5.02	1	2	8.79	.63	6.59	5.34	.13

An elbow injury killed his year, but he's been pretty effective over the years when healthy. Good strikeout rates, he keeps the ball in the park and has no significant platoon split. If he's healthy, a safe bet for 70 good innings.

MARK BRANDENBURG   RRP   1971   Age 26

YR	TEAM	Lge	IP	H	ER	HR	BB	K	ERA	W	L	H/9	HR/9	BB/9	K/9	KW
1993	Charleston, SC	S Atl	70.0	83	25	3	31	39	3.21	5	3	10.67	.39	3.99	5.01	.67
1994	Charlotte, FL	Flor	37.3	31	5	2	20	34	1.21	4	0	7.47	.48	4.82	8.20	1.53
1994	Tulsa	Texas	57.0	58	16	3	18	46	2.53	4	2	9.16	.47	2.84	7.26	1.71
1995	Oklahoma	AmA	55.3	55	14	2	23	45	2.28	5	1	8.95	.33	3.74	7.32	1.50
1995	Texas	AL	27.7	33	14	5	7	21	4.55	1	2	10.73	1.63	2.28	6.83	1.71
1996	Boston	AL	28.0	26	9	4	9	28	2.89	2	1	8.36	1.29	2.89	9.00	2.28
1996	Texas	AL	47.7	43	15	3	26	35	2.83	3	2	8.12	.57	4.91	6.61	.98

Brandenburg is a sidearming right-hander, despite which he doesn't get a lot of ground balls. He improved his strikeout rate this year, and he's capable of handling a large workload, both good things. He's not closer material at all, so this is as good as it gets. He'll have more good years.

KEVAN CANNON   LRP   1975   Age 22

YR	TEAM	Lge	IP	H	ER	HR	BB	K	ERA	W	L	H/9	HR/9	BB/9	K/9	KW
1995	Utica	NY-P	50.3	75	37	4	35	30	6.62	2	4	13.41	.72	6.26	5.36	.22
1996	Michigan	Midw	64.3	87	25	1	27	45	3.50	4	3	12.17	.14	3.78	6.30	1.15

Michigan is a good pitcher's park in a tough league for hitters, but no shots (unadjusted) in 73 innings gets your attention. Still has to maneuver through three levels, but keep an eye on him.

ROGER CLEMENS   RSP   1963   Age 34

YR	TEAM	Lge	IP	H	ER	HR	BB	K	ERA	W	L	H/9	HR/9	BB/9	K/9	KW
1993	Boston	AL	189.3	168	75	17	75	164	3.57	12	9	7.99	.81	3.57	7.80	1.71
1994	Boston	AL	167.0	123	43	14	76	164	2.32	14	5	6.63	.75	4.10	8.84	1.92
1995	Boston	AL	140.7	135	53	14	63	132	3.39	9	7	8.64	.90	4.03	8.45	1.81
1996	Boston	AL	241.3	198	70	16	110	247	2.61	19	8	7.38	.60	4.10	9.21	2.04

The inflated offense of the last few years has disguised his continued brilliance. Because of this, Clemens is now facing free agency with the Red Sox questioning his future. Dumb. He's a great pitcher, in fantastic shape and sucks up an enormous number of innings. I'd sign him in a minute. First-ballot Hall of Famer.

PAXTON CRAWFORD   RSP   1978   Age 19

YR	TEAM	Lge	IP	H	ER	HR	BB	K	ERA	W	L	H/9	HR/9	BB/9	K/9	KW
1996	Michigan	Midw	110.7	155	68	7	54	66	5.53	4	8	12.61	.57	4.39	5.37	.69

Crawford is one of a number of good-looking pitching prospects the Red Sox have at the lower levels. He was a 1995 draftee that the Red Sox are high on and handling properly: He averaged under six innings per start despite pitching well.

VAUGHN ESHELMAN   LBP   1969   Age 28

YR	TEAM	Lge	IP	H	ER	HR	BB	K	ERA	W	L	H/9	HR/9	BB/9	K/9	KW
1993	Frederick	Caro	124.0	161	80	11	87	77	5.81	5	9	11.69	.80	6.31	5.59	.28
1994	Bowie	East	150.3	202	82	14	80	97	4.91	7	10	12.09	.84	4.79	5.81	.74
1995	Boston	AL	81.3	84	36	3	38	41	3.98	5	4	9.30	.33	4.20	4.54	.46
1996	Pawtucket	Inter	42.0	40	17	6	24	23	3.64	3	2	8.57	1.29	5.14	4.93	.36
1996	Boston	AL	89.0	99	57	10	59	56	5.76	3	7	10.01	1.01	5.97	5.66	.40

The Red Sox' bad Vaughn is a stiff, still riding the 3-0 start in 1995 that helped the Red Sox start strong. There's nothing about him to like. OK, his name is fun to say. But nothing else.

JIM FARRELL   RSP   1974   Age 23

YR	TEAM	Lge	IP	H	ER	HR	BB	K	ERA	W	L	H/9	HR/9	BB/9	K/9	KW
1995	Michigan	Midw	59.7	80	36	11	32	46	5.43	2	5	12.07	1.66	4.83	6.94	1.11
1996	Michigan	Midw	38.0	50	16	3	22	20	3.79	2	2	11.84	.71	5.21	4.74	.28
1996	Sarasota	Flor	119.7	139	61	15	50	67	4.59	6	7	10.45	1.13	3.76	5.04	.74

Farrell is part of the Crawford class in the low minors. He's older than the rest, a college product, but like Crawford, Andy Yount and Bobby Rodgers, looked good in A ball. All four of these guys won't pan out, but you would expect at least one of them to end up having a career.

RICH GARCES   RRP   1971   Age 26

YR	TEAM	Lge	IP	H	ER	HR	BB	K	ERA	W	L	H/9	HR/9	BB/9	K/9	KW
1993	Portland, OR	PCL	49.3	66	46	4	73	38	8.39	1	4	12.04	.73	13.32	6.93	-1.02
1994	Nashville	South	69.7	85	45	6	45	60	5.81	3	5	10.98	.78	5.81	7.75	1.13
1995	Iowa	AmA	27.0	27	9	3	12	32	3.00	2	1	9.00	1.00	4.00	10.67	2.56
1995	Chicago Cubs	NL	11.0	11	5	0	4	5	4.09	0	1	9.00	.00	3.27	4.09	.55
1995	Florida	NL	13.3	14	8	1	9	14	5.40	0	1	9.45	.68	6.08	9.45	1.63
1996	Pawtucket	Inter	14.7	11	3	2	7	11	1.84	2	0	6.75	1.23	4.30	6.75	1.18
1996	Boston	AL	44.0	38	17	4	33	53	3.48	3	2	7.77	.82	6.75	10.84	1.93

It seems like forever since he was going to be the Twins closer. He's just 26, and may be about to start a nice career as a middle reliever. Throws very hard. Recommended.

TOM GORDON   RSP   1968   Age 29

YR	TEAM	Lge	IP	H	ER	HR	BB	K	ERA	W	L	H/9	HR/9	BB/9	K/9	KW
1993	Kansas City	AL	152.7	126	50	11	83	147	2.95	11	6	7.43	.65	4.89	8.67	1.67
1994	Kansas City	AL	154.3	125	54	13	91	122	3.15	10	7	7.29	.76	5.31	7.11	1.04
1995	Kansas City	AL	189.7	201	88	11	94	120	4.18	10	11	9.54	.52	4.46	5.69	.78
1996	Boston	AL	217.0	223	102	23	109	164	4.23	11	13	9.25	.95	4.52	6.80	1.14

Well, heck, I don't know. At least for a while you could count on him to be tough to hit, although he'd give up lots of walks. He even gave back that part of his game over the last two years. He's still got a good arm, and hasn't missed a start in three years. I don't think he can sustain this level, and will either revert to being fairly good or fall apart completely. Recommended, but roto players beware: Even when he's good, he kills your ratio.

REGGIE HARRIS   RRP   1969   Age 28

YR	TEAM	Lge	IP	H	ER	HR	BB	K	ERA	W	L	H/9	HR/9	BB/9	K/9	KW
1993	Jacksonville	South	34.0	38	25	5	28	22	6.62	1	3	10.06	1.32	7.41	5.82	.09
1993	Calgary	PCL	81.0	69	42	7	72	60	4.67	4	5	7.67	.78	8.00	6.67	.22
1994	Calgary	PCL	93.3	120	72	17	61	61	6.94	2	8	11.57	1.64	5.88	5.88	.49
1996	Trenton	East	34.3	21	5	3	23	32	1.31	4	0	5.50	.79	6.03	8.39	1.29

Ahem. Now hear this: Reggie Harris is going to be one of the great stories of 1997. The former first round pick of the Sox is back with them by way of Oakland, shoulder surgery, Kansas City and Taiwan. He was unhittable at Pawtucket. I wouldn't make him Mariano Rivera just yet, but I think he'll be one of the top middle relievers in the American League this year.

JOE HUDSON　　　　RRP　　1971　Age 26

YR	TEAM	Lge	IP	H	ER	HR	BB	K	ERA	W	L	H/9	HR/9	BB/9	K/9	KW
1993	Lynchburg	Caro	72.3	119	56	1	57	39	6.97	2	6	14.81	.12	7.09	4.85	-.16
1994	Sarasota	Flor	43.7	47	19	1	34	25	3.92	3	2	9.69	.21	7.01	5.15	-.03
1994	New Britain	East	35.0	59	20	0	24	18	5.14	2	2	15.17	.00	6.17	4.63	.00
1995	Trenton	East	29.0	26	8	0	21	19	2.48	2	1	8.07	.00	6.52	5.90	.34
1995	Boston	AL	46.3	51	16	2	24	29	3.11	3	2	9.91	.39	4.66	5.63	.71
1996	Pawtucket	Inter	31.7	29	15	0	25	15	4.26	2	2	8.24	.00	7.11	4.26	-.36
1996	Boston	AL	45.3	50	25	3	33	18	4.96	2	3	9.93	.60	6.55	3.57	-.45

I love guys who don't give up homers, but Hudson manages to still look lousy to me. He got 90 innings in Boston the last two years, mostly because the Sox bullpen had more turnover than the upper management at Apple.

KERRY LACY　　　　RRP　　1973　Age 24

YR	TEAM	Lge	IP	H	ER	HR	BB	K	ERA	W	L	H/9	HR/9	BB/9	K/9	KW
1993	Charleston, SC	S Atl	51.0	66	28	1	43	32	4.94	2	4	11.65	.18	7.59	5.65	-.01
1994	Tulsa	Texas	58.0	56	29	5	46	33	4.50	3	3	8.69	.78	7.14	5.12	-.08
1995	Tulsa	Texas	74.3	102	47	6	50	42	5.69	3	5	12.35	.73	6.05	5.09	.18
1996	Oklahoma	AmA	53.0	53	19	2	21	26	3.23	4	2	9.00	.34	3.57	4.42	.58
1996	Boston	AL	11.0	13	4	2	8	9	3.27	1	0	10.64	1.64	6.55	7.36	.82

Lacy, along with Brandenburg, was the booty for Mike Stanton at the trade deadline. He's a serviceable reliever, not overpowering, but better than, say, the guy above him. Seriously, he could do just about anything for 70 innings this year.

MIKE MADDUX　　　RRP　　1962　Age 35

YR	TEAM	Lge	IP	H	ER	HR	BB	K	ERA	W	L	H/9	HR/9	BB/9	K/9	KW
1993	NY Mets	NL	72.3	72	31	3	35	55	3.86	4	4	8.96	.37	4.35	6.84	1.19
1994	NY Mets	NL	43.3	44	21	7	17	30	4.36	2	3	9.14	1.45	3.53	6.23	1.19
1995	Boston	AL	88.7	85	30	5	17	65	3.05	6	4	8.63	.51	1.73	6.60	1.77
1996	Pawtucket	Inter	13.7	13	4	2	3	7	2.63	1	1	8.56	1.32	1.98	4.61	1.04
1996	Boston	AL	65.0	67	27	10	28	31	3.74	4	3	9.28	1.38	3.88	4.29	.46

He's performing in the biggest little-brother shadow since Frank Stallone released an album between "Rocky IV" and "Rambo." Maddux has been an effective pitcher in his own right the last five years in a setup/spot starter role, but battled elbow problems in 1996. He deserves at least a chance to regroup, but I think his run is over.

PAT MAHOMES　　　RRP　　1971　Age 26

YR	TEAM	Lge	IP	H	ER	HR	BB	K	ERA	W	L	H/9	HR/9	BB/9	K/9	KW
1993	Portland, OR	PCL	105.7	93	39	12	67	76	3.32	7	5	7.92	1.02	5.71	6.47	.73
1993	Minnesota	AL	37.7	45	28	8	18	24	6.69	1	3	10.75	1.91	4.30	5.73	.84
1994	Minnesota	AL	119.7	115	53	20	66	52	3.99	7	6	8.65	1.50	4.96	3.91	.06
1995	Minnesota	AL	96.0	92	57	20	49	67	5.34	4	7	8.62	1.88	4.59	6.28	.95
1996	Salt Lake City	PCL	31.7	32	11	0	15	33	3.13	2	2	9.09	.00	4.26	9.38	2.06
1996	Boston	AL	12.3	8	6	3	6	6	4.38	0	1	5.84	2.19	4.38	4.38	.36
1996	Minnesota	AL	46.0	55	28	8	28	29	5.48	2	3	10.76	1.57	5.48	5.67	.52

There has been some speculation, much of it racially tinged, that the failure of some of the Twin pitching prospects to develop has been the fault of Dick Such, the pitching coach in Minnesota. Mahomes and LaTroy Hawkins' failures are the primary evidence for this, particularly in light of their performance in the PCL. Mahomes is just 26 and his arm hasn't been abused, so he'll get the first chance to test this theory. Fenway isn't the best place for a young pitcher to suddenly find himself, and the Red Sox have about 12 better starting candidates, so Mahomes' next opportunity will probably come elsewhere.

RAFAEL ORELLANO　　LSP　　1973　Age 24

YR	TEAM	Lge	IP	H	ER	HR	BB	K	ERA	W	L	H/9	HR/9	BB/9	K/9	KW
1993	Utica	NY-P	14.7	29	16	4	12	7	9.82	0	2	17.80	2.45	7.36	4.30	-.41
1994	Sarasota	Flor	88.7	81	26	7	34	78	2.64	7	3	8.22	.71	3.45	7.92	1.78
1995	Trenton	East	173.0	180	71	23	90	124	3.69	10	9	9.36	1.20	4.68	6.45	.98
1996	Pawtucket	Inter	96.7	119	76	17	75	54	7.08	3	8	11.08	1.58	6.98	5.03	-.07

Orellano came into the season as the Sox' top pitching prospect. He battled an injury early on, and after posting a 16.47 ERA in his first six starts went on the DL. He pitched much better after returning (5.81 ERA in 16 appearances with improved control) and closed well (4.53 in six starts, better ratios), so I think he'll be back in 1997. Very thin.

CARL PAVANO RSP 1976 Age 21

YR	TEAM	Lge	IP	H	ER	HR	BB	K	ERA	W	L	H/9	HR/9	BB/9	K/9	KW
1995	Michigan	Midw	125.3	146	63	9	71	90	4.52	6	8	10.48	.65	5.10	6.46	.88
1996	Trenton	East	171.3	180	64	17	62	108	3.36	11	8	9.46	.89	3.26	5.67	1.08

Pavano sprinted past Orellano on the prospect lists with a great year at Trenton. The Thunder play in a good pitcher's park, but there's still a lot to like here. Pavano's a big guy (6' 5", 225) in the mold of this other pretty good Red Sox right-hander. He understands the value of conditioning, again like that other Sox starter, and he closed with a fury, going 10-1, 1.96 and allowing just one baserunner an inning. He and Suppan are going to be a great 1-2 punch around 1999.

JUAN PENA RSP 1977 Age 20

YR	TEAM	Lge	IP	H	ER	HR	BB	K	ERA	W	L	H/9	HR/9	BB/9	K/9	KW
1996	Michigan	Midw	167.0	192	72	20	45	97	3.88	10	9	10.35	1.08	2.43	5.23	1.14

Pena's a long way off radar, and just based on ability has a good chance to be the name on everyone's lips in two years. The one negative, and it's a big one, is that he averaged 7 1/3 innings a start this year, a frightening number for a 19-year-old. He'll probably get hurt in the next 16 months. This idiocy will end when some 21-year-old whose arm falls off sues and wins a monster worker's compensation award.

CHUCK RICCI RRP 1969 Age 28

YR	TEAM	Lge	IP	H	ER	HR	BB	K	ERA	W	L	H/9	HR/9	BB/9	K/9	KW
1993	Bowie	East	75.3	85	35	8	28	63	4.18	4	4	10.15	.96	3.35	7.53	1.67
1994	Reading	East	17.3	13	1	0	6	17	.52	2	0	6.75	.00	3.12	8.83	2.16
1994	Scranton-WB	Inter	61.0	66	28	7	28	60	4.13	3	4	9.74	1.03	4.13	8.85	1.92
1995	Scranton-WB	Inter	61.0	53	20	7	32	56	2.95	5	2	7.82	1.03	4.72	8.26	1.57
1996	Pawtucket	Inter	76.3	59	24	11	41	65	2.83	5	3	6.96	1.30	4.83	7.66	1.35

Ricci has bounced around some, and looked like he was the closer-in-waiting in Philadelphia before Bottalico lapped him. Left Scranton/Wilkes-Barre, undoubtedly at high speed, as a six-year free agent and was effective as the part-time Pawtucket closer. 2fi years at AAA tends to label a guy, so he's in a bad spot. Free agent again.

BRIAN ROSE RSP 1976 Age 21

YR	TEAM	Lge	IP	H	ER	HR	BB	K	ERA	W	L	H/9	HR/9	BB/9	K/9	KW
1995	Michigan	Midw	120.7	158	63	7	43	68	4.70	5	8	11.78	.52	3.21	5.07	.89
1996	Trenton	East	150.0	185	84	22	59	86	5.04	7	10	11.10	1.32	3.54	5.16	.83

Rose advanced a level without really developing, although simply staying healthy is a marker in his favor. Despite good walk/strikeout numbers, Rose hit 13 batters last year, on top of nine in 1995. Now, it's dangerous to read too much into that, but I'll do it anyway: It looks to me like Rose is not afraid to pitch inside. Rose also has a high HR/IP ratio, a possible indication that he works the inside half of the plate a lot. Recommended, despite the off year.

AARON SELE RSP 1970 Age 27

YR	TEAM	Lge	IP	H	ER	HR	BB	K	ERA	W	L	H/9	HR/9	BB/9	K/9	KW
1993	Pawtucket	Inter	89.0	79	26	8	33	70	2.63	7	3	7.99	.81	3.34	7.08	1.53
1993	Boston	AL	110.0	97	32	5	53	95	2.62	8	4	7.94	.41	4.34	7.77	1.51
1994	Boston	AL	142.7	132	49	12	64	102	3.09	10	6	8.33	.76	4.04	6.43	1.14
1995	Boston	AL	32.0	32	11	3	14	21	3.09	3	1	9.00	.84	3.94	5.91	.98
1996	Boston	AL	158.7	172	78	11	70	131	4.42	8	10	9.76	.62	3.97	7.43	1.48

OK, that was the post-surgery consolidation year. Now we have some fun. Sele wasn't at all terrible last year: only 14 homers in 29 starts and a 2-to-1 K/BB ratio, 3-to-1 after the All-Star break. The biggest thing he did was give up too many singles, correctable by 1) an improved Boston defense and 2) expected improvement in his pitching. He's going to have a very good year. Highly recommended.

HEATHCLIFF SLOCUMB   **RRP**   **1966**   **Age 31**

YR	TEAM	Lge	IP	H	ER	HR	BB	K	ERA	W	L	H/9	HR/9	BB/9	K/9	KW
1993	Charlotte, NC	Inter	28.7	28	13	2	15	20	4.08	1	2	8.79	.63	4.71	6.28	.92
1993	Iowa	AmA	11.0	8	2	0	9	9	1.64	1	0	6.55	.00	7.36	7.36	.61
1993	Chicago Cubs	NL	10.0	8	4	0	5	4	3.60	1	0	7.20	.00	4.50	3.60	.07
1993	Cleveland	AL	26.7	30	13	3	18	19	4.39	1	2	10.12	1.01	6.08	6.41	.62
1994	Philadelphia	NL	71.0	78	28	1	35	54	3.55	4	4	9.89	.13	4.44	6.85	1.17
1995	Philadelphia	NL	64.7	63	21	2	40	56	2.92	5	2	8.77	.28	5.57	7.79	1.21
1996	Boston	AL	82.3	63	20	2	57	85	2.19	7	2	6.89	.22	6.23	9.29	1.54

Slocumb is an odd closer package. He gets strikeouts and groundballs, but walks more batters than most pitchers with that combination, and many more than almost all closers. He also gives up no power at all, yielding just a .057 isolated power, 32 doubles and 10 homers in 275 innings over the last five years. This allows him to get away with putting more baserunners on than your typical closer. It's a neat trick, but I don't expect him to be able to keep it up. Avoid.

JEFF SUPPAN   **RBP**   **1975**   **Age 22**

YR	TEAM	Lge	IP	H	ER	HR	BB	K	ERA	W	L	H/9	HR/9	BB/9	K/9	KW
1994	Sarasota	Flor	159.7	172	71	15	69	131	4.00	9	9	9.70	.85	3.89	7.38	1.49
1995	Trenton	East	91.0	107	36	6	34	68	3.56	6	4	10.58	.59	3.36	6.73	1.40
1995	Pawtucket	Inter	43.0	53	27	9	14	27	5.65	2	3	11.09	1.88	2.93	5.65	1.15
1995	Boston	AL	23.3	27	11	4	5	19	4.24	1	2	10.41	1.54	1.93	7.33	1.96
1996	Pawtucket	Inter	138.7	134	53	15	38	116	3.44	9	6	8.70	.97	2.47	7.53	1.89
1996	Boston	AL	23.0	25	13	3	14	12	5.09	1	2	9.78	1.17	5.48	4.70	.20

There's not much I can tell you about Suppan that you don't already know. He's got good stuff, fantastic and still-improving control, a great pitcher's build and good mechanics. Deserved 30 starts in 1996, and should be the #4 or #5 starter in 1997, pending Clemens' status. Good thing: splitting the year between Boston and Pawtucket kept his innings down, after he threw 210 the year before at age 20. Suffered from an elbow problem late in 1996, watch him carefully in spring training.

TIM WAKEFIELD   **RSP**   **1967**   **Age 30**

YR	TEAM	Lge	IP	H	ER	HR	BB	K	ERA	W	L	H/9	HR/9	BB/9	K/9	KW
1993	Carolina	South	52.0	71	45	5	29	26	7.79	1	5	12.29	.87	5.02	4.50	.25
1993	Pittsburgh	NL	127.0	147	77	14	92	57	5.46	5	9	10.42	.99	6.52	4.04	-.28
1994	Buffalo	AmA	170.0	204	116	28	118	75	6.14	6	13	10.80	1.48	6.25	3.97	-.24
1995	Pawtucket	Inter	23.0	25	9	1	13	12	3.52	2	1	9.78	.39	5.09	4.70	.29
1995	Boston	AL	193.3	160	57	21	72	119	2.65	15	6	7.45	.98	3.35	5.54	1.01
1996	Boston	AL	213.3	211	107	31	94	134	4.51	11	13	8.90	1.31	3.97	5.65	.89

That's more like it. Wakefield's not a Cy Young threat in a normal year, but as an innings-munching #3 starter he could make some money. Knuckleball pitchers, in my opinion, are hurt more by the Incredible Shrinking Strike Zone [tm] because batters focus on a smaller and smaller hitting area. The threat of the knuckler being a strike is lessened, leading to more walks, more strikeouts, more cripple counts and more home runs. Recommended, but make sure he doesn't end up in Detroit or Colorado or something.

Player	Age	Team	Lge	AB	H	DB	TP	HR	BB	SB	CS	OUT	BA	OBA	SA	EQA	EQR	Peak
CHRIS ALLISON	24	Trenton	East	366	79	5	1	0	25	11	5	292	.216	.266	.235	.162	15	.174
JUAN BELL	28	Pawtucket	Inter	211	49	9	1	5	23	1	1	163	.232	.308	.355	.221	19	.221
JUNIOR BRADDY	24	Sarasota	Flor	352	80	11	2	9	24	4	1	273	.227	.277	.347	.207	27	.221
RANDY BROWN	26	Trenton	East	254	75	12	1	10	24	7	2	181	.295	.356	.469	.276	36	.287
JAMES CHAMBLEE	21	Michigan	Midw	312	62	10	1	2	12	1	1	251	.199	.228	.256	.143	10	.161
VIRGIL CHEVALIER	22	Michigan	Midw	501	119	18	1	9	24	6	2	384	.238	.272	.331	.201	35	.222
KEVIN CLARK	23	Michigan	Midw	492	129	18	1	11	22	2	3	366	.262	.294	.370	.221	42	.240
PHIL CLARK	28	Pawtucket	Inter	370	113	25	1	12	19	2	4	261	.305	.339	.476	.268	48	.270
ALEX COLE	30	Pawtucket	Inter	309	86	13	5	4	48	7	4	227	.278	.375	.392	.261	39	.255
MICHAEL COLEMAN	20	Sarasota	Flor	417	96	18	3	2	35	12	3	324	.230	.290	.302	.201	29	.229
KEVIN COUGHLIN	25	Trenton	East	176	45	2	1	0	20	4	2	133	.256	.332	.278	.210	13	.221
MILT CUYLER	27	Boston	AL	109	21	0	2	2	13	7	3	91	.193	.279	.284	.192	7	.198
ALEX DELGADO	25	Pawtucket	Inter	88	17	2	0	1	8	0	0	71	.193	.260	.250	.157	3	.166
	25	Trenton	East	83	18	3	0	3	8	1	0	65	.217	.286	.361	.216	7	.227
JOE DEPASTINO	22	Sarasota	Flor	352	84	10	1	7	27	1	1	269	.239	.293	.332	.208	26	.230
ETHAN FAGGETT	21	Sarasota	Flor	418	106	11	4	6	32	12	5	317	.254	.307	.342	.221	36	.247
DAVID GIBRALTER	21	Sarasota	Flor	462	123	18	2	14	28	5	4	343	.266	.308	.405	.237	47	.266
KEITH GOODWIN	21	Michigan	Midw	250	64	9	0	3	19	6	3	189	.256	.309	.328	.216	21	.242
JOE HAMILTON	21	Michigan	Midw	409	103	11	1	12	34	2	2	308	.252	.309	.372	.227	38	.254
RICK HOLIFIELD	26	Trenton	East	389	101	15	2	10	47	26	10	298	.260	.339	.386	.249	46	.259
DWAYNE HOSEY	29	Boston	AL	78	16	2	2	1	7	6	3	65	.205	.271	.321	.201	6	.203
	29	Pawtucket	Inter	370	105	20	2	13	40	13	5	270	.284	.354	.454	.270	51	.268
GAVIN JACKSON	22	Sarasota	Flor	284	61	10	1	1	30	2	3	226	.215	.290	.268	.181	16	.200
COLE LINIAK	19	Michigan	Midw	462	115	18	1	4	45	4	3	350	.249	.316	.318	.214	37	.246
LOU MERLONI	25	Pawtucket	Inter	116	27	4	0	1	10	0	1	90	.233	.294	.293	.191	7	.204
	25	Trenton	East	98	22	4	1	3	8	0	1	77	.224	.283	.378	.214	8	.226
NICK ORTIZ	22	Michigan	Midw	253	72	9	2	3	15	1	0	181	.285	.325	.372	.236	25	.260
	22	Trenton	East	134	29	2	0	3	11	2	1	106	.216	.276	.299	.189	8	.209
ROY PADILLA	20	Michigan	Midw	404	107	17	3	3	25	10	4	301	.265	.308	.344	.222	35	.253
GREG PATTON	24	Sarasota	Flor	284	64	11	1	4	31	1	1	221	.225	.302	.313	.204	21	.218
PORK CHOP POUGH	26	Pawtucket	Inter	244	55	11	1	11	32	2	1	190	.225	.315	.414	.241	27	.249
PETER PRODANOV	22	Michigan	Midw	154	34	4	1	3	14	1	1	121	.221	.286	.318	.199	11	.219
JOHN RAIFSTANGER	23	Michigan	Midw	369	102	10	0	6	49	3	2	269	.276	.361	.352	.244	40	.265
PAUL RAPPOLI	24	Trenton	East	200	41	6	0	3	24	3	2	162	.205	.290	.280	.187	12	.199
WILFREDO RIVERA	22	Michigan	Midw	154	36	7	1	2	5	0	0	118	.234	.258	.331	.193	10	.214
TONY RODRIGUEZ	25	Pawtucket	Inter	265	60	9	1	3	17	2	1	206	.226	.273	.302	.189	16	.200
TONY SHEFFIELD	22	Michigan	Midw	139	32	5	0	5	9	2	1	108	.230	.277	.374	.216	12	.238
DAVE SMITH	24	Sarasota	Flor	130	31	2	1	3	20	3	2	101	.238	.340	.338	.230	13	.245
GREG TIPPIN	23	Michigan	Midw	238	61	5	1	7	12	1	0	177	.256	.292	.374	.223	21	.243

Player	Age	Team	Lge	IP	H	ER	HR	BB	K	ERA	W	L	H/9	HR/9	BB/9	K/9	KW
SCOTT BAKKUM	26	Pawtucket	Inter	42.7	51	27	7	12	20	5.70	2	3	10.76	1.48	2.53	4.22	.77
BRIAN BARKLEY	20	Trenton	East	110.0	144	79	17	70	66	6.46	3	9	11.78	1.39	5.73	5.40	.37
JOE BARKSDALE	22	Michigan	Midw	37.7	50	31	4	42	10	7.41	1	3	11.95	.96	10.04	2.39	-1.71
	22	Sarasota	Flor	57.0	100	63	11	55	27	9.95	1	5	15.79	1.74	8.68	4.26	-.75
RICK BETTI	22	Trenton	East	73.7	83	40	7	54	48	4.89	3	5	10.14	.86	6.60	5.86	.31
MIKE BLAIS	24	Trenton	East	71.3	87	38	10	30	39	4.79	3	5	10.98	1.26	3.79	4.92	.69
BRETT CEDERBLAD	23	Trenton	East	53.3	69	28	8	21	36	4.72	3	3	11.64	1.35	3.54	6.08	1.14
JOHN DESILVA	28	Pawtucket	Inter	81.7	98	45	11	36	56	4.96	4	5	10.80	1.21	3.97	6.17	1.07
JOHN DOHERTY	29	Pawtucket	Inter	49.0	76	32	4	14	11	5.88	2	3	13.96	.73	2.57	2.02	.03
JARED FERNANDEZ	24	Trenton	East	163.7	213	116	19	104	70	6.38	5	13	11.71	1.04	5.72	3.85	-.15
GAR FINNVOLD	28	Pawtucket	Inter	34.7	48	23	6	15	29	5.97	1	3	12.46	1.56	3.89	7.53	1.54
KEN GRUNDT	26	Pawtucket	Inter	62.0	71	26	4	23	38	3.77	4	3	10.31	.58	3.34	5.52	1.00
ERIC GUNDERSON	30	Pawtucket	Inter	32.7	38	12	2	12	28	3.31	2	2	10.47	.55	3.31	7.71	1.74
CHAD HALE	24	Sarasota	Flor	53.3	69	36	3	25	27	6.08	2	4	11.64	.51	4.22	4.56	.46
DOUG HECKER	25	Sarasota	Flor	37.0	55	27	1	18	28	6.57	1	3	13.38	.24	4.38	6.81	1.18
BRENT KNACKERT	26	Pawtucket	Inter	45.3	47	26	10	32	28	5.16	2	3	9.33	1.99	6.35	5.56	.26
BRIAN LOONEY	26	Pawtucket	Inter	79.0	78	44	13	35	64	5.01	4	5	8.89	1.48	3.99	7.29	1.43
RON MAHAY	25	Sarasota	Flor	64.0	71	33	7	46	49	4.64	3	4	9.98	.98	6.47	6.89	.68
CESAR MARTINEZ	23	Sarasota	Flor	60.7	95	43	2	53	36	6.38	2	5	14.09	.30	7.86	5.34	-.19
TOM MCGRAW	28	Trenton	East	31.7	38	14	1	24	24	3.98	2	2	10.80	.28	6.82	6.82	.57
ETHAN MERRILL	24	Sarasota	Flor	77.3	116	55	2	37	39	6.40	3	6	13.50	.23	4.31	4.54	.44
	24	Trenton	East	55.3	80	54	12	33	31	8.78	1	5	13.01	1.95	5.37	5.04	.34
NATE MINCHEY	26	Pawtucket	Inter	93.0	91	26	8	30	50	2.52	7	3	8.81	.77	2.90	4.84	.89
PETER MUNRO	21	Sarasota	Flor	137.0	184	83	7	86	83	5.45	5	10	12.09	.46	5.65	5.45	.41
DEAN PETERSON	23	Sarasota	Flor	56.0	55	31	7	29	42	4.98	2	4	8.84	1.12	4.66	6.75	1.08
JEFF PIERCE	27	Pawtucket	Inter	30.0	36	15	5	12	18	4.50	1	2	10.80	1.50	3.60	5.40	.90
CURTIS ROMBOLI	23	Michigan	Midw	68.0	96	46	6	57	47	6.09	2	6	12.71	.79	7.54	6.22	.19
JEFF SAUVE	23	Michigan	Midw	54.3	63	34	5	34	34	5.63	2	4	10.44	.83	5.63	5.63	.47
ERIK SCHULLSTROM	27	Pawtucket	Inter	53.7	57	30	8	34	51	5.03	2	4	9.56	1.34	5.70	8.55	1.43
	27	Trenton	East	26.0	27	10	1	16	16	3.46	2	1	9.35	.35	5.54	5.54	.46
SHAWN SENIOR	24	Trenton	East	75.3	101	53	13	52	37	6.33	2	6	12.07	1.55	6.21	4.42	-.08
MICHAEL SPINELLI	19	Michigan	Midw	51.7	69	45	2	50	26	7.84	1	5	12.02	.35	8.71	4.53	-.67
DARRELL TILLMON	23	Michigan	Midw	32.3	48	26	5	22	17	7.24	1	3	13.36	1.39	6.12	4.73	.05
	23	Sarasota	Flor	100.7	123	43	7	42	43	3.84	6	5	11.00	.63	3.75	3.84	.34
LARRY WIMBERLY	20	Michigan	Midw	58.0	72	27	6	31	26	4.19	3	3	11.17	.93	4.81	4.03	.14
	20	Sarasota	Flor	26.7	43	27	3	22	12	9.11	0	3	14.51	1.01	7.43	4.05	-.51
JAY YENNACO	20	Michigan	Midw	145.7	238	118	17	89	73	7.29	4	12	14.70	1.05	5.50	4.51	.13

Prospect Profile: Carl Pavano

One of the top prospects in the Boston Red Sox organization is right-handed pitcher Carl Pavano. Although he was just named Eastern League Pitcher of the Year for 1996 and is one of the top pitching prospects in the game, success isn't his head.

His 6' 5", 225-pound frame may seem towering on the mound, but it has become more refined during his three years in professional ball; he has lost 20 pounds since graduating from high school in 1994. Scouts were reluctant to draft Pavano because of a belief that he would head to Louisiana State University (LSU). The Red Sox, as has been their policy of late, took a chance and soon worked out a deal with the Southington, Conn. native.

Pavano has a live sinking fastball with good movement and a good tail that tops out at 95 mph, a slider and a change-up. His smooth, slow motion is difficult for batters to read, and he's known as "deceptively fast"—the ball explodes on a hitter, making him that much harder to hit. He's just now working on a professional-caliber curve to complement this arsenal.

Pavano's first professional experience was in rookie ball, where he dominated the competition with a 1.84 ERA (less than half that of his Red Sox teammates), allowed only 31 hits in 44 innings and struck out 47 while walking only seven batters. "The Rookie League wasn't much different than high school," Pavano recalls. He was soon promoted to a middle level A ball team, Michigan in the Midwest League. This was Pavano's first full season, and it was during this time that he experienced his first and only professional injury, shoulder tendinitis.

"The mound in Michigan was on a downhill plane, but because I have a longer stride than most people, when my foot was landing, I was landing on flat ground. Instead of just throwing, it was as if I was pushing and putting pressure on my shoulder; both my shoulder and elbow were low, causing the tendinitis."

The Red Sox immediately sent Pavano, even though he hadn't established the top prospect status that would come in 1996, back for examination and rehabilitation. He returned to Michigan later in the season and put up numbers that showed his potential: 141 innings, 52 walks and 138 strikeouts. The best was yet to come, as Pavano jumped to Boston's double-A team, the Eastern League's Trenton Thunder, in 1996.

In 1996, Pavano had a 2.63 ERA with a 3-to-1 strikeout to walk ratio in 185 innings. And although the Trenton ballpark is a pitcher's park, there was no mistaking how well Pavano pitched; he started the All-Star Game and was named the Eastern League's Pitcher of the Year. This was all accomplished at the tender age of 20, when most pitchers are thinking about their junior year in college.

The most amazing part of 1996 was Pavano's second half performance; he pitched nearly shutout ball in his last 10 starts. He credits this success to hard work. "A lot of people wear down in the second half of a year because they don't properly condition themselves in the off-season. At no time during the year was I tired—I may have been mentally drained, but I was never at a point where I thought 'I'm out of shape.' I always felt ready to pitch, my arm was healthy."

The offseason routine for players is often overlooked by fans who feel that baseball is a three hours a day, six months a year game. Not so with Pavano, who does "Lots of running, watching what I eat and working out. My life now revolves around baseball, 24 hours a day. I work with free weights— some people don't believe in it, but I've been doing it the past two offseasons and it's worked for me."

Pavano believes that working out in the offseason is akin to putting money in the bank for a rainy day. "When you need something extra in the late innings of a game or during the year, and you're pitching 200 innings, it's there. During the regular season, I did a maintenance program to keep what I had developed. Whatever I worked towards in the off-season, I would keep my arm at that level, and not build it up any more."

According to Pavano, the hardest part of adjusting to the minor leagues is being away from home. "The first couple of years, I knew I would be going home after the season ended; now, I'm in Florida [at a camp with several other Red Sox prospects]. My family has always stuck by me. I never was able to properly express my gratitude, but they've always been good to me and helped out when I was down on my luck."

Pavano will be starting 1997 at the Red Sox big league training camp, where he'll get an opportunity to talk to one of his baseball idols, Roger Clemens. "I always like watching games with players like Clemens and Nolan Ryan, or old games with Mickey Mantle—power hitters and power pitchers. It's exciting to watch a person throw 100 miles per hour or hit a 500-foot home run."

While playing in AA, Pavano faced Vladimir Guerrero, who along with Andruw Jones was the top minor league prospect in 1996. When Guerrero got promoted, the big leagues did cross Pavano's mind. "I thought, 'Wait, I got this guy out. If he's ready for the big leagues, maybe I can be there as well. I want to excel in pitching—do well enough to be a quality big league pitcher. I don't want to go up to the majors and then get sent back down, but get called up and make a difference."

And since he won't be in the American League, what's the best way to get Vladimir Guerrero out? "Fastballs in, keep him off the plate—then some sliders and changing speeds. He's a really good hitter, but he'll swing at some bad pitches."

Watching a game has also become a completely different experience for Carl. "When I watch a game, I analyze it more; I look at things differently, to see how pitchers work the bat-ters, and what pitches they are throwing. Hitting is basically mistakes; if you don't make a mistake to a hitter, there's not much chance that he'll get a hit. They'll sometimes hit good pitches, but the percentages are with you for them not to hit good ones."

The combination of proper conditioning, talent and hard work can make or break many athletes. It looks like Carl Pavano has the right mix of all three, and he's on the right track to "The Show."

--Bob Gajarsky

Detroit Tigers

No team in baseball has a more clear-cut idea of the direction they need to take than the Detroit Tigers. Of course, no team came close to losing as many games as the Tigers did last year; focus comes with a price. Actually, no team had lost as many as 109 games since the 1979 Blue Jays, and you have to go back to the 1961 Phillies to find a non-expansion team with a worse record.

In fairness, the Tigers knew in the spring that their hopes for a successful season were slim, although a pitching staff that gave up 1103 runs—easily the highest total in AL history—put an exclamation point on the team's futility. But the Tigers were finally freed from Sparky Anderson's inability to write off a couple of seasons in the name of rebuilding. Under a new manager and GM, they were at long last able to take the hard first step of a journey they should have begun in 1989.

Seven years ago, the Tigers went 59-103 and were in much the same position they are now. Their once-dominant offense, which had led all of baseball in runs scored just two years before, was populated with has-beens (Fred Lynn, Chet Lemon, Dave Bergman), could-have-beens (Kenny Williams, Rob Richie) and never-wases (Mike Brumley, Rick Schu). But instead of wiping the slate clean and attempting to start over by building up a barren farm system, Sparky chose to put a Band-Aid over the offense, fill in the holes and pray. This would not have set the Tigers' rebuilding process back so much had it not been so successful. Cecil Fielder returned from Japan and hit 51 homers, Tony Phillips was signed as a free agent and Mickey Tettleton was acquired for Jeff Robinson's decaying carcass. The Tigers also benefited from the emergence of the only decent player their minor league system produced in the 1980s, Travis Fryman. Led by Tettleton and Phillips, the Tigers continued to draw walks—they ranked among the majors' top 3 every year from 1987 to 1994—and score runs, ranking among the top 3 every year from 1990 to 1994.

That the Tigers were prolific run scorers hid the fact that their pitching staff, which even in the Tigers heyday of 1984 was not particularly young, had rapidly aged and withered. Not that anyone in Detroit noticed: Bill Gullickson was a 20-game winner! Who cared if Frank Tanana was 37 years old and Walt Terrell—at any age—was in the rotation? Or that despite the majors' best offense in the first half of the 1990s, the Tigers never won more than 85 games?

The result was sad and predictable: the hitters got older, and either left town or lost their effectiveness. The entire rotation melted down and the Tigers were unable to develop any good starters to take their place. Despite valiant efforts from guys like David Wells and Mark Leiter, the Tigers slowly sank into a hopeless morass. Their offense was no longer able to compensate for an ever-worsening pitching staff, and the farm system that the Tigers neglected while they were just one starter away from contention was unable to help.

This time around the Tigers have tried to learn from their past. The painful, but correct, decision was made to let Sparky go, as well as incumbent GM Joe Klein. Faced with a long uphill battle back to respectability, the Tigers signed on with youth, hiring the still-wet-behind-the-ears Randy Smith from San Diego as GM and giving Buddy Bell his first managerial job. The Tigers' woeful record aside, both Smith and Bell did outstanding jobs in their first year in Detroit. Smith gambled on several trades in an attempt to bring young talent to the franchise, and Bell earned near-universal praise for his Showalter-esque calm discipline through a disastrous season.

The Tigers could easily look at 1996, which included a 4-37 stretch and no home wins after August, as a wasted season. But like most 100-loss teams, what the Tigers learned about their team and their personnel was far more important than what they accomplished. They learned that most of their players simply didn't belong in a major league uniform, but they also found some who they could attempt to rebuild around. In particular, they learned that:

• Bobby Higginson is a great, multitalented, player, the first great player the Tigers have developed since the Carter administration. Think of a calmer, more focused Kirk Gibson.

• Mark Lewis, who's been to hell and back as a prospect, may have finally found a home at second base.

• Mel Nieves and Tony Clark, when they actually make contact, have as much power as anyone in the division.

Toss in steady, if overrated, Travis Fryman, and the Tigers have the makings of a lineup that could be among baseball's best by 1999. And most importantly, only Fryman will have turned 30 by then, allowing the Tigers the luxury of not having to rework their offense every three years.

Of course, the Tigers have had great offenses before without winning. If the Tigers are ever to contend again, they simply have to learn how to build a pitching staff.

The Tigers have certainly written the book on how not to build a pitching staff, signing aging free-agent pitchers like Gullickson, Tim Belcher and Mike Moore over the years. But hidden by last season's disaster is that the Tigers have begun the slow process of developing their own pitchers and putting their feet to the fire. There have been notable failures along the way—the Tigers over-hyped Clint Sodowsky and Greg

Gohr before the season began—but also a number of successes. Felipe Lira has quietly established himself as a dependable starter, Jose Lima has given the Tigers hope of becoming a quality reliever and Justin Thompson finally arrived and justified the Tigers' faith in him over the years. And in the minor leagues, the Tigers have overcome years of wasted draft picks—anyone remember Matt Brunson?—to restock their system with pitching. In particular, 1995 #1 pick Mike Drumright could be in Detroit by September, and last year's #1, Seth Greisinger, outpitched everyone, including Kris Benson, on the U.S. Olympic Team.

The quick road back to respectability the Tigers tried to take in 1989 usually ends up back at the bottom. Lost in the amazing "Why Not?" season in Baltimore in 1989 was its aftermath: fooled into thinking that their terrible 1988 season was just a memory, the Orioles failed to show the patience necessary to rebuild their franchise properly, and it took them six long years to make a single wild-card appearance. The Tigers need to keep focused on the long, straight road to the top, or their 1996 season will have been in vain.

BRAD AUSMUS   C   1969   Age 28

Year	Team	Lge	AB	H	DB	TP	HR	BB	SB	CS	OUT	BA	OBA	SA	EQA	EQR	Peak
1993	Colo. Springs	PCL	235	51	7	2	2	24	6	3	187	.217	.290	.289	.194	15	.208
1993	San Diego	NL	162	43	7	1	5	8	2	0	119	.265	.300	.414	.240	17	.256
1994	San Diego	NL	331	85	12	1	7	35	4	1	247	.257	.328	.363	.234	33	.247
1995	San Diego	NL	339	106	17	3	6	36	14	4	237	.313	.379	.434	.278	48	.289
1996	Detroit	AL	226	56	10	0	5	26	3	4	174	.248	.325	.358	.227	21	.233
1996	San Diego	NL	151	28	4	0	1	15	1	4	127	.185	.259	.232	.141	5	.146
1997	*Houston*	*NL*	*172*	*41*	*8*	*1*	*4*	*17*	*6*	*2*	*133*	*.238*	*.307*	*.366*	*.247*	*20*	

Ausmus showed flashes of ability after the Tigers acquired him, but don't expect his 1995 production again. He would make a fine backup, but that's not the kind of endorsement you want of your starting catcher. Handles the defensive side of the game well, and will probably suck up 300 at bats in 1997 to tide the Tigers over until they can find someone who can play the position.

KIMERA BARTEE   CF   1973   Age 24

Year	Team	Lge	AB	H	DB	TP	HR	BB	SB	CS	OUT	BA	OBA	SA	EQA	EQR	Peak
1994	Frederick	Caro	534	146	17	2	8	48	24	6	394	.273	.333	.358	.240	56	.269
1995	Bowie	East	224	62	7	1	3	21	14	5	166	.277	.339	.357	.243	24	.269
1995	Rochester	Inter	52	7	2	1	0	0	0	0	45	.135	.135	.212	-.089	-1	-.087
1996	Detroit	AL	217	55	7	1	1	17	20	10	172	.253	.308	.309	.216	19	.234
1997	*Detroit*	*AL*	*252*	*71*	*7*	*2*	*4*	*16*	*27*	*14*	*195*	*.282*	*.325*	*.373*	*.243*	*28*	

Bartee has been a Rule V Ping-Pong ball the last two years - he's bounced from the Orioles to the Twins and back to Baltimore before the Tigers picked him up off waivers. He's a fine outfielder and a good baserunner, but he's probably always going to have problems with the stick. He has a huge platoon split: .378 vs. LHPs last year, .178 vs. RHPs, and there's talk of trying to make him a switch-hitter. Something about him reminds me of Milt Cuyler, but I wouldn't say that to his face.

RAUL CASANOVA   C   1973   Age 24

Year	Team	Lge	AB	H	DB	TP	HR	BB	SB	CS	OUT	BA	OBA	SA	EQA	EQR	Peak
1993	Waterloo	Midw	235	54	5	0	6	16	0	0	181	.230	.279	.328	.200	16	.228
1994	R. Cucamonga	Calif	475	144	15	1	18	35	1	2	333	.303	.351	.453	.267	62	.300
1995	Memphis	South	315	85	10	0	13	24	3	1	231	.270	.322	.425	.249	36	.276
1996	Toledo	Inter	164	43	7	0	8	20	0	1	122	.262	.342	.451	.260	21	.284
1996	Detroit	AL	85	16	1	0	4	6	0	0	69	.188	.242	.341	.186	5	.204
1997	*Detroit*	*AL*	*387*	*104*	*15*	*2*	*22*	*34*	*0*	*0*	*283*	*.269*	*.328*	*.488*	*.269*	*53*	

Casanova achieved prospect status with a monster 1994 season, but his numbers were inflated some by playing in the hitter-happy California League. Still, switch-hitting catchers with power are roughly as common as family fare on Fox, and the Tigers did well to get him in the Nieves deal. Threw out only 22% of basestealers last year. His Vlad is probably a bit optimistic, but the Tigers would be fools not to give him 400 at bats to find out.

FRANK CATALANOTTO   **2B**   **1974**   **Age 23**

Year	Team	Lge	AB	H	DB	TP	HR	BB	SB	CS	OUT	BA	OBA	SA	EQA	EQR	Peak
1994	Fayetteville	S Atl	482	143	18	4	4	32	2	2	341	.297	.340	.376	.243	50	.277
1995	Jacksonville	South	508	116	14	3	10	47	9	4	396	.228	.294	.327	.208	39	.233
1996	Jacksonville	South	511	145	24	3	17	63	11	7	373	.284	.362	.442	.268	69	.296
1997	*Oakland*	*AL*	*447*	*117*	*26*	*2*	*14*	*53*	*6*	*4*	*334*	*.262*	*.340*	*.423*	*.260*	*57*	

You have to love a left-handed hitting second baseman with broad offensive skills. When a hitter improves tremendously in his second year at a level, it's sometimes written off as a fluke, but I think Catalanotto's progress was legitimate. He was just 22 last season, and the breadth of his improvement is very impressive. The Tigers are making noises about giving Mark Lewis' job to someone else, so at the very least Catalanotto could be looking at a platoon role in Detroit next year. I like him a lot; he's in much the same position that Bobby Higginson was in two years ago, and we know how that turned out. A real sleeper.

TONY CLARK   **1B**   **1972**   **Age 25**

Year	Team	Lge	AB	H	DB	TP	HR	BB	SB	CS	OUT	BA	OBA	SA	EQA	EQR	Peak
1993	Lakeland	Flor	122	30	3	0	2	16	0	0	92	.246	.333	.320	.221	11	.249
1994	Trenton	East	406	110	13	0	19	36	1	2	298	.271	.330	.443	.255	49	.281
1994	Toledo	Inter	94	24	2	0	2	12	1	0	70	.255	.340	.340	.233	9	.257
1995	Toledo	Inter	421	105	14	1	15	52	0	1	317	.249	.332	.394	.242	46	.263
1995	Detroit	AL	101	24	6	1	3	8	0	0	77	.238	.294	.406	.231	10	.252
1996	Toledo	Inter	198	58	5	1	12	31	1	1	141	.293	.389	.510	.294	33	.315
1996	Detroit	AL	377	95	12	0	28	29	0	1	283	.252	.305	.507	.262	50	.280
1997	*Detroit*	*AL*	*568*	*150*	*15*	*2*	*34*	*73*	*0*	*0*	*418*	*.264*	*.348*	*.477*	*.273*	*82*	

One of the great stories in baseball. Clark was the #2 pick in all of baseball, right after Chipper Jones, in 1990, but his insistence on playing college basketball at San Diego State hindered his development for three years. His first pro manager called him a non-prospect after his first game, and after the 1993 season he looked like the mother of all blown draft picks. Since returning to baseball full time he has shown jaw-dropping power from both sides of the plate. He's a cripple hitter, hitting .437 with a .930 slugging average when ahead in the count last year.

He still has holes in his swing the size of a small satellite, but he also has a lot more potential to improve than most 25-year-olds. I won't guarantee that he will continue to improve, but I will say this: don't bet against him. He's been written off before, and the improvement in his game was borderline miraculous. The Vlad looks about right, but there's a lot of variance there.

JOHN COTTON   **OF**   **1971**   **Age 26**

Year	Team	Lge	AB	H	DB	TP	HR	BB	SB	CS	OUT	BA	OBA	SA	EQA	EQR	Peak
1993	Kinston	Caro	476	113	10	2	10	52	17	11	374	.237	.312	.330	.217	41	.239
1994	Springfield	Midw	85	19	3	2	1	9	3	1	67	.224	.298	.341	.217	7	.235
1994	R. Cucamonga	Calif	174	32	2	1	3	18	4	2	144	.184	.260	.259	.166	8	.180
1994	Wichita	Texas	88	17	2	0	3	11	1	0	71	.193	.283	.318	.199	6	.217
1995	Memphis	South	419	106	15	5	13	37	10	4	317	.253	.314	.406	.241	45	.258
1996	Jacksonville	South	221	53	4	2	12	16	10	2	170	.240	.291	.439	.245	25	.259
1996	Toledo	Inter	171	30	6	1	3	8	3	2	143	.175	.212	.275	.146	6	.155

Journeyman left-handed hitting outfielder who had a brief power surge at Jacksonville. You have to figure that anyone with even a grain of talent in the Tigers' organization has a chance to play in Detroit, but it's debatable whether Cotton has even that much.

FAUSTO CRUZ   **2B/SS**   **1972**   **Age 25**

Year	Team	Lge	AB	H	DB	TP	HR	BB	SB	CS	OUT	BA	OBA	SA	EQA	EQR	Peak
1993	Modesto	Calif	168	34	1	0	1	18	3	2	136	.202	.280	.226	.160	7	.178
1993	Huntsville	South	262	86	13	2	3	19	2	2	178	.328	.374	.427	.271	34	.303
1993	Tacoma	PCL	74	16	1	1	0	4	2	2	60	.216	.256	.257	.161	3	.183
1994	Tacoma	PCL	215	62	8	0	3	17	2	1	154	.288	.341	.367	.241	22	.266
1995	Edmonton	PCL	444	114	15	1	12	34	6	3	333	.257	.310	.376	.230	42	.250
1996	Toledo	Inter	388	92	14	1	11	34	8	6	302	.237	.299	.363	.220	34	.236

He's been touted as a talented middle infielder with Bret Boone-like potential, but with the exception of his torrid half-season with Huntsville in 1993, Cruz has never done anything to justify his reputation. He's overmatched as a shortstop, where he would have some value for the Tigers. He was unable to win a job with the A's when Brent Gates was nursing one of his many injuries, and he's unlikely to win a job now.

SEAN FREEMAN   **1B**   **1972**   **Age 25**

Year	Team	Lge	AB	H	DB	TP	HR	BB	SB	CS	OUT	BA	OBA	SA	EQA	EQR	Peak
1994	Jamestown	NY-P	230	56	7	1	2	14	1	1	175	.243	.287	.309	.197	15	.218
1995	Lakeland	Flor	437	124	16	1	8	43	2	2	315	.284	.348	.380	.247	48	.268
1996	Jacksonville	South	424	110	11	1	22	57	2	2	316	.259	.347	.446	.262	55	.281
1997	Detroit	AL	466	129	23	2	19	54	1	2	339	.277	.352	.457	.270	64	

A good hitter, and if he was two years younger he might have a 1000-game career in the major leagues to look forward to. As it is, he needs a hot start in 1997 or an injury to Clark if he wants major league meal money. Likely to be the proverbial AAA veteran in four years.

TRAVIS FRYMAN   **3B/SS**   **1969**   **Age 28**

Year	Team	Lge	AB	H	DB	TP	HR	BB	SB	CS	OUT	BA	OBA	SA	EQA	EQR	Peak
1993	Detroit	AL	619	196	38	5	27	82	9	3	426	.317	.397	.525	.303	108	.324
1994	Detroit	AL	466	124	34	5	18	45	2	2	344	.266	.331	.476	.264	62	.278
1995	Detroit	AL	569	158	22	5	16	63	4	2	413	.278	.350	.418	.258	70	.268
1996	Detroit	AL	617	166	33	3	22	57	4	3	454	.269	.331	.439	.255	75	.262
1997	*Detroit*	*AL*	*578*	*154*	*37*	*4*	*25*	*70*	*5*	*4*	*428*	*.266*	*.346*	*.474*	*.271*	*82*	

A steady everyday player, but after his 1993 season Fryman looked like a superstar-in-waiting, and his performance since then has been a tough pill to swallow in Detroit. He's still young enough for the Tigers to rebuild around him, and I suspect his numbers will improve some this year. Being the leader on a 53-109 ballclub has to be draining. He made the move back to shortstop better than anyone had the right to expect, and given their other options at the position, the Tigers should really keep him there and play Nevin at third.

LUIS GARCIA   **SS**   **1975**   **Age 22**

Year	Team	Lge	AB	H	DB	TP	HR	BB	SB	CS	OUT	BA	OBA	SA	EQA	EQR	Peak
1994	Jamestown	NY-P	242	37	5	1	1	7	3	3	209	.153	.177	.194	-.045	0	-.052
1995	Lakeland	Flor	371	98	10	2	3	8	6	5	278	.264	.280	.326	.202	25	.230
1996	Jacksonville	South	528	122	16	2	9	8	10	6	412	.231	.243	.320	.184	30	.206

Here's one of those options. Garcia is notable only for his age, and the fact that he can barely scribble a walk, let alone draw one. Wants to be Cedeno when he grows up, and even that's unlikely.

TERREL HANSEN   **OF**   **1967**   **Age 30**

Year	Team	Lge	AB	H	DB	TP	HR	BB	SB	CS	OUT	BA	OBA	SA	EQA	EQR	Peak
1993	Ottawa	Inter	355	78	10	0	11	21	1	1	278	.220	.263	.341	.197	24	.205
1994	Jacksonville	South	412	125	11	0	21	22	2	2	289	.303	.339	.483	.271	55	.278
1995	Jacksonville	South	183	42	4	0	9	11	0	1	142	.230	.273	.399	.219	16	.221
1995	Tacoma	PCL	50	11	0	0	3	3	0	0	39	.220	.264	.400	.217	4	.219
1996	Jacksonville	South	373	97	11	1	22	15	4	1	277	.260	.289	.472	.250	43	.248

If he wouldn't qualify for a pension the moment he made a major league roster, I'd advise Hansen to retire. Has to hope for a three-man collision in the Tigers outfield if he wants playing time at this point.

PHIL HIATT   **3B**   **1969**   **Age 28**

Year	Team	Lge	AB	H	DB	TP	HR	BB	SB	CS	OUT	BA	OBA	SA	EQA	EQR	Peak
1993	Omaha	AmA	51	12	0	0	3	4	0	0	39	.235	.291	.412	.231	5	.248
1993	Kansas City	AL	239	53	10	1	9	17	6	2	188	.222	.273	.385	.219	21	.235
1994	Memphis	South	418	125	18	2	18	40	8	4	297	.299	.360	.481	.278	61	.294
1995	Omaha	AmA	75	11	3	0	2	3	0	0	64	.147	.179	.267	.114	1	.116
1995	Kansas City	AL	114	25	4	0	5	9	1	0	89	.219	.276	.386	.219	10	.227
1996	Toledo	Inter	561	144	20	2	37	51	12	4	421	.257	.319	.497	.266	77	.273
1997	*Detroit*	*AL*	*471*	*117*	*17*	*2*	*28*	*42*	*8*	*1*	*355*	*.248*	*.310*	*.471*	*.260*	*61*	

Yeah, he hit 42 homers in Toledo last year. He also struck out 180 times in 555 at bats. I wouldn't say that's bad, but Tom Glavine has struck out 166 times in 632 career at bats. Strikeouts aren't worse than any other kind of out in the context of a game, but when projecting a player's future, that many whiffs should send out a real warning signal. He had good defensive numbers in AAA this year, but has a reputation for being less than agile. Unlikely to ever garner more than a platoon role in the majors again.

BOB HIGGINSON   **OF**   **1971**   **Age 26**

Year	Team	Lge	AB	H	DB	TP	HR	BB	SB	CS	OUT	BA	OBA	SA	EQA	EQR	Peak
1993	Lakeland	Flor	234	68	9	4	5	35	4	1	167	.291	.383	.427	.275	33	.304
1993	London	East	228	65	11	2	5	18	2	2	165	.285	.337	.417	.252	26	.278
1994	Toledo	Inter	485	130	21	2	21	44	12	5	360	.268	.329	.449	.259	61	.281
1995	Detroit	AL	411	93	18	5	15	62	6	4	322	.226	.328	.404	.242	47	.259
1996	Detroit	AL	441	142	28	1	28	65	6	3	302	.322	.409	.580	.319	87	.336
1997	*Detroit*	*AL*	*585*	*164*	*39*	*3*	*30*	*120*	*14*	*8*	*429*	*.280*	*.403*	*.511*	*.301*	*107*	

Wow. Higginson is yet another example of what happens when a young hitter with broad skills is given a full-time job in the major leagues and time to develop. Some decline in 1997 would be expected, but the walks and the power are likely here to stay. He's an excellent corner outfielder but was overmatched in center field. He does have a huge platoon split—he's a career .220 hitter against southpaws—but the Tigers have nothing to lose by playing him full time and hoping he learns to hit lefties with time. Vlad predicts a huge upswing in his walk total next year; if it happens, he will probably be an MVP candidate in three or four years.

TIM HYERS   **1B**   **1972**   **Age 25**

Year	Team	Lge	AB	H	DB	TP	HR	BB	SB	CS	OUT	BA	OBA	SA	EQA	EQR	Peak
1993	Knoxville	South	493	136	21	2	3	48	7	2	359	.276	.340	.345	.235	48	.263
1994	Las Vegas	PCL	46	10	0	0	1	4	0	0	36	.217	.280	.283	.183	3	.193
1994	San Diego	NL	119	31	2	0	0	11	3	0	88	.261	.323	.277	.210	9	.232
1995	Las Vegas	PCL	254	64	9	1	1	23	0	2	192	.252	.314	.307	.207	19	.225
1996	Toledo	Inter	442	109	14	4	7	41	5	1	334	.247	.311	.344	.221	39	.237

Considered a prospect with the Padres three years ago, but as a singles-hitting first baseman, he needs to hit .330 to have a shot. I doubt that will happen.

GABRIEL KAPLER   **OF**   **1976**   **Age 21**

Year	Team	Lge	AB	H	DB	TP	HR	BB	SB	CS	OUT	BA	OBA	SA	EQA	EQR	Peak
1995	Jamestown	NY-P	238	53	8	1	4	17	0	1	186	.223	.275	.315	.192	15	.220
1996	Fayetteville	S Atl	565	168	21	0	23	50	6	2	399	.297	.354	.457	.271	76	.308
1997	*Detroit*	*AL*	*525*	*152*	*28*	*1*	*17*	*47*	*6*	*4*	*377*	*.290*	*.348*	*.444*	*.266*	*69*	

Kapler was a 57th-round draft pick in 1995, but his low pedigree hasn't kept the Tigers from calling him one of their top prospects. He was an intense weightlifter, but has toned it down since he was drafted. Muscle-bound players typically are injury-prone, but Kapler has been durable so far. If he stays healthy, he could progress very, very quickly. He has all the skills you look for in a young hitter and he's only 21.

MARK LEWIS   **2B**   **1970**   **Age 27**

Year	Team	Lge	AB	H	DB	TP	HR	BB	SB	CS	OUT	BA	OBA	SA	EQA	EQR	Peak
1993	Charlotte-NC	Inter	518	145	24	1	18	37	7	3	376	.280	.328	.434	.255	62	.277
1993	Cleveland	AL	53	15	2	0	1	0	3	0	38	.283	.283	.377	.235	5	.254
1994	Charlotte-NC	Inter	335	83	11	1	8	34	2	2	254	.248	.317	.358	.226	31	.242
1994	Cleveland	AL	73	15	2	0	2	2	1	0	58	.205	.227	.315	.175	4	.187
1995	Cincinnati	NL	177	62	13	1	3	23	0	2	117	.350	.425	.486	.303	30	.319
1996	Detroit	AL	546	148	31	3	11	42	6	1	399	.271	.323	.399	.244	59	.254
1997	*San Francisco*	*NL*	*595*	*160*	*40*	*2*	*24*	*50*	*0*	*1*	*436*	*.269*	*.326*	*.464*	*.274*	*85*	

Lewis' career has been all over the map, and he needed a full season in Detroit to catch his breath. If he starts for the Tigers again next year, I suspect he'll improve, though Vlad is taking a leap of faith by predicting such a power surge. There are some flashing yellow lights around Lewis. He hit just .223 after the break, and the Tigers were reportedly disappointed with his defense. Proceed with caution; it's anyone's guess as to what he'll do this year. Traded to San Francisco, where he's in the mix for the second base job.

SCOTT MAKAREWICZ   **C**   **1967**   **Age 30**

Year	Team	Lge	AB	H	DB	TP	HR	BB	SB	CS	OUT	BA	OBA	SA	EQA	EQR	Peak
1993	Jackson	Texas	290	66	7	1	7	18	1	0	224	.228	.273	.331	.199	20	.207
1994	Tucson	PCL	168	42	6	1	3	13	0	0	126	.250	.304	.351	.219	14	.224
1995	Tucson	PCL	188	43	5	0	5	10	1	0	145	.229	.268	.335	.199	13	.201
1996	Jacksonville	South	263	80	9	1	13	14	3	2	185	.304	.339	.494	.274	36	.273

Makarewicz was a decent prospect for the Astros four years ago, and why Tony Eusebio made it to the majors over him is just the luck of the draw. He has some offensive skills, but at age 30 he's more a player-coach than anything else.

JUSTIN MASHORE   **OF**   **1972**   **Age 25**

Year	Team	Lge	AB	H	DB	TP	HR	BB	SB	CS	OUT	BA	OBA	SA	EQA	EQR	Peak
1993	Lakeland	Flor	453	110	10	1	5	33	14	6	349	.243	.294	.302	.203	32	.226
1994	Trenton	East	460	98	10	3	7	33	18	4	366	.213	.266	.293	.190	29	.209
1995	Jacksonville	South	151	38	5	2	4	7	4	1	114	.252	.285	.391	.228	14	.246
1995	Toledo	Inter	228	50	2	2	5	15	9	5	183	.219	.267	.311	.193	15	.211
1996	Jacksonville	South	462	125	22	5	7	26	11	7	344	.271	.309	.385	.233	45	.250

Mashore's speed and defense has made him a prospect for the last three years, but his hitting skills never developed the way the Tigers hoped. Not a prospect at this point.

TONY MITCHELL   **OF**   **1971**   **Age 26**

Year	Team	Lge	AB	H	DB	TP	HR	BB	SB	CS	OUT	BA	OBA	SA	EQA	EQR	Peak
1993	Kinston	Caro	330	74	9	1	7	30	3	2	258	.224	.289	.321	.202	24	.223
1994	Canton	East	511	135	12	0	24	38	4	1	377	.264	.315	.429	.248	58	.269
1995	Jackson	Texas	337	88	9	1	18	32	1	1	250	.261	.325	.454	.256	42	.274
1996	Jacksonville	South	177	54	6	0	11	18	1	0	123	.305	.369	.525	.293	29	.309
1996	Toledo	Inter	293	78	7	2	12	41	2	1	216	.266	.356	.427	.262	38	.276
1997	*Detroit*	*AL*	*429*	*121*	*15*	*0*	*26*	*49*	*2*	*0*	*308*	*.282*	*.356*	*.499*	*.283*	*66*	

Mitchell has been a minor league slugger for several years, but last year he raised his average enough to resurrect hopes of a major league career. He hits equally well from both sides of the plate and is adequate in the field, but he lacks any one great skill that could earn him a spot on a bench somewhere. The Vlad looks a little optimistic, but even if it's accurate, it will most likely be spent in AAA anyway.

PHIL NEVIN   **3B/C/LF**   **1971**   **Age 26**

Year	Team	Lge	AB	H	DB	TP	HR	BB	SB	CS	OUT	BA	OBA	SA	EQA	EQR	Peak
1993	Tucson	PCL	441	109	12	1	10	46	4	1	333	.247	.318	.347	.225	40	.248
1994	Tucson	PCL	439	101	10	1	11	52	2	1	339	.230	.312	.333	.216	37	.234
1995	Tucson	PCL	218	55	8	0	7	26	2	2	165	.252	.332	.385	.240	23	.257
1995	Detroit	AL	96	21	4	1	2	11	0	0	75	.219	.299	.344	.213	8	.228
1995	Houston	NL	61	7	2	0	0	8	1	0	54	.115	.217	.148	-.046	0	.013
1996	Jacksonville	South	355	103	11	0	22	51	4	1	253	.290	.379	.507	.292	58	.307
1996	Detroit	AL	120	35	6	0	8	8	1	0	85	.292	.336	.542	.285	18	.300
1997	*Detroit*	*AL*	*531*	*136*	*19*	*0*	*29*	*66*	*2*	*1*	*396*	*.256*	*.338*	*.456*	*.264*	*71*	

Nevin has resuscitated his career much the way Clark has. Like Clark, Nevin was a top draft pick, 1st in the nation in 1992, who looked like a waste of a roster spot for several years. Adding to his uninspired play was his juvenile tirade after being sent down to AAA by the Astros last year (he was hitting a robust .117 at the time). His stock had dropped like a junk bond when the Tigers acquired him last August.

But sometime during the offseason, the light bulb went on. Nevin, who always had a reputation of being a hard-nosed, hard-headed player, was the consummate company man when the Tigers asked him to 1) learn how to catch and 2) go down to AA to work on it. To the surprise of just about everyone, Nevin had easily his best season, showing more power and walking more than he had since college. His torrid hitting continued when the Tigers brought him up, even as the Tigers shuttled him around three different positions.

He's still a very intense, if more mature, player, and if the Tigers send him down again there's no telling how he'll react. But if they give him a starting job at any position in April, I'd bet on him keeping it into the next century.

MELVIN NIEVES   **RF/LF**   **1972**   **Age 25**

Year	Team	Lge	AB	H	DB	TP	HR	BB	SB	CS	OUT	BA	OBA	SA	EQA	EQR	Peak
1993	Las Vegas	PCL	154	40	5	0	6	16	1	1	115	.260	.329	.409	.246	17	.275
1993	Richmond	Inter	280	77	7	2	10	26	3	2	205	.275	.337	.421	.253	33	.284
1993	San Diego	NL	47	9	0	0	2	4	0	0	38	.191	.255	.319	.184	3	.205
1994	Las Vegas	PCL	394	104	9	3	20	53	1	1	291	.264	.351	.454	.266	53	.294
1995	San Diego	NL	238	52	6	1	15	22	2	3	189	.218	.285	.441	.234	25	.255
1996	Detroit	AL	432	107	24	4	24	44	1	2	327	.248	.317	.488	.261	57	.279
1997	*Detroit*	*AL*	*573*	*160*	*30*	*5*	*25*	*77*	*4*	*4*	*417*	*.279*	*.365*	*.480*	*.280*	*86*	

He finally hit in the majors the way his minor league numbers always said he would. He struck out even more than Clark, but lived it up early in the count: he hit .529 with a 1.020 slugging average on the first pitch. He's actually a much better outfielder than he's given credit for, but the Tigers' crowded outfield situation may push him to DH. Unless and until he learns to cut down on his strikeouts, he'll never reach the greatness that he's capable of. I like his chances; at the worst he'll be a switch-hitting Rob Deer, and in Tiger Stadium that's quite a player.

SHANNON PENN   **2B**   **1970**   **Age 27**

Year	Team	Lge	AB	H	DB	TP	HR	BB	SB	CS	OUT	BA	OBA	SA	EQA	EQR	Peak
1993	London	East	503	124	12	3	1	50	28	9	388	.247	.315	.288	.212	40	.230
1994	Toledo	Inter	450	122	14	4	2	30	30	10	338	.271	.317	.333	.228	42	.245
1995	Toledo	Inter	224	56	3	1	1	18	11	5	173	.250	.306	.286	.204	16	.215
1996	Toledo	Inter	359	97	11	2	6	28	14	7	269	.270	.323	.362	.234	36	.244

Penn was considered a top prospect by the Tigers two years ago. Ken Oberkfell would have been considered a top prospect two years ago by the Tigers.

CURTIS PRIDE   **LF/DH**   **1969**   **Age 28**

Year	Team	Lge	AB	H	DB	TP	HR	BB	SB	CS	OUT	BA	OBA	SA	EQA	EQR	Peak
1993	Harrisburg	East	185	66	5	2	13	12	13	4	123	.357	.396	.616	.325	37	.348
1993	Ottawa	Inter	270	79	9	3	6	34	21	8	199	.293	.372	.415	.270	38	.289
1994	Ottawa	Inter	312	83	13	3	10	38	16	4	233	.266	.346	.423	.262	41	.276
1995	Ottawa	Inter	158	44	6	2	5	13	6	3	117	.278	.333	.437	.257	20	.268
1995	Montreal	NL	64	12	1	0	0	5	2	2	54	.188	.246	.203	.127	2	.135
1996	Detroit	AL	268	81	17	5	10	31	11	6	193	.302	.375	.515	.290	44	.297
1997	*Detroit*	*AL*	*416*	*119*	*23*	*6*	*15*	*47*	*25*	*15*	*311*	*.286*	*.359*	*.478*	*.277*	*63*	

Pride, like Jim Abbott, has proven that your ability will eventually overshadow everything, even a disability. Pride is 95% deaf, but also a fine left-handed hitter, similar to Troy O'Leary but with better defense and speed. At the very least, he would be a terrific fourth outfielder for any team in baseball. As he continues to prove that he belongs in the major leagues, I suspect articles written about him will stop being prefaced with "Pride, who is 95% deaf...," and I suspect that's the way he wants it.

STEVE RODRIGUEZ   **2B**   **1971**   **Age 26**

Year	Team	Lge	AB	H	DB	TP	HR	BB	SB	CS	OUT	BA	OBA	SA	EQA	EQR	Peak
1993	Lynchburg	Caro	506	122	18	1	3	30	11	6	390	.241	.284	.298	.195	33	.214
1994	New Britain	East	164	45	4	2	0	9	5	2	121	.274	.312	.323	.219	14	.237
1994	Pawtucket	Inter	235	66	6	0	2	14	7	2	171	.281	.321	.332	.226	21	.245
1995	Pawtucket	Inter	327	72	15	2	1	27	9	5	260	.220	.280	.287	.188	20	.202
1996	Toledo	Inter	336	92	15	1	4	25	12	2	246	.274	.324	.360	.237	34	.250

He has a good glove, but his little ball skills at the plate aren't suited for a middle infielder in the '90s. A good insurance guy to have around in case the injury bug hits, but that's about it.

RUBEN SIERRA   **DH/OF**   **1966**   **Age 31**

Year	Team	Lge	AB	H	DB	TP	HR	BB	SB	CS	OUT	BA	OBA	SA	EQA	EQR	Peak
1993	Oakland	AL	642	164	24	5	28	56	23	4	482	.255	.315	.439	.254	78	.260
1994	Oakland	AL	432	121	21	1	25	23	8	5	316	.280	.316	.507	.268	59	.270
1995	Oakland	AL	269	76	15	0	15	25	4	4	197	.283	.344	.506	.275	39	.274
1995	NY Yankees	AL	216	58	11	0	9	23	1	0	158	.269	.339	.444	.261	27	.258
1996	NY Yankees	AL	360	93	17	1	11	40	1	3	270	.258	.333	.403	.244	40	.238
1996	Detroit	AL	158	35	10	1	1	20	3	1	124	.222	.309	.316	.212	13	.207
1997	*Cincinnati*	*NL*	*396*	*100*	*27*	*1*	*14*	*25*	*4*	*3*	*299*	*.253*	*.297*	*.432*	*.252*	*4*	

The Tigers were so desperate to dump him that they took two borderline prospects for him and are still paying over 80% of his salary. A classic Jim Bowden move, picking up a maligned veteran on the cheap and using his contract year as motivation for one good season. Sierra's collapse as a player is attributable to 1) the importance of plate discipline, 2) how difficult it is to master the game of baseball for very long and 3) how far over his head Sierra was playing in 1989.

DUANE SINGLETON   **CF**   **1973**   **Age 24**

Year	Team	Lge	AB	H	DB	TP	HR	BB	SB	CS	OUT	BA	OBA	SA	EQA	EQR	Peak
1993	El Paso	Texas	459	89	15	4	2	35	14	8	378	.194	.251	.257	.162	20	.184
1994	Stockton	Calif	139	38	2	0	4	15	8	3	104	.273	.344	.374	.248	16	.278
1994	El Paso	Texas	142	38	9	2	2	17	6	2	106	.268	.346	.401	.255	17	.284
1994	New Orleans	AmA	136	38	5	4	0	19	5	3	101	.279	.368	.375	.253	16	.285
1995	New Orleans	AmA	363	95	9	2	5	41	29	12	280	.262	.337	.339	.236	38	.261
1996	Toledo	Inter	298	64	11	4	8	36	12	5	239	.215	.299	.359	.222	28	.241
1996	Detroit	AL	56	9	1	0	0	4	0	2	49	.161	.217	.179	-.029	0	.020

Singleton looked like the solution to Milwaukee's center field problem after a swift ascent up the minor league chain in 1994, but he's a singles hitter who hasn't hit enough of them recently. In a way he's the mirror image of Bartee, and the two of them may get a chance to platoon in center, at least until the Tigers get fed up with their offense and try Higginson out there again.

JEFF TACKETT   **C**   **1966** **Age 31**

Year	Team	Lge	AB	H	DB	TP	HR	BB	SB	CS	OUT	BA	OBA	SA	EQA	EQR	Peak
1993	Baltimore	AL	87	15	4	0	0	14	0	0	72	.172	.287	.218	.157	4	.163
1994	Baltimore	AL	53	12	2	1	2	5	0	0	41	.226	.293	.415	.233	5	.237
1995	Toledo	Inter	313	86	8	0	8	36	2	1	228	.275	.350	.377	.247	34	.246
1996	Toledo	Inter	287	65	8	1	7	36	3	1	223	.226	.313	.334	.218	25	.213

Our obligatory AAA backup catcher reference. The Tigers could do worse than to give him the backup job in Detroit, but with Casanova and Ausmus they probably won't.

ALAN TRAMMELL   **SS/HoF**   **1958** **Age 39**

Year	Team	Lge	AB	H	DB	TP	HR	BB	SB	CS	OUT	BA	OBA	SA	EQA	EQR	Peak
1993	Detroit	AL	409	141	25	3	15	41	12	6	274	.345	.404	.531	.308	72	.292
1994	Detroit	AL	293	79	14	1	9	16	3	0	214	.270	.307	.416	.243	31	.231
1995	Detroit	AL	224	61	7	0	4	27	3	1	164	.272	.351	.357	.243	24	.231
1996	Detroit	AL	193	45	0	0	2	10	6	0	148	.233	.271	.264	.182	10	.173

It was sad watching Trammell end his career on this excuse for a team. At least it allowed him to get a head start on his coaching career, which should begin shortly. Looking forward to seeing Whitaker and him inducted in about 15 years.

BUBBA TRAMMELL   **OF**   **1972** **Age 25**

Year	Team	Lge	AB	H	DB	TP	HR	BB	SB	CS	OUT	BA	OBA	SA	EQA	EQR	Peak
1994	Jamestown	NY-P	244	63	8	1	6	18	4	3	184	.258	.309	.373	.228	23	.251
1995	Lakeland	Flor	478	138	20	1	18	42	8	2	342	.289	.346	.448	.266	63	.290
1996	Jacksonville	South	318	103	15	1	24	27	2	1	216	.324	.377	.604	.313	59	.335
1996	Toledo	Inter	183	52	10	1	6	22	3	1	132	.284	.361	.448	.271	25	.291
1997	*Detroit*	*AL*	*554*	*164*	*22*	*1*	*38*	*66*	*7*	*4*	*394*	*.296*	*.371*	*.545*	*.298*	*96*	

This Trammell (no relation) is exactly what you'd expect from a guy named Bubba: he's an adventure in the outfield—though he did make strides defensively this year—but an absolute monster at the plate. He deserves to play in the major leagues this year, and at some point he probably will. As long as the DH rule is still in place, Trammell is going to make a good living terrorizing pitchers for 300 at bats a year. Tore up the AFL.

DARYLE WARD   **1B**   **1975** **Age 22**

Year	Team	Lge	AB	H	DB	TP	HR	BB	SB	CS	OUT	BA	OBA	SA	EQA	EQR	Peak
1995	Fayetteville	S Atl	540	131	11	0	13	37	1	1	410	.243	.291	.335	.208	41	.237
1996	Lakeland	Flor	479	130	19	1	12	51	1	1	350	.271	.342	.390	.247	53	.276

Daryle is the son of former major leaguer Gary Ward, and the Tigers love his stroke. He was promoted to AAA briefly when the Tigers had an opening, indicating that they have him on the fast track. He's young and talented; he's also far from being ready. Check back a year from now.

ERIC WEDGE   **DH**   **1968** **Age 29**

Year	Team	Lge	AB	H	DB	TP	HR	BB	SB	CS	OUT	BA	OBA	SA	EQA	EQR	Peak
1993	Colo. Springs	PCL	88	19	2	0	3	14	0	0	69	.216	.324	.341	.222	8	.236
1994	Pawtucket	Inter	261	72	9	0	17	48	0	1	190	.276	.388	.506	.291	44	.304
1995	Pawtucket	Inter	385	87	10	1	19	61	1	2	300	.226	.332	.405	.243	44	.250
1996	Toledo	Inter	337	77	14	0	15	43	2	1	261	.228	.316	.404	.238	36	.240

Injuries ruined what could have been a great career. He can still hit, but he has absolutely no defensive value, and there are a lot of players just like him stuck in AAA.

EDDIE WILLIAMS   **DH/1B**   **1965** **Age 32**

Year	Team	Lge	AB	H	DB	TP	HR	BB	SB	CS	OUT	BA	OBA	SA	EQA	EQR	Peak
1993	Monterrey	Mex	206	62	7	0	9	15	0	1	145	.301	.348	.466	.269	27	.272
1994	Las Vegas	PCL	211	65	6	0	16	22	0	0	146	.308	.373	.564	.302	37	.301
1994	San Diego	NL	179	61	9	1	12	18	0	1	119	.341	.401	.603	.320	35	.318
1995	San Diego	NL	304	84	11	1	13	27	0	0	220	.276	.335	.447	.260	38	.255
1996	Detroit	AL	215	43	6	0	6	18	0	2	174	.200	.262	.312	.182	12	.175
1997	*Detroit*	*AL*	*164*	*42*	*3*	*1*	*9*	*16*	*0*	*0*	*122*	*.256*	*.322*	*.451*	*.257*	*20*	

Probably finished. Williams had a brutal season, and grounds into more double plays (one every 21.7 at bats for his career) than anyone else in baseball.

BRIAN BARNES   **LSP**   **1967**   **Age 30**

YR	TEAM	Lge	IP	H	ER	HR	BB	K	ERA	W	L	H/9	HR/9	BB/9	K/9	KW
1993	Montreal	NL	98.0	110	50	10	60	58	4.59	5	6	10.10	.92	5.51	5.33	.40
1994	Albuquerque	PCL	44.3	51	28	8	28	37	5.68	2	3	10.35	1.62	5.68	7.51	1.08
1994	Charlotte, NC	Inter	17.3	19	10	2	10	19	5.19	1	1	9.87	1.04	5.19	9.87	1.99
1994	Cleveland	AL	13.3	11	7	2	15	5	4.72	0	1	7.43	1.35	10.12	3.38	-1.41
1995	Pawtucket	Inter	100.0	113	58	13	43	76	5.22	4	7	10.17	1.17	3.87	6.84	1.31
1996	Jacksonville	South	68.7	85	35	8	29	54	4.59	3	5	11.14	1.05	3.80	7.08	1.41
1996	Toledo	Inter	84.0	88	41	7	39	58	4.39	4	5	9.43	.75	4.18	6.21	1.03

This is the same Brian Barnes who pitched well for the Expos in the early '90s. He's bounced around various organizations the last three years, but was healthy all season and pitched very well at both minor league stops. Ordinarily I wouldn't bet on a 30-year-old minor leaguer to get promoted, but he's a better pitcher than most of the stiffs the Tigers were trying last year, and he's left-handed. Deserves a shot.

CLAYTON BRUNER   **RSP**   **1977**   **Age 20**

YR	TEAM	Lge	IP	H	ER	HR	BB	K	ERA	W	L	H/9	HR/9	BB/9	K/9	KW
1996	Fayetteville	S Atl	131.7	172	78	8	110	83	5.33	5	10	11.76	.55	7.52	5.67	.01

Bruner was the best pitcher in the Fayetteville rotation, but all four main starters are good prospects: Bruner, David Borkowski, a smallish right-hander with a great sinking fastball, left-hander Justin Bettencourt and David Melendez. Bruner had the best numbers of the four, and like Borkowski was just 19. They're all too far from the majors to worry about right now, but in a year or two they should go a long way towards restoring what has been a barren farm system for some time.

BRYAN COREY   **RRP**   **1974**   **Age 23**

YR	TEAM	Lge	IP	H	ER	HR	BB	K	ERA	W	L	H/9	HR/9	BB/9	K/9	KW
1995	Jamestown	NY-P	23.7	27	15	3	18	24	5.70	1	2	10.27	1.14	6.85	9.13	1.33
1996	Fayetteville	S Atl	72.7	71	21	3	26	55	2.60	6	2	8.79	.37	3.22	6.81	1.47

A converted shortstop, Corey had an outstanding season in his first full year on the mound. He's only 6 feet, 160 pounds, but throws a heavy 92 miles an hour. He needs another good year before the comparisons to Trevor Hoffman (also a converted infielder) begin, but I like his chances. He was just too dominating last year to be a fluke.

JOHN CUMMINGS   **LRP**   **1969**   **Age 28**

YR	TEAM	Lge	IP	H	ER	HR	BB	K	ERA	W	L	H/9	HR/9	BB/9	K/9	KW
1993	Jacksonville	South	41.7	56	24	1	14	26	5.18	2	3	12.10	.22	3.02	5.62	1.12
1993	Calgary	PCL	60.0	67	31	6	27	33	4.65	3	4	10.05	.90	4.05	4.95	.64
1993	Seattle	AL	47.0	57	29	6	18	20	5.55	2	3	10.91	1.15	3.45	3.83	.41
1994	Seattle	AL	64.0	61	31	6	39	32	4.36	3	4	8.58	.84	5.48	4.50	.13
1995	San Antonio	Texas	24.3	33	14	0	10	11	5.18	1	2	12.21	.00	3.70	4.07	.43
1995	Los Angeles	NL	37.7	41	15	3	14	19	3.58	2	2	9.80	.72	3.35	4.54	.68
1996	Albuquerque	PCL	74.0	83	35	5	35	39	4.26	4	4	10.09	.61	4.26	4.74	.52
1996	Detroit	AL	31.7	34	15	2	21	23	4.26	2	2	9.66	.57	5.97	6.54	.69

Part of the haul the Tigers got for Chad Curtis. Maybe I'm stupid, but trading a center fielder in the prime of his career for two left-handers on the fringe of the major leagues doesn't seem like a fair trade. The Tigers were desperate for pitching help though, and Cummings wasn't terrible. For his career, lefties have hit better against him than right-handers (.313 vs. .280), so his chances of turning into a Tony Fossas-like specialist look slim. If he continues to get chances, I suspect he'll eventually improve his control and turn into a competent reliever.

MATT DREWS   **RSP**   **1975**   **Age 22**

YR	TEAM	Lge	IP	H	ER	HR	BB	K	ERA	W	L	H/9	HR/9	BB/9	K/9	KW
1994	Oneonta	NY-P	76.3	104	36	2	32	41	4.24	4	4	12.26	.24	3.77	4.83	.67
1995	Tampa	Flor	163.0	175	77	8	81	99	4.25	8	10	9.66	.44	4.47	5.47	.70
1996	Tampa	Flor	15.3	30	21	0	16	9	12.33	0	2	17.61	.00	9.39	5.28	-.59
1996	Norwich	East	42.0	47	27	4	40	28	5.79	2	3	10.07	.86	8.57	6.00	-.14
1996	Columbus, OH	Inter	19.7	17	22	4	30	6	10.07	0	2	7.78	1.83	13.73	2.75	-2.52
1996	Jacksonville	South	28.7	29	17	4	22	29	5.34	1	2	9.10	1.26	6.91	9.10	1.31

Let's face it: the Yankees over-hyped Drews before the season began. His terrific numbers at Tampa in 1995 were partly a result of playing in a great pitcher's league, and the Yankees failed to consider that when they jumped him to AAA. He's still got a great arm, and the Tigers were fortunate to get him while he was stuck in a slump. He's tall (6' 8"), durable and throws three pitches for strikes. If the Tigers are patient with him, he should be in their rotation by mid-1998.

MIKE DRUMRIGHT   **RSP**   **1974**   **Age 23**

YR	TEAM	Lge	IP	H	ER	HR	BB	K	ERA	W	L	H/9	HR/9	BB/9	K/9	KW
1995	Lakeland	Flor	18.3	25	13	3	12	14	6.38	1	1	12.27	1.47	5.89	6.87	.82
1995	Jacksonville	South	29.0	36	14	5	20	26	4.34	1	2	11.17	1.55	6.21	8.07	1.14
1996	Jacksonville	South	92.0	92	48	12	56	79	4.70	4	6	9.00	1.17	5.48	7.73	1.21

Drumright is the classic pitching prospect, a big right-hander with a mid-90s fastball and a deadly curveball. His breaking pitch was voted the best in the Southern League. He missed some time with a "weak shoulder;" he's not the first pitcher out of Wichita State to have arm trouble (Darren Dreifort, Tyler Green). The Tigers were extra cautious with him, and if his control continues to improve, he could turn into Jack McDowell.

JOEY EISCHEN   **LRP**   **1970**   **Age 27**

YR	TEAM	Lge	IP	H	ER	HR	BB	K	ERA	W	L	H/9	HR/9	BB/9	K/9	KW
1993	Harrisburg	East	108.7	141	63	13	77	84	5.22	4	8	11.68	1.08	6.38	6.96	.72
1993	Ottawa	Inter	38.3	37	16	3	20	23	3.76	2	2	8.69	.70	4.70	5.40	.63
1994	Ottawa	Inter	58.3	62	39	8	49	48	6.02	2	4	9.57	1.23	7.56	7.41	.58
1995	Albuquerque	PCL	15.3	8	0	0	5	13	.00	2	0	4.70	.00	2.93	7.63	1.81
1995	Ottawa	Inter	14.7	11	3	0	10	11	1.84	2	0	6.75	.00	6.14	6.75	.72
1995	Los Angeles	NL	20.3	20	8	1	13	14	3.54	1	1	8.85	.44	5.75	6.20	.63
1996	Detroit	AL	24.7	26	8	2	15	15	2.92	2	1	9.49	.73	5.47	5.47	.46
1996	Los Angeles	NL	42.7	52	24	4	25	32	5.06	2	3	10.97	.84	5.27	6.75	.93

The other half of the Curtis booty. Like Cummings, Eischen is a lefty whose numbers haven't yet caught up to his arm. Eischen was coveted by a number of teams—the Mariners reportedly offered Chris Widger for him—and his control has steadily improved. My gut feeling is that Eischen will have a decent career.

RAMON FERMIN   **RBP**   **1973**   **Age 24**

YR	TEAM	Lge	IP	H	ER	HR	BB	K	ERA	W	L	H/9	HR/9	BB/9	K/9	KW
1993	Modesto	Calif	58.7	87	51	7	41	33	7.82	1	6	13.35	1.07	6.29	5.06	.12
1994	Modesto	Calif	118.7	151	69	13	55	79	5.23	5	8	11.45	.99	4.17	5.99	.95
1995	Huntsville	South	91.3	124	56	5	59	45	5.52	3	7	12.22	.49	5.81	4.43	.02
1996	Jacksonville	South	77.0	92	53	6	53	35	6.19	3	6	10.75	.70	6.19	4.09	-.19

Acquired along with Fausto Cruz for Phil Plantier last winter, Fermin is about as nondescript as a prospect can be. He has decent stuff and numbers, but there's nothing in his record to suggest he'll ever be a major league pitcher.

EDDIE GAILLARD   **RRP**   **1971**   **Age 26**

YR	TEAM	Lge	IP	H	ER	HR	BB	K	ERA	W	L	H/9	HR/9	BB/9	K/9	KW
1993	Niagara	NY-P	11.7	23	9	0	7	6	6.94	0	1	17.74	.00	5.40	4.63	.19
1993	Fayetteville	S Atl	51.0	89	37	11	29	24	6.53	2	4	15.71	1.94	5.12	4.24	.13
1994	Lakeland	Flor	83.3	96	38	5	39	39	4.10	4	5	10.37	.54	4.21	4.21	.35
1995	Lakeland	Flor	48.3	64	15	1	25	37	2.79	3	2	11.92	.19	4.66	6.89	1.13
1996	Jacksonville	South	80.3	93	37	8	58	55	4.15	4	5	10.42	.90	6.50	6.16	.43

Gaillard has steadily moved up the Tigers' system despite not having one outstanding characteristic. His ERAs have been much better than his peripheral numbers would suggest, and he keeps the ball in the park. Grade C prospect; if the Tigers call him up, he'll probably walk a man an inning and be sent down faster than you can say "Clint Sodowsky."

RICK GREENE   **RSP**   **1971**   **Age 26**

YR	TEAM	Lge	IP	H	ER	HR	BB	K	ERA	W	L	H/9	HR/9	BB/9	K/9	KW
1993	Lakeland	Flor	34.7	68	31	2	23	25	8.05	1	3	17.65	.52	5.97	6.49	.67
1993	London	East	26.7	34	21	2	24	14	7.09	1	2	11.48	.68	8.10	4.72	-.45
1994	Lakeland	Flor	30.0	57	24	1	14	21	7.20	1	2	17.10	.30	4.20	6.30	1.05
1994	Trenton	East	17.3	20	18	0	25	4	9.35	0	2	10.38	.00	12.98	2.08	-2.55
1995	Jacksonville	South	35.7	53	20	4	20	22	5.05	2	2	13.37	1.01	5.05	5.55	.59
1996	Jacksonville	South	52.0	71	40	8	45	30	6.92	2	4	12.29	1.38	7.79	5.19	-.22

The Tigers' #1 pick in 1993, Greene has spent the better part of the last four seasons in double-A, but has never been even mildly effective. He was Jacksonville's closer last year, and somehow saved 30 games despite a 4.98 ERA. It's a tough pill to swallow, but if Greene doesn't turn the corner this year, the Tigers are going to have to admit they blew the pick and cut their losses.

GREG KEAGLE   **RBP**   **1971**   **Age 26**

YR	TEAM	Lge	IP	H	ER	HR	BB	K	ERA	W	L	H/9	HR/9	BB/9	K/9	KW
1993	Spokane	Nwern	69.3	108	40	3	43	43	5.19	3	5	14.02	.39	5.58	5.58	.47
1994	R. Cucamonga	Calif	82.7	72	20	2	52	59	2.18	7	2	7.84	.22	5.66	6.42	.73
1994	Wichita	Texas	64.3	93	53	7	41	41	7.41	2	5	13.01	.98	5.74	5.74	.48
1995	Memphis	South	75.0	94	53	12	53	63	6.36	2	6	11.28	1.44	6.36	7.56	.93
1995	Las Vegas	PCL	71.0	70	34	3	49	44	4.31	4	4	8.87	.38	6.21	5.58	.31
1996	Toledo	Inter	26.7	41	26	6	14	20	8.78	1	2	13.84	2.03	4.72	6.75	1.07
1996	Detroit	AL	89.0	95	57	11	70	68	5.76	3	7	9.61	1.11	7.08	6.88	.52

The only time Keagle pitched like a major leaguer was during the spring of 1994, but the Tigers liked his arm enough to keep him as a Rule V selection all season. He pitched much better after the Break, posting a 3.00 ERA in 24 innings, but still wasn't around the plate enough. His late surge not withstanding, he probably doesn't have enough command of his pitches to be consistently effective.

RICHIE LEWIS   **RRP**   **1966**   **Age 31**

YR	TEAM	Lge	IP	H	ER	HR	BB	K	ERA	W	L	H/9	HR/9	BB/9	K/9	KW
1993	Florida	NL	75.3	71	33	7	51	63	3.94	4	4	8.48	.84	6.09	7.53	.99
1994	Florida	NL	54.7	57	36	7	43	42	5.93	2	4	9.38	1.15	7.08	6.91	.54
1995	Charlotte, NC	Inter	55.3	55	21	6	28	38	3.42	3	3	8.95	.98	4.55	6.18	.92
1995	Florida	NL	35.3	31	13	9	18	29	3.31	2	2	7.90	2.29	4.58	7.39	1.32
1996	Detroit	AL	90.3	73	32	8	67	76	3.19	6	4	7.27	.80	6.68	7.57	.86

Arguably the only legitimate pitcher on the Tigers' staff all season. Lewis set an NCAA record for strikeouts while at Florida State, but at 5'10", most scouts were turned off by his height and he's been fighting an uphill battle ever since. He's been an effective, if wild, pitcher for the last four years, and his 72 appearances saved the bullpen from further abuse. As long as he keeps getting the ball and stays in his comfortable setup role, he should continue to pitch well. Released by Detroit in a roster space move, he'll be an NRI somewhere.

JOSE LIMA   **RRP**   **1973**   **Age 24**

YR	TEAM	Lge	IP	H	ER	HR	BB	K	ERA	W	L	H/9	HR/9	BB/9	K/9	KW
1993	London	East	163.7	177	90	21	78	104	4.95	7	11	9.73	1.15	4.29	5.72	.83
1994	Toledo	Inter	134.3	135	63	16	61	97	4.22	7	8	9.04	1.07	4.09	6.50	1.14
1995	Lakeland	Flor	18.3	30	14	3	2	14	6.87	1	1	14.73	1.47	.98	6.87	2.05
1995	Toledo	Inter	69.7	79	27	10	23	34	3.49	5	3	10.21	1.29	2.97	4.39	.72
1995	Detroit	AL	74.0	79	39	9	20	37	4.74	3	5	9.61	1.09	2.43	4.50	.89
1996	Toledo	Inter	67.0	93	44	10	19	47	5.91	2	5	12.49	1.34	2.55	6.31	1.47
1996	Detroit	AL	73.3	80	36	11	24	57	4.42	4	4	9.82	1.35	2.95	7.00	1.60

One of the Tigers' few home-grown pitchers, Lima is a control specialist who had no movement on his fastball as a starter. The Tigers tired of watching him surrender a .300 average and moved him to the bullpen. Not having to pace himself seems to have helped Lima's stuff; after the break, he gave up 47 hits in 46 innings strictly out of the bullpen. He also struck out a man an inning and his control improved. He still has problems with the gopher ball, but the Tigers consider him their closer of the future. His growing pains are probably not over, but his future is still bright.

FELIPE LIRA   **RSP**   **1972**   **Age 25**

YR	TEAM	Lge	IP	H	ER	HR	BB	K	ERA	W	L	H/9	HR/9	BB/9	K/9	KW
1993	London	East	139.3	177	61	18	54	92	3.94	8	7	11.43	1.16	3.49	5.94	1.11
1993	Toledo	Inter	29.7	35	18	5	15	19	5.46	1	2	10.62	1.52	4.55	5.76	.78
1994	Toledo	Inter	143.7	181	84	19	60	92	5.26	6	10	11.34	1.19	3.76	5.76	.98
1995	Detroit	AL	147.0	140	54	15	59	88	3.31	10	6	8.57	.92	3.61	5.39	.89
1996	Detroit	AL	195.3	188	90	25	71	109	4.15	11	11	8.66	1.15	3.27	5.02	.86

The ace of the staff. No one outside the state of Michigan has noticed that Lira has had two straight solid seasons and doesn't turn 25 until April. Despite going 0-7 after the break, he had a very respectable 4.73 ERA. He has kept his poise despite no assistance from his defense, which a pitcher like Lira needs, or his bullpen. If he ever does get that support, he could easily win 18 games.

TREVER MILLER LSP 1973 Age 24

YR	TEAM	Lge	IP	H	ER	HR	BB	K	ERA	W	L	H/9	HR/9	BB/9	K/9	KW
1993	Fayetteville	S Atl	132.7	214	126	11	94	69	8.55	3	12	14.52	.75	6.38	4.68	-.03
1994	Trenton	East	157.0	231	100	10	71	54	5.73	6	11	13.24	.57	4.07	3.10	.01
1995	Jacksonville	South	112.7	143	48	6	49	59	3.83	7	6	11.42	.48	3.91	4.71	.59
1996	Toledo	Inter	158.3	171	83	18	83	95	4.72	8	10	9.72	1.02	4.72	5.40	.62
1996	Detroit	AL	16.7	27	13	2	9	8	7.02	0	2	14.58	1.08	4.86	4.32	.22

The Tigers are looking at Miller to be the token lefty in their rotation next year, but I'm skeptical about his chances. He has neither great control nor high K rates, and he got the snot beaten out of him with the Tigers in September. I wouldn't give up on any 24-year-old left-hander, but Miller is at least a year or two away.

BRIAN MOEHLER RSP 1972 Age 25

YR	TEAM	Lge	IP	H	ER	HR	BB	K	ERA	W	L	H/9	HR/9	BB/9	K/9	KW
1993	Niagara	NY-P	46.0	77	45	5	43	20	8.80	1	4	15.07	.98	8.41	3.91	-.80
1994	Lakeland	Flor	149.0	177	67	6	86	70	4.05	8	9	10.69	.36	5.19	4.23	.11
1995	Jacksonville	South	147.3	210	102	16	73	69	6.23	5	11	12.83	.98	4.46	4.21	.29
1996	Jacksonville	South	159.0	211	76	10	59	87	4.30	8	10	11.94	.57	3.34	4.92	.81
1996	Detroit	AL	10.3	11	8	1	8	2	6.97	0	1	9.58	.87	6.97	1.74	-1.16

The Tigers also gave Moehler an audition last September, but he has even less talent than Miller. The Tigers assistant GM described Moehler as having "average big league stuff," and that was meant as a compliment. When words like "he's a real competitor" and "he eats up innings" are used to describe a pitcher, it's usually the kiss of death. Moehler's numbers certainly don't suggest he'll be anything more than a tenth man.

MIKE MYERS LRP 1969 Age 28

YR	TEAM	Lge	IP	H	ER	HR	BB	K	ERA	W	L	H/9	HR/9	BB/9	K/9	KW
1993	Edmonton	PCL	150.0	181	83	20	67	88	4.98	7	10	10.86	1.20	4.02	5.28	.75
1994	Brevard Cty	Flor	10.3	9	1	2	5	11	.87	1	0	7.84	1.74	4.35	9.58	2.10
1994	Edmonton	PCL	57.0	70	31	8	27	47	4.89	2	4	11.05	1.26	4.26	7.42	1.41
1995	Charlotte, NC	Inter	34.7	44	24	6	20	20	6.23	1	3	11.42	1.56	5.19	5.19	.43
1996	Detroit	AL	65.3	64	30	5	36	67	4.13	3	4	8.82	.69	4.96	9.23	1.84

Almost a mirror image of Richie Lewis. Another Marlin refugee, Myers had some control problems but was still the second-best reliever on the team. He appeared in more games (83) than any pitcher since 1987. It was only his second season as a reliever, and Myers struck out over a man an inning; any left-hander who can accomplish that has to be taken seriously. Held lefties to a .229 average. If you're in a roto league and looking for cheap saves, keep him in mind.

C.J. NITKOWSKI LSP 1973 Age 24

YR	TEAM	Lge	IP	H	ER	HR	BB	K	ERA	W	L	H/9	HR/9	BB/9	K/9	KW
1994	Chattanooga	South	68.3	72	32	5	54	47	4.21	4	4	9.48	.66	7.11	6.19	.29
1995	Chattanooga	South	46.0	47	19	0	26	40	3.72	3	2	9.20	.00	5.09	7.83	1.34
1995	Indianapolis	AmA	26.3	29	14	2	14	18	4.78	1	2	9.91	.68	4.78	6.15	.85
1995	Cincinnati	NL	32.3	41	22	4	18	16	6.12	1	3	11.41	1.11	5.01	4.45	.23
1995	Detroit	AL	40.3	48	24	6	21	13	5.36	1	3	10.71	1.34	4.69	2.90	-.20
1996	Toledo	Inter	106.3	107	51	12	66	85	4.32	6	6	9.06	1.02	5.59	7.19	1.00
1996	Detroit	AL	47.0	56	33	6	39	35	6.32	1	4	10.72	1.15	7.47	6.70	.37

A Seton Hall grad with a great changeup, Nitkowski is having more trouble with the major league transition than most pitchers. He has pitched very well in the minor leagues, but every time he's brought up he gets lit up like a Christmas tree. He'll probably be an effective starter some day, but it will be an upset if happens in 1997. Sent to Houston, same prognosis, but in a better situation.

OMAR OLIVARES | RSP | 1968 | Age 29

YR	TEAM	Lge	IP	H	ER	HR	BB	K	ERA	W	L	H/9	HR/9	BB/9	K/9	KW
1993	St. Louis	NL	116.3	143	59	11	69	62	4.56	6	7	11.06	.85	5.34	4.80	.26
1994	Louisville	AmA	45.3	47	20	4	20	34	3.97	3	2	9.33	.79	3.97	6.75	1.26
1994	St. Louis	NL	74.0	81	46	10	44	24	5.59	3	5	9.85	1.22	5.35	2.92	-.36
1995	Colo. Springs	PCL	11.0	13	5	1	3	5	4.09	0	1	10.64	.82	2.45	4.09	.75
1995	Scranton-WB	Inter	41.0	54	24	2	26	24	5.27	2	3	11.85	.44	5.71	5.27	.33
1995	Colorado	NL	32.3	37	20	3	23	13	5.57	1	3	10.30	.84	6.40	3.62	-.39
1996	Detroit	AL	160.3	157	66	13	78	78	3.70	10	8	8.81	.73	4.38	4.38	.36

Came back from the dead, or rather Coors Field, to post the best season of any Tigers starter. He's only a short-term solution, but he gets groundballs and has the experience to deal with the inevitable defensive mistakes that the Tigers will make as they improve. No star potential here, but he'll do as a #3 starter until Drumright, Greisinger and Drews are ready.

BRANDON REED | RRP | 1975 | Age 22

YR	TEAM	Lge	IP	H	ER	HR	BB	K	ERA	W	L	H/9	HR/9	BB/9	K/9	KW
1995	Fayetteville	S Atl	57.7	52	11	2	27	44	1.72	5	1	8.12	.31	4.21	6.87	1.24
1996	Jacksonville	South	24.0	22	5	1	3	13	1.88	2	1	8.25	.38	1.12	4.88	1.34

Reed's a sidearmer with deceptive stuff, frightening numbers and an equally frightening injury history. He's thin as a, well, reed and missed time all year with assorted ailments. Sidearm pitchers typically have trouble as they move up the ladder, but Reed didn't miss a beat while jumping from the Sally League to AA ball. If he stays healthy, he could be in Detroit by mid-season.

A.J. SAGER | RBP | 1965 | Age 32

YR	TEAM	Lge	IP	H	ER	HR	BB	K	ERA	W	L	H/9	HR/9	BB/9	K/9	KW
1993	Wichita	Texas	65.0	84	34	6	27	35	4.71	3	4	11.63	.83	3.74	4.85	.68
1993	Las Vegas	PCL	83.3	87	37	8	25	46	4.00	5	4	9.40	.86	2.70	4.97	.98
1994	Las Vegas	PCL	38.3	51	18	3	12	19	4.23	2	2	11.97	.70	2.82	4.46	.78
1994	San Diego	NL	46.7	61	30	4	21	24	5.79	2	3	11.76	.77	4.05	4.63	.53
1995	Colo. Springs	PCL	126.7	140	45	15	34	72	3.20	9	5	9.95	1.07	2.42	5.12	1.10
1995	Colorado	NL	14.7	17	12	1	8	9	7.36	0	2	10.43	.61	4.91	5.52	.61
1996	Toledo	Inter	36.0	40	12	5	6	20	3.00	3	1	10.00	1.25	1.50	5.00	1.29
1996	Detroit	AL	79.0	85	35	8	31	50	3.99	5	4	9.68	.91	3.53	5.70	1.02

This was one of Detroit's better pitchers this year. Honest.

CAM SMITH | RSP | 1974 | Age 23

YR	TEAM	Lge	IP	H	ER	HR	BB	K	ERA	W	L	H/9	HR/9	BB/9	K/9	KW
1994	Fayetteville	S Atl	113.3	176	118	12	120	77	9.37	2	11	13.98	.95	9.53	6.11	-.34
1995	Fayetteville	S Atl	129.3	137	80	8	121	94	5.57	5	9	9.53	.56	8.42	6.54	.08
1996	Lakeland	Flor	100.3	117	73	14	93	83	6.55	3	8	10.50	1.26	8.34	7.45	.40

A power arm, but if he's heard of the strike zone, he's keeping the secret to himself. Whether he can survive the jump to AA will tell us if he's got a future or not.

CLINT SODOWSKY | RSP | 1973 | Age 24

YR	TEAM	Lge	IP	H	ER	HR	BB	K	ERA	W	L	H/9	HR/9	BB/9	K/9	KW
1993	Fayetteville	S Atl	127.3	245	126	16	73	48	8.91	2	12	17.32	1.13	5.16	3.39	-.16
1994	Lakeland	Flor	98.7	131	61	8	47	56	5.56	4	7	11.95	.73	4.29	5.11	.63
1995	Jacksonville	South	113.7	121	47	5	66	59	3.72	7	6	9.58	.40	5.23	4.67	.25
1995	Toledo	Inter	56.0	54	21	6	39	27	3.38	4	2	8.68	.96	6.27	4.34	-.12
1995	Detroit	AL	23.7	22	11	4	18	14	4.18	1	2	8.37	1.52	6.85	5.32	.06
1996	Toledo	Inter	113.3	131	57	7	65	49	4.53	6	7	10.40	.56	5.16	3.89	.01
1996	Detroit	AL	25.0	37	26	4	20	9	9.36	0	3	13.32	1.44	7.20	3.24	-.72

Traded to Pittsburgh, where in all likelihood he'll make Pirate fans (the few that are left) cringe every time he takes the mound. I like sinkerball pitchers as much as anyone, but not this much.

JUSTIN THOMPSON   **LSP/Savior**   **1973**   **Age 24**

YR	TEAM	Lge	IP	H	ER	HR	BB	K	ERA	W	L	H/9	HR/9	BB/9	K/9	KW
1993	Lakeland	Flor	48.3	79	29	2	23	36	5.40	2	3	14.71	.37	4.28	6.70	1.16
1993	London	East	77.3	104	49	10	48	55	5.70	3	6	12.10	1.16	5.59	6.40	.74
1995	Lakeland	Flor	21.0	38	16	2	12	14	6.86	1	1	16.29	.86	5.14	6.00	.71
1995	Jacksonville	South	113.7	130	57	8	53	75	4.51	6	7	10.29	.63	4.20	5.94	.93
1996	Toledo	Inter	80.0	78	29	2	35	57	3.26	5	4	8.77	.22	3.94	6.41	1.15
1996	Detroit	AL	59.3	57	25	6	32	43	3.79	4	3	8.65	.91	4.85	6.52	.96

The Golden Boy. His elbow is held together with Scotch tape and yarn, but he has a riding fastball, a dandy overhand curve and the prayers of an entire fan base in his arsenal. The Tigers have babied him since his return from reconstructive surgery and if anything, his stuff is better than before. Thompson reminds me of John Tudor; he may never be able to throw 200 innings in a season, but when he's able to take the mound he'll cut up the opposition with surgical precision. Should win 150 games in his career.

TODD VAN POPPEL   **RBP/Enigma**   **1972**   **Age 25**

YR	TEAM	Lge	IP	H	ER	HR	BB	K	ERA	W	L	H/9	HR/9	BB/9	K/9	KW
1993	Tacoma	PCL	72.0	67	44	6	64	57	5.50	3	5	8.38	.75	8.00	7.12	.37
1993	Oakland	AL	83.3	80	45	10	67	49	4.86	4	5	8.64	1.08	7.24	5.29	-.04
1994	Oakland	AL	117.3	106	65	19	94	82	4.99	5	8	8.13	1.46	7.21	6.29	.29
1995	Oakland	AL	137.7	128	63	16	59	123	4.12	7	8	8.37	1.05	3.86	8.04	1.72
1996	Detroit	AL	37.7	46	38	9	30	15	9.08	1	3	10.99	2.15	7.17	3.58	-.60
1996	Oakland	AL	64.0	78	42	10	34	36	5.91	2	5	10.97	1.41	4.78	5.06	.49

His 9.06 ERA this year was the highest in baseball history (min: 90 IP). He still throws 95, though, he's just 25, and just a year ago he looked like a 15-game winner in the making. Why the Tigers placed him on waivers, with their pitching staff, is beyond me. The Angels claimed him on waivers, and combined with the presence of Jim Abbott, appear intent on making new pitching coach Marcel Lachemann pay dearly for the collapse of 1995.

BRIAN WILLIAMS   **RBP**   **1969**   **Age 28**

YR	TEAM	Lge	IP	H	ER	HR	BB	K	ERA	W	L	H/9	HR/9	BB/9	K/9	KW
1993	Houston	NL	79.7	81	44	7	47	54	4.97	4	5	9.15	.79	5.31	6.10	.71
1994	Tucson	PCL	19.0	20	4	0	12	15	1.89	2	0	9.47	.00	5.68	7.11	.95
1994	Houston	NL	80.0	111	58	9	50	47	6.53	2	7	12.49	1.01	5.62	5.29	.36
1995	San Diego	NL	71.3	85	51	3	45	68	6.43	2	6	10.72	.38	5.68	8.58	1.44
1996	Toledo	Inter	18.7	23	11	1	11	17	5.30	1	1	11.09	.48	5.30	8.20	1.41
1996	Detroit	AL	122.3	133	81	17	88	70	5.96	4	10	9.78	1.25	6.47	5.15	.10

If you're not part of the solution, you're part of the problem. Williams is not part of the solution.

Player	Age	Team	Lge	AB	H	DB	TP	HR	BB	SB	CS	OUT	BA	OBA	SA	EQA	EQR	Peak
RICHARD ALMANZAR	20	Lakeland	Flor	485	138	18	1	2	44	27	10	357	.285	.344	.338	.239	50	.272
ELOY ARANO	22	Lakeland	Flor	157	32	2	1	0	8	0	0	125	.204	.242	.229	.136	4	.151
KEVIN BAEZ	29	Toledo	Inter	304	71	9	1	11	26	2	0	233	.234	.294	.378	.224	28	.223
RYAN BALFE	20	Lakeland	Flor	354	92	10	0	12	22	2	0	262	.260	.303	.390	.233	34	.264
GLEN BARKER	25	Fayetteville	S Atl	142	39	1	0	1	13	8	3	106	.275	.335	.303	.225	13	.238
	25	Jacksonville	South	122	18	2	1	0	6	4	2	106	.148	.188	.180	.044	0	.042
	25	Toledo	Inter	81	19	1	1	0	9	4	4	66	.235	.311	.272	.193	5	.204
JAYSON BASS	22	Fayetteville	S Atl	321	73	7	1	10	43	8	4	252	.227	.319	.349	.225	30	.249
SCOTT BREAM	25	Jacksonville	South	110	26	2	0	3	8	1	1	85	.236	.288	.336	.207	8	.218
TARRIK BROCK	22	Fayetteville	S Atl	128	34	4	0	2	11	2	2	96	.266	.324	.344	.224	11	.248
	22	Jacksonville	South	104	12	2	0	0	8	2	1	93	.115	.179	.135	-.110	-2	-.108
	22	Lakeland	Flor	217	57	7	2	6	15	5	1	161	.263	.310	.396	.239	23	.263
RENE CAPELLAN	18	Fayetteville	S Atl	261	61	4	0	2	10	0	0	200	.234	.262	.272	.170	12	.199
JAVIER CARDONA	20	Fayetteville	S Atl	369	95	9	0	5	23	1	2	276	.257	.301	.322	.208	27	.237
MIKE DARR	20	Lakeland	Flor	318	72	14	4	1	25	3	2	248	.226	.283	.305	.194	21	.221
CARLOS DELACRUZ	20	Fayetteville	S Atl	333	73	13	2	5	16	8	4	264	.219	.255	.315	.188	20	.213
JAMIE DISMUKE	26	Jacksonville	South	81	21	1	1	4	13	0	0	60	.259	.362	.444	.268	11	.277
JUAN ENCARNACION	20	Lakeland	Flor	506	114	14	1	16	23	6	3	395	.225	.259	.352	.201	36	.229
MATT ENGLEKA	23	Fayetteville	S Atl	285	61	7	0	3	39	3	2	226	.214	.309	.270	.193	18	.209
ANTON FRENCH	20	Lakeland	Flor	257	66	10	3	1	11	12	5	196	.257	.287	.331	.212	20	.241
BRIAN FULLER	23	Fayetteville	S Atl	257	64	5	1	9	25	1	1	194	.249	.316	.381	.232	25	.253
APOSTOL GARCIA	19	Fayetteville	S Atl	254	47	3	1	2	16	5	1	208	.185	.233	.228	.137	7	.156
MIGUEL INZUNZA	23	Fayetteville	S Atl	248	56	7	0	1	21	1	1	193	.226	.286	.266	.180	13	.195
KEITH KIMSEY	23	Jacksonville	South	108	18	1	1	1	11	2	2	92	.167	.244	.222	.134	3	.144
GRAHAM KOONCE	21	Fayetteville	S Atl	520	116	13	1	8	46	3	3	407	.223	.286	.298	.192	33	.215
DEREK KOPACZ	21	Fayetteville	S Atl	196	43	8	1	3	10	1	1	154	.219	.257	.316	.186	11	.209
STEVE LACKEY	21	Fayetteville	S Atl	327	68	5	0	5	22	10	3	262	.208	.258	.269	.174	16	.194
JACQUES LANDRY	22	Fayetteville	S Atl	105	18	2	0	1	4	0	0	87	.171	.202	.219	.094	1	.107
LONNY LANDRY	23	Lakeland	Flor	298	66	7	3	5	22	10	2	234	.221	.275	.315	.201	21	.218
KEVIN LIDLE	24	Lakeland	Flor	327	65	9	0	9	27	1	1	263	.199	.260	.309	.183	19	.196
SANTIAGO PEREZ	20	Lakeland	Flor	423	95	14	1	2	16	3	2	330	.225	.253	.277	.169	19	.191
ADAM RODRIGUEZ	25	Lakeland	Flor	165	36	5	1	3	17	0	0	129	.218	.291	.315	.200	12	.212
JERRY SALZANO	21	Lakeland	Flor	436	105	20	1	8	34	3	3	334	.241	.296	.346	.213	35	.239
TOM SCHMIDT	23	Jacksonville	South	392	84	18	1	10	25	3	1	309	.214	.261	.342	.198	27	.215
BILLY THOMPSON	25	Jacksonville	South	114	25	3	0	3	5	1	1	90	.219	.252	.325	.187	7	.196
JAMES WAGGONER	23	Lakeland	Flor	197	42	2	0	1	10	1	1	156	.213	.251	.239	.148	7	.160
SCOTT WEAVER	22	Fayetteville	S Atl	462	101	8	0	4	48	11	8	369	.219	.292	.262	.183	26	.201

Player	Age	Team	Lge	IP	H	ER	HR	BB	K	ERA	W	L	H/9	HR/9	BB/9	K/9	KW
JUSTIN BETTENCOURT	22	Fayetteville	S Atl	132.0	168	88	10	85	81	6.00	5	10	11.45	.68	5.80	5.52	.39
BEN BLOMDAHL	25	Toledo	Inter	57.7	76	35	8	25	28	5.46	2	4	11.86	1.25	3.90	4.37	.48
DAVID BORKOWSKI	19	Fayetteville	S Atl	149.7	220	105	10	81	64	6.31	5	12	13.23	.60	4.87	3.85	.07
KEN CARLYLE	26	Jacksonville	South	142.7	189	88	9	60	65	5.55	5	11	11.92	.57	3.79	4.10	.42
BLAS CEDENO	23	Jacksonville	South	43.0	68	31	6	30	22	6.49	1	4	14.23	1.26	6.28	4.60	-.03
MIKE CHRISTOPHER	32	Detroit	AL	31.3	41	27	11	12	18	7.76	1	2	11.78	3.16	3.45	5.17	.86
	32	Toledo	Inter	37.7	50	18	5	9	33	4.30	2	2	11.95	1.19	2.15	7.88	2.09
DAVID DARWIN	22	Fayetteville	S Atl	51.0	72	25	3	19	27	4.41	3	3	12.71	.53	3.35	4.76	.75
ERIC DINYAR	22	Lakeland	Flor	58.7	56	21	1	46	40	3.22	4	3	8.59	.15	7.06	6.14	.28
PETER DURKOVIC	22	Fayetteville	S Atl	44.0	74	42	4	25	37	8.59	1	4	15.14	.82	5.11	7.57	1.24
MIKE EBY	24	Fayetteville	S Atl	47.3	38	12	0	41	32	2.47	4	1	7.83	.00	8.45	6.60	.09
JOHN FARRELL	33	Toledo	Inter	29.3	37	24	7	13	17	7.36	1	2	11.35	2.15	3.99	5.22	.74
JOHN FORAN	22	Fayetteville	S Atl	92.3	144	68	8	76	45	6.63	3	7	14.04	.78	7.41	4.39	-.39
MICHAEL GUILFOYLE	28	Toledo	Inter	47.3	59	29	6	38	35	5.51	2	3	11.22	1.14	7.23	6.65	.41
JIM GUTIERREZ	25	Jacksonville	South	96.3	111	52	7	63	52	4.86	4	5	10.37	.65	5.89	4.86	.15
KELTON JACOBSON	25	Lakeland	Flor	49.0	66	34	1	48	32	6.24	1	4	12.12	.18	8.82	5.88	-.24
DAVE MALENFANT	21	Fayetteville	S Atl	25.0	38	30	3	34	19	10.80	0	3	13.68	1.08	12.24	6.84	-.78
KENNY MARRERO	26	Lakeland	Flor	60.3	73	28	2	35	60	4.18	3	4	10.89	.30	5.22	8.95	1.68
RANDY MARSHALL	29	Toledo	Inter	91.0	100	41	7	34	49	4.05	5	5	9.89	.69	3.36	4.85	.77
JEFF MCCURRY	26	Toledo	Inter	56.7	67	31	2	33	46	4.92	2	4	10.64	.32	5.24	7.31	1.12
DAVID MELENDEZ	20	Fayetteville	S Atl	113.0	151	63	9	60	66	5.02	5	8	12.03	.72	4.78	5.26	.56
SCOTT NORMAN	23	Jacksonville	South	88.7	134	54	8	44	22	5.48	3	7	13.60	.81	4.47	2.23	-.37
WILLIAM PERUSEK	22	Fayetteville	S Atl	37.7	62	42	4	69	28	10.04	1	3	14.81	.96	16.49	6.69	-1.89
BRIAN POWELL	22	Lakeland	Flor	153.3	240	121	19	70	61	7.10	4	13	14.09	1.12	4.11	3.58	.17
WILLIS ROBERTS	21	Lakeland	Flor	130.7	169	69	9	93	77	4.75	6	9	11.64	.62	6.41	5.30	.17
JOHN ROSENGREN	23	Jacksonville	South	50.7	54	33	9	42	34	5.86	2	4	9.59	1.60	7.46	6.04	.15
MIKE SALAZAR	25	Jacksonville	South	26.7	39	24	3	16	14	8.10	1	2	13.16	1.01	5.40	4.72	.22
	25	Lakeland	Flor	32.3	38	17	2	10	17	4.73	2	2	10.58	.56	2.78	4.73	.88
VICTOR SANTOS	19	Lakeland	Flor	25.3	24	12	3	13	18	4.26	1	2	8.53	1.07	4.62	6.39	.98
BOB SCANLAN	29	Toledo	Inter	34.7	46	29	4	20	15	7.53	1	3	11.94	1.04	5.19	3.89	.00
JEFF SILER	25	Lakeland	Flor	52.3	63	22	5	26	33	3.78	3	3	10.83	.86	4.47	5.68	.77
MATT SKRMETTA	23	Lakeland	Flor	46.7	56	26	7	27	38	5.01	2	3	10.80	1.35	5.21	7.33	1.14
TRAD SOBIK	20	Lakeland	Flor	71.3	97	58	8	64	36	7.32	2	6	12.24	1.01	8.07	4.54	-.50
BRENT STENTZ	20	Fayetteville	S Atl	84.3	121	57	5	41	50	6.08	3	6	12.91	.53	4.38	5.34	.68
RANDY VERES	30	Detroit	AL	31.0	35	22	5	23	27	6.39	1	2	10.16	1.45	6.68	7.84	.94
MIKE WALKER	29	Detroit	AL	28.3	36	19	8	18	19	6.04	1	2	11.44	2.54	5.72	4.13	-.05
	29	Toledo	Inter	42.7	38	19	4	32	30	4.01	2	3	8.02	.84	6.75	6.33	.42
GREG WHITEMAN	23	Lakeland	Flor	132.0	168	75	9	117	89	5.11	6	9	11.45	.61	7.98	6.07	.03
SEAN WHITESIDE	25	Lakeland	Flor	90.3	129	59	10	46	46	5.88	3	7	12.85	1.00	4.58	4.58	.38

New York Yankees

Nobody wants to hear this, but the 1996 Yankees are the weakest World Champions since the 1988 Dodgers. Sure they made a great story, with the trials and tribulations of Joe Torre, Darryl Strawberry, Dwight Gooden and David Cone, but as a baseball team they were ordinary, carried by a few exceptional performances. At times in the past year, it has seemed like the Yankees, and in particular Bob Watson, were in a race to acquire as many stiffs as possible. In spite of this, they managed to climb on the backs of farm system products Bernie Williams, Derek Jeter and Mariano Rivera and ride to the Commissioner's Trophy.

Since midseason 1995, the Yankees have made a series of personnel moves that rivals the decision-making process at CBS for its embrace of mediocrity:

• Danny Tartabull, with one year left on his contract and some offensive value, was dealt straight up for Ruben Sierra, who had two years left on his deal and no hair.

• Darryl Strawberry was added to a roster already loaded down with corner outfielder/DH types.

• Buck Showalter, one of the best managers in baseball, was coerced into resigning and Joe Torre, one of the managers in baseball, hired.

• Bob Watson, whose decision-making acumen was key in the development of the Houston Astro dynasty, was brought in as the general manager.

• Mike Stanley, one of the best-hitting catchers in baseball, was allowed to leave as a free agent, and replaced by trading for Joe Girardi at the same salary.

• Wade Boggs, coming off two good years but 38 years old, was re-signed for two years.

• Two good young players, starting pitcher Sterling Hitchcock and third baseman Russ Davis, were traded to Seattle for Tino Martinez, Jeff Nelson and Jim Mecir. Martinez, coming off a career year at 27, was immediately signed for five years at $4 million a year, negating much of the gain anticipated by Don Mattingly's retirement.

• Mariano Duncan was signed to a two-year contract.

• Kenny Rogers, a serviceable left-handed starter, was given a ridiculous four-year $19 million contract.

• Jack McDowell, however, was let go and signed for two years with Cleveland for the same annual salary.

• Tim Raines was acquired from the Chicago White Sox and had his contract extended, squeezing Ruben Rivera and Matt Luke out of playing time.

• In the absence of Raines at the beginning of the season, Gerald Williams was given the bulk of the playing time in left field, despite the presence of better players in Rivera and Luke.

• In May, Felix Fermin was signed to a minor league deal, with the intent that if he played well as AAA, he would be brought up to play second base.

• For the second time, Darryl Strawberry was signed midseason.

• In a desperate attempt to get rid of Sierra, he was packaged with struggling-but-still-good prospect Matt Drews and sent to Detroit for Cecil Fielder, meaning the Yankees had managed to trade him for someone with less defensive value and a higher salary, a neat trick.

• Luis Sojo was claimed on waivers.

• Bob Wickman and Gerald Williams were sent to Milwaukee for Pat Listach and Graeme Lloyd. Now, the Yankees desperately needed a left-handed reliever, but adding Listach was inexplicable.

• When Watson discovered Listach was hurt, rather than count his blessings he insisted on compensation. The Brewers happily forked over Ricky Bones.

• Charlie Hayes was acquired from Pittsburgh.

• Despite the fact that he had been ineffective all year, Torre started Kenny Rogers in Game 4 of the Division Series, ALCS and World Series. All you need to know about the Yankee season is this: Rogers was horrid in all three starts; the Yankees won all three games.

• Between the Division Series and the ALCS Torre removed Ruben Rivera, a multi-purpose bench player, from the roster and replaced him with Mike Aldrete, an unnecessary and mediocre left-handed pinch-hitter. This despite the fact that Paul O'Neill's bad hamstring had slowed him to a crawl, and he desperately needed a defensive replacement. If O'Neill doesn't get to that ball at the end of Game 4, this move haunts the Yankees all winter.

16 months of ineffectual decision-making, and the team still got to do the big pile-on in late October. How? Three reasons: 1) Luck, 2) Mariano Rivera, 3) Luck. Everything that could possibly have broken right, short of a great comeback by Joe DiMaggio, did. The expected stiffs, Duncan and Girardi, hit way over their heads all season. Tony Fernandez broke his arm, ending a developing shortstop controversy. Derek Jeter got off to a good start offensively and defensively, removing the temptation to sign Spike Owen or someone.

Wade Boggs moved toward the cliff, but didn't fall off. The team's good players, Paul O'Neill, Bernie Williams and John Wetteland, all performed well. Andy Pettitte, although he wasn't the best pitcher in the league, was a rotation anchor while Jimmy Key and Dwight Gooden came back from different ailments and each provided good starting pitching for a time during David Cone's absence.

All of these things helped, but the single biggest reason the Yankees won was a 25-year-old Panamanian right-hander who had one of the greatest relief years ever. Mariano Rivera could have been a starter, but the Yankees had six other candidates. He could have been a closer, but John Wetteland was firmly entrenched. So he was sent to middle relief and became the most important player in the league. Because of Rivera's brilliance, the Yankees won almost all of the games they had a chance to win, posting a xx-x record when they led after X innings.

The importance of Rivera was made even clearer in the postseason, where the Yankees came from behind in their first five wins, thanks in part to his ability to shut down opponents in the 6th through 8th innings. Additionally, his presence increased the pressure on teams to beat the Yankees early: only one of the Yankees' four postseason defeats was a competitive game, and they outscored their opponents 26-8 from the seventh inning on.

Can it happen again? Probably not. One of the reasons teams have difficulty repeating is almost all good teams make bad decisions. When a team like the Yankees wins, however, the bad decisions go unrecognized and can even be compounded. Case in point: the Yankees picked up the option on Charlie Hayes' contract for $1.5 million. Hayes is a stiff, as is

Joe Girardi, who got a two-year deal for upwards of $2.5 million a year. When these players return to Earth, they're 1) using up cash and 2) blocking better players. The Yankees will not win the division in 1997, although they could hang around the wild card race on the strength of Williams, Jeter, Pettitte and Cone. Getting good value in trade for O'Neill, Raines, Fielder and Rogers would help as well, although only O'Neill has any market value.

Organization: Well, it's no secret that the Yankees have had turnover problems, prefer veterans to young players and like to spend money foolishly. Lost in this is that they've had a pretty good scouting and player development staff bringing quality players into and through the minors. Of course, the Yankees, thanks to their megabucks local cable contract with the MSG network, have the resources to put into scouting and signing bonuses, which helps.

Nothing is ever good enough for Steinbrenner though, so at the end of the 1995 season, he fired Vice President of Development and Scouting Bill Livesey, the architect of the system, along with two other player development executives and a host of scouts. The Yankee minor league system has been one of the most fruitful in baseball, and Livesey had been with the organization for 18 years, so the move to fire him can only be regarded as peculiar. Tampa Bay quickly snatched him up to be their director of player personnel, so it's worth noting that both expansion franchises have key management personnel who were quickly hired after being let go by the Yankees. A decision like this takes years to actually show up on the field at the major league level, and is something to be watched carefully.

CHRIS ASHBY	**C**		**1975**	**Age 22**													
Year Team	Lge	AB	H	DB	TP	HR	BB	SB	CS	OUT	BA	OBA	SA	EQA	EQR	Peak
1995 Greensboro	S Atl	314	82	11	1	9	50	1	1	233	.261	.363	.389	.254	38	.289
1996 Tampa	Flor	346	86	13	0	10	64	9	3	263	.249	.366	.373	.253	42	.284
1997 NY Yankees	*AL*	*355*	*87*	*12*	*0*	*9*	*68*	*11*	*4*	*272*	*.245*	*.366*	*.355*	*.252*	*43*	

Ashby continued to display discipline in A ball, while managing to avoid being converted to left field or something. 1997, and AA will be the telling point. I like his chances. Better than Girardi.

KURT BIEREK	**OF**		**1973**	**Age 24**													
Year Team	Lge	AB	H	DB	TP	HR	BB	SB	CS	OUT	BA	OBA	SA	EQA	EQR	Peak
1993 Oneonta	NY-P	285	56	3	2	4	14	2	2	231	.196	.234	.263	.150	10	.171
1994 Greensboro	S Atl	494	118	15	2	13	58	4	1	377	.239	.319	.356	.227	46	.255
1995 Tampa	Flor	465	106	11	0	6	52	2	2	361	.228	.306	.290	.198	32	.219
1996 Tampa	Flor	336	100	8	0	13	37	3	2	238	.298	.367	.438	.270	45	.294

Bierek's not a prospect. Remember this when he has a big spring training and gets the press and the spot that Matt Luke or Ricky Ledee deserves. Just another guy who mastered a level in his second year there.

WADE BOGGS 3B 1958 Age 39

Year	Team	Lge	AB	H	DB	TP	HR	BB	SB	CS	OUT	BA	OBA	SA	EQA	EQR	Peak
1993	NY Yankees	AL	577	191	27	2	3	80	0	1	387	.331	.412	.400	.280	81	.266
1994	NY Yankees	AL	376	135	18	1	13	62	2	1	242	.359	.450	.516	.324	72	.307
1995	NY Yankees	AL	465	155	22	4	6	75	1	1	311	.333	.426	.437	.295	73	.280
1996	NY Yankees	AL	501	156	28	2	2	67	1	2	347	.311	.393	.387	.268	64	.254
1997	*NY Yankees*	*AL*	*481*	*136*	*10*	*0*	*6*	*89*	*1*	*1*	*346*	*.283*	*.395*	*.341*	*.259*	*59*	

Boggs is beginning to test the value of getting on base, and will cross the line separating contributors from other players in 1997. An extra-base hit a week isn't getting it done at third base. His defense is now Lansfordesque, he can't hit lefties and he's slower than Jim Frey's thought process.

BRIAN BUCHANAN OF 1974 Age 23

Year	Team	Lge	AB	H	DB	TP	HR	BB	SB	CS	OUT	BA	OBA	SA	EQA	EQR	Peak
1994	Oneonta	NY-P	185	36	4	0	4	18	2	1	150	.195	.266	.281	.176	10	.199
1995	Greensboro	S Atl	101	29	0	0	3	8	3	1	73	.287	.339	.376	.246	11	.275
1996	Tampa	Flor	542	137	14	1	13	35	13	5	410	.253	.298	.354	.221	47	.244

A fantastic story, if not so much a baseball player. Buchanan was a first round pick in 1994, suffered a horrific ankle injury in 1995—a dislocation so bad it blew all the ligaments connecting the ankle to the leg—and returned to play full-time in 1996. He's a C, maybe C+ prospect, but he did improve across the board in 1996 and deserves to be watched.

NICK DELVECCHIO 1B 1970 Age 27

Year	Team	Lge	AB	H	DB	TP	HR	BB	SB	CS	OUT	BA	OBA	SA	EQA	EQR	Peak
1993	Greensboro	S Atl	512	127	13	0	18	61	2	1	386	.248	.328	.379	.237	53	.258
1994	Tampa	Flor	99	29	3	0	6	10	0	0	70	.293	.358	.505	.283	15	.304
1995	Norwich	East	460	131	17	2	23	66	1	1	330	.285	.375	.480	.282	70	.298
1996	Tampa	Flor	57	16	2	0	2	15	1	1	42	.281	.431	.421	.288	9	.298

A broken ankle ruined a crucial season for Delvecchio, who had moved to almost a prospect. Walk rate at four levels (mostly rehab stints) in 1996 was still great, and he didn't really have any speed to lose. He's not $4 million worse than Tino Martinez, that's for sure.

MARIANO DUNCAN 2B 1963 Age 34

Year	Team	Lge	AB	H	DB	TP	HR	BB	SB	CS	OUT	BA	OBA	SA	EQA	EQR	Peak
1993	Philadelphia	NL	501	143	24	3	12	21	5	4	362	.285	.314	.417	.244	53	.239
1994	Philadelphia	NL	352	98	20	1	9	22	9	2	256	.278	.321	.418	.250	40	.241
1995	Cincinnati	NL	70	21	2	1	3	6	0	1	50	.300	.355	.486	.273	10	.260
1995	Philadelphia	NL	196	55	10	1	3	3	1	2	143	.281	.291	.388	.225	17	.214
1996	NY Yankees	AL	400	136	33	3	8	9	4	3	267	.340	.355	.498	.282	57	.268
1997	*NY Yankees*	*AL*	*600*	*163*	*26*	*4*	*18*	*20*	*9*	*4*	*441*	*.272*	*.295*	*.418*	*.242*	*63*	

What, you didn't see this coming? Duncan was a big part of the Yankee offense this year, keeping an already so-so group from breaking down at the bottom of the lineup. He should return to a utility role in 1997, where he's serviceable. If he gets 600 AB, the Yankees are DOA.

CECIL FIELDER 1B 1964 Age 33

Year	Team	Lge	AB	H	DB	TP	HR	BB	SB	CS	OUT	BA	OBA	SA	EQA	EQR	Peak
1993	Detroit	AL	584	166	21	0	36	94	0	1	419	.284	.383	.505	.291	96	.289
1994	Detroit	AL	427	111	17	2	28	50	0	0	316	.260	.338	.506	.274	62	.268
1995	Detroit	AL	495	121	17	1	33	76	0	1	375	.244	.345	.483	.269	70	.260
1996	Detroit	AL	392	98	10	0	27	63	2	0	294	.250	.354	.482	.274	58	.260
1996	NY Yankees	AL	200	52	8	0	13	24	0	0	148	.260	.339	.495	.272	28	.258
1997	*NY Yankees*	*AL*	*602*	*150*	*19*	*0*	*38*	*80*	*0*	*1*	*453*	*.249*	*.337*	*.470*	*.267*	*84*	

Best thing he did all year: get Sierra off the roster. He hasn't been worthwhile since 1993, and is now an expensive mediocrity. His platoon split is negligible over the last few years, but is facing at least a pseudo-platoon role in New York. At $9 million a year, he's an awfully big albatross as a right-handed DH.

MIKE FIGGA   **C**   **1971**   **Age 26**

Year	Team	Lge	AB	H	DB	TP	HR	BB	SB	CS	OUT	BA	OBA	SA	EQA	EQR	Peak
1993	San Bernardino	Calif	307	72	7	1	17	9	1	1	236	.235	.256	.430	.224	28	.247
1994	Tampa	Flor	431	119	11	2	17	21	2	0	312	.276	.310	.429	.247	47	.268
1995	Norwich	East	422	123	17	2	16	39	1	0	299	.291	.351	.455	.269	56	.287

Blown ACL, blown season. His prognosis isn't good; although the basic skill set is still there—hitting for average, some power, some walks—his future as a catcher has to be in doubt. Watch closely, but if he struggles in 1997, it's probably over. Bat might support a move to third. Better than Girardi.

ANDY FOX   **UT**   **1971**   **Age 26**

Year	Team	Lge	AB	H	DB	TP	HR	BB	SB	CS	OUT	BA	OBA	SA	EQA	EQR	Peak
1993	Albany-NY	East	244	65	10	1	4	29	7	3	182	.266	.344	.365	.243	26	.267
1994	Albany-NY	East	490	107	15	1	11	56	14	7	390	.218	.299	.320	.208	39	.226
1995	Norwich	East	183	42	2	4	6	17	6	1	142	.230	.295	.383	.230	18	.245
1995	Columbus-OH	Inter	309	103	14	3	10	43	15	3	209	.333	.415	.495	.308	55	.329
1996	NY Yankees	AL	189	37	4	0	3	20	11	3	155	.196	.273	.265	.185	11	.194
1997	*NY Yankees*	*AL*	*486*	*130*	*22*	*3*	*15*	*53*	*18*	*7*	*363*	*.267*	*.340*	*.418*	*.259*	*62*	

Fox had a disappointing season. He showed the skills of a utility infielder, not what you like to see in a 25-year-old. There's no reason to think he can't be valuable as a platoon second baseman, and Fox/Duncan would be pretty cheap and no worse than league average. Recommended.

JOE GIRARDI   **C**   **1965**   **Age 32**

Year	Team	Lge	AB	H	DB	TP	HR	BB	SB	CS	OUT	BA	OBA	SA	EQA	EQR	Peak
1993	Colorado	NL	294	75	12	4	3	26	5	3	222	.255	.316	.354	.226	27	.228
1994	Colorado	NL	328	85	8	3	4	26	3	2	245	.259	.314	.338	.220	28	.219
1995	Colorado	NL	455	106	15	1	7	34	2	2	351	.233	.286	.316	.199	31	.195
1996	NY Yankees	AL	422	124	21	3	2	30	13	4	302	.294	.341	.372	.246	45	.238
1997	*NY Yankees*	*AL*	*409*	*108*	*18*	*2*	*1*	*27*	*9*	*4*	*305*	*.264*	*.310*	*.325*	*.220*	*35*	

A truly horrific signing, in the same category as the Disarcina or Snow deals. Yes, he had, by his standards, a good year. Yes, Torre loves him. But he's 33, has a history of execrable hitting and is, no matter what you may read, a bad defensive catcher. Trade for Chris Hoiles. Play Jorge Posada. Sign Darrell Porter. All better options than Girardi.

RUDY GOMEZ   **2B**   **1975**   **Age 22**

Year	Team	Lge	AB	H	DB	TP	HR	BB	SB	CS	OUT	BA	OBA	SA	EQA	EQR	Peak
1996	Tampa	Flor	139	40	7	1	2	23	2	1	100	.288	.389	.396	.268	19	.301
1997	*NY Yankees*	*AL*	*514*	*146*	*13*	*0*	*9*	*76*	*5*	*3*	*371*	*.284*	*.376*	*.362*	*.257*	*62*	

A pleasant surprise for the Yankees. Gomez was a ninth-round pick in the June draft, and played so well in rookie ball they jumped him to the Florida State League, where he continued to hit. In light of the Yankees' second base situation, Gomez needs about another six weeks at this level and he'll be listening to Bob Sheppard say his name. Probable ETA: mid-1998.

CHARLIE HAYES   **3B**   **1965**   **Age 32**

Year	Team	Lge	AB	H	DB	TP	HR	BB	SB	CS	OUT	BA	OBA	SA	EQA	EQR	Peak
1993	Colorado	NL	568	160	33	2	24	51	9	5	413	.282	.341	.474	.268	77	.271
1994	Colorado	NL	422	116	20	3	10	41	3	5	311	.275	.339	.408	.248	48	.246
1995	Philadelphia	NL	533	145	26	2	12	56	4	1	389	.272	.341	.396	.249	60	.243
1996	NY Yankees	AL	67	19	3	0	2	1	0	0	48	.284	.294	.418	.238	7	.229
1996	Pittsburgh	NL	466	117	20	2	10	41	5	0	349	.251	.312	.367	.230	44	.222
1997	*NY Yankees*	*AL*	*288*	*74*	*13*	*1*	*5*	*28*	*3*	*1*	*215*	*.257*	*.323*	*.361*	*.235*	*29*	

Sigh…. I don't think Wade Boggs is an everyday player anymore, either, but was it necessary to tie up $1.5 million and a roster spot to pick up this guy's option? I'll go out on a limb: he's a stiff. Demanded a trade, but is really just angling for a contract extension. If he gets it, I'll pay for Dr. Kevorkian's airfare to New York. "Hi, Bob; hi, George. My name is Jack. I heard you're having trouble sleeping…." He got it.

DEREK JETER   SS   1974   Age 23

Year	Team	Lge	AB	H	DB	TP	HR	BB	SB	CS	OUT	BA	OBA	SA	EQA	EQR	Peak
1993	Greensboro	S Atl	538	139	9	5	6	43	7	4	403	.258	.313	.327	.217	44	.250
1994	Tampa	Flor	303	101	14	5	2	22	16	2	204	.333	.378	.432	.283	43	.321
1994	Albany-NY	East	129	48	5	2	2	14	7	1	82	.372	.434	.488	.318	23	.361
1994	Columbus-OH	Inter	131	45	5	1	3	19	7	3	89	.344	.427	.466	.303	22	.344
1995	Columbus-OH	Inter	495	146	25	6	3	61	14	7	356	.295	.372	.388	.260	62	.291
1995	NY Yankees	AL	48	12	5	1	0	3	0	0	36	.250	.294	.396	.229	5	.257
1996	NY Yankees	AL	582	183	24	6	10	48	14	7	406	.314	.367	.428	.269	76	.297
1997	*NY Yankees*	*AL*	*617*	*180*	*28*	*6*	*10*	*60*	*21*	*3*	*440*	*.292*	*.355*	*.405*	*.265*	*80*	

Impressive debut, overshadowed by the historic season of Alex Rodriguez. Jeter hit a little better than expected and his defense, questioned in the minors, was steady all year. Odd development during the year: he hit .277 with a good walk rate and very little power in the first half, .350 with more power but few walks in the second. I expect him to keep the average and power, improve the strikeout and walk numbers and be a great player. Idle thought: could a Rickey Henderson/Tim Raines thing develop between Rodriguez and Jeter?

D'ANGELO JIMENEZ   SS   1978   Age 19

Year	Team	Lge	AB	H	DB	TP	HR	BB	SB	CS	OUT	BA	OBA	SA	EQA	EQR	Peak
1996	Greensboro	S Atl	568	124	17	2	6	43	6	6	450	.218	.273	.287	.182	32	.213

Scouts rave about Jimenez' tools, but the walks, for an 18-year-old, are what stand out. He's still got a lot of growing to do, and will play at high-A Tampa in 1997. Still two or three years away, but will begin showing up on radars this year. With Jeter at short and Rudy Gomez at second ahead of him, a lack of good third base prospects in the organization may eventually move him to third.

PAT KELLY   2B   1968   Age 29

Year	Team	Lge	AB	H	DB	TP	HR	BB	SB	CS	OUT	BA	OBA	SA	EQA	EQR	Peak
1993	NY Yankees	AL	414	122	23	1	10	27	15	8	300	.295	.338	.428	.257	50	.271
1994	NY Yankees	AL	290	85	23	2	3	20	6	5	210	.293	.339	.417	.253	34	.262
1995	NY Yankees	AL	272	67	13	1	4	23	8	3	208	.246	.305	.346	.221	24	.226
1997	*NY Yankees*	*AL*	*171*	*45*	*14*	*1*	*2*	*16*	*4*	*0*	*126*	*.263*	*.326*	*.392*	*.249*	*20*	

Gee, I guess he's never going to have that .280/.340/.440 season I predicted for him on r.s.b in 1993. Injuries have murdered his last two years, and while I like him better than Duncan, it's a marginal distinction. His career is just about over.

RICKY LEDEE   OF   1974   Age 23

Year	Team	Lge	AB	H	DB	TP	HR	BB	SB	CS	OUT	BA	OBA	SA	EQA	EQR	Peak
1993	Oneonta	NY-P	205	47	3	1	7	18	3	2	160	.229	.291	.356	.215	17	.248
1994	Greensboro	S Atl	517	124	13	3	19	77	5	5	398	.240	.338	.387	.242	57	.275
1995	Greensboro	S Atl	358	93	8	2	13	42	5	2	267	.260	.338	.402	.249	41	.279
1996	Norwich	East	143	52	8	1	7	15	2	1	92	.364	.424	.580	.327	28	.361
1996	Columbus-OH	Inter	361	97	18	3	19	44	4	2	266	.269	.348	.493	.275	53	.304
1997	*NY Yankees*	*AL*	*536*	*147*	*25*	*2*	*27*	*70*	*5*	*1*	*390*	*.274*	*.358*	*.479*	*.280*	*81*	

And I bet he thinks he's close to a big league job. Bzzzzt. While the left-handed hitting Ledee deserves the left field job in New York, or at least a clean shot at it, the Yankees already have Raines, O'Neill, Rivera, Luke and Strawberry vying for time at the outfield corners, with only O'Neill a good candidate to be elsewhere by spring training. Ledee will eventually get a job and have a nice little career, but not until 1998. Big platoon split.

JIM LEYRITZ   C   1964   Age 33

Year	Team	Lge	AB	H	DB	TP	HR	BB	SB	CS	OUT	BA	OBA	SA	EQA	EQR	Peak
1993	NY Yankees	AL	268	90	13	0	18	39	0	0	178	.336	.420	.586	.326	54	.323
1994	NY Yankees	AL	254	71	11	0	19	35	0	0	183	.280	.367	.547	.294	43	.288
1995	NY Yankees	AL	266	73	9	0	9	38	1	1	194	.274	.365	.410	.261	34	.252
1996	NY Yankees	AL	265	70	7	0	8	30	2	0	195	.264	.339	.381	.244	29	.232
1997	*California*	*AL*	*274*	*65*	*10*	*0*	*9*	*32*	*0*	*1*	*210*	*.237*	*.317*	*.372*	*.235*	*28*	

Hmmm…looks like a decline phase to me. Leyritz has a job for 1997 as Pettitte's personal catcher, and as the #2 guy and a utility player he's useful. The cliff is in sight, though. Better than Girardi. Given to California, he'll probably get more playing time than indicated above.

MIKE LOWELL 3B 1974 Age 23

Year	Team	Lge	AB	H	DB	TP	HR	BB	SB	CS	OUT	BA	OBA	SA	EQA	EQR	Peak
1995	Oneonta	NY-P	288	59	5	0	3	17	1	0	229	.205	.249	.253	.155	11	.173
1996	Greensboro	S Atl	460	120	15	0	9	37	4	1	341	.261	.316	.352	.226	42	.249
1996	Tampa	Flor	80	21	5	0	0	3	1	0	59	.262	.289	.325	.209	6	.228

He's not much of a third base prospect, but the Yankees are so thin at the position he actually looks halfway decent. Still two years away from any chance at a job.

MATT LUKE OF 1971 Age 26

Year	Team	Lge	AB	H	DB	TP	HR	BB	SB	CS	OUT	BA	OBA	SA	EQA	EQR	Peak
1993	Greensboro	S Atl	569	149	18	1	18	34	5	2	422	.262	.303	.392	.233	55	.257
1994	Tampa	Flor	232	73	5	1	17	26	3	1	160	.315	.384	.565	.307	42	.333
1994	Albany-NY	East	246	68	7	1	8	26	4	2	180	.276	.346	.411	.255	29	.277
1995	Norwich	East	381	105	14	3	10	18	4	3	279	.276	.308	.407	.239	39	.256
1995	Columbus-OH	Inter	77	22	3	0	3	3	1	1	56	.286	.312	.442	.249	9	.267
1996	Columbus-OH	Inter	265	71	10	1	17	18	1	1	195	.268	.314	.506	.266	36	.280
1997	*NY Yankees*	*AL*	*432*	*110*	*13*	*1*	*24*	*33*	*0*	*1*	*323*	*.255*	*.308*	*.456*	*.253*	*52*	

Luke is a left-handed hitter with power who fought a rib injury for most of the year that cost him at bats. He's not much of a fielder or runner, so he'll have to earn a job with his bat. Blocked badly at the major league level. No platoon differential, a good sign.

TINO MARTINEZ 1B 1968 Age 29

Year	Team	Lge	AB	H	DB	TP	HR	BB	SB	CS	OUT	BA	OBA	SA	EQA	EQR	Peak
1993	Seattle	AL	414	115	24	1	21	48	0	2	301	.278	.353	.493	.275	60	.291
1994	Seattle	AL	329	86	17	0	21	29	1	2	245	.261	.321	.505	.266	45	.276
1995	Seattle	AL	524	158	36	2	34	63	0	0	366	.302	.376	.573	.305	94	.312
1996	NY Yankees	AL	595	174	21	0	27	68	2	1	422	.292	.365	.464	.276	84	.278
1997	*NY Yankees*	*AL*	*518*	*140*	*20*	*0*	*28*	*59*	*1*	*1*	*379*	*.270*	*.345*	*.471*	*.272*	*73*	

But he drove in 117 runs, so it was a great year. When you get a free minute today, curse Harry Chadwick. Martinez' perceived value is higher than his real value by a factor of 10. He is at best the fourth-best first baseman in the division, tenth-best in the league, and he's already peaked. Martinez is a large albatross for the Yankees at $4M/year through the end of the century.

SHEA MORENZ OF 1974 Age 23

Year	Team	Lge	AB	H	DB	TP	HR	BB	SB	CS	OUT	BA	OBA	SA	EQA	EQR	Peak
1995	Oneonta	NY-P	120	26	3	1	1	12	0	1	95	.217	.288	.283	.184	7	.207
1996	Greensboro	S Atl	358	82	11	2	2	30	5	1	277	.229	.289	.288	.193	23	.212

Football player masquerading as prospect. Morenz has some speed and a good arm, but nothing else that makes baseball players good. A failed first-round draft pick, example N+1 why drafting athletes instead of baseball players is a bad idea.

CHRIS NORTON C 1971 Age 26

Year	Team	Lge	AB	H	DB	TP	HR	BB	SB	CS	OUT	BA	OBA	SA	EQA	EQR	Peak
1994	Savannah	S Atl	470	121	7	1	20	62	3	2	351	.257	.344	.404	.251	55	.273
1996	Norwich	East	177	49	10	1	6	14	2	1	129	.277	.330	.446	.258	22	.272

Norton resurrected his career by going to the independent Texas-Louisiana League and obliterating the ball for a year. He has a history of good walk rates, but is just minor league filler at this point. Better than Girardi.

PAUL O'NEILL RF 1963 Age 34

Year	Team	Lge	AB	H	DB	TP	HR	BB	SB	CS	OUT	BA	OBA	SA	EQA	EQR	Peak
1993	NY Yankees	AL	512	172	30	1	27	48	2	3	343	.336	.393	.557	.308	90	.301
1994	NY Yankees	AL	379	142	23	1	24	74	5	4	241	.375	.477	.631	.356	91	.344
1995	NY Yankees	AL	464	143	31	4	24	72	1	2	323	.308	.401	.547	.307	85	.292
1996	NY Yankees	AL	546	165	31	1	20	102	0	1	382	.302	.412	.473	.296	91	.281
1997	*NY Yankees*	*AL*	*487*	*125*	*21*	*0*	*25*	*91*	*0*	*0*	*362*	*.257*	*.374*	*.454*	*.278*	*74*	

Warning! Subjective evaluation ahead. O'Neill looked very awkward at the plate in the second half and the postseason. His leg kick hides the fact that he's swinging entirely with his arms and generating very little power. Way, way out in front on breaking balls, resulting in many 1-3 and 3-1 putouts, and he's just slapping at everything else. Loss in power compensated for by a soaring walk rate, but that often signifies an imminent decline. Hello, cliff.

JORGE POSADA C   1972 Age 25

Year	Team	Lge	AB	H	DB	TP	HR	BB	SB	CS	OUT	BA	OBA	SA	EQA	EQR	Peak
1993	Pr. William	Caro	435	109	17	1	14	58	10	3	329	.251	.339	.391	.247	50	.277
1994	Columbus-OH	Inter	319	74	10	1	11	31	4	3	248	.232	.300	.373	.223	29	.247
1995	Columbus-OH	Inter	375	91	26	3	8	53	3	2	286	.243	.336	.392	.244	42	.264
1996	Columbus-OH	Inter	361	92	16	4	11	76	2	2	271	.255	.384	.413	.268	50	.287
1997	*NY Yankees*	*AL*	*425*	*106*	*23*	*2*	*13*	*72*	*3*	*1*	*320*	*.249*	*.358*	*.405*	*.260*	*55*	

Yummy. Posada also has a good defensive reputation to go with the numbers above, and deserves at least a share of the catching job in New York. What the Yankees do at catcher will tell us a lot about their chances in 1997 and beyond. Posada is much cheaper and…better than Girardi.

TIM RAINES LF   1960 Age 37

Year	Team	Lge	AB	H	DB	TP	HR	BB	SB	CS	OUT	BA	OBA	SA	EQA	EQR	Peak
1993	Chi. White Sox	AL	424	137	15	4	20	68	20	5	292	.323	.417	.519	.312	79	.296
1994	Chi. White Sox	AL	389	107	15	5	11	62	12	0	282	.275	.375	.424	.274	56	.260
1995	Chi. White Sox	AL	510	153	27	4	14	71	13	2	359	.300	.386	.451	.284	77	.269
1996	NY Yankees	AL	201	57	10	0	9	34	10	1	145	.284	.387	.468	.291	33	.276
1997	*NY Yankees*	*AL*	*307*	*72*	*14*	*1*	*16*	*67*	*13*	*1*	*236*	*.235*	*.372*	*.443*	*.279*	*49*	

On one hand, Raines is 37 and holding back younger players. On the other, he's still 75% of the player he was, had a high OBP and is still the best leadoff option the Yankees have. A bad acquisition because of the other options available, but unlike Hayes and Girardi, helps the team anyway. Should be platooned (.206 SLG vs. LHP).

RUBEN RIVERA OF   1974 Age 23

Year	Team	Lge	AB	H	DB	TP	HR	BB	SB	CS	OUT	BA	OBA	SA	EQA	EQR	Peak
1993	Oneonta	NY-P	215	56	2	1	10	24	5	3	162	.260	.335	.419	.251	26	.290
1994	Greensboro	S Atl	422	121	13	1	23	39	18	4	305	.287	.347	.486	.278	62	.316
1994	Tampa	Flor	137	36	2	1	6	8	8	3	104	.263	.303	.423	.246	16	.280
1995	Norwich	East	274	87	14	6	11	34	12	6	193	.318	.393	.533	.302	48	.338
1995	Columbus-OH	Inter	177	47	6	1	13	26	6	3	133	.266	.360	.531	.287	29	.321
1996	Columbus-OH	Inter	364	79	17	2	9	41	10	6	291	.217	.296	.349	.215	31	.237
1996	NY Yankees	AL	88	25	6	1	2	13	6	2	65	.284	.376	.443	.278	13	.307
1997	*NY Yankees*	*AL*	*431*	*109*	*22*	*3*	*16*	*52*	*23*	*4*	*326*	*.253*	*.333*	*.429*	*.263*	*58*	

Rivera slipped a notch in the eyes of many this year due to a perceived "attitude problem." Frankly, if I'm the third-best outfielder in my organization, play well at the major league level in my short time and subsequently get sent down so Gerald Williams can play, I'll express some displeasure too. Deserves 600 at bats in New York, this year, but needs an O'Neill or Raines deal to get them.

ROD SMITH 2B   1976 Age 21

Year	Team	Lge	AB	H	DB	TP	HR	BB	SB	CS	OUT	BA	OBA	SA	EQA	EQR	Peak
1995	Oneonta	NY-P	195	38	5	1	1	23	8	3	160	.195	.280	.246	.176	10	.204
1995	Greensboro	S Atl	250	55	4	3	1	28	7	5	200	.220	.299	.272	.190	16	.220
1996	Greensboro	S Atl	511	105	12	4	5	50	21	6	412	.205	.276	.274	.186	31	.212

Smith is a speedy second baseman who had a high strikeout total (128), although some of that is attributable to taking lots of pitches. The steals will give him prospect status, but it's an open question whether the rest of the game will catch up. Even if it does, he's already been passed by Gomez, so I doubt he'll have a career.

LUIS SOJO 2B   1966 Age 31

Year	Team	Lge	AB	H	DB	TP	HR	BB	SB	CS	OUT	BA	OBA	SA	EQA	EQR	Peak
1993	Syracuse	Inter	144	31	7	1	1	9	2	1	114	.215	.261	.299	.183	8	.185
1993	Toronto	AL	47	8	3	0	0	4	0	0	39	.170	.235	.234	.132	1	.137
1994	Calgary	PCL	99	28	6	2	1	9	3	0	71	.283	.343	.414	.260	12	.263
1994	Seattle	AL	213	59	8	2	6	8	2	1	155	.277	.303	.418	.241	22	.243
1995	Seattle	AL	342	102	18	2	8	23	4	2	242	.298	.342	.433	.260	42	.259
1996	Seattle	AL	248	53	8	1	1	10	2	2	197	.214	.244	.266	.158	10	.155

In much the same way Dan Duquette is driven to acquire prospects two years past their best season, Bob Watson went after bad infielders last summer. Felix Fermin and Pat Listach didn't stick, Charlie Hayes and Sojo did. For some guys, the difference between a ring and nothing is dumb luck, for some, a dumb GM. Ask Bob Wickman. Sojo sucks.

SHANE SPENCER OF 1972 Age 25

Year	Team	Lge	AB	H	DB	TP	HR	BB	SB	CS	OUT	BA	OBA	SA	EQA	EQR	Peak
1993	Greensboro	S Atl	450	111	16	1	11	39	6	1	340	.247	.307	.360	.225	41	.252
1994	Tampa	Flor	346	100	14	1	11	28	3	2	248	.289	.342	.431	.259	42	.286
1995	Tampa	Flor	520	148	17	2	17	53	9	4	376	.285	.351	.423	.260	65	.283
1996	Norwich	East	468	121	12	0	26	62	3	1	348	.259	.345	.451	.264	62	.282

Spencer continued to build on his good 1995. He's a stocky guy with no speed but real power. As a corner outfielder with one trick, he'll need to improve the trick or the defense. A big 1997 would help.

DARYL STRAWBERRY DH/LF 1962 Age 35

Year	Team	Lge	AB	H	DB	TP	HR	BB	SB	CS	OUT	BA	OBA	SA	EQA	EQR	Peak
1993	Los Angeles	NL	102	15	3	0	5	17	1	0	87	.147	.269	.324	.192	7	.184
1994	San Francisco	NL	94	23	3	0	5	21	0	3	74	.245	.383	.436	.263	13	.249
1995	Columbus-OH	Inter	85	25	2	1	6	15	1	1	61	.294	.400	.553	.306	16	.291
1995	NY Yankees	AL	88	25	5	1	3	10	0	0	63	.284	.357	.466	.273	12	.259
1996	NY Yankees	AL	202	53	10	0	12	31	6	5	154	.262	.361	.490	.275	30	.261
1997	*NY Yankees*	*AL*	*246*	*61*	*5*	*0*	*14*	*37*	*4*	*3*	*188*	*.248*	*.346*	*.439*	*.262*	*33*	

All of the obvious problems keep him from getting a clean shot, but if put in a lineup and left alone Strawberry could still be one of the better DHs in the league. He's better than Cecil, for sure. The thing about his last two years is that his at bats have been widely scattered. If he just gets regular playing time, he'll hit .270 with walks and power.

CHRIS WILCOX OF 1974 Age 23

Year	Team	Lge	AB	H	DB	TP	HR	BB	SB	CS	OUT	BA	OBA	SA	EQA	EQR	Peak
1995	Oneonta	NY-P	229	62	12	2	2	15	3	1	168	.271	.316	.367	.231	22	.260
1996	Tampa	Flor	488	135	20	2	14	36	8	6	359	.277	.326	.412	.246	54	.272

A.K.A. Luke. He's a tweener outfield prospect, does everything OK but nothing stands out. In a horrid situation, with the Yankees hip-deep in better outfielders. Good enough to play forever in the minors, and a solid pick for your Eastern League rotisserie team.

BERNIE WILLIAMS CF 1969 Age 28

Year	Team	Lge	AB	H	DB	TP	HR	BB	SB	CS	OUT	BA	OBA	SA	EQA	EQR	Peak
1993	NY Yankees	AL	580	168	34	4	16	57	9	7	419	.290	.353	.445	.265	76	.284
1994	NY Yankees	AL	417	127	28	1	14	62	15	8	298	.305	.395	.477	.290	67	.305
1995	NY Yankees	AL	568	179	32	8	20	76	8	6	395	.315	.396	.505	.296	95	.308
1996	NY Yankees	AL	551	168	25	7	29	82	17	4	387	.305	.395	.534	.305	99	.312
1997	*NY Yankees*	*AL*	*662*	*206*	*31*	*7*	*37*	*86*	*16*	*4*	*460*	*.311*	*.390*	*.547*	*.310*	*123*	

Pssst…he's good. Bernie's been improving since the Yankees finally gave him a full-time job in 1993, but it took a monster postseason to get him some attention. He's better than Kenny Lofton, but you'd never know it. Two completely different hitters: left-handed, he's Luis Gonzalez; right-handed, Mike Piazza.

BRIAN BOEHRINGER RBP 1969 Age 28

YR	TEAM	Lge	IP	H	ER	HR	BB	K	ERA	W	L	H/9	HR/9	BB/9	K/9	KW
1993	Sarasota	Flor	104.7	123	51	4	69	72	4.39	5	7	10.58	.34	5.93	6.19	.58
1993	Birmingham	South	36.3	51	23	4	20	22	5.70	1	3	12.63	.99	4.95	5.45	.58
1994	Albany, NY	East	154.0	203	93	12	78	107	5.44	6	11	11.86	.70	4.56	6.25	.94
1995	Columbus, OH	Inter	97.0	107	36	7	44	49	3.34	6	5	9.93	.65	4.08	4.55	.49
1995	NY Yankees	AL	19.0	21	21	5	22	10	9.95	0	2	9.95	2.37	10.42	4.74	-1.03
1996	Columbus, OH	Inter	147.0	154	64	12	73	108	3.92	8	8	9.43	.73	4.47	6.61	1.09
1996	NY Yankees	AL	46.7	42	20	6	22	36	3.86	3	2	8.10	1.16	4.24	6.94	1.25

In three trips to New York over two years, Boehringer has gotten obliterated as a starter and pitched great out of the bullpen. The sample size is small, but he seems to be comfortable in the long relief role. Could be cheap help for a few years; his control will be the deciding factor.

RICKY BONES — RBP — 1969 — Age 28

YR	TEAM	Lge	IP	H	ER	HR	BB	K	ERA	W	L	H/9	HR/9	BB/9	K/9	KW
1993	Milwaukee	AL	203.0	218	104	29	73	65	4.61	10	13	9.67	1.29	3.24	2.88	.15
1994	Milwaukee	AL	169.0	155	54	15	50	55	2.88	13	6	8.25	.80	2.66	2.93	.31
1995	Milwaukee	AL	201.3	198	79	23	86	76	3.53	12	10	8.85	1.03	3.84	3.40	.17
1996	Milwaukee	AL	146.0	154	77	23	65	57	4.75	7	9	9.49	1.42	4.01	3.51	.17

Bones is another of the bad players Bob Watson was hell-bent on acquiring this year. Came over as "compensation" for Listach's injury. Bones is really, really bad. Future uncertain, but certainly slight.

MIKE BUDDIE — RSP — 1971 — Age 26

YR	TEAM	Lge	IP	H	ER	HR	BB	K	ERA	W	L	H/9	HR/9	BB/9	K/9	KW
1993	Greensboro	S Atl	129.3	185	120	23	121	84	8.35	3	11	12.87	1.60	8.42	5.85	-.16
1994	Tampa	Flor	133.7	176	84	11	87	87	5.66	5	10	11.85	.74	5.86	5.86	.49
1995	Norwich	East	135.0	201	119	6	101	84	7.93	3	12	13.40	.40	6.73	5.60	.18
1996	Norwich	East	146.0	204	104	10	90	77	6.41	4	12	12.58	.62	5.55	4.75	.20

He's a staff filler at Norwich, showed improvement in his second year. Buddie has chance to get beyond AAA, even though he keeps the ball in the park pretty well.

DAVID CONE — RSP — 1963 — Age 34

YR	TEAM	Lge	IP	H	ER	HR	BB	K	ERA	W	L	H/9	HR/9	BB/9	K/9	KW
1993	Kansas City	AL	249.3	204	79	21	124	196	2.85	19	9	7.36	.76	4.48	7.07	1.24
1994	Kansas City	AL	168.3	125	39	14	59	128	2.09	15	4	6.68	.75	3.15	6.84	1.49
1995	NY Yankees	AL	98.3	80	31	11	49	89	2.84	7	4	7.32	1.01	4.48	8.15	1.59
1995	Toronto	AL	129.0	112	40	11	44	102	2.79	9	5	7.81	.77	3.07	7.12	1.60
1996	NY Yankees	AL	70.3	50	16	3	36	69	2.05	6	2	6.40	.38	4.61	8.83	1.79

Cone had the best season ever for a player diagnosed with an aneurysm during it. Seriously, despite the seven no-hit innings in his return, he didn't pitch all that well after coming back. He's become increasingly reliant on his breaking pitches, particularly to left-handed batters, and seems unwilling to throw fastballs unless he absolutely has to. Throwing under 100 innings will help his career, and I expect two more years at his '93-'95 level, followed by a steep decline.

MATT DUNBAR — LBP — 1969 — Age 28

YR	TEAM	Lge	IP	H	ER	HR	BB	K	ERA	W	L	H/9	HR/9	BB/9	K/9	KW
1993	Pr. William	Caro	64.0	65	23	0	45	42	3.23	4	3	9.14	.00	6.33	5.91	.39
1993	Albany, NY	East	21.7	27	8	0	8	14	3.32	1	1	11.22	.00	3.32	5.82	1.11
1994	Albany, NY	East	36.0	37	10	1	19	30	2.50	3	1	9.25	.25	4.75	7.50	1.31
1994	Columbus, OH	Inter	24.3	23	5	1	12	17	1.85	2	1	8.51	.37	4.44	6.29	.99
1995	Columbus, OH	Inter	41.3	52	19	1	26	28	4.14	2	3	11.32	.22	5.66	6.10	.62
1996	Greensboro	S Atl	12.0	10	3	1	6	10	2.25	1	0	7.50	.75	4.50	7.50	1.37
1996	Norwich	East	65.3	69	32	3	35	44	4.41	3	4	9.51	.41	4.82	6.06	.82
1996	Columbus, OH	Inter	19.3	13	4	0	15	13	1.86	2	0	6.05	.00	6.98	6.05	.27

The Yankees have never taken him seriously as a prospect despite some good years out of the bullpen. Florida took him as a Rule V guy in 1995, but gave him back after seven bad innings. He throws ground balls, and if he gets the walks under control I think he can be Terry Leach for a few years, which would get him a decent pension.

DAVE EILAND — RSP — 1967 — Age 30

YR	TEAM	Lge	IP	H	ER	HR	BB	K	ERA	W	L	H/9	HR/9	BB/9	K/9	KW
1993	Charlotte, NC	Inter	34.0	45	21	8	16	11	5.56	1	3	11.91	2.12	4.24	2.91	-.09
1993	Oklahoma	AmA	34.0	39	15	1	12	14	3.97	2	2	10.32	.26	3.18	3.71	.44
1993	San Diego	NL	47.0	61	31	5	22	14	5.94	2	3	11.68	.96	4.21	2.68	-.16
1994	Columbus, OH	Inter	132.7	154	67	12	45	70	4.55	7	8	10.45	.81	3.05	4.75	.82
1995	Columbus, OH	Inter	102.0	115	39	1	35	52	3.44	6	5	10.15	.09	3.09	4.59	.76
1995	NY Yankees	AL	10.0	15	8	1	4	6	7.20	0	1	13.50	.90	3.60	5.40	.90
1996	Columbus, OH	Inter	87.3	81	30	9	21	62	3.09	6	4	8.35	.93	2.16	6.39	1.59
1996	Louisville	AmA	23.0	30	17	2	12	14	6.65	1	2	11.74	.78	4.70	5.48	.65

The new Mickey Weston. Eiland's career ERA in AAA is 3.50 in 864 innings, with a record of 65-38. He's only gotten two shots at a real MLB job, and pitched poorly both times. I expect him to show up with someone this season, and he could easily be the Devil Rays' #4 starter in 1998.

DWIGHT GOODEN   **RSP**   **1965**   **Age 32**

YR	TEAM	Lge	IP	H	ER	HR	BB	K	ERA	W	L	H/9	HR/9	BB/9	K/9	KW
1993	NY Mets	NL	201.7	199	81	17	83	144	3.61	12	10	8.88	.76	3.70	6.43	1.22
1994	NY Mets	NL	41.3	44	28	9	19	37	6.10	2	3	9.58	1.96	4.14	8.06	1.65
1996	NY Yankees	AL	171.0	155	72	16	92	122	3.79	10	9	8.16	.84	4.84	6.42	.93

Lost in the great comeback story was this: he didn't pitch all that well. He struggled with his control, and after a while just tried to get by on his fastball. Wrapped two horrendous stretches around two months of effectiveness. The time off—just 41 innings in two years—clearly hurt. A full winter of conditioning would help, and I expect him to be above average in 1997. He still has a fair shot at the Hall of Fame.

KEVIN HENTHORNE   **RBP**   **1970**   **Age 27**

YR	TEAM	Lge	IP	H	ER	HR	BB	K	ERA	W	L	H/9	HR/9	BB/9	K/9	KW
1996	Tampa	Flor	84.0	107	33	6	21	59	3.54	5	4	11.46	.64	2.25	6.32	1.54
1996	Norwich	East	55.0	59	25	3	28	35	4.09	3	3	9.65	.49	4.58	5.73	.76

Two years removed from the Northern League, he had a wonderful year splitting time between Norwich and Tampa. He needs another year like this to become a real prospect, and their jerking him around—no real role—shows they don't take him seriously, but he has a good grasp of the strike zone, and that's the skill to bet on.

JIMMY KEY   **LSP**   **1961**   **Age 36**

YR	TEAM	Lge	IP	H	ER	HR	BB	K	ERA	W	L	H/9	HR/9	BB/9	K/9	KW
1993	NY Yankees	AL	232.3	226	73	28	55	180	2.83	17	9	8.75	1.08	2.13	6.97	1.79
1994	NY Yankees	AL	166.0	179	55	9	58	96	2.98	12	6	9.70	.49	3.14	5.20	.95
1995	NY Yankees	AL	30.3	38	16	3	7	14	4.75	1	2	11.27	.89	2.08	4.15	.87
1996	Tampa	Flor	12.0	12	5	2	2	8	3.75	1	0	9.00	1.50	1.50	6.00	1.62
1996	NY Yankees	AL	169.3	158	66	17	62	112	3.51	11	8	8.40	.90	3.30	5.95	1.16

All those who thought he'd throw 170 innings raise their hands. Me neither. He returned too quickly from surgery and was killed for eight starts (7.14, 7 HR) before going on the DL. Posted a 3.91 ERA in 22 starts after he came off. The labor deal made him a free agent. I think he can help in 1997, but there's no way in hell I'd sign him for more than one year. Gets an enormous outside corner from umpires, similar to Tom Glavine.

GRAEME LLOYD   **LRP**   **1967**   **Age 30**

YR	TEAM	Lge	IP	H	ER	HR	BB	K	ERA	W	L	H/9	HR/9	BB/9	K/9	KW
1993	Milwaukee	AL	63.0	64	20	5	16	32	2.86	5	2	9.14	.71	2.29	4.57	.95
1994	Milwaukee	AL	46.7	46	20	4	16	30	3.86	3	2	8.87	.77	3.09	5.79	1.16
1995	Milwaukee	AL	31.3	27	11	4	8	13	3.16	2	1	7.76	1.15	2.30	3.73	.67
1996	Milwaukee	AL	50.0	47	13	2	19	23	2.34	4	2	8.46	.36	3.42	4.14	.52

The Life of a Lefty Specialist: Lloyd was going merrily along in Milwaukee, adding years to his pension as a nondescript player on baseball's faceless wonders. Then in the middle of his worst slump of the season, he was traded to New York, had five horrible appearances in the middle of the Yankees' meltdown and was at the center of a damaged goods controversy. Then he disappeared, throwing just four well-scattered innings in September.

Cut to October, and our tall Australian becomes a hero, pitching well in the Division Series and ALCS, then brilliantly in the World Series, shutting down the Braves' left-handed power. Go figure. Lloyd is the new Rick Honeycutt. He'll have a job as long as he wants one.

KATSUHIRO MAEDA   **RSP**   **1971**   **Age 26**

YR	TEAM	Lge	IP	H	ER	HR	BB	K	ERA	W	L	H/9	HR/9	BB/9	K/9	KW
1996	Norwich	East	49.3	56	24	4	27	22	4.38	2	3	10.22	.73	4.93	4.01	.11

The love child of Dennis Rodman and Hideo Nomo. OK, adopted love child. Maeda's an interesting character, and he had a serviceable half-season in the Yankee system while adjusting to a new culture, language, etc. He's no Nomo. Maeda has a good pitcher's build and a great fastball, but is still wild as all hell. If the Yankees are bad in 1997, he could get a callup; he won't be good until 1998, maybe 1999. Pitched well in the AFL.

JIM MECIR   **RRP**   **1970**   **Age 27**

YR	TEAM	Lge	IP	H	ER	HR	BB	K	ERA	W	L	H/9	HR/9	BB/9	K/9	KW
1993	Riverside	Calif	127.3	185	86	4	63	60	6.08	4	10	13.08	.28	4.45	4.24	.30
1994	Jacksonville	South	72.7	85	30	6	49	42	3.72	4	4	10.53	.74	6.07	5.20	.22
1995	Tacoma	PCL	64.7	69	26	4	35	43	3.62	4	3	9.60	.56	4.87	5.98	.78
1996	Columbus, OH	Inter	45.3	39	11	2	19	42	2.18	4	1	7.74	.40	3.77	8.34	1.84
1996	NY Yankees	AL	41.0	38	17	6	23	37	3.73	3	2	8.34	1.32	5.05	8.12	1.45

Mecir's a hard pitcher to watch in that his motion makes you think he's going to get hurt any second. He's a marginal middle reliever with a good story (he has a club foot) that may help him stand out in the middle relief crowd and get an extra opportunity. Random future, impossible to predict.

RAFAEL MEDINA   **RSP**   **1975**   **Age 22**

YR	TEAM	Lge	IP	H	ER	HR	BB	K	ERA	W	L	H/9	HR/9	BB/9	K/9	KW
1994	Oneonta	NY-P	59.0	93	65	10	53	35	9.92	1	6	14.19	1.53	8.08	5.34	-.24
1995	Greensboro	S Atl	82.7	123	62	11	56	62	6.75	2	7	13.39	1.20	6.10	6.75	.73
1995	Tampa	Flor	26.3	36	14	0	17	18	4.78	1	2	12.30	.00	5.81	6.15	.60
1996	Norwich	East	95.3	92	46	7	67	83	4.34	5	6	8.69	.66	6.33	7.84	1.03

Medina is a thin right-hander who fights the strike zone, although not so much that you can give up on him. He has low IP/GS numbers, but still throws a lot of pitches because he walks so many, making him a candidate for arm trouble. If he's healthy, I like him.

RAMIRO MENDOZA   **RSP**   **1972**   **Age 25**

YR	TEAM	Lge	IP	H	ER	HR	BB	K	ERA	W	L	H/9	HR/9	BB/9	K/9	KW
1994	Tampa	Flor	120.0	164	60	11	50	85	4.50	6	7	12.30	.82	3.75	6.38	1.19
1995	Norwich	East	83.0	108	42	6	42	54	4.55	4	5	11.71	.65	4.55	5.86	.81
1995	Columbus, OH	Inter	13.0	12	3	0	3	11	2.08	1	0	8.31	.00	2.08	7.62	2.02
1996	Columbus, OH	Inter	92.3	98	24	2	28	50	2.34	7	3	9.55	.19	2.73	4.87	.94
1996	NY Yankees	AL	53.7	74	32	4	11	33	5.37	2	4	12.41	.67	1.84	5.53	1.38

I love this kid. Mendoza was called up when the Yanks were desperate and showed he wasn't ready. Ignore it. He throws strikes and groundballs, has movement and knows what he's doing. When he finally gets a job, he's going to get hammered while he learns what works on major league hitters. When he does, he could be pre-injury Bill Swift for five years. Get him.

CASEY MITTAUER   **RRP**   **1973**   **Age 24**

YR	TEAM	Lge	IP	H	ER	HR	BB	K	ERA	W	L	H/9	HR/9	BB/9	K/9	KW
1994	Oneonta	NY-P	33.0	42	11	1	20	18	3.00	3	1	11.45	.27	5.45	4.91	.27
1995	Greensboro	S Atl	64.3	84	31	4	23	34	4.34	3	4	11.75	.56	3.22	4.76	.78
1996	Tampa	Flor	28.3	34	10	0	8	17	3.18	2	1	10.80	.00	2.54	5.40	1.16

Mittauer closed at Tampa when Jay Tessmer didn't. He's old for the league and has advanced slowly, but his arm is live and he doesn't throw gopher balls. Welcome to Norwich, kid, make or break your life.

JIM MUSSELWHITE   **RSP**   **1972**   **Age 25**

YR	TEAM	Lge	IP	H	ER	HR	BB	K	ERA	W	L	H/9	HR/9	BB/9	K/9	KW
1993	Oneonta	NY-P	16.3	22	9	0	13	9	4.96	1	1	12.12	.00	7.16	4.96	-.14
1993	Greensboro	S Atl	56.7	83	35	6	33	35	5.56	2	4	13.18	.95	5.24	5.56	.54
1994	Tampa	Flor	98.3	106	53	12	34	81	4.85	4	7	9.70	1.10	3.11	7.41	1.69
1994	Albany, NY	East	27.0	34	4	0	8	23	1.33	3	0	11.33	.00	2.67	7.67	1.89
1995	Norwich	East	119.0	176	87	15	44	75	6.58	4	9	13.31	1.13	3.33	5.67	1.06
1996	Tampa	Flor	13.3	27	17	3	8	4	11.48	0	1	18.23	2.03	5.40	2.70	-.45
1996	Norwich	East	33.3	33	9	5	13	19	2.43	3	1	8.91	1.35	3.51	5.13	.83

Injury problems derailed his year, after ineffectiveness killed 1995. It's too soon to tell if he'll make it back, and he has a number of things working against him, including his lack of a fastball. If he pitches well, he will begin running into the "he doesn't throw hard" bias. Up in the air, check on him in June.

JEFF NELSON   **RRP**   **1967**   **Age 30**

YR	TEAM	Lge	IP	H	ER	HR	BB	K	ERA	W	L	H/9	HR/9	BB/9	K/9	KW
1993	Seattle	AL	59.3	58	25	5	37	63	3.79	4	3	8.80	.76	5.61	9.56	1.78
1994	Calgary	PCL	23.3	21	6	1	9	26	2.31	2	1	8.10	.39	3.47	10.03	2.47
1994	Seattle	AL	42.0	34	13	3	21	43	2.79	3	2	7.29	.64	4.50	9.21	1.95
1995	Seattle	AL	77.0	60	15	4	28	96	1.75	8	1	7.01	.47	3.27	11.22	2.92
1996	NY Yankees	AL	74.3	70	27	5	37	88	3.27	5	3	8.48	.61	4.48	10.65	2.43

Nelson's the best player the Yankees got in the Hitchcock trade. He has nasty stuff, plus a three-quarters/sidearm delivery that kills righties. Except for 1995 though, lefties have had their way with him. Whether he can consistently get lefties out, by altering his delivery, adding a pitch, whatever, will determine if he's going to be a setup man or a specialist. I'm betting on specialist.

DAVE PAVLAS   **RRP**   **1963**   **Age 34**

YR	TEAM	Lge	IP	H	ER	HR	BB	K	ERA	W	L	H/9	HR/9	BB/9	K/9	KW
1995	Columbus, OH	Inter	55.0	46	16	3	27	43	2.62	4	2	7.53	.49	4.42	7.04	1.24
1996	Columbus, OH	Inter	73.3	66	16	5	20	53	1.96	6	2	8.10	.61	2.45	6.50	1.55
1996	NY Yankees	AL	22.7	22	5	0	8	17	1.99	2	1	8.74	.00	3.18	6.75	1.46

Scab, one of only three to log any significant time in majors this year. I repeat: we'll never know if he was really good enough, or just got in because he participated in the owners' sham.

MELIDO PEREZ   **RSP**   **1966**   **Age 31**

YR	TEAM	Lge	IP	H	ER	HR	BB	K	ERA	W	L	H/9	HR/9	BB/9	K/9	KW
1993	NY Yankees	AL	162.7	176	91	23	73	155	5.03	7	11	9.74	1.27	4.04	8.58	1.85
1994	NY Yankees	AL	149.3	137	59	15	63	108	3.56	9	8	8.26	.90	3.80	6.51	1.22
1995	NY Yankees	AL	69.7	66	35	9	33	44	4.52	4	4	8.53	1.16	4.26	5.68	.83

He missed almost the entire season after elbow surgery, shutting down his rehab after three starts when the elbow flared up. Perez is under contract for 1997, so if he's healthy he'll have a job. I expect little or no contribution.

ANDY PETTITTE   **LSP**   **1972**   **Age 25**

YR	TEAM	Lge	IP	H	ER	HR	BB	K	ERA	W	L	H/9	HR/9	BB/9	K/9	KW
1993	Pr. William	Caro	137.3	192	83	8	75	82	5.44	5	10	12.58	.52	4.92	5.37	.56
1994	Albany, NY	East	66.7	73	33	6	25	37	4.46	3	4	9.86	.81	3.38	5.00	.82
1994	Columbus, OH	Inter	91.3	109	37	3	30	51	3.65	5	5	10.74	.30	2.96	5.03	.94
1995	Columbus, OH	Inter	10.7	8	0	0	1	7	.00	1	0	6.75	.00	.84	5.91	1.76
1995	NY Yankees	AL	175.3	175	65	14	67	114	3.34	11	8	8.98	.72	3.44	5.85	1.09
1996	NY Yankees	AL	220.7	213	75	19	77	156	3.06	16	9	8.69	.77	3.14	6.36	1.34

Mercifully he did not win the Cy Young, one of the three awards the BBWAA got right this year, a fantastic job for them. Pettitte improved across the board, but threw a lot of pitches—five postseason starts on top of a heavy workload—and fought arm tenderness in midseason. I expect him to get injured this year, and return in mid-1998. Good long-term bet, lousy in the short term.

RAY RICKEN   **RBP**   **1974**   **Age 23**

YR	TEAM	Lge	IP	H	ER	HR	BB	K	ERA	W	L	H/9	HR/9	BB/9	K/9	KW
1994	Oneonta	NY-P	41.0	64	31	2	27	33	6.80	1	4	14.05	.44	5.93	7.24	.93
1994	Greensboro	S Atl	21.3	35	15	2	17	11	6.33	1	1	14.77	.84	7.17	4.64	-.25
1995	Greensboro	S Atl	57.0	59	23	3	25	44	3.63	3	3	9.32	.47	3.95	6.95	1.33
1995	Tampa	Flor	67.3	60	26	5	37	41	3.48	4	3	8.02	.67	4.95	5.48	.59
1995	Norwich	East	48.7	56	23	3	30	34	4.25	2	3	10.36	.55	5.55	6.29	.71
1996	Norwich	East	42.3	50	26	7	25	31	5.53	2	3	10.63	1.49	5.31	6.59	.87
1996	Columbus, OH	Inter	65.3	61	35	4	45	48	4.82	3	4	8.40	.55	6.20	6.61	.65

Ricken did not pitch well at Norwich, despite which he was moved up to Columbus, where he also did not pitch well and was removed from the rotation. This seems counterproductive: the kid's a starter, you know he's not ready for a higher level, you move him up, then take him out of the rotation at the higher level. This forces him to learn an entirely new routine and undermines his confidence, a neat player development exacta. He'll be back, he just needs time and innings.

DAN RIOS   RRP   1973   Age 24

YR	TEAM	Lge	IP	H	ER	HR	BB	K	ERA	W	L	H/9	HR/9	BB/9	K/9	KW
1994	Greensboro	S Atl	36.3	42	5	2	20	21	1.24	4	0	10.40	.50	4.95	5.20	.50
1995	Tampa	Flor	59.3	84	27	2	28	51	4.10	3	4	12.74	.30	4.25	7.74	1.52
1996	Norwich	East	39.7	40	13	0	26	28	2.95	3	1	9.08	.00	5.90	6.35	.64
1996	Columbus, OH	Inter	26.0	23	5	1	9	18	1.73	3	0	7.96	.35	3.12	6.23	1.30

I confess: pitchers who never give up homers turn me on. [Insert punch line here.] Rios has tossed just three in 228 innings over four years, despite which he's still not ready for the majors. He's got one pitch, a fastball, and it's not Troy Percival's. A second pitch and better control will both be necessary for Rios to reach New York.

MARIANO RIVERA   RRP   1970   Age 27

YR	TEAM	Lge	IP	H	ER	HR	BB	K	ERA	W	L	H/9	HR/9	BB/9	K/9	KW
1993	Greensboro	S Atl	34.0	41	14	0	21	19	3.71	2	2	10.85	.00	5.56	5.03	.29
1994	Tampa	Flor	33.0	41	13	3	17	21	3.55	2	2	11.18	.82	4.64	5.73	.75
1994	Albany, NY	East	57.7	70	21	5	14	29	3.28	4	2	10.92	.78	2.18	4.53	.96
1994	Columbus, OH	Inter	29.3	37	21	5	13	19	6.44	1	2	11.35	1.53	3.99	5.83	.95
1995	Columbus, OH	Inter	27.7	28	9	2	6	25	2.93	2	1	9.11	.65	1.95	8.13	2.22
1995	NY Yankees	AL	67.3	67	33	10	32	51	4.41	3	4	8.96	1.34	4.28	6.82	1.20
1996	NY Yankees	AL	104.7	75	14	1	36	126	1.20	11	1	6.45	.09	3.10	10.83	2.84

He had an amazing year. Started as a hard-throwing prospect, finished as quite possibly the most important player in baseball in that his dominance, or more accurately the threat of it, dictated the flow of the postseason. Rivera has a great fastball and not much else, which is why his current role may actually be perfect for him, allowing him to go through the lineup once but still be used more than a typical closer.

Recent history tells us that 100-inning relievers disappear quickly, but there are reasons to believe Rivera will be an exception: 1) despite the high IP total, he wasn't used in an abusive way. No 70-pitch outings or being used for 25 pitches four straight nights; 2) he was a starter, so he's used to a higher workload than the relievers who have burnt out and 3) he doesn't throw a dangerous pitch, like a split-finger or slider. Give Joe Torre credit for this one: Rivera was handled masterfully.

KENNY ROGERS   LSP   1965   Age 32

YR	TEAM	Lge	IP	H	ER	HR	BB	K	ERA	W	L	H/9	HR/9	BB/9	K/9	KW
1993	Texas	AL	206.0	214	93	19	82	146	4.06	11	12	9.35	.83	3.58	6.38	1.23
1994	Texas	AL	166.3	167	74	22	57	118	4.00	9	9	9.04	1.19	3.08	6.38	1.36
1995	Texas	AL	208.0	180	63	24	79	139	2.73	16	7	7.79	1.04	3.42	6.01	1.15
1996	NY Yankees	AL	178.3	166	69	13	87	89	3.48	11	9	8.38	.66	4.39	4.49	.40

Rogers returned to his level after a big 1995 in Texas. He pitched from behind all year, and pitched like he was scared to death in the postseason, absolutely refusing to throw a strike until he had to. Underwent surgery this winter to clean out his elbow. He's not a good bet, but his contract will keep him in the rotation for a while.

TIM RUMER   LBP   1970   Age 27

YR	TEAM	Lge	IP	H	ER	HR	BB	K	ERA	W	L	H/9	HR/9	BB/9	K/9	KW
1994	Albany, NY	East	135.3	157	67	12	98	96	4.46	7	8	10.44	.80	6.52	6.38	.50
1995	Columbus, OH	Inter	133.0	161	89	12	97	92	6.02	5	10	10.89	.81	6.56	6.23	.43
1996	Norwich	East	37.0	37	12	4	23	33	2.92	3	1	9.00	.97	5.59	8.03	1.28
1996	Columbus, OH	Inter	47.0	41	16	3	18	29	3.06	3	2	7.85	.57	3.45	5.55	.99

I heard he might be good, but he's just a…oh, never mind. Yankees, desperate for left-handed relief, could and did do worse (Dale Polley). He's started, too, so he can throw long relief, and double as the spot guy against the Thomes of the world.

ANTHONY SHELBY   LRP   1974   Age 23

YR	TEAM	Lge	IP	H	ER	HR	BB	K	ERA	W	L	H/9	HR/9	BB/9	K/9	KW
1994	Oneonta	NY-P	20.3	44	19	1	11	8	8.41	0	2	19.48	.44	4.87	3.54	-.04
1995	Greensboro	S Atl	75.3	122	70	8	43	47	8.36	1	7	14.58	.96	5.14	5.62	.59
1996	Greensboro	S Atl	22.7	23	6	0	14	14	2.38	2	1	9.13	.00	5.56	5.56	.46
1996	Tampa	Flor	27.0	32	13	2	10	13	4.33	1	2	10.67	.67	3.33	4.33	.61

Shelby was old for his league, and pitched well despite not having a clear role. He's probably not a prospect, but it's possible he'll take to relieving and become one. Regardless, he's two years away.

BOB ST. PIERRE   **RBP**   **1974**   **Age 23**

YR	TEAM	Lge	IP	H	ER	HR	BB	K	ERA	W	L	H/9	HR/9	BB/9	K/9	KW
1995	Oneonta	NY-P	73.0	113	47	7	40	54	5.79	3	5	13.93	.86	4.93	6.66	.99
1996	Tampa	Flor	124.0	164	77	13	55	78	5.59	5	9	11.90	.94	3.99	5.66	.89

St. Pierre held serve in high A ball, but he's the pitching version of Chris Norton. Sure he can play, but there's nothing about him that screams, "Play me!"

BRIEN TAYLOR   **LSP**   **1972**   **Age 25**

YR	TEAM	Lge	IP	H	ER	HR	BB	K	ERA	W	L	H/9	HR/9	BB/9	K/9	KW
1993	Albany, NY	East	149.3	147	81	9	126	114	4.88	7	10	8.86	.54	7.59	6.87	.39
1996	Greensboro	S Atl	13.0	26	43	3	57	6	29.77	0	1	18.00	2.08	39.46	4.15	-8.48

Scott Boras' folly, and arguably the worst #1 pick in history, surpassing Bill Bene. Taylor actually had a good career developing, but an off-season scuffle ruined his shoulder, chomped years out of his development and robbed him of, well, everything. Lesson: teenage kids are stupid, and throwing money and a #1 pick at them is more so, especially when, in the case of pitchers, it can so easily go wrong.

JAY TESSMER   **RRP**   **1973**   **Age 24**

YR	TEAM	Lge	IP	H	ER	HR	BB	K	ERA	W	L	H/9	HR/9	BB/9	K/9	KW
1995	Oneonta	NY-P	33.0	35	9	1	19	31	2.45	3	1	9.55	.27	5.18	8.45	1.52
1996	Tampa	Flor	87.7	86	18	4	29	75	1.85	8	2	8.83	.41	2.98	7.70	1.82

He's not the next Percival, as you may have seen him advertised. Tessmer is a sidearmer who doesn't throw hard but does throw strikes and groundballs. He's being groomed as a closer, but because he can pitch more often than a typical closer may be better suited for the Rivera role, or more appropriately, Steve Reed's job. Pitchers like this typically struggle against left-handed batters, and Tessmer's ability to get them out at the higher levels will determine how much money he ends up making.

DAVE WEATHERS   **RBP**   **1970**   **Age 27**

YR	TEAM	Lge	IP	H	ER	HR	BB	K	ERA	W	L	H/9	HR/9	BB/9	K/9	KW
1993	Edmonton	PCL	130.3	141	59	13	60	93	4.07	7	7	9.74	.90	4.14	6.42	1.10
1993	Florida	NL	45.0	58	24	3	18	33	4.80	2	3	11.60	.60	3.60	6.60	1.30
1994	Florida	NL	135.3	154	71	12	71	66	4.72	6	9	10.24	.80	4.72	4.39	.28
1995	Florida	NL	90.0	106	60	7	61	54	6.00	3	7	10.60	.70	6.10	5.40	.27
1996	Columbus, OH	Inter	16.0	20	10	1	6	6	5.62	1	1	11.25	.56	3.38	3.38	.28
1996	Florida	NL	71.0	89	38	7	35	35	4.82	3	5	11.28	.89	4.44	4.44	.37
1996	NY Yankees	AL	17.7	20	14	1	15	13	7.13	0	2	10.19	.51	7.64	6.62	.30

Like Boehringer, Weathers was murdered as a starter for the Yanks: 4 starts, 10.1 IP, 14.81 ERA, .492 opponents' OBP. He came back in September and pitched well out of the bullpen, with nine shutout innings, and in the postseason. The Yankees are deep in right-handed relievers, and Weathers isn't the best of the bunch. He'll get more chances, just not in New York.

JOHN WETTELAND   **RRP**   **1967**   **Age 30**

YR	TEAM	Lge	IP	H	ER	HR	BB	K	ERA	W	L	H/9	HR/9	BB/9	K/9	KW
1993	Montreal	NL	81.3	65	14	3	37	109	1.55	8	1	7.19	.33	4.09	12.06	3.00
1994	Montreal	NL	62.0	47	17	5	26	63	2.47	5	2	6.82	.73	3.77	9.15	2.10
1995	NY Yankees	AL	59.7	42	15	6	15	66	2.26	5	2	6.34	.91	2.26	9.96	2.75
1996	NY Yankees	AL	63.3	51	16	8	22	67	2.27	5	2	7.25	1.14	3.13	9.52	2.39

He slipped a notch this year, and fought some injury problems as the season went on. Wetteland is looking for a three-year deal in the $18 million range, and at this point I don't think he's worth it. The value of $15 million for 225 innings notwithstanding, I don't think he's a good risk. The Yankees have lots of relievers, including one closer candidate, and can use the money elsewhere (2B, 3B). I don't expect him to collapse, a la Thigpen or Dibble, but he'll be less effective, much like Randy Myers the last few years. Has the best chance of anyone for 500 saves.

Player	Age	Team	Lge	AB	H	DB	TP	HR	BB	SB	CS	OUT	BA	OBA	SA	EQA	EQR	Peak
TIM BARKER	28	Columbus-OH	Inter	406	101	25	5	2	56	15	5	310	.249	.340	.350	.238	43	.240
VICK BROWN	23	Greensboro	S Atl	98	30	1	0	2	8	4	1	69	.306	.358	.378	.257	12	.275
	23	Tampa	Flor	93	18	3	0	0	13	1	0	75	.194	.292	.226	.168	4	.184
ERIC CAMFIELD	23	Greensboro	S Atl	247	39	3	1	0	14	4	2	210	.158	.203	.178	.051	1	.058
BUBBA CARPENTER	27	Columbus-OH	Inter	469	106	19	2	6	48	7	4	367	.226	.298	.313	.204	35	.209
IVAN CRUZ	28	Columbus-OH	Inter	449	110	15	0	25	48	2	3	341	.245	.318	.445	.250	53	.252
MARK DALESANDRO	28	Columbus-OH	Inter	256	68	24	3	2	18	1	0	188	.266	.314	.406	.241	27	.243
DANIEL DONATO	23	Norwich	East	473	130	20	1	3	30	4	3	346	.275	.318	.340	.223	41	.242
DEREK DUKART	24	Tampa	Flor	200	60	9	0	4	8	1	1	141	.300	.327	.405	.246	21	.264
ROBERT EENHOORN	28	Columbus-OH	Inter	174	55	11	1	1	21	4	1	120	.316	.390	.408	.275	24	.278
GRANT FITHIAN	24	Norwich	East	182	35	4	1	5	10	1	0	147	.192	.234	.308	.172	9	.184
KRAIG HAWKINS	24	Tampa	Flor	282	82	2	3	2	31	7	3	203	.291	.361	.340	.243	30	.260
ROB HINDS	25	Norwich	East	186	41	2	1	2	18	7	3	148	.220	.289	.274	.191	12	.200
MATT HOWARD	28	Columbus-OH	Inter	203	66	10	1	2	19	6	2	139	.325	.383	.414	.274	27	.276
ERIC KNOWLES	22	Norwich	East	407	97	17	1	7	29	7	3	313	.238	.289	.337	.210	32	.231
JOSE LOBATON	22	Tampa	Flor	387	87	12	2	7	31	6	4	304	.225	.282	.320	.200	27	.220
R.D. LONG	25	Columbus-OH	Inter	125	26	4	1	0	15	3	1	100	.208	.293	.256	.183	7	.192
MARC MARINI	26	Columbus-OH	Inter	135	33	6	0	3	11	1	0	102	.244	.301	.356	.221	12	.229
CODY MCCORMICK	21	Greensboro	S Atl	180	33	3	0	5	9	0	0	147	.183	.222	.283	.152	7	.171
TIM MCINTOSH	31	Columbus-OH	Inter	206	54	8	0	9	12	0	0	152	.262	.303	.432	.243	22	.235
BRIAN MCLAMB	23	Tampa	Flor	274	55	6	0	4	21	4	3	222	.201	.258	.266	.166	12	.180
FRED MCNAIR	26	Norwich	East	252	69	8	1	6	10	1	0	183	.274	.302	.385	.231	23	.239
KEVIN NORTHRUP	26	Columbus-OH	Inter	169	45	9	1	4	12	3	1	125	.266	.315	.402	.241	18	.251
	26	Norwich	East	243	59	7	1	7	23	2	1	185	.243	.308	.366	.226	22	.235
SANDY PICHARDO	21	Tampa	Flor	303	72	6	4	4	19	2	3	234	.238	.283	.323	.199	21	.223
RENE PINTO	18	Greensboro	S Atl	169	31	6	0	1	4	1	0	138	.183	.202	.237	.115	3	.135
KINNIS PLEDGER	27	Norwich	East	463	124	23	3	18	59	15	3	342	.268	.351	.447	.268	64	.275
KEVIN RIGGS	27	Norwich	East	425	120	18	1	3	73	7	5	310	.282	.388	.351	.255	51	.261
SCOTT ROMANO	24	Norwich	East	111	32	1	0	3	9	1	0	79	.288	.342	.378	.246	12	.264
JEFFREY SAFFER	21	Greensboro	S Atl	160	40	7	1	3	6	0	0	120	.250	.277	.363	.212	12	.238
CODY SAMUEL	22	Greensboro	S Atl	500	118	8	0	15	29	0	1	383	.236	.278	.342	.204	36	.225
TATE SEEFRIED	24	Norwich	East	373	78	11	0	13	42	2	2	297	.209	.289	.343	.208	29	.222
DEREK SHUMPERT	20	Greensboro	S Atl	553	127	14	5	4	45	11	7	433	.230	.288	.295	.194	36	.220
SLOAN SMITH	23	Norwich	East	210	45	8	2	2	27	3	1	166	.214	.304	.300	.203	15	.221
	23	Tampa	Flor	207	45	5	1	5	41	3	3	165	.217	.347	.324	.226	20	.247
JAIME TORRES	23	Norwich	East	342	84	15	1	6	19	1	2	260	.246	.285	.348	.209	26	.227
JASON TROILO	23	Greensboro	S Atl	205	35	4	0	3	7	1	0	170	.171	.198	.234	.108	3	.117
DENNIS TWOMBLEY	21	Tampa	Flor	80	21	1	0	2	11	0	0	59	.262	.352	.350	.239	8	.270
JOSE VELAZQUEZ	20	Greensboro	S Atl	436	97	10	0	6	28	2	1	340	.222	.269	.287	.180	24	.205
TRACY WOODSON	33	Columbus-OH	Inter	420	115	25	2	19	19	3	0	305	.274	.305	.479	.258	52	.245
CARLOS YEDO	22	Tampa	Flor	484	108	9	1	13	57	1	0	376	.223	.305	.326	.211	38	.232

Player	Age	Team	Lge	IP	H	ER	HR	BB	K	ERA	W	L	H/9	HR/9	BB/9	K/9	KW
TOM BECKER	21	Greensboro	S Atl	104.7	163	88	10	107	54	7.57	3	9	14.02	.86	9.20	4.64	-.75
JASON BEVERLIN	22	Tampa	Flor	41.0	52	24	7	24	28	5.27	2	3	11.41	1.54	5.27	6.15	.73
ALEJANDRO BRACHO	20	Greensboro	S Atl	76.0	135	60	10	50	39	7.11	2	6	15.99	1.18	5.92	4.62	.06
MARK CARPER	27	Columbus, OH	Inter	34.0	42	24	6	20	13	6.35	1	3	11.12	1.59	5.29	3.44	-.18
CHRIS CORN	24	Tampa	Flor	153.0	176	71	15	58	79	4.18	8	9	10.35	.88	3.41	4.65	.70
ANDY CROGHAN	26	Norwich	East	37.7	48	24	4	21	37	5.73	1	3	11.47	.96	5.02	8.84	1.69
CHRIS CUMBERLAND	23	Columbus, OH	Inter	57.0	82	36	8	30	29	5.68	2	4	12.95	1.26	4.74	4.58	.34
	23	Norwich	East	87.7	129	74	13	47	33	7.60	2	8	13.24	1.33	4.83	3.39	-.08
LUIS DELOSSANTOS	18	Greensboro	S Atl	26.0	54	21	5	17	12	7.27	1	2	18.69	1.73	5.88	4.15	-.09
AL DRUMHELLER	24	Tampa	Flor	46.0	41	15	3	43	41	2.93	3	2	8.02	.59	8.41	8.02	.57
DARRELL EINERSTON	23	Greensboro	S Atl	58.0	99	38	2	29	26	5.90	2	4	15.36	.31	4.50	4.03	.22
BEN FORD	20	Greensboro	S Atl	68.3	109	63	4	48	46	8.30	2	6	14.36	.53	6.32	6.06	.44
RICH HINES	27	Columbus, OH	Inter	63.7	69	34	6	45	39	4.81	3	4	9.75	.85	6.36	5.51	.25
MIKE JERZEMBECK	24	Norwich	East	64.0	87	39	9	33	49	5.48	2	5	12.23	1.27	4.64	6.89	1.14
	24	Tampa	Flor	66.3	81	28	6	20	43	3.80	4	3	10.99	.81	2.71	5.83	1.27
SCOTT KAMIENIECKI	32	Columbus, OH	Inter	29.3	33	17	4	11	22	5.22	1	2	10.12	1.23	3.38	6.75	1.41
MIKE KOTARSKI	25	Norwich	East	66.0	86	41	3	37	49	5.59	2	5	11.73	.41	5.05	6.68	.97
DENNY LAIL	21	Tampa	Flor	31.7	43	11	1	19	15	3.13	2	2	12.22	.28	5.40	4.26	.07
FRANK LANKFORD	25	Norwich	East	81.3	94	41	4	50	46	4.54	4	5	10.40	.44	5.53	5.09	.31
DAVID MEYER	24	Tampa	Flor	33.7	55	18	3	23	13	4.81	2	2	14.70	.80	6.15	3.48	-.38
RICH OLIVIER	21	Greensboro	S Atl	38.0	72	35	3	33	24	8.29	1	3	17.05	.71	7.82	5.68	-.06
FRISCO PAROTTE	20	Greensboro	S Atl	44.0	52	31	3	49	23	6.34	1	4	10.64	.61	10.02	4.70	-.94
DALE POLLEY	30	Columbus, OH	Inter	30.3	30	9	1	12	24	2.67	2	1	8.90	.30	3.56	7.12	1.48
STEPHEN RANDOLPH	22	Greensboro	S Atl	82.7	95	58	10	130	62	6.31	3	6	10.34	1.09	14.15	6.75	-1.29
GREG RESZ	24	Norwich	East	36.0	44	17	1	22	28	4.25	2	2	11.00	.25	5.50	7.00	.96
JAKE ROBBINS	20	Greensboro	S Atl	60.0	110	73	7	70	28	10.95	1	6	16.50	1.05	10.50	4.20	-1.22
MARTIN ROBINSON	19	Greensboro	S Atl	39.7	81	53	2	43	21	12.03	0	4	18.38	.45	9.76	4.76	-.85
ERIC SCHAFFNER	21	Greensboro	S Atl	74.0	134	81	6	88	35	9.85	1	7	16.30	.73	10.70	4.26	-1.26
BRETT SCHLOMANN	21	Tampa	Flor	129.0	183	89	19	70	75	6.21	4	10	12.77	1.33	4.88	5.23	.52
MICHAEL SPENCE	21	Greensboro	S Atl	95.0	156	86	11	57	49	8.15	2	9	14.78	1.04	5.40	4.64	.20
	21	Tampa	Flor	36.0	59	34	5	18	15	8.50	1	3	14.75	1.25	4.50	3.75	.12
JOHN SUTHERLAND	27	Norwich	East	39.0	44	16	4	24	23	3.69	2	2	10.15	.92	5.54	5.31	.38
CESAR VERDIN	19	Greensboro	S Atl	56.0	82	44	7	36	39	7.07	1	5	13.18	1.12	5.79	6.27	.64
KENT WALLACE	25	Columbus, OH	Inter	64.3	69	30	13	22	28	4.20	3	4	9.65	1.82	3.08	3.92	.54
WALLY WHITEHURST	32	Columbus, OH	Inter	69.3	62	20	5	18	39	2.60	6	2	8.05	.65	2.34	5.06	1.10

Toronto Blue Jays

The Blue Jays are at a point that can be compared to the Royals during the few ugly years between the great Herzog teams of the late '70s, and the 1985 champions. Like those Royals teams of the early '80s, the Blue Jays are entering the first rebuilding effort of their history. Both franchises gave their fans a deliberate and progressive build-up from expansion to contention, relying on their minor league systems and a variety of the always-available talent that other organizations let slip through the cracks. After extended periods of contention, both organizations hit the downslopes of the careers of their important players or the overpriced free agency of others. They were both forced to confront the need for major roster overhauls. For both the Royals then and the Blue Jays now, some key veterans are in place and some young, talented, potentially great players have either arrived or are on the way. We've all seen this cycle: when winning begins to breed forgetfulness of what got a team into contention in the first place, leading to increasingly desperate acquisitions of veterans for that extra push to get that one more roll of the dice for postseason magic, pickups who usually wind up costing far more than they're worth.

You might expect serious rebuilding to involve lots of young players and high turnover. If the Blue Jays were a "rebuilding" team entering the '96 season, a team that slipped from five games under .500 in '94 to 22 under in '95, they did not show it, because they did not turn to their minor leagues. Gord Ash, replacing the highly respected Pat Gillick in the front office, made it clear he felt the franchise was in a distinct rebuilding phase. He talked about how the clubhouse now "belonged" to young players like Alex Gonzalez and Shawn Green, fresh off productive rookie seasons in '95. However, if Ash felt he was truly rebuilding the team, he had a strange way of showing it. In addition to the acquisitions of Hanson, Nixon, Quantrill, etc., Ash was further laying the foundations for the Blue Jays' future with moves like giving Ed Sprague a three-year contract. He announced that Sprague "is the type of player who's going to have to be part of the resurgence of this club...he makes the most of his skill." If a long-term commitment to a proven mediocrity is Gord Ash's idea of rebuilding, rebuilding might be more difficult than it has to be. The Blue Jays also retained Cito Gaston as manager. Gaston has strengths, but a healthy faith in the talent of young players has never been one of them. Whether or not Gaston would be capable and willing to direct the club through its rebuilding was, and still is, an open question.

Now, keeping in mind that this is supposed to be a rebuilding team, think about the Blue Jays' additions for the '96 season: Erik Hanson, Otis Nixon, Juan Samuel, Charlie O'Brien, Paul Quantrill and Frank Viola. Were these additions supposed to inspire confidence and bring the Blue Jays back from the disasters of '94 or '95? Or were they merely useful additions to tide the franchise over until the real talent arrives?

So the Blue Jays claimed they were in a rebuilding year, but spent most of 1996 avoiding the actual rebuilding. That means they may not have bottomed out yet, because they weren't willing to take their losses this year while investing in their future. Instead, they embarked on a miserable game of musical chairs for the over-30 crowd of always-available veterans, hoping that this would somehow produce respectability they were unwilling to earn with an honest rebuilding project. Perhaps the best measure of how the Blue Jays feel about their "rebuilding" year is that they scapegoated John Olerud, assigning him a disproportionate amount of blame for a disappointing season, while embracing the potentially devastating idea that Joe Carter is so integral to their future that they need to move him to first base. This would be disastrous. Despite the organization's satisfaction with the seasons Sprague and Carter put up, the Blue Jays had an awful offense in a great hitter's park, finishing 12th in the AL in runs. Singling out Olerud to blame for that, while ignoring the shortcomings of their other veterans, means the Jays will probably put an even worse offense on the field next year.

As it turned out, the only regular spots that opened up for new young players were DH (Carlos Delgado) and second base, and veteran Domingo Cedeno wound up getting the majority of playing time there over dubious prospects Tomas Perez, Miguel Cairo and Tilson Brito. The rotation and bullpen were entrusted to the aged, unless you consider giving the closer's role to a 30-year-old Mike Timlin a youth movement. As the obvious shortcomings of many of the veteran position players became obvious, rather than expand roles for many younger players the Blue Jays congratulated themselves that they had Juan Samuel and went out to acquire 31-year-old Jacob Brumfield. On the pitching staff, the predictable collapses of the Quantrills and Violas did create opportunities for prospects like Marty Janzen and Tim Crabtree, but down the stretch too much time was still being spent on guys like Woody Williams.

As unfortunate as the Blue Jays' inability to kick their sweet tooth for geezers has been, their bizarre decisions concerning who they actually select as "prospects" can be potentially far more troubling. Between the odd round-robin arrangement at second, which began and ended the season in confusion, the unfortunate trust placed in Sandy Martinez and the aforementioned faith in Sprague, Ash and Gaston seem to be making it clear that they can't separate the good young players from the bad. In particular, the Sprague decision might be particularly unfortunate, because the Jays have one of the best young prospects in baseball at third base, Tom Evans.

Despite all these shortcomings, the Blue Jays actually enjoyed a remarkable season, and it had nothing to do with the very old or the very young, the GM's "rebuilding" or Cito Gaston's on-field decisions. The credit for what successes there were belonged to a pair of starters bouncing back from ineffectiveness: Juan Guzman and Pat Hentgen. They were the best starting tandem in the league, and arguably in all of baseball. The misfortune is that their superb seasons were wasted on an organization which doesn't really seem to know how to improve itself, and it's dicey to count on their contributing anything as spectacular again.

The shape of the Blue Jays' future can be measured by the future of Cito Gaston as manager. Although his carefree tendencies towards on-field strategy seem to make him popular with his players, there is a legitimate question as to whether or not he will be the man to handle the swarms of prospects the Blue Jays will have to sort through in the next few years. His treatment of hitting prospects has already left much to be desired, particularly his handling of Carlos Delgado, Shawn Green and Alex Gonzalez in '94, and more recently Felipe Crespo.

If there's any doubt about how the Blue Jays envision their future, the acquisitions of Orlando Merced, Carlos Garcia and Dan Plesac from the Pirates spell it out. On acquiring these three mediocrities, all past their prime, the Blue Jays announced they were going to contend for the wild card. They'll be rudely disappointed, and the team now has a chance to be the worst team in the American League by '98.

In the past, the Blue Jays' farm system was infamous for its ability to mass-produce fool's gold. The list of pseudo-prospects (Junior Felix, Sil Campusano, Ryan Thompson, Mark Whiten, Howard Battle, Jose Herrera and even Derek Bell) is remarkable, as was the Jays' ability to put these men in other people's uniforms before their shortcomings were widely recognized. Now, however, the Blue Jays' system appears to be rich in talent, especially at the lower levels. Whereas they usually allow their position player prospects to move up a level at a time, the organization has shown a definite willingness to push pitching prospects up the ladder rapidly while not overusing them, like the Mets. This frightens some analysts, but it did not hinder the development of several pitchers this season, particularly Roy Halladay and Mark Sievert. If this ambitious handling of pitching prospects continues, don't be surprised if there's a growing debate in the organization to start making callups during the '97 season, assuming the Jays cut their losses with lost causes like Paul Quantrill.

The Blue Jays don't usually put much effort into fielding a winning team at Syracuse, frequently stocking the team with a blend of non-prospects (call them the Howard Battle group) or mediocre veterans (call them the Wes Chamberlain bunch). It's neither a particularly good or a particularly lousy team. That may change soon as a wave of solid prospects, especially on the left side of the infield, pushes its way up the chain. Knoxville had some top-notch hitting talent, leading the Southern League in OBP with a young team; similarly, Hagerstown posted the best OBP in the Sally League. The pitching staffs at both Knoxville and Dunedin finished near the top of their leagues in strikeouts. In general, the Jays seem to draft physically enormous right-handed pitchers and "tools"-oriented position players who wind up being lousy hitters. The organization has a pair of glaring weaknesses: catcher, where there have no decent prospects, and the outfield, where the ones the Jays have after Shannon Stewart are straight out of the Sil Campusano mold. However, by developing talented infielders and with a lot of lower level pitching, the Blue Jays' farm is a definite improvement over the past. It will be up to the big league club to put them to good use in the not-so-distant future.

TILSON BRITO   **2B/SS**   **1972**   **Age 25**

Year	Team	Lge	AB	H	DB	TP	HR	BB	SB	CS	OUT	BA	OBA	SA	EQA	EQR	Peak
1993	Dunedin	Flor	468	105	13	0	8	50	13	6	369	.224	.299	.303	.204	34	.228
1994	Knoxville	South	489	126	13	4	7	37	18	6	369	.258	.310	.344	.225	44	.248
1995	Syracuse	Inter	335	80	13	2	8	30	13	5	260	.239	.301	.361	.225	31	.245
1996	Syracuse	Inter	408	111	19	5	10	39	8	6	303	.272	.336	.417	.251	48	.268
1996	Toronto	AL	80	19	4	0	2	10	1	1	62	.237	.322	.362	.228	8	.243
1997	*Toronto*	*AL*	*414*	*105*	*22*	*2*	*8*	*39*	*9*	*2*	*311*	*.254*	*.318*	*.374*	*.239*	*43*	

Among the various second base prospects the Blue Jays have to sort through to find a good replacement for Roberto Alomar, Brito is neither the worst option (that was last year's winner, Domingo Cedeno) or the best (that would be last year's loser, "Creepy" Crespo). He's consistently shown surprising power for a middle infielder, some speed and is a good glove at short. His '94 season was marred by a season-long bout with undiagnosed tonsillitis, so his performance this past year at Syracuse could be reason for optimism. Basically, his upside is a useful backup.

JACOB BRUMFIELD   **OF**   **1965**   **Age 32**

Year	Team	Lge	AB	H	DB	TP	HR	BB	SB	CS	OUT	BA	OBA	SA	EQA	EQR	Peak
1993	Indianapolis	AmA	127	40	12	1	4	7	10	0	87	.315	.351	.520	.298	21	.301
1993	Cincinnati	NL	277	77	16	2	7	25	17	7	207	.278	.338	.426	.258	35	.260
1994	Cincinnati	NL	125	40	10	2	4	17	6	3	88	.320	.401	.528	.304	22	.302
1995	Pittsburgh	NL	407	111	22	2	4	41	17	10	306	.273	.339	.366	.240	43	.235
1996	Pittsburgh	NL	81	21	5	0	3	6	3	1	61	.259	.310	.432	.249	9	.239
1996	Toronto	AL	308	79	18	2	12	24	12	3	232	.256	.310	.445	.253	37	.244
1997	*Toronto*	*AL*	*350*	*91*	*19*	*1*	*14*	*32*	*19*	*7*	*266*	*.260*	*.322*	*.440*	*.265*	*48*	

You're a franchise that needs to rebuild, so who do you turn to? Somebody else's flop. Brumfield is your basic pain in the ass hustle player: he runs like a fool, shows poor range afield and doesn't have any single offensive strength good enough to give him anything like a regular job. Nevertheless, adding him was hailed as a good thing.

MIGUEL CAIRO   **IF**   **1974**   **Age 23**

Year	Team	Lge	AB	H	DB	TP	HR	BB	SB	CS	OUT	BA	OBA	SA	EQA	EQR	Peak
1993	Vero Beach	Flor	347	97	7	0	2	23	12	7	257	.280	.324	.317	.220	29	.254
1994	Bakersfield	Calif	538	136	18	2	2	28	21	11	413	.253	.290	.305	.202	38	.230
1995	San Antonio	Texas	444	120	15	1	2	25	25	9	333	.270	.309	.322	.221	38	.248
1996	Syracuse	Inter	471	127	13	3	3	29	18	6	350	.270	.312	.329	.222	41	.245

Although his defense wins rave reviews, Cairo's bat is so weak that he's in no better position to take hold of the second base position than any of the other Blue Jays' options. For whatever reason, Cairo was named a top 10 prospect in the California League in '94, which probably tells us more about how easy it is for Dodgers to make those lists than it does about Cairo's talent.

JOE CARTER   **OF/1B**   **1960**   **Age 37**

Year	Team	Lge	AB	H	DB	TP	HR	BB	SB	CS	OUT	BA	OBA	SA	EQA	EQR	Peak
1993	Toronto	AL	608	160	31	5	38	50	7	2	450	.263	.319	.518	.271	86	.258
1994	Toronto	AL	439	122	25	1	29	33	10	0	317	.278	.328	.538	.283	67	.269
1995	Toronto	AL	562	146	21	0	28	38	12	1	417	.260	.307	.447	.252	66	.240
1996	Toronto	AL	624	157	34	7	30	44	7	6	473	.252	.301	.473	.251	75	.239
1997	*Toronto*	*AL*	*529*	*134*	*18*	*1*	*25*	*39*	*8*	*7*	*402*	*.253*	*.305*	*.433*	*.246*	*60*	

The Blue Jays are half right about Joe Carter: he isn't good enough to play in the outfield any more. Unfortunately for Blue Jays fans, the logical conclusion Gord Ash draws from this is that he needs to be moved someplace else, when he really needs to start gathering splinters or calling it a career. At this point, if the Jays trade Olerud to play Carter at first, he'll be the most reliably crummy hitter at first base since Pete Rose or Steve Garvey. Of course, he's an extreme flyball hitter, so he'd still put up great numbers in Coors....

RICKEY CRADLE   **OF**   **1973**   **Age 24**

Year	Team	Lge	AB	H	DB	TP	HR	BB	SB	CS	OUT	BA	OBA	SA	EQA	EQR	Peak
1993	Hagerstown	SAtl	461	102	12	2	11	51	8	6	365	.221	.299	.328	.208	36	.236
1994	Dunedin	Flor	355	86	8	2	11	54	12	5	274	.242	.342	.369	.242	40	.271
1995	Dunedin	Flor	188	52	5	1	8	24	4	1	137	.277	.358	.441	.269	26	.296
1995	Knoxville	South	119	19	4	1	3	16	2	1	101	.160	.259	.286	.174	6	.192
1996	Knoxville	South	334	82	14	1	10	46	9	5	257	.246	.337	.383	.242	37	.264
1996	Syracuse	Inter	132	27	2	2	8	14	1	0	105	.205	.281	.432	.233	14	.253
1997	*Toronto*	*AL*	*369*	*92*	*21*	*1*	*14*	*47*	*11*	*7*	*284*	*.249*	*.334*	*.425*	*.255*	*47*	

Cradle's stock is on the rise, as he garnered one of the important AFL slots for the Blue Jays this winter. He'd be a more than adequate replacement for Jacob Brumfield.

FELIPE CRESPO   **2B/3B**   **1973**   **Age 24**

Year	Team	Lge	AB	H	DB	TP	HR	BB	SB	CS	OUT	BA	OBA	SA	EQA	EQR	Peak
1993	Dunedin	Flor	347	90	10	3	8	40	8	2	259	.259	.336	.375	.243	38	.275
1994	Knoxville	South	521	137	23	3	9	56	11	4	388	.263	.334	.370	.240	55	.268
1995	Syracuse	Inter	359	106	17	2	14	42	9	4	257	.295	.369	.471	.279	53	.308
1996	Syracuse	Inter	365	100	14	0	10	56	8	7	272	.274	.371	.395	.257	46	.279
1996	Toronto	AL	49	9	4	0	0	12	1	0	40	.184	.344	.265	.212	4	.229
1997	*Toronto*	*AL*	*462*	*131*	*27*	*3*	*10*	*59*	*14*	*6*	*337*	*.284*	*.365*	*.420*	*.269*	*63*	

Crespo is simply unlucky. Going into last spring, his major rivals career for playing time through most of his minor league, Chris Stynes and Joe Lis, had both been traded. He was clearly a better hitter than the puny horde of Britos and Cairos. Domingo Cedeno had shown only an ability to make outs and errors. Crespo even enjoyed a superb spring. But after all of that, a hamstring injury and the same snap judgments that Cito Gaston made about Alex Gonzalez, Shawn Green, and Carlos Delgado in '94 cost Crespo his job. A shoulder injury has produced a strange throwing motion that frightens scouts who twitter about these things. He may now be a year too late, because Jeff Patzke has moved into the second base picture, and should be the eventual winner.

BRANDON CROMER   **SS**   **1974**   **Age 23**

Year	Team	Lge	AB	H	DB	TP	HR	BB	SB	CS	OUT	BA	OBA	SA	EQA	EQR	Peak
1994	Hagerstown	SAtl	266	32	4	2	5	21	0	1	235	.120	.185	.207	.036	0	.024
1995	Dunedin	Flor	343	76	8	1	7	38	1	2	269	.222	.299	.312	.202	25	.227
1996	Knoxville	South	320	77	10	4	7	50	2	3	246	.241	.343	.363	.236	33	.260
1997	*Pittsburgh*	*NL*	*500*	*128*	*21*	*3*	*10*	*86*	*4*	*4*	*376*	*.256*	*.365*	*.370*	*.259*	*64*	

Cromer doesn't show up on many people's prospect lists, but he's shown a very good balance of power and patience for a shortstop. He's a left-handed hitter, and he seems to be platooned a lot, so this projection is pretty speculative. He could be a slower version of Andy Fox; in the AFL, he played second base. Cromer was one of the six players sent to Pittsburgh in the major deal in November.

JOHN CURL   **1B**   **1973**   **Age 24**

Year	Team	Lge	AB	H	DB	TP	HR	BB	SB	CS	OUT	BA	OBA	SA	EQA	EQR	Peak
1996	Dunedin	Flor	459	107	9	1	18	39	4	2	354	.233	.293	.375	.222	41	.241

When we talk in this book about minor league hitters who deserve to be considered prospects, don't think for a minute that we're talking about goofs like John Curl. Old for his league, in an organization laden with better first base prospects, he should be should be headed nowhere for years to come, sending amusing postcards to his friends from exotic locations like Knoxville.

LORENZO de la CRUZ   **OF**   **1972**   **Age 25**

Year	Team	Lge	AB	H	DB	TP	HR	BB	SB	CS	OUT	BA	OBA	SA	EQA	EQR	Peak
1994	Hagerstown	SAtl	468	102	10	2	14	26	6	4	370	.218	.259	.338	.195	31	.216
1995	Knoxville	South	511	125	15	7	9	36	7	5	391	.245	.294	.354	.216	43	.235
1996	Knoxville	South	441	97	14	2	15	29	5	2	346	.220	.268	.363	.208	34	.223

The organization thinks fondly (not necessarily highly) of de la Cruz for his spot in the organization's past: he was the top hitter on the most dominating team in Dominican Summer League history (the team finished 68-2). Since then, he's shown to be an impatient hitter and a lousy prospect, but the organization seems proud of him for his spot in history.

CARLOS DELGADO   **1B/DH**   **1972**   **Age 25**

Year	Team	Lge	AB	H	DB	TP	HR	BB	SB	CS	OUT	BA	OBA	SA	EQA	EQR	Peak
1993	Knoxville	South	480	135	14	1	22	92	6	2	347	.281	.397	.452	.285	75	.319
1994	Toronto	AL	131	29	3	0	9	25	1	1	103	.221	.346	.450	.260	18	.287
1994	Syracuse	Inter	316	99	6	0	18	40	1	0	217	.313	.390	.503	.296	52	.326
1995	Syracuse	Inter	347	112	16	2	23	46	1	2	237	.323	.402	.579	.315	66	.342
1995	Toronto	AL	91	16	3	0	3	6	0	0	75	.176	.227	.308	.165	4	.178
1996	Toronto	AL	487	131	27	2	25	58	0	0	356	.269	.347	.487	.273	69	.292
1997	*Toronto*	*AL*	*534*	*154*	*27*	*2*	*28*	*65*	*0*	*0*	*380*	*.288*	*.366*	*.504*	*.289*	*85*	

Exhibit A on how not to treat a top prospect. Delgado came up in '94 and was red hot. When the inevitable adjustment period came, the Blue Jays lacked the fortitude to ride it out, and Delgado was undone with extended time on the bench sprinkled with three weeks of spot starts. Then the organization decided it needed to show it was serious about the season by playing Mike Huff. Delgado was demoted, and was allowed to show that he still had nothing left to learn in the minors for almost two years before the team finally, grudgingly, handed him the lineup slot that should have been his all along. His days at catcher or in the outfield are over; he'll either get first base if the Jays come to their senses about Joe Carter or continue to DH.

TOM EVANS   **3B**   **1975**   **Age 22**

Year	Team	Lge	AB	H	DB	TP	HR	BB	SB	CS	OUT	BA	OBA	SA	EQA	EQR	Peak
1993	Hagerstown	SAtl	405	90	10	1	7	40	4	1	316	.222	.292	.304	.199	28	.232
1994	Hagerstown	SAtl	338	83	9	1	10	43	1	0	255	.246	.331	.367	.235	34	.272
1995	Dunedin	Flor	464	126	20	1	11	44	4	1	339	.272	.335	.390	.245	50	.278
1996	Knoxville	South	398	100	13	1	15	98	2	0	298	.251	.399	.402	.273	58	.306
1997	*Toronto*	*AL*	*519*	*121*	*16*	*0*	*20*	*119*	*1*	*1*	*399*	*.233*	*.376*	*.380*	*.259*	*68*	

One of the best prospects you may never have heard of. With a good throwing arm from the hot corner, Evans responded to questions about his defense by being named the best defensive third baseman in the Southern League this year. But what he really does is put runs on the board. Untranslated, Evans drew 115 walks and led all of the minor leagues in OBP. At worst, he could easily be the new Eddie "the Walking Man" Yost. Unfortunately, Sprague's signed to two more years, and the Blue Jays claim they can't trade Sprague because no one in the organization is ready to replace him. They're wrong.

ALEX GONZALEZ   **SS**   **1973**   **Age 24**

Year	Team	Lge	AB	H	DB	TP	HR	BB	SB	CS	OUT	BA	OBA	SA	EQA	EQR	Peak
1993	Knoxville	South	564	148	19	4	15	37	22	7	423	.262	.308	.390	.238	58	.270
1994	Syracuse	Inter	447	123	17	3	12	51	16	4	328	.275	.349	.407	.258	56	.290
1994	Toronto	AL	53	8	4	1	0	4	2	0	45	.151	.211	.264	.150	2	.172
1995	Toronto	AL	370	93	20	4	11	45	4	4	281	.251	.333	.416	.248	43	.273
1996	Toronto	AL	526	123	29	5	14	45	16	6	409	.234	.294	.388	.229	51	.249
1997	*Toronto*	*AL*	*545*	*143*	*38*	*4*	*16*	*45*	*14*	*8*	*410*	*.262*	*.319*	*.435*	*.253*	*66*	

After showing he could hit well enough to stick in '95, the big question going into this season was how well he'd field. By season's end, this was no longer a question: Gonzalez has been universally praised for his improved positioning, and he led all AL shortstops in deuces turned. There's been occasional speculation that he should be moved to third, which would not help either Gonzalez or the Blue Jays.

SHAWN GREEN   **RF**   **1973**   **Age 24**

Year	Team	Lge	AB	H	DB	TP	HR	BB	SB	CS	OUT	BA	OBA	SA	EQA	EQR	Peak
1993	Knoxville	South	362	89	10	1	4	25	3	4	277	.246	.295	.312	.201	25	.228
1994	Syracuse	Inter	443	148	21	2	13	39	13	5	300	.334	.388	.479	.291	69	.326
1995	Toronto	AL	382	113	31	4	17	20	1	2	271	.296	.331	.531	.279	56	.307
1996	Toronto	AL	421	117	32	3	11	33	5	1	305	.278	.330	.447	.259	52	.282
1997	*Toronto*	*AL*	*556*	*164*	*41*	*5*	*8*	*40*	*8*	*4*	*396*	*.295*	*.342*	*.430*	*.263*	*70*	

If Jesse Orosco had been raised in a weightless environment, he'd probably look a lot like Shawn Green. For two straight years, Green has had a miserable first half (.222/.286/.400 career), followed by a hot finish (.325/.363/.519). If he can hit like that second half all season, he could be the new Dave Parker; if not, there's always room for people like Luis Gonzalez. He's spent a lot of time in instructional league working on his defense, which seems to be improving.

MIKE HUFF   **OF**   **1964**   **Age 33**

Year	Team	Lge	AB	H	DB	TP	HR	BB	SB	CS	OUT	BA	OBA	SA	EQA	EQR	Peak
1993	Nashville	AmA	353	102	10	4	9	64	16	5	256	.289	.398	.416	.280	53	.278
1994	Toronto	AL	209	65	15	3	3	28	2	1	145	.311	.392	.455	.285	31	.279
1995	Toronto	AL	139	34	10	1	1	22	1	1	106	.245	.348	.353	.237	14	.227
1996	Syracuse	Inter	254	73	17	2	8	28	6	2	183	.287	.358	.465	.274	36	.261
1997	*Toronto*	*AL*	*232*	*63*	*10*	*2*	*5*	*32*	*6*	*3*	*172*	*.272*	*.360*	*.397*	*.260*	*30*	

Huff is a wasted talent on a AAA roster: he can play all three outfield positions, handle the infield in a pinch and he's a tough out and a good baserunner. You can't ask for much more from a bench player.

RYAN JONES   **1B**   **1975**   **Age 22**

Year	Team	Lge	AB	H	DB	TP	HR	BB	SB	CS	OUT	BA	OBA	SA	EQA	EQR	Peak
1994	Hagerstown	SAtl	416	91	13	0	14	38	0	0	325	.219	.284	.351	.209	33	.242
1995	Dunedin	Flor	494	120	12	0	19	36	1	1	375	.243	.294	.383	.224	45	.255
1996	Knoxville	South	507	121	16	1	17	49	1	1	387	.239	.306	.375	.226	47	.254
1997	*Toronto*	*AL*	*472*	*117*	*27*	*1*	*13*	*44*	*3*	*3*	*358*	*.248*	*.312*	*.392*	*.237*	*49*	

Jones is considered the best power-hitting prospect in the organization. He's also an awful glove at first, so he has to win attention with his bat. The Blue Jays, optimists that they are, compare him to Mark McGwire because he's huge and has bright red hair. Hitting like this, that means he has more in common with Gary Huckabay than with McGwire.

SANDY MARTINEZ   **C**   **1973**   **Age 24**

Year	Team	Lge	AB	H	DB	TP	HR	BB	SB	CS	OUT	BA	OBA	SA	EQA	EQR	Peak
1993	Hagerstown	SAtl	345	78	6	1	7	14	0	0	267	.226	.256	.310	.183	19	.208
1994	Dunedin	Flor	455	108	9	2	10	22	1	1	348	.237	.273	.332	.199	31	.224
1995	Knoxville	South	144	29	5	1	2	7	0	0	115	.201	.238	.292	.166	6	.182
1995	Toronto	AL	192	48	7	0	4	7	0	0	144	.250	.276	.349	.207	14	.228
1996	Toronto	AL	229	52	8	3	3	16	0	0	177	.227	.278	.328	.199	16	.217
1997	*Toronto*	*AL*	*281*	*66*	*5*	*0*	*7*	*18*	*0*	*0*	*215*	*.235*	*.281*	*.327*	*.205*	*20*	

Martinez is touted as the catcher of the future, and seldom is such a moniker wasted on somebody so ill-prepared. He's an offensive zero whose only use is his strong arm, a tool handicapped by his bad work behind the plate. He shouldn't be considered among the top hundred catchers in professional baseball right now, at all levels.

ADAM MELHUSE   **C**   **1972**   **Age 25**

Year	Team	Lge	AB	H	DB	TP	HR	BB	SB	CS	OUT	BA	OBA	SA	EQA	EQR	Peak
1996	Dunedin	Flor	331	80	12	1	14	61	2	1	252	.242	.360	.411	.258	43	.276
1996	Knoxville	South	95	17	2	0	1	11	0	0	78	.179	.264	.232	.150	3	.157

Melhuse is supposed to be the catcher of the future, but he's the same age as Martinez and Julio Mosquera. He's the best offensive prospect of the three was given an AFL assignment.

JULIO MOSQUERA   **C**   **1972**   **Age 25**

Year	Team	Lge	AB	H	DB	TP	HR	BB	SB	CS	OUT	BA	OBA	SA	EQA	EQR	Peak
1995	Hagerstown	SAtl	426	113	15	2	4	24	2	2	315	.265	.304	.338	.216	34	.234
1996	Knoxville	South	319	62	8	0	3	23	4	2	259	.194	.249	.248	.153	12	.164
1996	Syracuse	Inter	73	18	0	0	0	6	0	0	55	.247	.304	.247	.181	4	.192

The Blue Jays are calling him a prospect, but they're just being polite. Although he was named the best defensive catcher in the Southern League this year, his defensive work when he was called up was awful. He's as old as Sandy Martinez, and he's even more of an offensive zero. Non-prospect.

OTIS NIXON   CF   **1959**   **Age 38**

Year	Team	Lge	AB	H	DB	TP	HR	BB	SB	CS	OUT	BA	OBA	SA	EQA	EQR	Peak
1993	Atlanta	NL	474	133	12	3	1	67	39	11	352	.281	.370	.325	.250	55	.237
1994	Boston	AL	399	110	12	1	1	55	38	9	298	.276	.363	.318	.248	46	.236
1995	Texas	AL	590	176	17	3	1	58	49	20	434	.298	.361	.342	.249	67	.236
1996	Toronto	AL	495	141	14	1	1	71	54	13	367	.285	.375	.323	.256	61	.243
1997	*Toronto*	*AL*	*497*	*142*	*16*	*2*	*1*	*50*	*50*	*20*	*375*	*.286*	*.351*	*.332*	*.246*	*57*	

In a booming buyers' market for free agent center fielders, why did the Blue Jays sign the oldest one, the one least capable of handling center field anymore, the one with the least power (no easy feat in a market with Darren Lewis) to a two-year contract? Nixon does two things well: draw some walks and steal some bases. He has also become an inadequate center fielder with negligible ability to get the ball out of the infield. Yet like Boston and Texas before them, the Blue Jays don't think of Nixon as part of the problem; they're busy blaming John Olerud for Bosnia or something.

CHARLIE O'BRIEN   C   **1961**   **Age 36**

Year	Team	Lge	AB	H	DB	TP	HR	BB	SB	CS	OUT	BA	OBA	SA	EQA	EQR	Peak
1993	NY Mets	NL	191	50	8	0	5	17	1	1	142	.262	.322	.382	.236	19	.224
1994	Atlanta	NL	154	39	8	0	9	17	0	0	115	.253	.327	.481	.264	21	.250
1995	Atlanta	NL	201	46	4	0	10	31	0	1	156	.229	.332	.398	.241	22	.229
1996	Toronto	AL	324	77	13	0	14	29	0	1	248	.238	.300	.407	.233	32	.221
1997	*Toronto*	*AL*	*314*	*75*	*12*	*1*	*9*	*43*	*0*	*0*	*239*	*.239*	*.331*	*.369*	*.238*	*33*	

The Blue Jays are somewhat disappointed that O'Brien, a solid defender with some sock, had to play as much as he did. He couldn't really help it, what with his competition being Sandy Martinez. Although you might kvetch about how this is another example of how Gaston avoids developing the younger player, in this case he's right on, because Sandy Martinez has about as much chance of becoming a good major league regular as I do of being crowned King of Prussia. As part of the recriminations about the perceived shortcomings of the '96 season, it's rumored that O'Brien is on the trading block.

JOHN OLERUD   1B   **1969**   **Age 28**

Year	Team	Lge	AB	H	DB	TP	HR	BB	SB	CS	OUT	BA	OBA	SA	EQA	EQR	Peak
1993	Toronto	AL	563	211	50	2	31	119	0	1	353	.375	.484	.636	.362	139	.388
1994	Toronto	AL	389	118	28	2	13	61	1	2	273	.303	.398	.486	.292	63	.309
1995	Toronto	AL	497	149	22	0	13	86	0	0	348	.300	.403	.423	.281	73	.292
1996	Toronto	AL	397	108	19	1	19	60	1	0	289	.272	.368	.469	.277	58	.284
1997	*Toronto*	*AL*	*400*	*122*	*28*	*1*	*10*	*79*	*1*	*0*	*278*	*.305*	*.420*	*.455*	*.300*	*68*	

The scapegoat. Because of the memory of '93, the Blue Jays will forever be looking at him as a failure instead of a useful offensive player. He's not much good against left-handed pitching, but he's basically Wally Joyner: a good defensive first baseman who gets on base. Given the number of teams that will waste their time on Gregg Jefferies or J.R. Phillips, that should be more than enough.

JEFF PATZKE   2B   **1974**   **Age 23**

Year	Team	Lge	AB	H	DB	TP	HR	BB	SB	CS	OUT	BA	OBA	SA	EQA	EQR	Peak
1994	Hagerstown	SAtl	281	49	6	1	3	30	3	1	233	.174	.254	.235	.148	10	.168
1995	Dunedin	Flor	498	129	21	3	14	74	3	2	371	.259	.355	.398	.253	60	.284
1996	Knoxville	South	430	113	22	2	4	67	4	2	319	.263	.362	.351	.244	47	.269

After a very good AA campaign, Patzke's hat will be in the ring for the second base battle royal next spring. A switch-hitter, he finished third in the Southern League in OBP. If he looks like a "scrapper" in Gaston's eyes, he may suddenly become well-known.

ROBERT PEREZ   OF   1969   Age 28

Year	Team	Lge	AB	H	DB	TP	HR	BB	SB	CS	OUT	BA	OBA	SA	EQA	EQR	Peak
1993	Syracuse	Inter	534	152	24	5	13	28	11	9	391	.285	.320	.421	.247	59	.264
1994	Syracuse	Inter	517	149	22	2	10	28	3	4	372	.288	.325	.397	.242	53	.255
1995	Syracuse	Inter	513	173	33	3	11	19	6	3	343	.337	.361	.478	.281	71	.292
1996	Toronto	AL	202	66	6	0	3	8	3	0	136	.327	.352	.401	.260	23	.267
1997	*Toronto*	*AL*	*384*	*110*	*28*	*5*	*9*	*31*	*10*	*5*	*279*	*.286*	*.340*	*.456*	*.268*	*52*	

The Blue Jays finally gave one of their own outfielders an extended shot at some playing time, and Perez did not disappoint. He's really only cut out to play left field, and you can see he doesn't hit enough to merit a regular job; however, he should be a useful spare part for some time.

TOMAS PEREZ   2B   1974   Age 23

Year	Team	Lge	AB	H	DB	TP	HR	BB	SB	CS	OUT	BA	OBA	SA	EQA	EQR	Peak
1994	Burlington	Midw	476	107	12	1	7	40	4	4	373	.225	.285	.298	.191	30	.217
1995	Toronto	AL	99	25	4	1	1	7	0	1	75	.253	.302	.343	.213	8	.238
1996	Syracuse	Inter	125	35	8	1	1	7	6	1	91	.280	.318	.384	.244	13	.267
1996	Toronto	AL	295	74	12	4	1	25	1	2	223	.251	.309	.329	.213	23	.235
1997	*Toronto*	*AL*	*173*	*43*	*10*	*3*	*2*	*14*	*2*	*2*	*132*	*.249*	*.305*	*.376*	*.229*	*17*	

After having to spend the '95 season on the major league roster as a Rule V draftee, Perez wound up working his way into the jumbled second base picture.

ANGEL RAMIREZ   OF   1973   Age 24

Year	Team	Lge	AB	H	DB	TP	HR	BB	SB	CS	OUT	BA	OBA	SA	EQA	EQR	Peak
1994	Hagerstown	SAtl	463	114	11	5	9	19	10	6	355	.246	.276	.350	.209	35	.234
1995	Dunedin	Flor	554	143	14	2	10	20	10	6	417	.258	.284	.345	.211	43	.232
1996	Knoxville	South	390	96	18	4	5	11	9	3	297	.246	.267	.351	.208	29	.226

Another tools goof: his calling card is a throwing arm. That and two bucks will get him a warm glass of PBR in any dive in Syracuse.

LONELL ROBERTS   OF   1971   Age 26

Year	Team	Lge	AB	H	DB	TP	HR	BB	SB	CS	OUT	BA	OBA	SA	EQA	EQR	Peak
1993	Hagerstown	SAtl	518	109	13	1	4	39	21	7	416	.210	.266	.263	.177	27	.194
1994	Dunedin	Flor	497	129	14	1	5	31	34	7	375	.260	.303	.322	.222	44	.241
1995	Knoxville	South	456	98	11	2	1	27	32	9	367	.215	.259	.254	.178	25	.191
1996	Knoxville	South	237	58	0	0	1	27	14	6	185	.245	.322	.257	.204	17	.213

Roberts missed most of the season with a hamstring injury. He isn't really a prospect, but he's fast, so people who should know better keep putting him on prospect lists. He is routinely listed as the best baserunner in his league, and I'm sure he can double-bag groceries faster than the next guy too.

JUAN SAMUEL   DH   1961   Age 36

Year	Team	Lge	AB	H	DB	TP	HR	BB	SB	CS	OUT	BA	OBA	SA	EQA	EQR	Peak
1993	Cincinnati	NL	265	62	9	3	5	27	8	6	209	.234	.305	.347	.218	23	.207
1994	Detroit	AL	137	43	9	5	5	10	5	2	96	.314	.361	.562	.298	23	.282
1995	Detroit	AL	172	49	9	1	11	24	5	4	127	.285	.372	.541	.292	29	.276
1996	Toronto	AL	188	48	7	3	8	15	9	1	141	.255	.310	.452	.258	24	.245
1997	*Toronto*	*AL*	*198*	*52*	*8*	*1*	*7*	*16*	*6*	*0*	*146*	*.263*	*.318*	*.419*	*.255*	*24*	

Samuel was added to the Blue Jays to be a good bench bat, and he did that well enough. Carrying him for a year was indicative of the lofty ambitions the Blue Jays entered the season with, seriously talking about the wild card, when they were unlikely to do that counting on Carter, Nixon, Quantrill and the rest of the over-30 crowd of mediocrities.

ED SPRAGUE   **3B**   **1968**   **Age 29**

Year	Team	Lge	AB	H	DB	TP	HR	BB	SB	CS	OUT	BA	OBA	SA	EQA	EQR	Peak
1993	Toronto	AL	550	148	27	1	16	35	1	0	402	.269	.313	.409	.241	58	.255
1994	Toronto	AL	408	100	17	1	12	23	1	0	308	.245	.285	.380	.221	35	.230
1995	Toronto	AL	525	132	27	2	20	59	0	0	393	.251	.327	.425	.249	61	.256
1996	Toronto	AL	590	145	34	2	36	60	0	0	445	.246	.315	.493	.262	78	.264
1997	*Toronto*	*AL*	*545*	*139*	*21*	*1*	*34*	*46*	*0*	*0*	*406*	*.255*	*.313*	*.484*	*.263*	*72*	

Yippee. This is what Ed Sprague at his best looks like. It's adequate. Unfortunately for the Blue Jays, they're stuck with two more years of him, and their top position playing prospect is probably Tom Evans, who's akin to Sprague in the same way John Olerud is to Joe Carter. Knowing what we do about how the Blue Jays have evaluated that pair, it's pretty easy to guess that the Jays won't be clever enough to turn Sprague into prospects now, while the getting is good.

SHANNON STEWART   **CF**   **1974**   **Age 23**

Year	Team	Lge	AB	H	DB	TP	HR	BB	SB	CS	OUT	BA	OBA	SA	EQA	EQR	Peak
1993	St. Catherines	NY-P	322	79	8	1	3	25	10	5	248	.245	.300	.304	.205	24	.236
1994	Hagerstown	SAtl	234	66	7	2	4	19	7	5	173	.282	.336	.380	.242	25	.275
1995	Knoxville	South	509	133	20	3	6	82	24	8	384	.261	.364	.348	.248	59	.278
1996	Syracuse	Inter	431	127	24	5	7	55	23	5	309	.295	.374	.422	.275	61	.303
1997	*Toronto*	*AL*	*549*	*158*	*36*	*2*	*5*	*74*	*32*	*11*	*402*	*.288*	*.372*	*.388*	*.267*	*74*	

Stewart has spent much of his career as a DH, not out of his inability to field but because of a slow-healing high school football injury that has ruined his throwing arm. At this rate, he may wind up like Don Baylor, incapable of playing anywhere but left field. As a hitter, he's an excellent prospect who will add power with age. If he gets the leadoff job next spring, take it as a sign that the Blue Jays are getting serious about putting a good team on the field.

CRAIG STONE   **1B**   **1976**   **Age 21**

Year	Team	Lge	AB	H	DB	TP	HR	BB	SB	CS	OUT	BA	OBA	SA	EQA	EQR	Peak
1995	Hagerstown	SAtl	374	96	13	1	8	28	1	1	279	.257	.308	.361	.224	33	.260
1996	Hagerstown	SAtl	210	59	8	0	8	16	1	2	153	.281	.332	.433	.253	25	.288
1996	Dunedin	Flor	234	58	13	0	6	18	0	0	176	.248	.302	.380	.227	22	.258
1997	*Toronto*	*AL*	*427*	*116*	*23*	*1*	*18*	*34*	*2*	*1*	*312*	*.272*	*.325*	*.457*	*.262*	*55*	

He's a young Australian who the Blue Jays have cultivated slowly, and this year he began to pay off, thwacking 42 doubles between two levels. He's being pushed faster than Mike Whitlock, but probably isn't as good a prospect.

ANDY THOMPSON   **3B**   **1976**   **Age 21**

Year	Team	Lge	AB	H	DB	TP	HR	BB	SB	CS	OUT	BA	OBA	SA	EQA	EQR	Peak
1995	Hagerstown	SAtl	479	103	10	1	6	24	1	1	377	.215	.252	.278	.167	22	.193
1996	Dunedin	Flor	441	119	16	2	13	54	9	2	324	.270	.349	.404	.256	54	.290
1997	*Toronto*	*AL*	*490*	*124*	*28*	*3*	*13*	*69*	*12*	*4*	*370*	*.253*	*.345*	*.402*	*.256*	*61*	

Last year was only Thompson's second in pro ball since being picked as a high school shortstop in '94. He's already shown good control of the strike zone and some power. His misfortune is that he's a rung below Tom Evans on the chain, which should mean he'll wind up as trade bait.

CHRIS WEINKE   **1B**   **1973**   **Age 24**

Year	Team	Lge	AB	H	DB	TP	HR	BB	SB	CS	OUT	BA	OBA	SA	EQA	EQR	Peak
1993	Dunedin	Flor	479	116	7	0	16	56	4	2	365	.242	.321	.357	.228	45	.260
1994	Knoxville	South	541	132	16	1	9	46	7	2	411	.244	.303	.327	.213	43	.239
1995	Syracuse	Inter	351	79	9	1	11	44	3	2	274	.225	.311	.350	.221	31	.244
1996	Knoxville	South	267	63	9	1	13	44	1	1	205	.236	.344	.423	.254	33	.276
1996	Syracuse	Inter	164	30	5	1	3	19	0	1	135	.183	.268	.280	.172	8	.189

Weinke was a top draft choice as a corner infielder; he couldn't cut it at third. He was sent back to AA Knoxville to start '96 after having spent '95 at AAA Syracuse. Even then, he was a miserable offensive "force" as a first baseman. As a first base prospect, he's a godawful stiff, but the Blue Jays like him.

MIKE WHITLOCK   **1B**   **1977**   **Age 20**

Year	Team	Lge	AB	H	DB	TP	HR	BB	SB	CS	OUT	BA	OBA	SA	EQA	EQR	Peak
1996	Hagerstown	SAtl	462	107	8	1	16	86	1	1	356	.232	.352	.357	.240	50	.277

He had 20 homers, 108 walks and 132 strikeouts, numbers any fan of the great Rob Deer should love, and amazing figures from an A-ball hitter. Because the organization's focused on Weinke, Curl and Jones, Whitlock hasn't gotten brought up much yet as a first base prospect. Since the first three are bound for the same sort of success that came to Dann Howitt and Scott Cepicky, don't be surprised when Whitlock passes them.

KEVIN WITT   **SS**   **1976**   **Age 21**

Year	Team	Lge	AB	H	DB	TP	HR	BB	SB	CS	OUT	BA	OBA	SA	EQA	EQR	Peak
1995	Hagerstown	SAtl	496	107	14	1	13	24	1	2	391	.216	.252	.327	.186	29	.215
1996	Dunedin	Flor	458	117	9	2	15	35	5	2	343	.255	.308	.382	.232	44	.264

The Blue Jays' first-round pick in '94, Witt is a lefty-hitting shortstop with some power. He's tall and doesn't hit like a shortstop, so of course the talk is about moving him to a position where he may not hit well enough to make the majors. If he's at short, he could be the new Jose Valentin in two years; if he's moved to third, he'll be Josh Booty without the corked bat incident.

CARLOS ALMANZAR   **RRP**   **1974**   **Age 23**

YR	Team	Lge	IP	H	ER	HR	BB	K	ERA	W	L	H/9	HR/9	BB/9	K/9	KW
1995	Knoxville	South	118.0	151	70	11	46	70	5.34	5	8	11.52	.84	3.51	5.34	.90
1996	Knoxville	South	89.0	108	47	12	37	74	4.75	4	6	10.92	1.21	3.74	7.48	1.56

Unlike many of the young pitchers in the Jays' chain, Almanzar seems to be staying put. He spent '96 adapting to the role of long relief, and has shown good control.

LUIS ANDUJAR   **RSP**   **1973**   **Age 24**

YR	Team	Lge	IP	H	ER	HR	BB	K	ERA	W	L	H/9	HR/9	BB/9	K/9	KW
1993	Sarasota	Flor	77.0	80	28	4	39	56	3.27	5	4	9.35	.47	4.56	6.55	1.04
1993	Birmingham	South	35.7	40	10	4	24	36	2.52	3	1	10.09	1.01	6.06	9.08	1.51
1994	Birmingham	South	70.3	103	54	7	38	51	6.91	2	6	13.18	.90	4.86	6.53	.96
1995	Birmingham	South	151.7	166	60	12	61	110	3.56	9	8	9.85	.71	3.62	6.53	1.27
1995	Chi. WhiteSox	AL	30.0	26	9	4	14	9	2.70	2	1	7.80	1.20	4.20	2.70	-.15
1996	Nashville	AmA	36.7	54	26	4	13	20	6.38	1	3	13.25	.98	3.19	4.91	.84
1996	Chi. White Sox	AL	23.0	31	18	3	16	6	7.04	1	2	12.13	1.17	6.26	2.35	-.78
1996	Toronto	AL	14.3	13	6	4	1	5	3.77	1	1	8.16	2.51	.63	3.14	.89

The White Sox gave up on him quickly, and he may be a major surprise this year with the Jays. The times I've seen him, his fastball has been very lively. He was a Southern League All-Star in '95, and last year was wasted between the Sox' impatience and further injuries.

TRAVIS BAPTIST   **LBP**   **1972**   **Age 25**

YR	Team	Lge	IP	H	ER	HR	BB	K	ERA	W	L	H/9	HR/9	BB/9	K/9	KW
1993	Knoxville	South	30.3	39	16	3	11	18	4.75	1	2	11.57	.89	3.26	5.34	.96
1994	Syracuse	Inter	116.0	154	74	19	44	35	5.74	4	9	11.95	1.47	3.41	2.72	.05
1995	Syracuse	Inter	74.0	92	56	13	43	44	6.81	2	6	11.19	1.58	5.23	5.35	.48
1996	Syracuse	Inter	136.0	193	80	14	65	64	5.29	5	10	12.77	.93	4.30	4.24	.34

He has no real future: he's a soft-tosser who doesn't frighten left-handed batters, so his chances of eking out an existence as a spot reliever are unlikely. He's supposed to have a dandy curve, but it hasn't been too effective.

KURTISS BOGOTT   **LRP**   **1973**   **Age 24**

YR	TEAM	Lge	IP	H	ER	HR	BB	K	ERA	W	L	H/9	HR/9	BB/9	K/9	KW
1993	Utica	NY-P	45.3	84	42	6	37	27	8.34	1	4	16.68	1.19	7.35	5.36	-.05
1994	Lynchburg	Caro	23.7	35	21	1	18	9	7.99	1	2	13.31	.38	6.85	3.42	-.57
1995	Sarasota	Flor	77.0	112	51	5	55	44	5.96	3	6	13.09	.58	6.43	5.14	.11
1996	Dunedin	Flor	27.3	26	16	3	25	30	5.27	1	2	8.56	.99	8.23	9.88	1.23
1996	Knoxville	South	50.7	62	27	2	33	40	4.80	2	4	11.01	.36	5.86	7.11	.90

A refugee from the Red Sox organization. Lefty relievers who rack up more than a strikeout per inning usually wind up getting a shot.

BRIAN BOHANON   **LBP**   **1969** **Age 28**

YR	Team	Lge	IP	H	ER	HR	BB	K	ERA	W	L	H/9	HR/9	BB/9	K/9	KW
1993	Texas	AL	93.0	108	47	8	51	47	4.55	4	6	10.45	.77	4.94	4.55	.28
1994	Oklahoma	AmA	94.7	111	51	12	43	79	4.85	4	7	10.55	1.14	4.09	7.51	1.48
1994	Texas	AL	37.7	49	25	6	10	26	5.97	1	3	11.71	1.43	2.39	6.21	1.47
1995	Detroit	AL	106.3	113	51	9	43	63	4.32	6	6	9.56	.76	3.64	5.33	.87
1996	Syracuse	Inter	55.3	60	25	4	23	32	4.07	3	3	9.76	.65	3.74	5.20	.80
1996	Toronto	AL	22.3	25	14	3	19	16	5.64	1	1	10.07	1.21	7.66	6.45	.24

The '87 first-round pick of the Rangers, Bohanon is one of those ex-prospects who don't give up the ghost too easily. He's been surviving tossing garbage time for bad teams, but this meager existence is close to coming to an end.

DEREK BRANDOW   **RSP**   **1970** **Age 27**

YR	Team	Lge	IP	H	ER	HR	BB	K	ERA	W	L	H/9	HR/9	BB/9	K/9	KW
1993	Hagerstown	SAtl	64.3	98	43	7	47	36	6.02	2	5	13.71	.98	6.58	5.04	.03
1994	Dunedin	Flor	127.7	139	58	9	76	93	4.09	7	7	9.80	.63	5.36	6.56	.85
1995	Knoxville	South	99.3	101	54	12	64	80	4.89	4	7	9.15	1.09	5.80	7.25	.97
1996	Knoxville	South	11.0	11	8	3	6	4	6.55	0	1	9.00	2.45	4.91	3.27	-.14
1996	Syracuse	Inter	118.0	126	57	13	72	85	4.35	6	7	9.61	.99	5.49	6.48	.79

One thing you don't see here is that Brandow murders right-handed batters with his fastball and change (.213 avg.). He isn't touted by the Jays, but he does something well, has shown flashes where he just blows lineups away (especially in last winter's AFL) and could be a help in the pen in '97.

CHAD BROWN   **LRP**   **1972** **Age 25**

YR	Team	Lge	IP	H	ER	HR	BB	K	ERA	W	L	H/9	HR/9	BB/9	K/9	KW
1993	St. Catherines	NY-P	17.7	13	5	3	9	12	2.55	1	1	6.62	1.53	4.58	6.11	.89
1994	Dunedin	Flor	71.0	67	28	2	52	43	3.55	4	4	8.49	.25	6.59	5.45	.17
1995	Knoxville	South	38.3	40	21	3	28	26	4.93	2	2	9.39	.70	6.57	6.10	.39
1995	Syracuse	Inter	20.3	24	11	1	25	12	4.87	1	1	10.62	.44	11.07	5.31	-1.00
1996	Knoxville	South	60.3	72	27	2	27	45	4.03	3	4	10.74	.30	4.03	6.71	1.23

By no means an outstanding relief prospect, but he's a portsider, so he may show up.

CHRIS CARPENTER   **RSP**   **1975** **Age 22**

YR	Team	Lge	IP	H	ER	HR	BB	K	ERA	W	L	H/9	HR/9	BB/9	K/9	KW
1995	Dunedin	Flor	86.0	109	35	5	66	40	3.66	5	5	11.41	.52	6.91	4.19	-.33
1995	Knoxville	South	60.0	73	41	3	40	38	6.15	2	5	10.95	.45	6.00	5.70	.40
1996	Knoxville	South	159.0	163	76	13	104	107	4.30	8	10	9.23	.74	5.89	6.06	.55

Toronto's #1 pick in the '93 draft. Scouts drool about his makeup as much as his sinking fastball and power curve. He's extremely raw, but he's the best pitching prospect in the organization, and may surface in Toronto sometime in '97. Pitched well in the AFL.

TIM CRABTREE   **RRP**   **1970** **Age 27**

YR	Team	Lge	IP	H	ER	HR	BB	K	ERA	W	L	H/9	HR/9	BB/9	K/9	KW
1993	Knoxville	South	144.3	189	87	12	78	49	5.42	6	10	11.79	.75	4.86	3.06	-.20
1994	Syracuse	Inter	102.0	133	54	5	61	48	4.76	5	6	11.74	.44	5.38	4.24	.07
1995	Syracuse	Inter	29.7	43	27	0	17	19	8.19	1	2	13.04	.00	5.16	5.76	.63
1995	Toronto	AL	31.7	30	12	1	13	21	3.41	2	2	8.53	.28	3.69	5.97	1.07
1996	Toronto	AL	66.0	58	18	3	23	55	2.45	5	2	7.91	.41	3.14	7.50	1.72

Mixing a good slider and fastball, Crabtree became a crucial part of the Blue Jays' pen. He induces a ton of groundballs. Crabtree is a better pitcher than Timlin, but Timlin was first in line for the closer's job, and you wouldn't expect the Blue Jays to break up their routine, would you?

ROBERTO DURAN   **LBP**   **1973**   **Age 24**

YR	Team	Lge	IP	H	ER	HR	BB	K	ERA	W	L	H/9	HR/9	BB/9	K/9	KW
1993	Yakima	Nwern	32.7	48	37	4	51	28	10.19	1	3	13.22	1.10	14.05	7.71	-.94
1994	Bakersfield	Calif	57.7	69	40	5	59	56	6.24	2	4	10.77	.78	9.21	8.74	.61
1995	Vero Beach	Flor	88.7	102	46	11	90	81	4.67	4	6	10.35	1.12	9.14	8.22	.46
1996	Dunedin	Flor	43.3	38	9	2	26	39	1.87	4	1	7.89	.42	5.40	8.10	1.35
1996	Knoxville	South	74.7	71	41	7	68	52	4.94	3	5	8.56	.84	8.20	6.27	.04

Duran was claimed off waivers from the Dodger organization before the '96 season. He's got a 90+ fastball with extreme movement, but he hasn't really developed a second pitch.

KELVIM ESCOBAR   **RSP**   **1976**   **Age 21**

YR	Team	Lge	IP	H	ER	HR	BB	K	ERA	W	L	H/9	HR/9	BB/9	K/9	KW
1996	Dunedin	Flor	98.3	122	47	8	47	81	4.30	5	6	11.17	.73	4.30	7.41	1.40
1996	Knoxville	South	50.7	61	29	7	27	31	5.15	2	4	10.84	1.24	4.80	5.51	.64

Escobar is a young Venezuelan pitcher who exemplifies the Blue Jays' approach to pushing some of their pitchers hard. He skipped Hagerstown to start last season, having only pitched in the rookie leagues beforehand, and despite that earned a promotion to Knoxville. He mixes a 90+ fastball and a split-fingered fastball he uses as his changeup. Despite the speed with which he's moved up, he hasn't really thrown many innings or racked up high pitch counts.

HUCK FLENER   **LBP**   **1969**   **Age 28**

YR	Team	Lge	IP	H	ER	HR	BB	K	ERA	W	L	H/9	HR/9	BB/9	K/9	KW
1993	Knoxville	South	125.3	140	51	10	54	84	3.66	8	6	10.05	.72	3.88	6.03	1.04
1994	Syracuse	Inter	35.0	41	21	6	11	17	5.40	1	3	10.54	1.54	2.83	4.37	.75
1995	Syracuse	Inter	125.3	147	71	22	59	70	5.10	5	9	10.56	1.58	4.24	5.03	.62
1996	Syracuse	Inter	82.0	80	23	3	31	51	2.52	6	3	8.78	.33	3.40	5.60	1.02
1996	Toronto	AL	70.7	62	28	8	35	43	3.57	4	4	7.90	1.02	4.46	5.48	.71

Flener suffered a terrible elbow injury in '94, and has finally made it back as a junkballer with fine control. He got his chance this season as the Violas and Quantrills predictably flopped. Flener probably has a future in the bullpen: he was devastating against lefties at both Syracuse and Toronto.

JUAN GUZMAN   **RSP**   **1967**   **Age 30**

YR	Team	Lge	IP	H	ER	HR	BB	K	ERA	W	L	H/9	HR/9	BB/9	K/9	KW
1993	Toronto	AL	219.3	207	86	17	120	200	3.53	13	11	8.49	.70	4.92	8.21	1.50
1994	Toronto	AL	148.3	157	79	18	81	122	4.79	7	9	9.53	1.09	4.91	7.40	1.24
1995	Toronto	AL	136.3	144	79	12	76	94	5.22	6	9	9.51	.79	5.02	6.21	.81
1996	Toronto	AL	185.3	151	47	17	57	159	2.28	16	5	7.33	.83	2.77	7.72	1.88

After two years wasted on injuries, and recriminations from the Jays' front office about them, the Jays almost didn't sign Guzman for '96. It was fortunate they did; if not for a bout of appendicitis that ended his season a month early, it might be Guzman who'd spend this winter admiring the Cy Young Award in his trophy case. Knowing his injury history, the Jays treated him gingerly: he made no starts on three games' rest, and gave them 18 quality starts out of 27 total. Injuries have stolen some of his velocity, but his success could be compared to Dave Stieb's success after the trials of the '86 and '87 seasons. Guzman credited Charlie O'Brien for a large part of his success, noting his stabilizing influence.

ROY HALLADAY   **RSP**   **1977**   **Age 20**

YR	Team	Lge	IP	H	ER	HR	BB	K	ERA	W	L	H/9	HR/9	BB/9	K/9	KW
1996	Dunedin	Flor	146.0	189	80	11	67	79	4.93	6	10	11.65	.68	4.13	4.87	.59

Like Duran, Halladay skipped Hagerstown, going straight from the rookie leagues to high-A Dunedin, where he was the youngest player in the FSL. Keep in mind he was the Jays' first round pick out of high school in '95. He mixes that rare bird, the knuckle-curve, with a good fastball. The Jays want to see him develop a better breaking pitch.

ALLEN HALLEY   **RSP**   **1972**   **Age 25**

YR	Team	Lge	IP	H	ER	HR	BB	K	ERA	W	L	H/9	HR/9	BB/9	K/9	KW
1995	Hickory	SAtl	51.3	67	27	8	19	33	4.73	2	4	11.75	1.40	3.33	5.79	1.10
1996	Pr. William	Caro	121.7	153	76	18	68	91	5.62	5	9	11.32	1.33	5.03	6.73	.99

Halley came over as a throw-in in the deal that also brought the Blue Jays Andujar. He's a product of the Dutch Antilles who came to the U.S. to pitch college ball, and not an outstanding prospect.

MIKE HALPERIN   LSP   1974   Age 23

YR	Team	Lge	IP	H	ER	HR	BB	K	ERA	W	L	H/9	HR/9	BB/9	K/9	KW
1994	St. Catherines	NY-P	21.0	17	5	0	8	11	2.14	2	0	7.29	.00	3.43	4.71	.71
1994	Hagerstown	SAtl	27.0	31	4	2	11	16	1.33	3	0	10.33	.67	3.67	5.33	.86
1995	Dunedin	Flor	60.3	90	42	6	40	45	6.27	2	5	13.43	.90	5.97	6.71	.75
1996	Knoxville	South	143.7	159	54	6	81	80	3.38	9	7	9.96	.38	5.07	5.01	.40

While the Blue Jays have a huge assortment of right-handed starting pitcher prospects to sort through, Halperin is their top lefty starter. He's small, undoubtedly "crafty" and gets a lot of groundballs; he'll have to battle against the usual bias against short players, but he was successful at AA while people like Jose Pett were flailing. Don't be surprised if Halperin works his way into the mix.

ERIK HANSON   RSP   1965   Age 32

YR	Team	Lge	IP	H	ER	HR	BB	K	ERA	W	L	H/9	HR/9	BB/9	K/9	KW
1993	Seattle	AL	212.3	216	76	18	70	169	3.22	15	9	9.16	.76	2.97	7.16	1.65
1994	Cincinnati	NL	121.3	136	52	10	34	94	3.86	7	6	10.09	.74	2.52	6.97	1.69
1995	Boston	AL	186.3	181	71	16	63	139	3.43	12	9	8.74	.77	3.04	6.71	1.48
1996	Toronto	AL	215.7	223	105	21	106	150	4.38	11	13	9.31	.88	4.42	6.26	.98

The single most pointless acquisition, because Hanson he was signed to multi-year contract. Hanson was awful through July, putting up a 6.73 ERA. Losing his curveball for the second half of '95 may have hurt him; he resorted to the cut fastball as his change of pace, and neither it or the curve worked at all. At his best, he's a useful #3 starter, but for the Blue Jays, he's an expensive mistake and a roadblock to serious rebuilding.

PAT HENTGEN   RSP   1969   Age 28

YR	Team	Lge	IP	H	ER	HR	BB	K	ERA	W	L	H/9	HR/9	BB/9	K/9	KW
1993	Toronto	AL	214.3	209	84	27	84	126	3.53	14	10	8.78	1.13	3.53	5.29	.88
1994	Toronto	AL	172.7	155	56	19	65	144	2.92	12	7	8.08	.99	3.39	7.51	1.65
1995	Toronto	AL	203.0	224	101	22	95	135	4.48	10	13	9.93	.98	4.21	5.99	.94
1996	Toronto	AL	262.7	226	73	17	99	171	2.50	21	8	7.74	.58	3.39	5.86	1.10

Hurrah for the occasional smart choice from the media. Just to rehash, 22 out of 35 starts were quality starts, as opposed to Andy Pettitte's 18 of 34. Hentgen led the league in ERA, shutouts, complete games and innings pitched. Andy Pettitte led the AL in wins, supported by a better offense in an easier park for pitchers. Why should there even be any debate?

MARTY JANZEN   RBP   1973   Age 24

YR	Team	Lge	IP	H	ER	HR	BB	K	ERA	W	L	H/9	HR/9	BB/9	K/9	KW
1994	Greensboro	SAtl	89.3	133	69	10	40	55	6.95	2	8	13.40	1.01	4.03	5.54	.84
1995	Tampa	Flor	101.7	126	41	6	43	74	3.63	6	5	11.15	.53	3.81	6.55	1.23
1995	Knoxville	South	44.0	40	12	3	19	33	2.45	4	1	8.18	.61	3.89	6.75	1.28
1995	Norwich	East	18.0	23	13	3	8	12	6.50	1	1	11.50	1.50	4.00	6.00	1.00
1996	Syracuse	Inter	54.0	75	46	11	31	28	7.67	1	5	12.50	1.83	5.17	4.67	.26
1996	Toronto	AL	75.0	85	48	13	40	45	5.76	3	5	10.20	1.56	4.80	5.40	.60

Janzen is highly touted, and he does have the big fastball that is usually needed to make people pay attention in the first place. I don't really see him as a great pitching prospect. He's been fragile, has yet to develop a breaking pitch he can consistently throw for strikes, and his response to trouble on the mound is inevitably to try to throw harder. His fastball, for all it's heat, doesn't seem to have much movement, so that usually makes a bad situation worse as he starts over-throwing everything. He should be left alone in the rotation, and the Blue Jays need to take the pressure of expectations off of him.

JOSE PETT   RSP   1976   Age 21

YR	Team	Lge	IP	H	ER	HR	BB	K	ERA	W	L	H/9	HR/9	BB/9	K/9	KW
1994	Dunedin	Flor	81.7	117	48	2	30	37	5.29	3	6	12.89	.22	3.31	4.08	.53
1995	Knoxville	South	131.3	141	79	17	64	67	5.41	5	10	9.66	1.16	4.39	4.59	.43
1996	Knoxville	South	41.0	40	16	4	11	27	3.51	3	2	8.78	.88	2.41	5.93	1.37
1996	Syracuse	Inter	105.7	138	72	10	55	42	6.13	4	8	11.75	.85	4.68	3.58	.02

The biggest of the Blue Jays' enormous pitching prospects, you should remember Pett as the pricey surprise signing out of Brazil. He was pushed up to AA extremely quickly, and he's still goofy looking on the mound as he learns how to coordinate his 6' 6" frame. Rather than leave him alone in AA this year, the Blue Jays pushed him up early again, and he was a complete flop in Syracuse. As player personnel director Karl Kuehl is proud to point out, most pitchers Pett's age are in A ball or lower, so his "advances" are supposed to be a source of pride. Instead, it looks like Pett could be Portuguese for "David Clyde." He'll now be the Pirates' problem, as Pett was one of the six players traded to Pittsburgh for Merced, Plesac and Garcia.

PAUL QUANTRILL   RBP   1969   Age 28

YR	Team	Lge	IP	H	ER	HR	BB	K	ERA	W	L	H/9	HR/9	BB/9	K/9	KW
1993	Boston	AL	137.7	141	56	13	50	68	3.66	8	7	9.22	.85	3.27	4.45	.66
1994	Scranton-WB	Inter	53.7	60	22	5	10	30	3.69	3	3	10.06	.84	1.68	5.03	1.26
1994	Boston	AL	23.0	23	7	4	6	15	2.74	2	1	9.00	1.57	2.35	5.87	1.37
1994	Philadelphia	NL	30.0	39	19	3	13	12	5.70	1	2	11.70	.90	3.90	3.60	.22
1995	Philadelphia	NL	178.0	203	84	19	58	91	4.25	9	11	10.26	.96	2.93	4.60	.80
1996	Toronto	AL	136.0	156	67	22	54	83	4.43	7	8	10.32	1.46	3.57	5.49	.94

Apparently, one of the less well-known provisions of the Blue Jays' lease at the Skydome is that they're forced to hire a certain percentage of Canadian labor. A-shopping they went, landing "Bloody" Paul Quantrill, who contributed repeated atrocities to the '96 campaign. He had the lowest percentage of quality starts of anyone who started more than 20 games, a remarkable accomplishment for a non-Tiger.

BILL RISLEY   RRP   1967   Age 30

YR	Team	Lge	IP	H	ER	HR	BB	K	ERA	W	L	H/9	HR/9	BB/9	K/9	KW
1993	Ottawa	Inter	60.3	56	24	7	43	60	3.58	4	3	8.35	1.04	6.41	8.95	1.38
1994	Seattle	AL	51.0	31	13	7	21	60	2.29	5	1	5.47	1.24	3.71	10.59	2.60
1995	Seattle	AL	60.0	53	16	7	20	65	2.40	5	2	7.95	1.05	3.00	9.75	2.50
1996	Toronto	AL	41.0	32	14	6	25	28	3.07	3	2	7.02	1.32	5.49	6.15	.68

A fastball-slider pitcher, he's that rare that the Expos let get away before he became expensive. Toronto had hoped when Risley was acquired that he would be the closer, and enjoy the same success he had with Seattle the previous year. Unfortunately, a weak shoulder that had to be 'scoped at season's end kept him from pitching for any length of time. When he's on, his slider is murder on lefties.

MARK SIEVERT   RSP   1973   Age 24

YR	Team	Lge	IP	H	ER	HR	BB	K	ERA	W	L	H/9	HR/9	BB/9	K/9	KW
1994	St. Catherines	NY-P	69.7	81	35	7	43	48	4.52	4	4	10.46	.90	5.56	6.20	.68
1995	Hagerstown	SAtl	135.7	185	78	19	70	81	5.17	6	9	12.27	1.26	4.64	5.37	.63
1996	Knoxville	South	93.3	83	25	6	58	53	2.41	7	3	8.00	.58	5.59	5.11	.31
1996	Syracuse	Inter	53.3	63	35	6	40	38	5.91	2	4	10.63	1.01	6.75	6.41	.45

Undrafted in 1991, Sievert's career didn't begin until '93. He isn't overpowering, but these translations mask his good control and low batting averages allowed. He's come far fast, just ahead of the more highly regarded prospects, and he'll probably get a shot when the veterans in Toronto continue to get knocked around.

JOSE SILVA   RBP   1974   Age 23

YR	Team	Lge	IP	H	ER	HR	BB	K	ERA	W	L	H/9	HR/9	BB/9	K/9	KW
1993	Hagerstown	SAtl	124.3	133	53	8	85	94	3.84	7	7	9.63	.58	6.15	6.80	.73
1994	Dunedin	Flor	39.0	46	32	5	31	31	7.38	1	3	10.62	1.15	7.15	7.15	.60
1994	Knoxville	South	83.0	105	52	11	46	56	5.64	3	6	11.39	1.19	4.99	6.07	.78
1996	Knoxville	South	41.0	45	22	3	25	18	4.83	2	3	9.88	.66	5.49	3.95	-.05

This year was one of recovery for Silva, as he came back from a season lost to injuries sustained in a car accident. The accident hasn't removed the plus fastball, but the lost time showed. Still a top prospect, Silva will continue to rehab and pitch himself back into shape. He's been sent to Pittsburgh in the big nine-player trade, and the Pirates may give him a shot at the bullpen this spring.

BRIAN SMITH   **RRP**   **1973**   **Age 24**

YR	Team	Lge	IP	H	ER	HR	BB	K	ERA	W	L	H/9	HR/9	BB/9	K/9	KW
1995	Hagerstown	SAtl	91.3	108	22	2	28	58	2.17	8	2	10.64	.20	2.76	5.72	1.22
1996	Knoxville	South	70.7	76	34	7	36	41	4.33	4	4	9.68	.89	4.58	5.22	.59

You might think he's that biggest of turkeys, the closer prospect. However in '95, he tossed over 100 innings in relief, with a 101-16 strikeout to walk ratio. Someone to watch.

PAUL SPOLJARIC   **LRP**   **1971**   **Age 26**

YR	Team	Lge	IP	H	ER	HR	BB	K	ERA	W	L	H/9	HR/9	BB/9	K/9	KW
1993	Dunedin	Flor	23.3	18	5	2	16	22	1.93	2	1	6.94	.77	6.17	8.49	1.29
1993	Knoxville	South	40.0	33	11	4	27	37	2.47	3	1	7.43	.90	6.07	8.32	1.26
1993	Syracuse	Inter	90.3	106	61	14	66	72	6.08	3	7	10.56	1.39	6.58	7.17	.75
1994	Knoxville	South	92.3	105	55	14	66	62	5.36	4	6	10.23	1.36	6.43	6.04	.41
1994	Syracuse	Inter	45.0	50	34	7	33	32	6.80	1	4	10.00	1.40	6.60	6.40	.48
1995	Syracuse	Inter	81.7	79	51	14	68	92	5.62	3	6	8.71	1.54	7.49	10.14	1.51
1996	Syracuse	Inter	21.0	21	8	2	8	20	3.43	1	1	9.00	.86	3.43	8.57	2.00
1996	Toronto	AL	37.3	29	12	5	20	37	2.89	3	1	6.99	1.21	4.82	8.92	1.77

The Blue Jays have diddled, hemmed and hawed, and finally admitted to themselves that they probably need Spoljaric. He was supposed to have a short fuse in the minors, getting easily rattled by a bad pitch, but the move to the bullpen has apparently settled him down. Left-handers who rack up this many strikeouts have nothing left to prove in the minors. He should inherit Tony Castillo's role in the bullpen.

MIKE TIMLIN   **RRP**   **1966**   **Age 31**

YR	Team	Lge	IP	H	ER	HR	BB	K	ERA	W	L	H/9	HR/9	BB/9	K/9	KW
1993	Toronto	AL	56.0	60	26	7	30	51	4.18	3	3	9.64	1.12	4.82	8.20	1.53
1994	Toronto	AL	40.0	40	19	5	21	37	4.28	2	2	9.00	1.12	4.72	8.32	1.59
1995	Syracuse	Inter	16.3	14	6	3	6	11	3.31	1	1	7.71	1.65	3.31	6.06	1.19
1995	Toronto	AL	41.7	38	9	1	18	36	1.94	4	1	8.21	.22	3.89	7.78	1.62
1996	Toronto	AL	55.3	46	17	3	20	50	2.77	4	2	7.48	.49	3.25	8.13	1.90

The ultimate ersatz closer, or proof that the job doesn't take the "heart of a lion" or whatever bilge you'll hear about make-up. Jeff Reardon had makeup. He could lather it on from the compact he kept in his hip pocket instead of an emery board. It still didn't matter, because when push came to shove, he's paid to pitch, not be Tammy Faye Bakker. Timlin isn't that bad, but he's being generously rewarded for mediocrity and a rare bout of extended health.

FRANK VIOLA   **LSP**   **1960**   **Age 37**

YR	Team	Lge	IP	H	ER	HR	BB	K	ERA	W	L	H/9	HR/9	BB/9	K/9	KW
1993	Boston	AL	182.0	171	58	12	80	93	2.87	13	7	8.46	.59	3.96	4.60	.54
1994	Boston	AL	31.0	32	13	2	18	9	3.77	2	1	9.29	.58	5.23	2.61	-.44
1995	Dunedin	Flor	10.0	15	10	3	4	6	9.00	0	1	13.50	2.70	3.60	5.40	.90
1995	Indianapolis	AmA	31.3	35	16	4	10	22	4.60	1	2	10.05	1.15	2.87	6.32	1.39
1995	Cincinnati	NL	14.3	20	10	3	4	4	6.28	1	1	12.56	1.88	2.51	2.51	.21
1996	Knoxville	South	20.3	18	3	1	4	11	1.33	2	0	7.97	.44	1.77	4.87	1.18
1996	Toronto	AL	31.0	38	20	5	22	17	5.81	1	2	11.03	1.45	6.39	4.94	.05

It'd be a whole lot easier to be sympathetic towards Frank Viola about his career's end if he hadn't been such a self-centered jerk about it: he refused to go to the pen, demanded to be in the rotation and the Blue Jays blinked, reminded themselves that even if he was an ex-famous person he'd been awful, and showed him the door.

JEFF WARE   **RSP**   **1971**   **Age 26**

YR	Team	Lge	IP	H	ER	HR	BB	K	ERA	W	L	H/9	HR/9	BB/9	K/9	KW
1994	Knoxville	South	34.7	57	34	6	23	25	8.83	1	3	14.80	1.56	5.97	6.49	.67
1995	Syracuse	Inter	70.0	71	29	9	57	65	3.73	4	4	9.13	1.16	7.33	8.36	.95
1996	Syracuse	Inter	74.7	87	48	6	41	49	5.79	3	5	10.49	.72	4.94	5.91	.73
1996	Toronto	AL	33.3	30	24	5	32	11	6.48	1	3	8.10	1.35	8.64	2.97	-1.17

Jeff Ware is one of the great "Never Will Be's" around baseball: he never will be healthy, so he never will be successful for any length of time. The repeated injuries have taken the zip out of his fastball, and since his control hasn't improved he never will be someone the Blue Jays should count on.

WOODY WILLIAMS   **RBP**   **1967**   **Age 30**

YR	Team	Lge	IP	H	ER	HR	BB	K	ERA	W	L	H/9	HR/9	BB/9	K/9	KW
1993	Toronto	AL	36.7	40	15	2	24	25	3.68	2	2	9.82	.49	5.89	6.14	.57
1994	Toronto	AL	58.3	45	18	5	35	55	2.78	4	2	6.94	.77	5.40	8.49	1.48
1995	Toronto	AL	53.0	44	17	6	29	41	2.89	4	2	7.47	1.02	4.92	6.96	1.09
1996	Syracuse	Inter	30.0	25	4	3	10	27	1.20	3	0	7.50	.90	3.00	8.10	1.95
1996	Toronto	AL	59.7	58	24	7	22	41	3.62	4	3	8.75	1.06	3.32	6.18	1.23

The Blue Jays don't know what to do with Williams, and his cross-body throwing motion injures him often enough for them to avoid having to figure it out. Despite being a nibbler and an extreme flyball pitcher, he survives in Toronto. He'll continue to be a useful spare part whenever he's healthy.

Player	Age	Team	Lge	AB	H	DB	TP	HR	BB	SB	CS	OUT	BA	OBA	SA	EQA	EQR	Peak
SHARNOL ADRIANA	25	Syracuse	Inter	297	83	10	3	10	25	13	5	219	.279	.335	.434	.259	37	.272
CASEY BLAKE	22	Hagerstown	S Atl	178	39	6	1	2	8	2	1	140	.219	.253	.298	.178	9	.197
BEN CANDELARIA	21	Dunedin	Flor	128	23	3	0	1	11	1	2	107	.180	.245	.227	.133	3	.148
	21	Knoxville	South	162	39	7	1	3	15	2	1	124	.241	.305	.352	.220	14	.246
WES CHAMBERLAIN	30	Syracuse	Inter	135	47	4	0	9	19	1	1	89	.348	.429	.578	.326	27	.318
VIC DAVILA	23	Dunedin	Flor	408	102	15	0	10	30	1	1	307	.250	.301	.360	.221	35	.240
RYAN FREEL	20	Dunedin	Flor	390	91	16	1	6	30	10	8	307	.233	.288	.326	.204	29	.232
HERMAN GORDON	21	Hagerstown	S Atl	116	15	2	1	1	4	1	2	103	.129	.158	.190	-.089	-1	-.088
KRIS HARMES	25	Knoxville	South	123	23	6	0	2	10	1	0	100	.187	.248	.285	.169	6	.179
CHRIS HAYES	22	Dunedin	Flor	109	23	2	0	2	10	1	1	87	.211	.277	.284	.182	6	.202
	22	Hagerstown	S Atl	329	71	9	1	5	25	3	2	260	.216	.271	.295	.184	19	.203
SANTIAGO HENRY	23	Knoxville	South	370	86	11	3	4	14	6	3	287	.232	.260	.311	.188	22	.206
DAMON JOHNSON	20	Hagerstown	S Atl	131	20	3	1	1	8	1	1	112	.153	.201	.214	.090	1	.106
FELIX JOSE	31	Syracuse	Inter	333	85	11	1	15	33	2	0	248	.255	.322	.429	.250	39	.242
JOHN KEHOE	23	Hagerstown	S Atl	411	99	13	1	6	58	6	4	316	.241	.335	.321	.223	37	.242
BRIAN KOWITZ	26	Syracuse	Inter	110	26	6	2	1	9	1	1	85	.236	.294	.355	.215	9	.224
SELWYN LANGAIGNE	20	Dunedin	Flor	119	23	3	2	0	9	1	1	97	.193	.250	.252	.153	4	.174
ANDREW MCCORMICK	23	Dunedin	Flor	131	27	2	1	0	17	2	0	104	.206	.297	.237	.177	7	.191
	23	Hagerstown	S Atl	109	16	2	0	0	15	1	0	93	.147	.250	.165	.098	1	.109
DAVE MORGAN	24	Dunedin	Flor	92	23	2	0	4	16	0	0	69	.250	.361	.402	.256	11	.273
PAT MOULTRIE	23	Hagerstown	S Atl	135	33	2	1	1	9	4	1	103	.244	.292	.296	.201	9	.220
BOB MUMMAU	24	Dunedin	Flor	109	20	3	0	0	11	1	2	91	.183	.258	.211	.133	3	.140
	24	Knoxville	South	154	37	3	0	3	12	1	2	119	.240	.295	.318	.202	11	.216
MICHAEL PEEPLES	19	Hagerstown	S Atl	283	59	9	0	3	29	6	2	226	.208	.282	.272	.184	16	.212
SCOTT POSE	29	Syracuse	Inter	430	114	11	3	1	58	20	10	326	.265	.352	.312	.231	42	.230
JOHN RAMOS	30	Syracuse	Inter	324	77	9	0	9	41	1	1	248	.238	.323	.349	.225	30	.221
JONATHAN RIVERS	21	Dunedin	Flor	343	79	9	1	7	34	4	4	268	.230	.300	.324	.207	26	.231
LUIS RODRIGUEZ	22	Hagerstown	S Atl	266	46	4	1	1	19	2	1	221	.173	.228	.207	.111	5	.122
OMAR SANCHEZ	25	Dunedin	Flor	130	27	3	3	0	12	1	1	104	.208	.275	.277	.178	7	.188
	25	Hagerstown	S Atl	316	77	8	2	5	44	7	3	242	.244	.336	.329	.228	30	.240
ANTHONY SANDERS	22	Dunedin	Flor	427	105	10	0	17	31	10	7	329	.246	.297	.389	.228	41	.251
	22	Knoxville	South	133	31	2	0	2	5	1	1	103	.233	.261	.293	.179	7	.195
ANDY SHATLEY	20	Hagerstown	S Atl	201	34	0	0	3	22	1	0	167	.169	.251	.214	.133	5	.153
FAUSTO SOLANO	22	Hagerstown	S Atl	549	122	21	2	4	70	13	9	436	.222	.310	.290	.201	40	.222
MIKE STRANGE	22	Dunedin	Flor	161	47	2	1	1	23	3	2	116	.292	.380	.335	.248	18	.273
BRIAN TURANG	29	Syracuse	Inter	94	16	1	1	1	9	2	0	78	.170	.243	.234	.147	3	.146
CRAIG WILSON	19	Hagerstown	S Atl	513	118	13	2	10	24	7	4	399	.230	.264	.322	.193	33	.223
CHRIS WOODWARD	20	Hagerstown	S Atl	442	85	16	0	2	34	4	1	358	.192	.250	.242	.150	16	.171

Player	Age	Team	Lge	IP	H	ER	HR	BB	K	ERA	W	L	H/9	HR/9	BB/9	K/9	KW
TIM ADKINS	22	Dunedin	Flor	91.3	103	71	6	93	66	7.00	2	8	10.15	.59	9.16	6.50	-.12
SCOTT BROW	27	Syracuse	Inter	73.7	88	44	6	34	43	5.38	3	5	10.75	.73	4.15	5.25	.71
	27	Toronto	AL	38.7	42	18	4	25	22	4.19	2	2	9.78	.93	5.82	5.12	.25
GIOVANNI CARRARA	28	Syracuse	Inter	36.0	39	14	2	16	23	3.50	2	2	9.75	.50	4.00	5.75	.92
RUBEN CORRAL	20	Hagerstown	S Atl	34.7	69	38	4	31	20	9.87	1	3	17.91	1.04	8.05	5.19	-.28
JOHN CROWTHER	22	Hagerstown	S Atl	55.3	81	40	3	60	34	6.51	2	4	13.17	.49	9.76	5.53	-.60
JIM CZAJKOWSKI	32	Syracuse	Inter	85.3	90	45	4	47	59	4.75	4	5	9.49	.42	4.96	6.22	.83
TOM DAVEY	22	Hagerstown	S Atl	129.3	181	93	10	128	54	6.47	4	10	12.60	.70	8.91	3.76	-.97
ERNIE DELGADO	20	Hagerstown	S Atl	70.3	120	60	3	64	39	7.68	2	6	15.36	.38	8.19	4.99	-.38
ROGER DOMAN	23	Dunedin	Flor	26.7	41	23	3	19	14	7.76	1	2	13.84	1.01	6.41	4.72	-.03
	23	Knoxville	South	37.0	50	24	2	16	21	5.84	1	3	12.16	.49	3.89	5.11	.73
CHRIS FREEMAN	23	Knoxville	South	42.7	46	19	3	26	38	4.01	2	3	9.70	.63	5.48	8.02	1.30
MIGUEL GOMEZ	22	Dunedin	Flor	45.3	53	29	7	24	25	5.76	2	3	10.52	1.39	4.76	4.96	.46
MIKE GORDON	23	Dunedin	Flor	118.3	148	74	11	86	74	5.63	4	9	11.26	.84	6.54	5.63	.24
D.J. HARRIS	25	Dunedin	Flor	39.0	55	30	4	25	22	6.92	1	3	12.69	.92	5.77	5.08	.25
TYSON HARTSHORN	21	Hagerstown	S Atl	121.3	209	103	18	94	60	7.64	3	10	15.50	1.34	6.97	4.45	-.26
VINCE HORSMAN	29	Syracuse	Inter	33.7	39	19	7	14	17	5.08	2	2	10.43	1.87	3.74	4.54	.58
JASON JARVIS	22	Dunedin	Flor	99.3	138	70	8	56	47	6.34	3	8	12.50	.72	5.07	4.26	.15
MIKE JOHNSON	20	Hagerstown	S Atl	136.3	222	93	8	60	85	6.14	4	11	14.66	.53	3.96	5.61	.88
CLINT LAWRENCE	19	Hagerstown	S Atl	31.3	36	14	3	15	15	4.02	1	2	10.34	.86	4.31	4.31	.36
JEREMY LEE	21	Dunedin	Flor	45.0	78	39	3	26	20	7.80	1	4	15.60	.60	5.20	4.00	.03
	21	Hagerstown	S Atl	79.0	115	44	1	37	42	5.01	4	5	13.10	.11	4.22	4.78	.54
BEN LOWE	22	Hagerstown	S Atl	56.7	54	27	3	71	49	4.29	3	3	8.58	.48	11.28	7.78	-.22
MARK LUKASIEWICZ	23	Dunedin	Flor	27.7	32	20	2	29	22	6.51	1	2	10.41	.65	9.43	7.16	.03
CHRIS MCBRIDE	22	Hagerstown	S Atl	51.3	58	15	5	15	19	2.63	4	2	10.17	.88	2.63	3.33	.45
DOUG MEINERS	22	Dunedin	Flor	34.3	44	22	3	13	12	5.77	1	3	11.53	.79	3.41	3.15	.20
SCOTTY PACE	24	Dunedin	Flor	27.0	29	7	0	17	14	2.33	2	1	9.67	.00	5.67	4.67	.14
	24	Syracuse	Inter	49.0	56	33	4	34	29	6.06	2	3	10.29	.73	6.24	5.33	.21
KEN ROBINSON	26	Syracuse	Inter	61.7	55	32	14	47	65	4.67	3	4	8.03	2.04	6.86	9.49	1.45
MICHAEL ROMANO	24	Knoxville	South	121.0	145	79	16	82	65	5.88	4	9	10.79	1.19	6.10	4.83	.09
KEILAN SMITH	22	Dunedin	Flor	40.3	55	31	4	30	27	6.92	1	3	12.27	.89	6.69	6.02	.33
JAY VENIARD	21	Dunedin	Flor	57.7	74	39	9	28	29	6.09	2	4	11.55	1.40	4.37	4.53	.42
	21	Hagerstown	S Atl	37.3	50	34	6	34	24	8.20	1	3	12.05	1.45	8.20	5.79	-.12
ORESTE VOLKERT	21	Hagerstown	S Atl	54.7	72	33	4	28	24	5.43	2	4	11.85	.66	4.61	3.95	.16
JOE YOUNG	21	Dunedin	Flor	29.7	36	25	4	22	26	7.58	1	2	10.92	1.21	6.67	7.89	.96
	21	Hagerstown	S Atl	102.0	143	78	9	89	86	6.88	3	8	12.62	.79	7.85	7.59	.57

Toronto Blue Jays

Chicago White Sox

Because of their owner, Jerry Reinsdorf, the White Sox cannot help but be identified with the great game's labor woes. That doesn't necessarily mean that that's all the organization has to concern itself with. But when push came to shove, management and players united in Chicago in the labor war's ugliest repercussion: a blatant attempt to blame their failures, shortcomings, and incompetence on Chicago baseball fans. Who said the two sides can't cooperate?

1996 was supposed to be the year that the White Sox finally lived up to the promise of '93 and '94, and erased the bad memory of the collapse of '95. With the additions of free agents Tony Phillips, Harold Baines, Kevin Tapani, and Darren Lewis, and the acquisition through trade of ex-famous slugger Danny Tartabull, the team expected to finally push past the Indians. Before the season even began, the inevitably cocky Ozzie Guillen claimed that the Tribe was in trouble, because its pitching couldn't compare to the staff in Comiskey Park II. Other important changes included the release of famed hitting coach Walt Hriniak, whose "tyranny" apparently didn't jibe with a new generation of ballplayers. He was replaced by noted red-ass Bill Buckner. They'd chosen to retain goofy manager Terry Bevington, already ill-regarded for his bombastic promises, principles, threats and rules, all invariably ignored when push came to shove. Bevington was someone who was more than willing to go out of his way to antagonize the media and fans out of sheer orneriness.

Of course, there were major problems with this formula for success. The Sox were taking several gambles: their fourth starter was Jason Bere, coming off of one of the worst seasons for a starting pitcher without a Tigers affiliation since 1930, and their fifth starter on Opening Day was an even worse option, noted free agent flop Kirk McCaskill. Despite brave talk about how replacing Lance Johnson with Darren Lewis was actually improving the defense, they were taking on one of the worst offensive players in baseball. Danny Tartabull was a major injury risk. Harold Baines was ancient. They were trying a particularly dicey combination of an inexperienced manager with a pronounced tendency towards regarding pitchers, and a new bullpen of young pitchers. This last factor did not have to be a problem, in that the young middle relievers (particularly Simas, Karchner and Thomas) are all well-regarded prospects, but combined with a raw manager who would have to learn how to use them on the job it was potentially dangerous.

Early on, almost everything looked good for the Sox. Despite some camp hijinks involving Tony Phillips' prema-

ture retirement, the team was clicking offensively. Some things went wrong: Danny Tartabull proved to be an expensive waste in the #6 slot early on, and after a hot start Darren Lewis returned to showing why he'd been a transaction hot potato for the last few years. The pitching staff suffered a "setback" when Jason Bere totally broke down, but he was replaced by James Baldwin, who was exceptional. The bullpen was sturdy, as the young setup men were doing well handing leads off to Roberto Hernandez, who was enjoying an excellent comeback season. The Sox raced out to a 40-21 start. After a big weekend series in Cleveland during the first week of July, where the Sox took three of four games, they were only two back from Cleveland. Things were working out very well.

Then the first of several nails was driven into the Sox' coffin: Frank Thomas suffered a stress fracture in his foot. He missed most of July, and in his absence the team went 7-12. By itself, that shouldn't have been enough to take the Sox out of the wild card race. Terry Bevington was that extra edge. In Thomas' absence, Bevington's tendencies to overmanage, to overuse his pitching staff, to empty his bench by the seventh inning and to run his team out of potential big innings became that much more destructive. Without Thomas' steady offensive contributions, the White Sox were making a bad situation worse by scrabbling after runs with one-run strategies while still playing with a lineup that had sluggers like Ventura, Baines and Phillips.

The worst damage was done in the bullpen, as first Karchner and then Thomas imploded from quixotic usage patterns, and Simas slowly capsized. The open sore that was the #5 slot in the rotation became infected, and in the raging conflagration that was the pitching staff, the rotation slowly collapsed as well, overused and as Bevington overcompensated desperately for the damage he'd done in the pen. Rather than acknowledge his screwup, Bevington engaged in tepid week-long debates with incredulous sportswriters over the evils of "unfair" attributions of blown saves to middle relievers. Not even Thomas' return could undo Bevington's berserk destruction; from August 1 to the end of the season, the Sox were 27-28, hardly what a team in contention should expect to survive down the stretch.

Awash in disappointment as their season went down the tubes, the Sox players and management, unwilling to lay into one another in the wake of the strike, settled on a new scapegoat: the fans. Attendance at Comiskey was sparse, but the Sox still racked up over 1.6 million paying customers. As the July and August trade deadlines approached, GM Ron

Schueler fulminated about how the Sox were financially incapable of making any moves, because of poor attendance. He announced that if the team went down in flames, it was what people had paid, or more properly not paid, to see. Bevington, Thomas, Phillips, Guillen and others all joined the bleating pack baying for "loyalty" and commitment from fans, whining about betrayal, a lack of support and their inability to contend without fan dollars.

This behavior was simply disgusting. The media's willingness to cooperate was also ill-considered. But what was truly galling about this attempt to put a new spin on the season was that it failed to observe the real problem with the White Sox: they're about as public relations-impaired as your worst-imagined combination of the Moammar Gaddhafi, Madonna and Bob Dole. They've got an aesthetically challenged ballpark made worse with the loudest sound system in baseball, and instead of trying to make do and create a ballpark atmosphere, the organization insists it needs to "charge up" the fans. Bereft of any marketing ideas, the team recycled some old Bill Veeck ideas like "Dog Day," which revealed both how dated a Bill Veeck idea was, and how intellectually bankrupt Sox marketing is. The decision to resort to "challenging" the fans by boldly stating that this team wouldn't contend if the fans didn't show up was a bluff called by the fans, and the Sox did not contend. Who could possibly believe that a publicity campaign built around insulting the fans for not attending would somehow shame them into going to one of the worst major league venues for baseball?

As the final insult for the damages of '96, the Sox announced their decision to re-sign Terry Bevington to a two-year contract. If there was one thing that had excited Sox fans about the season as it collapsed, it was the hope that the inept manager would be sacked. In a classic gesture, the Sox told the fans to do the anatomically impossible, determined to stand by the ill-tempered crony who was more than willing to go after reporters and fans, but who wouldn't say boo about the team's need for a fifth starter, starting catcher or bullpen help. Jerry Reinsdorf, determined to put his ignorance on parade, has repeatedly tried to blame Don Fehr for his problems, but the problem lies with an organization that treats its fans more shabbily than any since the franchise shifts of decades long gone.

Trying to paper over their numerous self-inflicted wounds, the Sox have added slugger Albert Belle. This overinflates the Sox' great strength (offensive power), without doing anything to address the team's serious management problems, pitching problems or the "two outs in the lineup" problem with Guillen and Karkovice. Without addressing any of those problems, the Sox are in the same sad shape they were before they signed Belle. Albert can take solace in one thing: in Chicago, instead of being a big angry man, he'll be just another finger-pointing grump.

The Sox' farm system is not really in any better shape than it was a year ago. The organization is making one major change: it's dumping its South Bend affiliate to go with just two full-season A-ball teams. We pointed out last year that having three is simply wasting time and money on non-prospects in an organization awash in non-prospects, and diluting what little talent the Sox have. For example last season, the Sox' three A-ball affiliates were South Bend (54-82), Hickory (55-85) and Prince William (58-80). All three finished last, and these teams were almost entirely made up of Schueler draftees. Although winning isn't supposed to be critical in the minors, at the lower levels it's usually a sign of some talent, since you can't stock A-ball teams with minor league veterans.

The Sox created a major disaster out of the '96 draft. They botched their required offer of a contract to their first-round pick, Bobby Seay, within fifteen days of drafting him. They instead antagonized him and his agent, which led to a ripple effect where Seay and three other first-rounders were declared free agents, none of whom will be signing with Chicago.

As bleak as all of this sounds, the bad news won't really be hitting the Sox hard until three years from now, when most of the farm system will be running on empty. The upper levels have some players of note: Jeff Abbott is one of the best young hitters in baseball, and Mike Cameron would be going into spring with a shot at the center field job on most teams. Unfortunately both of them are outfielders, and the Sox are overstocked there for '97. The Sox also have a number of good 3B/SS candidates, notably Chris Snopek, but also Greg Norton and Olmedo Saenz. Again, the problem for these guys is several long-term contracts carried by current Sox veterans. Nowhere in the organization is there a catcher to replace Karkovice. There are several solid pitching prospects, but the organization already avoided Scott Ruffcorn one more time this year by resurrecting Joe Magrane from the dead and giving Kirk McCaskill a parting gift of a fifth wasted year in uniform. Whether or not the organization will have patience with any of them after last years' debacle involving Bill Simas or Matt Karchner remains to be seen, and even then, whether or not Terry Bevington has learned anything from his rampage through last year's staff is clearly unknown.

JEFF ABBOTT OF 1973 Age 24

Year	Team	Lge	AB	H	DB	TP	HR	BB	SB	CS	OUT	BA	OBA	SA	EQA	EQR	Peak
1994	Hickory	SAtl	240	87	11	3	6	32	1	0	153	.363	.438	.508	.319	44	.356
1995	Pr. William	Caro	281	100	9	0	6	26	4	1	182	.356	.410	.452	.295	43	.325
1995	Birmingham	South	205	65	9	1	3	19	1	2	142	.317	.375	.415	.266	26	.294
1996	Nashville	AmA	456	149	21	1	14	36	11	3	310	.327	.376	.469	.285	67	.310
1997	*Chi. White Sox*	*AL*	*609*	*187*	*28*	*2*	*17*	*65*	*14*	*5*	*427*	*.307*	*.374*	*.443*	*.285*	*93*	

The organization has decided to let Tartabull escape, so the Sox have several options in right field: They could keep Tony Phillips and move him there; they could (as rumored) trade Phillips and make Lyle Mouton the regular; or they could give a serious shot to either Jeff Abbott or Mike Cameron. Since Dave Martinez is a platoon player in center, Cameron or Abbott could also work their way into half a job there. All of these players are good options for the Sox, but all of them can't be kept: Belle, Martinez, Phillips and Lewis are all under contract. Abbott is one of the best young hitters in the minor leagues right now and was named the best batting prospect in the American Association. He's considered to have bad instincts for center, but he hasn't been moved permanently to one of the corners. Abbott missed his chance to shine in the AFL while recovering from an elbow injury.

HAROLD BAINES DH 1959 Age 38

Year	Team	Lge	AB	H	DB	TP	HR	BB	SB	CS	OUT	BA	OBA	SA	EQA	EQR	Peak
1993	Baltimore	AL	421	136	19	0	24	60	0	0	285	.323	.407	.539	.310	76	.294
1994	Baltimore	AL	326	95	10	1	16	30	0	0	231	.291	.351	.475	.273	45	.260
1995	Baltimore	AL	389	119	17	1	27	71	0	2	272	.306	.413	.563	.314	75	.298
1996	Chi. White Sox	AL	502	162	25	0	25	74	3	1	341	.323	.410	.522	.308	89	.292
1997	*Chi. White Sox*	*AL*	*468*	*132*	*11*	*0*	*21*	*64*	*0*	*0*	*336*	*.282*	*.368*	*.440*	*.280*	*69*	

He had a superb year, and if there's a tragedy in the White Sox' season, it's that Harold's return to Chicago was greeted with such profound indifference. His return should have been promoted as a moment of nostalgia for the "Winning Ugly" Sox of '83. Unfortunately, the team was busy recycling second-rate Bill Veeck promotions. Baines spent most of the year in the cleanup spot, and was not platooned as had been promised. Unfortunately, that meant less playing time for Chris Snopek. Buying Baines was a failure in one respect: despite Harold's good year, Frank Thomas was still issued 26 intentional walks.

PAT BORDERS C 1963 Age 34

Year	Team	Lge	AB	H	DB	TP	HR	BB	SB	CS	OUT	BA	OBA	SA	EQA	EQR	Peak
1993	Toronto	AL	491	129	21	0	14	23	2	2	364	.263	.296	.391	.229	45	.224
1994	Toronto	AL	297	75	14	1	3	15	1	1	223	.253	.288	.337	.208	22	.201
1995	Kansas City	AL	145	35	7	1	5	7	0	0	110	.241	.276	.407	.225	13	.216
1996	St. Louis	NL	70	23	3	0	0	2	0	1	48	.329	.347	.371	.242	7	.227
1996	California	AL	57	13	3	0	2	3	0	1	45	.228	.267	.386	.209	4	.200
1996	Chi. White Sox	AL	95	27	2	0	3	5	0	0	68	.284	.320	.400	.242	10	.230
1997	*Cleveland*	*AL*	*146*	*34*	*3*	*0*	*3*	*10*	*0*	*1*	*113*	*.233*	*.282*	*.315*	*.198*	*10*	

From World Series MVP to scrub. Of course, he started off as a scrub, so he shouldn't be unused to the feeling. His good defensive reputation has almost nothing to do with how he plays: he's a lousy plate blocker, and nobody ever pipes up with accolades for his game calling. He's a veteran, so he gets recycled.

DOUG BRADY 2B 1970 Age 27

Year	Team	Lge	AB	H	DB	TP	HR	BB	SB	CS	OUT	BA	OBA	SA	EQA	EQR	Peak
1993	Sarasota	Flor	462	110	12	2	8	48	13	4	356	.238	.310	.325	.217	39	.236
1994	Birmingham	South	528	127	16	5	5	40	19	6	407	.241	.294	.318	.210	41	.224
1995	Nashville	AmA	459	136	13	5	6	36	29	5	328	.296	.347	.386	.258	55	.272
1996	Nashville	AmA	437	105	16	6	6	35	18	5	337	.240	.297	.346	.220	38	.229

Scab. Now that he's not hitting around .300, the question of whether or not he deserved a look is moot. He's supposed to be close to earning his degree in psychology; he'll need it.

MIKE CAMERON **OF** **1973** **Age 24**

Year	Team	Lge	AB	H	DB	TP	HR	BB	SB	CS	OUT	BA	OBA	SA	EQA	EQR	Peak
1993	South Bend	Midw	421	88	10	2	1	21	8	4	337	.209	.247	.249	.155	16	.176
1994	Pr. William	Caro	489	115	11	11	6	51	13	6	380	.235	.307	.339	.219	43	.245
1995	Birmingham	South	366	93	15	3	12	51	14	7	280	.254	.345	.410	.254	45	.280
1996	Birmingham	South	490	147	24	6	28	60	27	9	352	.300	.376	.545	.300	87	.327
1997	Chi. White Sox	AL	532	136	29	2	17	59	23	11	407	.256	.330	.414	.258	69	

A top-notch center fielder and an excellent baserunner, Cameron was named the most exciting prospect in the Southern League. He should be the White Sox' center fielder right now, but there's talk of putting him in right, talk that unfortunately reflects the poor decision to sign both Darren Lewis and Dave Martinez. As dominating as he was last year, keep in mind it was his second year at Birmingham, which is usually a prompt for great-looking seasons.

CARMINE CAPPUCCIO **OF** **1970** **Age 27**

Year	Team	Lge	AB	H	DB	TP	HR	BB	SB	CS	OUT	BA	OBA	SA	EQA	EQR	Peak
1993	South Bend	Midw	398	108	19	2	4	32	1	2	292	.271	.326	.359	.231	37	.251
1994	Pr. William	Caro	414	114	18	1	10	22	5	2	302	.275	.312	.396	.238	42	.255
1995	Birmingham	South	257	71	11	2	5	21	1	1	187	.276	.331	.393	.243	27	.256
1995	Nashville	AmA	222	61	10	0	6	31	0	2	163	.275	.364	.401	.255	27	.269
1996	Nashville	AmA	417	113	19	2	10	29	1	2	306	.271	.318	.398	.239	43	.249
1997	Chi. White Sox	AL	319	81	19	1	6	37	2	2	240	.254	.331	.376	.246	36	

A beautifully mellifluous name, isn't it? He isn't a bad player, and most of his power is against RHPs, as you might have guessed. He should have the Joe Orsulak job on somebody's roster right now, instead of Joe Orsulak. He has a good throwing arm, so he can handle both OF corners.

DOMINGO CEDENO **2B/SS** **1969** **Age 28**

Year	Team	Lge	AB	H	DB	TP	HR	BB	SB	CS	OUT	BA	OBA	SA	EQA	EQR	Peak
1993	Syracuse	Inter	391	103	15	7	3	35	11	6	294	.263	.324	.361	.232	38	.250
1994	Syracuse	Inter	82	23	4	1	1	7	2	1	60	.280	.337	.390	.247	9	.257
1994	Toronto	AL	98	20	2	3	0	10	1	2	80	.204	.278	.286	.179	5	.188
1995	Toronto	AL	162	40	4	1	5	10	0	1	123	.247	.291	.377	.220	14	.227
1996	Toronto	AL	282	79	9	2	2	15	5	3	206	.280	.316	.348	.226	25	.231
1997	Chi. White Sox	AL	306	78	11	3	1	31	5	4	232	.255	.323	.320	.221	27	

Despite a strong arm, Cedeno is generally considered a poor defender. Those are his strong points. Only Cito Gaston would give a player of this caliber (lighter than a .22, I'm guessing Daisy air rifle range) almost 300 PA in the second slot. That the Sox weren't willing to make do with Snopek Norton, and even Paco Martin says something about their "brain trust."

GLENN DiSARCINA **IF** **1970** **Age 27**

Year	Team	Lge	AB	H	DB	TP	HR	BB	SB	CS	OUT	BA	OBA	SA	EQA	EQR	Peak
1993	Sarasota	Flor	486	128	22	2	7	30	6	2	360	.263	.306	.360	.225	43	.244
1994	Birmingham	South	461	113	18	1	8	28	6	2	350	.245	.288	.341	.211	36	.226
1996	Birmingham	South	179	64	7	2	7	5	2	0	115	.358	.375	.536	.303	29	.316
1996	Nashville	AmA	99	23	9	0	0	6	1	1	77	.232	.276	.323	.197	7	.203

The younger brother of Gary DiSarcina, Glenn is an awful defensive player who'd never hit a lick in previous seasons. After missing most of '95 due to injury, he was playing to keep his career alive. That done, I think he's more likely to go back to hitting like crap.

RAY DURHAM **2B** **1972** **Age 25**

Year	Team	Lge	AB	H	DB	TP	HR	BB	SB	CS	OUT	BA	OBA	SA	EQA	EQR	Peak
1993	Birmingham	South	548	147	21	7	4	41	26	13	414	.268	.319	.354	.230	53	.258
1994	Nashville	AmA	530	152	28	6	19	49	25	7	385	.287	.347	.470	.274	76	.302
1995	Chi. White Sox	AL	477	129	30	6	8	31	18	5	353	.270	.315	.409	.246	53	.268
1996	Chi. White Sox	AL	563	161	33	5	11	59	31	4	406	.286	.354	.421	.268	76	.287
1997	*Chi. White Sox*	*AL*	*617*	*178*	*47*	*8*	*13*	*60*	*47*	*8*	*447*	*.288*	*.352*	*.454*	*.285*	*97*	

Although these projections are working with the assumption that the current offensive levels will continue, this projection isn't out of Durham's reach in a good pitcher's season. Although he was prematurely named one of the best defensive second baseman in the league last season, he definitely improved in his second year. He also improved his hitting against right-handed pitching by leaps and bounds. If the Sox have a legitimate beef, it's that people aren't already acknowledging that Durham is the best second baseman in Chicago. It's unlikely that he'll ever reach Knoblauch-Alomar levels, but he's probably the third-best second baseman in the AL right now. In a world where Lance Johnson is considered a useful leadoff hitter, Durham will eventually succeed as a top of the order hitter.

OZZIE GUILLEN **SS** **1964** **Age 33**

Year	Team	Lge	AB	H	DB	TP	HR	BB	SB	CS	OUT	BA	OBA	SA	EQA	EQR	Peak
1993	Chi. White Sox	AL	462	136	26	4	5	13	5	3	329	.294	.314	.400	.241	47	.239
1994	Chi. White Sox	AL	369	109	10	5	1	14	5	4	264	.295	.321	.358	.230	34	.226
1995	Chi. White Sox	AL	419	110	22	3	1	13	6	7	316	.263	.285	.337	.206	30	.198
1996	Chi. White Sox	AL	503	137	26	8	4	10	6	5	371	.272	.287	.380	.222	43	.211
1997	*Chi. White Sox*	*AL*	*313*	*79*	*9*	*3*	*1*	*8*	*6*	*6*	*240*	*.252*	*.271*	*.310*	*.200*	*21*	

Bad. It's unfortunate that isn't a four-letter word, because by itself it doesn't come close to describing what a negative effect Ozzie Guillen has on his team. The world according to Ozzie is an interesting place. You want offense? He might be a notch above cross-town corpse Rey Sanchez. You want leadership? He's the guy in the clubhouse leading the charge against the fans, and the guy who at one point last season was talking about Joey Cora as the "missing man" whose absence had ruined their '95 season. You want arrogance? He's disappointed that not even his own children compare him with Cal Ripken. It isn't incredible that he rarely goes a game without a missed popup, a throw to the wrong base or a baserunning blunder; you name it, he'll blow it. The amazing thing is that its been this way for years, and only just now are the first rumbles of discontent occurring. Clearly a liability; fortunately for the Sox, his ludicrous contract runs out after this season.

JIMMY HURST **OF** **1972** **Age 25**

Year	Team	Lge	AB	H	DB	TP	HR	BB	SB	CS	OUT	BA	OBA	SA	EQA	EQR	Peak
1993	South Bend	Midw	477	108	10	0	17	29	7	1	370	.226	.271	.354	.209	37	.233
1994	Pr. William	Caro	480	131	23	2	20	62	9	5	354	.273	.356	.454	.269	66	.296
1995	Birmingham	South	310	60	7	0	12	31	8	3	253	.194	.267	.332	.198	22	.216
1996	Birmingham	South	485	125	14	0	18	45	13	6	366	.258	.321	.398	.242	53	.259
1997	*Chi. White Sox*	*AL*	*375*	*99*	*12*	*0*	*15*	*55*	*11*	*6*	*282*	*.264*	*.358*	*.416*	*.269*	*53*	

Yippee, the White Sox have their very own Glenn Braggs. When baseball needs someone to set a pick, Hurst could see the light of day. One of those "tools" prospects who's supposed to have unlimited power potential an Adonis-like build, the kind that usually litter the less-used portions of 40-man rosters. He's supposed to do everything well, but it hasn't translated to the baseball field. He got an AFL assignment, where he humiliated himself.

RON KARKOVICE **C** **1964** **Age 33**

Year	Team	Lge	AB	H	DB	TP	HR	BB	SB	CS	OUT	BA	OBA	SA	EQA	EQR	Peak
1993	Chi. White Sox	AL	407	98	17	1	23	32	2	1	310	.241	.296	.457	.246	47	.244
1994	Chi. White Sox	AL	209	46	8	1	12	37	0	3	166	.220	.337	.440	.251	26	.245
1995	Chi. White Sox	AL	327	75	15	0	15	39	2	3	255	.229	.311	.413	.237	35	.229
1996	Chi. White Sox	AL	358	82	18	0	12	24	0	0	276	.229	.277	.380	.217	30	.206
1997	*Chi. White Sox*	*AL*	*155*	*33*	*5*	*0*	*7*	*25*	*0*	*0*	*122*	*.213*	*.322*	*.381*	*.242*	*18*	

I suppose everyone has to have a favorite lousy player, and not even being a Sox fan, "Offisa Pupp" is probably mine. Sadly, his offensive contributions have fallen to the point that the Sox can't keep carrying his glove. Being an extreme flyball hitter, he could probably resurrect his career in Coors, but you could say that about a hundred other players. With Ozzie the out machine in the #9 spot, and Karko making outs three times out of four in the #8 slot, how did Tony Phillips drive in over 60 runs out of the leadoff slot?

CARLOS LEE   **3B**   **1976**   **Age 21**

Year	Team	Lge	AB	H	DB	TP	HR	BB	SB	CS	OUT	BA	OBA	SA	EQA	EQR	Peak
1995	Hickory	SAtl	224	48	4	0	4	6	1	2	178	.214	.235	.286	.161	9	.187
1996	Hickory	SAtl	501	140	13	3	8	18	7	5	366	.279	.304	.365	.226	44	.256

In an organization packed with third baseman, it seems almost silly that the Sox fielded an awful team at Hickory just to give Carlos Lee people to play with. In his second year at the level, it isn't too surprising he was successful.

DARREN LEWIS   **CF**   **1968**   **Age 29**

Year	Team	Lge	AB	H	DB	TP	HR	BB	SB	CS	OUT	BA	OBA	SA	EQA	EQR	Peak
1993	San Francisco	NL	534	144	20	5	3	38	40	13	403	.270	.318	.343	.233	53	.246
1994	San Francisco	NL	459	121	17	7	5	60	27	11	349	.264	.349	.364	.246	52	.256
1995	San Francisco	NL	315	85	10	3	1	21	18	6	236	.270	.315	.330	.226	29	.231
1995	Cincinnati	NL	166	42	3	0	0	19	9	9	133	.253	.330	.271	.202	12	.206
1996	Chi. White Sox	AL	340	81	13	2	4	46	22	5	264	.238	.329	.324	.231	34	.233
1997	*Chi. White Sox*	*AL*	*249*	*66*	*9*	*2*	*3*	*25*	*26*	*8*	*191*	*.265*	*.332*	*.353*	*.252*	*31*	

The great center fielder sweepstakes conducted after the '95 season had definite winners and definite losers. Darren Lewis was one of the winners: he got oodles of cash to play the greatest game around. The White Sox definitely lost: they had to play Lewis. Now they're stuck with having to pay him for another season.

JEFF LIEFER   **3B**   **1975**   **Age 22**

Year	Team	Lge	AB	H	DB	TP	HR	BB	SB	CS	OUT	BA	OBA	SA	EQA	EQR	Peak
1996	South Bend	Midw	289	88	5	0	13	22	3	3	203	.304	.354	.457	.269	38	.302
1996	Pr. William	Caro	150	29	2	0	1	10	0	0	121	.193	.244	.227	.135	4	.150
1997	*Chi. White Sox*	*AL*	*334*	*88*	*7*	*1*	*14*	*23*	*2*	*1*	*247*	*.263*	*.311*	*.416*	*.251*	*39*	

The Sox' '95 first-round pick, this was Liefer's first year in uniform. He committed a quick 23 errors in the Midwest League before his promotion to the Carolina League. Despite the defense, he was named to the league's All-Star team, and was named its best hitting prospect. He's usually compared to Robin Ventura because he's a left-handed hitter; it's too early to say whether the comparison will stick.

ROBERT MACHADO   **C**   **1973**   **Age 24**

Year	Team	Lge	AB	H	DB	TP	HR	BB	SB	CS	OUT	BA	OBA	SA	EQA	EQR	Peak
1993	South Bend	Midw	289	78	10	2	2	14	0	1	212	.270	.304	.339	.215	23	.245
1994	Pr. William	Caro	323	79	12	0	9	23	0	0	244	.245	.295	.365	.220	28	.246
1995	Pr. William	Caro	288	75	9	0	7	38	0	0	213	.260	.347	.365	.241	30	.266
1996	Birmingham	South	315	72	8	0	7	16	1	2	245	.229	.266	.321	.191	19	.208

Sometimes John Rooney, the radio play-by-play announcer for the Sox (that's right Sox fans: when it comes to Hawk and Wimpy, Just Say No), is an enormous goof. Machado stumbled into two hits in his first three at-bats for the Sox, after which when going through the Sox' lineup options, Rooney would immediately palaver about the ".667 hitter" on the Sox' bench. If it was a joke, it got tired faster than a Hawk monologue on umpire conspiracies or Wimpy's discussions of those yummy concessions. Machado, in case you haven't guessed, is about as much of a prospect as Nancy Faust.

NORBERTO MARTIN   **UT**   **1967**   **Age 30**

Year	Team	Lge	AB	H	DB	TP	HR	BB	SB	CS	OUT	BA	OBA	SA	EQA	EQR	Peak
1993	Nashville	AmA	585	177	17	4	10	32	27	4	412	.303	.339	.397	.256	68	.266
1994	Nashville	AmA	172	42	3	0	3	11	3	4	134	.244	.290	.314	.198	12	.202
1994	Chi. White Sox	AL	132	37	8	1	1	10	4	2	97	.280	.331	.379	.241	14	.247
1995	Chi. White Sox	AL	162	46	8	4	2	3	5	0	116	.284	.297	.420	.246	17	.248
1996	Chi. White Sox	AL	142	51	5	0	2	6	11	2	93	.359	.385	.437	.289	21	.287
1997	*Chi. White Sox*	*AL*	*282*	*79*	*8*	*5*	*4*	*12*	*14*	*0*	*203*	*.280*	*.310*	*.387*	*.253*	*33*	

The horror, the horror. Possibly Terry Bevington's favorite player, which tells you more than you need to know about Bevington. The number of times Bevington would have Martin pinch-run for Baines in the seventh, only to be stuck with having to let Martin hit with men aboard in the ninth, was probably more than most Sox fans want to remember.

DAVE MARTINEZ   **OF**   **1965**   **Age 32**

Year	Team	Lge	AB	H	DB	TP	HR	BB	SB	CS	OUT	BA	OBA	SA	EQA	EQR	Peak
1993	San Francisco	NL	248	64	10	1	6	31	5	3	187	.258	.341	.379	.243	27	.245
1994	San Francisco	NL	238	60	7	2	5	25	3	3	181	.252	.323	.361	.229	23	.228
1995	Chi. White Sox	AL	308	99	18	4	6	33	8	2	211	.321	.387	.464	.288	47	.282
1996	Chi. White Sox	AL	446	147	21	8	11	52	15	7	306	.330	.400	.487	.296	73	.286
1997	*Chi. White Sox*	*AL*	*505*	*138*	*29*	*5*	*10*	*62*	*14*	*9*	*376*	*.273*	*.353*	*.410*	*.265*	*68*	

The Sox, unfortunate winners of the Darren Lewis sweepstakes (Enter now! You'll be an instant loser!), could at least count their blessings in having retained Martinez. After Lewis' shortcomings became obvious, Martinez wound up starting 64 games in center, almost all after the All-Star break. Although he's been a top-notch spare part for the Sox, the rest of his career outside of has been decidedly mediocre. He's a good candidate to crash and burn.

FRANK MENECHINO   **2B**   **1971**   **Age 26**

Year	Team	Lge	AB	H	DB	TP	HR	BB	SB	CS	OUT	BA	OBA	SA	EQA	EQR	Peak
1993	Hickory	SAtl	190	49	3	2	4	25	4	1	142	.258	.344	.358	.241	20	.267
1994	South Bend	Midw	399	107	15	3	5	65	7	3	295	.268	.371	.358	.251	46	.272
1995	Pr. William	Caro	511	138	27	3	7	91	4	1	374	.270	.380	.376	.259	64	.277
1996	Birmingham	South	430	122	17	2	12	55	5	5	313	.284	.365	.416	.262	55	.276
1997	*Chi. White Sox*	*AL*	*526*	*143*	*28*	*3*	*17*	*82*	*6*	*4*	*387*	*.272*	*.370*	*.433*	*.277*	*78*	

This projection is a tad bit optimistic side, because mighty mite Menechino (5' 9") isn't likely to get the playing time with Durham around. He's old for a prospect, so his best shot is to be a throw-in in a deal that gets him to an organization that wants a man aboard the basepaths for its second baseman.

LYLE MOUTON   **OF**   **1969**   **Age 28**

Year	Team	Lge	AB	H	DB	TP	HR	BB	SB	CS	OUT	BA	OBA	SA	EQA	EQR	Peak
1993	Albany-NY	East	504	124	14	2	16	46	11	7	387	.246	.309	.377	.229	49	.245
1994	Albany-NY	East	285	86	12	1	12	25	5	3	202	.302	.358	.477	.276	41	.292
1994	Columbus-OH	Inter	208	64	12	4	4	14	3	1	145	.308	.351	.462	.272	28	.288
1995	Nashville	AmA	273	80	9	0	10	26	10	3	196	.293	.355	.436	.268	36	.279
1995	Chi. White Sox	AL	182	58	13	0	7	19	1	0	124	.319	.383	.505	.295	29	.305
1996	Chi. White Sox	AL	216	66	9	1	7	23	3	0	150	.306	.372	.454	.279	31	.286
1997	*Chi. White Sox*	*AL*	*349*	*97*	*17*	*1*	*16*	*35*	*5*	*1*	*253*	*.278*	*.344*	*.470*	*.279*	*52*	

The man who should have been the starting right fielder for the Sox all season, and like so many other things with the '96 Sox, a wasted opportunity. Mouton is an articulate, cheery player, so he's an oddity among the Sox. He's got a definite "Hriniak" swing that suits him well because he isn't really a power hitter. Although he lacks range in the field, he's got a good arm.

GREG NORTON   **3B/SS**   **1973**   **Age 24**

Year	Team	Lge	AB	H	DB	TP	HR	BB	SB	CS	OUT	BA	OBA	SA	EQA	EQR	Peak
1993	Hickory	SAtl	269	58	7	1	4	31	0	1	212	.216	.297	.294	.194	17	.220
1994	South Bend	Midw	494	126	13	1	6	52	2	1	369	.255	.326	.322	.220	42	.246
1995	Birmingham	South	488	121	17	2	7	62	13	7	373	.248	.333	.334	.228	46	.251
1996	Birmingham	South	295	81	9	2	8	28	4	3	217	.275	.337	.400	.247	33	.269
1996	Nashville	AmA	170	49	11	2	7	18	2	2	123	.288	.356	.500	.279	25	.304
1997	*Chi. White Sox*	*AL*	*378*	*99*	*19*	*2*	*15*	*39*	*7*	*4*	*283*	*.262*	*.331*	*.442*	*.265*	*51*	

A switch-hitter, Norton has been developed in the same fashion as Snopek was. A third baseman by trade, the Sox started using him at shortstop at the higher levels. It's an interesting organizational approach, because it gives the young player a shot at making the major league team as a utility player, or it gives him the easier task of trying to win playing time from the execrable Ozzie Guillen instead of Robin Ventura. Unfortunately, it just doesn't work out that way at the major league level.

MAGGLIO ORDONEZ   **OF**   **1974**   **Age 23**

Year	Team	Lge	AB	H	DB	TP	HR	BB	SB	CS	OUT	BA	OBA	SA	EQA	EQR	Peak
1993	Hickory	SAtl	284	54	8	1	4	19	2	2	232	.190	.241	.268	.156	11	.180
1994	Hickory	SAtl	509	134	15	2	10	38	7	3	378	.263	.314	.360	.228	47	.259
1995	Pr. William	Caro	507	124	18	2	12	39	7	3	386	.245	.299	.359	.221	44	.247
1996	Birmingham	South	491	127	22	0	19	31	7	6	370	.259	.303	.420	.239	51	.263

He isn't one of the prospects you hear about, but Ordonez looks like a nice little hitter. He's short, so he doesn't make prospect lists, but he can handle both outfield corners and was second in the Southern League in doubles.

TONY PHILLIPS   **LF**   **1959**   **Age 38**

Year	Team	Lge	AB	H	DB	TP	HR	BB	SB	CS	OUT	BA	OBA	SA	EQA	EQR	Peak
1993	Detroit	AL	582	193	18	0	13	138	16	8	397	.332	.460	.430	.307	104	.292
1994	Detroit	AL	441	125	19	2	20	95	12	4	320	.283	.410	.472	.295	76	.280
1995	California	AL	532	145	19	1	31	116	13	10	397	.273	.403	.487	.291	91	.277
1996	Chi. White Sox	AL	589	170	30	3	13	127	14	8	427	.289	.415	.416	.283	91	.269
1997	*Chi. White Sox*	*AL*	*597*	*143*	*21*	*2*	*12*	*133*	*12*	*9*	*463*	*.240*	*.378*	*.342*	*.256*	*76*	

What a season for Tony Phillips: retiring in spring training because of a meager contract, punching out a bigoted fan in Milwaukee, missing team autograph day, sparring with his manager. If the White Sox were looking for personality, they got it.

Hardly a week went by locally without an amazing diving catch by Tony Phillips. You can take that as impressive, or as a warning sign of the Dauer Effect: when a player is regularly making diving plays, it's probably a sign that he won't be making those plays when he gets older. As you can see from the projection, Phillips could start becoming less effective pronto. His speed is almost shot, and slugging under .400 while playing everyday should be considered a warning sign as well. Still, with his patience at the plate and his flexibility in playing several positions, Phillips is still one of the best lead-off hitters in the game.

One of the best reasons to fire a manager is when he puts his personality conflict with a player ahead of the good of the team, or lets it affect his judgment about putting the best team on the field. By all accounts, Terry Bevington wants Tony Phillips gone at any price, and with the acquisition of Albert Belle, Phillips is probably on the block.

MIKE ROBERTSON   **1B**   **1971**   **Age 26**

Year	Team	Lge	AB	H	DB	TP	HR	BB	SB	CS	OUT	BA	OBA	SA	EQA	EQR	Peak
1993	Birmingham	South	535	147	25	2	12	56	7	3	391	.275	.343	.396	.250	61	.276
1994	Birmingham	South	207	64	16	1	4	30	3	1	144	.309	.397	.454	.287	32	.312
1994	Nashville	AmA	213	46	6	0	8	17	0	2	169	.216	.274	.357	.204	16	.221
1995	Nashville	AmA	509	127	14	3	19	54	2	3	385	.250	.321	.401	.240	54	.257
1996	Nashville	AmA	462	121	14	2	20	42	1	2	343	.262	.323	.431	.249	53	.263

Imagine you're the big kid who always battered your Little League to pieces. Imagine the misfortune of finding out that there are people bigger and better than you'll ever be at the only position you can play. This sadness can lead to depression, weight gain and a career in insurance sales. So, give to the Victims of the Existence of Frank Thomas. Don't let another innocent suffer the fate of Scott Cepicky.

Robertson has been released, and despite having as much talent as cross-town hack Brant Brown, has zero future. Like all of these guys, he's supposed to field well, and he would probably even outhit Mike Squires. Once in awhile, a guy like this can wind up getting playing time (Wes Parker comes to mind), but that takes a lot of luck.

PETE ROSE Jr.   **3B**   **1970**   **Age 27**

Year	Team	Lge	AB	H	DB	TP	HR	BB	SB	CS	OUT	BA	OBA	SA	EQA	EQR	Peak
1993	Kinston	Caro	293	57	7	1	5	23	1	1	237	.195	.253	.276	.166	13	.180
1994	Hickory	SAtl	118	22	2	1	0	11	0	0	96	.186	.256	.220	.139	3	.149
1994	Pr. William	Caro	153	40	2	1	3	15	0	0	113	.261	.327	.346	.228	14	.243
1995	South Bend	Midw	442	111	16	3	5	43	1	0	331	.251	.318	.335	.220	38	.232
1996	Birmingham	South	408	94	10	1	3	26	1	1	315	.230	.276	.282	.182	22	.189

Ex-scab in an organization that won't begrudge him that. Carrying on the fine traditions of the Rose family in baseball, Pete Jr. was given his first extended taste of AA as a reward for his rallying to the owners' banner in the spring of '95. He won't be beating anyone out for a job based on what he does on the field.

OLMEDO SAENZ 3B 1971 Age 26

Year	Team	Lge	AB	H	DB	TP	HR	BB	SB	CS	OUT	BA	OBA	SA	EQA	EQR	Peak
1993	South Bend	Midw	52	16	3	1	0	6	0	0	36	.308	.379	.404	.267	7	.299
1993	Sarasota	Flor	123	30	7	2	1	8	2	1	93	.244	.290	.358	.218	10	.241
1993	Birmingham	South	183	65	12	2	7	19	1	1	119	.355	.416	.557	.318	34	.351
1994	Nashville	AmA	385	97	20	1	13	32	2	1	289	.252	.309	.410	.239	40	.260
1995	Nashville	AmA	427	130	18	1	15	49	0	2	299	.304	.376	.457	.277	60	.297
1996	Nashville	AmA	492	130	22	1	18	56	4	2	364	.264	.339	.423	.254	59	.268
1997	*Chi. White Sox*	*AL*	*328*	*88*	*19*	*1*	*14*	*36*	*0*	*2*	*242*	*.268*	*.341*	*.460*	*.271*	*46*	

Saenz was named the best defensive third baseman in the American Association and would be a very solid option at third for those teams that aren't lucky enough to have a Robin Ventura floating around. It'll be a shame if Saenz has to remain in the minors much longer.

BRIAN SIMMONS OF 1974 Age 23

Year	Team	Lge	AB	H	DB	TP	HR	BB	SB	CS	OUT	BA	OBA	SA	EQA	EQR	Peak
1995	Hickory	SAtl	170	28	2	1	2	16	2	2	144	.165	.237	.224	.128	4	.145
1996	South Bend	Midw	373	106	15	2	16	37	8	5	272	.284	.349	.464	.268	51	.296
1996	Pr. William	Caro	133	24	2	2	3	8	1	0	109	.180	.227	.293	.162	6	.178
1997	*Chi. White Sox*	*AL*	*454*	*114*	*24*	*2*	*19*	*44*	*9*	*6*	*346*	*.251*	*.317*	*.438*	*.257*	*58*	

A second-round pick from the University of Michigan in '95, Simmons has impressed the organization with his early strides in mastering hitting with wood. He should move up to AA in '97.

DON SLAUGHT C 1959 Age 38

Year	Team	Lge	AB	H	DB	TP	HR	BB	SB	CS	OUT	BA	OBA	SA	EQA	EQR	Peak
1993	Pittsburgh	NL	385	117	17	2	11	35	2	1	269	.304	.362	.444	.271	51	.257
1994	Pittsburgh	NL	245	71	5	0	3	38	0	0	174	.290	.385	.347	.254	28	.242
1995	Pittsburgh	NL	113	34	5	0	0	11	0	0	79	.301	.363	.345	.244	12	.233
1996	California	AL	208	68	6	0	7	13	0	0	140	.327	.367	.457	.277	28	.263
1997	*Chi. White Sox*	*AL*	*244*	*67*	*6*	*0*	*7*	*23*	*0*	*0*	*177*	*.275*	*.337*	*.385*	*.249*	*28*	

Although the onslaught of Don Slaught moves about as quickly as a knee-capped sloth, the man is still a good hitter. If the Sox choose to re-sign him, he'll be an excellent offense/defense platoon mate with Karkovice.

CHRIS SNOPEK IF 1971 Age 26

Year	Team	Lge	AB	H	DB	TP	HR	BB	SB	CS	OUT	BA	OBA	SA	EQA	EQR	Peak
1993	South Bend	Midw	77	28	4	1	4	12	1	0	49	.364	.449	.597	.343	17	.380
1993	Sarasota	Flor	385	91	13	1	12	57	2	1	295	.236	.335	.369	.237	40	.260
1994	Birmingham	South	382	98	20	2	7	56	5	2	286	.257	.352	.374	.247	43	.268
1995	Nashville	AmA	407	132	19	3	13	53	3	4	279	.324	.402	.482	.293	65	.314
1995	Chi. White Sox	AL	69	24	4	0	1	9	1	0	45	.348	.423	.449	.300	11	.319
1996	Nashville	AmA	159	40	3	0	3	22	2	2	121	.252	.343	.327	.227	15	.239
1996	Chi. White Sox	AL	105	28	6	2	6	6	0	1	78	.267	.306	.533	.267	14	.281
1997	*Chi. White Sox*	*AL*	*412*	*108*	*25*	*1*	*23*	*76*	*3*	*2*	*306*	*.262*	*.377*	*.495*	*.294*	*72*	

After being named the top prospect in the organization, he was treated in a fashion only Lou Piniella or Cito Gaston could truly appreciate: jerked in and out of the lineup, up and down from the minors, benched, cajoled and when playing, embarrassing the organization by outperforming Ozzie Guillen. The way Terry Bevington handled Snopek showed that Bev is ready to take his place with the masters when it comes to handling young hitting talent. He's considered a great defensive third baseman, and he didn't embarrass himself at short. The future is now for Snopek.

DANNY TARTABULL RF 1963 Age 34

Year	Team	Lge	AB	H	DB	TP	HR	BB	SB	CS	OUT	BA	OBA	SA	EQA	EQR	Peak
1993	NY Yankees	AL	528	144	33	2	39	97	0	0	384	.273	.386	.564	.304	98	.298
1994	NY Yankees	AL	407	110	21	1	22	67	1	1	298	.270	.373	.489	.283	63	.273
1995	NY Yankees	AL	193	44	8	0	8	34	0	0	149	.228	.344	.394	.246	22	.235
1995	Oakland	AL	90	25	3	0	3	10	0	2	67	.278	.350	.411	.249	10	.238
1996	Chi. White Sox	AL	477	126	25	3	28	65	1	2	353	.264	.352	.505	.278	72	.264
1997	*Chi. White Sox*	*AL*	*477*	*113*	*31*	*2*	*18*	*78*	*2*	*4*	*368*	*.237*	*.344*	*.423*	*.261*	*64*	

Danny Tartabull probably had the softest 100 RBI season ever. Since he didn't bother to start hitting well until the second half, when the pitching staff was a flaming wreck and the Sox were spiraling out of contention, his real contribution to the team wasn't even close to his season totals. However, playing the field for the first time for an entire season, he wasn't as bad as you'd think, although his arm was run on early and often. Whatever team signs him will regret it.

FRANK THOMAS 1B 1968 Age 29

Year	Team	Lge	AB	H	DB	TP	HR	BB	SB	CS	OUT	BA	OBA	SA	EQA	EQR	Peak
1993	Chi. White Sox	AL	564	189	31	0	50	117	4	1	376	.335	.449	.656	.350	136	.369
1994	Chi. White Sox	AL	408	149	28	1	42	111	2	3	262	.365	.501	.748	.386	121	.401
1995	Chi. White Sox	AL	504	163	24	0	46	140	3	2	343	.323	.470	.645	.354	128	.363
1996	Chi. White Sox	AL	536	193	22	0	44	111	1	1	344	.360	.470	.647	.357	131	.361
1997	*Chi. White Sox*	*AL*	*527*	*181*	*23*	*0*	*46*	*149*	*1*	*1*	*347*	*.343*	*.488*	*.649*	*.373*	*148*	

Thomas is still violently unpopular with carpenters for his unapologetic attitude towards having scabs build his home. It isn't a big deal, but it is symbolic of organizational unwillingness to apologize for anything. Thomas has been working hard to match Albert Belle's reputation for pointless surliness: he petulantly stopped talking to the media after it was mentioned that he went berserk after an ejection, going after Robin Ventura in the dugout for some unexplained reason. Not much was made of it in the press, certainly nothing to rival New York Post yellow journalism, but Thomas overreacted and pouted.

As far as baseball was concerned, Thomas really has improved light years in the field. He's still an awful fielder, but he's almost mastered the Steve Garvey "Pillar of Salt" technique.

JUAN THOMAS 1B 1972 Age 25

Year	Team	Lge	AB	H	DB	TP	HR	BB	SB	CS	OUT	BA	OBA	SA	EQA	EQR	Peak
1993	Hickory	SAtl	342	72	5	2	11	26	1	2	272	.211	.266	.333	.194	23	.218
1994	South Bend	Midw	455	105	11	2	15	22	2	2	352	.231	.266	.363	.206	34	.228
1995	Pr. William	Caro	483	119	15	2	25	38	3	3	367	.246	.301	.441	.243	54	.264
1996	Pr. William	Caro	510	140	11	3	17	47	4	2	372	.275	.336	.408	.250	58	.267

Four years in A ball is no way to earn prospect status. Nevertheless, his steady improvement up to this age means that he'll enjoy the best season of his life in Birmingham within the next two years, after which he can look forward to learning how to sell cars.

MARIO VALDEZ 1B 1975 Age 22

Year	Team	Lge	AB	H	DB	TP	HR	BB	SB	CS	OUT	BA	OBA	SA	EQA	EQR	Peak
1995	Hickory	SAtl	469	117	17	2	11	55	4	3	355	.249	.328	.365	.233	46	.265
1996	South Bend	Midw	214	75	8	0	10	29	1	2	141	.350	.428	.528	.315	39	.353
1996	Birmingham	South	175	47	9	0	4	27	0	0	128	.269	.366	.389	.256	21	.287
1997	*Chi. White Sox*	*AL*	*483*	*143*	*20*	*1*	*13*	*89*	*2*	*3*	*343*	*.296*	*.406*	*.422*	*.289*	*77*	

Another in the long list of people waiting for reincarnation with another organization, preferably of the Big Hurt-less variety. He has experience in the outfield, and has expressed an interest in catching. Smart guy. Valdez had an amazing first half with South Bend, and was named the best player on the team by the organization.

KERRY VALRIE   **OF**   **1969**   **Age 28**

Year	Team	Lge	AB	H	DB	TP	HR	BB	SB	CS	OUT	BA	OBA	SA	EQA	EQR	Peak
1993	Sarasota	Flor	390	79	7	1	12	16	11	4	315	.203	.234	.318	.181	22	.194
1994	Birmingham	South	436	121	22	2	4	35	16	5	320	.278	.331	.365	.240	45	.253
1995	Nashville	AmA	553	136	26	2	8	45	22	12	429	.246	.303	.344	.219	48	.228
1996	Nashville	AmA	510	139	28	3	13	33	10	7	378	.273	.317	.416	.244	56	.250

He's been mentioned as a prospect, and is usually held up as an example of a player who hurt his chances at the majors by scabbing. The problem is that he isn't a prospect, and you can't hurt your chance of getting something you'll never earn.

ROBIN VENTURA   **3B**   **1968**   **Age 29**

Year	Team	Lge	AB	H	DB	TP	HR	BB	SB	CS	OUT	BA	OBA	SA	EQA	EQR	Peak
1993	Chi. White Sox	AL	565	156	26	1	27	110	2	4	413	.276	.394	.469	.285	90	.301
1994	Chi. White Sox	AL	407	119	15	1	19	61	3	1	289	.292	.385	.474	.286	63	.297
1995	Chi. White Sox	AL	500	155	19	0	30	77	4	3	348	.310	.402	.528	.304	89	.311
1996	Chi. White Sox	AL	593	176	32	2	36	79	1	3	420	.297	.379	.540	.297	101	.300
1997	*Chi. White Sox*	*AL*	*561*	*157*	*22*	*1*	*29*	*100*	*2*	*3*	*407*	*.280*	*.389*	*.478*	*.295*	*96*	

The best third baseman in the AL, in franchise history, and the target of some of the most idiotic kvetching you'll ever hear about a great player. The foul Reinsdorf, unwilling to blame his staff for the attendance problems and on-field failures, spent his time taking potshots at Ventura in a September 20th interview: "He's kind of a laid-back guy... I think we need to get people with a little bit better personality." What the hell was that all about? This kind of dopey criticism only indicates an organization looking for scapegoats, and in the fine tradition of blaming great players, Ventura's the man.

JULIO VINAS   **C**   **1973**   **Age 24**

Year	Team	Lge	AB	H	DB	TP	HR	BB	SB	CS	OUT	BA	OBA	SA	EQA	EQR	Peak
1993	South Bend	Midw	193	57	7	1	7	9	1	0	136	.295	.327	.451	.260	23	.296
1993	Sarasota	Flor	66	15	1	1	1	5	0	0	51	.227	.282	.318	.198	4	.225
1994	South Bend	Midw	478	108	15	1	9	36	0	1	371	.226	.280	.318	.196	32	.219
1995	Birmingham	South	385	102	11	2	7	37	2	2	285	.265	.329	.358	.232	37	.257
1996	Nashville	AmA	348	83	16	2	10	38	1	3	268	.239	.313	.382	.230	34	.249

It was a bit of a surprise that Machado leapt past Vinas when Chad Kreuter went down. Vinas had already beaten out Scott Vollmer for the job as the starting catcher at AAA Nashville, so he might have expected to be the organization's top internal replacement. He isn't much of a hitter and his defensive reputation isn't outstanding, so he's gotten as far as he'll get: third catcher.

SCOTT VOLLMER   **C**   **1971**   **Age 26**

Year	Team	Lge	AB	H	DB	TP	HR	BB	SB	CS	OUT	BA	OBA	SA	EQA	EQR	Peak
1994	Hickory	SAtl	436	106	15	1	7	33	0	0	330	.243	.296	.330	.209	33	.226
1995	Birmingham	South	270	64	3	0	6	40	0	0	206	.237	.335	.315	.220	24	.236
1996	Birmingham	South	370	93	11	0	6	26	0	0	277	.251	.301	.330	.211	28	.222

He had a fine spring in '96, and carries a good defensive reputation. However, he was passed up by his rival, Vinas, last season, so the Sox have obviously started losing interest. The player to be named later in the Don Slaught deal, Vollmer is now Angels' property.

CRAIG WILSON   **IF**   **1971**   **Age 26**

Year	Team	Lge	AB	H	DB	TP	HR	BB	SB	CS	OUT	BA	OBA	SA	EQA	EQR	Peak
1993	South Bend	Midw	471	108	17	1	5	38	2	2	365	.229	.287	.301	.194	30	.214
1994	Pr. William	Caro	517	127	29	2	3	50	1	1	391	.246	.312	.327	.214	42	.233
1995	Birmingham	South	488	139	14	1	5	43	1	1	350	.285	.343	.348	.236	47	.253
1996	Birmingham	South	210	58	3	0	4	35	1	1	153	.276	.380	.348	.250	24	.264
1996	Nashville	AmA	125	22	3	1	1	11	0	0	103	.176	.243	.240	.141	4	.148

Although he has fairly good patience, Wilson is old, grounds into far too many double plays, and is probably going to be moved to second. No prospect.

WILSON ALVAREZ   **LSP**   **1970**   **Age 27**

YR	Team	Lge	IP	H	ER	HR	BB	K	ERA	W	L	H/9	HR/9	BB/9	K/9	KW
1993	Chi. White Sox	AL	204.7	172	64	15	132	161	2.81	15	8	7.56	.66	5.80	7.08	.91
1994	Chi. White Sox	AL	159.7	146	56	15	67	106	3.16	11	7	8.23	.85	3.78	5.97	1.05
1995	Chi. White Sox	AL	175.7	167	76	20	97	119	3.89	10	10	8.56	1.02	4.97	6.10	.79
1996	Chi. White Sox	AL	216.7	211	82	18	103	177	3.41	14	10	8.76	.75	4.28	7.35	1.38

One of baseball's great pitchers, Alvarez continued his wacky ways, this time having a great first half followed by a mediocre second half. He led AL left-handers in quality starts and quality starts as a percentage of starts (20/35). His curve can be devastating, and he's always entertaining to watch.

JAMES BALDWIN   **RSP**   **1972**   **Age 25**

YR	Team	Lge	IP	H	ER	HR	BB	K	ERA	W	L	H/9	HR/9	BB/9	K/9	KW
1993	Birmingham	South	108.7	117	51	7	58	80	4.22	6	6	9.69	.58	4.80	6.63	1.01
1993	Nashville	AmA	65.3	46	17	5	44	56	2.34	5	2	6.34	.69	6.06	7.71	1.06
1994	Nashville	AmA	156.0	143	62	15	98	138	3.58	9	8	8.25	.87	5.65	7.96	1.24
1995	Nashville	AmA	93.3	123	71	26	58	79	6.85	3	7	11.86	2.51	5.59	7.62	1.14
1995	Chi. White Sox	AL	15.7	30	17	5	10	10	9.77	0	2	17.23	2.87	5.74	5.74	.48
1996	Chi. White Sox	AL	168.3	164	68	21	61	124	3.64	10	9	8.77	1.12	3.26	6.63	1.39

Baldwin finally broke through when the Sox finally tiring of the Magrane-McCaskill disaster. As good as Alvarez' breaking stuff is, Baldwin's is better. With Uncle Charlie and a good heater, he works high in the strike zone, which is perfect for roomy Comiskey Park. He tired badly in the last two months of the season, but there are no concerns about his health.

JASON BERE   **RSP**   **1971**   **Age 26**

YR	Team	Lge	IP	H	ER	HR	BB	K	ERA	W	L	H/9	HR/9	BB/9	K/9	KW
1993	Nashville	AmA	46.7	39	16	1	30	48	3.09	3	2	7.52	.19	5.79	9.26	1.64
1993	Chi. White Sox	AL	140.7	112	49	13	87	133	3.14	10	6	7.17	.83	5.57	8.51	1.44
1994	Chi. White Sox	AL	140.3	118	50	16	85	125	3.21	10	6	7.57	1.03	5.45	8.02	1.31
1995	Chi. White Sox	AL	140.3	145	97	19	110	111	6.22	5	11	9.30	1.22	7.05	7.12	.61
1996	Nashville	AmA	12.0	10	2	1	6	12	1.50	1	0	7.50	.75	4.50	9.00	1.87
1996	Chi. White Sox	AL	17.7	24	15	3	18	19	7.64	0	2	12.23	1.53	9.17	9.68	.93

Considering the public blame game that surrounded whether his elbow was injured or if he had become Steve Blass, we may never see Jason Bere again. He had major surgery on his elbow near season's end, and even at his most successful, he had serious problems with control, holding baserunners and keeping the ball in the park. His breaking stuff was never that outstanding, and the injury may well take his fastball away.

MIKE BERTOTTI   **LBP**   **1970**   **Age 27**

YR	Team	Lge	IP	H	ER	HR	BB	K	ERA	W	L	H/9	HR/9	BB/9	K/9	KW
1993	Hickory	SAtl	51.7	57	22	3	40	45	3.83	3	3	9.93	.52	6.97	7.84	.87
1993	South Bend	Midw	97.7	117	53	6	59	63	4.88	4	7	10.78	.55	5.44	5.81	.58
1994	Pr. William	Caro	92.7	116	51	12	58	70	4.95	4	6	11.27	1.17	5.63	6.80	.86
1994	Birmingham	South	62.3	64	26	2	32	35	3.75	4	3	9.24	.29	4.62	5.05	.53
1995	Birmingham	South	57.7	71	40	5	46	41	6.24	2	4	11.08	.78	7.18	6.40	.34
1995	Nashville	AmA	31.3	42	31	8	22	31	8.90	1	2	12.06	2.30	6.32	8.90	1.39
1996	Nashville	AmA	79.0	88	42	10	55	61	4.78	4	5	10.03	1.14	6.27	6.95	.75
1996	Chi. White Sox	AL	28.0	28	14	4	20	19	4.50	1	2	9.00	1.29	6.43	6.11	.43

He's considered to have an above-average fastball for a left-hander, so he gets kept around despite the lack of success. It's possible that because he's a lefty and hasn't seriously hurt himself yet, he'll be around forever, and may break through with a pitching coach who knows what to do with him. It's also possible I might start eating avocados despite a passionate loathing for them.

TONY CASTILLO **LRP** **1963** **Age 34**

YR	Team	Lge	IP	H	ER	HR	BB	K	ERA	W	L	H/9	HR/9	BB/9	K/9	KW
1993	Toronto	AL	49.7	45	15	4	24	29	2.72	4	2	8.15	.72	4.35	5.26	.66
1994	Toronto	AL	67.3	65	17	6	30	42	2.27	5	2	8.69	.80	4.01	5.61	.87
1995	Toronto	AL	71.7	64	20	6	26	38	2.51	6	2	8.04	.75	3.27	4.77	.77
1996	Toronto	AL	72.0	67	27	8	21	46	3.38	5	3	8.38	1.00	2.62	5.75	1.26
1996	Chi. White Sox	AL	22.3	23	5	1	4	9	2.01	2	0	9.27	.40	1.61	3.63	.81

As a stretch move, few things were attacked more often than the Sox' acquisition of Castillo. The criticism came from the disappointment that the organization hadn't gone out and acquired people the way the Indians had, or the Yankees or the Orioles. To be fair to Castillo, he's one of the best left-handed long relievers in the game today. His arm is durable. Although '96 was the heaviest workload of his career, because he isn't being used as a spot reliever—being warmed up and shut down repeatedly over a week—he can probably handle the workload better than most. His stuff isn't outstanding, but he succeeds at his role, is durable and is now old enough now to not have to worry about being judged by his tools.

NELSON CRUZ **RBP** **1973** **Age 24**

YR	TEAM	Lge	IP	H	ER	HR	BB	K	ERA	W	L	H/9	HR/9	BB/9	K/9	KW
1995	Hickory	S Atl	56.7	94	40	8	24	39	6.35	2	4	14.93	1.27	3.81	6.19	1.11
1995	Pr. William	Caro	17.7	15	1	1	9	13	.51	2	0	7.64	.51	4.58	6.62	1.06
1996	Birmingham	South	137.0	175	64	12	49	103	4.20	7	8	11.50	.79	3.22	6.77	1.45

He literally came out of nowhere, pitching for the Expos in '91 and then disappearing until '95. I have no idea what his pitches are, but his strikeout rate was outstanding.

JEFF DARWIN **RBP** **1970** **Age 27**

YR	Team	Lge	IP	H	ER	HR	BB	K	ERA	W	L	H/9	HR/9	BB/9	K/9	KW
1993	Jacksonville	South	33.0	34	17	1	22	29	4.64	2	2	9.27	.27	6.00	7.91	1.14
1993	Edmonton	PCL	28.7	45	26	5	13	17	8.16	1	2	14.13	1.57	4.08	5.34	.76
1994	Calgary	PCL	66.0	56	22	8	34	46	3.00	4	3	7.64	1.09	4.64	6.27	.93
1995	Tacoma	PCL	58.7	57	19	3	26	47	2.91	5	2	8.74	.46	3.99	7.21	1.41
1996	Nashville	AmA	60.0	58	30	8	25	27	4.50	3	4	8.70	1.20	3.75	4.05	.41
1996	Chi. White Sox	AL	30.3	25	8	5	10	15	2.37	2	1	7.42	1.48	2.97	4.45	.74

The younger brother of Danny Darwin, and the compensation for Warren Newson. He's got a good heater and good breaking stuff that snaps in on the hands of left-handed batters. He was a good prospect with Seattle, and his performance down the stretch, as the rest of the pitching staff collapsed, should earn him a spot ahead of Matt Karchner or Bill Simas.

SCOTT EYRE **LSP** **1972** **Age 25**

YR	Team	Lge	IP	H	ER	HR	BB	K	ERA	W	L	H/9	HR/9	BB/9	K/9	KW
1993	Charleston,SC	SAtl	124.3	152	83	9	82	91	6.01	4	10	11.00	.65	5.94	6.59	.71
1994	South Bend	Midw	97.0	135	60	9	53	70	5.57	4	7	12.53	.84	4.92	6.49	.94
1996	Birmingham	South	145.3	193	87	13	92	100	5.39	6	10	11.95	.81	5.70	6.19	.64

After missing most of '95 to injury, Eyre is somebody the Sox are watching carefully. Despite pitching in Birmingham, a great pitcher's park, he didn't put up outstanding numbers. He had an AFL assignment and was lit up.

ALEX FERNANDEZ **RSP** **1970** **Age 27**

YR	Team	Lge	IP	H	ER	HR	BB	K	ERA	W	L	H/9	HR/9	BB/9	K/9	KW
1993	Chi. White Sox	AL	243.0	223	78	28	78	174	2.89	18	9	8.26	1.04	2.89	6.44	1.43
1994	Chi. White Sox	AL	169.0	160	65	23	55	120	3.46	11	8	8.52	1.22	2.93	6.39	1.40
1995	Chi. White Sox	AL	203.0	198	77	18	70	159	3.41	13	10	8.78	.80	3.10	7.05	1.57
1996	Chi. White Sox	AL	256.0	243	85	30	79	195	2.99	18	10	8.54	1.05	2.78	6.86	1.59

Fernandez is demanded a five-year contract and got it from the Marlins. A legitimate four-pitch starter, Fernandez might have been overused last year, as he led the American League in pitches per start. However, he finished strong. Fernandez stepped up this year and showed that he can be the ace starter the Sox expected him to be.

TOM FORDHAM   **LSP**   **1974**   **Age 23**

YR	Team	Lge	IP	H	ER	HR	BB	K	ERA	W	L	H/9	HR/9	BB/9	K/9	KW
1993	Hickory	SAtl	42.0	48	24	4	29	16	5.14	2	3	10.29	.86	6.21	3.43	-.41
1994	Hickory	SAtl	94.3	133	54	12	47	72	5.15	4	6	12.69	1.14	4.48	6.87	1.17
1994	South Bend	Midw	64.3	103	49	5	22	30	6.85	2	5	14.41	.70	3.08	4.20	.63
1995	Pr. William	Caro	75.7	85	23	8	47	57	2.74	5	3	10.11	.95	5.59	6.78	.86
1995	Birmingham	South	75.7	94	37	10	38	47	4.40	4	4	11.18	1.19	4.52	5.59	.73
1996	Birmingham	South	34.3	31	13	5	17	27	3.41	2	2	8.13	1.31	4.46	7.08	1.25
1996	Nashville	AmA	134.7	130	57	14	89	98	3.81	8	7	8.69	.94	5.95	6.55	.70

Success and more success, but Fordham still awaits the call. He has yet to allow more than a hit per inning pitched, has solid control, wins games hand over fist, and may have passed the better-known Scott Ruffcorn for next year's rotation.

MARVIN FREEMAN   **RBP**   **1963**   **Age 34**

YR	Team	Lge	IP	H	ER	HR	BB	K	ERA	W	L	H/9	HR/9	BB/9	K/9	KW
1993	Atlanta	NL	23.0	25	14	1	13	24	5.48	1	2	9.78	.39	5.09	9.39	1.86
1994	Colorado	NL	111.0	105	29	9	32	61	2.35	9	3	8.51	.73	2.59	4.95	1.00
1995	Colorado	NL	95.0	107	47	12	47	53	4.45	5	6	10.14	1.14	4.45	5.02	.56
1996	Colorado	NL	129.7	130	71	17	66	60	4.93	6	8	9.02	1.18	4.58	4.16	.24

If anyone will give him a shot, he can still help a team as a spot starter, long reliever or even fifth rotation starter. He's an extreme groundball pitcher, which contributed to his success in Coors. In a bigger ballpark, he'll be a useful addition to several teams.

STEVE GAJKOWSKI   **RRP**   **1970**   **Age 27**

YR	Team	Lge	IP	H	ER	HR	BB	K	ERA	W	L	H/9	HR/9	BB/9	K/9	KW
1993	Sarasota	Flor	61.3	65	22	2	25	35	3.23	4	3	9.54	.29	3.67	5.14	.79
1994	Birmingham	South	74.3	92	38	8	39	35	4.60	3	5	11.14	.97	4.72	4.24	.23
1995	Birmingham	South	48.0	73	28	5	22	22	5.25	2	3	13.69	.94	4.12	4.12	.34
1995	Nashville	AmA	23.0	30	15	2	11	11	5.87	1	2	11.74	.78	4.30	4.30	.36
1996	Nashville	AmA	102.0	126	61	10	56	39	5.38	4	7	11.12	.88	4.94	3.44	-.09

He doesn't fool too many people one way or another, but he's got health and a rubber arm, so he could turn up somewhere.

RUSS HERBERT   **RSP**   **1972**   **Age 25**

YR	Team	Lge	IP	H	ER	HR	BB	K	ERA	W	L	H/9	HR/9	BB/9	K/9	KW
1994	Hickory	SAtl	31.3	44	16	3	22	20	4.60	1	2	12.64	.86	6.32	5.74	.34
1995	Hickory	SAtl	100.0	112	56	12	67	66	5.04	4	7	10.08	1.08	6.03	5.94	.47
1995	South Bend	Midw	46.0	61	28	4	36	31	5.48	2	3	11.93	.78	7.04	6.07	.26
1996	Pr. William	Caro	127.3	160	80	14	84	102	5.65	5	9	11.31	.99	5.94	7.21	.92

Considered a tough-luck pitcher because his career record stands at 13-24, Herbert is probably a great sleeper with room for growth. He just took up the slider this year after leading the entire organization in strikeouts in '95. He had some trouble with tendinitis this year, and since that's the mystery injury, there's no telling if it's serious or not.

ROBERTO HERNANDEZ   **RRP**   **1965**   **Age 32**

YR	Team	Lge	IP	H	ER	HR	BB	K	ERA	W	L	H/9	HR/9	BB/9	K/9	KW
1993	Chi. White Sox	AL	77.0	68	17	6	24	73	1.99	7	2	7.95	.70	2.81	8.53	2.14
1994	Chi. White Sox	AL	47.0	44	22	5	21	49	4.21	2	3	8.43	.96	4.02	9.38	2.12
1995	Chi. White Sox	AL	60.3	61	24	9	30	85	3.58	4	3	9.10	1.34	4.48	12.68	3.11
1996	Chi. White Sox	AL	83.0	67	15	2	40	83	1.63	8	1	7.27	.22	4.34	9.00	1.92

There were complaints as the season went on that Hernandez was being overused. Although you didn't get it from his pitching 84 2/3 innings, Bevington had him warming up far more often than his 72 games tell you. Hernandez came apart in September (6.59 ERA, four losses). Unlike many closers, Hernandez actually throws three different pitches: fastball, slider and forkball. In the past, that was considered part of the problem: Hernandez would get too cute with his breaking stuff, instead of just gassing batters.

BARRY JOHNSON **RRP** **1970** **Age 27**

YR	Team	Lge	IP	H	ER	HR	BB	K	ERA	W	L	H/9	HR/9	BB/9	K/9	KW
1993	Sarasota	Flor	48.0	43	5	2	13	31	0.94	5	0	8.06	.38	2.44	5.81	1.33
1994	Birmingham	South	88.7	117	56	9	46	53	5.68	3	7	11.88	.91	4.67	5.38	.63
1995	Birmingham	South	72.3	75	21	2	23	41	2.61	6	2	9.33	.25	2.86	5.10	.98
1996	Nashville	AmA	97.7	105	38	11	53	57	3.50	6	5	9.68	1.01	4.88	5.25	.53

Apparently, the front office is still mad at Johnson for his having been the first minor leaguer to refuse to participate in 1995's invitation to scab. He's been very effective as a reliever, last season's Sox were screaming for bullpen help and Johnson kills left-handed batters with his breaking stuff, albeit with only an average fastball. Why did he start the year in Birmingham, after an excellent '95 campaign? On his career, he has an ERA of 2.70 and a 3-1 K:BB ratio. He has nothing left to prove in the minors.

MATT KARCHNER **RRP** **1967** **Age 30**

YR	Team	Lge	IP	H	ER	HR	BB	K	ERA	W	L	H/9	HR/9	BB/9	K/9	KW
1993	Memphis	South	27.3	39	17	3	6	10	5.60	1	2	12.84	.99	1.98	3.29	.60
1994	Birmingham	South	39.0	43	10	0	20	23	2.31	3	1	9.92	.00	4.62	5.31	.62
1994	Nashville	AmA	24.7	19	4	0	9	17	1.46	3	0	6.93	.00	3.28	6.20	1.25
1995	Nashville	AmA	35.3	42	7	4	15	26	1.78	3	1	10.70	1.02	3.82	6.62	1.25
1995	Chi. White Sox	AL	31.7	34	6	2	12	24	1.71	3	1	9.66	.57	3.41	6.82	1.42
1996	Chi. White Sox	AL	59.7	58	33	9	43	45	4.98	3	4	8.75	1.36	6.49	6.79	.64

Karchner is rarely healthy for any length of time, but last year's injuries probably had more to do with some major weight gain, which nobody would bring up. His fastball has little movement, but the real problem last year was his slider, which usually came home looking like a beach ball.

BRIAN KEYSER **RBP** **1967** **Age 30**

YR	Team	Lge	IP	H	ER	HR	BB	K	ERA	W	L	H/9	HR/9	BB/9	K/9	KW
1993	Nashville	AmA	116.7	144	62	8	39	40	4.78	5	8	11.11	.62	3.01	3.09	.28
1994	Nashville	AmA	129.3	124	40	10	48	67	2.78	9	5	8.63	.70	3.34	4.66	.72
1995	Nashville	AmA	67.3	56	21	5	18	35	2.81	5	2	7.49	.67	2.41	4.68	.96
1995	Chi. White Sox	AL	93.0	111	43	9	29	48	4.16	5	5	10.74	.87	2.81	4.65	.85
1996	Nashville	AmA	42.3	43	10	2	18	18	2.13	4	1	9.14	.43	3.83	3.83	.32
1996	Chi. White Sox	AL	60.0	75	28	3	30	19	4.20	3	4	11.25	.45	4.50	2.85	-.17

Keyser can't dent bread with any of his pitches from an overhand delivery. He's no threat to win a regular rotation spot, because the organization won't use him outside of the garbage-innings role.

AL LEVINE **RRP** **1968** **Age 29**

YR	Team	Lge	IP	H	ER	HR	BB	K	ERA	W	L	H/9	HR/9	BB/9	K/9	KW
1993	Sarasota	Flor	141.0	203	98	11	71	101	6.26	5	11	12.96	.70	4.53	6.45	1.02
1994	Birmingham	South	103.3	138	55	9	64	74	4.79	5	6	12.02	.78	5.57	6.45	.75
1994	Nashville	AmA	23.7	33	19	2	13	21	7.23	1	2	12.55	.76	4.94	7.99	1.43
1995	Birmingham	South	67.3	72	22	2	34	52	2.94	5	2	9.62	.27	4.54	6.95	1.18
1996	Nashville	AmA	59.0	64	26	3	33	38	3.97	4	3	9.76	.46	5.03	5.80	.67
1996	Chi. White Sox	AL	18.0	22	11	1	7	12	5.50	1	1	11.00	.50	3.50	6.00	1.12

Levine was given a shot in the Sox' bullpen in the wake of the failures of Karchner and others. He generates lots of grounders with a sinking fastball. He could be a useful pitcher in middle relief, but don't expect him to become a good closer, which is how the Sox are grooming him.

JOE MAGRANE **LBP** **1965** **Age 32**

YR	Team	Lge	IP	H	ER	HR	BB	K	ERA	W	L	H/9	HR/9	BB/9	K/9	KW
1993	California	AL	47.0	48	22	4	23	25	4.21	2	3	9.19	.77	4.40	4.79	.49
1993	St. Louis	NL	113.7	133	65	16	51	37	5.15	5	8	10.53	1.27	4.04	2.93	-.03
1994	California	AL	75.0	82	48	15	53	32	5.76	3	5	9.84	1.80	6.36	3.84	-.31
1995	Ottawa	Inter	62.0	78	44	6	41	32	6.39	2	5	11.32	.87	5.95	4.65	.06
1996	Nashville	AmA	25.3	31	16	5	12	22	5.68	1	2	11.01	1.78	4.26	7.82	1.54
1996	Chi. White Sox	AL	54.7	66	36	9	26	21	5.93	2	4	10.87	1.48	4.28	3.46	.08

One of two bad ideas for the fifth starter. Magrane hasn't been a major league pitcher in years, but one of the Sox' objectives has been to cultivate "characters of the game," and when the Sox signed Magrane, that was all he had left. Whether or not this means future tryouts for Buddy Hackett or Gallagher remains to be seen.

KIRK McCASKILL   **RBP**   **1961**   **Age 36**

YR	Team	Lge	IP	H	ER	HR	BB	K	ERA	W	L	H/9	HR/9	BB/9	K/9	KW
1993	Chi. White Sox	AL	114.0	141	60	12	42	67	4.74	5	8	11.13	.95	3.32	5.29	.93
1994	Chi. White Sox	AL	52.3	51	17	6	23	36	2.92	4	2	8.77	1.03	3.96	6.19	1.07
1995	Chi. White Sox	AL	82.0	94	40	9	35	50	4.39	4	5	10.32	.99	3.84	5.49	.87
1996	Chi. White Sox	AL	52.7	68	33	5	33	27	5.64	2	4	11.62	.85	5.64	4.61	.13

Signing Kirk McCaskill was probably Ron Schueler's second-worst decision in his career, the worst being the Sammy Sosa-George Bell trade. Signed to a four-year contract, McCaskill was supposed to be the team's #3 starter for the '92 season, but wound up being successful in only one year of the contract, that as a reliever. Why he was brought back for a fifth season is curious, and was probably done sheer stubbornness. Like a zillion guys, he could be useful as a reliever, but Bevington's insistence that McCaskill could be the fifth starter was as profound a bit of ignorance of a player's track record as you'll find.

JASON OLSEN   **RSP**   **1975**   **Age 22**

YR	Team	Lge	IP	H	ER	HR	BB	K	ERA	W	L	H/9	HR/9	BB/9	K/9	KW
1996	Hickory	SAtl	23.3	26	6	2	9	17	2.31	2	1	10.03	.77	3.47	6.56	1.32
1996	South Bend	Midw	50.3	52	16	4	17	34	2.86	4	2	9.30	.72	3.04	6.08	1.27
1996	Pr. William	Caro	69.7	91	43	6	42	38	5.56	3	5	11.76	.78	5.43	4.91	.28

A juco third baseman from Napa Valley who dabbled in some pitching, Olsen was not exactly highly-regarded as a 44th-round pick in '94. He racked up 162 innings in his first year as a professional, so I wouldn't be surprised if his arm fell off this year. He was named the organization's best player at Prince William this year.

RICH PRATT   **LSP**   **1971**   **Age 26**

YR	Team	Lge	IP	H	ER	HR	BB	K	ERA	W	L	H/9	HR/9	BB/9	K/9	KW
1993	Hickory	SAtl	36.7	49	28	4	33	17	6.87	1	3	12.03	.98	8.10	4.17	-.63
1994	Hickory	SAtl	146.7	176	55	11	49	91	3.38	9	7	10.80	.67	3.01	5.58	1.11
1995	Pr. William	Caro	136.7	177	77	14	61	88	5.07	6	9	11.66	.92	4.02	5.80	.93
1996	Birmingham	South	163.0	210	85	26	47	89	4.69	8	10	11.60	1.44	2.60	4.91	.99

A big, rangy lefty, Pratt has moved very slowly up the organizational chain. Although he's shown good control and some ability as a power pitcher, a warning sign for his future is that he was extremely homer-prone in one of the best pitcher's parks in the Southern League.

SCOTT RUFFCORN   **RSP**   **1970**   **Age 27**

YR	Team	Lge	IP	H	ER	HR	BB	K	ERA	W	L	H/9	HR/9	BB/9	K/9	KW
1993	Birmingham	South	123.0	133	50	7	70	106	3.66	8	6	9.73	.51	5.12	7.76	1.30
1993	Nashville	AmA	42.3	33	13	5	12	40	2.76	3	2	7.02	1.06	2.55	8.50	2.20
1994	Nashville	AmA	157.0	145	45	5	53	127	2.58	12	5	8.31	.29	3.04	7.28	1.67
1996	Nashville	AmA	142.0	158	70	17	82	108	4.44	7	9	10.01	1.08	5.20	6.85	.98

His attempts to pitch in the majors have become almost comic. Despite time lost to injury in '95, he still has the plus fastball, balanced by a circle change and a tepid slider. He was extremely wild early in the year, but settled down as it went along. At some point, the Sox are either going to pitch him or get tired of saving the spot on the 40-man roster for him. Rod Bolton's fate of being sold to Japan isn't too far off if Ruffcorn doesn't win a job this spring.

STEVE SCHRENK   **RSP**   **1969**   **Age 28**

YR	Team	Lge	IP	H	ER	HR	BB	K	ERA	W	L	H/9	HR/9	BB/9	K/9	KW
1993	Birmingham	South	56.0	42	10	3	12	38	1.61	5	1	6.75	.48	1.93	6.11	1.55
1993	Nashville	AmA	116.7	120	53	11	60	72	4.09	6	7	9.26	.85	4.63	5.55	.69
1994	Nashville	AmA	171.7	174	68	16	85	119	3.57	11	8	9.12	.84	4.46	6.24	.97
1996	Nashville	AmA	91.0	103	53	12	42	48	5.24	4	6	10.19	1.19	4.15	4.75	.54

He's finally recovered from his arm injuries, just in time for everyone to notice there isn't much left. It's fate, and it happens to the vast majority of bean-hurling bipeds.

BILL SIMAS **RRP** **1972** **Age 25**

YR	Team	Lge	IP	H	ER	HR	BB	K	ERA	W	L	H/9	HR/9	BB/9	K/9	KW
1993	Cedar Rapids	Midw	67.7	119	67	10	48	37	8.91	1	7	15.83	1.33	6.38	4.92	.04
1994	Lake Elsinore	Calif	42.3	51	16	2	14	22	3.40	3	2	10.84	.43	2.98	4.68	.81
1994	Midland	Texas	14.0	7	0	0	3	9	.00	2	0	4.50	.00	1.93	5.79	1.45
1995	Vancouver	PCL	35.3	51	19	2	18	41	4.84	2	2	12.99	.51	4.58	10.44	2.33
1995	Nashville	AmA	11.0	13	5	0	5	11	4.09	0	1	10.64	.00	4.09	9.00	1.98
1995	Chi. White Sox	AL	14.0	15	4	1	10	16	2.57	1	1	9.64	.64	6.43	10.29	1.82
1996	Chi. White Sox	AL	72.7	73	30	4	41	64	3.72	4	4	9.04	.50	5.08	7.93	1.37

Simas can be a fun pitcher to watch, although part of that could be the way he was used (usually being brought in with men on base). He'll rarely be healthy for any length of time (chronic elbow problems) and he's a bit heavy. He's not likely to enjoy a long career.

MIKE SIROTKA **LBP** **1971** **Age 26**

YR	Team	Lge	IP	H	ER	HR	BB	K	ERA	W	L	H/9	HR/9	BB/9	K/9	KW
1994	South Bend	Midw	171.0	231	106	14	83	108	5.58	6	13	12.16	.74	4.37	5.68	.80
1995	Birmingham	South	92.7	114	45	13	33	61	4.37	5	5	11.07	1.26	3.21	5.92	1.17
1995	Nashville	AmA	51.0	56	20	4	19	30	3.53	3	3	9.88	.71	3.35	5.29	.93
1995	Chi. White Sox	AL	34.3	39	13	2	18	19	3.41	2	2	10.22	.52	4.72	4.98	.48
1996	Nashville	AmA	85.3	100	43	10	36	48	4.54	4	5	10.55	1.05	3.80	5.06	.74
1996	Chi. White Sox	AL	26.7	32	21	3	13	11	7.09	1	2	10.80	1.01	4.39	3.71	.14

The Sox could probably get away with just plopping Sirotka into the rotation: he's got the classic lefty slider-fastball combo and excellent control. For whatever reason, the Sox try to give a final tryout to the Atlee Hammakers or Joe Magranes, but each of the last two years, they've come back to Sirotka as a long reliever and left-handed spot starter.

KEVIN TAPANI **RSP** **1964** **Age 33**

YR	Team	Lge	IP	H	ER	HR	BB	K	ERA	W	L	H/9	HR/9	BB/9	K/9	KW
1993	Minnesota	AL	224.3	235	99	21	67	154	3.97	13	12	9.43	.84	2.69	6.18	1.39
1994	Minnesota	AL	155.7	174	66	12	44	89	3.82	9	8	10.06	.69	2.54	5.15	1.08
1995	Minnesota	AL	134.7	145	61	19	38	88	4.08	7	8	9.69	1.27	2.54	5.88	1.33
1995	Los Angeles	NL	56.7	75	34	8	19	39	5.40	2	4	11.91	1.27	3.02	6.19	1.31
1996	Chi. White Sox	AL	225.0	228	96	30	82	146	3.84	13	12	9.12	1.20	3.28	5.84	1.13

Tapani was the most dramatic collapse down the stretch: his ERA over the last two months was 6.81. In years previous, Tapani had a reputation as someone who pitched better in the second half, so that, and his flop with the Dodgers the previous year, ends that. Overall, however, Tapani was an excellent bargain, putting up 19 quality starts. Although he has a broad repertoire of pitches, his forkball is his bread and butter. Tapani is being pursued by five different teams this off-season, with one rumor putting him in Wrigley. Moving out of spacious Comiskey would not be in his best interest. One reason he may not be back with the Sox is that Tapani was frank with the press, usually shooting down the front office's accusations of the perceived mellowness of the Sox clubhouse by pointing out that the great Twins' team he was on wasn't exactly filled with "rah-rah types." If there's one thing Jerry Reinsdorf can't tolerate, its honesty.

LARRY THOMAS **LRP** **1970** **Age 27**

YR	Team	Lge	IP	H	ER	HR	BB	K	ERA	W	L	H/9	HR/9	BB/9	K/9	KW
1993	Sarasota	Flor	54.7	62	21	5	22	21	3.46	3	3	10.21	.82	3.62	3.46	.25
1993	Nashville	AmA	97.3	114	63	14	43	62	5.83	4	7	10.54	1.29	3.98	5.73	.92
1994	Birmingham	South	130.3	185	104	20	78	61	7.18	3	11	12.77	1.38	5.39	4.21	.06
1995	Birmingham	South	37.0	30	8	0	20	36	1.95	3	1	7.30	.00	4.86	8.76	1.70
1996	Chi. White Sox	AL	30.3	32	9	1	15	20	2.67	2	1	9.49	.30	4.45	5.93	.87

Thomas was a major disappointment as a second-round draft pick in '91, totally flopping as a starter. The move to the bullpen was successful in '95, but in '96, he had a hard time adapting to major league usage patterns as a spot lefty. For his slider to be effective, he needs longer use in his outings, but expecting sensible usage of a reliever from Terry Bevington is right up there with world peace on God's list of "might happen soon."

STEVE WORRELL   **LRP**   **1970**   **Age 27**

YR	TEAM	Lge	IP	H	ER	HR	BB	K	ERA	W	L	H/9	HR/9	BB/9	K/9	KW
1993	South Bend	Midw	52.3	48	12	0	31	33	2.06	5	1	8.25	.00	5.33	5.68	.56
1994	Pr. William	Caro	42.7	48	25	6	26	32	5.27	2	3	10.12	1.27	5.48	6.75	.88
1995	Pr. William	Caro	43.3	41	11	4	11	38	2.28	4	1	8.52	.83	2.28	7.89	2.06
1995	Pr. William	Caro	47.3	47	16	6	15	40	3.04	3	2	8.94	1.14	2.85	7.61	1.82
1996	Birmingham	South	47.3	35	13	5	24	40	2.47	4	1	6.65	.95	4.56	7.61	1.39
1996	Nashville	AmA	19.0	21	8	2	8	9	3.79	1	1	9.95	.95	3.79	4.26	.47

Although Worrell isn't considered a prospect, lefties with these kinds of strikeout rates always wind up with their major league cup of coffee. Always.

Player	Age	Team	Lge	AB	H	DB	TP	HR	BB	SB	CS	OUT	BA	OBA	SA	EQA	EQR	Peak
MARK AVERY	26	Pr. William	Caro	278	60	6	1	8	27	0	0	218	.216	.285	.331	.203	20	.210
DARREN BAUGH	20	Hickory	S Atl	283	73	3	1	2	21	6	2	212	.258	.309	.297	.207	21	.236
BEN BOULWARE	24	Pr. William	Caro	451	100	8	0	5	25	7	3	354	.222	.263	.273	.174	22	.186
DAVID CANCEL	22	South Bend	Midw	322	72	4	1	2	9	6	4	254	.224	.245	.261	.159	13	.176
GLENN DISARCINA	26	Birmingham	South	179	64	7	2	7	5	2	0	115	.358	.375	.536	.303	29	.316
	26	Nashville	AmA	99	23	9	0	0	6	1	1	77	.232	.276	.323	.197	7	.203
BRIAN DOWNS	21	Hickory	S Atl	288	51	5	0	3	12	0	0	237	.177	.210	.226	.108	5	.121
BRIAN DRENT	22	South Bend	Midw	304	53	11	1	2	34	6	3	254	.174	.257	.237	.153	12	.169
JASON EVANS	25	Pr. William	Caro	343	80	12	2	4	50	2	1	264	.233	.331	.315	.219	30	.231
JOSHUA FAUSKE	22	Hickory	S Atl	437	96	7	0	9	40	0	0	341	.220	.285	.297	.191	27	.211
STEVE FRIEDRICH	23	South Bend	Midw	557	132	17	3	4	13	9	5	430	.237	.254	.300	.181	30	.197
LUIS GARCIA	20	Hickory	S Atl	300	73	12	1	3	11	4	2	229	.243	.270	.320	.196	19	.223
	20	South Bend	Midw	226	43	5	1	1	6	2	2	185	.190	.211	.235	.119	5	.137
RAMON GOMEZ	20	Hickory	S Atl	441	102	6	2	1	34	21	8	347	.231	.286	.261	.187	26	.213
CHRIS HEINTZ	21	South Bend	Midw	239	57	8	1	1	17	1	0	182	.238	.289	.293	.193	15	.215
JEFFREY JOHNSON	23	South Bend	Midw	354	57	5	0	3	15	5	3	300	.161	.195	.201	.074	2	.079
MARK JOHNSON	20	South Bend	Midw	226	53	11	2	2	30	2	1	174	.235	.324	.327	.220	20	.250
DAN KOPRIVA	26	Pr. William	Caro	351	79	9	1	7	51	0	0	272	.225	.323	.316	.215	29	.224
CHAD KREUTER	31	Chi. White Sox	AL	115	26	7	0	4	13	0	0	89	.226	.305	.391	.230	11	.221
ED LARREGUI	23	Birmingham	South	218	50	7	1	0	13	1	1	169	.229	.273	.271	.175	11	.190
CRAIG MCCLURE	20	Hickory	S Atl	222	41	6	1	2	15	2	1	182	.185	.236	.248	.144	7	.165
SANDY MCKINNON	22	Pr. William	Caro	417	98	12	3	8	21	10	5	324	.235	.272	.336	.203	30	.224
BRANDON MOORE	23	Pr. William	Caro	458	93	9	1	1	70	4	4	369	.203	.309	.234	.177	24	.193
JOSE MUNOZ	28	Nashville	AmA	301	71	13	1	6	23	7	1	231	.236	.290	.346	.216	25	.217
DAN OLSON	21	Hickory	S Atl	207	46	5	1	2	24	1	1	162	.222	.303	.285	.195	14	.219
JOSH PAUL	21	Hickory	S Atl	240	73	5	0	8	17	6	2	169	.304	.350	.425	.263	30	.295
EDDIE PEARSON	22	Birmingham	South	331	72	10	0	9	26	2	1	260	.218	.275	.329	.199	23	.219
WIL POLIDOR	22	Birmingham	South	82	18	2	0	0	2	0	0	64	.220	.238	.244	.143	2	.161
	22	Pr. William	Caro	280	55	2	2	2	14	1	2	227	.196	.235	.239	.136	8	.151
PETE PRYOR	22	Hickory	S Atl	223	65	10	0	6	28	1	1	159	.291	.371	.417	.266	29	.292
FERNANDO RAMSEY	30	Nashville	AmA	399	84	3	0	6	15	11	7	322	.211	.239	.263	.158	16	.155
NILSON ROBLEDO	27	Pr. William	Caro	319	73	6	0	7	19	0	0	246	.229	.272	.313	.192	20	.196
LIU RODRIGUEZ	19	Hickory	S Atl	458	99	10	0	1	48	6	5	364	.216	.291	.245	.173	23	.200
GREG SHEPPARD	21	South Bend	Midw	147	35	4	1	0	8	2	1	113	.238	.277	.279	.183	8	.207
RYAN TOPHAM	22	South Bend	Midw	409	87	12	3	6	41	9	4	326	.213	.284	.301	.195	27	.215
CHRIS TREMIE	26	Nashville	AmA	220	47	9	1	0	20	2	0	173	.214	.279	.264	.178	11	.185
JERRY WHITTAKER	22	Pr. William	Caro	310	72	5	2	8	21	6	2	240	.232	.281	.339	.208	24	.230
BRENT WILHELM	23	South Bend	Midw	398	87	12	1	5	44	4	4	315	.219	.296	.291	.194	26	.211

Player	Age	Team	Lge	IP	H	ER	HR	BB	K	ERA	W	L	H/9	HR/9	BB/9	K/9	KW
KEVIN BEIRNE	22	South Bend	Midw	124.0	196	95	7	78	69	6.90	4	10	14.23	.51	5.66	5.01	.25
CHAD BRADFORD	21	Hickory	S Atl	26.0	30	8	2	10	15	2.77	2	1	10.38	.69	3.46	5.19	.87
CURTIS BROOME	24	Pr. William	Caro	50.0	77	43	7	50	23	7.74	1	5	13.86	1.26	9.00	4.14	-.87
SHANE BUTEAUX	24	Pr. William	Caro	35.7	42	20	4	29	20	5.05	2	2	10.60	1.01	7.32	5.05	-.15
	24	South Bend	Midw	33.3	48	24	1	20	21	6.48	1	3	12.96	.27	5.40	5.67	.54
CARLOS CASTILLO	21	Pr. William	Caro	39.0	54	23	0	8	21	5.31	1	3	12.46	.00	1.85	4.85	1.15
	21	South Bend	Midw	115.3	173	84	16	39	80	6.55	4	9	13.50	1.25	3.04	6.24	1.32
CARLOS CHANTRES	20	Hickory	S Atl	100.0	154	80	13	57	51	7.20	3	8	13.86	1.17	5.13	4.59	.25
	20	South Bend	Midw	56.7	78	33	4	25	26	5.24	2	4	12.39	.64	3.97	4.13	.38
CHRIS CLEMONS	23	Birmingham	South	87.7	102	37	8	47	50	3.80	5	5	10.47	.82	4.83	5.13	.50
	23	Pr. William	Caro	31.7	45	17	7	12	18	4.83	2	2	12.79	1.99	3.41	5.12	.85
ERIK DESROSIERS	21	Pr. William	Caro	35.7	56	31	8	14	17	7.82	1	3	14.13	2.02	3.53	4.29	.55
	21	South Bend	Midw	58.3	90	46	10	25	24	7.10	1	5	13.89	1.54	3.86	3.70	.27
JIM DIXON	23	Pr. William	Caro	65.0	87	51	7	42	39	7.06	2	5	12.05	.97	5.82	5.40	.35
SEAN DUNCAN	23	South Bend	Midw	49.3	55	30	4	30	34	5.47	2	3	10.03	.73	5.47	6.20	.70
ROBERT ELLIS	25	Nashville	AmA	67.0	87	49	5	57	30	6.58	2	5	11.69	.67	7.66	4.03	-.57
JACK FORD	24	Pr. William	Caro	67.3	93	44	11	40	41	5.88	2	5	12.43	1.47	5.35	5.48	.49
JOEL GARBER	22	Hickory	S Atl	42.3	83	32	3	24	25	6.80	1	4	17.65	.64	5.10	5.31	.50
	22	South Bend	Midw	40.7	75	43	8	20	17	9.52	1	4	16.60	1.77	4.43	3.76	.15
ARIEL GARCIA	20	South Bend	Midw	129.3	205	108	15	63	48	7.52	3	11	14.27	1.04	4.38	3.34	.02
DEREK HASSELHOFF	22	South Bend	Midw	41.3	58	20	6	23	25	4.35	2	3	12.63	1.31	5.01	5.44	.56
MIKE HEATHCOTT	27	Birmingham	South	136.3	158	68	10	65	79	4.49	7	8	10.43	.66	4.29	5.22	.67
JON HUNT	22	Hickory	S Atl	117.7	189	107	4	101	44	8.18	3	10	14.46	.31	7.73	3.37	-.81
TIM KRAUS	23	South Bend	Midw	69.0	106	47	6	41	30	6.13	2	6	13.83	.78	5.35	3.91	-.03
MAXIMO NUNEZ	23	Hickory	S Atl	125.3	239	114	16	69	58	8.19	3	11	17.16	1.15	4.95	4.16	.15
MIKE PLACE	25	Birmingham	South	30.7	46	24	9	21	15	7.04	1	2	13.50	2.64	6.16	4.40	-.07
	25	Pr. William	Caro	35.3	37	18	2	11	21	4.58	2	2	9.42	.51	2.80	5.35	1.08
JOHN QUIRK	25	Pr. William	Caro	37.3	59	36	4	37	15	8.68	1	3	14.22	.96	8.92	3.62	-1.02
TODD RIZZO	25	Birmingham	South	63.0	69	26	1	47	35	3.71	4	3	9.86	.14	6.71	5.00	-.01
RICH SAUVEUR	32	Nashville	AmA	69.7	70	32	7	38	58	4.13	4	4	9.04	.90	4.91	7.49	1.27
BRIAN SCHMACK	22	Hickory	S Atl	51.7	88	30	5	24	31	5.23	2	4	15.33	.87	4.18	5.40	.75
JASON SECODA	21	South Bend	Midw	113.7	167	92	12	97	59	7.28	3	10	13.22	.95	7.68	4.67	-.36
CHUCK SMITH	26	Birmingham	South	28.3	29	10	1	17	22	3.18	2	1	9.21	.32	5.40	6.99	.98
	26	Pr. William	Caro	108.7	153	72	8	67	69	5.96	4	8	12.67	.66	5.55	5.71	.52
JOHN SNYDER	21	Birmingham	South	50.0	68	34	10	18	42	6.12	2	4	12.24	1.80	3.24	7.56	1.71
ROBERT THEODILE	23	Pr. William	Caro	116.7	161	81	7	77	63	6.25	4	9	12.42	.54	5.94	4.86	.13
ARCHIE VAZQUEZ	24	Birmingham	South	60.0	76	50	11	55	37	7.50	2	5	11.40	1.65	8.25	5.55	-.21
BRIAN WOODS	25	Birmingham	South	61.3	68	31	11	44	34	4.55	3	4	9.98	1.61	6.46	4.99	.05

Chicago White Sox

Cleveland Indians

Ah, what might have been. Tear in your beer? Thought that the Tribe had it all wrapped up with the McDowell signing, the over-the-top roster move intended to send a message to Atlanta? C'est la guerre.

In the wake of the failure of a good team to do as well as expected, there were many immediate cries for GM John Hart's head. After all, he'd traded some of the team's most popular players, only to have the new team fall short against Baltimore in the first round of the playoffs. Was it his fault? Were the moves good ones? Does Hart know what he's doing?

After the disappointment of falling short against the Braves in the 1995 World Series, the Indians went out of their way to make sure everyone knew they wouldn't be satisfied with that. They brought Julio Franco back from across the Pacific, letting Paul Sorrento go, hoping that would address a perceived weakness against left-handed pitching. They added mediot favorite Jack McDowell, gritty wacko that he is, to show that they wanted a "four aces" rotation to match against the Braves in their next big confrontation. They wanted to make sure everyone understood this team was not going to rest on the laurels of having won its division by 30 games. There was some concern that this was an old team, notably Eddie Murray, Dennis Martinez and Orel Hershiser. However, unlike the previous year's team, the bench was going to be stronger with the addition of Jeromy Burnitz.

The Indians busted out of the gate fast, disappointing no one. They raced out to a 35-17 record, scoring runs by the truckload. After building that lead, the team went into the doldrums, snoozily stumbling the rest of the way to the All-Star break with a 17-18 mark. Was it a sign of mediocrity? The pitching staff wasn't doing so well, as first Chad Ogea and then Jack McDowell struggled with injuries. Orel Hershiser endured a desperate period of ineffectiveness over the first two months. Dennis Martinez' elbow became a chronic concern. On top of this, Eddie Murray was almost worthless as a DH and Carlos Baerga had become the center of attention for his being out of shape and poor hitting; with those things on the table, noticing that his defense wasn't the best was bound to happen. Julio Franco began to suffer hamstring troubles, and Herb Perry's constant knee problems had already shelved the team's first choice to replace him. Hart had to guess: would the team snap out of it? Or did it need shaking up?

Hart gambled, making a series of daring trades. He quickly acquired Mark Carreon from a sinking Giants squad for Jim Poole, the Indians' second-string left-handed spot reliever. He sent a more important message by trading Eddie Murray, popular with the club's younger black players, for some needed pitching (Kent Mercker). Both trades were smart moves at the time: Carreon would be an adequate replacement for Franco at first, while Poole would be replaced easily enough by a younger pitcher like Alan Embree; Murray had been hitting .262/.326/.402 as a DH, and had effectively lost his playing time to Jeromy Burnitz, while Mercker was perceived to be having a hard time with Davey Johnson in Baltimore.

Then the bomb went off: chatty, popular Carlos Baerga (and scrub Alvaro Espinoza) were traded to the Mets for Jeff Kent and Jose Vizcaino. This deal had every look of a steal by the Indians, as Baerga seemed to be literally foundering (for those of you who know your fat horse afflictions). A wave of shrieking protest from fans and players erupted. As team chemistry guru Joe Carter put it, "I didn't think it could possibly happen to him... geez, this is his worst year and it's a pretty good year for a lot of other people." But the deal had given the Indians improved depth, defense, offense and had sent a clear message to the clubhouse that winning was to be accomplished at any price, in a manner only George Weiss of the old Yankees' dynasty of the '50s could have truly appreciated.

The hubbub didn't die down when the Indians took themselves out of the artificial Denny Neagle sweepstakes. John Schuerholz outbid himself while the Indians continued to protect their minor league talent. For all of the kvetching, bitching, moaning, and whining about how Hart had ruined a good thing, not a single Indians prospect had been surrendered in any of these trades. It could be argued that Hart's final stretch-drive deal, Jeromy Burnitz for Kevin Seitzer, was hardly a swap of a veteran for a young, promising player: Burnitz was rescued off the scrap heap, and will be 28 in '97. In all of the transactions made with an eye on winning this year, Hart had protected the Indians' future, keeping great prospects like Jaret Wright or Bartolo Colon, and even mediocre ones like Joe Roa. For a team that acquired so much veteran talent down the stretch, that's simply extraordinary.

The sad part of the story is that the Indians didn't win, as the Orioles stuck to their hot-hitting ways in the Division Series, Jim Thome broke his wrist but tried to play and Mike Hargrove again made a fool out of himself with his postseason managing. All of that was out of John Hart's control, with the possible argument that he could save himself some future heartache by axing Hargrove at his first opportunity. After the controversies of the past season, Hart hasn't lost his flair for the dramatic. He let Albert Belle walk away after swindling the Giants out of Matt Williams for none other than this year's stretch drive acquisitions, Jeff Kent and Jose Vizcaino, and tough luck pitcher Julian Tavarez. To sum up, that means a swap of a fat, injured Baerga, Tavarez and the always tasty Alvaro Espinoza, for Matt Williams and two months of Kent and Vizcaino. Unfortunately, the moves will be judged in terms of the forced non-signing of Belle, although it should also be mentioned that the move helps the Indians afford Kenny Lofton for a few years to come.

As Karl von Clausewitz put it, "only the intelligent are lucky." John Hart is a sharp guy, and he hasn't stopped being smart just because the crapshoot that the playoffs can be wound up going sour early this year. Unfortunately, he may be fighting for his job. If the Matt Williams deal goes bad because Williams goes on one of his two- or three-month hiatuses, and Chicago blows the Indians out of the water with Albert Belle mugging for the cameras in Sox black, don't be surprised if the cries for Hart's head on a stick reach a deafening pitch. If that happens, the sad thing is that they will have punished the man who, more than any other, is responsible for maneuvering the Indians from laughingstock to powerhouse.

As mentioned, the Indians survived a bevy of transactions without touching their fine assortment of minor league talent. They're blessed with middle infielders, power hitters (especially left-handed power), outfielders and a broad assortment of relievers and starting pitchers. Some of these players' strengths can be overstated: the young power hitters at Columbus in the Sally League were taking advantage of some remodeling that made the park a homer haven; the pitchers at Canton-Akron (AA) were helped by the Eastern League's general good nature for all pitchers. If there is a major orga-

nizational weakness, it's catcher, where the Tribe is counting on the development of converted infielder Einar Diaz for want of anyone else with a pulse at the position.

The Indians have had a very strange habit of drafting first basemen with their first-round picks lately, signing David Miller, Sean Casey and Danny Peoples. The strange thing is, with first base prospects like Richie Sexson already floating around, the Indians weren't exactly desperate at the position. Miller is enduring an embarrassing conversion to the outfield. These picks in the last two drafts may have led to the firing of scouting director Jay Robertson, whose tenure has been marred by controversy. His inability to work with longtime Indians' scouts and crosscheckers led to mass firings and resignations over the last three years; that kind of turmoil has hopefully played itself out with Robertson's dismissal. How badly this will affect the Indians' future is unknown; every A-ball team the Indians fielded posted a winning record, and all were stocked with some prospects.

At AAA, the Indians and the Rich family have a fine working arrangement. Anyone affiliated with Buffalo has to cooperate with the Rich family's drive to sell seats by giving them a solid core of talent to compete; the Indians have been in a unique position to staff Buffalo with some veteran spare parts (signed as insurance for major league injuries) and young talent. Not surprisingly, the Bisons handily led the American Association in wins, with a roster that combined prospects past (Nigel Wilson), present (Joe Roa, sort of) and future (Damian Jackson).

SANDY ALOMAR C 1966 Age 31

Year	Team	Lge	AB	H	DB	TP	HR	BB	SB	CS	OUT	BA	OBA	SA	EQA	EQR	Peak
1993	Cleveland	AL	219	64	8	0	8	13	3	1	156	.292	.332	.438	.258	26	.265
1994	Cleveland	AL	293	84	13	1	15	25	7	3	212	.287	.343	.491	.275	42	.277
1995	Cleveland	AL	206	65	4	0	12	7	3	1	142	.316	.338	.510	.280	29	.279
1996	Cleveland	AL	417	109	16	0	13	19	1	0	308	.261	.294	.393	.229	39	.224
1997	Cleveland	AL	460	125	14	0	17	28	3	2	337	.272	.314	.413	.246	51	

Not many players get to boast of having been one of the worst fan selections to the All-Star Game and one of the worst managerial selections to boot. Alomar's career has wound up being mostly reflected glory from his brother Roberto. The point where you might have claimed he was one of the AL's great catchers never came. Instead, you have one of the best GIDP men in baseball today, who just enjoyed his second healthy season of his career. Probably the most overrated player to never wear a Dodgers' or Mets' uniform.

BRUCE AVEN OF 1972 Age 25

Year	Team	Lge	AB	H	DB	TP	HR	BB	SB	CS	OUT	BA	OBA	SA	EQA	EQR	Peak
1994	Watertown	NY-P	228	66	6	1	6	16	5	2	164	.289	.336	.404	.251	26	.277
1995	Kinston	Caro	501	136	17	3	23	40	10	5	370	.271	.325	.455	.258	63	.281
1996	Canton	East	492	142	22	2	21	38	16	4	354	.289	.340	.470	.271	67	.290
1997	Cleveland	AL	624	181	26	1	36	57	23	9	452	.290	.349	.508	.285	98	

Aven isn't really considered a top prospect. He's a puny Doug Dascenzo clone with power, but he lacks range in the outfield. He hit well in the AFL, and he's considered a great hustler. He'll be an unheralded success like Brian Giles.

ALBERT BELLE   LF   1967   Age 30

Year	Team	Lge	AB	H	DB	TP	HR	BB	SB	CS	OUT	BA	OBA	SA	EQA	EQR	Peak
1993	Cleveland	AL	611	191	36	3	47	82	23	9	429	.313	.394	.612	.319	123	.332
1994	Cleveland	AL	414	148	31	2	37	58	8	5	271	.357	.436	.710	.354	101	.363
1995	Cleveland	AL	558	186	45	2	59	75	5	2	374	.333	.412	.738	.351	136	.354
1996	Cleveland	AL	600	185	38	3	47	98	11	0	415	.308	.405	.617	.327	126	.324
1997	*Chi. White Sox*	*AL*	*603*	*183*	*39*	*3*	*45*	*94*	*7*	*1*	*421*	*.303*	*.397*	*.602*	*.328*	*130*	

Well, as if those Chicago-Cleveland games weren't interesting enough, they just got much spicier. Albert will not hit 50 home runs in Chicago. It's a tougher home run park than Cleveland, probably the toughest park in the AL now that Oakland has been "remodeled" (butchered, sacrificed, whatever). Since Albert has already made it clear he does not like to DH, that means somebody or something in Chicago will have to give way or be traded, probably Tony Phillips. Concerns about Belle's personality in Chicago are pointless. Most of the team is surly with the media, so Albert will just be another schmoe in a room full of grumpy schmoes. He couldn't ask for a better situation than that.

TODD BETTS   3B   1973   Age 24

Year	Team	Lge	AB	H	DB	TP	HR	BB	SB	CS	OUT	BA	OBA	SA	EQA	EQR	Peak
1994	Watertown	NY-P	245	72	5	1	9	42	1	1	174	.294	.397	.433	.280	36	.313
1995	Kinston	Caro	362	103	14	2	10	84	1	1	260	.285	.419	.417	.285	56	.314
1996	Canton	East	245	58	7	0	2	34	0	0	187	.237	.330	.290	.210	19	.227

Injuries wrecked his '96 season, but hopefully the Indians won't be forgetting him already. Although he should regain his power with a full season, Betts is considered an awful defensive player. Before last season, the Indians had him work on catching in the instructional league, and a successful conversion would upgrade him from a mediocre third base prospect to an extremely useful player.

RUSSELL BRANYAN   3B   1976   Age 21

Year	Team	Lge	AB	H	DB	TP	HR	BB	SB	CS	OUT	BA	OBA	SA	EQA	EQR	Peak
1995	Columbus-GA	SAtl	287	69	3	2	14	21	1	0	218	.240	.292	.411	.233	29	.268
1996	Columbus-GA	SAtl	510	132	9	1	29	48	3	2	380	.259	.323	.451	.255	62	.290
1997	*Cleveland*	*AL*	*479*	*128*	*11*	*3*	*27*	*49*	*4*	*3*	*354*	*.267*	*.335*	*.472*	*.268*	*66*	

Branyan is very young, very streaky and very raw. He strikes out prodigiously, 286 times in the last two seasons alone. He led all A-ball players with 40 home runs, but Columbus shifted its fences this year, and was a very easy place to mash taters. He's considered absent-minded on defense, as in he forgets he has to play it.

MARK CARREON   1B/OF   1964   Age 33

Year	Team	Lge	AB	H	DB	TP	HR	BB	SB	CS	OUT	BA	OBA	SA	EQA	EQR	Peak
1993	San Francisco	NL	156	54	8	1	8	16	1	0	102	.346	.407	.564	.318	29	.315
1994	San Francisco	NL	101	28	4	0	3	9	0	0	73	.277	.336	.406	.249	11	.243
1995	San Francisco	NL	407	129	19	0	20	28	0	1	279	.317	.361	.511	.286	61	.276
1996	San Francisco	NL	297	79	22	3	9	26	2	3	221	.266	.325	.451	.254	36	.242
1996	Cleveland	AL	142	46	8	0	3	10	1	1	97	.324	.368	.444	.273	19	.260
1997	*Cleveland*	*AL*	*535*	*153*	*26*	*2*	*18*	*39*	*1*	*4*	*386*	*.286*	*.334*	*.443*	*.260*	*67*	

The pickup of Carreon for Jim Poole was a master stroke at replacing the fragile Julio Franco. Unfortunately, Carreon was quickly injured as well. He's effectively positionless, since he doesn't hit well enough to hold down first, and is a serious liability in the outfield. He also wouldn't be a great platoon player; for his career, he's consistently hit right-handed pitchers better than left-handers. He's a fine pinch-hitter and spare part, and those are the kinds of jobs he should be expecting as a free agent this offseason.

SEAN CASEY   1B   1975   Age 22

Year	Team	Lge	AB	H	DB	TP	HR	BB	SB	CS	OUT	BA	OBA	SA	EQA	EQR	Peak
1995	Watertown	NY-P	214	59	8	0	3	14	1	0	155	.276	.320	.355	.230	20	.262
1996	Kinston	Caro	360	113	15	2	11	31	1	0	247	.314	.368	.458	.277	50	.311

Casey is another example of the Indians' weird habit of drafting first basemen; he was their second-round pick in '95 after winning the NCAA batting title (their first-round pick was 1B David Miller). Although he looks like a fine left-handed hitter, he hasn't shown the power you want from a first baseman.

EINAR DIAZ   **C**   **1973**   **Age 24**

Year	Team	Lge	AB	H	DB	TP	HR	BB	SB	CS	OUT	BA	OBA	SA	EQA	EQR	Peak
1994	Columbus-GA	SAtl	497	119	11	1	12	16	2	2	380	.239	.263	.338	.197	33	.221
1995	Kinston	Caro	384	100	11	0	8	14	3	3	287	.260	.286	.352	.212	30	.234
1996	Canton	East	400	105	20	2	3	11	2	1	296	.262	.282	.345	.210	30	.228

Diaz is considered a top-notch defensive catcher, and this season might be the year that Tony Pena is finally run off the roster. The Indians have had real problems developing or drafting catchers, and Diaz is a converted infielder.

STEVE DUNN   **1B**   **1970**   **Age 27**

Year	Team	Lge	AB	H	DB	TP	HR	BB	SB	CS	OUT	BA	OBA	SA	EQA	EQR	Peak
1993	Nashville	South	375	95	14	1	13	33	1	1	281	.253	.314	.400	.237	39	.258
1994	Salt Lake City	PCL	321	87	13	1	12	23	0	0	234	.271	.320	.430	.249	36	.267
1995	Salt Lake City	PCL	397	116	15	1	14	31	3	1	282	.292	.343	.441	.263	50	.277
1996	Buffalo	AmA	311	92	15	1	12	32	2	1	220	.296	.362	.466	.275	44	.285
1997	*Cleveland*	*AL*	*320*	*91*	*14*	*1*	*12*	*44*	*2*	*2*	*231*	*.284*	*.371*	*.447*	*.276*	*46*	

The career objective for Steve Dunn is to carve out a Paul Sorrento-type role somewhere. He's hopeless against lefties, won't be mistaken for Mark Grace with the glove, and won't get a chance unless he winds up with a team whose manager pinch-hits a lot and wants to give that job to an "unproven" minor leaguer like Dunn (sort of like Tom Kelly with Sorrento). Unfortunately, not many teams actually do this, usually settling for retreads.

JULIO FRANCO   **1B**   **1962**   **Age 35**

Year	Team	Lge	AB	H	DB	TP	HR	BB	SB	CS	OUT	BA	OBA	SA	EQA	EQR	Peak
1993	Texas	AL	545	170	34	3	18	66	8	2	377	.312	.386	.484	.291	86	.280
1994	Chi. White Sox	AL	440	145	19	1	22	63	7	1	296	.330	.414	.527	.312	80	.296
1996	Cleveland	AL	430	137	19	1	14	61	8	8	301	.319	.403	.465	.288	67	.274
1997	*Cleveland*	*AL*	*489*	*143*	*26*	*2*	*17*	*83*	*1*	*0*	*346*	*.292*	*.395*	*.458*	*.290*	*78*	

The age is a guess; he could be anywhere between 35 and 38. Franco winning the Gold Glove in Japan tells us that either Japanese first basemen field like Dave Kinsman, or their selection process is as bad as ours. If you haven't noticed, his speed is shot.

One of the ongoing miseries of the Indians' season was Franc's ill health. His fragile hamstrings led to the acquisitions of first Mark Carreon and then Kevin Seitzer; fortunately, neither player cost them much talent. It may also have played a role in the acquisition of Jeff Kent; again, not costing much, but leading to a heap of complaints that put John Hart on the spot. If the Matt Williams trade flops because Williams remains unhealthy, the cries to punish Hart may be too harsh for ownership to resist. And at the root of the controversy was the acquisition of a fragile Julio Franco.

BRIAN GILES   **OF/DH**   **1971**   **Age 26**

Year	Team	Lge	AB	H	DB	TP	HR	BB	SB	CS	OUT	BA	OBA	SA	EQA	EQR	Peak
1993	Canton	East	443	140	14	3	9	53	10	6	309	.316	.389	.422	.275	62	.304
1994	Charlotte-NC	Inter	446	136	14	1	16	53	6	3	313	.305	.379	.448	.278	64	.302
1995	Buffalo	AmA	431	138	16	5	18	57	7	3	296	.320	.400	.506	.300	73	.321
1996	Buffalo	AmA	333	108	15	5	19	44	1	0	225	.324	.403	.571	.316	63	.333
1996	Cleveland	AL	120	42	14	1	5	19	3	0	78	.350	.439	.608	.341	27	.360
1997	*Cleveland*	*AL*	*615*	*208*	*29*	*2*	*16*	*81*	*6*	*4*	*411*	*.338*	*.415*	*.470*	*.302*	*103*	

With Albert Belle's departure, Giles should be the regular left fielder for the Indians in '97. The Indians are talking about platooning him, but that's unnecessary: his line-drive stroke works against both lefties and righties. Not every team is in a position to replace a great player like Belle with someone like Giles. To get attention, Giles pretty much has to hit .300 every year, because he's not a "tools" player: he's short, slow and lacks an outstanding throwing arm. He's got good range afield.

DAMIAN JACKSON   IF   1974   Age 23

Year	Team	Lge	AB	H	DB	TP	HR	BB	SB	CS	OUT	BA	OBA	SA	EQA	EQR	Peak
1993	Columbus-GA	SAtl	363	85	11	1	6	31	11	4	282	.234	.294	.320	.209	28	.241
1994	Canton	East	554	147	23	3	6	54	24	9	416	.265	.331	.350	.235	56	.267
1995	Canton	East	498	118	14	2	4	57	26	13	393	.237	.315	.297	.211	40	.236
1996	Buffalo	AmA	466	120	11	1	12	52	21	6	352	.258	.332	.363	.240	50	.265
1997	*Cleveland*	*AL*	*519*	*137*	*21*	*4*	*15*	*46*	*22*	*10*	*392*	*.264*	*.324*	*.407*	*.250*	*61*	

The Indians have begun looking at moving him to second, although he has been an excellent, if error-prone, shortstop. His power is growing with age. If the Indians have the courage to hand him the job at second, hats off to them.

TIM JORGENSEN   3B   1973   Age 24

Year	Team	Lge	AB	H	DB	TP	HR	BB	SB	CS	OUT	BA	OBA	SA	EQA	EQR	Peak
1995	Watertown	NY-P	307	88	8	2	9	25	2	1	220	.287	.340	.414	.254	36	.279
1996	Kinston	Caro	426	87	8	0	15	35	1	1	340	.204	.265	.329	.193	28	.209

Jorgensen is something of a longshot. He was Player of the Year in Division III ball for two years in a row at U. Wisconsin-Oshkosh. If he has another season like this, he won't be a worthwhile risk for much longer.

JEFF KENT   IF   1968   Age 29

Year	Team	Lge	AB	H	DB	TP	HR	BB	SB	CS	OUT	BA	OBA	SA	EQA	EQR	Peak
1993	NY Mets	NL	505	140	18	0	23	38	4	3	368	.277	.328	.450	.257	62	.272
1994	NY Mets	NL	419	122	22	4	15	29	1	3	300	.291	.337	.470	.265	54	.276
1995	NY Mets	NL	483	141	20	3	22	36	3	3	345	.292	.341	.482	.271	66	.277
1996	NY Mets	NL	346	107	19	1	10	26	3	3	242	.309	.358	.457	.271	46	.273
1996	Cleveland	AL	102	27	6	0	3	10	2	1	76	.265	.330	.412	.249	12	.251
1997	*San Francisco*	*NL*	*433*	*118*	*22*	*1*	*23*	*44*	*5*	*2*	*317*	*.273*	*.340*	*.487*	*.286*	*69*	

A fine little player who was misused by both the Indians and the Mets last year. He never has had the arm strength or instincts to handle third, but the Mets wanted to make their offense weaker by signing Jose Vizcaino to a ludicrous contract, so Kent had to be moved. It's fairly straightforward: as a second baseman, Kent is one of the better ones in his league, despite his defensive shortcomings. As a corner infielder, he's a light hitter and a defensive liability. If the Giants aren't any stupider than they have to be to have made the Matt Williams trade in the first place, they'll leave Kent at second. If Kent's hitting higher than sixth, it's another sign of an extremely weak lineup.

Kent's platoon splits have gone every direction imaginable over the last few years. He started his career with epic problems against left-handed pitchers, then crushed them and is now back to going homerless against them.

SCOTT LEIUS   IF   1966   Age 31

Year	Team	Lge	AB	H	DB	TP	HR	BB	SB	CS	OUT	BA	OBA	SA	EQA	EQR	Peak
1994	Minnesota	AL	352	88	14	1	15	38	2	4	268	.250	.323	.423	.245	40	.246
1995	Minnesota	AL	374	95	15	5	5	50	2	1	280	.254	.342	.361	.238	39	.236
1996	Buffalo	AmA	127	34	2	1	4	13	0	0	93	.268	.336	.394	.245	14	.240
1997	*Cleveland*	*AL*	*158*	*37*	*4*	*0*	*3*	*18*	*0*	*1*	*122*	*.234*	*.312*	*.316*	*.212*	*13*	

This is what a career coming to an end looks like. Leius never did anything else well enough to be forgiven for major slumps at the plate. Now that he's over 30, that may not be enough to keep Lou Piniella from being interested.

JOE LIS   IF   1969   Age 28

Year	Team	Lge	AB	H	DB	TP	HR	BB	SB	CS	OUT	BA	OBA	SA	EQA	EQR	Peak
1993	Knoxville	South	452	116	19	2	8	39	4	4	340	.257	.316	.361	.226	41	.243
1994	Syracuse	Inter	325	92	11	0	12	24	2	1	234	.283	.332	.428	.254	38	.268
1995	Syracuse	Inter	498	131	27	2	18	48	5	1	368	.263	.328	.434	.254	60	.264
1996	Buffalo	AmA	151	36	5	0	6	19	0	0	115	.238	.324	.391	.238	16	.244

Acquired for Scott Pose, an even greater disappointment. Lis can handle second or third, and has some pop for an infielder. He's a year removed from leading the International League in extra-base hits, but spending a year on Buffalo's bench may have ended his shot at a major league job.

KENNY LOFTON   CF   1967   Age 30

Year	Team	Lge	AB	H	DB	TP	HR	BB	SB	CS	OUT	BA	OBA	SA	EQA	EQR	Peak
1993	Cleveland	AL	589	210	34	9	2	87	66	11	390	.357	.439	.455	.316	109	.329
1994	Cleveland	AL	461	162	31	8	13	52	54	11	310	.351	.417	.538	.322	92	.330
1995	Cleveland	AL	490	161	26	14	8	41	54	15	344	.329	.380	.488	.295	82	.298
1996	Cleveland	AL	660	207	34	4	14	60	74	17	470	.314	.371	.441	.283	100	.282
1997	*Cleveland*	*AL*	*638*	*188*	*38*	*9*	*12*	*82*	*60*	*14*	*464*	*.295*	*.375*	*.439*	*.285*	*101*	

The overall trend has been consistently, incrementally downward, which isn't surprising considering Lofton's age. In the wake of what was considered a "story" in spring training (that the Indians defense was critically poor), Lofton came under some criticism for his play in center. Complaints about his defense usually focused on the number of errors he committed, but Lofton's range is still excellent. He's playing on an option for '97, after which he'll be a free agent. I'd expect his contract to make Marquis Grissom look like a piker.

ROD McCALL   1B   1972   Age 25

Year	Team	Lge	AB	H	DB	TP	HR	BB	SB	CS	OUT	BA	OBA	SA	EQA	EQR	Peak
1993	Kinston	Caro	255	50	5	0	8	28	2	1	206	.196	.276	.310	.191	16	.214
1994	High Desert	Calif	184	47	7	0	12	16	1	1	138	.255	.315	.489	.261	24	.287
1994	Kinston	Caro	212	44	9	0	8	22	1	1	169	.208	.282	.363	.211	17	.234
1995	Bakersfield	Calif	346	97	8	0	15	31	1	2	251	.280	.340	.434	.257	42	.279
1996	Canton	East	452	133	19	1	24	47	1	0	319	.294	.361	.500	.283	68	.303
1997	*Cleveland*	*AL*	*499*	*139*	*29*	*2*	*19*	*59*	*0*	*0*	*360*	*.279*	*.355*	*.459*	*.273*	*70*	

Playing on the same team as Richie Sexson, McCall played DH a lot. He's a huge slugger, but in an organization rich in left-handed power, he'll have a hard time carving out a future for himself with the Indians. He has already been given an invite for spring training, where he'll finally get the chance to open some eyes.

SCOTT MORGAN   OF   1974   Age 23

Year	Team	Lge	AB	H	DB	TP	HR	BB	SB	CS	OUT	BA	OBA	SA	EQA	EQR	Peak
1995	Watertown	NY-P	253	54	8	0	3	20	2	2	201	.213	.271	.281	.178	13	.199
1996	Columbus-GA	SAtl	326	97	9	1	17	36	4	2	231	.298	.367	.488	.282	49	.311
1997	*Cleveland*	*AL*	*555*	*141*	*19*	*0*	*22*	*60*	*5*	*4*	*418*	*.254*	*.327*	*.407*	*.248*	*64*	

Helped by a extremely easy park to hit homers, Morgan had a shot at winning the Sally League's Triple Crown before he missed almost two months with a slipped disc. He should be fine for '97.

GERONIMO PENA   UT   1967   Age 30

Year	Team	Lge	AB	H	DB	TP	HR	BB	SB	CS	OUT	BA	OBA	SA	EQA	EQR	Peak
1993	St. Louis	NL	261	70	18	2	6	29	11	4	195	.268	.341	.421	.258	33	.269
1994	St. Louis	NL	216	56	12	0	12	27	8	1	161	.259	.342	.481	.274	32	.281
1995	St. Louis	NL	103	28	6	1	1	18	2	2	77	.272	.380	.379	.257	13	.260
1996	Louisville	AmA	110	32	5	1	6	13	0	0	78	.291	.366	.518	.288	17	.286
1996	Buffalo	AmA	94	33	8	1	4	13	0	0	61	.351	.430	.585	.330	19	.330
1997	*Cleveland*	*AL*	*271*	*73*	*15*	*2*	*12*	*36*	*0*	*0*	*198*	*.269*	*.355*	*.472*	*.276*	*40*	

Fantasy baseball's answer to snark hunting. Even in his resurrections, Geronimo Pena is nothing if not unlucky or disappointing. He missed time this season for flying off to see his wife and newborn child, only to have his return delayed by visa problems.

TONY PENA   C   1957   Age 40

Year	Team	Lge	AB	H	DB	TP	HR	BB	SB	CS	OUT	BA	OBA	SA	EQA	EQR	Peak
1993	Boston	AL	304	55	7	0	6	27	1	2	251	.181	.248	.263	.155	12	.147
1994	Cleveland	AL	112	33	8	1	2	9	0	1	80	.295	.347	.438	.260	14	.247
1995	Cleveland	AL	267	74	10	0	8	14	1	0	193	.277	.313	.404	.241	28	.229
1996	Cleveland	AL	174	34	0	0	2	15	0	1	141	.195	.259	.230	.145	6	.137
1997	*Cleveland*	*AL*	*94*	*17*	*0*	*0*	*1*	*8*	*0*	*0*	*77*	*.181*	*.245*	*.213*	*.131*	*2*	

With Dennis Martinez' imminent departure, and Pena's outspokenness on behalf of Baerga, his career with the Indians is probably over. He may get signed as a caddy for someone who can still play baseball, but it'll be money down the drain.

HERB PERRY   **1B**   **1970**   **Age 27**

Year	Team	Lge	AB	H	DB	TP	HR	BB	SB	CS	OUT	BA	OBA	SA	EQA	EQR	Peak
1993	Canton	East	338	89	13	1	10	34	4	2	251	.263	.331	.396	.244	37	.265
1994	Charlotte-NC	Inter	386	123	17	2	13	40	6	3	266	.319	.383	.474	.286	58	.307
1995	Buffalo	AmA	186	60	11	1	3	17	1	0	126	.323	.379	.441	.278	26	.294
1995	Cleveland	AL	165	55	13	1	4	13	1	3	113	.333	.382	.497	.287	25	.302
1996	Buffalo	AmA	156	53	5	1	5	9	4	0	103	.340	.376	.481	.291	24	.302
1997	*Cleveland*	*AL*	*327*	*110*	*22*	*2*	*9*	*26*	*2*	*3*	*220*	*.336*	*.385*	*.498*	*.295*	*52*	

If Perry was a more durable player, the Indians would be in much, much better shape. They wouldn't have had to enter the cycle of trades that forced them to acquire first Mark Carreon, then Kevin Seitzer. But the two constants of Perry's career have been hitting and his being as durable as a fine china mouse. Perry is no longer an option at third base. At season's end, he was still having problems sorting out what needed to be done for a knee injury, so he isn't a good bet to be able to help the Tribe in '97.

ALEX RAMIREZ   **OF**   **1975**   **Age 22**

Year	Team	Lge	AB	H	DB	TP	HR	BB	SB	CS	OUT	BA	OBA	SA	EQA	EQR	Peak
1994	Columbus-GA	SAtl	465	101	12	0	14	23	3	2	366	.217	.254	.333	.191	29	.221
1995	Bakersfield	Calif	403	108	13	1	8	14	5	4	299	.268	.293	.365	.220	34	.249
1995	Canton	East	135	31	4	3	1	4	2	3	107	.230	.252	.326	.185	8	.211
1996	Canton	East	520	162	22	8	13	15	14	5	363	.312	.331	.460	.265	66	.297
1997	*Cleveland*	*AL*	*643*	*176*	*26*	*6*	*17*	*29*	*19*	*8*	*475*	*.274*	*.305*	*.412*	*.245*	*70*	

Ramirez has shown good power at a young age, but his terrible lack of patience at the plate will hold him back. He could be the man who inherits Lofton's center field job in '98 if the Tribe doesn't re-sign him.

MANNY RAMIREZ   **RF**   **1972**   **Age 25**

Year	Team	Lge	AB	H	DB	TP	HR	BB	SB	CS	OUT	BA	OBA	SA	EQA	EQR	Peak
1993	Canton	East	359	121	19	0	18	41	1	1	239	.337	.405	.540	.310	64	.348
1993	Charlotte-NC	Inter	152	50	9	0	13	27	1	1	103	.329	.430	.645	.338	34	.378
1993	Cleveland	AL	53	10	1	0	2	3	0	0	43	.189	.232	.321	.174	3	.195
1994	Cleveland	AL	291	78	17	0	19	42	4	2	215	.268	.360	.522	.286	47	.315
1995	Cleveland	AL	494	161	24	1	36	77	6	6	339	.326	.417	.597	.323	100	.351
1996	Cleveland	AL	548	168	43	3	33	84	8	5	385	.307	.399	.577	.312	105	.334
1997	*Cleveland*	*AL*	*584*	*203*	*39*	*3*	*42*	*113*	*7*	*5*	*386*	*.348*	*.453*	*.640*	*.351*	*141*	

For whatever reason, Ramirez gets belittled in the press for imagined weight problems, which one way or another haven't affected his hitting. Like Canseco or Strawberry, he also gets put down on defense far more than his actual skill justifies. Ramirez has an excellent throwing arm and enough range to survive; he's hardly a Sierra or Nieves in right field. One of Manny's best accomplishments this past season was his major improvement against right-handers.

KEVIN SEITZER   **1B/3B**   **1962**   **Age 35**

Year	Team	Lge	AB	H	DB	TP	HR	BB	SB	CS	OUT	BA	OBA	SA	EQA	EQR	Peak
1993	Oakland	AL	261	72	12	2	5	29	5	5	194	.276	.348	.395	.248	30	.239
1993	Milwaukee	AL	165	51	4	0	9	18	3	0	114	.309	.377	.497	.292	26	.281
1994	Milwaukee	AL	308	95	23	2	5	30	2	1	214	.308	.370	.445	.274	42	.261
1995	Milwaukee	AL	490	151	33	3	5	64	2	0	339	.308	.388	.418	.275	67	.261
1996	Milwaukee	AL	489	154	24	3	12	72	6	1	336	.315	.403	.450	.290	76	.275
1996	Cleveland	AL	83	32	7	0	2	13	0	0	51	.386	.469	.542	.339	17	.322
1997	*Cleveland*	*AL*	*450*	*126*	*15*	*1*	*22*	*47*	*3*	*2*	*326*	*.280*	*.348*	*.464*	*.272*	*63*	

Several years ago, Bill James grumped about how all the "Luke Appling types" weren't making it to the big leagues, or simply had ceased to exist. He was referring to right-handed high average hitters with good patience but poor power. The problem with that is that those players still do exist, and one of them had been playing in front of James for years in Kansas City: Kevin Seitzer. Seitzer gets too much regard for his bat control abilities, and he's a fine fill-in, spare part or regular if you've got a team that oozes power, like the Indians. He's effectively washed up on defense, only capable of an appearance of two per week at first. I'll be blunt: if Kevin Seitzer hits 22 home runs, equivalent or whatever, the moon's made of Roquefort.

RICHIE SEXSON	1B		1975	Age 22													
Year	Team	Lge	AB	H	DB	TP	HR	BB	SB	CS	OUT	BA	OBA	SA	EQA	EQR	Peak
1994	Columbus-GA	SAtl	499	117	12	1	11	31	3	1	383	.234	.279	.329	.202	35	.233
1995	Kinston	Caro	521	163	20	0	24	42	3	3	361	.313	.364	.489	.282	76	.321
1996	Canton	East	528	140	25	2	14	35	2	1	389	.265	.311	.400	.237	53	.265
1997	Cleveland	AL	609	171	26	1	23	51	4	2	440	.281	.336	.440	.262	78	

A spindly stork (6'6") with a short stroke, Sexson is young enough to be a great prospect. He has some power and should add more with age. However, he has yet to draw 40 walks under his own power in a season; if that doesn't change, he'll be the latest entry for the Dann Howitt All-Tall Goofballs. He had serious problems hitting in the AFL.

JIM THOME	3B		1971	Age 26													
Year	Team	Lge	AB	H	DB	TP	HR	BB	SB	CS	OUT	BA	OBA	SA	EQA	EQR	Peak
1993	Charlotte-NC	Inter	431	144	17	2	25	75	1	2	289	.334	.433	.557	.323	86	.356
1993	Cleveland	AL	159	46	9	0	10	31	2	1	114	.289	.405	.535	.306	29	.338
1994	Cleveland	AL	322	87	19	1	20	46	3	3	238	.270	.361	.522	.284	51	.309
1995	Cleveland	AL	463	154	30	3	29	100	4	3	312	.333	.451	.598	.338	104	.362
1996	Cleveland	AL	503	155	28	4	38	122	2	2	350	.308	.443	.606	.335	114	.353
1997	Cleveland	AL	545	182	30	3	40	160	6	5	368	.334	.485	.620	.359	142	

One of two players with an argument for being the best third baseman in the AL, the other being arch-rival Chicago's Robin Ventura. Unfortunately, with the addition of Matt Williams, Thome will have to settle for being a middle-of-the-pack first baseman, behind the McGwires and Thomases. Moving Thome across the infield is an overreaction to the perceived weakness of Cleveland's defense. One of the great misfortunes of Cleveland's season was Jim Thome breaking a bone in his wrist in the first playoff game against Baltimore. He tried to play through it, but he couldn't swing the bat adequately, and the absence of his hitting was probably the most damaging thing the Indians could have suffered.

RYAN THOMPSON	OF		1968	Age 29													
Year	Team	Lge	AB	H	DB	TP	HR	BB	SB	CS	OUT	BA	OBA	SA	EQA	EQR	Peak
1993	Norfolk	Inter	232	62	9	1	12	25	5	2	172	.267	.339	.470	.267	32	.282
1993	NY Mets	NL	293	75	18	1	12	23	2	6	224	.256	.310	.447	.244	33	.258
1994	NY Mets	NL	336	76	13	1	18	32	1	1	261	.226	.293	.432	.237	36	.246
1995	Norfolk	Inter	55	19	3	0	2	4	3	1	37	.345	.390	.509	.300	9	.310
1995	NY Mets	NL	273	72	9	0	9	22	3	1	202	.264	.319	.396	.240	29	.246
1996	Buffalo	AmA	549	143	22	2	20	28	12	4	410	.260	.296	.417	.239	57	.241

One of the great Blue Jays booby prizes, Thompson is at least a better player to have around than many of their famed crummy prospects. He can still handle center and hit with some pop. If a team needed someone to do those things (like the Astros or Giants or several others), Thompson would be a cheap and useful pickup.

JOSE VIZCAINO	IF		1968	Age 29													
Year	Team	Lge	AB	H	DB	TP	HR	BB	SB	CS	OUT	BA	OBA	SA	EQA	EQR	Peak
1993	Chicago Cubs	NL	561	161	20	2	5	54	10	7	407	.287	.350	.357	.241	58	.254
1994	NY Mets	NL	413	104	12	2	4	39	1	9	318	.252	.316	.320	.208	31	.216
1995	NY Mets	NL	523	158	22	4	4	41	7	3	368	.302	.353	.382	.252	58	.258
1996	Cleveland	AL	179	51	4	2	0	7	6	2	130	.285	.312	.330	.222	15	.223
1996	NY Mets	NL	377	122	14	6	1	33	7	5	260	.324	.378	.401	.266	47	.268
1997	San Francisco	NL	376	100	12	4	1	32	19	11	287	.266	.324	.327	.237	39	

I used to think Darren Daulton was the luckiest man in baseball. When he received his first enormous contract (before he'd blossomed), he was married to a Playmate of the Year and playing for a team with a reasonable future. Now, Daulton's divorced, semi-retired and can barely walk, so it's probably time to pick a new "luckiest man." My nominee might have to be Jose Vizcaino. Despite excellent arguments for Ozzie Guillen or Omar Vizquel, two oversized contracts for mediocrities (or worse), Vizcaino parlayed a few lucky breaks with the Cubs into a two-year contract signed before '96 for over $2M per year. If every replacement-level utility infielder got these kinds of breaks, Vizcaino wouldn't be quite so memorably lucky. An overrated defender for years, he's probably best compared to Jose Uribe Gonzalez Uribe Whatever, except he can shuttle around the infield, and he's luckier.

OMAR VIZQUEL   **SS**   **1967**   **Age 30**

Year	Team	Lge	AB	H	DB	TP	HR	BB	SB	CS	OUT	BA	OBA	SA	EQA	EQR	Peak
1993	Seattle	AL	567	153	14	2	3	54	13	10	424	.270	.333	.317	.222	49	.230
1994	Cleveland	AL	287	78	11	1	1	23	11	3	212	.272	.326	.328	.228	26	.233
1995	Cleveland	AL	551	156	19	0	11	60	30	11	406	.283	.354	.377	.253	65	.255
1996	Cleveland	AL	540	159	31	1	10	56	35	9	390	.294	.361	.411	.267	72	.266
1997	*Cleveland*	*AL*	*543*	*143*	*24*	*1*	*9*	*49*	*32*	*4*	*404*	*.263*	*.324*	*.361*	*.245*	*60*	

A close runner-up to Jose Vizcaino for the "luckiest man in baseball." What Vizquel really is is a lesson in the dangers of thinking that some intelligence in baseball management means intelligence in baseball management. When Cleveland initiated its policy of locking up young players to long-term contracts, before they had leverage to negotiate through arbitration or free agency, it was seen as a thoughtful adaptation to the excesses of those options, while usually retaining a player through the most productive period of his career. Signing the arguably past-prime Vizquel, after '95, to a deal through 2002, was not akin to those deals: as John Hart made it plain at the time, it was a reward. The misfortune is that giving Vizquel that kind of deal only helps create the expectation from others (especially Thome and Lofton) that they should receive that kind of deal, while also unfortunately creating a huge stumbling block to the futures of two very good shortstop prospects, Damian Jackson and Enrique Wilson.

All that aside, there are some reasons to be impressed with Vizquel of late. First, don't underestimate the influence of hitting coach Charlie Manuel. Unlike in his Seattle days, Vizquel can now hang in against left-handed pitchers, and has shown much better power and discipline at the plate. Second, he is a reliable shortstop. His need for shoulder surgery showed more and more as the season wore on, but he should be in full health next season. Third, understand that Vizquel is being judged by a generation of management that saw Bert Campaneris and Davey Concepcion as the great shortstops of their day. For such men to envision a future with Cal Ripken or Alex Rodriguez was dubious, any more than expecting them to understand competitive balance in a league where such players exist. The Indians, operating under old standards, are convinced they have a great shortstop, and while he's good, he'll wind up being a major disaster by the end of his contract.

ENRIQUE WILSON   **SS**   **1976**   **Age 21**

Year	Team	Lge	AB	H	DB	TP	HR	BB	SB	CS	OUT	BA	OBA	SA	EQA	EQR	Peak
1994	Columbus-GA	SAtl	525	126	17	4	10	37	9	6	405	.240	.290	.345	.212	42	.248
1995	Kinston	Caro	481	127	20	5	7	26	13	9	363	.264	.302	.370	.225	44	.260
1996	Canton	East	493	138	14	3	5	28	17	8	363	.280	.319	.351	.229	46	.261
1997	*Cleveland*	*AL*	*558*	*155*	*37*	*4*	*8*	*36*	*22*	*10*	*413*	*.278*	*.322*	*.401*	*.248*	*63*	

Just when you thought that the last thing baseball needs is another great shortstop prospect, Enrique Wilson starts clawing his was through the higher levels of an organization. Wilson is an excellent shortstop, switch-hits and can run a little. Unfortunately, the Tribe is committed to Omar Vizquel through 2002, so Wilson will be moving up to Buffalo in '97, and no farther. Because of Vizquel, there's been some offseason experimentation with moving Wilson to second, but so far he's still a shortstop. Named the best defensive shortstop in the Eastern League, with the best infield arm.

NIGEL WILSON   **OF/DH**   **1970**   **Age 27**

Year	Team	Lge	AB	H	DB	TP	HR	BB	SB	CS	OUT	BA	OBA	SA	EQA	EQR	Peak
1993	Edmonton	PCL	360	91	15	2	15	23	5	2	271	.253	.298	.431	.241	39	.262
1994	Edmonton	PCL	306	82	14	1	10	21	2	2	226	.268	.315	.418	.243	33	.261
1995	Indianapolis	AmA	307	95	21	2	17	17	5	3	215	.309	.346	.557	.291	49	.307
1996	Buffalo	AmA	500	153	21	4	28	54	4	3	350	.306	.374	.532	.294	82	.306

A canny grab off the waiver wire before the '96 season, it will be interesting to see if the Indians keep Wilson and give him a shot as the DH for '97. He's still a danger to himself and others with the glove, but last season was the best of his career, especially in showing some new-found plate discipline.

TOM WILSON   **C**   **1971**   **Age 26**

Year	Team	Lge	AB	H	DB	TP	HR	BB	SB	CS	OUT	BA	OBA	SA	EQA	EQR	Peak
1993	Greensboro	SAtl	422	93	8	1	9	70	1	2	331	.220	.331	.308	.215	35	.237
1994	Albany-NY	East	426	101	13	0	8	52	3	3	328	.237	.320	.324	.216	36	.235
1996	Buffalo	AmA	218	60	11	2	9	36	0	1	159	.275	.378	.468	.279	33	.295

In an organization with serious troubles at catcher, Wilson was a godsend from the Yankees' organization. Wilson has some power and some patience, and would give the team a much better option as a starter than Pena should Alomar go down with yet another injury.

BRIAN ANDERSON   **LSP**   **1972**   **Age 25**

YR	TEAM	Lge	IP	H	ER	HR	BB	K	ERA	W	L	H/9	HR/9	BB/9	K/9	KW
1994	California	AL	101.7	113	48	11	30	46	4.25	5	6	10.00	.97	2.66	4.07	.69
1995	California	AL	101.0	103	52	22	33	45	4.63	5	6	9.18	1.96	2.94	4.01	.60
1996	Buffalo	AmA	121.3	139	56	13	45	71	4.15	6	7	10.31	.96	3.34	5.27	.92
1996	Cleveland	AL	51.0	54	21	7	15	20	3.71	3	3	9.53	1.24	2.65	3.53	.51

After being rushed by the Angels, Anderson was left in the rotation at Buffalo and looked good. Unfortunately, Anderson is that breed of pitcher who has it especially rough in the AL, the flyball-tossing lefty. Cleveland is one of the better places for this type of pitcher to pitch, but it may not be enough. With Martinez' departure, Anderson is one of the top candidates to get a regular rotation job next spring, barring any major free agent pickups.

PAUL ASSENMACHER   **LRP**   **1961**   **Age 36**

YR	TEAM	Lge	IP	H	ER	HR	BB	K	ERA	W	L	H/9	HR/9	BB/9	K/9	KW
1993	ChicagoCubs	NL	38.0	44	13	5	18	33	3.08	3	1	10.42	1.18	4.26	7.82	1.54
1993	NY Yankees	AL	16.7	11	4	0	10	11	2.16	2	0	5.94	.00	5.40	5.94	.63
1994	Chi. White Sox	AL	32.3	27	10	2	14	29	2.78	3	1	7.52	.56	3.90	8.07	1.72
1995	Cleveland	AL	37.7	33	10	3	13	40	2.39	3	1	7.88	.72	3.11	9.56	2.41
1996	Cleveland	AL	46.0	44	12	1	15	42	2.35	4	1	8.61	.20	2.93	8.22	2.01

With usage like this, Assenmacher's career could go on another ten years. He used to be given 100 innings per year, but now, with the extreme patterns of the day dictating how lefty specialists are used, that's about three years' worth of work. Famed left-handed gunslingers like Rick Honeycutt aside, Assenmacher is probably the best in baseball today at this job, and since he's had two poor seasons in his entire career, there's little reason to expect that he won't keep mowing down Paul O'Neill or Mo Vaughn like they were Matt Walbeck for another year or two. The unfortunate part is that Assenmacher is capable of holding down a much larger role in the bullpen, but then the chances of injury would increase.

BARTOLO COLON   **RBP**   **1975**   **Age 22**

YR	TEAM	Lge	IP	H	ER	HR	BB	K	ERA	W	L	H/9	HR/9	BB/9	K/9	KW
1995	Kinston	Caro	118.0	116	33	9	54	111	2.52	9	4	8.85	.69	4.12	8.47	1.79
1996	Canton	East	57.3	51	15	2	31	41	2.35	4	2	8.01	.31	4.87	6.44	.93
1996	Buffalo	AmA	14.0	18	9	8	11	16	5.79	1	1	11.57	5.14	7.07	10.29	1.66

One of the best pitching prospects in baseball. He missed a lot of time this year with a bout of tendinitis and elbow problems; the Indians have come to the conclusion that Colon cannot go beyond 80 pitches in an outing without losing his control and damaging his arm, which is leading them to convert him to relief. Colon has complete mastery of the strike zone with a plus fastball, curve and changeup.

REID CORNELIUS   **RBP**   **1970**   **Age 27**

YR	TEAM	Lge	IP	H	ER	HR	BB	K	ERA	W	L	H/9	HR/9	BB/9	K/9	KW
1993	Harrisburg	East	143.3	171	98	12	104	91	6.15	5	11	10.74	.75	6.53	5.71	.27
1994	Ottawa	Inter	138.7	171	91	19	94	74	5.91	5	10	11.10	1.23	6.10	4.80	.08
1995	Norfolk	Inter	65.0	67	10	2	27	36	1.38	6	1	9.28	.28	3.74	4.98	.73
1995	NY Mets	NL	57.3	67	33	8	30	32	5.18	2	4	10.52	1.26	4.71	5.02	.50
1996	Buffalo	AmA	86.3	111	63	5	64	52	6.57	3	7	11.57	.52	6.67	5.42	.14

He's been an organizational hot potato, skipping from the Expos to the Mets to the Tribe. Cornelius lives off a curveball that he throws overhand. He's never been a prospect, but he's been with some sexy organizations.

ROLAND DELA MAZA **RBP** 1972 **Age 25**

YR	TEAM	Lge	IP	H	ER	HR	BB	K	ERA	W	L	H/9	HR/9	BB/9	K/9	KW
1993	Watertown	NY-P	80.7	137	52	11	29	42	5.80	3	6	15.29	1.23	3.24	4.69	.75
1994	Columbus, GA	SAtl	98.3	130	64	14	40	57	5.86	3	8	11.90	1.28	3.66	5.22	.82
1995	Kinston	Caro	99.3	126	36	15	42	74	3.26	7	4	11.42	1.36	3.81	6.70	1.28
1995	Canton	East	34.7	39	18	6	22	21	4.67	2	2	10.12	1.56	5.71	5.45	.39
1996	Canton	East	128.7	140	73	15	62	97	5.11	5	9	9.79	1.05	4.34	6.78	1.18

A soft-tosser out of Sacramento State, Dela Maza has been jerked into and out of roles, but still manages to keep his fine control and good strikeout numbers. However, because Canton is a great pitcher's park, I'd be wary of his proclivity for giving up the longball.

MAXIMO DE LA ROSA **RBP** 1972 **Age 25**

YR	TEAM	Lge	IP	H	ER	HR	BB	K	ERA	W	L	H/9	HR/9	BB/9	K/9	KW
1994	Columbus, GA	S Atl	66.7	61	33	2	52	42	4.46	3	4	8.24	.27	7.02	5.67	.13
1994	Kinston	Caro	62.7	95	57	7	50	36	8.19	1	6	13.64	1.01	7.18	5.17	-.07
1995	Kinston	Caro	56.7	57	25	0	48	45	3.97	3	3	9.05	.00	7.62	7.15	.48
1996	Canton	East	111.0	114	56	7	97	81	4.54	5	7	9.24	.57	7.86	6.57	.22

A converted outfielder, Maximo has been flip-flopped between the rotation and the bullpen. He throws a 90+ heater, and keeps the ball in the infield. He isn't an outstanding prospect, but he should be a useful spare part for a team.

TRAVIS DRISKILL **RBP** 1972 **Age 25**

YR	TEAM	Lge	IP	H	ER	HR	BB	K	ERA	W	L	H/9	HR/9	BB/9	K/9	KW
1993	Watertown	NY-P	50.0	90	49	6	36	28	8.82	1	5	16.20	1.08	6.48	5.04	.06
1994	Columbus, GA	S Atl	57.3	61	25	2	43	52	3.92	3	3	9.58	.31	6.75	8.16	1.03
1995	Kinston	Caro	21.0	21	7	3	8	18	3.00	1	1	9.00	1.29	3.43	7.71	1.71
1995	Canton	East	43.0	51	23	4	23	30	4.81	2	3	10.67	.84	4.81	6.28	.89
1996	Canton	East	159.3	188	83	8	80	109	4.69	8	10	10.62	.45	4.52	6.16	.92

Driskill has some of the best breaking stuff in the organization. This year, the Indians decided to see if they could turn him into a starting pitcher after he'd enjoyed some success as a reliever. He posted an ERA forty points better than league average, kept the ball in the yard and won 13 games. Overall, the Tribe has to be pleased.

ALAN EMBREE **LBP** 1970 **Age 27**

YR	TEAM	Lge	IP	H	ER	HR	BB	K	ERA	W	L	H/9	HR/9	BB/9	K/9	KW
1994	Canton	East	141.0	219	116	17	87	60	7.40	4	12	13.98	1.09	5.55	3.83	-.11
1995	Buffalo	AmA	38.7	36	9	0	24	50	2.09	3	1	8.38	.00	5.59	11.64	2.48
1995	Cleveland	AL	24.7	24	13	2	16	23	4.74	1	2	8.76	.73	5.84	8.39	1.34
1996	Buffalo	AmA	32.7	29	15	1	19	38	4.13	2	2	7.99	.28	5.23	10.47	2.18
1996	Cleveland	AL	31.3	26	19	9	22	32	5.46	1	2	7.47	2.59	6.32	9.19	1.48

That rare lefty with a plus fastball, Embree's career has stalled because he can't throw anything but a fastball, probably because of his past arm troubles. Other organizations would envy having a left-handed reliever with that sort of problem.

DANNY GRAVES **RRP** 1974 **Age 23**

YR	TEAM	Lge	IP	H	ER	HR	BB	K	ERA	W	L	H/9	HR/9	BB/9	K/9	KW
1994	Canton	East	21.3	14	1	0	3	8	.42	2	0	5.91	.00	1.27	3.38	.81
1996	Buffalo	AmA	74.3	66	13	1	33	38	1.57	7	1	7.99	.12	4.00	4.60	.53
1996	Cleveland	AL	29.7	27	12	2	11	21	3.64	2	1	8.19	.61	3.34	6.37	1.29

Named the best reliever in the American Association, Graves succeeds with a plus sinking fastball and a good slider. Graves is an outstanding reliever, and should be a major part of the Indians' bullpen in '97. He might be the first major league player of Vietnamese ancestry (his mother).

OREL HERSHISER | RSP | 1959 | Age 38

YR	TEAM	Lge	IP	H	ER	HR	BB	K	ERA	W	L	H/9	HR/9	BB/9	K/9	KW
1993	Los Angeles	NL	209.0	213	98	18	95	136	4.22	11	12	9.17	.78	4.09	5.86	.93
1994	Los Angeles	NL	133.3	152	63	15	55	68	4.25	7	8	10.26	1.01	3.71	4.59	.60
1995	Cleveland	AL	166.0	152	61	20	55	112	3.31	11	7	8.24	1.08	2.98	6.07	1.28
1996	Cleveland	AL	206.0	219	83	17	63	120	3.63	13	10	9.57	.74	2.75	5.24	1.06

The man whose face was made for Wheaties boxes endured some tough times this season. First, he was part of an off-season controversy involving whether or not he would retire to take up a broadcasting career. Then he staggered to a 4-4 mark with a 6.17 ERA in the opening months. He endured that, and more than made up for it, by logging 21 quality starts in 33 starts over the entire season. Third, and most ironically, after his midseason "comeback" a whispering campaign that Hershiser was cutting the ball began to circulate. It's probably Orel's just desserts, since back at the beginning of his career Orel was the straight-laced Dodger-blue whiner who hardly let an Astros-Dodgers series go by without shrieking about how Mike Scott was a cheater who cheated and who needed to be stopped from cheating, gollygeewillikers.

DARON KIRKREIT | RSP | 1973 | Age 24

YR	TEAM	Lge	IP	H	ER	HR	BB	K	ERA	W	L	H/9	HR/9	BB/9	K/9	KW
1994	Kinston	Caro	116.3	114	46	9	55	78	3.56	7	6	8.82	.70	4.26	6.03	.95
1994	Canton	East	42.0	63	38	6	33	40	8.14	1	4	13.50	1.29	7.07	8.57	1.09
1995	Canton	East	74.7	82	51	14	56	51	6.15	2	6	9.88	1.69	6.75	6.15	.36
1996	Kinston	Caro	29.3	28	7	4	14	13	2.15	2	1	8.59	1.23	4.30	3.99	.26

Kirkreit, once one of the top pitching prospects in the organization, is recovering slowly from surgery to repair a torn rotator cuff. His blazing fastball may have been left on the operating table, but we'll have to wait and see.

STEVEN KLINE | LSP | 1973 | Age 24

YR	TEAM	Lge	IP	H	ER	HR	BB	K	ERA	W	L	H/9	HR/9	BB/9	K/9	KW
1993	Watertown	NY-P	63.3	115	49	5	24	24	6.96	2	5	16.34	.71	3.41	3.41	.28
1994	Columbus,GA	SAtl	162.7	220	73	17	60	102	4.04	9	9	12.17	.94	3.32	5.64	1.05
1995	Canton	East	82.0	99	33	7	37	34	3.62	5	4	10.87	.77	4.06	3.73	.23
1996	Canton	East	135.7	185	94	16	70	79	6.24	4	11	12.27	1.06	4.64	5.24	.59

Elbow surgery before the season made this more of a trial of his arm's health than his future. He managed to survive, so it will be up to him to show something more in '97.

ALBIE LOPEZ | RSP | 1972 | Age 25

YR	TEAM	Lge	IP	H	ER	HR	BB	K	ERA	W	L	H/9	HR/9	BB/9	K/9	KW
1993	Canton	East	101.0	93	43	12	60	61	3.83	6	5	8.29	1.07	5.35	5.44	.48
1993	Cleveland	AL	50.0	50	31	8	35	26	5.58	2	4	9.00	1.44	6.30	4.68	-.01
1994	Charlotte, NC	Inter	135.3	149	64	20	56	87	4.26	7	8	9.91	1.33	3.72	5.79	1.00
1995	Buffalo	AmA	96.7	112	58	10	65	73	5.40	4	7	10.43	.93	6.05	6.80	.75
1995	Cleveland	AL	22.3	18	6	4	7	22	2.42	1	1	7.25	1.61	2.82	8.87	2.25
1996	Buffalo	AmA	99.3	101	53	13	55	74	4.80	5	6	9.15	1.18	4.98	6.70	.99
1996	Cleveland	AL	63.0	72	34	11	23	43	4.86	3	4	10.29	1.57	3.29	6.14	1.23

A test of Mike Hargrove's intestinal fortitude is whether or not he's finally going to give Albie Lopez a rotation spot. I'd say it's unlikely. The high, hard fastball, Lopez' primary weapon, is an especially frequent souvenir in the DH league, and the pressure to win now probably great enough on the Indians that waiting to see if Lopez can sort out his taterific troubles is doubtful. He'll be a fine starter for somebody else in some future year.

DENNIS MARTINEZ | RSP | 1955 | Age 42

YR	TEAM	Lge	IP	H	ER	HR	BB	K	ERA	W	L	H/9	HR/9	BB/9	K/9	KW
1993	Montreal	NL	218.3	220	102	29	88	133	4.20	11	13	9.07	1.20	3.63	5.48	.92
1994	Cleveland	AL	173.7	162	55	13	49	90	2.85	13	6	8.40	.67	2.54	4.66	.92
1995	Cleveland	AL	185.0	176	57	17	50	99	2.77	14	7	8.56	.83	2.43	4.82	1.00
1996	Cleveland	AL	112.3	111	45	10	39	46	3.61	7	5	8.89	.80	3.12	3.69	.45

"El Presidente" made it plain that trading a compadre was enough to make him hitch up his wagon and go. When Eddie Murray was traded, it bugged several of the black players, who simply made it plain. When Baerga left, Martinez led a bitter, nasty attack by the Tribe's Latino players against John Hart. He's announced he'd like to pitch at least one more year, but with his public attacks on the front office, he might be considered too much of a loose cannon by front office lackeys to have many options. The warning sign that he may be almost done, after years of expectation and prediction by so many, is the extra drop in his strikeout rates to go with the frayed tendon in his pitching elbow.

JACK McDOWELL   RSP   1966   Age 31

YR	TEAM	Lge	IP	H	ER	HR	BB	K	ERA	W	L	H/9	HR/9	BB/9	K/9	KW
1993	Chi. White Sox	AL	253.3	262	87	21	81	163	3.09	18	10	9.31	.75	2.88	5.79	1.21
1994	Chi. White Sox	AL	178.3	186	64	11	47	125	3.23	12	8	9.39	.56	2.37	6.31	1.51
1995	NY Yankees	AL	217.7	202	80	23	82	157	3.31	14	10	8.35	.95	3.39	6.49	1.32
1996	Cleveland	AL	192.0	197	86	18	71	136	4.03	10	11	9.23	.84	3.33	6.38	1.29

McDowell pitched through most of the season with a strained right forearm, which helps to explain the big drop-off. Either that, or he forgot all that "knowing how to win" garbage that got him his Cy Young Award. How bad of a season was it for McDowell? Despite an excellent beginning, he had only 14 quality starts in 30 attempts. If he's healthy, he should return to being a solid starter, but he'll never live up to the expectations that came with his contract.

KENT MERCKER   LBP   1968   Age 29

YR	TEAM	Lge	IP	H	ER	HR	BB	K	ERA	W	L	H/9	HR/9	BB/9	K/9	KW
1993	Atlanta	NL	63.7	56	21	2	44	57	2.97	5	2	7.92	.28	6.22	8.06	1.13
1994	Atlanta	NL	110.7	91	40	17	54	103	3.25	7	5	7.40	1.38	4.39	8.38	1.69
1995	Atlanta	NL	141.0	140	61	15	72	91	3.89	8	8	8.94	.96	4.60	5.81	.79
1996	Baltimore	AL	59.3	67	43	10	36	21	6.52	2	5	10.16	1.52	5.46	3.19	-.30
1996	Cleveland	AL	11.7	10	3	1	3	7	2.31	1	0	7.71	.77	2.31	5.40	1.22

Mercker was the latest example of the Orioles not understanding their league or their ballpark, both of which hurt left-handed pitching. He could still be a useful pitcher for many teams, but as an extreme flyball pitcher and a lefty, he has his limitations in the AL. Back in the NL with Cincinnati.

JOSE MESA   RRP   1966   Age 31

YR	TEAM	Lge	IP	H	ER	HR	BB	K	ERA	W	L	H/9	HR/9	BB/9	K/9	KW
1993	Cleveland	AL	207.3	237	109	22	73	123	4.73	10	13	10.29	.95	3.17	5.34	.99
1994	Cleveland	AL	72.0	69	24	3	28	62	3.00	5	3	8.62	.38	3.50	7.75	1.71
1995	Cleveland	AL	62.7	51	7	3	19	58	1.01	7	0	7.32	.43	2.73	8.33	2.09
1996	Cleveland	AL	71.7	65	22	5	29	62	2.76	5	3	8.16	.63	3.64	7.79	1.68

Not surprisingly, Joe Table did not remain almost untouchable. He really only suffered through a particularly brutal June (11.70 ERA for the month). The Indians are coming up to a tough decision with Mesa, because their farm system is filled with excellent bullpen options, and no closer is worth what Mesa is making. If the Indians flop in '97, don't be surprised to see Mesa as one of the first rats off the sinking ship.

CHARLES NAGY   RSP   1967   Age 30

YR	TEAM	Lge	IP	H	ER	HR	BB	K	ERA	W	L	H/9	HR/9	BB/9	K/9	KW
1993	Cleveland	AL	49.0	66	33	6	16	31	6.06	2	3	12.12	1.10	2.94	5.69	1.16
1994	Cleveland	AL	168.3	166	56	13	53	105	2.99	12	7	8.88	.70	2.83	5.61	1.16
1995	Cleveland	AL	179.0	191	77	19	65	140	3.87	10	10	9.60	.96	3.27	7.04	1.53
1996	Cleveland	AL	220.7	202	62	18	66	161	2.53	18	7	8.24	.73	2.69	6.57	1.52

Using his great power/groundball assortment, Nagy enjoyed a superb season, one that was certainly more impressive than the jilted Cy Young "candidate" Andy Pettitte. However, he does come with handicaps: because of his old arm injury, Hargrove has to use him carefully. Over half of Nagy's starts came on five or more days' rest, with good results (2.67 ERA). That careful usage may not be a luxury the Indians can afford this year with Martinez gone, and if McDowell continues to struggle. If Hargrove is tempted to expand Nagy's workload, watch out for trouble.

CHAD OGEA   RBP   1971   Age 26

YR	TEAM	Lge	IP	H	ER	HR	BB	K	ERA	W	L	H/9	HR/9	BB/9	K/9	KW
1993	Charlotte, NC	Inter	170.3	188	89	27	77	110	4.70	8	11	9.93	1.43	4.07	5.81	.92
1994	Charlotte, NC	Inter	154.7	159	73	21	48	94	4.25	8	9	9.25	1.22	2.79	5.47	1.12
1995	Cleveland	AL	105.0	96	30	11	32	57	2.57	8	4	8.23	.94	2.74	4.89	.94
1996	Cleveland	AL	146.7	139	58	18	45	97	3.56	9	7	8.53	1.10	2.76	5.95	1.29

One of the stupidest exercises of the season was the decision to demote Ogea, and the quibbling over whether or not he should be in the rotation. After an excellent '95 season, with McDowell coming apart at the seams and Hershiser struggling desperately in the early going, where was Ogea? He did miss time in May to tendinitis, but he wasn't back in the rotation regularly until late June. After the All-Star break, he posted a great ERA (4.23). Ogea impresses the hell out of some people, and frightens others with his reliance on the high strike, but the only way the Indians are going to sort out who's right is by pitching him.

ERIC PLUNK RRP 1964 Age 33

YR	TEAM	Lge	IP	H	ER	HR	BB	K	ERA	W	L	H/9	HR/9	BB/9	K/9	KW
1993	Cleveland	AL	70.3	63	25	6	34	80	3.20	5	3	8.06	.77	4.35	10.24	2.32
1994	Cleveland	AL	70.0	60	18	3	39	71	2.31	6	2	7.71	.39	5.01	9.13	1.79
1995	Cleveland	AL	63.0	50	14	5	28	71	2.00	6	1	7.14	.71	4.00	10.14	2.38
1996	Cleveland	AL	76.0	55	14	5	36	82	1.66	7	1	6.51	.59	4.26	9.71	2.17

The best middle reliever in baseball, one-year wonders like Barry Jones or Mariano Rivera be damned. To a certain extent, Plunk's status as the best relies on the fact that he'll never be moved out of the job; there's a widespread conviction that he lacks the "makeup" to close.

JOE ROA RSP 1972 Age 25

YR	TEAM	Lge	IP	H	ER	HR	BB	K	ERA	W	L	H/9	HR/9	BB/9	K/9	KW
1993	Binghamton	East	152.7	216	80	11	37	55	4.72	7	10	12.73	.65	2.18	3.24	.54
1994	Norfolk	Inter	155.7	217	87	17	49	63	5.03	7	10	12.55	.98	2.83	3.64	.51
1995	Buffalo	AmA	156.3	184	70	10	47	82	4.03	8	9	10.59	.58	2.71	4.72	.90
1996	Buffalo	AmA	156.7	179	65	18	57	68	3.73	9	8	10.28	1.03	3.27	3.91	.48

An extreme finesse pitcher, Roa has nothing left to prove in the minors. He'd be a fine addition to a number of major league rotations, and he's got a durable arm.

PAUL SHUEY RRP 1971 Age 26

YR	TEAM	Lge	IP	H	ER	HR	BB	K	ERA	W	L	H/9	HR/9	BB/9	K/9	KW
1993	Kinston	Caro	19.3	35	14	1	13	17	6.52	1	1	16.29	.47	6.05	7.91	1.12
1993	Canton	East	56.7	85	50	13	46	32	7.94	1	5	13.50	2.06	7.31	5.08	-.13
1994	Charlotte, NC	Inter	21.7	17	8	1	13	21	3.32	1	1	7.06	.42	5.40	8.72	1.56
1994	Cleveland	AL	12.0	13	8	1	12	16	6.00	0	1	9.75	.75	9.00	12.00	1.75
1995	Buffalo	AmA	25.7	24	9	3	10	24	3.16	2	1	8.42	1.05	3.51	8.42	1.93
1996	Buffalo	AmA	31.3	18	3	1	13	47	.86	3	0	5.17	.29	3.73	13.50	3.57
1996	Cleveland	AL	53.0	42	13	6	27	42	2.21	5	1	7.13	1.02	4.58	7.13	1.23

Shuey has finally turned the corner, learning to mix in an outstanding curve with his plus fastball. Although not many minor league relievers who are developed as closers every work out, Shuey may be the rare success.

GREG SWINDELL LBP 1965 Age 32

YR	TEAM	Lge	IP	H	ER	HR	BB	K	ERA	W	L	H/9	HR/9	BB/9	K/9	KW
1993	Houston	NL	186.0	223	93	26	61	120	4.50	9	12	10.79	1.26	2.95	5.81	1.20
1994	Houston	NL	147.0	174	72	20	40	69	4.41	7	9	10.65	1.22	2.45	4.22	.80
1995	Houston	NL	151.7	191	83	22	53	88	4.93	7	10	11.33	1.31	3.15	5.22	.95
1996	Houston	NL	23.3	36	23	5	14	13	8.87	1	2	13.89	1.93	5.40	5.01	.32
1996	Cleveland	AL	29.3	27	15	7	9	20	4.60	1	2	8.28	2.15	2.76	6.14	1.36

What was the worst roster move the Indians made all year? Trading Eddie Murray? No, there were good reasons for that. Carlos Baerga? Nope. No, the most idiotic waste of time involving the Tribe was the nostalgic acquisition of the dregs, no, the offal that's left of "Flounder's" career. Take what happened to Kent Mercker, or Sid Fernandez when he went to Baltimore, and imagine that scenario at its worst, and that's what you get with trying to resuscitate Swindell's career out of pity.

JULIAN TAVAREZ RBP 1973 Age 24

YR	TEAM	Lge	IP	H	ER	HR	BB	K	ERA	W	L	H/9	HR/9	BB/9	K/9	KW
1993	Kinston	Caro	105.3	128	54	7	47	67	4.61	5	7	10.94	.60	4.02	5.72	.90
1993	Cleveland	AL	37.7	53	26	7	15	20	6.21	1	3	12.66	1.67	3.58	4.78	.70
1994	Charlotte, NC	Inter	166.3	181	73	16	59	85	3.95	9	9	9.79	.87	3.19	4.60	.73
1995	Cleveland	AL	84.0	77	28	7	23	68	3.00	6	3	8.25	.75	2.46	7.29	1.81
1996	Cleveland	AL	81.0	93	36	7	24	44	4.00	5	4	10.33	.78	2.67	4.89	.96

Tavarez was probably doomed in the AL after his run-in with an umpire during a brawl in Milwaukee. The Giants apparently plan to keep him in the bullpen, which is a good idea for a few more years at least, since there are major concerns over whether Tavarez' slight build can hold up to regular rotation work. What he has to work on changing is finding a breaking pitch that works against left-handed batters; good times or bad, Tavarez has real problems against them (they've hit .329/.383/.514 against him on his career).

CASEY WHITTEN   LSP   1972   Age 25

YR	TEAM	Lge	IP	H	ER	HR	BB	K	ERA	W	L	H/9	HR/9	BB/9	K/9	KW
1993	Watertown	NY-P	65.0	114	37	11	32	42	5.12	3	4	15.78	1.52	4.43	5.82	.83
1994	Kinston	Caro	137.0	159	81	20	86	100	5.32	5	10	10.45	1.31	5.65	6.57	.78
1995	Canton	East	106.7	113	45	11	47	70	3.80	6	6	9.53	.93	3.97	5.91	.98
1996	Canton	East	34.7	28	7	2	17	33	1.82	3	1	7.27	.52	4.41	8.57	1.75
1996	Buffalo	AmA	42.0	59	45	7	32	30	9.64	1	4	12.64	1.50	6.86	6.43	.43

The best left-handed pitching prospect in the organization. Whitten has had recurring shoulder troubles, which just this year were diagnosed as an uncommon vascular condition where clotting occurs spontaneously. With blood thinners, Whitten should be fine for the future. Another lefty with a plus fastball, the Indians plan on letting Whitten get a full season under his belt at Buffalo in '97, to demonstrate his ability to pitch with his condition while erasing this year's failure to succeed there.

JARET WRIGHT   RSP   1976   Age 21

YR	TEAM	Lge	IP	H	ER	HR	BB	K	ERA	W	L	H/9	HR/9	BB/9	K/9	KW
1995	Columbus,GA	SAtl	111.3	118	60	11	109	64	4.85	5	7	9.54	.89	8.81	5.17	-.48
1996	Kinston	Caro	91.3	79	32	2	72	75	3.15	6	4	7.78	.20	7.09	7.39	.69

Wright is almost as outstanding a pitching prospect as Colon, although his attempts to develop a breaking pitch he can throw for strikes haven't been too successful. With a fastball that regularly tops 95, the Indians can afford to be patient. Although he was injured this year, it wasn't an arm problem: at an All-Star game, he was hit in the face with a bat and had to have his jaw wired shut. He looked good in the AFL, and could move up the organizational ladder very quickly.

Player	Age	Team	Lge	AB	H	DB	TP	HR	BB	SB	CS	OUT	BA	OBA	SA	EQA	EQR	Peak
MILT ANDERSON	23	Columbus-GA	S Atl	267	57	7	0	5	33	11	4	214	.213	.300	.296	.204	20	.222
JAMES BETZSOLD	23	Canton	East	274	62	10	3	3	27	3	1	213	.226	.296	.318	.205	20	.223
PAT BRYANT	23	Canton	East	112	21	2	0	3	15	5	1	92	.188	.283	.286	.195	8	.211
MARK BUDZINSKI	22	Columbus-GA	S Atl	282	67	9	2	3	47	4	1	216	.238	.347	.316	.228	27	.251
CASEY CANDAELE	35	Buffalo	AmA	405	125	18	2	6	31	3	4	284	.309	.358	.407	.258	48	.245
GERAD CAWHORN	24	Kinston	Caro	181	40	7	1	2	19	1	1	142	.221	.295	.304	.198	12	.212
PATRICIO CLAUDIO	24	Kinston	Caro	378	101	10	2	1	41	15	7	284	.267	.339	.312	.226	34	.243
TIM COSTO	27	Buffalo	AmA	257	55	9	0	8	21	1	2	204	.214	.273	.342	.200	18	.205
JOHN DONATI	23	Columbus-GA	S Atl	151	39	3	1	4	8	0	0	112	.258	.296	.371	.223	13	.242
PAUL FARIES	31	Buffalo	AmA	176	44	7	1	2	14	3	1	133	.250	.305	.335	.217	15	.208
CHIP GLASS	25	Kinston	Caro	495	121	10	6	5	35	5	3	377	.244	.294	.319	.205	36	.216
MICHAEL GLAVINE	23	Columbus-GA	S Atl	130	34	1	0	5	22	0	0	96	.262	.368	.385	.255	16	.277
RICKY GONZALEZ	21	Columbus-GA	S Atl	256	51	3	0	2	13	0	0	205	.199	.238	.234	.136	7	.152
GARY HAGY	27	Kinston	Caro	185	38	5	0	5	35	2	1	148	.205	.332	.314	.218	16	.222
ROBIN HARRISS	24	Kinston	Caro	268	53	2	1	4	14	1	1	216	.198	.238	.257	.149	9	.158
HEATH HAYES	24	Columbus-GA	S Atl	364	80	6	0	15	28	1	0	284	.220	.276	.360	.209	29	.224
ERIC HELFAND	27	Buffalo	AmA	268	56	5	0	6	47	0	2	214	.209	.327	.295	.207	21	.212
TOM MARSH	30	Buffalo	AmA	401	93	14	1	9	21	8	4	312	.232	.270	.339	.203	29	.199
GUILLERMO MERCEDES	22	Kinston	Caro	394	86	4	1	1	26	1	1	309	.218	.267	.241	.158	15	.174
DAVID MILLER	22	Kinston	Caro	503	117	9	1	7	34	6	3	389	.233	.281	.296	.191	31	.211
JASON MINICI	22	Columbus-GA	S Atl	348	65	10	1	4	24	3	2	285	.187	.239	.256	.150	12	.165
CRISTIAN MOTA	20	Columbus-GA	S Atl	127	24	2	0	2	7	0	1	104	.189	.231	.252	.139	4	.159
MIKE MOYLE	24	Kinston	Caro	207	53	5	1	6	26	1	1	155	.256	.339	.377	.241	22	.257
MIKE NEAL	24	Canton	East	261	55	6	2	4	35	2	1	207	.211	.304	.295	.199	18	.213
CHAN PERRY	23	Kinston	Caro	372	100	10	1	10	32	1	1	273	.269	.327	.382	.238	38	.259
LUIS RAVEN	27	Canton	East	276	83	11	0	18	34	0	0	193	.301	.377	.536	.297	46	.304
MARCOS SCUTARO	20	Columbus-GA	S Atl	332	75	7	1	8	29	2	1	258	.226	.288	.325	.203	24	.232
STEVE SOLIZ	25	Canton	East	146	35	4	1	2	10	1	1	112	.240	.288	.322	.202	10	.212
DON SPARKS	30	Buffalo	AmA	530	157	29	4	8	59	2	2	375	.296	.367	.411	.263	66	.257
DARREN STUMBERGER	23	Columbus-GA	S Atl	498	142	14	1	18	41	0	0	356	.285	.340	.426	.256	59	.279
JERRY TAYLOR	23	Kinston	Caro	159	38	6	1	1	42	0	0	121	.239	.398	.308	.247	18	.270
GREG THOMAS	23	Canton	East	307	83	10	3	11	24	2	1	225	.270	.323	.430	.251	35	.272
CHAD THORNHILL	23	Columbus-GA	S Atl	171	27	1	0	2	23	0	1	145	.158	.258	.199	.123	4	.135
WILLY VALERA	20	Columbus-GA	S Atl	404	74	8	1	4	15	4	3	333	.183	.212	.238	.123	9	.139
BRYAN WARNER	21	Columbus-GA	S Atl	340	78	6	0	4	14	3	2	264	.229	.260	.282	.175	17	.196
	21	Kinston	Caro	114	23	0	0	1	7	1	0	91	.202	.248	.228	.143	4	.159
CHAD WHITAKER	19	Columbus-GA	S Atl	245	53	4	0	9	20	1	1	193	.216	.275	.343	.203	18	.235
ERIC WHITE	23	Kinston	Caro	434	94	13	0	5	28	1	2	342	.217	.264	.281	.174	22	.189

Player	Age	Team	Lge	IP	H	ER	HR	BB	K	ERA	W	L	H/9	HR/9	BB/9	K/9	KW
DANNON ATKINS	22	Columbus, GA	S Atl	141.7	213	100	22	93	70	6.35	5	11	13.53	1.40	5.91	4.45	.01
JASON BENNETT	21	Columbus, GA	S Atl	60.7	67	34	3	36	28	5.04	3	4	9.94	.45	5.34	4.15	.05
DAN BRABANT	23	Kinston	Caro	53.3	63	37	9	39	35	6.24	2	4	10.63	1.52	6.58	5.91	.32
JOSE CABRERA	24	Canton	East	58.0	85	43	10	22	30	6.67	2	4	13.19	1.55	3.41	4.66	.70
GREG CADARET	34	Buffalo	AmA	60.7	67	28	3	38	37	4.15	3	4	9.94	.45	5.64	5.49	.42
DAVID CALDWELL	21	Kinston	Caro	122.7	174	73	13	54	55	5.36	5	9	12.77	.95	3.96	4.04	.35
JIM CROWELL	22	Columbus, GA	S Atl	137.3	218	103	19	100	57	6.75	4	11	14.29	1.25	6.55	3.74	-.39
MARC DESCHENES	23	Columbus, GA	S Atl	63.7	94	44	10	58	37	6.22	2	5	13.29	1.41	8.20	5.23	-.31
SCOT DONOVAN	23	Kinston	Caro	47.3	69	41	7	34	25	7.80	1	4	13.12	1.33	6.46	4.75	-.03
TONY DOUGHERTY	23	Columbus, GA	S Atl	43.0	40	17	4	31	24	3.56	3	2	8.37	.84	6.49	5.02	.05
	23	Kinston	Caro	30.3	34	6	3	16	22	1.78	5	0	10.09	.89	4.75	6.53	.99
CHRIS GRANATA	24	Kinston	Caro	84.3	125	56	6	58	40	5.98	3	6	13.34	.64	6.19	4.27	-.12
GREG GRANGER	23	Columbus, GA	S Atl	70.0	120	49	6	42	37	6.30	2	6	15.43	.77	5.40	4.76	.24
RICHARD GRIFE	24	Columbus, GA	S Atl	48.3	77	35	1	29	23	6.52	1	4	14.34	.19	5.40	4.28	.08
BENJI GRIGSBY	25	Canton	East	26.3	25	10	0	14	16	3.42	2	1	8.54	.00	4.78	5.47	.63
KRIS HANSON	25	Kinston	Caro	41.7	56	34	7	22	18	7.34	1	4	12.10	1.51	4.75	3.89	.11
TERRY HARVEY	23	Kinston	Caro	61.7	96	42	5	24	24	6.13	2	5	14.01	.73	3.50	3.50	.29
KEITH HORN	22	Columbus, GA	S Atl	75.7	111	57	9	36	42	6.78	2	6	13.20	1.07	4.28	5.00	.59
JIM LEWIS	26	Buffalo	AmA	115.0	148	78	9	67	60	6.10	4	9	11.58	.70	5.24	4.70	.25
SAMMIE MATHIS	23	Columbus, GA	S Atl	71.7	112	51	8	46	37	6.40	2	6	14.07	1.00	5.78	4.65	.10
MIKE MATTHEWS	22	Canton	East	149.7	196	92	13	92	83	5.53	6	11	11.79	.78	5.53	4.99	.28
BRETT MERRICK	22	Columbus, GA	S Atl	47.3	47	23	3	35	28	4.37	2	3	8.94	.57	6.65	5.32	.11
RAFAEL MESA	22	Kinston	Caro	73.3	71	27	5	38	39	3.31	5	3	8.71	.61	4.66	4.79	.43
WILMER MONTOYA	22	Canton	East	46.7	46	22	2	35	31	4.24	2	3	8.87	.39	6.75	5.98	.31
NOE NAJERA	25	Kinston	Caro	124.0	152	57	14	84	91	4.14	7	7	11.03	1.02	6.10	6.60	.68
JULIO PEREZ	22	Kinston	Caro	38.0	54	24	3	24	15	5.68	1	3	12.79	.71	5.68	3.55	-.24
ERIK PLANTENBERG	27	Buffalo	AmA	32.0	39	16	2	19	24	4.50	2	2	10.97	.56	5.34	6.75	.91
JASON RAKERS	23	Columbus, GA	S Atl	64.7	114	44	6	26	35	6.12	2	5	15.87	.84	3.62	4.87	.72
FRANKIE SANDERS	20	Columbus, GA	S Atl	105.3	135	57	10	55	59	4.87	5	7	11.53	.85	4.70	5.04	.51
DARRYL SCOTT	27	Buffalo	AmA	77.0	68	27	11	34	60	3.16	6	3	7.95	1.29	3.97	7.01	1.34
JEFF SEXTON	24	Canton	East	45.3	51	28	6	28	25	5.56	2	3	10.12	1.19	5.56	4.96	.26
KEVIN TOLAR	25	Canton	East	41.3	46	18	1	32	29	3.92	3	3	10.02	.22	6.97	6.31	.36
JAY VAUGHT	24	Canton	East	87.0	113	56	10	44	58	5.79	3	7	11.69	1.03	4.55	6.00	.86
TEDDY WARRECKER	23	Kinston	Caro	116.3	160	112	14	114	61	8.66	2	11	12.38	1.08	8.82	4.72	-.63
LENNY WEBER	23	Kinston	Caro	53.0	52	12	0	47	34	2.04	5	1	8.83	.00	7.98	5.77	-.07
BILL WERTZ	29	Buffalo	AmA	28.0	35	16	3	24	19	5.14	1	2	11.25	.96	7.71	6.11	.11
JIMMY WILLIAMS	31	Buffalo	AmA	108.7	128	59	13	61	80	4.89	5	7	10.60	1.08	5.05	6.63	.95
SCOTT WINCHESTER	23	Columbus, GA	S Atl	52.0	71	32	9	24	33	5.54	2	4	12.29	1.56	4.15	5.71	.87

Kansas City Royals

There are many variables which govern a team's fortunes, like money, front office competence and the vagaries of fate which cause one star pitcher (let's call him Jose Rijo) to blow out his arm while elsewhere, a struggling slugger (we'll call him Matt Williams) suddenly raises his average 70 points. For most teams, the first two factors remain relatively constant from year to year, and the third determines most of the transient changes in a franchise's success. Every so often, a team will reach a crossroads, when their personnel arrives at a collective age such that the rapidly-diminishing returns on retaining them forces wholesale changes to be made, and the team rebuilds. But even such a drastic change is rarely more than a ripple in the undulating river that guides the organization's overall course.

Rarely, though, will an organization undergo genuine turmoil, with each component of success pulling in a different direction. The Kansas City Royals are enduring such an upheaval. Name an ingredient for a team's success, and the Royals have a question mark the size of the Washington Monument next to it. Ownership? The Royals don't have an owner. What they do have is David Glass, a Wal-Mart executive who has done a damn fine job of getting his name in the news as one of the leaders of the hard-line owners in the labor dispute, despite not having a cent invested in the team. Front office? Bob Boone, like his mentor Gene Mauch, is a spectacular riddle of a manager; he's a brilliant baseball man, but for the life of him doesn't know how to exploit that brilliance to make rational baseball decisions. Personnel? The Royals have a surfeit of mediocre veterans (Bip Roberts, Tim Belcher) holding down jobs while the waves of talent from the farm system, promising but still unproven hitters like Michael Tucker, Jon Nunnally, and Joe Vitiello, try to erode a shoreline of moderately useful but vastly overrated players like Tom Goodwin and Craig Paquette.

What is so chaotic about having a burgeoning farm system, you may ask? Young talent is like your grandmother's vegetable garden; if it's nurtured carefully and patiently, it will ripen beautifully, but in the hands of a neglectful or foolish caretaker, weeds will overgrow and ruin a promising crop. The evil winds that swirl at the Royals' top are threatening to devastate the harvest below. Start with Glass, who has had de facto control of the team since the death of long-time owner Ewing Kauffman in 1994. With no financial stake in the Royals' success, Glass has been content to let an obtuse general manager, Herk Robinson, continue to sacrifice long-term goals for short-term respectability. The signings of Belcher and Roberts were supposed to be temporary buffers that bought the farm system another year to develop talent without a sense of urgency. But now, both have been re-signed for at least another year, despite the availability of better—and certainly cheaper—options from within the organization.

This disingenuous activity in the front office trickled down to the dugout. Boone had a stated goal at the beginning of the year to "bring on the young players slowly and find out what they can do." He then decided to accomplish the task by moving those players all over the diamond and the lineup card, giving them neither a feeling of security nor a role they could grow comfortable with. Johnny Damon, who was already battling higher expectations than any young Royals hitter since Clint Hurdle, batted in every spot in the lineup by the end of May, and was moved back and forth from center to right field constantly.

Without any better options, the Royals' youth movement moved forward haltingly. Damon played every day, and despite criminal mismanagement showed considerable promise for a 22-year-old. Tucker showed tantalizing bat speed and finished with a flourish, hitting .363 in August before ending his season with a broken ring finger. Joe Randa hit .303 at third base, and promising catcher Mike Sweeney posted a .770 OPS after a mid-season promotion.

But some of the Royals' other fine prospects were stunted by Boone's decision to let undeserving veterans play. The bizarre decision to move Jose Offerman to first, which was prompted by the desire to have perennial stiff David Howard play every day, cut into the playing time of both Joe Vitiello and Bob Hamelin. Boone would habitually start Vitiello at DH for four games, then whimsically switch the two to see if Hamelin had learned anything by watching Vitiello bat. With neither a steady rhythm of playing time nor hope of a regular job, both of them suffered through disappointing seasons. By year's end, the hostility between Hamelin and Boone all but guaranteed that Hamelin, whose .391 OBP led the team, would not return next year. Boone's weak spot for reclamation projects led to the coronation of Craig Paquette as the new Great White Hope. Royals fans were treated to rave reviews of Paquette's team-leading HR and RBI totals; what they were not told about was his .296 OBP and erratic defense.

Boone's treatment of the pitching staff was not nearly as senseless. He gave Kevin Appier, Belcher and Chris Haney the ball every fifth day and seamlessly worked Jose Rosado into the rotation when Mark Gubicza went down with a broken leg. In the bullpen, though, Boone impeded the development of promising relievers Jamie Bluma and Rick Huisman by leaving them in AAA too long while continuing to use old, ineffective pitchers like Mike Magnante and Tim Pugh instead. In any case, the Royals' pitching staff has never been a disaster like the Royals' offense, which has finished last in the AL in runs scored three of the last four years.

It is all too clear now that the Royals erred in picking Boone to oversee the franchise's rebirth. Unlike the Tigers' Buddy Bell, whose commitment to the five-year plan resulted in a season that was terrible on the surface but planted the seeds for future success, Boone's unwillingness to make a long-term commitment has endangered what looked like a bright future in Kansas City. Half-hearted rebuilding is no better than not rebuilding, and Boone's straddle-the-fence attitude has alienated the entire team's scouting department. Many of the Royals' top scouts, angered with the misuse of the talent they worked so hard to find, have begun to defect en masse to other organizations. If players like Damon, Sweeney and Rosado break through in 1997 and post All-Star-caliber seasons, all may be forgiven. But if the Royals, who have not had a winning April in eight years, get off to another poor start, sweeping and reckless changes may be in store, changes that could set back the Royals' rebuilding process for years.

To describe 1997 as a pivotal year in Kansas City would be a laughable understatement. The AL Central has a clear demarcation between the haves and have-nots. Albert Belle's change of address from Cleveland to Chicago leaves the division with a pair of 500-pound gorillas and three small-market teams trying to find an alternate way to the top. Baseball has proven to us that money is no substitute for intelligence, and that a small-market team can win by patiently nurturing its own talent and filling the holes with inexpensive veterans when the team is ready to contend.

For all the mistakes made along the way, the Royals had the right idea last year. They made the necessary sacrifices for their future and finished last for the first time in their history. But if life can teach us anything about baseball, it is that while success rarely comes soon, if you remain committed to your plan, it usually does come. The Royals' front office showed last year how impatient they were when their highly touted minor leaguers initially struggled in the majors. They need to change their approach this year from finding out what their players can do to letting them do it. If they do, the Royals can still be on course to put a contending team on the field as early as 1998. If they don't, and players struggle to reach expectations this year, the backlash may set off a chain reaction that no one who believed in the Royals' plan for revival is prepared to see.

DARREN BURTON   **OF**   **1973**   **Age 24**

Year	Team	Lge	AB	H	DB	TP	HR	BB	SB	CS	OUT	BA	OBA	SA	EQA	EQR	Peak
1993	Wilmington	Caro	570	145	15	2	9	44	16	5	430	.254	.308	.335	.220	49	.250
1994	Memphis	South	386	95	9	2	4	36	6	3	294	.246	.310	.311	.210	30	.236
1995	Orlando	South	230	69	12	1	5	26	5	2	163	.300	.371	.426	.270	31	.297
1995	Wichita	Texas	163	34	6	1	1	11	5	3	132	.209	.259	.276	.174	8	.191
1996	Omaha	AmA	476	125	24	3	14	61	7	5	356	.263	.346	.414	.254	58	.276

The Royals had been enamored with his tools for years, but only in the last two years has he done anything with them. Not coincidentally, he started to hit for the first time in 1995 when the Royals tired of his slow development and waived him, and the Cubs picked him up. After the season, the Royals frantically tried to re-acquire him, making room on the 40-man roster when the Cubs didn't. He had a middling season in AAA, and has a great arm in right field, but still needs another year or two of development before he shows up on any major league roster. Just released by the Royals to make room on the 40-man roster; he should have no trouble finding a AAA job somewhere.

JEREMY CARR   **OF**   **1971**   **Age 26**

Year	Team	Lge	AB	H	DB	TP	HR	BB	SB	CS	OUT	BA	OBA	SA	EQA	EQR	Peak
1993	Eugene	Nwern	144	34	3	2	1	13	12	2	112	.236	.299	.306	.218	12	.238
1994	Rockford	Midw	455	107	8	3	1	50	24	10	358	.235	.311	.273	.203	33	.220
1995	Bakersfield	Calif	505	106	14	1	1	63	20	9	408	.210	.298	.248	.184	30	.198
1996	Wichita	Texas	458	108	16	1	6	44	27	6	356	.236	.303	.314	.217	39	.229

A speed merchant who was considered so expendable that he was loaned to Bakersfield, a co-op club, in 1995. But nothing perks up the Royals' attention like a few stolen bases, and Carr racked up 52 of them, swaying the Royals to re-evaluate him and promote him to AA. His knowledge of the strike zone is such that he's not an automatic out, but at his age, he's going to need a miracle to get a chance.

JOHNNY DAMON   **CF/RF**   **1974**   **Age 23**

Year	Team	Lge	AB	H	DB	TP	HR	BB	SB	CS	OUT	BA	OBA	SA	EQA	EQR	Peak
1993	Rockford	Midw	530	142	20	6	6	39	25	9	397	.268	.318	.362	.234	53	.270
1994	Wilmington	Caro	499	153	20	8	6	53	25	6	352	.307	.373	.415	.272	68	.310
1995	Wichita	Texas	425	132	10	3	16	61	18	7	300	.311	.397	.461	.289	68	.324
1995	Kansas City	AL	191	57	11	5	4	12	7	0	134	.298	.340	.471	.275	27	.308
1996	Kansas City	AL	518	142	22	5	6	31	25	5	381	.274	.315	.371	.239	53	.263
1997	*Kansas City*	*AL*	*473*	*140*	*32*	*5*	*6*	*38*	*40*	*8*	*341*	*.296*	*.348*	*.423*	*.276*	*68*	

It's easy to blame Boone for not allowing Damon to get comfortable in one batting spot and one position last year, and it's partially true. But Bobby Higginson batted 1 through 9, played all three outfield spots last year and had a terrific season. Damon's problems were exacerbated by an overly aggressive approach at the plate. His tendency to swing at the first pitch, no matter where it was, got him in trouble by putting him behind in the count too often. When he was ahead in the count, his overzealousness was easily exploited by pitchers. Damon batted .298 with a .394 slugging average with the count in his favor; the AL average was .348 and .595, respectively.

Damon has a fairly unique batting style; when he makes contact with the ball, so much weight is on his front foot that his back foot hardly touches the ground. It's been very successful for him and the Royals have been loath to change it, but it also requires that all his mechanics be in sync. It also gives Damon trouble hitting the outside pitch, and his impatience last year meant that too often, he was swinging at pitches he had no chance of doing anything with. If he narrows his personal strike zone this year, I suspect he'll recover. He has an awkward running motion, but he's a terrific center fielder and basestealer.

LINO DIAZ   **3B**   **1971**   **Age 26**

Year	Team	Lge	AB	H	DB	TP	HR	BB	SB	CS	OUT	BA	OBA	SA	EQA	EQR	Peak
1993	Eugene	Nwern	192	44	4	1	1	5	2	1	149	.229	.249	.276	.168	9	.186
1994	Rockford	Midw	427	122	15	1	4	27	5	3	308	.286	.328	.354	.232	40	.252
1995	Wilmington	Caro	184	56	6	2	2	11	1	2	130	.304	.344	.391	.247	20	.266
1995	Wichita	Texas	225	71	9	2	6	13	1	1	155	.316	.353	.453	.270	29	.288
1996	Wichita	Texas	159	36	6	1	2	10	1	1	124	.226	.272	.314	.192	10	.203
1996	Omaha	AmA	270	69	10	2	3	20	0	2	203	.256	.307	.341	.215	22	.227

Slick-fielding third baseman who hits nothing but singles. In 1995, he hit enough of them that Kevin Seitzer comparisons were not just valid, but inevitable, but last year his Bill Pecota impersonation didn't impress anyone. His opportunity for major league playing time is hanging by a thread.

SAL FASANO   **C**   **1972**   **Age 25**

Year	Team	Lge	AB	H	DB	TP	HR	BB	SB	CS	OUT	BA	OBA	SA	EQA	EQR	Peak
1993	Eugene	Nwern	186	48	4	1	8	10	2	2	140	.258	.296	.419	.236	19	.264
1994	Rockford	Midw	357	97	6	1	20	27	4	2	262	.272	.323	.462	.259	45	.286
1994	Wilmington	Caro	95	30	4	0	6	12	0	0	65	.316	.393	.547	.306	17	.338
1995	Wilmington	Caro	92	22	2	1	2	5	0	0	70	.239	.278	.348	.207	7	.226
1995	Wichita	Texas	317	85	10	1	17	24	3	3	235	.268	.320	.467	.257	39	.279
1996	Omaha	AmA	105	23	2	0	4	7	0	1	83	.219	.268	.352	.200	7	.217
1996	Kansas City	AL	143	29	3	0	6	14	1	1	115	.203	.274	.350	.203	11	.218
1997	*Kansas City*	*AL*	*207*	*54*	*4*	*0*	*11*	*19*	*0*	*2*	*155*	*.261*	*.323*	*.440*	*.256*	*26*	

A better player than he showed last year. He has big-time power and his catching skills have improved so much that Nichols' Law no longer applies to him. He had trouble keeping his average afloat last year, and in his words, "They told me to hit about .200 and play good defense. The problem is, that's exactly what I did." Actually, Sal, the problem was Mike Sweeney. He should have a good career, and if the Royals don't move one of them to first base, between Fasano and Sweeney the Royals will have a very marketable player to trade in a year or two.

CARLOS FEBLES   **2B**   **1976**   **Age 21**

Year	Team	Lge	AB	H	DB	TP	HR	BB	SB	CS	OUT	BA	OBA	SA	EQA	EQR	Peak
1996	Lansing	Midw	376	96	13	2	6	50	14	7	287	.255	.343	.348	.237	39	.268
1997	*Kansas City*	*AL*	*545*	*155*	*21*	*5*	*7*	*82*	*23*	*12*	*402*	*.284*	*.378*	*.380*	*.267*	*74*	

It's not very shrewd to project a player from low A-ball to the major leagues, especially one with little power. But Febles is a terrific fielder—he was voted the best defensive second baseman in the Midwest League - and posted a .403 OBP last year. For a Royals' hitter to show that kind of discipline is unusual—when you consider the free-swinging tendencies of most Latin players, it's almost unheard of. A similar player to Jed Hansen, who is the heir apparent at second base, but he's three years younger and has a much higher upside.

RAUL GONZALEZ   **OF**   **1974**   **Age 23**

Year	Team	Lge	AB	H	DB	TP	HR	BB	SB	CS	OUT	BA	OBA	SA	EQA	EQR	Peak
1993	Wilmington	Caro	482	121	20	2	9	48	7	3	364	.251	.319	.357	.228	45	.263
1994	Wilmington	Caro	432	107	14	4	8	39	0	2	327	.248	.310	.354	.221	38	.251
1995	Wilmington	Caro	325	101	15	2	12	15	4	2	226	.311	.341	.480	.272	44	.305
1995	Wichita	Texas	79	21	2	1	2	7	2	0	58	.266	.326	.392	.246	9	.282
1996	Wichita	Texas	84	21	3	1	1	5	1	1	64	.250	.292	.345	.212	7	.234

Could be an everyday player in the major leagues by now if the Royals had used some common sense. He had a fine season at Wilmington in 1993, a tremendous accomplishment for a 19-year-old playing in a pitcher's park in the Carolina League. The Royals sent him back to Wilmington the following season, and not surprisingly he brooded and had an off-season. Finally he was promoted to AA in 1995, but despite a fast start he was sent down when the Royals had to make room for Vince Coleman (do you sense a trend here?). Last year his season was ended by a broken thumb in May. The luster is off him now, but he's still only 23 and he's right-handed, so if he gets off to a fast start he could find himself in a platoon role in Kansas City before long.

TOM GOODWIN   **CF**   **1969**   **Age 28**

Year	Team	Lge	AB	H	DB	TP	HR	BB	SB	CS	OUT	BA	OBA	SA	EQA	EQR	Peak
1993	Albuquerque	PCL	280	57	6	2	1	27	10	3	226	.204	.274	.250	.174	14	.186
1994	Omaha	AmA	434	132	16	5	3	26	37	13	315	.304	.343	.385	.255	52	.268
1995	Kansas City	AL	487	148	17	3	5	39	51	18	357	.304	.356	.382	.259	61	.270
1996	Kansas City	AL	525	150	14	4	1	40	67	22	397	.286	.336	.333	.243	58	.248
1997	*Kansas City*	*AL*	*513*	*142*	*13*	*8*	*3*	*50*	*58*	*15*	*386*	*.277*	*.341*	*.351*	*.256*	*64*	

If the Royals had a GM that was a better judge of talent than the immortal Lou Gorman, they would push hard to trade Goodwin to the Red Sox for John Valentin. The Royals have five legitimate candidates for their starting outfield and all of them are left-handed. Goodwin is the oldest and most over-rated, which is precisely why the Royals would never trade him. He's not completely bereft of talent; he matches Damon step for step in the outfield and is a wonderful basestealer, which makes him one of the game's best fourth outfielders. Unfortunately, as a starter he's barely average, and the Royals don't have any big bombers in the outfield to compensate for his weaknesses. He'll probably get a huge raise once he's eligible for arbitration next year, but he won't be worth it.

JEFF GROTEWOLD   **1B/DH**   **1966**   **Age 31**

Year	Team	Lge	AB	H	DB	TP	HR	BB	SB	CS	OUT	BA	OBA	SA	EQA	EQR	Peak
1993	Portland-OR	PCL	152	36	3	1	6	24	1	1	117	.237	.341	.388	.243	17	.249
1994	San Bernardino	Calif	120	33	6	0	5	12	0	1	88	.275	.341	.450	.260	15	.262
1995	Omaha	AmA	358	100	11	0	17	80	0	1	259	.279	.411	.453	.289	58	.287
1996	Omaha	AmA	350	95	11	0	11	59	1	2	257	.271	.377	.397	.261	45	.255

Good AAA hitter who could easily cover first base in the major leagues for a month while the regular mends from an injury. There are a dozen guys just like him, and none of them ever gets the call because the mysticism of being a "major leaguer" still permeates the air in 28 dugouts across North America.

BOB HAMELIN | **1B** | **1968** | **Age 29**

Year	Team	Lge	AB	H	DB	TP	HR	BB	SB	CS	OUT	BA	OBA	SA	EQA	EQR	Peak
1993	Omaha	AmA	486	123	14	1	28	82	7	2	365	.253	.361	.459	.272	70	.287
1993	Kansas City	AL	49	11	1	0	3	7	0	0	38	.224	.321	.429	.247	6	.260
1994	Kansas City	AL	310	85	21	1	24	56	4	3	228	.274	.385	.581	.306	59	.318
1995	Omaha	AmA	122	35	6	0	10	30	2	2	89	.287	.428	.582	.320	26	.326
1995	Kansas City	AL	210	38	7	1	8	26	0	1	173	.181	.271	.338	.196	15	.200
1996	Kansas City	AL	240	62	15	1	9	54	5	2	180	.258	.395	.442	.280	37	.283
1997	*Kansas City*	*AL*	*343*	*83*	*9*	*0*	*17*	*69*	*3*	*1*	*261*	*.242*	*.369*	*.417*	*.270*	*50*	

Likely to be traded, released or in Japan by the time you read this. No one could have predicted such a bizarre turn of events for the 1994 Rookie of the Year, but then no one thought that after his terrible slump to start 1995, Boone would never give him more than two weeks to re-establish himself. The disappearance of his power stemmed in part from an inability to pull the trigger on hittable pitches; Hamelin may have become too patient for his own good. He rebounded last year, but you have to wonder what Boone was thinking when he decided that the best way for Hamelin to regain his confidence was to come to the ballpark not knowing if he would be in the starting lineup. An extreme flyball hitter; could still hit 50 homers if the Rockies picked him up.

JED HANSEN | **2B** | **1973** | **Age 24**

Year	Team	Lge	AB	H	DB	TP	HR	BB	SB	CS	OUT	BA	OBA	SA	EQA	EQR	Peak
1994	Eugene	Nwern	245	51	4	1	3	16	2	2	196	.208	.257	.269	.166	11	.184
1995	Springfield	Midw	432	102	17	3	9	62	17	6	336	.236	.332	.352	.234	45	.259
1996	Wichita	Texas	407	106	16	2	11	29	11	5	306	.260	.310	.391	.236	41	.256
1996	Omaha	AmA	101	22	3	0	3	13	2	0	79	.218	.307	.337	.219	9	.240

A heady player, smooth around the bag and with a variety of offensive skills. Exhibit #973 in the importance of plate discipline: Hansen was hitting over .330 at Wichita through mid-June, despite jumping a level, at which point his walks began to taper off as he got more aggressive; he then went into a horrendous slump which lasted through a promotion to AAA. He began to take more pitches and saw his average rise towards the end of the year. Needs a consolidation year at AAA, and then we'll see what he can do.

DAVID HOWARD | **SS** | **1967** | **Age 30**

Year	Team	Lge	AB	H	DB	TP	HR	BB	SB	CS	OUT	BA	OBA	SA	EQA	EQR	Peak
1993	Omaha	AmA	157	38	7	2	0	8	3	1	120	.242	.279	.312	.198	11	.205
1994	Kansas City	AL	83	18	1	0	2	11	3	2	67	.217	.309	.301	.205	6	.212
1995	Kansas City	AL	258	66	13	4	1	25	6	1	193	.256	.322	.349	.230	25	.232
1996	Kansas City	AL	421	93	15	5	4	40	5	6	334	.221	.289	.309	.196	28	.195
1997	*Kansas City*	*AL*	*331*	*80*	*12*	*3*	*2*	*27*	*3*	*2*	*253*	*.242*	*.299*	*.314*	*.212*	*26*	

The longest-running joke in baseball continues unabated. When Howard hangs up his spikes at the age of 53, no doubt we'll see him giving lectures around the country on "How to keep your job without doing any work by hypnotizing your boss." Surreal. After years as the weakest-hitting backup in the league, he was given 400 at-bats to prove that he could be the weakest-hitting regular in the league. You want a weak stick? When Howard put the first pitch in play, he hit a hardy .205.

A legitimately good defensive shortstop, but he created barely half as many runs per out as Tom Goodwin. Ozzie Smith in his prime would not have been an above-average shortstop with offensive numbers like these. Yet the Royals do nothing but rave about his defense, and even the local sportswriters have blinders on to his offense. The Kansas City Star gave end-of-season grades to each player, and Howard was awarded a B. The same grade Kevin Appier got.

KEITH LOCKHART   2B/3B   1965   Age 32

Year	Team	Lge	AB	H	DB	TP	HR	BB	SB	CS	OUT	BA	OBA	SA	EQA	EQR	Peak
1993	Louisville	AmA	479	144	19	2	14	62	3	2	337	.301	.381	.436	.275	67	.277
1994	Las Vegas	PCL	320	86	10	3	6	25	2	2	236	.269	.322	.375	.234	31	.232
1995	Omaha	AmA	150	53	5	1	5	17	1	2	99	.353	.419	.500	.304	25	.298
1995	Kansas City	AL	278	93	21	3	7	15	8	1	186	.335	.369	.507	.293	43	.288
1996	Kansas City	AL	434	120	33	3	7	30	11	6	320	.276	.323	.415	.247	49	.239
1997	*Kansas City*	*AL*	*325*	*91*	*18*	*1*	*8*	*34*	*8*	*4*	*238*	*.280*	*.348*	*.415*	*.264*	*43*	

Valuable bench player, because he plays two infield positions adequately, bats left-handed and hits doubles. The Royals have about five candidates to play the two positions on Lockhart's résumé, but they love his quiet demeanor in KC and he figures to wedge his way into the lineup long enough to get 300 at-bats again this year. Could hit .320 again at any time, because he hits the ball according to how he's pitched.

RYAN LONG   OF   1973   Age 24

Year	Team	Lge	AB	H	DB	TP	HR	BB	SB	CS	OUT	BA	OBA	SA	EQA	EQR	Peak
1993	Rockford	Midw	405	107	18	2	8	12	7	3	301	.264	.285	.378	.223	35	.254
1994	Wilmington	Caro	506	126	19	2	9	15	4	2	382	.249	.271	.348	.206	37	.230
1995	Wichita	Texas	340	70	11	0	7	10	4	2	272	.206	.229	.300	.167	16	.183
1996	Wichita	Texas	442	115	14	1	17	19	5	3	330	.260	.291	.412	.233	43	.253
1997	*Kansas City*	*AL*	*450*	*108*	*25*	*1*	*14*	*20*	*4*	*3*	*345*	*.240*	*.272*	*.393*	*.226*	*42*	

Even by Royals standards, he's a hack. Long didn't draw his first walk until June, and in over 2000 at bats, he's walked 72 times. Barry Bonds drew 86 walks after the All-Star break last year. The power surge can be attributed to playing at the same level, in a generous home park for two straight years.

MENDY LOPEZ   3B   1975   Age 22

Year	Team	Lge	AB	H	DB	TP	HR	BB	SB	CS	OUT	BA	OBA	SA	EQA	EQR	Peak
1995	Wilmington	Caro	452	129	28	2	3	28	12	5	328	.285	.327	.376	.240	46	.273
1996	Wichita	Texas	329	84	13	3	6	25	10	3	247	.255	.308	.368	.231	32	.259

A fine prospect. Lopez jumped from rookie ball, where he hit .362 in 1994, to AA in little over a year. He was voted the best defensive third baseman in the Texas League, and his range factor was off the charts. His patience improved as the season went on before a broken finger ended it. The Royals have so many third basemen (Randa, Paquette) to sort through that Lopez shouldn't see playing time before mid-1998, but he could be a good one when he arrives.

MIKE MACFARLANE   C   1964   Age 33

Year	Team	Lge	AB	H	DB	TP	HR	BB	SB	CS	OUT	BA	OBA	SA	EQA	EQR	Peak
1993	Kansas City	AL	391	110	22	0	24	42	2	4	285	.281	.351	.522	.281	59	.279
1994	Kansas City	AL	313	78	16	2	14	35	1	0	235	.249	.325	.447	.255	38	.249
1995	Boston	AL	367	86	16	1	17	38	2	1	282	.234	.306	.422	.240	40	.231
1996	Kansas City	AL	380	105	26	2	19	31	3	3	278	.276	.331	.505	.271	53	.258
1997	*Kansas City*	*AL*	*383*	*95*	*17*	*0*	*17*	*41*	*4*	*2*	*290*	*.248*	*.321*	*.426*	*.254*	*47*	

Playing in Kansas City, he's been one of the more underrated catchers in the game for several years. He's a fly-ball hitter and the perception is that he would be a far more respected power hitter in another ballpark, but he's such a pull hitter that most of his homers are straight down the line, where the dimensions at Kauffman Stadium are unlikely to affect them. His off season with the Red Sox is an indication of that, though that may have been the Green Monster messing with his head and his batting style. Still has two or three years left, but the Royals should consider trading him, because Sweeney is ready to start and Fasano is overqualified as a backup.

FELIX MARTINEZ   SS   1974   Age 23

Year	Team	Lge	AB	H	DB	TP	HR	BB	SB	CS	OUT	BA	OBA	SA	EQA	EQR	Peak
1994	Wilmington	Caro	414	103	13	2	2	26	10	4	315	.249	.293	.304	.203	29	.231
1995	Wichita	Texas	425	98	12	2	3	29	29	10	337	.231	.280	.289	.199	30	.222
1996	Omaha	AmA	403	90	10	2	5	46	16	7	320	.223	.303	.295	.204	30	.226

A year ago, he was ranked the #6 prospect in the organization by Baseball America. Mike Sweeney was ranked #7. If this doesn't convince you that tools players get too much respect, nothing will. Great range, erratic throwing arm, but unless his bat develops his fielding won't matter.

RAMON MARTINEZ **2B** **1973** **Age 24**

Year	Team	Lge	AB	H	DB	TP	HR	BB	SB	CS	OUT	BA	OBA	SA	EQA	EQR	Peak
1993	Wilmington	Caro	79	17	3	0	0	10	1	2	64	.215	.303	.253	.179	4	.202
1994	Wilmington	Caro	339	84	10	1	2	31	3	2	257	.248	.311	.301	.206	25	.231
1995	Wichita	Texas	394	96	15	1	3	38	8	4	302	.244	.310	.310	.210	31	.232
1996	Lynchburg	Caro	314	85	4	4	1	21	5	2	231	.271	.316	.318	.217	25	.236
1996	Wichita	Texas	94	30	2	1	1	6	3	1	65	.319	.360	.394	.260	11	.281

Generic second base prospect in an organization full of them. A demotion to AA in mid-season—the Royals flip-flopped him with Hansen—suggests the honeymoon is over for Martinez. Doesn't do anything poorly, but neither does he have any outstanding skills to attract attention with.

ANTHONY MEDRANO **SS** **1975** **Age 22**

Year	Team	Lge	AB	H	DB	TP	HR	BB	SB	CS	OUT	BA	OBA	SA	EQA	EQR	Peak
1994	Dunedin	Flor	202	44	4	2	5	11	2	1	159	.218	.258	.332	.193	13	.223
1995	Wilmington	Caro	488	146	19	5	4	34	7	3	345	.299	.345	.383	.249	53	.283
1996	Wichita	Texas	474	115	14	1	8	20	8	4	363	.243	.273	.327	.200	33	.224

Picked up with Chris Stynes in the David Cone trade, and an intriguing player. Medrano is young, an extraordinarily fluid shortstop and can hit for a good average. His development will continue to lag until he learns to take more pitches. He has a long, loopy swing, but struck out only 36 times all season. The Royals have never had a great shortstop, and there's a chance Medrano might become one, but until he starts to walk more he doesn't look any better than a right-handed Ozzie Guillen.

HENRY MERCEDES **C** **1970** **Age 27**

Year	Team	Lge	AB	H	DB	TP	HR	BB	SB	CS	OUT	BA	OBA	SA	EQA	EQR	Peak
1993	Tacoma	PCL	256	54	8	1	4	28	1	1	203	.211	.289	.297	.192	16	.209
1993	Oakland	AL	48	11	3	0	0	2	1	1	38	.229	.260	.292	.178	3	.195
1994	Tacoma	PCL	203	34	3	1	1	13	1	1	170	.167	.218	.207	.100	3	.103
1995	Omaha	AmA	275	55	8	0	10	24	2	0	220	.200	.264	.338	.198	19	.209
1995	Kansas City	AL	44	12	2	0	0	8	0	0	32	.273	.385	.318	.245	5	.261
1996	Omaha	AmA	228	48	7	1	7	29	0	0	180	.211	.300	.342	.212	19	.221

The living, breathing definition of a AAA catcher, with maybe a smidgen more power than most. Good defensive rep, but that may just be Nichols' Law in effect.

MARK MERCHANT **OF** **1969** **Age 28**

Year	Team	Lge	AB	H	DB	TP	HR	BB	SB	CS	OUT	BA	OBA	SA	EQA	EQR	Peak
1993	Chattanooga	South	345	97	10	0	15	45	2	2	250	.281	.364	.441	.268	47	.287
1994	Chattanooga	South	345	104	10	1	6	39	1	1	242	.301	.372	.388	.260	42	.274
1996	Nashville	AmA	135	29	5	0	4	18	1	0	106	.215	.307	.341	.217	12	.221
1996	Omaha	AmA	123	34	5	0	4	22	1	1	90	.276	.386	.415	.270	17	.275

He was the second overall pick in the draft in 1987. Drafting high school hitters in the first round has always been a chancy proposition; sometimes they turn into Derek Jeter, sometimes they turn into Merchant. He improved significantly as a hitter in 1993, but after six years with the "failed draft pick" label over his head, he wasn't likely to get a chance then. Also wrote the theme music for "Mad About You."

ROD MYERS **CF/LF** **1973** **Age 24**

Year	Team	Lge	AB	H	DB	TP	HR	BB	SB	CS	OUT	BA	OBA	SA	EQA	EQR	Peak
1993	Rockford	Midw	493	118	16	2	9	46	21	8	383	.239	.304	.335	.219	43	.249
1994	Wilmington	Caro	481	122	15	2	10	58	18	6	365	.254	.334	.356	.237	50	.265
1995	Wichita	Texas	497	135	16	2	8	32	20	8	370	.272	.316	.360	.232	48	.256
1996	Omaha	AmA	423	121	21	1	15	51	32	7	309	.286	.363	.447	.278	63	.303
1996	Kansas City	AL	63	18	5	0	2	7	3	2	47	.286	.357	.460	.269	9	.291
_1997_	_Kansas City_	_AL_	_383_	_104_	_17_	_0_	_19_	_43_	_39_	_6_	_285_	_.272_	_.345_	_.465_	_.286_	_62_	

Plays like a poor man's Johnny Damon, and Myers was Damon's teammate for three straight years coming through the system. Freed from Damon's shadow this year, he took a big leap forward as a hitter, adding legitimate power to his arsenal of speed and defense. He's at an age where sudden improvements are usually not flukes, and Vlad thinks he can play. He impressed the Royals in his September debut, but like Damon, Goodwin, Nunnally and Tucker, he's left-handed. It should be very interesting to see how Boone handles the five-headed hydra in his outfield.

LES NORMAN   **OF**   **1969**   **Age 28**

Year	Team	Lge	AB	H	DB	TP	HR	BB	SB	CS	OUT	BA	OBA	SA	EQA	EQR	Peak
1993	Memphis	South	497	139	23	2	17	47	8	5	363	.280	.342	.437	.259	62	.278
1994	Memphis	South	397	103	12	2	14	37	5	3	297	.259	.323	.406	.243	43	.257
1995	Omaha	AmA	313	83	14	2	9	21	5	2	232	.265	.311	.409	.241	33	.251
1996	Omaha	AmA	78	19	2	0	2	7	0	1	60	.244	.306	.346	.214	6	.221
1996	Kansas City	AL	49	6	0	0	0	6	1	1	44	.122	.218	.122	-.088	-1	-.084

The Royals' need for a right-handed caddy for all their left-handed starting outfielders led them to keep Norman on the roster for much of the season. Don't count on that happening again. NRI, Cleveland.

SERGIO NUNEZ   **2B**   **1975**   **Age 22**

Year	Team	Lge	AB	H	DB	TP	HR	BB	SB	CS	OUT	BA	OBA	SA	EQA	EQR	Peak
1995	Wilmington	Caro	488	123	10	1	5	50	21	10	375	.252	.322	.307	.217	41	.247
1996	Wilmington	Caro	413	103	13	4	3	33	19	6	316	.249	.305	.322	.217	35	.243

Hit .394 in rookie ball two years ago, and his great defense was prompting comparisons to Roberto Alomar. Assorted ailments and an unexplained intestinal problem have plagued him the last two seasons, and he's about to be passed by Febles on the organizational depth chart. If the Royals challenge him with a promotion to AA, I suspect he'll succeed, but he needs to hit the ball with more authority if he's going to survive past that.

JON NUNNALLY   **RF**   **1972**   **Age 25**

Year	Team	Lge	AB	H	DB	TP	HR	BB	SB	CS	OUT	BA	OBA	SA	EQA	EQR	Peak
1993	Columbus-GA	S Atl	457	100	5	1	12	47	7	5	362	.219	.292	.313	.200	33	.224
1994	Kinston	Caro	503	127	18	1	17	54	14	6	382	.252	.325	.394	.242	55	.267
1995	Kansas City	AL	308	80	16	6	16	52	6	4	232	.260	.367	.506	.283	49	.307
1996	Omaha	AmA	355	99	17	2	23	49	10	7	263	.279	.366	.532	.288	59	.309
1996	Kansas City	AL	90	19	6	1	5	13	0	0	71	.211	.311	.467	.251	11	.269
1997	*Kansas City*	*AL*	*555*	*142*	*41*	*5*	*27*	*112*	*6*	*4*	*417*	*.256*	*.381*	*.494*	*.292*	*96*	

His career has taken more twists and turns than the plot of "General Hospital," but he's emerged as a hell of a player. His tremendous debut as a Rule V draftee in 1995 was clouded by a prolonged slump at the end of the year, and following more struggles in the Arizona Fall League the Royals sent him down to AAA early in the year. After a slow start, though, Nunnally learned to lay off the breaking pitches he couldn't hit and began to feast on mistakes. He has the most power in the organization and absolutely deserves to start in right field next season, but he'll have to hit for power from the get-go or he may end up with the same fate as Hamelin, because the front office isn't impressed by gaudy walk totals.

JOSE OFFERMAN   **1B/2B/SS**   **1969**   **Age 28**

Year	Team	Lge	AB	H	DB	TP	HR	BB	SB	CS	OUT	BA	OBA	SA	EQA	EQR	Peak
1993	Los Angeles	NL	607	170	23	4	2	80	25	11	448	.280	.364	.341	.245	67	.263
1994	Albuquerque	PCL	218	61	5	3	1	34	6	2	159	.280	.377	.344	.252	25	.266
1994	Los Angeles	NL	250	57	9	4	1	41	2	1	194	.228	.337	.308	.219	22	.230
1995	Los Angeles	NL	448	137	14	6	5	75	2	6	317	.306	.405	.397	.272	61	.283
1996	Kansas City	AL	563	173	33	8	5	74	24	10	400	.307	.388	.421	.276	80	.283
1997	*Kansas City*	*AL*	*556*	*162*	*27*	*8*	*8*	*102*	*19*	*11*	*405*	*.291*	*.401*	*.412*	*.283*	*86*	

This may be hard to believe, but Offerman is an excellent defensive first baseman. Scooping up throws, turning the 3-6-3 double play...he almost made Royals fans forget Wally Joyner out there. It still doesn't excuse the move, because it forced David Howard to play everyday and Offerman simply doesn't hit enough to play first. After three months of experimenting, Boone finally moved him to second base, where he seems to belong. His defense was much better than at shortstop—where the long throws seemed to bother him—and a second baseman with a .390 OBP has a lot of value. Could still move back to first base to make room for one of the Royals' second base prospects, which would be a mistake.

CRAIG PAQUETTE **3B/LF** **1969** **Age 28**

Year	Team	Lge	AB	H	DB	TP	HR	BB	SB	CS	OUT	BA	OBA	SA	EQA	EQR	Peak
1993	Tacoma	PCL	183	44	5	0	7	26	2	2	141	.240	.335	.383	.239	20	.256
1993	Oakland	AL	398	94	22	4	15	17	4	2	306	.236	.267	.425	.227	38	.244
1994	Tacoma	PCL	242	64	7	1	15	14	3	2	180	.264	.305	.488	.258	30	.272
1995	Oakland	AL	287	70	13	1	15	12	5	2	219	.244	.274	.453	.239	31	.248
1996	Omaha	AmA	65	21	2	0	4	9	1	0	44	.323	.405	.538	.312	12	.319
1996	Kansas City	AL	430	112	14	1	23	23	5	3	321	.260	.298	.458	.248	49	.254
1997	*Kansas City*	*AL*	*199*	*51*	*2*	*0*	*9*	*7*	*4*	*3*	*151*	*.256*	*.282*	*.402*	*.233*	*20*	

Led the Royals in homers, more an indication of the team's lack of power than any ability on Paquette's part. He was touted as a great find by the Royals, but he had a 101-23 strikeout-to-walk ratio and is an awkward fielder. All you need to know about Bob Boone is that he started Paquette at shortstop six times last year, rather than move Offerman back there. Hit .312 with a .885 OPS against left-handers last year, and would have genuine value as a platoon player. Chances are, though, he'll be used more than his abilities dictate.

JOE RANDA **3B/2B** **1970** **Age 27**

Year	Team	Lge	AB	H	DB	TP	HR	BB	SB	CS	OUT	BA	OBA	SA	EQA	EQR	Peak
1993	Memphis	South	516	144	22	3	12	38	5	4	376	.279	.329	.403	.245	56	.267
1994	Omaha	AmA	460	125	20	1	12	33	4	1	336	.272	.320	.398	.242	48	.259
1995	Omaha	AmA	234	60	7	1	8	24	2	2	176	.256	.326	.397	.241	25	.254
1995	Kansas City	AL	71	13	0	0	2	6	0	1	59	.183	.247	.268	.153	3	.158
1996	Kansas City	AL	338	103	25	1	6	26	13	4	239	.305	.354	.438	.269	45	.280
1997	*Pittsburgh*	*NL*	*433*	*124*	*37*	*2*	*15*	*27*	*11*	*5*	*314*	*.286*	*.328*	*.485*	*.278*	*64*	

Quietly had a very good season. Randa is a good average hitter who hits lots of doubles, and he has shown flashes of power at times in the minor leagues. Unfortunately, he attended the Carney Lansford School of Third Base Defense; he dives at everything, and consequently he has a great reputation but terrible defensive numbers. Deserves to start next season, if only so the Royals can find out if he can develop the power that Vlad says he will. Dealt with a lot last season, including the death of his mother in a car crash, and if his life is less chaotic this year, his bat may come alive. Despite being named to a few All-Rookie teams in 1996, he actually lost his rookie status in 1995. Probable second baseman in Pittsburgh after the King/Bell trade.

BIP ROBERTS **2B/LF** **1964** **Age 33**

Year	Team	Lge	AB	H	DB	TP	HR	BB	SB	CS	OUT	BA	OBA	SA	EQA	EQR	Peak
1993	Cincinnati	NL	299	74	8	0	3	42	22	5	230	.247	.340	.304	.232	30	.231
1994	San Diego	NL	412	135	14	4	3	45	19	6	283	.328	.394	.403	.277	57	.272
1995	San Diego	NL	305	99	10	0	4	21	17	2	208	.325	.368	.397	.270	39	.261
1996	Kansas City	AL	340	97	16	3	1	25	13	9	252	.285	.334	.359	.235	34	.224
1997	*Kansas City*	*AL*	*258*	*76*	*10*	*4*	*0*	*20*	*14*	*1*	*183*	*.295*	*.345*	*.364*	*.259*	*31*	

The Royals made an inexplicable, inexcusable decision to re-sign him. Last year Roberts had a job waiting for him at second base, but this year…what exactly is his role on this team? There are only three positions he has any ability to play: second base, the property of Jose Offerman, and where the Royals have more prospects than at any other position; third base, where Paquette, Randa and Lockhart are all in contention; and left field, where the Royals have Michael Tucker. Wild and fanciful rumors around KC have Roberts playing left field and Tucker moving to first base, which is an abominable idea. Rumors also have Boone sending Damon down to AAA for "more seasoning." And Royals fans wonder why they haven't been to the postseason in 11 years….

STEVE SISCO **OF/2B** **1970** **Age 27**

Year	Team	Lge	AB	H	DB	TP	HR	BB	SB	CS	OUT	BA	OBA	SA	EQA	EQR	Peak
1993	Rockford	Midw	476	122	18	2	2	32	10	4	358	.256	.303	.315	.210	36	.229
1994	Wilmington	Caro	284	73	9	3	2	32	3	3	214	.257	.332	.331	.224	25	.239
1995	Wichita	Texas	208	56	9	1	3	14	2	1	153	.269	.315	.365	.230	19	.242
1996	Wichita	Texas	466	125	13	1	12	38	3	1	342	.268	.323	.378	.237	47	.246

Good collegiate player who has acquitted himself reasonably in the pros. Not a prospect, but a good, knowledgeable baseball man who could easily find work as a college coach when he hangs up his spikes.

MATT SMITH   1B/P   1976   Age 21

Year	Team	Lge	AB	H	DB	TP	HR	BB	SB	CS	OUT	BA	OBA	SA	EQA	EQR	Peak
1995	Springfield	Midw	419	80	9	0	6	18	3	2	341	.191	.224	.255	.141	13	.162
1996	Wilmington	Caro	463	100	7	1	5	36	1	2	365	.216	.273	.268	.172	23	.196

The Royals' first-round pick out of an Oregon high school in 1994, but while most teams liked him as a left-handed pitcher, the Royals liked his power potential more. Looking at the numbers, it's pretty obvious they made the wrong decision, but Smith is not nearly as bad as the numbers indicate. Twenty-year-olds who play a full season in high A-ball are fairly rare, and his offense improved as the season wore on. He's very smooth around the bag, and the Blue Rocks' stadium shaved a lot of his power. The Royals should continue to be aggressive and promote him to AA this year; playing in the bandbox in Wichita, he could hit 20 homers and make everyone take notice.

ANDY STEWART   C/1B   1971   Age 26

Year	Team	Lge	AB	H	DB	TP	HR	BB	SB	CS	OUT	BA	OBA	SA	EQA	EQR	Peak
1993	Wilmington	Caro	373	96	13	1	7	24	4	1	278	.257	.302	.354	.222	32	.244
1994	Wilmington	Caro	376	115	17	1	14	26	0	1	262	.306	.351	.468	.272	50	.296
1994	Memphis	South	73	16	1	0	0	4	0	0	57	.219	.260	.233	.149	2	.163
1995	Wichita	Texas	215	49	10	0	4	11	1	1	167	.228	.265	.330	.195	14	.209
1995	Omaha	AmA	156	44	5	0	4	14	0	1	113	.282	.341	.391	.245	17	.262
1996	Wichita	Texas	203	56	11	2	3	14	2	1	148	.276	.323	.394	.241	21	.254
1996	Omaha	AmA	183	37	7	2	2	17	0	1	147	.202	.270	.295	.181	10	.191

Not enough defense to catch, not enough offense to play first base. Stewart's been in that bind for several years now, and it appears unlikely that he'll find his way out.

CHRIS STYNES   2B/3B/LF   1973   Age 24

Year	Team	Lge	AB	H	DB	TP	HR	BB	SB	CS	OUT	BA	OBA	SA	EQA	EQR	Peak
1993	Dunedin	Flor	493	127	18	2	9	22	9	4	370	.258	.289	.357	.218	41	.248
1994	Knoxville	South	559	171	24	3	9	28	16	6	394	.306	.339	.408	.255	65	.285
1995	Omaha	AmA	307	78	10	3	9	29	4	4	233	.254	.318	.394	.237	32	.262
1996	Omaha	AmA	291	101	18	2	9	21	6	2	192	.347	.391	.515	.302	48	.328
1996	Kansas City	AL	92	27	7	0	0	2	5	2	67	.293	.309	.370	.234	9	.254
1997	*Kansas City*	*AL*	*414*	*127*	*23*	*3*	*8*	*20*	*6*	*3*	*290*	*.307*	*.339*	*.435*	*.267*	*53*	

Still learning with the glove, and being moved around the diamond incessantly isn't helping. He can positively hit, and the Royals seriously need his bat in the lineup next season. Stynes was a good average hitter when he was acquired from the Blue Jays, and he's added power since then. He's not a very patient hitter, but his walk totals have crept up slowly, and he doesn't strike out much either. Still 24, coming off a batting title in AAA, and if he's given 400 at bats this year he'll be a surprise contender for Rookie of the Year. How much he plays will be a reflection of Boone's faith in continuing the youth movement. Sadly, I suspect it won't be much.

LARRY SUTTON   1B   1970   Age 27

Year	Team	Lge	AB	H	DB	TP	HR	BB	SB	CS	OUT	BA	OBA	SA	EQA	EQR	Peak
1993	Rockford	Midw	387	95	13	1	7	77	1	2	294	.245	.371	.339	.242	42	.262
1994	Wilmington	Caro	511	154	20	1	22	70	1	1	358	.301	.386	.474	.286	78	.306
1995	Wichita	Texas	198	48	5	1	5	23	1	0	150	.242	.321	.354	.228	19	.241
1996	Wichita	Texas	473	130	12	1	19	70	3	1	344	.275	.368	.425	.267	63	.278

A very good hitter, but he's a year or two older than he needs to be to get a shot. An elbow injury ruined his 1995 season, and that setback may have cost him the chance at a productive career. He's a short guy and has a very compact stroke, which makes his power that much more impressive. Sensationally patient at the plate, and the best defensive first baseman in the Texas League. The best comparison I can think of is to the Cardinals' Mark Sweeney; if he gets an opportunity with the right manager, he'll make a good platoon first baseman and deadly pinch-hitter. It likely will not happen with the Royals.

MIKE SWEENEY   C   1974   Age 23

Year	Team	Lge	AB	H	DB	TP	HR	BB	SB	CS	OUT	BA	OBA	SA	EQA	EQR	Peak
1993	Eugene	Nwern	187	43	6	1	5	19	0	0	144	.230	.301	.353	.217	16	.252
1994	Rockford	Midw	292	83	11	2	9	46	0	0	209	.284	.382	.428	.273	41	.310
1995	Wilmington	Caro	366	125	18	1	20	59	4	1	242	.342	.433	.560	.326	73	.365
1996	Wichita	Texas	239	72	9	1	12	29	2	1	168	.301	.377	.498	.288	38	.317
1996	Omaha	AmA	102	26	6	0	3	7	0	0	76	.255	.303	.402	.234	10	.256
1996	Kansas City	AL	165	46	8	0	5	19	1	2	121	.279	.353	.418	.256	20	.282
1997	*Kansas City*	*AL*	*588*	*183*	*31*	*2*	*27*	*88*	*1*	*1*	*406*	*.311*	*.401*	*.509*	*.307*	*106*	

Handled correctly, he's a superstar in the making. He has the complete package as a hitter—power, average and patience—and is possibly the first prospect in Royals' history that can make that claim. He had a sore elbow that limited his catching the first half of the season, but he threw out 8 of 19 would-be basestealers in Kansas City. The Royals seem committed to playing him every day next year, and if they do he will have a season worthy of the Rookie of the Year award if he was eligible. There is some talk of moving him to first base, though, and letting Fasano catch, yet another example of why the Royals have finished in the bottom half of the AL in runs scored 12 of the last 14 years.

MIKE TUCKER   LF   1971   Age 26

Year	Team	Lge	AB	H	DB	TP	HR	BB	SB	CS	OUT	BA	OBA	SA	EQA	EQR	Peak
1993	Wilmington	Caro	253	73	10	1	5	30	6	1	181	.289	.364	.395	.261	32	.288
1993	Memphis	South	254	69	6	2	9	38	7	3	188	.272	.366	.417	.265	34	.292
1994	Omaha	AmA	494	137	11	4	23	71	8	2	359	.277	.368	.455	.275	71	.299
1995	Omaha	AmA	276	78	16	3	4	26	10	3	201	.283	.344	.406	.256	33	.275
1995	Kansas City	AL	179	49	9	0	5	19	2	3	133	.274	.343	.408	.249	21	.267
1996	Kansas City	AL	340	89	20	4	12	40	10	4	255	.262	.339	.450	.262	45	.277
1997	*Kansas City*	*AL*	*505*	*141*	*25*	*5*	*21*	*66*	*11*	*5*	*369*	*.279*	*.363*	*.473*	*.283*	*79*	

More likely to have a breakout season than anyone else in the division. He has a beautiful swing, and it's easy to see why the Royals were so excited to get him in the first round in 1992. He has a pronounced uppercut and he struggled against off-speed pitches his first year in the league, but he was able to lay off those pitches last year and his walk-to-strikeout rate nearly doubled. He didn't fall off at all against southpaws, and his strong finish may be a harbinger of things to come. He's 26, probably the most common age for an established major league hitter to raise the level of his game a notch or two. Grounded into only seven double plays all year, but that was as many as Damon and Goodwin combined. As a team the Royals only hit into 99 twin killings, the lowest in baseball.

JOE VITIELLO   1B   1970   Age 27

Year	Team	Lge	AB	H	DB	TP	HR	BB	SB	CS	OUT	BA	OBA	SA	EQA	EQR	Peak
1993	Memphis	South	427	120	16	1	15	52	1	0	307	.281	.359	.429	.265	55	.287
1994	Omaha	AmA	362	124	23	2	12	56	2	1	239	.343	.431	.517	.315	67	.338
1995	Omaha	AmA	229	61	11	1	11	14	0	1	169	.266	.309	.467	.253	27	.267
1995	Kansas City	AL	132	35	4	0	8	8	0	0	97	.265	.307	.477	.257	16	.271
1996	Omaha	AmA	136	38	6	0	8	16	1	0	98	.279	.355	.500	.281	21	.292
1996	Kansas City	AL	258	63	16	1	8	38	2	0	195	.244	.341	.407	.251	31	.261
1997	*Kansas City*	*AL*	*281*	*82*	*20*	*1*	*13*	*35*	*2*	*1*	*200*	*.292*	*.370*	*.509*	*.295*	*47*	

Like Stynes, he could have a terrific season if he's just given a job in spring training and told to run with it. He's had consistent success at AAA, but instead of hitting balls into the alleys last year, he was hitting balls into the ground, and Vitiello is as slow as molasses on a winter morning. The first base job is unsettled, and Vitiello still has an opportunity. Vlad loves him, but the neural wiring can't take the strain of trying to factor Boone's whimsy into the equation.

KEVIN YOUNG   **3B/1B**   **1969**   **Age 28**

Year	Team	Lge	AB	H	DB	TP	HR	BB	SB	CS	OUT	BA	OBA	SA	EQA	EQR	Peak
1993	Pittsburgh	NL	455	109	22	2	7	43	2	2	348	.240	.305	.343	.216	38	.231
1994	Buffalo	AmA	232	65	11	3	7	17	5	1	168	.280	.329	.444	.260	29	.275
1994	Pittsburgh	NL	123	26	7	2	1	9	0	2	99	.211	.265	.325	.187	7	.195
1995	Calgary	PCL	160	52	12	1	9	14	5	2	110	.325	.379	.581	.309	29	.322
1995	Pittsburgh	NL	182	42	5	0	7	10	1	3	143	.231	.271	.374	.208	14	.217
1996	Omaha	AmA	190	58	10	1	11	14	3	0	132	.305	.353	.542	.293	31	.299
1996	Kansas City	AL	132	32	4	0	9	11	3	3	103	.242	.301	.477	.250	16	.256
1997	*Kansas City*	*AL*	*269*	*67*	*16*	*1*	*15*	*27*	*4*	*5*	*207*	*.249*	*.318*	*.483*	*.264*	*37*	

No one knows what happened to Young, who in 1992 looked like one of the ten best hitting prospects in baseball. But the Royals, in a rare moment of lucidity, claimed him off waivers from Pittsburgh, and for the first time he actually brought his bat with him to the majors. Smoked left-handers for a 1.034 OPS, and the Royals, who have been a predominantly left-handed club for several years, could definitely use his bat on the bench. His talents are almost identical to Paquette's, though, and the Royals may decide to keep only one of them. He's been released.

KEVIN APPIER   **RSP**   **1968**   **Age 29**

YR	TEAM	Lge	IP	H	ER	HR	BB	K	ERA	W	L	H/9	HR/9	BB/9	K/9	KW
1993	Kansas City	AL	232.0	187	54	8	91	191	2.09	20	6	7.25	.31	3.53	7.41	1.59
1994	Kansas City	AL	153.3	128	46	10	67	141	2.70	12	5	7.51	.59	3.93	8.28	1.78
1995	Kansas City	AL	198.7	167	69	14	84	186	3.13	14	8	7.57	.63	3.81	8.43	1.86
1996	Kansas City	AL	209.3	185	62	15	80	201	2.67	16	7	7.95	.64	3.44	8.64	2.02

The Man. The three-year contract he signed in July, after months of wrangling and rumors that he was headed elsewhere in trade, was the single most important event in the Royals' season. Appier is one of the ten best pitchers in baseball. He's consistently effective and hasn't missed more than five starts in any season since he joined the rotation for good in 1990. His sometimes-eccentric outbursts have prompted sportswriters in KC to refer to him as "Planet Appier," one of the better nicknames in the game.

He's been up and down the last three years, bothered by a change in pitching coaches and—more importantly—sinful abuse by Boone in 1995. Boone finally got the message last year and lowered his pitch counts, and there's every reason to think Appier will be in the top five in ERA again this year. If the Royals finally score some runs, that could get him 20 wins and a Cy Young bid.

TIM BELCHER   **RSP**   **1962**   **Age 35**

YR	TEAM	Lge	IP	H	ER	HR	BB	K	ERA	W	L	H/9	HR/9	BB/9	K/9	KW
1993	Cincinnati	NL	133.0	140	66	12	62	98	4.47	7	8	9.47	.81	4.20	6.63	1.16
1993	Chi. White Sox	AL	70.7	65	30	8	30	35	3.82	4	4	8.28	1.02	3.82	4.46	.53
1994	Detroit	AL	162.7	180	96	19	83	74	5.31	7	11	9.96	1.05	4.59	4.09	.22
1995	Seattle	AL	179.7	180	78	18	92	96	3.91	10	10	9.02	.90	4.61	4.81	.45
1996	Kansas City	AL	238.0	247	88	24	74	110	3.33	15	11	9.34	.91	2.80	4.16	.69

What provoked Belcher's best season in years? He developed a changeup in spring training and threw it often, getting more groundball outs than ever before, although he gave up a career-high 28 homers. Kauffman Stadium, which since the introduction of grass in 1995 has been a marked pitcher's park, probably helped, but his road ERA (3.88) was actually better than his mark at home (3.97). Most importantly he had his best control since his rookie season. His control continued to improve as the season wore on, and his ERA was 3.49 from July 1st on. Don't be surprised if he remains effective, as long as he's given more rest than the younger members of the staff.

BRIAN BEVIL   **RSP**   **1972**   **Age 25**

YR	TEAM	Lge	IP	H	ER	HR	BB	K	ERA	W	L	H/9	HR/9	BB/9	K/9	KW
1993	Wilmington	Caro	65.7	61	23	2	35	38	3.15	4	3	8.36	.27	4.80	5.21	.54
1993	Memphis	South	30.0	41	17	5	18	19	5.10	1	2	12.30	1.50	5.40	5.70	.55
1994	Memphis	South	91.7	89	45	8	57	61	4.42	5	5	8.74	.79	5.60	5.99	.60
1995	Wichita	Texas	68.3	84	46	8	44	48	6.06	2	6	11.06	1.05	5.80	6.32	.66
1995	Omaha	AmA	22.0	37	26	6	18	9	10.64	0	2	15.14	2.45	7.36	3.68	-.61
1996	Wichita	Texas	69.3	62	19	4	36	61	2.47	6	2	8.05	.52	4.67	7.92	1.47
1996	Omaha	AmA	64.7	66	32	9	28	60	4.45	3	4	9.19	1.25	3.90	8.35	1.81
1996	Kansas City	AL	10.7	9	5	2	5	7	4.22	0	1	7.59	1.69	4.22	5.91	.91

Finally made good on the promise he's shown the Royals for years. After injuries ruined what was supposed to be his breakout season in 1995, he was nearly released during the offseason. He re-established himself as a presence this year, and was impressive in three outings with the big club, two against the Indians. He's a pure power pitcher, and impossible for right-handed batters to pick up. He's in contention with Pittsley and Rusch for the #5 spot in the rotation, and even if he loses he might get moved to the bullpen, where the Royals lack depth.

JAMIE BLUMA   **RRP**   **1972**   **Age 25**

YR	TEAM	Lge	IP	H	ER	HR	BB	K	ERA	W	L	H/9	HR/9	BB/9	K/9	KW
1994	Eugene	Nwern	32.0	30	5	0	7	17	1.41	4	0	8.44	.00	1.97	4.78	1.10
1995	Wichita	Texas	50.7	42	17	9	13	26	3.02	4	2	7.46	1.60	2.31	4.62	.96
1995	Omaha	AmA	22.7	21	11	2	17	10	4.37	1	2	8.34	.79	6.75	3.97	-.36
1996	Omaha	AmA	55.3	60	20	7	28	33	3.25	4	2	9.76	1.14	4.55	5.37	.65
1996	Kansas City	AL	19.7	17	6	2	5	14	2.75	1	1	7.78	.92	2.29	6.41	1.56

Drafted out of Wichita State, where he was only the 3rd-best closer - behind Darren Dreifort and Braden Looper - they've had in the last 5 years. Throws a good fastball, but his slider is his out pitch, getting groundballs for his infielders to scoop up. After breezing through the low minors, he struggled for a period in AAA until he learned to mix his pitches better and throw to both sides of the plate. He was very effective for Omaha right before his callup, and was a perfect 5-for-5 in save opportunities while subbing for Jeff Montgomery. I like him a lot; he strikes me as a Roger McDowell-type innings eater and groundball machine, but with a higher upside than McDowell.

MEL BUNCH   **RSP**   **1972**   **Age 25**

YR	TEAM	Lge	IP	H	ER	HR	BB	K	ERA	W	L	H/9	HR/9	BB/9	K/9	KW
1993	Rockford	Midw	73.3	105	28	6	25	41	3.44	5	3	12.89	.74	3.07	5.03	.91
1993	Wilmington	Caro	58.3	66	25	3	24	34	3.86	3	3	10.18	.46	3.70	5.25	.82
1994	Wilmington	Caro	54.7	68	33	8	22	42	5.43	2	4	11.20	1.32	3.62	6.91	1.40
1995	Omaha	AmA	62.3	63	32	10	27	43	4.62	3	4	9.10	1.44	3.90	6.21	1.09
1995	Kansas City	AL	40.7	40	20	11	15	19	4.43	2	3	8.85	2.43	3.32	4.20	.57
1996	Omaha	AmA	143.0	185	95	28	80	78	5.98	5	11	11.64	1.76	5.03	4.91	.38

Seemed to make an impressive leap from A-ball to the major leagues in 1995, but regressed badly last year. AAA hitters lit him up like the Aurora Borealis all season, and there doesn't seem to be any explanation for it. Pitched well in the Arizona Fall League, but the Gopher Syndrome frequently lies latent for a time before recurring.

TIM BYRDAK   **LSP**   **1974**   **Age 23**

YR	TEAM	Lge	IP	H	ER	HR	BB	K	ERA	W	L	H/9	HR/9	BB/9	K/9	KW
1994	Eugene	Nwern	60.3	92	43	8	26	38	6.41	2	5	13.72	1.19	3.88	5.67	.92
1995	Wilmington	Caro	151.3	157	54	9	65	94	3.21	10	7	9.34	.54	3.87	5.59	.90
1996	Wichita	Texas	78.3	114	65	14	57	39	7.47	2	7	13.10	1.61	6.55	4.48	-.14

Listed only to teach a lesson about the unpredictability of pitchers. A year ago, Byrdak and Jose Rosado were virtually indistinguishable; both were left-handed starters who were effective by throwing strikes and changing speeds. Rosado is all the rage in Kansas City, while Byrdak languishes in AA, recovering from a terrible season and arm trouble. But anyone who claims they could differentiate between the two last year is lying.

JEFF GRANGER   **LRP**   **1972**   **Age 25**

YR	TEAM	Lge	IP	H	ER	HR	BB	K	ERA	W	L	H/9	HR/9	BB/9	K/9	KW
1993	Eugene	Nwern	31.7	42	19	3	9	32	5.40	1	3	11.94	.85	2.56	9.09	2.39
1994	Memphis	South	126.0	185	80	10	88	89	5.71	5	9	13.21	.71	6.29	6.36	.55
1995	Wichita	Texas	88.3	122	67	10	50	69	6.83	3	7	12.43	1.02	5.09	7.03	1.07
1996	Omaha	AmA	73.7	69	21	9	39	56	2.57	6	2	8.43	1.10	4.76	6.84	1.09
1996	Kansas City	AL	16.7	19	10	3	10	11	5.40	1	1	10.26	1.62	5.40	5.94	.63

Chalk up another victory for Royals do-it-all bullpen coach Guy Hansen, who took Granger, then just another failed first-round draft pick, to Puerto Rico last year for winter ball and converted him into a reliever. The results were dramatic; Granger throws harder now and is more aggressive on the inside part of the plate. He still has a tendency to throw gimme fastballs, and that could hinder his development. Should start the year as the Royals' #1 lefty out of the bullpen; if he survives the entire year in Kansas City, he'll pitch 10 years in the major leagues.

TIM GRIEVE   **RRP**   **1972**   **Age 25**

YR	TEAM	Lge	IP	H	ER	HR	BB	K	ERA	W	L	H/9	HR/9	BB/9	K/9	KW
1994	Eugene	Nwern	50.3	43	13	2	34	42	2.32	4	2	7.69	.36	6.08	7.51	.98
1996	Wilmington	Caro	31.0	34	10	2	18	21	2.90	2	1	9.87	.58	5.23	6.10	.73

Not nearly as heralded as his younger brother Ben, Grieve is a potentially outstanding pitcher. One of the few pitchers active today who can claim to have a strikeout-to-hit ratio of 3-to-1, as he did with Eugene in 1994. A ligament tear in his elbow forced him to sit out all of 1995, but he was brought along gingerly this year and pitched very well. Elbow injuries, if given enough time to heal, usually don't recur, so as long as the Royals watch him carefully he should continue to be effective. Whether he can make up for lost time is unknown.

MARK GUBICZA   **RSP**   **1963**   **Age 34**

YR	TEAM	Lge	IP	H	ER	HR	BB	K	ERA	W	L	H/9	HR/9	BB/9	K/9	KW
1993	Kansas City	AL	104.7	123	49	2	48	82	4.21	6	6	10.58	.17	4.13	7.05	1.32
1994	Kansas City	AL	129.3	146	54	9	30	57	3.76	7	7	10.16	.63	2.09	3.97	.80
1995	Kansas City	AL	212.3	219	77	20	67	81	3.26	14	10	9.28	.85	2.84	3.43	.43
1996	Kansas City	AL	119.7	123	53	19	37	53	3.99	7	6	9.25	1.43	2.78	3.99	.63

Gubicza had the longest continuous tenure with one team of any pitcher in the American League, and trading him to Anaheim for Chili Davis was a difficult decision emotionally. But he hasn't been the same pitcher since his shoulder blew out in 1990 and the Royals have many better and younger alternatives for the #5 spot. Last year was a reaction to the workload he received in 1995, when he led the AL in starts. He's fully recovered from the broken leg that ended his season, and as long as his pitch counts are kept in double digits this year he can be counted on as a safety net to keep the Angels' rotation from imploding.

CHRIS HANEY   **LSP**   **1969**   **Age 28**

YR	TEAM	Lge	IP	H	ER	HR	BB	K	ERA	W	L	H/9	HR/9	BB/9	K/9	KW
1993	Omaha	AmA	45.3	44	11	2	19	29	2.18	4	1	8.74	.40	3.77	5.76	.98
1993	Kansas City	AL	124.3	134	71	13	59	67	5.14	5	9	9.70	.94	4.27	4.85	.55
1994	Omaha	AmA	101.7	125	67	12	47	70	5.93	3	8	11.07	1.06	4.16	6.20	1.03
1994	Kansas City	AL	28.3	33	18	2	12	17	5.72	1	2	10.48	.64	3.81	5.40	.85
1995	Kansas City	AL	81.0	78	28	7	34	31	3.11	6	3	8.67	.78	3.78	3.44	.20
1996	Kansas City	AL	227.7	251	103	24	57	111	4.07	12	13	9.92	.95	2.25	4.39	.90

After a potential breakout season in 1995 was derailed by back problems, Haney stayed healthy in 1996 and…and…the jury is still out. Every start he made came back as either a 7-5-2-2-0-4 gem or a 3-8-6-6-2-1 cubic zirconia. If I were a mathematician, I'd say Haney's career lies at the edge of chaos; he simply can't sustain last year's performance for long. Either he learns to throw his pitches on the corners of the plate and turns into Denny Neagle, or he doesn't and hitters will turn him into Charlie Hudson. A gamble, but not a bad one for the Royals to take because if he doesn't pan out, they have half a dozen capable youngsters waiting for a rotation spot to open up.

RICK HUISMAN   **RRP**   **1969**   **Age 28**

YR	TEAM	Lge	IP	H	ER	HR	BB	K	ERA	W	L	H/9	HR/9	BB/9	K/9	KW
1993	San Jose	Calif	20.7	23	6	0	13	11	2.61	1	1	10.02	.00	5.66	4.79	.18
1993	Phoenix	PCL	66.7	72	41	5	53	47	5.54	2	5	9.72	.68	7.16	6.35	.33
1994	Jackson	Texas	46.3	38	9	2	30	46	1.75	4	1	7.38	.39	5.83	8.94	1.52
1995	Tucson	PCL	51.7	52	23	1	33	42	4.01	3	3	9.06	.17	5.75	7.32	1.00
1995	Kansas City	AL	10.0	13	6	2	1	12	5.40	0	1	11.70	1.80	.90	10.80	3.37
1996	Omaha	AmA	54.7	58	29	8	32	41	4.77	2	4	9.55	1.32	5.27	6.75	.93
1996	Kansas City	AL	29.3	24	11	4	18	22	3.38	2	1	7.36	1.23	5.52	6.75	.87

Huisman was once a top prospect with the Giants, but they ruined his arm even worse than Salomon Torres', and eventually released him. He doesn't throw as hard as he once did, and his once-deadly sinker is only a shadow of itself. He does still have a great slider and his fastball darts, and with those two pitches he has carved a niche for himself as a short reliever. The Royals brought Bluma and Huisman up at about the same time, and they were collectively the best relievers in Kansas City all season. Should get a full season with the Royals, and if he doesn't start nibbling he'll have a career.

JASON JACOME   **LRP**   **1971**   **Age 26**

YR	TEAM	Lge	IP	H	ER	HR	BB	K	ERA	W	L	H/9	HR/9	BB/9	K/9	KW
1993	St. Lucie	Flor	85.7	132	43	4	34	52	4.52	4	6	13.87	.42	3.57	5.46	.93
1993	Binghamton	East	79.3	96	35	7	49	42	3.97	5	4	10.89	.79	5.56	4.76	.20
1994	Norfolk	Inter	118.7	161	61	9	56	68	4.63	6	7	12.21	.68	4.25	5.16	.66
1994	NY Mets	NL	53.0	53	14	3	22	28	2.38	4	2	9.00	.51	3.74	4.75	.65
1995	Norfolk	Inter	40.3	46	22	6	19	26	4.91	2	2	10.26	1.34	4.24	5.80	.87
1995	Kansas City	AL	85.3	96	41	14	23	39	4.32	4	5	10.12	1.48	2.43	4.11	.76
1995	NY Mets	NL	21.3	35	22	3	17	10	9.28	0	2	14.77	1.27	7.17	4.22	-.39
1996	Kansas City	AL	48.3	62	20	4	23	31	3.72	3	2	11.54	.74	4.28	5.77	.85

His ERA makes no sense in light of his other numbers. Hitters tattooed him for a .337 average, but he had a respectable 4.72 ERA, the result of coming in with two outs and giving up a pair of singles before getting out of the inning. Boone made him his lefty specialist as the season went on, and he was mildly effective, holding left-handers to a .276 average with only 1 homer. There's no reason to think he can handle a larger role; he's strained to capacity in his current one.

MARK KIEFER   **RBP**   **1969**   **Age 28**

YR	TEAM	Lge	IP	H	ER	HR	BB	K	ERA	W	L	H/9	HR/9	BB/9	K/9	KW
1993	El Paso	Texas	46.7	53	28	5	27	31	5.40	2	3	10.22	.96	5.21	5.98	.69
1993	New Orleans	AmA	27.0	30	18	4	20	21	6.00	1	2	10.00	1.33	6.67	7.00	.67
1994	New Orleans	AmA	119.3	117	55	18	60	104	4.15	6	7	8.82	1.36	4.53	7.84	1.48
1994	Milwaukee	AL	11.0	13	9	4	8	8	7.36	0	1	10.64	3.27	6.55	6.55	.55
1995	New Orleans	AmA	66.3	65	20	5	27	46	2.71	5	2	8.82	.68	3.66	6.24	1.16
1995	Milwaukee	AL	49.3	35	14	6	27	40	2.55	4	1	6.39	1.09	4.93	7.30	1.20
1996	New Orleans	AmA	69.7	64	37	14	43	55	4.78	3	5	8.27	1.81	5.56	7.11	.98
1996	Omaha	AmA	44.0	51	29	7	15	27	5.93	2	3	10.43	1.43	3.07	5.52	1.07
1996	Milwaukee	AL	10.0	14	7	1	5	5	6.30	0	1	12.60	.90	4.50	4.50	.37

A long-time Brewers hopeful who the Royals acquired in a minor-league trade. Kiefer seems to think the strike zone extends from the belt to the shoulders and gets a lot of hitters to climb the ladder, but also gives up the occasional roof job. If he gets an opportunity to pitch for the Royals, in a spacious park with an outfield that can run down anything, he could be surprisingly effective.

DOUG LINTON   **RBP**   **1966**   **Age 31**

YR	TEAM	Lge	IP	H	ER	HR	BB	K	ERA	W	L	H/9	HR/9	BB/9	K/9	KW
1993	Syracuse	Inter	44.3	53	28	11	20	34	5.68	2	3	10.76	2.23	4.06	6.90	1.29
1993	California	AL	26.3	32	18	8	16	20	6.15	1	2	10.94	2.73	5.47	6.84	.91
1993	Toronto	AL	11.0	11	7	0	10	4	5.73	0	1	9.00	.00	8.18	3.27	-.95
1994	Norfolk	Inter	16.7	14	5	1	2	12	2.70	1	1	7.56	.54	1.08	6.48	1.89
1994	NY Mets	NL	51.0	71	23	4	25	27	4.06	3	3	12.53	.71	4.41	4.76	.49
1995	Omaha	AmA	104.3	127	52	9	37	74	4.49	5	7	10.96	.78	3.19	6.38	1.33
1995	Kansas City	AL	22.3	22	17	4	10	13	6.85	1	1	8.87	1.61	4.03	5.24	.74
1996	Omaha	AmA	22.0	27	12	1	10	12	4.91	1	1	11.05	.41	4.09	4.91	.61
1996	Kansas City	AL	103.7	105	49	11	29	84	4.25	6	6	9.12	.95	2.52	7.29	1.80

He's a significantly better pitcher than he was with the Blue Jays, which still makes him no better than a 9th or 10th man. He handled that role wonderfully for the Royals last year, resurfacing when the Royals needed a fifth starter and making an emergency relief outing or two. The Royals have too much young pitching to keep Linton around anymore.

MIKE MAGNANTE   **LRP**   **1965**   **Age 32**

YR	TEAM	Lge	IP	H	ER	HR	BB	K	ERA	W	L	H/9	HR/9	BB/9	K/9	KW
1993	Omaha	AmA	100.3	99	38	7	39	67	3.41	6	5	8.88	.63	3.50	6.01	1.13
1993	Kansas City	AL	35.0	36	13	3	12	16	3.34	2	2	9.26	.77	3.09	4.11	.60
1994	Kansas City	AL	47.0	51	20	4	17	20	3.83	3	2	9.77	.77	3.26	3.83	.46
1995	Omaha	AmA	54.3	55	19	3	20	32	3.15	4	2	9.11	.50	3.31	5.30	.94
1995	Kansas City	AL	44.7	45	18	6	17	28	3.63	3	2	9.07	1.21	3.43	5.64	1.02
1996	Kansas City	AL	54.0	54	28	4	26	31	4.67	3	3	9.00	.67	4.33	5.17	.64

The perfect symbol of the mediocrity of Royals baseball. He has been with the team for six years despite little talent, no sub-4.00 ERAs since his rookie year and no platoon split for a pitcher whose assigned job was to get out left-handed hitters. The emergence of Granger has finally allowed the Royals to release him and mercifully end his career.

JEFF MONTGOMERY   **RRP**   **1962**   **Age 35**

YR	TEAM	Lge	IP	H	ER	HR	BB	K	ERA	W	L	H/9	HR/9	BB/9	K/9	KW
1993	Kansas City	AL	84.3	67	16	3	27	68	1.71	8	1	7.15	.32	2.88	7.26	1.70
1994	Kansas City	AL	45.0	44	14	4	16	49	2.80	3	2	8.80	.80	3.20	9.80	2.47
1995	Kansas City	AL	65.3	60	21	7	26	49	2.89	5	2	8.27	.96	3.58	6.75	1.35
1996	Kansas City	AL	63.3	55	23	13	20	44	3.27	4	3	7.82	1.85	2.84	6.25	1.37

He's had a run of three straight disappointing seasons, and not surprisingly he finally admitted that his chronic bursitis was only going to be cured by surgery. How many pitchers have lost their effectiveness because they won't admit they're hurt? The healthy Montgomery was the AL's best closer for a time, and while he's unlikely to reach that form again, a 2.70 ERA and 40 saves are certainly both possibilities.

STEVE OLSEN   **RBP**   **1970**   **Age 27**

YR	TEAM	Lge	IP	H	ER	HR	BB	K	ERA	W	L	H/9	HR/9	BB/9	K/9	KW
1993	Birmingham	South	127.0	191	97	25	72	70	6.87	4	10	13.54	1.77	5.10	4.96	.38
1994	Birmingham	South	92.3	120	52	10	43	54	5.07	4	6	11.70	.97	4.19	5.26	.71
1994	Nashville	AmA	69.0	68	25	5	24	51	3.26	5	3	8.87	.65	3.13	6.65	1.43
1995	Birmingham	South	77.7	100	47	5	31	43	5.45	3	6	11.59	.58	3.59	4.98	.76
1995	Nashville	AmA	73.0	90	43	9	25	40	5.30	3	5	11.10	1.11	3.08	4.93	.87
1996	Wichita	Texas	50.7	45	17	9	20	32	3.02	4	2	7.99	1.60	3.55	5.68	1.01
1996	Omaha	AmA	62.7	74	36	6	32	34	5.17	3	4	10.63	.86	4.60	4.88	.48

Taken from the White Sox in the minor league portion of the Rule V draft. He's a "crafty righty," and comes from a three-quarters delivery that is tough for right-handers to pick up, but he just doesn't throw hard enough to have a significant major league career.

HIPOLITO PICHARDO   **RRP**   **1970**   **Age 27**

YR	TEAM	Lge	IP	H	ER	HR	BB	K	ERA	W	L	H/9	HR/9	BB/9	K/9	KW
1993	Kansas City	AL	163.7	177	68	10	60	72	3.74	10	8	9.73	.55	3.30	3.96	.49
1994	Kansas City	AL	67.7	75	30	3	26	35	3.99	4	4	9.98	.40	3.46	4.66	.69
1995	Kansas City	AL	64.0	65	27	4	32	43	3.80	4	3	9.14	.56	4.50	6.05	.89
1996	Kansas City	AL	68.0	70	30	4	27	42	3.97	4	4	9.26	.53	3.57	5.56	.96

As expected, the downgrade in the Royals' infield defense last year, with the departures of Gary Gaetti, Greg Gagne and Wally Joyner, affected Pichardo more than anyone. His fastball drops like a stone when it reaches the plate, but those groundballs were rolling past guys like Randa, Paquette, and Hamelin all season. He should recover; he throws too hard and his pitches dance too much not to. He's probably still five years away from his peak.

JIM PITTSLEY **RSP** **1974** **Age 23**

YR	TEAM	Lge	IP	H	ER	HR	BB	K	ERA	W	L	H/9	HR/9	BB/9	K/9	KW
1993	Rockford	Midw	68.3	100	48	4	43	51	6.32	2	6	13.17	.53	5.66	6.72	.82
1994	Wilmington	Caro	144.0	199	81	15	60	116	5.06	6	10	12.44	.94	3.75	7.25	1.48
1995	Omaha	AmA	45.3	39	17	5	22	34	3.38	3	2	7.74	.99	4.37	6.75	1.16
1996	Wichita	Texas	19.7	12	1	0	7	6	.46	2	0	5.49	.00	3.20	2.75	.11
1996	Omaha	AmA	68.0	77	31	7	50	44	4.10	4	4	10.19	.93	6.62	5.82	.29

A much-ballyhooed prospect who returned from surgery that repaired a ligament in his elbow. Pittsley looked like a potential 200-game winner before he went down, but it's still unknown if he's back at 100%. He threw very well at times last year, but his sharpness was off, not unusual following surgery. Pittsley threw eight shutout innings for Omaha in the playoffs, and the Royals wisely decided to shut him down and give him the winter off. He's the potential #5 starter come spring training, but the Royals would be better advised to put him the bullpen and make him a long reliever, much like the Indians did with Julian Tavarez two years ago. A big, barrel-chested guy, but his arms look like twigs in comparison, making me wonder if the elbow problems will recur.

STEPHEN PRIHODA **LRP** **1973** **Age 24**

YR	TEAM	Lge	IP	H	ER	HR	BB	K	ERA	W	L	H/9	HR/9	BB/9	K/9	KW
1995	Spokane	Nwern	58.3	90	42	9	23	35	6.48	2	4	13.89	1.39	3.55	5.40	.91
1996	Wilmington	Caro	71.7	65	18	2	31	62	2.26	6	2	8.16	.25	3.89	7.79	1.62

Prihoda gets no respect as a prospect because he throws 84 on a good day, but he carved up Carolina League hitters like Thanksgiving turkey all season. He's a tall, gangly pitcher, and when he comes to the plate it's all arms and legs. Yeah, he gets by on deception, but ask Sid Fernandez what that's done for his career. He struck out nine straight hitters at one point last year, and I don't care if his fastball wouldn't get pulled over in a school zone, Prihoda can pitch.

KEN RAY **RSP** **1975** **Age 22**

YR	TEAM	Lge	IP	H	ER	HR	BB	K	ERA	W	L	H/9	HR/9	BB/9	K/9	KW
1994	Rockford	Midw	113.3	120	35	6	76	80	2.78	9	4	9.53	.48	6.04	6.35	.61
1995	Wilmington	Caro	68.7	100	41	4	32	47	5.37	3	5	13.11	.52	4.19	6.16	1.00
1995	Wichita	Texas	68.7	83	49	7	55	45	6.42	2	6	10.88	.92	7.21	5.90	.16
1996	Wichita	Texas	111.3	156	85	16	75	65	6.87	3	9	12.61	1.29	6.06	5.25	.24

Ray's just a kid, still growing into his body, and the growing pains have been evident the last two seasons. He's a southern boy who throws hard but has a bit of trouble with that thing they call the strike zone. The Royals love his arm, and they've been aggressive in promoting him through the system. Ray pitched well in the AFL, but his control problems linger. Needs at least two more years before he's ready for the major leagues.

JOSE ROSADO **LSP** **1975** **Age 22**

YR	TEAM	Lge	IP	H	ER	HR	BB	K	ERA	W	L	H/9	HR/9	BB/9	K/9	KW
1995	Wilmington	Caro	123.0	172	68	12	46	87	4.98	5	9	12.59	.88	3.37	6.37	1.28
1996	Wichita	Texas	11.7	12	0	0	2	10	.00	1	0	9.26	.00	1.54	7.71	2.19
1996	Omaha	AmA	92.0	86	35	15	51	68	3.42	6	4	8.41	1.47	4.99	6.65	.97
1996	Kansas City	AL	105.3	98	28	6	28	62	2.39	9	3	8.37	.51	2.39	5.30	1.17

The new Tom Glavine. Like Glavine, Rosado has trouble getting left-handers out, but has a terrific riding fastball and no fear busting right-handed hitters in at their fists. He was the Junior College Player of the Year in 1994, but lasted until the 12th round, yet another reminder that scouts, in general, refuse to take a player's performance into consideration at all when evaluating his potential. Rosado jumped from rookie ball to the major leagues in barely 18 months, and showed an almost preternatural poise. He pitches with complete faith in his defense's ability to make the plays behind him, holds baserunners well and can throw his fastball, slider or changeup for strikes regardless of the count. If it sounds like I like Rosado, I do. The Royals haven't developed a good southpaw since Danny Jackson, but they've got one now.

GLENDON RUSCH   **LSP**   **1975**   **Age 22**

YR	TEAM	Lge	IP	H	ER	HR	BB	K	ERA	W	L	H/9	HR/9	BB/9	K/9	KW
1994	Rockford	Midw	99.0	142	67	7	49	77	6.09	3	8	12.91	.64	4.45	7.00	1.22
1995	Wilmington	Caro	150.7	148	46	6	52	108	2.75	12	5	8.84	.36	3.11	6.45	1.37
1996	Omaha	AmA	161.7	189	81	13	62	97	4.51	8	10	10.52	.72	3.45	5.40	.94

Rusch is a similar pitcher to Rosado in many ways; he's left-handed, has an average fastball and throws strikes with all his pitches. His control is impeccable, especially with his fastball, which he can throw "into a teacup," according to the Royals. Struggled to make the adjustment to AAA after skipping a level, but he was still named the best pitching prospect in the American Association. His time is near, but probably not in April. The Royals want him to "work on a few things," but his only real weakness is that he sometimes leaves a hittable fastball in the batter's wheelhouse.

TOBY SMITH   **RRP**   **1972**   **Age 25**

YR	TEAM	Lge	IP	H	ER	HR	BB	K	ERA	W	L	H/9	HR/9	BB/9	K/9	KW
1993	Eugene	Nwern	20.3	22	9	2	6	18	3.98	1	1	9.74	.89	2.66	7.97	1.99
1994	Rockford	Midw	107.0	130	52	10	45	57	4.37	5	7	10.93	.84	3.79	4.79	.65
1995	Wilmington	Caro	70.7	91	41	11	29	48	5.22	3	5	11.59	1.40	3.69	6.11	1.11
1996	Wichita	Texas	47.7	51	23	7	26	36	4.34	2	3	9.63	1.32	4.91	6.80	1.04

A first baseman in college, largely the result of attending Wichita State while Bluma and Dreifort manned the bullpen there. He throws as hard as anyone in the organization, but he's unpolished. Smith has moved through the system slowly, but he's been effective everywhere he's pitched and probably has a lot more development left in him than most players his age. Unlikely to surface this year, but someone to keep an eye on.

DILSON TORRES   **RBP**   **1970**   **Age 27**

YR	TEAM	Lge	IP	H	ER	HR	BB	K	ERA	W	L	H/9	HR/9	BB/9	K/9	KW
1993	St. Catherine's	NY-P	17.7	34	18	4	11	12	9.17	0	2	17.32	2.04	5.60	6.11	.64
1994	Wilmington	Caro	54.0	59	15	5	22	33	2.50	4	2	9.83	.83	3.67	5.50	.92
1994	Memphis	South	54.0	56	16	4	18	37	2.67	4	2	9.33	.67	3.00	6.17	1.31
1995	Omaha	AmA	26.0	28	9	2	11	10	3.12	2	1	9.69	.69	3.81	3.46	.20
1995	Kansas City	AL	45.0	54	24	6	18	28	4.80	2	3	10.80	1.20	3.60	5.60	.97
1996	Wichita	Texas	51.0	66	25	6	20	22	4.41	3	3	11.65	1.06	3.53	3.88	.41
1996	Omaha	AmA	83.0	106	50	10	30	30	5.42	3	6	11.49	1.08	3.25	3.25	.27

Let's say this one more time: pitchers are inherently unpredictable. Two years ago, Torres was a sensation, with numbers as jaw-dropping as his sinker. Now he can't get anyone out. He has no injury history to report, but most of the time a pitcher's unexplained collapse stems from trying to pitch through pain. He can always come back, but not until he figures out what's wrong with him, and I doubt he will this year.

ROBERT TOTH   **RSP**   **1973**   **Age 24**

YR	TEAM	Lge	IP	H	ER	HR	BB	K	ERA	W	L	H/9	HR/9	BB/9	K/9	KW
1993	Wilmington	Caro	130.7	171	69	14	65	81	4.75	6	9	11.78	.96	4.48	5.58	.74
1994	Wilmington	Caro	54.3	64	14	3	15	24	2.32	4	2	10.60	.50	2.48	3.98	.70
1994	Memphis	South	80.7	106	52	16	38	48	5.80	3	6	11.83	1.79	4.24	5.36	.73
1995	Wichita	Texas	94.7	101	27	7	36	65	2.57	8	3	9.60	.67	3.42	6.18	1.20
1995	Omaha	AmA	45.7	52	21	7	13	27	4.14	2	3	10.25	1.38	2.56	5.32	1.13
1996	Wichita	Texas	95.7	109	43	5	35	42	4.05	5	6	10.25	.47	3.29	3.95	.49
1996	Omaha	AmA	44.7	65	37	5	23	17	7.46	1	4	13.10	1.01	4.63	3.43	-.02

Poor Toth. After years of trying to gain respect as a pitching prospect, he finally opened eyes with an excellent 1995 season and was on the cusp of the majors. But nothing worked for him last year, and it may have cost him his best opportunity at a job. Brian Bevil came back from a similar setback last year, but Toth isn't nearly the hard thrower that Bevil is.

JULIO VALERA   **RRP**   **1969**   **Age 28**

YR	TEAM	Lge	IP	H	ER	HR	BB	K	ERA	W	L	H/9	HR/9	BB/9	K/9	KW
1993	California	AL	54.0	72	36	8	17	29	6.00	2	4	12.00	1.33	2.83	4.83	.90
1994	Midland	Texas	17.3	18	7	3	12	11	3.63	1	1	9.35	1.56	6.23	5.71	.35
1994	Vancouver	PCL	56.0	68	32	8	26	37	5.14	2	4	10.93	1.29	4.18	5.95	.94
1995	Vancouver	PCL	65.7	97	55	3	29	41	7.54	2	5	13.29	.41	3.97	5.62	.88
1996	Omaha	AmA	15.3	22	12	0	8	8	7.04	0	2	12.91	.00	4.70	4.70	.39
1996	Kansas City	AL	61.3	70	34	6	29	30	4.99	3	4	10.27	.88	4.26	4.40	.40

Saying the Royals could have used better relief early last year is like saying the Titanic could have used more lifeboats. Valera, Jacome, Tim Pugh and Magnante combined to give the Royals one of the most execrable middle relief corps in recent memory. Unless he suddenly regains his pre-injury form, he's through.

Player	Age	Team	Lge	AB	H	DB	TP	HR	BB	SB	CS	OUT	BA	OBA	SA	EQA	EQR	Peak
JOSE AMADO	21	Lansing	Midw	215	65	8	1	5	13	4	2	152	.302	.342	.419	.257	25	.288
DOUG BLOSSER	19	Lansing	Midw	120	22	1	0	4	12	1	0	98	.183	.258	.292	.177	6	.202
RAMY BROOKS	26	Wilmington	Caro	375	86	9	1	13	39	2	1	290	.229	.302	.363	.221	33	.230
JIMMIE BYINGTON	22	Wilmington	Caro	304	79	12	2	1	16	5	3	228	.260	.297	.322	.209	23	.230
EDUARDO CEDENO	23	Wilmington	Caro	167	31	0	0	2	12	5	2	138	.186	.240	.222	.140	5	.152
JOSE CEPEDA	21	Lansing	Midw	566	138	18	1	4	27	4	2	430	.244	.278	.300	.191	34	.215
GARY COFFEE	21	Lansing	Midw	404	81	8	0	10	40	3	1	324	.200	.273	.295	.185	24	.207
DONOVAN DELANEY	22	Wilmington	Caro	393	95	9	2	4	19	8	3	301	.242	.277	.305	.195	25	.214
EMILIANO ESCANDON	21	Lansing	Midw	381	87	11	3	4	35	4	2	296	.228	.293	.304	.199	26	.224
MICHAEL EVANS	23	Wilmington	Caro	290	50	4	0	8	48	0	1	241	.172	.290	.269	.179	16	.195
ADAM FINNIESTON	23	Lansing	Midw	196	30	2	1	2	9	2	1	167	.153	.190	.204	.068	1	.075
PATRICK HALLMARK	22	Lansing	Midw	460	111	16	2	2	25	15	5	354	.241	.280	.298	.196	30	.216
SHANE HALTER	26	Omaha	AmA	305	76	14	0	5	33	6	2	231	.249	.322	.344	.227	28	.235
JASON LAYNE	23	Lansing	Midw	94	20	2	0	1	10	0	0	74	.213	.288	.266	.180	5	.198
KEVIN LONG	29	Wichita	Texas	442	106	21	2	3	52	8	7	343	.240	.320	.317	.214	36	.213
TONY LONGUEIRA	21	Lansing	Midw	156	24	0	1	1	10	2	1	133	.154	.205	.186	.065	1	.075
RAMON MARTINEZ	26	Omaha	AmA	324	78	9	2	6	25	3	2	248	.241	.295	.336	.211	25	.220
SEAN MCNALLY	23	Wilmington	Caro	443	109	10	1	8	49	1	1	335	.246	.321	.327	.218	37	.237
MARK MELITO	24	Lansing	Midw	207	45	7	1	1	20	4	1	163	.217	.286	.275	.188	12	.199
CARLOS MENDEZ	22	Wilmington	Caro	414	107	14	2	4	20	1	0	307	.258	.293	.331	.209	31	.230
TONY MIRANDA	23	Lansing	Midw	139	34	3	1	2	13	1	0	105	.245	.309	.324	.214	11	.233
JULIO MONTILLA	23	Wilmington	Caro	153	35	6	0	0	8	1	0	118	.229	.267	.268	.173	7	.188
CESAR MORILLO	22	Wichita	Texas	119	25	1	1	2	7	2	0	94	.210	.254	.286	.177	6	.194
JOSE MOTA	31	Omaha	AmA	232	53	3	2	3	19	6	4	183	.228	.287	.297	.195	15	.188
ALEJANDRO PRIETO	20	Wilmington	Caro	457	114	12	4	1	27	11	7	350	.249	.291	.300	.198	31	.225
MARK QUINN	22	Lansing	Midw	446	115	11	1	9	32	7	4	335	.258	.308	.348	.221	38	.244
KEIFER RACKLEY	25	Wilmington	Caro	302	76	4	1	9	40	2	1	227	.252	.339	.361	.237	31	.250
JUAN ROCHA	22	Lansing	Midw	473	111	10	3	13	51	7	4	366	.235	.309	.351	.221	42	.244
DON SHEPPARD	25	Wichita	Texas	98	19	2	0	2	8	2	2	81	.194	.255	.276	.167	5	.175
AL SHIRLEY	22	Wilmington	Caro	354	74	6	1	13	49	4	3	283	.209	.305	.342	.215	30	.237
CHAD STRICKLAND	24	Wichita	Texas	240	49	8	1	5	16	1	1	192	.204	.254	.308	.180	13	.194
BRIAN TEETERS	23	Wilmington	Caro	180	37	5	2	2	28	8	2	145	.206	.312	.289	.209	14	.226
MATT TREANOR	20	Lansing	Midw	392	87	8	1	6	25	2	1	306	.222	.269	.293	.183	22	.207

Player	Age	Team	Lge	IP	H	ER	HR	BB	K	ERA	W	L	H/9	HR/9	BB/9	K/9	KW
JUSTIN ADAM	21	Lansing	Midw	67.7	103	62	9	74	38	8.25	2	6	13.70	1.20	9.84	5.05	-.78
ERIC ANDERSON	21	Wilmington	Caro	139.0	202	92	22	64	48	5.96	5	10	13.08	1.42	4.14	3.11	.00
MANUEL BERNAL	22	Lansing	Midw	81.0	156	60	9	21	26	6.67	2	7	17.33	1.00	2.33	2.89	.38
MIKE BOVEE	22	Wichita	Texas	162.3	236	104	20	61	84	5.77	6	12	13.08	1.11	3.38	4.66	.71
DUSTIN BRIXEY	22	Wilmington	Caro	100.7	138	68	5	57	26	6.08	3	8	12.34	.45	5.10	2.32	-.50
LANCE CARTER	21	Wilmington	Caro	58.0	99	56	10	25	34	8.69	1	5	15.36	1.55	3.88	5.28	.79
TERRY CLARK	35	Omaha	AmA	44.0	44	14	12	19	30	2.86	3	2	9.00	2.45	3.89	6.14	1.07
CHRIS EDDY	26	Wichita	Texas	28.3	33	14	6	23	18	4.45	1	2	10.48	1.91	7.31	5.72	.08
PAT FLURY	23	Wilmington	Caro	76.0	82	24	3	40	47	2.84	5	3	9.71	.36	4.74	5.57	.67
JAVIER GAMBOA	22	Wichita	Texas	84.0	121	61	18	46	32	6.54	2	7	12.96	1.93	4.93	3.43	-.09
	22	Wilmington	Caro	30.0	47	14	4	4	17	4.20	1	2	14.10	1.20	1.20	5.10	1.40
PHILLIP GRUNDY	23	Wilmington	Caro	145.3	196	100	21	70	81	6.19	5	11	12.14	1.30	4.33	5.02	.59
BRIAN HARRISON	27	Wichita	Texas	108.3	129	49	11	25	66	4.07	6	6	10.72	.91	2.08	5.48	1.31
KEVIN HODGES	23	Lansing	Midw	41.7	59	36	5	25	14	7.78	1	4	12.74	1.08	5.40	3.02	-.34
	23	Wilmington	Caro	34.0	55	34	3	24	10	9.00	1	3	14.56	.79	6.35	2.65	-.71
BRENT KAYSNER	22	Lansing	Midw	37.7	44	35	4	71	25	8.36	1	3	10.51	.96	16.96	5.97	-2.25
SCOTT KEY	19	Lansing	Midw	52.7	65	49	5	59	38	8.37	1	5	11.11	.85	10.08	6.49	-.36
ALLEN MCDILL	24	Wichita	Texas	60.3	82	39	10	29	51	5.82	2	5	12.23	1.49	4.33	7.61	1.45
GENO MORONES	25	Wichita	Texas	35.0	51	29	6	25	20	7.46	1	3	13.11	1.54	6.43	5.14	.11
	25	Wilmington	Caro	84.7	110	46	10	39	42	4.89	4	5	11.69	1.06	4.15	4.46	.45
BLAINE MULL	19	Lansing	Midw	149.7	242	102	10	53	72	6.13	5	12	14.55	.78	3.19	4.33	.65
CARLOS PAREDES	20	Lansing	Midw	100.3	170	81	3	89	45	7.27	3	8	15.25	.27	7.98	4.04	-.65
MARC PHILLIPS	24	Wilmington	Caro	43.7	71	37	5	27	13	7.63	1	4	14.63	1.03	5.56	2.68	-.50
TIM PUGH	29	Kansas City	AL	36.7	39	18	8	13	26	4.42	2	2	9.57	1.96	3.19	6.38	1.33
KEVIN RAWITZER	25	Wichita	Texas	62.7	80	47	7	50	40	6.75	2	5	11.49	1.01	7.18	5.74	.12
MICHAEL ROBBINS	22	Lansing	Midw	99.3	158	63	7	48	48	5.71	4	7	14.32	.63	4.35	4.35	.36
RICH RODRIGUEZ	33	Omaha	AmA	67.3	79	37	10	29	56	4.95	3	4	10.56	1.34	3.88	7.49	1.53
MATTHEW SAIER	23	Wilmington	Caro	118.7	169	84	12	72	90	6.37	4	9	12.82	.91	5.46	6.83	.91
ALLEN SANDERS	21	Lansing	Midw	26.7	49	20	4	3	3	6.75	1	2	16.54	1.35	1.01	1.01	.08
JOSE SANTIAGO	21	Lansing	Midw	66.0	102	38	6	28	35	5.18	3	4	13.91	.82	3.82	4.77	.64
JIM TELGHEDER	25	Wilmington	Caro	66.7	76	26	9	21	35	3.51	4	3	10.26	1.22	2.84	4.73	.87
TODD THORN	19	Lansing	Midw	147.7	213	80	18	45	67	4.88	6	10	12.98	1.10	2.74	4.08	.68
MODESTO VILLARREAL	20	Lansing	Midw	36.0	67	39	8	16	18	9.75	1	3	16.75	2.00	4.00	4.50	.50
JEFF WALLACE	20	Lansing	Midw	104.0	172	84	13	86	53	7.27	3	9	14.88	1.12	7.44	4.59	-.33
BRYAN WOLFF	24	Wilmington	Caro	55.0	62	40	3	50	39	6.55	2	4	10.15	.49	8.18	6.38	.08

Milwaukee Brewers

I tried to hold off on writing this chapter as long as I could so I'd be able to say a few nice words about Bud Selig. But try as I might, I couldn't hold off long enough for Bud to actually do something worth some positive words. I'm already 30; the average male lives to be 72 or so; a guy in my physical condition usually doesn't see 65, so I figured I might as well go ahead and write it. I mean, in the midst of a labor dispute, it's going to be pretty hard to concentrate on the Brewers when their owner is such an icon in the labor wars, but hey, Brewer fans deserve a few words about their team, not about the ignominious and embarrassing activities of the shameless owner. So let's get on to the Brewers.

Lots of corporations have mission statements. Microsoft's is "A computer on every desktop." I called the Milwaukee Brewers front office to find out theirs, and they put me on hold. Then a tape recording of some music came on and after a while, I was disconnected. I'm going to assume that "Love to Love You Baby" is not the mission statement of the Brewers, but rather a somewhat vapid disco hit from Donna Summer. My confusion is probably understandable. Anyway…I think I've managed to figure out the Brewer mission statement. It's down to two contenders. Here they are:

"Gimme."

It's simple, straightforward, focused and tells you everything you need to know about the Brewers as a team and an organization. Gimme a new stadium. You pay for it, we'll lease it for virtually nothing. We need it to compete. Gimme revenue sharing. You pay for it, we'll use the cash to increase our margin. We need it to compete. Of course, this mission statement only has full effect if spoken with a French accent.

Our second contender is….

"It's a Family Business."

From Maharajah Bud Selig down to In-Law Randy Levine, this is a family affair. Ask Sal Bando someday about the qualifications of his brother Chris to be on a major league professional staff. If Sal can't give you an answer, why not ask club general counsel Wendy Selig-Prieb? Yes, thanks to the wonders of family relationships, corporate profits can be turned into illicit and fully deductible salaries and overhead.

It's kind of an unfair gripe, but the nepotism in this organization is affecting the club for the worse. Are we really to believe that Chris Bando was the best person for the incredibly difficult job of bench coach? He might be, but do you think that had any bearing on whether or not he got the job? This sort of organizational maneuvering sends a clear message to everyone in the organization—quality doesn't matter.

Change your name to Selig, Bando or Prieb and you've got a future in this organization. Kiss ass. Performance is secondary. Actually, for the players, I should have capitalized ass, because I'm talking about one in particular—Phil Garner.

Garner used to be known as a stealing freak. At random, players would get a good lead and then bolt for second base from the depths of the clubhouse, like some sort of misplaced Monty Python sketch. Many basestealers made it, many others didn't. Big innings were converted into hit and runs blown harder than Charlie Sheen. "Ol' Scrap Iron" has since turned into something of a vengeful postal worker, undersized and overstressed. Despite looking like the protein version of Ned Flanders, Garner has trained his Brewers to be a bunch of thugs. Opposing players don't much care for the Brewers, and apparently neither does the Milwaukee fan base. Brewer players get involved in a lot of talking on the field, and more Brewers showed up on Baseball Tonight for their fisticuffs than did for their play.

1997 will be the start of another cycle of whining for the club. They're poised, as far as they know, to make a play for the wild card, which is a slightly smarter strategy than repeatedly kissing a belt sander. They'll fall a little short of course, and it'll take approximately 15 seconds for Sal Bando-Prieb to feed Peter Gammons a line about Milwaukee not being able to make a play for an impact player like Garret Anderson for the stretch run. Gammons might use that line, or he might not. Either way, it won't be accurate.

The Brewers are going to have trouble because they've got tough holes to fill. They've got a few decent hitters; Jaha, Nilsson, Newfield, Cirillo and Valentin. But only Valentin and Cirillo are likely to be well above average for their positions, and outside of Valentin they're weak up the middle, with or without Chuck E. Carr and his ghastly-lookin' knee injuries. The rotation's not all that bad and the bullpen's a strength, but Garner can't be trusted to keep people healthy. The offense is good enough to contend if everything breaks their way, but that usually doesn't happen. The pitching staff could be great if D'Amico breaks out (unlikely at his young age), McDonald stays healthy and one of the seven dwarfs steps up. But by and large, there's just enough here to contend for the wild card spot. This organization has made that their goal. Was achieving it really a good idea?

Sal Bando has no plan for this club, and Phil Garner cannot implement a coherent plan if he's handed one. This team has a bunch of good, replaceable players. That's not the way to build a champion. And it's not very becoming to blame it on all your surroundings when you fail under the weight of your own incompetence.

Bud Selig is making money here, but he's doing so in a thoroughly beige way. Until he realizes that everything that he does causes waves throughout the organization, he's doomed to continue owning an annuity that plays baseball.

Organization: One of the brightest stars of the organization is not being recognized. Tim Ireland has consistently outperformed expectations with his teams and laid out a clear, coherent vision of what a baseball team should do to improve on the field. Why organizations go out and hire the carcass of

John McNamara while Ireland rots in obscurity is lost on me. Ireland deserves a major league job, and it's nothing short of a shame that he hasn't had that opportunity. Until people like Tim Ireland have a shot to do their jobs in the big leagues, there is no reason to believe that MLB is anything close to a meritocracy—it is nothing more than an inbred hiring network, where who you know matters infinitely more than what you're capable of, what you know and what you've demonstrated you can do.

BRIAN BANKS OF 1971 Age 26

Year	Team	Lge	AB	H	DB	TP	HR	BB	SB	CS	OUT	BA	OBA	SA	EQA	EQR	Peak
1994	Beloit	Midw	148	30	2	1	3	6	1	1	119	.203	.234	.291	.163	6	.179
1994	Beloit	Midw	242	64	7	1	7	24	5	1	179	.264	.331	.388	.245	26	.267
1994	Stockton	Calif	255	54	6	0	4	32	2	4	205	.212	.300	.282	.189	16	.207
1995	El Paso	Texas	442	121	27	4	13	71	7	4	325	.274	.374	.441	.272	63	.291
1996	New Orleans	AmA	502	134	25	5	15	69	16	6	374	.267	.356	.426	.263	66	.277
1997	*Milwaukee*	*AL*	*561*	*148*	*29*	*4*	*18*	*71*	*15*	*9*	*422*	*.264*	*.347*	*.426*	*.258*	*71*	

Replicis Rangies, the replacement outfielder of the Lactate Serengeti. Best noted for his colorful indigo and goldenrod plumage, his acceptable defense and his league average bat. Known to go into feeding frenzies throughout the central United States and eastern Canada. Not endangered.

RONNIE BELLIARD 2B 1975 Age 22

Year	Team	Lge	AB	H	DB	TP	HR	BB	SB	CS	OUT	BA	OBA	SA	EQA	EQR	Peak
1995	Beloit	Midw	474	126	15	2	12	28	6	6	354	.266	.307	.382	.229	45	.260
1996	El Paso	Texas	417	99	15	4	3	54	17	5	323	.237	.325	.314	.222	37	.249

This next sentence could end my baseball career if taken out of context. Belliard's a good-hitting middle infielder, showing good range in both directions. His bat is above average for a prospect at his position and his secondary skills make him a very good bet to have some value in the majors. If everything breaks precisely right for him he could grow up to be Bobby Grich, and that's a pretty good top end.

JEROMY BURNITZ OF 1969 Age 28

Year	Team	Lge	AB	H	DB	TP	HR	BB	SB	CS	OUT	BA	OBA	SA	EQA	EQR	Peak
1993	Norfolk	Inter	262	61	13	2	8	26	8	5	206	.233	.302	.389	.230	26	.247
1993	NY Mets	NL	270	68	10	5	14	42	3	5	207	.252	.353	.481	.268	39	.287
1994	Norfolk	Inter	329	84	14	3	15	47	13	4	249	.255	.348	.453	.267	46	.282
1994	NY Mets	NL	145	35	3	0	3	25	1	1	111	.241	.353	.324	.231	14	.242
1995	Buffalo	AmA	459	135	24	4	21	54	13	4	328	.294	.368	.501	.287	73	.299
1996	Cleveland	AL	127	35	7	0	8	25	2	1	93	.276	.395	.520	.298	22	.305
1996	Milwaukee	AL	72	17	1	0	3	8	2	0	55	.236	.312	.375	.235	7	.239
1997	*Milwaukee*	*AL*	*392*	*110*	*19*	*2*	*25*	*60*	*2*	*1*	*283*	*.281*	*.376*	*.531*	*.294*	*67*	

A member of the Ken Phelps All-Star team, for those of you who remember the Bill James concept from the '80s. Hits for power, draws some walks, won't kill you in the field. A perfect platoon partner who's been passed over for playing time by the likes of David Hulse, George Wendt and the Mets' "Five-Tool Outfielder Who Can't Hit of the Week." [tm]

CHUCK CARR CF 1969 Age 28

Year	Team	Lge	AB	H	DB	TP	HR	BB	SB	CS	OUT	BA	OBA	SA	EQA	EQR	Peak
1993	Florida	NL	560	151	19	2	4	57	47	18	427	.270	.337	.332	.236	58	.254
1994	Florida	NL	432	110	18	2	2	28	27	6	328	.255	.300	.319	.219	37	.230
1995	Florida	NL	315	75	13	0	5	49	21	10	250	.238	.341	.327	.232	32	.240
1996	Milwaukee	AL	106	29	5	1	1	6	5	4	81	.274	.312	.368	.228	10	.234
1997	*Milwaukee*	*AL*	*AL*	*246*	*66*	*9*	*3*	*1*	*34*	*17*	*10*	*190*	*.268*	*.357*	*.341*	*.241*	*27*

Last year, my software thought he'd have a real breakout year, so naturally I went in to debug. Instead of breaking out, he was this year's unfortunate TheismannCam victim, his ligaments serving as object lessons in slow motion on SportsCenter. He's not a great ballplayer, a lot of people don't particularly like him, but there's something about watching someone who can play this kind of defense. I hope he makes it back and fills out a few more "Plays of the Week" reels.

JEFF CIRILLO   **3B/2B**   **1970**   **Age 27**

Year	Team	Lge	AB	H	DB	TP	HR	BB	SB	CS	OUT	BA	OBA	SA	EQA	EQR	Peak
1993	El Paso	Texas	253	78	9	1	8	25	1	1	176	.308	.371	.447	.274	35	.297
1993	New Orleans	AmA	221	65	12	1	4	31	2	1	157	.294	.381	.412	.269	30	.293
1994	New Orleans	AmA	242	77	15	1	11	29	3	0	165	.318	.391	.525	.303	42	.324
1994	Milwaukee	AL	126	29	6	0	4	11	0	1	98	.230	.292	.373	.218	11	.235
1995	Milwaukee	AL	327	89	17	4	10	47	7	2	240	.272	.364	.440	.270	45	.286
1996	Milwaukee	AL	565	183	45	5	15	57	4	9	391	.324	.386	.501	.289	88	.301
1997	*Milwaukee*	*AL*	*566*	*178*	*37*	*3*	*21*	*67*	*6*	*6*	*394*	*.314*	*.387*	*.502*	*.292*	*91*	

This is a championship caliber ballplayer. Cirillo helps a team at either third base or second base with a good glove and a good mixture of batting average and secondary skills. It wouldn't surprise me to see him slug .500 for a few years in a row. He's been good enough to help a team in the majors for some time. Good batting eye; I expect he'll walk quite a bit more than projected.

JOHN JAHA   **1B**   **1966**   **Age 31**

Year	Team	Lge	AB	H	DB	TP	HR	BB	SB	CS	OUT	BA	OBA	SA	EQA	EQR	Peak
1993	Milwaukee	AL	523	146	17	0	24	55	13	7	384	.279	.348	.449	.265	69	.272
1994	New Orleans	AmA	65	26	6	0	3	12	1	0	39	.400	.494	.631	.370	16	.383
1994	Milwaukee	AL	291	69	9	0	13	32	3	3	225	.237	.313	.402	.236	30	.238
1995	Milwaukee	AL	315	97	19	2	21	36	2	1	219	.308	.379	.581	.308	57	.306
1996	Milwaukee	AL	542	162	24	1	35	84	3	1	381	.299	.393	.541	.304	97	.297
1997	*Milwaukee*	*AL*	*600*	*172*	*28*	*2*	*32*	*77*	*3*	*2*	*430*	*.287*	*.368*	*.500*	*.285*	*93*	

One of many lumbering hitters the Brewers have acquired. Jaha's an acceptable major league first baseman, and he'll be one for another couple of years. I like his defense at first base, but I'm in the minority.

GEOFF JENKINS   **1B/DH**   **1975**   **Age 22**

Year	Team	Lge	AB	H	DB	TP	HR	BB	SB	CS	OUT	BA	OBA	SA	EQA	EQR	Peak
1995	Stockton	Calif	49	12	2	0	2	8	1	0	37	.245	.351	.408	.258	6	.295
1995	El Paso	Texas	79	20	3	1	1	7	2	1	60	.253	.314	.354	.226	7	.257
1996	Stockton	Calif	140	43	5	2	3	15	2	1	98	.307	.374	.436	.273	19	.307
1996	El Paso	Texas	77	19	4	2	1	11	1	1	59	.247	.341	.390	.243	9	.272
1997	*Milwaukee*	*AL*	*437*	*123*	*18*	*2*	*6*	*52*	*4*	*3*	*317*	*.281*	*.358*	*.373*	*.249*	*49*	

Jenkins is a very strange player. It's not often that a player can't find a defensive position at this point in his career. His stroke looks very sharp to me; he waits back exceptionally well, then explodes into the ball nice and smooth. Then again, I've always been a fan of Doug Jennings' swing, too. Not a fast man; can barely outrun continental drift or Robin Ventura.

JESSE LEVIS   **C**   **1968**   **Age 29**

Year	Team	Lge	AB	H	DB	TP	HR	BB	SB	CS	OUT	BA	OBA	SA	EQA	EQR	Peak
1993	Charlotte-NC	Inter	132	31	5	1	2	16	0	1	102	.235	.318	.333	.216	11	.229
1993	Cleveland	AL	64	12	3	0	0	2	0	0	52	.188	.212	.234	.117	1	.126
1994	Charlotte-NC	Inter	386	107	13	0	11	52	1	0	279	.277	.363	.396	.258	47	.268
1995	Buffalo	AmA	196	62	10	0	6	32	0	2	136	.316	.412	.459	.290	31	.297
1996	Milwaukee	AL	233	55	5	1	1	38	0	0	178	.236	.343	.279	.212	19	.214
1997	*Milwaukee*	*AL*	*228*	*61*	*5*	*0*	*7*	*33*	*0*	*0*	*167*	*.268*	*.360*	*.382*	*.252*	*27*	

Forced to sign with Milwaukee following the 104th Congress' "Tools of Ignorance Act," compelling all catchers who are about to become Brian Dorsett to sign with either Milwaukee or go to Kintetsu in a cultural exchange. Levis is a perfectly good starting catcher; a good parallel would probably be Mike LaValliere at the same age. Levis has more power and probably isn't quite the defensive catcher Spanky was. A guy who can really help a team as a backup and may be doing that for many years to come.

PAT LISTACH   **2B/SS**   **1968**   **Age 29**

Year	Team	Lge	AB	H	DB	TP	HR	BB	SB	CS	OUT	BA	OBA	SA	EQA	EQR	Peak
1993	Milwaukee	AL	361	94	16	1	4	40	17	7	274	.260	.334	.343	.234	36	.247
1994	Milwaukee	AL	54	16	2	0	0	3	2	1	39	.296	.333	.333	.231	5	.241
1995	Milwaukee	AL	333	72	9	2	0	25	12	3	264	.216	.271	.255	.176	17	.180
1996	Milwaukee	AL	316	75	16	2	1	36	25	5	246	.237	.315	.310	.224	29	.226
1997	*Houston*	*NL*	*184*	*40*	*6*	*1*	*0*	*13*	*31*	*7*	*151*	*.217*	*.269*	*.261*	*.223*	*18*	

Damaged, bad goods. Any team that signs him just isn't thinking. The Brewers tried valiantly to dump him on George and the Yankees, but they returned him as damaged goods. Of course, Listach completely sucks when he's healthy, and is only slightly more likely to be in the majors in two years than Morganna's ever-dropping gravity eggs. Signed with Houston.

MARK LORETTA   **IF**   **1972**   **Age 25**

Year	Team	Lge	AB	H	DB	TP	HR	BB	SB	CS	OUT	BA	OBA	SA	EQA	EQR	Peak
1993	Stockton	Calif	202	65	3	1	3	15	3	1	138	.322	.369	.391	.262	24	.294
1994	El Paso	Texas	307	88	13	3	1	25	5	2	221	.287	.340	.358	.240	31	.264
1994	New Orleans	AmA	140	30	3	0	2	12	2	1	111	.214	.276	.279	.182	8	.201
1995	New Orleans	AmA	487	136	17	4	8	39	9	7	358	.279	.333	.380	.240	51	.261
1995	Milwaukee	AL	50	13	0	0	2	4	1	1	38	.260	.315	.380	.231	5	.249
1996	New Orleans	AmA	73	18	4	1	0	9	1	1	56	.247	.329	.329	.222	6	.239
1996	Milwaukee	AL	154	43	2	0	1	14	2	1	112	.279	.339	.312	.224	13	.240
1997	*Milwaukee*	*AL*	*250*	*70*	*11*	*1*	*5*	*22*	*4*	*2*	*182*	*.280*	*.338*	*.392*	*.248*	*28*	

Not a bad utility guy to have. If he can hang on and be perceived as a major leaguer, perhaps find the occasional spotlight, he might be Mike Gallego or Dick Schofield with a bit more of a bat. Not a long-term solution in the infield, but certainly no worse a player than the Joey Coras of the world.

KEVIN MAAS   **1B**   **1965**   **Age 32**

Year	Team	Lge	AB	H	DB	TP	HR	BB	SB	CS	OUT	BA	OBA	SA	EQA	EQR	Peak
1993	Columbus-OH	Inter	109	31	4	0	4	18	0	1	79	.284	.386	.431	.272	15	.274
1993	NY Yankees	AL	154	35	3	0	11	26	1	1	120	.227	.339	.461	.260	21	.262
1994	Indianapolis	AmA	288	84	12	1	20	30	2	2	206	.292	.358	.549	.291	47	.290
1994	Las Vegas	PCL	88	19	4	1	3	8	1	0	69	.216	.281	.386	.222	8	.220
1995	Columbus-OH	Inter	164	44	4	1	9	23	0	0	120	.268	.358	.470	.273	23	.267
1995	Minnesota	AL	57	11	2	0	2	7	0	0	46	.193	.281	.333	.201	4	.197
1996	New Orleans	AmA	120	31	7	0	7	15	0	0	89	.258	.341	.492	.271	17	.261
1997	*Milwaukee*	*AL*	*165*	*40*	*2*	*0*	*10*	*20*	*0*	*0*	*125*	*.242*	*.324*	*.436*	*.251*	*20*	

If you need a big left-handed bat on the bench to scare the opposing manager, this might be the guy. If you need that bat to make contact, however, make sure it's in someone else's hands. Sam Horn without the charisma or talent, and with an extra helping of jawbone.

MIKE MATHENY   **C**   **1971**   **Age 26**

Year	Team	Lge	AB	H	DB	TP	HR	BB	SB	CS	OUT	BA	OBA	SA	EQA	EQR	Peak
1993	El Paso	Texas	340	74	15	1	2	19	1	2	268	.218	.259	.285	.173	17	.190
1994	New Orleans	AmA	179	40	9	1	4	17	1	1	140	.223	.291	.352	.212	15	.230
1994	Milwaukee	AL	53	12	2	0	1	3	0	1	42	.226	.268	.321	.187	3	.205
1995	Milwaukee	AL	166	40	10	1	0	12	2	1	127	.241	.292	.313	.203	12	.218
1996	New Orleans	AmA	66	14	3	0	1	3	1	0	52	.212	.246	.303	.180	4	.194
1996	Milwaukee	AL	313	64	14	2	8	14	3	2	251	.204	.239	.339	.186	19	.196
1997	*Milwaukee*	*AL*	*233*	*50*	*13*	*1*	*5*	*16*	*2*	*2*	*185*	*.215*	*.265*	*.343*	*.199*	*16*	

Not a sure bet to outhit the average National League pitcher. Hence, he has great defensive skills. Kind of the Tracy Jones of catchers.

MATT MIESKE — RF/CF — 1968 — Age 29

Year	Team	Lge	AB	H	DB	TP	HR	BB	SB	CS	OUT	BA	OBA	SA	EQA	EQR	Peak
1993	New Orleans	AmA	224	59	11	1	9	29	6	3	168	.263	.348	.442	.263	30	.277
1993	Milwaukee	AL	59	15	1	0	3	4	0	1	45	.254	.302	.424	.234	6	.246
1994	Milwaukee	AL	259	66	11	1	10	21	3	4	197	.255	.311	.421	.240	28	.249
1995	Milwaukee	AL	266	66	13	1	12	27	2	4	204	.248	.317	.440	.246	31	.252
1996	Milwaukee	AL	373	103	23	3	14	26	1	5	275	.276	.323	.466	.256	46	.259
1997	Milwaukee	AL	388	103	22	1	14	51	2	4	289	.265	.351	.436	.260	50	

Yet another generic outfielder. Mieske's basically a minor league Mike Huff, and he'll be dancing for jobs for the next several years. Probably will be able to help a team as a fourth outfielder/pinch-hitter, but his job security is roughly the same as the cast of "Homeboys in Outer Space."

MARC NEWFIELD — OF — 1973 — Age 24

Year	Team	Lge	AB	H	DB	TP	HR	BB	SB	CS	OUT	BA	OBA	SA	EQA	EQR	Peak
1993	Jacksonville	South	345	103	9	0	18	31	1	1	243	.299	.356	.481	.277	49	.314
1993	Seattle	AL	66	16	3	0	1	3	0	1	51	.242	.275	.333	.196	4	.222
1994	Calgary	PCL	415	126	23	1	17	40	0	2	291	.304	.365	.487	.280	60	.313
1995	Las Vegas	PCL	68	21	4	0	3	3	1	0	47	.309	.338	.500	.279	10	.310
1995	Tacoma	PCL	201	56	5	0	7	19	1	0	145	.279	.341	.408	.253	23	.278
1995	San Diego	NL	57	19	5	1	1	2	0	0	38	.333	.356	.509	.286	8	.317
1995	Seattle	AL	85	16	4	0	3	3	0	0	69	.188	.216	.341	.175	4	.197
1996	Milwaukee	AL	179	55	11	0	8	11	0	1	125	.307	.347	.503	.278	25	.302
1996	San Diego	NL	195	51	8	0	6	19	1	1	145	.262	.327	.395	.241	21	.263
1997	Milwaukee	AL	578	179	20	0	25	43	5	3	402	.310	.357	.474	.277	81	

If he has a typical year he'll battle for playing time, get criticized for not being Andruw Jones and get traded, along with Ron Villone, for some generic outfielder having a year over his head. Glenallen Hill, for example. Newfield is actually a pretty good ballplayer, and could get better given some stability and consistent playing time. He's not going to be a super-star, but he could certainly be a better player than Joe Carter. Watch Newfield set up to field singles into the outfield; he needs coaching there as he pulls his hips and head early. Singles will skip by this guy more often than they should.

DAVE NILSSON — RF/DH/1B/C — 1970 — Age 27

Year	Team	Lge	AB	H	DB	TP	HR	BB	SB	CS	OUT	BA	OBA	SA	EQA	EQR	Peak
1993	New Orleans	AmA	63	22	3	0	2	5	0	1	42	.349	.397	.492	.292	10	.317
1993	Milwaukee	AL	301	81	9	2	9	39	4	4	224	.269	.353	.402	.252	36	.276
1994	Milwaukee	AL	396	107	26	3	12	34	1	0	289	.270	.328	.442	.256	48	.274
1995	Milwaukee	AL	262	72	12	1	12	24	2	0	190	.275	.336	.466	.266	35	.280
1996	Milwaukee	AL	452	149	32	2	17	57	2	3	306	.330	.405	.522	.304	78	.316
1997	Milwaukee	AL	626	204	51	3	24	64	2	2	424	.326	.388	.532	.302	106	

Had the Mickey Tettleton conversion a few years early. Not enormously valuable at first base or in the outfield, but certainly a batter player than guys like Cecil Fielder. He'll be a solid player for several years. Health should no longer be an issue.

MIKE RENNHACK — UT — 1975 — Age 22

Year	Team	Lge	AB	H	DB	TP	HR	BB	SB	CS	OUT	BA	OBA	SA	EQA	EQR	Peak
1993	Asheville	S Atl	454	107	15	1	9	27	7	5	352	.236	.279	.333	.203	33	.237
1994	Quad Cities	Midw	462	93	7	0	9	41	6	2	371	.201	.266	.275	.175	24	.202
1995	Quad Cities	Midw	315	80	10	1	1	31	6	2	237	.254	.321	.302	.213	25	.242
1996	Stockton	Calif	462	133	20	1	14	39	4	5	334	.288	.343	.426	.256	55	.286
1997	Milwaukee	AL	479	132	19	1	15	35	6	5	352	.276	.325	.413	.247	53	

I've only seen this guy hit on tape. He's got a very strange swing, but it looks normal in most ways. If you get a chance to watch him, watch his torso during the middle of his stroke. His lower body leads into the hitting zone, and then out of nowhere his whole upper body kind of follows. I don't think I've ever seen anything quite like it from a successful hitter, but it's certainly worked for him so far. I guess the closest thing I've seen is actually Kirby Puckett, but Rennhack probably won't have that kind of career.

KELLY STINNETT **C** **1970** **Age 27**

Year	Team	Lge	AB	H	DB	TP	HR	BB	SB	CS	OUT	BA	OBA	SA	EQA	EQR	Peak
1993	Charlotte-NC	Inter	293	78	9	2	6	20	0	0	215	.266	.313	.372	.230	27	.250
1994	NY Mets	NL	151	38	6	2	2	13	2	0	113	.252	.311	.358	.227	14	.244
1995	NY Mets	NL	201	47	9	1	4	32	2	0	154	.234	.339	.348	.234	20	.247
1996	New Orleans	AmA	342	98	16	0	25	34	3	2	246	.287	.351	.553	.290	56	.302
1997	*Milwaukee*	*AL*	*464*	*124*	*16*	*0*	*15*	*37*	*0*	*0*	*340*	*.267*	*.321*	*.399*	*.242*	*49*	

Another catcher snagged by Sal Bando. Might be good enough to start for a few years; if not, certainly a capable back-up. If Pat Borders has a job, there's no reason Kelly shouldn't have one.

JOSH TYLER **IF** **1974** **Age 23**

Year	Team	Lge	AB	H	DB	TP	HR	BB	SB	CS	OUT	BA	OBA	SA	EQA	EQR	Peak
1995	Beloit	Midw	195	39	2	0	2	29	1	2	158	.200	.304	.241	.176	10	.196
1996	Stockton	Calif	276	77	9	1	2	18	2	4	203	.279	.323	.341	.222	24	.246
1997	*Milwaukee*	*AL*	*405*	*113*	*20*	*1*	*5*	*33*	*3*	*2*	*294*	*.279*	*.333*	*.370*	*.239*	*41*	

Hit .320 unadjusted in Stockton last year, and supposedly has the tools to play several positions, but isn't polished at any of them. Given time, he could develop; most scouts like him better than the numbers indicate, but when it's scouts vs. numbers, I almost always bet on the numbers.

TIM UNROE **1B/3B** **1971** **Age 26**

Year	Team	Lge	AB	H	DB	TP	HR	BB	SB	CS	OUT	BA	OBA	SA	EQA	EQR	Peak
1993	Stockton	Calif	388	87	12	2	11	23	5	4	305	.224	.268	.351	.203	28	.224
1994	El Paso	Texas	481	140	23	2	17	39	9	3	344	.291	.344	.453	.267	63	.290
1995	New Orleans	AmA	375	96	18	2	6	22	4	0	279	.256	.297	.363	.223	33	.240
1996	New Orleans	AmA	413	112	20	3	23	39	8	3	304	.271	.334	.501	.273	59	.288
1997	*Milwaukee*	*AL*	*502*	*141*	*27*	*2*	*18*	*42*	*11*	*5*	*366*	*.281*	*.336*	*.450*	*.262*	*65*	

Milwaukee's somewhat soggy version of Jason Giambi; a good hitter for a third baseman, but can't play enough defense to hold the position, at least in the eyes of the coaching staff. No star potential, but might be able to stick if he can find a team where there's a big hole at third base. Leo Gomez at age 26 without quite as much power and probably slightly better defense. The Brewers are big on acquiring guys like this, and they develop them at a pretty good clip too.

JOSE VALENTIN **SS** **1970** **Age 27**

Year	Team	Lge	AB	H	DB	TP	HR	BB	SB	CS	OUT	BA	OBA	SA	EQA	EQR	Peak
1993	New Orleans	AmA	398	99	19	3	10	49	10	7	306	.249	.331	.387	.240	43	.261
1993	Milwaukee	AL	54	14	1	3	1	7	1	0	40	.259	.344	.444	.265	7	.288
1994	Milwaukee	AL	285	67	14	1	12	37	11	3	221	.235	.323	.418	.249	34	.266
1995	Milwaukee	AL	337	72	21	3	12	37	15	7	272	.214	.291	.401	.230	35	.243
1996	Milwaukee	AL	551	142	31	7	24	66	17	4	413	.258	.337	.470	.268	77	.278
1997	*Milwaukee*	*AL*	*607*	*152*	*43*	*4*	*20*	*79*	*18*	*5*	*460*	*.250*	*.337*	*.433*	*.258*	*78*	

A very fine ballplayer, and probably the second best shortstop in the American League in 1997. He doesn't hit for average, but does everything else pretty well and has some genuine power. Like most switch-hitters, not particularly good from one side; he probably should sit against lefties now and then. His defense is probably the best in the American League, febrile rantings of Omar Vizquel boosters notwithstanding. Of course, that's strictly a subjective view on my part. If you want to know more about defense, see Sherri Nichols' excellent work on defensive average.

FERNANDO VINA **2B** **1969** **Age 28**

Year	Team	Lge	AB	H	DB	TP	HR	BB	SB	CS	OUT	BA	OBA	SA	EQA	EQR	Peak
1993	Norfolk	Inter	291	66	6	3	4	10	13	7	232	.227	.252	.309	.188	18	.201
1993	Seattle	AL	45	11	2	0	0	5	6	0	34	.244	.320	.289	.237	5	.249
1994	NY Mets	NL	125	31	6	0	0	14	3	1	95	.248	.324	.296	.213	10	.225
1995	Milwaukee	AL	287	73	9	6	3	22	6	3	217	.254	.307	.359	.225	26	.234
1996	Milwaukee	AL	553	156	18	10	7	38	16	7	404	.282	.328	.389	.244	59	.249
1997	*Milwaukee*	*AL*	*470*	*115*	*15*	*11*	*4*	*31*	*15*	*8*	*363*	*.245*	*.291*	*.349*	*.216*	*39*	

Getting clubbed by Albert Belle might be the best thing that ever happened to him: managers will remember his name when filling that all-important "guy that can't hit" spot on the roster. Pretty much the incarnation of the Phil Garner Brewers: scrappy, harboring a borderline Napoleonic Complex, but basically ineffectual.

TURNER WARD   **OF**   **1965**   **Age 32**

Year	Team	Lge	AB	H	DB	TP	HR	BB	SB	CS	OUT	BA	OBA	SA	EQA	EQR	Peak
1993	Toronto	AL	168	33	3	2	5	24	3	2	137	.196	.297	.327	.207	13	.210
1994	Milwaukee	AL	366	83	15	2	9	52	5	2	285	.227	.323	.352	.228	35	.226
1995	Milwaukee	AL	129	34	3	1	4	14	6	1	96	.264	.336	.395	.252	15	.245
1996	Milwaukee	AL	67	12	2	1	2	13	3	0	55	.179	.312	.328	.223	6	.213

Brewers more likely to help the club in 1997 include Gorman Thomas, Don Money, Moose Haas and Augie Busch.

GERALD WILLIAMS   **OF**   **1967**   **Age 30**

Year	Team	Lge	AB	H	DB	TP	HR	BB	SB	CS	OUT	BA	OBA	SA	EQA	EQR	Peak
1993	Columbus-OH	Inter	343	95	17	3	9	22	22	8	256	.277	.321	.423	.253	41	.263
1993	NY Yankees	AL	67	11	3	3	0	2	2	0	56	.164	.188	.299	.153	3	.155
1994	NY Yankees	AL	87	26	7	0	5	4	1	3	64	.299	.330	.552	.274	13	.282
1995	NY Yankees	AL	183	46	18	2	7	23	4	2	139	.251	.335	.486	.268	26	.270
1996	Milwaukee	AL	92	19	4	0	0	4	3	1	74	.207	.240	.250	.156	4	.154
1996	NY Yankees	AL	233	63	15	4	5	15	7	8	178	.270	.315	.433	.243	26	.241
1997	*Milwaukee*	*AL*	*244*	*65*	*15*	*2*	*5*	*19*	*11*	*6*	*185*	*.266*	*.319*	*.406*	*.244*	*27*	

Spare part who can play a few roles decently: pinch runner, pinch hitter, defensive sub…. He'll be fighting for a job the rest of his career. Of course, if Dave Gallagher can find work, Gerald's not much different, so he should be able to find something.

ANTONE WILLIAMSON   **1B/DH**   **1974**   **Age 23**

Year	Team	Lge	AB	H	DB	TP	HR	BB	SB	CS	OUT	BA	OBA	SA	EQA	EQR	Peak
1994	Stockton	Calif	87	18	1	0	3	6	0	1	70	.207	.258	.322	.184	5	.210
1994	El Paso	Texas	49	11	0	0	2	6	0	0	38	.224	.309	.347	.219	4	.249
1995	El Paso	Texas	390	107	22	2	8	42	2	1	284	.274	.345	.403	.252	45	.282
1996	New Orleans	AmA	203	52	9	1	4	21	1	0	151	.256	.326	.369	.235	20	.258
1997	*Milwaukee*	*AL*	*576*	*163*	*36*	*4*	*13*	*49*	*4*	*0*	*413*	*.283*	*.339*	*.427*	*.258*	*70*	

Willliamson is a tools player, hyped by many, and has fought some serious battles for playing time. His numbers aren't really anything to get excited about, but his supporters point to David Justice as a parallel; his playing time in the minors was diminished for several reasons, and they insist Antone will develop similarly. I doubt it, but it is the responsible opposing viewpoint.

WAGNER ARIAS   **RBP**   **1975**   **Age 22**

YR	TEAM	Lge	IP	H	ER	HR	BB	K	ERA	W	L	H/9	HR/9	BB/9	K/9	KW
1994	Beloit	Midw	145.7	163	75	22	90	84	4.63	7	9	10.07	1.36	5.56	5.19	.34
1996	Beloit	Midw	61.3	64	25	3	32	36	3.67	4	3	9.39	.44	4.70	5.28	.59

Pitched fairly well in Beloit, but not well enough to hang a star on him. Likely to lose a little of that control he found in 1996. If he doesn't, he'll be in the majors in 1998.

RYAN BOWEN   **RBP**   **1968**   **Age 29**

YR	TEAM	Lge	IP	H	ER	HR	BB	K	ERA	W	L	H/9	HR/9	BB/9	K/9	KW
1993	Florida	NL	153.3	160	75	12	105	95	4.40	8	9	9.39	.70	6.16	5.58	.32
1994	Edmonton	PCL	17.7	20	10	3	13	11	5.09	1	1	10.19	1.53	6.62	5.60	.21
1994	Florida	NL	47.3	46	22	8	23	30	4.18	2	3	8.75	1.52	4.37	5.70	.81
1995	Florida	NL	17.0	23	10	3	14	14	5.29	1	1	12.18	1.59	7.41	7.41	.62
1996	New Orleans	AmA	26.3	28	17	4	24	19	5.81	1	2	9.57	1.37	8.20	6.49	.11

Sometimes, that second column tells you all you need to know. Bowen's arm has been tired for some time, and it's unlikely that this year will be the year he gets healthy and learns to pitch.

MARSHALL BOZE   **RBP**   **1971**   **Age 26**

YR	TEAM	Lge	IP	H	ER	HR	BB	K	ERA	W	L	H/9	HR/9	BB/9	K/9	KW
1993	Stockton	Calif	77.3	97	35	5	46	38	4.07	4	5	11.29	.58	5.35	4.42	.14
1993	El Paso	Texas	78.0	85	34	5	46	34	3.92	5	4	9.81	.58	5.31	3.92	-.02
1994	New Orleans	AmA	164.3	189	92	19	91	73	5.04	7	11	10.35	1.04	4.98	4.00	.09
1995	New Orleans	AmA	107.0	140	62	10	60	42	5.21	4	8	11.78	.84	5.05	3.53	-.08
1996	New Orleans	AmA	37.0	38	20	5	36	27	4.86	2	2	9.24	1.22	8.76	6.57	.00
1996	Milwaukee	AL	32.7	43	22	4	25	18	6.06	1	3	11.85	1.10	6.89	4.96	-.07

One of the gaggle of questionable fifth starters that seem to be more and more prevalent. Perhaps a little saltpeter in the water supply would help. Then again, jokes about the water supply in Milwaukee aren't going over too big these days. Well, chill out and have an Odwalla, guys.

BYRON BROWNE   **RSP**   **1971**   **Age 26**

YR	TEAM	Lge	IP	H	ER	HR	BB	K	ERA	W	L	H/9	HR/9	BB/9	K/9	KW
1993	Stockton	Calif	124.3	134	69	10	134	77	4.99	5	9	9.70	.72	9.70	5.57	-.57
1994	Stockton	Calif	55.7	56	29	5	38	44	4.69	3	3	9.05	.81	6.14	7.11	.84
1994	El Paso	Texas	26.3	29	10	3	17	24	3.42	2	1	9.91	1.03	5.81	8.20	1.28
1995	El Paso	Texas	114.7	107	47	8	94	93	3.69	7	6	8.40	.63	7.38	7.30	.59
1996	New Orleans	AmA	103.3	110	74	16	91	67	6.45	3	8	9.58	1.39	7.93	5.84	-.04

Striking out a guy an inning isn't particularly great if you're also walking one. More common than all the fine political ads we've been privy to. Watch Browne for fifteen minutes, and you'll instantly understand why he won't make the majors. Never the same delivery twice.

JEFF D'AMICO   **RSP**   **1976**   **Age 21**

YR	TEAM	Lge	IP	H	ER	HR	BB	K	ERA	W	L	H/9	HR/9	BB/9	K/9	KW
1995	Beloit	Midw	118.0	130	40	9	43	77	3.05	8	5	9.92	.69	3.28	5.87	1.14
1996	El Paso	Texas	88.7	93	36	10	23	62	3.65	5	5	9.44	1.02	2.33	6.29	1.51
1996	Milwaukee	AL	85.7	81	39	17	33	51	4.10	5	5	8.51	1.79	3.47	5.36	.92

Young flamethrower with great control and great stuff. He's 21 years old, and being handed over to the man who made Cal Eldred a Jello-armed retread. Cal Eldred may come back, if he can hang around the majors for a few years and his arm heals. I hope he and D'Amico have had many long talks. If you've got him in a perpetual league and he gets hot, see if you can trade him for comparable prospects that don't work as pitchers.

JASON DAWSEY   **LSP**   **1974**   **Age 23**

YR	TEAM	Lge	IP	H	ER	HR	BB	K	ERA	W	L	H/9	HR/9	BB/9	K/9	KW
1996	Beloit	Midw	90.3	88	20	6	55	74	1.99	8	2	8.77	.60	5.48	7.37	1.09

Pitched pretty well at Beloit; will spend the summer in glorious El Paso, Texas. While there, he'll enjoy temperatures of 140-150 degrees while being pelted by the musical stylings of Marty Robbins. In business, we call this "motivationally dissonant."

VALERIO DE LOS SANTOS   **LSP**   **1976**   **Age 21**

YR	TEAM	Lge	IP	H	ER	HR	BB	K	ERA	W	L	H/9	HR/9	BB/9	K/9	KW
1996	Beloit	Midw	142.7	204	88	15	76	85	5.55	5	11	12.87	.95	4.79	5.36	.59

Pitched 165 innings for Beloit last year, and probably another 50-100 in other leagues around the continent. He pitched well, but how long can he hold up? Supposedly has a great fastball and forkball, so his arm will probably implode in New Orleans in May of 1998.

CAL ELDRED   **RSP**   **1968**   **Age 29**

YR	TEAM	Lge	IP	H	ER	HR	BB	K	ERA	W	L	H/9	HR/9	BB/9	K/9	KW
1993	Milwaukee	AL	255.0	233	101	33	103	186	3.56	16	12	8.22	1.16	3.64	6.56	1.28
1994	Milwaukee	AL	177.7	146	68	20	89	95	3.44	11	9	7.40	1.01	4.51	4.81	.48
1995	Milwaukee	AL	24.0	21	7	4	11	18	2.62	2	1	7.88	1.50	4.12	6.75	1.22
1996	New Orleans	AmA	31.0	26	11	2	22	25	3.19	2	1	7.55	.58	6.39	7.26	.82
1996	Milwaukee	AL	84.3	76	30	7	39	48	3.20	5	4	8.11	.75	4.16	5.12	.67

Threw just over 5000 pitches in 1993 and faced nearly 1100 batters, despite complaining of a dead arm and shoulder pain in late August. In 1994 he led the majors in starts with 25, and didn't pitch nearly as well as he did the year before. In the two full years since, he's had 19 starts.

HORACIO ESTRADA   **LBP**   **1976**   **Age 21**

YR	TEAM	Lge	IP	H	ER	HR	BB	K	ERA	W	L	H/9	HR/9	BB/9	K/9	KW
1996	Beloit	Midw	26.0	27	8	3	14	21	2.77	2	1	9.35	1.04	4.85	7.27	1.21
1996	Stockton	Calif	45.7	50	26	7	25	39	5.12	2	3	9.85	1.38	4.93	7.69	1.33

Young reliever who the Brewers are high on. Has a 3-to-1 K/W ratio, hasn't been overworked and doesn't demonstrate his belief in Libertarian conflict resolution on the side of the highway in Venezuela. Another relatively recent Milwaukee pitcher showed two of those three virtues, but it's unlikely he'll be in the bigs anytime soon. Besides, if Julio Machado did show up on the outer shores of MLB, he'd have to go where he's needed most—to the bargaining table with Selig and Reinsdorf.

MIKE FETTERS   **RRP**   **1965**   **Age 32**

YR	TEAM	Lge	IP	H	ER	HR	BB	K	ERA	W	L	H/9	HR/9	BB/9	K/9	KW
1993	Milwaukee	AL	58.3	60	25	4	25	24	3.86	3	3	9.26	.62	3.86	3.70	.27
1994	Milwaukee	AL	45.3	39	11	0	28	30	2.18	4	1	7.74	.00	5.56	5.96	.60
1995	Milwaukee	AL	35.0	37	12	3	20	33	3.09	3	1	9.51	.77	5.14	8.49	1.54
1996	Milwaukee	AL	61.3	60	20	3	27	51	2.93	5	2	8.80	.44	3.96	7.48	1.50

Consistently effective and entertaining reliever who greatly resembles character actor Abraham Benrubi, best known as Jerry on ER. Fetters is effective against both righties and lefties; a valuable pitcher to have in any bullpen.

MICK FIELDBINDER   **RSP**   **1974**   **Age 23**

YR	TEAM	Lge	IP	H	ER	HR	BB	K	ERA	W	L	H/9	HR/9	BB/9	K/9	KW
1996	Beloit	Midw	66.7	96	36	3	23	41	4.86	3	4	12.96	.41	3.11	5.54	1.07

Pretty much diced up younger competition in the Midwest League, but will move up quickly if he's a real prospect. Peripheral numbers are promising; Fieldbinder could make it to the majors as a good steady reliever without excessive progress.

BRYCE FLORIE   **RRP**   **1970**   **Age 27**

YR	TEAM	Lge	IP	H	ER	HR	BB	K	ERA	W	L	H/9	HR/9	BB/9	K/9	KW
1993	Wichita	Texas	139.0	151	85	9	134	96	5.50	5	10	9.78	.58	8.68	6.22	-.10
1994	Las Vegas	PCL	68.0	64	32	3	54	56	4.24	4	4	8.47	.40	7.15	7.41	.68
1995	San Diego	NL	67.7	53	27	9	44	61	3.59	4	4	7.05	1.20	5.85	8.11	1.24
1996	Milwaukee	AL	19.0	18	12	3	13	12	5.68	1	1	8.53	1.42	6.16	5.68	.36
1996	San Diego	NL	48.3	49	21	1	31	45	3.91	3	2	9.12	.19	5.77	8.38	1.35

Part of Sal Bando's saving grace, the fleecing of San Diego. Not a great pitcher, but he has great stuff and his perceived value is higher than his performance should indicate. Not likely to be a great closer any time soon, but his stuff is good enough that he could turn into Bill Taylor late in his career.

RAMON GARCIA   **RBP**   **1970**   **Age 27**

YR	TEAM	Lge	IP	H	ER	HR	BB	K	ERA	W	L	H/9	HR/9	BB/9	K/9	KW
1996	New Orleans	AmA	36.3	35	9	2	16	26	2.23	3	1	8.67	.50	3.96	6.44	1.16
1996	Milwaukee	AL	75.7	77	43	14	23	39	5.11	3	5	9.16	1.67	2.74	4.64	.86

Look for Garcia to take a big step forward in 1997; his minor league performance indicates to me that he should pitch a lot better than he did in 1996. I wouldn't be surprised to see him break out and have a really big season or ten, even at his advanced age. Other authors disagree with me on this point, but I'm much more affable and bright than they are.

BRIAN GIVENS   **LSP**   **1966**   **Age 31**

YR	TEAM	Lge	IP	H	ER	HR	BB	K	ERA	W	L	H/9	HR/9	BB/9	K/9	KW
1993	Memphis	South	32.0	42	22	5	16	22	6.19	1	3	11.81	1.41	4.50	6.19	.94
1994	Birmingham	South	99.7	123	62	10	72	88	5.60	4	7	11.11	.90	6.50	7.95	1.02
1995	New Orleans	AmA	74.0	72	25	2	43	66	3.04	5	3	8.76	.24	5.23	8.03	1.37
1995	Milwaukee	AL	108.0	106	52	10	55	72	4.33	6	6	8.83	.83	4.58	6.00	.85
1996	New Orleans	AmA	131.0	133	55	10	76	97	3.78	8	7	9.14	.69	5.22	6.66	.92
1996	Milwaukee	AL	14.7	29	16	2	7	10	9.82	0	2	17.80	1.23	4.30	6.14	.97

What you see is what you get. He's not going to suddenly find his control and be the great pitcher someone thought he might become 12 or 15 years ago, but he's been pretty durable, reasonably consistent and can be used well in the right spots.

DOUG JONES　　**RRP**　　**1957**　**Age 40**

YR	TEAM	Lge	IP	H	ER	HR	BB	K	ERA	W	L	H/9	HR/9	BB/9	K/9	KW
1993	Houston	NL	83.3	107	44	7	31	64	4.75	4	5	11.56	.76	3.35	6.91	1.47
1994	Philadelphia	NL	52.7	57	12	2	10	35	2.05	5	1	9.74	.34	1.71	5.98	1.57
1995	Baltimore	AL	46.7	53	23	5	17	42	4.44	2	3	10.22	.96	3.28	8.10	1.88
1996	New Orleans	AmA	23.0	30	9	2	9	14	3.52	2	1	11.74	.78	3.52	5.48	.95
1996	Chicago Cubs	NL	32.0	41	17	4	10	23	4.78	2	2	11.53	1.12	2.81	6.47	1.45
1996	Milwaukee	AL	31.3	29	9	3	14	33	2.59	2	1	8.33	.86	4.02	9.48	2.15

Baseball's Yosemite Sam has probably finished up a career. It finished like it started—later than expected. His performance in 1996 was pretty good, but I think he's going to have a hard time finding a place to take the mound in 1997, what with Tony LaRussa being in the NL and all. This just in: The Cardinals have signed Matt Keough to a three-year deal.

SCOTT KARL　　**LSP**　　**1972**　**Age 25**

YR	TEAM	Lge	IP	H	ER	HR	BB	K	ERA	W	L	H/9	HR/9	BB/9	K/9	KW
1993	El Paso	Texas	163.0	188	64	10	61	67	3.53	10	8	10.38	.55	3.37	3.70	.39
1994	El Paso	Texas	49.7	51	20	3	20	37	3.62	3	3	9.24	.54	3.62	6.70	1.33
1994	New Orleans	AmA	85.0	96	34	11	42	48	3.60	5	4	10.16	1.16	4.45	5.08	.58
1995	New Orleans	AmA	44.3	49	17	4	18	26	3.45	3	2	9.95	.81	3.65	5.28	.85
1995	Milwaukee	AL	124.3	129	47	9	52	58	3.40	8	6	9.34	.65	3.76	4.20	.46
1996	Milwaukee	AL	208.3	200	88	24	76	117	3.80	12	11	8.64	1.04	3.28	5.05	.86

Pretty decent control pitcher; there's no difference between Scott Karl and Bob Tewksbury circa 1989, except Karl's got better stuff. Smart pitcher; might even be smart enough to ignore Phil Garner.

SEAN MALONEY　　**RRP**　　**1971**　**Age 26**

YR	TEAM	Lge	IP	H	ER	HR	BB	K	ERA	W	L	H/9	HR/9	BB/9	K/9	KW
1994	Beloit	Midw	52.0	85	41	4	16	33	7.10	1	5	14.71	.69	2.77	5.71	1.21
1995	El Paso	Texas	59.7	68	36	5	35	46	5.43	2	5	10.26	.75	5.28	6.94	.99
1996	El Paso	Texas	52.3	52	9	1	18	47	1.55	5	1	8.94	.17	3.10	8.08	1.92

More Irish sounding than Ramon Garcia. Good stuff, and really took a step forward at El Paso. If he holds this pattern steady, he'll have a good but brief major league career starting in about two years. Might be the closer at El Paso this year.

BEN McDONALD　　**RSP**　　**1968**　**Age 29**

YR	TEAM	Lge	IP	H	ER	HR	BB	K	ERA	W	L	H/9	HR/9	BB/9	K/9	KW
1993	Baltimore	AL	216.0	185	72	17	96	176	3.00	15	9	7.71	.71	4.00	7.33	1.44
1994	Baltimore	AL	156.0	142	53	12	58	91	3.06	11	6	8.19	.69	3.35	5.25	.91
1995	Baltimore	AL	79.7	65	30	9	40	62	3.39	5	4	7.34	1.02	4.52	7.00	1.20
1996	Milwaukee	AL	221.3	210	73	21	72	141	2.97	16	9	8.54	.85	2.93	5.73	1.18

The gamble worked out pretty well. I thought his arm was deader than Jerry Reinsdorf's honeymoon, but I was wrong. Pitched about as well as Andy Pettitte, a front-runner for the Cy Young. That contract's got a couple more years, and I still think he's hurt in some way, despite his fine year. Don't know if he's still eating mustard sardines before each start. I know I'm not.

JOSE MERCEDES　　**RSP**　　**1971**　**Age 26**

YR	TEAM	Lge	IP	H	ER	HR	BB	K	ERA	W	L	H/9	HR/9	BB/9	K/9	KW
1993	Bowie	East	133.3	199	91	15	85	58	6.14	4	11	13.43	1.01	5.74	3.92	-.13
1994	New Orleans	AmA	17.7	20	9	1	10	6	4.58	1	1	10.19	.51	5.09	3.06	-.25
1994	Milwaukee	AL	30.3	21	6	4	17	11	1.78	3	0	6.23	1.19	5.04	3.26	-.17
1996	New Orleans	AmA	97.3	114	54	13	41	39	4.99	4	7	10.54	1.20	3.79	3.61	.25
1996	Milwaukee	AL	17.0	17	13	6	6	6	6.88	1	1	9.00	3.18	3.18	3.18	.26

In English, his name translates as "No Prospect." Surely we can't just dismiss that as coincidence.

ANGEL MIRANDA   **LBP**   **1970**   **Age 27**

YR	TEAM	Lge	IP	H	ER	HR	BB	K	ERA	W	L	H/9	HR/9	BB/9	K/9	KW
1993	New Orleans	AmA	17.7	12	7	3	12	22	3.57	1	1	6.11	1.53	6.11	11.21	2.21
1993	Milwaukee	AL	118.0	102	44	13	57	91	3.36	8	5	7.78	.99	4.35	6.94	1.23
1994	New Orleans	AmA	12.7	11	4	0	9	8	2.84	1	0	7.82	.00	6.39	5.68	.30
1994	Milwaukee	AL	45.3	37	20	7	28	23	3.97	3	2	7.35	1.39	5.56	4.57	.13
1995	Milwaukee	AL	74.7	75	34	7	50	44	4.10	4	4	9.04	.84	6.03	5.30	.26
1996	Milwaukee	AL	109.7	106	50	10	71	75	4.10	6	6	8.70	.82	5.83	6.16	.59

A consistently good, consistently injured pitcher. I'm going to go out on a limb and suggest that if he's healthy, he'll be good. I bet you're feeling pretty good about plunking down $19.95 right about now, huh? He completely fools batters with his motion; even without strikeouts, Miranda could be effective for a long time if he can somehow stay healthy.

AL REYES   **RRP**   **1971**   **Age 26**

YR	TEAM	Lge	IP	H	ER	HR	BB	K	ERA	W	L	H/9	HR/9	BB/9	K/9	KW
1993	Burlington	Midw	65.7	66	33	8	35	47	4.52	3	4	9.05	1.10	4.80	6.44	.95
1994	Harrisburg	East	64.0	77	25	5	19	44	3.52	4	3	10.83	.70	2.67	6.19	1.39
1995	Milwaukee	AL	32.7	19	6	3	18	29	1.65	3	1	5.23	.83	4.96	7.99	1.42
1996	Beloit	Midw	17.3	21	7	2	8	14	3.63	1	1	10.90	1.04	4.15	7.27	1.38

Reyes can absolutely pitch. The only question is his health. But don't worry—Phil Garner will be watching over him. [Shudder.]

SID ROBERSON   **LSP**   **1972**   **Age 25**

YR	TEAM	Lge	IP	H	ER	HR	BB	K	ERA	W	L	H/9	HR/9	BB/9	K/9	KW
1993	Stockton	Calif	148.3	189	64	10	32	61	3.88	8	8	11.47	.61	1.94	3.70	.75
1994	El Paso	Texas	164.3	211	67	9	67	86	3.67	10	8	11.56	.49	3.67	4.71	.65
1995	New Orleans	AmA	13.0	20	10	1	12	7	6.92	0	1	13.85	.69	8.31	4.85	-.46
1995	Milwaukee	AL	85.3	92	41	14	38	39	4.32	4	5	9.70	1.48	4.01	4.11	.37
1996	New Orleans	AmA	10.7	11	6	2	11	3	5.06	0	1	9.28	1.69	9.28	2.53	-1.48

Smallish lefty; doesn't impress scouts, and probably isn't the next John Tudor, but he's pitched well enough to at least warrant a look in spring training, health permitting.

TRAVIS SMITH   **RSP**   **1973**   **Age 24**

YR	TEAM	Lge	IP	H	ER	HR	BB	K	ERA	W	L	H/9	HR/9	BB/9	K/9	KW
1996	Stockton	Calif	52.3	65	16	4	25	30	2.75	4	2	11.18	.69	4.30	5.16	.64
1996	El Paso	Texas	99.3	119	48	6	53	55	4.35	5	6	10.78	.54	4.80	4.98	.46

Pitched huge in Stockton in 1995; fumbled a bit as he moved up, but I expect he'll pull it together pretty well next year, probably at some combination of El Paso and New Orleans. I like Smith a lot; that K rate will likely come up some, even though he is moving up a level.

STEVE SPARKS   **RSP**   **1966**   **Age 31**

YR	TEAM	Lge	IP	H	ER	HR	BB	K	ERA	W	L	H/9	HR/9	BB/9	K/9	KW
1993	New Orleans	AmA	171.7	186	83	17	100	96	4.35	9	10	9.75	.89	5.24	5.03	.37
1994	New Orleans	AmA	176.0	191	91	24	85	94	4.65	8	12	9.77	1.23	4.35	4.81	.52
1995	Milwaukee	AL	203.3	189	77	15	89	95	3.41	13	10	8.37	.66	3.94	4.20	.42
1996	New Orleans	AmA	55.7	67	40	7	45	23	6.47	2	4	10.83	1.13	7.28	3.72	-.58
1996	Milwaukee	AL	89.7	92	49	16	54	20	4.92	4	6	9.23	1.61	5.42	2.01	-.69

A knuckleballer. What else do you really need to know?

BRIAN TOLLBERG   **RSP**   **1973**   **Age 24**

YR	TEAM	Lge	IP	H	ER	HR	BB	K	ERA	W	L	H/9	HR/9	BB/9	K/9	KW
1995	Beloit	Midw	115.0	157	65	13	38	72	5.09	5	8	12.29	1.02	2.97	5.63	1.13
1996	El Paso	Texas	143.0	187	78	15	39	89	4.91	6	10	11.77	.94	2.45	5.60	1.25

Anybody that walks 23 guys and strikes out 109 gets serious development attention in my organization. Tollberg moved up levels with grace, showing little sign of overuse or fatigue. Not a grade A prospect, but definitely a grade B worth watching. Could be in Cheesetown by July if he gets hot.

TIM VANEGMOND RBP   1969   Age 28

YR	TEAM	Lge	IP	H	ER	HR	BB	K	ERA	W	L	H/9	HR/9	BB/9	K/9	KW
1993	New Britain	East	173.0	221	107	22	62	125	5.57	6	13	11.50	1.14	3.23	6.50	1.36
1994	Pawtucket	Inter	113.0	115	51	9	54	72	4.06	6	7	9.16	.72	4.30	5.73	.84
1994	Boston	AL	38.0	36	20	6	22	21	4.74	2	2	8.53	1.42	5.21	4.97	.36
1995	Pawtucket	Inter	62.3	70	30	10	30	40	4.33	3	4	10.11	1.44	4.33	5.78	.84
1996	New Orleans	AmA	45.0	33	6	2	16	26	1.20	5	0	6.60	.40	3.20	5.20	.93
1996	Pawtucket	Inter	59.7	65	30	8	31	38	4.53	3	4	9.80	1.21	4.68	5.73	.74
1996	Milwaukee	AL	54.7	53	25	5	24	32	4.12	3	3	8.73	.82	3.95	5.27	.77

Consistent journeyman; probably could be making a lot of money if someone were to give him a shot in a rotation for 10-15 starts. Probably the most consistent pitcher in baseball over the last three years. Not great, but consistent, and generally pretty healthy.

RON VILLONE LRP   1970   Age 27

YR	TEAM	Lge	IP	H	ER	HR	BB	K	ERA	W	L	H/9	HR/9	BB/9	K/9	KW
1993	Riverside	Calif	72.3	85	44	6	70	57	5.47	3	5	10.58	.75	8.71	7.09	.19
1993	Jacksonville	South	58.3	55	33	7	52	49	5.09	2	4	8.49	1.08	8.02	7.56	.51
1994	Jacksonville	South	72.7	65	37	8	85	74	4.58	3	5	8.05	.99	10.53	9.17	.42
1995	Tacoma	PCL	27.7	11	4	3	23	42	1.30	3	0	3.58	.98	7.48	13.66	2.68
1995	San Diego	NL	25.7	25	11	6	13	33	3.86	2	1	8.77	2.10	4.56	11.57	2.72
1995	Seattle	AL	20.0	18	15	6	24	26	6.75	1	1	8.10	2.70	10.80	11.70	1.20
1996	Las Vegas	PCL	20.3	14	3	0	11	23	1.33	2	0	6.20	.00	4.87	10.18	2.18
1996	Milwaukee	AL	24.3	13	6	4	19	18	2.22	2	1	4.81	1.48	7.03	6.66	.46
1996	San Diego	NL	18.0	18	5	2	9	17	2.50	1	1	9.00	1.00	4.50	8.50	1.71

Hard throwing lefties, no matter what they do, will be coveted. Villone can pitch, but should never be allowed to pitch to right-handers who crush high fastballs. This isn't a large number of players, but Rickey Henderson should definitely not be pitched to by this man. Control used to be nonexistent; now it comes and goes. He has been effective, and will continue to be so as long as he's healthy. Mitch Williams with good mechanics and a greater desire to learn.

KEVIN WICKANDER LRP   1965   Age 32

YR	TEAM	Lge	IP	H	ER	HR	BB	K	ERA	W	L	H/9	HR/9	BB/9	K/9	KW
1993	Cincinnati	NL	25.3	33	18	5	22	20	6.39	1	2	11.72	1.78	7.82	7.11	.41
1995	Toledo	Inter	12.0	13	3	1	6	7	2.25	1	0	9.75	.75	4.50	5.25	.62
1995	Detroit	AL	17.3	17	4	1	9	9	2.08	2	0	8.83	.52	4.67	4.67	.39
1996	Milwaukee	AL	25.3	24	11	2	17	18	3.91	2	1	8.53	.71	6.04	6.39	.62

Bounced back big, but will have to fight for a job every year for the rest of his career. Will likely tire of it in about three to four years.

BOB WICKMAN RRP   1969   Age 28

YR	TEAM	Lge	IP	H	ER	HR	BB	K	ERA	W	L	H/9	HR/9	BB/9	K/9	KW
1993	NY Yankees	AL	140.0	159	73	14	77	73	4.69	7	9	10.22	.90	4.95	4.69	.33
1994	NY Yankees	AL	68.3	57	20	3	29	55	2.63	6	2	7.51	.40	3.82	7.24	1.46
1995	NY Yankees	AL	79.7	74	28	6	35	51	3.16	6	3	8.36	.68	3.95	5.76	.93
1996	Milwaukee	AL	16.7	11	6	3	10	13	3.24	1	1	5.94	1.62	5.40	7.02	.99
1996	NY Yankees	AL	79.3	87	30	6	36	59	3.40	5	4	9.87	.68	4.08	6.69	1.21

The Rodney Dangerfield of the Yankee organization. He has pitched well enough to do a very good job in the majors, and yet doesn't get much attention or respect. Wickman knows how to pitch and will continue to be effective. Many more batters will get the opportunity to scream out "$#@%#$@%!!!" as they ground into a DP and pound their bat in the turf.

STEVE WOODARD RSP   1975   Age 22

YR	TEAM	Lge	IP	H	ER	HR	BB	K	ERA	W	L	H/9	HR/9	BB/9	K/9	KW
1995	Beloit	Midw	99.7	145	73	15	44	61	6.59	3	8	13.09	1.35	3.97	5.51	.84
1996	Stockton	Calif	162.3	233	82	14	38	90	4.55	8	10	12.92	.78	2.11	4.99	1.14

Worked pretty hard, but a very good prospect. He'll anchor the El Paso rotation this year, and I expect him to tear the league a new Reinsdorf. Mechanics are grade A excellent. This gentleman can pitch.

Player	Age	Team	Lge	AB	H	DB	TP	HR	BB	SB	CS	OUT	BA	OBA	SA	EQA	EQR	Peak
ALEX ANDREOPOULOS	23	Stockton	Calif	296	80	12	0	5	30	5	2	218	.270	.337	.361	.238	30	.259
JUNIOR BETANCES	23	Stockton	Calif	465	102	7	4	1	38	7	5	368	.219	.278	.258	.174	23	.189
EDGAR CACERES	32	New Orleans	AmA	403	104	9	2	3	28	7	4	303	.258	.306	.313	.209	30	.199
CARLOS CAMPUSANO	20	Beloit	Midw	343	75	12	1	2	6	2	1	269	.219	.232	.277	.158	13	.180
ROBINSON CANCEL	20	Beloit	Midw	224	44	1	1	1	10	6	2	182	.196	.231	.223	.135	6	.154
JOE DEBERRY	26	Stockton	Calif	193	47	4	1	6	17	1	0	146	.244	.305	.368	.226	18	.234
BILL DOBROLSKY	26	El Paso	Texas	201	48	7	0	2	16	1	2	155	.239	.295	.303	.197	13	.204
TODD DUNN	25	El Paso	Texas	359	109	14	2	16	40	9	2	252	.304	.373	.487	.287	56	.303
DAVID ELLIOTT	22	Beloit	Midw	384	95	6	1	11	48	9	5	294	.247	.331	.354	.232	38	.256
KEN FELDER	25	New Orleans	AmA	435	92	15	1	15	32	2	3	346	.211	.266	.354	.201	31	.213
LAURO FELIX	26	El Paso	Texas	305	71	10	1	8	66	7	3	237	.233	.369	.351	.247	36	.257
JONAS HAMLIN	26	El Paso	Texas	512	128	21	4	17	36	7	4	388	.250	.299	.406	.234	52	.243
MIKE HARRIS	26	El Paso	Texas	260	70	10	3	6	26	3	1	191	.269	.336	.400	.248	29	.258
	26	New Orleans	AmA	151	27	1	1	2	8	1	1	125	.179	.220	.238	.127	4	.130
BOBBY HUGHES	25	El Paso	Texas	237	65	9	1	12	27	2	2	174	.274	.348	.473	.269	33	.282
	25	New Orleans	AmA	125	24	2	0	4	6	1	1	102	.192	.229	.304	.166	6	.176
DAVID HULSE	28	Milwaukee	AL	117	26	2	0	0	8	4	1	92	.222	.272	.239	.170	5	.173
ANTHONY IAPOCE	22	Beloit	Midw	283	74	4	2	1	34	11	6	215	.261	.341	.300	.222	25	.244
MIKE KINKADE	23	Beloit	Midw	514	144	17	1	15	34	12	6	376	.280	.325	.405	.246	56	.267
DANNY KLASSEN	20	Stockton	Calif	437	103	16	2	2	24	7	4	338	.236	.275	.295	.189	26	.214
TOBY KOMINEK	23	Stockton	Calif	364	96	13	3	6	37	5	3	271	.264	.332	.365	.236	37	.256
KEVIN KOSLOFSKI	29	New Orleans	AmA	244	55	7	2	4	32	4	2	191	.225	.315	.320	.214	20	.213
SCOTT KRAUSE	22	El Paso	Texas	84	24	2	1	3	2	1	0	60	.286	.302	.440	.249	9	.275
	22	Stockton	Calif	431	119	13	2	15	22	13	4	316	.276	.311	.420	.247	48	.272
TODD LANDRY	23	New Orleans	AmA	398	92	17	1	5	35	12	3	309	.231	.293	.317	.208	30	.226
MICKEY LOPEZ	22	Beloit	Midw	245	59	6	1	1	22	6	4	190	.241	.303	.286	.198	17	.218
	22	Stockton	Calif	220	54	6	1	0	17	3	2	168	.245	.300	.282	.194	14	.215
ROBERTO LOPEZ	24	New Orleans	AmA	450	101	17	2	7	64	7	4	353	.224	.321	.318	.216	38	.231
JAMIE LOPICCOLO	23	Beloit	Midw	317	75	13	1	4	29	2	3	245	.237	.301	.322	.206	24	.224
GABBY MARTINEZ	22	El Paso	Texas	336	70	8	4	1	18	6	4	270	.208	.249	.265	.162	14	.179
GREG MARTINEZ	24	El Paso	Texas	165	44	2	1	1	12	8	2	123	.267	.316	.309	.220	14	.237
	24	Stockton	Calif	290	74	3	1	0	21	14	5	221	.255	.305	.272	.201	20	.216
BILL MCGONIGLE	24	Stockton	Calif	229	53	5	0	2	13	1	2	178	.231	.273	.279	.177	12	.190
AL MEALING	22	Beloit	Midw	282	66	8	2	6	14	7	6	222	.234	.270	.340	.201	20	.222
DARRELL NICHOLAS	24	El Paso	Texas	237	54	8	2	2	25	5	4	187	.228	.302	.304	.202	17	.217
KEVIN NORIEGA	22	Beloit	Midw	428	102	15	1	4	29	3	2	328	.238	.287	.306	.197	28	.217
HECTOR ORTEGA	23	El Paso	Texas	350	72	8	2	6	25	7	3	281	.206	.259	.291	.180	19	.195
DANNY PEREZ	25	El Paso	Texas	153	48	13	3	2	12	3	1	106	.314	.364	.477	.281	22	.297
	25	New Orleans	AmA	203	36	3	0	2	33	4	1	168	.177	.292	.222	.168	10	.176
RYAN RITTER	22	Beloit	Midw	357	79	8	2	7	17	10	3	281	.221	.257	.314	.190	22	.211
CECIL RODRIQUES	24	El Paso	Texas	387	93	16	2	5	31	4	4	298	.240	.297	.331	.208	30	.223
BRAD SEITZER	26	El Paso	Texas	432	121	15	0	15	47	4	2	313	.280	.351	.419	.259	53	.269
RICK SMITH	24	Beloit	Midw	385	85	13	0	8	30	2	2	302	.221	.277	.317	.195	25	.209
JERMAINE SWINTON	23	Stockton	Calif	166	43	3	0	8	9	0	0	123	.259	.297	.422	.238	17	.259
WES WEGER	25	New Orleans	AmA	213	43	5	0	5	20	0	0	170	.202	.270	.296	.183	12	.192
DREW WILLIAMS	24	Stockton	Calif	440	122	16	2	18	50	4	4	322	.277	.351	.445	.264	57	.282

Player	Age	Team	Lge	IP	H	ER	HR	BB	K	ERA	W	L	H/9	HR/9	BB/9	K/9	KW
KURT ARCHER	27	New Orleans	AmA	30.3	40	18	5	14	13	5.34	1	2	11.87	1.48	4.15	3.86	.25
GREG BECK	23	Stockton	Calif	135.7	217	105	17	62	61	6.97	4	11	14.40	1.13	4.11	4.05	.32
PETER BENNY	20	Beloit	Midw	135.0	169	84	14	111	94	5.60	5	10	11.27	.93	7.40	6.27	.24
JOSHUA BISHOP	21	Beloit	Midw	146.7	218	88	18	80	69	5.40	6	10	13.38	1.10	4.91	4.23	.18
TERRY BURROWS	27	New Orleans	AmA	27.0	22	8	1	11	14	2.67	2	1	7.33	.33	3.67	4.67	.64
NELSON CANA	20	Beloit	Midw	30.3	41	16	3	27	24	4.75	1	2	12.16	.89	8.01	7.12	.37
	20	Stockton	Calif	46.3	52	27	4	43	23	5.24	2	3	10.10	.78	8.35	4.47	-.60
RON CARIDAD	24	Stockton	Calif	27.0	32	8	2	16	12	2.67	2	1	10.67	.67	5.33	4.00	.00
CRIS CARPENTER	31	New Orleans	AmA	47.7	50	15	4	12	34	2.83	3	2	9.44	.76	2.27	6.42	1.57
BROOKS DRYSDALE	25	Stockton	Calif	54.0	67	31	10	33	39	5.17	2	4	11.17	1.67	5.50	6.50	.79
MIKE FARRELL	27	New Orleans	AmA	61.3	77	29	6	21	32	4.26	3	4	11.30	.88	3.08	4.70	.79
JOE GANOTE	28	New Orleans	AmA	105.0	128	72	15	60	54	6.17	4	8	10.97	1.29	5.14	4.63	.26
SCOTT GARDNER	24	Stockton	Calif	130.3	145	66	11	61	94	4.56	6	8	10.01	.76	4.21	6.49	1.11
ADAM HOUSLEY	24	Beloit	Midw	59.7	90	34	7	37	31	5.13	3	4	13.58	1.06	5.58	4.68	.16
SCOTT HUNTSMAN	23	Stockton	Calif	43.3	42	18	3	32	35	3.74	3	2	8.72	.62	6.65	7.27	.76
KEVIN KLOEK	25	El Paso	Texas	49.7	58	25	7	25	37	4.53	3	3	10.51	1.27	4.53	6.70	1.10
JEFF KRAMER	22	El Paso	Texas	55.7	73	48	5	38	29	7.76	1	5	11.80	.81	6.14	4.69	.03
	22	Stockton	Calif	52.7	68	38	4	37	29	6.49	2	4	11.62	.68	6.32	4.96	.07
MIKE MISURACA	27	New Orleans	AmA	78.0	97	39	10	43	47	4.50	4	5	11.19	1.15	4.96	5.42	.57
NORM MONTOYA	25	El Paso	Texas	116.0	154	64	6	42	59	4.97	5	8	11.95	.47	3.26	4.58	.71
M. PASQUALICCHIO	21	Stockton	Calif	63.3	77	32	3	42	44	4.55	3	4	10.94	.43	5.97	6.25	.59
ANDY PAUL	24	El Paso	Texas	87.7	105	51	4	56	59	5.24	4	6	10.78	.41	5.75	6.06	.58
TONY PAVLOVICH	21	Beloit	Midw	29.7	32	12	2	20	19	3.64	2	1	9.71	.61	6.07	5.76	.40
TONY PHILLIPS	27	New Orleans	AmA	50.0	55	24	6	13	26	4.32	3	3	9.90	1.08	2.34	4.68	.97
MIKE POTTS	25	Milwaukee	AL	45.7	52	29	6	31	20	5.72	2	3	10.25	1.18	6.11	3.94	-.21
LUIS SALAZAR	21	Stockton	Calif	50.7	55	21	9	19	22	3.73	3	3	9.77	1.60	3.38	3.91	.46
HENRY SANTOS	23	El Paso	Texas	92.3	122	64	10	64	59	6.24	3	7	11.89	.97	6.24	5.75	.36
JOE SLUSARSKI	29	New Orleans	AmA	57.7	74	36	3	33	30	5.62	2	4	11.55	.47	5.15	4.68	.27
JOE WAGNER	24	Stockton	Calif	148.3	191	91	16	101	65	5.52	6	10	11.59	.97	6.13	3.94	-.22
STEVE WHITAKER	26	El Paso	Texas	133.3	155	78	8	108	69	5.27	5	10	10.46	.54	7.29	4.66	-.27

Minnesota Twins

Little was expected from the Twins in 1996. The team was coming off of a '95 season in which they finished with the worst record in baseball and been accused of dumping most of their major league talent. The collection of unknowns and lightly-regardeds, at least as far as card-carrying BBWAA types were concerned, that they'd gathered to go with a "veteran" core was supposed to give Twins fans a lousy season. Focusing on the team's problems in getting its spring training games broadcast back home, one columnist in the Minneapolis-St. Paul Star Tribune accused the team of being "bush league," leading to GM Terry Ryan's angry proclamation that "this isn't a second-rate baseball organization."

Those problems aside, the organization had other controversies. First, there were a lot of public complaints about pitching coach Dick Such. Such has been accused of being a poor teacher, with Scott Erickson being used as the classic example of his failure to develop a pitcher. That only works if you really think Erickson can be much better than he's been, a dubious proposition. Other examples were held up: Eddie Guardado, Pat Mahomes, LaTroy Hawkins. Whether the accusations were fair can't be proven one way or another. The cries for Such's head reached the point that apparently Ryan asked manager Tom Kelly to fire Such. Kelly left Such in place, remaining loyal to his pitching coach and indifferent to radio call-in idiots and media kvetching. Naturally, this was treated as a bad sign by those interested parties.

The bigger problem by far was the devastating news that Kirby Puckett's vision problems were going to keep him off the field. The notion that baseball could even be played in Minnesota without Kirby bordered on sacrilege, but more critically was Kirby's effect on the bottom line: would people still want to come to the Hubert H. Humphrey Metrodome without Kirby, or would they notice that beanbagball is considered downright ugly in most of the rest of the country?

So most predictions buried the Twins in last place, behind scrappy Brewers and Royals squads that had media-anointed geniuses running their teams. When looking over the Twins' future, speculation centered on where they'd be sending Chuck Knoblauch, and for what. But as we pointed out last year, the Twins had already hit bottom during the first half of the '95 season, and had done nothing but improve after trading Scott Erickson, Kevin Tapani and Mark Guthrie, and renting out Rick Aguilera to Boston. The team went 36-44 to finish the '95 season; not greatness, but a good mark with several young players and an almost entirely new pitching staff.

Knowing that, the '96 season was hardly a surprise if you actually follow the Twins instead of just the big names. What was particularly gratifying about their success is that it was season-long. They were a .477 team before the All-Star break and a .487 team after it. They won on the road as well as they did at home. They were on the outskirts of the wild card race into mid-September, although they fortunately didn't let that dictate any ill-considered trades for stretch drive help. They were in third for most of the season, falling behind the Brewers only after both teams had been eliminated. They won by playing rookies like Matt Lawton, or sophomores like Rich Becker or Marty Cordova or Frankie Rodriguez or Brad Radke or Scott Stahoviak, and young veterans like Knoblauch. They had window dressing like Paul Molitor and Roberto Kelly so mediots would know who to credit, but the Twins' success was homegrown.

In August, the Twins' also-ran status was killed off with the signing of Knoblauch to a five-year, $30 million contract extension. Particularly satisfying were the young pitchers who broke through: Rodriguez in particular, but Brad Radke improved over his rookie year, and Rich Robertson and Scott Aldred came out of nowhere to give the Twins a rotation that was about league average. Not surprisingly, the cries for Dick Such' head seem to have subsided.

So where do the Twins go from here? The organization has a fine farm system that has been exceptionally productive of late. They have a fine manager in taciturn Tom Kelly, a GM who has picked some good talent in recent drafts and one of the best frameworks of young talent with major league experience in baseball today. They've already learned the major lesson that the Indians had to offer: sign your young talent to multi-year contracts to avoid arbitration and inspire confidence. The Twins signed Marty Cordova to a four-year deal after his rookie season; don't be surprised if Todd Walker gets a similar deal after the '97 season. The expectation should be that this year the Twins finish above .500. They'll be on the outskirts of the wild card race, but unlike many of the contenders for the honor, they won't be dead without it. With a major addition or two, the chances are very good that the Twins could surprise and pass either the White Sox or the Indians. Making a free agent splash or two is expected because the Twins' owner, Carl Pohlad, wants to rally support for a publicly-funded stadium, and as the results in Seattle from two years ago scream, nothing gets votes like wins.

Here's hoping the Twins keep shorting the beat writers their cocktail weenies and continue running a baseball organization. In a very short time, they'll be squashing the "small market teams can't compete" myth again.

The Twins' farm system is deep in pitching. Although most of the upper level pitchers aren't great prospects, many of them can pitch at the major league level. Further down, the top picks of the '95 draft, Mark Redman and Jason Bell, are quickly clawing their way up the chain. The other thing noticeable about the Twins farm system are some very rough, but potentially great, young players. Jose Valentin might be the best catching prospect in baseball. You should already know about Todd Walker, the Twins' third baseman right now. Torii Hunter is raw, but a great defensive outfielder who hit well for a 20-year-old in the Eastern League. The downside is that the Twins have an extreme lack of power among their minor league players.

As an organization, the Twins seem to always try to put winning teams on the field for their minor league affiliates. At AAA, part of that can be explained by Salt Lake owner Joe Buzas' drive to keep a new stadium filled in one of the best minor league markets in the country. This year was somewhat different in that the Buzz were stocked with fewer minor

league veterans than usual, but still managed to post the second-best record in the PCL. Like any PCL park, Salt Lake distorts offensive statistics hiding the fact that the Buzz probably won more with a fine pitching staff than they did with hitting prospects; beyond Todd Walker, no Buzz regular will be a Twins regular in the future. New Britain was the Twins' lone losing team, finishing 20 games under .500. Again, the story was pitching, except in this case it was the failure of several pitchers to develop in the pitcher-friendly Eastern League. Besides Hunter, the team had one outstanding offensive performer in Ryan Radmanovich, recovering from a knee injury that had shelved him for all of '95. At Fort Myers in the Florida State League, Twins' prospects led the circuit in strikeouts as the team finished with the second-best record in the league.

RICH BECKER   **OF**   **1972**   **Age 25**

Year	Team	Lge	AB	H	DB	TP	HR	BB	SB	CS	OUT	BA	OBA	SA	EQA	EQR	Peak
1993	Nashville	South	538	151	18	4	16	86	17	4	391	.281	.380	.418	.273	76	.305
1994	Salt Lake City	PCL	275	75	14	2	2	36	5	1	201	.273	.357	.360	.247	31	.272
1994	Minnesota	AL	99	27	3	0	1	13	5	1	73	.273	.357	.333	.245	11	.271
1995	Salt Lake City	PCL	123	36	4	0	6	24	5	1	88	.293	.408	.472	.297	21	.322
1995	Minnesota	AL	394	96	16	1	2	34	8	9	306	.244	.304	.305	.202	28	.220
1996	Minnesota	AL	522	149	30	4	12	67	19	5	378	.285	.367	.427	.270	72	.289
1997	*Minnesota*	*AL*	*519*	*150*	*33*	*5*	*13*	*82*	*13*	*5*	*374*	*.289*	*.386*	*.447*	*.281*	*78*	

After a career plagued with knee injuries, '96 was a "make or break" season for Becker. He made it, even with a slow start. Although you might credit the Twins with patience, remember that outfielders who could do anything were at a premium for the Twins after Puckett's eye problems surfaced. He has an excellent arm and is generally solid in center. His major shortcoming is that he'll probably never hit left-handed pitching. His attempts to hit them from either side of the plate have been pathetic. This will keep him from being a superstar, but then finding players who do what he does against right-handed pitching is fairly rare, and you'll always find Roberto Kelly types willing to work for spare change to pound lefties.

BRENT BREDE   **OF**   **1972**   **Age 25**

Year	Team	Lge	AB	H	DB	TP	HR	BB	SB	CS	OUT	BA	OBA	SA	EQA	EQR	Peak
1993	Ft. Myers	Flor	191	60	7	1	1	28	4	2	133	.314	.402	.377	.270	25	.302
1994	Ft. Myers	Flor	442	120	21	2	4	58	10	2	324	.271	.356	.355	.246	49	.271
1995	New Britain	East	469	128	23	2	4	62	9	4	345	.273	.358	.356	.245	51	.267
1996	Salt Lake City	PCL	481	153	28	4	12	80	11	4	332	.318	.415	.468	.298	80	.319
1997	*Minnesota*	*AL*	*597*	*175*	*29*	*5*	*15*	*76*	*15*	*8*	*430*	*.293*	*.373*	*.434*	*.272*	*83*	

A PCL slugger, Brede is probably entertaining delusions of grandeur while angling for the honorary Randy Bush roster spot that Tom Kelly always keeps open for a left-handed bat of overwhelming mediocrity.

RON COOMER   **1B/3B/OF**   **1967**   **Age 30**

Year	Team	Lge	AB	H	DB	TP	HR	BB	SB	CS	OUT	BA	OBA	SA	EQA	EQR	Peak
1993	Birmingham	South	273	90	10	0	14	15	1	1	184	.330	.365	.520	.291	42	.303
1993	Nashville	AmA	213	66	14	0	13	12	1	2	149	.310	.347	.559	.290	34	.302
1994	Albuquerque	PCL	518	153	22	2	19	27	3	2	367	.295	.330	.456	.261	64	.268
1995	Albuquerque	PCL	317	94	12	1	16	19	4	2	224	.297	.336	.492	.273	44	.274
1995	Minnesota	AL	102	27	4	1	5	9	0	1	76	.265	.324	.471	.258	13	.259
1996	Minnesota	AL	232	67	11	1	12	17	3	0	165	.289	.337	.500	.277	33	.276
1997	*Minnesota*	*AL*	*316*	*94*	*11*	*1*	*16*	*20*	*3*	*2*	*224*	*.297*	*.339*	*.491*	*.273*	*44*	

Coomer has turned out to be an extremely useful spare part for a Twins team that's becoming heavy in left-handed hitters, because he crushes left-handed pitching. A line drive hitter who can play either infield corner, Coomer also put in a shaky 17 starts in right field. Think Mickey Hatcher with power and a legitimate ability to handle third.

MARTY CORDOVA   **LF**   **1970**   **Age 27**

Year	Team	Lge	AB	H	DB	TP	HR	BB	SB	CS	OUT	BA	OBA	SA	EQA	EQR	Peak
1993	Nashville	South	523	128	20	2	19	59	7	3	398	.245	.321	.400	.241	57	.261
1994	Salt Lake City	PCL	372	116	15	2	16	37	12	4	260	.312	.374	.492	.288	58	.309
1995	Minnesota	AL	515	146	28	3	26	53	20	7	376	.283	.350	.501	.280	78	.296
1996	Minnesota	AL	566	172	39	2	17	52	11	5	399	.304	.362	.470	.277	81	.288
1997	*Minnesota*	*AL*	*641*	*210*	*46*	*3*	*20*	*55*	*16*	*8*	*439*	*.328*	*.381*	*.502*	*.293*	*102*	

Signed to a four-year deal before the '96 season, Cordova is a player who could easily frustrate a dumb team, because he has few weaknesses: he's got a fine swing, a good eye, gets a great jump on the ball, throws well and runs the bases intelligently. For all of that, you'd think he was a great player, but he'll have to settle for being a very good one.

MIKE DURANT   **C**   **1970**   **Age 27**

Year	Team	Lge	AB	H	DB	TP	HR	BB	SB	CS	OUT	BA	OBA	SA	EQA	EQR	Peak
1993	Nashville	South	447	104	15	0	9	41	10	2	345	.233	.297	.327	.212	36	.230
1994	Salt Lake City	PCL	334	85	16	2	4	33	6	2	251	.254	.322	.350	.229	31	.245
1995	Salt Lake City	PCL	292	66	11	2	3	21	9	5	231	.226	.278	.308	.196	20	.206
1996	Salt Lake City	PCL	100	26	5	0	1	11	5	1	75	.260	.333	.340	.236	10	.243
1996	Minnesota	AL	81	17	2	0	0	10	3	0	64	.210	.297	.235	.184	5	.191

Durant showed a good arm in his short trial as Greg Myers' backup. His patience was much better at lower levels, and his speed, once his finest offensive asset, is now gone. Durant probably won't get either back. Released.

CHIP HALE   **PH**   **1965**   **Age 32**

Year	Team	Lge	AB	H	DB	TP	HR	BB	SB	CS	OUT	BA	OBA	SA	EQA	EQR	Peak
1993	Portland-OR	PCL	210	53	15	1	1	20	1	1	158	.252	.317	.348	.223	19	.225
1993	Minnesota	AL	188	65	5	1	4	20	2	1	124	.346	.409	.447	.291	28	.294
1994	Minnesota	AL	119	32	6	0	2	16	0	2	89	.269	.356	.370	.241	13	.239
1995	Salt Lake City	PCL	49	13	4	0	0	6	0	1	37	.265	.345	.347	.229	5	.223
1995	Minnesota	AL	104	28	2	0	3	11	0	0	76	.269	.339	.375	.241	11	.235
1996	Minnesota	AL	87	24	4	0	1	9	0	0	63	.276	.344	.356	.238	9	.231

The Twins have took him off of the 40-man roster, and he was picked up by the Dodgers. It should say something about Tom Kelly and the Twins' ability to maximize their talent when they were able to take a replacement-level second baseman and turn him into one of the best-regarded pinch-hitters around.

STEVE HAZLETT   **OF**   **1970**   **Age 27**

Year	Team	Lge	AB	H	DB	TP	HR	BB	SB	CS	OUT	BA	OBA	SA	EQA	EQR	Peak
1993	Ft. Myers	Flor	119	38	3	1	1	14	6	2	83	.319	.391	.387	.272	16	.295
1994	Nashville	South	474	138	18	1	16	38	5	2	338	.291	.344	.435	.261	59	.280
1995	Salt Lake City	PCL	423	115	21	2	6	41	7	7	315	.272	.336	.374	.238	44	.251
1996	Salt Lake City	PCL	300	55	8	2	10	31	6	1	246	.183	.260	.323	.192	20	.200

A short fireplug of a player, Hazlett is a right-handed hitter without much sock who endured a miserable '96 season. He didn't even rack up good platoon numbers, so his shot to work into the Twins' outfield rotation is limited, if he isn't just cut free as a minor league free agent.

DENNY HOCKING   **UT**   **1970**   **Age 27**

Year	Team	Lge	AB	H	DB	TP	HR	BB	SB	CS	OUT	BA	OBA	SA	EQA	EQR	Peak
1993	Nashville	South	418	106	8	2	8	32	9	3	315	.254	.307	.340	.220	36	.239
1994	Salt Lake City	PCL	384	90	9	3	5	28	9	4	298	.234	.286	.312	.201	27	.216
1995	Salt Lake City	PCL	393	101	17	1	9	26	10	6	298	.257	.303	.374	.227	37	.240
1996	Salt Lake City	PCL	129	32	4	1	3	10	2	1	98	.248	.302	.364	.224	12	.232
1996	Minnesota	AL	127	25	5	0	1	8	3	3	105	.197	.244	.260	.155	5	.160

Hocking is a well-regarded shortstop with no bat and a tendency for bad luck. There was a lot of well-intentioned grousing by Twins fans that Tom Kelly had to be free-basing his Skoal if he thought giving Hocking 30 starts in right field was a good idea. In retrospect, of course it looked like a bad idea, but the organization did want to find out if Hocking could hit, and there really wasn't any other position to put him at (short of benching Meares, Hocking's direct competitor). So the Twins burned some outfield playing time on Hocking, who not only didn't hit well enough to push Meares, but hit badly enough to probably end any shot he had at earning a job with the team ever again. Clunky as it sounds, sometimes a team needs to figure this sort of thing out, and it hardly cost the Twins that shot at the Yankees.

TORII HUNTER   **OF**   **1976**   **Age 21**

Year	Team	Lge	AB	H	DB	TP	HR	BB	SB	CS	OUT	BA	OBA	SA	EQA	EQR	Peak
1994	Ft. Wayne	Midw	344	90	9	0	9	21	5	4	258	.262	.304	.366	.224	31	.263
1995	Ft. Myers	Flor	415	106	11	1	9	34	5	2	311	.255	.312	.352	.224	37	.259
1996	New Britain	East	354	93	16	2	7	25	6	4	265	.263	.311	.379	.231	34	.262
1997	*Minnesota*	*AL*	*446*	*121*	*20*	*4*	*7*	*35*	*8*	*5*	*330*	*.271*	*.324*	*.381*	*.238*	*46*	

Hunter is an excellent defensive outfielder with a superb throwing arm who hasn't figured out the hitting part of his job description yet. As the Twins' first-round pick in '93, he'll be given every opportunity to learn. Although there are reasons to be suspicious of "tools" players getting chances to learn how to hit (since they usually don't), Hunter is extremely young, and has been hitting in pitcher's leagues.

J.J. JOHNSON   **OF**   **1974**   **Age 23**

Year	Team	Lge	AB	H	DB	TP	HR	BB	SB	CS	OUT	BA	OBA	SA	EQA	EQR	Peak
1994	Lynchburg	Caro	521	104	17	2	10	31	3	3	420	.200	.245	.298	.171	25	.195
1995	Sarasota	Flor	402	104	9	2	11	23	5	4	302	.259	.299	.373	.224	36	.251
1996	New Britain	East	456	124	17	2	15	37	9	6	338	.272	.327	.417	.248	52	.274
1996	Salt Lake City	PCL	55	17	2	1	1	1	0	1	39	.309	.321	.436	.248	6	.273
1997	*Minnesota*	*AL*	*495*	*136*	*25*	*4*	*14*	*37*	*8*	*5*	*364*	*.275*	*.325*	*.426*	*.251*	*57*	

Part of the compensation from the Red Sox for Aguilera, Johnson is a typical minor league outfield prospect: he doesn't hit well enough yet to be good prospect for either outfield corner, but he isn't a top-notch center fielder either. He's young enough to start making major gains at the plate, enough to make a career for himself, but he has to start doing it soon.

ROBERTO KELLY   **OF**   **1965**   **Age 32**

Year	Team	Lge	AB	H	DB	TP	HR	BB	SB	CS	OUT	BA	OBA	SA	EQA	EQR	Peak
1993	Cincinnati	NL	327	107	16	2	10	23	18	4	224	.327	.371	.480	.289	50	.291
1994	Cincinnati	NL	182	56	5	0	4	13	8	7	133	.308	.354	.401	.252	21	.250
1994	Atlanta	NL	260	77	15	2	7	27	9	3	186	.296	.362	.450	.274	36	.272
1995	Montreal	NL	97	28	1	0	2	8	3	3	72	.289	.343	.361	.237	10	.231
1995	Los Angeles	NL	418	123	18	2	7	21	13	6	301	.294	.328	.397	.246	45	.242
1996	Minnesota	AL	320	101	16	4	6	23	10	2	221	.316	.362	.447	.275	44	.266
1997	*Minnesota*	*AL*	*424*	*125*	*25*	*2*	*9*	*30*	*14*	*4*	*303*	*.295*	*.341*	*.427*	*.261*	*53*	

Re-signed for '97, Kelly was a fine part-timer and spare part for the Twins. He can't handle center any longer, and his only real use these days is to help a little against left-handers. If Kelly starts playing on an everyday basis, it's a very bad sign because he can't hit well enough to justify the playing time, and it would mean the Twins have given up on several prospects at once.

CHUCK KNOBLAUCH   **2B**   **1969**   **Age 28**

Year	Team	Lge	AB	H	DB	TP	HR	BB	SB	CS	OUT	BA	OBA	SA	EQA	EQR	Peak
1993	Minnesota	AL	608	176	29	4	3	69	27	8	440	.289	.362	.365	.254	71	.271
1994	Minnesota	AL	449	143	46	3	5	41	32	5	311	.318	.376	.468	.290	70	.306
1995	Minnesota	AL	542	184	36	7	13	79	45	17	375	.339	.424	.504	.310	100	.322
1996	Minnesota	AL	573	191	32	14	13	98	44	14	396	.333	.431	.506	.315	110	.323
1997	*Minnesota*	*AL*	*588*	*186*	*32*	*11*	*10*	*102*	*30*	*2*	*404*	*.316*	*.417*	*.459*	*.303*	*102*	

Just when Knoblauch had gotten to the point where you might say he was the best player in the American League, Alex Rodriguez arrives to stay. There are some warning signs for Knoblauch: second base is always a tough position to stay healthy at and he was pelted with19 pitches last year. Few players can endure the running, baserunners breaking up the double play, and the rest of the punishment, while putting up numbers as good as these. On the other hand, the Twins were in a situation where failure to re-sign Knoblauch would signal that they weren't serious about their future after Puckett's retirement.

COREY KOSKIE   **3B**   **1973**   **Age 24**

Year	Team	Lge	AB	H	DB	TP	HR	BB	SB	CS	OUT	BA	OBA	SA	EQA	EQR	Peak
1995	Ft. Wayne	Midw	479	137	21	2	15	29	1	2	344	.286	.327	.432	.252	55	.278
1996	Ft. Myers	Flor	351	89	12	1	11	36	1	1	263	.254	.323	.387	.237	36	.258

Koskie has not shown the kind of pop the Twins were hoping to see, and his defense has also raised alarms. With the re-signing of Knoblauch and the shift of Todd Walker, Koskie's future is as trade bait or minor league free agent.

RYAN LANE   **2B/SS**   **1975**   **Age 22**

Year	Team	Lge	AB	H	DB	TP	HR	BB	SB	CS	OUT	BA	OBA	SA	EQA	EQR	Peak
1995	Ft. Wayne	Midw	453	110	20	1	7	52	7	4	347	.243	.321	.338	.222	41	.253
1996	Ft. Myers	Flor	423	112	13	3	12	54	11	5	316	.265	.348	.395	.251	50	.282
1996	New Britain	East	120	26	3	1	2	7	3	2	96	.217	.260	.308	.186	7	.209

A patient hitter, Lane can look forward to one of two career paths: he can wind up pushing Meares at short in the spring of '98, or he can settle for being groomed for the inevitable Cookie Newman roster spot. His offensive skills are such that he probably deserves a full-blown shot at the shortstop job, but the question is whether he's cut out for full time work at the position.

CHRIS LATHAM   **OF**   **1973**   **Age 24**

Year	Team	Lge	AB	H	DB	TP	HR	BB	SB	CS	OUT	BA	OBA	SA	EQA	EQR	Peak
1993	Yakima	Nwern	205	50	1	3	4	25	9	4	159	.244	.326	.337	.227	20	.258
1994	Yakima	Nwern	304	88	12	3	5	38	12	9	225	.289	.368	.398	.258	38	.289
1994	Bakersfield	Calif	196	39	4	1	2	23	14	4	161	.199	.283	.260	.190	13	.211
1995	Vero Beach	Flor	274	76	9	2	7	48	24	6	204	.277	.385	.401	.275	41	.304
1995	SanAntonio	Texas	223	66	11	2	10	30	10	6	163	.296	.379	.498	.287	36	.316
1996	Salt Lake City	PCL	373	92	11	2	10	35	20	6	287	.247	.311	.367	.234	38	.254
1997	*Minnesota*	*AL*	*434*	*121*	*21*	*3*	*15*	*39*	*21*	*5*	*318*	*.279*	*.338*	*.445*	*.266*	*58*	

After drawing 90 walks in 1995, Latham showed much less patience in a Salt Lake this year. However, with Rich Becker in need of a platoon-mate come rain or shine, Latham will have a shot to work his way into a role on the Twins' bench.

MATT LAWTON   **OF**   **1972**   **Age 25**

Year	Team	Lge	AB	H	DB	TP	HR	BB	SB	CS	OUT	BA	OBA	SA	EQA	EQR	Peak
1993	Ft. Wayne	Midw	363	97	13	1	9	52	10	7	273	.267	.359	.383	.251	43	.281
1994	Ft. Myers	Flor	476	146	19	1	12	74	26	11	341	.307	.400	.426	.282	72	.312
1995	New Britain	East	429	117	13	3	15	50	18	6	318	.273	.349	.422	.261	55	.283
1995	Minnesota	AL	60	19	5	1	1	8	1	1	42	.317	.397	.483	.290	10	.315
1996	Salt Lake City	PCL	211	57	10	0	7	24	2	2	156	.270	.345	.417	.254	25	.271
1996	Minnesota	AL	251	63	7	1	6	28	4	4	192	.251	.326	.359	.229	24	.246
1997	*Minnesota*	*AL*	*438*	*119*	*21*	*2*	*16*	*69*	*9*	*8*	*327*	*.272*	*.371*	*.438*	*.268*	*61*	

Lawton can be a very frustrating player to watch. A converted infielder, he hasn't mastered his footwork in the outfield, which results in very uneven quality of work, especially on his throws. Competing with another left-handed hitting center fielder (Becker), that can be a major handicap. Unlike Becker, he isn't strictly a platoon player, and has a fine track record of hitting lefties in the minors. He might win the regular right field job this year, especially since he was much improved in his second go-round with the Twins after the All-Star break (.292/.369/.442).

PAT MEARES   SS   1969   Age 28

Year	Team	Lge	AB	H	DB	TP	HR	BB	SB	CS	OUT	BA	OBA	SA	EQA	EQR	Peak
1993	Minnesota	AL	348	90	12	4	1	9	4	4	262	.259	.277	.325	.199	23	.214
1994	Minnesota	AL	230	62	12	1	2	15	5	1	169	.270	.314	.357	.230	21	.243
1995	Minnesota	AL	392	108	19	4	13	15	10	4	288	.276	.302	.444	.249	44	.259
1996	Minnesota	AL	515	135	24	7	8	17	9	4	384	.262	.286	.383	.224	46	.230
1997	*Minnesota*	*AL*	*526*	*137*	*20*	*4*	*9*	*29*	*11*	*4*	*393*	*.260*	*.299*	*.365*	*.225*	*47*	

Meares has shown better power with age, but he's failed to show increased patience. His career high in walks is 16, drawn last year (not counting the lone intentional walk some doofus issued to him). By comparison, back in '88 Ozzie Guillen drew his career high 22. There are not many professional baseball players that can't do something Ozzie Guillen has. Meares hasn't shown greatly improved range afield, so he's pretty average at almost everything. If he's making a fraction of what Guillen or DiSarcina or Bordick are making he's a steal, but he isn't really helping the Twins.

DOUG MIENTKIEWICZ   1B   1974   Age 23

Year	Team	Lge	AB	H	DB	TP	HR	BB	SB	CS	OUT	BA	OBA	SA	EQA	EQR	Peak
1995	Ft. Myers	Flor	119	31	6	1	1	16	1	1	89	.261	.348	.353	.238	12	.266
1996	Ft. Myers	Flor	515	145	29	1	8	59	6	1	371	.282	.355	.388	.254	60	.280
1997	*Minnesota*	*AL*	*465*	*133*	*32*	*3*	*11*	*44*	*8*	*3*	*335*	*.286*	*.348*	*.439*	*.264*	*60*	

A contact hitter drafted out of the University of Florida, Mientkiewicz has to show plenty of power to make it. A good comparison for his best-possible future would be Hal Morris; if he's only 95% as good as Morris, he'll wind up being Brant Brown, i.e., a hack.

DAMIAN MILLER   C   1970   Age 27

Year	Team	Lge	AB	H	DB	TP	HR	BB	SB	CS	OUT	BA	OBA	SA	EQA	EQR	Peak
1993	Ft. Myers	Flor	333	66	10	0	2	27	3	1	268	.198	.258	.246	.157	13	.170
1994	Nashville	South	341	88	5	0	9	35	3	3	256	.258	.327	.352	.228	32	.245
1995	Salt Lake City	PCL	291	75	16	1	4	17	2	3	219	.258	.299	.361	.219	25	.231
1996	Salt Lake City	PCL	381	97	16	1	8	25	1	2	286	.255	.300	.365	.221	33	.230

Miller isn't a prospect, but as a catcher in an organization dealing with the Curse of Walbeck, he could wind up with playing time. Durant received and flubbed his opportunity, so if the Twins don't sign Terry Steinbach, Miller has a chance.

PAUL MOLITOR   DH/1B   1957   Age 40

Year	Team	Lge	AB	H	DB	TP	HR	BB	SB	CS	OUT	BA	OBA	SA	EQA	EQR	Peak
1993	Toronto	AL	645	222	36	5	27	82	20	3	426	.344	.418	.541	.319	122	.303
1994	Toronto	AL	t460	161	30	4	15	55	18	0	299	.350	.419	.530	.320	87	.305
1995	Toronto	AL	530	148	32	2	17	62	12	0	382	.279	.355	.443	.270	72	.257
1996	Minnesota	AL	656	220	39	8	9	55	18	6	442	.335	.387	.460	.287	98	.273
1997	*Minnesota*	*AL*	*617*	*189*	*32*	*5*	*13*	*73*	*11*	*0*	*428*	*.306*	*.380*	*.438*	*.279*	*88*	

Molitor enjoyed a fine season, but one that wasn't really that much better than his final Toronto season. His power has taken a major drop, and a DH who slugs .468 in a league that slugs .445 isn't a top hitter. But Molitor has shown he has almost as many lives as a left-handed reliever, so his ability to stay at this level, or even to enjoy a year as good as his earlier campaigns, isn't inconceivable. He was much stronger in the second half (.359/.406/.500).

GREG MYERS   C   1966   Age 31

Year	Team	Lge	AB	H	DB	TP	HR	BB	SB	CS	OUT	BA	OBA	SA	EQA	EQR	Peak
1993	California	AL	292	77	7	0	9	18	3	2	217	.264	.306	.380	.230	28	.236
1994	California	AL	126	31	3	0	3	10	0	2	97	.246	.301	.341	.210	10	.212
1995	California	AL	276	75	12	2	10	17	0	1	202	.272	.314	.438	.248	31	.247
1996	Minnesota	AL	327	92	20	3	6	19	0	0	235	.281	.321	.416	.247	35	.242
1997	*Minnesota*	*AL*	*291*	*78*	*12*	*1*	*9*	*25*	*0*	*0*	*213*	*.268*	*.326*	*.409*	*.246*	*32*	

One of the less well-advertised roster moves the Twins made before last season was the addition of Greg Myers. We live in a baseball age where the third-biggest lie is "there just aren't as many catchers around as there used to be." (The first is "We're going bankrupt"; the second, "Pitching sucks because of expansion.") Greg Myers is an example of how wrong-headed this idea is. He was available because there are plenty of solid catching options, and he was cheap. He has a good throwing arm, he's been a popular receiver with his pitchers and how many teams couldn't use a left-handed stick with some pop out of the position?

What's silly about the "good old days" version of lie #3 is that good catchers have probably never been as plentiful as they are today. The '27 Yankees could have used Greg Myers. But in the modern game, almost nobody gets stuck with Joe Astroth or Jim Hegan anymore. When Ned Yost pops up, he doesn't stick around, despite more major league teams and more major league jobs. Sure, some teams will screw around with Matt Walbeck for awhile, but that's because they don't know better. Once they figure it out, a good player like Myers is easily available.

JAMIE OGDEN   **1B/OF**   **1972**   **Age 25**

Year	Team	Lge	AB	H	DB	TP	HR	BB	SB	CS	OUT	BA	OBA	SA	EQA	EQR	Peak
1993	Ft. Myers	Flor	405	94	13	1	11	30	4	1	312	.232	.285	.351	.212	32	.237
1994	Ft. Myers	Flor	259	68	5	0	9	16	8	4	195	.263	.305	.386	.233	26	.257
1995	New Britain	East	399	113	14	1	14	43	4	3	289	.283	.353	.429	.261	50	.284
1996	Salt Lake City	PCL	445	107	13	1	17	43	13	2	340	.240	.307	.389	.236	46	.253

A tall, strapping Twin Cities local, Ogden has almost no chance of earning a major league at bat on merit. He's a "tools" first baseman, in that he cuts a fine figure in cleats. Playing first, all that matters is the ability to hit extremely well, and he doesn't have that tool.

ISRAEL PAEZ   **IF**   **1977**   **Age 20**

Year	Team	Lge	AB	H	DB	TP	HR	BB	SB	CS	OUT	BA	OBA	SA	EQA	EQR	Peak
1995	Ft. Wayne	Midw	402	92	9	1	2	27	4	5	315	.229	.277	.271	.177	21	.207
1996	Ft. Wayne	Midw	470	114	14	2	6	38	6	4	360	.243	.299	.319	.207	35	.239

Paez is an extremely young infielder who's spent time at second, short and third. Although he's shown good patience and pop for his age and position, he hits into a ton of double plays (18 last year). He's not an outstanding prospect, but he'll eventually be in the utility infielder mix.

A.J. PIERZYNSKI   **C**   **1977**   **Age 20**

Year	Team	Lge	AB	H	DB	TP	HR	BB	SB	CS	OUT	BA	OBA	SA	EQA	EQR	Peak
1995	Ft. Wayne	Midw	86	24	2	1	2	1	0	0	62	.279	.287	.395	.228	8	.269
1996	Ft. Wayne	Midw	443	110	17	1	8	15	0	2	335	.248	.273	.345	.203	31	.234

A good catching prospect with the misfortune of being in an organization with a better one (Jose Valentin). He's a good prospect in his own right, having shown good power at an early age.

TOM QUINLAN   **3B**   **1968**   **Age 29**

Year	Team	Lge	AB	H	DB	TP	HR	BB	SB	CS	OUT	BA	OBA	SA	EQA	EQR	Peak
1993	Syracuse	Inter	474	113	16	3	16	56	4	1	362	.238	.319	.386	.236	49	.249
1994	Scranton-WB	Inter	267	62	8	1	9	27	3	1	206	.232	.303	.371	.225	25	.235
1995	Salt Lake City	PCL	462	119	13	3	18	39	5	2	345	.258	.315	.416	.244	51	.250
1996	Salt Lake City	PCL	487	124	22	1	15	37	4	5	368	.255	.307	.396	.233	48	.235

Quinlan is an excellent defensive third baseman. That and some box tops could get him a decoder ring if he's patient.

BRIAN RAABE   **2B**   **1968**   **Age 29**

Year	Team	Lge	AB	H	DB	TP	HR	BB	SB	CS	OUT	BA	OBA	SA	EQA	EQR	Peak
1993	Nashville	South	539	146	19	0	7	52	11	4	397	.271	.335	.345	.233	52	.246
1994	Salt Lake City	PCL	461	125	19	1	3	46	7	5	341	.271	.337	.336	.229	43	.239
1995	Salt Lake City	PCL	436	123	26	3	5	44	11	0	313	.282	.348	.390	.255	51	.261
1996	Salt Lake City	PCL	477	153	27	2	17	45	7	5	329	.321	.379	.493	.288	73	.290

One of the toughest players to strike out at any level, about once every 32 plate appearance over the last three years. Like most purported utility infielders, Raabe is a second baseman who won't win the major league job, so he volunteers to move around the infield. He's popular in the organization for his work ethic. With the release of Chip Hale and the uncertain status of Jeff Reboulet, Raabe may finally make the Twins in '97. The team has reportedly been contacted by several Japanese teams about his availability.

RYAN RADMANOVICH   **OF**   **1972**   **Age 25**

Year	Team	Lge	AB	H	DB	TP	HR	BB	SB	CS	OUT	BA	OBA	SA	EQA	EQR	Peak
1993	Ft. Wayne	Midw	216	60	3	2	8	23	4	1	157	.278	.347	.421	.260	27	.292
1994	Ft. Wayne	Midw	397	102	10	3	16	37	11	7	302	.257	.320	.418	.245	45	.270
1994	Ft. Myers	Flor	87	17	3	0	2	7	2	1	71	.195	.255	.299	.180	5	.200
1996	New Britain	East	472	134	21	2	23	44	5	6	344	.284	.345	.483	.270	65	.289
1997	*Minnesota*	*AL*	*540*	*139*	*27*	*2*	*13*	*47*	*3*	*2*	*403*	*.257*	*.317*	*.387*	*.236*	*54*	

After he missed the '95 season to a terrible knee injury, the Twins could have left Radmanovich in A ball; many teams would have done so. Instead, the Twins pushed him up to AA. It was an inspired decision. Radmanovich has some experience at third, but that position is covered with Walker, Koskie and Chad Roper in the organization. Radmanovich is a left-handed power hitter whose future is now; with the confused right field situation at the big league level, a good spring could get him into the mix immediately.

JEFF REBOULET   **IF**   **1964**   **Age 33**

Year	Team	Lge	AB	H	DB	TP	HR	BB	SB	CS	OUT	BA	OBA	SA	EQA	EQR	Peak
1993	Minnesota	AL	243	66	3	0	3	36	5	4	181	.272	.366	.321	.236	25	.234
1994	Minnesota	AL	190	50	12	1	3	18	0	0	140	.263	.327	.384	.239	20	.233
1995	Minnesota	AL	217	65	9	0	5	28	1	2	154	.300	.380	.410	.266	28	.256
1996	Minnesota	AL	233	51	8	0	0	25	4	2	184	.219	.295	.253	.181	13	.172
1997	*Minnesota*	*AL*	*190*	*46*	*5*	*1*	*3*	*22*	*5*	*3*	*147*	*.242*	*.321*	*.326*	*.220*	*17*	

There's a sort of spooky consistency to Kelly's Twins in their ability to develop almost perfect replacements for certain role players. For example, Jeff Reboulet has been an excellent replacement for Cookie Newman: he can easily handle second, short or third, has some patience at the plate and will chip in enough on offense to keep himself around. Before '96, Reboulet was probably the best utility infielder in baseball, but his disappointing season last year has the Twins wondering whether they want him; he's been taken off the 40-man roster, and his status is up in the air.

CHAD ROPER   **3B**   **1974**   **Age 23**

Year	Team	Lge	AB	H	DB	TP	HR	BB	SB	CS	OUT	BA	OBA	SA	EQA	EQR	Peak
1993	Ft. Myers	Flor	463	108	9	1	11	38	1	1	356	.233	.291	.328	.205	34	.237
1994	Ft. Myers	Flor	350	84	8	0	7	30	5	4	270	.240	.300	.323	.208	27	.236
1995	New Britain	East	453	101	15	2	12	24	2	2	354	.223	.262	.344	.198	31	.222
1996	New Britain	East	482	120	14	2	9	38	4	4	366	.249	.304	.342	.216	40	.238

Usually, when a player logs consecutive years at a level, it's a chance to make some major gains as a hitter, or at least to put up a fine season the second time around. Roper's gotten the shot to do it twice in the last four years, and neither time did he earn a promotion in-season. With Walker's shift to third, Roper's future is basically dead.

MITCH SIMONS   **2B**   **1969**   **Age 28**

Year	Team	Lge	AB	H	DB	TP	HR	BB	SB	CS	OUT	BA	OBA	SA	EQA	EQR	Peak
1993	West Palm Bch	Flor	164	43	3	0	2	17	8	4	125	.262	.331	.317	.224	15	.239
1993	Harrisburg	East	79	18	1	1	0	6	1	0	61	.228	.282	.266	.182	4	.193
1994	Nashville	South	409	128	12	0	7	40	17	5	286	.313	.374	.394	.266	52	.281
1995	Salt Lake City	PCL	475	141	28	2	4	47	25	11	345	.297	.360	.389	.258	58	.268
1996	Salt Lake City	PCL	508	120	22	4	6	42	26	7	395	.236	.295	.331	.216	43	.222

Simons was voted the best baserunner in the PCL this year, and like every scrappy second baseman on his way to begging for a utility job, that's worth more to his pride than it is to his job prospects.

SCOTT STAHOVIAK   **1B**   **1970**   **Age 27**

Year	Team	Lge	AB	H	DB	TP	HR	BB	SB	CS	OUT	BA	OBA	SA	EQA	EQR	Peak
1993	Nashville	South	344	92	16	1	12	51	6	1	253	.267	.362	.424	.266	46	.289
1993	Minnesota	AL	57	11	4	0	0	4	0	2	47	.193	.246	.263	.146	2	.164
1994	Salt Lake City	PCL	425	116	28	3	11	64	5	5	314	.273	.368	.431	.266	57	.285
1995	Minnesota	AL	265	72	12	0	6	30	5	1	194	.272	.346	.385	.250	30	.264
1996	Minnesota	AL	403	112	29	3	13	58	3	3	294	.278	.369	.462	.274	58	.285
1997	*Minnesota*	*AL*	*438*	*122*	*16*	*1*	*30*	*82*	*3*	*2*	*318*	*.279*	*.392*	*.525*	*.299*	*77*	

Yowza! That projection goes beyond happy and right into delirious. When he was drafted as one of the best college hitters in the country out of Creighton, his biggest booster in the Twins front office might have believed such a thing possible, but I doubt it. Hell, I loved him out of Creighton, and I don't think he can turn half his doubles into home runs. The Rott Stahovimer platoon at first is exactly what the Twins can afford, and it's better at putting up runs and playing the position than somebody famous, like Cecil Fielder.

JOSE VALENTIN   **C**   **1976**   **Age 21**

Year	Team	Lge	AB	H	DB	TP	HR	BB	SB	CS	OUT	BA	OBA	SA	EQA	EQR	Peak
1995	Ft. Wayne	Midw	401	120	12	2	17	37	0	2	283	.299	.358	.466	.273	55	.315
1996	Ft. Myers	Flor	350	89	14	1	9	29	1	0	261	.254	.311	.377	.231	33	.262
1996	New Britain	East	171	40	6	0	3	14	1	1	133	.234	.292	.322	.203	12	.228
1997	*Minnesota*	*AL*	*471*	*129*	*26*	*2*	*10*	*33*	*3*	*1*	*343*	*.274*	*.321*	*.401*	*.243*	*50*	

The best young catching prospect in baseball, and younger brother of Milwaukee's Jose Valentin. Valentin is a short switch-hitter with power. Despite being a converted third baseman, he's already been dubbed a top defensive player. He still needs to work on his footwork to speed up his release times, but that should be ironed out by the time he's ready for the majors at some point in '98.

MATT WALBECK   **C**   **1970**   **Age 27**

Year	Team	Lge	AB	H	DB	TP	HR	BB	SB	CS	OUT	BA	OBA	SA	EQA	EQR	Peak
1993	Iowa	AmA	333	90	14	1	7	21	1	1	244	.270	.314	.381	.233	32	.253
1994	Minnesota	AL	339	70	9	0	6	18	1	1	270	.206	.246	.286	.168	16	.180
1995	Minnesota	AL	395	104	20	1	1	25	3	1	292	.263	.307	.327	.214	31	.226
1996	Minnesota	AL	214	47	6	0	3	9	3	1	168	.220	.251	.290	.175	11	.183
1997	*Detroit*	*AL*	*266*	*71*	*13*	*2*	*5*	*16*	*2*	*1*	*196*	*.267*	*.309*	*.387*	*.236*	*26*	

Does Terry Ryan have nightmares?

"Weren't you Omlet, Prince of Thieves or something?"

"That was Hamlet, mate. Now, you'll notice I've chained you to Matt Walbeck, who by his very existence happens to create a small offensive implosion that has the effect of a tactical nuclear weapon. If you wait long enough, you'll be destroyed."

"What's this hacksaw for?"

"Well, Mr. Ryan, you can saw through the chains in a bit, but there's no guarantee that the Walbeck won't go off. That, or you could saw through your leg in about five minutes."

"Wait, what are you doing! For god's sake man, don't give Walbeck a bat, that'll trigger the explosion for sure! This is a death sentence, you bastard!"

"Remember, Mr. Ryan, only you could have stopped the Walbeck from existing in the first place."

TODD WALKER   **3B**   **1973**   **Age 24**

Year	Team	Lge	AB	H	DB	TP	HR	BB	SB	CS	OUT	BA	OBA	SA	EQA	EQR	Peak
1994	Ft. Myers	Flor	183	58	4	1	11	30	4	2	127	.317	.413	.530	.309	34	.346
1995	New Britain	East	533	155	19	2	22	57	16	6	384	.291	.359	.458	.273	75	.302
1996	Salt Lake City	PCL	546	171	26	4	27	54	11	5	380	.313	.375	.524	.294	89	.320
1996	Minnesota	AL	82	21	5	0	0	4	2	0	61	.256	.291	.317	.209	6	.227
1997	*Minnesota*	*AL*	*621*	*175*	*20*	*4*	*24*	*61*	*13*	*6*	*452*	*.282*	*.346*	*.443*	*.264*	*81*	

By all accounts, a miserable defender at the hot corner. That's the bad news. The good news is the boy can kill right-handed pitching. Unless the Twins sign Steinbach or the right field situation suddenly produces a winner who hits the bejeezuz out of the ball, the one spot in the lineup where the Twins can make a major gain over 1996 is Walker over Dave Hollins. Fairly or not, much of Twins' ability to improve on offense will rely on Walker's ability to have a great rookie season.

RICK AGUILERA   **RBP**   **1962**   **Age 35**

YR	TEAM	Lge	IP	H	ER	HR	BB	K	ERA	W	L	H/9	HR/9	BB/9	K/9	KW
1993	Minnesota	AL	70.3	61	20	9	17	61	2.56	6	2	7.81	1.15	2.18	7.81	2.06
1994	Minnesota	AL	45.0	54	18	6	12	45	3.60	3	2	10.80	1.20	2.40	9.00	2.40
1995	Minnesota	AL	24.3	20	5	2	7	29	1.85	2	1	7.40	.74	2.59	10.73	2.93
1995	Boston	AL	30.0	26	7	4	8	23	2.10	2	1	7.80	1.20	2.40	6.90	1.70
1996	Minnesota	AL	111.3	113	49	16	30	80	3.96	6	6	9.13	1.29	2.43	6.47	1.55

The experiment was a success, although Aggie did suffer the rash of injuries that has always plagued him with the heavier workload of being a starter. He started the season with a bout of tendinitis and finished early with a sore hamstring; he did not suffer a major arm injury. He pitched particularly poorly at home (7.13 ERA), and as an extreme flyball pitcher might have been bad off in the Humpdome. Continuing a trend we pointed out last year, Twins pitchers were the most flyball- (vs. groundball) oriented pitching staff in the American League. Among the Twins' regular pitchers, Aguilera, Aldred, Guardado and Radke are all extreme flyball pitchers, and all but Radke had extreme problems pitching in the Twin Cities. The problem is inextricably linked to the ballpark, and is a major challenge to overcome if the Twins want to move up to serious contenders.

SCOTT ALDRED   **LBP**   **1968**   **Age 29**

YR	TEAM	Lge	IP	H	ER	HR	BB	K	ERA	W	L	H/9	HR/9	BB/9	K/9	KW
1995	Lakeland	Flor	60.0	75	29	5	27	46	4.35	3	4	11.25	.75	4.05	6.90	1.29
1996	Detroit	AL	44.0	55	39	7	27	35	7.98	1	4	11.25	1.43	5.52	7.16	1.01
1996	Minnesota	AL	122.0	122	53	16	45	72	3.91	7	7	9.00	1.18	3.32	5.31	.94

Rescued on waivers from the Tigers on May 28, Aldred looked like a bad idea. He'd gone 0-4 (9.35 ERA) with the Tigers, so it hardly looked like he'd be a useful contributor to the Twins. However, Aldred wound up being a very solid starter for the Twins. In the second half, he posted a 4.61 ERA in a league where anything under 5.00 was good. I was impressed by what I saw: he works his fastball low and hard for strikes; if he has one of the normal AL umpires, calling a different strike zone for "Scott Who?" as opposed to somebody famous, he is forced to work higher in the zone and gets hammered. If the mound gets raised or the strike zone starts getting called consistently, I could see Aldred being a very solid starter. On the other hand, he's been very injury-prone, so he could just as easily disappear.

MARC BARCELO   **RSP**   **1972**   **Age 25**

YR	TEAM	Lge	IP	H	ER	HR	BB	K	ERA	W	L	H/9	HR/9	BB/9	K/9	KW
1994	Nashville	South	167.3	198	79	14	72	120	4.25	9	10	10.65	.75	3.87	6.45	1.18
1995	Salt Lake City	PCL	136.0	200	105	20	75	57	6.95	4	11	13.24	1.32	4.96	3.77	.02
1996	Salt Lake City	PCL	56.7	77	37	8	23	28	5.88	2	4	12.23	1.27	3.65	4.45	.57
1996	New Britain	East	72.7	116	55	7	48	45	6.81	2	6	14.37	.87	5.94	5.57	.37

His disastrous introduction to Salt Lake City has dropped Barcelo from one of the Twins' top prospects to the mystery pitching flop answer to Brad Komminsk. It got so bad this year that he had to be dropped back to AA. He still has a good fastball and hard slider, and could still sort himself out, but as things stand now he's an even more dramatic failure for the organization than Pat Mahomes.

JASON BELL   RSP   1975   Age 22

YR	TEAM	Lge	IP	H	ER	HR	BB	K	ERA	W	L	H/9	HR/9	BB/9	K/9	KW
1995	Ft. Wayne	Midw	30.7	35	11	0	9	26	3.23	2	1	10.27	.00	2.64	7.63	1.88
1996	Ft. Myers	Flor	81.3	79	22	2	33	60	2.43	7	2	8.74	.22	3.65	6.64	1.30
1996	New Britain	East	85.7	113	57	13	48	71	5.99	3	7	11.87	1.37	5.04	7.46	1.23

Bell has excellent command of three pitches (fastball, slider, change), but no single one is dominating. As a top draft choice from '95, he's moving up the ladder very quickly.

SHANE BOWERS   RBP   1972   Age 25

YR	TEAM	Lge	IP	H	ER	HR	BB	K	ERA	W	L	H/9	HR/9	BB/9	K/9	KW
1994	Ft. Wayne	Midw	72.3	94	33	4	27	45	4.11	4	4	11.70	.50	3.36	5.60	1.03
1995	Ft. Myers	Flor	129.0	164	55	11	48	74	3.84	7	7	11.44	.77	3.35	5.16	.88
1996	New Britain	East	119.7	161	75	16	55	72	5.64	4	9	12.11	1.20	4.14	5.42	.77

Bowers looks like one of those people for whom AA may be the cutoff. He's got a nice curve and an OK fastball, but he pitched poorly in a pitcher's park in a pitcher's league.

EDDIE GUARDADO   LRP   1971   Age 26

YR	TEAM	Lge	IP	H	ER	HR	BB	K	ERA	W	L	H/9	HR/9	BB/9	K/9	KW
1993	Nashville	South	59.3	63	9	1	16	42	1.37	6	1	9.56	.15	2.43	6.37	1.52
1993	Minnesota	AL	95.7	116	56	13	41	48	5.27	4	7	10.91	1.22	3.86	4.52	.54
1994	Salt Lake City	PCL	141.7	156	67	20	65	74	4.26	8	8	9.91	1.27	4.13	4.70	.53
1995	Minnesota	AL	92.0	93	41	12	47	71	4.01	5	5	9.10	1.17	4.60	6.95	1.17
1996	Minnesota	AL	73.0	57	31	10	34	71	3.82	4	4	7.03	1.23	4.19	8.75	1.87

Guardado enjoyed an excellent season as the Twins' main left-handed reliever. Although his ERA was superficially bad (5.25), he was able to pitch frequently, tying for the AL lead in games (83). He continued his excellence against left-handed batters, holding them to .198/.254/.288. He fiddles with his delivery, mixing four pitches with frequent changes of his throwing motion. In particular, he'll drop down to sidearm against lefties. He appeared in 35 games after having pitched the previous day, which led the American League, so few people deserve the reputation for having a rubber arm as much as Eddie.

GREG HANSELL   RRP   1971   Age 26

YR	TEAM	Lge	IP	H	ER	HR	BB	K	ERA	W	L	H/9	HR/9	BB/9	K/9	KW
1993	Albuquerque	PCL	93.3	112	61	9	70	46	5.88	3	7	10.80	.87	6.75	4.44	-.21
1994	Albuquerque	PCL	115.3	104	31	7	42	86	2.42	10	3	8.12	.55	3.28	6.71	1.42
1995	Los Angeles	NL	19.7	30	15	5	8	12	6.86	1	1	13.73	2.29	3.66	5.49	.92
1995	Salt Lake City	PCL	30.3	38	16	3	7	16	4.75	1	2	11.27	.89	2.08	4.75	1.06
1996	Minnesota	AL	74.3	76	35	11	32	44	4.24	4	4	9.20	1.33	3.87	5.33	.81

He's been claimed off of waivers by the Red Sox. Hansell was given up on by the Dodgers because he could not throw a useful curve. With a good fastball and little else, he'll remain in the bullpen.

LATROY HAWKINS   RSP   1973   Age 24

YR	TEAM	Lge	IP	H	ER	HR	BB	K	ERA	W	L	H/9	HR/9	BB/9	K/9	KW
1993	Ft. Wayne	Midw	139.7	148	57	7	57	105	3.67	9	7	9.54	.45	3.67	6.77	1.34
1994	Ft. Myers	Flor	35.0	40	11	2	10	28	2.83	3	1	10.29	.51	2.57	7.20	1.76
1994	Nashville	South	67.0	60	24	3	40	42	3.22	4	3	8.06	.40	5.37	5.64	.54
1994	Salt Lake City	PCL	76.3	84	31	7	41	31	3.66	4	4	9.90	.83	4.83	3.66	.01
1995	Salt Lake City	PCL	135.7	147	50	9	53	68	3.32	9	6	9.75	.60	3.52	4.51	.62
1995	Minnesota	AL	27.7	36	23	3	13	9	7.48	1	2	11.71	.98	4.23	2.93	-.08
1996	Salt Lake City	PCL	130.0	136	54	12	42	80	3.74	7	7	9.42	.83	2.91	5.54	1.12
1996	Minnesota	AL	27.3	36	17	7	10	23	5.60	1	2	11.85	2.30	3.29	7.57	1.70

Hawkins probably has reason to feel confused. After his first shot with the Twins in '95, he was told he was being too fine and nibbling too much. So this year he came into spring training firing strikes, but was also still getting pasted, to the point that Tom Kelly said he was throwing too many strikes. To go with a good fastball, Hawkins has a good curve and slider.

SCOTT KLINGENBECK **RSP** **1971** **Age 26**

YR	TEAM	Lge	IP	H	ER	HR	BB	K	ERA	W	L	H/9	HR/9	BB/9	K/9	KW
1993	Frederick	Caro	120.0	190	71	7	58	92	5.32	5	8	14.25	.52	4.35	6.90	1.21
1994	Bowie	East	130.7	174	77	16	53	88	5.30	5	10	11.98	1.10	3.65	6.06	1.11
1995	Rochester	Inter	40.0	49	13	2	15	24	2.92	3	1	11.02	.45	3.38	5.40	.96
1995	Baltimore	AL	31.7	29	13	6	19	15	3.69	2	2	8.24	1.71	5.40	4.26	.07
1995	Minnesota	AL	50.7	61	37	14	25	27	6.57	2	4	10.84	2.49	4.44	4.80	.49
1996	Salt Lake City	PCL	141.3	158	52	8	54	81	3.31	9	7	10.06	.51	3.44	5.16	.86
1996	Minnesota	AL	29.0	38	20	4	11	14	6.21	1	2	11.79	1.24	3.41	4.34	.59

Klingenbeck has been an enormous pain in the ass for the Twins. They've tried to teach him how to set up hitters and have confidence in his defense. Just when they think he's figured it out, and they call him up to show that he's learned, he tries pumping gas with a poor fastball, spots the opposition a half-dozen runs or so and leaves the Twins apoplectic. If he gets a pitching coach he'll pay attention to, or goes to a team where he'll find one, he could succeed. Right now, there's little reason for confidence.

TRAVIS MILLER **LSP** **1973** **Age 24**

YR	TEAM	Lge	IP	H	ER	HR	BB	K	ERA	W	L	H/9	HR/9	BB/9	K/9	KW
1994	Ft. Wayne	Midw	48.3	66	18	2	18	31	3.35	3	2	12.29	.37	3.35	5.77	1.09
1995	New Britain	East	149.7	202	94	20	80	117	5.65	6	11	12.15	1.20	4.81	7.04	1.14
1996	Salt Lake City	PCL	151.7	181	79	17	73	116	4.69	7	10	10.74	1.01	4.33	6.88	1.21
1996	Minnesota	AL	27.3	39	21	6	10	14	6.91	1	2	12.84	1.98	3.29	4.61	.71

Miller's calling card is a wicked slider, considered the best breaking pitch thrown by anyone in the Twins' chain. He's been durable, and he managed to pitch effectively in Salt Lake, no easy feat. He'll be given an opportunity to win a spot at the bottom of the rotation, along with Dan Serafini and LaTroy Hawkins.

DAN NAULTY **RBP** **1970** **Age 27**

YR	TEAM	Lge	IP	H	ER	HR	BB	K	ERA	W	L	H/9	HR/9	BB/9	K/9	KW
1993	Ft. Wayne	Midw	101.0	130	49	7	65	57	4.37	5	6	11.58	.62	5.79	5.08	.25
1993	Ft. Myers	Flor	26.3	46	23	6	19	16	7.86	1	2	15.72	2.05	6.49	5.47	.20
1994	Ft. Myers	Flor	78.7	100	41	10	43	64	4.69	4	5	11.44	1.14	4.92	7.32	1.21
1994	Nashville	South	42.7	58	36	5	30	23	7.59	1	4	12.23	1.05	6.33	4.85	.04
1995	Salt Lake City	PCL	85.0	88	44	11	57	69	4.66	4	5	9.32	1.16	6.04	7.31	.93
1996	Minnesota	AL	56.3	40	17	5	36	54	2.72	4	2	6.39	.80	5.75	8.63	1.44

After a good AFL campaign before the season, making the big leagues was pretty likely. A huge flamethrower, Naulty has exceptional movement on his stuff, which leads to severe control problems from time to time. Naulty was the object of an early attempt by some mediots to whine Dave Stevens out of the closer job (often the same guys who just a few short months before had been comparing Stevens to Gossage), but anointing Naulty would have been premature. His season ended early when he had to have surgery to remove part of a rib to reduce circulation problems in his right arm. It isn't expected to make him lose any time this season.

JOSE PARRA **RBP** **1973** **Age 24**

YR	TEAM	Lge	IP	H	ER	HR	BB	K	ERA	W	L	H/9	HR/9	BB/9	K/9	KW
1993	SanAntonio	Texas	100.0	126	52	12	27	63	4.68	5	6	11.34	1.08	2.43	5.67	1.28
1994	Albuquerque	PCL	136.3	174	69	9	52	76	4.56	7	8	11.49	.59	3.43	5.02	.81
1995	Albuquerque	PCL	50.0	58	26	8	22	30	4.68	3	3	10.44	1.44	3.96	5.40	.81
1995	Minnesota	AL	63.0	77	46	10	23	29	6.57	2	5	11.00	1.43	3.29	4.14	.56
1996	Salt Lake City	PCL	41.3	50	20	2	17	21	4.35	2	3	10.89	.44	3.70	4.57	.60
1996	Minnesota	AL	70.7	79	35	12	29	48	4.46	4	4	10.06	1.53	3.69	6.11	1.11

Parra throws three different pitches well, all of them from three different angles. That's enough to wow people, but it hasn't yielded consistent results. Tom Kelly and Dick Such don't have much confidence in him so far: in 22 relief appearances, he did not record a single "hold," meaning he wasn't being handed many leads and was usually used to mop up lost causes, like a Scott Klingenbeck start. Whether or not he'll live up to the expectations that had him billed as the central player in the Tapani deal with the Dodgers is up in the air.

BRAD RADKE   RSP   1973   Age 24

YR	TEAM	Lge	IP	H	ER	HR	BB	K	ERA	W	L	H/9	HR/9	BB/9	K/9	KW
1993	Ft. Myers	Flor	80.0	106	49	6	32	54	5.51	3	6	11.93	.68	3.60	6.07	1.12
1993	Nashville	South	69.0	94	43	7	24	57	5.61	3	5	12.26	.91	3.13	7.43	1.70
1994	Nashville	South	170.0	198	71	12	60	97	3.76	10	9	10.48	.64	3.18	5.14	.92
1995	Minnesota	AL	181.3	184	86	29	51	75	4.27	9	11	9.13	1.44	2.53	3.72	.61
1996	Minnesota	AL	232.0	209	86	33	62	142	3.34	15	11	8.11	1.28	2.41	5.51	1.23

The best pitcher few people have heard of. The major change from his rookie season was that Radke learned how often and when he could get away with his high leg kick, and how to throw his assortment of pitches effectively from the stretch. He's got a fastball with late action, tailing away from righties, to go with a good slider and the inevitable change-up. He logged 20 quality starts in 35 attempts, and was seventh in the AL in opponents' batting average. If the Twins start putting better-than-average offensive teams on the field, Radke should start winning a huge number of games.

MARK REDMAN   LSP   1974   Age 23

YR	TEAM	Lge	IP	H	ER	HR	BB	K	ERA	W	L	H/9	HR/9	BB/9	K/9	KW
1995	Ft. Myers	Midw	28.0	40	16	6	18	17	5.14	1	2	12.86	1.93	5.79	5.46	.37
1996	Ft. Myers	Flor	74.3	79	26	2	47	55	3.15	5	3	9.57	.24	5.69	6.66	.80
1996	New Britain	East	96.7	123	55	6	63	72	5.12	4	7	11.45	.56	5.87	6.70	.77

A soft-tosser whose out pitch is his changeup, Redman helps himself with a distracting delivery. He's one of those people for whom the term "savvy" gets waved around a lot, scout-ese for "we think he'll succeed, but we can't tell you why because we don't know."

TODD RITCHIE   RBP   1972   Age 25

YR	TEAM	Lge	IP	H	ER	HR	BB	K	ERA	W	L	H/9	HR/9	BB/9	K/9	KW
1993	Nashville	South	42.3	53	21	2	21	31	4.46	2	3	11.27	.43	4.46	6.59	1.08
1994	Nashville	South	15.3	28	11	2	10	7	6.46	1	1	16.43	1.17	5.87	4.11	-.10
1995	New Britain	East	103.7	155	78	14	67	47	6.77	3	9	13.46	1.22	5.82	4.08	-.09
1996	New Britain	East	75.0	120	58	6	39	40	6.96	2	6	14.40	.72	4.68	4.80	.43
1996	Salt Lake City	PCL	23.0	27	12	4	13	15	4.70	1	2	10.57	1.57	5.09	5.87	.68

Despite injuries, Ritchie is still considered to have the best fastball in the organization. For 1997, the Twins will be forced to keep him on the big league roster or pass him through waivers, so he'll probably have to be kept in the bullpen.

BRETT ROBERTS   RSP   1970   Age 27

YR	TEAM	Lge	IP	H	ER	HR	BB	K	ERA	W	L	H/9	HR/9	BB/9	K/9	KW
1993	Ft. Myers	Flor	149.7	222	105	9	115	85	6.31	5	12	13.35	.54	6.92	5.11	-.03
1994	Ft. Myers	Flor	103.7	154	83	9	63	58	7.21	3	9	13.37	.78	5.47	5.04	.31
1995	New Britain	East	161.3	189	70	11	63	104	3.90	9	9	10.54	.61	3.51	5.80	1.06
1996	Salt Lake City	PCL	159.0	201	93	26	87	70	5.26	7	11	11.38	1.47	4.92	3.96	.09

Ah, the differences between low and high altitudes. After giving up only nine homers in New Britain, Roberts waved 28 pitches goodbye at Salt Lake City. His strikeout rate also plummeted. Although Roberts is hardly an example of a great pitching prospect handicapped by a tough park, his fate illustrates how a pitcher's boneyard (say, most of the PCL) can lead to development problems.

RICH ROBERTSON   LBP   1969   Age 28

YR	TEAM	Lge	IP	H	ER	HR	BB	K	ERA	W	L	H/9	HR/9	BB/9	K/9	KW
1993	Buffalo	AmA	126.0	151	63	9	67	66	4.50	6	8	10.79	.64	4.79	4.71	.37
1994	Buffalo	AmA	113.3	119	42	7	46	64	3.34	8	5	9.45	.56	3.65	5.08	.78
1995	Salt Lake City	PCL	41.7	31	10	3	16	37	2.16	4	1	6.70	.65	3.46	7.99	1.80
1995	Minnesota	AL	51.7	46	21	4	32	38	3.66	3	3	8.01	.70	5.57	6.62	.81
1996	Minnesota	AL	186.7	178	81	18	119	109	3.91	11	10	8.58	.87	5.74	5.26	.32

Before the nifty find of Scott Aldred, the major surprise on the season for the Twins was Rich Robertson. A typical lefty junkballer, Robertson had been allowed to languish in the Pirates' organization. When the Twins gave him an audition in September of '95, he put up three excellent starts. In a full season, Robertson was the modern version of 1950s Yankees' starter Tommy Byrne. Byrne was to pitching what Ted Williams was to hitting: if there was somebody he thought could hurt him at the plate, he'd put that man on first; if the next guy looked pretty tough, he'd get a pass too. Maybe the next guy as well. Although Robertson was pulled from the rotation to keep him from making a run at Brian Kingman's corner of history as the last 20-game loser, his record was the product of lousy run support (3.67 runs per game). Robertson is a good example of what a team can get from the waiver wire if it's clever.

FRANKIE RODRIGUEZ   RBP   1973   Age 24

YR	TEAM	Lge	IP	H	ER	HR	BB	K	ERA	W	L	H/9	HR/9	BB/9	K/9	KW
1993	New Britain	East	157.0	173	81	20	100	116	4.64	7	10	9.92	1.15	5.73	6.65	.78
1994	Pawtucket	Inter	176.0	192	84	18	77	132	4.30	9	11	9.82	.92	3.94	6.75	1.27
1995	Pawtucket	Inter	25.0	21	10	3	11	15	3.60	2	1	7.56	1.08	3.96	5.40	.81
1995	Boston	AL	16.0	19	14	3	10	14	7.88	0	2	10.69	1.69	5.62	7.88	1.22
1995	Minnesota	AL	90.3	88	48	7	49	45	4.78	4	6	8.77	.70	4.88	4.48	.27
1996	Minnesota	AL	206.3	199	93	22	82	106	4.06	11	12	8.68	.96	3.58	4.62	.65

Rodriguez is just fun to watch. Maybe the indelible image of Terry Forster on the mound is hard to shake, but seeing a pitcher as active as Rodriguez when it comes to fielding is a fun change of pace. On top of that, the guy can pitch. He had to put up with some midseason strangeness, when he was shuttled out of the rotation and into the bullpen to close while Stevens was being erratic and Naulty had gone down. Like Radke, I wouldn't be surprised if this year Rodriguez explodes onto the national stage and wins a passel of games.

DAN SERAFINI   LSP   1974   Age 23

YR	TEAM	Lge	IP	H	ER	HR	BB	K	ERA	W	L	H/9	HR/9	BB/9	K/9	KW
1993	Ft. Wayne	Midw	119.7	158	84	7	109	87	6.32	4	9	11.88	.53	8.20	6.54	.13
1994	Ft. Myers	Flor	122.3	184	96	17	77	101	7.06	3	11	13.54	1.25	5.66	7.43	1.06
1995	New Britain	East	150.7	180	72	9	89	95	4.30	8	9	10.75	.54	5.32	5.67	.56
1996	Salt Lake City	PCL	124.0	156	68	19	72	88	4.94	6	8	11.32	1.38	5.23	6.39	.82

Since being picked in the first round in '92, Serafini hasn't missed a start in his professional career. Pitching in Utah is tough, but Serafini showed that he can fool people with four pitches, the best of which are a fastball with good movement and an overhand curve. He'll be given every opportunity to win a rotation job with the Twins this year.

DAVE STEVENS   RRP   1970   Age 27

YR	TEAM	Lge	IP	H	ER	HR	BB	K	ERA	W	L	H/9	HR/9	BB/9	K/9	KW
1993	Orlando	South	63.3	80	37	8	45	37	5.26	3	4	11.37	1.14	6.39	5.26	.15
1993	Iowa	AmA	32.3	26	14	3	17	26	3.90	2	2	7.24	.84	4.73	7.24	1.23
1994	Salt Lake City	PCL	40.3	38	9	2	20	26	2.01	3	1	8.48	.45	4.46	5.80	.82
1994	Minnesota	AL	45.3	52	27	5	24	24	5.36	2	3	10.32	.99	4.76	4.76	.40
1995	Minnesota	AL	66.7	68	31	13	34	47	4.18	3	4	9.18	1.76	4.59	6.35	.97
1996	Minnesota	AL	58.0	52	22	10	26	28	3.41	3	3	8.07	1.55	4.03	4.34	.44

This was a tough season for Stevens. He lost his claim to the closer's spot in between shoulder tenderness at the start of the season and a self-inflicted hand injury he got from hitting a wall after a poor outing in July. The early returns on his new forkball (replacing the slider as his off-speed pitch) are incomplete, since Stevens missed time to injury, but did pitch better than he had before.

HECTOR TRINIDAD   RSP   1974   Age 23

YR	TEAM	Lge	IP	H	ER	HR	BB	K	ERA	W	L	H/9	HR/9	BB/9	K/9	KW
1993	Peoria	Midw	134.7	181	60	8	41	69	4.01	7	8	12.10	.53	2.74	4.61	.85
1994	Daytona	Flor	157.0	212	82	13	59	109	4.70	7	10	12.15	.75	3.38	6.25	1.24
1995	New Britain	East	110.7	163	69	7	29	71	5.61	4	8	13.26	.57	2.36	5.77	1.34
1996	New Britain	East	127.7	162	77	7	42	70	5.43	5	9	11.42	.49	2.96	4.93	.90

A control artist who came over as compensation from the Cubs for GM Andy MacPhail, Trinidad isn't an outstanding prospect. Since he's a righty without a good fastball, his shot at the majors is pretty slim; for every Bob Tewksbury, there are a dozen Dave Eilands.

MIKE TROMBLEY   **RBP**   **1967**   **Age 30**

YR	TEAM	Lge	IP	H	ER	HR	BB	K	ERA	W	L	H/9	HR/9	BB/9	K/9	KW
1993	Minnesota	AL	114.7	125	59	15	47	88	4.63	6	7	9.81	1.18	3.69	6.91	1.38
1994	Salt Lake City	PCL	57.7	68	27	6	26	53	4.21	3	3	10.61	.94	4.06	8.27	1.74
1994	Minnesota	AL	48.7	52	28	9	20	31	5.18	2	3	9.62	1.66	3.70	5.73	.99
1995	Salt Lake City	PCL	66.0	68	25	4	33	54	3.41	4	3	9.27	.55	4.50	7.36	1.33
1995	Minnesota	AL	99.0	100	52	16	44	68	4.73	5	6	9.09	1.45	4.00	6.18	1.06
1996	Salt Lake City	PCL	34.0	26	9	3	13	31	2.38	3	1	6.88	.79	3.44	8.21	1.87
1996	Minnesota	AL	67.7	58	16	2	26	55	2.13	6	2	7.71	.27	3.46	7.32	1.57

This year was Trombley's last chance with the organization and he made the best of it. Two factors turned his career around. First, despite his resistance, he finally accepted a job in the pen. Second, he picked up a split-fingered fastball, junking the slider that was racking up frequent flier mileage. Throwing from the bullpen, the usual overreactions to the split-finger should be less troublesome, and Trombley should be a very effective long reliever for the Twins in '97.

SCOTT WATKINS   **LRP**   **1970**   **Age 27**

YR	TEAM	Lge	IP	H	ER	HR	BB	K	ERA	W	L	H/9	HR/9	BB/9	K/9	KW
1993	Ft. Wayne	Midw	26.7	34	14	0	12	18	4.72	1	2	11.48	.00	4.05	6.08	1.01
1993	Ft. Myers	Flor	24.7	32	15	0	16	32	5.47	1	2	11.68	.00	5.84	11.68	2.43
1994	Salt Lake City	PCL	54.0	65	34	8	34	40	5.67	2	4	10.83	1.33	5.67	6.67	.81
1995	Salt Lake City	PCL	51.0	46	14	5	18	53	2.47	4	2	8.12	.88	3.18	9.35	2.32
1995	Minnesota	AL	21.7	21	11	2	12	11	4.57	1	1	8.72	.83	4.98	4.57	.28
1996	Salt Lake City	PCL	47.7	56	37	6	40	35	6.99	1	4	10.57	1.13	7.55	6.61	.31

A soft-tosser with a strange delayed delivery, Watkins has probably already missed his big chance. He could have made a role for himself in '96 after an excellent '95, but he lost out to guys like Mike Milchin. Because he's a lefty, he has more lives than a cat, but that doesn't mean his next one will be in the Twin Cities.

Player	Age	Team	Lge	AB	H	DB	TP	HR	BB	SB	CS	OUT	BA	OBA	SA	EQA	EQR	Peak
RAFAEL ALVAREZ	19	Ft Wayne	Midw	491	134	23	3	5	32	6	4	361	.273	.317	.363	.230	46	.265
ARMANN BROWN	23	Ft Myers	Flor	422	102	11	4	6	58	19	8	328	.242	.333	.329	.229	41	.248
ANTUAN BUNKLEY	20	Ft Wayne	Midw	178	38	7	1	1	12	0	0	140	.213	.263	.281	.174	9	.196
TONY BYRD	25	New Britain	East	201	48	7	1	1	16	9	5	158	.239	.295	.299	.202	14	.214
GARY CARABALLO	24	New Britain	East	302	73	8	0	8	24	1	2	231	.242	.298	.348	.214	24	.229
DAN CEY	20	Ft Wayne	Midw	88	20	3	0	0	6	1	0	68	.227	.277	.261	.177	4	.204
JOE CRANFORD	21	Ft Myers	Flor	107	22	2	1	0	7	2	1	86	.206	.254	.243	.156	4	.176
CLEATUS DAVIDSON	19	Ft Wayne	Midw	211	33	7	2	0	17	1	1	179	.156	.219	.209	.102	3	.119
ANTHONY FELSTON	21	Ft Wayne	Midw	214	63	3	1	0	34	10	2	153	.294	.391	.318	.255	25	.286
JEFF FERGUSON	23	New Britain	East	297	84	13	2	5	34	4	2	215	.283	.356	.391	.254	35	.276
TROY FORTIN	21	Ft Myers	Flor	369	87	6	1	8	26	1	1	283	.236	.286	.322	.201	26	.226
JOE FRASER	21	Ft Wayne	Midw	341	70	8	1	6	19	4	1	272	.205	.247	.287	.172	17	.191
CARLOS GARCIA	20	Ft Myers	Flor	92	14	1	0	1	5	5	1	79	.152	.196	.196	.104	1	.114
	20	Ft Wayne	Midw	134	26	2	0	1	16	6	2	110	.194	.280	.231	.171	7	.194
ADRIAN GORDON	22	Ft Wayne	Midw	360	96	12	4	2	36	5	4	268	.267	.333	.339	.228	33	.252
SHANE GUNDERSON	22	Ft Myers	Flor	429	104	16	2	7	56	6	4	329	.242	.330	.338	.226	40	.249
SCOTT HILT	23	New Britain	East	189	37	5	1	2	30	2	1	153	.196	.306	.265	.189	12	.206
JEFF HORN	25	Salt Lake City	PCL	82	25	3	0	3	12	0	1	58	.305	.394	.451	.280	12	.294
STEVE HULS	21	Ft Wayne	Midw	206	39	2	0	1	9	1	1	168	.189	.223	.214	.112	3	.125
TRAVIS JOHNSON	22	Ft Wayne	Midw	194	58	12	0	4	25	3	2	138	.299	.379	.423	.271	26	.300
BEN JONES	22	Ft Myers	Flor	167	35	1	0	0	15	9	2	134	.210	.275	.216	.167	8	.184
IVORY JONES	23	Ft Myers	Flor	150	33	7	1	0	19	5	3	120	.220	.308	.280	.199	11	.215
RAUL JUAREZ	20	Ft Wayne	Midw	177	35	1	0	3	15	1	1	143	.198	.260	.254	.160	7	.181
TOM KNAUSS	22	Ft Myers	Flor	120	22	2	0	4	11	1	1	99	.183	.252	.300	.175	6	.192
	22	Ft Wayne	Midw	216	61	9	1	7	19	1	0	155	.282	.340	.431	.259	26	.286
GREG LAKOVIC	21	Ft Wayne	Midw	99	23	2	0	0	12	1	1	77	.232	.315	.253	.189	6	.211
KEITH LEGREE	24	Ft Myers	Flor	210	56	4	1	6	38	1	1	155	.267	.379	.381	.258	26	.276
MARK LEONARD	31	Salt Lake City	PCL	192	43	3	1	5	38	0	1	150	.224	.352	.328	.230	19	.222
ANTHONY LEWIS	25	New Britain	East	475	122	10	1	22	43	6	5	358	.257	.319	.421	.245	53	.258
RENE LOPEZ	24	New Britain	East	187	43	4	0	4	19	1	2	146	.230	.301	.316	.203	14	.218
JIM MCCALMONT	24	Ft Myers	Flor	90	17	2	0	0	4	1	0	73	.189	.223	.211	.116	2	.122
MIKE MORIARTY	22	Ft Myers	Flor	446	104	14	0	5	53	8	7	349	.233	.315	.298	.205	33	.227
KELCEY MUCKER	21	Ft Myers	Flor	343	78	6	2	3	32	3	1	266	.227	.293	.283	.192	21	.214
TOM NEVERS	24	New Britain	East	477	124	23	4	8	41	4	5	358	.260	.319	.375	.231	46	.248
TOMMY PETERMAN	21	Ft Wayne	Midw	180	41	6	0	3	7	0	0	139	.228	.257	.311	.184	10	.205
CHAD RUPP	24	New Britain	East	285	74	9	0	16	12	3	1	212	.260	.290	.460	.247	32	.264
JOHN SCHROEDER	20	Ft Wayne	Midw	435	105	10	1	12	12	2	2	332	.241	.262	.352	.202	30	.229
JEFF SMITH	22	Ft Wayne	Midw	216	46	3	0	2	16	1	0	170	.213	.267	.255	.166	10	.182
BRIAN TURNER	25	New Britain	East	162	40	4	0	6	12	4	1	123	.247	.299	.383	.230	16	.242

Player	Age	Team	Lge	IP	H	ER	HR	BB	K	ERA	W	L	H/9	HR/9	BB/9	K/9	KW
TODD BARTELS	22	Ft Wayne	Midw	45.3	68	33	7	14	21	6.55	1	4	13.50	1.39	2.78	4.17	.69
ERIK BENNETT	27	Minnesota	AL	28.0	28	17	6	17	13	5.46	1	2	9.00	1.93	5.46	4.18	.03
ROBERT BOGGS	21	Ft Wayne	Midw	128.0	197	90	11	84	84	6.33	4	10	13.85	.77	5.91	5.91	.49
RON CARIDAD	24	New Britain	East	29.0	36	22	3	29	16	6.83	1	2	11.17	.93	9.00	4.97	-.59
TROY CARRASCO	21	New Britain	East	100.3	134	78	9	82	52	7.00	3	8	12.02	.81	7.36	4.66	-.28
WALKER CHAPMAN	20	Ft Wayne	Midw	81.7	138	68	4	54	38	7.49	2	7	15.21	.44	5.95	4.19	-.09
TREVOR COBB	22	Ft Myers	Flor	112.7	130	49	2	60	72	3.91	7	6	10.38	.16	4.79	5.75	.72
DERON DOWHOWER	24	Ft Myers	Flor	66.3	82	44	8	60	61	5.97	2	5	11.13	1.09	8.14	8.28	.72
SEAN GAVAGHAN	26	New Britain	East	36.0	49	29	5	35	33	7.25	1	3	12.25	1.25	8.75	8.25	.56
TOM GOURDIN	23	Ft Myers	Flor	55.0	82	44	9	40	32	7.20	1	5	13.42	1.47	6.55	5.24	.11
PHIL HAIGLER	22	Ft Wayne	Midw	57.3	103	47	4	33	22	7.38	1	5	16.17	.63	5.18	3.45	-.14
JEFF HARRIS	21	Ft Wayne	Midw	77.0	117	39	6	43	53	4.56	4	5	13.68	.70	5.03	6.19	.81
DAVID HOOTEN	21	Ft Wayne	Midw	32.7	39	12	0	17	24	3.31	2	2	10.74	.00	4.68	6.61	1.03
DOM KONIECZKI	27	New Britain	East	31.3	38	20	3	28	17	5.74	1	2	10.91	.86	8.04	4.88	-.38
TOM LAROSA	21	Ft Wayne	Midw	76.7	103	52	10	43	57	6.10	3	6	12.09	1.17	5.05	6.69	.97
KEVIN LEGAULT	25	Salt Lake City	PCL	76.3	97	42	10	31	46	4.95	3	5	11.44	1.18	3.66	5.42	.89
MIKE LINCOLN	21	Ft Myers	Flor	52.0	82	37	8	34	18	6.40	2	4	14.19	1.38	5.88	3.12	-.43
KEITH LINEBARGER	25	New Britain	East	90.3	118	57	10	42	52	5.68	3	7	11.76	1.00	4.18	5.18	.68
ALAN MAHAFFEY	22	Ft Wayne	Midw	108.0	179	94	17	47	47	7.83	2	10	14.92	1.42	3.92	3.92	.33
JASON MCKENZIE	22	Ft Wayne	Midw	32.7	49	27	3	19	18	7.44	1	3	13.50	.83	5.23	4.96	.34
MIKE MISURACA	27	Salt Lake City	PCL	35.7	47	27	4	20	20	6.81	1	3	11.86	1.01	5.05	5.05	.42
PAUL MORSE	23	New Britain	East	50.7	66	38	5	33	36	6.75	2	4	11.72	.89	5.86	6.39	.67
TOM MOTT	22	Ft Myers	Flor	65.0	102	51	8	51	36	7.06	2	5	14.12	1.11	7.06	4.98	-.10
BRAD NIEDERMAIER	23	Ft Wayne	Midw	59.0	85	44	4	38	45	6.71	2	5	12.97	.61	5.80	6.86	.84
JOE NORRIS	25	Salt Lake City	PCL	35.3	46	22	3	21	31	5.60	1	3	11.72	.76	5.35	7.90	1.29
KEVIN OHME	25	New Britain	East	74.0	98	52	8	42	32	6.32	2	6	11.92	.97	5.11	3.89	.02
PAUL PAVICICH	23	Ft Myers	Flor	37.3	62	35	6	19	21	8.44	1	3	14.95	1.45	4.58	5.06	.54
DAN PERKINS	21	Ft Myers	Flor	119.7	164	63	9	55	81	4.74	2	8	12.33	.68	4.14	6.09	1.00
ROB RADLOSKY	22	Ft Myers	Flor	91.0	146	81	16	64	59	8.01	2	8	14.44	1.58	6.33	5.84	.36
FRED RATH	23	Ft Myers	Flor	26.0	31	11	2	15	21	3.81	2	1	10.73	.69	5.19	7.27	1.12
	23	Ft Wayne	Midw	37.3	36	12	2	13	39	2.89	3	1	8.68	.48	3.13	9.40	2.35
KASEY RICHARDSON	19	Ft Wayne	Midw	95.3	148	64	7	51	51	6.04	3	8	13.97	.66	4.81	4.81	.40
WILL RUSHING	23	Ft Myers	Flor	144.3	202	86	16	101	82	5.36	6	10	12.60	1.00	6.30	5.11	.13
BENJ SAMPSON	21	Ft Myers	Flor	62.7	70	31	7	37	48	4.45	3	4	10.05	1.01	5.31	6.89	.97
	21	New Britain	East	69.3	124	56	8	33	39	7.27	2	6	16.10	1.04	4.28	5.06	.62
PHIL STIDHAM	27	Salt Lake City	PCL	74.0	95	51	8	48	44	6.20	2	6	11.55	.97	5.84	5.35	.32
SCOTT TANKSLEY	22	Ft Wayne	Midw	25.3	31	17	0	10	16	6.04	1	2	11.01	.00	3.55	5.68	1.01

Minnesota Twins

Anaheim Angels

When Disney bought the Angels, I made a promise to myself that I wouldn't take the huge, obvious openings this marriage created. I promised the other authors that I wouldn't stoop to depths like calling them a Mickey Mouse organization, or call the front office "nothing short of Goofy." I swore that there would be no sketches of Jorge Fabregas with mouse, nor pen and ink art of signs that say "You must be at least this tall to ride Ms. Autry." No, you'll find none of that. What you will find is a lot of speculation, a quick thought experiment or two, and a surprisingly positive outlook for a team that many think is lost at sea.

Memories of Donnie Moore and Dave Henderson are gone now. The ghosts of the great '95 gaspfest are irrelevant and absent; this is an entirely new organization under control of one of the most frighteningly efficient corporations on earth. Where in the past, the management of the Angels has focused on winning a title for Gene Autry before he dies, the management can now simply focus on making money. Does this mean that they won't focus on winning? Not at all. The Angels are a very healthy franchise, despite lukewarm fan support and the perception of malaise. They were unhealthy for many years, but if I were to pick a franchise that could become the next Atlanta Braves, this would be it. Why?

Accountability.

No longer is "we tried" sufficient. Disney doesn't play that way. If there's a management team in Anaheim that doesn't do the job, they'll be gone. Disney isn't impatient or impetuous; they're generally a well-managed company and I expect that organizational tendency to bleed over to the ballclub. Quickly and thoroughly. With an Autry in charge, the Angel management could never really look beyond a one-year time horizon; they're no longer constrained by that issue. They need to make money, and what's the best way to do that? Simple. Win ballgames and make sure people know about it.

Don't be surprised to find Angel games all over satellite and cable systems in one form or another fairly quickly. Disney is pretty much the fourth reich of distribution, and a large part of the Braves' success comes from the synergy with TBS and the resulting national exposure. Disney will likely engage in lots of cross-promotional deals; they'll get people into the park, no matter what part of Anaheim you're talking about. Their revenue stream is going to grow over the next few years, and Walt's Frozen Head Corps [tm] understands the value of investing in its business units.

The Angels are a lot better off than most clubs right now, and probably better off than they were a year ago, at least as far as long-term organization prospects go. It's going to be a good decade for Angel fans, provided they can keep Gene Mauch at a distance.

My optimism is organizational, rather than on-field, but I think the Angels are the team to beat in the AL West next year—or at least they can be. We'll have to see how new manager Terry Collins chooses to use his players, but I think this club has an excellent opportunity to jump out and grab this division by the throat.

Don't misunderstand me—there are problems with this team. However, the problems are generally easy to fix. The Angels can dramatically improve their team at little or no cost; the real question is whether or not they see the problems. I think they see at least one of them, and will catch on to the second quickly enough to win the division.

The first easily fixable problem is third base. Last year, the Angels ran Tim Wallach, Jack Howell and Leaky, the incontinent dwarf, out to third base for a good part of the season. They absolutely, predictably sucked, except for a hot stretch in August by Leaky. The Angels have George Arias, a decent third base prospect with nothing left to prove in the minors. He'll get them at least 30 runs over the human flotsam they had at third base in 1996. There's a conservative three wins. Next, the Angels upgrade their 1B/OF flotilla. Instead of polluting first base with J.T. Snow's flaccid bat, they'll add Darin Erstad to the Anderson/Edmonds/Salmon mix. Salmon should rebound a bit from a disappointing 1996, and Garret Anderson, entering his prime, should provide a significant (20 run) increase over Snow's alleged production. Hell, Garrett Morris would probably hit better and work cheaper. That's another couple of wins, and this team is right back to "respectable," which these days is enough to contend.

The pitching doesn't show any signs of faltering; Langston and Finley have good health records, there's some decent depth and the acquisitions of Gubicza and Watson give them two more shots at a good starting pitcher. For now, there's nothing that can be done about the imbecilic signing of Gary DiSarcina, but not even his contract lasts forever. The talent that's here on the offense isn't old, and it should be enough to sustain them until the revolution in management that I'm talking about starts to kick in three years down the road. By then, maybe they'll be ready to thaw Walt's head.

Organization: It's virtually all new. Terry Collins has been brought in to manage, presumably because he's really good at making it look like his eyes are going to bug out of his head. Personally, I think they should have stolen Tim Ireland from the Brewers, but I guess that's nit-picking. The Angels' brass has been taking some pretty bad people off the waiver wire and trying to scrape the mucus off of them. You can acquire some quality that way, but not in the form of Mike Harkey, ferchrissake! If they can dig up a generic dweeb to replace J. T. Snow, that'd go a long way towards heartening the Angel faithful.

GARRET ANDERSON — LF — 1972 — Age 25

Year	Team	Lge	AB	H	DB	TP	HR	BB	SB	CS	OUT	BA	OBA	SA	EQA	EQR	Peak
1993	Vancouver	PCL	468	128	26	2	5	30	2	2	342	.274	.317	.370	.231	44	.258
1994	Vancouver	PCL	498	146	29	3	12	29	3	2	354	.293	.332	.436	.257	59	.283
1995	Vancouver	PCL	63	20	8	0	0	5	0	0	43	.317	.368	.444	.274	8	.299
1995	California	AL	379	126	20	1	18	19	6	2	255	.332	.364	.533	.295	60	.321
1996	California	AL	608	175	33	2	12	27	7	9	442	.288	.318	.408	.241	63	.258
1997	*California*	*AL*	*555*	*174*	*39*	*3*	*15*	*31*	*6*	*4*	*385*	*.314*	*.350*	*.476*	*.280*	*80*	

The very definition of a tradable player. Anderson's skill, hitting for average, is extremely visible and does a lot to hide his inability to get on base. The Angels should probably let him get hot for half a season, then unload him for the best available offer. This team's biggest strength is outfield depth, and Anderson's the odd man out.

GEORGE ARIAS — 3B — 1972 — Age 25

Year	Team	Lge	AB	H	DB	TP	HR	BB	SB	CS	OUT	BA	OBA	SA	EQA	EQR	Peak
1993	Cedar Rapids	Midw	264	55	8	1	8	24	3	1	210	.208	.274	.337	.202	19	.227
1994	Lake Elsinore	Calif	523	133	16	1	19	48	3	2	392	.254	.317	.398	.238	54	.263
1995	Midland	Texas	511	122	9	3	25	55	2	1	390	.239	.313	.415	.241	55	.261
1996	Vancouver	PCL	250	86	14	0	11	20	2	1	165	.344	.393	.532	.305	42	.327
1996	California	AL	252	61	8	1	6	16	2	0	191	.242	.287	.353	.215	20	.229
1997	*California*	*AL*	*430*	*110*	*21*	*1*	*18*	*38*	*3*	*1*	*321*	*.256*	*.316*	*.435*	*.254*	*52*	

Probably going to be a good one. In 1996, while the Angels were deciding which carcass—Wallach or Howell—was less worm-eaten, Arias whittled in Canada and watched from the bench. Personally, I think his defensive skills are excellent. He doesn't leave his feet unnecessarily and his glove is always in position to make the play. I believe he can be a slightly better player than Dean Palmer–slightly inferior with the bat, and greatly superior with the glove. A keeper.

LARRY BARNES — OF/1B — 1975 — Age 22

Year	Team	Lge	AB	H	DB	TP	HR	BB	SB	CS	OUT	BA	OBA	SA	EQA	EQR	Peak
1996	Cedar Rapids	Midw	502	144	16	1	23	44	5	3	361	.287	.344	.460	.267	66	.299
1997	*California*	*AL*	*621*	*187*	*28*	*2*	*21*	*45*	*6*	*4*	*438*	*.301*	*.348*	*.454*	*.273*	*85*	

Good enough hitter to play in the bigs right now. His fielding is holding him back. The Angels need to somehow transplant Barnes' hitting ability into DiSarcina's body. He'll be a better than league average hitter with some power some day, but probably not for a couple of years.

DANNY BUXBAUM — 1B — 1973 — Age 24

Year	Team	Lge	AB	H	DB	TP	HR	BB	SB	CS	OUT	BA	OBA	SA	EQA	EQR	Peak
1995	Boise	Nwern	257	82	7	0	8	38	0	0	175	.319	.407	.440	.288	39	.317
1996	Lake Elsinore	Calif	300	78	8	1	11	23	0	0	222	.260	.313	.403	.239	31	.260
1997	*California*	*AL*	*446*	*128*	*16*	*1*	*11*	*39*	*0*	*0*	*318*	*.287*	*.344*	*.401*	*.257*	*53*	

A bit old for the level he played at last year, but he played well. Now onto Midland. If he can take a step up there, and not just stay level, he's probably in for a good, solid major league career. If not, he's probably on the Crash Davis career track.

VINCE COLEMAN   **OF**   **1962**   **Age 35**

Year	Team	Lge	AB	H	DB	TP	HR	BB	SB	CS	OUT	BA	OBA	SA	EQA	EQR	Peak
1993	NY Mets	NL	380	110	15	6	3	27	32	11	281	.289	.337	.384	.251	45	.242
1994	Kansas City	AL	436	102	15	11	2	29	43	7	341	.234	.282	.333	.222	40	.212
1995	Kansas City	AL	297	90	14	4	5	28	26	9	216	.303	.363	.428	.272	42	.258
1995	Seattle	AL	163	49	11	2	1	10	16	7	121	.301	.341	.411	.258	20	.245
1996	Vancouver	PCL	89	19	1	1	0	9	3	1	71	.213	.286	.247	.179	5	.172
1996	Cincinnati	NL	85	14	1	1	1	10	10	2	73	.165	.253	.235	.179	5	.170
1997	*California*	*AL*	*104*	*25*	*1*	*0*	*0*	*7*	*18*	*1*	*80*	*.240*	*.288*	*.250*	*.226*	*10*	

Like a strain of the flu, Coleman keeps popping up year after year, infecting some unwilling and unhappy host. He's useless at this point, except perhaps as a modern-day Herb Washington or a pastry chef. If Vince Coleman shows up in your town as an NRI, you are legally entitled to make threatening phone calls to the front office of the club in question.

CHILI DAVIS   **DH**   **1960**   **Age 37**

Year	Team	Lge	AB	H	DB	TP	HR	BB	SB	CS	OUT	BA	OBA	SA	EQA	EQR	Peak
1993	California	AL	578	145	26	0	33	74	4	1	434	.251	.336	.467	.264	78	.251
1994	California	AL	394	123	16	1	27	69	3	2	273	.312	.415	.563	.316	77	.301
1995	California	AL	431	143	19	0	24	91	3	3	291	.332	.448	.543	.326	88	.309
1996	California	AL	532	157	19	0	30	86	5	2	377	.295	.393	.500	.295	89	.280
1997	*Kansas City*	*AL*	*485*	*115*	*22*	*0*	*23*	*116*	*0*	*0*	*370*	*.237*	*.384*	*.425*	*.278*	*7*	

Has established himself as a very good, consistent hitter at a very late age. Vladimir projects he's going to plummet off the face of the earth, which means he'll meld nicely with Bob Boone's plans for the KC offense. Will likely outperform the projection above, as well as sing a really bitchin' Karoake rendition of "Daddy, Don't You Walk So Fast."

GARY DISARCINA   **SS**   **1968**   **Age 29**

Year	Team	Lge	AB	H	DB	TP	HR	BB	SB	CS	OUT	BA	OBA	SA	EQA	EQR	Peak
1993	California	AL	418	102	21	1	4	17	5	5	321	.244	.274	.328	.198	28	.209
1994	California	AL	390	101	14	2	3	18	3	6	295	.259	.292	.328	.204	28	.212
1995	California	AL	366	116	30	6	6	21	7	4	254	.317	.354	.481	.277	51	.284
1996	California	AL	537	138	27	4	5	21	2	1	400	.257	.285	.350	.212	41	.214
1997	*California*	*AL*	*582*	*158*	*22*	*2*	*7*	*18*	*4*	*2*	*426*	*.271*	*.293*	*.352*	*.223*	*50*	

An organization that sees this player as a strength rather than a weakness is nothing short of diseased. Average with the glove, and you see how he hits. Yet the Angels, in their mercy, signed him to a three-year deal worth $9 million. Hopefully for Angels' fans, Disney will bring in some new people with active neurons.

JIM EDMONDS   **CF**   **1970**   **Age 27**

Year	Team	Lge	AB	H	DB	TP	HR	BB	SB	CS	OUT	BA	OBA	SA	EQA	EQR	Peak
1993	Vancouver	PCL	359	106	18	2	10	38	4	5	258	.295	.363	.440	.266	47	.290
1993	California	AL	61	15	4	1	0	3	0	1	47	.246	.281	.344	.202	4	.221
1994	California	AL	290	79	14	1	5	30	4	2	213	.272	.341	.379	.244	31	.262
1995	California	AL	565	170	30	4	37	52	1	4	399	.301	.360	.565	.295	94	.311
1996	California	AL	432	132	28	4	27	46	4	0	300	.306	.372	.576	.306	78	.318
1997	*California*	*AL*	*623*	*200*	*53*	*4*	*44*	*71*	*5*	*3*	*426*	*.321*	*.390*	*.631*	*.328*	*131*	

A darn good outfielder. One of the top two defensive outfielders in the AL, along with Bernie Williams, and a similar player overall. Like the rest of the Angel outfield, definitely a championship caliber player. That projection up there is huge, but I'm not going to bet against it.

DARIN ERSTAD   **OF**   **1974**   **Age 23**

Year	Team	Lge	AB	H	DB	TP	HR	BB	SB	CS	OUT	BA	OBA	SA	EQA	EQR	Peak
1995	Lake Elsinore	Calif	115	39	4	2	4	5	1	0	76	.339	.367	.513	.293	18	.328
1996	Vancouver	PCL	362	111	18	3	8	43	10	4	255	.307	.380	.439	.277	52	.306
1996	California	AL	208	59	6	1	4	18	3	3	152	.284	.341	.380	.242	22	.267
1997	*California*	*AL*	*574*	*199*	*32*	*7*	*17*	*52*	*22*	*6*	*381*	*.347*	*.401*	*.516*	*.312*	*104*	

Another excellent outfielder. One scout called him "The Jerry Rice of Baseball;" he doesn't clock as particularly fast, but when the ball's in the air he gets to it better than anybody. Defensive technique is excellent, batting stroke is extremely quick and vicious; the numbers and scouts agree. This guy will have a nice career, making a few appearances at the All-Star Game.

JORGE FABREGAS **C** **1970** **Age 27**

Year	Team	Lge	AB	H	DB	TP	HR	BB	SB	CS	OUT	BA	OBA	SA	EQA	EQR	Peak
1993	Midland	Texas	409	99	17	1	6	30	1	0	310	.242	.294	.333	.209	31	.227
1994	Vancouver	PCL	209	41	4	1	1	12	1	1	169	.196	.240	.239	.140	6	.152
1994	California	AL	127	36	3	0	0	7	2	1	92	.283	.321	.307	.215	10	.231
1995	Vancouver	PCL	75	20	0	0	5	9	0	0	55	.267	.345	.467	.267	10	.280
1995	California	AL	229	59	5	0	3	17	0	2	172	.258	.309	.319	.208	17	.221
1996	California	AL	255	74	3	0	3	17	0	1	182	.290	.335	.337	.228	23	.237
1997	*California*	*AL*	*307*	*79*	*5*	*0*	*6*	*19*	*0*	*1*	*229*	*.257*	*.301*	*.332*	*.217*	*25*	

A remarkably consistent player. He hits like lint.

TODD GREENE **C/DH** **1971** **Age 26**

Year	Team	Lge	AB	H	DB	TP	HR	BB	SB	CS	OUT	BA	OBA	SA	EQA	EQR	Peak
1993	Boise	Nwern	315	74	6	1	11	18	2	1	242	.235	.276	.365	.212	25	.234
1994	Lake Elsinore	Calif	534	150	20	1	28	52	6	2	386	.281	.345	.479	.272	74	.296
1995	Midland	Texas	309	86	7	1	20	16	3	2	225	.278	.314	.502	.266	41	.285
1995	Vancouver	PCL	172	46	2	1	14	11	1	0	126	.267	.311	.535	.273	25	.293
1996	Vancouver	PCL	228	70	10	0	7	16	0	1	159	.307	.352	.443	.265	29	.280
1996	California	AL	79	15	1	0	2	4	2	0	64	.190	.229	.278	.164	3	.175
1997	*California*	*AL*	*469*	*134*	*10*	*1*	*23*	*33*	*0*	*1*	*336*	*.286*	*.333*	*.458*	*.267*	*62*	

More power than the numbers above indicate. He'll probably slug .600 for a couple of years in the majors. Doesn't walk much, and has prospect's disease–it's doubtful his defense (or at least his defensive reputation) will allow him to stay at catcher, where he'd be exceptionally valuable. At first base or DH, he's not nearly as valuable. If I'm the Angels' GM, he catches and Jorge Fabregas gets transferred to EuroDisney.

JASON HERRICK **UT** **1974** **Age 23**

Year	Team	Lge	AB	H	DB	TP	HR	BB	SB	CS	OUT	BA	OBA	SA	EQA	EQR	Peak
1994	Cedar Rapids	Midw	353	84	13	2	7	35	5	2	271	.238	.307	.346	.220	31	.249
1995	Cedar Rapids	Midw	369	96	12	1	10	30	8	2	275	.260	.316	.379	.236	37	.264
1996	Lake Elsinore	Calif	211	58	9	0	5	19	2	2	155	.275	.335	.389	.243	22	.270
1997	*California*	*AL*	*504*	*142*	*21*	*1*	*17*	*32*	*15*	*7*	*369*	*.282*	*.325*	*.429*	*.258*	*62*	

I'll tell you this about the projections in this book: They're generally excellent. Generally. There are a few bugs to work out, particularly when tracking people through Greenville and also through Lake Elsinore. Herrick is a decent hitter, but he won't do that well this coming year. Needs to find a position where the Angels are happy with him.

REX HUDLER **UT** **1961** **Age 36**

Year	Team	Lge	AB	H	DB	TP	HR	BB	SB	CS	OUT	BA	OBA	SA	EQA	EQR	Peak
1994	California	AL	124	37	8	0	8	6	2	2	89	.298	.331	.556	.283	19	.269
1995	California	AL	225	62	13	0	8	10	12	0	163	.276	.306	.440	.258	28	.245
1996	California	AL	303	95	21	3	16	9	14	5	213	.314	.333	.561	.290	48	.276
1997	*Philadelphia*	*NL*	*325*	*81*	*19*	*2*	*7*	*6*	*19*	*7*	*251*	*.249*	*.263*	*.385*	*.232*	*33*	

Doing his best Tony Phillips impersonation, sans those irritating walks. Good guy to have on a club, provided the price is right. Not likely to keep up the 1996 pace with the bat, obviously. Signed an absurd deal with Philadelphia, where he'll play mostly outfield.

ORLANDO PALMEIRO **OF** **1969** **Age 28**

Year	Team	Lge	AB	H	DB	TP	HR	BB	SB	CS	OUT	BA	OBA	SA	EQA	EQR	Peak
1993	Midland	Texas	535	134	11	3	1	41	10	5	406	.250	.304	.288	.200	36	.214
1994	Vancouver	PCL	454	133	24	2	1	54	16	10	331	.293	.368	.361	.250	52	.264
1995	Vancouver	PCL	412	132	19	4	1	42	14	6	286	.320	.383	.393	.268	53	.278
1996	Vancouver	PCL	253	78	11	3	1	29	6	2	177	.308	.379	.387	.265	32	.272
1996	California	AL	87	25	7	1	0	8	0	1	63	.287	.347	.391	.246	9	.251

Line drive hitting outfielder, hoping to catch on somewhere as a fourth outfielder. Dwight Smith lite. America fell in love with him as "Chesperito."

CHRIS PRITCHETT   **1B**   **1970**   **Age 27**

Year	Team	Lge	AB	H	DB	TP	HR	BB	SB	CS	OUT	BA	OBA	SA	EQA	EQR	Peak
1993	Midland	Texas	468	121	22	3	2	56	2	3	350	.259	.338	.331	.226	43	.246
1994	Midland	Texas	473	134	18	2	7	82	3	1	340	.283	.389	.374	.263	60	.282
1995	Vancouver	PCL	450	130	22	2	12	56	2	2	322	.289	.368	.427	.267	59	.281
1996	Vancouver	PCL	502	151	26	1	19	69	5	3	354	.301	.385	.470	.285	77	.296
1997	*California*	*AL*	*492*	*144*	*29*	*2*	*17*	*83*	*6*	*4*	*352*	*.293*	*.395*	*.463*	*.292*	*81*	

The best first baseman in the Angel organization. Hits well, gets on base, plays good defense at first base and yet J.T. Snow. When an organization continuously demonstrates that it can't gauge on-field talent, that's not just a sign of bad on-field management; it's a sign that upper management isn't doing the job. I believe this organization will greatly benefit from being purchased by The Great Happy Corporate Conformity or Death Kingdom. Accountability has to come into play at some point.

TIM SALMON   **RF**   **1969**   **Age 28**

Year	Team	Lge	AB	H	DB	TP	HR	BB	SB	CS	OUT	BA	OBA	SA	EQA	EQR	Peak
1993	California	AL	521	152	29	1	37	86	5	4	373	.292	.392	.564	.306	97	.328
1994	California	AL	375	108	19	2	23	54	1	3	270	.288	.378	.533	.293	63	.309
1995	California	AL	546	187	36	2	38	93	5	5	364	.342	.438	.625	.338	121	.351
1996	California	AL	583	168	27	5	30	93	4	2	417	.288	.386	.506	.293	97	.300
1997	*California*	*AL*	*614*	*193*	*37*	*4*	*41*	*90*	*3*	*2*	*423*	*.314*	*.402*	*.588*	*.323*	*125*	

1996 had to be a huge disappointment for Salmon. Hitting his peak during a big hitters' era, he barely managed to be above average for league outfielders. He's capable of much more, but his 1996 leads me to believe that perhaps he's not going to take that next step up in production. Even if he doesn't, he's an excellent right fielder, but he probably could use one or two more days off throughout the year.

J.T. SNOW   **1B**   **1968**   **Age 29**

Year	Team	Lge	AB	H	DB	TP	HR	BB	SB	CS	OUT	BA	OBA	SA	EQA	EQR	Peak
1993	Vancouver	PCL	95	31	4	0	6	9	0	0	64	.326	.385	.558	.306	17	.324
1993	California	AL	423	106	18	1	19	57	3	0	317	.251	.340	.433	.257	53	.272
1994	Vancouver	PCL	187	51	9	1	7	21	1	1	137	.273	.346	.444	.262	24	.271
1994	California	AL	224	49	5	0	8	19	0	1	176	.219	.280	.348	.205	17	.213
1995	California	AL	551	165	22	1	27	53	2	1	387	.299	.361	.490	.281	81	.288
1996	California	AL	576	150	17	1	18	56	1	6	432	.260	.326	.387	.236	59	.238
1997	*San Francisco*	*NL*	*439*	*115*	*22*	*1*	*17*	*44*	*3*	*5*	*329*	*.262*	*.329*	*.433*	*.264*	*59*	

Well, you've seen his peak. What did you think? And that defensive rep? A joke. Snow's an absolutely miserable ballplayer, and probably costs his team more than anyone else on the roster. The Angels have an interesting talent structure: a fantastic outfield and a lousy infield. That might make the club fairly easy to fix, especially if Arias and Pritchett get some playing time and pan out. J.T. Snow is approximately as useful to a ballclub as a large sack of wheat…that's gone bad…and already been eaten by a bulldog with colonic cysts. Better than Ozzie Guillen.

RANDY VELARDE   **2B/UT**   **1963**   **Age 34**

Year	Team	Lge	AB	H	DB	TP	HR	BB	SB	CS	OUT	BA	OBA	SA	EQA	EQR	Peak
1993	NY Yankees	AL	232	75	14	2	9	20	2	2	158	.323	.377	.517	.293	37	.288
1994	NY Yankees	AL	285	83	17	1	10	22	4	2	204	.291	.342	.463	.267	38	.258
1995	NY Yankees	AL	370	106	19	1	8	56	5	1	265	.286	.380	.408	.269	50	.256
1996	California	AL	531	152	28	3	14	71	7	7	386	.286	.370	.429	.267	71	.254
1997	*California*	*AL*	*442*	*116*	*22*	*1*	*15*	*62*	*6*	*5*	*331*	*.262*	*.353*	*.419*	*.263*	*59*	

Great utility guy to have. Can play a few defensive positions, hits for a decent average, will take a walk and occasionally belt a ball out of the park. Has a few years left before vamping for a spot on that Norm Hitzges/Paul White fantasy baseball show. Probably not ugly enough to make that cast, though.

TIM WALLACH   3B   1958   Age 39

Year	Team	Lge	AB	H	DB	TP	HR	BB	SB	CS	OUT	BA	OBA	SA	EQA	EQR	Peak
1993	Los Angeles	NL	484	111	16	1	13	39	0	2	375	.229	.287	.347	.208	37	.198
1994	Los Angeles	NL	427	128	17	1	26	53	0	2	301	.300	.377	.527	.293	70	.278
1995	Los Angeles	NL	336	95	23	2	10	31	0	0	241	.283	.343	.452	.264	43	.251
1996	California	AL	190	45	5	0	9	18	1	0	145	.237	.303	.405	.235	19	.224
1996	Los Angeles	NL	166	40	3	0	5	14	0	1	127	.241	.300	.349	.215	14	.205

Not with the organization any more, but I've included him as an object lesson. The Angels had no clue that they over-performed in 1995, so they went out and got this guy as a stopgap until Arias was ready in a pathetic bid to get into the postseason in 1996. Is this an organization that does adequate research and gets information before making decisions, or is it knee-jerk and reactionary? Retired.

MIKE WOLFF   OF   1971   Age 26

Year	Team	Lge	AB	H	DB	TP	HR	BB	SB	CS	OUT	BA	OBA	SA	EQA	EQR	Peak
1993	Cedar Rapids	Midw	431	100	9	2	15	59	4	3	334	.232	.324	.367	.231	43	.255
1994	Midland	Texas	404	107	13	1	14	49	7	4	301	.265	.344	.406	.252	48	.274
1995	Midland	Texas	436	108	16	1	12	57	7	4	332	.248	.335	.372	.238	46	.255
1996	Lake Elsinore	Calif	43	11	0	0	2	7	2	0	32	.256	.360	.395	.263	6	.281
1996	Vancouver	PCL	263	67	12	1	11	33	6	3	199	.255	.338	.433	.256	33	.272
1997	*California*	*AL*	*360*	*98*	*18*	*1*	*14*	*48*	*4*	*1*	*263*	*.272*	*.358*	*.444*	*.274*	*52*	

He won't hit that well. No prospect. Mentioned by some as a potential future manager; that could well be, but it's some time off.

JIM ABBOTT   LSP   1968   Age 29

YR	TEAM	Lge	IP	H	ER	HR	BB	K	ERA	W	L	H/9	HR/9	BB/9	K/9	KW
1993	NY Yankees	AL	211.7	227	102	23	84	99	4.34	11	13	9.65	.98	3.57	4.21	.51
1994	NY Yankees	AL	159.7	166	72	22	70	89	4.06	9	9	9.36	1.24	3.95	5.02	.69
1995	California	AL	84.7	91	34	4	31	41	3.61	5	4	9.67	.43	3.30	4.36	.63
1995	Chi. White Sox	AL	112.3	113	40	10	38	45	3.20	7	5	9.05	.80	3.04	3.61	.44
1996	Vancouver	PCL	26.7	19	12	4	24	17	4.05	1	2	6.41	1.35	8.10	5.74	-.11
1996	California	AL	143.3	157	97	19	81	56	6.09	5	11	9.86	1.19	5.09	3.52	-.10

Lefty who's lost his fastball and his confidence. Could be reborn as a spot left-hander out of the pen, but I think his days as a decent starter are past.

KYLE ABBOTT   LSP   1968   Age 29

YR	TEAM	Lge	IP	H	ER	HR	BB	K	ERA	W	L	H/9	HR/9	BB/9	K/9	KW
1993	Scranton-WB	Inter	162.3	180	83	22	85	89	4.60	8	10	9.98	1.22	4.71	4.93	.47
1995	Philadelphia	NL	28.3	27	10	3	18	19	3.18	2	1	8.58	.95	5.72	6.04	.58
1996	Midland	Texas	81.0	92	43	10	45	39	4.78	4	5	10.22	1.11	5.00	4.33	.19

Consistently has his K/W ratio right around one. This is not a good thing. His best career move probably involves a tacky gold jacket.

ROB BONANNO   RBP   1971   Age 26

YR	TEAM	Lge	IP	H	ER	HR	BB	K	ERA	W	L	H/9	HR/9	BB/9	K/9	KW
1994	Boise	Nwern	35.0	34	12	2	13	20	3.09	3	1	8.74	.51	3.34	5.14	.88
1994	Cedar Rapids	Midw	43.7	72	28	5	23	25	5.77	2	3	14.84	1.03	4.74	5.15	.53
1995	Lake Elsinore	Calif	97.0	140	52	12	25	47	4.82	4	7	12.99	1.11	2.32	4.36	.87
1995	Midland	Texas	12.3	22	12	4	7	5	8.76	0	1	16.05	2.92	5.11	3.65	-.06
1996	Lake Elsinore	Calif	29.7	38	10	0	12	21	3.03	2	1	11.53	.00	3.64	6.37	1.21
1996	Midland	Texas	60.0	76	36	7	32	42	5.40	2	5	11.40	1.05	4.80	6.30	.90

A better pitcher than say, Randy Lerch, Charles Nelson Reilly or Disco Stu. He's been trying to combine decent stuff with control for several years and hasn't succeeded yet. He probably won't.

SHAWN BOSKIE   RBP   1967   Age 30

YR	TEAM	Lge	IP	H	ER	HR	BB	K	ERA	W	L	H/9	HR/9	BB/9	K/9	KW
1993	Iowa	AmA	68.3	71	30	4	28	32	3.95	4	4	9.35	.53	3.69	4.21	.48
1993	Chicago Cubs	NL	63.7	64	27	7	28	37	3.82	4	3	9.05	.99	3.96	5.23	.75
1994	Philadelphia	NL	83.7	85	50	14	37	55	5.38	3	6	9.14	1.51	3.98	5.92	.98
1995	California	AL	112.3	122	58	15	28	51	4.65	5	7	9.77	1.20	2.24	4.09	.80
1996	California	AL	191.3	207	95	34	72	129	4.47	9	12	9.74	1.60	3.39	6.07	1.18

That was a pleasant surprise. Boskie pitched very well all year for the Angels, and basically was a Steve Ontiveros substitute. Looked far better on the mound than in previous years, and seemed to have much more zip on his fastball. Certainly worth keeping and putting in the rotation for next year. Sometimes, the mud sticks to the wall. Expected to sign with the Orioles.

JOSE CINTRON   RSP   1976   Age 21

YR	TEAM	Lge	IP	H	ER	HR	BB	K	ERA	W	L	H/9	HR/9	BB/9	K/9	KW
1994	Boise	Nwern	62.3	97	46	7	28	26	6.64	2	5	14.01	1.01	4.04	3.75	.24
1995	Cedar Rapids	Midw	59.3	84	39	5	14	25	5.92	2	5	12.74	.76	2.12	3.79	.73
1996	Cedar Rapids	Midw	153.7	248	98	20	55	80	5.74	6	11	14.52	1.17	3.22	4.69	.76

Not pitching particularly well yet, but improving each year, hasn't been overworked yet and is supposedly a very bright young man who knows how to pitch. Doesn't strike many guys out yet, but if that K rate can jump about one per nine innings, Cintron could be a real prospect. Dark horse, young enough to break out.

JASON DICKSON   RSP   1973   Age 24

YR	TEAM	Lge	IP	H	ER	HR	BB	K	ERA	W	L	H/9	HR/9	BB/9	K/9	KW
1994	Boise	Nwern	36.3	56	27	4	24	18	6.69	1	3	13.87	.99	5.94	4.46	.00
1995	Cedar Rapids	Midw	153.7	188	71	15	62	87	4.16	8	9	11.01	.88	3.63	5.10	.79
1996	Midland	Texas	51.3	56	22	3	16	33	3.86	3	3	9.82	.53	2.81	5.79	1.23
1996	Vancouver	PCL	120.3	152	73	11	53	58	5.46	5	8	11.37	.82	3.96	4.34	.45
1996	California	AL	44.0	47	16	6	19	19	3.27	3	2	9.61	1.23	3.89	3.89	.32

Young control pitcher; if he's going to be successful in the majors, it could happen now or it could happen six years from now. Not a good candidate for consistent success.

KEN EDENFIELD   RRP   1967   Age 30

YR	TEAM	Lge	IP	H	ER	HR	BB	K	ERA	W	L	H/9	HR/9	BB/9	K/9	KW
1993	Midland	Texas	85.0	97	51	10	51	59	5.40	3	6	10.27	1.06	5.40	6.25	.73
1994	Vancouver	PCL	81.7	69	30	7	45	72	3.31	5	4	7.60	.77	4.96	7.93	1.41
1995	Vancouver	PCL	56.0	63	23	3	33	42	3.70	3	3	10.12	.48	5.30	6.75	.92
1995	California	AL	12.7	15	6	1	5	6	4.26	0	1	10.66	.71	3.55	4.26	.53
1996	Columbus, OH	Inter	39.7	34	9	1	19	23	2.04	3	1	7.71	.23	4.31	5.22	.66
1996	Vancouver	PCL	29.3	30	13	1	24	15	3.99	2	1	9.20	.31	7.36	4.60	-.31

Doing his best to make sure his walk rate and strikeout rate combine to make a constant. Career near its end. Second career, interestingly, is likely to involve karaoke, but I've already told you too much. If I said any more, I'd have to kill you.

MARK EICHHORN   RRP   1961   Age 36

YR	TEAM	Lge	IP	H	ER	HR	BB	K	ERA	W	L	H/9	HR/9	BB/9	K/9	KW
1993	Toronto	AL	71.7	75	21	3	26	48	2.64	6	2	9.42	.38	3.27	6.03	1.19
1994	Baltimore	AL	69.0	61	13	1	21	34	1.70	7	1	7.96	.13	2.74	4.43	.79
1996	Lake Elsinore	Calif	14.0	18	8	1	2	13	5.14	1	1	11.57	.64	1.29	8.36	2.46
1996	California	AL	30.3	34	13	3	12	23	3.86	2	1	10.09	.89	3.56	6.82	1.38

A personal favorite of mine, and should have won the Rookie of the Year award in 1986. His submarine delivery freezes lots of right-handers, but he can get hurt if he leaves a pitch up in the zone. No longer throws hard enough to get the ball past anyone, but can still fool people. Spot reliever versus righties at this point; I'll always be rooting for him.

CHUCK FINLEY　　　**LSP**　　**1963**　**Age 34**

YR	TEAM	Lge	IP	H	ER	HR	BB	K	ERA	W	L	H/9	HR/9	BB/9	K/9	KW
1993	California	AL	248.3	238	86	22	93	192	3.12	17	11	8.63	.80	3.37	6.96	1.48
1994	California	AL	182.0	170	71	19	77	145	3.51	11	9	8.41	.94	3.81	7.17	1.44
1995	California	AL	203.3	188	82	19	97	195	3.63	13	10	8.32	.84	4.29	8.63	1.80
1996	California	AL	238.3	226	90	23	99	208	3.40	15	11	8.53	.87	3.74	7.85	1.68

One of the most underrated players in baseball–Chuck is a very effective and durable starting pitcher who's spent his entire career on teams that hit like Carol Channing. A good bet to maintain his level of performance for some time, and you can also assume that when he pitches, Terry Collins will choose that day to make Jorge Fabregas the DH.

TODD FROHWIRTH　　　**RRP**　　**1963**　**Age 34**

YR	TEAM	Lge	IP	H	ER	HR	BB	K	ERA	W	L	H/9	HR/9	BB/9	K/9	KW
1993	Baltimore	AL	95.3	89	37	7	48	51	3.49	6	5	8.40	.66	4.53	4.81	.47
1994	Pawtucket	Inter	49.7	51	18	5	24	45	3.26	4	2	9.24	.91	4.35	8.15	1.63
1994	Boston	AL	27.3	37	28	3	17	13	9.22	0	3	12.18	.99	5.60	4.28	.03
1995	Buffalo	AmA	30.7	34	13	5	16	29	3.82	2	1	9.98	1.47	4.70	8.51	1.66
1996	Rochester	Inter	15.3	12	7	2	6	13	4.11	1	1	7.04	1.17	3.52	7.63	1.66
1996	Vancouver	PCL	13.0	13	5	2	4	11	3.46	1	0	9.00	1.38	2.77	7.62	1.85

Another submarining right-hander scrambling to find a roster spot somewhere in the bigs. Career is probably over. Strong anti-tobacco advocate back in the '80s, if memory serves. Didn't Todd used to chew dirt soaked in Hawaiian Punch or something? Be the first to e-mail some verification to info@baseballprospectus.com and we'll send you a Baseball Prospectus T-shirt. And no, contrary to the wishes of our clientele, the T-shirt does not come filled with Tiffani-Amber Thiessen.

GREG GOHR　　　**RBP**　　**1968**　**Age 29**

YR	TEAM	Lge	IP	H	ER	HR	BB	K	ERA	W	L	H/9	HR/9	BB/9	K/9	KW
1993	Toledo	Inter	101.3	138	72	16	52	63	6.39	3	8	12.26	1.42	4.62	5.60	.71
1993	Detroit	AL	22.7	26	13	1	15	24	5.16	1	2	10.32	.40	5.96	9.53	1.69
1994	Toledo	Inter	69.3	81	32	7	24	46	4.15	4	4	10.51	.91	3.12	5.97	1.21
1994	Detroit	AL	33.7	35	14	3	22	21	3.74	2	2	9.36	.80	5.88	5.61	.40
1995	Toledo	Inter	14.7	19	10	1	10	13	6.14	1	1	11.66	.61	6.14	7.98	1.12
1995	Detroit	AL	10.0	9	1	0	4	12	.90	1	0	8.10	.00	3.60	10.80	2.70
1996	Toledo	Inter	11.7	17	8	1	6	12	6.17	0	1	13.11	.77	4.63	9.26	1.93
1996	California	AL	24.3	31	15	6	11	15	5.55	1	2	11.47	2.22	4.07	5.55	.83
1996	Detroit	AL	94.0	116	57	20	36	58	5.46	3	7	11.11	1.91	3.45	5.55	.99

Toledo. Detroit. Toledo. Detroit. Toledo. Detroit. If a guy doesn't pitch well enough to hang on as a mopup guy for the Tigers, who jumped at the chance to grab Todd Van Poppel off the waiver wire, you probably don't want him on your team. I saw Gary DiSarcina actually salivate in the on-deck circle with Gohr pitching. Dreadful.

JASON GRIMSLEY　　　**RBP**　　**1968**　**Age 29**

YR	TEAM	Lge	IP	H	ER	HR	BB	K	ERA	W	L	H/9	HR/9	BB/9	K/9	KW
1993	Charlotte, NC	Inter	126.7	154	63	10	67	83	4.48	6	8	10.94	.71	4.76	5.90	.78
1993	Cleveland	AL	42.3	53	23	3	23	28	4.89	2	3	11.27	.64	4.89	5.95	.76
1994	Charlotte, NC	Inter	66.7	65	34	10	23	50	4.59	3	4	8.78	1.35	3.11	6.75	1.47
1994	Cleveland	AL	82.7	85	34	6	37	58	3.70	5	4	9.25	.65	4.03	6.31	1.10
1995	Buffalo	AmA	64.3	68	25	4	27	35	3.50	4	3	9.51	.56	3.78	4.90	.69
1995	Cleveland	AL	34.7	36	19	4	33	25	4.93	2	2	9.35	1.04	8.57	6.49	.02
1996	Vancouver	PCL	14.0	10	2	0	4	9	1.29	2	0	6.43	.00	2.57	5.79	1.29
1996	California	AL	130.7	140	83	12	77	79	5.72	5	10	9.64	.83	5.30	5.44	.49

There's a theme throughout this book when it comes to marginal pitchers, particularly ones who throw hard: If this guy can eliminate one walk per nine innings, he'll be good. So it goes with Jason, who actually had some pretty good outings this year. He's going to have to get lucky to have a career now, but he could put together a couple of valuable years. Don't count him completely out. And yet, there's something oddly karmic about writing "BP" after his name.

RYAN HANCOCK **RBP** **1972** **Age 25**

YR	TEAM	Lge	IP	H	ER	HR	BB	K	ERA	W	L	H/9	HR/9	BB/9	K/9	KW
1993	Boise	Nwern	14.0	19	9	1	8	10	5.79	1	1	12.21	.64	5.14	6.43	.86
1994	Lake Elsinore	Calif	104.0	131	59	11	47	62	5.11	5	7	11.34	.95	4.07	5.37	.77
1994	Midland	Texas	44.3	66	31	2	16	25	6.29	1	4	13.40	.41	3.25	5.08	.88
1995	Midland	Texas	162.0	208	87	18	61	66	4.83	7	11	11.56	1.00	3.39	3.67	.37
1996	Vancouver	PCL	75.0	77	36	8	47	54	4.32	4	4	9.24	.96	5.64	6.48	.75
1996	California	AL	28.0	32	18	2	17	18	5.79	1	2	10.29	.64	5.46	5.79	.56

He hasn't adjusted real well as he's moved up in the organization. For hitters, that's troubling; for pitchers, it doesn't really tell you much. Hancock's not a major prospect. One guy out of 100 like this will turn into Bob Tewksbury. The other 99 utilize handy phrases like "Price Check on Jumbo Depends...."

HEATH HAYNES **RRP** **1969** **Age 28**

YR	TEAM	Lge	IP	H	ER	HR	BB	K	ERA	W	L	H/9	HR/9	BB/9	K/9	KW
1993	Harrisburg	East	60.7	56	25	2	26	59	3.71	4	3	8.31	.30	3.86	8.75	1.95
1994	Ottawa	Inter	82.0	83	31	8	22	63	3.40	5	4	9.11	.88	2.41	6.91	1.70
1996	Lake Elsinore	Calif	35.0	36	7	1	2	28	1.80	3	1	9.26	.26	.51	7.20	2.27

This guy can pitch. He has always been able to pitch. He doesn't have the great stuff he had before his unplanned hiatus, but he's already a quality reliever. The Angels have a lot of bullpen depth, and Haynes only adds to it. Could be a real boon if he gets called up mid-season. Sometimes, a strong bullpen is enough to overcome the DiSarcinas and Fabregases of the world. Usually not, but sometimes.

MIKE HOLTZ **LRP** **1973** **Age 24**

YR	TEAM	Lge	IP	H	ER	HR	BB	K	ERA	W	L	H/9	HR/9	BB/9	K/9	KW
1994	Boise	Nwern	30.3	32	4	0	15	29	1.19	3	0	9.49	.00	4.45	8.60	1.76
1995	Lake Elsinore	Calif	73.0	87	26	8	31	65	3.21	5	3	10.73	.99	3.82	8.01	1.72
1996	Midland	Texas	38.7	50	28	6	14	33	6.52	1	3	11.64	1.40	3.26	7.68	1.75
1996	California	AL	28.7	21	7	1	20	30	2.20	2	1	6.59	.31	6.28	9.42	1.57

More bullpen depth. A quality reliever right now, and likely to get better. Holtz throws a heavy ball and knows how to pitch. Outside of this organization, an excellent closer prospect, despite the suspect control.

MIKE JAMES **RRP** **1968** **Age 29**

YR	TEAM	Lge	IP	H	ER	HR	BB	K	ERA	W	L	H/9	HR/9	BB/9	K/9	KW
1993	Vero Beach	Flor	53.0	62	39	4	43	47	6.62	2	4	10.53	.68	7.30	7.98	.83
1993	Albuquerque	PCL	29.0	32	19	5	22	25	5.90	1	2	9.93	1.55	6.83	7.76	.88
1994	Vancouver	PCL	85.7	98	45	14	43	57	4.73	4	6	10.30	1.47	4.52	5.99	.87
1995	California	AL	55.3	48	21	6	28	36	3.42	3	3	7.81	.98	4.55	5.86	.81
1996	California	AL	79.7	61	19	6	44	63	2.15	7	2	6.89	.68	4.97	7.12	1.13

Skinnier than my right thigh. Rescued from the Dodger chain, he's found enough control to make him effective in the majors. One of these pitchers who really has a hard time against guys that draw a walk and just owns the Ruben Sierras of the world. That may sound tautological, but it really plays out. I've always thought that platooning the type of pitcher against the type of hitter could be even more effective than normal platooning.

MARK LANGSTON **LSP** **1961** **Age 36**

YR	TEAM	Lge	IP	H	ER	HR	BB	K	ERA	W	L	H/9	HR/9	BB/9	K/9	KW
1993	California	AL	251.7	218	78	23	97	201	2.79	19	9	7.80	.82	3.47	7.19	1.53
1994	California	AL	119.3	114	51	17	58	107	3.85	7	6	8.60	1.28	4.37	8.07	1.60
1995	California	AL	200.3	207	86	20	68	142	3.86	11	11	9.30	.90	3.05	6.38	1.36
1996	California	AL	122.7	110	50	15	48	80	3.67	8	6	8.07	1.10	3.52	5.87	1.08

Basically the same pitcher as Chuck Finley, with ever so slightly less durability. Should not be allowed to pitch to Jose Canseco. His K rate took a notable downturn last year, so don't be stunned if he falls off a cliff in 1997.

PHIL LEFTWICH   **RSP**   **1969**   **Age 28**

YR	TEAM	Lge	IP	H	ER	HR	BB	K	ERA	W	L	H/9	HR/9	BB/9	K/9	KW
1993	Vancouver	PCL	115.0	147	68	10	59	83	5.32	5	8	11.50	.78	4.62	6.50	1.01
1993	California	AL	79.3	80	28	5	30	32	3.18	6	3	9.08	.57	3.40	3.63	.36
1994	California	AL	114.0	119	57	14	46	66	4.50	6	7	9.39	1.11	3.63	5.21	.83
1995	Vancouver	PCL	33.7	33	12	5	13	24	3.21	2	2	8.82	1.34	3.48	6.42	1.27
1996	Midland	Texas	37.3	35	12	4	8	27	2.89	3	1	8.44	.96	1.93	6.51	1.69
1996	Vancouver	PCL	102.7	126	74	16	53	73	6.49	3	8	11.05	1.40	4.65	6.40	.97

Crap shoot. Some days, he's working spots and no one can hit him. Most days, he struggles a bit. His control went south last year, and without that he's selling cars somewhere.

DARRELL MAY   **LBP**   **1972**   **Age 25**

YR	TEAM	Lge	IP	H	ER	HR	BB	K	ERA	W	L	H/9	HR/9	BB/9	K/9	KW
1993	Macon	S Atl	91.3	110	33	9	32	65	3.25	6	4	10.84	.89	3.15	6.41	1.35
1993	Durham	Caro	45.7	53	19	4	25	29	3.74	3	2	10.45	.79	4.93	5.72	.67
1994	Durham	Caro	68.7	85	27	5	25	49	3.54	4	4	11.14	.66	3.28	6.42	1.32
1994	Greenville	South	57.7	73	28	5	26	33	4.37	3	3	11.39	.78	4.06	5.15	.70
1995	Greenville	South	83.7	94	43	18	29	60	4.63	4	5	10.11	1.94	3.12	6.45	1.37
1995	Richmond	Inter	47.7	62	22	1	23	36	4.15	2	3	11.71	.19	4.34	6.80	1.18
1996	Calgary	PCL	124.0	144	53	17	48	61	3.85	7	7	10.45	1.23	3.48	4.43	.60

May has consistently pitched well enough to earn a serious major league trial, and with Terry Collins and his new regime coming in, he just might get it. I really like this guy, despite all the obvious problems in his statistical record. I think that Earl Weaver could make him a mighty valuable pitcher. I don't know if Terry Collins is up to that task. Will probably start the year in AAA.

CHUCK McELROY   **LRP**   **1968**   **Age 29**

YR	TEAM	Lge	IP	H	ER	HR	BB	K	ERA	W	L	H/9	HR/9	BB/9	K/9	KW
1993	Iowa	AmA	15.3	19	9	1	11	12	5.28	1	1	11.15	.59	6.46	7.04	.73
1993	Chicago Cubs	NL	46.7	51	27	5	31	30	5.21	2	3	9.84	.96	5.98	5.79	.43
1994	Cincinnati	NL	56.0	53	13	3	20	35	2.09	5	1	8.52	.48	3.21	5.62	1.07
1995	Cincinnati	NL	40.0	47	26	5	18	24	5.85	1	3	10.57	1.12	4.05	5.40	.79
1996	Indianapolis	AmA	12.7	13	4	0	5	8	2.84	1	0	9.24	.00	3.55	5.68	1.01
1996	California	AL	36.0	31	8	2	14	31	2.00	3	1	7.75	.50	3.50	7.75	1.71
1996	Cincinnati	NL	12.3	13	8	2	11	11	5.84	0	1	9.49	1.46	8.03	8.03	.67

Hard throwing left-hander who likes to work high in the strike zone. On days when he's got his good stuff, that's a winning strategy. On days when he doesn't, it's blunt trauma wounds to bleacher dwellers. McElroy had trouble making the adjustment to the American League, where the strike zones are short and fat. Will struggle early in the year, and will be pitching well by the end of it, if management has patience.

RICH MONTELEONE   **RRP**   **1963**   **Age 34**

YR	TEAM	Lge	IP	H	ER	HR	BB	K	ERA	W	L	H/9	HR/9	BB/9	K/9	KW
1993	NY Yankees	AL	85.3	86	46	15	40	52	4.85	4	5	9.07	1.58	4.22	5.48	.77
1994	San Francisco	NL	44.3	43	16	6	17	15	3.25	3	2	8.73	1.22	3.45	3.05	.15
1995	Vancouver	PCL	15.3	22	7	2	4	7	4.11	1	1	12.91	1.17	2.35	4.11	.78
1996	Columbus, OH	Inter	33.7	42	14	1	11	17	3.74	2	2	11.23	.27	2.94	4.54	.78
1996	California	AL	15.3	21	8	4	3	5	4.70	1	1	12.33	2.35	1.76	2.93	.54

Rich is at the point now where he doesn't even unpack his bags. Shows flashes of brilliance, but the interval between those flashes seems to grow longer with each passing day. Indistinguishable from a hundred other guys fighting for the #9 and #10 spots on a pitching staff.

RAFAEL NOVOA   **LRP**   **1968**   **Age 29**

YR	TEAM	Lge	IP	H	ER	HR	BB	K	ERA	W	L	H/9	HR/9	BB/9	K/9	KW
1993	New Orleans	AmA	108.0	111	51	20	49	68	4.25	6	6	9.25	1.67	4.08	5.67	.87
1993	Milwaukee	AL	55.3	58	27	7	25	18	4.39	3	3	9.43	1.14	4.07	2.93	-.04
1994	Iowa	AmA	131.7	153	79	12	81	48	5.40	5	10	10.46	.82	5.54	3.28	-.29
1996	Lake Elsinore	Calif	24.0	32	12	6	14	20	4.50	1	2	12.00	2.25	5.25	7.50	1.19
1996	Midland	Texas	22.3	27	17	0	16	13	6.85	1	1	10.88	.00	6.45	5.24	.13
1996	Vancouver	PCL	12.7	19	9	4	6	8	6.39	0	1	13.50	2.84	4.26	5.68	.83

Often strikes out even more guys than he walks. But not always. Has never once been caught rolling nude in a Sizzler salad bar, to the best of my knowledge.

STEVE ONTIVEROS RSP 1961 Age 36

YR	TEAM	Lge	IP	H	ER	HR	BB	K	ERA	W	L	H/9	HR/9	BB/9	K/9	KW
1993	Portland, OR	PCL	94.7	96	34	6	28	59	3.23	7	4	9.13	.57	2.66	5.61	1.20
1993	Seattle	AL	17.7	18	2	0	7	13	1.02	2	0	9.17	.00	3.57	6.62	1.32
1994	Oakland	AL	112.0	97	30	7	30	55	2.41	9	3	7.79	.56	2.41	4.42	.87
1995	Oakland	AL	129.3	146	62	11	41	78	4.31	6	8	10.16	.77	2.85	5.43	1.10

A master illusionist; throws his fastball about 80 mph, and the m stands for meters. Nonetheless, when he's healthy he's an excellent pitcher for six or seven innings. Of course, he's only healthy 40% of the time, and since he can't bounce back quickly after throwing, you can only use him in the rotation. And it's hard to put a guy in the rotation when you know he's going to be out at least half the time. Difficult but tempting pitcher. I know it's difficult, but think of Steve as the Anna Nicole Smith of starting pitchers. But without the goatee.

BRAD PENNINGTON LRP 1969 Age 28

YR	TEAM	Lge	IP	H	ER	HR	BB	K	ERA	W	L	H/9	HR/9	BB/9	K/9	KW
1993	Rochester	Inter	15.0	13	10	0	15	15	6.00	1	1	7.80	.00	9.00	9.00	.75
1993	Baltimore	AL	33.3	32	20	7	27	40	5.40	1	3	8.64	1.89	7.29	10.80	1.78
1994	Rochester	Inter	81.0	74	54	10	86	74	6.00	3	6	8.22	1.11	9.56	8.22	.35
1995	Indianapolis	AmA	14.0	17	17	3	24	10	10.93	0	2	10.93	1.93	15.43	6.43	-1.71
1996	Vancouver	PCL	25.7	23	19	3	26	36	6.66	1	2	8.06	1.05	9.12	12.62	1.93
1996	Boston	AL	12.3	6	3	1	15	12	2.19	1	0	4.38	.73	10.95	8.76	.18

When people see Brad Pennington, they don't see him properly. He is, in fact, just a plain old bad pitcher who throws hard. And yet, one team's scout always sees him throw two strikes in a row, and is arrogant enough to think that his organization can turn him into…

TROY PERCIVAL RRP 1970 Age 27

YR	TEAM	Lge	IP	H	ER	HR	BB	K	ERA	W	L	H/9	HR/9	BB/9	K/9	KW
1993	Vancouver	PCL	17.3	24	12	0	16	16	6.23	1	1	12.46	.00	8.31	8.31	.69
1994	Vancouver	PCL	57.3	61	24	4	36	63	3.77	3	3	9.58	.63	5.65	9.89	1.88
1995	California	AL	72.3	40	12	7	27	94	1.49	7	1	4.98	.87	3.36	11.70	3.06
1996	California	AL	72.3	39	12	8	33	97	1.49	7	1	4.85	1.00	4.11	12.07	3.00

The best pitcher in baseball, bar none. Throws hard, works quickly and people just can't catch up to it. A catcher to pitcher conversion that worked beyond anyone's wildest dreams, and he didn't even have to go to Sweden.

JOE ROSSELLI LRP 1972 Age 25

YR	TEAM	Lge	IP	H	ER	HR	BB	K	ERA	W	L	H/9	HR/9	BB/9	K/9	KW
1993	Shreveport	Texas	20.7	27	10	1	11	14	4.35	1	1	11.76	.44	4.79	6.10	.83
1994	Shreveport	Texas	82.0	81	24	3	26	39	2.63	6	3	8.89	.33	2.85	4.28	.71
1994	Phoenix	PCL	70.3	91	36	9	22	30	4.61	3	5	11.64	1.15	2.82	3.84	.58
1995	Phoenix	PCL	75.0	91	38	9	19	31	4.56	3	5	10.92	1.08	2.28	3.72	.67
1995	San Francisco	NL	30.3	41	27	5	23	6	8.01	1	2	12.16	1.48	6.82	1.78	-1.11
1996	Vancouver	PCL	54.3	60	21	4	32	31	3.48	3	3	9.94	.66	5.30	5.13	.39

Might as well be throwing underhand; there might be a softer tosser who doesn't throw a knuckler, but I've never seen him. No prospect, so he'll be in the Detroit rotation by May.

DENNIS SPRINGER RSP 1965 Age 32

YR	TEAM	Lge	IP	H	ER	HR	BB	K	ERA	W	L	H/9	HR/9	BB/9	K/9	KW
1993	Albuquerque	PCL	121.3	152	75	17	51	54	5.56	4	9	11.27	1.26	3.78	4.01	.39
1994	Reading	East	124.0	139	69	12	59	85	5.01	5	9	10.09	.87	4.28	6.17	.99
1995	Scranton-WB	Inter	159.0	180	98	21	68	97	5.55	6	12	10.19	1.19	3.85	5.49	.87
1995	Philadelphia	NL	22.0	20	12	3	11	13	4.91	1	1	8.18	1.23	4.50	5.32	.65
1996	Vancouver	PCL	102.3	99	33	11	47	65	2.90	7	4	8.71	.97	4.13	5.72	.87
1996	California	AL	95.0	84	49	21	45	62	4.64	5	6	7.96	1.99	4.26	5.87	.89

His career might just be beginning; throws two different and distinct knuckleballs. For purposes of future performance, there is no difference between Dennis Springer and Tim Wakefield. I'd like to have him on a staff for one simple reason: knuckleballs can generally work big workloads without devastating side effects. This gives you some flexibility in terms of working with your other starters.

PAUL SWINGLE   **RRP**   **1967**   **Age 30**

YR	TEAM	Lge	IP	H	ER	HR	BB	K	ERA	W	L	H/9	HR/9	BB/9	K/9	KW
1993	Vancouver	PCL	62.7	87	54	5	41	50	7.76	1	6	12.49	.72	5.89	7.18	.92
1993	California	AL	43.0	41	20	7	17	42	4.19	2	3	8.58	1.47	3.56	8.79	2.04
1995	New Orleans	AmA	41.3	45	24	7	20	36	5.23	2	3	9.80	1.52	4.35	7.84	1.52
1996	Vancouver	PCL	22.3	23	10	1	14	20	4.03	1	1	9.27	.40	5.64	8.06	1.28

He's earned at least a shot. If someone has an arm this good, and they haven't completely stunk up the joint in the minors, they deserve at least a shot with the big league team. Unfortunately for Paul, the Angels have an amazing amount of bullpen depth. He'll have to move on in order to really get a shot.

Player	Age	Team	Lge	AB	H	DB	TP	HR	BB	SB	CS	OUT	BA	OBA	SA	EQA	EQR	Peak
EDGAR ALFONZO	29	Midland	Texas	307	70	12	1	4	23	1	1	238	.228	.282	.313	.196	20	.194
JUSTIN BAUGHMAN	21	Cedar Rapids	Midw	475	104	11	3	6	33	23	9	380	.219	.270	.293	.191	30	.214
RANDY BETTEN	24	Lake Elsinore	Calif	276	63	11	2	2	15	5	2	215	.228	.268	.304	.190	17	.202
TYRONE BOYKIN	28	Midland	Texas	129	28	6	0	5	31	0	1	102	.217	.369	.380	.250	16	.253
JAMIE BURKE	24	Midland	Texas	143	39	4	1	2	18	1	1	105	.273	.354	.357	.242	15	.260
	24	Vancouver	PCL	158	39	2	0	2	8	2	1	120	.247	.283	.297	.193	10	.208
JOVINO CARVAJAL	27	Midland	Texas	158	34	2	1	2	10	5	3	127	.215	.262	.278	.177	8	.183
	27	Vancouver	PCL	276	66	4	1	5	15	15	5	215	.239	.278	.315	.205	20	.210
EDDIE CHRISTIAN	24	Midland	Texas	422	108	19	2	5	34	5	4	318	.256	.311	.346	.221	36	.236
JED DALTON	23	Cedar Rapids	Midw	310	77	6	1	10	16	10	4	237	.248	.285	.371	.222	27	.241
	23	Lake Elsinore	Calif	122	27	2	1	1	8	3	1	96	.221	.269	.279	.182	7	.197
DAVID DAVALILLO	21	Cedar Rapids	Midw	385	89	8	0	5	20	2	3	299	.231	.269	.291	.181	21	.203
	21	Midland	Texas	81	11	1	0	0	4	1	0	70	.136	.176	.148	-.103	-1	-.107
FREDDY DIAZ	23	Midland	Texas	155	25	3	1	3	13	1	1	131	.161	.226	.252	.137	5	.151
	23	Vancouver	PCL	126	34	9	1	3	14	0	0	92	.270	.343	.429	.257	15	.279
TRENT DURRINGTON	20	Cedar Rapids	Midw	82	19	0	0	0	27	7	1	64	.232	.422	.232	.252	10	.288
PAUL FAILLA	23	Lake Elsinore	Calif	290	51	8	2	1	39	6	4	243	.176	.274	.228	.157	12	.171
P.J. FORBES	28	Vancouver	PCL	420	116	20	2	1	41	4	2	306	.276	.341	.340	.233	40	.235
LEON GLENN	26	Midland	Texas	317	56	7	1	8	22	6	5	266	.177	.230	.281	.157	13	.163
BRIAN GREBECK	28	Vancouver	PCL	244	58	8	2	2	33	1	1	187	.238	.329	.311	.216	20	.218
AARON GUIEL	23	Midland	Texas	438	100	18	3	9	50	8	4	342	.228	.307	.345	.219	38	.238
BRET HEMPHILL	24	Lake Elsinore	Calif	403	93	13	1	13	40	2	1	311	.231	.300	.365	.221	36	.237
JACK HOWELL	34	California	AL	126	34	5	1	8	10	0	1	93	.270	.324	.516	.269	17	.256
NORM HUTCHINS	20	Cedar Rapids	Midw	474	93	11	8	3	19	10	4	385	.196	.227	.272	.156	19	.178
RYAN KANE	22	Cedar Rapids	Midw	495	111	13	0	13	29	3	2	386	.224	.267	.329	.196	33	.216
AARON LEDESMA	25	Vancouver	PCL	450	137	25	3	2	33	2	2	315	.304	.352	.387	.251	50	.265
KEITH LUULOA	21	Midland	Texas	527	113	14	1	6	44	3	3	417	.214	.275	.279	.179	28	.200
JOHN MCANINCH	22	Cedar Rapids	Midw	304	66	7	1	8	14	0	1	239	.217	.252	.326	.186	18	.206
TONY MOEDER	24	Lake Elsinore	Calif	341	92	11	1	11	28	2	1	250	.270	.325	.405	.245	37	.262
	24	Midland	Texas	85	17	1	0	4	11	0	0	68	.200	.292	.353	.212	7	.226
BEN MOLINA	21	Midland	Texas	361	83	12	1	7	24	0	0	278	.230	.278	.327	.199	25	.223
BO ORTIZ	26	Midland	Texas	501	126	19	3	9	31	8	4	379	.251	.295	.355	.218	42	.227
GREG SHOCKEY	26	Midland	Texas	324	88	17	2	7	42	2	1	237	.272	.355	.401	.255	39	.266
CHRIS SMITH	22	Lake Elsinore	Calif	243	57	7	0	8	17	1	0	186	.235	.285	.362	.215	20	.237
TODD TAKAYOSHI	25	Lake Elsinore	Calif	315	85	9	0	9	58	0	0	230	.270	.383	.384	.262	40	.277
CHRIS TURNER	27	Vancouver	PCL	403	105	15	1	3	59	1	2	300	.261	.355	.325	.232	39	.238
JOE URSO	25	Lake Elsinore	Calif	479	122	26	2	8	58	3	1	358	.255	.335	.367	.238	49	.251
TY VAN BURKLEO	32	Lake Elsinore	Calif	206	59	8	1	11	46	2	1	148	.286	.417	.495	.302	37	.287
JON VANDERGRIEND	24	Cedar Rapids	Midw	446	106	13	1	16	39	5	3	343	.238	.298	.379	.225	41	.241
KEVIN YOUNG	24	Lake Elsinore	Calif	465	114	13	1	2	37	11	6	357	.245	.301	.290	.200	32	.214

Player	Age	Team	Lge	IP	H	ER	HR	BB	K	ERA	W	L	H/9	HR/9	BB/9	K/9	KW
STEVENSON AGOSTO	20	Cedar Rapids	Midw	134.3	181	99	16	111	76	6.63	4	11	12.13	1.07	7.44	5.09	-.16
MATT BEAUMONT	23	Midland	Texas	150.0	191	102	18	93	107	6.12	5	12	11.46	1.08	5.58	6.42	.74
CARLOS CASTILLO	25	Lake Elsinore	Calif	26.3	30	13	2	10	17	4.44	1	2	10.25	.68	3.42	5.81	1.08
	25	Midland	Texas	35.0	36	16	4	26	12	4.11	2	2	9.26	1.03	6.69	3.09	-.64
TONY CHAVEZ	25	Midland	Texas	67.3	80	33	4	33	45	4.41	3	4	10.69	.53	4.41	6.01	.90
BRIAN COOPER	21	Lake Elsinore	Calif	146.0	202	90	17	46	98	5.55	5	11	12.45	1.05	2.84	6.04	1.30
JOSH DEAKMAN	22	Lake Elsinore	Calif	145.7	209	97	16	66	73	5.99	5	11	12.91	.99	4.08	4.51	.48
JON DECLUE	25	Midland	Texas	103.3	133	69	10	66	62	6.01	3	8	11.58	.87	5.75	5.40	.36
GEOFF EDSELL	24	Midland	Texas	81.0	82	44	9	60	49	4.89	4	5	9.11	1.00	6.67	5.44	.15
	24	Vancouver	PCL	98.0	103	43	8	56	40	3.95	6	5	9.46	.73	5.14	3.67	-.06
ROBERT ELLIS	25	Vancouver	PCL	40.7	35	18	3	34	24	3.98	3	2	7.75	.66	7.52	5.31	-.11
MIKE FREEHILL	25	Midland	Texas	46.0	49	21	4	27	39	4.11	2	3	9.59	.78	5.28	7.63	1.22
PEP HARRIS	23	California	AL	32.3	29	12	4	17	19	3.34	2	2	8.07	1.11	4.73	5.29	.58
	23	Midland	Texas	36.3	46	22	2	14	23	5.45	1	3	11.39	.50	3.47	5.70	1.03
	23	Vancouver	PCL	110.0	149	66	14	59	51	5.40	4	8	12.19	1.15	4.83	4.17	.18
JASON HILL	24	Cedar Rapids	Midw	37.0	48	21	3	40	16	5.11	2	2	11.68	.73	9.73	3.89	-1.14
	24	Lake Elsinore	Calif	35.3	45	15	4	16	18	3.82	2	2	11.46	1.02	4.08	4.58	.51
MARK HOLZEMER	26	California	AL	25.7	31	20	6	8	19	7.01	1	2	10.87	2.10	2.81	6.66	1.52
PETE JANICKI	25	Midland	Texas	28.3	37	23	3	14	14	7.31	1	2	11.75	.95	4.45	4.45	.37
	25	Vancouver	PCL	98.0	146	79	17	49	72	7.26	3	8	13.41	1.56	4.50	6.61	1.08
JOHN LLOYD	22	Cedar Rapids	Midw	85.0	123	67	16	74	40	7.09	2	7	13.02	1.69	7.84	4.24	-.55
MATT PERISHO	21	Lake Elsinore	Calif	114.3	147	64	9	68	61	5.04	5	8	11.57	.71	5.35	4.80	.26
	21	Midland	Texas	49.3	48	18	4	27	41	3.28	3	2	8.76	.73	4.93	7.48	1.26
JEFF SCHMIDT	25	Vancouver	PCL	35.0	33	11	0	30	16	2.83	3	1	8.49	.00	7.71	4.11	-.56
SCOTT SCHOENEWEIS	22	Lake Elsinore	Calif	84.7	99	41	6	31	53	4.36	4	5	10.52	.64	3.30	5.63	1.05
BRIAN SCUTERO	22	Cedar Rapids	Midw	74.7	98	42	11	55	33	5.06	3	5	11.81	1.33	6.63	3.98	-.33
KYLE SEBACH	24	Lake Elsinore	Calif	98.7	140	65	15	36	66	5.93	3	8	12.77	1.37	3.28	6.02	1.19
NICK SKUSE	24	Cedar Rapids	Midw	81.0	99	52	13	74	31	5.78	3	6	11.00	1.44	8.22	3.44	-.91
TRAVIS THURMOND	22	Cedar Rapids	Midw	25.0	27	7	2	18	18	2.52	2	1	9.72	.72	6.48	6.48	.54
	22	Lake Elsinore	Calif	32.7	41	16	4	20	25	4.41	2	2	11.30	1.10	5.51	6.89	.92
BEN VANRYN	24	Vancouver	PCL	32.3	39	17	3	17	23	4.73	2	2	10.86	.84	4.73	6.40	.95
GRANT VERMILLION	24	Cedar Rapids	Midw	52.3	75	37	6	41	34	6.36	2	4	12.90	1.03	7.05	5.85	.19
JARROD WASHBURN	21	Lake Elsinore	Calif	84.0	91	33	5	38	59	3.54	5	4	9.75	.54	4.07	6.32	1.09
	21	Midland	Texas	81.0	79	37	10	35	47	4.11	4	5	8.78	1.11	3.89	5.22	.77
SHAD WILLIAMS	25	California	AL	29.0	38	25	6	22	25	7.76	1	2	11.79	1.86	6.83	7.76	.88
	25	Vancouver	PCL	69.3	83	36	9	36	48	4.67	3	5	10.77	1.17	4.67	6.23	.91

Oakland A's

Last season, the A's bit the bullet and started over. The timing of the changes on the field was directly related to a number of good-byes off of it: the death of owner Walter Haas, and the subsequent, relatively unmourned departure of manager Tony LaRussa, whose assumption of more and more responsibility for personnel moves contributed greatly to the dismal performances of '93, '94, and '95.

With his personal loyalty to Haas no longer an issue upon the owner's death, Tony LaRussa left town, taking away with him many of the overvalued veterans that had generated so many unrealistic expectations and unjustified reputations. This led to quick predictions that the A's franchise was doomed to a return of the miseries of the late '70s, when their last "dynasty" had fizzled out in the wake of free agency and universal disgust with Charlie Finley's panache. Always willing to inflate the reputation of LaRussa, an overwhelming majority of commentators condemned the A's franchise as incapable of rising to the heights to which he had led them, and bereft of his inspiring leadership, doomed to total collapse. In forecasting the '96 season of the A's, 110 losses came up a lot.

As is often the case with preseason judgments based on exaggerated reputations, the A's disappointed those who had left them for dead in February. The reasons were straightforward enough: whatever courtiers like Tom Boswell or George Will might say, the Oakland A's that arose from the ashes of Finley's self-immolation and the false promise of Billyball weren't the "LaRussa A's," they were the product of the hard work of an organization, starting with Sandy Alderson and organizational soldiers like Walt Jocketty and Ron Schueler (long since graduated to GM jobs elsewhere), on down to scouts and coaches who rebuilt a farm system that through Finley's penury resembled a vacant lot. Sandy Alderson, reappointed team president after the '96 season, is the rock of the franchise, even though for years he has been overshadowed by the never-ending "LaRussa for genius" campaign.

Freed from LaRussa's public dominance, Alderson moved with the same decisiveness that brought the A's out of the Age of Chris Codiroli into respectability in the first place. He dumped his old manager's favorites, and the overpriced, over-30 talent. Famous "stars" like Todd Stottlemyre, Dennis Eckersley, Danny Tartabull, Rick Honeycutt, Mike Gallego and Ron Darling were shown the door, years late in some cases. What the mainstream media missed was that these players weren't only easily replaceable, they'd been downright lousy. Improvement wasn't merely possible, it was pretty likely. With the addition of a patient, successful and available Art Howe to ride through the bumps of recovery as he

had in Houston, the Oakland A's were in great shape to start sorting through what was left, taking a good look at their upper level minor league talent while hoping for the best from veterans like McGwire, Bordick and Steinbach. Change came, and the A's learned a lot about what their future might look like.

First, they learned who's still able to contribute to the team's future, and who isn't. Mark McGwire showed that his remarkable '95 season was no fluke, and that he has indeed become an even more dangerous hitter than he was in his youth. Terry Steinbach gave them a final season that made a dandy parting gift prior to his expected departure as a free agent. Younger players like Jason Giambi and Ernie Young proved they belong, receiving their major chances in '96 after rotten handling in LaRussa's hands in past seasons.

What is important to stress about these players, however, is that they aren't really that young, and neither are many of the "new" players in this first year of honest rebuilding. Giambi, Young, Scott Brosius, Bill Taylor, Mike Mohler, George Williams...even Damon Mashore or Brian Lesher; not only is the future now for these guys, but none of them are especially young or likely to be the foundations of the A's three years from now. In 1996, these players were important elements in showing that there is life after LaRussa, but the chance that any of them will be significant parts of a rosy A's future is doubtful. However, the foundation of the next great A's team has already been drafted. Before Alderson locks up the current crop of major league talent to multi-year contracts (especially Mike Bordick), he'll hopefully realize that the team's future will depend on what Ben Grieve, Miguel Tejada, David Newhan and Scott Spiezio can do, not only four years from now, but within the next two years.

Second, the future probably won't be in Oakland. One of the major stories of the '96 season in the East Bay was the "remodeling" of the Coliseum that made a travesty of much of the season. The team had to accept construction during games as local government made a relatively pleasant bowl into a football mausoleum dedicated to the greater glory of Al Davis' insatiable, predatory greed. The mayor of Sacramento, in discussing his city's stadium plans, has already made it clear that his target is to land the A's. Other locations around Northern California, aware that the A's can escape from their lease in Oakland easily enough in the near future, are dusting off plans to bring the A's to their town. The new owners, some of the few wealthy men left in Northern California still willing to take the plunge and buy into baseball, seem wet behind the ears. They make the occasional silly public statement, but seem willing to let their baseball people drive the bus.

As for media "analysis" of the A's "surprising" success, rather than learning a lesson from their ludicrous 110-loss projections, they're now clamoring for the A's to add valuable veterans like Kirt Manwaring or Tom Goodwin, either of whom would be a step down from suiting up a roadside squeegee beggar.

What will be especially critical in the next year will be the ability of Art Howe, Sandy Alderson, and Bob Cluck to sort through the A's various pitching options. In '96, they showed admirable courage in starting the season with a rotation of Reyes, Johns, Prieto, Wojciechowski and Van Poppel. Unfortunately, like many organizations with several "options" and no established pitchers, they lost their patience quickly with their struggling young starters. This isn't a recent development: Sandy Alderson was around to lose patience with a young Jose Rijo, and the A's track record in developing young starters (since Curt Young, of all people) has been absolutely abominable. There is one thing that bugs me about Art Howe's handling of the staff: he seemed to blow quality starts away by trying to stretch a good outing by a starter into one extra inning. Since I don't have the boxscores for the entire season handy, it's a gut-level guess, but something that bears watching.

Times are a-changin' in the A's farm system. For years, the A's would push their prospects up the chain slowly, and would favor drafting college talent, which seemed to reinforce two common perceptions of the A's farm system: the tendency of A's minor league offenses to draw plenty of walks, and the high number of injuries among their pitchers.

In recent years, the A's have shown they aren't afraid to take risks with their higher draft choices (like Todd Van Poppel, Ariel Prieto or Eric Chavez), even having outstanding prospects like Miguel Tejada skip levels in consecutive years, or pushing Ben Grieve up the ladder quickly. They still generally draft solid talent rather than "tools" players with high potential upsides (or more usually, disastrous downsides). Those few "tool" types they draft seem to have washed out very quickly, such as Benji Grigsby or Gary Hust. This approach leads to winning minor league teams remarkable for their balance, but it also hasn't produced multiple superstars. With the recent selections or development of Grieve, Chavez and Tejada, that may soon change. Overall, the organization is deep in middle infielders and catchers, and has a solid group of young right-handed pitchers.

As an organization, the A's seem to suffer more than their fair share of injuries to young pitchers. Despite asking for nothing approaching the workloads of Mets minor league pitchers, injuries to minor league pitchers had become so numerous that the A's have begun a few innovations in pitcher usage at the lower levels. Some critics of minor league development (Johnny Sain, for example) have pointed out that the five-man rotation can be a bad thing for developing arms; however, the dangers of racking up big pitch counts could be made worse in four-man rotations. The A's began trying a new method aimed at combining player development with building good pitching staffs: at both Western Michigan and Modesto they were using six- or seven-man rotations, with every pitcher getting both starts and middle relief jobs, so that the top half-dozen pitchers on each team wound up racking up the most innings, but fewer innings overall than they would have under regular rotation work. So far, the results have been mixed, but the team has seen fewer injuries than they had previously.

The '96 season was very good for the A's chain overall. Edmonton, moving into a new park (which early on seems to be one of the better pitcher's parks in the Pacific Coast League) handily won its division in both halves of the season, and then took the league championship. The Trappers pulled this off despite some heavy personnel turnover (losing most of their rotation and several regulars to the A's at one time), and were using several players who'd begun the year at Huntsville or Modesto by the time the playoffs rolled around. Those of you familiar with Bill James' notion that good AAA teams are a good indicator for success for the parent club the next season, take note. Another happy sign was that the Trappers' pitching staff allowed the fewest walks in the PCL, while also leading in ERA. Both of the A's full-season A-ball teams, Modesto and West Michigan, posted winning seasons en route to making the playoffs; both clubs also had some of the best pitching staffs in their leagues, being near the top in ERA and strikeouts. This season will see the A's out of the Midwest League, as the A-ball affiliation shuffle left the A's having to put both of their full season A-ball teams in the California League in 1997.

TONY BATISTA   2B/SS   1974   Age 23

Year	Team	Lge	AB	H	DB	TP	HR	BB	SB	CS	OUT	BA	OBA	SA	EQA	EQR	Peak
1994	Modesto	Calif	475	120	16	1	14	45	4	3	358	.253	.317	.379	.233	47	.265
1995	Huntsville	South	430	109	15	1	16	29	5	4	325	.253	.301	.405	.234	43	.261
1996	Edmonton	PCL	205	63	13	2	8	14	2	1	143	.307	.352	.507	.282	30	.312
1996	Oakland	AL	238	71	9	2	6	19	7	3	170	.298	.350	.429	.263	30	.290
1997	*Oakland*	*AL*	*486*	*133*	*24*	*1*	*14*	*47*	*10*	*5*	*358*	*.274*	*.338*	*.414*	*.258*	*60*	

Coming out of relative obscurity, Batista has gotten rave reviews for his defense at second, where he was moved during the course of the season. Although his hitting record indicates another impatient Latin shortstop, he was very good at taking or fouling off pitches, but so far that hasn't translated into walks. However, his control of the strike zone is something that may improve dramatically in the near future. One of the toughest questions for the A's going into next season is whether or not they'll even bother with Brent Gates getting a shot at the job; at this point, handing it to Batista is the best thing the organization can do, especially considering the number of shortstops the A's have coming up.

ALLEN BATTLE   OF   1969   Age 28

Year	Team	Lge	AB	H	DB	TP	HR	BB	SB	CS	OUT	BA	OBA	SA	EQA	EQR	Peak
1993	Arkansas	Texas	405	106	21	7	4	44	13	6	305	.262	.334	.378	.242	44	.259
1994	Louisville	AmA	524	158	38	4	8	60	16	5	371	.302	.373	.435	.274	73	.289
1995	Louisville	AmA	168	46	10	1	3	28	6	1	123	.274	.378	.399	.268	23	.278
1995	St. Louis	NL	120	33	5	0	0	17	2	2	90	.275	.365	.317	.233	12	.242
1996	Oakland	AL	130	25	2	0	1	17	10	2	107	.192	.286	.231	.184	8	.190
1996	Edmonton	PCL	226	64	10	2	4	34	7	2	164	.283	.377	.398	.266	30	.273

People who blow their big chance rarely get another when they have as many shortcomings as Battle. With an arm too weak for center and nowhere near enough power to handle one of the outfield corners, he's praying to have a career like Milt Thompson's, filling in as a pinch-hitter and pinch-runner.

MARK BELLHORN   2B/SS   1975   Age 22

Year	Team	Lge	AB	H	DB	TP	HR	BB	SB	CS	OUT	BA	OBA	SA	EQA	EQR	Peak
1995	Modesto	Calif	235	54	5	0	6	22	2	1	182	.230	.296	.328	.208	18	.236
1996	Huntsville	South	479	114	17	3	10	62	11	1	366	.238	.325	.349	.231	47	.259
1997	*Oakland*	*AL*	*451*	*111*	*22*	*4*	*8*	*74*	*15*	*4*	*344*	*.246*	*.352*	*.366*	*.253*	*55*	

Part of the ripple effect of the emergence of Miguel Tejada seems to be the shift of the shortstops ahead of him over to second base. Like Batista, Bellhorn was moved to second during the last season. He isn't considered a great prospect, but switch-hitting middle infielders who do a bit of everything usually get shots at a job. Bellhorn was the A's second round pick out of Auburn in '95, and has been pushed quickly up the ladder. He has yet to disappoint, but '97 may have to be his year to show enough to stick around before Tejada arrives.

GERONIMO BERROA   DH/OF   1965   Age 32

Year	Team	Lge	AB	H	DB	TP	HR	BB	SB	CS	OUT	BA	OBA	SA	EQA	EQR	Peak
1993	Edmonton	PCL	318	90	17	2	14	32	1	1	229	.283	.349	.481	.273	44	.275
1994	Oakland	AL	347	111	17	2	15	42	7	2	238	.320	.393	.510	.300	58	.298
1995	Oakland	AL	558	167	24	2	26	65	7	4	395	.299	.372	.489	.284	85	.278
1996	Oakland	AL	585	169	27	1	37	47	0	3	419	.289	.342	.528	.281	87	.271
1997	*Oakland*	*AL*	*595*	*155*	*22*	*1*	*27*	*56*	*0*	*1*	*441*	*.261*	*.324*	*.437*	*.257*	*74*	

The classic example of the "minor league hitter" who finally gets his chance. Hopefully, he's done more than enough good work to dispel major league biases against minor league performance, but never overestimate front offices. With a vicious-looking stroke he sprays balls all over the outfield, and is a fun hitter to watch take his cuts. Sadly, he's reaching the point where he's going to start hurting the A's if he continues to play regularly: he's arbitration-eligible, so he'll be getting expensive when he's too old to get any better.

MIKE BORDICK SS 1966 Age 31

Year	Team	Lge	AB	H	DB	TP	HR	BB	SB	CS	OUT	BA	OBA	SA	EQA	EQR	Peak
1993	Oakland	AL	558	152	25	2	4	65	11	8	414	.272	.348	.346	.237	56	.242
1994	Oakland	AL	397	106	20	4	2	39	7	2	293	.267	.333	.353	.235	39	.236
1995	Oakland	AL	436	124	9	0	11	36	12	3	315	.284	.339	.381	.247	48	.246
1996	Oakland	AL	524	125	17	4	5	52	5	6	405	.239	.307	.315	.207	40	.203
1997	*Baltimore*	*AL*	*381*	*98*	*16*	*4*	*2*	*39*	*6*	*4*	*287*	*.257*	*.326*	*.336*	*.225*	*34*	

Mike Bordick went from being Sports Illustrated's "Most Underrated Player" in baseball to "Dramatically Overvalued Hack" in record time, roughly within a half-hour after SI hit the stands. He's old, his offensive contributions crashed and burned in a peak offensive season, and the A's are rich in shortstops. In another season he could be almost worthless, so a challenge for the A's front office is if they're smart enough to let him go now.

RAFAEL BOURNIGAL 2B/SS 1966 Age 31

Year	Team	Lge	AB	H	DB	TP	HR	BB	SB	CS	OUT	BA	OBA	SA	EQA	EQR	Peak
1993	Albuquerque	PCL	449	96	8	0	6	27	2	2	355	.214	.258	.272	.168	20	.172
1994	Albuquerque	PCL	201	56	2	0	2	10	2	2	147	.279	.313	.318	.213	15	.216
1994	Los Angeles	NL	118	28	3	1	0	11	0	0	90	.237	.302	.280	.193	7	.194
1995	Harrisburg	East	98	22	2	1	0	10	1	0	76	.224	.296	.265	.188	6	.185
1996	Oakland	AL	252	61	11	3	0	16	4	3	194	.242	.287	.310	.198	17	.194

By all accounts, wears his cup well. When given a choice between playing Jose Offerman and a hole in the head, leave it to Tommy Lasorda to go one worse and play Raffy Bournigal. Leave it to major league habits that this odd decision produces more spring training invites for Bournigal. If there was one thing wrong with the A's season that they could have easily avoided, it was Raffy Bournigal starting 51 games at second.

SCOTT BROSIUS 3B/UT 1967 Age 30

Year	Team	Lge	AB	H	DB	TP	HR	BB	SB	CS	OUT	BA	OBA	SA	EQA	EQR	Peak
1993	Tacoma	PCL	208	56	8	0	8	19	5	3	155	.269	.330	.423	.251	25	.262
1993	Oakland	AL	217	59	10	1	8	15	5	0	158	.272	.319	.438	.256	26	.266
1994	Oakland	AL	328	81	15	1	15	25	2	5	252	.247	.300	.436	.239	35	.244
1995	Oakland	AL	396	112	21	1	20	42	4	2	286	.283	.352	.492	.277	58	.280
1996	Oakland	AL	427	129	21	0	23	59	7	2	300	.302	.387	.513	.296	72	.295
1997	*Oakland*	*AL*	*521*	*132*	*14*	*0*	*26*	*69*	*6*	*4*	*393*	*.253*	*.341*	*.430*	*.261*	*68*	

Scott Brosius blossomed with regular playing time at a single position, after being released from the endless cycle of shuffling around the field to suit his old manager's whims. He's one of the best defenders at the hot corner in the AL. He generates a lot of fly balls with a long swing that seems to look more and more like McGwire's over time. His defensive work in the past in the outfield has been very similar to Giambi's: play deep and hope nothing gets over his head. There's no happy solution with what to do with both of them, McGwire at first and Berroa at DH, except to trade one of them to make room for a real outfielder.

EMIL BROWN OF 1975 Age 22

Year	Team	Lge	AB	H	DB	TP	HR	BB	SB	CS	OUT	BA	OBA	SA	EQA	EQR	Peak
1995	W. Michigan	Midw	488	121	13	1	4	43	15	10	377	.248	.309	.303	.207	37	.235
1996	Modesto	Calif	213	57	6	0	8	25	6	3	159	.268	.345	.408	.253	26	.284
1997	*Oakland*	*AL*	*413*	*96*	*15*	*2*	*12*	*62*	*11*	*7*	*324*	*.232*	*.333*	*.366*	*.240*	*46*	

Sometimes referred to as "Emile." He's credited with having the strongest outfield arm in the organization, but he lost much of '96 to a broken hamate bone at the beginning of the season.

STEVE COX 1B 1975 Age 22

Year	Team	Lge	AB	H	DB	TP	HR	BB	SB	CS	OUT	BA	OBA	SA	EQA	EQR	Peak
1994	W. Michigan	Midw	327	74	13	1	6	34	1	2	255	.226	.299	.327	.207	25	.239
1995	Modesto	Calif	501	140	15	2	23	69	2	2	363	.279	.367	.455	.273	71	.310
1996	Huntsville	South	389	103	13	1	11	43	1	1	287	.265	.338	.388	.244	42	.273
1997	*Oakland*	*AL*	*474*	*119*	*25*	*1*	*16*	*63*	*1*	*4*	*359*	*.251*	*.339*	*.409*	*.253*	*58*	

Cox took a major step forward in '95 when he finally enjoyed a healthy season. He's young enough to be a solid prospect, and the A's showed their hopes for him sending him to the AFL, where he looked good. He was named the Southern League's best defensive first baseman this year. He'll have to hit for more power than he did in '96 to separate himself from the Steve Dunns of the world.

D.T. CROMER   **1B**   **1971**   **Age 26**

Year	Team	Lge	AB	H	DB	TP	HR	BB	SB	CS	OUT	BA	OBA	SA	EQA	EQR	Peak
1993	Madison	Midw	332	80	13	2	4	16	4	3	255	.241	.276	.328	.200	23	.220
1994	W. Michigan	Midw	364	89	12	2	10	27	6	5	280	.245	.297	.371	.222	32	.241
1995	Modesto	Calif	386	91	11	2	11	29	2	3	298	.236	.289	.360	.214	32	.229
1996	Modesto	Calif	505	151	25	4	23	21	11	4	358	.299	.327	.501	.273	70	.288

Named the best defensive first baseman in the California League and the A's minor league player of the year, he's a good bet to wind up having a career like Jim Bowie's: a fine minor league player, but a non-prospect because of his age; despite being four years older, he's behind Cox in the chain.

ROB DeBOER   **C**   **1971**   **Age 26**

Year	Team	Lge	AB	H	DB	TP	HR	BB	SB	CS	OUT	BA	OBA	SA	EQA	EQR	Peak
1995	W. Michigan	Midw	366	90	16	1	7	48	5	3	279	.246	.333	.352	.232	36	.248
1996	Modesto	Calif	255	65	5	2	10	59	6	3	193	.255	.395	.408	.272	37	.287
1996	Huntsville	South	125	32	2	0	5	22	1	1	94	.256	.367	.392	.256	16	.269

A dark horse in the catching mix in a post-Steinbach world, DeBoer has displayed the classic organizational patience and good power. He's also short, and although there's usually a prejudice against small catchers, DeBoer offers enough on offense to avoid being ignored.

BRENT GATES   **2B**   **1970**   **Age 27**

Year	Team	Lge	AB	H	DB	TP	HR	BB	SB	CS	OUT	BA	OBA	SA	EQA	EQR	Peak
1993	Oakland	AL	550	174	32	1	10	60	7	2	378	.316	.384	.433	.278	77	.302
1994	Oakland	AL	237	71	12	1	2	21	3	0	166	.300	.357	.384	.255	27	.272
1995	Oakland	AL	534	146	28	4	6	47	3	3	391	.273	.332	.375	.238	54	.251
1996	Oakland	AL	247	65	18	2	2	18	1	1	183	.263	.313	.377	.231	23	.240
1997	*Oakland*	*AL*	*387*	*106*	*37*	*2*	*5*	*33*	*2*	*2*	*283*	*.274*	*.331*	*.419*	*.255*	*47*	

What could have been? It's increasingly irrelevant. Gates has shown good range but has been consistently mediocre turning the deuce. His offense never developed, and while he might eventually put up a fine campaign approaching this projection, it probably won't be in Oakland.

JASON GIAMBI   **3B/1B/LF**   **1971**   **Age 26**

Year	Team	Lge	AB	H	DB	TP	HR	BB	SB	CS	OUT	BA	OBA	SA	EQA	EQR	Peak
1993	Modesto	Calif	319	82	8	1	10	54	1	1	238	.257	.365	.382	.253	38	.278
1994	Huntsville	South	201	44	4	0	7	26	0	0	157	.219	.308	.343	.217	17	.236
1994	Tacoma	PCL	175	51	11	0	5	23	1	0	124	.291	.374	.440	.274	24	.298
1995	Edmonton	PCL	189	60	19	1	4	32	0	0	129	.317	.416	.492	.303	33	.326
1995	Oakland	AL	180	50	7	0	7	29	2	1	131	.278	.378	.433	.272	25	.291
1996	Oakland	AL	535	155	36	1	21	51	0	1	381	.290	.352	.479	.274	75	.288
1997	*Oakland*	*AL*	*560*	*165*	*25*	*1*	*14*	*96*	*0*	*1*	*396*	*.295*	*.398*	*.418*	*.283*	*84*	

He's accused of being all sorts of things: lazy, crazy, unwilling to play with injuries. Beyond all the clubhouse chicanery, gossip, and having incurred the open hostility of Tony LaRussa and Mike Gallego—NONE OF WHICH MEANS A DAMN THING about his ability as a baseball player—what Giambi is is the best left-handed bat the A's have developed since Dwayne Murphy. He's good at lofting the ball, and although he's too old to really be outstanding for years to come, he's a fine hitter. He's probably someone who probably needs to wear catching gear to protect himself in the outfield After taking a fall playing on a field that had been ruined by a Raiders' game, he was severely hampered at the plate over the last two months of the season.

BEN GRIEVE   **OF**   **1976**   **Age 21**

Year	Team	Lge	AB	H	DB	TP	HR	BB	SB	CS	OUT	BA	OBA	SA	EQA	EQR	Peak
1995	W. Michigan	Midw	401	104	10	1	5	50	5	2	299	.259	.341	.327	.229	38	.264
1995	Modesto	Calif	110	26	2	0	2	12	1	0	84	.236	.311	.309	.210	9	.242
1996	Modesto	Calif	282	87	10	1	9	29	4	3	198	.309	.373	.447	.274	39	.312
1996	Huntsville	South	237	52	5	1	7	30	0	1	186	.219	.307	.338	.213	20	.242
1997	*Oakland*	*AL*	*570*	*157*	*24*	*1*	*16*	*70*	*5*	*6*	*419*	*.275*	*.355*	*.405*	*.260*	*72*	

So far, the highly touted Grieve has been less than advertised. He's been pushed hard up the chain, usually getting promoted at the first sign of success. At his age, that means few great-looking seasons, and probably trouble perfecting the timing of the beautiful swing scouts drool over. There's been some speculation that he's easily frustrated by pitchers' tendency to pitch around him. By all accounts, a mediocre defender with poor range but a strong arm.

CREIGHTON GUBANICH   C   1972   Age 25

Year	Team	Lge	AB	H	DB	TP	HR	BB	SB	CS	OUT	BA	OBA	SA	EQA	EQR	Peak
1993	Madison	Midw	395	101	10	1	16	50	1	1	295	.256	.339	.408	.249	46	.279
1994	Modesto	Calif	384	82	13	1	12	45	3	2	304	.214	.296	.346	.213	32	.235
1995	Huntsville	South	286	64	3	1	13	45	1	0	222	.224	.329	.378	.237	30	.257
1996	Huntsville	South	222	59	10	0	9	26	1	0	163	.266	.343	.432	.259	28	.277
1996	Edmonton	PCL	117	27	4	1	4	6	2	0	90	.231	.268	.385	.219	10	.237
1997	*Oakland*	*AL*	*416*	*96*	*10*	*0*	*19*	*57*	*0*	*0*	*320*	*.231*	*.323*	*.392*	*.243*	*47*	

One of the heroes of Edmonton's championship season, Gubanich should get a long look next spring. He's supposed to have a strong arm behind the plate, and has also played the infield corners.

RAMON HERNANDEZ   C   1976   Age 21

Year	Team	Lge	AB	H	DB	TP	HR	BB	SB	CS	OUT	BA	OBA	SA	EQA	EQR	Peak
1996	W. Michigan	Midw	469	111	12	1	12	54	1	1	359	.237	.315	.343	.221	41	.250

One of the reasons the A's probably aren't too worried about how their numerous young catchers in the upper levels of the system turn out is Hernandez. He won the batting title in his rookie league in '95, and was rated the A's sixth-best prospect entering the '96 season. He's shown a lot of patience at the plate for a young player. He's potentially a very good catcher, but needs work; for that reason, the A's will be bringing him along slowly as the upper level prospects sort themselves out.

JOSE HERRERA   OF   1973   Age 24

Year	Team	Lge	AB	H	DB	TP	HR	BB	SB	CS	OUT	BA	OBA	SA	EQA	EQR	Peak
1993	Hagerstown	SAtl	398	107	11	2	6	19	15	9	300	.269	.302	.352	.222	35	.252
1994	Modesto	Calif	377	97	12	2	9	31	11	6	286	.257	.314	.371	.231	37	.259
1995	Huntsville	South	369	102	9	2	7	27	6	4	271	.276	.326	.369	.235	36	.258
1996	Oakland	AL	320	86	14	1	6	20	8	2	236	.269	.312	.375	.234	31	.254
1997	*Oakland*	*AL*	*254*	*71*	*14*	*3*	*1*	*13*	*16*	*5*	*188*	*.280*	*.315*	*.370*	*.244*	*28*	

Sure to go down in history as another Blue Jays' tools goof who got more ink than he deserved. Herrera does nothing particularly well, but he's a nice physical specimen with a strong arm, so people think he'll learn how to play baseball. There's a damning, consistent mediocrity about his numbers, which don't bring to light that he's also supposed to be very skittish about going to the wall in the outfield.

PATRICK LENNON   OF   1968   Age 29

Year	Team	Lge	AB	H	DB	TP	HR	BB	SB	CS	OUT	BA	OBA	SA	EQA	EQR	Peak
1993	Canton	East	159	40	5	1	4	28	2	1	120	.252	.364	.371	.250	19	.264
1994	New Britain	East	452	147	22	2	18	44	9	5	310	.325	.385	.502	.293	72	.305
1995	Trenton	East	106	44	4	0	2	13	5	1	63	.415	.479	.509	.341	21	.344
1995	Pawtucket	Inter	131	34	6	1	3	16	4	2	99	.260	.340	.389	.247	15	.251
1995	Salt Lake City	PCL	114	43	8	0	7	11	2	1	72	.377	.432	.632	.341	24	.350
1996	Edmonton	PCL	251	77	10	1	12	27	3	2	176	.307	.374	.498	.287	39	.289
1997	*Oakland*	*AL*	*427*	*120*	*23*	*3*	*18*	*53*	*2*	*2*	*309*	*.281*	*.360*	*.475*	*.282*	*65*	

Should the A's trade away Berroa or Brosius or Giambi, freeing up one of the outfield corners, Lennon could easily be the man who takes the job. His career has mirrored Danny Tartabull's: he was originally a middle infielder and moved to the outfield as he got older. Wherever he's played, he's hit, and given the chance could easily be the new Geronimo Berroa.

BRIAN LESHER   OF   1971   Age 26

Year	Team	Lge	AB	H	DB	TP	HR	BB	SB	CS	OUT	BA	OBA	SA	EQA	EQR	Peak
1993	Madison	Midw	412	104	8	2	6	36	8	4	312	.252	.312	.325	.216	34	.238
1994	Modesto	Calif	406	105	10	0	12	68	6	5	306	.259	.365	.372	.250	48	.271
1995	Huntsville	South	490	128	18	1	19	61	5	4	366	.261	.343	.418	.254	59	.271
1996	Edmonton	PCL	414	112	18	0	18	35	6	3	305	.271	.327	.444	.256	51	.270
1996	Oakland	AL	82	19	3	0	5	5	0	0	63	.232	.276	.451	.237	9	.249
1997	*Oakland*	*AL*	*444*	*109*	*13*	*0*	*28*	*36*	*8*	*5*	*340*	*.245*	*.302*	*.464*	*.255*	*56*	

Wow, that's a interesting projection. Lesher is someone who manages to impress scouts and managers despite his perceived lack of "tools." He's also worked out at first base. He may not have a role as a platoon player: on his career, he's hit right-handers much better.

DAMON MASHORE OF 1970 Age 27

Year	Team	Lge	AB	H	DB	TP	HR	BB	SB	CS	OUT	BA	OBA	SA	EQA	EQR	Peak
1993	Huntsville	South	262	62	5	1	4	23	11	2	202	.237	.298	.309	.211	21	.229
1994	Huntsville	South	214	47	7	1	4	15	3	1	168	.220	.271	.318	.195	14	.209
1995	Edmonton	PCL	335	93	16	3	2	40	13	4	246	.278	.355	.361	.248	38	.262
1996	Edmonton	PCL	183	46	6	1	7	19	5	1	138	.251	.322	.410	.247	21	.256
1996	Oakland	AL	105	28	6	1	3	16	4	0	77	.267	.364	.429	.272	15	.283
1997	*Oakland*	*AL*	*260*	*64*	*13*	*1*	*5*	*32*	*8*	*0*	*196*	*.246*	*.329*	*.362*	*.245*	*29*	

Maybe it's just me, but with his goatee and hair, Mashore looks like "King Tut," the pharaonic bad guy Adam West used to battle on "Batman." Mashore used to be a prospect, but serious knee injuries pretty much ended his shot at being an exciting center fielder. Like many A's, he's very patient at the plate, working the count and fouling off pitches. When the A's were desperate enough to try anyone in the leadoff slot they gave Mashore a chance, and started scoring runs by the truckload; naturally Mashore got injured, ending that. Whether or not he has much of a future, he should be a useful spare part.

JASON McDONALD 2B/UT 1972 Age 25

Year	Team	Lge	AB	H	DB	TP	HR	BB	SB	CS	OUT	BA	OBA	SA	EQA	EQR	Peak
1994	W. Michigan	Midw	431	100	9	6	3	68	25	11	342	.232	.337	.302	.223	40	.245
1995	Modesto	Calif	516	125	19	3	7	90	29	10	401	.242	.355	.331	.240	57	.261
1996	Edmonton	PCL	481	105	5	2	9	60	25	8	384	.218	.305	.293	.207	38	.222
1997	*Oakland*	*AL*	*448*	*106*	*7*	*8*	*14*	*85*	*32*	*18*	*360*	*.237*	*.358*	*.382*	*.256*	*60*	

The A's almost kept him out of spring training. McDonald was finally allowed to remain at a single position last year, playing second. He's also spent a lot of time at shortstop and center field. He's essentially the middle infield version of Kerwin Moore.

MARK McGWIRE 1B 1964 Age 33

Year	Team	Lge	AB	H	DB	TP	HR	BB	SB	CS	OUT	BA	OBA	SA	EQA	EQR	Peak
1993	Oakland	AL	88	32	6	0	11	22	0	1	57	.364	.491	.807	.389	27	.387
1994	Oakland	AL	138	37	2	0	10	38	0	0	101	.268	.426	.500	.306	26	.299
1995	Oakland	AL	327	96	16	0	44	91	1	1	232	.294	.447	.746	.360	90	.348
1996	Oakland	AL	422	131	19	0	52	116	0	0	291	.310	.459	.725	.363	116	.345
1997	*Oakland*	*AL*	*424*	*118*	*15*	*0*	*43*	*139*	*0*	*0*	*306*	*.278*	*.456*	*.618*	*.347*	*109*	

The best offensive player in baseball today, bar none. Among some analysts, there's a debate about whether McGwire has reached a new level of ability or not. Sign me up with the "has" group. Before the injuries he was less patient, and now there's almost a Ted Williams-like quality to him at the plate: give him his pitch, or give him first base. He's not the superior first baseman he used to be, but the foot injuries should be a thing of the past. More troublesome is his back; he had surgery this offseason, but should be in fine shape for the spring.

IZZY MOLINA C 1971 Age 26

Year	Team	Lge	AB	H	DB	TP	HR	BB	SB	CS	OUT	BA	OBA	SA	EQA	EQR	Peak
1993	Modesto	Calif	449	101	16	2	6	28	1	3	351	.225	.270	.310	.188	27	.207
1994	Huntsville	South	394	83	12	0	9	19	3	1	312	.211	.247	.310	.180	21	.195
1995	Huntsville	South	310	79	11	0	9	26	2	2	233	.255	.312	.377	.230	30	.247
1996	Edmonton	PCL	342	84	8	2	11	24	2	3	261	.246	.295	.377	.222	30	.234

Steinbach signed with Minnesota, and Izzy Molina is the man who's been expected for the last few years to replace him. His defense is well-regarded. Molina is considered a crank; he apparently didn't care to spend a second season in Huntsville in '95. Since the A's are deep in catching options, Molina's got his weak bat and his reputation going against him.

KERWIN MOORE CF 1971 Age 26

Year	Team	Lge	AB	H	DB	TP	HR	BB	SB	CS	OUT	BA	OBA	SA	EQA	EQR	Peak
1993	High Desert	Calif	508	110	13	4	6	83	28	7	405	.217	.327	.293	.218	45	.241
1994	Huntsville	South	522	128	13	3	7	92	29	10	403	.245	.358	.322	.239	56	.260
1995	Edmonton	PCL	264	67	12	2	3	45	8	2	199	.254	.362	.348	.247	30	.265
1996	Edmonton	PCL	457	98	12	7	3	89	29	8	367	.214	.342	.291	.225	44	.236

The minor leagues' answer to Gary Pettis. He can fly in the outfield, is extremely patient at the plate and is basically a better prospect than Allen Battle ever could be. However, he isn't a better player than Ernie Young, and he isn't young. Acquiring him wasn't worth giving up Kurt Abbott.

WILLIE MORALES   C   1973   Age 24

Year	Team	Lge	AB	H	DB	TP	HR	BB	SB	CS	OUT	BA	OBA	SA	EQA	EQR	Peak
1993	So.Oregon	Nwern	214	47	7	0	2	9	0	1	168	.220	.251	.280	.166	10	.190
1994	W. Michigan	Midw	396	101	13	0	12	31	2	2	297	.255	.309	.379	.229	37	.257
1995	Modesto	Calif	426	103	15	0	6	22	1	2	325	.242	.279	.319	.197	28	.217
1996	Huntsville	South	383	106	14	0	16	32	0	1	278	.277	.333	.439	.256	46	.278
1997	*Oakland*	*AL*	*410*	*103*	*15*	*0*	*16*	*38*	*0*	*1*	*308*	*.251*	*.315*	*.405*	*.244*	*45*	

Another of the A's catching prospects, and the one nobody talks about. He's a better hitter than Molina, but his defense doesn't get much attention one way or another.

PEDRO MUNOZ   DH/OF   1969   Age 28

Year	Team	Lge	AB	H	DB	TP	HR	BB	SB	CS	OUT	BA	OBA	SA	EQA	EQR	Peak
1993	Minnesota	AL	328	79	10	1	15	27	1	1	250	.241	.299	.415	.235	33	.251
1994	Minnesota	AL	246	74	15	2	11	19	0	0	172	.301	.351	.512	.283	37	.299
1995	Minnesota	AL	378	116	15	0	20	19	0	3	265	.307	.340	.505	.275	53	.286
1996	Oakland	AL	121	31	4	0	6	9	0	0	90	.256	.308	.438	.246	14	.253

The knee injuries that have turned him into a DH ruined his '96 season. The knees will never get better, and when he's healthy he isn't the best DH around. If you want an example of a slow player's career fizzling early, here it is.

DAVID NEWHAN   OF   1974   Age 23

Year	Team	Lge	AB	H	DB	TP	HR	BB	SB	CS	OUT	BA	OBA	SA	EQA	EQR	Peak
1995	So.Oregon	Nwern	153	35	3	0	5	21	3	2	120	.229	.322	.346	.224	14	.253
1995	W. Michigan	Midw	102	23	2	0	3	11	1	1	80	.225	.301	.333	.210	8	.234
1996	Modesto	Calif	459	124	15	2	18	47	9	4	339	.270	.338	.429	.257	56	.283

A 17th-round pick out of Pepperdine whose power was supposed to be aluminum-dependent, Newhan has already been a happy surprise. He was red-hot during the second half, which could be a good sign that he's ready to advance up the chain quickly.

PHIL PLANTIER   LF   1969   Age 28

Year	Team	Lge	AB	H	DB	TP	HR	BB	SB	CS	OUT	BA	OBA	SA	EQA	EQR	Peak
1993	San Diego	NL	473	118	17	1	35	67	4	4	359	.249	.343	.512	.274	71	.294
1994	San Diego	NL	345	78	16	0	20	41	3	1	268	.226	.308	.446	.247	41	.261
1995	Houston	NL	71	19	1	0	5	12	0	0	52	.268	.373	.493	.284	11	.298
1995	San Diego	NL	153	42	2	0	6	19	1	1	112	.275	.355	.405	.255	18	.266
1996	Edmonton	PCL	122	41	4	1	8	12	1	0	81	.336	.396	.582	.317	23	.326
1996	Oakland	AL	231	49	7	1	7	28	2	2	184	.212	.297	.342	.211	19	.216
1997	*Oakland*	*AL*	*227*	*54*	*8*	*0*	*14*	*33*	*2*	*1*	*174*	*.238*	*.335*	*.458*	*.265*	*32*	

Plantier probably would have gotten more playing time in Oakland if he hadn't had an incentive-based contract that kicked in at 75 games; he was sent down to stay at 73. He's in the same situation as Munoz: injury-prone, near useless afield and close to washed up before 30 because his wrists have slowed.

CHARLES POE   LF/DH   1972   Age 25

Year	Team	Lge	AB	H	DB	TP	HR	BB	SB	CS	OUT	BA	OBA	SA	EQA	EQR	Peak
1993	Sarasota	Flor	321	76	9	1	13	29	3	4	249	.237	.300	.393	.228	31	.256
1994	Pr. William	Caro	488	125	16	1	11	44	8	1	364	.256	.318	.361	.231	47	.255
1995	Birmingham	South	445	129	20	2	14	49	12	3	319	.290	.360	.438	.270	60	.293
1996	Huntsville	South	423	104	13	2	11	39	3	2	321	.246	.310	.364	.225	39	.241

The man who lost a year of his life to Michael Jordan's curiosity, rotting in A ball for an extra season while His Tongueness proved he couldn't play baseball. Poe came to the A's along with Andrew Lorraine in exchange for the last year of Danny Tartabull's contract. Non-prospect.

DEMOND SMITH   OF   1973   Age 24

Year	Team	Lge	AB	H	DB	TP	HR	BB	SB	CS	OUT	BA	OBA	SA	EQA	EQR	Peak
1995	Cedar Rapids	Midw	327	101	17	3	7	25	15	6	232	.309	.358	.443	.271	44	.299
1995	Lake Elsinore	Calif	151	49	5	1	6	9	6	2	104	.325	.363	.490	.285	23	.316
1996	Huntsville	South	456	111	13	8	10	46	19	8	353	.243	.313	.373	.233	46	.253

Getting Smith from the Angels for Mike Aldrete is almost reason enough to keep guys like Mike Aldrete in uniform. He's a speed player, but he didn't shine in his first season above A-ball, so whether or not he'll be good enough soon enough is an open question.

SCOTT SPIEZIO   **3B**   **1973**   **Age 24**

Year	Team	Lge	AB	H	DB	TP	HR	BB	SB	CS	OUT	BA	OBA	SA	EQA	EQR	Peak
1994	Modesto	Calif	467	120	20	3	12	74	2	0	347	.257	.359	.390	.253	56	.284
1995	Huntsville	South	550	156	27	5	15	64	6	2	396	.284	.358	.433	.266	72	.294
1996	Edmonton	PCL	524	129	21	2	19	54	5	3	398	.246	.317	.403	.239	56	.260
1997	*Oakland*	*AL*	*558*	*148*	*30*	*3*	*22*	*69*	*4*	*2*	*412*	*.265*	*.346*	*.448*	*.269*	*77*	

Spiezio has become the player who could make Scott Brosius or Jason Giambi expendable: a switch-hitter with pop, patience and a good glove, he's ready to enter his offensive prime right now. He started slowly at Edmonton, but improved as the season went along.

MATT STAIRS   **DH/OF**   **1969**   **Age 28**

Year	Team	Lge	AB	H	DB	TP	HR	BB	SB	CS	OUT	BA	OBA	SA	EQA	EQR	Peak
1994	New Britain	East	337	104	19	2	9	49	7	4	237	.309	.396	.457	.286	52	.302
1995	Pawtucket	Inter	276	76	9	0	13	29	3	2	202	.275	.344	.449	.263	36	.273
1996	Edmonton	PCL	180	59	10	1	8	20	0	0	121	.328	.395	.528	.304	31	.310
1996	Oakland	AL	137	38	4	1	10	19	1	1	100	.277	.365	.540	.291	23	.298
1997	*Oakland*	*AL*	*393*	*110*	*16*	*1*	*25*	*44*	*1*	*2*	*285*	*.280*	*.352*	*.517*	*.287*	*63*	

Having learned their lesson with Geronimo Berroa, the A's snatched Matt Stairs off the scrap pile, gave him some playing time and weren't disappointed. Another very good minor league hitter, Stairs was given up on when it was decided he'd never make a good infielder. Now he's an outfielder with a good, accurate arm who can give a team excellent left-handed pop. Hopefully, his role will expand next season.

TERRY STEINBACH   **C**   **1962**   **Age 35**

Year	Team	Lge	AB	H	DB	TP	HR	BB	SB	CS	OUT	BA	OBA	SA	EQA	EQR	Peak
1993	Oakland	AL	398	123	19	1	13	28	3	2	277	.309	.354	.460	.272	53	.262
1994	Oakland	AL	375	112	22	2	12	26	2	1	264	.299	.344	.464	.269	49	.255
1995	Oakland	AL	414	123	27	1	18	25	1	3	294	.297	.337	.498	.272	57	.259
1996	Oakland	AL	513	139	24	1	35	49	0	1	375	.271	.335	.526	.277	76	.263
1997	*Minnesota*	*AL*	*538*	*148*	*27*	*1*	*24*	*50*	*0*	*0*	*390*	*.275*	*.337*	*.463*	*.265*	*70*	

This was probably his last season in an A's uniform before he signs with his home state Twins to die as so many other distinguished veterans do. The finest A's catcher since Mickey Cochrane, and robbed of a spot on this year's All-Star team by the perpetually dim Mike Hargrove. I'm not alone in saying A's fans will miss him. However, he's old, expensive and a good bet to crash and burn relative to a season like this last one.

MIGUEL TEJADA   **SS**   **1976**   **Age 21**

Year	Team	Lge	AB	H	DB	TP	HR	BB	SB	CS	OUT	BA	OBA	SA	EQA	EQR	Peak
1995	So.Oregon	Nwern	281	61	6	2	7	29	7	1	221	.217	.290	.327	.209	22	.242
1996	Modesto	Calif	462	113	7	2	15	38	13	8	357	.245	.302	.366	.224	42	.255
1997	*Oakland*	*AL*	*464*	*121*	*10*	*3*	*12*	*43*	*17*	*9*	*352*	*.261*	*.323*	*.373*	*.241*	*50*	

Named the most exciting prospect in the California League. For the second year in a row the A's had him skip a level, and it didn't slow him down in the least. He's got one of the strongest infield arms in the minors, he's fast and he can already hit for power. Prospects that look this good this fast can wind up in the majors far sooner than you might expect. If Bordick is gone and Tejada puts on a show in the spring, don't be surprised if he's on the major league roster at some point in '97. If there's a reason for caution, it's the season-ending ankle injury he suffered in August, but it isn't supposed to be major.

GEORGE WILLIAMS C 1969 Age 28

Year	Team	Lge	AB	H	DB	TP	HR	BB	SB	CS	OUT	BA	OBA	SA	EQA	EQR	Peak
1993	Huntsville	South	458	137	18	2	15	62	4	2	323	.299	.383	.445	.278	66	.298
1994	W. Michigan	Midw	238	71	12	1	8	37	3	2	169	.298	.393	.458	.284	36	.300
1995	Edmonton	PCL	289	83	10	0	14	47	0	3	209	.287	.387	.467	.281	44	.292
1996	Oakland	AL	132	20	4	0	3	28	0	0	112	.152	.300	.250	.177	7	.183
1997	*Oakland*	*AL*	*343*	*95*	*15*	*1*	*11*	*58*	*0*	*0*	*248*	*.277*	*.382*	*.423*	*.277*	*50*	

When the A's released Mickey Tettleton (to keep Ron Hassey, of all people) in 1988, he was a 28-year-old switch-hitting catcher with sock. Williams, like Tettleton before him, has endured some questions about his defense. To my eyes, the problem seems to be one of working on his release, which slows down a good arm. At any rate, Williams is a patient hitter with power, and matched with some defensive whiz could make a fine replacement for Steinbach. His struggles this year probably had more to do with a lack of playing time, for the first time in his career, than anything else.

JASON WOOD UT 1970 Age 27

Year	Team	Lge	AB	H	DB	TP	HR	BB	SB	CS	OUT	BA	OBA	SA	EQA	EQR	Peak
1993	Huntsville	South	382	86	18	2	3	31	2	2	298	.225	.283	.306	.194	25	.211
1994	Huntsville	South	485	128	21	2	7	47	2	3	360	.264	.329	.359	.231	46	.248
1995	Edmonton	PCL	417	89	16	3	3	30	1	3	331	.213	.266	.288	.177	22	.186
1996	Huntsville	South	502	123	11	1	18	60	2	2	381	.245	.326	.378	.235	51	.245

LaRussa took a liking to him because he had that ineffable Gallego quality of scrappiness. Sadly for him, he was so limited defensively that not even LaRussa could overlook it. He's moving backward, and although he has some patience and some pop, he's playing third more and more, and second and short less and less, so he may not even have a future as a utility player. Don't be surprised if he winds up managing.

ERNIE YOUNG CF 1970 Age 27

Year	Team	Lge	AB	H	DB	TP	HR	BB	SB	CS	OUT	BA	OBA	SA	EQA	EQR	Peak
1993	Modesto	Calif	306	87	10	2	18	54	11	4	223	.284	.392	.507	.296	53	.321
1993	Huntsville	South	126	27	3	0	5	22	5	3	102	.214	.331	.357	.232	13	.253
1994	Huntsville	South	273	94	12	2	15	37	4	3	182	.344	.423	.568	.321	53	.344
1994	Tacoma	PCL	101	26	1	0	5	12	1	3	78	.257	.336	.416	.243	11	.259
1995	Edmonton	PCL	345	89	13	1	16	47	2	1	257	.258	.347	.441	.261	45	.275
1996	Oakland	AL	461	111	18	4	19	52	7	5	355	.241	.318	.421	.244	52	.254
1997	*Oakland*	*AL*	*339*	*81*	*24*	*1*	*20*	*55*	*8*	*6*	*264*	*.239*	*.345*	*.493*	*.275*	*53*	

While Ernie didn't hit well enough to guarantee his immediate future with the A's, he did squelch criticisms of his defense. Like Marty Cordova the year before, Young came up with questions about his defense that turned out to be ludicrous. Young gets a superb jump on the ball and has a good arm. While he'll never grow into a middle of the order power threat, he showed that he's a useful player who can contribute as the regular center fielder or fourth outfielder for a few years to come.

MARK ACRE RRP 1969 Age 28

YR	TEAM	Lge	IP	H	ER	HR	BB	K	ERA	W	L	H/9	HR/9	BB/9	K/9	KW
1993	Madison	Midw	28.0	14	1	2	18	24	.32	3	0	4.50	.64	5.79	7.71	1.12
1993	Huntsville	South	20.0	27	11	3	5	16	4.95	1	1	12.15	1.35	2.25	7.20	1.84
1994	Tacoma	PCL	26.7	25	5	1	13	27	1.69	3	0	8.44	.34	4.39	9.11	1.94
1994	Oakland	AL	33.3	26	10	4	24	21	2.70	3	1	7.02	1.08	6.48	5.67	.27
1995	Oakland	AL	52.3	52	29	7	30	48	4.99	2	4	8.94	1.20	5.16	8.25	1.46
1996	Edmonton	PCL	40.0	35	9	1	20	41	2.03	3	1	7.88	.22	4.50	9.23	1.95
1996	Oakland	AL	25.7	34	12	4	9	17	4.21	1	2	11.92	1.40	3.16	5.96	1.20

At 6' 8" with a big forkball, Acre might be right out of central casting as the prototypical fire-breathing closer. Unfortunately he's only cut out for "Gentle Ben."

WILLIE ADAMS — RSP — 1973 — Age 24

YR	TEAM	Lge	IP	H	ER	HR	BB	K	ERA	W	L	H/9	HR/9	BB/9	K/9	KW
1994	Modesto	Calif	40.3	50	17	7	13	27	3.79	2	2	11.16	1.56	2.90	6.02	1.28
1994	Huntsville	South	54.7	70	36	4	33	26	5.93	2	4	11.52	.66	5.43	4.28	.07
1995	Huntsville	South	75.0	86	33	10	26	55	3.96	4	4	10.32	1.20	3.12	6.60	1.42
1995	Edmonton	PCL	64.3	70	28	3	21	37	3.92	4	3	9.79	.42	2.94	5.18	.99
1996	Edmonton	PCL	105.0	98	41	13	49	65	3.51	7	5	8.40	1.11	4.20	5.57	.81
1996	Oakland	AL	76.3	70	28	9	25	66	3.30	5	3	8.25	1.06	2.95	7.78	1.86

Adams is another giant with a mean forkball, but he's a four-pitch starter out of Stanford. As predicted in last year's Prospectus, Adams got a shot at midseason as the first mystery man rotation (Van Poppel, Reyes, Johns, Wojo and Prieto) fell apart. According to some in the organization, Adams figured out that if guys like Bobby Chouinard were getting called up, he wasn't far off, and he seemed to get serious. Whatever, he's now a lock for next year's rotation. There are times when he just gets creamed; this is usually tipped off very early in the game when he's missing high.

JOHN BRISCOE — RRP — 1968 — Age 29

YR	TEAM	Lge	IP	H	ER	HR	BB	K	ERA	W	L	H/9	HR/9	BB/9	K/9	KW
1993	Huntsville	South	35.7	34	14	4	21	46	3.53	2	2	8.58	1.01	5.30	11.61	2.54
1993	Oakland	AL	25.0	27	22	2	28	25	7.92	1	2	9.72	.72	10.08	9.00	.48
1994	Oakland	AL	48.7	33	19	7	40	44	3.51	3	2	6.10	1.29	7.40	8.14	.86
1996	Oakland	AL	25.7	17	8	2	25	14	2.81	2	1	5.96	.70	8.77	4.91	-.56
1996	Edmonton	PCL	52.0	68	28	6	29	51	4.85	2	4	11.77	1.04	5.02	8.83	1.69

Maybe Art Howe's more susceptible to ulcers than Tony LaRussa, but he couldn't stomach the wild ride that is the Briscoe Kid.

BOBBY CHOUINARD — RSP — 1972 — Age 25

YR	TEAM	Lge	IP	H	ER	HR	BB	K	ERA	W	L	H/9	HR/9	BB/9	K/9	KW
1993	Modesto	Calif	128.0	177	70	16	61	57	4.92	6	8	12.45	1.12	4.29	4.01	.26
1994	Modesto	Calif	130.7	170	50	5	43	48	3.44	9	6	11.71	.34	2.96	3.31	.36
1995	Huntsville	South	154.3	178	80	12	70	81	4.67	7	10	10.38	.70	4.08	4.72	.55
1996	Edmonton	PCL	78.3	74	27	7	31	37	3.10	6	3	8.50	.80	3.56	4.25	.53
1996	Oakland	AL	59.7	68	31	8	33	31	4.68	3	4	10.26	1.21	4.98	4.68	.31

Part of the payment for Harold Baines from the Orioles, Chouinard finally broke through this season. He's been reliably healthy and keeps the ball down. He'll be in the starter mix, but that doesn't make him a tasty option.

JIM CORSI — RRP — 1962 — Age 35

YR	TEAM	Lge	IP	H	ER	HR	BB	K	ERA	W	L	H/9	HR/9	BB/9	K/9	KW
1994	Edmonton	PCL	21.0	26	11	1	12	13	4.71	1	1	11.14	.43	5.14	5.57	.57
1995	Oakland	AL	44.0	34	11	2	27	26	2.25	4	1	6.95	.41	5.52	5.32	.39
1996	Oakland	AL	73.3	66	23	5	36	42	2.82	5	3	8.10	.61	4.42	5.15	.61

Whereas Mark Acre looks the part, Jim Corsi is the genuine article: a major league reliever with a wicked sinker that batters mostly just kill worms with. He's probably a good bet to get injured this year, because he rarely enjoys seasons as healthy as his last one. As someone who had an ex-girlfriend say I bear an uncanny resemblance to Jim Corsi, I resent last year's physical comparison of Corsi to Chris "Big Bundle of Love" Bosio.

JIMMY DASPIT — RBP — 1970 — Age 27

YR	TEAM	Lge	IP	H	ER	HR	BB	K	ERA	W	L	H/9	HR/9	BB/9	K/9	KW
1993	SanAntonio	Texas	71.0	115	56	6	49	42	7.10	2	6	14.58	.76	6.21	5.32	.22
1994	Jackson	Texas	65.0	58	21	2	30	54	2.91	5	2	8.03	.28	4.15	7.48	1.45
1995	Tucson	PCL	59.0	59	21	3	28	44	3.20	4	3	9.00	.46	4.27	6.71	1.17
1996	Edmonton	PCL	84.0	98	43	5	37	62	4.61	4	5	10.50	.54	3.96	6.64	1.22

Daspit has been a successful reliever in the PCL for two years, no easy feat, but he rarely gets any consideration because he succeeds with a deceptive delivery and no outstanding pitch. He'd be an improvement over the Briscoe Kid.

KIRK DRESSENDORFER   RRP   1969   Age 28

YR	TEAM	Lge	IP	H	ER	HR	BB	K	ERA	W	L	H/9	HR/9	BB/9	K/9	KW
1993	Modesto	Calif	10.0	16	4	2	5	10	3.60	1	0	14.40	1.80	4.50	9.00	1.87
1995	Modesto	Calif	32.3	46	24	5	24	32	6.68	1	3	12.80	1.39	6.68	8.91	1.30
1995	Huntsville	South	18.3	16	7	2	7	14	3.44	1	1	7.85	.98	3.44	6.87	1.43
1996	Huntsville	South	48.0	60	35	3	24	31	6.56	1	4	11.25	.56	4.50	5.81	.81
1996	Edmonton	PCL	12.7	22	9	1	4	8	6.39	0	1	15.63	.71	2.84	5.68	1.18

Kirk is the only guy left from the "Four Aces." Dressendorfer has never recovered for any length of time from the arm abuse he endured at Texas as an amateur. He's a dubious prospect as a reliever who will be given a shot on the basis of who he was. Sadly, that's just a memory.

BUDDY GROOM   LRP   1966   Age 31

YR	TEAM	Lge	IP	H	ER	HR	BB	K	ERA	W	L	H/9	HR/9	BB/9	K/9	KW
1993	Toledo	Inter	96.0	108	32	5	43	63	3.00	7	4	10.12	.47	4.03	5.91	.96
1993	Detroit	AL	36.7	47	21	4	15	16	5.15	2	2	11.54	.98	3.68	3.93	.39
1994	Detroit	AL	31.7	30	10	4	14	26	2.84	3	1	8.53	1.14	3.98	7.39	1.47
1995	Toledo	Inter	30.3	37	15	5	7	20	4.45	1	2	10.98	1.48	2.08	5.93	1.46
1995	Detroit	AL	41.7	51	27	5	26	23	5.83	2	3	11.02	1.08	5.62	4.97	.25
1996	Oakland	AL	78.0	77	26	7	36	55	3.00	6	3	8.88	.81	4.15	6.35	1.08

Old Buddy Groom showed that he could be just as successful as he was in '94. He's strictly a junkballer who induces lots of groundballs, and with a good interior defense, like the '96 A's had, he can survive. Unlike the Assenmachers of the world, Groom doesn't really fare well against left-handed batters, so he's more a genuine middle reliever, than an 8th-inning setup man.

STACY HOLLINS   RBP   1973   Age 24

YR	TEAM	Lge	IP	H	ER	HR	BB	K	ERA	W	L	H/9	HR/9	BB/9	K/9	KW
1993	Madison	Midw	128.3	193	115	25	71	62	8.06	3	11	13.54	1.75	4.98	4.35	.20
1994	Modesto	Calif	127.3	156	55	11	71	86	3.89	7	7	11.03	.78	5.02	6.08	.77
1995	Huntsville	South	75.7	94	54	11	55	48	6.42	2	6	11.18	1.31	6.54	5.71	.27
1995	Edmonton	PCL	28.3	43	34	4	25	23	10.80	0	3	13.66	1.27	7.94	7.31	.45
1996	Huntsville	South	130.0	163	91	18	65	74	6.30	4	10	11.28	1.25	4.50	5.12	.58

What doesn't show up here is that after that big season at Modesto, he had an excellent season in the Arizona Fall League and got labeled as a top prospect. He's a fastball-change starter, and it isn't working. A shift to the pen may be the only way to get him back on track.

DOUG JOHNS   LBP   1968   Age 29

YR	TEAM	Lge	IP	H	ER	HR	BB	K	ERA	W	L	H/9	HR/9	BB/9	K/9	KW
1993	Huntsville	South	82.3	99	44	4	42	42	4.81	4	5	10.82	.44	4.59	4.59	.38
1994	Tacoma	PCL	124.3	114	44	10	61	56	3.18	9	5	8.25	.72	4.42	4.05	.25
1995	Edmonton	PCL	124.0	144	44	9	56	64	3.19	9	5	10.45	.65	4.06	4.65	.53
1995	Oakland	AL	53.7	46	26	5	28	25	4.36	3	3	7.71	.84	4.70	4.19	.22
1996	Oakland	AL	158.3	172	83	17	72	68	4.72	8	10	9.78	.97	4.09	3.87	.27

After two superb seasons and an ERA title in the PCL, it was time to find out if the soft-tossing Johns could handle a regular spot in the rotation. The A's gave it a shot and it didn't work, as Johns put up only eight quality starts in 23 attempts. Basically, Johns is a younger edition of Buddy Groom who got an extended shot to show what he could do as a starter.

DANE JOHNSON   RRP   1963   Age 34

YR	TEAM	Lge	IP	H	ER	HR	BB	K	ERA	W	L	H/9	HR/9	BB/9	K/9	KW
1994	Nashville	AmA	42.3	40	11	2	22	36	2.34	4	1	8.50	.43	4.68	7.65	1.38
1994	Chi. White Sox	AL	12.7	15	7	2	12	7	4.97	0	1	10.66	1.42	8.53	4.97	-.47
1995	Nashville	AmA	53.3	52	22	2	35	45	3.71	3	3	8.78	.34	5.91	7.59	1.05
1996	Syracuse	Inter	48.7	41	12	4	22	42	2.22	4	1	7.58	.74	4.07	7.77	1.57

Picked up during the offseason on waivers from the Blue Jays, Johnson is an ex-community college pitching coach who turned an invite from the Brewers in '93 into a second career. At this point, he's a reliable AAA closer, sparing an organization from wasting the overrated spotlight role on someone with actual talent.

STEVE KARSAY   **RBP**   **1972**   **Age 25**

YR	TEAM	Lge	IP	H	ER	HR	BB	K	ERA	W	L	H/9	HR/9	BB/9	K/9	KW
1993	Knoxville	South	95.3	107	39	10	43	73	3.68	6	5	10.10	.94	4.06	6.89	1.28
1993	Oakland	AL	48.3	51	20	4	18	34	3.72	3	2	9.50	.74	3.35	6.33	1.27
1994	Oakland	AL	27.3	27	6	1	9	15	1.98	2	1	8.89	.33	2.96	4.94	.91
1996	Modesto	Calif	31.0	41	14	2	0	20	4.06	1	2	11.90	.58	.00	5.81	1.94

When the A's originally pulled the trigger on the "Rent-A-Henderson" deal with the Blue Jays, it looked like a steal: two months of Rickey for a genuine pitching prospect and a tools-laden outfielder. Now, with Herrera looking like fifth outfielder scrap and Karsay scarcely more healthy than Dressendorfer, it looks like a waste of time. His curveball is apparently self-destructive, so he spent last season throwing his fastball (back up to 92) and a changeup. The A's say he's in the mix for next year; given his injuries, it should be in the pen.

BILL KING   **RSP**   **1973**   **Age 24**

YR	TEAM	Lge	IP	H	ER	HR	BB	K	ERA	W	L	H/9	HR/9	BB/9	K/9	KW
1995	W. Michigan	Midw	124.0	221	97	9	59	64	7.04	3	11	16.04	.65	4.28	4.65	.48
1996	Modesto	Calif	146.3	213	89	11	46	63	5.47	6	10	13.10	.68	2.83	3.87	.58

Modesto's contribution to why run support, and not "knowing how to win," makes some people look better than they are. In reality, King racked up a record of 16-4, and his future is probably slightly worse than that of the A's last 16-4 minor leaguer, Steve Lemke, whose career ended last season in injuries and disappointment. There are far better prospects among the A's A-ball pitchers (Kevin Mlodik, for example), but with young pitchers, surviving is usually a better measure of talent than tools. This is why it's dicey to talk about great futures or total hopelessness for any A-ball pitcher.

TIM KUBINSKI   **LRP**   **1972**   **Age 25**

YR	TEAM	Lge	IP	H	ER	HR	BB	K	ERA	W	L	H/9	HR/9	BB/9	K/9	KW
1993	So. Oregon	Nwern	59.3	95	40	6	15	29	6.07	2	5	14.41	.91	2.28	4.40	.90
1994	W. Michigan	Midw	136.0	223	97	11	55	80	6.42	4	11	14.76	.73	3.64	5.29	.85
1995	Modesto	Calif	94.3	153	76	13	34	54	7.25	2	8	14.60	1.24	3.24	5.15	.91
1995	Edmonton	PCL	30.0	33	15	4	13	11	4.50	1	2	9.90	1.20	3.90	3.30	.12
1996	Huntsville	South	94.0	95	36	7	42	56	3.45	6	4	9.10	.67	4.02	5.36	.78

The conversion to the pen last year suited him, and the A's think he'll push for a job in '97. He's another lefty junkballer, living off of a cut fastball and changeup.

ANDREW LORRAINE   **LBP**   **1973**   **Age 24**

YR	TEAM	Lge	IP	H	ER	HR	BB	K	ERA	W	L	H/9	HR/9	BB/9	K/9	KW
1994	Vancouver	PCL	133.3	153	51	12	47	78	3.44	9	6	10.33	.81	3.17	5.27	.96
1995	Vancouver	PCL	90.0	121	50	9	40	48	5.00	4	6	12.10	.90	4.00	4.80	.60
1995	Nashville	AmA	37.3	54	28	4	19	23	6.75	1	3	13.02	.96	4.58	5.54	.70
1996	Edmonton	PCL	133.7	178	80	19	59	60	5.39	5	10	11.99	1.28	3.97	4.04	.35

Acquired along with the luckless Charlie Poe from the White Sox for Danny Tartabull's last contract year, Lorraine has gone from being a highly-regarded pitching prospect to someone easily confused with Dana Allison or Curtis Shaw. He's yet another lefty junkballer, and unlike Doug Johns, he can't even prove that once upon a time he fooled somebody. It may be early to write him off, but he's been a major flop to this point.

MIKE MOHLER   **LRP**   **1969**   **Age 28**

YR	TEAM	Lge	IP	H	ER	HR	BB	K	ERA	W	L	H/9	HR/9	BB/9	K/9	KW
1993	Oakland	AL	64.3	58	40	11	48	44	5.60	2	5	8.11	1.54	6.72	6.16	.37
1994	Modesto	Calif	26.3	26	8	1	8	19	2.73	2	1	8.89	.34	2.73	6.49	1.48
1994	Tacoma	PCL	59.0	66	25	6	27	43	3.81	4	3	10.07	.92	4.12	6.56	1.16
1995	Edmonton	PCL	41.7	39	12	0	25	26	2.59	4	1	8.42	.00	5.40	5.62	.52
1995	Oakland	AL	23.3	17	6	0	19	15	2.31	2	1	6.56	.00	7.33	5.79	.10
1996	Oakland	AL	81.0	73	25	7	42	62	2.78	6	3	8.11	.78	4.67	6.89	1.13

He was probably set back more than he had to be by LaRussa's insane decision to turn him into a rotation starter in '93, when he went 0-6 with a 6.94 ERA. On his career, he's got an ERA of 3.67 as a reliever. Like Groom, Mohler was used as a long reliever instead of in the spot role and succeeded at it. His success surprised many, including me: when I first saw him in April, he didn't seem to be throwing anything like he used to, and he'd come up with a sinking fastball with extraordinary movement.

STEVE MONTGOMERY   **RRP**   **1971**   **Age 26**

YR	TEAM	Lge	IP	H	ER	HR	BB	K	ERA	W	L	H/9	HR/9	BB/9	K/9	KW
1993	St. Petersburg	Flor	35.7	42	15	3	13	27	3.79	2	2	10.60	.76	3.28	6.81	1.45
1993	Arkansas	Texas	28.0	42	19	2	18	14	6.11	1	2	13.50	.64	5.79	4.50	.05
1994	Arkansas	Texas	96.3	114	44	12	45	53	4.11	5	6	10.65	1.12	4.20	4.95	.60
1996	Edmonton	PCL	52.7	52	16	7	17	33	2.73	4	2	8.89	1.20	2.91	5.64	1.15
1996	Oakland	AL	14.3	15	10	5	13	8	6.28	1	1	9.42	3.14	8.16	5.02	-.37

The payment from the Cardinals for Dennis Eckersley, Montgomery is a product of that organization's strange decision to "develop" closers. After piling up 36 saves at Arkansas in '95, Steve took his fine-tuned "closer mentality" to the mound in Oakland, and was shellacked back to Edmonton before May Day. He should still have a future as a setup man.

ARIEL PRIETO   **RSP**   **1967**   **Age 30?**

YR	TEAM	Lge	IP	H	ER	HR	BB	K	ERA	W	L	H/9	HR/9	BB/9	K/9	KW
1995	Oakland	AL	58.3	58	29	4	33	37	4.47	3	3	8.95	.62	5.09	5.71	.63
1996	Oakland	AL	125.7	120	47	7	57	72	3.37	8	6	8.59	.50	4.08	5.16	.70

After struggling through the first half of '96, Prieto finally got used to pitching with newfound bulk gained thanks to American cuisine. No word on whether Gary Huckabay was consulted on how to "play big." Whereas earlier in the season he seemed to be overthrowing everything, by the end of the year he was mechanically sound and throwing his slider for strikes. He may be 27, as is claimed, or 30, or even older; he'd been scouted on the Cuban national team for over ten years.

CARLOS REYES   **RBP**   **1969**   **Age 28**

YR	TEAM	Lge	IP	H	ER	HR	BB	K	ERA	W	L	H/9	HR/9	BB/9	K/9	KW
1993	Greenville	South	63.3	72	21	5	32	42	2.98	4	3	10.23	.71	4.55	5.97	.85
1994	Oakland	AL	77.7	71	31	9	47	56	3.59	5	4	8.23	1.04	5.45	6.49	.80
1995	Oakland	AL	69.3	71	36	10	30	49	4.67	3	5	9.22	1.30	3.89	6.36	1.15
1996	Oakland	AL	122.7	123	52	16	63	75	3.82	7	7	9.02	1.17	4.62	5.50	.68

Reyes was the A's Opening Day starter in '96, and was unfairly yanked from the rotation early on. He was very effective in long relief, and should be around next season in the long relief/spot starter role. Like too many of the A's possible starters he lives on junk, in this case throwing one of the nicest changeups you'll see from someone not named Doug Jones.

BRAD RIGBY   **RSP**   **1973**   **Age 24**

YR	TEAM	Lge	IP	H	ER	HR	BB	K	ERA	W	L	H/9	HR/9	BB/9	K/9	KW
1995	Modesto	Calif	136.3	163	78	6	66	94	5.15	6	9	10.76	.40	4.36	6.21	.98
1996	Huntsville	South	146.7	179	81	14	68	92	4.97	6	10	10.98	.86	4.17	5.65	.84

Currently considered the A's best pitching prospect, Rigby has actually been gaining velocity with age while retaining command of both the slider and curve that got him noticed in the first place at Georgia Tech. All summer long people were asking about his availability, and the A's invariably shut down the discussions at that point.

MICHAEL ROSSITER   **RSP**   **1973**   **Age 24**

YR	TEAM	Lge	IP	H	ER	HR	BB	K	ERA	W	L	H/9	HR/9	BB/9	K/9	KW
1993	Modesto	Calif	99.0	137	58	15	49	67	5.27	4	7	12.45	1.36	4.45	6.09	.92
1995	Modesto	Calif	59.3	85	35	6	26	45	5.31	3	4	12.89	.91	3.94	6.83	1.29
1996	Huntsville	South	135.0	181	83	16	51	84	5.53	5	10	12.07	1.07	3.40	5.60	1.02

It's generally forgotten that Rossiter was a first-round sandwich pick, but he was once a good prospect, since derailed by injuries. Last season was his first full year in a rotation since '92. He's filled out his 6'6" frame with age, and has fine control when he's healthy. He could wind up being very successful in the bullpen.

AARON SMALL   RBP   1972   Age 25

YR	TEAM	Lge	IP	H	ER	HR	BB	K	ERA	W	L	H/9	HR/9	BB/9	K/9	KW
1993	Knoxville	South	84.3	106	41	5	52	32	4.38	4	5	11.31	.53	5.55	3.42	-.25
1994	Knoxville	South	88.0	106	39	5	55	59	3.99	5	5	10.84	.51	5.62	6.03	.61
1995	Charlotte, NC	Inter	37.7	41	14	2	14	26	3.35	2	2	9.80	.48	3.35	6.21	1.23
1996	Edmonton	PCL	112.0	115	55	9	38	68	4.42	5	7	9.24	.72	3.05	5.46	1.06
1996	Oakland	AL	29.0	34	20	2	22	16	6.21	1	2	10.55	.62	6.83	4.97	-.05

This big man enjoyed something of a remarkable redirection of his career last year. He had been developed as a curve-balling bullpen ace by the Blue Jays and Marlins. Snagged on waivers by the A's, his pitching coach at Edmonton, Pete Richert, had him scrap the curve, take up the slider and polish a change to go with his good fastball. He tossed a no-hitter, and in a season where most of the Trappers' rotation was called up to Oakland, managed to fill the gaps on the roster. The A's front office has been very impressed with him, and seems to think they can count on him for next season.

BILLY TAYLOR   RRP   1962   Age 35

YR	TEAM	Lge	IP	H	ER	HR	BB	K	ERA	W	L	H/9	HR/9	BB/9	K/9	KW
1993	Richmond	Inter	64.3	63	18	3	35	66	2.52	5	2	8.81	.42	4.90	9.23	1.85
1994	Oakland	AL	45.3	40	19	4	20	48	3.77	3	2	7.94	.79	3.97	9.53	2.18
1996	Oakland	AL	59.3	50	21	4	27	65	3.19	4	3	7.58	.61	4.10	9.86	2.26

Taylor returned from the dead, having missed the '95 season with torn knee ligaments. He was back in shape sooner than expected, and was back as the A's bullpen ace by May. He can be absolutely unhittable at times, and if healthy could crank out a monster season if there was ever a good collection of starters ahead of him.

DAVE TELGHEDER   RSP   1967   Age 30

YR	TEAM	Lge	IP	H	ER	HR	BB	K	ERA	W	L	H/9	HR/9	BB/9	K/9	KW
1993	Norfolk	Inter	71.3	92	30	7	29	43	3.79	4	4	11.61	.88	3.66	5.43	.89
1993	NY Mets	NL	74.0	84	37	10	29	34	4.50	4	4	10.22	1.22	3.53	4.14	.50
1994	Norfolk	Inter	147.0	186	70	16	39	70	4.29	7	9	11.39	.98	2.39	4.29	.83
1995	Norfolk	Inter	86.0	89	34	8	17	63	3.56	6	4	9.31	.84	1.78	6.59	1.75
1996	Edmonton	PCL	95.0	104	45	8	32	48	4.26	5	6	9.85	.76	3.03	4.55	.76
1996	Oakland	AL	79.7	84	31	10	28	41	3.50	5	4	9.49	1.13	3.16	4.63	.75

You can look at Dave Telgheder in one of two ways: either you see having to turn to a Dave Telgheder by season's end as a disappointment, or if you like Dave Telgheder, he had a nice little season. He could be an effective fifth starter, not hurting your team or the opposition, if everything breaks right for him.

BRET WAGNER   LSP   1973   Age 24

YR	TEAM	Lge	IP	H	ER	HR	BB	K	ERA	W	L	H/9	HR/9	BB/9	K/9	KW
1994	New Jersey	NY-P	10.3	13	10	0	7	6	8.71	0	1	11.32	.00	6.10	5.23	.22
1994	Savannah	S Atl	39.3	38	9	3	10	25	2.06	3	1	8.69	.69	2.29	5.72	1.33
1995	St Petersburg	Flor	82.7	98	40	5	40	42	4.35	4	5	10.67	.54	4.35	4.57	.44
1995	Arkansas	Texas	33.3	35	12	1	23	26	3.24	2	2	9.45	.27	6.21	7.02	.79
1996	Huntsville	South	123.7	135	68	7	88	71	4.95	6	8	9.82	.51	6.40	5.17	.12

Part of the payment for Todd Stottlemyre, Wagner is a very solid prospect because he's one of those rare left-handers with a real fastball. Although he's still being used as a starter, the A's may move him to the bullpen, depending on how the other lefties in the organization shape up. He pitched poorly in the Arizona Fall League.

JOHN WASDIN   RSP   1973   Age 24

YR	TEAM	Lge	IP	H	ER	HR	BB	K	ERA	W	L	H/9	HR/9	BB/9	K/9	KW
1993	Madison	Midw	43.0	44	12	2	12	23	2.51	4	1	9.21	.42	2.51	4.81	.98
1994	Modesto	Calif	24.0	22	6	3	7	20	2.25	2	1	8.25	1.12	2.62	7.50	1.84
1994	Huntsville	South	129.7	149	65	16	49	85	4.51	6	8	10.34	1.11	3.40	5.90	1.12
1995	Edmonton	PCL	165.0	186	94	28	54	101	5.13	7	11	10.15	1.53	2.95	5.51	1.10
1996	Edmonton	PCL	47.0	52	19	6	22	25	3.64	3	2	9.96	1.15	4.21	4.79	.54
1996	Oakland	AL	131.7	133	71	20	53	72	4.85	6	9	9.09	1.37	3.62	4.92	.73

The Braves have apparently been trying to get Wasdin from the A's, so somebody who knows what they're doing sees something to like. Wasdin seemed desperate to get the high strike called, which with AL umps left him behind in the count early and often. Working high in the zone, he's a homer-prone flyball pitcher. Regardless, he's one of the A's best potential starters, and hopefully they won't lose patience with him as they did with Van Poppel. He dominated in a brief AFL stint.

DON WENGERT   **RBP**   **1970**   **Age 27**

YR	TEAM	Lge	IP	H	ER	HR	BB	K	ERA	W	L	H/9	HR/9	BB/9	K/9	KW
1993	Madison	Midw	67.7	104	35	7	26	27	4.66	3	5	13.83	.93	3.46	3.59	.33
1993	Modesto	Calif	62.0	85	39	8	32	30	5.66	2	5	12.34	1.16	4.65	4.35	.29
1994	Modesto	Calif	39.0	46	14	1	15	34	3.23	2	2	10.62	.23	3.46	7.85	1.75
1994	Huntsville	South	90.3	103	48	17	49	72	4.78	4	6	10.26	1.69	4.88	7.17	1.17
1995	Edmonton	PCL	37.0	52	25	5	20	18	6.08	1	3	12.65	1.22	4.86	4.38	.24
1995	Oakland	AL	29.3	31	12	3	13	16	3.68	2	1	9.51	.92	3.99	4.91	.64
1996	Oakland	AL	162.7	182	76	24	64	72	4.20	9	9	10.07	1.33	3.54	3.98	.44

The new Walt Terrell, right down to the fast pace, assortment of pitches, funny little ears and the unibrow. He throws a 90 mph fastball with no movement and a slider, despite which the A's think he'll be a rotation starter, usually citing his workmanlike attitude. They might be right: for whatever reason, when he started with more than four days' rest, he was awful (7.35 ERA).

JAY WITASICK   **RBP**   **1973**   **Age 24**

YR	TEAM	Lge	IP	H	ER	HR	BB	K	ERA	W	L	H/9	HR/9	BB/9	K/9	KW
1994	Madison	Midw	100.3	97	37	7	58	89	3.32	7	4	8.70	.63	5.20	7.98	1.36
1995	Arkansas	Texas	31.3	45	25	4	20	22	7.18	1	2	12.93	1.15	5.74	6.32	.67
1996	Huntsville	South	62.3	52	18	4	31	46	2.60	5	2	7.51	.58	4.48	6.64	1.09
1996	Oakland	AL	13.3	11	6	4	5	12	4.05	0	1	7.43	2.70	3.38	8.10	1.86

Part of the payment for Stottlemyre, the A's converted him to closer during the season, and the early returns have been good. He has a tendency to try too hard to blow hitters away with his fastball, which can lead to embarrassments like the game he lost on Joe Carter's mammoth game-winning home run in Toronto.

STEVE WOJCIECHOWSKI LSP   **1971**   **Age 26**

YR	TEAM	Lge	IP	H	ER	HR	BB	K	ERA	W	L	H/9	HR/9	BB/9	K/9	KW
1993	Modesto	Calif	75.3	75	26	4	40	37	3.11	5	3	8.96	.48	4.78	4.42	.28
1993	Huntsville	South	61.0	107	54	7	41	40	7.97	1	6	15.79	1.03	6.05	5.90	.45
1994	Huntsville	South	161.7	175	75	9	90	90	4.18	9	9	9.74	.50	5.01	5.01	.42
1995	Edmonton	PCL	73.0	73	29	6	28	36	3.58	4	4	9.00	.74	3.45	4.44	.62
1995	Oakland	AL	49.0	51	23	7	29	13	4.22	2	3	9.37	1.29	5.33	2.39	-.54
1996	Oakland	AL	80.0	89	42	8	30	29	4.72	4	5	10.01	.90	3.38	3.26	.24
1996	Edmonton	PCL	56.7	57	27	4	26	38	4.29	3	3	9.05	.64	4.13	6.04	.98

In case you didn't get the point, the A's pitching staff had serious velocity problems in '96. Wojo is a particularly stark example of this, because his best pitch is a changeup. He's younger than Doug Johns, but the A's got frustrated with him very quickly, and he's never enjoyed consistent control.

Player	Age	Team	Lge	AB	H	DB	TP	HR	BB	SB	CS	OUT	BA	OBA	SA	EQA	EQR	Peak
DANNY ARDOIN	21	Modesto	Calif	321	72	8	1	5	36	3	3	252	.224	.303	.302	.201	23	.224
JOSE CASTRO	21	Modesto	Calif	367	72	9	0	7	32	12	6	301	.196	.261	.278	.176	20	.197
RYAN CHRISTENSON	22	W. Michigan	Midw	127	35	2	1	2	10	1	2	94	.276	.328	.354	.228	12	.252
ROD CORREIA	28	Huntsville	South	245	58	7	1	2	24	6	1	188	.237	.305	.298	.207	18	.208
JEFFREY D'AMICO	21	Modesto	Calif	174	41	4	1	3	14	1	1	134	.236	.293	.322	.204	13	.227
JEFF DAVANON	22	W. Michigan	Midw	304	66	10	3	2	38	3	3	241	.217	.304	.289	.197	21	.217
ROB DEBOER	25	Huntsville	South	125	32	2	0	5	22	1	1	94	.256	.367	.392	.256	16	.269
	25	Modesto	Calif	255	65	5	2	10	59	6	3	193	.255	.395	.408	.272	37	.287
JUAN DILONE	23	Modesto	Calif	408	96	9	0	11	33	15	5	317	.235	.293	.338	.215	34	.234
MARIO ENCARNACION	18	W. Michigan	Midw	418	89	9	1	7	37	11	4	333	.213	.277	.289	.189	26	.222
DUANE FILCHNER	23	W. Michigan	Midw	501	121	15	1	8	57	1	0	380	.242	.319	.323	.217	42	.236
DAVID FRANCISCO	24	Huntsville	South	391	93	9	1	3	23	8	2	300	.238	.280	.289	.191	24	.205
WEBSTER GARRISON	30	Edmonton	PCL	295	84	11	0	10	39	2	1	212	.285	.368	.424	.267	39	.261
	30	Huntsville	South	181	48	7	1	7	19	1	1	134	.265	.335	.431	.254	22	.250
TYRONE HORNE	25	Edmonton	PCL	205	44	5	1	4	30	4	2	163	.215	.315	.307	.210	16	.221
GARY HUST	24	Huntsville	South	200	42	7	0	3	15	2	0	158	.210	.265	.290	.182	11	.193
EDWARD LARA	20	W. Michigan	Midw	268	53	4	0	1	19	8	3	218	.198	.251	.224	.148	9	.166
TOREY LOVULLO	30	Edmonton	PCL	94	25	1	0	4	17	0	0	69	.266	.378	.404	.265	12	.259
	30	Oakland	AL	82	18	4	0	3	11	1	2	66	.220	.312	.378	.224	8	.218
DAVE MADSEN	24	Modesto	Calif	177	37	4	0	3	24	1	0	140	.209	.303	.282	.195	12	.210
ERIC MARTINS	23	Huntsville	South	395	92	19	1	1	40	5	3	306	.233	.303	.294	.200	27	.218
ALEX MIRANDA	24	W. Michigan	Midw	439	90	4	1	6	68	1	0	349	.205	.312	.273	.195	29	.208
MARK MOORE	26	Modesto	Calif	97	16	3	0	3	13	0	0	81	.165	.264	.289	.175	5	.180
WILLIAM MORALES	23	Huntsville	South	383	106	14	0	16	32	0	1	278	.277	.333	.439	.256	46	.278
MIKE NEILL	26	Modesto	Calif	445	135	11	2	16	52	13	4	314	.303	.376	.445	.278	64	.289
RANDY ORTEGA	23	W. Michigan	Midw	147	34	1	0	2	19	0	0	113	.231	.319	.279	.201	10	.218
ARTURO PAULINO	21	W. Michigan	Midw	240	47	3	1	2	18	5	4	197	.196	.252	.242	.152	9	.169
SCOTT SHELDON	27	Edmonton	PCL	351	99	19	1	11	41	4	2	254	.282	.357	.436	.265	46	.271
DAVE SLEMMER	23	Modesto	Calif	86	22	4	0	3	8	1	1	65	.256	.319	.407	.241	9	.262
FRED SORIANO	21	Modesto	Calif	127	29	1	0	2	11	6	2	100	.228	.290	.283	.197	9	.223
JOSE SORIANO	22	W. Michigan	Midw	447	99	13	1	5	23	10	5	353	.221	.260	.289	.180	24	.199
JON VALENTI	22	W. Michigan	Midw	476	113	10	1	11	24	3	1	364	.237	.274	.332	.201	33	.222
WILFREDO VENTURA	19	Modesto	Calif	101	24	0	1	3	5	0	0	77	.238	.274	.347	.205	7	.236
DANE WALKER	26	W. Michigan	Midw	509	129	17	1	8	90	7	5	385	.253	.366	.338	.241	55	.251
DERRICK WHITE	26	Modesto	Calif	199	52	7	1	6	22	4	2	149	.261	.335	.397	.246	22	.256
	26	W. Michigan	Midw	277	70	8	0	9	34	6	2	209	.253	.334	.379	.242	30	.252

Player	Age	Team	Lge	IP	H	ER	HR	BB	K	ERA	W	L	H/9	HR/9	BB/9	K/9	KW
TODD ABBOTT	22	W. Michigan	Midw	110.7	188	81	12	54	66	6.59	3	9	15.29	.98	4.39	5.37	.69
BENITO BAEZ	19	W. Michigan	Midw	109.3	172	74	9	69	59	6.09	4	8	14.16	.74	5.68	4.86	.20
BOB BENNETT	25	Huntsville	South	77.7	99	49	10	42	60	5.68	3	6	11.47	1.16	4.87	6.95	1.10
CHRIS COCHRANE	23	Modesto	Calif	67.0	83	33	6	25	43	4.43	3	4	11.15	.81	3.36	5.78	1.09
STEVEN CONNELLY	22	Modesto	Calif	58.0	64	28	5	37	41	4.34	3	3	9.93	.78	5.74	6.36	.69
CARL DALE	23	Modesto	Calif	114.3	134	67	11	84	64	5.27	5	8	10.55	.87	6.61	5.04	.03
PAUL FLETCHER	29	Edmonton	PCL	77.7	68	23	8	50	62	2.67	6	3	7.88	.93	5.79	7.18	.95
KEVIN GUNTHER	23	W. Michigan	Midw	81.3	120	47	9	33	57	5.20	3	6	13.28	1.00	3.65	6.31	1.19
GARY HAUGHT	25	Huntsville	South	62.3	73	29	4	28	38	4.19	3	4	10.54	.58	4.04	5.49	.82
MIGUEL JIMENEZ	26	Huntsville	South	34.7	46	32	6	31	20	8.31	1	3	11.94	1.56	8.05	5.19	-.28
	26	Modesto	Calif	64.0	92	34	6	33	47	4.78	3	4	12.94	.84	4.64	6.61	1.04
ROBERT KAZMIRSKI	24	W. Michigan	Midw	46.3	60	22	3	37	24	4.27	2	3	11.65	.58	7.19	4.66	-.24
STEVE LEMKE	26	Modesto	Calif	40.3	66	28	2	20	18	6.25	1	3	14.73	.45	4.46	4.02	.22
DEREK MANNING	25	Huntsville	South	67.3	101	52	10	26	37	6.95	2	5	13.50	1.34	3.48	4.95	.78
MIKE MAURER	23	Huntsville	South	59.7	72	28	3	41	33	4.22	3	4	10.86	.45	6.18	4.98	.11
CHRIS MICHALAK	25	Modesto	Calif	34.7	41	18	4	20	25	4.67	2	2	10.64	1.04	5.19	6.49	.87
KEVIN MLODIK	21	W. Michigan	Midw	119.3	158	60	5	70	86	4.53	6	7	11.92	.38	5.28	6.49	.84
JUAN MORENO	21	W. Michigan	Midw	89.7	135	72	9	90	62	7.23	2	8	13.55	.90	9.03	6.22	-.18
CHRIS MORRISON	24	W. Michigan	Midw	48.7	89	45	9	26	33	8.32	1	4	16.46	1.66	4.81	6.10	.83
CHRIS NELSON	23	Modesto	Calif	57.7	91	41	6	19	39	6.40	2	4	14.20	.94	2.97	6.09	1.29
	23	W. Michigan	Midw	62.0	74	22	4	27	50	3.19	4	3	10.74	.58	3.92	7.26	1.44
JUAN PEREZ	23	Modesto	Calif	88.3	130	57	11	40	56	5.81	3	7	13.25	1.12	4.08	5.71	.88
JAMEY PRICE	24	W. Michigan	Midw	78.3	109	25	2	26	56	2.87	6	3	12.52	.23	2.99	6.43	1.40
JASON RAJOTTE	23	Modesto	Calif	67.7	58	20	4	33	36	2.66	6	2	7.71	.53	4.39	4.79	.50
SCOTT RIVETTE	22	W. Michigan	Midw	130.0	203	99	11	68	91	6.85	4	10	14.05	.76	4.71	6.30	.92
SCOTT ROSE	26	Edmonton	PCL	52.0	58	18	3	21	16	3.12	4	2	10.04	.52	3.63	2.77	.01
CURTIS SHAW	26	Modesto	Calif	95.3	110	54	5	74	56	5.10	4	7	10.38	.47	6.99	5.29	.02
ANDY SMITH	21	W. Michigan	Midw	97.7	153	86	11	89	60	7.92	2	9	14.10	1.01	8.20	5.53	-.21
MATTHEW WALSH	23	Modesto	Calif	63.0	60	32	5	37	43	4.57	3	4	8.57	.71	5.29	6.14	.73
TODD WEINBERG	24	W. Michigan	Midw	48.7	68	31	6	40	41	5.73	2	3	12.58	1.11	7.40	7.58	.68
RYAN WHITAKER	24	Modesto	Calif	102.3	152	71	8	46	55	6.24	3	8	13.37	.70	4.05	4.84	.60
TODD WILLIAMS	25	Edmonton	PCL	86.7	122	61	4	47	27	6.33	3	7	12.67	.42	4.88	2.80	-.29
DAVE ZANCANARO	27	Huntsville	South	40.0	57	28	4	30	26	6.30	1	3	12.82	.90	6.75	5.85	.26
	27	Modesto	Calif	69.0	69	33	8	44	42	4.30	4	4	9.00	1.04	5.74	5.48	.39

Seattle Mariners

Whoever coined the phrase "pitching is 90% of baseball" must have had the 1996 Mariners in mind. How else could you explain how the Mariners, who scored more runs (993) than any team since the 1950 Red Sox, finished with a thoroughly disappointing 85-76 record? It must have been the pitching staff, right?

Anyone who doesn't think that preventing runs and scoring runs are equally important can go to the back of the class. Success demands that a team do both, and the Mariners prevented runs last year like a bad pair of pantyhose.

What happened in Seattle that made the "Refuse to Lose" endless summer a dim memory? For starters, the Mariners are the most dichotomous team in baseball: the difference in quality between their good players and the rest of the team is immense. Consider who their top four hitters were: 21-year-old Uberphenom Alex Rodriguez, Ken Griffey Jr., Edgar Martinez and Jay Buhner. All four scored and drove in 100 runs apiece, three of them are deserving All-Stars and two of them are probably headed to Cooperstown. But all of them except Buhner also spent time on the DL last year. Now consider the production the Mariners got from third base and left field. After the injury to Russ Davis the Mariners were forced to audition everyone from Doug Strange to the outrageously-expensive Jeff Manto at third base. And the potentially terrific platoon of Bragg and Rich Amaral in left field vaporized when Piniella refused to make Bragg the starter, then finally let him go in the Moyer trade. Amaral played well in a utility role, but along with Brian Hunter gave the Mariners marginal production from left field.

The Mariners finally addressed both problems by acquiring Mark Whiten and Dave Hollins in a pair of late-season trades, but the damage had already been done. It sounds silly to chastise the best offense of the last 40 years for not scoring more runs, but as amazing as it sounds there was still room for improvement in Seattle. When you consider that Paul Sorrento posted an .877 OPS—and it was only the fifth-best mark on the team—993 runs doesn't sound so unlikely. If the Mariners had started Bragg in left field full-time and used better judgment in finding a replacement for Davis, they could have scored closer to 1050 runs, which might have dragged the pitching staff, kicking and screaming, into the postseason once again.

Ah, their pitching staff. The staff that features one great pitcher and a motley crew of young pitchers called up after one good month in Double-A. Is there any question of who the Mariners' Most Valuable Player is? The Mariners were able to regroup after Griffey's injury in 1995, and with Randy Johnson pitching every other day for the season's last six weeks they thrilled Seattlites into October. But when Johnson went down for most of last year—no doubt a result of the abuse he took down the stretch in '95—the Mariners lurched forward painfully, dragging a 5.21 team ERA behind them, and were unable to prevent the Rangers from holding on for the division.

It would be unfair to make a dig at the Mariners' pitching staff without mentioning the culprit behind their ineptitude. Lou Piniella is an unconventional manager who does many things well: he can put together a lineup, and runs a bullpen to get the platoon advantage better than most. But he absolutely has no idea how to develop a young starting pitcher. His idea of putting together the back end of his rotation is to scour the organizational reports, see if anybody in AA or AAA has had a decent month and then anoint them as Seattle's new red-blooded phenom. Never mind that the "phenom" is 21 years old and was pitching in rookie ball last April—you're ready for the big time, son! After getting blasted in six starts for the big club, the poor kid is sent down, his confidence shot, while Piniella calls him "timid" and claims he "doesn't have what it takes to succeed in the big leagues." The Mariners have had a number of fine pitching prospects over the last few years, but most were promoted before they were ready, and Piniella had neither the patience nor the confidence to let them develop fully.

All this is precisely why the loss of Johnson was felt so acutely. Without the Big Unit, the only established starters in Seattle were Sterling Hitchcock and Chris Bosio. Hitchcock was a disappointment all season and Bosio's knees all but fell off while he was pitching. The rotation's inexperience was so acute that Bob Wells, a 28-year-old journeyman rookie the year before, was hailed as the staff's anchor for much of the summer. As the season progressed, it became clear that as an anchor, Wells was doing a fine job of keeping the Mariners in place. Throw in Bob Wolcott, whose win in Game 1 of the 1995 ALCS meant that he was guaranteed to start no matter how badly he pitched, and you have a pretty ugly top four. The role of fifth starter on this team was passed around like a bong at Woodstock all year. Paul Menhart, Edwin Hurtado, Matt Wagner, Bob Milacki, Rusty Meacham and Salomon Torres all made at least four starts, and only Torres was at least mildly effective. The rotation was so bad that even the late-season trades for Moyer and Terry Mulholland only made the problem more obvious, because they were forced to occupy the #1 and #2 spots in the rotation, a ludicrous assignment. In retrospect, it is almost surprising that the Mariners played as well as they did without one truly above-average starter in their rotation for most of the season.

Can the Mariners contend again next season? If they do, it will be despite some of the ridiculously short-term decisions they have made over the last two years. The trade of Ron Villone and Marc Newfield in 1995, while it paid immediate dividends, deprived Seattle of their best young arm and the solution to their woes in left field. And last year, GM Woody Woodward pawned off blue-chipper Arquimedez Pozo for Jeff Manto—Jeff Manto!—which should cut into the Mariners depth up the middle this year.

As the Mariners have proven, depth isn't necessary if your front line players are good enough. The trade of Wagner and catcher Chris Widger to Montreal for Jeff Fassero gives the Mariners even more of a disparity between their wheat and their chaff. But if Johnson returns to health, he and Fassero will give Seattle two of the AL's five best left-handers. Throw in four of the 20 best hitters in the league, and even a supporting cast as uninspiring as the Mariners' can provide enough help to lead the franchise back to the postseason.

RICH AMARAL UT 1962 Age 35

Year	Team	Lge	AB	H	DB	TP	HR	BB	SB	CS	OUT	BA	OBA	SA	EQA	EQR	Peak
1993	Seattle	AL	379	116	28	1	1	36	18	8	271	.306	.366	.393	.261	47	.251
1994	Calgary	PCL	54	15	5	0	0	4	1	0	39	.278	.328	.370	.240	6	.228
1994	Seattle	AL	228	60	9	2	4	24	4	1	169	.263	.333	.373	.241	24	.229
1995	Seattle	AL	240	70	16	2	2	21	20	2	172	.292	.349	.400	.266	31	.254
1996	Seattle	AL	313	92	11	3	1	48	25	6	227	.294	.388	.358	.267	42	.254
1997	*Seattle*	*AL*	*259*	*71*	*10*	*1*	*1*	*31*	*23*	*10*	*198*	*.274*	*.352*	*.332*	*.245*	*29*	

Amaral has had a heck of a career for a guy who was buried in the minors until he was 31. Absolutely should not be a starter, but he's a great insurance policy in case Cora goes down or Jose Cruz isn't ready. The decline phase starts now, but his improved plate discipline and ability to hit left-handers (.303 lifetime) should hold him a job for another few years. Ironically, the same forces of inertia which forced him to languish in the minors for so long should help him prolong his career.

DAVID ARIAS 1B 1976 Age 21

Year	Team	Lge	AB	H	DB	TP	HR	BB	SB	CS	OUT	BA	OBA	SA	EQA	EQR	Peak
1996	Wisconsin	Midw	502	148	14	1	17	39	2	2	356	.295	.346	.428	.259	61	.294
1997	*Seattle*	*AL*	*551*	*153*	*18*	*1*	*17*	*57*	*3*	*2*	*400*	*.278*	*.345*	*.407*	*.256*	*67*	

Arias was voted the Midwest League's best defensive first baseman and #6 prospect, and the Mariners likely will start him in AA next year. He showed a lot of different skills for a guy so young, so ignore him at your own risk.

JAMES BONNICI 1B 1972 Age 25

Year	Team	Lge	AB	H	DB	TP	HR	BB	SB	CS	OUT	BA	OBA	SA	EQA	EQR	Peak
1993	Riverside	Calif	380	103	11	1	8	42	0	0	277	.271	.344	.368	.241	40	.270
1994	Riverside	Calif	412	107	15	1	10	48	1	1	306	.260	.337	.374	.239	43	.265
1995	Port City	South	540	162	28	1	23	74	2	1	379	.300	.384	.483	.288	84	.312
1996	Tacoma	PCL	508	148	16	0	26	57	1	2	362	.291	.363	.476	.277	73	.296
1997	*Seattle*	*AL*	*583*	*181*	*21*	*1*	*36*	*66*	*0*	*2*	*404*	*.310*	*.381*	*.535*	*.301*	*101*	

Bonnici is a big, lumbering guy and a 58th-round draft pick, but he can put runs on the board. He's a converted catcher and is still unpolished around the bag. He's as good a hitter as Sorrento, but if the Mariners didn't give Greg Pirkl a job, why would they give Bonnici one? Should get a chance somewhere before too long.

SCOTT BRYANT OF 1968 Age 29

Year	Team	Lge	AB	H	DB	TP	HR	BB	SB	CS	OUT	BA	OBA	SA	EQA	EQR	Peak
1993	Ottawa	Inter	375	103	13	1	12	53	1	1	273	.275	.364	.411	.261	47	.275
1994	Calgary	PCL	403	111	20	2	16	37	1	1	293	.275	.336	.454	.261	51	.272
1995	Edmonton	PCL	403	107	22	1	12	48	1	2	298	.266	.344	.414	.253	48	.258
1996	Tacoma	PCL	216	56	9	2	2	14	1	2	162	.259	.304	.347	.217	18	.218

Bryant hasn't spent consecutive years in the same organization since 1990-91. There's a good reason for that.

JAY BUHNER   RF   1965   Age 32

Year	Team	Lge	AB	H	DB	TP	HR	BB	SB	CS	OUT	BA	OBA	SA	EQA	EQR	Peak
1993	Seattle	AL	574	165	29	2	33	105	2	4	413	.287	.398	.517	.298	100	.300
1994	Seattle	AL	359	100	22	4	21	66	0	1	260	.279	.391	.538	.300	64	.298
1995	Seattle	AL	474	127	21	0	44	61	0	1	348	.268	.351	.591	.297	83	.291
1996	Seattle	AL	566	156	25	0	46	85	0	1	411	.276	.370	.564	.298	100	.287
1997	Seattle	AL	527	135	20	0	38	90	0	1	393	.256	.365	.510	.287	87	

He led the AL in strikeouts, but he's the best .270 hitter in the game. A real flyball hitter, and you have to wonder what his home run totals would be like if the Mariners hadn't moved their fences out two years ago. His Gold Glove was a complete joke. Anyone who thinks Buhner is the best right fielder in the AL should be punished by having to watch footage of every one of the 6,814 balls that fell between him and Griffey last year.

JOEY CORA   2B   1965   Age 32

Year	Team	Lge	AB	H	DB	TP	HR	BB	SB	CS	OUT	BA	OBA	SA	EQA	EQR	Peak
1993	Chi. White Sox	AL	588	167	18	14	3	72	19	6	427	.284	.362	.378	.255	70	.257
1994	Chi. White Sox	AL	316	90	15	4	2	38	7	3	230	.285	.362	.377	.253	37	.251
1995	Seattle	AL	431	133	21	2	3	37	18	7	305	.309	.363	.387	.259	52	.254
1996	Seattle	AL	532	157	38	6	6	35	5	5	380	.295	.339	.423	.255	62	.245
1997	Seattle	AL	471	126	28	5	4	34	12	8	353	.268	.317	.374	.236	48	

Re-signing him was a huge mistake, but it was forced on the Mariners because Woody Woodward can't discern a ballplayer from a bowl of Campbell's soup. Seattle could have enjoyed a Rodriguez-Pozo double play combination for years, but making a statement to the fans that the Mariners were "serious about winning" was a higher priority. Cora is 32, the most common age for a player to suddenly collapse offensively, and he was never that good to begin with.

JOSE CRUZ   OF   1974   Age 23

Year	Team	Lge	AB	H	DB	TP	HR	BB	SB	CS	OUT	BA	OBA	SA	EQA	EQR	Peak
1995	Riverside	Calif	149	35	4	0	6	19	1	1	115	.235	.321	.383	.234	15	.263
1996	Lancaster	Calif	200	54	9	1	4	30	3	1	147	.270	.365	.385	.256	24	.283
1996	Port City	South	187	52	9	1	3	24	3	0	135	.278	.360	.385	.256	22	.283
1996	Tacoma	PCL	79	19	2	1	6	17	1	1	61	.241	.375	.519	.286	13	.316
1997	Seattle	AL	580	167	38	5	21	108	10	4	417	.288	.400	.479	.296	99	

Despite Mark Whiten's great stretch run, the Mariners have been reluctant to re-sign him and put an end to their revolving door in left field. Look up and see why. Cruz was the #3 overall pick in the 1995 draft, and at the plate was better in college than even Darin Erstad. His terrific walk totals at Rice have carried over professionally; one day we should be able to convert Division I stats into DTs. A serious contender for Rookie of the Year.

RUSS DAVIS   3B   1970   Age 27

Year	Team	Lge	AB	H	DB	TP	HR	BB	SB	CS	OUT	BA	OBA	SA	EQA	EQR	Peak
1993	Columbus-OH	Inter	434	112	16	0	25	42	1	1	323	.258	.324	.468	.259	55	.282
1994	Columbus-OH	Inter	428	117	20	1	24	60	3	5	315	.273	.363	.493	.278	64	.298
1995	NY Yankees	AL	99	28	6	2	2	10	0	0	71	.283	.349	.444	.264	13	.279
1996	Seattle	AL	168	40	6	0	6	17	2	0	128	.238	.308	.381	.232	17	.241
1997	Seattle	AL	326	88	18	2	14	39	5	4	242	.270	.348	.466	.271	46	

His career was put on hiatus almost before it started. Davis has waited a long time for his opportunity and he probably won't let a broken leg take it away from him. Vlad is forgiving, but it remains to be seen if Piniella will be.

ALEX DIAZ   OF   1969   Age 28

Year	Team	Lge	AB	H	DB	TP	HR	BB	SB	CS	OUT	BA	OBA	SA	EQA	EQR	Peak
1993	New Orleans	AmA	56	17	1	0	0	3	6	0	39	.304	.339	.321	.251	6	.271
1993	Milwaukee	AL	70	23	3	0	0	0	5	2	49	.329	.329	.371	.245	7	.264
1994	Milwaukee	AL	187	46	5	7	1	10	4	4	145	.246	.284	.364	.214	15	.225
1995	Seattle	AL	272	70	9	0	5	13	19	8	210	.257	.291	.346	.220	24	.229
1996	Tacoma	PCL	177	41	4	0	0	8	5	4	140	.232	.265	.254	.167	8	.172
1996	Seattle	AL	79	19	0	0	2	2	6	3	63	.241	.259	.316	.198	5	.202
1997	Seattle	AL	93	23	2	0	0	6	10	3	73	.247	.293	.269	.209	7	

The Mariners' idea of a bench player. And we wonder why they lost to the Rangers? Signed by the Mets.

EDDY DIAZ   SS   1972   Age 25

Year	Team	Lge	AB	H	DB	TP	HR	BB	SB	CS	OUT	BA	OBA	SA	EQA	EQR	Peak
1993	Appleton	Midw	193	55	9	1	3	12	5	4	142	.285	.327	.389	.240	20	.269
1993	Jacksonville	South	263	62	8	0	7	17	4	2	203	.236	.282	.346	.209	20	.235
1994	Jacksonville	South	346	81	11	0	9	23	8	3	268	.234	.282	.344	.210	27	.232
1995	Port City	South	440	119	13	0	18	40	7	4	325	.270	.331	.423	.252	52	.274
1996	Tacoma	PCL	425	117	21	2	14	17	3	3	311	.275	.303	.433	.244	46	.261

A shortstop in the Mariners' organization, which must rank as the most ill-advised career choice since Jordan retired from the Bulls.

CHARLES GIPSON   OF/SS   1973   Age 24

Year	Team	Lge	AB	H	DB	TP	HR	BB	SB	CS	OUT	BA	OBA	SA	EQA	EQR	Peak
1993	Appleton	Midw	362	78	8	0	1	48	8	6	290	.215	.307	.246	.184	21	.208
1994	Riverside	Calif	500	135	10	2	1	63	17	8	373	.270	.352	.304	.229	47	.256
1995	Port City	South	404	90	8	2	1	30	7	6	320	.223	.276	.260	.173	20	.192
1996	Port City	South	418	107	11	2	1	35	17	8	319	.256	.313	.299	.211	33	.230

Gipson is a step ahead of Diaz, already learning a new position. With offensive skills like his, though, it doesn't really matter where he plays.

CRAIG GRIFFEY   OF/BoC   1971   Age 26

Year	Team	Lge	AB	H	DB	TP	HR	BB	SB	CS	OUT	BA	OBA	SA	EQA	EQR	Peak
1993	Appleton	Midw	105	24	3	0	2	9	4	1	82	.229	.289	.314	.207	8	.226
1993	Riverside	Calif	194	42	3	2	3	10	4	1	153	.216	.255	.299	.183	11	.202
1994	Jacksonville	South	335	69	8	1	4	33	11	5	271	.206	.277	.272	.182	19	.198
1995	Port City	South	313	59	9	1	1	44	8	2	256	.188	.289	.233	.172	16	.185
1996	Port City	South	407	89	13	4	3	39	12	4	322	.219	.287	.292	.196	27	.206

"BoC" stands for Brother of Celebrity. The Griffeys' talent level difference makes Tony and Chris Gwynn look like the Niekro brothers. Ken keeps talking about how great it would be for him and his brother to play in the same outfield. Keep going on the DL, Junior, and eventually you'll run into Craig while on rehab.

KEN GRIFFEY, JR.   CF   1970   Age 27

Year	Team	Lge	AB	H	DB	TP	HR	BB	SB	CS	OUT	BA	OBA	SA	EQA	EQR	Peak
1993	Seattle	AL	595	194	36	3	53	102	16	7	408	.326	.425	.664	.340	137	.369
1994	Seattle	AL	434	140	23	4	40	56	10	3	297	.323	.400	.671	.334	96	.358
1995	Seattle	AL	262	70	7	0	18	53	4	2	194	.267	.390	.500	.292	45	.307
1996	Seattle	AL	548	168	27	2	50	78	16	1	381	.307	.393	.637	.327	116	.340
1997 Seattle		_AL_	_599_	_216_	_37_	_4_	_57_	_116_	_12_	_1_	_384_	_.361_	_.464_	_.721_	_.375_	_165_	

His defense has finally improved to the point where he actually deserves to play center field. He's still seven miles from being the best defensive outfielder in the league. 27 this year, so look out.

GIOMAR GUEVARA   SS/2B   1973   Age 24

Year	Team	Lge	AB	H	DB	TP	HR	BB	SB	CS	OUT	BA	OBA	SA	EQA	EQR	Peak
1993	Bellingham	Nwern	223	44	5	2	1	21	1	3	182	.197	.266	.251	.159	9	.182
1994	Appleton	Midw	394	100	15	1	7	34	5	6	300	.254	.313	.350	.221	34	.248
1995	Riverside	Calif	298	63	9	1	2	24	3	2	237	.211	.270	.268	.173	15	.191
1996	Port City	South	427	111	16	0	3	46	13	4	320	.260	.332	.319	.225	39	.244

He's a shortstop by trade, but with Pozo and Relaford out of the organization, Guevara will probably be groomed to replace Cora at second base down the line. He's a poor man's Cora at the plate, but he makes up for it with better defense. Out of ten players like Guevara, one will turn into Omar Vizquel, and the other nine end up like Manny Alexander.

MIKE HICKEY   3B/2B   1970   Age 27

Year	Team	Lge	AB	H	DB	TP	HR	BB	SB	CS	OUT	BA	OBA	SA	EQA	EQR	Peak
1993	Appleton	Midw	264	65	11	1	2	30	6	3	202	.246	.323	.318	.219	23	.238
1994	Riverside	Calif	504	132	15	4	10	57	8	4	376	.262	.337	.367	.239	52	.255
1995	Port City	South	472	129	18	1	8	58	4	2	345	.273	.353	.367	.245	51	.258
1996	Port City	South	258	64	14	2	1	51	6	3	197	.248	.372	.329	.243	29	.252
1996	Wisconsin	Midw	91	27	5	0	0	18	0	0	64	.297	.413	.352	.267	12	.278

When you're 26 years old and your manager tells you that you've been demoted to A ball, a little light bulb should go off in your head, the one that says, "if they offer me a coaching job, take it." Only listed because of his cool walk totals.

DAVE HOLLINS   **3B**   **1966**   **Age 31**

Year	Team	Lge	AB	H	DB	TP	HR	BB	SB	CS	OUT	BA	OBA	SA	EQA	EQR	Peak
1993	Philadelphia	NL	559	156	27	3	20	93	2	2	405	.279	.382	.445	.276	81	.283
1994	Philadelphia	NL	165	38	5	1	5	26	1	0	127	.230	.335	.364	.236	17	.237
1995	Philadelphia	NL	208	47	11	2	7	55	1	1	162	.226	.388	.399	.265	29	.263
1996	Minnesota	AL	420	99	19	0	15	70	6	4	325	.236	.345	.388	.245	48	.241
1996	Seattle	AL	95	34	3	0	3	13	0	2	63	.358	.435	.484	.303	16	.297
1997	*Seattle*	*AL*	*508*	*134*	*23*	*1*	*17*	*94*	*3*	*2*	*376*	*.264*	*.379*	*.413*	*.270*	*71*	

There are some things Hollins doesn't do well. He's never hit for a great average and he has a reputation for being less than fluid at third base. But he has terrific secondary skills and his defense is better than advertised. After he was made the scapegoat for the Phillies' problems in 1995, he rubbed some members of the front office the wrong way. That's all behind him now. Fragile as a Ming vase, but a really valuable player when he's in the lineup. He signed a two-year deal with Anaheim, and will see time at both corners and DH.

BRIAN R. HUNTER   **1B/LF**   **1968**   **Age 29**

Year	Team	Lge	AB	H	DB	TP	HR	BB	SB	CS	OUT	BA	OBA	SA	EQA	EQR	Peak
1993	Richmond	Inter	101	25	3	0	6	11	4	2	78	.248	.321	.455	.256	13	.269
1993	Atlanta	NL	80	11	3	1	0	3	0	0	69	.138	.169	.200	-.065	0	-.072
1994	Pittsburgh	NL	235	55	11	1	12	18	0	0	180	.234	.289	.443	.239	25	.249
1995	Cincinnati	NL	81	18	4	0	2	12	2	1	64	.222	.323	.346	.226	8	.229
1996	Tacoma	PCL	94	33	3	1	7	9	1	0	61	.351	.408	.628	.332	19	.335
1996	Seattle	AL	199	54	8	0	8	15	0	1	146	.271	.322	.432	.249	23	.251
1997	*Seattle*	*AL*	*245*	*65*	*13*	*1*	*12*	*18*	*2*	*2*	*182*	*.265*	*.316*	*.473*	*.261*	*32*	

A one-dimensional player, but it's a good dimension. Hunter uppercuts on everything, hitting the occasional 450-foot homer but leaving himself vulnerable to pitches on the black. Sorrento has never been able to hit left-handers, and Hunter was a nice caddy for the first half of the season. He went into the tank after the break though, and the Mariners are loaded with right-handed first basemen just waiting for him to falter.

RAUL IBANEZ   **DH/1B**   **1972**   **Age 25**

Year	Team	Lge	AB	H	DB	TP	HR	BB	SB	CS	OUT	BA	OBA	SA	EQA	EQR	Peak
1993	Bellingham	Nwern	141	34	5	1	0	13	0	1	108	.241	.305	.291	.197	9	.219
1993	Appleton	Midw	163	39	4	0	4	19	0	1	125	.239	.319	.337	.218	14	.245
1994	Appleton	Midw	334	92	18	1	7	26	5	2	244	.275	.328	.398	.245	36	.270
1995	Riverside	Calif	369	113	13	4	16	33	2	1	257	.306	.363	.493	.283	55	.308
1996	Port City	South	79	28	7	1	1	6	2	1	52	.354	.400	.506	.302	13	.325
1996	Tacoma	PCL	413	115	14	2	12	43	7	5	302	.278	.346	.409	.254	49	.272
1997	*Seattle*	*AL*	*459*	*129*	*24*	*1*	*12*	*45*	*11*	*5*	*335*	*.281*	*.345*	*.416*	*.260*	*58*	

He made all the prospect charts with a monster 1995, but it was in a great hitter's park, he was way too old for the league and his defense got him moved from catcher to first base. Got a taste with the big club last year, but his new-found power disappeared, and a first baseman with gap power is about as rare as a cellular phone in Manhattan. Vlad doesn't like him either.

RANDY JORGENSEN   **1B**   **1972**   **Age 25**

Year	Team	Lge	AB	H	DB	TP	HR	BB	SB	CS	OUT	BA	OBA	SA	EQA	EQR	Peak
1993	Bellingham	Nwern	241	57	5	0	5	23	3	2	186	.237	.303	.320	.208	18	.233
1994	Riverside	Calif	378	90	8	1	3	33	1	1	289	.238	.299	.288	.195	24	.215
1995	Riverside	Calif	504	133	17	1	11	37	2	1	372	.264	.314	.367	.229	47	.249
1996	Port City	South	475	130	23	1	9	49	1	1	346	.274	.342	.383	.245	51	.262

His power makes Ibanez look like Harmon Killebrew. Ken Phelps has as much chance to play in Seattle next year.

RICK LADJEVICH   **3B**   **1972**   **Age 25**

Year	Team	Lge	AB	H	DB	TP	HR	BB	SB	CS	OUT	BA	OBA	SA	EQA	EQR	Peak
1994	Bellingham	Nwern	247	67	4	0	2	14	1	2	182	.271	.310	.312	.208	18	.230
1995	Riverside	Calif	475	128	9	0	8	21	1	1	348	.269	.300	.339	.215	37	.233
1996	Port City	South	425	116	16	1	7	29	1	2	311	.273	.319	.365	.230	39	.246

Nice trend, but he better speed up his progress if he wants to reach the major leagues before he's 40. He's not really a prospect, although every so often a guy like this develops suddenly in his mid-twenties.

EDGAR MARTINEZ   DH   1963   Age 34

Year	Team	Lge	AB	H	DB	TP	HR	BB	SB	CS	OUT	BA	OBA	SA	EQA	EQR	Peak
1993	Seattle	AL	138	35	5	0	6	29	0	0	103	.254	.383	.420	.270	20	.263
1994	Seattle	AL	327	93	20	1	14	53	5	2	236	.284	.384	.480	.286	52	.276
1995	Seattle	AL	518	190	43	0	35	118	4	3	331	.367	.484	.653	.364	132	.346
1996	Seattle	AL	502	166	49	2	28	124	3	3	339	.331	.463	.604	.343	117	.326
1997	*Seattle*	*AL*	*542*	*171*	*38*	*0*	*29*	*111*	*2*	*3*	*374*	*.315*	*.432*	*.546*	*.323*	*111*	

Despite Seattle's prominence on the baseball landscape the last two years, Martinez remains the most unknown great hitter in baseball. Like Wade Boggs, incompetent team management kept him in AAA years after he was ready for the major leagues. He had a legitimate chance for 60 doubles before he strained his ribs while making an emergency start at third base. Few star players have to jump through the hurdles he did to make it, and his early snub may motivate him to stick around, posting a .400 OBP every year into his 40s.

JOHN MARZANO   C   1963   Age 34

Year	Team	Lge	AB	H	DB	TP	HR	BB	SB	CS	OUT	BA	OBA	SA	EQA	EQR	Peak
1994	Scranton-WB	Inter	284	57	17	1	1	23	2	2	229	.201	.261	.278	.171	14	.164
1995	Oklahoma	AmA	434	131	35	2	10	37	3	3	306	.302	.357	.461	.271	59	.258
1996	Seattle	AL	106	26	7	0	0	7	0	0	80	.245	.292	.311	.201	7	.190

No doubt relieved that Widger was traded. He'll probably volunteer in spring training to be Fassero's personal catcher.

KEVIN REIMER   DH   1964   Age 33

Year	Team	Lge	AB	H	DB	TP	HR	BB	SB	CS	OUT	BA	OBA	SA	EQA	EQR	Peak
1993	Milwaukee	AL	443	117	22	1	16	32	5	3	329	.264	.314	.427	.246	49	.245
1996	Salt Lake City	PCL	191	50	5	0	9	11	3	1	142	.262	.302	.429	.244	21	.231
1996	Tacoma	PCL	94	26	2	0	3	3	0	0	68	.277	.299	.394	.232	9	.220

He's back to re-establish the standard to which inept outfielders are compared. No one plays the outfield like Reimer, nobody. Sam Horn, "The Anvil," hit his one and only major league triple off Reimer's glove one lovely spring day in Baltimore. It takes a special kind of player to redefine the way we watch baseball, but Reimer helped us all appreciate the joys of watching the coordination-challenged play the field.

ALEX RODRIGUEZ   SS   1976   Age 21

Year	Team	Lge	AB	H	DB	TP	HR	BB	SB	CS	OUT	BA	OBA	SA	EQA	EQR	Peak
1994	Appleton	Midw	253	74	9	2	12	20	8	3	182	.292	.344	.486	.275	36	.323
1994	Jacksonville	South	62	17	3	1	1	9	1	0	45	.274	.366	.403	.263	8	.310
1994	Calgary	PCL	115	31	4	2	5	8	2	3	87	.270	.317	.470	.253	14	.296
1994	Seattle	AL	54	11	0	0	0	3	3	0	43	.204	.246	.204	.150	2	.172
1995	Tacoma	PCL	218	79	7	2	16	19	2	3	142	.362	.414	.633	.330	45	.381
1995	Seattle	AL	143	34	5	2	6	6	4	2	111	.238	.268	.427	.230	14	.265
1996	Seattle	AL	604	219	46	2	39	59	16	4	389	.363	.419	.639	.339	130	.384
1997	*Seattle*	*AL*	*626*	*210*	*54*	*3*	*31*	*71*	*19*	*8*	*424*	*.335*	*.403*	*.580*	*.321*	*124*	

Rodriguez could be a pretty good player someday if he lives up to his potential.

Seriously, is there anything left to say about Rodriguez? He'll probably hold four or five significant major league records by the time he hangs up his spikes, and he proved this year that his defense really is good enough that any talk of him moving elsewhere is just jealous sniping. His MVP snub is the worst decision made by the BBWAA voters since George Bell was given Alan Trammell's trophy in 1987. He could be Honus Wagner, Ernie Banks and Cal Ripken all wrapped into one. Or he could really surprise us.

ANDY SHEETS   **INF**   **1972**   **Age 25**

Year	Team	Lge	AB	H	DB	TP	HR	BB	SB	CS	OUT	BA	OBA	SA	EQA	EQR	Peak
1993	Appleton	Midw	265	59	7	2	1	15	3	3	209	.223	.264	.275	.173	13	.194
1993	Riverside	Calif	179	30	5	1	1	11	1	1	150	.168	.216	.223	.112	3	.127
1994	Riverside	Calif	104	27	3	1	2	13	3	1	78	.260	.342	.365	.242	11	.266
1994	Jacksonville	South	237	47	8	0	1	20	2	2	192	.198	.261	.245	.156	9	.172
1994	Calgary	PCL	90	27	5	0	2	10	1	1	64	.300	.370	.422	.266	12	.293
1995	Tacoma	PCL	443	129	31	6	3	34	7	2	316	.291	.342	.409	.255	52	.277
1996	Tacoma	PCL	238	84	15	3	6	24	5	3	157	.353	.412	.517	.308	41	.329
1996	Seattle	AL	110	21	9	0	0	10	2	0	89	.191	.258	.273	.173	6	.185
1997	*Seattle*	*AL*	*351*	*101*	*21*	*3*	*7*	*34*	*6*	*4*	*254*	*.288*	*.351*	*.425*	*.263*	*45*	

A pretty good hitter who can play three infield positions, which at the least should earn him a job on the bench. Sheets really should platoon with Cora, who can't hit left-handers at all. Whether he has a productive career or not depends on how well he gets along with Piniella.

PAUL SORRENTO   **1B**   **1966**   **Age 31**

Year	Team	Lge	AB	H	DB	TP	HR	BB	SB	CS	OUT	BA	OBA	SA	EQA	EQR	Peak
1993	Cleveland	AL	475	133	24	1	24	62	3	1	343	.280	.363	.486	.280	71	.287
1994	Cleveland	AL	323	90	12	0	15	34	0	1	234	.279	.347	.455	.265	42	.268
1995	Cleveland	AL	328	82	12	0	29	52	1	1	247	.250	.353	.552	.288	55	.286
1996	Seattle	AL	473	139	30	1	24	57	0	2	336	.294	.370	.514	.288	75	.281
1997	*Seattle*	*AL*	*506*	*130*	*15*	*0*	*32*	*71*	*0*	*0*	*376*	*.257*	*.348*	*.476*	*.274*	*74*	

Well, you'd have to say he did a pretty good job replacing Tino Martinez. Strictly a platoon player, but a very dangerous hitter whose flyball tendencies fit well in this lineup.

DOUG STRANGE   **3B/LF**   **1964**   **Age 33**

Year	Team	Lge	AB	H	DB	TP	HR	BB	SB	CS	OUT	BA	OBA	SA	EQA	EQR	Peak
1993	Texas	AL	493	136	23	0	12	46	6	3	360	.276	.338	.396	.247	55	.246
1994	Texas	AL	228	50	11	1	6	15	1	3	181	.219	.267	.355	.201	16	.198
1995	Seattle	AL	156	44	10	2	2	10	0	3	115	.282	.325	.410	.240	16	.231
1996	Seattle	AL	184	44	7	1	3	14	1	0	140	.239	.293	.337	.211	14	.201
1997	*Seattle*	*AL*	*94*	*23*	*3*	*0*	*3*	*7*	*1*	*0*	*71*	*.245*	*.297*	*.372*	*.229*	*9*	

Look no further if you want to know how tough the loss of Russ Davis was. He's a switch-hitter in name only, with a .198 average against southpaws the last five years. Strange is an underrated fielder, but he really doesn't belong on a major league roster anymore.

MARCUS STURDIVANT   **OF**   **1974**   **Age 23**

Year	Team	Lge	AB	H	DB	TP	HR	BB	SB	CS	OUT	BA	OBA	SA	EQA	EQR	Peak
1993	Bellingham	Nwern	248	56	5	1	4	11	3	2	194	.226	.259	.302	.183	14	.211
1994	Appleton	Midw	420	89	9	4	2	27	9	7	338	.212	.260	.267	.168	20	.191
1995	Riverside	Calif	355	86	10	3	1	31	13	6	275	.242	.303	.296	.205	26	.228
1996	Lancaster	Calif	289	66	13	2	1	23	10	4	227	.228	.285	.298	.197	20	.218
1996	Port City	South	250	69	9	3	2	22	9	4	185	.276	.335	.360	.238	26	.263

A classic fourth outfielder/pinch-runner/defensive replacement. Sturdivant was voted the best defensive outfielder and baserunner in the California League, but at the plate he's a Luis Polonia clone with an almost embarrassing lack of power. Similar to the Marlins' Jesus Tavarez, who was drafted out of the Mariner organization.

JASON VARITEK   **C**   **1972**   **Age 25**

Year	Team	Lge	AB	H	DB	TP	HR	BB	SB	CS	OUT	BA	OBA	SA	EQA	EQR	Peak
1995	Port City	South	372	88	11	2	11	59	0	1	285	.237	.341	.366	.237	39	.258
1996	Port City	South	519	133	22	1	13	56	5	3	389	.256	.329	.378	.238	53	.254
1997	*Seattle*	*AL*	*425*	*112*	*25*	*1*	*13*	*56*	*4*	*3*	*316*	*.264*	*.349*	*.419*	*.260*	*54*	

The next time a team drafts a player represented by Scott Boras and the negotiations get tough, they should put the kid in touch with Varitek. Boras' hard-line tactics turned away the Twins, who drafted him as a junior, and when the Mariners drafted him the following year, he insisted on marquee money. As a senior Varitek had no leverage, and held out until the following March. He eventually got $650,000, about average money for a late first-round pick, but lost about two years of development. His second season with a wood bat was discouragingly like his first, not what anyone expected from one of the greatest catchers in collegiate history. He'll probably take a step forward this year, but he's 25, and his star potential is almost gone.

MARK WHITEN   **LF/RF**   **1967**   **Age 30**

Year	Team	Lge	AB	H	DB	TP	HR	BB	SB	CS	OUT	BA	OBA	SA	EQA	EQR	Peak
1993	St. Louis	NL	578	154	11	3	28	67	13	7	431	.266	.343	.441	.260	75	.271
1994	St. Louis	NL	340	101	16	2	15	41	9	4	243	.297	.373	.488	.285	53	.292
1995	Pawtucket	Inter	105	28	2	1	4	19	3	1	78	.267	.379	.419	.271	15	.273
1995	Boston	AL	109	21	1	0	2	8	1	0	88	.193	.248	.257	.157	4	.157
1995	Philadelphia	NL	214	57	8	1	11	34	6	0	157	.266	.367	.467	.280	33	.283
1996	Philadelphia	NL	188	48	6	0	8	35	11	3	143	.255	.372	.415	.269	27	.267
1996	Atlanta	NL	92	24	4	1	3	17	1	4	72	.261	.376	.424	.256	12	.254
1996	Seattle	AL	141	43	5	0	13	21	2	1	99	.305	.395	.617	.320	29	.317
1997	*Seattle*	*AL*	*303*	*77*	*12*	*3*	*15*	*51*	*11*	*5*	*231*	*.254*	*.362*	*.462*	*.285*	*50*	

Buhner's presence in right field made Whiten the strongest-armed left fielder in recent memory. If he ever tames his weakness for pitches down and away, he may be an All-Star. Overqualified to be a bench player, but he's been labeled a journeyman and is not going to have a starting job handed to him.

CHRIS WIDGER   **C**   **1971**   **Age 26**

Year	Team	Lge	AB	H	DB	TP	HR	BB	SB	CS	OUT	BA	OBA	SA	EQA	EQR	Peak
1993	Riverside	Calif	363	85	16	1	8	10	3	2	280	.234	.255	.350	.199	25	.219
1994	Jacksonville	South	399	99	9	2	15	39	5	3	303	.248	.315	.393	.236	41	.257
1995	Tacoma	PCL	176	49	6	1	10	10	0	0	127	.278	.317	.494	.265	23	.284
1996	Tacoma	PCL	358	108	14	1	14	27	6	1	251	.302	.351	.464	.273	49	.288
1997	*Montreal*	*NL*	*421*	*107*	*22*	*1*	*15*	*29*	*6*	*2*	*316*	*.254*	*.302*	*.418*	*.251*	*50*	

The Expos have the small market treadmill turned up to top speed each off-season, and forced to move Fassero, GM Jim Beattie explored familiar haunts in Seattle by trading for Widger. Widger has little star potential, but he has a nice mix of skills for a catcher. He'll probably get the bulk of the playing time behind the plate once the Expos find someone to take Darrin Fletcher off their hands. Good defense, Grade B power, but potentially an Ed Sprague-caliber out-maker.

DAN WILSON   **C**   **1969**   **Age 28**

Year	Team	Lge	AB	H	DB	TP	HR	BB	SB	CS	OUT	BA	OBA	SA	EQA	EQR	Peak
1993	Indianapolis	AmA	192	48	9	1	1	20	1	0	144	.250	.321	.323	.219	16	.234
1993	Cincinnati	NL	77	17	3	0	0	11	0	0	60	.221	.318	.260	.193	5	.208
1994	Seattle	AL	281	61	13	2	3	10	1	2	222	.217	.244	.310	.176	14	.185
1995	Seattle	AL	402	115	23	3	10	34	2	1	288	.286	.342	.433	.259	49	.269
1996	Seattle	AL	493	142	20	0	20	32	1	2	353	.288	.331	.450	.259	60	.266
1997	*Seattle*	*AL*	*451*	*116*	*16*	*0*	*18*	*51*	*3*	*3*	*338*	*.257*	*.333*	*.412*	*.251*	*53*	

Give Piniella some credit here. His trade of Erik Hanson and Bret Boone for Wilson and Bobby Ayala looked like something Timothy Leary (the other one) concocted, but Wilson has developed into a pretty good hitter, and his catching skills were never questioned. Unlikely to ever exceed his 1995-96 performance.

BOBBY AYALA   **RRP**   **1970**   **Age 27**

YR	TEAM	Lge	IP	H	ER	HR	BB	K	ERA	W	L	H/9	HR/9	BB/9	K/9	KW
1993	Indianapolis	AmA	26.0	35	16	1	16	17	5.54	1	2	12.12	.35	5.54	5.88	.58
1993	Cincinnati	NL	96.3	109	67	16	56	63	6.26	3	8	10.18	1.49	5.23	5.89	.65
1994	Seattle	AL	55.3	43	17	2	27	74	2.77	4	2	6.99	.33	4.39	12.04	2.91
1995	Seattle	AL	71.7	70	32	8	31	77	4.02	4	4	8.79	1.00	3.89	9.67	2.25
1996	Seattle	AL	67.3	61	33	9	27	59	4.41	3	4	8.15	1.20	3.61	7.89	1.73

A bit of an enigma; Ayala has had two straight underachieving seasons, and every time he begins to straighten himself out he gives up a game-tying homer in the eighth. His biggest problem is that injuries have robbed him of his once-devastating sinker. There's nothing wrong with his other pitches, but he can't finish hitters off and his pitches are up in the strike zone too much. If he's healthy this year, he'll be close to his 1994 numbers again.

CHRIS BOSIO   **RSP**   **1963**   **Age 34**

YR	TEAM	Lge	IP	H	ER	HR	BB	K	ERA	W	L	H/9	HR/9	BB/9	K/9	KW
1993	Seattle	AL	161.3	141	61	15	66	123	3.40	10	8	7.87	.84	3.68	6.86	1.37
1994	Seattle	AL	124.7	128	54	13	44	65	3.90	7	7	9.24	.94	3.18	4.69	.77
1995	Seattle	AL	172.0	200	77	16	73	85	4.03	9	10	10.47	.84	3.82	4.45	.53
1996	Seattle	AL	61.0	68	34	7	25	38	5.02	3	4	10.03	1.03	3.69	5.61	.95

Only 34, but his knees are collecting Social Security checks. Bosio probably has one more good season left in him, but only if he's moved to the bullpen.

JASON BROSNAN   **LRP**   **1968**   **Age 29**

YR	TEAM	Lge	IP	H	ER	HR	BB	K	ERA	W	L	H/9	HR/9	BB/9	K/9	KW
1993	Bakersfield	Calif	32.0	43	19	2	16	24	5.34	1	3	12.09	.56	4.50	6.75	1.12
1993	Vero Beach	Flor	22.3	33	22	2	24	25	8.87	0	2	13.30	.81	9.67	10.07	.94
1993	San Antonio	Texas	17.3	27	13	1	11	7	6.75	1	1	14.02	.52	5.71	3.63	-.22
1994	San Antonio	Texas	27.7	41	18	4	16	21	5.86	1	2	13.34	1.30	5.20	6.83	.98
1994	Albuquerque	PCL	58.0	68	27	3	36	36	4.19	3	3	10.55	.47	5.59	5.59	.47
1995	San Antonio	Texas	20.3	28	10	2	6	18	4.43	1	1	12.39	.89	2.66	7.97	1.99
1995	Albuquerque	PCL	28.7	30	12	3	12	16	3.77	2	1	9.42	.94	3.77	5.02	.73
1996	Port City	South	71.0	83	33	9	37	55	4.18	4	4	10.52	1.14	4.69	6.97	1.15
1996	Tacoma	PCL	29.3	22	13	3	19	22	3.99	2	1	6.75	.92	5.83	6.75	.79

Has left arm, will travel. He has had to rent an apartment 14 times in the last six years, none in a major league city. He's not really all that bad a pitcher, but to get a chance he needs to throw 10 perfect innings in spring training or hope that one of his old managers gets hired as a pitching coach somewhere.

RAFAEL CARMONA   **RRP**   **1973**   **Age 24**

YR	TEAM	Lge	IP	H	ER	HR	BB	K	ERA	W	L	H/9	HR/9	BB/9	K/9	KW
1993	Bellingham	Nwern	30.7	45	20	2	15	17	5.87	1	2	13.21	.59	4.40	4.99	.56
1994	Riverside	Calif	61.0	59	21	4	25	42	3.10	4	3	8.70	.59	3.69	6.20	1.14
1995	Port City	South	13.0	14	5	0	3	11	3.46	1	0	9.69	.00	2.08	7.62	2.02
1995	Tacoma	PCL	45.0	55	27	8	24	35	5.40	2	3	11.00	1.60	4.80	7.00	1.13
1995	Seattle	AL	48.7	51	24	8	35	28	4.44	2	3	9.43	1.48	6.47	5.18	.11
1996	Seattle	AL	90.3	90	36	9	57	60	3.59	6	4	8.97	.90	5.68	5.98	.57

Carmona is developing into quite a pitcher. He somehow survived the Piniella Escalator, and young pitchers who survive in the big leagues despite poor control are a rarity. Can't get left-handers out, and his stamina is still a question mark - batters hit .357 after he threw 45 pitches. But with Mike Jackson probably leaving, Carmona could take over the role of setup man for Charlton. He may have reached the point where he won't be set down if he goes through a bad stretch, and that should help his pitching.

NORM CHARLTON **LRP** **1963** **Age 34**

YR	TEAM	Lge	IP	H	ER	HR	BB	K	ERA	W	L	H/9	HR/9	BB/9	K/9	KW
1993	Seattle	AL	33.7	24	9	4	19	50	2.41	3	1	6.42	1.07	5.08	13.37	3.19
1995	Philadelphia	NL	22.0	22	16	2	17	11	6.55	1	1	9.00	.82	6.95	4.50	-.24
1995	Seattle	AL	46.0	26	6	2	16	58	1.17	5	0	5.09	.39	3.13	11.35	3.00
1996	Seattle	AL	75.0	66	27	6	39	71	3.24	5	3	7.92	.72	4.68	8.52	1.67

One of the best left-handed relievers in baseball. His 4.04 ERA last year was the worst of his career, which can be completely attributed to a six-week stretch in mid-summer when he couldn't get anybody out. His elbow is a constant worry, and Piniella didn't do him any favors by using him five times a week during the 1995 postseason. If nothing in his arm snaps, he'll save 30 games this year.

KEN CLOUDE **RSP** **1975** **Age 22**

YR	TEAM	Lge	IP	H	ER	HR	BB	K	ERA	W	L	H/9	HR/9	BB/9	K/9	KW
1995	Wisconsin	Midw	142.3	169	64	10	85	91	4.05	8	8	10.69	.63	5.37	5.75	.57
1996	Lancaster	Calif	151.3	184	80	15	71	101	4.76	7	10	10.94	.89	4.22	6.01	.95

This is the kind of guy you need to know about if you really want the edge in a fantasy league. Drafted out of a prep school outside Baltimore in 1994, Cloude has steadily moved up the ranks, a level a year, and this season was voted the best pitching prospect in the California League at midseason. His mediocre raw numbers this year were a product of the high altitude at Lancaster, so don't be fooled. He's got four pitches and Piniella loves him. In a normal organization he'd be two years away from a rotation spot, but in Seattle he's a legitimate candidate for the rotation by August.

DEAN CROW **RRP** **1973** **Age 24**

YR	TEAM	Lge	IP	H	ER	HR	BB	K	ERA	W	L	H/9	HR/9	BB/9	K/9	KW
1993	Bellingham	Nwern	41.3	46	15	1	23	22	3.27	3	2	10.02	.22	5.01	4.79	.34
1994	Appleton	Midw	13.3	28	14	4	9	7	9.45	0	1	18.90	2.70	6.08	4.72	.06
1995	Riverside	Calif	54.3	65	20	1	19	30	3.31	4	2	10.77	.17	3.15	4.97	.87
1996	Port City	South	63.0	74	33	4	23	31	4.71	3	4	10.57	.57	3.29	4.43	.65

Was the closer at Port City, and his 26 saves are sure to impress someone in the front office. He's got as much chance as any good minor league reliever; some make it, some don't, and you'd be a fool to predict who will and who won't.

TIM DAVIS **LRP** **1971** **Age 26**

YR	TEAM	Lge	IP	H	ER	HR	BB	K	ERA	W	L	H/9	HR/9	BB/9	K/9	KW
1993	Appleton	Midw	69.3	67	20	6	43	52	2.60	6	2	8.70	.78	5.58	6.75	.85
1993	Riverside	Calif	28.0	19	5	2	10	40	1.61	3	0	6.11	.64	3.21	12.86	3.48
1994	Calgary	PCL	37.3	33	9	1	12	37	2.17	3	1	7.96	.24	2.89	8.92	2.25
1994	Seattle	AL	49.3	53	19	3	27	27	3.47	3	2	9.67	.55	4.93	4.93	.41
1995	Tacoma	PCL	12.0	17	7	2	6	12	5.25	0	1	12.75	1.50	4.50	9.00	1.87
1995	Seattle	AL	24.3	29	17	2	18	19	6.29	1	2	10.73	.74	6.66	7.03	.68
1996	Tacoma	PCL	16.0	20	11	1	13	16	6.19	1	1	11.25	.56	7.31	9.00	1.17
1996	Seattle	AL	42.0	42	16	3	18	33	3.43	3	2	9.00	.64	3.86	7.07	1.39

Quietly had a breakthrough season. Davis is probably miscast as a reliever—he has no platoon split and he pitched brilliantly last year with long rest. Like everyone else on this staff he has a checkered health record, but he can pitch. With Johnson, Moyer, Fassero and Sanders around he probably won't get the opportunity to show it in Seattle.

RYAN FRANKLIN **RSP** **1973** **Age 24**

YR	TEAM	Lge	IP	H	ER	HR	BB	K	ERA	W	L	H/9	HR/9	BB/9	K/9	KW
1993	Bellingham	Nwern	61.0	106	45	3	27	31	6.64	2	5	15.64	.44	3.98	4.57	.53
1994	Appleton	Midw	105.0	127	58	7	35	63	4.97	5	7	10.89	.60	3.00	5.40	1.05
1994	Riverside	Calif	54.7	76	27	5	12	23	4.45	3	3	12.51	.82	1.98	3.79	.77
1995	Port City	South	132.3	189	95	16	62	79	6.46	4	11	12.85	1.09	4.22	5.37	.74
1996	Port City	South	167.0	218	98	25	44	93	5.28	7	12	11.75	1.35	2.37	5.01	1.08

Extreme control specialist who has had a predictably difficult adjustment to AA. He could always turn into Bob Tewksbury, but far more likely to turn into Nate Minchey.

TIM HARIKKALA   **RSP**   **1972**   **Age 25**

YR	TEAM	Lge	IP	H	ER	HR	BB	K	ERA	W	L	H/9	HR/9	BB/9	K/9	KW
1993	Appleton	Midw	33.3	60	31	4	16	19	8.37	1	3	16.20	1.08	4.32	5.13	.63
1994	Appleton	Midw	83.7	84	30	7	35	39	3.23	5	4	9.04	.75	3.76	4.20	.46
1994	Riverside	Calif	25.7	22	6	2	13	20	2.10	2	1	7.71	.70	4.56	7.01	1.20
1994	Jacksonville	South	49.7	77	31	5	29	17	5.62	2	4	13.95	.91	5.26	3.08	-.29
1995	Tacoma	PCL	136.3	163	73	16	71	68	4.82	6	9	10.76	1.06	4.69	4.49	.32
1996	Tacoma	PCL	148.7	216	92	14	65	96	5.57	6	11	13.08	.85	3.93	5.81	.95

Take out the first half of 1994, and there is not a single piece of evidence that suggests Harikkala is a prospect. There are better pitchers to take a chance on.

STERLING HITCHCOCK   **LSP**   **1971**   **Age 26**

YR	TEAM	Lge	IP	H	ER	HR	BB	K	ERA	W	L	H/9	HR/9	BB/9	K/9	KW
1993	Columbus, OH	Inter	72.0	89	42	8	39	69	5.25	3	5	11.12	1.00	4.88	8.62	1.66
1993	NY Yankees	AL	31.0	33	16	4	16	27	4.65	1	2	9.58	1.16	4.65	7.84	1.45
1994	Columbus, OH	Inter	47.0	59	28	4	23	39	5.36	2	3	11.30	.77	4.40	7.47	1.39
1994	NY Yankees	AL	49.0	48	19	3	31	37	3.49	3	2	8.82	.55	5.69	6.80	.84
1995	NY Yankees	AL	168.3	148	68	20	71	121	3.64	10	9	7.91	1.07	3.80	6.47	1.21
1996	Seattle	AL	198.3	229	100	23	78	128	4.54	10	12	10.39	1.04	3.54	5.81	1.05

A very, very disappointing season. Hitchcock was beaten up all season, and there's very little in his 1996 campaign to build on. He got worse as the season wore on, with a 6.14 ERA after the break. He's a flyball pitcher working in a unforgiving ballpark, and the Griffey-Buhner gap in right-center had something to do with the 50 doubles he surrendered in just 197 innings. He's got another chance, but there may not be a third. Traded to San Diego, where he'll be the fourth starter.

EDWIN HURTADO   **RBP**   **1970**   **Age 27**

YR	TEAM	Lge	IP	H	ER	HR	BB	K	ERA	W	L	H/9	HR/9	BB/9	K/9	KW
1993	St. Catherine's	NY-P	84.3	104	44	9	57	46	4.70	4	5	11.10	.96	6.08	4.91	.12
1994	Hagerstown	S Atl	119.0	145	56	10	69	72	4.24	6	7	10.97	.76	5.22	5.45	.51
1995	Knoxville	South	50.7	57	31	7	32	29	5.51	2	4	10.12	1.24	5.68	5.15	.30
1995	Toronto	AL	78.0	77	39	10	42	33	4.50	4	5	8.88	1.15	4.85	3.81	.06
1996	Tacoma	PCL	29.3	26	12	6	15	22	3.68	2	1	7.98	1.84	4.60	6.75	1.10
1996	Seattle	AL	49.0	55	32	9	31	35	5.88	2	3	10.10	1.65	5.69	6.43	.72

Counted on to fill the #4 starter role, Hurtado was laughed out of the American League by midseason. He managed to regroup in the PCL, but he's 27 and he has more walks than strikeouts in his big league career. He's a latecomer to the mound, not pitching professionally until he was 23, and he might resurface as a reliever in a year or two. I doubt it will be in Seattle.

MIKE JACKSON   **RRP**   **1965**   **Age 32**

YR	TEAM	Lge	IP	H	ER	HR	BB	K	ERA	W	L	H/9	HR/9	BB/9	K/9	KW
1993	San Francisco	NL	74.7	64	26	8	32	68	3.13	5	3	7.71	.96	3.86	8.20	1.77
1994	San Francisco	NL	40.7	25	6	5	14	47	1.33	5	0	5.53	1.11	3.10	10.40	2.69
1995	Cincinnati	NL	48.0	40	11	6	22	37	2.06	4	1	7.50	1.12	4.12	6.94	1.28
1996	Seattle	AL	71.3	59	23	10	25	68	2.90	5	3	7.44	1.26	3.15	8.58	2.07

One of the more underrated relievers in the game, but problems with the long ball ruined the first half of his season. The Mariners have not done a very good job assembling their staff; most of their pitchers get flyball outs, which is a recipe for disaster in the Kingdome. Jackson was almost untouchable after the break, but the Mariners aren't keen on asking him back. He should land on his feet somewhere and be very effective for at least three more years.

RANDY JOHNSON   **LSP**   **1964**   **Age 33**

YR	TEAM	Lge	IP	H	ER	HR	BB	K	ERA	W	L	H/9	HR/9	BB/9	K/9	KW
1993	Seattle	AL	250.3	192	76	24	110	318	2.73	19	9	6.90	.86	3.95	11.43	2.82
1994	Seattle	AL	169.3	129	45	13	77	199	2.39	14	5	6.86	.69	4.09	10.58	2.50
1995	Seattle	AL	210.7	163	45	12	69	293	1.92	19	4	6.96	.51	2.95	12.52	3.44
1996	Seattle	AL	60.7	47	19	8	26	82	2.82	5	2	6.97	1.19	3.86	12.16	3.09

Commenting on Johnson is like commenting on Sandy Koufax in the mid-60s: you know he's the best left-handed pitcher of his generation, you know if he's healthy he could win 25 games in any given year and you know there isn't a pitcher in baseball that batters would rather face less. How important has his improved control been? Over the last five years, batters have spanked Johnson for a .139 average when he gets ahead in the count. His back may continue to give him trouble, but when he can take the mound he should be as unhittable as ever.

DEREK LOWE   **RSP**   **1973**   **Age 24**

YR	TEAM	Lge	IP	H	ER	HR	BB	K	ERA	W	L	H/9	HR/9	BB/9	K/9	KW
1993	Riverside	Calif	134.3	215	98	10	65	56	6.57	4	11	14.40	.67	4.35	3.75	.16
1994	Jacksonville	South	137.0	201	97	9	76	59	6.37	4	11	13.20	.59	4.99	3.88	.04
1996	Port City	South	60.3	65	26	7	20	24	3.88	4	3	9.70	1.04	2.98	3.58	.45
1996	Tacoma	PCL	98.0	127	61	8	48	45	5.60	4	7	11.66	.73	4.41	4.13	.28

A former first-round pick who peaked in AA. Like most high school pitchers who don't live up to expectations, injuries have played a role. His draft position may give him a few extra opportunities, but it's unlikely he'll do anything with them.

GREG McCARTHY   **LRP**   **1969**   **Age 28**

YR	TEAM	Lge	IP	H	ER	HR	BB	K	ERA	W	L	H/9	HR/9	BB/9	K/9	KW
1993	Canton	East	31.0	33	18	2	44	30	5.23	1	2	9.58	.58	12.77	8.71	-.29
1994	Canton	East	29.0	24	12	0	29	29	3.72	2	1	7.45	.00	9.00	9.00	.75
1994	Charlotte, NC	Inter	22.3	18	20	1	32	18	8.06	0	2	7.25	.40	12.90	7.25	-.81
1996	Tacoma	PCL	63.7	64	28	2	62	75	3.96	4	3	9.05	.28	8.76	10.60	1.34

Journeyman who finally got a cup of coffee when the Mariners were desperate for someone who could get left-handers out. Like Brosnan, if his control had been even average five years ago he could have made a few million dollars.

RUSTY MEACHAM   **RBP**   **1968**   **Age 29**

YR	TEAM	Lge	IP	H	ER	HR	BB	K	ERA	W	L	H/9	HR/9	BB/9	K/9	KW
1993	Kansas City	AL	21.3	29	12	2	6	13	5.06	1	1	12.23	.84	2.53	5.48	1.20
1994	Kansas City	AL	50.3	47	16	6	13	35	2.86	4	2	8.40	1.07	2.32	6.26	1.50
1995	Kansas City	AL	60.0	70	29	6	21	30	4.35	3	4	10.50	.90	3.15	4.50	.71
1996	Omaha	AmA	50.7	58	27	6	25	32	4.80	2	4	10.30	1.07	4.44	5.68	.78
1996	Tacoma	PCL	18.3	15	6	0	7	17	2.95	1	1	7.36	.00	3.44	8.35	1.92
1996	Seattle	AL	43.0	53	21	7	14	24	4.40	2	3	11.09	1.47	2.93	5.02	.94

One of the more entertaining pitchers in baseball. He pitches like a bomb is going to go off on the mound any second. Very good control, and his pitches move enough to compensate for a complete lack of velocity. Meacham was buried by the Royals when the forkball he had been developing wasn't ready, and pitched much better after the Mariners traded for him. He's running out of chances to re-establish himself, but I suspect he just might.

PAUL MENHART   **RBP**   **1969**   **Age 28**

YR	TEAM	Lge	IP	H	ER	HR	BB	K	ERA	W	L	H/9	HR/9	BB/9	K/9	KW
1993	Syracuse	Inter	142.3	158	73	17	88	88	4.62	7	9	9.99	1.07	5.56	5.56	.46
1995	Syracuse	Inter	48.7	67	42	6	33	26	7.77	1	4	12.39	1.11	6.10	4.81	.08
1995	Toronto	AL	78.7	70	38	8	48	50	4.35	4	5	8.01	.92	5.49	5.72	.53
1996	Tacoma	PCL	25.3	53	29	4	20	10	10.30	0	3	18.83	1.42	7.11	3.55	-.59
1996	Seattle	AL	42.7	51	27	7	26	18	5.70	2	3	10.76	1.48	5.48	3.80	-.11

Acquired from the Blue Jays along with Hurtado, and pitched even worse. Once again folks: pitchers with poor strike-out-to-walk ratios won't be successful for long. I doubt his résumé lists the .431 average AAA hitters lit him up for this year.

JAMIE MOYER   **LSP**   **1963**   **Age 34**

YR	TEAM	Lge	IP	H	ER	HR	BB	K	ERA	W	L	H/9	HR/9	BB/9	K/9	KW
1993	Rochester	Inter	50.3	46	11	2	20	33	1.97	5	1	8.23	.36	3.58	5.90	1.07
1993	Baltimore	AL	150.0	151	50	11	45	93	3.00	11	6	9.06	.66	2.70	5.58	1.18
1994	Baltimore	AL	148.3	147	60	20	43	85	3.64	9	7	8.92	1.21	2.61	5.16	1.07
1995	Baltimore	AL	115.7	111	54	17	33	65	4.20	6	7	8.64	1.32	2.57	5.06	1.04
1996	Boston	AL	90.3	100	36	11	29	48	3.59	6	4	9.96	1.10	2.89	4.78	.87
1996	Seattle	AL	70.0	63	27	8	21	28	3.47	5	3	8.10	1.03	2.70	3.60	.52

Throws so slow it's a wonder he's survived this long without a knuckleball. One of the better quotes this season came from Piniella, who commented on Moyer by saying, "All young pitchers can learn from watching Moyer. When he gets into a jam, he doesn't try to get out of it by throwing harder." Despite a good season, he's not a safe bet; he's 34 and if his control isn't perfect, he's liable to get bombed.

TERRY MULHOLLAND   **LSP**   **1963**   **Age 34**

YR	TEAM	Lge	IP	H	ER	HR	BB	K	ERA	W	L	H/9	HR/9	BB/9	K/9	KW
1993	Philadelphia	NL	184.7	183	72	21	60	112	3.51	12	9	8.92	1.02	2.92	5.46	1.09
1994	NY Yankees	AL	122.0	145	77	22	42	71	5.68	5	9	10.70	1.62	3.10	5.24	.97
1995	San Francisco	NL	149.3	192	103	25	52	59	6.21	5	12	11.57	1.51	3.13	3.56	.40
1996	Philadelphia	NL	131.3	162	67	17	32	46	4.59	6	9	11.10	1.16	2.19	3.15	.50
1996	Seattle	AL	69.3	71	28	4	29	33	3.63	4	4	9.22	.52	3.76	4.28	.49

Mulholland never fully recovered from having Jim Fregosi as a manager. In the early '90s Fregosi decided that bullpens were a luxury and worked Mulholland, Curt Schilling and Tommy Greene to death, along with whoever else was unfortunate enough to be in the rotation at the time. Only Schilling has kept his effectiveness, and even he can't pitch more than four months at a time without breaking down. For the nth time, managers, pay attention to pitch counts. Mulholland signed with the Cubs, where he'll start the year in rotation.

ALEX PACHECO   **RRP**   **1974**   **Age 23**

YR	TEAM	Lge	IP	H	ER	HR	BB	K	ERA	W	L	H/9	HR/9	BB/9	K/9	KW
1993	Jamestown	NY-P	12.0	15	8	0	7	8	6.00	0	1	11.25	.00	5.25	6.00	.69
1993	Burlington	Midw	36.7	59	34	4	17	14	8.35	1	3	14.48	.98	4.17	3.44	.10
1994	Burlington	Midw	59.7	93	51	7	32	43	7.69	1	6	14.03	1.06	4.83	6.49	.96
1994	West Palm Bch	Flor	11.0	10	3	2	6	9	2.45	1	0	8.18	1.64	4.91	7.36	1.23
1995	Harrisburg	East	79.0	93	47	10	39	68	5.35	3	6	10.59	1.14	4.44	7.75	1.47
1996	Harrisburg	East	24.3	29	10	2	15	20	3.70	2	1	10.73	.74	5.55	7.40	1.08
1996	Ottawa	Inter	40.0	49	28	6	23	28	6.30	1	3	11.02	1.35	5.18	6.30	.81

Pacheco was a throw-in in the Fassero deal, but he's young and has had intermittent success in the high minors over the last two years. The departure of Mike Jackson leaves the Mariners a little thin in right-handed relief, and Pacheco could provide some depth. The Piniella shuttle beckons; he ought to stop Tim Davis in spring training and ask him for advice on short-term lodging in Tacoma.

RYAN SMITH   **RRP**   **1972**   **Age 25**

YR	TEAM	Lge	IP	H	ER	HR	BB	K	ERA	W	L	H/9	HR/9	BB/9	K/9	KW
1994	Appleton	Midw	128.3	154	53	12	43	51	3.72	8	6	10.80	.84	3.02	3.58	.44
1995	Riverside	Calif	122.3	171	70	8	67	70	5.15	5	9	12.58	.59	4.93	5.15	.48
1996	Port City	South	90.3	105	39	6	43	47	3.89	5	5	10.46	.60	4.28	4.68	.49

Survived both the jump to AA and a conversion to the bullpen. Very stingy with the home run, and he might handle the PCL better than you'd expect. He'll probably be able to drive both ways on the Tacoma-Seattle route with his eyes closed before long.

MAC SUZUKI   **RBP**   **1975**   **Age 22**

YR	TEAM	Lge	IP	H	ER	HR	BB	K	ERA	W	L	H/9	HR/9	BB/9	K/9	KW
1993	San Bernardino	Calif	71.3	64	30	5	63	60	3.79	4	4	8.07	.63	7.95	7.57	.54
1994	Jacksonville	South	12.0	16	4	1	9	8	3.00	1	0	12.00	.75	6.75	6.00	.31
1995	Riverside	Calif	10.0	17	8	1	8	6	7.20	0	1	15.30	.90	7.20	5.40	.00
1996	Port City	South	68.7	80	40	11	37	48	5.24	3	5	10.49	1.44	4.85	6.29	.88
1996	Tacoma	PCL	20.7	34	18	3	14	12	7.84	0	2	14.81	1.31	6.10	5.23	.22

Still a curiosity at this point. He's missed the better part of the last three seasons with injuries, which may have been the best thing for his arm in the long run. He's still only 22, and should eventually be a very good, if erratic, major league pitcher. The Mariners tried him in the rotation last year, but his future most likely lies in the bullpen.

SALOMON TORRES   **RBP**   **1972**   **Age 25**

YR	TEAM	Lge	IP	H	ER	HR	BB	K	ERA	W	L	H/9	HR/9	BB/9	K/9	KW
1993	Shreveport	Texas	75.0	82	29	7	23	48	3.48	5	3	9.84	.84	2.76	5.76	1.23
1993	Phoenix	PCL	97.3	104	34	6	36	79	3.14	7	4	9.62	.55	3.33	7.30	1.60
1993	San Francisco	NL	43.3	41	21	6	33	23	4.36	2	3	8.52	1.25	6.85	4.78	-.12
1994	Phoenix	PCL	74.3	80	37	6	39	55	4.48	4	4	9.69	.73	4.72	6.66	1.04
1994	San Francisco	NL	84.0	94	49	10	42	39	5.25	3	6	10.07	1.07	4.50	4.18	.27
1995	Tacoma	PCL	26.0	22	9	3	16	18	3.12	2	1	7.62	1.04	5.54	6.23	.69
1995	Seattle	AL	73.7	81	41	11	43	45	5.01	3	5	9.90	1.34	5.25	5.50	.52
1996	Tacoma	PCL	125.7	161	81	17	67	101	5.80	5	9	11.53	1.22	4.80	7.23	1.21
1996	Seattle	AL	48.7	42	20	5	24	35	3.70	3	2	7.77	.92	4.44	6.47	1.05

He's only 25? Torres is going into his fifth season in the majors and has been a prospect since 1990...he never missed time on the DL, but there isn't a doubt in my mind that he has pitched through serious arm miseries over the last few years. The Giants should be ashamed of themselves for making him throw 211 innings when he was just 19, and 233 innings two years later.

His fastball and slider began to show their old movement towards the end of last year, and he gave the Mariners a sign that he might be on the way back. Before the arm problems his stuff was electric, darting all over the place, and if he ever returns to that form he'll be an All-Star. He's a two-pitch pitcher and his future is probably as a closer; for now the Mariners will give him the #5 starter job and see if he can run with it.

SAL URSO   **LRP**   **1972**   **Age 25**

YR	TEAM	Lge	IP	H	ER	HR	BB	K	ERA	W	L	H/9	HR/9	BB/9	K/9	KW
1993	Appleton	Midw	46.3	69	25	2	32	29	4.86	2	3	13.40	.39	6.22	5.63	.32
1994	Riverside	Calif	31.0	50	27	5	18	17	7.84	1	2	14.52	1.45	5.23	4.94	.34
1995	Port City	South	41.7	51	14	0	28	34	3.02	3	2	11.02	.00	6.05	7.34	.94
1996	Tacoma	PCL	67.3	76	21	6	40	37	2.81	5	2	10.16	.80	5.35	4.95	.31

Diminutive southpaw who has a significant backward platoon split: lefties smoked him for a .387 average, but right-handers hit just .223 with no power. Being left-handed will give him opportunities he wouldn't otherwise get, but he has to rely on his manager doing his homework and not trying him as a one-batter specialist.

MATT WAGNER   **RSP**   **1972**   **Age 25**

YR	TEAM	Lge	IP	H	ER	HR	BB	K	ERA	W	L	H/9	HR/9	BB/9	K/9	KW
1994	Appleton	Midw	29.0	30	8	3	11	30	2.48	2	1	9.31	.93	3.41	9.31	2.25
1995	Port City	South	126.3	147	61	12	49	86	4.35	6	8	10.47	.85	3.49	6.13	1.17
1995	Tacoma	PCL	31.3	44	26	4	21	31	7.47	1	2	12.64	1.15	6.03	8.90	1.46
1996	Tacoma	PCL	87.0	98	29	9	39	68	3.00	6	4	10.14	.93	4.03	7.03	1.34
1996	Seattle	AL	80.7	84	47	13	40	40	5.24	3	6	9.37	1.45	4.46	4.46	.37

Another fast-moving pitching prospect who was rushed to Seattle and got his brains beat in. Wagner has a great arm and a prototype pitcher's body, and still has a bright future. Dealt in the Fassero trade, the Expos need to give him another half-season in AAA. If Carlos Perez isn't ready to come back in April, he may get a shot at the rotation before he's ready, and that could hinder his progress.

BOB WELLS **RBP** **1966** **Age 31**

YR	TEAM	Lge	IP	H	ER	HR	BB	K	ERA	W	L	H/9	HR/9	BB/9	K/9	KW
1993	Clearwater	Flor	24.7	28	5	0	9	19	1.82	2	1	10.22	.00	3.28	6.93	1.49
1993	Scranton-WB	Inter	18.0	22	7	1	7	7	3.50	1	1	11.00	.50	3.50	3.50	.29
1994	Reading	East	17.7	21	6	3	4	14	3.06	1	1	10.70	1.53	2.04	7.13	1.87
1994	Calgary	PCL	30.0	38	19	7	12	14	5.70	1	2	11.40	2.10	3.60	4.20	.50
1994	Scranton-WB	Inter	14.0	19	5	1	8	11	3.21	1	1	12.21	.64	5.14	7.07	1.07
1995	Seattle	AL	77.7	83	40	10	41	38	4.64	4	5	9.62	1.16	4.75	4.40	.28
1996	Seattle	AL	130.7	133	59	21	49	91	4.06	7	8	9.16	1.45	3.37	6.27	1.25

Not all that good a pitcher, but going 12-7 should provide job security for some time. The trade for Fassero kills his chances of making the rotation, meaning the job of long man is his to lose. Given where his career was two years ago, Wells would answer the bullpen phone and fetch sunflower seeds from the clubhouse to stay in the major leagues.

BOB WOLCOTT **RSP** **1974** **Age 23**

YR	TEAM	Lge	IP	H	ER	HR	BB	K	ERA	W	L	H/9	HR/9	BB/9	K/9	KW
1993	Bellingham	Nwern	83.7	103	34	10	23	45	3.66	5	4	11.08	1.08	2.47	4.84	.99
1994	Riverside	Calif	162.0	206	73	12	67	94	4.06	9	9	11.44	.67	3.72	5.22	.81
1995	Port City	South	78.7	76	27	7	21	41	3.09	6	3	8.69	.80	2.40	4.69	.96
1995	Tacoma	PCL	74.3	100	45	12	24	40	5.45	3	5	12.11	1.45	2.91	4.84	.89
1995	Seattle	AL	37.3	40	14	6	15	19	3.38	2	2	9.64	1.45	3.62	4.58	.62
1996	Tacoma	PCL	11.7	18	11	5	4	13	8.49	0	1	13.89	3.86	3.09	10.03	2.57
1996	Seattle	AL	150.7	166	77	22	58	76	4.60	7	10	9.92	1.31	3.46	4.54	.65

He was given the entire season to prove that his ALCS performance wasn't a fluke, and failed miserably. Would have been better served by a full season in AAA, but the Mariners' other options were so bad they couldn't afford to spare him. The abuse inflicted on him was a good lesson, and he's man enough to learn from it. His future is still bright.

Player	Age	Team	Lge	AB	H	DB	TP	HR	BB	SB	CS	OUT	BA	OBA	SA	EQA	EQR	Peak
JOSE AMADO	21	Wisconsin	Midw	239	61	6	0	5	15	3	2	180	.255	.299	.343	.215	19	.241
ANDY AUGUSTINE	23	Lancaster	Calif	114	25	2	1	0	17	1	0	89	.219	.321	.254	.195	7	.212
MIKE BARGER	25	Port City	South	374	75	13	3	1	21	12	2	301	.201	.243	.259	.164	16	.173
SHAWN BUHNER	23	Lancaster	Calif	238	40	10	1	2	15	0	0	198	.168	.217	.244	.126	6	.137
DOUG CARROLL	22	Lancaster	Calif	110	24	2	0	3	9	0	0	86	.218	.277	.318	.195	7	.214
JOSE CASTRO	20	Wisconsin	Midw	114	20	3	0	0	7	1	2	96	.175	.223	.202	.098	1	.112
JIM CLIFFORD	26	Lancaster	Calif	387	83	10	2	14	40	2	2	306	.214	.288	.359	.213	32	.221
JASON COOK	24	Lancaster	Calif	447	103	12	2	4	68	2	1	345	.230	.332	.293	.212	36	.227
FARUQ DARCUIEL	23	Wisconsin	Midw	217	41	3	1	1	13	3	2	178	.189	.235	.226	.132	6	.142
CHRIS DEAN	22	Lancaster	Calif	172	39	6	0	4	12	3	1	134	.227	.277	.331	.203	12	.223
	22	Wisconsin	Midw	216	52	4	1	4	13	5	3	167	.241	.284	.324	.203	16	.225
SEAN DRINKWATER	25	Port City	South	104	27	4	0	2	11	1	2	79	.260	.330	.356	.228	10	.240
LUIS FIGUEROA	19	Wisconsin	Midw	141	36	5	0	2	4	1	0	105	.255	.276	.333	.204	10	.235
JASON FRIEDMAN	26	Port City	South	136	25	5	2	1	6	0	0	111	.184	.218	.272	.144	4	.150
ADONIS HARRISON	19	Wisconsin	Midw	202	48	11	1	1	14	2	1	155	.238	.287	.317	.201	14	.232
MIKE KNAPP	31	Tacoma	PCL	187	35	9	1	3	20	1	1	153	.187	.266	.294	.179	10	.172
MIKE LANZA	22	Lancaster	Calif	376	79	8	2	3	11	1	2	299	.210	.233	.266	.150	13	.165
JESUS MARQUEZ	23	Lancaster	Calif	483	121	16	4	15	33	9	4	366	.251	.298	.393	.231	47	.251
MANUEL MARTINEZ	25	Tacoma	PCL	282	86	10	1	5	23	12	7	203	.305	.357	.401	.257	34	.272
JOE MATHIS	21	Wisconsin	Midw	486	125	11	4	6	26	9	3	364	.257	.295	.333	.213	38	.238
TEODORO MEDRANO	20	Wisconsin	Midw	177	32	3	1	4	11	2	1	146	.181	.229	.277	.155	7	.175
LUIS MOLINA	22	Lancaster	Calif	121	24	2	0	0	11	1	1	98	.198	.265	.215	.143	4	.156
SHANE MONAHAN	21	Lancaster	Calif	576	134	18	5	11	19	9	3	445	.233	.257	.339	.198	39	.221
MANNY PATEL	24	Port City	South	381	81	8	1	1	48	7	3	303	.213	.301	.247	.182	21	.195
JULIO PEGUERO	27	Tacoma	PCL	332	90	14	1	1	20	6	4	246	.271	.312	.328	.217	27	.222
JOEL RAMIREZ	22	Wisconsin	Midw	374	77	6	0	2	22	3	3	300	.206	.250	.238	.147	12	.162
ROBERTO RAMIREZ	26	Port City	South	186	41	8	1	3	13	1	1	146	.220	.271	.323	.194	12	.202
EDWARD RANDOLPH	21	Wisconsin	Midw	203	32	6	1	1	17	1	0	171	.158	.223	.212	.110	3	.123
DOUG SAUNDERS	26	Tacoma	PCL	134	34	2	0	4	18	1	0	100	.254	.342	.358	.239	14	.246
SCOT SEALY	25	Lancaster	Calif	253	57	11	1	7	31	1	1	197	.225	.310	.360	.223	23	.235
CHAD SHEFFER	22	Wisconsin	Midw	332	58	5	0	4	49	6	4	278	.175	.281	.226	.160	14	.176
SCOTT SMITH	24	Lancaster	Calif	248	61	8	0	8	11	4	1	188	.246	.278	.375	.219	21	.235
	24	Wisconsin	Midw	249	75	7	1	9	18	6	3	177	.301	.348	.446	.266	32	.284
KARL THOMPSON	22	Wisconsin	Midw	454	119	16	1	10	25	1	1	336	.262	.301	.368	.224	40	.246
LUIS TINOCO	21	Wisconsin	Midw	448	127	16	2	12	40	3	4	325	.283	.342	.408	.251	51	.280
RANDY VICKERS	20	Wisconsin	Midw	185	41	5	0	6	9	1	2	146	.222	.258	.346	.195	12	.223
CARLOS VILLALOBOS	22	Lancaster	Calif	411	96	14	2	4	36	4	2	317	.234	.295	.307	.201	29	.222
DUSTY WATHAN	22	Lancaster	Calif	244	51	5	0	6	19	0	0	193	.209	.266	.303	.184	14	.204

Player	Age	Team	Lge	IP	H	ER	HR	BB	K	ERA	W	L	H/9	HR/9	BB/9	K/9	KW
MATT APANA	25	Port City	South	87.7	99	57	9	80	40	5.85	3	7	10.16	.92	8.21	4.11	-.68
CHRIS BECK	24	Lancaster	Calif	77.3	96	38	6	51	36	4.42	4	5	11.17	.70	5.94	4.19	-.09
DENYS BONILLA	22	Wisconsin	Midw	62.0	70	21	2	32	39	3.05	4	3	10.16	.29	4.65	5.66	.73
DUFF BRUMLEY	25	Port City	South	25.7	31	13	1	24	12	4.56	1	2	10.87	.35	8.42	4.21	-.70
MIKE BUTCHER	31	Tacoma	PCL	41.0	70	51	13	33	35	11.20	1	4	15.37	2.85	7.24	7.68	.75
ANDY COLLETT	22	Wisconsin	Midw	31.7	40	19	3	29	19	5.40	1	3	11.37	.85	8.24	5.40	-.26
JOHN DANIELS	22	Lancaster	Calif	86.0	102	44	9	35	63	4.60	4	6	10.67	.94	3.66	6.59	1.28
CLINT GOULD	24	Lancaster	Calif	30.0	37	18	0	20	11	5.40	1	2	11.10	.00	6.00	3.30	-.40
KEVIN GRYBOSKI	22	Wisconsin	Midw	118.3	182	96	9	80	63	7.30	3	10	13.84	.68	6.08	4.79	.08
LEE GUETTERMAN	37	Tacoma	PCL	27.0	29	13	3	13	23	4.33	1	2	9.67	1.00	4.33	7.67	1.47
BRETT HINCHLIFFE	21	Lancaster	Calif	147.0	192	88	18	75	91	5.39	6	10	11.76	1.10	4.59	5.57	.71
BRENT IDDON	20	Wisconsin	Midw	85.7	101	32	6	53	71	3.36	6	4	10.61	.63	5.57	7.46	1.09
RUSSELL JACOBS	21	Wisconsin	Midw	58.0	81	50	3	67	39	7.76	1	5	12.57	.47	10.40	6.05	-.58
DAMASO MARTE	22	Wisconsin	Midw	122.0	167	87	11	96	72	6.42	4	10	12.32	.81	7.08	5.31	.00
BOB MILACKI	31	Tacoma	PCL	153.0	146	57	14	53	97	3.35	10	7	8.59	.82	3.12	5.71	1.12
BLAS MINOR	30	Seattle	AL	25.3	25	10	5	11	14	3.55	2	1	8.88	1.78	3.91	4.97	.68
IVAN MONTANE	23	Lancaster	Calif	53.0	59	30	2	50	34	5.09	2	4	10.02	.34	8.49	5.77	-.20
	23	Port City	South	91.3	110	65	6	87	59	6.41	3	7	10.84	.59	8.57	5.81	-.21
TREY MOORE	23	Lancaster	Calif	84.7	115	48	9	36	48	5.10	3	6	12.22	.96	3.83	5.10	.74
	23	Port City	South	49.7	79	50	6	39	31	9.06	1	5	14.32	1.09	7.07	5.62	.11
GERONIMO NEWTON	22	Port City	South	42.0	51	16	7	26	18	3.43	3	2	10.93	1.50	5.57	3.86	-.11
TONY PHILLIPS	27	Tacoma	PCL	49.0	74	37	10	13	20	6.80	1	4	13.59	1.84	2.39	3.67	.63
LEE RUSSELL	25	Port City	South	108.3	146	69	9	59	65	5.73	4	8	12.13	.75	4.90	5.40	.57
MARINO SANTANA	24	Lancaster	Calif	142.0	179	88	24	67	105	5.58	5	11	11.35	1.52	4.25	6.65	1.16
AARON SCHEFFER	20	Wisconsin	Midw	59.7	68	35	6	44	56	5.28	3	4	10.26	.91	6.64	8.45	1.16
ROY SMITH	20	Wisconsin	Midw	125.0	198	118	12	94	62	8.50	3	11	14.26	.86	6.77	4.46	-.20
CHAD SODEN	22	Wisconsin	Midw	25.0	32	10	3	13	13	3.60	2	1	11.52	1.08	4.68	4.68	.39
TOM SZIMANSKI	23	Lancaster	Calif	38.7	59	20	3	14	29	4.66	2	2	13.73	.70	3.26	6.75	1.44
JOHN THOMPSON	23	Lancaster	Calif	55.7	75	40	10	34	33	6.47	2	4	12.13	1.62	5.50	5.34	.40
TIM TRAWICK	24	Lancaster	Calif	28.3	44	21	4	11	13	6.67	1	2	13.98	1.27	3.49	4.13	.50
	24	Wisconsin	Midw	67.7	110	45	5	36	32	5.99	2	6	14.63	.67	4.79	4.26	.22
JOHN VANHOF	22	Wisconsin	Midw	79.3	117	87	11	130	36	9.87	1	8	13.27	1.25	14.75	4.08	-2.33
BILL WERTZ	29	Port City	South	26.0	32	9	1	10	19	3.12	2	1	11.08	.35	3.46	6.58	1.33
	29	Tacoma	PCL	30.3	48	19	2	28	21	5.64	1	2	14.24	.59	8.31	6.23	.00
TREY WITTE	26	Tacoma	PCL	42.7	51	11	2	18	18	2.32	4	1	10.76	.42	3.80	3.80	.32
GREG WOOTEN	22	Lancaster	Calif	87.0	113	41	7	29	45	4.24	5	5	11.69	.72	3.00	4.66	.80
	22	Wisconsin	Midw	74.0	75	27	4	38	43	3.28	5	3	9.12	.49	4.62	5.23	.59
ROBERT WORLEY	25	Port City	South	60.3	76	39	3	45	29	5.82	2	5	11.34	.45	6.71	4.33	-.24

Texas Rangers

The 1996 Texas Rangers did something their franchise had never done before: they made the playoffs.

They did it, moreover, with a core of homegrown talent on the front side of 30: Juan Gonzalez, Ivan Rodriguez, Rusty Greer, Dean Palmer, Roger Pavlik and Darren Oliver. The remaining regulars were a free agent bust (Clark) and some glovemen, two of whom, McLemore and Elster, came through with surprisingly good offensive seasons. A key free agent signing, Ken Hill, put them over the top.

The task for management now becomes staying on top, and they're going to face one real problem: The farm system is barren. It hasn't produced a major league regular in three years, and there's no one who looks ready to step in. They have been able to make some trades with, of all things, minor league pitchers, but the only player in the system who looks even close to ready is a catcher. That won't help a lot; they've got that position sort of covered.

This winter, the Rangers took one step forward and two steps back almost every day. They turned loose aging veterans Mike Henneman, Kevin Elster and Darryl Hamilton despite their contributions to a successful season. But they followed decisions like that with inexplicable ones like signing Mark McLemore, a well-past-prime second baseman, to a three-year contract. The core of 1996's team is intact, and if they can stave off continued declines from Mickey Tettleton and Will Clark, keep Ivan Rodriguez and Juan Gonzalez healthy and assemble a bullpen, they're in decent shape for a wild card, taking into account that their schedule will be weaker than that of the East and Central contenders.

The Minor Leagues: Despite all of what I said above, the Rangers had three league MVPs and three playoff teams. Oklahoma City won the American Association championship after compiling only the fifth-best record in the league, 74-70. While they had the league MVP in Lee Stevens, they only had one regular player, Benji Gil, under 26 years old; the team was developed expressly for backing up the Rangers in the event of injury, not developing talent. Rick Helling had a big year in the rotation but is now a Marlin; Patterson was an exceptional reliever, while Alberro and Santana may have shots at the majors. The Tulsa Drillers had the bulk of Texas' prospects and the second-best record in the Texas League at 75-64 before losing in the first round of the playoffs. A strong infield, led by 26-year-old MVP Bubba Smith, carried the team, but catcher Kevin Brown was their only good prospect. Second baseman Edwin Diaz, third baseman Mike Bell and outfielders Marc Sagmoen and Mark Little have chances.

The Charlotte Rangers, in Florida, play in a pitcher's park in a pitcher's league that makes the jump to the high-offense Texas League very deceiving. The team finished a poor 63-76, as tools prospect Andrew Vessel collapsed and a number of old players tearing up the league were promoted to Tulsa. Third baseman Fernando Tatis is the best hitting prospect in the system, and they had one pitcher, Danny Kolb, who's highly touted and another, Ted Silva, who's good. The SAL's Charleston (SC) River Dogs finished just 63-78, but featured four Dominican teenagers making their U.S. debuts, three of whom—outfielders Ruben Mateo and Juan Nunez, and pitcher Henry Mota—bear close watching.

ANDY BARKETT   **1B**   **1974**   **Age 23**

Year	Team	Lge	AB	H	DB	TP	HR	BB	SB	CS	OUT	BA	OBA	SA	EQA	EQR	Peak
1995	Charleston-SC	S Atl	82	15	4	0	0	8	0	1	68	.183	.256	.232	.141	3	.163
1996	Charlotte-FL	Flor	414	116	16	1	9	51	2	1	299	.280	.359	.389	.254	49	.284
1997	*Texas*	*AL*	*389*	*107*	*23*	*1*	*11*	*39*	*5*	*2*	*284*	*.275*	*.341*	*.424*	*.254*	*46*	

A totally unheralded first baseman, he spent most of 1995 at Butte, a co-op club in the Pioneer League. This is not a sign your organization has big plans for you. Still, he's hit for a good average with moderate power and a good eye.

MIKE BELL   **3B**   **1975**   **Age 22**

Year	Team	Lge	AB	H	DB	TP	HR	BB	SB	CS	OUT	BA	OBA	SA	EQA	EQR	Peak
1994	Charleston-SC	S Atl	493	114	15	2	6	39	7	5	384	.231	.288	.306	.197	33	.227
1995	Charlotte-FL	Flor	493	125	12	1	7	42	6	4	372	.254	.312	.325	.215	40	.244
1996	Tulsa	Texas	489	120	20	2	14	40	2	1	370	.245	.302	.380	.228	46	.255
1997	*Texas*	*AL*	*474*	*120*	*22*	*1*	*17*	*46*	*2*	*2*	*356*	*.253*	*.319*	*.411*	*.240*	*50*	

Of the Bells, he ranks well below his relatives. While he stepped up nicely in power, he hasn't displayed good range in the field, makes a lot of errors and doesn't get on base. He has shown gradual improvement, though.

KEVIN BROWN   **C**   **1973**   **Age 24**

Year	Team	Lge	AB	H	DB	TP	HR	BB	SB	CS	OUT	BA	OBA	SA	EQA	EQR	Peak
1994	Hudson Valley	NY-P	240	51	5	0	6	18	0	0	189	.213	.267	.308	.187	14	.209
1995	Charlotte-FL	Flor	376	101	13	1	13	44	2	2	277	.269	.345	.412	.253	45	.279
1996	Tulsa	Texas	470	116	14	1	22	66	1	2	356	.247	.340	.421	.252	57	.274

Of the real prospects in the Texas system, he's probably the second best hitter behind Tatis. He had some trouble with wood bats in 1994, but followed with two nearly identical seasons. He's got some major weaknesses yet: he strikes out a lot, and he's been poor at stopping basestealers, even though he has a strong arm and his defense gets praised first. With Valle gone and no catcher worth mentioning at Oklahoma City, he'll have a chance to back up Rodriguez in 1997.

DAMON BUFORD   **CF**   **1970**   **Age 27**

Year	Team	Lge	AB	H	DB	TP	HR	BB	SB	CS	OUT	BA	OBA	SA	EQA	EQR	Peak
1993	Rochester	Inter	117	32	4	1	1	8	7	1	86	.274	.320	.350	.237	12	.257
1993	Baltimore	AL	80	19	3	0	3	9	2	2	63	.237	.315	.387	.231	8	.253
1994	Rochester	Inter	458	120	15	2	16	35	21	4	342	.262	.314	.408	.247	52	.265
1995	Rochester	Inter	191	57	11	2	4	17	12	3	137	.298	.356	.440	.273	27	.286
1995	NY Mets	NL	140	35	3	0	5	21	6	6	111	.250	.348	.379	.240	16	.253
1996	Texas	AL	144	39	5	0	7	15	8	5	110	.271	.340	.451	.260	19	.272
1997	*Texas*	*AL*	*388*	*111*	*13*	*3*	*14*	*37*	*18*	*7*	*284*	*.286*	*.348*	*.443*	*.264*	*51*	

One of many former Orioles with the Rangers, he was picked up for Terrell Lowery. He relies on speed and defense, while infuriating coaches by hitting balls into the air and not taking advantage of his speed. He is perfectly adequate as a reserve outfielder, and would probably be an improvement over Hamilton both offensively and defensively in '97.

WILL CLARK   **1B**   **1964**   **Age 33**

Year	Team	Lge	AB	H	DB	TP	HR	BB	SB	CS	OUT	BA	OBA	SA	EQA	EQR	Peak
1993	San Francisco	NL	511	154	26	2	16	71	2	2	359	.301	.387	.454	.281	75	.279
1994	Texas	AL	397	136	24	2	14	73	5	1	262	.343	.445	.519	.322	77	.316
1995	Texas	AL	455	138	28	3	17	68	0	1	318	.303	.394	.490	.292	74	.282
1996	Texas	AL	432	119	22	1	13	63	2	1	314	.275	.368	.421	.265	57	.252
1997	*Texas*	*AL*	*432*	*127*	*23*	*1*	*12*	*69*	*0*	*0*	*305*	*.294*	*.391*	*.435*	*.276*	*61*	

Clark's slide to mediocrity continued as he posted career lows in virtually every category. Once a consistent .300 EQA/100 EQR guy, he hasn't met both those marks since 1992. Vlad's guess looks about right to me, although it will be worse if he makes three trips to the DL again.

MIKE COOLBAUGH   **SS/1B**   **1972**   **Age 25**

Year	Team	Lge	AB	H	DB	TP	HR	BB	SB	CS	OUT	BA	OBA	SA	EQA	EQR	Peak
1993	Hagerstown	S Atl	400	85	8	0	13	23	2	1	316	.213	.255	.330	.190	25	.214
1994	Dunedin	Flor	462	115	18	1	18	27	2	2	349	.249	.290	.409	.231	45	.255
1995	Knoxville	South	503	107	22	1	9	36	5	5	401	.213	.265	.314	.188	31	.204
1996	Charlotte-FL	Flor	468	133	19	1	18	38	5	6	341	.284	.338	.444	.258	58	.276

Although he shouldn't be confused with longtime journeyman Scott Coolbaugh, Mike's not a whole lot better, beating up on the Florida State League at age 24. He also played a lot of third base and DH, his best position.

EDWIN DIAZ   **2B**   **1975**   **Age 22**

Year	Team	Lge	AB	H	DB	TP	HR	BB	SB	CS	OUT	BA	OBA	SA	EQA	EQR	Peak
1994	Charleston-SC	S Atl	423	99	13	3	9	19	6	6	330	.234	.267	.343	.200	29	.230
1995	Charlotte-FL	Flor	470	130	18	2	11	29	6	7	347	.277	.319	.394	.237	47	.269
1996	Tulsa	Texas	502	121	22	3	14	25	7	5	386	.241	.277	.380	.218	43	.244

The differences between the Texas and Florida Leagues being what they are, people talk like he stepped up this year, when I believe he really took a step backwards. While he continues to show good power for a middle infielder, it wasn't any different from what he did at Charlotte. He's a poor fielder, poor baserunner and has no batting eye at all: 80 walks and 323 strikeouts in three years, with no improvement at all. He really should repeat AA.

KEVIN ELSTER   **SS**   **1965**   **Age 32**

Year	Team	Lge	AB	H	DB	TP	HR	BB	SB	CS	OUT	BA	OBA	SA	EQA	EQR	Peak
1994	Albany-NY	East	141	34	5	0	2	19	1	0	107	.241	.331	.319	.222	12	.221
1995	Philadelphia	NL	53	11	3	1	1	8	0	0	42	.208	.311	.358	.222	5	.215
1996	Texas	AL	511	125	30	2	23	52	4	1	387	.245	.314	.446	.251	61	.242
1997	*Texas*	*AL*	*405*	*97*	*23*	*2*	*19*	*36*	*5*	*3*	*311*	*.240*	*.302*	*.447*	*.243*	*45*	

Back from a shoulder injury, and how. He was even better for most of the year, hitting just .208 over the final two months. He provided the Rangers with adequate defense and far more offense than they would have gotten from Gil. The final power numbers are not totally shocking: he averaged 22 doubles and 16 HR per 511 AB in 1988-90, if you translated those seasons to the 1996 AL. Recovering a level of play one had five years ago, or even raising it a modest amount as Elster did, is rare, but there's always at least one player a year who does it. This is the kind of season Elster's minor league career indicated he could have, but it should have happened in 1986, not 1996.

HANLEY FRIAS   **SS**   **1974**   **Age 23**

Year	Team	Lge	AB	H	DB	TP	HR	BB	SB	CS	OUT	BA	OBA	SA	EQA	EQR	Peak
1993	Charleston-SC	S Atl	490	100	11	1	5	29	11	6	396	.204	.249	.261	.162	21	.187
1994	High Desert	Calif	453	97	11	3	3	34	17	6	362	.214	.269	.272	.181	25	.205
1995	Charlotte-FL	Flor	128	41	5	2	1	13	5	3	90	.320	.383	.414	.271	17	.305
1995	Tulsa	Texas	368	97	15	2	1	41	11	6	277	.264	.337	.323	.227	34	.254
1996	Tulsa	Texas	508	130	21	6	3	30	7	5	383	.256	.297	.339	.213	40	.236

This guy, on the other hand, is a terrific fielder, and in 1995 showed a real knack for working out a walk. He too went backwards in '96, again despite a superficial increase in power produced by the league. With his slight (6'0", 160) build, he's going to need to concentrate on walks to buttress his offense.

BENJI GIL   **SS**   **1973**   **Age 24**

Year	Team	Lge	AB	H	DB	TP	HR	BB	SB	CS	OUT	BA	OBA	SA	EQA	EQR	Peak
1993	Tulsa	Texas	350	88	4	1	14	34	12	5	267	.251	.318	.389	.239	37	.271
1993	Texas	AL	57	8	0	0	0	6	1	2	51	.140	.222	.140	-.070	0	-.090
1994	Oklahoma	AmA	495	125	17	4	12	36	11	5	375	.253	.303	.376	.228	47	.256
1995	Texas	AL	416	92	19	3	10	26	2	4	328	.221	.267	.353	.202	30	.222
1996	Oklahoma	AmA	296	63	13	1	5	24	4	4	237	.213	.272	.314	.191	19	.208
1997	*Texas*	*AL*	*333*	*83*	*12*	*1*	*10*	*27*	*4*	*3*	*253*	*.249*	*.306*	*.381*	*.226*	*31*	

Benji suffered a herniated disk in his back that required surgery this spring, and subsequently lost his job to Kevin Elster. His offense continues to decline as pitchers exploit his willingness to swing at anything. He still rates as an outstanding defender, but his offense is getting too bad to take.

JUAN GONZALEZ   RF   1970   Age 27

Year	Team	Lge	AB	H	DB	TP	HR	BB	SB	CS	OUT	BA	OBA	SA	EQA	EQR	Peak
1993	Texas	AL	548	181	28	1	56	41	4	1	368	.330	.377	.692	.331	116	.360
1994	Texas	AL	427	122	18	4	20	31	6	4	309	.286	.334	.487	.269	58	.288
1995	Texas	AL	353	105	20	2	28	17	0	0	248	.297	.330	.603	.296	59	.312
1996	Texas	AL	536	164	32	2	45	44	2	0	372	.306	.359	.625	.311	100	.323
1997	*Texas*	*AL*	*587*	*184*	*25*	*2*	*55*	*31*	*1*	*0*	*403*	*.313*	*.348*	*.644*	*.309*	*107*	

The AL MVP. I'm pretty sure he got the award because he came in second in RBIs despite missing 28 games. As we have argued in the case of Joe Carter—RBIs are as much a function of opportunity as skill—so it goes here. Take everybody in a league, and if you know two things, slugging average and AB with RISP, you can predict RBI with an average error of less than 10.

The point is that despite the missed games, Juan Gonzalez had more at bats with runners in scoring position than Albert Belle, the man who won the RBI title. His RBI/AB-RISP ratio was 86%, only sixth-best among AL players with 100 RBI, behind Ken Griffey (90%), Frank Thomas (92%), Albert Belle (96%), Brady Anderson (99%) and Mark McGwire (an astounding 110%). He had more RBIs than them because he had more chances, not because he was better in the clutch or anything like that. Alex Rodriguez was close to Juan, with an 83% rate; given Juan's RBI chances, he would have had two less. I don't think it's as bad as the 1987 choices, since there is the further argument that Texas won and Seattle didn't, but Gonzalez' performance, looking at what he did himself and without the aid of The Ballpark (+197 points of OPS at home), is nowhere near MVP caliber.

RUSTY GREER   LF   1969   Age 28

Year	Team	Lge	AB	H	DB	TP	HR	BB	SB	CS	OUT	BA	OBA	SA	EQA	EQR	Peak
1993	Tulsa	Texas	486	131	16	3	14	51	6	2	357	.270	.339	.401	.250	56	.268
1994	Oklahoma	AmA	115	37	9	1	4	19	1	1	79	.322	.418	.522	.308	21	.327
1994	Texas	AL	282	92	16	1	11	47	0	0	190	.326	.422	.507	.309	51	.326
1995	Texas	AL	418	114	21	2	14	55	3	1	305	.273	.357	.433	.265	55	.275
1996	Texas	AL	536	173	39	6	17	61	9	0	363	.323	.392	.513	.302	91	.309
1997	*Texas*	*AL*	*531*	*161*	*44*	*5*	*19*	*69*	*7*	*2*	*372*	*.303*	*.383*	*.512*	*.292*	*86*	

He's a player everyone should love: a left-handed hitter who doesn't need to be platooned, hits for average and power, takes a walk, is a smart baserunner and an outstanding fielder who makes flamboyant diving catches. It's a shame he was nursing a broken rib into the playoffs. I think he'll exceed Vlad's projection.

DARRYL HAMILTON   CF   1965   Age 32

Year	Team	Lge	AB	H	DB	TP	HR	BB	SB	CS	OUT	BA	OBA	SA	EQA	EQR	Peak
1993	Milwaukee	AL	530	173	20	1	12	49	21	10	367	.326	.383	.436	.278	75	.281
1994	Milwaukee	AL	141	36	10	1	1	15	3	0	105	.255	.327	.362	.237	14	.236
1995	Milwaukee	AL	397	107	22	5	5	47	10	1	291	.270	.347	.388	.252	47	.247
1996	Texas	AL	621	176	27	4	6	54	15	5	450	.283	.341	.369	.244	66	.235
1997	*Texas*	*AL*	*615*	*175*	*30*	*5*	*7*	*57*	*14*	*5*	*445*	*.285*	*.345*	*.384*	*.246*	*67*	

The offensive level of 1996 and the friendliness of The Ballpark disguises how far Hamilton has fallen since the glorious days of 1992-93. A very old 32.

DEREK LEE   OF   1967   Age 30

Year	Team	Lge	AB	H	DB	TP	HR	BB	SB	CS	OUT	BA	OBA	SA	EQA	EQR	Peak
1993	Portland-OR	PCL	381	111	20	3	11	54	10	3	273	.291	.379	.446	.279	56	.289
1994	Ottawa	Inter	485	150	30	6	15	65	9	4	339	.309	.391	.489	.292	78	.299
1995	Norfolk	Inter	365	95	11	0	19	48	9	4	274	.260	.346	.447	.263	49	.266
1996	Oklahoma	AmA	423	125	27	2	12	53	6	7	305	.296	.374	.454	.274	60	.272

Even though he's hit everywhere he's played for the last five years, he's been in six organizations and gotten a grand total of 34 major league plate appearances. He could have been Geronimo Berroa, and could still play a better DH than several teams are planning for '97. Don't confuse him with Derrek Lee, the young Padre prospect.

MARK LITTLE   **CF**   **1973**   **Age 24**

Year	Team	Lge	AB	H	DB	TP	HR	BB	SB	CS	OUT	BA	OBA	SA	EQA	EQR	Peak
1994	Hudson Valley	NY-P	216	55	9	1	4	17	6	3	164	.255	.309	.361	.227	20	.253
1995	Charlotte-FL	Flor	461	118	22	4	12	45	13	8	351	.256	.322	.399	.241	50	.267
1996	Tulsa	Texas	415	110	14	1	12	45	16	6	311	.265	.337	.390	.248	48	.269
1997	*Texas*	*AL*	*350*	*94*	*17*	*1*	*11*	*38*	*16*	*8*	*264*	*.269*	*.340*	*.417*	*.252*	*42*	

He was the best defensive outfielder in the Texas League in Baseball America's Tools survey, runs well and spikes his OBA with 24 HBPs the last two seasons. He missed the last month of 1996 with an injured shoulder.

RUBEN MATEO   **RF/CF**   **1978**   **Age 19**

Year	Team	Lge	AB	H	DB	TP	HR	BB	SB	CS	OUT	BA	OBA	SA	EQA	EQR	Peak
1996	Charleston-SC	S Atl	518	128	19	4	8	21	13	5	395	.247	.276	.346	.210	40	.245

The best of four teenagers Texas brought to Charleston from the Dominican Summer League, scouts rave over him as a five-tooler. He's fast, has a great arm (best in the league) and lacks plate discipline, but has age clearly on his side.

MARK McLEMORE   **2B**   **1965**   **Age 32**

Year	Team	Lge	AB	H	DB	TP	HR	BB	SB	CS	OUT	BA	OBA	SA	EQA	EQR	Peak
1993	Baltimore	AL	586	171	30	5	5	68	20	11	426	.292	.365	.386	.256	71	.259
1994	Baltimore	AL	343	87	10	1	3	51	18	4	260	.254	.350	.315	.236	35	.234
1995	Texas	AL	468	123	22	5	5	59	20	10	355	.263	.345	.363	.242	51	.238
1996	Texas	AL	511	143	21	4	5	87	26	10	378	.280	.385	.366	.261	66	.252
1997	*Texas*	*AL*	*538*	*144*	*24*	*3*	*2*	*89*	*26*	*12*	*406*	*.268*	*.372*	*.335*	*.244*	*59*	

The surprise in Texas was that Mac didn't fold as the season went on. He's always been an excellent defensive second baseman and a good basestealer. He's learned how to get on base consistently.

MIKE MURPHY   **OF**   **1972**   **Age 25**

Year	Team	Lge	AB	H	DB	TP	HR	BB	SB	CS	OUT	BA	OBA	SA	EQA	EQR	Peak
1993	Spartanburg	S Atl	524	131	20	2	4	26	14	6	399	.250	.285	.319	.204	38	.229
1994	Dunedin	Flor	481	125	11	2	2	50	17	5	361	.260	.330	.304	.221	41	.243
1995	Kinston	Caro	184	44	2	0	2	15	8	2	142	.239	.296	.283	.201	13	.217
1996	Charlotte-FL	Flor	375	122	15	3	10	30	12	5	258	.325	.375	.461	.282	54	.302
1996	Tulsa	Texas	124	27	3	1	4	19	1	0	97	.218	.322	.355	.228	12	.244

Another false prospect: 24-year-old in the Florida State League, in his third year at high A and he beats up on young pitching.

WARREN NEWSON   **OF**   **1965**   **Age 32**

Year	Team	Lge	AB	H	DB	TP	HR	BB	SB	CS	OUT	BA	OBA	SA	EQA	EQR	Peak
1993	Nashville	AmA	182	61	7	2	4	38	4	1	122	.335	.450	.462	.312	33	.316
1993	Chi. White Sox	AL	41	14	1	0	2	9	0	0	27	.341	.460	.512	.326	8	.318
1994	Chi. White Sox	AL	103	27	3	0	3	14	1	0	76	.262	.350	.379	.249	12	.247
1995	Chi. White Sox	AL	86	21	2	2	3	24	1	1	66	.244	.409	.419	.278	13	.273
1995	Seattle	AL	73	22	3	0	2	16	1	0	51	.301	.427	.425	.294	12	.288
1996	Texas	AL	233	58	12	1	10	36	3	0	175	.249	.349	.438	.263	31	.253
1997	*Texas*	*AL*	*249*	*69*	*12*	*1*	*7*	*63*	*4*	*2*	*182*	*.277*	*.423*	*.418*	*.284*	*39*	

Some of us have been pushing him as a good, unnoticed hitter for some time. He excelled while Juan Gonzalez was injured and he was playing regularly, but really dropped off after the All-Star break.

JUAN NUNEZ   **CF**   **1977**   **Age 20**

Year	Team	Lge	AB	H	DB	TP	HR	BB	SB	CS	OUT	BA	OBA	SA	EQA	EQR	Peak
1996	Charleston-SC	S Atl	348	90	7	2	1	28	20	6	264	.259	.314	.299	.216	29	.249

Another of Charleston's Dominican dandies, he's small (5' 10", 160), very fast, switch-hits and has no power at all.

LUIS ORTIZ   **1B**   **1970**   **Age 27**

Year	Team	Lge	AB	H	DB	TP	HR	BB	SB	CS	OUT	BA	OBA	SA	EQA	EQR	Peak
1993	Pawtucket	Inter	403	112	16	1	17	16	1	1	292	.278	.305	.449	.250	45	.271
1994	Pawtucket	Inter	321	93	11	2	6	28	1	2	230	.290	.347	.393	.249	36	.267
1995	Oklahoma	AmA	172	51	8	4	3	10	1	1	122	.297	.335	.442	.259	21	.273
1995	Texas	AL	108	25	6	2	1	6	0	1	84	.231	.272	.352	.203	8	.213
1996	Oklahoma	AmA	511	158	14	1	14	28	1	4	357	.309	.345	.423	.257	60	.267
1997	*Texas*	*AL*	*436*	*137*	*16*	*1*	*20*	*26*	*2*	*4*	*303*	*.314*	*.353*	*.493*	*.275*	*60*	

He doesn't really bring anything special to the table, but he is being talked about as a backup to Will Clark in '97. I think Vladimir is getting a little carried away with the age 27 thing, and find a .260 EQA far more likely than .275. Sold to Japan.

DEAN PALMER   **3B**   **1969**   **Age 28**

Year	Team	Lge	AB	H	DB	TP	HR	BB	SB	CS	OUT	BA	OBA	SA	EQA	EQR	Peak
1993	Texas	AL	528	139	31	2	39	57	11	8	397	.263	.335	.551	.281	83	.301
1994	Texas	AL	346	89	14	2	20	26	3	4	261	.257	.309	.483	.256	43	.270
1995	Texas	AL	119	40	5	0	10	21	1	1	80	.336	.436	.630	.338	26	.351
1996	Texas	AL	577	157	26	2	36	58	2	0	420	.272	.339	.511	.277	85	.283
1997	*Texas*	*AL*	*526*	*151*	*23*	*2*	*35*	*52*	*1*	*2*	*377*	*.287*	*.351*	*.538*	*.284*	*81*	

He recovered fully from an ugly arm injury in 1995 to have a perfectly normal Dean Palmer season, featuring lots of home runs and wretched defense.

IVAN RODRIGUEZ   **C**   **1972**   **Age 25**

Year	Team	Lge	AB	H	DB	TP	HR	BB	SB	CS	OUT	BA	OBA	SA	EQA	EQR	Peak
1993	Texas	AL	481	140	29	4	13	33	8	5	346	.291	.337	.449	.261	60	.293
1994	Texas	AL	368	114	18	0	18	32	6	3	257	.310	.365	.505	.286	56	.315
1995	Texas	AL	493	150	32	2	13	16	0	2	345	.304	.326	.456	.259	59	.282
1996	Texas	AL	634	185	46	3	18	37	5	0	449	.292	.331	.459	.264	80	.282
1997	*Texas*	*AL*	*639*	*204*	*34*	*2*	*18*	*35*	*4*	*3*	*438*	*.319*	*.355*	*.463*	*.271*	*83*	

You can't catch 147 games without fading in September, the second year in a row he's collapsed under the workload down the stretch. He—of course—led all major league catchers in CS and CS%. And while Hundley was getting a lot of attention for the all-time catchers' home run record, Pudge was busy shredding the all-time catchers' doubles record of 41.

MARC SAGMOEN   **OF**   **1971**   **Age 26**

Year	Team	Lge	AB	H	DB	TP	HR	BB	SB	CS	OUT	BA	OBA	SA	EQA	EQR	Peak
1993	Charleston-SC	S Atl	244	66	8	1	6	17	7	2	180	.270	.318	.385	.240	25	.265
1994	Charlotte-FL	Flor	497	147	26	6	6	35	10	5	355	.296	.342	.408	.254	58	.277
1995	Tulsa	Texas	246	55	5	2	7	21	4	2	193	.224	.285	.346	.210	19	.224
1995	Oklahoma	AmA	190	41	8	2	4	18	5	2	151	.216	.284	.342	.209	15	.225
1996	Tulsa	Texas	391	100	14	3	9	31	4	4	295	.256	.310	.376	.229	37	.242
1996	Oklahoma	AmA	118	34	4	0	5	5	1	0	84	.288	.317	.449	.256	14	.270

He was making decent progress before he got caught up in trying to hit for more power and ruined his swing. He claims to have recovered his stroke by looking at old tapes; we'll see if Oklahoma City was more than a temporary aberration.

BUBBA SMITH   **1B**   **1970**   **Age 27**

Year	Team	Lge	AB	H	DB	TP	HR	BB	SB	CS	OUT	BA	OBA	SA	EQA	EQR	Peak
1993	Winston-Salem	Caro	350	96	9	0	18	31	1	0	254	.274	.333	.454	.261	44	.284
1993	Jacksonville	South	139	29	3	0	6	7	0	2	112	.209	.247	.360	.192	9	.209
1994	Charleston-WV	S Atl	363	79	11	1	12	17	1	1	285	.218	.253	.353	.197	25	.211
1995	Ft Myers	Flor	190	67	8	0	14	14	1	1	124	.353	.397	.616	.323	37	.341
1995	New Britain	East	151	37	5	0	7	5	0	0	114	.245	.269	.417	.226	14	.238
1996	Tulsa	Texas	519	143	14	1	26	45	0	1	377	.276	.333	.457	.261	65	.271

Bubba—from California—is a big, slow guy with the physique of John Kruk. A fan favorite, he's a two-time MVP of the Carolina League who washed out of his first two tries at AA. He's hit a lot of home runs—34 per 162 games played—but would strike out 160 times in those games.

LEE STEVENS 1B 1967 **Age 30**

Year	Team	Lge	AB	H	DB	TP	HR	BB	SB	CS	OUT	BA	OBA	SA	EQA	EQR	Peak
1993	Syracuse	Inter	411	108	20	0	15	41	2	3	306	.263	.330	.421	.249	47	.258
1996	Oklahoma	AmA	448	147	29	2	30	61	3	0	301	.328	.409	.603	.325	91	.323
1996	Texas	AL	77	17	1	3	3	6	0	0	60	.221	.277	.429	.230	8	.231

He intended to play another year in Japan, but Kintetsu, his team of the past two years, released their gaijin players this spring, so he came back looking for work. He came back to be the AA's MVP, leading the league in homers, doubles, on-base percentage and slugging, coming in second in RBIs and third in batting average.

FERNANDO TATIS 3B 1975 **Age 22**

Year	Team	Lge	AB	H	DB	TP	HR	BB	SB	CS	OUT	BA	OBA	SA	EQA	EQR	Peak
1995	Charleston-SC	S Atl	523	144	22	2	14	37	11	9	388	.275	.323	.405	.243	56	.276
1996	Charlotte-FL	Flor	339	97	12	0	14	27	5	2	244	.286	.339	.445	.262	43	.293

Tatis, a slugging third baseman from San Pedro de Macoris, is the best hitting prospect in the organization. He missed the first two months of the season with a broken hamate bone that required surgery, but came back much sooner than expected. He can certainly hit, and he's got room to get stronger. He hasn't displayed either range or hands at third base.

MICKEY TETTLETON DH 1961 **Age 36**

Year	Team	Lge	AB	H	DB	TP	HR	BB	SB	CS	OUT	BA	OBA	SA	EQA	EQR	Peak
1993	Detroit	AL	532	138	24	4	38	114	4	5	399	.259	.390	.534	.296	95	.281
1994	Detroit	AL	342	86	18	2	17	97	0	1	257	.251	.417	.465	.293	60	.278
1995	Texas	AL	430	103	17	1	34	107	0	0	327	.240	.391	.521	.295	77	.280
1996	Texas	AL	486	115	22	1	24	94	2	1	372	.237	.360	.434	.263	66	.251
1997	Texas	AL	340	71	9	0	21	73	0	0	269	.209	.349	.421	.251	43	

The Looper was an offensive zero for three months of the season, and eventually revealed he'd been playing with torn cartilage in one knee.

ANDREW VESSEL LF 1975 **Age 22**

Year	Team	Lge	AB	H	DB	TP	HR	BB	SB	CS	OUT	BA	OBA	SA	EQA	EQR	Peak
1994	Charleston-WV	S Atl	423	89	13	1	7	25	3	4	338	.210	.254	.296	.175	22	.203
1995	Charlotte-FL	Flor	517	130	17	1	11	29	4	8	395	.251	.291	.352	.211	41	.241
1996	Charlotte-FL	Flor	501	110	21	3	5	41	1	3	394	.220	.279	.303	.189	31	.211

Vessel is the kind of athlete scouts adore: he's strong, he's fast, he's big...and he has no idea how to hit. He reported overweight, pulled a groin in the spring and watched his prospect status evaporate faster than Congressional pledges of campaign reform.

JACK VOIGT OF/1B 1966 **Age 31**

Year	Team	Lge	AB	H	DB	TP	HR	BB	SB	CS	OUT	BA	OBA	SA	EQA	EQR	Peak
1993	Rochester	Inter	63	22	5	1	3	9	0	1	42	.349	.431	.603	.328	13	.334
1993	Baltimore	AL	154	47	12	1	7	26	1	0	107	.305	.406	.532	.308	28	.315
1994	Bowie	East	160	46	7	1	5	23	3	2	116	.287	.377	.438	.273	23	.276
1994	Baltimore	AL	141	33	2	0	4	18	0	0	108	.234	.321	.333	.220	12	.223
1995	Texas	AL	62	10	3	0	2	10	0	0	52	.161	.278	.306	.188	4	.189
1996	Oklahoma	AmA	446	132	18	0	20	75	5	4	318	.296	.397	.471	.288	71	.282

Before the season he was traded to Boston, non-tendered by Boston, signed with San Diego, assigned to Las Vegas and cut the day before the season started. He said he'd play for anybody, anywhere and so he started the year with Charlotte—the one in Florida, not North Carolina. He's 30, but hits well, especially against left-handers, and can fill a first base/DH/outfield role. Six-year free agent.

JOSE ALBERRO   RSP   1969   Age 28

YR	TEAM	Lge	IP	H	ER	HR	BB	K	ERA	W	L	H/9	HR/9	BB/9	K/9	KW
1993	Tulsa	Texas	17.0	14	2	2	11	17	1.06	2	0	7.41	1.06	5.82	9.00	1.54
1993	Oklahoma	AmA	16.7	24	12	2	13	13	6.48	1	1	12.96	1.08	7.02	7.02	.58
1994	Oklahoma	AmA	67.7	82	37	7	44	45	4.92	3	5	10.91	.93	5.85	5.99	.53
1995	Oklahoma	AmA	72.7	77	31	4	37	48	3.84	4	4	9.54	.50	4.58	5.94	.84
1995	Texas	AL	21.0	24	14	2	12	10	6.00	1	1	10.29	.86	5.14	4.29	.14
1996	Oklahoma	AmA	162.7	168	67	11	79	116	3.71	10	8	9.30	.61	4.37	6.42	1.05

Groomed as a closer his entire career, he first tried starting in late 1995 and enjoyed his first full season in the rotation this year. An advantage to all the years as a closer is that, at 28, his arm is probably in better shape than a lot of younger pitchers.

JOHN BURKETT   RSP   1965   Age 32

YR	TEAM	Lge	IP	H	ER	HR	BB	K	ERA	W	L	H/9	HR/9	BB/9	K/9	KW
1993	San Francisco	NL	223.7	241	95	20	65	141	3.82	13	12	9.70	.80	2.62	5.67	1.24
1994	San Francisco	NL	156.7	176	63	14	51	79	3.62	9	8	10.11	.80	2.93	4.54	.78
1995	Florida	NL	186.7	209	83	22	73	113	4.00	10	11	10.08	1.06	3.52	5.45	.94
1996	Florida	NL	151.3	163	77	15	55	95	4.58	7	10	9.69	.89	3.27	5.65	1.07
1996	Texas	AL	68.7	68	22	3	17	45	2.88	5	3	8.91	.39	2.23	5.90	1.41

Burkett is finally with Texas, who traded for him after the '94 season and let him go as a free agent before the next season started. He pitched well after joining the Rangers and recorded the only playoff win in their history.

DENNIS COOK   LRP   1963   Age 34

YR	TEAM	Lge	IP	H	ER	HR	BB	K	ERA	W	L	H/9	HR/9	BB/9	K/9	KW
1993	Charlotte, NC	Inter	40.3	51	26	6	10	32	5.80	1	3	11.38	1.34	2.23	7.14	1.82
1993	Cleveland	AL	54.3	62	32	10	19	36	5.30	2	4	10.27	1.66	3.15	5.96	1.20
1994	Chi. White Sox	AL	32.7	29	13	4	15	26	3.58	2	2	7.99	1.10	4.13	7.16	1.35
1995	Cleveland	AL	13.0	15	7	3	11	13	4.85	0	1	10.38	2.08	7.62	9.00	1.10
1995	Texas	AL	45.0	44	17	5	17	40	3.40	3	2	8.80	1.00	3.40	8.00	1.82
1996	Texas	AL	68.7	51	21	2	36	61	2.75	5	3	6.68	.26	4.72	8.00	1.49

He did an exceptional job as a lefty setup man, especially when limited to one inning of work: .154/.217/.302 in his first inning, .295/.351/.438 in subsequent innings. Cook still throws a high fastball that occasionally gets drilled.

CLINT DAVIS   RRP   1970   Age 27

YR	TEAM	Lge	IP	H	ER	HR	BB	K	ERA	W	L	H/9	HR/9	BB/9	K/9	KW
1993	St Petersburg	Flor	24.7	32	9	0	14	35	3.28	2	1	11.68	.00	5.11	12.77	2.98
1993	Arkansas	Texas	33.0	29	11	2	15	26	3.00	3	1	7.91	.55	4.09	7.09	1.34
1996	Tulsa	Texas	43.7	36	10	4	17	33	2.06	4	1	7.42	.82	3.50	6.80	1.39
1996	Oklahoma	AmA	12.3	15	5	1	8	13	3.65	1	0	10.95	.73	5.84	9.49	1.70

An aging but effective pitcher who spent 1995 in the Texas-Louisiana League, earning 21 saves and striking out 59 batters in 40 innings.

BRYAN EVERSGERD   LRP   1969   Age 28

YR	TEAM	Lge	IP	H	ER	HR	BB	K	ERA	W	L	H/9	HR/9	BB/9	K/9	KW
1993	Arkansas	Texas	59.3	72	26	4	29	49	3.94	4	3	10.92	.61	4.40	7.43	1.38
1994	Louisville	AmA	11.7	11	6	0	9	7	4.63	0	1	8.49	.00	6.94	5.40	.06
1994	St Louis	NL	67.3	73	31	8	26	44	4.14	3	4	9.76	1.07	3.48	5.88	1.09
1995	Ottawa	Inter	49.7	55	20	0	34	38	3.62	3	3	9.97	.00	6.16	6.89	.76
1995	Montreal	NL	20.7	23	12	2	11	7	5.23	1	1	10.02	.87	4.79	3.05	-.18
1996	Oklahoma	AmA	62.7	62	19	3	22	50	2.73	5	2	8.90	.43	3.16	7.18	1.60

An undrafted pitcher who worked his way up from a Cardinal tryout camp, he is the prototypical Oklahoma pitcher: an aging journeyman.

KEVIN GROSS   RBP   1961   Age 36

YR	TEAM	Lge	IP	H	ER	HR	BB	K	ERA	W	L	H/9	HR/9	BB/9	K/9	KW
1993	Los Angeles	NL	197.0	237	104	16	97	146	4.75	9	13	10.83	.73	4.43	6.67	1.12
1994	Los Angeles	NL	155.0	168	59	12	58	117	3.43	10	7	9.75	.70	3.37	6.79	1.42
1995	Texas	AL	185.0	185	94	24	93	105	4.57	9	12	9.00	1.17	4.52	5.11	.57
1996	Texas	AL	129.3	136	56	15	52	75	3.90	7	7	9.46	1.04	3.62	5.22	.84

Gross started the year in the rotation, but in June suffered a torn ligament in his back and lost his effectiveness. He went to the bullpen for the last month and a half of the season and did extremely well before it flared up again, knocking him out of the playoffs.

MIKE HENNEMAN   RRP   1962   Age 35

YR	TEAM	Lge	IP	H	ER	HR	BB	K	ERA	W	L	H/9	HR/9	BB/9	K/9	KW
1993	Detroit	AL	70.7	70	23	4	35	60	2.93	5	3	8.92	.51	4.46	7.64	1.43
1994	Detroit	AL	34.7	41	20	4	18	26	5.19	1	3	10.64	1.04	4.67	6.75	1.08
1995	Detroit	AL	28.7	24	3	0	9	24	.94	3	0	7.53	.00	2.83	7.53	1.81
1995	Houston	NL	20.3	23	6	1	6	17	2.66	1	1	10.18	.44	2.66	7.52	1.84
1996	Texas	AL	41.7	38	19	5	17	33	4.10	2	3	8.21	1.08	3.67	7.13	1.46

He either has it or he doesn't, and when he doesn't he gets creamed. Not re-signed for '97.

KEN HILL   RSP   1966   Age 31

YR	TEAM	Lge	IP	H	ER	HR	BB	K	ERA	W	L	H/9	HR/9	BB/9	K/9	KW
1993	Montreal	NL	177.0	175	77	7	94	87	3.92	10	10	8.90	.36	4.78	4.42	.28
1994	Montreal	NL	151.0	144	51	12	57	79	3.04	11	6	8.58	.72	3.40	4.71	.72
1995	Cleveland	AL	74.7	77	29	5	34	48	3.50	5	3	9.28	.60	4.10	5.79	.90
1995	St Louis	NL	110.0	124	62	15	54	45	5.07	5	7	10.15	1.23	4.42	3.68	.12
1996	Texas	AL	250.0	225	73	15	100	163	2.63	20	8	8.10	.54	3.60	5.87	1.06

Easily the best season of his career, closely comparable to Pat Hentgen's: better than Hentgen if you only look at road games, since he was absolutely killed by The Ballpark.

JONATHAN JOHNSON   RSP   1975   Age 22

YR	TEAM	Lge	IP	H	ER	HR	BB	K	ERA	W	L	H/9	HR/9	BB/9	K/9	KW
1995	Charlotte, FL	Flor	38.3	44	16	4	22	18	3.76	2	2	10.33	.94	5.17	4.23	.12
1996	Tulsa	Texas	158.7	194	82	15	61	80	4.65	8	10	11.00	.85	3.46	4.54	.65

The Rangers best hope for a pitching prospect, he's their first-round pick from 1995. His pitches, a mediocre fastball and a great curve, aren't the stuff that inspires confidence, and he was only moderately successful at Tulsa.

DANNY KOLB   RSP   1975   Age 22

YR	TEAM	Lge	IP	H	ER	HR	BB	K	ERA	W	L	H/9	HR/9	BB/9	K/9	KW
1996	Charleston, SC	SAL	108.3	117	62	7	86	70	5.15	5	7	9.72	.58	7.14	5.82	.15
1996	Charlotte, FL	Flor	33.3	48	21	2	20	21	5.67	1	3	12.96	.54	5.40	5.67	.54
1996	Tulsa	Texas	10.3	6	1	0	10	6	.87	1	0	5.23	.00	8.71	5.23	-.44

This guy is the pitcher the Rangers are highest on. Their sixth-round pick from 1995, he throws a mid-90s fastball, but his control isn't up to major league standards yet.

ERIC MOODY   RRP   1971   Age 26

YR	TEAM	Lge	IP	H	ER	HR	BB	K	ERA	W	L	H/9	HR/9	BB/9	K/9	KW
1993	Erie	NY-P	43.3	76	37	4	23	17	7.68	1	4	15.78	.83	4.78	3.53	-.02
1994	Hudson Valley	NY-P	73.0	118	41	4	31	40	5.05	3	5	14.55	.49	3.82	4.93	.69
1995	Charlotte, FL	Flor	78.7	108	35	4	22	41	4.00	4	5	12.36	.46	2.52	4.69	.93
1996	Tulsa	Texas	88.0	100	36	4	34	66	3.68	5	5	10.23	.41	3.48	6.75	1.38

Even though he'd been successful as a starter, in 1996 he was converted to a closer. His strikeout rate took off and he collected 16 saves.

HENRY MOTA   RBP   1978   Age 19

YR	TEAM	Lge	IP	H	ER	HR	BB	K	ERA	W	L	H/9	HR/9	BB/9	K/9	KW
1996	Charleston, SC	S Atl	84.0	99	46	10	42	37	4.93	4	5	10.61	1.07	4.50	3.96	.20

He pitched to a 1.85 ERA in the Dominican Summer League at age 17 in 1995. Starting in the bullpen this year, he made a spot start and won, so he got another one, and won…. He wound up going 6-0 with a 2.00 ERA in the second half of the season.

DARREN OLIVER   LSP   1971   Age 26

YR	TEAM	Lge	IP	H	ER	HR	BB	K	ERA	W	L	H/9	HR/9	BB/9	K/9	KW
1993	Tulsa	Texas	66.0	59	18	2	55	55	2.45	5	2	8.05	.27	7.50	7.50	.62
1994	Texas	AL	49.0	42	19	4	36	49	3.49	3	2	7.71	.73	6.61	9.00	1.35
1995	Texas	AL	49.3	43	18	3	33	39	3.28	3	2	7.84	.55	6.02	7.11	.87
1996	Charlotte, FL	Flor	11.0	9	4	2	5	7	3.27	1	0	7.36	1.64	4.09	5.73	.89
1996	Texas	AL	173.7	171	68	16	79	107	3.52	11	8	8.86	.83	4.09	5.55	.82

Oliver was one of the Rangers biggest question marks coming into the year: that he was a good pitcher was unquestioned, but how long could he hold up following arm surgeries each of the last two years? As it turned out, all year.

DANNY PATTERSON   RRP   1971   Age 26

YR	TEAM	Lge	IP	H	ER	HR	BB	K	ERA	W	L	H/9	HR/9	BB/9	K/9	KW
1993	Charlotte, FL	Flor	58.7	71	26	4	38	32	3.99	4	3	10.89	.61	5.83	4.91	.18
1994	Charlotte, FL	Flor	12.3	17	9	2	6	7	6.57	0	1	12.41	1.46	4.38	5.11	.61
1994	Tulsa	Texas	40.0	40	13	3	22	24	2.92	3	1	9.00	.68	4.95	5.40	.56
1995	Tulsa	Texas	32.3	50	27	2	18	21	7.52	1	3	13.92	.56	5.01	5.85	.70
1995	Oklahoma	AmA	25.7	25	7	0	12	8	2.45	2	1	8.77	.00	4.21	2.81	-.12
1996	Oklahoma	AmA	76.3	86	20	4	24	44	2.36	6	2	10.14	.47	2.83	5.19	1.02

Totally unheralded, coming out of the 47th round in 1989, he's been extremely effective in the minors for three years. He throws a big sinker that produces a ton of ground balls, which has led to a lot of errors and unearned runs in the minors.

ROGER PAVLIK   RSP   1968   Age 29

YR	TEAM	Lge	IP	H	ER	HR	BB	K	ERA	W	L	H/9	HR/9	BB/9	K/9	KW
1993	Oklahoma	AmA	35.0	27	9	1	17	29	2.31	3	1	6.94	.26	4.37	7.46	1.39
1993	Texas	AL	165.0	154	57	19	89	136	3.11	11	7	8.40	1.04	4.85	7.42	1.26
1994	Charlotte, FL	Flor	15.3	16	2	2	4	12	1.17	2	0	9.39	1.17	2.35	7.04	1.76
1994	Oklahoma	AmA	28.0	28	10	4	9	34	3.21	2	1	9.00	1.29	2.89	10.93	2.92
1994	Texas	AL	51.3	59	36	7	32	31	6.31	2	4	10.34	1.23	5.61	5.44	.41
1995	Texas	AL	191.3	164	69	17	93	148	3.25	13	8	7.71	.80	4.37	6.96	1.23
1996	Texas	AL	201.0	194	84	23	84	122	3.76	12	10	8.69	1.03	3.76	5.46	.88

He got off to a great start, and piled up a gaudy 11-2 record at the break thanks to outstanding run support. He collapsed in September and October, yet thanks again to run support was charged with only one loss in six terrible outings.

JEFF RUSSELL   RRP   1962   Age 35

YR	TEAM	Lge	IP	H	ER	HR	BB	K	ERA	W	L	H/9	HR/9	BB/9	K/9	KW
1993	Boston	AL	45.7	39	11	1	16	46	2.17	4	1	7.69	.20	3.15	9.07	2.23
1994	Boston	AL	28.0	28	13	3	14	18	4.18	1	2	9.00	.96	4.50	5.79	.80
1994	Cleveland	AL	13.0	12	6	2	3	10	4.15	0	1	8.31	1.38	2.08	6.92	1.79
1995	Texas	AL	32.7	34	9	3	9	21	2.48	3	1	9.37	.83	2.48	5.79	1.31
1996	Texas	AL	56.0	52	15	4	23	22	2.41	4	2	8.36	.64	3.70	3.54	.25

The right-handed setup man for Henneman, he killed right handed hitters (holding them to a .622 OPS) but was killed by lefties (.859). Like Cook, he was usually used for only one inning at a time; unlike Cook, he had no problems going longer.

JULIO SANTANA   RSP   1973   Age 24

YR	TEAM	Lge	IP	H	ER	HR	BB	K	ERA	W	L	H/9	HR/9	BB/9	K/9	KW
1994	Charleston, SC	S Atl	81.3	81	40	4	62	61	4.43	4	5	8.96	.44	6.86	6.75	.53
1994	Tulsa	Texas	64.7	58	25	2	51	33	3.48	4	3	8.07	.28	7.10	4.59	-.24
1995	Charoltte, FL	Flor	27.0	42	16	2	22	20	5.33	1	2	14.00	.67	7.33	6.67	.39
1995	Tulsa	Texas	92.7	103	40	9	65	61	3.88	5	5	10.00	.87	6.31	5.92	.40
1996	Oklahoma	AmA	177.3	184	94	11	91	94	4.77	8	12	9.34	.56	4.62	4.77	.44

Santana is a converted shortstop who, a year ago, was widely regarded as their best pitching prospect. He's got a very strong arm—that is, after all, why they made him a pitcher—but he's still very much a thrower with a lot to learn about pitching. His control showed a lot of improvement; unfortunately, his strikeouts fell precipitously.

TED SILVA   **RSP**   **1975**   **Age 22**

YR	TEAM	Lge	IP	H	ER	HR	BB	K	ERA	W	L	H/9	HR/9	BB/9	K/9	KW
1995	Charleston, SC	S Atl	56.3	84	33	6	20	38	5.27	2	4	13.42	.96	3.20	6.07	1.22
1996	Charlotte, FL	Flor	100.0	128	47	14	41	69	4.23	5	6	11.52	1.26	3.69	6.21	1.15
1996	Tulsa	Texas	69.0	78	25	5	24	22	3.26	5	3	10.17	.65	3.13	2.87	.17

At Cal State Fullerton in 1995, he went 18-1 and pitched the deciding game of the College World Series. Then, because he wasn't really big (6', 170 passes for small among pitchers these days), and didn't throw 90, he lingered until the 21st round. He's now 22-8 as a professional. Despite a perceived lack of tools, he knows how to pitch.

MIKE STANTON   **LRP**   **1967**   **Age 30**

YR	TEAM	Lge	IP	H	ER	HR	BB	K	ERA	W	L	H/9	HR/9	BB/9	K/9	KW
1993	Atlanta	NL	50.7	54	33	5	35	42	5.86	2	4	9.59	.89	6.22	7.46	.93
1994	Atlanta	NL	45.0	42	16	2	30	33	3.20	3	2	8.40	.40	6.00	6.60	.70
1995	Atlanta	NL	20.0	29	12	3	8	12	5.40	1	1	13.05	1.35	3.60	5.40	.90
1995	Boston	AL	20.7	17	7	3	9	10	3.05	1	1	7.40	1.31	3.92	4.35	.47
1996	Boston	AL	56.7	51	16	7	25	44	2.54	4	2	8.10	1.11	3.97	6.99	1.34
1996	Texas	AL	22.0	19	5	2	4	13	2.05	2	0	7.77	.82	1.64	5.32	1.36

Stanton was picked up for Mark Brandenburg, because as a Proven Veteran he would be more reliable down the stretch. He certainly was effective, but so was Brandenburg, and the two were virtually identical in ERA: Mike was at 3.83 for Boston, 3.22 for Texas, while Mark was 3.81 and 3.21. Signed with the Yankees. Could get 10-15 saves as #1 lefty.

ED VOSBERG   **LRP**   **1962**   **Age 35**

YR	TEAM	Lge	IP	H	ER	HR	BB	K	ERA	W	L	H/9	HR/9	BB/9	K/9	KW
1993	Iowa	AmA	60.7	68	28	6	29	59	4.15	3	4	10.09	.89	4.30	8.75	1.84
1994	Tacoma	PCL	50.0	40	16	4	24	47	2.88	4	2	7.20	.72	4.32	8.46	1.74
1994	Oakland	AL	13.7	16	6	2	6	12	3.95	1	1	10.54	1.32	3.95	7.90	1.65
1995	Texas	AL	36.0	30	11	3	17	36	2.75	3	1	7.50	.75	4.25	9.00	1.94
1996	Texas	AL	43.7	47	12	3	21	31	2.47	4	1	9.69	.62	4.33	6.39	1.05

Very quietly he's been a good reliever for several years now.

MATT WHITESIDE   **RRP**   **1968**   **Age 29**

YR	TEAM	Lge	IP	H	ER	HR	BB	K	ERA	W	L	H/9	HR/9	BB/9	K/9	KW
1993	Oklahoma	AmA	11.0	16	6	1	9	9	4.91	0	1	13.09	.82	7.36	7.36	.61
1993	Texas	AL	72.3	79	32	7	27	41	3.98	4	4	9.83	.87	3.36	5.10	.86
1994	Texas	AL	60.7	68	32	5	30	37	4.75	3	4	10.09	.74	4.45	5.49	.72
1995	Texas	AL	52.7	46	17	5	20	46	2.91	4	2	7.86	.85	3.42	7.86	1.77
1996	Oklahoma	AmA	89.7	102	38	7	36	43	3.81	5	5	10.24	.70	3.61	4.32	.54
1996	Texas	AL	33.0	37	17	7	12	14	4.64	2	2	10.09	1.91	3.27	3.82	.45

After three seasons in Arlington, he gave up eight home runs in 32 innings and found himself on a bus to Oklahoma City.

BOBBY WITT   **RSP**   **1965**   **Age 32**

YR	TEAM	Lge	IP	H	ER	HR	BB	K	ERA	W	L	H/9	HR/9	BB/9	K/9	KW
1993	Oakland	AL	218.0	233	99	17	103	137	4.09	12	12	9.62	.70	4.25	5.66	.82
1994	Oakland	AL	136.3	148	72	20	76	110	4.75	6	9	9.77	1.32	5.02	7.26	1.17
1995	Florida	NL	109.0	107	45	8	56	85	3.72	6	6	8.83	.66	4.62	7.02	1.18
1995	Texas	AL	62.3	75	26	4	22	46	3.75	4	3	10.83	.58	3.18	6.64	1.42
1996	Texas	AL	200.7	210	92	22	100	150	4.13	11	11	9.42	.99	4.49	6.73	1.12

When your fifth starter is a pitcher of Bobby Witt's caliber, and has a DT-ERA just over 4, you've got a heck of a pitching staff. He still throws hard and figures to be back in '97.

Player	Age	Team	Lge	AB	H	DB	TP	HR	BB	SB	CS	OUT	BA	OBA	SA	EQA	EQR	Peak
TOMMY ADAMS	26	Charlotte-FL	Flor	192	48	5	0	3	24	4	2	146	.250	.333	.323	.224	17	.234
DEREK BAKER	20	Charleston-SC	S Atl	170	39	5	1	4	15	0	0	131	.229	.292	.341	.210	13	.238
ANDY BARKETT	21	Charlotte-FL	Flor	414	116	16	1	9	51	2	1	299	.280	.359	.389	.254	49	.284
BRIAN BLAIR	24	Tulsa	Texas	384	84	19	2	3	42	6	4	304	.219	.296	.302	.199	27	.213
MATT BOKEMEIER	23	Charlotte-FL	Flor	518	139	27	3	3	27	9	2	381	.268	.305	.349	.223	45	.243
CHRIS BRIONES	23	Charleston-SC	S Atl	81	13	3	1	0	2	0	0	68	.160	.181	.222	.073	0	.071
CLIFF BRUMBAUGH	22	Charleston-SC	S Atl	494	114	16	3	7	57	8	3	383	.231	.310	.318	.212	40	.234
FRANK CHARLES	27	Oklahoma	AmA	113	20	4	2	1	6	1	3	96	.177	.218	.274	.141	4	.144
	27	Tulsa	Texas	148	36	4	0	4	10	1	0	112	.243	.291	.351	.215	12	.221
TIM COSSINS	26	Charlotte-FL	Flor	240	56	8	0	5	13	1	1	185	.233	.273	.329	.198	16	.205
OSMANI ESTRADA	27	Oklahoma	AmA	133	34	4	1	1	15	3	1	100	.256	.331	.323	.225	12	.230
	27	Tulsa	Texas	86	20	2	0	2	8	1	1	67	.233	.298	.326	.207	7	.213
RIKKERT FANEYTE	27	Oklahoma	AmA	371	85	9	0	11	37	13	7	293	.229	.299	.342	.216	32	.221
CARY FENTON	23	Charlotte-FL	Flor	303	80	8	0	1	28	11	6	229	.264	.326	.300	.216	25	.235
TONY FISHER	21	Charleston-SC	S Atl	115	25	0	0	3	2	2	1	91	.217	.231	.296	.168	5	.186
LOU FRAZIER	31	Oklahoma	AmA	211	50	7	2	3	16	11	3	164	.237	.291	.332	.215	18	.209
SHAWN GALLAGHER	19	Charleston-SC	S Atl	316	67	6	1	7	14	2	1	250	.212	.245	.304	.176	16	.203
RENE GONZALES	34	Oklahoma	AmA	160	41	6	2	3	26	1	1	120	.256	.360	.375	.249	18	.237
	34	Texas	AL	91	19	1	0	3	10	0	0	72	.209	.287	.319	.199	6	.188
JOE GOODWIN	22	Charleston-SC	S Atl	270	63	8	0	1	25	1	2	209	.233	.298	.274	.188	16	.207
RYAN GORECKI	22	Charlotte-FL	Flor	298	81	5	0	0	19	1	1	218	.272	.315	.289	.204	20	.225
FRANCISCO JARAMILLO	21	Charleston-SC	S Atl	137	24	3	0	1	7	1	0	113	.175	.215	.219	.112	2	.122
JASON JOHNSON	20	Charleston-SC	S Atl	414	83	14	2	1	34	4	3	334	.200	.261	.251	.160	17	.181
CESAR KING	18	Charleston-SC	S Atl	290	67	4	1	6	17	3	2	225	.231	.274	.314	.194	19	.227
LELAND MACON	23	Charlotte-FL	Flor	352	83	9	2	3	36	5	6	275	.236	.307	.298	.201	25	.219
JOHN MCAULAY	23	Charlotte-FL	Flor	129	25	4	0	3	20	0	0	104	.194	.302	.295	.197	9	.214
CRAIG MONROE	19	Charleston-SC	S Atl	161	22	8	1	0	14	1	1	140	.137	.206	.199	.075	1	.084
ASBEL ORTIZ	20	Charleston-SC	S Atl	321	61	8	2	1	10	0	1	261	.190	.215	.237	.120	6	.136
ERIK PAPPAS	30	Oklahoma	AmA	341	67	9	0	6	64	4	6	280	.196	.323	.276	.198	25	.194
JOSE PARRA	19	Charleston-SC	S Atl	90	12	0	0	0	6	2	1	79	.133	.188	.133	-.102	-1	-.098
ROWAN RICHARDS	22	Charlotte-FL	Flor	119	18	3	1	1	5	1	1	102	.151	.185	.218	.078	1	.086
TRACY SANDERS	26	Tulsa	Texas	172	37	7	0	6	30	1	1	136	.215	.332	.360	.231	17	.240
JOSE SANTO	18	Charleston-SC	S Atl	143	27	3	1	3	10	1	1	117	.189	.242	.287	.165	6	.193
JON SHAVE	28	Oklahoma	AmA	424	109	15	2	7	44	7	4	319	.257	.327	.351	.230	40	.232
STEVE SMELLA	22	Charleston-SC	S Atl	134	20	0	0	3	13	2	1	115	.149	.224	.216	.117	3	.132
ALEX SMITH	26	Oklahoma	AmA	204	45	8	0	6	24	4	2	161	.221	.303	.348	.218	18	.226
KURT STILLWELL	31	Texas	AL	76	20	1	0	2	10	0	0	56	.263	.349	.355	.239	8	.230
JOSE TEXIDOR	24	Tulsa	Texas	302	71	6	0	10	18	2	1	232	.235	.278	.354	.210	23	.224
BRIAN THOMAS	25	Oklahoma	AmA	254	66	11	3	7	33	1	0	188	.260	.345	.409	.253	30	.267
CHRIS UNRAT	25	Charlotte-FL	Flor	144	38	5	0	3	24	1	1	107	.264	.369	.361	.249	17	.263
DAVE VALLE	35	Texas	AL	85	25	5	1	3	9	0	0	60	.294	.362	.482	.279	12	.265
DANNY VASQUEZ	22	Charlotte-FL	Flor	260	51	8	0	7	7	2	3	212	.196	.217	.308	.162	11	.178
NATE VOPATA	23	Charleston-SC	S Atl	532	123	13	4	8	30	5	4	413	.231	.272	.316	.193	34	.210

Player	Age	Team	Lge	IP	H	ER	HR	BB	K	ERA	W	L	H/9	HR/9	BB/9	K/9	KW
CHUCK BAUER	23	Charleston, SCS	Atl	85.0	151	69	3	56	39	7.31	2	7	15.99	.32	5.93	4.13	-.11
JIM BROWER	23	Charlotte, FL	Flor	127.0	188	79	17	60	63	5.60	5	9	13.32	1.20	4.25	4.46	.43
	23	Tulsa	Texas	30.3	38	15	4	14	13	4.45	1	2	11.27	1.19	4.15	3.86	.25
BUCKY BUCKLES	23	Charlotte, FL	Flor	48.0	71	30	5	20	31	5.62	2	3	13.31	.94	3.75	5.81	1.00
JUAN CASTILLO	26	Tulsa	Texas	82.0	98	59	11	63	31	6.48	2	7	10.76	1.21	6.91	3.40	-.59
DAVID CHAVARRIA	23	Charlotte, FL	Flor	71.7	98	54	7	57	56	6.78	2	6	12.31	.88	7.16	7.03	.55
RODNEY COOK	25	Charlotte, FL	Flor	69.3	101	36	4	37	35	4.67	3	5	13.11	.52	4.80	4.54	.31
CHRIS CURTIS	25	Oklahoma	AmA	72.7	97	47	5	45	32	5.82	3	5	12.01	.62	5.57	3.96	-.07
JEFF DAVIS	23	Tulsa	Texas	89.3	119	54	10	31	42	5.44	4	6	11.99	1.01	3.12	4.23	.63
RYAN DEMPSTER	19	Charleston, SCS	Atl	120.7	173	89	16	84	77	6.64	3	10	12.90	1.19	6.27	5.74	.35
STEVE DREYER	26	Oklahoma	AmA	112.7	140	52	5	47	66	4.15	6	7	11.18	.40	3.75	5.27	.82
JAIME ESCAMILLA	24	Charlotte, FL	Flor	54.3	84	36	7	38	29	5.96	2	4	13.91	1.16	6.29	4.80	.03
DAVE GEEVE	26	Tulsa	Texas	76.0	111	49	11	34	50	5.80	3	5	13.14	1.30	4.03	5.92	.97
RYAN GLYNN	21	Charleston, SCS	Atl	99.7	163	86	13	85	40	7.77	2	9	14.71	1.17	7.68	3.61	-.71
GIL HEREDIA	30	Texas	AL	74.0	81	36	10	15	41	4.38	4	4	9.85	1.22	1.82	4.99	1.21
ROB KELL	25	Charlotte, FL	Flor	68.7	92	47	7	27	45	6.16	2	6	12.06	.92	3.54	5.90	1.08
BRANDON KNIGHT	20	Charlotte, FL	Flor	89.7	146	75	14	63	55	7.53	2	8	14.65	1.41	6.32	5.52	.26
BRYAN LINK	23	Charlotte, FL	Flor	65.3	101	48	11	28	46	6.61	2	5	13.91	1.52	3.86	6.34	1.15
DAVID MANNING	24	Tulsa	Texas	82.7	96	34	5	58	40	3.70	5	4	10.45	.54	6.31	4.35	-.13
JERRY MARTIN	24	Tulsa	Texas	79.0	102	52	11	55	41	5.92	3	6	11.62	1.25	6.27	4.67	-.01
MIKE MCHUGH	23	Charleston, SCS	Atl	44.7	63	51	5	75	29	10.28	1	4	12.69	1.01	15.11	5.84	-1.83
BOBBY MOORE	23	Charleston, SCS	Atl	118.7	183	104	14	67	69	7.89	3	10	13.88	1.06	5.08	5.23	.47
DONALD MORILLO	22	Charlotte, FL	Flor	44.0	65	38	3	52	25	7.77	1	4	13.30	.61	10.64	5.11	-.95
JOE MORVAY	25	Tulsa	Texas	42.0	59	30	3	26	22	6.43	1	4	12.64	.64	5.57	4.71	.18
SCOTT MUDD	23	Charleston, SCS	Atl	150.0	274	117	16	76	63	7.02	4	13	16.44	.96	4.56	3.78	.12
JOHN O'DONOGHUE	27	Tulsa	Texas	73.0	95	44	9	33	38	5.42	3	5	11.71	1.11	4.07	4.68	.54
GARDNER O'FLYNN	24	Charlotte, FL	Flor	95.7	161	83	14	47	27	7.81	2	9	15.15	1.32	4.42	2.54	-.26
JOHN POWELL	25	Tulsa	Texas	104.7	130	66	18	45	65	5.68	4	4	11.18	1.55	3.87	5.59	.90
MO SANFORD	29	Oklahoma	AmA	138.0	164	72	17	69	108	4.70	6	9	10.70	1.11	4.50	7.04	1.22
CARLOS SIMMONS	22	Charleston, SCS	Atl	46.3	78	51	10	47	19	9.91	1	4	15.15	1.94	9.13	3.69	-1.05
DAN SMITH	20	Charlotte, FL	Flor	75.7	126	71	9	53	41	8.44	1	7	14.99	1.07	6.30	4.88	.05
	26	Tulsa	Texas	46.0	56	25	6	28	24	4.89	2	3	10.96	1.17	5.48	4.70	.20
MIKE VENAFRO	22	Charleston, SCS	Atl	49.0	80	34	1	32	34	6.24	1	4	14.69	.18	5.88	6.24	.61

Arizona Diamondbacks

Despite being a good year and a half away from existing, the Arizona Diamondbacks have already made a few major splashes. In the last year, they've unveiled their retractable-roof stadium, a glib management team and their first minor league affiliates. In particular, the Diamondbacks have gotten good marks for the organizational team that they've put together of Buck Showalter, Joe Garagiola, Jr. and Rollie Hemond. Owner Jerry Colangelo appeared diplomatic during the labor crisis, stressing the need for a cooperative relationship with the players. There was an immediate rush to call this "the basketball approach" by sportswriters eager to see some benefit to Colangelo's ownership of the NBA Phoenix Suns.

Most of this book is devoted, in one way or another, to trashing the ways major league organizations habitually do things, so you might think that the way the D-backs are operated represents a breath of fresh air. The problem is that the D-backs don't appear to be paying attention to what really makes a great farm system great: not the successes of top draft picks, but the ones of mid- and late-round picks, or strong overseas scouting and development. The other problem is that the money is far from guaranteed as well spent. Travis Lee has fine credentials as a hitter, and he is only 20, but with a wooden bat in his hands he could easily be the next Tim Costo. As for the money blown on the pitchers, the survival rate of pitchers, high draft pick or low, is poor (ask Dan Opperman, Kiki Jones, Kirk Dressendorfer, Lance Dickson, Brien Taylor and hundreds of others). Even if they avoid injury, the survivor's subsequent success is rarely guaranteed (such as with Todd Van Poppel).

So be very cautious about believing in the future of the Diamondbacks. The brain trust, such as it is, could wind up being very disappointing. Garagiola is an ex-agent, a pedigree that shows up in the way the D-backs are quick to cough up oodles of cash to potential nobodies. If he mistakes big signings with real accomplishments, his tenure as GM may be very unhappy. Hemond endured a fairly miserable reign as the Orioles' GM, helping to perpetuate one of the worst minor league systems known to man, yet the D-backs are convinced that "40 years of baseball experience" will somehow erase Hemond's record as the man who brought Glenn Davis to Baltimore. Buck Showalter has a fine record of success in the Yankees' organization, but there are reasons to be worried. Although he racked up a superb record in the minors, it's hard to say how important his role was in the development of minor league talent; he obviously had little input in who was selected or signed.

As a major league manager running an offense, Showalter was notable for shutting down the running game and deriding the perceived virtues of the "useful" out. As far as handling a pitching staff, I think we're all left with the indelible image of his blowing the Yankees out of the '95 postseason with his decision to leave an exhausted David Cone on the mound. Showalter is a fine manager, but the way he runs a team has almost nothing in common with the "accepted" National League style. If Buck is heavily criticized for this during the D-backs first year or two, the organization's willingness to ignore the criticism while waiting for a good team will be tested.

The Diamondbacks have been very aggressive in creating a farm system that will eventually sustain the major league organization. Defying expectations that they would only operate one A-ball franchise in '97, they've already established affiliations with both South Bend in the Midwest League and High Desert in the California League.

Significant as this early hoarding of affiliates might be, the Diamondbacks made a much larger national impression with their acquisition of notorious first-round free agents Travis Lee and John Patterson. The D-backs also displayed their aggressive approach to acquiring amateur talent with the signings of two Cuban defectors, Vladimir Nunez and Larry Rodriguez. Arizona spent nearly $20 million in bonuses to sign these four players. These signings were again cited as examples of an "NBA attitude," as the Diamondbacks shake up the baseball world with lots of youth and lots of cash.

For all of their lip service to a belief in minor league development, the results from their first two minor league teams were mixed. Lethbridge dominated the Pioneer League in wins and almost every statistical category (only to get squashed in the playoffs). Whether or not hitters like Kevin Sweeney are as good as they showed isn't certain, and moving up to the California League's version of Coors Field (High Desert) won't clear things up. Vlad Nunez lived up to expectations, leading the league in ERA, strikeouts and wins. He proved what we probably already knew: Cuban baseball is probably a cut above the Pioneer League. The D-backs' team in the Arizona rookie league (not to be confused with the AFL) was the worst team in the circuit.

In short, the Diamondbacks have shown a flair for the dramatic. That may help season ticket sales, and it may mean they'll be buying pricey free agents as soon as they can, but it probably isn't a formula for success.

Tampa Bay Devil Rays

Pity the poor denizens of the Tampa Bay area. They have put up with one of the NFL's most laughable franchises for close to two decades. In their desperation for a sports team they could have pride in, they sacrificed their dignity, groveling repeatedly as they courted countless existing baseball teams looking for leverage to get a new stadium from Chicago, Cleveland, Seattle or <insert city here>. Their lust for a team—any team—led them to build a state-of-the-art ballpark at the end of an era in which new ballparks were called "stadiums" and "state-of-the-art" meant domes, artificial turf and easy highway access. They made it to the altar more times than Elizabeth Taylor, but were stranded there each time. And now, after one last jilting by the San Francisco Giants gave Tampa enough ammunition to hijack the expansion process and insure a team of their own, they have the misfortune of trying to keep up with an expansion brother that has more resources, more brainpower and much, much more money.

Indeed, the best way to describe the Devil Rays is to show how they differ from their sibling, the Arizona Diamondbacks. The Diamondbacks have a beautiful, corporate-sponsored, revenue-factory ballpark under construction; the Devil Rays get to play in western Florida's tribute to 1971 architecture. The Diamondbacks hired one of baseball's most respected managers, Buck Showalter, a year ago; the Devil Rays were spurned this winter by Terry Collins and appear unlikely to have a manager in place until shortly before the Expansion Draft this November. And in perhaps the defining difference between the two teams, the Diamondbacks' financial stability enabled them to blow everyone out of the water in the Travis Lee sweepstakes. The Devil Rays, feeling compelled to respond, countered by offering high school phenom Matt White an eight-figure contract of their own.

There are two main problems with a deal of this sort. Lee is a 21-year-old collegiate hitter who, in all likelihood, could make a AA All-Star team right now. White is an 18-year-old schoolboy who still has to prove he can get hitters out in rookie ball. Year after year, college players prove to be better investments in the draft's first round than high school players, and hitters are better bets than pitchers. True, White has been called the best high school pitcher in decades, and likely would have been picked first had he not been represented by Scott Boras, the Agent Guild's answer to Jerry Reinsdorf. But the last high school pitcher to be picked #1 overall was Brien Taylor. Giving an untested pitcher $10 million in the hope that he will pan out sometime in the next century seems like a risky proposition.

That brings up the second problem: the Devil Rays felt obliged to take the gamble on White, not just because they felt his talent justified it, but for the short-lived PR gain on the Diamondbacks that he provided. What does it say about the Devil Rays' philosophy on franchise-building that their boldest move to date has simply been to follow the Diamondbacks' lead? The contracts given to White and fellow high school pitcher Bobby Seay may yet prove to be money well spent, regardless of the motives behind them. It is certainly true that the Devil Rays, as much as the Diamondbacks, are committed to patiently constructing a winning franchise by scouting and developing their own players. But with fewer assets to work with than their comrades in Arizona, the Devil Rays need to surpass them in guile and courage. They can't expect to forge new ground when they keep stumbling over the footprints of the behemoth they're trying to catch.

Labor

A Look the Labor War

It has been two years since the baseball strike began, a year and a half since it ended under a court injunction, three months since a resolution seemed imminent and two weeks after the deadline, but baseball's labor war has finally been resolved. For two years, the owners were unwilling to deal with their internal differences, while the union had been unwilling to give in to unreasonable demands. This has been the situation in previous labor negotiations; however, some owners seemed to be more determined than ever to break the union, rather than work to resolve the situation. That is why baseball suffered the prolonged strike, and why the final agreement took so long and was resolved only when the signing of Albert Belle exposed the internal problems.

The most important issue in the dispute is money. Baseball generates a lot of money, and it's natural for the players and owners to both want larger pieces of the pie. The main issue in the negotiations, and in almost every labor negotiation, has been the structure of player salaries as determined by arbitration eligibility, free-agent eligibility and restrictions, and now caps and taxes. Both sides have gained from the increase in revenues in the 1980s. Before the strike, many owners claimed they were losing money, but this was primarily the result of accounting practices; this explains why money-losing businesses could still sell for eighty million dollars. Even by the owners' own figures, 1993 was the eighth consecutive year that MLB had operated at a profit, following eleven years of losses.

The owners have internal problems that contributed to the strike. Small-market owners would like a larger share of the revenue; large-market owners are not willing to give it up, but would be happy if instead the players had to give it up. Meanwhile, some owners wanted to break the union, although it hasn't broken in any of the previous strikes or lockouts; others preferred to have an agreement. The owners made this worse by agreeing to require a 3/4 vote to approve any labor action after the strike started; this allowed a minority of owners to threaten any deal.

Despite what you may read, concern for the fans was never an issue in the strike, other than concern for fans' dollars. Baseball owners, like all business owners, set prices to maximize profit, not to break even; therefore, any change in payrolls from a new agreement will go into or out of owners' pockets, not to the fans as higher or lower ticket prices. (Despite the jump in salaries under free agency, ticket prices have been essentially constant in real value for 50 years.) The union set the strike date when it was thought a strike would be most effective; the possibility of a settlement in time for the World Series was a strong incentive for the owners to set-

tle, but the union was willing to give up on the World Series if the owners didn't settle. The strike was a calculated risk by both sides, with the expectations that the gains at the negotiating table would outweigh the losses from alienating fans. The owners lost the gamble when the imposed salary cap was overturned.

The salary cap that started the trouble was primarily an attempt to reduce salaries. The cap would have placed the same limit on all teams' salaries, and would have forced salaries down from 58% to 50% of revenues. Individual teams have been working on publicly announced budgets for several years, but they have set their budgets as appropriate for their own situations; the cap and accompanying salary "floor" would force many teams to spend less than they want, and some to spend more. The owners' early tax plans were attempts to create the same situation without forcing it; the tax rates on high payrolls were around 75%, which would mean that a team over the threshold would have to pay $7 million to match a $4 million offer from a low-payroll team. Current proposals have tax rates around 35%, which will discourage, but not prevent, significant spending over the salary cap threshold. Other proposals have included small across-the-board taxes, which would lower all salaries by the same small factor.

Revenue sharing is another method for redistributing the owners' money, which would have similar effects on salaries. It is different in principle because it represents an actual effect; when the Yankees play in Seattle, there is no reason that the Yankees should get all of the revenue for broadcasting the game in New York. Revenue sharing gives the Mariners a share of the New York TV revenue, and the Yankees a share of the Seattle revenue; this will help low-revenue teams at the expense of high-revenue teams. Note that it will reduce salaries, which is why it concerns the union. If a player will generate $1 million in extra revenue, but his team must pay 5% of the extra revenue to other teams, he might only be offered $950,000.

In contrast, the most recent sticking point, service time, is not directly a financial issue. A player receives credit for the time he is on a major-league roster; this time is used to determine his eligibility for arbitration, free agency and a pension. It is common for service time to be a negotiated issue in strike resolution. It is particularly important to the baseball players' union, because a loss of service time would have a serious effect on those players who lose free-agent eligibility. In every previous in-season strike, the players received service time for the strike, and the union insisted on it for this one as well. The owners tried to divide the union's membership by offering service time to all but the players who needed it for free agency, but the union did not accept this.

With an understanding of the issues, we can now follow the history of the labor negotiations. The problem began when the owners agreed to increase revenue sharing, but the large-market owners, who would lose money from such a plan, would agree to it only with a salary cap. This led to the owners' plan in 1994: they offered the salary cap as a proposal, and if the players did not accept it, the owners intended to declare an impasse in collective bargaining, impose their last offer and use replacements if the players struck. Imposition of the last offer and use of replacements are allowed under labor law, provided that management negotiates in good faith. However, making an offer involving major concessions by the union, refusing to budge from it and adding insult to injury by skipping a pension payment before the strike date did not seem to be negotiating in good faith.

The union's response was essentially forced, given that surrender was not an option. If the salary cap was imposed in December, the players could strike during spring training and the early season, but this would not cause a loss to the owners; spring training loses money, and revenues increase as the season goes on while salaries remain constant. Therefore, the union set a late-season date for the strike, August 12. To strike on this date threatened the playoffs, but did not kill them; the owners could have tried to work out a deal in late August, resumed the season in September and played the playoffs as scheduled. Instead, the owners chose to sacrifice the profits from the playoffs and stick to their plan. The union was also willing to continue negotiation with an agreement of no strike, no lockout and no unilateral imposition; this had been agreed to in 1993, but the owners refused in 1994.

The union had opened negotiations with its own plan asking for substantial gains, but unlike the owners, it was willing to make concessions. In July, the union proposed a continuation of the status quo. In September, the union proposed its own tax plan, with 1.5% taxes on revenues and payrolls; in November, the union proposed 5% taxes across the board and increased rates on very high payrolls. The owners responded with their own tax plan, but that was a plan designed to work like a cap, with very high tax rates on the portion of payrolls over the desired cap level. The owners also made it clear that the cap would be the imposed plan if the union refused this tax offer.

The union did refuse it, and the owners imposed the cap on December 22, 1994. The union immediately filed a charge of failure to bargain in good faith with the National Labor Relations Board; simultaneously, the union announced a signing freeze, so that players would not sign contracts under conditions it considered unfair. The NLRB issued a complaint, the first step towards getting a court ruling; the own-

ers chose to settle by withdrawing the cap rather than fighting this charge. However, the owners then initiated their own signing freeze, and renewed contracts by changing the language to deny players arbitration and free agency. Since this would have had the same effect as imposing the changes, the union filed a new charge.

Meanwhile, negotiations resumed in February, 1995 with the help of federal mediator William Usery. Usery was able to get the two sides to talk, but no mediator can bring together two parties who don't want to bargain; both sides were waiting for the NLRB, and the union felt it had already conceded enough. Both sides made new tax proposals similar to their November plans. Usery did not actually offer a plan; what was reported as Usery's plan was a leaked set of proposals. It included some elements under discussion, such as a 50% tax on payrolls over $40 million, unrestricted free agency after four years and a phase-out of arbitration, but also several concessions to the owners which had not been discussed or adequately studied. The owners accepted this plan, but the union refused it because of the high tax rate and other concessions.

The owners came up with another plan, which they claimed was based on Usery's plan but which may have been a step backwards; the tax was 50% on payrolls above the league average, and Usery's concession to the players on free agency was removed. The players made a new plan which accepted the Fort Lauderdale revenue-sharing plan, with a trivial tax compared to the owners' high taxes. It still seemed that both sides were waiting for the NLRB.

The NLRB issued its new complaint, and asked Judge Sonia Sotomayor to grant an injunction restoring the old work rules. The owners immediately made a proposal with a tax of 50% on payrolls over $44M and no phase-out of arbitration; the players responded with a tax of 25% on payrolls over $50M. Judge Sotomayor then granted the preliminary injunction on March 31, 1995. The owners could have attempted to lock the players out, but the 3/4 rule came back to haunt them; no vote was even called. The 1995 season started, and a deal seemed possible for the first time.

However, nothing happened at the bargaining table. Neither side made a proposal during the 1995 season. The injunction was upheld on appeal, essentially ensuring that the solution would have to be worked out at the bargaining table. Both sides made small concessions on their tax plans in the offseason, but they were still almost as far apart in February, 1996 as they had been in March, 1995.

In March, serious bargaining finally began. The union offered to raise the tax rate from 25% to 30%; the owners offered to lower the rate to 40% and raise the threshold closer to the union's level. This time, productive negotiations continued during the season. The owners made a new proposal on May 23 that eliminated the tax in the final year; this is important because the final year's agreement would remain in effect if negotiations continued after the expiration of the agreement.

There was still a gap to be bridged, and owners impatient to bridge it announced in late July that they would make a "last offer" and ask Judge Sotomayor to declare an impasse if the players rejected it, allowing the owners to impose it. No impasse or "last offer" occurred; instead, the next two weeks were filled with productive bargaining.

On August 11, at the end of those two weeks, the negotiators had a deal. The tax rate of 35% in 1997 and 1998, and 34% in 1999, would be imposed on the portion of payrolls over $51M in 1997, $55M in 1998 and $58.9M in 1999. There would be no tax in 2000; the union had the option to extend the agreement to 2001 with no tax in return for a payment. The union agreed to waive any right to legal action against the owners for actions during the strike in return for service time for all players.

The deal still had to be approved by both sides, and the owners refused without calling a vote. Several owners did not want to lose players who would become free agents with the additional service time. Other owners wanted to extract additional concessions from the union. Still others preferred to play under the old system, without revenue sharing. A counterproposal was made to grant service time to all but the 19 players who needed it for free agency; the union rejected this offer, insisting on full service time for all players.

In order to take effect for 1997, any deal would need approval by November 15, the day on which free agents could sign with new teams, so this date represented a deadline. In an effort to leave options open even after the players went home at the end of the season, the union obtained approval from the players for the August 11 proposal, allowing the owners to approve it later and have it take effect. Any significant change would still require player approval, which would prevent implementation until the players returned in 1997.

On November 6, the owners rejected the plan by an 18-12 vote. The actual reported preferences were 16-14 in favor, which would not have been enough to approve the agreement under the 3/4 rules; four owners changed their votes to "no" at Bud Selig's request, in a show of owner solidarity. The owners talked about modifying the agreement, but this was already known to be impossible. The November 15 deadline had now passed. A new meeting was set for November 26, but this seemed to be just a procedural meeting.

However, the subsequent free agent signings exposed the internal problems between owners, and gave the deal new life. White Sox owner Jerry Reinsdorf, who had led the hardline movement to put tighter controls on salaries, signed Albert Belle to the largest contract in baseball history. This created the perception among his fellow owners that Reinsdorf had been acting out of his own self-interest, rather than genuine interest in helping owners as a group. This contract put the Sox well over the tax threshold under the rejected deal, and the failure to restore service time had also conveniently prevented their star pitcher, Alex Fernandez, from filing for free agency.

With many owners angry at Reinsdorf, and with the active support of acting commissioner Bud Selig, the deal which had been rejected on November 6 was accepted on November 26. All necessary changes were made retroactively; players who became eligible for free agency with the added service time were allowed to become free agents, including those who had re-signed with their original teams before the agreement. Reinsdorf was the big loser in the settlement; he had signed Belle under the assumption that there would be no tax, and now he would have to pay the tax as well as the salary.

The passage of the new agreement also allows the secondary proposals to take effect. The new revenue-sharing plan will be phased in as scheduled, which means that the small-market owners who tried to kill the deal will now reap its benefits. Interleague play was also dependent on the agreement.

The failure of the plan would have had major effects on the players and owners, but it wouldn't have been very noticeable to most fans. When the owners rejected their own negotiator's deal, they probably gave up any claim to having negotiated in good faith if they had wanted to lock the players out, so the chances of a lockout or strike endangering the '97 season were already slim. Interleague play will begin. Fourteen players became free agents. There will still be trades made for economic reasons, as has happened throughout baseball's history and would have happened with any cap, tax or revenue-sharing plans.

The most important difference may simply be the fact that there is now an agreement, instead of a sword hanging over the game. MLB reported that many licensing and marketing deals were contingent on a labor agreement. The off-season news will now all be about trades, prospects, signings and new ballparks, instead of about taxes and legal arguments. Baseball has bought itself four years to re-establish its image. Let hope they get started.

--David Grabiner

115 Years of Chicken Little: The Business of Baseball

Professional baseball is on the wane. Salaries must come down, or the interest of the public must be increased in some way. If one or the other does not happen, bankruptcy stares every team in the face.

— Albert Spalding, 1881

Doomsayers have been predicting baseball's demise since before Strom Thurmond was born. Today is no different: fans are continually being told that rising player salaries will destroy the sport, that small market teams will be driven under, that families will be priced out of the ballpark, that baseball, burdened with such high player salaries, will not be able to compete with basketball and the like.

Sportswriters happily repeat these fears unquestioningly. Baseless scaremongering is hardly unique to baseball; ask any apple-grower about Alar, or note that Ravi Batra can still find an ear with a presidential candidate (albeit Pat Buchanan) even after his "The Great Depression of 1990." Yet somehow, no one ever says that R.E.M.'s $80 million record contract will keep the average citizen from listening to top music, or that Stephen King's $30 million advance will devastate the publishing industry, or that Demi Moore's $25-million-a-movie deal will keep smaller studios from being able to compete. But San Francisco Giants owner Peter Magowan keeps a straight face and claims that player salaries are putting baseball through a serious economic crisis.

This essay looks at the various jeremiads and comes to the conclusion that they're bunk. Along the way, we'll take a look at some of the various interesting claims that have been made about the economics of baseball, and why a well-run team can be successful and profitable even if it is in a "small market" that allegedly cannot compete with the big-market clubs.

Is Baseball Losing Money?

The standard claim by many owners is that their teams are losing money. Therefore, the argument follows, they should receive a subsidy from taxpayers to build them a new stadium, or they should be allowed to move the team to a municipality that wants to subsidize them, or players should accept a labor deal that reduces their salaries.

The sky has been falling for decades. Recall that before the 1994 strike, it was explained that many teams were on the verge of bankruptcy. Since then, there has been a disastrous strike, a halving of the value of the television contract, a decline in attendance, no corresponding decline in salaries — yet not a single team has gone under. Recall also that the Houston franchise, supposedly losing $10 million a year, has no shortage of suitors wishing to pay well over $100 million to own the team—$100 million that could, with next to no risk whatsoever, be put into short-term bonds and earn a $6 million profit. There is also no shortage of suitors wishing to pay nine-digit expansion fees for the privilege of losing this money. Now, if baseball was really in trouble, why are so many trying to get into the business?

The answer is simple: baseball is not in the financial trouble it claims to be. A baseball team may be losing money—but the owner of that baseball team almost never is.

When a team is showing losses on paper, the books don't always tell the whole story. In 1991, Turner Broadcasting System paid $9 million to the Atlanta Braves to show nearly a full season of games to a national cable television audience—well over 400 hours of programming. (By comparison, Columbia Pictures fetches about $2 million for each half-hour "Seinfeld" rerun that it sells nationwide.) That's a hugely profitable deal for TBS, and a not-so-hot deal for the Atlanta Braves—but their common owner, Ted Turner, is indifferent about who shows the profit.

Or perhaps not so indifferent. There are advantages to jiggering contracts between a commonly-owned baseball team and an affiliate. The affiliate might be publicly traded, while the baseball team does not have the pressure of producing profits on paper. Indeed, the paper losses can produce nice tax write-offs for the owner. A team that shows losses on paper cuts a more sympathetic figure when they ask for a government-funded stadium or other subsidy. And if teams were showing large paper profits, it would be hard to plead poverty at labor negotiations or in the court of public opinion.

So the St. Louis Cardinals, in their Anheuser-Busch days, received no money from beer sales at Cardinal games. Teams finance themselves with loans from their owners—and then show the huge interest expenses on their books. In the NFL, a number of teams pay their owners higher salaries than most of their players. Money is going from the left-hand pocket into the right-hand pocket—but then the owner of the pants turns out only one of the pockets when claiming to be losing money.

The most telling indication of this came in the 1994 labor dispute. The owners made public statement after public statement that they were losing money—but then would not publicly open their books for inspection of their claims. (Labor laws required them to show the books to representatives of the players, who were required to keep the information confidential.) Baseball is a monopoly, so allowing an audit of its books—something that every public corporation does—is not going to reveal competitive secrets. But it would likely reveal what it revealed in 1985, when the owners allowed the players to have Stanford economist Roger Noll inspect the records: owners overstating their economic losses by tens of millions of dollars. This is entirely proper from a legal and accounting perspective: the numbers aren't lying. Some of the baseball teams really are "losing money." But the baseball team owners aren't.

Can "Small-Market" Teams Succeed?

It depends on how you define "small market."

The media definition (as well as that of the baseball preachers of doom) seems to be teams that have just won pennants and have lots of attendance as a result are "large market." Teams that are poorly run and have ended up in the basement with empty stadiums cannot possibly compete against these franchises. Everyone ignores the fact that the largest crowds in baseball come from the fourth-smallest SMSA in the major leagues, Colorado. St. Louis, a market that once drew fewer fans in a season for its AL club than the Yankees drew for a doubleheader, and a market that has lost a football and a basketball team, is sometimes called a "large market," even though it is the sixth-smallest SMSA in the majors. "Large market" Atlanta has an SMSA smaller than at least sixteen other major league teams (including small-market Seattle, Houston and Detroit) and has trouble selling out playoff games.

In the heat of the 1995 pennant race, Peter Gammons was complaining how the Cincinnati Reds' trade for David Wells was an example of the rich getting richer—but now, of course, we hear of the Reds as a small-market team.

Up through 1995—indeed, well into 1995, as the "large-market" Angels looked to run away with the division—we were told how the Seattle Mariners simply had no chance of ever competing with the New York Yankees of the world. Indeed, it was surprising that anyone in Seattle ever showed up to a baseball game, they were told so often that they just couldn't compete, which made "small market" a bit of a self-fulfilling prophecy. In 1991, Commissioner Fay Vincent was announcing that Seattle could not hope to compete with Oakland and Boston. The standard argument during the lead-up to the 1994 strike, repeated verbatim by so many sports-writers that it almost certainly came from a representative of the owners, was that "small-market clubs such as...San Diego and Seattle cannot compete with big-market clubs such as...Toronto."

After the 1995 playoffs, we heard less about Seattle as such a non-competitive small-market team and more about the San Diego Padres. Presumably there will be a new poster child for small markets for 1997. Perhaps it will be the Milwaukee Brewers, whose recent youth movement might result in baseball Chicken Littles being embarrassed for a third straight year. (In the 1950's, of course, Milwaukee was

the large-market franchise drawing two million fans a year that had moved from Boston, and whose success had forced the Brooklyn Dodgers to head west in hopes of competing.)

Meanwhile, Boston, according to an October 1996 Will McDonough column, has magically transformed into one of the have-not teams that cannot compete against Baltimore, the new large-market team. Never mind that the Orioles finished behind the Red Sox in 1995.

No less a luminary than Bill James has fallen prey to the paranoia. In his 1992 *Baseball Book*, one of his team comments looked at the competitive balance of baseball. He correctly noted that the balance was much better since free agency—with nearly every team making the playoffs at least once, and World Series winners such as Minnesota, Detroit, Philadelphia, Kansas City and Pittsburgh instead of the monotony of the New York Yankees dynasty. Despite this, he saw a grim future for baseball, and one franchise in particular. In the face of the large-market Toronto bulldozer, this small-market franchise had traded away one of its top pitchers, was playing to empty stadiums and going with a strategy of youth. According to James:

> Major league baseball is entering a very rough period. The Cleveland Indians are the canary in baseball's coal mine, and the canary just dropped off his perch.
>
> *--Bill James, 1992,* The Baseball Book

Keep in mind that when James wrote this, the core of Belle-Thome-Ramirez-Lofton was already in the organization. The Atlanta Braves had just demonstrated that a decade of futility and recent last place finish with a team of improving youngsters hardly mandated future doom. But James apparently fell for the drumbeat of fifteen years of Chicken Littles saying that free agency would doom baseball. We all know what happened next. The Indians are now one of the large-market teams the Boston Red Sox and Toronto Blue Jays have no hope of competing against.

And the Indians didn't do anything that any other team couldn't do:

Get good prospects. The Indians didn't succeed by buying up every free agent in sight; indeed, their recent shift in strategy to let languish or unload the Mark Clarks, Herb Perrys and Brian Gileses in favor of Jeff Kents and Kevin Seitzers has probably hurt the club. The stars of the Indians are players the Indians developed. The stars of the Braves, with the exception of Greg Maddux, are players the Braves developed or traded prospects for. For all you hear about the money of the Yankees, they wouldn't have won anything without the players they developed, such as Derek Jeter, Bernie Williams and Mariano Rivera. The Yankees' World Series victory is hardly an example of the haves beating the have-nots: the

Yankees' dollars resulted in millions devoted to mediocrities such as Kenny Rogers, Joe Girardi, part-time DH Cecil Fielder and Tino Martinez. While the Milwaukee Brewers are the latest example of a team that allegedly cannot succeed without more money, the reality is that throughout the 1980s, the Brewers produced precisely one top-notch prospect in Gary Sheffield, and then promptly traded him away for a buy-one-get-one-free Big Mac coupon. All the money in the world isn't going to help a team that poor in prospects win. The 1996 Orioles are perhaps the best example in the history of baseball of a team devoted almost entirely to free agents, and they barely eked their way into the playoffs. And even the Orioles had three critical stars, Cal Ripken, Mike Mussina and Brady Anderson, that they essentially developed, plus one, Bobby Bonilla, whom they could not have acquired without trading prospects.

Free agents are investments, not expenses. Good players cost money, but good players produce results and results put fannies in the seats. Barry Bonds gets $7 million a year because Barry Bonds increases team revenues at least $7 million a year. Consider the situation where Barry Bonds only generated $5 million of revenue a year: why would an owner offer to pay him more than that? The question is not how the Pirates can afford to sign Barry Bonds, but how the Pirates can afford not to sign Barry Bonds. The corollary to this is:

Invest wisely. When all was said and done, nothing stopped the Pirates from signing Barry Bonds—they chose not to do so when he was asking for a contract of the same magnitude that they signed Andy Van Slyke to. After Bonds left, they signed Jay Bell to a huge contract, and ended up blowing a large sum of money on the likes of the eminently forgettable Mike Kingery. The Pirates were a small-market team that was succeeding quite nicely, but then blew its money on the wrong horse. Sure, the Yankees and Mets can make costly mistakes like this and still run a profit, even though mistakes like spending $3 million a year on Lance Johnson are just as expensive and foolish.

The Pirates are on the right track now, believe it or not: instead of spending millions on Denny Neagle, a pitcher who was never going to help them win a pennant, they got a pitcher far more likely to be around when the Pirates start winning and one of the top power-hitting prospects in the minors. They're selling high and buying low, always a good move. Similarly, the early 1990's Indians took a pass on Greg Swindell so that he could play for large markets such as Cincinnati and Houston, and concentrated on paying the players who could be helpful to them when they were ready to compete. The Milwaukee Brewers recently made a good trade in unloading overrated power hitter Greg Vaughn for three solid prospects (from the small-market San Diego Padres, no less), putting themselves in contention for 1997

and potentially embarrassing their owner, Bud Selig, who seems to have staked his career on the failure of the Brewers. The Pirates' current problem is their failure to abide by the following rule:

Sign instead of whine. You have a young Kenny Lofton or Manny Ramirez? Instead of complaining how you're a small market and have no hope of ever retaining him once he becomes a free agent, give him a long-term contract now. You'll improve morale, save money on arbitration, promote loyalty to the team that could pay off when the player does become a free agent and demonstrate to fans you're committed to winning. If you're constantly telling fans you have no hope of competing, they're going to start to believe you—and start staying home. You also hurt your chances of rebuilding. The Padres made a good investment decision to unload Fred McGriff a few years back, trading him when his stock was high, but also when he was at an age where he was unlikely to be a cost-effective contributor when the Padres' rebuilding was finished. But by announcing that they were holding a fire sale and that they couldn't compete or afford McGriff, they lost any leverage in trade negotiations: instead of trading McGriff for Ryan Klesko, they got Melvin Nieves. In conjunction with bad-mouthing the team's chances, this dump alienated thousands of fans. Despite this disaster, they've made it to the playoffs in the 1990s more often than the large-market New York Mets. The Houston Astros are currently suffering from a similar problem. They have two of the best players in baseball in Jeff Bagwell and Craig Biggio, but management chooses to emphasize the high salaries and low performance of Doug Drabek and Greg Swindell instead.

There's a final point one should realize in this whole large-market/small-market controversy, aside from the fact that the size of the market is within the power of most team's marketing departments. The vast majority of teams have been purchased in the last ten years. Any benefits of being in a large market have already been extracted by the previous owners of the baseball franchise when they sold the franchise to the current owner—that price presumably reflected the size of the market. Just as one has to pay higher rent to get a store in the middle of the Manhattan theater district than one does to get the same square footage in Waukegan, Illinois, the Orioles current ownership paid three times what the Pirates ownership did to get their respective franchises.

Do Long-Term Guaranteed Contracts Hurt Performance?
We've all heard, or even perhaps thought of the charge: Of course So-And-So is having a career year. He's up for free agency next year. And once So-And-So signs a long-term contract, he'll go back to being the bum he always was.

The conventional wisdom seems to make common sense. The player up for free agency has a lot more to play for than someone in the first year of a guaranteed long-term contract.

Heck, standard economic theory would predict as much: that's why executives get stock options instead of tenure.

The problem is that the sentiment is so often expressed by the "Those greedy bums should be paying us to get to play a game" yahoo crowd, that those of us sympathetic to the free market and free agency wince when we hear these sentiments and want to refute them immediately.

The counterexamples are numerous: Andre Dawson (1987), Kirk Gibson (1988), Terry Pendleton (1991) and Barry Bonds (1993) all won MVP awards after signing long-term multi-million free agency contracts. The argument against the counter-counter-anecdotes is strong, too. Yeah, you can name Glenn Davis, Bruce Sutter, Vince Coleman, Greg Swindell, Cecil Fielder and other free agent flops, but face it, free agents have to have six years of service time, and these guys all became free agents past their prime, when injuries are more likely and career years less likely. Besides, Vince Coleman always sucked.

I'm not convinced by the battle of the anecdotes. The first three of those four MVPs were terrible choices. Andre Dawson won on Wrigley-inflated HR/RBI numbers, beating out many better-qualified candidates. The last three almost certainly won their awards for post hoc, ergo propter hoc reasons: Terry Pendleton joins the Braves, the Braves suddenly improve from last to first and win the division, therefore Terry Pendleton made the difference and is the MVP, never mind that Barry Bonds had a better season. (Barry Bonds was helped by this reasoning in 1993 even though he deserved his award; I suspect that had he stayed in Pittsburgh and posted the same numbers, Gary Sheffield would have won the MVP for his Triple Crown run that year. But I digress.)

Now, professional athletes are at the top of their field, and they couldn't get there without a strong competitive desire. And perhaps it is the case that that competitive desire is so strong that players' utility function is influenced more by winning and performance than by money. But still, millions of dollars at stake are millions of dollars at stake. Can one really say that players aren't influenced by this factor?

But teams have utility functions, too. They know that players might slack, and take this into account when they make their offers, discounting the price of long-term contracts. A player who signs a long-term contract is almost certainly getting less than if he signed a series of one-year contracts, stayed healthy and continued to perform at the top of his game—even if he had no intention of slacking when he got the long-term contract.

So does that mean that players who sign long-term contracts are necessarily the ones who will slack? No. Players are risk-averse. Signing the long-term contract for a million less a year is like buying an insurance policy against injury. The team is selling that insurance policy: it's taking a risk too, but unlike a player, it has the ability to spread that risk around several players over several years. Over the long run, the team breaks even—or comes out ahead.

Now, obviously this problem is going to be less serious for the 29-year-old in the middle of his career than the 36-year-old at the end of his career. The 29-year-old is going to come up for free agency again, and isn't going to want a reputation as a slacker. Then again, an eight-figure contract is enough for anyone to retire on, even with the hope of an additional eight-figure contract in the future. And teams still cannot distinguish the slackers from the non-slackers: even after two long-term contracts where the player plays at his top form, there's going to be that last contract where the player has no financial incentive to excel—and a team can rarely tell in advance when a player's last contract will be.

There are some mechanisms to avoid this. Option years are the most commonly used in baseball. If a player plays well in the last year of his contract, a team can pick up the option for an additional one-year contract. A team with such a contract structure would then get two or more "last years" of the contract if it felt that playing for a contract was a problem. Similarly, buyout clauses in contracts allow teams to get out of contracts for a price: one could make a strong argument that the magnitude of these buyout prices is an indicator of the difference between the value per year of a one-year and a long-term contract.

Would a solution to the ostensible problem be to abolish the guaranteed contract? Not in the financial sense — doing so would not save teams a penny. The only result of abolishing the guaranteed contract (assuming those players with existing guaranteed contracts are grandfathered) would be to shift risk from the owners to the players. But the players would want to be compensated for accepting that risk, and in a free market, they would be, through contracts that had higher signing bonuses or larger per-year averages.

Perhaps the problem isn't a problem: the only players who get long-term contracts are those who have sensational years; because players who don't have sensational years don't usually get long-term contracts, the players with long-term contracts are disproportionately likely to have huge falloffs in performance because they have further to fall.

The real answer is that the issue hasn't been studied yet, and what the baseball analyst should say in such a case is that the question is more complex than it seems and that we don't yet know the answer. Someone someday will blow a weekend going through Gary Huckabay's Vladimir projections and seeing if Vladimir systematically underestimates players playing in the last year of their contracts and overestimates players in the first year of long-term contracts. The Vladimir system would be optimal for this, because it takes into account age and park effects already and discounts for the likelihood of injury. But until then, beware of knee-jerk (or even not-so-knee-jerk) answers by someone who hasn't seen such a study: the conclusion they've reached more likely reflects their opinion of "players are/aren't greedy" than the reality of the situation.

Does Arbitration Inflate Salaries?

No. And it's ridiculous to claim otherwise, even though owners and sportswriters often point to arbitration as evidence that the sky is falling for baseball.

Well, okay, it depends on your baseline point. Against a reserve clause or a rule that all players must be paid $5.25/hour, arbitration increases salaries. But against the free market, they most certainly do not. As a group, owners make profits on the collection of players who are offered arbitration, even if the occasional arbitration results in an "overpaid" player.

Yes, arbitration often doubles or triples a player's salary. But that isn't a function of the arbitration overvaluing the player — it is a function of a player tied by the reserve clause to negotiating with a single team being underpaid before he is eligible for arbitration.

The truth of this simple point is demonstrated by the fact that under the current collective bargaining agreement, a player cannot go to arbitration unless the owner wants that player to. If the owner truly believed that arbitration would result in a player being "overpaid," the owner could simply release the player, making that player a free agent, and then sign the player in the free market for less than what arbitration would offer him. With the exception of the occasional injury and player who didn't reach his service time until he was well into his decline phase of his career, arbitration has consistently resulted in lower salaries for players than they later earned by becoming free agents. A beautiful example of this came in April 1995, when the Yankees paid $1 million to the Expos for the rights to John Wetteland, whose salary was to be determined by arbitration. If arbitration really resulted in anything close to, much less above, market value salaries, this was a surefire money-losing proposition for the Yankees.

Are High Salaries Caused By A "Shortage" Of Free Agents?

This is a theory one hears from time to time; its most notable proponent is former baseball labor leader Marvin Miller. As Miller tells it, Charles O. Finley proposed making everyone a free agent, and asked owners to abolish the reserve clause completely. Miller was frightened by this proposal, because the "glut" of free agents would flood the market and reduce salaries. Fortunately the owners were too foolish to recognize this, and Miller is a genius for encouraging them to retain part of the reserve clause.

If this somewhat self-serving theory still sounds counter-intuitive to you, it's because it's wrong. Miller talks about the "glut" in the free agent market that would result from universal free agency, but somehow forgets that if everyone were a free agent, there would also be a shortage of players to sign. Imagine a situation where there are only ten good shortstops in the majors. Yes, under the current situation, if there are only one or two shortstops who are free agents, there are going to be twenty teams bidding for their services. But if all ten were free agents, then there would also be an additional eight teams needing shortstops. Supply has gone up, but so has demand. Eventually eight of these free agent shortstops are going to sign—and then the market will be right back where it would have been, with twenty teams chasing two shortstops. The only difference being that Derek Jeter will have signed for a lot more than the six-figure salary he made under the reserve clause last year with the Yankees.

A Digression on Production Per Dollar

Every once in a while, a Murray Chass or some other sportswriter will take a look at player salaries, add up batting average and home runs and some other statistics, divide them into the salaries, and meet his weekly quota of columns by talking about production per dollar or some other such nonsense. Invariably, the column is nonsense.

Never mind that Dante Bichette's 40 home runs in Colorado mean something different than Barry Bonds' 40 home runs in San Francisco. Never mind that some Mike Piazza or Manny Ramirez stuck under the reserve clause with a salary a quarter of their market worth is bound to be more productive than an Andre Dawson at the end of his career, essentially being paid to cut ribbons.

The measure is nonsense because it starts off with a player producing nothing being worth zero, and that's the wrong baseline. A 19-9 starting pitcher is (at least) a five-million dollar player; a 9-19 starting pitcher, if one lasts in the rotation that long, is a minimum wager. But it's certainly not the case that the latter player is the better bargain.

This is because sportswriters, along with many in baseball management, are often unaware of the basic economic concept of opportunity cost. Opportunity cost is the value of the next-best opportunity foregone. The cost to the Yankees in playing Darryl Strawberry in left field is not just the money they pay Darryl Strawberry; they also lose the opportunity to play Ruben Rivera in left field. So they're not really paying Strawberry's salary for Strawberry's production; they're actually paying the difference between Strawberry's and Rivera's salary for the difference between Strawberry's and Rivera's production. One will often find for teams with more dollars than sense that this ratio is a negative number: Billy McMillon will sit so Greg Colbrunn can play, Shannon

Stewart for Otis Nixon, Ryan Klesko for Terry Pendleton and so on.

But the reality is that if you were to stitch together a team of minimum-wagers, players just at the cusp of major-league ability, and call them, say, the Detroit Tigers, they'd still win fifty games and hit .230. That 9-19 pitcher can be replaced with another minimum-wage stiff that goes 9-19: those pitchers with a 6.00 ERA are a dime a dozen. The 20-8 pitcher isn't twice as good as a 10-18 pitcher; the first one generated eleven wins and the second one generated one win above the opportunity cost of a minimum wage scrub. It also explains why a 14-14 pitcher might get paid millions of dollars a year; sure, he's an average pitcher, but an average pitcher is worth a heck of a lot more than a scrub. If pitchers who could win half their games were free, then everyone would be, as in Garrison Keillor's town, above-average.

Murray Chass shouldn't feel too bad; I've seen peer-reviewed economic journal articles make the same basic measurement mistake to predict salaries, and then express confusion when the resulting model produces strange results. Then again, I've also seen numerous peer-reviewed economic journal articles attempt regression of attendance as caused by wins and pennants — even though the most devoted theoretical physicist would be hard-pressed to demonstrate that an event that occurred in September caused an event to occur the previous April. But perhaps that's a subject for next year's *Prospectus*.

When the correct baseline is worked in, one finds that there is a lot less variance from free agent to free agent in production per dollar. That is not to say that there are not systematic errors being made in the market. I would hypothesize that the free agent market consistently overvalues the speedsters like Otis Nixon, Vince Coleman and Lance Johnson, and high-RBI, low-OBP players like Joe Carter and Cecil Fielder, while undervaluing high-OBP players like Mickey Tettleton and Tony Phillips. It also fails to adequately account for distortions in statistics caused by ballpark effects. An interesting study could be done with the salary numbers and Clay Davenport's Equivalent Averages; the first team to take advantage of these market distortions would make a killing on both the baseball diamond and the financial books. In a world where Andres Galarraga is talked of as an MVP candidate with a straight face, the Colorado Rockies could make exceptionally shrewd trades, but for the fact that their management seems to be as unaware of the impact of altitude on batting average as anybody.

--Ted Frank

Extra
Innings

Support-Neutral Win-Loss Records

When John Smoltz got an "L" next to his name after giving up only one run (unearned, no less) in eight innings in Game 5 of the World Series, we heard the moniker that's been attached to countless starters: "tough luck loser." But just how tough was his luck? I mean, a starter who gives up only a run in eight innings will certainly lose occasionally. The question is: how often?

That's one of the questions that a collection of measures I've been working with attempts to answer. I've given the measures the heading "support-neutral" (SN) because they measure a starter's contribution to winning and losing regardless of the support he receives from his team's offense and relief corps. A starter's Support-Neutral W/L record (SNW/SNL) is his expected (in the statistical sense) W/L record—how many games he would be expected to win and lose given his pitching performances, assuming he had a league-average offense and bullpen behind him. And a starter's Support-Neutral Value Added (SNVA) measures the total number of extra games his team would be expected to win with his pitching performances instead of an average pitcher's.

It's fun that SNW/SNL allows us to measure a pitcher's "luck" with his real W/L record, as with the Smoltz example above. But these stats' real strength is as a measure of the total value of a starter's pitching over a season or career. What distinguishes support-neutral stats from other measures is that the support-neutral stats look at each start's contribution to winning individually, rather than estimating his winning contribution by looking at cumulative run prevention over a bunch of starts or an entire season. This game-by-game perspective of the support-neutral stats removes distortions that can be introduced in cumulative run prevention statistics like ERA and Thorn and Palmer's Adjusted Pitching Runs (APR). As a result, I think that SN stats give a more accurate pitcher of a starter's value than APR.

How They're Calculated

The basic idea behind the calculation of the SN stats is pretty simple. I'll use SNW to illustrate. A starter's SNW total is calculated by determining, for each start he makes over the season, the probability that he would get the win given the way he pitched in that game, and then summing up the individual probabilities over all of his starts. The sum gives you the number of wins a pitcher could expect to get for an average team given his performances. A "performance" here consists only of the number of innings pitched, the number of runs (not earned runs) given up, the park in which the game was played and whether the pitcher was at home or on the road. SNW assumes that these are the only things that influence whether the pitcher wins or loses.

Getting these probabilities is a little complicated. The starter gets a win when two things happen: (1) he leaves the game with the lead and (2) his team holds it without ever giving it up. To get the probability of a pitcher getting a win for an average team, I look at all the different possible sequences of innings that could lead to a win. For example, a start like Smoltz' Game 5 start (8 IP, 1 R at home) would result in a win if...

- his team scored 2 in the first 8 innings and his relievers gave up 0 in the 9th, or
- his team scored 3 in the first 8 innings and his relievers gave up 0 in the 9th, or
- his team scored 3 in the first 8 innings and his relievers gave up 1 in the 9th, or
- etc., etc., etc....

I figure out each of the individual probabilities above, substituting "league average" for "his," and then combine them using the simplest laws of probability, i.e., multiplying whenever it says "and" and adding whenever it says "or." The individual inning probabilities (e.g., the probability of "average relievers gave up 1 in the 9th") just come from the league single inning scoring distribution for that year. For example, in the National League in 1996, teams scored zero runs in 71.3% of the innings, one run in 15.3% of the innings, two runs in 7.3% of the innings, etc. Park effects are figured in by changing the definition of "average team." For example, an average team will score more runs in Coors and fewer in Dodger Stadium, and the run scoring distribution is altered to reflect that.

The end results of all the calculations are three probabilities: the start resulting in a win for the pitcher (SNW), the start resulting in an loss for the pitcher (SNL), and the start resulting in a win for an average team (SNVA). Smoltz' start calculates to a 0.75 SNW and a 0.05 SNL. This start will result in a team win 85% of the time; since SNVA is concerned with comparing a starter to a league average pitcher, and since an average pitcher's starts will presumably result in 50% wins, Smoltz's start gets an SNVA rating of 0.85 - 0.5 = 0.35 games above average.

Why They're Good Measures of Pitcher Value

That's a lot of calculation to go through to get a measure of pitching value. Is it worth it? In particular, do the SN stats tell us anything that Thorn and Palmer's Adjusted Pitching

Runs (APR) weren't already telling us? In fact, they do. Consider the following two pitchers:

Pitcher A			Pitcher B		
Start	**IP**	**R**	**Start**	**IP**	**R**
Game 1	4	8	Game 1	0	14
Game 2	4	8	Game 2	8	2
TOTAL	8	16	TOTAL	8	16

Any stat that measures run prevention cumulatively (e.g., ERA and APR) will rate these two pitchers even. But baseball intuition tells us that Pitcher B has helped his team more. An average team is very likely to go 0-2 behind Pitcher A's two starts, but that same average team has a pretty good shot at winning Pitcher B's second game. And the SN stats accurately measure what our intuition tells us: Pitcher A's SNW/L record is right around 0-2 (more accurately, 0.0-1.8) while Pitcher B's SNW/L record is closer to 1-1 (0.6-1.1). Pitcher A's SNVA mark shows him 0.86 games below average, while Pitcher B's SNVA is a much more tolerable 0.27 games below average.

The key insight that causes SN stats to work in this case is: All runs are not created equal. Pitcher B's Game 1 isn't a whole lot worse than Pitcher A's Game 1, even though he gave up a bunch more runs in fewer innings. Cumulative run prevention stats (ERA, APR) treat run number 14 in that game as equal to run number 1, and that's where they go wrong. In fact, Thorn and Palmer's measurements conclude that Pitcher B's start in Game 1 cost his team well over a full game in the standings, an absolute impossibility. SNVA's conclusion is a much more reasonable .5 game cost; he guaranteed them a single loss, and that's all.

That's easy to show on hypothetical examples, but do SN stats and APR tell us anything different about the value of real pitchers? Yes, quite often. Here's a pronounced example—the 1992 records of Charlie Leibrandt and Melido Perez:

	APR	SNVA
Leibrandt	11.8	2.02
Perez,M	26.3	1.90

APR evaluates Perez as being 14.5 runs—about one-and-a-half games—better than Leibrandt. However, SNVA shows that, when the pitchers' performance is evaluated game-by-game, Leibrandt was actually a little better than Perez. The key here again is how the runs fell start-by-start. Perez was Mr. Steady during 1992, never getting bombed, but also rarely dominating his opponents. Leibrandt, on the other hand, had his share of disastrous outings, but pitched exceptionally most of the rest of the time. Those awful starts showed up disproportionately in Leibrandt's ERA and APR, but the SN measurements give a more balanced and accurate view of Leibrandt's contribution to the Braves that year.

1996 SNW/L Report

Enough with the explanation, let's get to the numbers. On page 467 are the best and worst starting pitchers from 1996 according to the SN measures. They're ranked by Support Neutral Wins Above Replacement (SNWAR), which is the number of SNWs a pitcher got above what a .425 pitcher would get in the same number of Support-Neutral decisions.

The AL list shows Pat Hentgen as the league's best pitcher. Amazingly, the BBWAA got the AL Cy Young Award right. Andy Pettitte, the close runner-up in the Cy Young voting, wasn't particularly close by the SN measures, despite having a fine season. (Remember that the lists show only performance as starters. Pettitte has only 20 wins on this list because one of his 21 wins came in relief.) Ken Hill was actually quite close to Hentgen in value, closer than their ERAs or APRs would have you believe. Two rookie starters had excellent seasons: Jose Rosado of Kansas City, who finished 13th in the league despite having only a half-season; and James Baldwin of the White Sox, who pitched well all year.

The NL list shows Kevin Brown with a significant lead over John Smoltz for top starter. However, as was the case with Hentgen/Hill in the AL, the gap between them was significantly less under the SN measurements than it was under cumulative run support measurements (APR and RA). Still, Brown's lead over Smoltz was significant, and I think it's a shame it wasn't rewarded with more recognition in the Cy Young voting. Unfortunately, Brown's teammates didn't provide the run support, and the BBWAA loves run support. The run support, and the Cy, went to Smoltz. At season's end, the league's top six starters were all Braves or Marlins.

[A note to those of you who read my year-end report on rec.sport.baseball, which had a much wider gap between Brown and Smoltz: I switched from Total Baseball's 1995 park factors to the 1996 factors as soon as they were released. Joe Robbie Stadium changed dramatically from a slight hitter's park to a solid pitcher's park in '96.]

The tables show:

- each pitcher's Support-Neutral W/L record (SNW, SNL)
- his Support-Neutral Winning Percentage (SNPct): SNW/(SNW+SNL)
- his actual W/L record (W, L)
- his runs allowed per nine innings (RA)
- his Adjusted Pitching Runs (APR): the number of runs he prevented that a league average pitcher would have allowed. Same as the Total Baseball measure except using runs rather than earned runs
- his Support-Neutral Value Added (SNVA)
- his Support-Neutral Wins Above Replacement (SNWAR)

Top 30 AL Starters (ranked by SNWs over a .425 pitcher):

Pitcher	Team	SNW	SNL	SNPct	W	L	RA	APR	SNVA	SNWAR
Hentgen	TOR	18.6	9.0	.675	20	10	3.56	55.3	4.78	6.89
Hill	TEX	18.2	9.0	.669	16	10	3.95	46.5	4.60	6.64
Guzman	TOR	14.5	5.4	.726	11	8	3.26	45.2	4.15	6.00
Clemens	BOS	16.6	9.2	.644	10	13	3.93	42.6	3.48	5.64
Fernandez	CHI	17.2	10.3	.625	16	10	3.84	37.6	3.37	5.51
Nagy	CLE	15.5	8.1	.658	17	5	3.61	42.3	3.72	5.48
McDonald	MIL	15.6	8.8	.638	12	10	4.19	34.8	3.23	5.20
Appier	KCR	15.0	8.1	.648	14	11	3.71	37.9	3.20	5.18
Pettitte	NYY	15.1	9.1	.623	20	8	4.33	26.7	2.86	4.81
Alvarez	CHI	14.2	10.4	.577	15	10	4.39	17.5	1.74	3.74
Belcher	KCR	14.7	11.1	.570	15	11	4.41	23.7	1.98	3.73
Radke	MIN	14.4	11.1	.565	11	16	4.85	17.7	1.53	3.58
Finley	CAL	14.8	11.7	.558	15	16	4.69	16.1	1.55	3.52
Rosado	KCR	7.8	3.7	.681	8	6	3.29	24.1	2.06	2.94
Hershiser	CLE	13.1	10.8	.547	15	9	5.02	6.1	0.91	2.93
Rogers	NYY	11.7	9.1	.563	12	8	4.88	11.2	1.39	2.86
Key	NYY	11.3	8.6	.566	12	11	4.94	9.4	1.06	2.80
Pavlik	TEX	13.0	11.1	.539	15	8	5.37	7.3	1.05	2.75
Mussina	BAL	14.2	13.0	.522	19	11	5.07	6.0	0.60	2.63
Oliver	TEX	11.1	8.9	.556	14	6	5.03	12.6	1.24	2.61
Karl	MIL	12.2	10.7	.533	13	9	5.38	6.2	0.74	2.47
Cone	NYY	5.8	2.1	.733	7	2	3.12	18.4	1.71	2.45
Tapani	CHI	12.8	11.8	.520	13	10	4.91	4.2	0.43	2.34
Wells	BAL	12.9	12.4	.510	11	14	5.30	-0.2	0.36	2.15
Ogea	CLE	8.1	6.0	.574	7	6	4.37	13.4	1.05	2.11
Haney	KCR	13.3	13.4	.498	10	14	5.37	-2.1	-0.04	1.96
Gooden	NYY	10.7	9.8	.520	11	7	5.33	2.3	0.49	1.95
Prieto	OAK	8.2	6.5	.557	6	7	4.73	6.6	0.70	1.94
Baldwin	CHI	10.0	9.1	.524	11	6	4.69	7.7	0.43	1.90
Olivares	DET	9.7	8.7	.527	7	11	5.06	6.8	0.47	1.89

Top 30 NL Starters (ranked by SNWs over a .425 pitcher):

Pitcher	Team	SNW	SNL	SNPct	W	L	RA	APR	SNVA	SNWAR
Brown	FLA	17.5	6.2	.739	17	11	2.32	59.9	5.47	7.46
Smoltz	ATL	18.5	8.7	.681	24	8	3.30	43.8	4.69	6.94
G. Maddux	ATL	17.6	8.1	.686	15	11	3.12	47.0	4.51	6.72
Glavine	ATL	16.8	8.6	.663	15	10	3.48	36.1	3.88	6.04
A. Leiter	FLA	14.9	8.1	.650	16	12	3.09	36.0	3.34	5.17
Neagle	P/A	14.5	8.7	.626	16	9	3.78	26.8	2.80	4.65
Schilling	PHI	13.2	6.9	.655	9	10	3.39	29.9	2.83	4.62
Trachsel	CHI	13.8	8.3	.624	13	9	3.60	26.4	2.56	4.40
Fassero	MON	15.4	10.5	.594	16	11	3.76	27.2	2.36	4.37
An. Benes	STL	14.4	10.4	.580	18	10	4.12	16.4	1.80	3.86
Stottlemyre	STL	13.8	10.5	.567	14	11	4.07	17.1	1.63	3.44
Martinez,P	MON	13.7	10.5	.567	13	10	4.15	15.6	1.50	3.44
Reynolds	HOU	14.6	11.8	.554	16	10	3.88	12.1	1.29	3.41
Valdes	LAD	13.5	10.2	.568	15	7	3.76	14.7	1.42	3.40
Osborne	STL	12.3	9.0	.578	13	9	3.94	18.1	1.52	3.25
Smiley	CIN	13.5	11.0	.552	13	14	4.11	13.8	1.20	3.11
Nomo	LAD	13.4	10.9	.552	16	11	3.67	17.6	1.18	3.09
Astacio	LAD	11.9	9.6	.553	8	8	3.91	9.2	1.05	2.76
Ashby	SDP	9.4	6.5	.590	9	5	3.58	15.9	1.22	2.63
Reynoso	COL	10.3	7.9	.566	8	9	5.18	13.4	1.22	2.57
Hamilton	SDP	12.8	11.4	.528	15	9	4.27	5.2	0.63	2.49
Navarro	CHI	13.3	12.5	.516	15	12	4.41	9.3	0.37	2.33
Darwin	P/H	9.7	7.9	.553	8	11	4.23	9.4	0.86	2.25
Valenzuela	SDP	10.7	9.4	.534	13	8	4.05	8.6	0.84	2.19
Avery	ATL	9.0	7.1	.558	7	9	4.42	6.8	0.93	2.14
Ritz	COL	12.3	11.9	.508	17	11	5.70	7.2	0.27	2.01
M. Clark	NYM	11.8	11.2	.512	14	11	4.15	5.9	0.18	2.00
S. Sanders	SDP	6.7	4.4	.605	8	3	3.59	10.7	1.11	2.00
Burba	CIN	11.3	10.8	.512	11	13	4.48	4.2	0.28	1.92
Portugal	CIN	9.0	8.2	.523	8	9	4.30	6.5	0.35	1.68

Bottom 10 AL Starters (ranked by SNWs over a .425 pitcher):

Pitcher	Team	SNW	SNL	SNPct	W	L	RA	APR	SNVA	SNWAR
J. Abbott	CAL	4.6	12.3	.271	2	18	8.39	-44.9	-3.76	-2.59
VanPoppel	O/D	2.3	9.1	.200	2	7	11.79	-46.0	-3.34	-2.57
Haynes	BAL	1.5	6.1	.202	1	6	10.08	-27.2	-2.10	-1.70
Janzen	TOR	2.0	5.9	.249	2	6	8.70	-21.9	-1.91	-1.39
Nitkowski	DET	1.2	4.5	.215	2	3	9.80	-18.0	-1.52	-1.19
B. Williams	DET	4.0	8.2	.328	3	9	7.71	-23.3	-1.95	-1.18
Kamieniecki	NYY	0.3	3.2	.088	1	2	14.02	-16.4	-1.32	-1.18
Mercker	BAL	2.3	5.9	.282	3	5	8.94	-22.6	-1.67	-1.18
Sodowsky	DET	0.9	3.9	.185	1	3	12.58	-19.1	-1.48	-1.15
Keagle	DET	0.7	3.4	.163	0	5	11.63	-16.3	-1.32	-1.08

Bottom 10 AL Starters (ranked by SNWs over a .425 pitcher):

Pitcher	Team	SNW	SNL	SNPct	W	L	RA	APR	SNVA	SNWAR
Bullinger	CHI	4.4	10.3	.301	5	9	7.93	-36.1	-2.82	-1.83
Jarvis	CIN	4.5	10.2	.306	8	8	7.23	-31.2	-2.79	-1.75
Hammond	FLA	1.2	5.7	.171	2	6	12.11	-31.5	-2.22	-1.73
VanLandingham	SFG	8.6	14.4	.375	9	14	6.09	-31.7	-2.81	-1.14
P. Wilson	NYM	7.1	12.1	.371	5	12	6.16	-31.8	-2.43	-1.03
Woodall	ATL	0.1	2.2	.036	0	2	16.62	-10.9	-1.03	-0.88
Ericks	PIT	0.3	2.4	.124	0	3	11.40	-10.5	-0.98	-0.81
Munoz	PHI	0.9	3.1	.229	0	3	9.95	-13.7	-1.05	-0.79
Dessens	PIT	0.1	1.9	.057	0	2	14.46	-9.6	-0.87	-0.76
Schmidt	A/P	4.0	7.2	.359	5	6	6.03	-11.3	-1.47	-0.74

As mentioned above, since SNW/SNL represents an expected or deserved W/L record, they allow us to measure how lucky or unlucky a pitcher was with his actual record. The tables below show this, with E(W) and E(L) representing Expected Wins and Expected Losses. E(W) is the same as SNW, except it awards 0 to a starter who goes fewer than five innings in a game. E(L) is the same as SNL.

It's no surprise to see Texas and Seattle starters, who were supported by excellent offenses, well-represented in the AL Luckiest list. And Ramon Martinez accomplished the improbable feat of finishing on top of the NL Luckiest list for the second year in a row. On the Unluckiest side, Jim Abbott and Roger Clemens continued their recent streaks of bad luck: they are #1 and #2 (respectively) among unlucky pitchers over the past 5 years. And Kevin Brown's record exhibited the lack of run support that may have cost him the Cy Young vote; he was just edged out by the even-more-victimized Curt Schilling for the league Unluckiest crown.

Luckiest 10 AL Starters (ranked by (W - E(W)) + (E(L) - L)):

Pitcher	Team	E(W)	E(L)	W	L	Diff.
Moyer	B/S	7.4	7.0	11	3	7.6
Hitchcock	SEA	10.0	13.4	13	9	7.3
Mussina	BAL	14.1	13.0	19	11	6.9
Oliver	TEX	10.3	8.9	14	6	6.6
Pettitte	NYY	14.8	9.1	20	8	6.4
Pavlik	TEX	11.9	11.1	15	8	6.2
Gordon	BOS	11.1	13.3	12	9	5.2
McDowell	CLE	10.8	11.8	13	9	5.1
Nagy	CLE	15.5	8.1	17	5	4.6
Wakefield	BOS	10.7	14.2	14	13	4.5

Luckiest 10 NL Starters (ranked by (W - E(W)) + (E(L) - L)):

Pitcher	Team	E(W)	E(L)	W	L	Diff.
R. Martinez	LAD	8.8	8.7	15	5	10.0
Gardner	SFG	8.2	12.2	12	7	9.0
Smoltz	ATL	18.4	8.7	24	8	6.3
Al. Benes	STL	9.9	13.0	12	9	6.0
Jarvis	CIN	4.3	10.2	8	8	5.9
Ritz	COL	12.3	11.9	17	11	5.7
B. Jones	NYM	10.3	11.9	12	8	5.6
Hamilton	SDP	12.6	11.4	15	9	4.8
Valdes	LAD	13.4	10.2	15	7	4.8
Salkeld	CIN	4.5	7.9	6	5	4.4

Unluckiest 10 AL Starters (ranked by (W - E(W)) + (E(L) - L)):

Pitcher	Team	E(W)	E(L)	W	L	Diff.
Clemens	BOS	16.5	9.2	10	13	-10.4
R. Robertson	MIN	9.5	11.1	6	16	-8.4
Radke	MIN	14.3	11.1	11	16	-8.3
J. Abbott	CAL	4.5	12.3	2	18	-8.2
Gubicza	KCR	6.3	6.7	4	12	-7.6
Lira	DET	10.7	11.9	6	14	-6.8
Guzman	TOR	13.7	5.4	11	8	-5.3
McDonald	MIL	15.3	8.8	12	10	-4.5
Olivares	DET	9.1	8.7	7	11	-4.4
J. Thompson	DET	2.8	3.6	1	6	-4.2

Unluckiest 10 NL Starters (ranked by (W - E(W)) + (E(L) - L)):

Pitcher	Team	E(W)	E(L)	W	L	Diff.
Schilling	PHI	13.1	6.9	9	10	-7.1
Castillo	CHI	9.8	12.9	7	16	-5.9
G. Maddux	ATL	17.3	8.1	15	11	-5.2
S. Fernandez	PHI	4.8	2.7	3	6	-5.1
Morgan	S/C	7.6	7.5	6	11	-5.1
Brown	FLA	17.2	6.2	17	11	-5.0
Mk. Williams	PHI	8.0	11.2	6	14	-4.8
Darwin	P/H	9.6	7.9	8	11	-4.8
Mimbs	PHI	4.9	6.2	3	9	-4.7
Rapp	FLA	8.6	11.0	8	15	-4.6

At the team level, the Texas Rangers, surprisingly, ended up with the top-ranked starting rotation in the AL. They were boosted by the outstanding performance of Ken Hill, of course, but something that distinguished them even more was the fact that they had no absolutely awful performances from any of their starters. Another no-dogs staff, the Kansas City Royals, finished a close second, while a staff made up almost entirely of dogs, the Detroit Tigers, ended up setting a new standard in ineptitude, burrowing past everyone for the bottom spot.

In the NL, the Atlanta Braves put together the top starting staff in the league, or for that matter in the majors, for the umpteenth year in a row (OK, fifth). With the late-season addition of Neagle and the offseason re-signing of Smoltz, they look good to maintain that streak through next year at least. The San Francisco Giants had the NL's worst rotation. Early in the season they looked to match the Tigers in the "embarrassment" category, but less-than-awful late-season performances from Shawn Estes, Osvaldo Fernandez and William VanLandingham rescued their season from going down in the annals of stiff history, and raised it to a "merely terrible" classification.

I don't usually care too much about how well the SN model predicts wins and losses at a league level. I think wins and losses are affected by many factors (e.g., managers trying to get their starter the win) that I don't want to include in the model. Nevertheless, I'm always curious to see how league SNW/L matches with league W/L. For what it's worth, SNW/L generally seems to underpredict the number of decisions in the American League somewhat, and predict the W/L record in the National League pretty well. That pattern held true this year. In the AL, the SN model predicted league starters to be 70 games below .500, at 750-820; league starters actually finished 48 games under, at 780-828. In the NL, the prediction was 32 games below .500, 762-794; league starters' real cumulative record was just eight games under, 780-788.

--Michael Wolverton

Run Support

One of the game's great chestnuts is the theory that some pitchers "pitch to the score" and "know how to win" in a way other than always allowing the fewest runs possible. The reverse, that some pitchers tend to give up runs more often in close games, is also a popular theory, though it's invoked less often. This, some say, makes it worthwhile to look at a pitcher's won-loss record in addition to his ERA to judge his effectiveness. The number of runs a pitcher allows would not be completely indicative of his value to his team if he gives up those runs in a way that contributes to more wins than the average pitcher with the same rate of runs allowed.

Over the years, I've seen virtually no evidence that would lead me to believe that this theory holds water for modern-day pitchers. However, just because it was clear that this theory was not applicable to the performances of most pitchers didn't mean that it might not be applicable to a few pitchers. I decided to look at the careers of individual pitchers and look at the relationship between their run support and runs allowed totals and their won-loss records, to see if that might tell us something about "pitching to the score."

It's pretty obvious to everyone that there's a relationship between wins and the difference between the number of runs a team scores and allows. Baseball researcher Pete Palmer has found that about 10 extra runs usually leads to an extra victory. However, a better tool exists with which to estimate how many wins and losses to expect from the runs a team scores and allows. This method, made popular by Bill James, involves squaring the number of runs scored by a team and dividing that result by the addition of the squaring of the team's runs scored to the squaring of the team's runs allowed. In other words:

$$\frac{\text{Runs Scored Squared}}{\text{Runs Scored Squared} + \text{Runs Allowed Squared}}$$

This results in a winning percentage, which you would then multiply by the number of games the team has played to get the number of wins, and subtract the number of wins from the total games played to get the number of losses. You now have a good estimate of how an average team that scores and allows a certain number of runs would do in terms of wins and losses. In general, teams finish fairly close to the result you would get from the formula. Teams that win an unusually high percentage of close games will usually win more than the formula projects, and teams that lose an unusual percentage of close games (compared, in both cases, to how they do in non-close games) will do worse than the formula projects. The best recent example of this on a team level is the 1984 New York Mets. That team went 54-31 in games decided by a margin of one or two runs, and 36-41 in all other games.

Because they did so much better in close games than in other games, thus putting their runs scored and runs allowed to more efficient use, they finished with a won-loss record of 90-72, while the formula predicted a record of 78-84.

Note that it has been found that a power of 1.83 works a bit better than a power of 2 for this formula. Since a button with a power of 1.83 is not found on most calculators, and since that kind of exactness isn't required for these kind of estimates, I'll stick with using 2.

In the past, this formula has been used mostly with teams. However, we can also estimate the expected winning percentage of a pitcher by using the number of runs he allows and his run support. If a pitcher really "pitches to the score," allowing fewer runs in close games than in games in which he is granted a large lead, his won-loss record should be better than the record projected for the average pitcher with that pitcher's runs allowed and run support totals. That pitcher's career should show a pattern of him winning more games than we would expect. And, of course, the opposite should be true for a pitcher who allows more runs in close games than in blowouts.

Over the past few years, I've tested many pitchers to who have a "pitch to the score" reputation, including Jack Morris, Jack McDowell, Doc Gooden and Dave Stewart. I have also followed the careers of two pitchers with the opposite reputation, Dave Stieb and Jose DeLeon. In no case have I found any pattern whatsoever of a pitcher winning or losing more games during his career than the formula projects. In all these cases I found pitchers who tended to win and lose the number of games that their runs allowed and run support totals project them to win and lose.

The pitchers who get a reputation of "pitching to the score" have one thing in common: they have all gotten good run support during most of their careers. It seems apparent that pitchers get this reputation because they get better run support than other pitchers and thus have a W-L record that looks better than their ERA or runs allowed. In general, these pitchers get this support because they are on good offensive teams for a number of years. Jack Morris is the best example of this; in his entire career, he was on only one below-average offensive team (1989), and he pitched for several great offensive teams. The "pitch to the score" theory seems to be an effort to imbue a pitchers' won-loss record with a value other than luck.

Another thing that pitchers with this reputation have in common is that they pitch a lot of innings. This leads to more wins (as well as losses), and the number of wins seems to impress people more than the won-loss record itself, if Cy Young voting is used as a measure. Of course, pitching more innings is generally a good thing, and makes a pitcher (especially an effective one) more valuable, but it has little to do with the issue at hand.

Note that in these career examinations, we estimated a player's projected won-loss record by multiplying the formula's estimation of expected winning percentage by the number of decisions a pitcher actually had. This solution isn't perfect—obviously a good or bad bullpen can greatly affect the number of decisions a pitcher has—but it is the best one available, and I don't think it presents a serious problem. Also note that no positive correlation has been found between a pitchers' run support compared to team runs scored from year to year in the AL, so there is no evidence that pitchers have an ability to inspire teams to score more runs in their starts. Of course in the NL, pitchers' batting affects run support, but that has no real bearing on the issue at hand.

Here is the data on the recent pitchers I've studied. First, on Jack Morris, through 1993: The first column is Morris' projected record based on the runs he allowed and the run support he received. The second column is Morris' actual won-loss record. The third column indicates how many more wins his actual record credits him with compared to the projection based on his run support. The fourth column is Morris' projected record based on the runs he allowed and the league average run support. The fifth column indicates how many more wins his actual record credits him with compared to the projection based on league average run support.

Year	Proj.	Actual	Diff.	Proj.	Diff.
1979	16-8	17-7	+1	16-8	+1
1980	16-15	16-15	0	16-15	0
1981	16-5	14-7	-2	13-8	+1
1982	15-18	17-16	+2	17-16	0
1983	21-12	20-13	-1	20-13	0
1984	18-12	19-11	+1	16-14	+3
1985	17-10	16-11	-1	17-10	-1
1986	20-9	21-8	+1	18-11	+3
1987	19-10	18-11	-1	18-11	0
1988	14-14	15-13	+1	14-14	+1
1989	6-14	6-14	0	8-12	-2
1990	15-18	15-18	0	14-19	+1
1991	19-11	18-12	-1	17-13	+1
1992	18-9	21-6	+3	14-13	+7
1993	6-13	7-12	+1	6-13	+1
Total	**236-178**	**240-174**	**+4**	**224-190**	**+16**

The conclusion is obvious. Morris' records are the result of how many runs he allows and how many runs are scored in his starts. Thus, his ERA (or RA) and innings pitched are a perfectly accurate measure of how valuable Jack has been to his teams.

Now, a look at the projected records (based on his actual run support and runs allowed) and actual records of another pitcher who reputedly "pitches to the score."

Jack McDowell (through 1994):

Year	Proj W-L	Act W-L
1988	5-10	5-10
1990	14-9	14-9
1991	19-8	17-10
1992	22-8	20-10
1993	22-10	22-10
1994	10-9	10-9
Total	**92-54**	**88-58**

The year McDowell won the Cy Young, 1993, he had a very high ERA early in the year but a good won-loss record, and a number of commentators claimed that he had accomplished this by pitching to the score. Midway through the season, I took a look at McDowell's performances and recorded when he allowed runs and when the White Sox scored for him. Here are the results:

• 4/6/93 - Chicago scores three in the top of the 1st. McDowell blows the lead by allowing four runs in the 1st and 3rd innings. Chicago scores six in the 4th. McDowell pitches six innings, gets the win.
• 4/11 - McDowell allows one run in the top of the 1st. Chicago scores one in the bottom of the 1st. McDowell allows two runs in the 5th. Chicago scores four in the 6th. McDowell allows one in the 7th, is taken out and gets the win.
• 4/16 - Chicago scores one in the top of the 2nd. McDowell allows two in the bottom of the 2nd. The Sox score one in the top of the 3rd, tying it. McDowell allows two in the bottom of the 3rd. Chicago scores seven in the rest of the game. McDowell pitches seven innings, gets the win.
• 4/22 - McDowell allows one run in the 2nd inning, one more in the 6th. Chicago scores three in the 8th and 9th innings to give McDowell the victory.
• 4/27 - McDowell allows three runs in the 2nd. Chicago scores nine in the next five innings. McDowell allows one more run in the 8th, but wins.
• 5/2 - McDowell allows three runs in the first two innings. Chicago scores one in the 6th. McDowell allows three more runs in the 7th and gets the loss.
• 5/8 - Chicago scores five runs in the 1st. McDowell gives up six runs in the 2nd and 3rd. The White Sox score five more in the 4th and 5th innings. McDowell allows one more in the 6th, finishes and gets the win.
• 5/14 - McDowell pitches nine innings, shuts out the

Rangers, and wins. Chicago scores three in the first two innings and another in the 8th.

- 5/19 - Chicago gets shut out. McDowell allows two runs in the 8th and loses.

In these nine starts, McDowell allowed the go-ahead run to score ten times. Six times McDowell had at least a three-run lead, and one of two things always happened. Either he blew the lead, or he shut the other team down by allowing only one run or none. Not once did he get a large lead and then allow the other team some runs but not enough to catch up. His ERA with large leads that he didn't blow is minuscule; 30 of the 33 runs he allowed enabled the opposition to either catch up or take a bigger lead over the White Sox. Not only is that not "pitching to the score," but it's the exact opposite. Only if you believe that McDowell is psychic and knew that it didn't matter if he put his team three or five runs down, or blew a lead, that he knew his teammates would come back, can you argue that McDowell was "pitching to the score"—the score that would be, that is.

Two other pitchers who frequently were tagged with the "pitches to the score" label are Dave Stewart and Doc Gooden, both of whom often had won-loss records that didn't seem to go with their ERAs.

Dave Stewart:

Year	Proj W-L	Act W-L
1984	7-14	7-14
1987	19-14	20-13
1988	21-12	21-12
1989	19-11	21-9
1990-94	67-45	64-48
Total	**133-96**	**133-96**

Doc Gooden:

Year	Proj W-L	Act W-L
1984	16-10	17-9
1985	25-3	24-4
1986	15-8	17-6
1987	15-7	15-7
1988	19-8	18-9
1990	19-7	19-7
1991	13-7	13-7
1992	10-13	10-13
1993	16-11	12-15
Total	**148-74**	**145-77**

What both Stewart and Gooden had in common was not that they "pitched to the score" but that they pitched in pitcher's parks and received excellent run support year after year.

A pitcher with the opposite reputation is Dave Stieb. I looked at the bulk of his career in the same way:

Year	Run Supp.	Runs Alld.	Proj. W-L	Act. W-L
1979	4.56	4.88	8-8	8-8
1980	3.88	4.00	13-14	12-15
1981	2.80	3.42	9-12	11-10
1982	3.92	3.62	17-14	17-14
1983	4.53	3.40	19-10	17-12
1984	4.46	2.93	17-7	16-8
1985	4.44	3.02	18-9	14-13
1986	4.71	5.62	8-11	7-12
1987	5.97	4.48	14-8	13-9
1988	4.71	3.30	16-8	16-8
1989	5.18	3.61	17-8	17-8
1990	4.52	3.15	16-8	18-6
Total			**172-117**	**166-123**

Stieb didn't "win" quite as many games as the runs figures indicate he should have, but the difference of six victories is clearly within the range of normal random variation, and there is no visible pattern of Stieb consistently "losing" more than he should have.

We also should look at Jose DeLeon, the pitcher probably most identified with a "pitching well enough to lose" syndrome recently. Note that DeLeon's 1985 and several other seasons are not included in this study because of either too few starts or too many relief appearances. (Years missing from the analyses of other pitchers may be absent because of the same reasons or because the analysis was in some cases done several years ago, thus not including those pitchers' most recent season or two.)

Year	Run Supp.	Runs Alld.	Proj. W-L	Act. W-L
1983	4.33	3.00	7-3	7-3
1984	3.32	4.03	8-12	7-13
1985	2.32	5.15	4-17	2-19
1987	4.55	4.63	11-12	11-12
1988	3.79	3.79	11.5-11.5	13-10
1989	3.33	3.53	13-15	16-12
1990	3.13	4.73	8-18	7-19
1991	4.00	3.15	9-5	5-9
Total			**71.5-93.5**	**68-97**

Once again, no real pattern. DeLeon's record is slightly worse than it is projected to be, but the amount is nowhere close to being statistically significant. In fact, the whole difference between his projected and actual records can be said to be the result of just one year, 1991, DeLeon's last year as a full-time starter. Out of curiosity, I went back and looked at DeLeon's box scores for that year, and found the reason for the large discrepancy. Evidently, by 1991, DeLeon had lost a lot of his stamina. However, Joe Torre took about three months to realize this. In that time, Torre consistently left DeLeon in the game just long enough to give up the go-ahead run in the 5th, 6th or 7th innings. Eventually, Torre stopped leaving DeLeon in that long, and by the end of the season he had moved DeLeon to the bullpen.

None of this should imply that DeLeon was a good pitcher. He was a lot better than his "record" indicates, but that doesn't mean that he was particularly good. In DeLeon's case, his reputation of "knowing how to lose" got intertwined with an additional reputation of "having great stuff but not using it well." That latter reputation may very well be true, but is a separate issue.

In addition to studying pitchers from 1980 to the present, I've been interested in looking at pitchers of the past to see if maybe a "pitch to the score" ability did exist in the past. I believe that it did exist in the distant past, when baseball was a less competitive game, but I'm more interested in the recent past. Sandy Koufax is one pitcher who it has been speculated "pitched to the score," and thus was even better at contributing to winning than his great ERAs indicate. Thanks to David Smith and Retrosheet, I now have run support data as well as an ability to separate Koufax's starting performances from his relief performances, and I was able to examine the prime of his career to see if he "pitched to the score." The following is a chart of his run support, his average runs allowed per nine innings in his starts, the W-L records that the formula projects for his starts, and his actual W-L record in his starts. The run support figures used are his run support per nine innings when Koufax was in the game. Run support per start is also available (and in some cases, though not for Koufax, the only information that's been published for pitchers), and has the advantage of including runs scored after Koufax was relieved. These certainly do affect his records, but overall I think the run support for the innings when Koufax was still in games is slightly more indicative of the quality of his support. Note that Koufax had one win in relief in 1961, so his record here differs from what's in baseball encyclopedias.

Year	Run Supp.	Runs Alld.	Proj. W-L	Act. W-L
1961	4.11	3.89	16-14	17-13
1962	5.00	2.98	15-6	14-
1963	4.18	1.97	25-5	25-5
1964	3.48	2.00	18-6	19-5
1965	3.70	2.43	24-10	26-8
1966	4.26	2.06	29-7	27-9
Total			127-48	128-47

Obviously, it doesn't look like Koufax "pitched to the score" either, so his ERAs are indicative of his value.

Catfish Hunter is another pitcher of recent times I wanted to look at. Hunter's ERA relative to the league during his career (only 4% better, after park adjustment) makes him look like a very poor choice for the Hall of Fame despite the fact that he was easily voted in. So the question of whether Hunter won more games than his ERA and run support suggests he should have is an important one. Thanks again to David Smith and Retrosheet, I was able to obtain Hunter's run support figures and other data necessary to look at Hunter's career through the Pythagorean prism.

Year	Run Supp.	Runs Alld.	Proj. W-L	Act. W-L
1965	4.10	4.58	7-8	7-8
1966	3.68	4.34	8-12	9-11
1967	3.31	3.15	16-14	13-17
1968	4.09	3.86	14-12	13-13
1969	3.60	3.61	13-14	12-15
1970	4.20	4.26	16-16	18-14
1971	4.11	3.38	19-13	21-11
1972	3.95	2.27	20-7	20-7
1973	5.50	3.69	18-8	21-5
1974	4.61	2.75	27-10	25-12
1975	4.62	2.94	26-11	23-14
1976	4.53	3.80	19-13	17-15
1977	5.59	5.22	10-8	9-9
1978	4.95	3.61	12-6	12-6
1979	3.95	5.83	3-8	2-9
Total			228-160	222-166

Once again, we find no evidence that W-L record shows anything that adjusted ERA doesn't. Hunter in fact finishes six games under his projected record, but that is unlikely to have any significance other than randomness.

None of this proves that there are no pitchers who "pitch to the score," or win or lose more than their ERAs suggest they would. This is obviously not a systematic study of all pitchers, present or past. But I think the evidence presented does suggest that anytime a pitcher is tagged with a reputation that indicates that his (adjusted) ERA is not indicative of his contributions, we should take it with many grains of salt, and not believe it unless there is clear evidence that it is true.

--Greg Spira

Clutch: Myth or Adjective?

It is widely reported that clutch hitting exists, and that certain players can be defined as having that something extra in the big moments. Statistics are trotted out on a routine basis to defend a player, by showing how he's always hit well in the clutch, and can be expected to continue as a "clutch performer." However, is this true? If so, we can say that clutch hitters exist. However, if there is no correlation from one year to the next, we can say that clutch hitters probably do not exist, and that this is another baseball myth.

For the purposes of this study, I only used players who had more than 300 at bats in both 1995 and 1996. This means that only players who are in the lineup almost 50% of the time in both years will be counted. There were a total of 170 players who met these requirements.

What I did was simple: I took a player's total batting average in 1995, and then compared that to his batting average with runners in scoring position (RISP) in 1995. If a player's RISP batting average was higher than normal, he received a "+"; if it was lower, he received a "-"; two players received "0" and were eliminated from this part of the study. Because the major leagues as a whole hit 1% higher with RISP in 1995, I actually compared a player's RISP batting average to 101% of his normal batting average. The 1996 RISP was compared to 100.5% of the player's normal batting average. If the batting averages were within .0005 of each other, the player was assigned a "0."

I performed the same comparisons for 1996. If clutch hitters exist—if past clutch performance would be a good predictor for future clutch performance—a "+" one season would more than likely lead to a "+" in the following season, while a "-" in one season should lead to a "-" in the next year. Based on the 168 players, a distribution consistent with the theory "There are clutch hitters" would mean that there should be significantly more players in the "double plus" and "double minus" categories.

If clutch hitters are random, and clutch hitting is not an ability, then the distribution of players should resemble that of a coin flip. If a coin is flipped two times, there is a .25 chance that there will be two heads; a .5 chance that there will be one head and one tail; and a .25 chance that there will be two tails. Therefore, if clutch hitting is not random, the distribution for these 168 players should wind up roughly being that 42 players have two "+"; 84 have one "+" and one "-"; and 42 have 2 "-".

The actual distribution turned out to be 48 players with two "+", 82 with one of each and 38 with 2 "-". These results indicate that if a player hits better than his average with RISP

one year, it means absolutely nothing about whether his average with RISP will be better or worse than his normal performance in the following season.

Let's try it in situations defined as close & late (C&L): when the game is in the 7th inning or later, the batting team is up by one run, tied or has the potential tying run on base, at bat or on deck. The same principles apply here as with the RISP test with 164 players in the study. Because the major leagues as a whole hit 4% lower in 1995 C&L situations, I actually compared a player's C&L batting average to 96% of his normal batting average. The 1996 C&L average was compared to 95% of his normal batting average. If the batting averages were within .0005 of each other, the player was assigned a "0". This occurred with six players in the study. The actual distribution turned out to be: 35 players with 2 "+"; 92 with one of each, and 37 with 2 "-". Again, the close and late situations have no relation to future performance.

How about another breakdown? Maybe the absolute best hitters in those situations know how to pour it on each year. The top 10 hitters with runners in scoring position in 1995 were Rickey Henderson, Tony Gwynn, Kenny Lofton, Edgar Martinez, B.J. Surhoff, Kevin Seitzer, Dante Bichette, Chuck Knoblauch, Carlos Baerga and Delino DeShields. In 1996, that group had five players hit better than their norm with RISP and five hit worse with RISP.

Looking at the top 10 in C&L situations, we find something that should surprise even most "experts." Of the batters who were in the top 10 in C&L average, seven of them performed WORSE than their normal average in those situations.

And while the National League MVPs were performing above and beyond the call of duty in C&L situations, even in their MVP seasons Mo Vaughn (1995: 164 average; one double, two homers in 67 at bats) and Juan Gonzalez (1996: 239 average; six doubles, three homers in 67 at bats) weren't quite living up to the standards others had established for them.

Well, it's still looking like a coin flip - not even remotely close to supporting the "Clutch hitting exists" argument. Let's look further:

Maybe older players hit better than young ones. We'll look at every player who was born before July 1, 1964; everyone who was at least 30 or 31 years old during 1995. There were 45 such players during these years. One of these players fell into the "0" category for RISP situations and one was a "0" for C&L situations. With runners in scoring position, 11 of them did better than their average in both seasons, nine did worse and 24 players alternated. Similarly, in C&L situations,

11 players did better than their average, seven worse, with 26 alternating. If there is anything to be gained by being a veteran player, it doesn't show up in these situations.

Before making any general conclusions, there are a few precautions to be aware of; these results are only for major league baseball, and shouldn't be applied uniformly to the minor leagues or other levels of competition. Also, the results may be slightly biased in that certain star players, such as Jim Edmonds, have a large platoon differential, making them especially vulnerable to that lefty reliever who comes in to retire the one tough lefty batter. This could skew the results of this study to a certain degree.

Clutch hitting may exist at the major league level. If so, it's not in any of the traditional statistics that some people have started to embrace. And the conclusion here is obvious: past performance with runners in scoring position and performance in "close and late" situations (which are those statistics usually used to prove the point) are not a good indicator to a player's performance in those situations in the future.

--Bob Gajarsky

Defensive Average

developed by Sherri Nichols

What is Defensive Average, you ask? Its inventor, Sherri Nichols, explains:

"Defensive Average (or DA) is the number of balls fielded by a player at a position divided by the number of balls hit to that fielder's zone of responsibility while he's playing that position. It's similar in concept to STATS' Zone Rating, though the zones for DA seem to be quite a bit larger than STATS. The zones cover the entire field, and overlap one another. DA is based on the Baseball Workshop's data, which contains location data for batted balls; these locations are recorded to a finer degree of granularity than is used in determining DA. The location of a batted ball is determined by where it is caught or lands if it's a fly ball, or where it is either fielded or goes through the infield for a ground ball. The Project Scoresheet scoring system, which is used by the Baseball Workshop, includes a diagram of the field with the field divided into sections (see page 495). Multiple sections are lumped together to form zones of responsibility.

"Defensive Average does have some shortcomings. One is that there are a fair number of easy flyballs that could be caught without difficulty by more than one outfielder. We don't know if there are biases in the outfield data concerning this; we don't know if on some teams, the center fielder just takes all of those, inflating his DA, while on other teams they are spread more evenly. There's also the issue of the relationship between the pitching staff and the defense. Will a bad pitching staff make a good fielder look bad? How do you tell if the defense is bad because the pitching staff is bad, or if the pitching staff is good because the defense is good?"

That said, although Defensive Average isn't the perfect defensive statistic, it's as good as you're going to see from any source, especially considering that it's pretty unlikely that anyone will ever be able to totally separate pitching from defense. Unlike STATS' Range Factor (RF) stat, DA is a rate-based statistic, measuring opportunities instead of raw play totals, so it isn't nearly as dependent on the vagaries of what kinds of pitchers a defender plays behind. It also doesn't give a fielder double credit for having participated in an assisted double play (one the player didn't complete on his own). Unlike STATS' Zone Rating (ZR), DA zones cover the whole field, so a player doesn't get a free boost to his DA for making a play beyond his assigned range, as happens with ZR. Finally, DA measures an infielder's ability to turn the double play well, as well as giving us an image of how many extra-base hits any fielder may have helped create for opponents, better than any other defensive statistic.

We've listed every regular at a position in each league, as well as several semi-regular players and the occasional statis-

tical tease, like Cal Ripken's totals in this year's third base experiment. We've also nominated a Gold Glove at each position, based on regular playing time and DA. Beyond listings and team totals for the individual infield and outfield positions, Sherri also calculates the team totals for defensive "units": the outfield, the infield and combinations of infielders, which can give you a broader picture of what a team's defensive shortcomings or strengths were as a team.

Defensive Average glossary:

Name:	Obvious
G:	Games played at that position
GOps:	Groundball opportunities; the number of ground balls hit to the area of responsibility for that position when this player was playing that position.
AGOps:	An adjustment to the GOps to account for batted balls for which there was no location data.
GO:	Groundballs turned into outs by this player.
AGDA:	GO/AGOps
FOps:	Flyball opportunities (anything that's not a groundball).
AFOps:	Adjusted fly ball opportunities
FO:	Fly balls converted into outs
AFDA:	FO/AFOps
FE:	Fielding errors
TE:	Throwing errors
1B:	Number of singles through the area of responsibility. (on groundballs for infielders, flyballs for outfielders)
2B:	Number of doubles through the area of responsibility.
AGO/2B:	AGOps per double allowed.
AFO/2B:	AFOps per double allowed.
3B:	Number of triples through the area of responsibility.
AGO/3B:	AGOps per triple allowed.
AFO/3B:	AFOps per triple allowed.
DPOps:	Number of double play opportunities, defined as runner on at least first, less than two out, ground ball to area of responsibility.
DPI:	Number of double plays successfully initiated on these opportunities.
DP%:	DPI/DPOps

AMERICAN LEAGUE

—First Base—

Team	G	GOps	AGOps	GO	AGDA	FE	TE	1B	2B	AGO/2B	3B	AGO/3B	DPOps	DPI	DP%
League	1133	4855	5014.2	3094	.617	122	35	1885	298	16.8	24	208.9	1496	123	0.082
BAL	163	331	351.0	206	.587	7	2	132	19	18.5	1	351.0	104	14	0.135
BOS	162	328	333.6	200	.599	11	5	130	9	37.1	1	333.6	117	10	0.085
CAL	161	305	319.8	187	.585	10	2	126	22	14.5	1	319.8	92	12	0.130
CHA	162	323	341.4	205	.601	9	4	125	21	16.3	5	68.3	108	4	0.037
CLE	161	429	447.2	293	.655	11	2	134	21	21.3	1	447.2	110	12	0.109
DET	162	335	338.7	203	.599	8	5	130	29	11.7	0	0.0	107	5	0.047
KCA	161	404	415.8	272	.654	7	2	156	21	19.8	1	415.8	104	14	0.135
MIL	162	355	359.8	234	.650	10	2	126	23	15.6	0	0.0	120	9	0.075
MIN	162	354	369.4	239	.647	7	1	135	26	14.2	4	92.3	99	7	0.071
NYA	162	318	333.2	195	.585	5	0	123	26	12.8	2	166.6	95	9	0.095
OAK	162	347	359.1	231	.643	11	2	120	19	18.9	3	119.7	110	7	0.064
SEA	161	329	334.9	181	.540	9	5	157	29	11.5	2	167.4	101	5	0.050
TEX	163	352	356.1	226	.635	8	2	156	14	25.4	2	178.1	125	6	0.048
TOR	162	345	357.1	222	.622	9	1	135	19	18.8	1	357.1	104	9	0.087

Name	G	GOps	AGOps	GO	AGDA	FE	TE	1B	2B	AGO/2B	3B	AGO/3B	DPOps	DPI	DP%
Giambi, Jason	45	85	86.4	71	.822	3	0	18	2	43.2	0	0.0	28	3	0.107
Olerud, John	**101**	**189**	**194.1**	**139**	**.716**	**2**	**0**	**62**	**11**	**17.6**	**1**	**194.1**	**48**	**8**	**0.167**
Offerman, Jose	96	202	205.8	146	.710	4	1	67	10	20.6	0	0.0	52	6	0.115
Coomer, Ron	57	85	87.4	59	.675	2	0	29	4	21.8	1	87.4	22	2	0.091
Clark, Will	117	247	248.9	167	.671	3	1	102	11	22.6	2	124.4	82	2	0.024
Jaha, John	85	170	171.9	114	.663	6	0	61	11	15.6	0	0.0	72	5	0.069
Seitzer, Kevin	70	153	156.3	103	.659	1	1	50	10	15.6	0	0.0	41	3	0.073
Stahoviak, Scott	114	217	227.4	146	.642	4	1	83	18	12.6	3	75.8	58	4	0.069
Franco, Julio	97	234	242.0	153	.632	9	0	81	7	34.6	0	0.0	65	9	0.138
Vaughn, Mo	146	283	287.3	177	.616	10	5	108	7	41.0	1	287.3	101	10	0.099
Fielder, Cecil	79	170	172.1	106	.616	3	4	67	16	10.8	0	0.0	55	1	0.018
Snow, J.T.	154	289	302.6	180	.595	8	2	116	20	15.1	1	302.6	87	12	0.138
Thomas, Frank	139	263	278.3	165	.593	6	3	105	18	15.5	4	69.6	94	3	0.032
McGwire, Mark	109	218	226.2	134	.592	8	2	86	12	18.9	3	75.4	68	4	0.059
Martinez, Tino	151	289	303.2	179	.590	5	0	105	23	13.2	2	151.6	84	9	0.107
Palmeiro, Rafael	159	322	342.0	201	.588	6	2	130	18	19.0	1	342.0	100	13	0.130
Clark, Tony	87	175	175.8	101	.574	5	1	74	15	11.7	0	0.0	55	3	0.055
Sorrento, Paul	138	270	275.2	149	.541	7	4	125	23	12.0	2	137.6	82	4	0.049
Hunter, Brian R.	41	44	44.5	23	.517	1	1	22	4	11.1	0	0.0	15	1	0.067
Carter, Joe	41	68	74.5	32	.430	2	0	36	3	24.8	0	0.0	26	0	0.000

For the second time in three years, John Olerud led the AL in DA among regulars. Interestingly enough Joe Carter, the man who may have his job, ranks about where you'd expect an outfielder playing out of position to rank. Frank Thomas improved considerably, but improvement has gotten him to simply bad with the leather, as opposed to catastrophic. Palmeiro's season marked a major dropoff from seasons past, so it will be interesting to see if this year is the beginning of something worse, or simply an aberration. Although he's the Gold Glove winner for the AL, JT Snow has consistently ranked below average. AL Gold Glove, 1B: John Olerud.

—Second Base—

Team	G	GOps	AGOps	GO	AGDA	FE	TE	1B	2B	AGO/2B	3B	AGO/3B	DPOps	DPI	DP%
League	1133	8328	8569.3	5655	.660	167	70	3360	50	171.4	4	2142.3	1809	586	0.324
BAL	163	631	662.7	432	.652	10	5	246	1	662.7	0	0.0	143	51	0.357
BOS	162	656	666.3	429	.644	19	6	254	6	111.0	1	666.3	130	30	0.231
CAL	161	465	484.5	311	.642	10	5	200	0	0.0	0	0.0	111	37	0.333
CHA	162	586	614.6	407	.662	10	4	237	2	307.3	0	0.0	107	33	0.308
CLE	161	646	675.3	431	.638	15	4	251	6	112.6	0	0.0	136	39	0.287
DET	162	631	637.4	414	.650	10	5	267	4	159.3	0	0.0	139	38	0.273
KCA	161	633	649.5	445	.685	7	7	263	0	0.0	0	0.0	132	55	0.417
MIL	162	604	611.3	420	.687	14	4	257	2	305.7	0	0.0	138	51	0.370
MIN	162	512	531.7	364	.685	5	3	207	9	59.1	0	0.0	108	31	0.287
NYA	162	556	577.4	371	.643	14	7	213	3	192.5	0	0.0	127	33	0.260
OAK	162	638	659.6	435	.660	9	6	235	2	329.8	0	0.0	141	42	0.298
SEA	161	556	564.0	355	.629	10	7	254	3	188.0	2	282.0	117	44	0.376
TEX	163	613	618.9	433	.700	11	4	248	7	88.4	0	0.0	145	47	0.324
TOR	162	601	618.9	408	.659	23	3	228	5	123.8	1	618.9	135	55	0.407

Name	G	GOps	AGOps	GO	AGDA	FE	TE	1B	2B	AGO/2B	3B	AGO/3B	DPOps	DPI	DP%
Roberts, Bip	63	225	230.6	166	.720	1	3	91	0	0.0	0	0.0	43	17	0.395
Lockhart, Keith	84	242	248.4	178	.717	5	3	83	0	0.0	0	0.0	49	22	0.449
Hudler, Rex	53	126	131.3	93	.708	2	2	41	0	0.0	0	0.0	31	12	0.387
Batista, Tony	52	193	199.8	141	.706	2	1	62	0	0.0	0	0.0	49	15	0.306
McLemore, Mark	**147**	**551**	**556.2**	**390**	**.701**	**9**	**3**	**223**	**7**	**79.5**	**0**	**0.0**	**133**	**45**	**0.338**
Vina, Fernando	137	494	499.0	345	.691	13	3	205	2	249.5	0	0.0	114	45	0.395
Knoblauch, Chuck	151	462	480.7	327	.680	5	3	188	8	60.1	0	0.0	99	29	0.293
Perez, Tomas	75	268	274.0	185	.675	11	1	98	2	137.0	1	274.0	61	26	0.426
Frye, Jeff	100	400	400.9	269	.671	8	1	152	2	200.4	0	0.0	84	22	0.262
Lewis, Mark	144	534	540.1	358	.663	7	3	214	3	180.0	0	0.0	117	36	0.308
Duncan, Mariano	104	289	299.5	198	.661	6	5	108	1	299.5	0	0.0	70	18	0.257
Durham, Ray	150	518	544.9	359	.659	8	3	212	1	544.9	0	0.0	95	28	0.295
Alomar, Roberto	142	537	565.9	371	.656	6	5	209	1	565.9	0	0.0	118	42	0.356
Gates, Brent	64	227	234.7	151	.644	6	3	86	1	234.7	0	0.0	55	19	0.345
Bournigal, Rafael	64	212	219.2	140	.639	1	1	84	1	219.2	0	0.0	37	8	0.216
Cedeno, Domingo	64	212	219.9	139	.632	7	2	94	3	73.3	0	0.0	43	18	0.419
Baerga, Carlos	100	400	415.3	260	.626	10	4	156	5	83.1	0	0.0	85	25	0.294
Cordero, Wil	37	144	149.3	93	.623	7	3	51	1	149.3	0	0.0	30	5	0.167
Velarde, Randy	114	313	326.4	201	.616	7	2	147	0	0.0	0	0.0	74	25	0.338
Fox, Andy	72	147	154.5	94	.609	7	1	60	1	154.5	0	0.0	32	7	0.219
Cora, Joey	140	419	425.8	258	.606	8	5	196	3	141.9	1	425.8	87	29	0.333
Offerman, Jose	38	103	105.9	64	.604	0	1	55	0	0.0	0	0.0	20	10	0.500

If you've followed the debates about the relative merits of Roberto Alomar's defensive skill over the years, you won't be surprised by these numbers. Yet again, he finished below average in DA; however, teaming with Cal Ripken did lead to his best figures in starting the deuce in years. One of the biggest improvements was Ray Durham, who went from last in the AL in '95 to the middle of the pack. Keith Lockhart's DP% was the highest in the last three years of any major league second baseman who played in 80 games, but it looks like Jose Offerman has some work to do. AL Gold Glove, 2B: Mark McLemore, because of regular playing time.

—Third Base—

Team	G	GOps	AGOps	GO	AGDA	FE	TE	1B	2BAGO/2B		3B	AGO/3B	DPOps	DPI	DP%
League	1133	6675	6900.9	4122	.597	153	115	2464	463	14.9	6	1150.1	1769	348	0.197
BAL	163	482	511.5	296	.579	11	7	182	26	19.7	0	0.0	117	31	0.265
BOS	162	461	469.0	286	.610	12	6	176	18	26.1	0	0.0	144	18	0.125
CAL	161	574	599.0	363	.606	26	5	199	40	15.0	0	0.0	161	28	0.174
CHA	162	443	469.7	275	.585	9	4	164	18	26.1	2	234.9	108	30	0.278
CLE	161	469	493.4	287	.582	9	10	170	36	13.7	0	0.0	101	24	0.238
DET	162	569	575.6	345	.599	6	7	213	52	11.1	1	575.6	160	27	0.169
KCA	161	468	483.3	280	.579	19	7	179	40	12.1	0	0.0	107	18	0.168
MIL	162	466	473.0	288	.609	12	8	179	36	13.1	1	473.0	119	17	0.143
MIN	162	443	461.5	294	.637	5	14	159	29	15.9	1	461.5	118	22	0.186
NYA	162	455	475.2	285	.600	6	7	156	29	16.4	0	0.0	124	26	0.210
OAK	162	537	556.4	343	.616	11	12	175	37	15.0	0	0.0	139	36	0.259
SEA	161	490	497.9	285	.572	12	9	190	37	13.5	1	497.9	151	26	0.172
TEX	163	417	422.6	244	.577	8	9	176	38	11.1	0	0.0	116	17	0.147
TOR	162	401	415.2	251	.605	7	10	146	27	15.4	0	0.0	104	28	0.269

Name	G	GOps	AGOps	GO	AGDA	FE	TE	1B	2BAGO/2B		3B	AGO/3B	DPOps	DPI	DP%
Ripken, Cal	6	22	22.0	16	.727	0	0	6	2	11.0	0	0.0	4	1	0.250
Brosius, Scott	**109**	**337**	**346.9**	**229**	**.660**	**5**	**5**	**102**	**24**	**14.5**	**0**	**0.0**	**89**	**23**	**0.258**
Hollins, Dave	144	400	414.0	271	.655	7	10	133	22	18.8	1	414.0	112	19	0.170
Arias, George	83	279	293.1	186	.635	9	1	93	16	18.3	0	0.0	73	17	0.233
Naehring, Tim	116	326	331.2	208	.628	7	4	121	9	36.8	0	0.0	103	16	0.155
Fryman, Travis	128	445	450.0	270	.600	4	4	169	41	11.0	1	450.0	114	18	0.158
Lockhart, Keith	55	124	126.6	76	.600	4	1	49	11	11.5	0	0.0	24	4	0.167
Sprague, Ed	148	347	360.7	216	.599	7	8	130	20	18.0	0	0.0	90	23	0.256
Cirillo, Jeff	154	392	397.4	236	.594	12	5	156	27	14.7	1	397.4	98	13	0.133
Ventura, Robin	150	386	409.4	239	.584	7	3	141	16	25.6	2	204.7	94	26	0.277
Thome, Jim	150	425	447.3	260	.581	9	8	153	32	14.0	0	0.0	94	22	0.234
Boggs, Wade	123	320	335.2	194	.579	3	4	113	23	14.6	0	0.0	81	19	0.235
Surhoff, B.J.	106	293	310.3	179	.577	9	5	113	15	20.7	0	0.0	76	21	0.276
Randa, Joe	92	221	231.2	133	.575	6	3	78	19	12.2	0	0.0	51	10	0.196
Palmer, Dean	154	376	381.4	219	.574	8	8	157	37	10.3	0	0.0	107	13	0.121
Wallach, Tim	46	141	143.3	82	.572	6	1	57	16	9.0	0	0.0	46	3	0.065
Paquette, Craig	51	115	117.6	67	.570	8	3	44	10	11.8	0	0.0	29	4	0.138
Howell, Jack	43	77	82.5	46	.558	6	2	27	4	20.6	0	0.0	29	4	0.138
Giambi, Jason	39	140	142.6	79	.554	3	5	50	12	11.9	0	0.0	34	8	0.235
Davis, Russ	51	131	136.6	70	.512	4	3	51	14	9.8	1	136.6	32	4	0.125
Valentin, John	12	22	22.0	11	.500	1	0	15	2	11.0	0	0.0	8	0	0.000

Ripken's here as a gag, or as a sop to Orioles fans who will have to get used to the arrival of Mike Bordick. By midseason '96, many people in baseball were buzzing about how good Scott Brosius looked at third, and he was a favorite for most-improved player. However, he's been among the league leaders in DA for several years. Dave Hollins' performance was something of a surprise, and Travis Fryman and Tim Naehring managed to show that their gains in '95 were real improvements. Wade Boggs suffered his first below-average season in some time, while it looks like concerns about Jason Giambi's glovework at the hot corner are deserved. AL Gold Glove, 3B: Scott Brosius.

—Shortstop—

Team	G	GOps	AGOps	GO	AGDA	FE	TE	1B	2BAGO/2B	3B AGO/3B	DPOps	DPI	DP%
League	1133	8846	9113.4	5825	.639	179	135	3689	27 337.5	0 0.0	1972	685	0.347
BAL	163	630	663.4	423	.638	12	5	242	1 663.4	0 0.0	121	42	0.347
BOS	162	644	653.9	426	.651	14	7	253	2 327.0	0 0.0	166	53	0.319
CAL	161	652	677.5	444	.655	20	5	254	1 677.5	0 0.0	140	48	0.343
CHA	162	592	626.2	373	.596	13	8	255	3 208.7	0 0.0	105	33	0.314
CLE	161	644	671.1	441	.657	9	12	247	0 0.0	0 0.0	125	48	0.384
DET	162	668	674.8	422	.625	20	8	304	1 674.8	0 0.0	156	50	0.321
KCA	161	630	648.0	416	.642	7	15	276	2 324.0	0 0.0	150	58	0.387
MIL	162	659	667.0	444	.666	17	22	274	1 667.0	0 0.0	151	68	0.450
MIN	162	509	531.1	330	.621	14	10	233	3 177.0	0 0.0	124	46	0.371
NYA	162	677	706.2	424	.600	11	14	267	1 706.2	0 0.0	131	40	0.305
OAK	162	683	706.2	460	.651	11	5	261	2 353.1	0 0.0	166	59	0.355
SEA	161	618	627.0	391	.624	8	8	289	2 313.5	0 0.0	150	43	0.287
TEX	163	630	637.3	410	.643	9	8	303	5 127.5	0 0.0	146	46	0.315
TOR	162	610	627.6	421	.671	14	8	231	3 209.2	0 0.0	141	51	0.362

Name	G	GOps	AGOps	GO	AGDA	FE	TE	1B	2BAGO/2B	3B AGO/3B	DPOps	DPI	DP%
Valentin, Jose	**151**	**593**	**600.3**	**410**	**.683**	**15**	**22**	**235**	**1 600.3**	**0 0.0**	**133**	**62**	**0.466**
Trammell, Alan	43	143	144.8	98	.677	3	1	55	0 0.0	0 0.0	27	6	0.222
Fryman, Travis	29	107	108.0	73	.676	1	1	43	0 0.0	0 0.0	29	8	0.276
Gonzalez, Alex	147	566	582.9	393	.674	13	7	207	3 194.3	0 0.0	132	48	0.364
Howard, David	135	492	507.2	332	.655	3	8	217	1 507.2	0 0.0	110	40	0.364
Vizquel, Omar	150	583	605.0	395	.653	9	11	225	0 0.0	0 0.0	109	37	0.339
DiSarcina, Gary	150	604	628.7	408	.649	16	4	242	1 628.7	0 0.0	129	41	0.318
Bordick, Mike	155	629	650.8	421	.647	11	5	243	2 325.4	0 0.0	157	55	0.350
Valentin, John	118	473	480.6	310	.645	10	6	187	1 480.6	0 0.0	137	45	0.328
Elster, Kevin	157	586	592.5	380	.641	6	8	285	5 118.5	0 0.0	139	45	0.324
Meares, Pat	150	434	452.2	288	.637	14	8	195	2 226.1	0 0.0	104	35	0.337
Ripken, Cal	158	588	620.4	394	.635	10	4	228	0 0.0	0 0.0	115	40	0.348
Cedeno, Andujar	51	208	208.2	131	.629	11	1	97	0 0.0	0 0.0	39	12	0.308
Rodriguez, Alex	146	549	555.7	347	.624	7	8	249	2 277.8	0 0.0	135	37	0.274
Guillen, Ozzie	146	475	503.2	304	.604	9	2	206	2 251.6	0 0.0	85	28	0.329
Jeter, Derek	157	643	670.9	403	.601	10	12	255	1 670.9	0 0.0	126	38	0.302
Offerman, Jose	37	114	117.0	69	.590	4	6	48	1 117.0	0 0.0	35	15	0.429

For the first time in three years, somebody other than John Valentin led AL shortstops, as Jose V. put together a brilliant season. Just as sophomore Ray Durham showed the most improvement among second basemen, Alex Gonzalez of the Blue Jays made huge strides in his second season. Hopefully, Derek Jeter will show the same kind of improvement as he learns the hitters. The decay of Ozzie Guillen has been obvious on the field recently, and these numbers don't do anything to discount that. AL Gold Glove, SS: Jose Valentin.

—Left Field—

Team	G	FOps	AFOps	FO	AFDA	FE	TE	1B	2B	AFO/2B	3B	AFO/3B
League	1133	8187	8514.9	4753	.558	83	22	1881	1548	5.5	67	127.1
BAL	163	562	601.6	327	.544	5	2	158	86	7.0	5	120.3
BOS	162	641	657.1	312	.475	9	0	172	148	4.4	7	93.9
CAL	161	559	588.5	340	.578	3	5	122	105	5.6	5	117.7
CHA	162	597	633.4	377	.595	7	1	109	116	5.5	4	158.4
CLE	161	562	594.4	338	.569	7	3	116	118	5.0	2	297.2
DET	162	609	617.2	334	.541	11	3	149	115	5.4	5	123.4
KCA	161	550	570.0	327	.574	9	0	120	99	5.8	4	142.5
MIL	162	598	609.0	344	.565	4	1	135	113	5.4	8	76.1
MIN	162	606	638.7	370	.579	2	2	124	118	5.4	4	159.7
NYA	162	511	539.6	284	.526	4	0	131	103	5.2	1	539.6
OAK	162	636	666.4	357	.536	6	2	147	126	5.3	6	111.1
SEA	161	633	643.7	380	.590	3	1	146	106	6.1	4	160.9
TEX	163	606	614.1	371	.604	5	1	126	97	6.3	7	87.7
TOR	162	517	539.7	292	.541	8	1	126	98	5.5	5	107.9

Name	G	FOps	AFOps	FO	AFDA	FE	TE	1B	2B	AFO/2B	3B	AFO/3B
Goodwin, Tom	75	199	207.7	128	.616	2	0	36	36	5.8	1	207.7
Amaral, Rich	63	171	174.8	105	.601	0	0	41	25	7.0	3	58.3
Phillips, Tony	**150**	**547**	**578.8**	**346**	**.598**	**5**	**1**	**102**	**103**	**5.6**	**3**	**192.9**
Greer, Rusty	136	499	507.4	303	.597	4	1	103	83	6.1	6	84.6
Newfield, Marc	49	162	162.7	97	.596	1	0	32	31	5.2	2	81.3
Perez, Robert	59	146	154.3	90	.583	2	0	34	20	7.7	1	154.3
Anderson, Garret	140	485	513.7	299	.582	3	4	105	88	5.8	5	102.7
Cordova, Marty	145	536	564.5	327	.579	2	1	112	103	5.5	3	188.2
Bragg, Darren	54	142	147.2	85	.577	0	0	32	25	5.9	0	0.0
Hammonds, Jeffrey	64	192	208.6	119	.570	2	0	52	25	8.3	4	52.2
Belle, Albert	152	516	544.8	310	.569	7	3	109	107	5.1	2	272.4
Plantier, Phil	67	240	245.4	136	.554	3	1	52	47	5.2	3	81.8
Vaughn, Greg	98	343	349.9	189	.540	3	1	85	67	5.2	3	116.6
Carter, Joe	115	304	316.9	165	.521	6	1	78	61	5.2	4	79.2
Williams, Gerald	70	165	175.1	90	.514	2	0	46	30	5.8	1	175.1
Raines, Tim	51	147	157.5	80	.508	1	0	34	35	4.5	0	0.0
Higginson, Bob	63	186	186.2	94	.505	2	1	54	34	5.5	2	93.1
O'Leary, Troy	66	139	139.0	69	.496	3	0	38	28	5.0	1	139.0
Greenwell, Mike	75	265	279.7	138	.493	4	0	58	67	4.2	4	69.9
Giambi, Jason	44	142	152.3	66	.433	0	0	33	41	3.7	2	76.1
Jefferson, Reggie	45	144	144.3	62	.430	2	0	46	33	4.4	2	72.1

It took a couple of players playing out of position to finally underwhelm Mike Greenwell, the perennial cellar dweller hereabouts. Red Sox left fielders as a group have finished last in the AL in DA for years, but with Greenwell's departure it will be interesting to see how much of that is park illusion, and how much of it was Greenwell's limitations. Marty Cordova didn't enjoy quite the amazing campaign he had in his rookie year, when he posted an excellent .634 DA, but he's clearly an above-average defender. After a mediocre season in RF in '95, Rusty Greer looked fine in left. AL Gold Glove, LF: Tony Phillips.

—Center Field—

Team	G	FOps	AFOps	FO	AFDA	FE	TE	1B	2B	AFO/2B	3B	AFO/3B
League	1133	10164	10555.6	6107	.579	54	11	2511	1449	7.3	240	44.0
BAL	163	668	711.2	415	.583	2	1	172	98	7.3	17	41.8
BOS	162	753	770.5	401	.520	2	1	221	112	6.9	21	36.7
CAL	161	672	705.7	424	.601	2	1	167	85	8.3	9	78.4
CHA	162	693	732.6	456	.622	3	1	141	101	7.3	13	56.4
CLE	161	643	678.2	398	.587	7	3	148	100	6.8	12	56.5
DET	162	784	794.1	450	.567	9	1	225	82	9.7	23	34.5
KCA	161	715	741.8	425	.573	6	0	165	113	6.6	23	32.3
MIL	162	784	797.5	470	.589	5	1	186	104	7.7	25	31.9
MIN	162	750	788.9	473	.600	2	0	168	113	7.0	13	60.7
NYA	162	679	713.6	403	.565	5	0	166	107	6.7	11	64.9
OAK	162	762	797.1	446	.560	2	0	193	114	7.0	19	42.0
SEA	161	739	750.7	462	.615	5	0	169	99	7.6	12	62.6
TEX	163	795	807.3	449	.556	0	0	204	113	7.1	31	26.0
TOR	162	727	757.0	435	.575	4	2	186	108	7.0	11	68.8

Name	G	FOps	AFOps	FO	AFDA	FE	TE	1B	2B	AFO/2B	3B	AFO/3B
Erstad, Darin	36	150	154.0	101	.656	1	0	27	20	7.7	1	154.0
Lewis, Darren	137	427	452.0	285	.631	2	1	83	58	7.8	7	64.6
Griffey Jr., Ken	**137**	**595**	**606.1**	**378**	**.624**	**4**	**0**	**131**	**81**	**7.5**	**9**	**67.3**
Becker, Rich	121	524	549.1	337	.614	2	0	115	73	7.5	8	68.6
Bartee, Kimera	95	341	341.0	209	.613	2	0	94	26	13.1	10	34.1
Damon, Johnny	89	321	336.9	206	.611	3	0	60	52	6.5	11	30.6
Martinez, Dave	73	257	270.8	165	.609	1	0	56	41	6.6	5	54.2
Lofton, Kenny	153	599	630.0	375	.595	7	3	136	93	6.8	10	63.0
Edmonds, Jim	111	446	473.1	278	.588	0	1	116	58	8.2	6	78.8
Young, Ernie	133	551	582.3	341	.586	1	0	135	75	7.8	11	52.9
Nixon, Otis	125	563	591.7	342	.578	1	1	146	79	7.5	10	59.2
Anderson, Brady	143	560	597.2	341	.571	2	1	145	87	6.9	16	37.3
Williams, Bernie	140	572	599.6	334	.557	5	0	139	94	6.4	11	54.5
Hamilton, Darryl	147	694	703.7	384	.546	0	0	184	106	6.6	22	32.0
Goodwin, Tom	81	308	315.4	172	.545	3	0	84	46	6.9	9	35.0
Bragg, Darren	52	200	203.3	110	.541	0	0	54	34	6.0	5	40.7
Listach, Pat	66	282	289.2	156	.539	2	1	77	39	7.4	8	36.1
Kelly, Roberto	40	152	161.6	87	.538	0	0	38	30	5.4	3	53.9
Curtis, Chad	80	344	349.0	182	.522	6	1	101	48	7.3	11	31.7
Tinsley, Lee	78	268	272.2	131	.481	0	1	84	45	6.0	8	34.0

Erstad is posted just as a tease, although he may not be at this level consistently. The real story has been the improvement of Ken Griffey Jr. over the last few years. As recently as '94, he was last in the AL in DA, but he was above average in '95 and excellent in '96. Another notable improvement was by Rich Becker, while Bernie Williams seems to have slowed down dramatically over the last two years. Jim Edmonds continued to be the one of the best center fielders at preventing extra-base hits. AL Gold Glove, CF: Ken Griffey Jr.

—Right Field—

Team	G	FOps	AFOps	FO	AFDA	FE	TE	1B	2B	AFO/2B	3B	AFO/3B
League	1133	8214	8547.5	4731	.553	84	19	1962	1335	6.4	227	37.7
BAL	163	575	615.1	337	.548	7	1	132	105	5.9	15	41.0
BOS	162	599	613.5	300	.489	11	1	187	89	6.9	15	40.9
CAL	161	540	568.8	325	.571	6	3	128	78	7.3	10	56.9
CHA	162	589	626.8	360	.574	8	1	129	91	6.9	12	52.2
CLE	161	526	557.7	310	.556	7	2	129	84	6.6	13	42.9
DET	162	624	632.3	341	.539	15	3	156	92	6.9	22	28.7
KCA	161	623	644.7	386	.599	5	1	133	84	7.7	26	24.8
MIL	162	625	636.0	370	.582	3	3	125	113	5.6	19	33.5
MIN	162	621	654.3	381	.582	7	1	117	114	5.7	19	34.4
NYA	162	573	601.7	347	.577	1	0	134	89	6.8	8	75.2
OAK	162	590	618.8	328	.530	6	0	161	85	7.3	20	30.9
SEA	161	554	564.8	297	.526	3	3	130	114	5.0	12	47.1
TEX	163	586	596.1	299	.502	3	0	168	94	6.3	24	24.8
TOR	162	589	613.8	350	.570	2	0	133	103	6.0	12	51.1

Name	G	FOps	AFOps	FO	AFDA	FE	TE	1B	2B	AFO/2B	3B	AFO/3B
Martinez, Dave	73	95	103.8	69	.665	2	0	21	4	25.9	0	0.0
Devereaux, Mike	64	98	103.3	68	.658	2	0	20	13	7.9	0	0.0
Mieske, Matt	**108**	**323**	**330.2**	**205**	**.621**	**1**	**0**	**55**	**59**	**5.6**	**8**	**41.3**
Lawton, Matt	60	232	240.4	147	.612	3	0	39	41	5.9	9	26.7
Damon, Johnny	63	234	238.7	145	.607	2	1	64	22	10.9	3	79.6
Green, Shawn	127	418	433.4	254	.586	2	0	92	68	6.4	9	48.2
Tucker, Michael	73	221	233.9	137	.586	1	0	39	37	6.3	14	16.7
O'Neill, Paul	146	479	504.5	295	.585	0	0	105	78	6.5	7	72.1
Kelly, Roberto	54	168	179.4	105	.585	0	1	25	38	4.7	6	29.9
Herrera, Jose	92	273	280.8	160	.570	4	0	71	36	7.8	6	46.8
Newson, Warren	58	187	189.7	108	.569	1	0	46	27	7.0	6	31.6
Salmon, Tim	153	512	539.4	304	.564	5	3	123	77	7.0	9	59.9
Ramirez, Manny	149	469	498.2	274	.550	7	2	117	76	6.6	12	41.5
Tartabull, Danny	122	439	465.5	253	.543	6	1	99	80	5.8	11	42.3
Berroa, Geronimo	54	145	151.8	80	.527	2	0	34	27	5.6	5	30.4
Buhner, Jay	142	468	478.9	252	.526	2	1	111	97	4.9	10	47.9
Higginson, Bob	57	188	191.8	101	.526	3	2	51	29	6.6	4	48.0
Nieves, Melvin	84	305	308.3	160	.519	7	1	73	54	5.7	13	23.7
Nilsson, Dave	55	188	190.9	96	.503	1	3	46	38	5.0	7	27.3
Bonilla, Bobby	107	340	368.3	184	.500	5	0	79	75	4.9	11	33.5
Gonzalez, Juan	102	336	342.0	161	.471	2	0	103	57	6.0	14	24.4
O'Leary, Troy	110	296	303.6	143	.471	3	1	90	57	5.3	5	60.7

We've mentioned that several sophomores showed dramatic improvements in '96; add Shawn Green to the list. The annual joke in right continues to be Jay Buhner who, strong arm or no, has seen an incredible number of doubles skip past him, as he yet again was one of the worst outfielders in the majors in allowing extra-base hits to drop around him. Since he actually improved this year (when Randy Johnson was injured), it doesn't seem to be the pitching staff's fault. One of the big disappointments has to be the dropoff Tim Salmon endured. For somebody who's been kept off the field a lot, Danny Tartabull didn't humiliate himself, but he was hardly an asset. AL Gold Glove, RF: Matt Mieske.

—Infield—

Team	G	GOps	AGOps	GO	AGDA	FE	TE	1B	2B	AGO/2B	3B	AGO/3B	DPOps	DPI	DP%
League	1133	26140	26783.3	18696	.698	621	355	8112	810	33.1	34	787.7	6046	1742	0.288
BAL	163	1873	1952.9	1357	.695	40	19	558	46	42.5	1	1952.9	423	138	0.326
BOS	162	1902	1926.4	1341	.696	56	24	588	31	62.1	2	963.2	463	111	0.240
CAL	161	1823	1884.0	1305	.693	66	17	558	62	30.4	1	1884.0	432	125	0.289
CHA	162	1766	1843.6	1260	.683	41	20	567	41	45.0	7	263.4	388	100	0.258
CLE	161	1992	2062.0	1452	.704	44	28	566	59	34.9	1	2062.0	415	123	0.296
DET	162	2008	2025.5	1384	.683	44	25	661	83	24.4	1	2025.5	480	120	0.250
KCA	161	1951	1995.5	1413	.708	40	31	624	63	31.7	1	1995.5	437	145	0.332
MIL	162	1919	1938.9	1386	.715	53	36	606	62	31.3	1	1938.9	453	145	0.320
MIN	162	1657	1710.0	1227	.718	31	28	501	64	26.7	5	342.0	377	106	0.281
NYA	162	1817	1878.9	1275	.679	36	28	541	56	33.6	2	939.4	411	108	0.263
OAK	162	2018	2073.4	1469	.708	42	25	563	60	34.6	3	691.1	476	144	0.303
SEA	161	1781	1802.7	1212	.672	39	29	622	69	26.1	5	360.5	430	118	0.274
TEX	163	1838	1854.7	1313	.708	36	23	632	61	30.4	2	927.4	437	116	0.265
TOR	162	1795	1839.8	1302	.708	53	22	525	53	34.7	2	919.9	424	143	0.337

—Outfield—

Team	G	FOps	AFOps	FO	AFDA	FE	TE	1B	2B	AFO/2B	3B	AFO/3B
League	1133	23995	24796.9	15591	.629	221	52	4986	3117	8.0	356	69.7
BAL	163	1634	1727.5	1079	.625	14	4	355	203	8.5	23	75.1
BOS	162	1755	1791.2	1013	.566	22	2	449	253	7.1	27	66.3
CAL	161	1616	1686.7	1089	.646	11	9	328	195	8.6	16	105.4
CHA	162	1726	1813.8	1193	.658	18	3	301	219	8.3	21	86.4
CLE	161	1579	1655.8	1046	.632	21	8	304	224	7.4	20	82.8
DET	162	1817	1837.5	1125	.612	35	7	408	222	8.3	36	51.0
KCA	161	1707	1758.6	1138	.647	20	1	322	215	8.2	36	48.9
MIL	162	1813	1840.1	1184	.643	12	5	352	240	7.7	35	52.6
MIN	162	1796	1875.3	1224	.653	11	3	324	244	7.7	23	81.5
NYA	162	1601	1672.2	1034	.618	10	0	346	216	7.7	13	128.6
OAK	162	1787	1858.8	1131	.608	14	2	398	228	8.2	32	58.1
SEA	161	1732	1757.0	1139	.648	11	4	343	231	7.6	19	92.5
TEX	163	1779	1802.1	1119	.621	8	1	406	211	8.5	37	48.7
TOR	162	1653	1711.6	1077	.629	14	3	350	216	7.9	18	95.1

—First Base/Second Base—

Team	G	GOps	AGOps	GO	AGDA	FE	TE	1B	2B	AGO/2B	3B	AGO/3B	DPOps	DPI	DP%
League	1133	12015	12301.4	8749	.711	289	105	3728	326	37.7	28	439.3	2684	709	0.264
BAL	163	875	911.7	638	.700	17	7	267	19	48.0	1	911.7	200	65	0.325
BOS	162	894	905.4	629	.695	30	11	276	13	69.6	2	452.7	197	40	0.203
CAL	161	702	727.0	498	.685	20	7	237	22	33.0	1	727.0	164	49	0.299
CHA	162	837	871.7	612	.702	19	8	266	21	41.5	5	174.3	175	37	0.211
CLE	161	981	1014.6	724	.714	26	6	277	23	44.1	1	1014.6	196	51	0.260
DET	162	884	891.6	617	.692	18	10	294	30	29.7	0	0.0	205	43	0.210
KCA	161	947	966.9	717	.742	14	9	298	21	46.0	1	966.9	196	69	0.352
MIL	162	890	899.1	654	.727	24	6	284	25	36.0	0	0.0	219	60	0.274
MIN	162	789	813.2	603	.741	12	4	231	32	25.4	4	203.3	161	38	0.236
NYA	162	787	812.5	566	.697	19	7	235	26	31.3	2	406.3	181	42	0.232
OAK	162	907	931.9	666	.715	20	8	257	21	44.4	3	310.6	203	49	0.241
SEA	161	783	792.5	536	.676	19	12	278	30	26.4	4	198.1	177	49	0.277
TEX	163	880	887.0	659	.743	19	6	276	20	44.3	2	443.5	215	53	0.247
TOR	162	859	879.9	630	.716	32	4	252	23	38.3	2	440.0	195	64	0.328

—Second Base/Shortstop—

Team	G	GOps	AGOps	GO	AGDA	FE	TE	1B	2B	AGO/2B	3B	AGO/3B	DPOps	DPI	DP%
League	1133	16323	16748.6	11480	.685	346	205	5671	212	79.0	6	2791.4	3359	1271	0.378
BAL	163	1214	1271.0	855	.673	22	10	420	8	158.9	0	0.0	249	93	0.373
BOS	162	1236	1252.9	855	.682	33	13	413	10	125.3	1	1252.9	264	83	0.314
CAL	161	1076	1115.3	755	.677	30	10	384	14	79.7	0	0.0	244	85	0.348
CHA	162	1118	1170.6	780	.666	23	12	395	11	106.4	0	0.0	198	66	0.333
CLE	161	1239	1287.9	872	.677	24	16	408	20	64.4	0	0.0	230	87	0.378
DET	162	1249	1260.7	836	.663	30	13	472	23	54.8	0	0.0	271	88	0.325
KCA	161	1195	1223.2	861	.704	14	22	433	8	152.9	0	0.0	232	113	0.487
MIL	162	1211	1224.0	864	.706	31	26	424	18	68.0	1	1224.0	239	119	0.498
MIN	162	970	1004.7	694	.691	19	13	356	21	47.8	1	1004.7	210	77	0.367
NYA	162	1135	1173.1	795	.678	25	21	358	15	78.2	0	0.0	232	73	0.315
OAK	162	1256	1293.5	895	.692	20	11	396	18	71.9	0	0.0	272	101	0.371
SEA	161	1109	1123.2	746	.664	18	15	431	13	86.4	2	561.6	242	87	0.360
TEX	163	1164	1174.4	843	.718	20	12	416	20	58.7	0	0.0	247	93	0.377
TOR	162	1151	1180.2	829	.702	37	11	365	13	90.8	1	1180.2	229	106	0.463

—Shortstop/Third Base—

Team	G	GOps	AGOps	GO	AGDA	FE	TE	1B	2B	AGO/2B	3B	AGO/3B	DPOps	DPI	DP%
League	1133	14168	14529.1	9947	.685	332	250	4427	484	30.0	6	2421.5	3107	1033	0.332
BAL	163	1002	1045.9	719	.687	23	12	295	27	38.7	0	0.0	196	73	0.372
BOS	162	1015	1028.4	712	.692	26	13	319	18	57.1	0	0.0	256	71	0.277
CAL	161	1125	1161.6	807	.695	46	10	325	40	29.0	0	0.0	252	76	0.302
CHA	162	930	973.0	648	.666	22	12	302	20	48.7	2	486.5	179	63	0.352
CLE	161	1018	1055.5	728	.690	18	22	296	36	29.3	0	0.0	193	72	0.373
DET	162	1127	1137.0	767	.675	26	15	370	53	21.5	1	1137.0	264	77	0.292
KCA	161	1007	1031.9	696	.674	26	22	329	42	24.6	0	0.0	216	76	0.352
MIL	162	1030	1040.8	732	.703	29	30	323	37	28.1	1	1040.8	228	85	0.373
MIN	162	870	899.0	624	.694	19	24	272	32	28.1	1	899.0	200	68	0.340
NYA	162	1033	1069.7	709	.663	17	21	309	30	35.7	0	0.0	208	66	0.317
OAK	162	1116	1147.1	803	.700	22	17	311	39	29.4	0	0.0	247	95	0.385
SEA	161	999	1011.2	676	.668	20	17	345	39	25.9	1	1011.2	242	69	0.285
TEX	163	958	967.8	654	.676	17	17	356	41	23.6	0	0.0	217	63	0.290
TOR	162	938	962.1	672	.698	21	18	275	30	32.1	0	0.0	209	79	0.378

NATIONAL LEAGUE

—First Base—

Team	G	GOps	AGOps	GO	AGDA	FE	TE	1B	2B	AGO/2B	3B	AGO/3B	DPOps	DPI	DP%
League	1134	5002	5144.8	3237	.629	138	28	1935	249	20.7	45	114.3	1677	105	0.063
ATL	162	306	316.6	183	.578	11	2	139	18	17.6	2	158.3	123	7	0.057
CHN	162	389	396.6	273	.688	3	1	141	21	18.9	4	99.2	131	8	0.061
CIN	162	344	354.6	226	.637	9	2	127	16	22.2	1	354.6	128	8	0.062
COL	162	410	416.2	261	.627	13	2	174	22	18.9	7	59.5	106	4	0.038
FLO	162	426	431.7	290	.672	9	0	152	19	22.7	3	143.9	121	14	0.116
HOU	162	369	387.1	240	.620	11	5	139	10	38.7	1	387.1	127	10	0.079
LAN	162	362	379.0	242	.639	13	2	131	15	25.3	2	189.5	110	7	0.064
MON	162	315	324.6	178	.548	12	1	131	22	14.8	3	108.2	99	4	0.040
NYN	162	369	372.5	233	.625	12	2	157	19	19.6	7	53.2	137	9	0.066
PHI	162	360	385.3	217	.563	9	1	140	19	20.3	3	128.4	99	6	0.061
PIT	162	376	379.9	257	.676	5	3	143	15	25.3	2	190.0	135	13	0.096
SDN	162	342	350.5	231	.659	7	2	119	17	20.6	3	116.8	126	6	0.048
SFN	162	323	332.0	206	.620	16	1	111	20	16.6	5	66.4	120	4	0.033
SLN	162	311	321.3	200	.622	8	4	131	16	20.1	2	160.7	115	5	0.043

Name	G	GOps	AGOps	GO	AGDA	FE	TE	1B	2B	AGO/2B	3B	AGO/3B	DPOps	DPI	DP%
Joyner, Wally	119	226	232.5	166	.714	2	1	71	11	21.1	3	77.5	73	3	0.041
McCarty, Dave	51	56	57.5	41	.713	2	1	15	2	28.7	0	0.0	24	1	0.042
King, Jeff	92	174	175.0	123	.703	1	1	61	8	21.9	1	175.0	65	8	0.123
Colbrunn, Greg	134	324	329.6	222	.673	6	0	115	18	18.3	2	164.8	90	10	0.111
Grace, Mark	141	317	324.2	218	.672	3	1	120	17	19.1	4	81.0	108	7	0.065
Conine, Jeff	48	100	100.0	67	.670	2	0	36	1	100.0	1	100.0	27	4	0.148
Johnson, Mark	100	192	195.0	129	.662	4	1	77	7	27.9	1	195.0	68	5	0.074
Jefferies, Gregg	53	118	122.5	80	.653	1	0	39	6	20.4	2	61.3	29	3	0.103
Mabry, John	146	254	262.6	171	.651	5	3	103	15	17.5	2	131.3	91	4	0.044
Karros, Eric	154	347	363.2	229	.630	13	2	128	14	25.9	2	181.6	105	6	0.057
Galarraga, Andres	159	402	408.3	256	.627	12	2	170	22	18.6	7	58.3	101	4	0.040
Morris, Hal	140	278	287.0	180	.627	7	2	102	14	20.5	0	0.0	104	6	0.058
Brogna, Rico	52	97	98.4	61	.620	2	0	43	6	16.4	5	19.7	25	2	0.080
Bagwell, Jeff	162	365	383.1	236	.616	11	5	139	10	38.3	1	383.1	125	10	0.080
McGriff, Fred	158	292	301.7	176	.583	10	2	133	18	16.8	2	150.9	116	6	0.052
Huskey, Butch	75	163	163.7	95	.580	8	2	71	10	16.4	2	81.9	70	5	0.071
Segui, David	114	214	219.7	123	.560	6	1	89	16	13.7	1	219.7	58	3	0.052
Rodriguez, Henry	51	97	100.6	55	.547	5	0	39	5	20.1	2	50.3	38	1	0.026
Carreon, Mark	72	122	127.5	69	.541	8	0	42	12	10.6	2	63.7	43	0	0.000

Perhaps the big surprise here is the continuing lackluster showing of reputed gloveman David Segui. As a regular, he has never posted a league-average DA. Jeff Bagwell seems to have endured a setback and Fred McGriff's decline continued. You might be surprised that Mark Grace isn't the leader, but he's consistently finished among the league leaders, so his reputation seems justified. NL Gold Glove, 1B: Wally Joyner.

—Second Base—

Team	G	GOps	AGOps	GO	AGDA	FE	TE	1B	2BAGO/2B	3B	AGO/3B	DPOps	DPI	DP%
League	1134	8193	8405.3	5587	.665	173	50	3330	49 171.5	7	1200.8	1658	489	0.295
ATL	162	636	651.0	455	.699	18	3	231	4 162.8	1	651.0	117	39	0.333
CHN	162	632	643.7	450	.699	7	2	260	3 214.6	0	0.0	122	39	0.320
CIN	162	542	557.4	376	.675	6	4	216	4 139.4	1	557.4	106	28	0.264
COL	162	636	644.4	433	.672	12	4	289	5 128.9	0	0.0	130	41	0.315
FLO	162	574	581.5	389	.669	11	5	229	2 290.8	0	0.0	126	45	0.357
HOU	162	575	604.5	381	.630	7	4	245	3 201.5	1	604.5	107	19	0.178
LAN	162	568	593.9	390	.657	16	2	220	3 198.0	0	0.0	93	36	0.387
MON	162	540	552.8	361	.653	11	2	224	4 138.2	0	0.0	96	29	0.302
NYN	162	606	611.5	403	.659	8	6	288	2 305.7	1	611.5	141	41	0.291
PHI	162	554	586.3	372	.634	11	3	209	4 146.6	0	0.0	110	45	0.409
PIT	162	629	636.4	406	.638	15	3	288	3 212.1	1	636.4	132	21	0.159
SDN	162	625	640.5	423	.660	11	2	231	5 128.1	1	640.5	138	37	0.268
SFN	162	530	543.5	360	.662	19	3	211	4 135.9	1	543.5	121	38	0.314
SLN	162	546	559.8	388	.693	21	7	189	3 186.6	0	0.0	119	31	0.261

Name	G	GOps	AGOps	GO	AGDA	FE	TE	1B	2BAGO/2B	3B	AGO/3B	DPOps	DPI	DP%
Thompson, Robby	62	184	186.4	132	.708	5	2	70	1 186.4	1	186.4	39	16	0.410
Lemke, Mark	**133**	**498**	**509.9**	**360**	**.706**	**14**	**2**	**175**	**3 170.0**	**0**	**0.0**	**92**	**31**	**0.337**
Boone, Bret	141	451	461.5	322	.698	4	2	179	4 115.4	1	461.5	82	25	0.305
Sandberg, Ryne	146	518	527.7	367	.696	6	0	220	3 175.9	0	0.0	95	30	0.316
Alicea, Luis	125	338	348.7	237	.680	18	6	120	3 116.2	0	0.0	80	17	0.213
Castillo, Luis	41	140	141.2	96	.680	1	2	53	0 0.0	0	0.0	29	13	0.448
Reed, Jody	145	509	522.6	353	.675	7	2	183	2 261.3	1	522.6	114	33	0.289
Young, Eric	139	529	535.9	362	.675	8	4	244	3 178.6	0	0.0	110	38	0.345
Gallego, Mike	43	150	152.6	102	.669	2	1	58	0 0.0	0	0.0	28	10	0.357
Vizcaino, Jose	93	320	322.8	215	.666	5	1	154	1 322.8	1	322.8	63	18	0.286
King, Jeff	71	229	231.3	151	.653	7	0	104	0 0.0	0	0.0	49	11	0.224
Lansing, Mike	159	512	523.4	339	.648	10	2	219	4 130.9	0	0.0	93	28	0.301
DeShields, Delino	154	522	545.9	351	.643	15	2	211	3 182.0	0	0.0	87	33	0.379
Garcia, Carlos	77	258	259.5	166	.640	5	0	117	2 129.8	1	259.5	56	6	0.107
Alfonzo, Edgardo	66	228	230.1	146	.635	3	5	108	1 230.1	0	0.0	62	15	0.242
Veras, Quilvio	67	236	239.7	151	.630	5	1	100	1 239.7	0	0.0	52	14	0.269
Biggio, Craig	162	565	594.4	374	.629	6	4	240	3 198.1	1	594.4	103	17	0.165
Morandini, Mickey	137	454	479.4	300	.626	8	3	182	3 159.8	0	0.0	94	37	0.394
Scarsone, Steve	74	205	212.5	133	.626	8	1	89	1 212.5	0	0.0	49	10	0.204

Several surprises among NL second basemen: Mickey Morandini continues to plummet, Ryne Sandberg put up a pretty solid season after a year and a half off and two-time reigning league DA champ Delino DeShields had a season in the field to match his awful year at the plate. Mark Lemke had rated second behind DeShields among regulars each of the last two years, so his lead this year isn't shocking. Meanwhile, it would seem a certain gold-plated ex-catcher continues to play second about as well as you'd expect an ex-catcher: Biggio finished near the bottom, as he always has since he gave up a chest protector. Particularly ugly was his appalling DP%, which along with Carlos Garcia's mark this year, ranks among the worst ever. NL Gold Glove, 2B: Mark Lemke.

—Third Base—

Team	G	GOps	AGOps	GO	AGDA	FE	TE	1B	2B	AGO/2B	3B	AGO/3B	DPOps	DPI	DP%
League	1134	7476	7708.6	4513	.585	230	108	2868	532	14.5	8	963.6	1738	288	0.166
ATL	162	467	482.8	273	.565	16	5	186	38	12.7	0	0.0	92	14	0.152
CHN	162	461	471.9	286	.606	8	6	177	45	10.5	0	0.0	112	19	0.170
CIN	162	576	595.7	348	.584	22	9	211	51	11.7	1	595.7	127	22	0.173
COL	162	622	631.5	387	.613	18	4	240	43	14.7	0	0.0	140	35	0.250
FLO	162	553	562.1	329	.585	17	4	197	42	13.4	1	562.1	146	24	0.164
HOU	162	563	596.2	327	.548	16	13	222	45	13.2	0	0.0	146	19	0.130
LAN	162	418	445.9	224	.502	13	4	188	31	14.4	1	445.9	110	8	0.073
MON	162	595	609.6	377	.618	14	15	191	45	13.5	0	0.0	125	18	0.144
NYN	162	555	560.2	333	.594	21	19	229	29	19.3	0	0.0	128	19	0.148
PHI	162	445	474.5	269	.567	15	6	161	27	17.6	1	474.5	86	18	0.209
PIT	162	635	642.5	397	.618	18	8	248	38	16.9	2	321.3	145	27	0.186
SDN	162	572	588.4	351	.597	18	5	216	41	14.4	0	0.0	130	23	0.177
SFN	162	524	540.4	309	.572	23	7	197	27	20.0	1	540.4	150	28	0.187
SLN	162	490	508.5	303	.596	11	3	205	30	16.9	1	508.5	101	14	0.139

Name	G	GOps	AGOps	GO	AGDA	FE	TE	1B	2B	AGO/2B	3B	AGO/3B	DPOps	DPI	DP%
Andrews, Shane	**123**	**385**	**392.8**	**256**	**.652**	**8**	**7**	**116**	**30**	**13.1**	**0**	**0.0**	**76**	**11**	**.145**
Spiers, Bill	76	133	140.9	90	.639	1	4	39	9	15.7	0	0.0	37	7	.189
Castilla, Vinny	160	598	606.5	377	.622	17	3	228	41	14.8	0	0.0	134	34	.254
Gomez, Leo	124	280	285.9	175	.612	4	3	105	28	10.2	0	0.0	68	14	.206
Kent, Jeff	89	302	304.1	185	.608	12	9	127	19	16.0	0	0.0	67	13	.194
Pendleton, Terry	149	473	481.1	292	.607	17	2	160	36	13.4	1	481.1	116	20	.172
Caminiti, Ken	145	498	510.6	309	.605	16	4	181	37	13.8	0	0.0	113	20	.177
Magadan, Dave	51	95	97.9	59	.602	2	1	38	9	10.9	0	0.0	27	4	.148
Hayes, Charlie	124	456	461.2	277	.601	11	7	177	26	17.7	2	230.6	106	20	.189
Greene, Willie	74	231	237.5	140	.589	9	5	75	20	11.9	0	0.0	48	9	.188
Gaetti, Gary	133	364	376.6	220	.584	8	1	157	24	15.7	1	376.6	84	13	.155
Branson, Jeff	64	151	154.7	90	.582	6	3	57	14	11.1	0	0.0	35	6	.171
Arias, Alex	59	111	112.4	65	.578	2	1	46	5	22.5	0	0.0	31	6	.194
Williams, Matt	92	292	301.8	173	.573	10	3	111	19	15.9	1	301.8	91	12	.132
Zeile, Todd	106	293	317.4	180	.567	7	3	107	19	16.7	1	317.4	61	10	.164
Jones, Chipper	118	314	327.2	183	.559	9	4	132	25	13.1	0	0.0	61	9	.148
Berry, Sean	110	364	385.1	201	.522	14	8	152	28	13.8	0	0.0	94	11	.117
Blowers, Mike	90	221	238.1	118	.496	7	2	107	15	15.9	0	0.0	56	4	.071

After finishing last in the AL in '95 and last in the NL in '96, I think its fair to say Mike Blowers is one of the worst in the business. Sean Berry and Todd Zeile annually bring up the rear as well. Perhaps the biggest surprise was the performance of Chipper Jones, who after being near the top in '95, fell off dramatically. Most of the NL leaders are surprises, so knowing who among Andrews, Castilla or Gomez had a good year, and who will be consistently good is chancy. NL Gold Glove, 3B: Shane Andrews.

Defensive Average

—Shortstop—

Team	G	GOps	AGOps	GO	AGDA	FE	TE	1B	2B	AGO/2B	3B	AGO/3B	DPOps	DPI	DP%
League	1134	9619	9885.0	6264	.634	227	129	4115	51	193.8	2	4942.5	1987	683	0.344
ATL	162	644	660.8	429	.649	18	13	263	2	330.4	0	0.0	118	42	0.356
CHN	162	682	694.6	467	.672	20	10	264	1	694.6	0	0.0	115	42	0.365
CIN	162	677	698.6	441	.631	14	6	294	6	116.4	0	0.0	155	47	0.303
COL	162	702	712.4	443	.622	15	17	326	4	178.1	0	0.0	136	45	0.331
FLO	162	709	718.8	468	.651	12	8	270	2	359.4	0	0.0	163	62	0.380
HOU	162	704	745.0	418	.561	21	9	337	6	124.2	0	0.0	145	50	0.345
LAN	162	676	706.9	455	.644	18	8	259	1	706.9	0	0.0	156	60	0.385
MON	162	678	694.7	434	.625	17	10	287	3	231.6	1	694.7	139	36	0.259
NYN	162	676	682.2	436	.639	15	12	329	2	341.1	0	0.0	149	55	0.369
PHI	162	617	648.2	431	.665	14	8	228	3	216.1	0	0.0	117	41	0.350
PIT	162	754	762.9	489	.641	10	4	355	7	109.0	0	0.0	157	44	0.280
SDN	162	738	759.6	450	.592	19	6	334	5	151.9	0	0.0	147	44	0.299
SFN	162	680	699.5	435	.622	16	12	279	6	116.6	1	699.5	158	58	0.367
SLN	162	682	702.0	468	.667	18	6	290	3	234.0	0	0.0	132	57	0.432

Name	G	GOps	AGOps	GO	AGDA	FE	TE	1B	2B	AGO/2B	3B	AGO/3B	DPOps	DPI	DP%
Belliard, Rafael	63	146	151.8	108	.712	2	1	53	0	0.0	0	0.0	25	9	.360
Sanchez, Rey	**92**	**384**	**390.6**	**274**	**.701**	**9**	**2**	**139**	**1**	**390.6**	**0**	**0.0**	**63**	**22**	**.349**
Jones, Chipper	38	133	133.5	93	.697	2	2	53	0	0.0	0	0.0	33	11	.333
Smith, Ozzie	52	211	220.3	151	.685	7	1	76	2	110.2	0	0.0	43	22	.512
Stocker, Kevin	118	433	455.0	300	.659	8	5	160	3	151.7	0	0.0	89	30	.337
Clayton, Royce	113	467	477.4	314	.658	11	5	212	1	477.4	0	0.0	89	35	.393
Renteria, Edgar	106	453	457.3	301	.658	8	3	169	2	228.7	0	0.0	102	36	.353
Gagne, Greg	127	534	558.8	367	.657	14	7	196	1	558.8	0	0.0	121	48	.397
Bell, Jay	151	660	668.6	435	.651	7	4	309	7	95.5	0	0.0	133	35	.263
Aurilia, Rich	93	309	319.0	206	.646	7	3	116	2	159.5	0	0.0	70	22	.314
Hernandez, Jose	87	289	295.0	188	.637	11	8	119	0	0.0	0	0.0	51	19	.373
Larkin, Barry	151	585	605.2	385	.636	12	5	251	6	100.9	0	0.0	130	37	.285
Ordonez, Rey	150	600	606.3	383	.632	15	12	289	2	303.1	0	0.0	126	46	.365
Grudzielanek, Mark	153	634	649.5	405	.624	16	10	263	3	216.5	1	649.5	129	34	.264
Dunston, Shawon	78	320	326.3	202	.619	7	8	131	4	81.6	1	326.3	74	31	.419
Weiss, Walt	155	643	652.6	403	.618	13	16	293	4	163.2	0	0.0	123	41	.333
Blauser, Jeff	79	310	317.7	191	.601	14	9	137	2	158.9	0	0.0	51	20	.392
Gomez, Chris	89	393	402.6	237	.589	11	2	182	4	100.6	0	0.0	89	27	.303
Miller, Orlando	116	453	477.9	277	.580	12	7	209	5	95.6	0	0.0	91	32	.352
Gutierrez, Ricky	74	224	239.5	128	.534	9	2	109	1	239.5	0	0.0	48	16	.333

Well how about that? Raffy Belliard's reputation seems to be grounded in fact. As bad as Jeff Blauser seems here, he's two years removed from leading the NL, and he had a good '95 as well. In more ways than one, his year was washed out by injuries. Wunderkind Rey Ordonez didn't do particularly well away from SportsCenter, but he turned the deuce well and he might improve in '97 as he learns to position himself. Barry Larkin's year might seem to be a disappointment, but it's actually an improvement over '95, when he finished last in the league. Since he usually winds up around average, it would be premature to read too much into that '95 season. NL Gold Glove, SS: Rey Sanchez.

—Left Field—

Team	G	FOps	AFOps	FO	AFDA	FE	TE	1B	2B	AFO/2B	3B	AFO/3B
League	1134	6762	6995.5	4028	.576	93	13	1466	1269	5.5	68	102.9
ATL	162	441	458.6	240	.523	9	1	100	94	4.9	7	65.5
CHN	162	498	510.4	309	.605	4	1	97	90	5.7	3	170.1
CIN	162	484	503.7	278	.552	4	2	96	106	4.8	12	42.0
COL	162	464	472.3	276	.584	2	3	103	80	5.9	7	67.5
FLO	162	488	497.8	260	.522	6	2	138	84	5.9	2	248.9
HOU	162	478	504.3	310	.615	7	1	74	100	5.0	4	126.1
LAN	162	446	472.1	274	.580	9	2	106	70	6.7	8	59.0
MON	162	446	460.1	252	.548	10	1	104	82	5.6	2	230.0
NYN	162	574	580.4	345	.594	9	0	140	84	6.9	3	193.5
PHI	162	455	485.4	289	.595	5	0	87	95	5.1	4	121.4
PIT	162	467	474.4	251	.529	8	0	103	112	4.2	8	59.3
SDN	162	488	501.2	323	.644	5	0	88	80	6.3	3	167.1
SFN	162	544	564.2	311	.551	6	0	127	112	5.0	2	282.1
SLN	162	489	506.9	310	.612	9	0	103	80	6.3	3	169.0

Name	G	FOps	AFOps	FO	AFDA	FE	TE	1B	2B	AFO/2B	3B	AFO/3B
Jefferies, Gregg	51	155	160.7	110	.684	0	0	28	25	6.4	1	160.7
Henderson, Rickey	**114**	**289**	**296.4**	**199**	**.671**	**3**	**0**	**52**	**43**	**6.9**	**0**	**0.0**
May, Derrick	70	184	190.4	124	.651	2	1	29	36	5.3	2	95.2
Gant, Ron	116	337	348.1	215	.618	5	0	73	52	6.7	3	116.0
Mouton, James	79	155	166.6	100	.600	4	0	27	28	5.9	0	0.0
Burks, Ellis	129	344	348.6	209	.599	2	3	72	60	5.8	5	69.7
Gilkey, Bernard	151	516	522.0	310	.594	6	0	127	76	6.9	3	174.0
Gonzalez, Luis	139	380	388.6	229	.589	3	0	75	76	5.1	3	129.5
Floyd, Cliff	69	118	119.9	70	.584	3	0	28	16	7.5	1	119.9
Cangelosi, John	53	97	104.5	61	.584	1	0	12	25	4.2	1	104.5
Hollandsworth, Todd	122	289	304.0	175	.576	4	1	75	44	6.9	5	60.8
Bonds, Barry	148	483	499.4	281	.563	6	0	112	92	5.4	2	249.7
Klesko, Ryan	144	349	362.2	192	.530	4	1	77	76	4.8	5	72.4
Conine, Jeff	128	348	357.3	188	.526	5	0	94	64	5.6	1	357.3
Martin, Al	142	342	346.9	179	.516	6	0	79	82	4.2	6	57.8
Incaviglia, Pete	70	161	172.2	88	.511	3	0	36	40	4.3	2	86.1
Rodriguez, Henry	89	195	200.3	101	.504	6	0	48	43	4.7	0	0.0

For all the flak Ryan Klesko has to deal with, it would seem he's adequate compared to Al Martin, who usually finishes right around the bottom year after year. Despite a new league, and coming off of a poor '95, Rickey Henderson adapted pretty quickly. There's been some concern in the past that DA is unfair to Colorado outfielders, but if that's the case, it certainly didn't affect Ellis Burks' ability. Also, it's getting to the point that we can't just laugh off Derrick May; for the second time in three years, he was among the league's leaders, so he has to be doing something right. NL Gold Glove, LF: Rickey Henderson.

—Center Field—

Team	G	FOps	AFOps	FO	AFDA	FE	TE	1B	2B	AFO/2B	3B	AFO/3B
League	1134	9262	9586.8	5496	.573	74	19	2283	1375	7.0	246	39.0
ATL	162	616	638.4	370	.580	1	0	147	98	6.5	19	33.6
CHN	162	621	637.7	371	.582	4	1	146	91	7.0	18	35.4
CIN	162	645	669.6	387	.578	3	4	142	99	6.8	28	23.9
COL	162	657	670.0	362	.540	5	1	156	112	6.0	26	25.8
FLO	162	644	656.5	356	.542	4	1	190	85	7.7	15	43.8
HOU	162	645	685.2	383	.559	13	2	129	124	5.5	19	36.1
LAN	162	593	626.3	378	.604	4	1	144	75	8.4	13	48.2
MON	162	627	643.8	403	.626	3	4	146	68	9.5	12	53.6
NYN	162	721	729.3	419	.574	10	3	205	83	8.8	11	66.3
PHI	162	722	776.4	430	.554	4	1	176	120	6.5	19	40.9
PIT	162	695	706.3	365	.517	10	0	195	118	6.0	23	30.7
SDN	162	654	674.7	398	.590	7	1	162	96	7.0	13	51.9
SFN	162	757	783.8	451	.575	4	0	175	123	6.4	20	39.2
SLN	162	665	690.0	423	.613	2	0	170	83	8.3	10	69.0

Name	G	FOps	AFOps	FO	AFDA	FE	TE	1B	2B	AFO/2B	3B	AFO/3B
Santangelo, F.P.	76	286	291.6	185	.634	2	2	68	26	11.2	7	41.7
Lankford, Ray	**144**	**563**	**583.7**	**360**	**.617**	**1**	**0**	**142**	**68**	**8.6**	**10**	**58.4**
White, Rondell	86	295	304.1	186	.612	1	1	71	36	8.4	5	60.8
Javier, Stan	53	232	241.5	147	.609	1	0	44	35	6.9	7	34.5
Cedeno, Roger	50	136	147.7	89	.603	1	0	35	18	8.2	2	73.9
Finley, Steve	160	630	650.8	387	.595	6	1	157	91	7.2	11	59.2
McRae, Brian	155	581	597.3	348	.583	4	1	131	89	6.7	16	37.3
Davis, Eric	115	419	435.7	253	.581	2	1	97	63	6.9	16	27.2
Grissom, Marquis	158	564	584.2	338	.579	1	0	134	91	6.4	17	34.4
Johnson, Lance	157	678	686.5	392	.571	10	2	196	78	8.8	10	68.7
Hunter, Brian Lee	127	460	491.8	277	.563	11	1	93	87	5.7	11	44.7
Allensworth, J.	61	246	251.2	140	.557	3	0	67	39	6.4	5	50.2
Benard, Marvin	102	440	455.8	253	.555	3	0	108	77	5.9	9	50.6
Walker, Larry	54	214	222.2	120	.540	1	0	46	43	5.2	7	31.7
White, Devon	139	541	551.3	296	.537	3	1	162	70	7.9	12	45.9
Otero, Ricky	100	449	470.8	248	.527	2	1	108	85	5.5	16	29.4
McCracken, Q.	85	246	247.7	128	.517	4	1	64	37	6.7	13	19.1
Kingery, Mike	64	215	217.0	106	.489	2	0	60	42	5.2	8	27.1

How about Mike Kingery, folks? Not just anybody gets to finish last in his league three years in a row. Lance Johnson's showing shouldn't surprise you, since he was in the middle of the pack in the AL in '95. After a very good '94, Marquis Grissom has been pretty average each of the last two seasons, but Ray Lankford's '96 was one of the greatest full-seasons for a NL center fielder in some time. NL Gold Glove, CF: Ray Lankford.

—Right Field—

Team	G	FOps	AFOps	FO	AFDA	FE	TE	1B	2B	AFO/2B	3B	AFO/3B
League	1134	7463	7715.0	4504	.584	95	28	1613	1170	6.6	217	35.6
ATL	162	560	576.5	372	0.645	8	3	114	64	9.0	11	52.4
CHN	162	572	586.8	344	0.586	9	2	118	89	6.6	16	36.7
CIN	162	485	502.5	302	0.601	6	0	100	69	7.3	20	25.1
COL	162	523	533.7	279	0.523	8	2	105	117	4.6	24	22.2
FLO	162	515	525.8	266	0.506	4	3	134	90	5.8	24	21.9
HOU	162	490	519.5	298	0.574	4	3	87	93	5.6	16	32.5
LAN	162	575	608.0	355	0.584	11	1	137	73	8.3	6	101.3
MON	162	493	507.2	303	0.597	5	1	109	72	7.0	11	46.1
NYN	162	536	542.0	318	0.587	12	3	121	78	6.9	18	30.1
PHI	162	588	625.2	381	0.609	9	4	112	95	6.6	13	48.1
PIT	162	555	562.5	339	0.603	3	1	111	86	6.5	23	24.5
SDN	162	480	496.4	274	0.552	5	1	125	77	6.4	12	41.4
SFN	162	539	558.2	314	0.563	10	1	122	91	6.1	11	50.7
SLN	162	552	571.8	359	0.628	1	3	118	76	7.5	12	47.7

Name	G	FOps	AFOps	FO	AFDA	FE	TE	1B	2B	AFO/2B	3B	AFO/3B
Sanders, Reggie	**80**	**232**	**241.4**	**158**	**.654**	**2**	**0**	**44**	**25**	**9.7**	**10**	**24.1**
Walker, Larry	32	52	52.1	34	.652	0	0	8	9	5.8	1	52.1
Jordan, Brian	128	422	435.5	279	.641	1	1	83	60	7.3	10	43.5
Whiten, Mark	73	194	206.2	132	.640	5	4	36	24	8.6	3	68.7
Merced, Orlando	115	382	387.0	240	.620	2	1	71	56	6.9	18	21.5
Alou, Moises	123	319	327.3	202	.617	1	1	73	39	8.4	5	65.5
Dye, Jermaine	71	199	202.7	125	.617	2	2	49	22	9.2	3	67.6
Sosa, Sammy	124	417	428.6	253	.590	9	1	90	58	7.4	10	42.9
Obando, Sherman	47	122	125.9	74	.588	3	0	26	20	6.3	5	25.2
McGee, Willie	42	95	98.8	58	.587	0	2	25	10	9.9	2	49.4
Bell, Derek	157	462	489.2	284	.581	4	3	81	84	5.8	16	30.6
Mondesi, Raul	157	553	583.2	338	.580	11	1	134	71	8.2	5	116.6
Gwynn, Tony	111	307	318.3	183	.575	1	1	80	45	7.1	6	53.0
Ochoa, Alex	75	233	235.1	134	.570	3	2	56	32	7.3	9	26.1
Eisenreich, Jim	51	156	163.1	90	.552	3	0	36	25	6.5	7	23.3
Hill, Glenallen	97	289	304.7	160	.525	6	1	69	50	6.1	9	33.9
Bichette, Dante	139	453	464.3	235	.506	7	2	92	105	4.4	23	20.2
Sheffield, Gary	161	468	478.8	239	.499	3	3	124	83	5.8	22	21.8

Reggie Sanders is regularly among the league leaders in right, so this year was no surprise. We're showing Larry Walker here (and in center) to point out how badly out of position he was, rather than suffering from a park illusion. No such luck for Dante Bichette. With the year Gary Sheffield had with the glove, he's not just a threat to others, but to himself. Raul Mondesi might be pleased with his new Gold Glove, but he has yet to rank above average during any season of his career. Meanwhile, Brian Jordan griped publicly about not getting the Gold Glove, and it would seem he had a point. NL Gold Glove, RF: Reggie Sanders.

—Infield—

Team	G	GOps	AGOps	GO	AGDA	FE	TE	1B	2B	AGO/2B	3B	AGO/3B	DPOps	DPI	DP%
League	1134	27424	28026.0	19601	.699	768	315	8542	848	33.0	61	459.4	6090	1565	0.257
ATL	162	1873	1914.8	1340	.700	63	23	587	60	31.9	3	638.3	406	102	0.251
CHN	162	1991	2022.2	1476	.730	38	19	603	67	30.2	4	505.5	418	108	0.258
CIN	162	1936	1983.5	1391	.701	51	21	593	73	27.2	3	661.2	426	105	0.246
COL	162	2129	2152.7	1524	.708	58	27	702	72	29.9	7	307.5	449	125	0.278
FLO	162	2062	2085.3	1476	.708	49	17	594	65	32.1	4	521.3	471	145	0.308
HOU	162	1989	2075.5	1366	.658	55	31	664	62	33.5	2	1037.8	457	98	0.214
LAN	162	1818	1887.4	1311	.695	60	16	542	48	39.3	3	629.1	436	111	0.255
MON	162	1914	1951.4	1350	.692	54	28	575	70	27.9	4	487.8	393	87	0.221
NYN	162	1995	2009.4	1405	.699	56	39	694	52	38.6	8	251.2	453	124	0.274
PHI	162	1783	1864.8	1289	.691	49	18	510	50	37.3	4	466.2	380	110	0.289
PIT	162	2170	2189.8	1549	.707	48	18	725	62	35.3	5	438.0	467	105	0.225
SDN	162	2054	2097.7	1455	.694	55	15	621	63	33.3	4	524.4	450	110	0.244
SFN	162	1872	1914.0	1310	.684	74	23	575	54	35.4	7	273.4	475	128	0.269
SLN	162	1838	1880.7	1359	.723	58	20	557	50	37.6	3	626.9	409	107	0.262

—Outfield—

Team	G	FOps	AFOps	FO	AFDA	FE	TE	1B	2B	AFO/2B	3B	AFO/3B
League	1134	21201	21810.4	14028	0.643	262	60	4163	2712	8.0	351	62.1
ATL	162	1474	1517.4	982	.647	18	4	287	184	8.2	24	63.2
CHN	162	1537	1570.5	1024	.652	17	4	278	200	7.9	28	56.1
CIN	162	1454	1500.1	967	.645	13	6	262	196	7.7	37	40.5
COL	162	1472	1496.3	917	.613	15	6	290	226	6.6	38	39.4
FLO	162	1445	1469.1	882	.600	14	6	344	183	8.0	26	56.5
HOU	162	1453	1523.6	991	.650	24	6	232	211	7.2	25	60.9
LAN	162	1488	1560.5	1007	.645	24	4	312	159	9.8	16	97.5
MON	162	1431	1465.7	958	.654	18	6	284	163	9.0	18	81.4
NYN	162	1657	1672.7	1082	.647	31	6	359	180	9.3	22	76.0
PHI	162	1599	1689.7	1100	.651	18	5	289	217	7.8	25	67.6
PIT	162	1528	1547.5	955	.617	21	1	312	230	6.7	34	45.5
SDN	162	1456	1492.8	995	.667	17	2	284	169	8.8	19	78.6
SFN	162	1651	1700.4	1076	.633	20	1	337	222	7.7	22	77.3
SLN	162	1556	1603.1	1092	.681	12	3	293	172	9.3	17	94.3

—First Base/Second Base—

Team	G	GOps	AGOps	GO	AGDA	FE	TE	1B	2B	AGO/2B	3B	AGO/3B	DPOps	DPI	DP%
League	1134	11969	12216.4	8824	.722	311	78	3668	281	43.5	51	239.5	2715	594	0.219
ATL	162	862	880.3	638	.725	29	5	265	20	44.0	3	293.4	198	46	0.232
CHN	162	936	949.6	723	.761	10	3	280	22	43.2	4	237.4	211	47	0.223
CIN	162	805	823.1	602	.731	15	6	243	19	43.3	2	411.5	185	36	0.195
COL	162	938	947.8	694	.732	25	6	313	26	36.5	7	135.4	196	45	0.230
FLO	162	912	921.3	679	.737	20	5	263	21	43.9	3	307.1	201	59	0.294
HOU	162	851	883.9	621	.703	18	9	267	12	73.7	2	441.9	190	29	0.153
LAN	162	842	871.0	632	.726	29	4	243	17	51.2	2	435.5	169	43	0.254
MON	162	761	776.2	539	.694	23	3	243	24	32.3	3	258.7	160	33	0.206
NYN	162	884	890.4	636	.714	20	8	312	21	42.4	8	111.3	218	50	0.229
PHI	162	815	853.9	589	.690	20	4	235	21	40.7	3	284.6	173	51	0.295
PIT	162	912	920.0	663	.721	20	6	304	18	51.1	3	306.7	214	34	0.159
SDN	162	886	903.3	654	.724	18	4	249	20	45.2	4	225.8	209	43	0.206
SFN	162	785	801.5	566	.706	35	4	235	22	36.4	5	160.3	201	42	0.209
SLN	162	780	796.1	588	.739	29	11	216	18	44.2	2	398.0	190	36	0.189

—Second Base/Shortstop—

Team	G	GOps	AGOps	GO	AGDA	FE	TE	1B	2B	AGO/2B	3B	AGO/3B	DPOps	DPI	DP%
League	1134	16969	17373.3	11851	.682	400	179	6039	243	71.5	9	1930.4	3167	1172	0.370
ATL	162	1238	1266.0	884	.698	36	16	406	17	74.5	1	1266.0	197	81	0.411
CHN	162	1264	1285.0	917	.714	27	12	427	31	41.5	0	0.0	218	81	0.372
CIN	162	1167	1199.0	817	.681	20	10	417	28	42.8	1	1199.0	214	75	0.350
COL	162	1276	1292.0	876	.678	27	21	515	18	71.8	0	0.0	246	86	0.350
FLO	162	1220	1234.6	857	.694	23	13	413	10	123.5	1	1234.6	246	107	0.435
HOU	162	1197	1254.5	799	.637	28	13	458	22	57.0	1	1254.5	232	69	0.297
LAN	162	1196	1245.3	845	.679	34	10	397	16	77.8	0	0.0	199	96	0.482
MON	162	1150	1174.3	795	.677	28	12	403	19	61.8	0	0.0	206	65	0.316
NYN	162	1220	1229.9	839	.682	23	18	504	8	153.7	1	1229.9	251	96	0.382
PHI	162	1136	1192.8	803	.673	25	11	362	12	99.4	0	0.0	192	86	0.448
PIT	162	1304	1317.4	895	.679	25	7	521	12	109.8	1	1317.4	253	65	0.257
SDN	162	1266	1295.1	873	.674	30	8	436	21	61.7	1	1295.1	252	81	0.321
SFN	162	1149	1176.6	795	.676	35	15	395	15	78.4	2	588.3	248	96	0.387
SLN	162	1186	1215.4	856	.704	39	13	385	14	86.8	0	0.0	213	88	0.413

—Shortstop/Third Base—

Team	G	GOps	AGOps	GO	AGDA	FE	TE	1B	2B	AGO/2B	3B	AGO/3B	DPOps	DPI	DP%
League	1134	15473	15829.2	10777	.681	457	237	4893	567	27.9	10	1582.9	3107	971	0.313
ATL	162	1013	1036.7	702	.677	34	18	324	40	25.9	0	0.0	187	56	0.299
CHN	162	1056	1073.7	753	.701	28	16	324	45	23.9	0	0.0	193	61	0.316
CIN	162	1133	1162.6	789	.679	36	15	353	54	21.5	1	1162.6	231	69	0.299
COL	162	1191	1205.0	830	.689	33	21	389	46	26.2	0	0.0	235	80	0.340
FLO	162	1151	1165.0	797	.684	29	12	332	44	26.5	1	1165.0	260	86	0.331
HOU	162	1140	1194.0	745	.624	37	22	399	50	23.9	0	0.0	240	69	0.287
LAN	162	976	1016.3	679	.668	31	12	299	31	32.8	1	1016.3	225	68	0.302
MON	162	1153	1175.2	811	.690	31	25	332	46	25.5	1	1175.2	222	54	0.243
NYN	162	1116	1124.1	769	.684	36	31	387	31	36.3	0	0.0	227	74	0.326
PHI	162	968	1010.9	700	.692	29	14	275	29	34.9	1	1010.9	167	59	0.353
PIT	162	1259	1270.8	886	.697	28	12	422	44	28.9	2	635.4	247	71	0.287
SDN	162	1169	1195.4	801	.670	37	11	373	43	27.8	0	0.0	226	67	0.296
SFN	162	1090	1115.8	744	.667	39	19	343	32	34.9	2	557.9	254	86	0.339
SLN	162	1058	1084.6	771	.711	29	9	341	32	33.9	1	1084.6	193	71	0.368

Defensive Average Areas of Responsibility

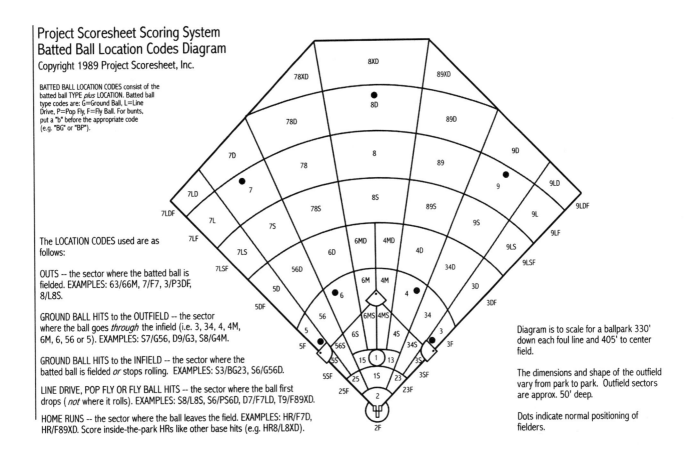

Project Scoresheet Scoring System
Batted Ball Location Codes Diagram

Copyright 1989 Project Scoresheet, Inc.

BATTED BALL LOCATION CODES consist of the batted ball TYPE *plus* LOCATION. Batted ball type codes are: G=Ground Ball, L=Line Drive, P=Pop Fly, F=Fly Ball. For bunts, put a "b" before the appropriate code (e.g. "BG" or "BP").

The LOCATION CODES used are as follows:

OUTS -- the sector where the batted ball is fielded. EXAMPLES: 63/66M, 7/F7, 3/P3DF, 8/L8S.

GROUND BALL HITS to the OUTFIELD -- the sector where the ball goes *through* the infield (i.e. 3, 34, 4, 4M, 6M, 6, 56 or 5). EXAMPLES: S7/G56, D9/G3, S8/G4M.

GROUND BALL HITS to the INFIELD -- the sector where the batted ball is fielded *or* stops rolling. EXAMPLES: S3/BG23, S6/G56D.

LINE DRIVE, POP FLY OR FLY BALL HITS -- the sector where the ball first drops (*not* where it rolls). EXAMPLES: S8/L8S, S6/PS6D, D7/F7LD, T9/F89XD.

HOME RUNS -- the sector where the ball leaves the field. EXAMPLES: HR/F7D, HR/F89XD. Score inside-the-park HRs like other base hits (e.g. HR8/L8XD).

Diagram is to scale for a ballpark 330' down each foul line and 405' to center field.

The dimensions and shape of the outfield vary from park to park. Outfield sectors are approx. 50' deep.

Dots indicate normal positioning of fielders.

Internet Baseball Awards

The following is the results of the fifth annual Internet Baseball Awards, as voted on by the denizens of the Usenet rec.sport.baseball newsgroups and other cyberspace baseball fans. Although members of the BBWAA are not explicitly forbidden from voting, we do require at least 11 functional synapses for MVP, Cy Young and RoY suffrage.

120 ballots were cast this year from around the United States and Canada. We asked all participants to give some serious critical thought to their ballots, costing us the votes of John Hickey and Zsa Zsa Gabor. Our apologies to the Gabor family.

The point system for the balloting was as follows:

MVP Ballots: 14 points for 1st place votes, 9 points for 2nd place votes, 8 for 3rd, etc., down to 1 for 10th.

Cy Young Ballots: 10 points for 1st place votes, 7 points for 2nd place votes, 5 for 3rd, 3 for fourth and 1 for 5th. (This is the one award where our point system differs from the BBWAA point system, since we have a longer ballot here)

Rookie of the Year Ballots: 5 points for 1st place votes, 3 points for 2nd place votes and 1 point for 3rd place votes.

Thanks to Steven Carter, David Pease and Dave "Bordick Boy" Nieporent for their assistance and encouragement, and special thanks to the voters, who took the matter seriously and spent the time to fill out complete and thoughtful ballots.

AL Most Valuable Player

The AL MVP was about as close as a Chicago alderman election. Alex Rodriguez grabbed the award easily. Last year's Internet AL MVP, Albert Belle, finished fourth. Frank Thomas finished fifth; he's finished in the top six every year we've held these awards. The highest ranking pitcher, Mariano Rivera, finished twelfth. Inexplicably, Juan Gonzalez finished in the top three here as well.

NL Most Valuable Player

The NL MVP race was extremely tight, with Mike Piazza edging Ken Caminiti by less than a hundred points. Barry Bonds, who has never finished lower than fourth in this balloting, wasn't that far off in third place, another hundred points back. Last year's BBWAA MVP winner, Barry Larkin, finished 5th, while last year's Internet MVP Winner, Greg Maddux, finished 15th. The highest ranking pitcher in the balloting this year was Kevin Brown, who nudged Todd Hundley out of the #9 spot.

AL Cy Young

The Internet AL Cy Young race was a laugher, as Pat Hentgen easily outdistanced all competitors. Mariano Rivera posted the best year ever by a middle reliever in the voting,

finishing second. The top eight candidates received over 95% of the points, indicating widespread agreement on the top pitchers in the league.

NL Cy Young

The Internet NL Cy Young race was a bit more competitive, but Kevin Brown still won handily over the runner-up, John Smoltz. Greg Maddux, the incumbent, finished third. The top five finishers came from only two teams, the Atlanta Braves and the Florida Marlins. Many more pitchers in the NL than in the AL recieved at least one vote.

AL Rookie of the Year

Derek Jeter bashed and gloved his way to the highest point total in Internet Rookie of the Year voting history. He overwhelmed the competition with an incredible 505 points, and took 98 of 105 first place votes. The second-place dogfight was considerably more suspensful, where Chicago's James Baldwin beat out KC's Jose Rosado by a mere 5.5 points. Rosado actually had more first and second place points, but Baldwin's fuller season must have earned him enough third place votes to edge out Rosado.

NL Rookie of the Year

Los Angeles may be perpetually awarded the BBWAA NL Rookie of the Year, but they lost out again in the Internet Awards as Florida's Edgar Renteria handily won the voting, with Dodger and BBWAA favorite Todd Hollandsworth finishing back in third. Coming in second was Jason Kendall, with a rather bizarre distribution of votes; people really didn't know where to put him on their ballots. A point of pride for the InetBA: Rey Ordonez was never in the running.

One more balloting note. This is the first year of these awards (except, obviously, for the first) that none of the winners had won their awards in previous years. It certainly was a unique baseball season. (Of course, the winner of the Internet NL MVP this year, Mike Piazza, did win the Internet NL Rookie of the Year award back in 1993.)

Here's a brief history of the Internet Baseball Awards. Next year's balloting begins in the last three weeks of the season at: http://www.baseballprospectus.com.

Year	AL MVP	NL MVP	AL Cy	NL Cy	AL RotY	NL RotY
1995	A.Belle	G.Maddux	R.Johnson	G.Maddux	G.Anderson	H.Nomo
1993	F.Thomas	B.Bonds	K.Appier	G.Maddux	T.Salmon	M.Piazza
1992	F.Thomas	B.Bonds	R.Clemens	G.Maddux	P.Listach	R.Sanders
1991	C.Ripken	B.Bonds	R.Clemens	T.Glavine	C.Knoblauch	J.Bagwell

The Internet Baseball Awards are the extremely hazardous project of Greg Spira, with help from Steven Carter, Dave Kirsch, David Pease, and David Nieporent. These award results may be excerpted from *Baseball Prospectus 1997* in any form provided credit is fully disclosed.

AL Most Valuable Player Voting

Rank	Player	1	2	3	4	5	6	7	8	9	10	B	P
1	**Rodriguez, A**	**87**	**15**	**8**	**3**	**1**	**1**	**1**	**0**	**0**	**0**	**116.0**	**1453.0**
2	McGwire, M	9	40	22	10	8	5	5	5	1	1	106.0	843.0
3	Gonzalez, J	8	17	14	9	4	5	7	3	6	7	80.0	545.0
4	Belle, A	3	8	15	11	16	9	8	11	7	8	96.0	539.0
5	Thomas, F	0	5	10	13	20	15	10	10	2	4	89.0	489.0
6	Anderson, B	2	6	12	16	13	9	8	8	2	5	81.0	462.0
7	Thome, J	2	11	16	14	6	5	5	4	7	2	72.0	462.0
8	Griffey, K	0	2	4	10	11	10	12	9	13	4	75.5	341.5
9	Knoblauch, C	1	2	4	10	6	9	7	10	9	5	63.0	296.0
10	Vaughn, M	1	3	1	2	9	8	8	13	8	6	59.0	250.0
11	Martinez, E	0	1	1	3	3	4	8	8	7	11	46.0	157.0
12	Rivera, M	3	2	1	2	3	5	3	2	5	4	29.5	156.5
13	Williams, B	0	1	0	2	3	4	5	0	3	5	23.0	92.0
14	Rodriguez, I	1	0	2	0	0	3	3	2	4	6	21.0	77.0
15	Hentgen, P	0	1	2	0	2	2	1	3	1	3	15.0	65.0
16	Alomar, R	0	0	0	0	1	1	4	3	10	7	26.0	63.0
17	Palmeiro, R	0	1	0	3	0	2	1	2	4	2	15.0	60.0
18	Pettitte, A	0	0	0	0	1	5	2	0	0	3	11.0	42.0
19	Lofton, K	0	0	0	1	1	1	1	3	2	0	9.0	35.0
20	Molitor, P	0	0	0	0	1	0	0	1	3	1	6.0	16.0
20	Murray, E	0	0	2	0	0	0	0	0	0	0	2.0	16.0
22	Fielder, C	1	0	0	0	0	0	0	0	0	0	1.0	14.0
23	Fernandez, A	0	0	0	1	0	0	1	0	1	0	3.0	13.0
24	Phillips, T	0	0	0	0	0	2	0	0	1	0	3.0	12.0
25	Greer, R	0	0	0	0	0	0	1	1	2	0	4.0	11.0
26	Jeter, D	0	0	0	0	0	0	1	1	0	2	4.0	9.0
27	Clemens, R	0	0	0	0	0	0	1	0	2	0	3.0	8.0
27	Hernandez, R	0	0	0	0	0	0	2	0	0	0	2.0	8.0
29	Hill, K	0	0	0	0	0	0	0	1	0	3	4.0	6.0
30	Edmonds, J	0	0	0	0	0	1	0	0	0	0	1.0	5.0
31	Baines, H	0	0	0	0	0	0	0	1	0	0	1.0	3.0
31	McLemore, M	0	0	0	0	0	0	0	1	0	0	1.0	3.0
31	Nagy, C	0	0	0	0	0	0	0	1	0	0	1.0	3.0
34	Buhner, J	0	0	0	0	0	0	0	0	1	0	1.0	2.0
34	Clark, W	0	0	0	0	0	0	0	0	1	0	1.0	2.0
34	Ripken, C	0	0	0	0	0	0	0	0	0	2	2.0	2.0
37	Higginson, B	0	0	0	0	0	0	0	0	0	1	1.0	1.0
37	Jaha, J	0	0	0	0	0	0	0	0	0	1	1.0	1.0
37	Martinez, T	0	0	0	0	0	0	0	0	0	1	1.0	1.0
37	Marzano, J	0	0	0	0	0	0	0	0	0	1	1.0	1.0
37	Ramirez, M	0	0	0	0	0	0	0	0	0	1	1.0	1.0
37	Vaughn, G	0	0	0	0	0	0	0	0	0	1	1.0	1.0
	Totals	*118*	*115*	*114*	*110*	*109*	*106*	*105*	*103*	*102*	*97*	*1079.0*	*6583.0*

NL Most Valuable Player Voting

Rank	Player	1	2	3	4	5	6	7	8	9	10	B	P
1	**Piazza, M**	**45**	**28**	**16**	**11**	**6**	**4**	**0**	**1**	**0**	**0**	**111.0**	**1146.0**
2	Caminiti, K	35	21	18	22	9	6	0	0	1	0	112.0	1063.0
3	Bonds, B	23	28	29	12	6	3	2	4	0	0	107.0	961.0
4	Sheffield, G	10	18	15	20	16	8	4	1	3	3	98.0	726.0
5	Larkin, B	0	6	9	10	22	14	10	6	7	2	86.0	472.0
6	Bagwell, J	0	0	4	6	15	20	17	12	6	4	84.0	384.0
7	Jones, C	0	1	4	9	5	15	20	12	14	7	87.0	360.0
8	Burks, E	0	5	6	3	4	2	12	11	10	10	63.0	259.0
9	Brown, K	1	4	4	4	8	8	8	4	4	7	52.0	257.0
10	Hundley, T	0	0	1	2	2	4	6	18	7	10	50.0	156.0
11	Smoltz, J	0	1	4	5	2	3	5	4	2	9	35.0	148.0
12	Gilkey, B	0	0	0	0	3	0	2	41	41	6	39.0	82.0
13	Galarraga, A	1	0	1	1	2	4	2	0	3	4	18.0	79.0
14	Finley, S	0	0	1	1	1	4	1	5	2	4	19.0	68.0
15	Maddux, G	0	0	0	0	1	2	0	6	5	3	17.0	47.0
16	Gwynn, T	0	0	0	1	1	0	2	1	2	1	8.0	29.0
17	Lankford, R	0	0	0	0	0	2	1	2	3	2	10.0	28.0
17	Sosa, S	0	0	0	0	0	0	2	3	4	3	12.0	28.0
19	Benes, An	0	0	0	0	2	1	1	1	1	0	6.0	26.0
20	Rodriguez, H	0	0	0	1	0	1	1	0	3	1	7.0	23.0
21	Jordan, B	0	0	0	0	0	1	1	2	1	1	6.0	18.0
22	Grissom, M	0	0	1	1	0	0	0	0	0	0	2.0	15.0
23	Glavine, T	0	0	0	1	0	0	1	0	0	0	2.0	11.0
24	Bichette, D	0	0	0	0	0	1	0	1	1	0	3.0	10.0
24	Davis, E	0	0	0	1	0	0	0	0	1	1	3.0	10.0
26	Hoffman, T	0	1	0	0	0	0	0	0	0	0	1.0	9.0
26	McGriff, F	0	0	0	0	1	0	0	0	1	1	3.0	9.0
28	Grudzielanek	0	0	0	0	0	1	0	0	1	1	3.0	8.0
28	Nen, R	0	0	0	0	1	0	0	0	1	0	2.0	8.0
30	Johnson, L	0	0	0	0	0	0	0	1	1	2	4.0	7.0
31	Karros, E	0	0	0	0	0	0	1	0	1	0	2.0	6.0
32	Biggio, C	0	0	0	0	0	0	0	1	0	2	3.0	5.0
33	Bell, D	0	0	0	0	0	0	1	0	0	0	1.0	4.0
33	Gant, R	0	0	0	0	0	0	1	0	0	0	1.0	4.0
33	Klesko, R	0	0	0	0	0	0	0	0	1	2	3.0	4.0
33	Mondesi, R	0	0	0	0	0	0	1	0	0	0	1.0	4.0
37	Brantley, J	0	0	0	0	0	0	0	0	1	1	2.0	3.0
37	Rojas, M	0	0	0	0	0	0	0	1	0	0	1.0	3.0
37	Young, E	0	0	0	0	0	0	0	1	0	0	1.0	3.0
	Totals	*115*	*113*	*113*	*111*	*107*	*104*	*102*	*102*	*101*	*97*	*1065.0*	*6483.0*

AL Cy Young Award Voting

Rank	Player	1	2	3	4	5	B	P
1	Hentgen	88	13	8	2	1	112	1018
2	Rivera	11	25	11	8	12.5	68	376.5
3	Pettitte	11	15	13	10	7	56	317
4	Nagy	4	20	14	15	13	66	308
5	Hill	2	10	12	18	19	61	223
6	Fernandez	1	13	13	15	9.5	52	220.5
7	Guzman	1	15	12	10	9.5	48	214.5
8	Clemens	1	4	13	18	16.5	53	173.5
9	Appier	0	0	7	1	4	12	42
10	Mussina	0	1	5	3	0	9	41
11	Hernandez	0	1	2	2	5	10	28
12	Wetteland	0	0	2	4	3	9	25
13	Percival	0	0	1	2	1	4	12
14	Cone	0	0	0	0	1	1	1
14	Pavlik	0	0	0	0	1	1	1
14	Mesa	0	0	0	0	1	1	1
	Totals	*119*	*117*	*113*	*108*	*104*	*563*	*3002*

NL Cy Young Award Voting

Rank	Player	1	2	3	4	5	B	P
1	Brown	87.5	18	5	1	0	112	1032.5
2	Smoltz	27.5	42	36	5	2	113	769.5
3	Maddux	0	46	37	10	1	94	538
4	Glavine	0	0	6	34	19	59	151
5	ALeiter	0	1	2	23	25	51	111
6	AnBenes	0	4	5	2	5	16	64
7	Hoffman	0	1	6	4	3	14	52
8	Nomo	0	1	4	3	11	19	47
9	Fassero	0	0	3	4	4	11	31
10	RMartinez	0	0	4	2	0	6	26
11	Trachsel	0	0	1	4	4	9	21
12	Schilling	0	0	1	2	1	4	12
13	Valdez	0	0	1	0	6	7	11
14	Neagle	0	0	0	1	4	5	7
15	Reynolds	0	0	0	1	3	4	6
15	Brantley	0	0	0	2	0	2	6
15	ToWorrell	0	0	0	1	3	4	6
15	Nen	0	0	0	1	3	4	6
19	Wohlers	0	0	0	1	1	2	4
20	Kile	0	0	0	1	0	1	3
20	Hamilton	0	0	0	1	0	1	3
20	AlBenes	0	0	0	1	0	1	3
20	Ritz	0	0	0	0	3	3	3
20	Stottlemyre	0	0	0	1	0	1	3
21	PJMartinez	0	0	0	0	1	1	1
21	Valenzuela	0	0	0	0	1	1	1
21	Darwin	0	0	0	0	1	1	1
	Totals	*116*	*113*	*111*	*105*	*101*	*546*	*2919*

AL Rookie of the Year Voting

Rank	Player	1	2	3	B	P
1	Jeter, D	98	5	0	103	505
2	Baldwin, J	2	31	23.5	57	126.5
3	Rosado, J	4	29	14	47	121
4	Clark, J	0	10	8	18	38
5	Giles, B	0	4	4	8	16
6	Coppinger, R	0	2	5	7	11
7	Batista, T	1	1	2	4	10
8	Brandenburg, M	0	2	2	4	8
8	Erstad, D	0	2	2	4	8
10	Wolcott, B	0	2	1	3	7
11	Coomer, R	0	1	3	4	6
12	D'Amico, J	0	1	1	2	4
12	Springer, D	0	1	1	2	4
14	Boehringer, B	0	1	0	1	3
14	Wasdin, J	0	1	0	1	3
16	Adams, W	0	0	2	2	2
16	Snopek, C	0	0	2	2	2
18	Bartee, K	0	0	1	1	1
18	Flener, H	0	0	1	1	1
18	Fox, A	0	0	1	1	1
18	Keagle, G	0	0	1	1	1
18	Lawton, M	0	0	1	1	1
18	Myers, M	0	0	1	1	1
18	Perez, R	0	0	1	1	1
18	Thompson, J	0	0	1	1	1
26	Herrera, J	0	0	0.5	1	0.5
	Totals	*105*	*93*	*79*	*278*	*883*

NL Rookie of the Year Award Voting

Rank	Player	1	2	3	B	P
1	Renteria, E	60	15	7	82	352
2	Kendall, J	21	21	19	61	187
3	Hollandsworth, T	8.5	31	18	58	153.5
4	Wagner, B	2	5	11	18	36
5	Benes, Al	3.5	3	8	15	34.5
6	Santangelo, F	3	4	7	14	34
7	Adams, T	3	4	2	9	29
8	Ordonez, R	4	2	0.5	7	26.5
9	Urbina, U	1	4	6	11	23
10	Dye, J	0	3	4	7	13
10	Wade, T	1	2	2	5	13
12	Grace, M	0	3	2	5	11
13	Mathews, T	0	2	4	6	10
14	Cordova, F	1	1	0	2	8
15	Park, C	1	0	0	1	5
16	McCracken, Q	0	1	0	1	3
17	Person, R	0	0	1	1	1
17	Wall, D	0	0	1	1	1
17	Wilson, P	0	0	1	1	1
17	Wright, J	0	0	1	1	1
21	Ochoa, A	0	0	0.5	1	0.5
	Total	*109*	*101*	*95*	*307*	*909*

Index

The following is an index of all 1,643 players listed in this book with a full DT and a comment. Following each player's name is their organization and the pages you can find that organization's players on.

-A-

Name	Org	Pages
ANDY ABAD	BOS	239-253
JEFF ABBOTT	CHW	305-323
JIM ABBOTT	ANA	389-401
KURT ABBOTT	FLA	37-53
KYLE ABBOTT	ANA	389-401
BOB ABREU	HOU	126-139
JUAN ACEVEDO	NYM	68-81
MARK ACRE	OAK	402-419
TERRY ADAMS	CHC	97-111
WILLIE ADAMS	OAK	402-419
JOEL ADAMSON	FLA	37-53
BENNY AGBAYANI	MON	54-67
RICK AGUILERA	MIN	373-388
JOSE ALBERRO	TEX	436-447
ISRAEL ALCANTARA	MON	54-67
SCOTT ALDRED	MIN	373-388
MANNY ALEXANDER	BAL	225-238
ANTONIO ALFONSECA	FLA	37-53
EDGARDO ALFONZO	MON	54-67
LUIS ALICEA	STL	154-168
DUSTIN ALLEN	SDP	198-210
JERMAINE ALLENSWORTH	PIT	140-153
CARLOS ALMANZAR	TOR	288-304
ROBERTO ALOMAR	BAL	225-238
SANDY ALOMAR	CLE	324-339
MOISES ALOU	MON	54-67
GARVIN ALSTON	COL	169-182
GABE ALVAREZ	SDP	198-210
TAVO ALVAREZ	MON	54-67
WILSON ALVAREZ	CHW	305-323
MANUEL AMADOR	PHI	82-95
RICH AMARAL	SEA	420-435
RUBEN AMARO	PHI	82-95
BRADY ANDERSON	BAL	225-238
BRIAN ANDERSON	CLE	324-339
GARRET ANDERSON	ANA	389-401
JIMMY ANDERSON	PIT	140-153
MARLON ANDERSON	PHI	82-95
SHANE ANDREWS	MON	54-67
LUIS ANDUJAR	TOR	288-304
ERIC ANTHONY	COL	169-182
KEVIN APPIER	KCR	340-359
ALEX ARIAS	FLA	37-53
DAVID ARIAS	SEA	420-435
GEORGE ARIAS	ANA	389-401
WAGNER ARIAS	MIL	360-372
JAMIE ARNOLD	ATL	23-36
ANDY ASHBY	SDP	198-210
CHRIS ASHBY	NYY	272-287
BILLY ASHLEY	LAD	183-197
PAUL ASSENMACHER	CLE	324-339
PEDRO ASTACIO	LAD	183-197
DEREK AUCOIN	MON	54-67
RICH AUDE	PIT	140-153
RICH AURILIA	SFG	211-224
BRAD AUSMUS	DET	256-271
BRUCE AVEN	CLE	324-339
STEVE AVERY	ATL	23-36
BOBBY AYALA	SEA	420-435
MANUEL AYBAR	STL	154-168

-B-

CARLOS BAERGA	MON	54-67
JEFF BAGWELL	HOU	126-139
BEN BAILEY	CIN	112-125
CORY BAILEY	STL	154-168
PHILIP BAILEY	SFG	211-224
ROGER BAILEY	COL	169-182
HAROLD BAINES	CHW	305-323
DENNIS BAIR	CHC	97-111
PAUL BAKO	CIN	112-125
JAMES BALDWIN	CHW	305-323
JEFF BALL	HOU	126-139
BRIAN BANKS	MIL	360-372
TRAVIS BAPTIST	TOR	288-304
BRIAN BARBER	STL	154-168
BRET BARBERIE	CHC	97-111
LORENZO BARCELO	SFG	211-224
MARC BARCELO	MIN	373-388
ANDY BARKETT	STL	154-168
BRIAN BARNES	DET	256-271
LARRY BARNES	ANA	389-401
MANUEL BARRIOS	HOU	126-139
TONY BARRON	MON	54-67
KIMERA BARTEE	DET	256-271
RICHARD BATCHELOR	STL	154-168
FLETCHER BATES	MON	54-67
JASON BATES	COL	169-182
TONY BATISTA	OAK	402-419
KIM BATISTE	SFG	211-224
ALLEN BATTLE	OAK	402-419
DANNY BAUTISTA	ATL	23-36
JOSE BAUTISTA	SFG	211-224
TREY BEAMON	PIT	140-153
BLAINE BEATTY	PIT	140-153
ROD BECK	SFG	211-224
RICH BECKER	MIN	373-388
MATT BEECH	PHI	82-95
TIM BELCHER	KCR	340-359
STAN BELINDA	BOS	239-253
TIM BELK	CIN	112-125
DAVID BELL	STL	154-168
DEREK BELL	HOU	126-139
JASON BELL	MIN	373-388
JAY BELL	PIT	140-153
MIKE BELL	TEX	436-447
ALBERT BELLE	CLE	324-339
MARK BELLHORN	OAK	402-419
RAFAEL BELLIARD	ATL	23-36
RONNIE BELLIARD	MIL	360-372
CLAY BELLINGER	BAL	225-238
RIGO BELTRAN	STL	154-168
ADRIAN BELTRE	LAD	183-197
ESTEBAN BELTRE	ATL	23-36
MARVIN BENARD	SFG	211-224
ALAN BENES	STL	154-168
ANDY BENES	STL	154-168
ARMANDO BENITEZ	BAL	225-238
YAMIL BENITEZ	MON	54-67
MIKE BENJAMIN	PHI	82-95
SHAYNE BENNETT	MON	54-67
JEFF BERBLINGER	STL	154-168
JASON BERE	CHW	305-323
DAVID BERG	FLA	37-53

Name	Org	Pages
SEAN BERGMAN	SDP	198-210
GERONIMO BERROA	OAK	402-419
MIKE BERRY	BAL	225-238
SEAN BERRY	HOU	126-139
MIKE BERTOTTI	CHW	305-323
ANDRES BERUMEN	SDP	198-210
TODD BETTS	CLE	324-339
BOBBY BEVEL	COL	169-182
BRIAN BEVIL	KCR	340-359
DANTE BICHETTE	COL	169-182
MIKE BIELECKI	ATL	23-36
KURT BIEREK	NYY	272-287
STEVE BIESER	MON	54-67
CRAIG BIGGIO	HOU	126-139
WILLIE BLAIR	SDP	198-210
NATE BLAND	LAD	183-197
JEFF BLAUSER	ATL	23-36
RON BLAZIER	PHI	82-95
DARIN BLOOD	SFG	211-224
MIKE BLOWERS	LAD	183-197
GEOFFREY BLUM	MON	54-67
JAMIE BLUMA	KCR	340-359
HIRAM BOCACHICA	MON	54-67
DOUG BOCHTLER	SDP	198-210
BRIAN BOEHRINGER	NYY	272-287
JOE BOEVER	PIT	140-153
WADE BOGGS	NYY	272-287
KURTISS BOGOTT	TOR	288-304
BRIAN BOHANON	TOR	288-304
TOM BOLTON	PIT	140-153
ROB BONANNO	ANA	389-401
BARRY BONDS	SFG	211-224
RICKY BONES	NYY	272-287
BOBBY BONILLA	BAL	225-238
JAMES BONNICI	SEA	420-435
AARON BOONE	CIN	112-125
BRET BOONE	CIN	112-125
JOSH BOOTY	FLA	37-53
PEDRO BORBON	ATL	23-36
PAT BORDERS	CHW	305-323
MIKE BORDICK	OAK	402-419
TOBY BORLAND	PHI	82-95
RICHIE BORRERO	BOS	239-253
CHRIS BOSIO	SEA	420-435
SHAWN BOSKIE	ANA	389-401
HEATH BOST	COL	169-182
D.J. BOSTON	PIT	140-153
RICKY BOTTALICO	PHI	82-95
KENT BOTTENFIELD	CHC	97-111
STEVE BOURGEOIS	SFG	211-224
RAFAEL BOURNIGAL	OAK	402-419
RYAN BOWEN	MIL	360-372
BRENT BOWERS	BAL	225-238
SHANE BOWERS	MIN	373-388
MARSHALL BOZE	MIL	360-372
TERRY BRADSHAW	STL	154-168
DOUG BRADY	CHW	305-323
DARREN BRAGG	BOS	239-253
MARK BRANDENBURG	BOS	239-253
DEREK BRANDOW	TOR	288-304
JEFF BRANSON	CIN	112-125
JEFF BRANTLEY	CIN	112-125
RUSSELL BRANYAN	CLE	324-339
BRENT BREDE	MIN	373-388

Name	Team	Pages
BILLY BREWER	LAD	183-197
KARY BRIDGES	HOU	126-139
STONEY BRIGGS	SDP	198-210
JOHN BRISCOE	OAK	402-419
TILSON BRITO	TOR	288-304
DOUG BROCAIL	HOU	126-139
RICO BROGNA	MON	54-67
JERRY BROOKS	FLA	37-53
SCOTT BROSIUS	OAK	402-419
JASON BROSNAN	SEA	420-435
ADRIAN BROWN	PIT	140-153
BRANT BROWN	CHC	97-111
CHAD BROWN	TOR	288-304
EMIL BROWN	OAK	402-419
KEVIN BROWN	FLA	37-53
KEVIN BROWN	TEX	436-447
RAY BROWN	CIN	112-125
BYRON BROWNE	MIL	360-372
MARK BROWNSON	COL	169-182
JACOB BRUMFIELD	TOR	288-304
CLAYTON BRUNER	DET	256-271
JULIO BRUNO	SDP	198-210
WILLIAM BRUNSON	LAD	183-197
JIM BRUSKE	LAD	183-197
ADAM BRYANT	CIN	112-125
SCOTT BRYANT	SEA	420-435
JIM BUCCHERI	MON	54-67
BRIAN BUCHANAN	NYY	272-287
MIKE BUDDIE	NYY	272-287
DAMON BUFORD	TEX	436-447
JAY BUHNER	SEA	420-435
SCOTT BULLETT	CHC	97-111
JIM BULLINGER	CHC	97-111
KIRK BULLINGER	MON	54-67
MEL BUNCH	KCR	340-359
DAVE BURBA	CIN	112-125
JOHN BURKETT	TEX	436-447
ELLIS BURKS	COL	169-182
JEROMY BURNITZ	MIL	360-372
DARREN BURTON	KCR	340-359
HOMER BUSH	SDP	198-210
ALBERT BUSTILLOS	COL	169-182
ADAM BUTLER	ATL	23-36
BRETT BUTLER	LAD	183-197
DANNY BUXBAUM	ANA	389-401
PAUL BYRD	NYM	68-81
TIM BYRDAK	KCR	340-359

-C-

MIGUEL CAIRO	TOR	288-304
DAN CAMACHO	LAD	183-197
MIKE CAMERON	CHW	305-323
KEN CAMINITI	SDP	198-210
TOM CANDIOTTI	LAD	183-197
JOHN CANGELOSI	HOU	126-139
JAY CANIZARO	SFG	211-224
KEVAN CANNON	BOS	239-253
JOSE CANSECO	BOS	239-253
CARMINE CAPPUCCIO	CHW	305-323
TODD CAREY	BOS	239-253
DAN CARLSON	SFG	211-224
RAFAEL CARMONA	SEA	420-435
CHRIS CARPENTER	TOR	288-304
CHUCK CARR	MIL	360-372
JEREMY CARR	KCR	340-359
HECTOR CARRASCO	CIN	112-125
MARK CARREON	CLE	324-339
JOE CARTER	TOR	288-304
MIKE CARTER	CHC	97-111
STEVE CARVER	PHI	82-95
RAUL CASANOVA	DET	256-271
SEAN CASEY	CLE	324-339
LARRY CASIAN	CHC	97-111
͢TE CASTELLANO	COL	169-182
͢STILLA	COL	169-182

Name	Team	Pages
BERTO CASTILLO	NYM	68-81
FRANK CASTILLO	CHC	97-111
LUIS CASTILLO	FLA	37-53
MARINO CASTILLO	SFG	211-224
TONY CASTILLO	CHW	305-323
KEVIN CASTLEBERRY	MON	54-67
RAMON CASTRO	HOU	126-139
FRANK CATALANOTTO	DET	256-271
ANDUJAR CEDENO	HOU	126-139
DOMINGO CEDENO	CHW	305-323
ROGER CEDENO	LAD	183-197
SCOTT CHAMBERS	LAD	183-197
NORM CHARLTON	SEA	420-435
CARLOS CHAVEZ	BAL	225-238
RAUL CHAVEZ	MON	54-67
BOBBY CHOUINARD	OAK	402-419
JASON CHRISTIANSEN	PIT	140-153
ERIC CHRISTOPHERSON	HOU	126-139
ARCHI CIANFROCCO	SDP	198-210
JOSE CINTRON	ANA	389-401
JEFF CIRILLO	MIL	360-372
CHRIS CLAPINSKI	FLA	37-53
DAVE CLARK	LAD	183-197
MARK CLARK	NYM	68-81
TONY CLARK	DET	256-271
WILL CLARK	TEX	436-447
STEVE CLAYBROOK	CIN	112-125
ROYCE CLAYTON	STL	154-168
ROGER CLEMENS	BOS	239-253
PAT CLINE	CHC	97-111
BRAD CLONTZ	ATL	23-36
KEN CLOUDE	SEA	420-435
DANNY CLYBURN	BAL	225-238
ALAN COCKRELL	COL	169-182
GREG COLBRUNN	FLA	37-53
VINCE COLEMAN	ANA	389-401
LOU COLLIER	PIT	140-153
BARTOLO COLON	CLE	324-339
DENNIS COLON	HOU	126-139
DAVID CONE	NYY	272-287
JEFF CONINE	FLA	37-53
DECOMBA CONNER	CIN	112-125
MATT CONNOLLY	CHC	97-111
DENNIS COOK	TEX	436-447
STEVE COOKE	PIT	140-153
BRENT COOKSON	BAL	225-238
MIKE COOLBAUGH	TEX	436-447
RON COOMER	MIN	373-388
ROCKY COPPINGER	BAL	225-238
JOEY CORA	SEA	420-435
ARCHIE CORBIN	BAL	225-238
WIL CORDERO	BOS	239-253
FRANCISCO CORDOVA	PIT	140-153
MARTY CORDOVA	MIN	373-388
BRYAN COREY	DET	256-271
RHEAL CORMIER	MON	54-67
REID CORNELIUS	CLE	324-339
JIM CORSI	OAK	402-419
JOHN COTTON	DET	256-271
STEVE COX	OAK	402-419
TIM CRABTREE	TOR	288-304
RICKEY CRADLE	TOR	288-304
CARLOS CRAWFORD	PHI	82-95
JOE CRAWFORD	NYM	68-81
PAXTON CRAWFORD	BOS	239-253
DOUG CREEK	SFG	211-224
FELIPE CRESPO	TOR	288-304
BRANDON CROMER	TOR	288-304
D.T. CROMER	OAK	402-419
TRIPP CROMER	STL	154-168
DEAN CROW	SEA	420-435
FAUSTO CRUZ	DET	256-271
JACOB CRUZ	SFG	211-224
JOSE CRUZ	SEA	420-435
NELSON CRUZ	CHW	305-323

Name	Team	Pages
JOHN CUMMINGS	DET	256-271
MIDRE CUMMINGS	PIT	140-153
WILL CUNNANE	FLA	37-53
JOHN CURL	TOR	288-304
CHAD CURTIS	LAD	183-197
KEVIN CURTIS	BAL	225-238

-D-

OMAR DAAL	MON	54-67
JEFF D'AMICO	MIL	360-372
JOHNNY DAMON	KCR	340-359
VIC DARENSBOURG	FLA	37-53
DANNY DARWIN	HOU	126-139
JEFF DARWIN	CHW	305-323
JIMMY DASPIT	OAK	402-419
BRIAN DAUBACH	NYM	68-81
BEN DAVIS	SDP	198-210
CHILI DAVIS	ANA	389-401
CLINT DAVIS	TEX	436-447
ERIC DAVIS	CIN	112-125
RUSS DAVIS	SEA	420-435
TIM DAVIS	SEA	420-435
TOMMY DAVIS	BAL	225-238
WALT DAWKINS	PHI	82-95
JASON DAWSEY	MIL	360-372
ANDRE DAWSON	FLA	37-53
LORENZO de la CRUZ	TOR	288-304
ROLAND DE LA MAZA	CLE	324-339
MAXIMO DE LA ROSA	CLE	324-339
MARIANO DE LOS SANTOS	PIT	140-153
VALERIO DE LOS SANTOS	MIL	360-372
DARREL DEAK	STL	154-168
ROB DeBOER	OAK	402-419
STEVE DECKER	COL	169-182
ROB DEER	SDP	198-210
MIKE DeJEAN	COL	169-182
CARLOS DELGADO	TOR	288-304
DAVID DELLUCCI	BAL	225-238
RICH DeLUCIA	SFG	211-224
NICK DELVECCHIO	NYY	272-287
DON DENBOW	SFG	211-224
SHANE DENNIS	SDP	198-210
TONY DeROSSO	BOS	239-253
DELINO DeSHIELDS	LAD	183-197
ELMER DESSENS	PIT	140-153
KRIS DETMERS	STL	154-168
JOHN DETTMER	ATL	23-36
CESAR DEVAREZ	BAL	225-238
MIKE DEVEREAUX	BAL	225-238
MARK DEWEY	SFG	211-224
ALEX DIAZ	SEA	420-435
EDDY DIAZ	SEA	420-435
EDWIN DIAZ	TEX	436-447
EINAR DIAZ	CLE	324-339
LINO DIAZ	KCR	340-359
JASON DICKSON	ANA	389-401
MIKE DiFELICE	STL	154-168
JERRY DiPOTO	NYM	68-81
GARY DiSARCINA	ANA	389-401
GLENN DiSARCINA	CHW	305-323
GLENN DISHMAN	PHI	82-95
BUBBA DIXON	SDP	198-210
BO DODSON	BOS	239-253
BRIAN DORSETT	CHC	97-111
DAVID DOSTER	PHI	82-95
OCTAVIO DOTEL	NYM	68-81
DOUG DRABEK	HOU	126-139
DARREN DREIFORT	LAD	183-197
KIRK DRESSENDORFER	OAK	402-419
MATT DREWS	DET	256-271
TRAVIS DRISKILL	CLE	324-339
JUSTIN DRIZOS	COL	169-182
MIKE DRUMRIGHT	DET	256-271
MATT DUNBAR	NYY	272-287
MARIANO DUNCAN	NYY	272-287

STEVE DUNN	CLE	324-339
SHAWON DUNSTON	SFG	211-224
TODD DUNWOODY	FLA	37-53
ROBERTO DURAN	TOR	288-304
MIKE DURANT	MIN	373-388
RAY DURHAM	CHW	305-323
JERMAINE DYE	ATL	23-36
MIKE DYER	MON	54-67
LEN DYKSTRA	PHI	82-95

-E-

ANGEL ECHEVARRIA	COL	169-182
DENNIS ECKERSLEY	STL	154-168
KEN EDENFIELD	ANA	389-401
JIM EDMONDS	ANA	389-401
KURT EHMANN	SFG	211-224
MARK EICHHORN	ANA	389-401
DAVE EILAND	NYY	272-287
JOEY EISCHEN	DET	256-271
JOEY EISCHEN	LAD	183-197
JIM EISENREICH	PHI	82-95
SCOTT ELARTON	HOU	126-139
CAL ELDRED	MIL	360-372
KEVIN ELSTER	TEX	436-447
ALAN EMBREE	CLE	324-339
ANGELO ENCARNACION	PIT	140-153
JOHN ERICKS	PIT	140-153
SCOTT ERICKSON	BAL	225-238
DARIN ERSTAD	ANA	389-401
KELVIM ESCOBAR	TOR	288-304
VAUGHN ESHELMAN	BOS	239-253
ALVARO ESPINOZA	NYM	68-81
BOBBY ESTALELLA	PHI	82-95
SHAWN ESTES	SFG	211-224
HORACIO ESTRADA	MIL	360-372
TONY EUSEBIO	HOU	126-139
TOM EVANS	TOR	288-304
CARL EVERETT	NYM	68-81
BRYAN EVERSGERD	TEX	436-447
SCOTT EYRE	CHW	305-323

-F-

JORGE FABREGAS	ANA	389-401
MIKE FARMER	COL	169-182
JIM FARRELL	BOS	239-253
SAL FASANO	KCR	340-359
JEFF FASSERO	MON	54-67
CARLOS FEBLES	KCR	340-359
RAMON FERMIN	DET	256-271
ALEX FERNANDEZ	CHW	305-323
OSVALDO FERNANDEZ	SFG	211-224
SID FERNANDEZ	PHI	82-95
MIKE FETTERS	MIL	360-372
MICK FIELDBINDER	MIL	360-372
CECIL FIELDER	NYY	272-287
MIKE FIGGA	NYY	272-287
NELSON FIGUEROA	NYM	68-81
CHUCK FINLEY	ANA	389-401
STEVE FINLEY	SDP	198-210
JOHN FLAHERTY	SDP	198-210
BEN FLEETHAM	MON	54-67
HUCK FLENER	TOR	288-304
DARRIN FLETCHER	MON	54-67
BRYCE FLORIE	MIL	360-372
CLIFF FLOYD	MON	54-67
CHAD FONVILLE	LAD	183-197
TOM FORDHAM	CHW	305-323
BROOK FORDYCE	CIN	112-125
TIM FORKNER	HOU	126-139
TIM FORTUGNO	CIN	112-125
TONY FOSSAS	STL	154-168
JIM FOSTER	BAL	225-238
KEVIN FOSTER	CHC	97-111
KRIS FOSTER	LAD	183-197

KEITH FOULKE	SFG	211-224
ANDY FOX	NYY	272-287
JOHN FRANCO	NYM	68-81
JULIO FRANCO	CLE	324-339
MATT FRANCO	NYM	68-81
MICAH FRANKLIN	STL	154-168
RYAN FRANKLIN	SEA	420-435
JOHN FRASCATORE	STL	154-168
SCOTT FREDRICKSON	COL	169-182
MARVIN FREEMAN	CHW	305-323
RICKY FREEMAN	CHC	97-111
SEAN FREEMAN	DET	256-271
STEVE FREY	PHI	82-95
HANLEY FRIAS	TEX	436-447
TODD FROHWIRTH	ANA	389-401
JEFF FRYE	BOS	239-253
TRAVIS FRYMAN	DET	256-271
AARON FULLER	BOS	239-253
BRAD FULLMER	MON	54-67
AARON FULTZ	SFG	211-224
CHRIS FUSSELL	BAL	225-238
MIKE FYHRIE	NYM	68-81

-G-

GARY GAETTI	STL	154-168
GREG GAGNE	LAD	183-197
EDDIE GAILLARD	DET	256-271
JAY GAINER	COL	169-182
BRYON GAINEY	NYM	68-81
STEVE GAJKOWSKI	CHW	305-323
ANDRES GALARRAGA	COL	169-182
MIKE GALLEGO	STL	154-168
RON GANT	STL	154-168
RICH GARCES	BOS	239-253
CARLOS GARCIA	PIT	140-153
FREDDY GARCIA	PIT	140-153
KARIM GARCIA	LAD	183-197
LUIS GARCIA	DET	256-271
OMAR GARCIA	ATL	23-36
RAMON GARCIA	MIL	360-372
NOMAR GARCIAPARRA	BOS	239-253
MIKE GARDINER	NYM	68-81
MARK GARDNER	SFG	211-224
CADE GASPAR	SDP	198-210
BRENT GATES	OAK	402-419
TODD GENKE	COL	169-182
SCOTT GENTILE	MON	54-67
JASON GIAMBI	OAK	402-419
STEVE GIBRALTER	CIN	112-125
DERRICK GIBSON	COL	169-182
BENJI GIL	TEX	436-447
BRIAN GILES	CLE	324-339
BERNARD GILKEY	NYM	68-81
CHARLES GIPSON	SEA	420-435
JOE GIRARDI	NYY	272-287
BRIAN GIVENS	MIL	360-372
DOUG GLANVILLE	CHC	97-111
TOM GLAVINE	ATL	23-36
GREG GOHR	ANA	389-401
WAYNE GOMES	PHI	82-95
CHRIS GOMEZ	SDP	198-210
LEO GOMEZ	CHC	97-111
RUDY GOMEZ	NYY	272-287
ALEX GONZALEZ	TOR	288-304
GEREMIS GONZALEZ	CHC	97-111
JUAN GONZALEZ	TEX	436-447
LUIS GONZALEZ	CHC	97-111
RAUL GONZALEZ	KCR	340-359
ARNOLD GOOCH	NYM	68-81
DWIGHT GOODEN	NYY	272-287
CURTIS GOODWIN	CIN	112-125
TOM GOODWIN	KCR	340-359
TOM GORDON	BOS	239-253
MARK GRACE	CHC	97-111
MIKE GRACE	PHI	82-95

TONY GRAFFANINO	ATL	23-36
JEFF GRANGER	KCR	340-359
DANNY GRAVES	CLE	324-339
CRAIG GREBECK	FLA	37-53
SHAWN GREEN	TOR	288-304
RICK GREENE	DET	256-271
TODD GREENE	ANA	389-401
TOMMY GREENE	PHI	82-95
WILLIE GREENE	CIN	112-125
MIKE GREENWELL	BOS	239-253
RUSTY GREER	TEX	436-447
TOMMY GREGG	FLA	37-53
BEN GRIEVE	OAK	402-419
TIM GRIEVE	KCR	340-359
CRAIG GRIFFEY	SEA	420-435
KEN GRIFFEY, JR.	SEA	420-435
KEVIN GRIJAK	ATL	23-36
JASON GRIMSLEY	ANA	389-401
MARQUIS GRISSOM	ATL	23-36
BUDDY GROOM	OAK	402-419
KEVIN GROSS	TEX	436-447
JEFF GROTEWOLD	KCR	340-359
MARK GRUDZIELANEK	MON	54-67
MIKE GRZANICH	HOU	126-139
EDDIE GUARDADO	MIN	373-388
CREIGHTON GUBANICH	OAK	402-419
MARK GUBICZA	KCR	340-359
MARK GUERRA	NYM	68-81
VLADIMIR GUERRERO	MON	54-67
WILTON GUERRERO	LAD	183-197
GIOMAR GUEVARA	SEA	420-435
CARLOS GUILLEN	HOU	126-139
JOSE GUILLEN	PIT	140-153
OZZIE GUILLEN	CHW	305-323
MIKE GULAN	STL	154-168
LINDSAY GULIN	NYM	68-81
MARK GUTHRIE	LAD	183-197
RICKY GUTIERREZ	HOU	126-139
JUAN GUZMAN	TOR	288-304
TONY GWYNN	SDP	198-210

-H-

CHRIS HAAS	STL	154-168
JOHN HABYAN	COL	169-182
DAVE HAJEK	HOU	126-139
JOHN HALAMA	HOU	126-139
CHIP HALE	MIN	373-388
JOE HALL	BAL	225-238
ROY HALLADAY	TOR	288-304
ALLEN HALLEY	TOR	288-304
MIKE HALPERIN	TOR	288-304
BOB HAMELIN	KCR	340-359
DARRYL HAMILTON	TEX	436-447
JOEY HAMILTON	SDP	198-210
CHRIS HAMMOND	FLA	37-53
JEFFREY HAMMONDS	BAL	225-238
MIKE HAMPTON	HOU	126-139
RYAN HANCOCK	ANA	389-401
CHRIS HANEY	KCR	340-359
TODD HANEY	CHC	97-111
GREG HANSELL	MIN	373-388
DAVE HANSEN	LAD	183-197
JED HANSEN	KCR	340-359
TERREL HANSEN	DET	256-271
ERIK HANSON	TOR	288-304
JASON HARDTKE	NYM	68-81
TIM HARIKKALA	SEA	420-435
MIKE HARKEY	LAD	183-197
BRIAN HARMON	LAD	183-197
PETE HARNISCH	NYM	68-81
DENNY HARRIGER	SDP	198-210
LENNY HARRIS	CIN	112-125
REGGIE HARRIS	BOS	239-253
JASON HART	CHC	97-111
CHAD HARTVIGSON	SFG	211-224

BILL HASELMAN BOS 239-253
CHRIS HATCHER HOU 126-139
SCOTT HATTEBERG BOS 239-253
RYAN HAWBLITZEL COL 169-182
LATROY HAWKINS MIN 373-388
CHARLIE HAYES NYY 272-287
HEATH HAYNES ANA 389-401
JIMMY HAYNES BAL 225-238
STEVE HAZLETT MIN 373-388
BRONSON HEFLIN PHI 82-95
RICK HELLING FLA 37-53
WES HELMS ATL 23-36
TODD HELTON COL 169-182
SCOTT HEMOND STL 154-168
KENNY HENDERSON SDP 198-210
RICKEY HENDERSON SDP 198-210
ROD HENDERSON MON 54-67
BOB HENLEY MON 54-67
MIKE HENNEMAN TEX 436-447
DOUG HENRY NYM 68-81
DWAYNE HENRY COL 169-182
PAT HENTGEN TOR 288-304
KEVIN HENTHORNE NYY 272-287
RUSS HERBERT CHW 305-323
FELIX HEREDIA FLA 37-53
JULIAN HEREDIA SFG 211-224
MATT HERGES LAD 183-197
CHAD HERMANSEN PIT 140-153
DUSTIN HERMANSON SDP 198-210
ELVIN HERNANDEZ PIT 140-153
FERNANDO HERNANDEZ SDP 198-210
JOSE HERNANDEZ CHC 97-111
LIVAN HERNANDEZ FLA 37-53
RAMON HERNANDEZ OAK 402-419
ROBERTO HERNANDEZ CHW 305-323
SANTOS HERNANDEZ SFG 211-224
XAVIER HERNANDEZ HOU 126-139
JOSE HERRERA OAK 402-419
JASON HERRICK ANA 389-401
OREL HERSHISER CLE 324-339
PHIL HIATT DET 256-271
MIKE HICKEY SEA 420-435
RICHARD HIDALGO HOU 126-139
BOB HIGGINSON DET 256-271
VEE HIGHTOWER CHC 97-111
GLENALLEN HILL SFG 211-224
KEN HILL TEX 436-447
STERLING HITCHCOCK SEA 420-435
DENNY HOCKING MIN 373-388
TREVOR HOFFMAN SDP 198-210
CHRIS HOILES BAL 225-238
AARON HOLBERT STL 154-168
TODD HOLLANDSWORTH LAD 183-197
DAMON HOLLINS ATL 23-36
DAVE HOLLINS SEA 420-435
STACY HOLLINS OAK 402-419
DARREN HOLMES COL 169-182
CHRIS HOLT HOU 126-139
MIKE HOLTZ ANA 389-401
RICK HONEYCUTT STL 154-168
CHRIS HOOK SFG 211-224
JOHN HOPE PIT 140-153
TYLER HOUSTON CHC 97-111
DAVID HOWARD KCR 340-359
THOMAS HOWARD CIN 112-125
MIKE HUBBARD CHC 97-111
JOHN HUDEK HOU 126-139
REX HUDLER ANA 389-401
JOE HUDSON BOS 239-253
MIKE HUFF TOR 288-304
TROY HUGHES CHC 97-111
RICK HUISMAN KCR 340-359
TODD HUNDLEY NYM 68-81
BRIAN R. HUNTER SEA 420-435
'ANL HUNTER HOU 126-139

RICH HUNTER PHI 82-95
TORII HUNTER MIN 373-388
BILL HURST FLA 37-53
JIMMY HURST CHW 305-323
EDWIN HURTADO SEA 420-435
BUTCH HUSKEY NYM 68-81
MARK HUTTON FLA 37-53
TIM HYERS DET 256-271
ADAM HYZDU BOS 239-253

-I-

RAUL IBANEZ SEA 420-435
JESUS IBARRA SFG 211-224
PETE INCAVIGLIA BAL 225-238
JOHNNY ISOM BAL 225-238
JASON ISRINGHAUSEN NYM 68-81

-J-

DAMIAN JACKSON CLE 324-339
DANNY JACKSON STL 154-168
MIKE JACKSON SEA 420-435
JASON JACOME KCR 340-359
JOHN JAHA MIL 360-372
MIKE JAMES ANA 389-401
MARTY JANZEN TOR 288-304
KEVIN JARVIS CIN 112-125
ELINTON JASCO CHC 97-111
STAN JAVIER SFG 211-224
DOMINGO JEAN CIN 112-125
GREGG JEFFERIES PHI 82-95
REGGIE JEFFERSON BOS 239-253
GEOFF JENKINS MIL 360-372
ROBIN JENNINGS CHC 97-111
MARCUS JENSEN SFG 211-224
DEREK JETER NYY 272-287
D'ANGELO JIMENEZ NYY 272-287
DOUG JOHNS OAK 402-419
KEITH JOHNS STL 154-168
BARRY JOHNSON CHW 305-323
BRIAN JOHNSON SDP 198-210
CHARLES JOHNSON FLA 37-53
DANE JOHNSON OAK 402-419
J.J. JOHNSON MIN 373-388
JONATHAN JOHNSON TEX 436-447
LANCE JOHNSON NYM 68-81
MARK JOHNSON PIT 140-153
RANDY JOHNSON SEA 420-435
RUSS JOHNSON HOU 126-139
ANDRUW JONES ATL 23-36
BOBBY JONES COL 169-182
BOBBY JONES NYM 68-81
CHIPPER JONES ATL 23-36
CHRIS JONES NYM 68-81
DAX JONES SFG 211-224
DOUG JONES MIL 360-372
RYAN JONES TOR 288-304
TODD JONES HOU 126-139
BRIAN JORDAN STL 154-168
KEVIN JORDAN PHI 82-95
RICARDO JORDAN PHI 82-95
RANDY JORGENSEN SEA 420-435
TIM JORGENSEN CLE 324-339
TERRY JOSEPH CHC 97-111
WALLY JOYNER SDP 198-210
JEFF JUDEN MON 54-67
DAVE JUSTICE ATL 23-36

-K-

JAMES KAMMERER COL 169-182
GABRIEL KAPLER DET 256-271
MATT KARCHNER CHW 305-323
RON KARKOVICE CHW 305-323
SCOTT KARL MIL 360-372

RYAN KARP PHI 82-95
ERIC KARROS LAD 183-197
STEVE KARSAY OAK 402-419
BRAD KAUFMAN SDP 198-210
GREG KEAGLE DET 256-271
MIKE KELLY CIN 112-125
PAT KELLY NYY 272-287
ROBERTO KELLY MIN 373-388
JASON KENDALL PIT 140-153
DARRYL KENNEDY SFG 211-224
DAVID KENNEDY COL 169-182
GUS KENNEDY ATL 23-36
JEFF KENT CLE 324-339
TIM KESTER HOU 126-139
JIMMY KEY NYY 272-287
BRIAN KEYSER CHW 305-323
MARK KIEFER KCR 340-359
BROOKS KIESCHNICK CHC 97-111
DARRYL KILE HOU 126-139
TIM KILLEEN SDP 198-210
BILL KING OAK 402-419
JEFF KING PIT 140-153
MIKE KINGERY PIT 140-153
EUGENE KINGSALE BAL 225-238
WAYNE KIRBY LAD 183-197
DARON KIRKREIT CLE 324-339
RYAN KLESKO ATL 23-36
STEVEN KLINE CLE 324-339
SCOTT KLINGENBECK MIN 373-388
CHUCK KNOBLAUCH MIN 373-388
RANDY KNOLL PHI 82-95
DANNY KOLB TEX 436-447
PAUL KONERKO LAD 183-197
CLINT KOPPE CIN 112-125
COREY KOSKIE MIN 373-388
MARK KOTSAY FLA 37-53
RICK KRIVDA BAL 225-238
MARC KROON SDP 198-210
TIM KUBINSKI OAK 402-419
MIKE KUSIEWICZ COL 169-182

-L-

KERRY LACY BOS 239-253
RICK LADJEVICH SEA 420-435
JOE LAGARDE LAD 183-197
TOM LAMPKIN SFG 211-224
RYAN LANE MIN 373-388
MARK LANGSTON ANA 389-401
RAY LANKFORD STL 154-168
MIKE LANSING MON 54-67
ANDY LARKIN FLA 37-53
BARRY LARKIN CIN 112-125
GREG LAROCCA SDP 198-210
CHRIS LATHAM MIN 373-388
MATT LAWTON MIN 373-388
JALAL LEACH MON 54-67
RICKY LEDEE NYY 272-287
CARLOS LEE CHW 305-323
DEREK LEE TEX 436-447
DEREK LEE SDP 198-210
PHIL LEFTWICH ANA 389-401
AL LEITER FLA 37-53
MARK LEITER MON 54-67
SCOTT LEIUS CLE 324-339
MARK LEMKE ATL 23-36
PATRICK LENNON OAK 402-419
BRIAN LESHER OAK 402-419
CURT LESKANIC COL 169-182
AL LEVINE CHW 305-323
JESSE LEVIS MIL 360-372
DARREN LEWIS CHW 305-323
MARC LEWIS ATL 23-36
MARK LEWIS DET 256-271
RICHIE LEWIS DET 256-271
T.R. LEWIS BOS 239-253

Name	Team	Pages
JIM LEYRITZ	NYY	272-287
CORY LIDLE	NYM	68-81
JON LIEBER	PIT	140-153
MIKE LIEBERTHAL	PHI	82-95
JEFF LIEFER	CHW	305-323
KERRY LIGTENBERG	ATL	23-36
DEREK LILLIQUIST	CIN	112-125
JOSE LIMA	DET	256-271
RICH LINARES	LAD	183-197
DOUG LINTON	KCR	340-359
FELIPE LIRA	DET	256-271
NELSON LIRIANO	PIT	140-153
JOE LIS	CLE	324-339
PAT LISTACH	MIL	360-372
MARK LITTLE	TEX	436-447
SCOTT LIVINGSTONE	SDP	198-210
GRAEME LLOYD	NYY	272-287
ESTEBAN LOAIZA	PIT	140-153
KEITH LOCKHART	KCR	340-359
KENNY LOFTON	CLE	324-339
MARCUS LOGAN	STL	154-168
RICH LOISELLE	PIT	140-153
KEVIN LOMON	ATL	23-36
RYAN LONG	KCR	340-359
TERRENCE LONG	NYM	68-81
ALBIE LOPEZ	CLE	324-339
JAVY LOPEZ	ATL	23-36
JOSE LOPEZ	NYM	68-81
LUIS LOPEZ	SDP	198-210
MENDY LOPEZ	KCR	340-359
MARK LORETTA	MIL	360-372
ANDREW LORRAINE	OAK	402-419
KEVIN LOVINGIER	STL	154-168
DEREK LOWE	SEA	420-435
SEAN LOWE	STL	154-168
MIKE LOWELL	NYY	272-287
TERRELL LOWERY	NYM	68-81
LOU LUCCA	FLA	37-53
ERIC LUDWICK	STL	154-168
ROB LUKACHYK	MON	54-67
MATT LUKE	NYY	272-287
RYAN LUZINSKI	LAD	183-197
CURT LYONS	CIN	112-125

-M-

KEVIN MAAS	MIL	360-372
JOHN MABRY	STL	154-168
CHRIS MACCA	COL	169-182
BOB MACDONALD	NYM	68-81
FAUSTO MACEY	SFG	211-224
MIKE MACFARLANE	KCR	340-359
ROBERT MACHADO	CHW	305-323
GREG MADDUX	ATL	23-36
MIKE MADDUX	BOS	239-253
CALVIN MADURO	PHI	82-95
KATSUHIRO MAEDA	NYY	272-287
DAVE MAGADAN	CHC	97-111
DANNY MAGEE	ATL	23-36
WENDELL MAGEE	PHI	82-95
MIKE MAGNANTE	KCR	340-359
JOE MAGRANE	CHW	305-323
PAT MAHOMES	BOS	239-253
SCOTT MAKAREWICZ	DET	256-271
JOSE MALAVE	BOS	239-253
SEAN MALONEY	MIL	360-372
MATT MANTEI	FLA	37-53
BARRY MANUEL	MON	54-67
KIRT MANWARING	HOU	126-139
ELIESER MARRERO	STL	154-168
AL MARTIN	PIT	140-153
CHRIS MARTIN	MON	54-67
NORBERTO MARTIN	CHW	305-323
DAVE MARTINEZ	CHW	305-323
DENNIS MARTINEZ	CLE	324-339
EDDY MARTINEZ	BAL	225-238
EDGAR MARTINEZ	SEA	420-435
FELIX MARTINEZ	KCR	340-359
JESUS MARTINEZ	LAD	183-197
PEDRO MARTINEZ	CIN	112-125
PEDRO MARTINEZ	MON	54-67
RAMON MARTINEZ	KCR	340-359
RAMON MARTINEZ	LAD	183-197
SANDY MARTINEZ	TOR	288-304
TINO MARTINEZ	NYY	272-287
TIM MARX	PIT	140-153
JOHN MARZANO	SEA	420-435
ONAN MASAOKA	LAD	183-197
DAMON MASHORE	OAK	402-419
JUSTIN MASHORE	DET	256-271
DAN MASTELLER	MON	54-67
RUBEN MATEO	TEX	436-447
MIKE MATHENY	MIL	360-372
T.J. MATHEWS	STL	154-168
TERRY MATHEWS	BAL	225-238
JEFF MATRANGA	STL	154-168
GARY MATTHEWS	SDP	198-210
JASON MAXWELL	CHC	97-111
DARRELL MAY	ANA	389-401
DERRICK MAY	HOU	126-139
BRENT MAYNE	NYM	68-81
ROD McCALL	CLE	324-339
GREG McCARTHY	SEA	420-435
DAVE McCARTY	SFG	211-224
KIRK McCASKILL	CHW	305-323
SCOTT McCLAIN	BAL	225-238
QUINTON McCRACKEN	COL	169-182
BEN McDONALD	MIL	360-372
JASON McDONALD	OAK	402-419
JACK McDOWELL	CLE	324-339
ROGER McDOWELL	BAL	225-238
CHUCK McELROY	ANA	389-401
ETHAN McENTIRE	NYM	68-81
WILLIE McGEE	STL	154-168
FRED McGRIFF	ATL	23-36
RYAN McGUIRE	MON	54-67
MARK McGWIRE	OAK	402-419
WALT McKEEL	BOS	239-253
MARK McLEMORE	TEX	436-447
GREG McMICHAEL	ATL	23-36
BILLY McMILLON	FLA	37-53
MITCH McNEELY	LAD	183-197
BRIAN McRAE	CHC	97-111
RUSTY MEACHAM	SEA	420-435
BRIAN MEADOWS	FLA	37-53
PAT MEARES	MIN	373-388
JIM MECIR	NYY	272-287
RAFAEL MEDINA	NYY	272-287
ANTHONY MEDRANO	KCR	340-359
ROBERTO MEJIA	BOS	239-253
ADAM MELHUSE	TOR	288-304
JUAN MELO	SDP	198-210
MITCH MELUSKEY	HOU	126-139
CARLOS MENDOZA	NYM	68-81
RAMIRO MENDOZA	NYY	272-287
FRANK MENECHINO	CHW	305-323
PAUL MENHART	SEA	420-435
ORLANDO MERCED	PIT	140-153
HENRY MERCEDES	KCR	340-359
JOSE MERCEDES	MIL	360-372
MARK MERCHANT	KCR	340-359
KENT MERCKER	CLE	324-339
JOSE MESA	CLE	324-339
NELSON METHENEY	PHI	82-95
DANNY MICELI	PIT	140-153
DOUG MIENTKIEWICZ	MIN	373-388
MATT MIESKE	MIL	360-372
MIKE MILCHIN	BAL	225-238
KEVIN MILLAR	FLA	37-53
DAMIAN MILLER	MIN	373-388
KURT MILLER	FLA	37-53
ORLANDO MILLER	HOU	126-139
TRAVIS MILLER	MIN	373-388
TREVER MILLER	DET	256-271
RALPH MILLIARD	FLA	37-53
DOUG MILLION	COL	169-182
ALAN MILLS	BAL	225-238
KEVIN MILLWOOD	ATL	23-36
MARK MIMBS	LAD	183-197
MICHAEL MIMBS	PHI	82-95
DOUG MIRABELLI	SFG	211-224
ANGEL MIRANDA	MIL	360-372
KEITH MITCHELL	CIN	112-125
KEVIN MITCHELL	CIN	112-125
LARRY MITCHELL	PHI	82-95
TONY MITCHELL	DET	256-271
CASEY MITTAUER	NYY	272-287
DAVE MLICKI	NYM	68-81
DOUG MLICKI	HOU	126-139
BRIAN MOEHLER	DET	256-271
MIKE MOHLER	OAK	402-419
IZZY MOLINA	OAK	402-419
PAUL MOLITOR	MIN	373-388
RAUL MONDESI	LAD	183-197
WONDERFUL MONDS	ATL	23-36
RICH MONTELEONE	ANA	389-401
JEFF MONTGOMERY	KCR	340-359
RAY MONTGOMERY	HOU	126-139
STEVE MONTGOMERY	OAK	402-419
ERIC MOODY	TEX	436-447
JOEL MOORE	COL	169-182
KERWIN MOORE	OAK	402-419
VINCE MOORE	SDP	198-210
ALEX MORALES	SFG	211-224
WILLIE MORALES	OAK	402-419
MICKEY MORANDINI	PHI	82-95
MIKE MORDECAI	ATL	23-36
RAMON MOREL	PIT	140-153
SHEA MORENZ	NYY	272-287
MIKE MORGAN	CIN	112-125
SCOTT MORGAN	CLE	324-339
ALVIN MORMAN	HOU	126-139
RUSS MORMAN	FLA	37-53
BOBBY MORRIS	CHC	97-111
HAL MORRIS	CIN	112-125
MATT MORRIS	STL	154-168
JULIO MOSQUERA	TOR	288-304
DAMIAN MOSS	ATL	23-36
HENRY MOTA	TEX	436-447
TONY MOUNCE	HOU	126-139
JAMES MOUTON	HOU	126-139
LYLE MOUTON	CHW	305-323
JAMIE MOYER	SEA	420-435
BILL MUELLER	SFG	211-224
TERRY MULHOLLAND	SEA	420-435
SEAN MULLIGAN	SDP	198-210
BOBBY MUNOZ	PHI	82-95
MIKE MUNOZ	COL	169-182
PEDRO MUNOZ	OAK	402-419
MIKE MURPHY	TEX	436-447
EDDIE MURRAY	BAL	225-238
GLENN MURRAY	PHI	82-95
HEATH MURRAY	SDP	198-210
JIM MUSSELWHITE	NYY	272-287
MIKE MUSSINA	BAL	225-238
GREG MYERS	MIN	373-388
JIMMY MYERS	BAL	225-238
MIKE MYERS	DET	256-271
RANDY MYERS	BAL	225-238
ROD MYERS	CHC	97-111
ROD MYERS	KCR	340-359

-N-

TIM NAEHRING	BOS	239-253
CHARLES NAGY	CLE	324-339
TONY NAKASHIMA	LAD	183-197

TYRONE NARCISSE	HOU	126-139
BOB NATAL	FLA	37-53
DAN NAULTY	MIN	373-388
JAIME NAVARRO	CHC	97-111
DENNY NEAGLE	ATL	23-36
BRY NELSON	HOU	126-139
JEFF NELSON	NYY	272-287
ROBB NEN	FLA	37-53
PHIL NEVIN	DET	256-271
MARC NEWFIELD	MIL	360-372
DAVID NEWHAN	OAK	402-419
WARREN NEWSON	TEX	436-447
DAVID NIED	COL	169-182
MELVIN NIEVES	DET	256-271
DAVE NILSSON	MIL	360-372
C.J. NITKOWSKI	DET	256-271
OTIS NIXON	TOR	288-304
TROT NIXON	BOS	239-253
HIDEO NOMO	LAD	183-197
LES NORMAN	KCR	340-359
JAMIE NORTHEIMER	PHI	82-95
CHRIS NORTON	NYY	272-287
GREG NORTON	CHW	305-323
RAFAEL NOVOA	ANA	389-401
CLEMENTE NUNEZ	FLA	37-53
JUAN NUNEZ	TEX	436-447
SERGIO NUNEZ	KCR	340-359
JON NUNNALLY	KCR	340-359
RYAN NYE	PHI	82-95

-O-

TROY O'LEARY	BOS	239-253
SHERMAN OBANDO	MON	54-67
CHARLIE O'BRIEN	TOR	288-304
ALEX OCHOA	NYM	68-81
JOSE OFFERMAN	KCR	340-359
JAMIE OGDEN	MIN	373-388
CHAD OGEA	CLE	324-339
KIRT OJALA	CIN	112-125
JOHN OLERUD	TOR	288-304
JOSE OLIVA	STL	154-168
OMAR OLIVARES	DET	256-271
DARREN OLIVER	TEX	436-447
JOE OLIVER	CIN	112-125
JOSE OLMEDA	FLA	37-53
JASON OLSEN	CHW	305-323
STEVE OLSEN	KCR	340-359
GREGG OLSON	HOU	126-139
ERIC OLSZEWSKI	ATL	23-36
PAUL O'NEILL	NYY	272-287
STEVE ONTIVEROS	ANA	389-401
MIKE OQUIST	SDP	198-210
MAGGLIO ORDONEZ	CHW	305-323
REY ORDONEZ	NYM	68-81
RAFAEL ORELLANO	BOS	239-253
KEVIN ORIE	CHC	97-111
JESSE OROSCO	BAL	225-238
JOE ORSULAK	FLA	37-53
LUIS ORTIZ	TEX	436-447
RUSS ORTIZ	SFG	211-224
DONOVAN OSBORNE	STL	154-168
KEITH OSIK	PIT	140-153
ANTONIO OSUNA	LAD	183-197
WILLIS OTANEZ	BAL	225-238
RICKY OTERO	PHI	82-95
ERIC OWENS	CIN	112-125
JAYHAWK OWENS	COL	169-182
ALEX PACHECO	SEA	420-435

-P-

ISRAEL PAEZ	MIN	373-388
TOM PAGNOZZI	STL	154-168
LANCE PAINTER	COL	169-182
PALL	FLA	37-53

ORLANDO PALMEIRO	ANA	389-401
RAFAEL PALMEIRO	BAL	225-238
DEAN PALMER	TEX	436-447
JOSE PANIAGUA	MON	54-67
CRAIG PAQUETTE	KCR	340-359
MARK PARENT	BAL	225-238
CHAN HO PARK	LAD	183-197
JOSE PARRA	MIN	373-388
JULIO PARRA	LAD	183-197
JEFF PARRETT	PHI	82-95
STEVE PARRIS	PIT	140-153
BRONSWELL PATRICK	HOU	126-139
BOB PATTERSON	CHC	97-111
DANNY PATTERSON	TEX	436-447
JEFF PATZKE	TOR	288-304
CARL PAVANO	BOS	239-253
DAVE PAVLAS	NYY	272-287
ROGER PAVLIK	TEX	436-447
JAY PAYTON	NYM	68-81
ALDO PECORILLI	ATL	23-36
RUDY PEMBERTON	BOS	239-253
GERONIMO PENA	CLE	324-339
JUAN PENA	BOS	239-253
TONY PENA	CLE	324-339
TERRY PENDLETON	ATL	23-36
SHANNON PENN	DET	256-271
BRAD PENNINGTON	ANA	389-401
BILLY PERCIBAL	BAL	225-238
TROY PERCIVAL	ANA	389-401
EDDIE PEREZ	ATL	23-36
EDDIE PEREZ	CIN	112-125
JHONNY PEREZ	HOU	126-139
MELIDO PEREZ	NYY	272-287
MIKE PEREZ	CHC	97-111
NEIFI PEREZ	COL	169-182
ROBERT PEREZ	TOR	288-304
TOMAS PEREZ	TOR	288-304
YORKIS PEREZ	FLA	37-53
HERB PERRY	CLE	324-339
ROBERT PERSON	NYM	68-81
ROBERTO PETAGINE	NYM	68-81
CHRIS PETERS	PIT	140-153
CHRIS PETERSEN	CHC	97-111
CHARLES PETERSON	PIT	140-153
MARK PETERSON	SFG	211-224
MARK PETKOVSEK	STL	154-168
BEN PETRICK	COL	169-182
JOSE PETT	TOR	288-304
ANDY PETTITTE	NYY	272-287
J.R. PHILLIPS	PHI	82-95
TONY PHILLIPS	CHW	305-323
MIKE PIAZZA	LAD	183-197
HIPOLITO PICHARDO	KCR	340-359
A.J. PIERZYNSKI	MIN	373-388
GREG PIRKL	BOS	239-253
JIM PITTSLEY	KCR	340-359
PHIL PLANTIER	OAK	402-419
DAN PLESAC	PIT	140-153
ERIC PLUNK	CLE	324-339
CHARLES POE	OAK	402-419
PLACIDO POLANCO	STL	154-168
LUIS POLONIA	ATL	23-36
JIM POOLE	SFG	211-224
MARK PORTUGAL	CIN	112-125
JORGE POSADA	NYY	272-287
DANTE POWELL	SFG	211-224
JAY POWELL	FLA	37-53
ARQUIMEDEZ POZO	BOS	239-253
JOSE PRADO	LAD	183-197
RICH PRATT	CHW	305-323
CURTIS PRIDE	DET	256-271
ARIEL PRIETO	OAK	402-419
STEPHEN PRIHODA	KCR	340-359
CHRIS PRITCHETT	ANA	389-401
BILL PULSIPHER	NYM	68-81

-Q-

PAUL QUANTRILL	TOR	288-304
TOM QUINLAN	MIN	373-388

-R-

BRIAN RAABE	MIN	373-388
SCOTT RADINSKY	LAD	183-197
BRAD RADKE	MIN	373-388
RYAN RADMANOVICH	MIN	373-388
BRADY RAGGIO	STL	154-168
STEVE RAIN	CHC	97-111
TIM RAINES	NYY	272-287
ALEX RAMIREZ	CLE	324-339
ANGEL RAMIREZ	TOR	288-304
MANNY RAMIREZ	CLE	324-339
EDGAR RAMOS	HOU	126-139
JOE RANDA	KCR	340-359
PAT RAPP	FLA	37-53
GARY RATH	LAD	183-197
JON RATLIFF	CHC	97-111
KEN RAY	KCR	340-359
BRITT REAMES	STL	154-168
JEFF REBOULET	MIN	373-388
BOBBY RECTOR	SFG	211-224
MARK REDMAN	MIN	373-388
MIKE REDMOND	FLA	37-53
BRANDON REED	DET	256-271
JEFF REED	COL	169-182
JODY REED	SDP	198-210
RICK REED	NYM	68-81
STEVE REED	COL	169-182
POKEY REESE	CIN	112-125
KEVIN REIMER	SEA	420-435
BRYAN REKAR	COL	169-182
DESI RELAFORD	PHI	82-95
MIKE RENNHACK	MIL	360-372
EDGAR RENTERIA	FLA	37-53
AL REYES	MIL	360-372
CARLOS REYES	OAK	402-419
SHANE REYNOLDS	HOU	126-139
ARMANDO REYNOSO	COL	169-182
ARTHUR RHODES	BAL	225-238
DAN RICABAL	LAD	183-197
CHUCK RICCI	BOS	239-253
CHRIS RICHARD	STL	154-168
RAY RICKEN	NYY	272-287
BRAD RIGBY	OAK	402-419
ADAM RIGGS	LAD	183-197
DAN RIOS	NYY	272-287
BILLY RIPKEN	BAL	225-238
CAL RIPKEN	BAL	225-238
BILL RISLEY	TOR	288-304
TODD RITCHIE	MIN	373-388
KEVIN RITZ	COL	169-182
MARIANO RIVERA	NYY	272-287
ROBERTO RIVERA	CHC	97-111
RUBEN RIVERA	NYY	272-287
JOE ROA	CLE	324-339
JASON ROBBINS	CIN	112-125
J.P. ROBERGE	LAD	183-197
SID ROBERSON	MIL	360-372
BIP ROBERTS	KCR	340-359
BRETT ROBERTS	MIN	373-388
CHRIS ROBERTS	NYM	68-81
LONELL ROBERTS	TOR	288-304
JASON ROBERTSON	FLA	37-53
MIKE ROBERTSON	CHW	305-323
RICH ROBERTSON	MIN	373-388
KERRY ROBINSON	STL	154-168
OSCAR ROBLES	HOU	126-139
ALEX RODRIGUEZ	SEA	420-435
FELIX RODRIGUEZ	LAD	183-197
FRANKIE RODRIGUEZ	MIN	373-388

Name	Team	Pages
HENRY RODRIGUEZ	MON	54-67
IVAN RODRIGUEZ	TEX	436-447
NERIO RODRIGUEZ	BAL	225-238
STEVE RODRIGUEZ	DET	256-271
VICTOR RODRIGUEZ	FLA	37-53
KENNY ROGERS	NYY	272-287
CHRISTIAN ROJAS	CIN	112-125
MEL ROJAS	MON	54-67
SCOTT ROLEN	PHI	82-95
NATE ROLISON	FLA	37-53
WILLIE ROMERO	LAD	183-197
MARC RONAN	FLA	37-53
CHAD ROPER	MIN	373-388
JOHN ROPER	CIN	112-125
JOSE ROSADO	KCR	340-359
MEL ROSARIO	BAL	225-238
BRIAN ROSE	BOS	239-253
PETE ROSE Jr.	CHW	305-323
JOHN ROSKOS	FLA	37-53
JOE ROSSELLI	ANA	389-401
MICHAEL ROSSITER	OAK	402-419
MATT RUEBEL	PIT	140-153
KIRK RUETER	SFG	211-224
SCOTT RUFFCORN	CHW	305-323
BRUCE RUFFIN	COL	169-182
JOHNNY RUFFIN	CIN	112-125
TIM RUMER	NYY	272-287
TOBY RUMFIELD	CIN	112-125
GLENDON RUSCH	KCR	340-359
JEFF RUSSELL	TEX	436-447
KEN RYAN	PHI	82-95
MATT RYAN	PIT	140-153

-S-

DONNIE SADLER	BOS	239-253
OLMEDO SAENZ	CHW	305-323
JON SAFFER	MON	54-67
A.J. SAGER	DET	256-271
MARC SAGMOEN	TEX	436-447
MIKE SAIPE	COL	169-182
ROGER SALKELD	CIN	112-125
TIM SALMON	ANA	389-401
JUAN SAMUEL	TOR	288-304
JESUS SANCHEZ	NYM	68-81
REY SANCHEZ	CHC	97-111
RYNE SANDBERG	CHC	97-111
REGGIE SANDERS	CIN	112-125
SCOTT SANDERS	SDP	198-210
JULIO SANTANA	TEX	436-447
RUBEN SANTANA	CIN	112-125
F.P. SANTANGELO	MON	54-67
BENITO SANTIAGO	PHI	82-95
DAMIAN SAPP	BOS	239-253
ROB SASSER	ATL	23-36
CHRIS SAUNDERS	NYM	68-81
TONY SAUNDERS	FLA	37-53
STEVE SCARSONE	SFG	211-224
GENE SCHALL	PHI	82-95
CURT SCHILLING	PHI	82-95
CURT SCHMIDT	MON	54-67
JASON SCHMIDT	PIT	140-153
PETE SCHOUREK	CIN	112-125
STEVE SCHRENK	CHW	305-323
RICK SCHU	MON	54-67
TIM SCOTT	SFG	211-224
RUDY SEANEZ	LAD	183-197
REED SECRIST	PIT	140-153
CHRIS SEELBACH	FLA	37-53
KEVIN SEFCIK	PHI	82-95
DAVID SEGUI	MON	54-67
KEVIN SEITZER	CLE	324-339
BILL SELBY	BOS	239-253
AARON SELE	BOS	239-253
DAN SERAFINI	MIN	373-388
SCOTT SERVAIS	CHC	97-111

SCOTT SERVICE	CIN	112-125
RICHIE SEXSON	CLE	324-339
JEFF SHAW	CIN	112-125
DANNY SHEAFFER	STL	154-168
ANDY SHEETS	SEA	420-435
CHRIS SHEFF	FLA	37-53
GARY SHEFFIELD	FLA	37-53
ANTHONY SHELBY	NYY	272-287
ALVIE SHEPHERD	BAL	225-238
CRAIG SHIPLEY	SDP	198-210
BARRY SHORT	NYM	68-81
PAUL SHUEY	CLE	324-339
RUBEN SIERRA	DET	256-271
MARK SIEVERT	TOR	288-304
JOSE SILVA	TOR	288-304
TED SILVA	TEX	436-447
DAVE SILVESTRI	MON	54-67
BILL SIMAS	CHW	305-323
BRIAN SIMMONS	CHW	305-323
RANDALL SIMON	ATL	23-36
MITCH SIMONS	MIN	373-388
BENJI SIMONTON	SFG	211-224
DUANE SINGLETON	DET	256-271
MIKE SIROTKA	CHW	305-323
STEVE SISCO	KCR	340-359
DON SLAUGHT	CHW	305-323
HEATHCLIFF SLOCUMB	BOS	239-253
AARON SMALL	OAK	402-419
MARK SMALL	HOU	126-139
JOHN SMILEY	CIN	112-125
BRIAN SMITH	TOR	288-304
BUBBA SMITH	TEX	436-447
CAM SMITH	DET	256-271
DEMOND SMITH	OAK	402-419
DWIGHT SMITH	ATL	23-36
LEE SMITH	CIN	112-125
MARK SMITH	BAL	225-238
MATT SMITH	KCR	340-359
OZZIE SMITH	STL	154-168
ROD SMITH	NYY	272-287
RYAN SMITH	SEA	420-435
TOBY SMITH	KCR	340-359
TRAVIS SMITH	MIL	360-372
ZANE SMITH	PIT	140-153
JOHN SMOLTZ	ATL	23-36
CHRIS SNOPEK	CHW	305-323
J.T. SNOW	ANA	389-401
MATT SNYDER	BAL	225-238
STEVE SODERSTROM	SFG	211-224
CLINT SODOWSKY	DET	256-271
LUIS SOJO	NYY	272-287
PAUL SORRENTO	SEA	420-435
SAMMY SOSA	CHC	97-111
STEVE SPARKS	MIL	360-372
SHANE SPENCER	NYY	272-287
BILL SPIERS	HOU	126-139
SCOTT SPIEZIO	OAK	402-419
PAUL SPOLJARIC	TOR	288-304
ED SPRAGUE	TOR	288-304
DENNIS SPRINGER	ANA	389-401
RUSS SPRINGER	PHI	82-95
BOB ST. PIERRE	NYY	272-287
SCOTT STAHOVIAK	MIN	373-388
MATT STAIRS	OAK	402-419
ANDY STANKIEWICZ	MON	54-67
MIKE STANLEY	BOS	239-253
MIKE STANTON	TEX	436-447
T.J. STATON	PIT	140-153
KENNIE STEENSTRA	CHC	97-111
BLAKE STEIN	STL	154-168
TERRY STEINBACH	OAK	402-419
BRIAN STEPHENSON	CHC	97-111
GARRETT STEPHENSON	PHI	82-95
DAVE STEVENS	MIN	373-388
LEE STEVENS	TEX	436-447

TODD STEVERSON	SDP	198-210
ANDY STEWART	KCR	340-359
SHANNON STEWART	TOR	288-304
KELLY STINNETT	MIL	360-372
KEVIN STOCKER	PHI	82-95
CRAIG STONE	TOR	288-304
TODD STOTTLEMYRE	STL	154-168
DOUG STRANGE	SEA	420-435
DARYL STRAWBERRY	NYY	272-287
ERIC STUCKENSCHNEIDER	LAD	183-197
EVERETT STULL	MON	54-67
MARCUS STURDIVANT	SEA	420-435
TANYON STURTZE	CHC	97-111
CHRIS STYNES	KCR	340-359
JEFF SUPPAN	BSO	
B.J. SURHOFF	BAL	225-238
LARRY SUTTON	KCR	340-359
MAC SUZUKI	SEA	420-435
DALE SVEUM	PIT	140-153
DEREK SWAFFORD	PIT	140-153
PEDRO SWANN	ATL	23-36
DAVE SWARTZBAUGH	CHC	97-111
MARK SWEENEY	STL	154-168
MIKE SWEENEY	KCR	340-359
BILL SWIFT	COL	169-182
GREG SWINDELL	CLE	324-339
PAUL SWINGLE	ANA	389-401

-T-

JEFF TACKETT	DET	256-271
SCOTT TALANOA	MON	54-67
JEFF TAM	NYM	68-81
KEVIN TAPANI	CHW	305-323
TONY TARASCO	BAL	225-238
DANNY TARTABULL	CHW	305-323
FERNANDO TATIS	TEX	436-447
JIM TATUM	SDP	198-210
EDDIE TAUBENSEE	CIN	112-125
JESUS TAVAREZ	FLA	37-53
JULIAN TAVAREZ	CLE	324-339
BILLY TAYLOR	OAK	402-419
BRIEN TAYLOR	NYY	272-287
REGGIE TAYLOR	PHI	82-95
MIGUEL TEJADA	OAK	402-419
AMAURY TELEMACO	CHC	97-111
DAVE TELGHEDER	OAK	402-419
JAY TESSMER	NYY	272-287
MICKEY TETTLETON	TEX	436-447
BOB TEWKSBURY	SDP	198-210
FRANK THOMAS	CHW	305-323
JUAN THOMAS	CHW	305-323
LARRY THOMAS	CHW	305-323
JIM THOME	CLE	324-339
ANDY THOMPSON	TOR	288-304
JASON THOMPSON	SDP	198-210
JUSTIN THOMPSON	DET	256-271
MARK THOMPSON	COL	169-182
MILT THOMPSON	LAD	183-197
ROBBY THOMPSON	SFG	211-224
RYAN THOMPSON	CLE	324-339
JOHN THOMSON	COL	169-182
MIKE TIMLIN	TOR	288-304
OZZIE TIMMONS	CHC	97-111
LEE TINSLEY	BOS	239-253
BRIAN TOLLBERG	MIL	360-372
DILSON TORRES	KCR	340-359
SALOMON TORRES	SEA	420-435
ROBERT TOTH	KCR	340-359
JUSTIN TOWLE	CIN	112-125
STEVE TRACHSEL	CHC	97-111
ALAN TRAMMELL	DET	256-271
BUBBA TRAMMELL	DET	256-271
JODY TREADWELL	LAD	183-197
HECTOR TRINIDAD	MIN	373-388
RICKY TRLICEK	NYM	68-81

MIKE TROMBLEY	MIN	373-388
MIKE TUCKER	KCR	340-359
BRAD TYLER	BAL	225-238
JOSH TYLER	MIL	360-372

-U-

TIM UNROE	MIL	360-372
UGUETH URBINA	MON	54-67
SAL URSO	SEA	420-435

-V-

ISMAEL VALDES	LAD	183-197
MARC VALDES	FLA	37-53
PEDRO VALDES	CHC	97-111
MARIO VALDEZ	CHW	305-323
JOHN VALENTIN	BOS	239-253
JOSE VALENTIN	MIL	360-372
JOSE VALENTIN	MIN	373-388
FERNANDO VALENZUELA	SDP	198-210
JULIO VALERA	KCR	340-359
KERRY VALRIE	CHW	305-323
TODD VAN POPPEL	DET	256-271
JOHN VANDERWAL	COL	169-182
TIM VANEGMOND	MIL	360-372
WILLIAM VANLANDINGHAM	SFG	211-224
JASON VARITEK	SEA	420-435
GREG VAUGHN	SDP	198-210
MO VAUGHN	BOS	239-253
RANDY VELARDE	ANA	389-401
EDGARD VELAZQUEZ	COL	169-182
ROBIN VENTURA	CHW	305-323
DARIO VERAS	SDP	198-210
QUILVIO VERAS	FLA	37-53
DAVE VERES	MON	54-67
ANDREW VESSEL	TEX	436-447
JOSE VIDRO	MON	54-67
SCOTT VIEIRA	CHC	97-111
RON VILLONE	MIL	360-372
FERNANDO VINA	MIL	360-372
JULIO VINAS	CHW	305-323
FRANK VIOLA	TOR	288-304
JOE VITIELLO	KCR	340-359
JOSE VIZCAINO	CLE	324-339
OMAR VIZQUEL	CLE	324-339
JACK VOIGT	TEX	436-447
SCOTT VOLLMER	CHW	305-323
ED VOSBERG	TEX	436-447

-W-

TERRELL WADE	ATL	23-36
BILLY WAGNER	HOU	126-139
BRET WAGNER	OAK	402-419

MATT WAGNER	SEA	420-435
PAUL WAGNER	PIT	140-153
DAVID WAINHOUSE	PIT	140-153
TIM WAKEFIELD	BOS	239-253
MATT WALBECK	MIN	373-388
JAMIE WALKER	HOU	126-139
LARRY WALKER	COL	169-182
SHON WALKER	PIT	140-153
TODD WALKER	MIN	373-388
WADE WALKER	CHC	97-111
DONNE WALL	HOU	126-139
DEREK WALLACE	NYM	68-81
TIM WALLACH	ANA	389-401
JEROME WALTON	ATL	23-36
BRYAN WARD	FLA	37-53
DARYLE WARD	DET	256-271
TURNER WARD	MIL	360-372
JEFF WARE	TOR	288-304
JOHN WASDIN	OAK	402-419
B.J. WASZGIS	BAL	225-238
PAT WATKINS	CIN	112-125
SCOTT WATKINS	MIN	373-388
SEAN WATKINS	SDP	198-210
ALLEN WATSON	SFG	211-224
DAVE WEATHERS	NYY	272-287
NEIL WEBER	MON	54-67
LENNY WEBSTER	MON	54-67
ERIC WEDGE	DET	256-271
JOHN WEHNER	PIT	140-153
CHRIS WEINKE	TOR	288-304
WALT WEISS	COL	169-182
BOB WELLS	SEA	420-435
DAVID WELLS	BAL	225-238
TURK WENDELL	CHC	97-111
DON WENGERT	OAK	402-419
DAVID WEST	PHI	82-95
JOHN WETTELAND	NYY	272-287
MATT WHISENANT	FLA	37-53
DEVON WHITE	FLA	37-53
GABE WHITE	CIN	112-125
JIMMY WHITE	CIN	112-125
RONDELL WHITE	MON	54-67
MARK WHITEN	SEA	420-435
MATT WHITESIDE	TEX	436-447
MIKE WHITLOCK	TOR	288-304
DARRELL WHITMORE	FLA	37-53
CASEY WHITTEN	CLE	324-339
KEVIN WICKANDER	MIL	360-372
BOB WICKMAN	MIL	360-372
CHRIS WIDGER	SEA	420-435
SCOTT WIEGANDT	PHI	82-95
CHRIS WILCOX	NYY	272-287
MARC WILKINS	PIT	140-153
RICK WILKINS	SFG	211-224

BERNIE WILLIAMS	NYY	272-287
BRIAN WILLIAMS	DET	256-271
EDDIE WILLIAMS	DET	256-271
GEORGE WILLIAMS	OAK	402-419
GERALD WILLIAMS	MIL	360-372
JUAN WILLIAMS	ATL	23-36
KEITH WILLIAMS	SFG	211-224
MATT WILLIAMS	SFG	211-224
MIKE WILLIAMS	PHI	82-95
WOODY WILLIAMS	TOR	288-304
ANTONE WILLIAMSON	MIL	360-372
CRAIG WILSON	CHW	305-323
DAN WILSON	SEA	420-435
DESI WILSON	SFG	211-224
ENRIQUE WILSON	CLE	324-339
NIGEL WILSON	CLE	324-339
PAUL WILSON	NYM	68-81
PRESTON WILSON	NYM	68-81
TOM WILSON	CLE	324-339
JAY WITASICK	OAK	402-419
BOBBY WITT	TEX	436-447
KEVIN WITT	TOR	288-304
MARK WOHLERS	ATL	23-36
STEVE WOJCIECHOWSKI	OAK	402-419
BOB WOLCOTT	SEA	420-435
MIKE WOLFF	ANA	389-401
TONY WOMACK	PIT	140-153
JASON WOOD	OAK	402-419
KERRY WOOD	CHC	97-111
BRAD WOODALL	ATL	23-36
STEVE WOODARD	MIL	360-372
TYRONE WOODS	BOS	239-253
STEVE WORRELL	CHW	305-323
TIM WORRELL	SDP	198-210
TODD WORRELL	LAD	183-197
JAMEY WRIGHT	COL	169-182
JARET WRIGHT	CLE	324-339
RON WRIGHT	PIT	140-153

-X, Y, Z-

ESTEBAN YAN	BAL	225-238
ANTHONY YOUNG	HOU	126-139
DMITRI YOUNG	STL	154-168
ERIC YOUNG	COL	169-182
ERNIE YOUNG	OAK	402-419
KEVIN YOUNG	KCR	340-359
GREG ZAUN	FLA	37-53
TODD ZEILE	BAL	225-238
ALAN ZINTER	BOS	239-253
JON ZUBER	PHI	82-95

All Fantasy Games are *NOT* the Same!

Scoresheet Baseball is a fantasy game that was developed 11 years ago as an alternative to traditional 'Rotisserie' games. At *Scoresheet,* we don't just total stats. Instead, each week of the upcoming 1997 baseball season your team will play **complete simulated ballgames, at-bat by at-bat, inning by inning, using your player's actual major league stats from that week**. All done on <u>our</u> computer!

MAKE *ALL* THE DECISIONS

* PLATOON   * PINCH HIT

* BUNT   * STEAL   * RELIEVE

SCORESHEET SPORTS

Using a lineup card **you** fill out, our computer simulates pitcher & fielder vs. batter matchups to play **real ballgames**. With *Scoresheet Baseball* every baseball statistic imaginable gets used, not just a few 'categories'. Your team will play a full **162-game head to head** schedule against the other teams in your league. You can **join alone** (we will put you in a league with other owners), **or** you can join with a group of friends and **form your own complete league**.

Throughout the 1997 major league season you'll receive weekly mailings, including scoresheets like the sample below, for every game your team plays, along with league standings, scores of all other games in your league, individual and team stats, trade information and offers, league leaders, a newsletter, and more. You can choose to receive your weekly results by **postal mail, fax, or e-mail.**

As author Gary Huckabay says: "*Scoresheet* is the most entertaining and realistic fantasy game there is." If you'd like more information about *Scoresheet Baseball*, just call the number below, or check out our web page at http://www.scoresheet.com. Have a great 1997 season!

in the U.S.
P.O. Box 2420
Berkeley, CA 94702
(510) 526-3954
FAX: (510) 526-3899
staff@scoresheet.com
http://www.scoresheet.com

in CANADA
P.O. Box 188
Grimsby, Ont L3M 4G3
(905) 945-5919
FAX: (905) 945-1399
scocan@netaccess.on.ca

WEEK 16 - GAME 4	1	2	3	4	5	6	7	8	9		IP	H	R	ER	BB	K
CF Bra Anderson	O		1B			1B		O	O	Dave Wells	4.2	6	4	3	4	5
2B Ch Knoblauch	K		O			O+		1B		Jim Corsi	2.1	3	2	2	0	2
LF Marty Cordova	O			O		1B*		SF*		Eric Plunk	1	0	0	0	1	0
DH Chili Davis		BB		K		O		1B+								
1B Cecil Fielder		O		K		K		/1B*								
3B Robin Ventura		K			HR		O	K								
SS Dave Howard																
RF Tim Salmon		O			K		BB		1B							
C Mark Parent			O		O					(this is part of						
PH Scott Stahoviak						DP				a sample game)						
C Charlie O'Brien																
PH Lee Tinsley								O+								
SS Mike Bordick			K		O											
PH-3B M Pagliarulo								2B	K							

	1	2	3	4	5	6	7	8	9		IP	H	R	ER	BB	K
DH Paul Molitor	O	E5		BB	O			DP		Pat Hentgen	7.2	7	4	4	2	7
RF Ger Williams	O	+1B*		SH++	O					R Hernandez	1.1	2	0	0	0	2
CF Ber Williams	1B	-O		BB		1B										

11th Year!

For a FREE brochure, call: 1-800-934-7265